MOON HANDBOOKS®

PERU

FIRST EDITION

ROSS WEHNER & RENÉE DEL GAUDIO

D0976370

AVALON TRAVEL

CONTENTS

Discover Peru

Explore Peru

MAPS

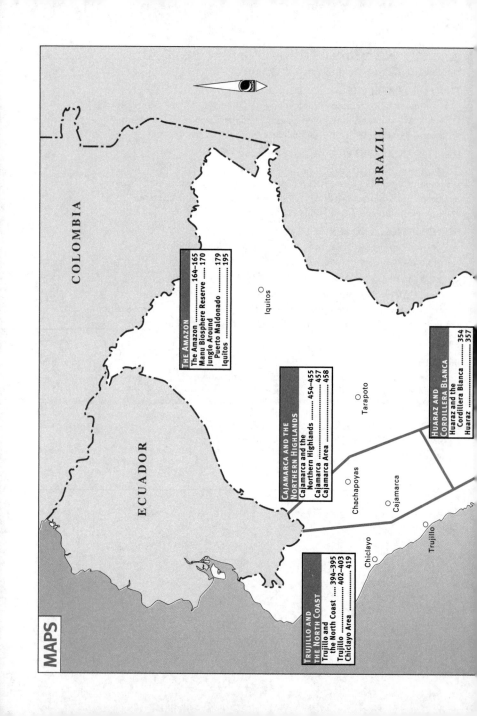

COLOMBIA

BRAZIL

ECUADOR

Iquitos ○

Tarapoto ○

Chachapoyas ○

Cajamarca ○

Chiclayo ○

Trujillo ○

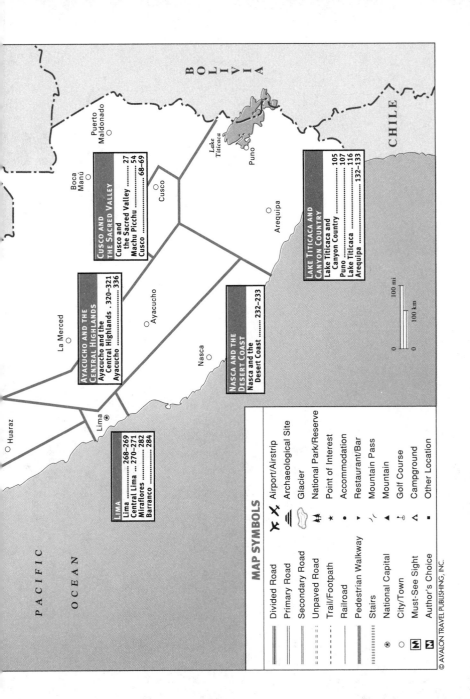

PACIFIC

OCEAN

O Huaraz

La Merced
O

Boca
Manú
O

Puerto
Maldonado
O

Lima ⊕

O Ayacucho

O Cusco

O
Cusco

Lake
Titicaca

O Puno

Nasca
O

O Arequipa

B
O
L
I
V
I
A

CHILE

0   100 mi

0   100 km

MAP SYMBOLS

▮▮ Divided Road	✈ ✈ Airport/Airstrip
▮ Primary Road	☆ Archaeological Site
▮ Secondary Road	🖙 Glacier
▬ ▬ ▬ Unpaved Road	⛟ National Park/Reserve
- - - Trail/Footpath	★ Point of Interest
▬▬ Railroad	● Accommodation
▬ Pedestrian Walkway	▼ Restaurant/Bar
▥▥▥▥▥ Stairs	⌇ Mountain Pass
⊛ National Capital	▲ Mountain
O City/Town	⛳ Golf Course
Ⓜ Must-See Sight	⋀ Campground
ⓩ Author's Choice	▪ Other Location

© AVALON TRAVEL PUBLISHING, INC.

Discover
Peru

The Spaniards' first impressions of Peru, when they sailed down its coast for the first time in 1528, were of barren beaches and man-eating savages. It was not until they began their now-legendary journey to the interior, through ochre desert and lush river valleys, up and over snowy passes, and into the sublime, magical realm of the *altiplano* that they realized what they had stumbled upon: a people every bit as advanced as the ancient Egyptians, with the most intricate stone construction in the history of the world and an abundance of what the Spaniards most wanted: gold. In Cusco, the capital of the Inca empire, the Spaniards found miniature gold figurines in the shape of jungle insects, four-inch-thick temple walls made of gold, shields and vases and even hand plows—all made of gold. Even before reaching Cusco, the Spaniards had shipped home gold that would be worth between $30 million and $50 million today.

Despite the conquistadors' toll, Peru's people and their connection to the land have remained remarkably intact over the centuries. Travelers who stumble off the beaten path in Peru's *altiplano,* or high plains, will journey back in time to the stone huts, the fields of quinoa, and the brightly clothed Quechuan people first encountered by the Spaniards. On the eastern slope of the Andes, where the mountains cede to the Amazon basin, the time warp is even greater: traveling along any of Peru's jungle rivers is like watching a movie roll backwards from the 19th century to the Stone Age.

Cusco remains the primary destination for most travelers to Peru, who come to wander the city's cobblestone streets, marvel at the Spanish cathedral and monasteries built atop massive Inca walls, eat alpaca steaks and fat ears of sweet corn and party until dawn at the city's nightclubs. Nearby but reachable only by train—or by a multi-day trek through some of the world's most breathtaking scenery—is the other world of the Incas: Machu Picchu, the mountaintop city on the edge of the Amazon jungle.

Yet Cusco is just the beginning of what Peru offers, a secret that is jealously guarded by Peru's experienced travelers. There is a well-swept room to visit in Cajamarca that the Inca emperor Atahualpa filled with gold in an (unsuccessful) attempt to free himself from the Spaniards; perfect breaks to be surfed and heaping bowls of cebiche to be eaten in the northern beach towns; snow-covered mountains to be climbed against a backdrop of sparkling jungle rivers; freeze-dried-potato soup to be eaten in a stone hut with a Quechuan family; and miles of Amazon to be floated with nothing more than a hammock and a bunch of bananas.

Of special interest is Peru's desert coast, which is rubbing shoulders with India and Egypt as a must-see destination for those drawn to the ancient and mysterious. A series of advanced, though poorly understood, cultures including the Nasca, Moche, Chimu, and Sicán flourished here thousands of years before the Incas. They left their mark with huge adobe pyramids, stone carvings, brightly painted murals, and, most important, tombs.

In 1987, archaeologists shocked the world by unearthing a series of royal Moche tombs near present-day Chiclayo. The Lords of Sipán exhibit, now back at Chiclayo's Museo Tumbas Reales after a world tour, includes mummies, elaborate textiles, ceramics, and hundreds of treasures made from gold, silver, and precious stones. Further south in Trujillo, archaeologists are uncovering murals depicting human sacrifice in the uppermost levels of the Moche pyramid known as Huaca de la Luna ("The Pyramid of the Moon"). Even further south are the Nasca Lines, a perplexing dialect of hummingbirds, monkeys, and mythical beings etched for miles into the timeless sands of the desert. The only way to see the images these lines form is from an airplane, an enigma that modern experts have been unable to explain.

Seeing most of Peru in one trip is impossible. Even if you planned on visiting the country for two months, you would still have to be selective. Take it from us—after a few years of living in Peru, and eight months of traveling full time, there is still plenty we have not seen.

The country's major sites, like its geography, can be divided into three zones. The desert coast contains the main pre-Inca sites, such as the Lords of Sipán exhibit in Chiclayo, the Moche pyramids and Chimu citadel near Trujillo, and the enigmatic Nasca Lines.

Peru's Andean highlands are rich in both Inca and Spanish history and are most famous for a circuit that leads through the Sacred Valley, Machu Picchu, and Cusco. From here a train leads through high grasslands to Lake Titicaca, one of a half-dozen other areas in Peru's highlands that boast a vibrant Andean culture and deep shadow of history.

Finally, the Amazon jungle contains a host of excellent lodges, which are grouped in three main areas: Iquitos, Puerto Maldonado, and the Parque Nacional Manu. As a bare minimum, visiting the Cusco area requires at least five days, though visitors could jet into Peru's northern coast and Amazon for as little as three days each and still have a worthwhile visit.

Peru's leading resource for up-to-date information is South American Explorers Club (SAE), a non-profit organization with clubhouses in Cusco (Choquechaca 188, #4, tel. 084/24-5484, cuscoclub@saexplorers.org, 9:30 A.M.–5 P.M. Mon.–Fri., 10 A.M.–1 P.M. Saturday) and Lima (Piura 135, Miraflores, tel. 01/445-3306, limaclub@saexplorers.org, 9:30 A.M.–5 P.M. Mon.–Fri., 9:30 A.M.–1 P.M. Saturday). Many outfitters, restaurants, and hotels in Peru offer discounts for SAE members, as noted in listings throughout this book.

WHEN TO GO

The traditional time to visit Peru is in the South American winter, from June through August, when dry, sunny weather opens up over the mountains and the Amazon. Because Peru's dry months coincide perfectly with summer vacation in North America and Europe, this is also when most tourists visit Peru. Prices for lodging tend to go up during these months, and hot spots like Machu Picchu can be crowded. Especially crowded times are Inti Raymi, the June 24th sun festival in Cusco, and Fiestas Patrias, the national Peruvian holiday at the end of July.

The bulk of the rainy season is between December and April, when trekking and other outdoor activities are hampered by muddy paths and soggy skies. To avoid crowds, we heartily recommend squeezing your trip in between the rainy season and the high tourist months. May, September, October, and even November are excellent times to visit Peru. The weather is usually fine and prices for lodging tend to be lower.

There are some dry spots in the country, however, even during the wettest months. Peru's largest jungle city, Iquitos, is far enough down the Amazon basin to have a less-pronounced wet season. Clouds move in most afternoons throughout the year, drop a load of water, and then shuffle away again to reveal sun. The only thing that fluctuates in Iquitos year-round is the Amazon River itself, which heaves up and down in tune with highland rains. So Iquitos is a year-round option for visiting the Amazon.

Peru's desert coast can also be visited year-round because hardly any rain ever falls here. Ironically, the sunniest months on the coast are the wettest in the highlands, from December to March. The weather is especially bright and sunny in Peru's extreme north coast, where surfers congregate for the white-sand beaches and huge seasonal breaks.

WHAT TO TAKE

Travel light and have a carefree vacation—drop-off laundry is common throughout Peru's cities, so you don't need to bring more than five days' clothing. Try to fit everything into a medium-sized backpack, which will allow you to walk around easily and spring in and out of jungle boats.

For Peru's hot climates of the coast and jungle, we recommend light, fast-drying clothing that protects your arms and legs from sun and mosquitoes. A wide-brimmed hat, with a string to keep it from blowing off your head, is essential. Bandannas to protect the neck from sun are a good idea as well. And of course sunscreen and dark sunglasses. In case your shoes get wet, bring along an extra pair of lightweight shoes or Teva-like sandals—most jungle lodges will lend you rubber boots for tromping through the mud.

These same clothes can be worn on most days in the highlands, though you will want to fortify your wardrobe with a lightweight rain jacket, a fleece jacket, and some silk-weight long underwear for sleeping at night. Buy an alpaca wool hat when you get to Peru. If you are planning on doing the Inca Trail, we recommend a sleeping bag rated for freezing temperatures, lightweight pair of fleece gloves, light hiking boots, and a pair of trekking poles. Your guide will most likely provide you with a tent.

Miscellaneous items include a Leatherman-type folding knife (remember to place it in checked luggage so it will not get confiscated), a lighter wrapped with a bit of duct tape for repairs, a mending kit, Purell hand sanitizer, a head lamp with extra bulb and batteries, a camera, a voltage adapter, a Nalgene bottle or two, a roll of toilet paper (Peru's public bathrooms are always out), binoculars, a pocket English-Spanish dictionary, and a tiny calculator for confirming money exchange rates.

Don't forget your medical kit, which contains among other things insect repellent, water purification tablets, and anti-malarial medication. Most people bring a journal, a few pens, and a book (there are English-language book exchanges in many Peruvian cities).

In terms of paperwork, you should have a valid passport, plane ticket, student card if you have one, a yellow card listing your vaccinations, travelers checks, ATM card and credit card, and a copy of your travel insurance details. In a separate place, list the numbers of your travelers checks and passport, and the phone numbers for replacing your cards—or, better yet, email this information to yourself. A photocopy of the first few pages of your passport and your plane ticket is also a good idea.

What you should not bring are items that will be confiscated by the airlines, including white gas or previously used camping stoves. Ice axes are fine, as long as they are placed in checked luggage. Leave your jewelry and fancy watch at home too.

CUSCO AND THE SACRED VALLEY

The heart and soul of Peru is the Cusco area, which was the Inca homeland for two centuries before the Spaniards built Peru's first capital here in the 16th century. Avoid the heights of Cusco (3,400 meters, or 11,150 feet) by beginning with the Sacred Valley, which the Incas considered paradise on earth for its sunny weather, rolling rivers, and fertile earth. The Incas built a string of sacred temples and fortresses up and down the valley, including Pisac and Ollantaytambo. The valley is cut by the Río Urubamba, which tumbles from here through steep gorges and toward the most fabled achievement of the Incas, Machu Picchu. The only way to get to Machu Picchu is via train or the Inca Trail, a paved stone highway that culminates in a bird's-eye view of Machu Picchu's temples, palaces, and workers' quarters. After seeing the Inca ruins, travelers are primed for Cusco, an imperial city that is still caught in a tug-of-war between the New World and European mindset. Atop the flawless stone walls built by the Incas, the Spaniards erected more than a dozen baroque churches and filled them with religious paintings, saints, and gold-plated altars. Other highlights of a Cusco tour including the artisan barrio of San Blas and the fortress of Sacsayhuamán.

LAKE TITICACA AND CANYON COUNTRY

Life proceeds according to the earthy rhythms of ancient times at Lake Titicaca, the world's highest navigable lake, which stretches from golden grasslands to the snow-covered peaks of Bolivia. For many visitors, the highlight of a Lake Titicaca visit is journeying across the lake to stay with a family on either Isla Taquile or Isla Anapia, where despite the altitude of 4,200 meters (13,780 feet) villagers cultivate potatoes and quinoa on rock terraces that drop steeply toward the lake's waters. Perched more than two and a half miles above the world's oceans,

Lake Titicaca feels at times like a sea on a planet that is not Earth. Its waters glow orange with the rising and setting of the sun and become transparent and azure at midday. From here, a new highway brings travelers in only five hours to **Arequipa,** a sophisticated colonial city where the **Plaza de Armas, Catedral,** and **Monasterio Santa Catalina** are built entirely of the local *sillar,* a sparkling white volcanic stone. A few hours away, ancient stone villages dot the rim of the awesome **Colca Canyon,** where the **Cruz del Cóndor** is the best spot on earth to see the world's largest flying bird.

THE AMAZON

If you fly above the Amazon, you will see clouds and an endless emerald blanket of vegetation, interrupted only by the muddy squiggles of jungle rivers. Because there are very few roads in the Amazon basin, you will travel by motorized dugout canoe, which is one of the best ways to see toucans, tanagers, and other rainforest birds. The forest is strangely hushed and dark underneath the rainforest canopy, which rustles as troops of monkeys pass overhead. The tropical sun comes back in full force as you paddle over the waters of an oxbow lake. Near **Iquitos,** gateway to the **Reserva Nacional Pacaya-Samiria,** it is common to see pink river dolphins and lily pads the size of dinner tables. Around **Puerto Maldonado** or **Parque Nacional Manu** you have a good chance of seeing giant otters.

NASCA AND THE DESERT COAST

Few ancient mysteries have stumped scientists, and sparked such a bizarre collection of theories, as the **Nasca Lines.** Dug into the landscape a thousand years ago and preserved by the area's peculiar climate, the lines include hummingbirds, whales and a series of intersecting grids and trapezoids, some of which are 10 km long. Even from a three-story observation tower along the highway, visitors can see a lizard, a tree, and an odd pair of outstretched hands—but the view is best from an airplane. Some researchers think these shapes were used in ceremonies to ask the gods for rain; others believe they were landing strips for Martians.

Nearby is the Ica Desert, an unexplored area of rolling sand dunes, wilderness beaches, and an astounding variety of marine fossils, including long-extinct porpoises and gigantic sharks. One of the best launch pads for exploring is the palm-fringed Lago Huacachina, where travelers can slide down dunes on sandboards. The next stop on the way to Lima is the Reserva Nacional Paracas, Peru's most important stretch of protected coastline and home to sea lions, two hundred bird species, and the endangered Humboldt penguin. Further on is Chincha, home to Peru's small but outspoken Afro-Peruvian culture and Hacienda San José, the country's best-preserved colonial plantation. From here Lima is just a few hours away along a route that passes a string of ocean beaches.

LIMA

Peru's capital has been avoided by travelers in the past because of its gray weather, grimy downtown, and chaotic feel. But the country's capital, christened *City of the Kings* when Francisco Pizarro founded it in 1535, is making a roaring comeback. Upscale restaurants and cafés have cropped up alongside the renovated Plaza Mayor, which is surrounded by the country's most important colonial Catedral and the palaces of the president and archbishop. The historic center is packed with 16th- and 17th-century marvels, including immaculately restored homes such as the Casa de Aliaga and the Palacio Torre Tagle. There are unique things to see at all of the dozen colonial churches in Lima, including the catacombs of San Francisco and the lavishly decorated facade of San Pedro. The outlying districts of Miraflores and San Isidro offer a range of lodging, bars, and a chance to sample the full spectrum of Peruvian cuisine. Bohemian Barranco, tucked on the edge of Lima's crescent-shaped bay, is the nightlife district and favored backpacker's den. The country's best museums are also here, including the Museo Larco and Museo de la Nación.

AYACUCHO AND THE CENTRAL HIGHLANDS

Ayacucho means *corner of death* in Spanish, and this tucked-away corner of the Andes has seen plenty of bloodshed over the last five centuries, from the Incas battling the local Chancas to the 1980s uprising of the Shining Path, Peru's most notorious terrorist movement. After a decade of peace, Ayacucho—and the surrounding region—is once again safe to visit. Nowhere is Peru's colonial past more palpable than Ayacucho, the most stunning city of Peru's Andes, with a gorgeous Catedral and nearly 30 other colonial churches, not to mention the charming village of Quinua and the ancient ruins of Wari. Further north the mountains give way to the Mantaro Valley, where villages built of rammed earth, tiles, and wooden beams blend in with the chocolate-brown fields. The villages in the Mantaro Valley such as Hualhuas and Cochas Grande are the best place in Peru to buy handicrafts, which range from weavings to carved gourds. If you come here, you are bound to see religious processions and dances—there are more traditional festivals in the Mantaro Valley than days in the year.

HUARAZ AND THE CORDILLERA BLANCA

Trekkers who make it over Punta Unión, a pass at 4,750 meters in the Cordillera Blanca, rub their eyes in disbelief when they first see Alpamayo. This pyramid of fluted snow lures climbers from around the world. It is but one of dozens of majestic snow giants that spring from Peru's high grasslands to form a spectacular tumble of broken glaciers, jagged peaks, and emerald lakes such as Lagunas Llanganuco. Besides trekking, the gentle valleys that thread the range also lure both horse packers and mountain bikers, while rafters test their mettle on the Class IV waters of the Río Santa. Further south, and separated by an area of high-altitude grasslands, the Cordillera Huayhuash rises in even more dramatic shapes. This remote range can be circumnavigated along a trail that includes eight passes over 4,600 meters.

TRUJILLO AND THE NORTH COAST

The Huaca de la Luna is a ten-story adobe pyramid that rises above the arid countryside and colonial mansions of old Trujillo. Archaeologists continue to unearth the bright murals that once decorated the pyramid, which was built over seven centuries by the Moche culture. The long line of Moche rulers included the Lords of Sipán, whose tombs were unearthed in 1987 near Chiclayo. The gold masks, huge earrings inlaid with turquoise, scepters, and other items from the tombs are on display at Chiclayo's new museum, Museo Tumbas Reales de Sipán. The cultures that followed the Moche also left a string of impressive cities on the north coast. Chan Chan, near Trujillo, is a 5,000-acre complex of adobe walls and esplanades that has been partially restored. The Sicán culture built the huge stepped platforms at Túcume and Batán Grande near Chiclayo, where precious objects recovered from their tombs are on display at the Museo Sicán.

CAJAMARCA AND THE NORTHERN HIGHLANDS

From Peru's north coast a road leads to Cajamarca, an overlooked gem of Peru's Andes where *campesinos* come to sell their cheese and barley on Sunday mornings. The countryside here is gorgeous and is crisscrossed with Inca paths, or Qhapah Ñan, and the enigmatic irrigation canals at Cumbemayo. One of the country's best baroque churches is in Cajamarca at the Complejo Belén, which also includes Atahualpa's famous ransom room, or Cuarto de Rescate. From Cajamarca the road leads inland, rougher now, through spectacular green grasslands before plunging down into the ochre landscape of the Marañón Canyon. From the subtropical climate at river's edge, the road on the other side climbs 3,030 meters (10,000 feet) to a whole new ecosystem. Dense cloud forest covers the mountain slopes where the Chachapoya culture built a series of stone cities that are still being discovered. Their crowning achievement was Kuélap, a stone fortress perched on a limestone cliff. The city's 400 round stone homes were protected by massive defense walls that can only be entered through three narrow passageways.

You've heard of the Eco-Challenge and the Ironman, so we now present the Peru Challenge. This 21-day tour is for the extraordinarily ambitious and energetic. More than anything, it is proof of all that Peru has to offer—and it still leaves out a lot. The odyssey unfolds chronologically among Peru's ancient ruins and colonial cities, with a dab of Amazon and a dash through the desert for balance. Getting around is accomplished via a straightforward combination of planes, trains, buses, and *combis*.

DAY 1

Begin by flying into Lima and catching a connecting flight to Peru's north, where you will spend two nights at Huanchaco Beach near Trujillo.

DAY 2

During the day you can see colonial Trujillo, the Moche pyramid of Huaca de la Luna, and the Chimu city of Chan Chan.

DAY 3

In the morning see Trujillo's Museo Cassineli, then hop on a bus for Chiclayo (three hours). Hire a private car and head to a country inn at Túcume (45 minutes), where you will stay two nights sleeping in the bucolic countryside near the pyramids.

DAY 4

After seeing the Lords of Sipán treasures at the Museos Tumbas Reales, visit the Sicán pyramids at Batán Grande and the new Museo Sicán.

DAY 5

Fly from Chiclayo to Lima. Here you begin the Gringo Trail, the time-honored backpacker's route to Cusco. Take bus to Pisco (three hours) and short *combi* ride to the beach town of El Chaco, where you stay two nights.

DAY 6

Explore Reserva Nacional Paracas. Watch sea lions and perhaps endangered Humboldt Penguins, picnic on a wilderness beach and return to your hotel for sunset over the Pacific Ocean.

DAY 7

Take bus to Nasca (2.5 hours) to visit Museo Antonini and aqueducts and stay the night. Or take a bus to Ica (one hour), for tour of pisco bodegas and sandboarding on the dunes above Lake Huacachina, where you stay the night. You choose.

DAY 8

Morning overflight of the Nasca Lines from either Nasca or Ica. Take the bus to Arequipa from Ica (eight hours) or Nasca (6.5 hours). Check in for two-night stay in Arequipa.

DAY 9

Tour sophisticated Arequipa, a sparkling white

city best known for the 17th-century Monasterio Santa Catalina.

DAY 10
Flight or bus trip from Arequipa to Puno (seven hours).

DAYS 11–12
Explore Lake Titicaca with a day tour of Amantaní and the Uros islands. Return to Puno for the night, or consider a stay with a family on Amantaní.

DAY 13
Continue onward to Cusco. From Puno you can either take a direct, nonstop train or a tour bus that allows you to see the ruins along the way (nine hours).

DAY 14
Take a *combi* from Cusco down to the Sacred Valley to see the ruins and market of Pisac, where you will stay the night.

DAY 15
Head to the ruins of Moray and Ollantaytambo. Tour Ollantaytambo, then take an afternoon train to Machu Picchu and overnight in Aguas Calientes.

Arequipa's Cathedral at sunset

DAY 16
From your base in the nearby town of Aguas Calientes, rise at dawn to be alone for sunrise at Machu Picchu. Full day at Machu Picchu, then hop on the afternoon train to Cusco.

DAYS 17–18
Tour the Cusco area, where you will have two days to soak in the churches, the artisan neighborhood of San Blas, and the fortress of Sacsayhuamán.

DAYS 19–20
As a final treat, take a morning flight (30 minutes) to Puerto Maldonado for a two-night stay at a jungle lodge.

DAY 21
From Puerto Maldonado catch a morning flight to Lima's airport, where you can leave your bags for a quick peek at the city center and a gourmet dinner in Miraflores. Then hop a red-eye for home.

ceremonial Chan Chan figure with stylized sea otters in background

Outdoor Adventure

This trip combines the most spectacular adventures that we can imagine in Peru—mountain biking in the Cordillera Negra, a walk along the wild side of the Cordillera Huayhuash, and an epic whitewater descent from Lake Titicaca, the world's highest navigable lake, to the Amazon jungle. In the process you will experience Peru's thin air, its most extraordinary alpine panoramas, Andean villages rooted in centuries of tradition, the villages of Lake Titicaca, and world-class Amazon rain forest. Between the two expeditions, you will have a chance to rest weary legs by touring the fabulous circuit of the Sacred Valley, Machu Pichu, and Cusco.

The final days of your trip include floating on torpid, muddy waters through the pristine rainforest of the Parque Nacional Bahuaja-Sonene. Floating silently, as opposed to cruising on a motorboat, is an excellent way to see a huge range of birds and other jungle animals (your chances of seeing a jaguar here are equal to those at the Parque Nacional Manu). You will need to contract an experienced operator, such as Amazonas Explorer (see *Sports and Recreation* in the *Cusco* chapter), for this rafting trip.

A similar sequence that would be shorter and less expensive begins with the five-day Santa Cruz trek in the Cordillera Blanca and takes in the best scenery of the world's second-highest mountain chain, including perfect views of snow pyramid Alpamayo. Then it's off to Cusco for a four-day wild ride through the Class IV Río Apurimac, considered one of the world's best whitewater rivers.

DAY 1
Arrive in Lima, bus to Huaraz (seven hours)

DAY 2
Downhill mountain-bike cruise through the Cordillera Negra.

DAY 3
Depart for the village of Huallanca, passing the Glacier Pastoruri and the giant *puya raimondi* plants en route (four–five hours).

DAYS 4–8
Early-morning *combi* to Huallanca and on to Ishpac (5.5 hours) to begin Huayhuash trek. Make your first camp a few kilometers from Ishpac.

Machu Picchu with Huayna Picchu in the background

DAY 13
Cusco tour.

DAY 14
Bus to Lake Titicaca, with ruins along the way.

DAY 15
Lake Titicaca tour.

DAY 16
Drive to raft put-in on Río Tambopata.

DAYS 17–23
Raft whitewater during the day and camp on wilderness beaches at night.

DAY 24
Short motorboat ride to the Tambopata Research Center for overnight stay—within minutes of the world's largest macaw clay lick, where dozens of species of macaws, parrots, and parakeets gather each morning.

DAY 9
Transport from Cajatambo to Pativilca and on to Lima (nine hours). Overnight in Lima.

DAY 25
Boat ride to Puerto Maldonado and flight to Lima to return home.

DAY 10
Early-morning flight to Cusco. Take *combi* to Ollantaytambo for a one-night stay.

DAY 11
Sacred Valley tour with evening train to Aguas Calientes.

DAY 12
Tour Machu Picchu and take afternoon train to Cusco.

This trip is designed for fans of ancient history and ruins who are willing to leaf through history books, sit in lectures, and spend hours wandering around ancient ruins. This trip will allow you to understand the achievements of the Incas by first examining the Moche, Chimu, and Sicán cultures that preceded them.

The only part of this tour that requires private transportation is the visit to San José de Moro. Specialty operators like Far Horizons Archaeological & Cultural Trips offer this basic itinerary spiced up with expert archaeologist tour guides and a series of exclusive lectures.

DAY 1

Arrive in Lima. Begin with a grounding at the Museo Nacional de Arqueología in Lima.

DAY 2

Fly to Trujillo and transfer to Huanchaco Beach for two-night stay.

DAY 3

Tour the Trujillo area. During the day you will see the Moche murals at the Huaca de la Luna, the Chimu citadel of Chan Chan, the ceramics at Museo Cassineli, and the city's colonial mansions.

DAY 4

Head north to Chiclayo. Stop to see the Moche site of El Brujo along the way. Then check into a country inn near the Sicán pyramids of Túcume, where you will spend two nights.

DAY 5

Tour the Chiclayo area. See the Lords of Sipán exhibit at the Museo Tumbas Reales, the Sicán pyramids of Batán Grande, and the new Museo Sicán.

DAY 6

Fly back to Lima for a day tour of Pachacámac, an adobe temple that once housed the most revered oracle in the Andes.

DAY 7

Catch a morning flight to Cusco and transfer to Ollantaytambo for a two-night stay. In the afternoon, begin your tour of the Sacred Valley with a detailed visit to the sun temple at Ollantaytambo.

DAY 8

Continue your tour of the Sacred Valley with visits to the fortress of Pisac and odd terraced pits of Moray.

DAY 9

Visit the traditional market at Chinchero, with plenty of time to examine the town's Inca walls and ruins scattered throughout the countryside.

DAY 10

At dawn, board a train for Aguas Calientes, which will serve as your base for exploring Machu Picchu for the next two days.

DAYS 12–13

Tour Cusco area: See the Inca walls, Sacsayhuamán and the other ruins outside the city, colonial churches, and the artisan barrio of San Blas.

DAY 14

Take a morning flight to Lima. Visit the Museo Larco and have a farewell oceanside dinner before catching your flight home.

The Incas may have developed new crop varieties at Moray.

© RENÉE DEL GAUDIO AND ROSS WEHNER

DAY 11

Second day at Machu Picchu. The adventurous can climb to the summit of Putukusi, a forest rock dome that overlooks the Inca citadel. In the afternoon, take the train to Cusco.

At Túcume, 26 eroded pyramids are spread throughout the desert.

© RENÉE DEL GAUDIO AND ROSS WEHNER

This overland odyssey through Peru's northern highlands is for those who want to get off the Gringo Trail and experience a mind-blowing cross-section of Peru's geography.

DAY 1

Arrive in Lima, fly to Trujillo, and take a taxi to Huanchaco Beach for a two-night stay.

DAY 2

Tour Trujillo area: see colonial mansions, the Huaca de la Luna, and the Museo Cassineli.

DAY 3

Morning visit to the Chimu capital of Chan Chan. Take an afternoon bus to Cajamarca (four–five hours).

DAY 4

Tour Cajamarca, where Francisco Pizarro captured Inca emperor Atahualpa and ransomed him for a room of gold. Besides Atahualpa's chamber (called the *Cuarto de Rescate*), Cajamarca offers baroque churches, the carved aqueducts at Cumbemayo, and a stunning pastoral setting.

DAY 5

After a morning visit to Cumbemayo, begin the rough overland journey to the cloud forest of the Chachapoya. The first leg of the trip involves an afternoon bus to the charming country town of Celendín (four hours).

DAY 6

Bus ride to Leimebamba (eight hours)—a spectacular, bumpy ride down and up the Marañon Canyon, which is deeper than Arizona's Grand Canyon and ranges from high-altitude grasslands to the subtropical valley floor.

DAY 7

Explore Leimebamba with a visit to the Museo Leimebamba and a hike to the lost city of La Congona. That afternoon, take a *colectivo* down the

Archaeologists have no idea how, or when, the aqueducts at Cumbemayo were made.

© RENÉE DEL GAUDIO AND ROSS WEHNER

© RENÉE DEL GAUDIO AND ROSS WEHNER

Yarapa River Lodge in Iquitos

Utcubamba Valley to Chillo or Tingo (1.5 hours). Plan on a two-night stay at one of the charming country lodges at the foot of Kuélap.

DAY 8
Hike to the Chachapoya citadel of Kuélap.

DAY 9
Take a *colectivo* to Pedro Ruiz (one hour) to get back on paved highway, and hop on a bus for Tarapoto (eight hours).

DAY 10
Relax in Tarapoto by visiting Laguna Sauce or hiking to the local waterfalls.

DAY 11
The most adventurous part of the trip begins with an early-morning *colectivo* over the muddy, potholed road to Yurimaguas (six–eight hours). That afternoon, board a cargo boat down the Río Huallaga bound for Iquitos.

DAY 12
Rest up in Iquitos by swinging on a hammock, eating bananas, and watching the Amazon float by.

DAY 13
Disembark at riverside village of Nauta. Or you can choose to disembark before Iquitos and cap off your stay at one of the excellent lodges upriver—or head all the way to Iquitos and meet your boat to a jungle lodge there.

DAYS 14–15
Jungle tour.

DAY 16
Return to Iquitos for celebration dinner—or keep floating on into Brazil!

DAY 17
Fly to Lima and return home

Several days can be chopped off this trip by starting from Chiclayo, from where a newly paved highway leads into Peru's interior. In Chiclayo you can see the Treasures of Sipán at the Museo Tumbas Reales and pyramids left behind by the Moche and Sicán cultures. Smooth pavement leads from here to the lodges beneath Kuélap, a journey of 10 hours up spectacular cloud-forest valleys. Then the itinerary would proceed as in the original version.

If you are hankering to visit the Reserva Nacional Pacaya-Samiria, get off the Yurimaguas-Iquitos cargo boat in the middle of the first night at the town of Lagunas. Here guides can be hired for a week of paddling in a dugout canoe and camping in the reserve.

10 Days in Peru

This 10-day tour hits the high points of southern Peru in a schedule that allows for gradual acclimatization to altitude.

DAY 1
Early-morning arrival in Lima, fly to Cusco, and head to Pisac, where you'll overnight.

DAY 2
Tour Sacred Valley, with visits to Moray and Ollantaytambo.

DAY 3
Wander around Ollantaytambo and catch the evening Backpacker train to Aguas Calientes, your base for seeing Machu Picchu.

DAY 4
Rise early to explore the ruins of Machu Picchu. In the afternoon, you can either hike to Huayna

Temple of Ten Niches, Ollantaytambo

© RENÉE DEL GAUDIO AND ROSS WEHNER

Picchu or indulge in a gourmet lunch at the Sanctuary Lodge. Then take the train for a two-day stay in Cusco.

DAYS 5–6

Tour Cusco, taking two days to soak in the sights. Travelers with a bit more time may want to extend this trip from Cusco with a visit to biodiverse Parque Nacional Manu (five–seven days) or a visit to Lake Titicaca (three–five days).

DAY 7

Hop a morning flight to Arequipa to see the city's elegant Monasterio Santa Catalina and Plaza de Armas.

DAY 8

Leave early the next morning for Colca Canyon and keep a sharp eye out for herds of vicuña along the way. The adventurous can mountain-bike the final descent to the Colca Lodge, where you will star-gaze that night and soak your weary feet in riverside hot springs

DAY 9

Rise the next morning to tour Colca. See Andean condors and stone villages before returning to Arequipa.

colonial architecture in Lima

© RENÉE DEL GAUDIO AND ROSS WEHNER

DAY 10

Catch a morning flight from Arequipa to Lima, where you have a chance to see colonial architecture, shop, and have a gourmet meal before catching your flight home.

Explore
Peru

Cusco and the Sacred Valley

It is difficult to think of any country in the world that has a destination with the magnetic pull of **Machu Picchu,** the legendary *lost city of the Incas* discovered by American explorer Hiram Bingham in 1911. Visiting Machu Picchu is an essential part of any Peru trip—nearly nine out of ten foreigners visiting the country make it to this citadel of sculpted stone, cloaked in clouds high on a jungle ridge. It is the clearest example of how the Incas built in harmony with extraordinary natural settings.

The river that runs past Machu Picchu is the Río Urubamba, which the Incas considered a sacred reflection of the Milky Way. Before reaching Macchu Picchu, it flows through the **Sacred Valley,** a breathtaking landscape of snow-capped mountains, red granite cliffs, and lush green terraces. The Sacred Valley runs roughly from Pisac

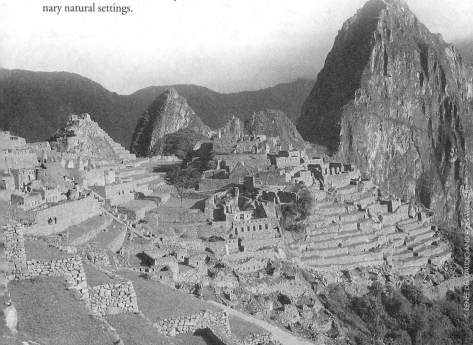

to Ollantaytambo, the Inca breadbasket that still produces much of the grains, vegetables, and fruits consumed in Cusco. Compared to the chilly, thin air of Cusco, the Sacred Valley is balmy and lush and the Incas considered it paradise on earth. Inca palaces, fortresses, and temples are dotted throughout this valley, along with charming Andean villages that produce and sell some of the country's finest handicrafts. Along with Machu Picchu, the Sacred Valley is near the top of Peru's must-see list.

Much of the Sacred Valley has been sculpted by the Incas with the movements of the suns and stars in mind. The temple-fortresses of Pisac and Ollantaytambo both correspond very precisely to lunar and solar events. Moray, an area of terraced natural depressions, was probably designed to use sun and shade to work as an agricultural laboratory. The Incas went to great effort to redirect the Río Urubamba into a stone channel—to maximize farming land, but also probably to reflect the straight shape of the Milky Way.

The Urubamba gorge running from the Sacred Valley to Machu Picchu is so treacherous and serpentine that the Incas built a paved stone highway up into the mountains. This route, known today as the **Inca Trail,** rises and falls through ecosystems and high passes before making a dramatic entry at Machu Picchu's legendary Intipunko (*Sun Gate*). There are shorter options for hiking parts of the Inca Trail, though most people prefer to do the full four-day route, which begins with high plains and views of snow-covered mountains and ends in high jungle.

The Incas' capital city was **Cusco,** which in Quechua means *belly button of the world.* Though the Spaniards did their best to destroy it, there is no ignoring the perfect Inca walls that run alongside the city's cobblestone streets. On top of these walls, the Spaniards built a dozen baroque churches and convents. With every earthquake, the Spanish buildings cracked and tumbled while the Inca walls stood strong. The standoff between these two cultures makes Cusco seem like a Jerusalem of the New World.

PLANNING YOUR TIME

The traditional way to visit Machu Picchu is all wrong. Most travelers arrive in Cusco and spend a night or two seeing the city. Then they take a whirlwind day tour of the Sacred Valley and then take the train from Cusco to Machu Picchu in one day.

The first thing wrong with this plan is that Cusco is at 3,400 meters (11,150 feet). Most people feel at least some discomfort from altitude sickness, which can feel like the flu and is a heck of a way to start a vacation. A much better plan is to head first for the Sacred Valley, a pastoral paradise with Southern California–like weather that is, most important, 500 meters lower. Few people get altitude sickness here.

Visiting the Sacred Valley first makes sense from a chronological perspective as well. Seeing the ruins of Ollantaytambo and Pisac are a good introduction to Machu Picchu. After understanding the Inca side of the equation, travelers then can return by train to Cusco, which is a Jerusalem-like blend of two opposing cultures, Spanish colonial and Inca imperial.

The one-day Sacred Valley tours take place on Pisac market days (Tuesday, Thursday, or Sunday) and include lunch in Urubamba and a visit to the Ollantaytambo ruins. Visitors usually miss the Pisac ruins, some of the finest in Peru, and also get shortchanged on Ollantaytambo, which contains Inca ruins second only to Machu Picchu. This is also Peru's best-preserved Inca village and a major center for hiking and rafting. Shorter trains for Machu Picchu leave from here and from a more pleasant station in nearby Urubamba.

If at all possible, travelers should overnight at Aguas Calientes, the closest town to Machu Picchu, and the best way to do this is with Ollantaytambo's new evening Backpacker trains. Day-trippers from Cusco have only several hours at the ruins in the middle of the day. But those who stay in Aguas Calientes can arrive at the ruins at sunrise or linger late in the afternoon with the ruins all to themselves. Midday, when Machu Picchu is most crowded, is a good

Must-Sees

Look for **M** to find the sights and activities you can't miss and **M** for the best dining and lodging.

Pisac

M Pisac Market: Peru's most famous crafts market takes place Tuesday, Thursday, and Sunday in this ancient Inca village, nestled in the shadow of an imposing Inca fortress and temple (page 28).

Ollantaytambo

M Ollantaytambo Temple: Second in importance only to Machu Picchu, Ollantaytambo includes some of the Incas' best stonework, including a series of ceremonial baths, elegant trapezoidal doorways, and a sun temple that faces the rising sun (page 46).

Machu Picchu

M Temple of the Moon and Huayna Picchu: Apart from the royal palaces and exquisite sun temple, Machu Picchu also stands out for its exquisite Temple of the Moon. This natural cave, sculpted with curving stone walls, is well worth the 45-minute hike to Huayna Picchu (page 58).

M Inca Trail: For those who hike it, this sacred path is part trek, part religious pilgrimage. It winds down from the windswept mountains to lush cloud forest, passing 30 ruins along the way, until reaching Machu Picchu (page 59).

Cusco

M Catedral: Cusco's baroque cathedral, built atop

© RENEE DEL GAUDIO AND ROSS WEHNER

day two of the Inca Trail

a former Inca palace, dominates the town's Plaza de Armas and is filled with a huge range of paintings from the Cusco School, elegant carved choir stalls, and a gold-covered Renaissance altar (page 71).

M Coricancha and Santo Domingo: Coricancha, the Inca Sun Temple, was once covered with thick plates of solid gold. After sacking it, the Spaniards built a Dominican church atop its seamless walls, a bizarre juxtaposition that illustrates the religious conflict that continues to drive Cusco today (page 73).

M Sacsayhuamán: This stone fortress of massive zigzag walls, fashioned from stone blocks weighing hundreds of tons, towers over Cusco and is the maximum expression of the Incas' military strength (page 76).

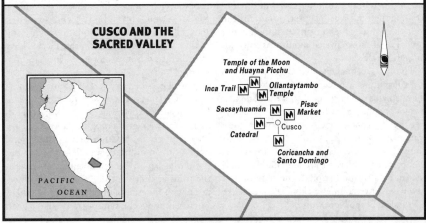

CUSCO AND THE SACRED VALLEY

Temple of the Moon and Huayna Picchu

Inca Trail **M** **M** Ollantaytambo Temple

Sacsayhuamán **M** **M** Pisac Market

Catedral **M** ○ Cusco

M

Coricancha and Santo Domingo

PACIFIC OCEAN

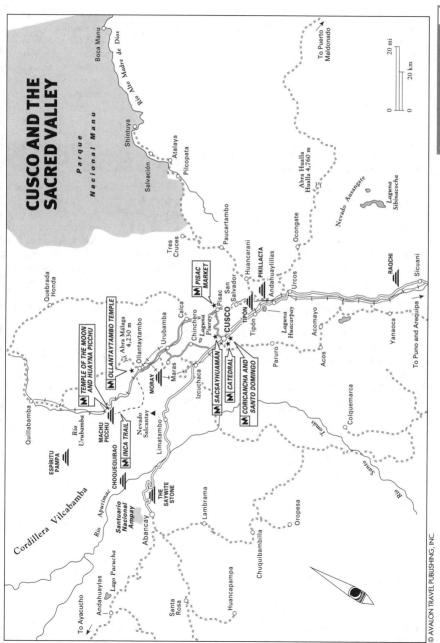

CUSCO AND THE SACRED VALLEY

Parque Nacional Manu

20 mi

20 km

© AVALON TRAVEL PUBLISHING, INC.

time to explore outlying sites such as Huaynu Picchu, the Moon Temple, the Inca Bridge, or the Sun Gate.

A four-hour train ride leads from Aguas Calientes to Cusco, where travelers may spend at least two days admiring Inca stonework and colonial architecture, touring the museums, and enjoying great food and lodging. Many people continue on for the spectacular train or bus jour-ney to Lake Titicaca, where it is possible to stay with families on Taquile or Anapia Islands. A lesser-known option is a 40-minute flight to Puerto Maldonado, in the heart of Peru's Amazon. In three or four days, visitors can see a range of animals and get an excellent introduction to the Amazon. Even more biodiversity can be seen in the longer, and more expensive, trips to the Parque Nacional Manu.

Pisac

This quaint Andean town, nestled near the top of the Sacred Valley, is best known for a huge crafts market that is probably Peru's number two tourist draw behind Machu Picchu. During market days on Tuesday, Thursday, and Sunday, hundreds of travelers descend upon this village as part of a whirlwind day tour from Cusco that begins here in the morning and continues on for lunch at Urubamba and a tour of the ruins at Ollantaytambo.

But there is a lot more to Pisac, and an increasing number of travelers are staying here for a night or two to explore further afield. On non-market days, the town's main square is a peaceful place with a huge pisonay tree and an ancient colonial church built atop Inca foundations. The **Inca fortress** above town represents the most important Inca ruins in the valley besides Ollantaytambo. The ruins contain a rare combination of residential, military, and religious construction that sheds a deep light onto the daily life of the Incas.

In the high plains beyond the fortress, there are a series of remote villages that can be reached only on foot. Roman and Fielding Vizcarra, owners of Hotel Pisaq, lead recommended trips into the surrounding countryside to visit these Quechuan villages along with the remote ruins of Cuyo Chico and Cuyo Grande.

ⓜ PISAC MARKET

Pisac has evolved into one of the biggest, certainly the most famous, *artesanía* markets in all of South America. It begins every Sunday, Tuesday, and Thursday at 9 A.M. when the first tour buses arrive from Cusco and winds down around 5 P.M. when the last tourists leave. The town's main square is filled wall-to-wall on these days with stalls selling the full range of Peruvian *artesanía:* carved gourds (*mates burilados*), ceramics, felt hats, alpaca sweaters and mittens, musical instruments, paintings, antiques, a huge variety of trinkets, and, most of all, weavings and jewelry. Even if you are not buying, the café balconies overlooking the market offer superb people-watching: hundreds of camera-toting tourists, from every conceivable country on earth, haggle with Quechuan-speaking merchants, all to the beat of drum-and-juggling sessions put on by a scraggly band of local hippies. Quality tends to be in the low to middle range—the good stuff is found in the homes of the *artesanos* themselves or in upscale city galleries—but prices are very reasonable, especially when buying in quantity.

Though touristy beyond belief, the Pisac market has a remarkably deeper side that is rooted in its colonial past and has proven resilient to mass tourism. On Sundays only, *campesinos* from surrounding villages set up a barter market, or *mercado de treque,* which is an ancient Peruvian custom and an interesting example of the informal economies upon which highlanders depend. Quechuan-speaking Indians sit behind huge piles of potatoes, carrots, herbs, and other vegetables in one corner of the square. They sell these products to buy essentials (salt, sugar, kerosene, matches, medicines) but also trade to acquire other foods, such as oranges from the Quillabamba Valley. It exists side-by-side to the Pisac market but ends by 3 P.M. so that villagers can walk home before dark.

Also on Sundays only, masses in Quechua are held at 6 and 11 A.M. in **San Pedro Apóstol de Pisac,** the colonial church on the main square that was rebuilt after the 1955 earthquake. The early mass is held for townspeople, and the later one is reserved for the *varayocs* and *regidores* (elected mayors and their appointed deputies) of the 13 villages that are a two- to five-hour walk away through the mountains. After mass, the officials proceed around the square in their Sunday best before a series of baptisms, and sometimes a wedding, are held in the church. Between services, it is possible to enter the church for a glimpse at the Inca foundations and an interesting collection of colonial paintings.

PISAC RUINS

Pisac is one of Cusco's few great Inca ruins that feature all types of architecture—agricultural, hydraulic, military, residential, and religious. It probably began as a military garrison to guard against incursion from the Anti Indians, who occupied the easternmost corner of the empire known as *Antisuyo* (present-day Paucartambo and the Manu jungle). Pachacútec probably built Pisac's imperial architecture, though oddly there is no mention of Pisac in the Spanish chronicles.

There are several ways to see the **Pisac ruins** (7 A.M.–3 P.M., admission with Cusco ruins ticket), but the best is to take a $3–4 taxi up the 8 km highway to the ruins. Instead of going to the main entrance, tell your taxi to head right on the switchback and head further up to the Pisac ruins of **Qanchisracay.** From here a trail leads along a ridge, through a tunnel, and down into the **Intihuatana,** or the main sun temple. The walk is steep and exposed to heights, but safe. Or arrive at the Intihuatana via the main path from the main entrance. Allow for one or two hours for Pisac (return to town via taxi) and another two hours for walking downhill all the way to town.

the finely built temples around Pisac's Intihuatana

THE INCAS' SACRED STEPS

Step designs are found everywhere in important Inca ruins. At the sacred rocks near Qenco and Sacsayhuaman, there are staircases leading nowhere. The famous walls of Ollantaytambo are decorated with faint step patterns. At Pisac, there is an especially interesting step pattern in the shape of a *chacana,* a diamond symbol with three steps on each side.

Like the crucifix for Christians, the *chacana* is a sacred symbol for Quechuan-speaking people. Conventional wisdom holds that the four points of the *chacana* correspond to the four corners of the Inca Empire. The three steps on each side of the *chacana* correspond to the trilogy of the Inca world. The bottom step corresponds to below the earth *(uju pacha),* associated with the serpent and wisdom. The middle step is the earth *(key pacha),* associated with the puma and force. And the top level is the sky *(yanam pacha),* linked to the condor and the future.

At Pisac, there is a half-*chacana* symbol in front of the Intihuatana, or the sacred stone pillar used to measure the sun's movement. Above the *chacana,* sculpted out of rock, is another stone pillar that is easy to miss if you aren't looking for it. During the June 21 winter solstice, the sun casts a shadow from this pillar that hits the *chacana.* The resulting shadow completes the bottom half of the *chacana,* marking the beginning of the harvest season.

Qanchisracay is one of three residential areas in Pisac. It is composed of rough stone buildings, walls with niches, and small squares. These were probably military garrisons and, in the style of a medieval castle, shelter for villagers in times of war. An easier residential area to visit, below the Intihuatana, is named after the Andean partridge **P'isaqa**—the namesake of the Pisac itself.

From Qanchisracay an Inca trail traverses the hillside, arrives at a small pass, then heads up and over a rocky summit to the sun temple, behind and out of sight. At the pass, four purification baths flow with water brought down from a lake at 4,500 meters. Below are five agricultural terraces, once planted with potatoes and *olluco,* the Andean tuber. On the opposing cliff wall, thousands of holes left by grave robbers are all that is left of what was once the Incas' largest cemetery. On the other side of the pass to the left, a 10-minute detour around the corner reveals Inca buttresses, which were once spanned by a hanging bridge made of plant fibers. This is an alternate trail to the Intihuatana and passes a series of fine irrigation canals.

The main path from the pass crosses through a military wall with a perfect trapezoidal door, known as the **Door of the Serpent.** Above is the second residential area, **Hanam P'isaq** (upper Pisac). The path now climbs up steep staircases and niches carved out of the rock itself, alongside a cliff and through the **Q'alla Q'asa** (Split Rock) tunnel. Faced with a vertical rock face, Inca engineers decided to enlarge a rock fissure and *bore* through the entire cliff—how they did this, with no iron or steel implements, boggles the mind.

The best view of the Intihuatana is from above. Like the sun temple at Machu Picchu, the Intihuatana is an oval building of perfect masonry encasing a votive rock. The pillar atop the rock was used to track the sun's movements. (Most of the finely carved pillar was recently chopped off by thieves—not long before the one in Machu Picchu was chipped during the filming of a beer commercial.) The walls of five other temples surround the temple, including one that was probably devoted to the moon. To the right are a series of restored baths that flow into an underground canal. In front of the Intihuatana is a sacred *chacana* symbol.

Off the easier trail back to the main entrance of the ruins is **P'isaqa,** the third and finest residential area, with its own ritual bath. These were probably homes for the elite, as opposed to the military garrisons closer to the pass. Most people head back at this point to the main entrance, though there are two trails from here that make for pleasant two-hour walks back to Pisac. One descends directly to the Río Quitamayo, with spectacular views, while the other drops through lookout towers of Coriwayrachina and an area of steep terracing. Both trails merge on the other side of the river for the final descent into town.

ENTERTAINMENT AND EVENTS

Pisac's big festival is **La Virgen del Carmen**, which begins on July 15 and runs for five days. The first day includes a horse-riding contest followed by a series of religious procession and dances.

There are no discos in Pisac, but the cafés around the square serve beer and cocktails.

SHOPPING

Apart from the Pisac Market, there are crafts shops open all week long on all the main streets leading from the square, especially **Mariscal Castilla**, **San Francisco**, and **Bolognesi**. Contemporary art is sold in the first floor of the **Mullu Café Restaurant** (Plaza Constitución 352) and in a related gallery a block from the square on San Francisco.

ACCOMMODATIONS

Under $10

At **Parador Turístico de Pisac** (Plaza Constitución, tel. 084/20-3061, $6 s, $10 d) the wood-floored rooms are so huge that there is even space for a table, a few chairs, and a floor weaving. The windows offer the best views in town of the main square and market—a great place to sit and have a drink (but there are only four rooms, so book ahead!). Rooms in the back, with private bathrooms, are coming soon, and a simple restaurant is downstairs. (This hotel found new management in 2004, so prices, and even the name, may change.)

The next best budget option is **Hostal Kinsa Ccocha** (Arequipa 307, tel. 084/20-3101, $5 s, $9 d), which has several plain, clean rooms a block from the Plaza Constitución. The shared bathrooms have wood-heated hot water, so throw on a couple of logs before showering.

The last-resort options include **Hospedaje Samana Wasi** (Plaza Constitución, tel. 084/20-

3018, $5 s, $9 d), which offers shoebox-sized rooms overlooking the plaza, shared bathrooms, and a restaurant (7 A.M.–9 P.M.). **Hospedaje Buho** (Intihuatana 114, tel. 084/20-3001, $5 s, $9 d) does a lot of advertising but its rooms are disappointing.

$10–25

Hotel Pisaq (Plaza Constitución, tel. 084/20-3062, htpisaq@mail.terra.com.pe, www .aart.com/aart/HOTELPISAQ.html, $10 pp shared bath, $13 pp private bath, breakfast $3 extra) is a labor of love for Roman Vizcarra and Fielding Wood-Vizcarra, a Peruvian-American couple who founded the hotel a decade ago. The front of their adobe building, covered in bright murals, includes an excellent café and restaurant with balconies overlooking the market square. Past the building's threshold is a hushed, contemplative atmosphere that recalls Fielding's hometown of Taos, New Mexico. Friezes of turquoise and scarlet fringe the sand-colored walls, and the atmosphere—neither Inca nor Navajo—is billed as a *celebration of indigenous culture all over the Americas.* Additional perks include a rock-heated sauna, laundry, and a constant supply of water from the hotel's own well—a big advantage, given Pisac's sporadic water supply. Roman speaks Spanish, Quechua, Italian, and German and leads tours throughout the area that combine culture with spirituality. The 10-day trip, described on the website, is based in Pisac and includes Cusco, Machu Picchu, and a communal workday in Amaru, a Quechuan village.

$25–50

The American-run **Paz y Luz** (off the road to ruins 2 km outside of town, tel. 084/20-3204, dianedunn@terra.com.pe, www.maxart.com/window/gateway.html, $15 pp including breakfast) is a collection of earth-colored lodges on the edge of the Río Urubamba above Pisac. There are no roads here, only fields, and there are spectacular walks in every direction through the countryside. The rooms are comfortable and tastefully decorated and have brand-new bathrooms. A central area has a wood stove, dining table, and polished wood staircase. In the back, in a separate building, is a one-bedroom apartment with its own kitchen—it is also $15 pp though breakfast is not included.

$50–100

On the outside, **Hotel Royal Inka III Pisac** (on road to ruins 1 km outside of town, tel. 084/20-3064, royalin@terra.com.pe, www.royalinkahotel.com, $54 s, $78 d) is a charming, converted hacienda with a mid-19th-century chapel. Unfortunately, most of the rooms are in a cold and charmless modern addition. Some rooms have wood stoves, however, and the second and third floors offer views out over the fields. There are a range of services, mostly included in the price, which include pool, private Jacuzzi, sauna, tennis court with rented rackets, horses, bikes, game room, restaurant, bar, and videos. There is also a spa, where you can get a massage for $25 and other treatments. Without a deep discount, this hotel may seem overpriced when compared to other, more charming and considerably cheaper options nearby.

FOOD
Cafés and Desserts

The best café in the Sacred Valley is **N Ulrike's Café** (Plaza Constitución, tel. 084/20-3195, ulrikescafe@terra.com.pe, 7 A.M.–8 P.M.). Ulrike Simic, the classy German owner of this newly opened establishment, offers the most creative lunch *menús* in town ($4, including vegetarian options) and personally makes a delectable array of cheesecakes, including chocolate chip, coffee, and lemon. Art adorns the walls and baroque music drifts through the air, making every sitting nook a perfect respite from the bustling world of commerce outside. **Mullu Café-Restaurant** (Plaza Constitución 352, 9 A.M.–8 P.M.) has an interesting collection of contemporary art on the first floor and a café, with nice market views, on the second. Its service and food, however, pales in comparison to Ulrike's Café.

Local Favorites

The best place for trout in Pisac, and maybe the whole Cusco area, is **N Restaurant Valle Sagrado** (Amazonas 116, tel. 084/20-3009, 8 A.M.–10 P.M., $2–5), operated over the last 10 years by the motherly Carmen Luz. During lunch, this place is packed with locals who come not only for the trout but for chicken, soups, sandwiches, and lamb ribs. Restaurant Valle Sagrado is right on the main drag, along with many other lesser restaurants; look for its faux-Inca walls.

Despite its humble entrance, **Doña Clorinda** (Plaza Constitución next to Hotel Pisaq, tel. 084/20-3051, 7 A.M.–7 P.M., $2–5) serves up safe, delectable *comida típica* ranging from *lomo saltado* ($3) to *rocoto relleno* ($4). There is a basic lunch menu for $2 or a more luxurious version for $5.

If you are in the mood for something quick, tasty, and cheap, try the *empanadas* made in a few old, wood-fired ovens around town. The bready concoction—stuffed with cheese, sliced onion, tomato, olives, and oregano—can be had for $0.50 each on the corner of the main square near the Hotel Pisaq or on Mariscal Castilla 372, one block away on the other end of the square.

For dessert, get homemade ice cream at **Helados Misk'y** (Puno, near Hotel Pisaq, 8 A.M.–7 P.M.).

Markets

The best supermarkets are **Sofis Market** (Bolognesi s/n, tel. 084/20-3017, 6:30 A.M.–10 P.M.) and **La Baratura** (Manuel Prado 105, 6 A.M.–10 P.M.).

INFORMATION AND SERVICES

The best info about Pisac is available from **Ulrike's Café**, **Paz y Luz**, or **Hotel Pisaq**, which also offers laundry, money exchange, and faxing.

There is a clinic and pharmacy above the plaza near the public parking area.

A better pharmacay is **Botica Claudio** (Amazonas 214, 9 A.M.–8 P.M.).

There is an **ATM machine** on the corner of the main square, near the Parador Turístico, and a store that changes foreign currency and travelers checks on the square near the church.

A **mailbox** is located on the main square inside the Restaurant Samana Wasi, which also sells

The high trail at Pisac skirts two residential areas.

stamps. There are **phone booths** at Sofis Market on Bolognesi and near the municipality on the main square. **Internet** is available in the Restaurant Valle Sagrado and on the corner of the plaza near the Parador Turístico de Pisac.

GETTING THERE AND AROUND

Buses for Pisac leave Cusco from below Tullumayo and Garcilaso every 20 minutes and charge $0.75 for the one-hour journey. For a 45-minute ride, hire a taxi in the Cusco's Plaza de Armas for $10. Buses drop passengers off at the bridge on the main highway, from which it is a three-block walk uphill to the market and main square. Return buses to Cusco leave from same spot every 15 minutes up until 7 P.M. Buses heading the opposite direction also stop here on the way to Yucay and then Urubamba (30–40 minutes, $0.50). Once in Pisac, taxis can be taken 8 km to the main Pisac ruins entrance ($3) or the upper level ($4).

HUCHUY CUSCO

After Ollantaytambo and Pisac, Huchuy Cusco is the next most important Inca ruin in the Sacred Valley. This site features a two-story *kallanka,* or Inca hall, that is nearly 40 meters long and topped off by a well-preserved third story of adobe—it is easy to imagine this adobe painted, as were the buildings in Cusco, and topped off with a pyramid of thick thatch. There are also terraces, a square, an Inca gate, and many other rougher buildings within a few hundred yards of the hall. The whole site commands a small plateau, 800 meters above the Sacred Valley, with spectacular views.

This was probably the royal estate once known as Caquia Jaquijahuana where, according to myth, Inca Viracocha hid when the Chancas threatened to invade Cusco in 1438. One of his sons, who later renamed himself Pachacútec, rose up and defeated the Chancas, thus beginning the meteoric rise of the Incas. After the conquest, the Spaniards found a mummy at this site—said to be that of Viracocha.

Reaching Huchuy Cusco is not easy, but it's worth the effort. The shortest way to get there is a three-hour, uphill hike from Lamay, a village between Pisac and Urubamba. The entrance to the footbridge that crosses the Río Urubamba is marked with a large blue sign from the National Institute of Culture.

Another highly recommended option is to approach Huchuy Cusco from the opposite direction in a two-day hike across the high plains from Cusco. The trip starts at Sacsayhuamán and Cusco and follows the original Inca trail to Calca, heading past finely wrought canals, villages, and several 4,000-meter passes. The total trip is 17 miles, including the final descent to Lamay, where you can catch a bus back to Cusco via Pisac. Both trips are described in detail in Peter Frost's *Exploring Cusco.* For either route, bring plenty of water and food as there is little along the way.

YUCAY

This quiet town, a few kilometers east of Urubamba, consists of a large, grassy plaza where soccer games are played in the shade of two massive pisonay trees reputed to be 450 years old. Various colonial homes, now hotels, front the square along with the restored colonial church of Santiago Apóstol. On the far end of the square, near the highway, lies the adobe palace of Sayri Túpac, who settled here after emerging from Vilcabamba in 1558. Away from the main square lie quiet, dusty streets and extensive Inca terracing on the hillsides near town. There are few services outside the hotels clustered around the square.

Accommodations

$25–50 The unpretentious **Hostal Y'llary** (Plaza Manco II 107, tel. 084/20-1112, $25 s, $30 d, includes breakfast) has rustic, large rooms with high ceilings and comfortable beds. The views from the flower garden are amazing, and it is also possible to pitch a tent in the yard ($5 pp).

$50–100: The luxurious **Sonesta Posada del Inca** (Plaza Manco II, Yucay 123, tel. 084/20-1107, reserves@sonestaperu.com, www.sonesta.com, $85, $99, includes breakfast) is like a small village with rooms spread out among plazas and gardens, courtyard fountains, a miniature crafts market, and a chapel. The hotel is built around the charming 16th-century Santa Catalina de Sena monastery, where 21 rooms are located. The modern, though colonial-style, building next door has another 40 rooms or so with high ceilings, cable TV, lock boxes, and bathrooms with tubs. There is also a nice restaurant ($15 lunch buffet), jewelry shop, ATM, and a full spa. Even if you don't stay here, stop in and see the excellent museum, which has a range of ceramics, *quipus,* and weavings from most of Peru's cultures, from the Chavín to the Inca.

The well-decorated **La Casona de Yucay** (Plaza Manco II 104, tel. 084/20-1455, casonayucay@terra.com.pe, $60 s, $80 d, includes buffet breakfast) is a colonial hacienda that has been converted into a hotel with large rooms and great views. The colonial sitting room is elegant, though the gardens need some work.

Mirador de los Inkas (Km 60.5 of the Pisac-Ollantaytambo highway, tel. 084/81-2409, miradorcollaguas@infonegocio.net.pe, www.miradordeloscollaguas.com, $80 s, $80 d) is a new riverside hotel owned by the Vellutino family, which runs a similar lodge in the Colca Canyon. The hotel occupies a magic spot next to the Río Urubamba's roaring Huarán rapids and just upstream from the foundations of an Inca hanging bridge. The rooms are built of stone and adobe and have exposed beams, carpeted floors, reading tables, and bathrooms with tiles brought all the way from Sabandía, a village near Arequipa. There is a good restaurant with river views, a terrace, cool bungalows for families, and a hot tub with bar for star viewing.

Food

Cusco's best-kept gastronomical secret is **Huayoccari Hacienda Restaurant** (Km. 64 of the Pisac-Ollantaytambo highway, call for directions beforehand, tel. 084/962-2224 or 084/22-6241, hsilabrador@latinmail.com, $35 pp). This elegant gourmet retreat, 2 km up a dirt road near

Yucay, is a converted country manor perched high on a ridge overlooking the Sacred Valley. Past a rustic courtyard, the restaurant's walls are lined with colonial paintings, altars, and ceramics collected by José Ignacio Lambarri, whose family has owned the land and nearby hacienda for more than three centuries. The garden terraces offer dazzling views, and digestive walks, past roses and fuchsias to Inca terraces and some of the most fertile farmland in Peru.

Apart from its privileged location, Huayoccari has the most sophisticated cuisine in all of Cusco. It is completely organic and, best of all, based on the hacienda's original recipes. Lunch begins with *sara lagua,* a cream soup made of local white corn, fresh cheese, and the herb huacatay. Main courses include steamed river trout with a sauce of herbs and fresh capers, or chicken rolled with fresh cheese and country bacon and covered with sauco-berry sauce. The whole meal builds toward the desserts, made of delectable fruits found only in Peru: cheese cake with aguaymanto marmelade, chirimoya meringue, or a sachatomate compote. Though off the beaten path, Huayoccari is well worth the trek for the food, the country setting, and the private collection of art. There are only a handful of tables, so make reservations well in advance. Huayocarri is between Pisac and Urubamba and can be reached via taxi from either town.

Getting There

From Cusco, buses leave for Yucay from the first block of Grau. Frequent buses pass Yucay's main square going one direction to Pisac (30 minutes) or to Urubamba (10 minutes) in the other.

Urubamba

Urubamba lies smack in the center of the Sacred Valley and thus makes a good base for exploring the valley. Ollantaytambo is 20 minutes down the valley one way and Pisac is 40 minutes the other. From here another highway climbs onto the high plains toward Chinchero, a weaving center with a Sunday market and Inca ruins, and Cusco.

Despite an atrocious highway strip, Urubamba is a relaxed and friendly town that grows on people who spend time there. The massive flow of tourism through the Sacred Valley—especially strong on the Pisac market days, Sunday, Tuesday, and Thursday—mostly bypasses Urubamba, which has just one good ruin and little else to attract tourists besides its pleasant square and a colonial cathedral (now, unfortunately, condemned and propped up in back with beams). Other towns like Ollantaytambo, or even Pisac, have more of a Quechua flavor, but none are as mellow as Urubamba. Recently several hip bars and cafés have sprung up in response to a stream of college students brought here by ProPeru and other student organizations.

The plains above Urubamba are spectacular: the snow-covered Cordillera Urubamba rises over a patchwork of russet and chocolate-brown fields. In the middle is Maras, a dense cluster of red tile roofs, and two other startling visual anomalies. Moray is a set of huge natural depressions in the earth that were elaborately terraced by the Incas. Salinas is a blinding-white salt mine that sprawls across the mountain slope.

With these sights plus mountain biking, rafting, and horseback riding, it is no surprise that Urubamba is home to the valley's best hotels—Incaland, Sol y Luna, and Sonesta Posada del Inca (in nearby Yucay). Because the day tours through the valley stop here for lunch, Urubamba also has the greatest concentration of good restaurants. A final Urubamba highlight worth mentioning is the Seminario ceramics studio (see *Shopping*).

MORAY AND SALINAS

If you want to soak in the Sacred Valley's spectacular scenery, spend time wandering around the high plains above Urubamba. First stop is Maras, a dusty town with a few colonial churches and *chicherías,* fermented corn-beer shops advertised by red or blue plastic bags tied to the end of wooden poles. There is also an ancient hatmaker

looking across the Sacred Valley from Maras

named Teodosio Argandaño Caviedes—his shop is near the corner of Leguía and Jesus. About 5 km further, or a half hour along a good dirt road, lie the four natural depressions of Moray (7:30 A.M.–5:15 P.M., daily, $2). These sinkholes, 150 meters deep, were caused by rain eroding the calcium-rich soil.

With its perfect terrracing, Moray appears at first glance to be a ceremonial center or a Greek-style ampitheater. But researchers have discovered that the pits harbor a cluster of microclimates. Graduations of sun, shade, and elevation among the terraces create dramatic differences in temperature. Irrigation canals and the discovery of different seeds on the terraces are additional clues that Moray was once a gigantic crops laboratory. It was here, perhaps, that the Incas learned to grow corn and potatoes in a variety of elevations, fueling the expansion of the empire.

On the nearby hills that lead down to the Urubamba Valley, the Incas once again transformed nature: a spring of warm, salty water was diverted into thousands of pools, where sunlight evaporates the water and leaves a thin crust of salt. The salt mines, or *Salinas,* continue to be worked by a collective of 260 salt miners from the nearby villages of Maras and Pichinjoto. (You may see this salt marketed overseas as "Peruvian pink salt.") Today there are 5,740 pools, or *pocitos,* each of which yield 150 kilos of unrefined salt per month. There is a dazzling, and oft-photographed, contrast between the barren hillsides and the snow-white salt pools, which visitors can explore along narrow, crunchy paths.

To reach Moray, take a Cusco-Urubamba bus and get off at the Máras turnoff (say *ramal a Maras, por favor*). *Colectivos* wait here and charge $6–9 for a half-day tour of Maras, Moray, and Salinas. A recommended company is Empresa Transporte Moray. To get from Moray to Salinas, car-bound travelers must return to Maras and then proceed another 5 km downhill to the salt mines. Another option is to get a ride to Maras (4 km) and then walk the remaining 7 km to Moray (two hours, mostly uphill), through a patchwork of fields. From Moray, it is a two-hour walk—ask for directions along the way—to the salt mines. A steep but beautiful path continues for another kilometer or two from Salinas to the Urubamba Valley, ending 5 km down from Urubamba and at the doorstep of the recommended Tunupa Restaurant. This whole circuit makes for an excellent full-day circuit on horse, bike, or foot, though many travelers elect to be dropped off at Salinas and take the scenic, one-hour walk to Urubamba.

ENTERTAINMENT AND EVENTS

Urubamba erupts in bullfights, dancing, and partying during the Pentecostal celebration of Señor Torrechayoc in late May or early June and then once again for Urubamba Day on November 9. An even better party, however, is Huayllabamba's Virgen de la Natividad, held September 7–10. This party gets better and better every year, thanks to sponsorship from Incaland owner Nick Asheshov and friends.

Urubamba's nightlife has improved with students. The best way to begin an evening is with an *empanada* and a beer at **La Esquina** on the main square. The owner of this pizza-and-empanada bar, a Lima transplant named Lucy, sings

---

WHERE FIESTAS ARE SERIOUS BUSINESS

With a final burst of drinking, dancing, and eating this past weekend we have at last wound up our annual participation in the fiesta of Our Lady of the Nativity, at Huallabamba, a pueblo just upstream from Urubamba.

It's serious business. We had to scour our section of the Sacred Valley for guinea pigs and barnyard fowl, because the tasteless supermarket chicken is not acceptable to Our Lady. We had been fattening up a flock of ducks and a handful of free-range pigs and earmarked suckling piglets for the fiesta. A steer was dispatched, and many of our guests undertook to bring along sheep, more piglets, maize, and the scores of other items that go into endless days and nights of jolly breakfasts, lunches, suppers, and non-stop Andean music and dancing. Each of the meals is a banquet, some attended by hundreds of guests.

We were *mayordomos,* or sponsors, for one of the dozen groups that, each with its own elaborate costume, its own music, its own ancient tradition, danced for Our Lady. Her dressed-up statue was paraded round town, up the hill to a chapel, all in a tradition-ridden timetable organized by no one. There's no coordinating committee and if anyone owns an electronic watch, they don't spend much time looking at it.

It would be misleading to say, though, that it's a clockwork operation. When my 12-year-old boy goes along for the rehearsals for the Capac Negro (*Millionaire Slaves of the Virgin*) dance group, in the weeks leading up to the fiesta, he has to wait till everyone else, including the fellow with the taped practice music, arrives. But on the day, you saw a score or so of lads each in elaborate uniform, danc-

ing with military precision to ancient Quechua tunes and rhythms, with dirges and chants that reach back thousands of years. Our Lady is just the latest in a long line of Apus, the Andean gods who reside on the snow peaks, some of them visible from Huallabamba.

A dozen more dance groups come along, with colorful costumes representing jungle Indians fighting the Incas, or the Incas fighting the Spaniards, or even, rather boring this one, barbers in top hats and morning coats, foot-long noses and scissors going snip-snip in time to weird Andean-medieval flute music.

One wonders what the contribution of these fiestas is to the gross domestic product. What do the World Bank people who drift by from time to time in their chauffeur-driven, lap-topped Toyota 4x4s think of all this? What say the Inter-American Development Bank, USAID, and the European Union development people with their tax-free incomes and diplomatic passports?

We can be pretty sure that they switch off their satellite-feed cell phones and join in. They may not be having much luck solving our poverty, but that doesn't mean they can't spot the kind of party that, as they would be the first to recognize, none of them could begin to organize for themselves. Huallabamba's *Virgen de la Natividad* is held September 7–10.

(Contributed by Nicholas Asheshov, a British journalist who has covered Peru for four decades. Asheshov heads the Planning Division of the Incaland Hotel and the Sacred Valley Railway, in Urubamba.)

whenever the spirit moves her (and her musician friends show up).

Other spots for sporadic night action include **Chez Mary,** across the street from La Esquina, and the nearby **Café Pintacha** at Bolognesi 523. The upstairs of the new **Uversa Bar** (Comercio and Arica, tel. 084/80-9729, 6 P.M. onwards), with its couches, blue walls, and elegant metal art, feels like a New York lounge.

The best watering hole and weekend dance spot is **Tequila Bar** (third block of Mariscal Castilla, tel. 084/80-1646, tequilaclub@hotmail.com, noon onwards). Within the course of a night, this Jeckyl-and-Hyde place can swing from mellow artist pub to Wild West bar, with fists (and beer bottles!) flying.

SHOPPING

When in Urubamba, do not miss **Seminario Ceramics** (Barriózabal 111, tel. 084/20-1002, kupa@terra.com.pe, www.ceramicseminario.com, 8 A.M.–5 P.M.). With Pablo Seminario focusing on form and Marilú Behar on color, this husband-and-wife team began to crank out ceramics out of a small home in Urubamba two decades ago. Thanks to international recognition and lucrative contracts (including a deal with Pier One Imports), their original adobe workshop has blossomed into an expansive, garden-filled complex where visitors can pet llamas, watch an educational video, and see the whole ceramics-making process. The couple's workshop produces a range of objects from compotes and coffee cups to sculptures and large painting frames adorned with delicate touches of silver. Everything is handmade, painted with natural mineral oxides, and kiln-fired.

For upscale shopping, head to an outlet of **Alpaca Mon Repos** (Conchatupac s/n, across from El Maizal, tel. 084/20-1174, monrepos@qnet.com.pe, www.monrepos-peru.com), a Cucsobased clothing store.

SPORTS AND RECREATION
Hiking, Biking, and Horseback Riding

Urubamba is a fast-growing center of adventure sports, including horseback riding, mountain biking, rafting, trekking, and parapenting. There are some highly recommended horseback rides—that can also be done on foot or mountain bike—on both sides of the Urubamba Valley. The sun in the Sacred Valley is intensely bright, so bring sun hat and lotion. It is best to get an early start to avoid the often cloudy (sometimes rainy) afternoons.

To the north (snow-covered mountain side), several mule tracks lead up valleys to high passes on the Cordillera Vilcabamba. On the other side are remote Quechuan villages in the Lares Valley, a journey of several days with an option of returning by car at the end.

One of these valleys, the Pumahuanca, is a pleasant half-day trip that combines streams glinting in the morning sun, a series of microclimes including forests of rhododendrons and native quenua trees and, at the turnaround point, ruins of several two-story Inca buildings. The other valley above Urubamba dead-ends at Chicón, the glaciated peak (5,530 m) that looms above the village. This peak is rarely climbed, even though it is one of the easier summits in the Cusco area—see Cusco agencies for more info.

For those who can take a full day on a horse or on a bike, there is a breathtaking circuit on the south side of the valley that traverses the high plains around Maras and Moray and then descends via the salt mines to Urubamba. The scenery is spectacular.

Good Peruvian *paso* horses in the valley are owned, and cared for, by Edward van Brunschot, a Peruvian-Dutch equestrian expert with a tour company named **Perol Chico** (Grau 203, tel. 084/62-4475, info@perolchico.com, www.perolchico.com, 10 percent SAE discount). The pampering begins at 5 A.M. when horses are given a mixture of foods that include oats, wheat, corn, soya, molasses, minerals, and salt. By 6 A.M. they have digested that and by 7 A.M. they are fed more grass. By 8 A.M. grooming begins, before clients take their first riding lessons—even experienced riders must pass a competency test—at 9 A.M. In the style of Spanish *hacendados,* Brunschot outfits riders with a large-brimmed straw hat, a poncho, and a gourmet lunch.

Incaland rents mountain bikes and a half-

Salinas has over 5,740 salt pools.

dozen trail horses, which are especially suited for the steep ride up the Pumahuanca Valley. Owner Nicholas Asheshov, together with Colorado horse packer Gary Ziegler, designs custom horse trips throughout the surrounding mountains. Contact Nick Asheshov at tel. 084/20-1126 to arrange a trip.

Sol y Luna also rents mountain bikes and easily has the biggest and best collection of *paso* horses in the valley. These elegant animals, which kick their feet out to one side for a smooth ride, are best for the Maras-Moray-Salinas loop or a flat loop around the valley (they are not well-suited, however, for the steep Pumahuanca ride).

All of the Cusco rafting agencies descend the Río Urubamba, which is at its wildest during the high-water months from December to May. As the river drops between June and November, the agencies run the steeper, lower section that ends just past Ollantaytambo, though the rapids rarely exceed Class II. The water itself, unfortunately, is somewhat polluted, with plastic festooning the banks. A better, though further out, option is the Río Apurímac (see Cusco agencies).

Paragliding

Apart from running the Valley's best hotel, Marie-Hélène Miribel and Franz Schilter also offer parapent lessons and are the only instructors in Cusco with international certification. They charge $100 for a tandem one-hour flight, taking off from a nearby mountain and landing in the valley itself.

ACCOMMODATIONS
Under $10

There is a good camping spot by where the salt mines hit the road. Urubamba offers few budget options, outside of several seedy hostels that cater mainly to truck drivers. **La Casa de la Abuela** (Bolivar 272, tel. 084/962-2975, lacasadelaabuela@hotmail.com, $9) has a few pleasant bunk rooms, with shared bathroom, in an enclosed yard behind their restaurant. A final option, in an unfortunate modern building with restaurant, is **Hostal Torrechayoc** (second block of Mariscal Castilla, tel. 084/20-1033, d $9).

$10–25

Los Geranios (Cabo Conchatupa s/n, tel. 084/20-1093, $12 s, $15 d), best known for its lunch buffets, has recently built a few rooms with lots of sunlight, private baths, and hot water. These are an excellent value for Urubamba.

$50–100

Incaland (Ferrocarril s/n, tel. 084/20-1126, ventasurubamba@sacredvalleyrail.com, www.sacredvalleyrailway.com, $68 s, $80 d, includes buffet breakfast) is the only hotel in Peru, and one of the few in the world, to have its own train station. Guests awaken to breakfast, board a train at 6:10 A.M., and arrive in Machu Picchu two hours later—an hour or two before everyone else arrives from Cusco. Apart from this notable advantage, Incaland has humongous bungalows with separate sitting rooms, new bathrooms, and wood floors, spread out in a 26-acred, lush botanical garden of native Andean fauna on the banks of the Río Urubamba.

The restaurant offers buffets both at breakfast (fresh fruit, eggs, quinoa porridge, corn bread,

afternoon shadows on Moray

etc.) and lunch (alpaca medallions, fried trout, tomato-basil-cheese salads), with local musicians playing in the evenings. Other perks include friendly staff, Olympic-size pool, herd of alpacas, and a half-dozen sturdy trail horses perfect for a jaunt to the salt mines or the Pumahuanca Valley. The owner, British journalist Nicholas Asheshov, lives with his family at the hotel and is a gold mine of information on Peru, which he has written about for four decades.

The **Hotel San Agustín Monasterio de la Recoleta** (Recoleta s/n, tel. 084/20-1004, $75 s, $80 d) occupies a stunning, 16th-century Franciscan monastery, though erratic service continues to keep guests away. There is a modern addition with a few spectacular rooms upstairs, outfitted with exposed beams, stone showers, and sun windows ($100 d). Rooms in the old section ($60 d) are surrounded by a stone courtyard and cannot be renovated because of historical restrictions—they are nicer than the bland modern rooms ($80 d). All rooms have private baths.

The **Hotel San Agustín Urubamba** (Ferrocarril s/n, tel. 084/20-1443, $69 s, $79 d) is livelier than its sister hotel next door, but rooms are smaller and not well decorated. There are touches of colonial architecture, but mostly this hotel is characterized by manicured gardens, a small but crystal-clear pool, and a full spa with sauna and massage services ($15 per hour). The one drawback is the proximity (10 yards) to the highway, so ask for a room in back. Both Agustín hotels offer deep discounts—more than half—for guests traveling without an agency.

Over $100
Our vote for the most elegant, luxurious hotel in the Sacred Valley goes to the **M Sol y Luna Hotel** (tel. 084/20-1620, www.hotelsolyluna.com, solluna@terra.com.pe, $100 s, $115 d, includes buffet breakfast, 10 percent SAE discount), opened in 1998 by Marie-Hélène Miribel and Franz Schilter. This French-Swiss couple have carefully designed every last detail of their 28 round bungalows, in-

cluding terra-cotta tiles, exposed beams, marble bathrooms, king-size beds, and stained-glass windows in the shape of the moon. The $14.50 poolside buffet is exquisite, featuring a range of fresh vegetables, pastas, alpaca and chicken dishes, and a dessert spread that includes cake made from lúcuma, the intoxicatingly tasty fruit. Groups are often treated to *pachamanca* cooking with *marinera* dance demonstrations. Plan on spending time here to stroll through the hotel's gardens, play tennis, lounge by the pool, work out at the gym, or check into the spa, which includes Jacuzzi and massage. Nearly two dozen Peruvian horses (*caballos de paso*) are lodged in elegant stables in the back and available for half- and full-day rides. If that weren't enough, the hotel also rents mountain bikes, and the owners are the only parapent instructors in Cusco with international certification. One downside of the hotel is the extreme cost of long-distance calls ($3 per minute to Lima) and extremely slow Internet connection($18 per hour)—for these services consider taking a five-minute *motocar* into town ($1).

FOOD

International

The unpretentious **La Casa de la Abuela** (Bolivar 272, tel. 084/962-2975, lacasadelaabuela@hotmail.com, $4) has wood-fired pizzas, pastas that go far beyond your typical bolognesi, and a highly recommended chicken curry. It all comes out of a tiny kitchen run by Señora Yoni Carpio, a very kind and professionally trained cook. She also makes a range of Andean and vegetarian dishes. The atmosphere is quirky but charming with Charlie Chaplin posters, disco lights, and family photos on windowsills. You can play ping-pong while you wait for your food to be served. Another pizza place that gets high marks in Urubamba is **Finestra** (Mariscal Castilla).

Three student cafés are also nightspots. **Café Pintacha** (Bolognesi 523, tel. 084/74-8525, 11 A.M.–11 P.M.) offers frozen lemonade, hamburgers, grilled chicken sandwiches, *taquitos,* and hot chocolate with bay leaves. **Chez Mary** (main square, tel. 084/43-4771, 7 A.M.–10 P.M.) is a funky pub-restaurant serving *cebiche,* garlic trout,

sandwiches, soups, ice creams, and vegetarian food. Across the street, **La Esquina** (main square, 7:30 A.M.–10:30 P.M.) serves breakfast as well as empanadas and pizza, and is one of the few places in all of Peru to make guacamole (called *ensalada de palta*). These places come alive at night.

Peruvian

The Sacred Valley day tours use Urubamba as a lunch spot, so there are a half dozen restaurants that offer good lunch buffets. The best, and newest, of these is **Tunupa,** which is just past Urubamba on a dirt road that leads to the salt mines. **Los Geranios** (Cabo Conchatupa s/n, tel. 084/20-1093, noon–5 P.M. daily, $9 buffet) is the least pretentious and most authentic of a group of restaurants on Urubamba's main drag. Other excellent buffets are available at **Incaland** ($12) and **Sol y Luna Hotel** ($14.50)—see *Accommodations.* For inexpensive, good Peruvian food locals head to **Las Ñustas** (Mariscal Castilla).

INFORMATION AND SERVICES

There's a **police station** on Palacio s/n (tel. 084/20-1012)

The **town clinic** is on 9 de Noviembre s/n (tel. 084/20-1032, lab open 8 A.M.–1 P.M.). The best healthcare option is to call Dr. Fernando Dávilos, a specialist in natural remedies, on his cell phone, tel. 084/69-0223.

There is an **ATM** on the highway in front of Urubamba, near the **Banco de la Nación** in the first block of Mariscal de Castilla (tel. 084/20-1291). Money and travelers checks can be exchanged at the **Western Union** on Comercio 131 (tel. 084/20-1737).

The **post office** is located on the main square, along with several pay phones under the municipality awning. Painfully slow Internet is available at **Pintacha Café** and at another locale beyond the main square set up by an American exchange student with ProPeru.

ProPeru

This highly recommended organization, run by a Peruvian named Richard Webb, organizes home stays for college students (and older folk too) in

Urubamba, Calca, and other areas in Peru. Students take classes in art, history, anthropology, and Spanish and work on service projects that range from reforestation to setting up a women's shelter or the town's first Internet café. ProPeru receives rave reviews from its students and is surely one of the better foreign study programs in Peru. For more information, contact Richard Webb at 212/353-6158, richard@properu.org, or www.properu.org. Other volunteer organizations in Urubamba include Casa de los Milagros, which works with disabled children.

Massages and Ayahuasca Sessions

There are a number of masseuses and alterna-
tive therapy practitioners in Urubamba. Gabriela Jiménez (cell phone tel. 084/968-9707) advertises an esoteric massage that includes natural healing oils made from local herbs. Mario Orihuela Fort (tel. 084/20-1455) was trained at Norway's Moravia Monastic University in the art of Kineirgy, which he describes as "the art and science of moving energies with the help of the hands." An English-speaking couple named Gerardo and Diana (tel. 084/63-6959) are the masseuses at the Hotel San Agustín spa. Shamanic Healing (shamanic_healing@yahoo .com, tel. 084/9-65-5509) offers hallucinogenic ayahuasca and San Pedro ceremonies at a riverside *Inipi,* or sweat lodge.

AYAHUASCA: VINE OF THE SOUL

Ayahuasca (pronounced "ah-yah-waska") is a Quechuan word meaning "vine of the soul," though it is called by dozens of names, including *yagé* in Colombia and *caapi* in Brazil. A ceremonial stone cup found in the jungle of Ecuador is proof that the mind-altering brew has been used in Amazon rituals for at least 2,500 years. At least 72 cultural groups in the Amazon use it for rituals today, and there are even a handful of modern-day religious movements that use ayahuasca in their sacraments, most notably Santo Daime, www.santodaime.org, which is active in Europe and the San Francisco Bay Area in the United States.

Modern-day chemist J. C. Callaway calls ayahuasca "one of the most sophisticated drug delivery systems in existence." The ayahuasca experience is the result of a precise interaction of chemicals contained in different plants, including harmala and dimethyl-tryptamine (DMT) alkaloids. Though DMT would usually be metabolized and deactivated by an enzyme in the human stomach, certain chemicals from another plant knock out the enzyme and allow DMT to circulate freely into the brain, triggering powerful visions. How Amazon *curanderos* stumbled on this complex combination of plants and vines is a mystery.

But ayahuasca is much more than just a chemical synergy. Research has shown repeatedly that ayahuasca sessions outside of the jungle, and without a *curandero,* are nowhere near as powerful as those conducted inside the Amazon. The experience is fed, and seemingly magnified, by the life and power of the Amazon.

The *curandero* is also an integral part of the ayahuasca ceremony. He controls every step of the experience through *ícaros,* the magical songs that are used only in ayahuasca sessions. A *curandero* is measured by the *ícaros* that he knows, which can be in a variety of languages (Spanish, Quechua, Cocama and other Amazon dialects) and have different purposes. *ícaros,* sometimes referted to as "painted songs," control the substance of ayahuasca visions. They can be used to intensify a vision, produce joy or feelings of love, or return a wandering soul back to its owner. When a person wants an ayahuasca experience to end, the *curandero* uses an *ícaro* to bring that person back down to earth.

Though unpleasant, vomiting is essential to the ayahuasca experience. *Curanderos* say vomiting purges participants of their bad energies and allows them to proceed with their visions, which often involve regressions to long-forgotten traumas. Beat Generation intellectuals William S. Burroughs and Allen Ginsberg (authors of the *Yage Letters*) began the Western trivialization of ayahuasca in the 1950s and early 1960s when they treated it as just another psychedelic drug. This has led to by U.S. travelers who come to the Amazon for short and easy experiences and often leave disappointed.

GETTING THERE

From Cusco, *combis* for Urubamba leave from the first block of Grau near the bridge (1.5 hours, $1.25). *Combis* drop passengers at Urubamba's gas station on the main drag, where frequent transport continues for the 20-minute ride to Ollantaytambo and Pisac (40 minutes).

Urubamba is also home to a new train that runs from here to Machu Picchu each day, passing Ollantaytambo en route. The **Vistadome train** ($69 round trip, $42 one-way) leaves from Inca-land at 6:10 A.M. each morning and arrives in Aguas Calientes at 8:20 A.M. The train leaves Aguas Calientes at 4:45 P.M. and is one of the later after-noon trains, leaving visitors more times at the ruins. It arrives back in Urubamba at 7:10 P.M.

GETTING AROUND

Motocars are ubiquitous in Urubamba and can be contracted cheaply to arrive at the Chicón or Pumahuanca roadheads or for getting to Yucay. **Sol y Luna** offers a full-day valley tour to Ollantaytambo and Pisac, in private car with lunch included, for $95 per day. Another op-tion is to contract a private driver and car—Ollantaytambo and Pisac together is $35, while one or the other is $20. Ask your hotel for recommendations.

The western fascination with psychedelics and cool drug trips is absolutely foreign to Amazon *curanderos*. For them ayahuasca is a sacred sub-stance—*el remedio,* the ultimate medicine that can heal anything from a snakebite or depres-sion to the poor welfare of an entire tribe. A mas-ter *curandero* can also use it to see into the future, invoke magical powers, and communicate with the spirit world.

Maestro curanderos ingest ayahuasca and a se-ries of other hallucinogenic and purgative jungle medicines, such as tobacco juice, during a rigorous diet that can last months, even years. This diet often involves nothing more than plantains, rice, and perhaps fish, with absolutely no salt, spices, fat, alcohol, or caffeine. Sexual abstinence is key to the experience as well. Ayahuasca and other med-icines are taken repeatedly, perhaps once a week or every few days.

Foreigners who want to try ayahuasca should first visit www.biopark.org, an informative web-site with links to the California-based quarterly *Ayahuasca* and the highly responsible **El Tigre Journeys** (tel. 065/22-3595, 303/449-5479 in the U.S., otorongo_blanco@terra.com.pe). This agency offers weeklong "SpiritQuests" run by Howard Lawler, also known as Otorongo Blanco, an Amer-ican who used to run the Desert Museum in Tuc-son, Arizona, before moving nearly a decade ago to the Iquitos area. El Tigre Journeys uses only *maestro*

curanderos and has participants follow a strict diet during a week that typically includes three cere-monies. There are also a range of special trips around Peru and during solstice and other special times of the year.

We also highly recommend the Takiwasi Center (www.takiwasi.com), which offers week-long ayahuasca seminars that involve *maestro curanderos* and meticulous preparation. A benefit of trying ayahuasca at the Takiwasi Center is that the funds are used to supplement the center's remarkable mission of treatment for drug addiction.

Both of these organizations run medical checks on all participants in order to ensure a safe experi-ence. When combined with ayahuasca, anti-de-pressants such as Prozac, Effexor, Zoloft or Wellbutrin can cause elevated levels of serotonin, leading to elevated blood pressure, coma, and even death. At least six weeks should pass between end-ing these drugs and taking ayahuasca. Other med-icines requiring caution include St. John's Wort and any sedatives, tranquilizers, antihistamines, amphetamines, diet pills and medicines for allergy, cold, or hypertension. Those with high blood pres-sure, heart conditions, or a history of schizophrenia should not take ayahuasca.

When performed properly, an ayahuasca cere-mony can be a life-changing experience. Ultimately, this is why in the Amazon ayahuasca has always been considered powerful medicine.

Ollantaytambo

Ollantaytambo is the last town in the Sacred Valley before the Río Urubamba plunges through steep gorges toward Machu Picchu. It is the best preserved Inca village in Peru, with its narrow alleys, street water canals, and trapezoidal doorways. The Inca temple and fortress above town is second in beauty only to Machu Picchu. In the terraced fields entering town, men still use foot plows, or *chaquitacllas*, to till fields and plant potatoes. There are endless things to explore in and around Ollantaytambo, which is framed by the snow-capped Verónica mountain and surrounded on all sides by Inca ruins, highways, and terraces. Whisking through Ollantaytambo, as most travelers do, is a great shame. Stay and get to know the place.

Ollantaytambo is also in the throes of a tremendous struggle to save its way of life against the mass forces of tourism and development. Trinket sellers have crowded the areas in front of the Inca temple and the train station. Non-descript pizzerias are creeping onto the main square, which is continually shaken by the passing of massive trucks bound for the Camisea pipeline in the jungle around Quillabamba. One solution to these problems, as resident Wendy Weeks suggests, is to move the train station outside of town and have visitors enter as the Incas did—through the main gate and *on foot*.

The town's saving grace, and what should carry it through its present crisis, is the tremendous sense of community that is palpable to anyone who pauses here. A cadre of researchers, lead by English archaeologist Anne Kendall, have spent considerable time researching Inca farming technology and have restored hundreds of farming terraces and aqueducts. A new museum, founded by Kendall and directed by Joaquín Randall, has blossomed into a showcase of local life and includes a ceramics workshop and a program to recover lost weaving techniques.

HISTORY

Ollantaytambo was occupied long before the Incas by the Quillques, who built some of the rougher buildings at Pumamarca and on the ridge near the Ollantaytambo temple itself. After Inca emperor Pachacútec conquered this area around 1440, construction began on a ceremonial center and royal estate that housed an estimated 1,000 workers year-round. What Ollantaytambo is most famous for, however, is a 1537 battle in which the Incas defeated a Spanish army—and nearly massacred it altogether.

The battle happened during the 1536–37 Inca rebellion, when Manco Inca was forced to withdraw his troops to Ollantaytambo after being defeated by the Spanish at Sacsayhuamán. Hernando Pizarro arrived at Ollantaytambo one morning at dawn with 70 cavalry and 30 foot soldiers. But Manco Inca's men were waiting on the terraces of the sun temple, which had been hastily converted into a fort. Pedro Pizarro wrote afterward, "We found it so well fortified that it was a thing of horror."

From high on the upper terraces, Manco Inca commanded his troops from horseback—co-

© RENÉE DEL GAUDIO AND ROSS WEHNER

imperial Inca lintel at Ollantaytambo

opting the symbol of Spanish strength—as jungle archers shot volleys of arrows and Inca soldiers fired off slingshots and rolled boulders. Sensing defeat, the Spaniards retreated, but Manco Inca pulled a final surprise. On cue, he diverted the Río Urubamba and flooded the plains below Ollantaytambo, causing the Spaniards' horses to founder in the mud. Manco's forces fought the Spanish all the way to Cusco, where Pizarro waited for Diego de Almagro to return from his Chile campaign with reinforcements. Manco Inca meanwhile recognized the growing strength of the Spaniards and withdrew to Vilcabamba.

After Manco's departure, the whole valley became an *encomienda* for Hernando Pizarro, who pursued Manco deep into Vilcabamba and raided his camp in 1539. Manco narrowly escaped, but his wife and sister, Cura Ocllo, was captured and brought to Ollantaytambo. After Manco refused to surrender, Francisco Pizarro had Cura Ocllo stripped, whipped, and killed with arrows. To make sure Manco got the message, they floated her body down the Río Urubamba toward Vilcabamba, where Manco's troops found her.

About two-thirds of the inhabitants of the Sacred Valley died of diseases brought by the Spanish. The descendants of the survivors were put to work in the haciendas that sprung up in the valley, often the result of Spaniards marrying Inca elite. One of these, the Hacienda Sillque, is today a ruin of adobe walls and arched doorways, about 20 km west of Ollantaytambo. A road down the Urubamba Valley to Quillabamba was begun in 1895. It was this road that Hiram Bingham took to *discover* Machu Picchu in 1911. In the 1920s, the road was converted into the train line that now carries travelers to Machu Picchu.

SIGHTS

Ask your bus driver to let you off 1 km before Ollantaytambo at the original Inca trail, which follows the hillside on the right (north) side of town. To your left is the plain that Manco Inca flooded in the 1537 battle against the Spanish. The path leads up to the town's restored terraces and through a massive Inca gate, through which a water channel still runs. The path then joins with the road past the Wall of 100 Niches, whose inward slant indicates this was the inside—not the outside—of a roadside building (or maybe the road went through the building).

day one on the Inca Trail with Verónica in the background

Once in the main plaza, head a half block north to the **Museo CATCCO** (tel. 084/20-4024, www.catcco.org, 8 A.M.–10 P.M. Mon.–Fri., 8 A.M.–8 P.M. Sat.–Sun., $1, donations welcome), which is one of the best ethnographical museums in the Andes. Guides for day hikes can also be hired at the museum, which offers a tourist information center, Internet, a store, and a ceramics workshop and hosts a variety of lectures, concerts, and other events. Ask to see the best book yet written on Ollantaytambo, J. P. Protzen's *Inca Architecture and Construction at Ollantaytambo.*

Behind the museum is the original Inca town, named *Qozqo Ayllu,* which is laid out in the form of a trapezoid and bisected by narrow, irrigated alleys. Oversized trapezoidal doorways open in the courtyards of homes, or *kanchas,* occupied continuously ever since Pachacútec's time.

Ⓜ OLLANTAYTAMBO TEMPLE

The other half of Ollantaytambo, *Araqama Ayllu,* is across the Río Patacancha. The main square is fronted with a series of monumental buildings, and above is the temple that was being constructed when the Spaniards arrived—and was later converted into a fortress by Manco Inca.

Two hundred steps lead up terraces to a double-jamb gateway and the **Temple of Ten Niches,** a long wall with odd protuberances. Some say these bumps draw heat away from the slabs, preventing them from expanding. Others say they somehow served in the transport of the blocks. Or perhaps the Incas valued them as we do today, for the graceful shadows they cast across the stone.

Above is the unfinished **Temple of the Sun,** considered one of the masterpieces of Inca stonework. Six giant monoliths of pink rhyolite are perfectly slotted together with thin slices of stone and oriented to glow with the rising sun. Traces of the *chacana* symbols and pumas that once decorated the walls can still be seen. What is unusual about the wall are the long straight lines—and the molten bronze that was poured in the T-joints to hold the wall together. These features indicate the wall was probably the handiwork of the Lake Titicaca's Colla Indians, who were brought to work here by Pachacútec as part of the forced labor system known as *mitimayo.* According to J. P. Protzen, the wall was probably intended to be one side of a great platform, which

Temple of Ten Niches, Ollantaytambo

OLLANTAYTAMBO'S WINTER STARS

May can get off to a warm start in the Sacred Valley, so warm that even within a few weeks of June's winter solstice, it seems like summer.

Summery, green-season clouds wrap round the folds of the mountains in the early morning, but the snow peaks appear against a blue sky before midday and the bright, clear nights of winter start soon afternoon. You get a wonderful star show from 6 P.M. onwards.

The moon comes over the mountains to the east like a searchlight. When it's half or quarter-size, or not yet up, you get a gallery view of thousands of stars. It's a planetarium, and the Incas and their predecessors thought of it that way, too.

The Incas saw the Sacred Valley, which is separated from Cusco by the high rolling farmland and llama pastures of the Chinchero massif, as the reflection of the Milky Way. And the valley, at 2,900 meters, with what's known as an Andean subtropical climate, was literally heaven on Earth. Cold, complex Cusco, at 3,400 meters, was the political capital, where they went to work.

Edgar Elorietta, an amiable agronomist born and bred in Urubamba, has devoted much of his free time over the past several years to an effort to relate the silent stones of the great Inca ruins in the Sacred Valley, especially Ollantaytambo, to the movements of the stars and the planets. These mystic connections, he says, were destroyed by the conquistadores four and a half centuries ago. Edgar also tries to tie in the remaining stories and myths of the Quechua descendents of the Incas who live in the highland communities beneath the snow peaks of the Cordillera Urubamba.

Edgar's efforts so far have already produced the discovery of a massive pyramid-like series of terraces, walls, and underground structures at Ollantaytambo that not even the Spaniards, much less today's archaeologists, had spotted.

According to Edgar, this was the original Pacaritambo, from where the four Ayar brothers emerged to found the Inca empire.

Edgar is no romantic New Age visionary seeking into past and future lives. He says he is the only person in the Sacred Valley who *hasn't* seen any UFOs—Sky Brothers, as the shaman set nicely calls them—in his thousands of sky-gazing hours, though he has occasionally seen some lights zig-zagging across the night sky that were clearly not aircraft or satellites. "But I wouldn't call them UFOs," he says.

One of the most impressive sights in the Andes is the moment just after first light on the day of the winter solstice, June 21, when a first sharp ray of sunlight suddenly hits a walled tennis court–sized section of Edgar's Ollantaytambo Pyramid. A few moments later another ray picks out another walled section of the ruin, which runs for nearly 750 meters.

It's a show and it's dramatic. It was clearly carefully designed and planned hundreds or thousands of years ago by people who had an extraordinary grasp of architecture, engineering, astronomy—all things that we can understand and appreciate—together with a highly developed social, political, and religious sensibility—all things that we no longer have.

To watch the June solstice show, you have to be high on the other side of the river from Ollantaytambo. It's an easy hour or so walking from the Inca bridge just upstream from town. A mule path leads west and downstream, rising past Inca terraces to a point where you have a gallery view of a fine slice of the Sacred Valley.

(Contributed by Nicholas Asheshov, a British journalist who has covered Peru for four decades. Asheshov heads the Planning Division of the Incaland Hotel and the Sacred Valley Railway, in Urubamba.)

Giant slabs of pink rhyolite form the unfinished Temple of the Sun.

seems likely with the unfinished blocks, rough walls, and plaza nearby. It is uncertain why the construction stopped—perhaps it was Pachacútec's death, a rebellion of the Colla Indians, the smallpox epidemic of 1527, or the arrival of the Spaniards.

To the left of the plaza, the **Cachicata quarry** appears high on the hillside. The Incas dragged boulders weighing up to 52 tons down the mountain, across the Río Urubamba and the valley floor, and then up a steep ramp—the top of which is at a 25-degree angle, three times that allowed on most U.S. highways! Ollantaytambo expert Vincent Lee used sleds and levers to show how the Incas moved such blocks up the ramp, which still leads up the hillside to the temple. On the ridge above the temple are rougher buildings and the **Incahuatana,** the hitching place of the Inca, where prisoners may have been lashed into the human-sized portals.

At the base of the ruins are the **Princess Baths,** a half dozen fountains adorned with *chacana* symbols. Some of the fountains are engineered in such a way as to cause a whirlpool that allows sediment to drop before the water continues over a delicately shaped spout. On the steep flanks of Pinculluna, the sacred hill that rises above the Inca town, are the ruins of several granaries, which glow in the afternoon sun.

WALKS AROUND OLLANTAYTAMBO

There are many walks along Inca trails in the Sacred Valley above town, the Inca breadbasket that produced food for 100,000 people. A good hike begins at the village of Huilloq and descends the valley along the dirt road back to Ollantaytambo. This hike passes through the town of Markaqocha, with its beautiful chapel and pre-Hispanic ruins. Along the way, a two-hour side hike leads up an Inca trail to Pumamarca, a complex of buildings centered around a courtyard that shows both Inca and pre-Inca building styles. There are also high walls built in the typical zigzag fasion, fashioned out of stones set in adobe. This route leads above the huge, and recently restored, terraces of Sima Pukio.

Another fine walk begins at the Inca bridge near town and follows a fairly well-preserved Inca trail to Cachicata, the stone quarry perched 700 to 900 meters above the valley floor across from Ollantaytambo. It was here that the great stone blocks were slid down the hillside and hauled across the river to Ollantaytambo. There are three separate stone quarries, within half a kilometer of one another, littered with massive chiseled blocks and small *chullpas,* or burial towers. The western and highest quarry contains mysterious needle-shaped blocks that are up to 7 meters long. From Cachicata, it is possible to see that the terraces below the Ollantaytambo ruins form a pyramid shape, with one 750-meter-long wall aligning with the rays of the winter solstice. New Age theorists Fernando and Edgar Elorieta believe this is the original Pakaritampu, where the four original Inca brothers emerged to found Cusco. A few hours' walk above the Cachicata is a perfect Inca gate that frames Salcantay in the background.

ENTERTAINMENT AND EVENTS

During the **Fiesta de Reyes** (the Celebration of the Kings), a revered image of Jesus is brought down to Ollantaytambo from Marcaqocha, a town high up in the Patacancha Valley. The event includes a solemn procession around Ollantaytambo's main square, which involves images of the three wise men.

During the eight-day *carnaval* season in late January and early February the upper Patacancha Valley explodes into a series of traditions: cow branding, offerings to mountain *apus* by local priests, *wallata* (the dance of the condor), and ritual battles between towns that are now fought with mature fruit instead of rocks.

The town's most important celebration is the **Señor de Choquequilca**, which happens during the Pentecost at the end of May or early June.

The festival dates back to the miraculous appearance of a wooden cross near the town's Inca bridge. A chapel dedicated to El Señor de Choquequilca was completed in the main square in 1995.

Nightlife
The **Bar Amazónico La Puzanga** (Calle de Medio, 5–11 P.M. daily) is half a block north of the main square in the Inca town. Though it sits more than 2,700 meters up, this eccentric bar somehow bills itself as *a mystery of the jungle.*

CUSCO'S BATTLE WITH THE BOTTLE

Every time travelers buy a plastic water bottle, they are contributing to a solid waste problem that is reaching epic proportions not only in Cusco but all over Peru. The best way to understand the problem is to raft along Cusco's Río Urubamba, where tree roots are blanketed in thick gobs of plastic bags and beaches are completely covered with plastic bottles.

What resources Peru's municipal governments have are used to fight poverty, not improve the environment. There is no plastic recycling in Peru, so everything ends up in open landfills or, as is the case with the Urubamba, floating downstream to the Amazon. Nearly 200 million plastic bottles are produced every month in Peru alone, and a good chunk of these are consumed by tourists—who need a few liters of purified water for each day in Peru.

Recently a plastic boycott campaign has been started by longtime Ollantaytambo resident Joaquín Randall (for more information, visit the Museo CATCCO or www.catcco.org).
Here's how travelers can do their part to resolve Peru's plastic addiction:
- Carry a Nalgene or other water bottle and fill it with treated or boiled water
- Buy sodas and water in refillable glass bottles
- Demand that your hotel provide water tanks (*bidones*) or at the very least boiled water for refilling bottles
- Re-use plastic bags over and over and do not accept new ones.
- Spread the word.

The owner is from the jungle city of Pucallpa and makes a variety of drinks involving local sugarcane and jungle roots. There are several other bars nearby, including **Kusikuy Bar** (further along on Medio) and **Señor Ganso** (Lares, three blocks from square, 9 A.M.–11 P.M.).

SHOPPING

On Calle del Medio in Inca town, Julio Farfán Fuentes carves picture frames out of cedar and has Inca tools and weapons on exhibition. There is a ceramics shop and a few crafts shops between the two squares that sell weavings, marble carvings, wood masks, and older weavings (40 years old, apparently). The nonprofit store at Museo CATCCO sells weavings and ceramics, and profits go directly back to the instruction workshops. El Albergue—see *Accommodations*—has an eclectic store. The Ollantaytambo train station and ruins parking lot are clogged with vendors hawking cheap weavings and other touristy trinkets.

SPORTS AND RECREATION

Cusco's rafting agencies head past Ollantaytambo down the Class II–III rapids of Río Urubamba (see *Sports and Recreation* in the *Cusco* section). More information about the walks described above is available from the Museo CATCCO. The bar Señor Ganso (Lares, three blocks from square, 9 A.M.–11 P.M.) leads horseback trips in the area. A favorite mountain biking route is the long downhill from *Abra Malaga,* the high pass above town leading to Quillabamba.

ACCOMMODATIONS
Under $10
Unlike Urubamba, Ollantaytambo has plenty of good budget options for backpackers taking the morning or afternoon train to Machu Picchu. **Hostal Ollanta** (Plaza de Armas, tel. 084/20-4116, $4.50 s, $9 d) is the town's best budget option. Rooms are clean, with wood floors, and arranged around a cement courtyard. The shared bathrooms are new and have hot water. At **Hostal La Ñusta** (Ocubamba, tel. 084/20-4035, $4.50,

$9), the rooms are dark and basic but have great views of the ruins from a rickety balcony. Owner Ruben Ponce is friendly and knowledgeable about the town's ruins. **Restaurant Miranda** (near main bridge between plazas, tel. 084/20-4091, $5 s, $9 d) has a few clean rooms with stone walls and shared bathrooms. There are other rooms with private bath, and prices are negotiable.

In the Inca town, **Hostal Chaskawasa** (at corner of Medio and Atoq K'ikllu, $3 for shared bunkroom, $9 for private double) has several clean rooms, with wooden floors, arranged around a tiny courtyard. The terrace on the top of the building is a good place to drink beer and look at the Inca granaries. Walking through town, and following the road left (toward the ruins) to the San Isidro neighborhood, you'll find a few families that have turned their homes into hostels under a now-defunct government program. Rooms here cost around $3–5 pp.

$10–25
A very comfortable option is **Hostal Las Orquideas** (Estación s/n, tel. 084/20-4032, $10 s, $20 d, includes breakfast), with small, plain rooms with private bath around a courtyard and garden. The funky, colorful **Hostal Munay Tika** (Estación s/n, tel. 084/20-4111, munaytika@latinmail.com, $15 s, $25 d, includes breakfast) needs some work but is clean and friendly. The 25 rooms, with hard beds, front a flower garden and include clean private bath. There is also a sauna, though it is a bit grimy.

$25–50
Ollantaytambo's most charming, and best known, lodging is **N El Albergue** (Casilla 784, tel. 084/20-4014, albergue@rumbosperu.com, www.rumbosperu.com/elalbergue/, $25 s, $30 d, shared bathrooms, includes breakfast). The lodge is operated by Wendy Weeks, a painter from Seattle who arrived here in 1976 after an overland journey with her husband, writer Robert Randall. After her husband's death in 1990, Wendy stayed to raise her two sons here—Joaquín is the driving force behind the town's new museum and an anti-plastics campaign while Ishmael is a New York–based sculp-

tor. Wendy Weeks is a beloved member of the community and a passionate spokeswoman for its preservation.

To reach El Albergue, head to the train station, through the gate, and down the tracks in the direction of an arrow and large sign for El Albergue painted on a wall. Compared to the mayhem of the station, El Albergue is a hushed paradise. Blue-and-yellow tanagers flit among datura flowers and a huge Canary Island palm that was planted in the 1920s. The eight rooms are huge, with whitewashed walls, wood tables and beds, and an uncluttered grace. Decorations include local weavings, Wendy's paintings, a vase of flowers, and a river stone or two. After a breakfast of coffee and French toast, guests browse through the eclectic store that includes books, weavings, bottles of Matacuy (a homemade *digestif* for guinea pig meals), and a sundry of hard-to-find objects—Ekeko dolls, Waq'ullu dance masks, and all the metal fittings for a *zappo* table, the colonial game that is like horseshoes with a twist. Days end with a book on the wood balconies above the garden, followed by an evening steam in the wood-fired sauna.

$50–100

Hostal Sauce (Ventiderio 248, tel. 084/20-4044, hostalsauce@viabcp.com, www.hostalsauce.com.pe, $59 s, $69 d) is a serene, upscale establishment with eight sun-filled rooms overlooking the Ollantaytambo ruins. The restaurant, serving salads, meats, and pastas, has a cozy sitting area with a fireplace and couches.

Over $100

Built in 2000, the luxury **Hotel Pakaritampu** (Ferrocarril s/n, tel. 084/20-4020, hotel@pakaritampu.com, www.pakaritampu.com, $99 s, $104 d, includes buffet breakfast) seems a bit out of place in Ollantaytambo. The two-story concrete block buildings stick out like a sore thumb and, from the ruins above, it is easy to see that this hotel takes up more than its share of space. If you don't mind these things, the hotel does have pleasant gardens and large rooms with wood floors, spring mattresses, goosedown duvets, telephones, and a small balcony. There are nice

couches and a fireplace for having a drink, and an interesting library, though the restaurant is not recommended. Other services include laundry, free Internet and $1/day luggage storage available for non-guests.

FOOD
Cafés and Desserts
Ollanta's best café is **Il Capuccino** (Ventiderio s/n, 7 A.M.–10 P.M. daily), which also serves wine, coffee, and a variety of desserts. There is a small book exchange.

International
A good, inexpensive place for an early breakfast is **Restaurant La Ñusta** (Plaza de Armas, tel. 084/20-4035, 6 A.M.–9 P.M., $2) serving 12 types of pancakes (including *kiwicha* and chocolate) along with fruit, yogurt, and granola. **Mayupata** (tel. 084/20-4009, 6 A.M.–10 P.M., $3–8) overlooks the Río Patacancha and has the best food in town. They serve thin-crust pizzas, huge burgers smothered in mozzarella, and an excellent *lomo saltado*. The fireplace is great for cold nights. The outdoor tables at **Gran Tunupa** overlook the main street (Bentinerio s/n, tel. 084/20-4077, 6 A.M.–10 P.M. daily, $5) and are a good place to linger with a beer. This restaurant serves pancakes and omelets in the morning and wood-fired pizzas ($8 for large) during lunch and dinner. A bit cheaper, but also good, are the **Fortaleza** restaurants (one by ruins and other in main square, tel. 084/20-4047, 7:30 A.M.–8 P.M., $3),which serve cocktails along with sandwiches, pizza, and various beef and chicken dishes.

Vegetarian
Alcázar (Calle del Medio, one block from main square) is a simple place with inexpensive breakfast and vegetarian lunch options, including French toast, honey-and-banana pancakes, and fresh juices.

Peruvian
Kusicoyllor Café-Bar (Plaza Araccama s/n, tel. 084/20-4114, 8 A.M.–10 P.M., $5–8), located directly in front of the ruins, serves New Andean

and international food, ice cream (only place in Ollanta!), homemade croissants, and real espresso. They have a surprisingly good wine selection, full bar, friendly service, and a few interesting plates, like *chicarrón novoandino* (chunks of deep-fried chicken and bananas). With all the tourist restaurants around, **Restaurant Miranda** (near Patacancha bridge between plazas, tel. 084/20-4091, 6 A.M.–10 P.M., $5 s, $9 d) has a refreshing local feel. Alicia Miranda serves up $2 breakfast with juice, eggs, *tamal,* and coffee and a good $3 lunch menu, with vegetarian options.

Markets

The best mini-market for snacks or a picnic is **Abarrotes Shely** on the Plaza de Armas.

INFORMATION AND SERVICES

The best source for information on Ollantaytambo is the **CATCCO Tourist Information Center** (tel. 084/20-4024, www.catcco.org, 8 A.M.–10 P.M., Mon.–Fri., 8 A.M.–8 P.M., Sat.–Sun.). The best book on the ruins, available at El Albergue, is J. P. Protzen's *Inca Architecture and Construction at Ollantaytambo.*

Police and a **phone center** are located on the main square along with the **Virgen del Carmen pharmacy** (with three-hour laundry service), **post office**, and **public clinic** (tel. 084/200-2090).

Internet is expensive in Ollantaytambo. The options are **Internet Ollanta** (8 A.M.–9:30 P.M., $2/hour) and the **Museo CATCCO** with a reduced fee of $1/hour from 8–10 P.M. Mon.–Fri. and 8 A.M.–8 P.M. Sat.–Sun.

There are no banks nor ATM machines in Ollantaytambo.

GETTING THERE AND AROUND

To get to Ollantaytambo from Cusco, take the bus from the first block of Grau near the bridge (90 minutes, $1.25) to Urubamba and then hop another *combi* for the 20-minute, $0.75 ride to Ollantaytambo. The station where you catch the train to Aguas Calientes is a 10- or 15-minute walk from the main square along the Río Patacancha. From Ollantaytambo. A variety of **Back-**

packer ($48 round trip only) and **Vistadome** ($69 round trip, $42 one-way) trains either leave from here or stop here on the way from Cusco between 8 A.M. and 9 A.M. The most popular option is a Backpacker train that leaves Ollantaytambo at 9:05 P.M. All these trains take about 1.5 hours to reach Aguas Calientes. The Aguas Calientes–Cusco trains stop in Ollantaytambo in the afternoon between 5 and 6 P.M.

One advantage of taking the train from Ollantaytambo—besides the shorter and cheaper ride—is the ability to reach Aguas Calientes at different times of the day. Vistadome trains leave Ollantaytambo for Aguas Calientes throughout the day, including 10:30 A.M., 2:55 P.M., with a popular Backpacker option leaving at 7:45 P.M. Trains from Aguas Calientes also stop in Ollantaytambo throughout the day. For up-to-date prices and times, see www.perurail.com.

Reaching Cusco from Ollantaytambo is easy. Combis leave Ollantaytambo's main square for Urubamba, where another combi can be taken to Cusco. Direct buses for Cusco ($1.75, 1 hour and 20 minutes) leave from Ollantaytambo when the evening trains arrive.

Buses from Cusco also pass through Ollantaytambo on their way up-and-over the high pass at Abra Máalaga and onto the jungle city of Quillabamba, which is the gateway to the bio-diverse Lower Urubamba Basin. Trucks, and a few buses, headed in this direction stop in Ollantaytambo's main square at A.M. and 8 P.M. Ask local *combi* drivers for more details.

Taxis can be rented for quick trips to Urubamba ($6) or to the town of Huilloq for a day hike.

CHINCHERO

Chinchero is a small Andean village, off the beaten tourist track, that lies along the shortest driving route between Cusco and the Sacred Valley. Chinchero is perched on the high plains at 3,800 meters above sea level and has great views over the snow-capped Urubamba range. It is nearly 400 meters above Cusco, so visitors should be aware of altitude sickness.

Past Chinchero's less-than-appealing street front is the main square, where a handicrafts market is held on the same day as Pisac's (Tuesdays, Thursdays, and Sundays). There are a number of talented weavers in Chinchero who exhibit their wares at this market, which is smaller and less touristy than Pisac. The highlight of the square is an Inca wall with huge niches, which probably formed part of an Inca palace. Above the square is a 17th-century adobe church that was built on Inca foundations, which has deteriorated floral designs painted on its interior. It is open for visitors on market days only.

Chinchero sits on the edge of a plateau that drops suddenly into the Sacred Valley. If you can leave Chinchero by noon, you'll have time for a nice four-hour hike that drops along an old Inca trail into this valley and ends at Huayllabamba, where *combis* pass in the late afternoon for Urubamba or Pisac. From the church, there is a wide trail that leads up the opposite side of the valley and then gradually descends into the Sacred Valley. Once you arrive at the Río Urubamba, the Sacred Valley's main river, head right (downstream) toward the bridge at Huayllabamba.

There's a hostel or two in Chinchero, but they are very basic and the town's high altitude and bone-chilling nights make the Sacred Valley—almost 1,000 meters lower—a much better option. In Cusco, *colectivos* for Chinchero can be taken from the first block of Grau near the bridge (45 minutes, $0.75).

Machu Picchu

Though many photographers have tried, no glossy postcard can capture the sweep and majesty of Machu Picchu. Viewed from the switchbacks near the original main entrance, the city's streets, temples, and stairways sprawl across a jungle ridge that drops more than 300 meters into the Río Urubamba below. Andean peaks, including the horn-shaped Huayna Picchu, rise in the background and frame this mist-drenched island in the sky.

A visit to Machu Picchu is many visitors' main motivation for coming to Peru. The place has a vibrant, spiritual feel and is probably the world's best example of architecture integrating with the landscape. It is in some respects the Incas' lesson to the western world, teaching us how to build our world around nature, not against it.

There is not a stone out of place at Machu Picchu. Terraces, gardens, temples, staircases, and aqueducts all have purpose and grace. Shapes mimic the silhouettes of surrounding mountains. Windows and instruments track the sun during the June and December solstices. At sunrise, rows of ruins are illuminated one by one as the sun creeps over the mountain peaks. The sun, moon, water, and earth were revered by the Incas, and they drive the city's layout.

Adding to Machu Picchu's mystery is the fact that archaeologists still do not know when or why it was built. There is no mention of it in any of the colonial chronicles, and it lay forgotten for centuries until Yale archaeologist Hiram Bingham stumbled across it in 1911.

Bingham, a 36-year-old adventurer who ended up being both a U.S. Senator and the inspiration for Indiana Jones, came to Peru to find Vilcabamba, the legendary lost city of the Incas. This was the jungle enclave, well-described by Spanish soldiers, to which Manco Inca and his followers retreated following their unsuccessful rebellion against the Spanish in 1537. Bingham began his search walking down the newly built road along the Río Urubamba (now the train line) and asking locals if they knew of any ruins along the way.

It was in this way that local resident Melchor Arteaga led Bingham to the vine-covered site, which Bingham would return to in 1912 and 1915 to excavate. He was convinced, to the end of his life, that Mahcu Picchu was the *lost city of the Incas*. But historians are now certain he was incorrect. A wealth of supporting evidence indicates the real Vilcabamba was further into the jungle at Espíritu Pampa, which Bingham also visited but dismissed at the time as too insignificant.

Bingham discovered more than 100 human skeletons in cemeteries around Machu Picchu,

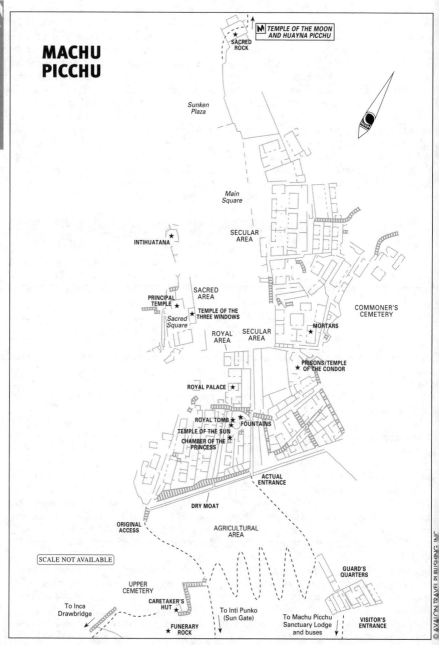

MACHU PICCHU

TEMPLE OF THE MOON AND HUAYNA PICCHU

SACRED ROCK

Sunken Plaza

Main Square

SECULAR AREA

INTIHUATANA

PRINCIPAL TEMPLE

SACRED AREA

TEMPLE OF THE THREE WINDOWS

Sacred Square

ROYAL AREA

SECULAR AREA

COMMONER'S CEMETERY

MORTARS

PRISONS/TEMPLE OF THE CONDOR

ROYAL PALACE

ROYAL TOMB

FOUNTAINS

TEMPLE OF THE SUN

CHAMBER OF THE PRINCESS

ACTUAL ENTRANCE

DRY MOAT

ORIGINAL ACCESS

AGRICULTURAL AREA

SCALE NOT AVAILABLE

UPPER CEMETERY

CARETAKER'S HUT

To Inca Drawbridge

FUNERARY ROCK

To Inti Punko (Sun Gate)

To Machu Picchu Sanctuary Lodge and buses

GUARD'S QUARTERS

VISITOR'S ENTRANCE

and an inexperienced scientist on his team incorrectly concluded that 80 of them belonged to women. The finding prompted the idea of Machu Picchu as a giant *acllahuasi* or a house for the Inca's chosen "virgins of the sun." Subsequent research on the skeletons proved that half were men and half women, but the sexy idea blazes on (and is still repeated today by Machu Picchu tour guides).

Part of Machu Picchu's power is that it is a riddle, a blank slate upon which generations of historians and explorers have scribbled their pet theories. Some claimed Machu Picchu was an exclusive religious complex or a giant coca plantation. Others said it was a boarding school for brainwashing the children of leaders conquered by the Incas.

The latest theory, which is gaining widespread acceptance, is that Machu Picchu was a winter retreat built by Inca Pachacútec in the mid-15th century. Scholars had long believed this, but concrete proof came in the form of a 16th-century suit filed by the descendants of Pachacútec, which University of California, Berkeley, anthropologist Dr. John Rowe found while searching through archives in Cusco. In the suit, the family sought the return of the lands, including a retreat called Picchu.

Though Machu Picchu certainly had a religious sector, and probably an *acllahuasi* too, its primary purpose was pleasure. The Incas could come here to escape the chill rains of Cusco, enjoy the jungle fruits of nearby Quillabamba, and hunt in the surrounding jungle.

VISITING THE RUINS

As many as two thousand people a day visit Machu Picchu during the high season from June to September and a total of 400,000 visited in 2003. The National Insitute of Culture (INC), the Peruvian government agency in charge of Machu Picchu, says the five hectares (12 acres) of the ruins easily absorbs this many visitors. But UNESCO, the United National cultural agency, disagrees and threatens to list the lost city on its list of endangered sites if the INC does not curtail the number of visitors to Machu Picchu.

For the moment there are no restrictions on how many tourists can visit Machu Picchu in a single day. Nevertheless, the large package tours with a megaphone-style guide take away from

© RENÉE DEL GAUDIO AND RUSS WEHNER

Machu Picchu seen from Huayna Picchu

the magic of the place. Here are a few tips for having Machu Picchu all to yourself:

- Avoid the busiest months of June to August. The cusp months of April–May and Sept.–Oct. are usually sunny as well.
- Avoid the Peruvian holidays from July 28 to August 10. The days around Cusco's Inti Raymi festival, June 24, are also busy.
- Visit on a Sunday, when most package tours are at the Pisac or Chincheros markets. Tuesdays, Wednesdays, or Thursdays tend to be low days as well.
- Stay the night at Aguas Calientes and beat the train crowds, which arrive at the ruins around 10 A.M. and start departing around 2 P.M. Either arrive early in the morning or linger in the late afternoon. During midday, when Machu Picchu is most crowded, you can hike to Huayna Picchu, the Temple of the Moon, and the Inca Bridge.

Machu Picchu admission is expensive by Peruvian standards and only lasts one day, though a second day is half-price. Foreigners pay $20, and nationals and students under 26 with ISIC card pay $10. The ruins are open 7 A.M.–5 P.M. daily. Evening hours are also available—6–10 P.M. nightly. Unless you are staying at the Sanctuary Lodge next door, visiting at night is difficult because no transportation is available and walking down the road at night is not a good idea. The best way to visit at night is with an agency, such as Rikuni Sacred Experience (see *Sports and Recreation* in *Aguas Calientes*). During the day there are always guides, of varying quality, waiting at the entrance to the ruins. Top-notch, though expensive, guides can be hired at the Sanctuary Lodge. Rikuni Sacred Experience in Aguas Calientes charges $45–50 for a three-hour tour of Machu Picchu for groups of five or more.

Outside the gate of the ruins, there are bathrooms and, usually, piles of free walking sticks. **El Mirador Snack Bar** ($4) sells bottled water, sandwiches, and hamburgers for eating at picnic tables overlooking the ruins. The gourmet **Sanctuary Lodge Restaurant** (tel. 084/21-1039) serves an extraordinary buffet breakfast to the public (5:30–9:30 A.M., $15) and a buffet lunch (11:30 A.M.–3 P.M., $22) that is worth the price

if you have a good appetite and want to spoil yourself. There is also a separate dining room with an à la carte menu serving international and Peruvian food (the ginger iced parfait is especially good). Bring plenty of cash when visiting Machu Picchu, as there are no ATMs, though Visa card cash advances with heavy commissions are possible at the Sanctuary Lodge.

RUINS TOUR

From the ticket booth, the path enters the south side of Machu Picchu through the **Guards' Quarters,** which now serve as the modern-day entrance. Take the nearby path marked with white arrows, which switchbacks in the forest alongside the terraces and gains the classic postcard view over the ruins. From here it is possible to understand that Machu Picchu is divided by a large grassy square in two areas. To the left are the **Royal and Sacred Areas,** which were probably reserved for the Inca emperor and his court. To the right is the **Secular Area,** where the workers lived.

Two paths from above meet at this point. The first, which can be seen traversing the mountain slopes, is the Inca Trail; the high pass is the **Sun Gate,** or *Inti Punko* in Quechua. The other path is a dead-end track toward the Inca Bridge. The nearby terraces, known as the **Agricultural Area,** once provided food for up to one thousand residents. Amazingly, the terraces never needed to be reconstructed, even after centuries of being covered with ivy, thanks to elaborate drainage and support systems below the surface. Much of Machu Picchu, in fact, is built on top of a giant landfill that is terraced underneath for support.

Above is a small thatched hut known as the **Caretaker's Hut** and an oddly shaped **Funerary Rock,** where Inca nobles may once have been prepared for burial. Bingham found the greatest number of skeletons in the **Upper Cemetery** above. From just below the Caretaker's Hut, follow the Inca Trail toward the trapezoidal doorway that served as the original gate.

At the edge of the terraces, descend the long flight of stairs alongside a dry moat, which Bingham thought was used for defensive purposes but was probably a drain for the terraces. (If you

on the summit rock of Huayna Picchu

did not climb to the **Caretaker's Hut,** then proceed along the level path from the modern-day entrance.) At the bottom of the staircase, head left and you will reach a series of 16 small **fountains,** the finest of which is at the top. These fountains were most likely used for ceremonial purposes and are fed by a natural spring that sends water along a stone channel.

Next to the **Main Fountain** stands the **Temple of the Sun,** the only round building at Machu Picchu. Though cordoned off, its interior can be appreciated from above. Its sinuous shape wraps around a boulder with a tapered tower that served as a solar observatory. During sunrise on the June solstice, the sun's rays shine through the window and perfectly illuminate this tower. Below is a cave-like space called the **Royal Tomb** (though no mummy was ever found here), which contains some of the finest stonework at Machu Picchu. There are tall niches here for offerings, and stone blocks are perfectly fitted with the shape of the cave, complementing an elegant stepped altar.

Adjacent to the temple is a two-story structure that was likely used for Inca nobility. Bingham named it the **Chamber of the Princess,** and the name stuck. The three-walled house

nearby has been restored with a thatched roof as an example of how Inca buildings once looked.

From here another staircase ascends to a jumble of rocks that was once the quarry for the city. As you ascend, the buildings to the right are called the **Royal Area** because of the massive lintels and spacious rooms characteristic of imperial Inca architecture. At the quarry, turn right to arrive at a small square with two of the most impressive buildings in the city. First is the **Temple of Three Windows,** which is elegantly built on top of a boulder, with windows that perfectly frame distant mountains. Next to it is the **Principal Temple,** another three-walled building with immense foundation stones and skillfully cut masonry. The kite-shaped sacred stone in the small square may represent the Southern Cross constellation.

Climbing the mounds above this temple leads to what was probably the most important shrine at Machu Picchu, the **Intihuatana,** or *Hitching Post of the Sun.* This device was clearly used to make astronomical observations and calculate the passing seasons. Its shape mimics that of Huayna Picchu in the background and appears to be powerfully aligned with mountains in all directions. All major Inca temples had such a stone,

There is a marked difference between sacred and secular walls at Machu Picchu.

though this is one of the few that was not desecrated by the Spaniards.

Walking down from the mounds and across the grassy plaza, you'll see a huge **Sacred Rock,** which echoes the form of the mountains in the back. This is the gateway to **Huayna Picchu,** the huge mountain that looms over Machu Picchu, and the **Temple of the Moon.**

Continuing back now into the other side of the city, you enter the **Secular Area,** where rougher homes probably served as workers' lodging. Near the back of this area is a large room with shallow round depressions, which are often filled with water and are called the **Mortars,** though their real use stumps archaeologists. Farther down the slope, Bingham found other skeletons in an area dubbed the **Commoners' Cemetery.**

On the other side of the passageway from the Mortars room is the extraordinary **Temple of the Condor,** named for a faint covering on the floor of the rock that may represent the head and neck of a stylized condor. Bingham called this area the **Prisons** because of niches where pris-

oners may once have been lashed, but modern-day historians have dismissed that as romantic hyperbole. There is a bizarre cavern nearby with stone blocks fitted perfectly to the surrounding rock. Though it looks like a place to store mummies, it was probably used as a solar observatory. During the December solstice, sunlight enters the window that is partly carved out of the boulder and illuminates the back of the cave. From here, cross the main square and exit the ruins via the **Guards' Quarters.**

◪ TEMPLE OF THE MOON AND HUAYNA PICCHU

The hike to Huayna Picchu starts at the Sacred Rock and passes through a gate that is open from 7 A.M.–1 P.M. (though no one seems to mind if you are late in descending). This one- to two-hour walk is steep but the path is in excellent shape, though the last 20 meters include a steep rock slab that is climbed with a ladder and a rope. The Incas built terraces here, and the airy summit offers a perfect view of the entire complex, which spreads out before the summit like a map. Behind the summit, a trail leads down an alternate route to the **Temple of the Moon,** a construction equally as exquisite as the Temple of the Sun but with an entirely different mood. The temple is a large natural cave, where rocks have been fitted perfectly in flowing, gentle shapes. Instead of the tower and bright sunlight of the Temple of the Sun, everything here is recessed, dark, with sinuous lines. Nearby there is a lower cave with rougher stonework and, above, a magnificent recessed doorway and gallery, to which the alternate route from Huayna Picchu descends. This route contains a short but near-vertical section climbed with a lashed wooden ladder and is not good for those nervous about heights. The easier, though slightly longer, way to reach the Temple of the Moon is to retrace your steps down from Huayna Picchu and take the marked trail turn-off halfway down, which leads right to the side of the main cave. Visiting the Temple of the Moon adds at least an hour onto the Huayna Picchu hike.

The path to the summit of Huayna Picchu looks steeper than it is.

INCA BRIDGE AND INTI PUNKO

If you have the time and the energy, head to the Caretaker's Hut and hike up the Inca Trail, which arcs across the mountain slope to a high pass. It takes about 45 minutes to walk to this pass, where there is a stone construction known as the Sun Gate, or **Inti Punko.** Another path, only for those good with heights, leads west from the Caretaker's Hut through the cemetery. The path becomes quite narrow and exposed and at one point passes over a manmade ledge like that found on the upper route at the Pisac ruins. The trail ends near a gap in the stone ledge, where the Incas evidently placed a drawbridge. Past the drawbridge, the path oddly peters out into steep, dangerous terrain. Some take this as evidence that Machu Picchu was a summer retreat and this was a trail to a hunting area, not a highway to anywhere in particular.

 INCA TRAIL

Though at times crowded, the hike to Machu Picchu is an unforgettable experience—both a backpacking trip and a religious pilgrimage. There are lots of ways to do it, including walks of one to four days, with or without a pack on your back. All trail hikers must go with an agency, to ensure everyone's safety and keep trash off the trail. (The Inca Trail is part of the Machu Picchu Historical Sanctuary, administered by the National Institute of Culture.) There is a wide range in price and quality among Inca Trail agencies (see *Sports and Recreation* in the *Cusco* section) and reservations should be made at least one month in advance.

The two- or even one-day option begins at Km 104 of the railroad line and includes a steep hike to reach the final stretch of the Inca Trail, including the ruins at Wiñay Wayna. Some agencies continue the same day to Machu Picchu and stay overnight in Aguas Calientes, while others camp near Wiñay Wayna to enter Machu Picchu the following morning.

We highly recommend the four-day trip, which passes more than 30 Inca sites along the way and includes the most spectacular scenery. This trip traditionally begins with an early-morning three-hour bus ride to Piscacucho, which is at Km 82 of the train line at 2,700 meters (some agencies use the train instead, which drops backpackers a bit further down at Km 84). The trail begins in a subtropical ecosystem, with lots of agave plants and Spanish moss hanging from the trees. Many of the cacti along the trail have a parasite that turns crimson when you crush it in your fingers, a trick local woman use for lipstick. The first ruins you pass are **Patallacta,** meaning *city above terraces* in Quechua, a middle-class residential complex used as a staging ground for Machu Picchu. There is 12 km of hiking this first day with an elevation gain of 500 meters to Wayllabamba, where most groups camp the first night with stunning views of the Huayluro Valley.

Day two is a much more strenuous 12 km, because you gain 1,200 meters in elevation and climb two mountain passes back to back. On the backside of the first pass, at 4,200 meters, you will pass by the ruins of **Runkurakay,** a round food storehouse strategically located at a lookout point. This site has an incredible view over a valley and nearby waterfall. The second pass, at 3,950 meters, is named *Dead Woman's*

Pass after a mummy discovered there. In the late afternoon you will see the ruins of **Sayaqmarka** (3,625 meters) with good views of the Vilcabamba range. Sayaqmarka was probably used as a *tambo,* or resting spot for priests and others journeying to Machu Picchu. The complex is divided into a rough lower section and a more elaborate upper area that was probably used for ceremonial purposes. Most trekkers camp this second night at Pacaymayo, with views of snow-covered peaks including Humantay (5,850 meters) and Salcantay (6,271 meters), the highest peak in the area.

Day three, the most unforgettable day of the trek, is a relatively easy day with plenty of time for meandering. You enter the cloud forest, full of orchids, ferns, and bromeliads, to reach the ruins of **Phuyupatamarka,** a ceremonial site from where you first see the backside of Machu Picchu, marked with a flag. Look out for hummingbirds, finches, parrots, and the crimson Andean cock of the rock. Most groups rest at a halfway lookout point that is often shrouded

Runkurakay, a round storehouse, on day two of the Inca Trail

by clouds. From here, it is a two-hour hike straight down, dropping 1,000 meters to the third campsite at 2,650 meters, where there are hot showers, cold beers, and a restaurant. There is usually plenty of time in the afternoon to see the ruins of **Wiñay Wayna,** a spectacular ceremonial and agricultural site that is about a 10-minute walk away. We were lucky enough to see these ruins under the light of a full moon, which was truly mesmerizing. This complex is divided into two sectors, with religious temples at the top and rustic dwellings below. The hillside is carved into spectacular terraces and the Río Urubamba flows far below.

The fourth day is all about getting to Machu Picchu. Most groups rise very early in the morning in an attempt to reach the sanctuary before sunrise, and it can feel like walking in a herd of cattle. The walk is flat at the start and then inclines steeply up to the **Sun Gate,** from where you will be rewarded with a 180-degree view of Machu Picchu. Your guide will take you through the ruins, leaving you time to wander on your own and to climb Huayna Picchu if you haven't had enough.

GETTING THERE

The only way to reach Machu Picchu is to walk the Inca Trail or ride the train from Cusco (four hours), Urubamba (two hours and 10 minutes), or Ollantaytambo (one hour and 15 minutes). During the 1990s, a company named HeliCusco operated huge Russian helicopters to Machu Picchu, blowing many of Aguas Calientes' sheet-metal roofs off in the process. Thankfully, helicopters have been banned inside the Machu Picchu Historical Sanctuary and condors are slowly returning to the area. We saw one cruising in the air underneath the ruins: watch for finger-like feathers at the ends of the wings, whitish upper wings, and a white neck.

PeruRail (tel. 084/22-1992 for reservations or reservas@perurail.com, www.perurail.com) offers three train services from Cusco to Machu Picchu via its train station in nearby Aguas Calientes; the **Backpacker** ($60 round trip, $42 one-way), the **Vistadome** ($89 round trip, $60 one-way), and the new, luxury **Hiram Bingham service** ($417 round trip only). The Backpacker train is nearly as comfortable as the Vistadome, with large, soft seats and plenty of leg room. Food for sale includes sandwiches ($2) and candy bars ($1.50). The perks of the Vistadome include large viewing windows in the ceilings, shows put on by train attendants (including fashion walks to promote alpaca clothing), luxurious seats, lights snacks and beverages, and live Andean music.

The Hiram Bingham service is in a whole different league. A full brunch is served on the ride from Poroy (15 minutes outside Cusco) to Machu Picchu, where guests are treated to a deluxe ruins tour and a full tea at the Sanctuary Lodge. On the ride home, pre-dinner Pisco sours are served in the elegant dark wood bar, accompanied by a live band and dancing. A gourmet four-course dinner follows at your private table, accompanied by a selection of wines. Afterwards, there is live music and dancing for those with energy. This is the most luxurious train service in Latin America, hands down. If it feels like the Orient Express, it is—PeruRail has been operated by Orient Express Ltd. since the late 1990s.

Depending on the season, two or three Backpacker and Vistadome trains leave from the San Pedro Station (Cascaparo and Santa Clara, tel. 084/22-1291) in Cusco, a five-minute taxi ride from the center of Cusco. They all leave around 6 and 6:30 A.M. and arrive in Aguas Calientes roughly four hours later. Some stop briefly in Poroy and Ollantaytambo en route. On the way to Machu Picchu, try to get a seat on the left side of the train to see the raucous Río Urubamba. The trains leave for Cusco between 3:30 and 4:20 P.M., also arriving roughly four hours later.

Many travelers are now arriving in Machu Picchu via trains that run back and forth throughout the day between Ollantaytambo and Machu Picchu, a 80-minute journey made by Vistadome ($69 round trip, $42 one-way) and Backpacker ($48, round-trip only) trains. The Vistadomes arrive in Aguas Calientes at 8:20 A.M., 11:45 A.M., and 4:15 P.M., and the late-evening Backpacker ar-

day three on the Inca Trail

© RENÉE DEL GAUDIO AND ROSS WEHNER

rives at 11 P.M. The earliest of these trains originates in a new station in Urubamba, farther up the valley. These Vistadomes leave Aguas Calientes for Ollantaytambo at 8:35 A.M., 1:20 P.M., and 4:45 P.M. This last train continues all the way to Urubamba, and there is also a Backpacker train for Ollantaytambo that leaves at 5 P.M. (See www.perurail.com for up-to-date timetable.)

The Hiram Bingham luxury train avoids the famous (or infamous) switchbacks out of Cusco by leaving from the Poroy station, which is a 15-minute drive from Cusco. It departs at 9 A.M. and arrives in Aguas Calientes at 12:30 P.M. On the return, the train departs Aguas Calientes at 6:30 P.M. and gets to Poroy at 10 P.M.

The Cusco–Machu Picchu train ride begins with a series of switchbacks that gradually reveal Cusco's expanse of red-tiled roofs. The train crosses high, desolate plains before descending to meet the Urubamaba Valley. Once past Ollantaytambo, the rail enters a gorge that grows narrower and deeper as it continues its descent. Look for occasional glimpses of snow-covered Verónica (5,750 m) to the right. At Km 88 there is a modern bridge built on Inca foundations. As the vegetation grows thicker, and the air thicker, the train descends into what the Peruvians call the *ceja de selva,* or the eyebrow of the jungle, and the Río Urubamba starts crashing over house-sized boulders. The train continues until reaching the ramshackle town of Aguas Calientes.

Aguas Calientes

Ever since a landslide destroyed the train line past Machu Picchu to Quillabamba, Aguas Calientes is literally the end of the line for the Cusco–Machu Picchu train. This ramshackle, unappealing town is the Kathmandu of Peru's Inca Trail, where trekkers stagger down from the heights for a cooked meal, a hot bath, and a good night's sleep. Except for those who can afford the two fancy hotels nearby, everyone who overnights at Machu Picchu ends up here. Long called a tropical slum, Aguas Calientes is slowly reshaping itself with a new plaza for selling crafts next to the river. Even so, do not stay for more than one night, and stick to recommended restaurants. Food poisoning is a big problem here.

The town spreads uphill from the tracks, past a square and up the main drag of Pachacútec alongside the Río Aguas Calientes. On the other side of the river is the Orquideas neighborhood with a few peaceful, good lodging options.

At the top of Pachacútec are the town's **thermal baths** ($2, with towels and even bathing suits for rent). The baths are cleanest in the morning and are usually quite grimy by evening. On a dirt trail uphill past the baths are a few spectacular waterfalls for bathing. This path leads uphill for several hours to a string of remote waterfalls.

SPORTS AND RECREATION

Putukusi, a forested rock dome 1,000 meters above Aguas Calientes, is a superb half-day hike that offers great views of Machu Picchu and a chance to see many different cloud forest birds. The highlight is 400 meters (1,200 feet) of wooden ladders nailed to the near-vertical cliff face. The trailhead is signed and is 150 meters past the control point on the railroad tracks. A less demanding hike leads to the **Mandor waterfalls,** a 15-minute hike through a banana plantation and jungle that leads from Km 115 of the tracks. Neither of these hikes require a guide.

The Machu Picchu Pueblo Hotel leads guided tours to Putukusi ($15 guests, $30 nonguests). A recommended Aguas Calientes agency is **Rikuni Sacred Experience** (Imperio de los Inkas 119, on the train tracks, tel. 084/21-1036, rikunis@yahoo.ar), which leads trips to Mandor and Putukusi and spiritual night tours of Machu Picchu for energy sessions and *pachamama* offerings.

ENTERTAINMENT AND EVENTS

The best bar in town, hands down, is **Blues Bar Café** (Pachacútec s/n, tel. 084/21-1125, victoremar@hotmail.com, 9:30 A.M.–midnight), a two-story wooden building with a porch overlooking the town. The menu includes *empanadas* and hamburgers. There is a candlelit couch surrounded by antiques, a book exchange, and a stack of *Caretas* magazines from the 1970s. Happy hour is from 6–7 P.M. and 9:30–10 P.M. and includes a two-for-one special on the "mega Pisco sour," which comes in a milk glass.

The two discos in town are **Sagra's Pub Bar** and **Wasicha,** both next to the Indio Feliz Restaurant on Lloqueyupanqui. For pool and cheap beers, head to **Bobby's** (1 P.M.–midnight), which is on the Las Orquideas promenade above Puente Los Presidentes.

ACCOMMODATIONS

Compared to the rest of the country, lodging in Augas Calientes is exorbitantly expensive. The cleanest budget places are in the Orquideas neighborhood, across from the Río Aguas Calientes that flows from the hot baths and cleaves the town in two. In Aguas Calientes, forking over a bit more dough to be in the $25–50 range buys a lot of extra comfort, hot water, and river views. All of the hotels are in Aguas Calientes except for the two nicest ones. The Machu Picchu Pueblo Hotel is upstream from town and the Machu Picchu Sanctuary Lodge is next to the ruins themselves.

Under $10

Hospedaje Inti Wasi (Las Orquideas M-23, tel. 084/21-1036, hanan65@latinmail.com, $5 s, $9 d) is the nicest budget place in terms of natural surroundings. To get there, walk from the train station all the way up the right side of the Río Aguas Calientes until it dead-ends at a point a few hundred yards below the hot baths. The main sitting area is a plant-filled courtyard, diffused with yellow light from a yellow, semi-transparent roof and echoing with the sounds of the river nearby. The bunkrooms are small and sparse, with foam beds, and have a tendency to heat up in the sun. Bathrooms are clean, with water heated by electric showerheads. Also in the Orquideas neighborhood is **Hospedaje Q'ente** (tel. 084/21-1110, $4 s, $9 d). Rooms here are basic but clean with shared bathrooms. The main appeal is the neighborhood itself, which is a bit dirty but has a soccer field and a small-town feel that is a welcome respite from the hustle of Aguas Calientes.

Down by the tracks on the other side of town is the decrepit but classic **Hostal Los Caminantes** (Imperio de los Incas 140, tel. 084/21-2007, $5 s, $10 d). This old wooden building has been receiving backpackers for decades and has friendly management, even if the rooms have foam beds and are badly in need of renovation. Hot water and rooms with private bath are available ($10 s, $15 d).

$10–25

Hostal Quilla (tel. 084/21-1009, $15 s, $18) is on Pachacútec between Wiracocha and Tupac Inca Yupanqui. Rooms are plain with tile floors but service is friendly.

$25–50

A company named Invermac operates three hotels in Aguas Calientes, all lined up next to one another on both sides of the tracks. The best of these is the **Machupicchu Hostal** (tel. 084/21-

1034, $26 s, $30 d, includes breakfast), where rooms are arranged around a plant-filled courtyard overlooking the river. There is a sitting area with a great river view, and the rooms themselves are plain, clean, and comfortable. Next door is the sister **Presidente Hostal** (tel. 084/21-1034, presidente@terra.com.pe, www.presidente.com.pe, $45 s, $50 d, includes breakfast), a similar production with carpeted, bigger rooms. This place has the look and feel of a real hotel and rooms are pleasant, with earth-colored walls—ask for one that overlooks the river. The third and least impressive in the Invermac trinity is **Continental Hostal** (tel. 084/21-1078, $20 s, $30 d), which is brand-new, a bit sterile, and located on the side of the tracks away from the river (three rooms have river views). Reservations for all three hotels can be made at presidente@terra.com.pe.

The most charming hostel in town is **Gringo Bill's** (off one corner of main square, look for signs, tel. 084/21-1046, gringobills@yahoo.com, www.machupicchugringobills.com, $25 s, $35 d, includes breakfast), with a treehouse atmosphere and large rooms with balconies and great showers. The downside is that the room windows do not lock, there are overpowering New Age fluorescent paintings, and guests have to make an advance down payment at an office in Cusco.

Hostal Restaurant La Cabaña (Pachacútec M-20, tel. 084/21-1048, lacabana_mapi@latinmail.com, www.cabanahostal.com, $25 s, $35 d, includes breakfast) is a friendly place at the top of the main street. Rooms have tile floors, exposed wood beams, and whitewashed cement walls. The owners, Beto and Marta, take an eco-sensitive approach. ("We're trying to return to what we've destroyed," Beto told us.) Additional services include guides for walks, security boxes, laundry, and a DVD player with 150 movies.

Hotel Urpi (Las Orquideas above Puente los Presidentes, tel. 084/21-1127, ferminurpi@hotmail.com, $39 s, $49 d) is in a quiet spot on the far bank of the Río Aguas Calientes. This peaceful place is new and clean, with lúcuma-colored walls.

$50–100

If you walk up the main street above the plaza, you cannot miss the yellow **Machu Picchu Inn** (tel.

084/21-1011, ventas-sales@peruhotel.com.pe, www.peruhotel.com.pe, $93 s, $93 d, includes breakfast). Like many former state-owned hotels, this one seems a bit sterile and overpriced. It does, however, have all the amenities: large, tile-floored rooms, comfortable beds, cable TV, restaurant, bar, pool table, and patios with a view.

Over $100

M The Machu Picchu Pueblo Hotel (tel. 084/21-1032 or 084/24-5314 for reservations, www.inkaterra.com.pe, central@inkaterra.com) is one of Peru's most elegant hotels and has been aptly described a *paradise at Machu Picchu's feet*. A short walk from the hustle and bustle of Aguas Calientes, this peaceful patch of rainforest echoes the tumbling of the nearby Río Urubamba and the sounds of some 150 different tropical birds. Stone paths wind through the forest past fountains and pools and up to secluded bungalows. Large rooms feature rustic colonial-style furniture, rough tile floors, luxury bathrooms, recessed reading areas, and nice details like thick bathrobes, fruit, and the hotel's own line of organic shampoos and conditioners. The hotel has grown since 1978 with an eco-philosophy that includes building all of its furniture on site. It received the Sustainable Travel award from *National Geographic Traveler* in 2002.

Pueblo Hotel is the only Machu Picchu hotel to give visitors a taste of the jungle, and it's the best substitute for those not planning to visit the Amazon. The biologist guides lead early-morning bird watching walks (we saw a range of tanagers, hummingbirds, motmots, and the Andean cock of the rock in two hours). The hotel's nature walks include the biggest orchid collection in Peru (372 species), a butterfly house, miniature tea plantation, and a pool for viewing native fish. The hotel has re-introduced the *Osso anteojos* (Andean spectacled bear) to the area, and one bear, which was found too tame to release after years in the Cusco zoo, lives in a hut near the hotel. There is an excellent restaurant, a bar, a spa ($60 for massage and sauna), and a spring-fed swimming pool. Guests also pay $10 for the excellent lunch buffet at InkaTerra, the sister restaurant next to the train station (normal price is $15). Guides also lead a two-hour walk up into the forest to waterfalls and pre-Inca stone carvings and other day hikes in the area.

If you have deep pockets and want to stay within a stone's throw of the lost Inca city, check out the **Machu Picchu Sanctuary Lodge** (tel. 084/21-1039, res-mapi@peruorienteexpress.com.pe, www.orient-express.com, $455 s, $547 d, includes breakfast, lunch, and dinner). The lodge began as a state-owned hotel in the 1970s, but it was privatized in 1995 and ultimately acquired by Orient-Express Hotels, which also operates Cusco's finest hotel, El Monasterio, and Peru Rail. Orient-Express is not allowed to make any additions to the building, so it remains a small, modest hotel on the outside with an elegant interior. The 31 rooms have been outfitted with antiques, king-size beds, and cable TV, and the slightly more expensive rooms have views over the ruins. One advantage of staying here is a night excursion to the ruins, hosted by a local shaman, which is difficult to do from Aguas Calientes. There are two restaurants, one serving gourmet à la carte items ($13), and the other an extraordinary buffet ($22). The hotel also offers trekking, river rafting, and mountain biking trips, and walking paths behind the hotel lead through an orchid garden. In high season, this hotel is booked solid, so make reservations at least three months in advance.

FOOD

Along the railroad tracks and up on the main Pachacútec street, Aguas Calientes is awash with pizzerias and their street salespeople. Choose carefully—many are not as good a bargain (nor as clean) as advertised.

Local Favorites

The French/Peruvian-owned **M Indio Feliz** (Lloque Yupanqui Lote 4–12, tel. 084/21-1090, Mon.–Sat., $9) serves up the best and safest food in town, best described as Peruvian cuisine with French touches, served in American portions. The two-story restaurant has a peaceful, homey feel, with tables in a sunny upstairs dining room. The four-course set menu is huge and, when we were there, included quiche Lorraine, *sopa criolla,* lemon or garlic trout, ginger chicken, and apple pie. There is so much food, in fact, that a single meal can be divided for two people, something the kitchen is happy to do. There is real espresso, calla lilies on all the tables, and opera music in the background.

Pueblo Viejo (Pachacútec s/n, tel. 084/21-1193, noon–11 P.M., $3–6) is at the bottom of the restaurant row and has a cozy atmosphere, including live music and fireplace. There is a huge range of food here, from vegetarian and pizza to grilled meats. There are affordable lunchtime menus here as well. If you like this place, check out **Toto's House** (tel. 084/21-1020, 8:30 A.M.–11 P.M.), a more upscale restaurant on the tracks nearby with an $11 lunch buffet and river views.

Pizza

Restaurant-Pizzeria Inka Wasi (Pachacútec 112, tel. 084/21-1010, 9 A.M.–10 P.M. Mon.–Sat., 1–10 P.M. Sun., $7) serves trout, chicken brochettes, *cebiche,* pastas, and pizzas on picnic tables on the Plaza de Armas. Also on the plaza is **Inka's Pizzeria Restaurant** (Plaza de Armas, tel. 084/21-1063, $7). Along Pachacútec, recommended places include **Pizzeria Inka Planet** (Pachacútec s/n, $2–8) and **Pizzeria Keros** (Pachacútec 116, tel. 084/74-0819, 9 A.M.–11 P.M. daily), which also serve Peruvian dishes like guinea pig, *cebiche,* and grilled alpaca. **Chez Maggy** (Pachacútec 156, tel. 084/21-1006, 11 A.M.–4 P.M. and 6–11 P.M.) is a bit further up the street. Along with its sister restaurant in Cusco, it has an established reputation for pastas and wood-fired pizzas. Avoid a pizzeria named Big Brother—we have received two reports of food poisoning.

Vegetarian

Excellent vegetarian food is available at **Govinda** (Pachacútec 20, tel. 084/21-1021, 7 A.M.–10 P.M.), which has a variety of lunch menus ranging from $2–8.

Markets

The biggest mini-market, and a good place to put together a picnic, is **El Pueblo,** with juices, yogurts, fresh bread, deli meats, and cheeses. A variety of places prepare bag lunches, including Gringo Bill's (off one corner of the main square, tel. 084/21-1046).

INFORMATION AND SERVICES

There is a helpful **tourist office** (Pachacútec s/n, tel. 084/21-1104) just up the main street from the square that hands out free maps.

Police are located on the tracks right across from Hostal Presidente.

Where the tracks cross the Río Aguas Calientes is an **EsSalud** clinic with emergency 24-hour service (tel. 084/21-1037) and, on the other side, the **Ministerio de Salud clinic. Señor de Huanca drugstore** is on the tracks across from the Hostal Presidente. If they don't have what you need, the **Pharmacy Popular** (Puputi s/n, tel. 084/22-8787) is just off the plaza.

There are no ATMs in Aguas Calientes or Machu Picchu, though in a pinch the **Machu Picchu Sanctuary Lodge** will charge you $10 for a cash advance on your Visa card. There is also a **Western Union** (tel. 084/422-0014) just off the Plaza de Armas.

The **post office** is up Pachacútec and open 10 A.M.–2 P.M. and 4–8 P.M.

There are a smattering of **Internet** places around the main square.

Laundry Angela (Pachacútec 150, tel. 084/21-2205, $2 per kilo) will wash clothes the same day.

Massage Services

There are many places along Pachacútec that advertise Thai and other type of massages. The best masseuse in town is Sergio, a Chilean who spent a year learning the art of massage in the old medicine hospital in Chiang Mai, Thailand. His shop, which he runs with girlfriend Jessica, is on Pachacútec across from La Cabaña. They charge $20 for a 45-minute massage or $5 for a five-minute backpacker's foot rub.

Cusco and the Sacred Valley

Cusco

Along with the Aztec capital of Tenochtitlán (now swallowed by modern-day Mexico City), Cusco was the other imperial capital in the Americas at the start of the Spanish conquest. Cusco was a dazzling sight, with its temples of elegantly fitted stone, colossal plazas, royal palaces, and the hilltop fortress of Sacsayhuamán, which the Incas somehow built from house-sized stones. This was the capital of the New World's Roman Empire and, like Rome, paved highways fanned out from here through an empire that had stretched in a mere century between southern Chile and Colombia. As Francisco Pizarro marched wide-eyed through this kingdom in 1533, Cusco became the holy grail of his conquest. Two scouts he sent ahead told him the city was as elegant as a European city and literally covered in gold. Before the scouts left Cusco, they used crowbars to pry 700 plates of gold off the walls of Coricancha, the sun temple.

Despite four centuries of Spanish domination, Cusco still seems to be in a tug-of-war between Spanish and Inca cultures. Though the Spaniards destroyed the Inca buildings in an act of domination, they had enough common sense to leave many of the bulging, seamless stone walls as foundations. These walls line many of Cusco's narrow cobblestone alleys, which thread among the many baroque churches and convents the Spaniards built here. Part of Cusco's power, and the reason visitors linger here, is the uneasy cultural tension evident in places like Coricancha and even hotel lobbies, where seamless Inca walls are nestled incongruously among arcades of Spanish arches.

With its proximity to the standout attractions of Machu Picchu and the Sacred Valley, Cusco is one of the top destinations in Latin America and the mecca of the Gringo Trail, the well-trod backpacker's route through Latin America. The sheer quantity of restaurants, hotels, and cafés indicates the city's dependence on tourism, which somehow has not diminished Cusco's charm. Schoolchildren run through the street yelling in Quechua, and villagers in the surrounding countryside retain their native dress, festivals, and love of *chicha,* the local brew of fermented corn.

Cusco is at 3,400 meters (11,150 feet), and most people who arrive here feel some form of *soroche,* or altitude sickness, which can range from a headache and the chills to more serious ailments. The best plan is to visit the Sacred Valley and Machu Picchu first and return to Cusco after becoming used to the altitude. Cusco's *boleto turístico* gets you into most of the major sites of Cusco and the Sacred Valley for a mere $10 (see the sidebar *Cusco's Tourist Ticket*).

The heart of Cusco is its Plaza de Armas, which stands out for its huge, 16th-century cathedral. Beyond the Plaza de Armas, and opposite the cathedral, are two charming squares, Plaza Regocijo and Plaza San Francisco. Further along in this direction lie the Market of San Pedro and the train station for Machu Picchu. To the side of the cathedral, a narrow pedestrian street named Procuradores is lined wall-to-wall with restaurants, bars, and cafés. This is Cusco's *Gringo Alley,* which is crowded with aggressive salespeople. Behind the cathedral, steep alleys lead to San Blas, a bohemian neighborhood that contains most of our favorite hostels, cafés, and bars.

HISTORY

Like most empires, the foundation of the Inca empire is shrouded in myth. The best-known version is that the empire began around 1100 A.D., when Manco Capac and Mama Oclla, children of the sun and the moon, arose from the waters of Lake Titicaca and searched the land for a place to found their kingdom. When they reached the fertile valley of Cusco, Manco Capac was able, for the first time, to plunge his golden staff into the ground. This was the divine sign that showed them where to found the Inca capital city, which was christened Q'osqo, or "navel of the world."

The seeds of truth in this legend are that the **Tiwanaku** (200–1000 A.D.), from the south shores of Lake Titicaca, were the first advanced culture to reach the Cusco area. Around 700 A.D. an even more potent culture, the **Wari** (700–1100 A.D.) from Ayacucho, spread here and built aqueducts, the large city of Pikillacta, and probably, as some archaeologists believe, the first water temple at Pisac. The Incas, sandwiched between these two advanced cultures, rose out of the vacum created when both collapsed. The Incas combined the Tiwanakus' stonework and farming techniques on one hand with the Waris' highway system and mummy worship on the other. The result was a potent system of economic and political organization.

Little is known about Inca history, though it is believed Manco Capac probably existed and was indeed the first Inca. There were a total of thirteen Inca emperors, though the empire for all practical purposes began with Inca Yunpanqui, the ninth Inca leader and one of the younger sons of **Inca Viracocha.** Around 1440 the Chancas, the tribe that toppled the Wari, had amassed a large army that was poised to overrun Cusco. Inca Viracocha fled, probably to his estate at Huchuy Cusco in the Sacred Valley, but Inca Yupanqui stayed on to defend Cusco. Of the ensuing battle, mestizo chronicler Inca Garcilaso de la Vega reports that even the stones of Cusco rose up and became soldiers. Against overwhelming odds, Inca Yupanqui and a team of seasoned generals beat back the Chancas.

After the battle, Inca Yupanqui changed his name to **Pachacútec** ("shaker of the earth" in Quechuan), took over Cusco from his disgraced father, and launched the Incas' unprecedented period of expansion. Pachacútec created a vision of the Inca people as a people of power, ruled over by a class of elites who were allowed the privilege of chewing coca leaves and wearing large ear plugs. He used a stick-and-carrot strategy, learned from the Wari, of conquering territories peacefully by bearing down on them with overwhelmingly large armies on one hand, and by offering the rich benefits of being integrated into a well-functioning web of commerce on the other.

In the Cusco area, what is most obvious about Pachacútec is that he was a master builder. He fashioned the city of Cusco into the shape of a puma, a sacred animal admired for its grace and strength, with Sacsayhuamán as the head, the city as the body, and the Coricancha sun temple as the tail. He built a huge central plaza, which included both today's Plaza de Armas and the Plaza Regocijo, and also somehow devised a way to move the stones to begin construction of Sacsayhuamán. He is credited for building nearly all of the other major Inca monuments in the area, including Pisac, Ollantaytambo and probably even Machu Picchu. Pachacútec's armies conquered the entire area between Cusco and Lake Titicaca and also spread north through the central highlands.

His son, **Túpac Yupanqui,** was less of a builder and even more of a warrior. He spent most of his life away from Cusco in long, brutal campaigns in northern Peru against the stubborn Chachapoyans. He dominated the entire coastline, including the Chimú empire based at Chan Chan, and pushed all the way to Quito, in present-day Ecuador.

His son **Hauyna Capac,** the last Inca to rule over a unified empire, seemed to be ruling over a

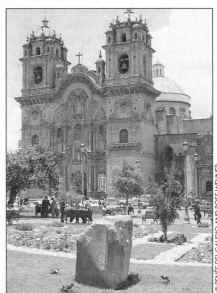

© RENÉE DEL GAUDIO AND ROSS WEHNER

This lone rock is the last trace of Inca stonework in Cusco's Plaza de Armas.

territory that had extended itself almost to the breaking point. Nevertheless he continued the campaign in the north, fathering a son named **Atahualpa** in Quito, and pushed the Inca empire to its last limits, up against what is now the Ecuador-Columbia border. After his death Atahualpa challenged **Huascar,** the legitimate heir in Cusco, and a disastrous civil war broke out, killing thousands of Incas and badly damaging the empire's infrastructure.

In the end, **Atahualpa** was victorious. He might have been able to unify the empire again if it were not for the fact that **Francisco Pizarro** and a small Spanish army had begun their march across Peru. Pizarro and his men took Atahualpa hostage in November 1532 and held him until an entire room was filled with gold, much of which was taken from Cusco and carried by llama trains to Cajamarca. Then the Spaniards murdered Atahualpa anyway and continued their march to Cusco.

To maintain stability, Pizarro needed to find a new Inca ruler, and befriended **Manco Inca,** another son of Huayna Capac in Cusco, who was grateful to Pizarro for having routed Atahualpa's army of Quito-based Incas. Under the guise of liberators and with Manco Inca's blessing, Pizarro and his men entered Cusco and took full and peaceful possession of the city in November 1533.

It didn't take long, however, for Manco Inca to grow resentful. The Spaniards had sacked Cusco for all of its gold and silver in the first month, picking clean the gold-filled sun temple and even the sacred Inca mummies and melting everything into bars for shipping to Spain. They lived in the palaces of the former Inca emperors and forced Inca nobles to hand over their wives.

Manco Inca escaped from Cusco and by May 1536 had amassed an army estimated at 100,000 to 200,000 soldiers, who used slingshots to throw red-hot coals onto Cusco's thatched roofs, burning their beloved city to the ground. Trapped, the Spaniards made a last-ditch effort against the Incas, who had occupied the fortress of Sacsayhuamán. During a battle that raged for more than a week, the Spaniards prevailed against overwhelming odds, causing Manco Inca to retreat to Ollantaytambo

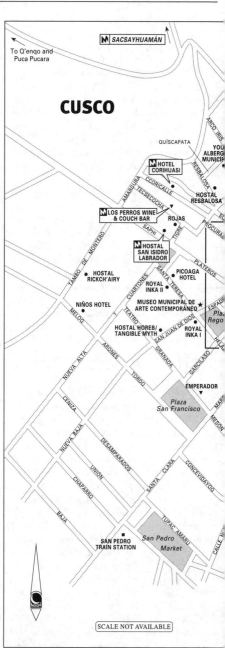

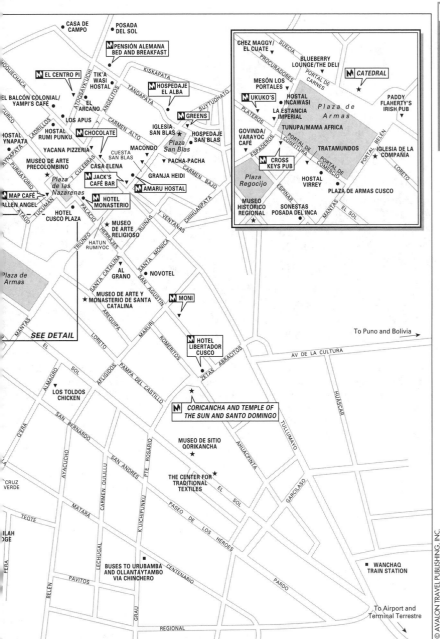

© AVALON TRAVEL PUBLISHING, INC.

Iglesia de la Compañía on Cusco's Plaza de Armas

and then later to the jungle enclave of **Vilcabamba.** The Incas resisted for more than three decades until their last leader, Inca **Túpac Amaru,** was captured in the Amazon and executed in Cusco's main square in 1573.

By this time, Cusco had already faded from prominence. After its gold was gone, Francisco Pizarro left for the coast and made Lima the capital of the new viceroyalty. More than two centuries later, an Indian who claimed Inca descent and called himself Túpac Amaru II would rally Inca fervor once again and launch another siege of Cusco. But the Spaniards quickly captured him and hung him in Cusco's main square. His body was quartered and pieces of it were left in the squares of surrounding Inca villages as a warning for the future.

Cusco would have ended up another quiet Andean city like Cajamarca and Ayacucho were it not for Hiram Bingham's discovery of Machu Picchu in 1911. That discovery sparked an in-

ternational interest in Cusco, which flourished in the 1920s with a glittering café society and a generation of intellectuals that included photographer **Martín Chambi.** During the 1920s the train line was built past Machu Picchu that still carries travelers today.

A **1950 earthquake,** the most severe in three centuries, destroyed the homes of 35,000 people in Cusco but had the unexpected benefit of clearing away colonial facades that had covered up Inca stonework for centuries. Much of the Inca stonework visible today around Cusco, including the long wall at Coricancha, was discovered thanks to the earthquake. Based on these ruins, and Cusco's colonial architecture, Cusco was declared a **UNESCO World Heritage site** in 1983.

PLAZA DE ARMAS

Cusco's Plaza de Armas is surrounded by colonial stone arcades and graced with two extraordinary

CUSCO'S TOURIST TICKET

You will go broke if you pay to get into each museum, church, and archaeological site around Cusco. Even if you are going to visit a few places, buy a *boleto turístico* for $10 ($5 for students under age 26 with ISIC card). The ticket covers 16 sites in and around Cusco, including must-sees like Sacsayhuamán, Pisac, Ollantaytambo, and Cusco's Catedral. The tickets can be bought at the entrance to most major sites or in two offices in Cusco: OFEC (Av. El Sol 103, #106, tel. 084/22-7037, 8 A.M.–6 P.M. Mon.–Fri.) or Casa Garcilaso (corner of Garcilaso and Heladeros, tel. 084/22-6919, 8 A.M.–5 P.M. Mon.–Fri., 8 A.M.–4 P.M. Sat., 8 A.M.– noon Sun.). Unfortunately, the pass only lasts 10 days. There is a process for extending expired passes

but—take it from us—it's not worth wasting a day navigating the halls of the Instituto Nacional de Cultura, which is a harrowing bureaucracy even by Peruvian standards. Sites not covered by the ticket include the Qorichanca Temple ($1.25), Iglesia de La Merced ($1.25), Inca's Museum ($1.25), and the Museo de Arte Precolumbino ($5).

The ticket covers the following 16 sites: Sacsayhuamán, Cusco Cathedral, Pikillacta, Museo de Arte Religioso, Tipón, Iglesia San Blas, Ollantaytambo, Museo Histórico Regional, Pisac, Chinchero ruins, Q'enqo, Museo de Arte y Monasterio de Santa Catalina, Puca Pucara, Museo Palacio Municipal, Tambo Machay, and Museo de Sitio Corichanca (though not Corichanca Temple).

churches, the Catedral and the Jesuit Iglesia de la Compañía. Though a grove of native trees was unfortunately ripped out in the late 1990s, Cusco's main square is a lively place for locals and tourists alike—full of child shoe shiners, hand-holding schoolgirls, and old men sharing crossword puzzles. Two flags fly over the square, the red-and-white flag of Peru and the rainbow-colored flag of the Inca nation, which is nearly identical to the gay pride flag. It is much older, of course, and its eight colors represent the four corners of Tahuantinsuyo, the Inca empire.

M Catedral

Cusco's baroque Catedral (Plaza de Armas, 10–11:30 A.M. Mon.–Thurs. and Sat., 2–5:30 P.M. daily, entry with *boleto turístico*) sits between the more recent church of **Jesús María** (1733) on its right and, on its left, **El Triunfo** (1539), the first Christian church in Cusco, built to celebrate the victory over Manco Inca. The cathedral was built on top of Inca Viracocha's palace using blocks of red granite taken from Sacsayhuamán and took more than a century to construct from 1560 onwards. At least four earthquakes from 1650 to 1986, along with damp and neglect, had taken a serious toll on the building. Fortunately, Cusco's archbishop acquired financial backing from Telefónica for a complete renovation from 1997 to 2002, which removed much of time's

grime that had covered chapels and paintings. For the first time in a century perhaps, it is possible to make out the unique **Cusco School** paintings, including odd works such as Christ eating a guinea pig at the Last Supper and a (very) pregnant Virgin Mary. There is also an interesting painting, reported to be the oldest in Cusco, showing Cusco during the 1650 earthquake with the townspeople praying in the Plaza de Armas. The church also contains considerable gold- and silverwork, including a silver bier for the **Señor de los Temblores** (Lord of the Earthquakes), patron of Cusco. There is also 17th-century carved pulpit and choir stalls and an original gold-covered Renaissance altar. In the bell tower is the huge Maria Angola bell, one of the largest bells in the world and made with 27 kg of gold.

Iglesia de La Compañía

Across the corner from the cathedral is the 17th-century **Iglesia de la Compañía** (no set hours, free admission), which was built on top of the palace of Inca Huayna Capac. This church was built by the Jesuits, who were expelled from Latin America in 1767 but not before they built a series of churches in Peru's principal cities that outshine even the cathedral. This graceful, highly ornate facade is a case in point, behind which is a single nave leading to a spectacular baroque altar. Near the main door is a 17th-century painting depicting the wedding of Inca princess Beatriz Clara Coya to Spanish *captín* Martín García de Loyola, grandnephew of San Ignacio de Loyola.

NORTHEAST OF THE PLAZA DE ARMAS

Museo Inka

Head down the alley to the left of the Cathedral to reach this museum (corner of Ataúd and

Túcuman, tel. 084/23-7380, 9 A.M.–5 P.M. Mon.–Fri., 9 A.M.–4 P.M. Sat., $1.50). This ornate colonial home contains an interesting collection of Inca objects, including jewelry, ceramics, textiles, mummies, and a variety of metal and gold artifacts. It also has the world's largest collection of *qeros,* wooden cups the Incas used for drinking.

Museo de Arte Precolombino

Head in the same direction up the alley toward the Plaza de las Nazarenas and the fabulous new private museum (Plaza de las Nazarenas 231, tel. 084/23-3210, 9 A.M.–11 P.M. daily, $5). MAP opened its doors in June 2003 and contains an exquisite array of ceramics, painting, jewelry, and objects made of silver and gold. Unlike at other archaeological museums, the pieces here are not meant to be viewed as artifacts representative of their cultures. They are ancient works of art, pieces of elaborate craftsmanship and beauty that were handpicked from the Museo Larco in Lima. The museum has an elegant layout designed by Federick Syszlo, one of Peru's most respected contemporary painters, and in the courtyard is an interesting glass box containing the MAP café, Cusco's most upscale restaurant. Near the end of the plaza is the 400-year-old **Seminario San Antonio Abad,** which has been converted into **Hotel Monasterio,** Cusco's leading five-star hotel. Even if you are not a guest, sneak a peak at the courtyard and the 17th-century **Iglesia San Antonio Abad.**

Museo de Arte Religioso

Just one block downhill along Palacio, this museum (Palacio and Hatun Rumiyoc, 8–11:30 A.M. and 3–5:30 P.M. Mon.–Sat., entry with *boleto turístico*) resides in a colonial building that was built by the Marquis of Buenavista and later occupied by Cusco's archbishop. These days its handsome salons showcase religious paintings from the 17th and 18th centuries. Walk up the alleyway Hatun Rumiyoc and you will see that the entire museum is built upon a foundation of Inca stones that fit perfectly into one another. This was the foundation of an early ruler of Cusco, **Inca Roca,** and near the end of the street you will find the famous stone with 12 sides, all of which conforms perfectly to its neighbor.

TAXI SAFETY

It is a common misconception that traveling through Peru's remote countryside is risky while spending time in a tourist town like Cusco is safe. In fact, the exact opposite is true. The number of taxi assaults, where cab drivers rob their passengers, are on the rise in Cusco. Most of these are simple robberies, though some have involved violence. Here are some tips for staying out of trouble:

- Only take newer-looking taxis with a golden registry emblem on the front windshield, along with a red insurance sticker.
- Look at the taxi driver and decide whether you feel comfortable with him. If you feel nervous, wave the taxi on and choose another.
- Always take a taxi late at night, especially after drinking.
- Walk in a group at night.
- Carry your wallet in your front pocket and keep your backpack in front of you in a market or other crowded areas. In markets, it is often better to leave most of your money and passport at home.
- Walk with purpose and confidence.
- Do not buy drugs.
- When riding on a bus, store your luggage below or keep it on your lap. Do not put it on the racks above you where others can reach it as you sleep.
- Be leery of new friends at bars and on the street—many scams involve misplaced trust or the lure of drugs and sex and are hatched over the space of hours. Think twice before you go somewhere out-of-the-way with someone you just met.

Sadly the stone was badly chipped and scarred by a group of unknown vandals in April 2004.

Walk to the end of this street (which changes names three times in three blocks!) and you will reach Choquechaca, where many of Cusco's best restaurants and cafés—and the South American Explorer's Club—are located. Cross Choquechaca and continue up Cuesta San Blas, which leads to Cusco's **San Blas** neighborhood. This square, known as Plaza San Blas, is home to several artisan families who have been operating here for decades. Its steep cobblestone alleys offer excellent views over Cusco.

Iglesia San Blas (Plaza San Blas, 8–11:30 A.M. Mon.–Thurs. and Sat., 2–5:30 P.M. daily, entry with *boleto turístico*) is a small, white-washed adobe church built in 1563. One of the New World's most famous works of art is found here, a carved pulpit made from the trunk of a single tree. There is also a gold-covered baroque altar. If you are hungry, San Blas is a great place for lunch: Head to Greens on Tandapata or the Pie Shop on Atoqsayk'uchi.

EAST OF THE PLAZA DE ARMAS

Museo de Arte y Monasterio de Santa Catalina

From the Plaza de Armas, head down Arequipa to this museum (Arequipa, 9 A.M.–5:30 P.M. Mon.–Thurs. and Sat., 9 A.M.–3 P.M. Fri., entry with *boleto turístico*), which was built on top of the enclosure where the chosen virgins of the Inca lived, known as the **Acllahuasi,** or "house of the chosen ones." In a strange historical twist, the Spaniards converted the building into a convent, where 30 nuns remain cloistered to this day. Holy women have thus lived in this building for at least five centuries. The museum has a good collection of Cusco School paintings and an impressive Renaissance altar. A highlight is a trunk containing miniature figurines depicting the life of Christ, which was used by Catholic missionaries for proselytizing in far-flung regions of Peru.

Coricancha and Santo Domingo

The greatest prize in the Spaniards' 1533 sacking of Cusco was Coricancha (Plazoleta Santo Domingo, 8 A.M.–5 P.M. Mon.–Sat., 2–4 P.M. Sun., $3, $1.50 students), the sun temple. For the Incas, the building had many functions. It was foremost a place where offerings were burnt in thanks to the sun, though there were also rooms devoted to the moon, stars, lightning, thunder, and rainbows. Like so much of Inca ceremonial architecture, the building also served as a solar observatory and mummy storehouse.

The south-facing walls of the temple were covered with gold in order to reflect the light of the sun and illuminate the temple. Inside was the **Punchaco,** a solid-gold disk inlaid with precious stones, which represented the sun and was probably the most sacred object in the Inca Empire. Pizarro's scouts had already produced approximately a ton and a half of gold by stripping the inner walls of Coricancha. When the main Spanish force gained Cusco, they gathered hundreds of gold sculptures and objects from the temple, including an altar big enough to hold two men and an extraordinary artificial garden made of gold, including cornstalks with silver stems and ears of gold. Tragically, everything was melted down within a month—except for the Punchaco. It disappeared from the temple and its whereabouts are unknown to this day.

The Dominicans took over the Coricancha and dismantled most of it, using the polished ashlar to build their church and convent of Santa Domingo on top of the sun temple's walls. For centuries, many of the Coricancha's walls were hidden beneath the convent. But in 1950 an earthquake caused large sections of the convent to crumble, exposing Inca walls of the highest quality.

It requires considerable imagination today to imagine how the Inca's most important temple must have once looked. The eight-sided sacrificial font, stripped of the 55 kg of gold that once covered it, stands in the middle of the Coricancha's main square. The rooms that surround it may once have been covered with silver and dedicated to the moon, stars, and thunder. The wall running along the temple's eastern side is 60 meters long and 5 meters high, and each block is perfectly interlocked with its neighbor. But the highlight is the curved retaining wall beneath

COLONIAL PAINTING: THE CUSCO SCHOOL

The religious paintings that cover the walls of Peru's colonial churches are more than decoration. For centuries after the conquest, painting was the Catholic church's main tool for converting Peru's native peoples, who for the most part did not read or speak Spanish. The church's religious campaign produced thousands of now-priceless works and renowned schools of painting in Cusco and Quito, in present-day Ecuador.

Shortly after the conquest, the different orders of the Catholic church began importing paintings into Lima from well-known painters of the ongoing European Renaissance. The museum at Iglesia San Francisco in Lima contains works by European painters who influenced the American schools of painting, collectively known as the Spanish American Baroque. These 16th-century European masters included the Spanish painters Francisco de Zurbarán and Bartolomé Esteban Murillo and Flemish master Peter Paul Rubens.

By 1580, demand for European paintings had so outstripped supply that European painters began arriving Lima in search of lucrative commissions. One of these was Italian Jesuit Bernardo Bitti (1548–1610), who was a disciple of Caravaggio and the brightly colored, emotional works of the Italian Baroque. He was probably the single most influential European painter to work in Peru, and his paintings can be seen at La Merced in Cusco, La Compañía in Arequipa, and Lima's San Francisco museum. With the guidance of Bitti and other European masters, the church orders set up convent studios around Peru where Indian and *mestizo* artisans cranked out a staggering quantity of paintings in serial fashion—one painter would specialize in clothing, another in landscape, and still another in face and hands.

Right from the start, the workshops in Cusco began developing a unique style that blended the European Baroque with images from Peru, including local trees, plants, animals, and foods. Cusco's cathedral, for instance, contains a painting that shows the Last Supper served with roasted guinea pig and *chicha,* the local corn beer. In another painting nearby, there is a pregnant Virgin Mary with the lustrous, smooth hair of Andean women. Often the dress of the Virgin Mary has a triangular shape, which art scholars believe is a transformation of the ancient Andean practice of worshipping *apus,* or sacred mountains.

The painters of the Cusco School also used a lot of gold to highlight their paintings and create a richly decorated surface. Most paintings pictured the Virgin Mary, scenes from the life of a saint, or panoramas of devils and angels. An entirely unique invention of Cusco's painters was the archangels, flying through the air with ornate Spanish clothing and armed with muskets. Far from the tranquil realism of the Flemish Baroque, these paintings portrayed a dazzling otherworld, filled with powerful spiritual beings, which were meant to awe, stun, and frighten Indian viewers into accepting Catholicism. The most famous painters of the Cusco School were Diego Quispe Tito, Juan Espinosa de los Monteros, and Antonio Sinchi Roca, though it is difficult to decipher who did what because paintings were rarely signed.

In Quito, new-world painters embarked on a different course. The founder of the Quito School was Father Bedón, who studied with Bitti in Lima but quickly dropped the Italian Mannerist style upon returning to Quito. Instead he ushered in a type of religious painting that combined the gold decorations of the Cusco School with the colder colors and shadowy depths favored by Peter Paul Rubens and other Flemish painters. The cathedrals in northern Peru, including Cajamarca and Trujillo, often feature paintings from both schools side by side.

the facade of the church, which has not budged an inch in all of Cusco's earthquakes.

Museo de Sitio Corikancha

Reached through an underground entrance across the garden from the temple is this rather unimpressive museum (Avenida de Sol, 9 A.M.–5:30 P.M. daily, $3) that exhibits a few artifacts from the excavation of Coricancha. There is also a model of the sun temple and blueprints of its floor plans. There are no guides available here, and explanations are in Spanish only.

On your way back to the Plaza de Armas, walk down the narrow alley of Loreto. To your right are the Inca walls of the Acllahuasi, now the Santa Catalina convent. To the left are the walls of the palace of Huayna Capaca, now the Iglesia de la Compañía.

SOUTHWEST OF THE PLAZA DE ARMAS

From the Plaza de Armas, walk up Mantas for one block to the **Iglesia de la Merced** (tel. 084/23-1821, 9 A.M.–noon and 2–5 P.M. Mon.–Sat., $1), which was completely rebuilt following the 1650 earthquake. Inside the church lay two conquistadores, a father and a son, who were executed by the Spanish shortly after the conquest. Diego de Almagro the Elder was hung after he rebelled against Francisco Pizarro's authority, and his son, Diego de Almagro the Younger, was executed four years later for murdering Francisco Pizarro in revenge. Hanging on the walls nearby the tombs are paintings by the 16th-century master Bernardo Bitti. The church's elegant cloisters contain a small museum, which showcases a magnificent monstrance made of gold, silver, and precious stones.

From here, head down Heladeros to the **Plaza Regocijo** and the **Museo Histórico Regional** (Heladeros, tel. 084/22-5211, 8:30 A.M.–5 P.M. Mon.–Sat., entry with *boleto turístico*), which was once the home of colonial Peru's most famous and eloquent writers, the mestizo Inca Garcilaso de la Vega. The museum provides a fine survey of Peru's pre-Inca cultures, starting with pre-ceramic arrow heads and continuing with artifacts from

the Chavín, Moche, Chimú, Chancay, and Inca cultures. The holdings include a Nasca mummy and, on the second floor, colonial furniture and paintings from the Cusco School. Across the Plaza Regocijo in the municipality is the **Museo Municipal de Arte Contemporáneo** (Plaza Regocijo, 9 A.M.–5:30 P.M. Mon.–Fri., free), which contains contemporary art of varying quality.

From Plaza Regocijo, walk down Garcilaso to **San Francisco,** a convent and church that stands above the plaza of the same name. This church, with three naves and the shape of a Latin cross, was built in 1572 and is one of the few churches in Cusco to survive the 1650 earthquake. As a result, its convent is one of the few remaining examples of the highly ornate 16th-century plateresque style, complemented here by *azulejo* tiles imported from Seville. There are two smaller colonial churches down Santa Clara from here toward the market and the train station: the first is **Santa Clara,** which is open only for early-morning mass from 6–7 A.M., and the second is **San Pedro,** which is open 2–5:30 P.M. Mon.–Sat.

OUTSIDE THE CITY

There are four highly recommended Inca ruins outside of Cusco, which many Cusco agencies offer as part of a rushed, half-day tour. The ruins all accept the *boleto turístico* and are open 7 A.M.–6 P.M.; after-hours visits are possible at Sacsayhuamán, the ruins closest to Cusco. Peter Frost's excellent guide to Cusco, *Exploring Cusco,* details a few interesting walks around this spectacular landscape between the four sites, which are littered with aqueducts, Inca roads, caves, shrines, and carvings.

All the ruins lie close to the road that runs between Cusco and Pisac. An enjoyable way to see the ruins is to take a Pisac bus or taxi to the farthest ruins, Tambomachay, and walk the 8 km back to Cusco, visiting all the ruins along the way (this walk can be shortened considerably by just walking between Q'enqo and Sacsayhuamán, a distance of 1 km). Occasional robberies have been reported in this area, so it is better to walk in a group of two or more during the early part of the day.

Sacsayhuamán

Looming over Cusco to the north are the ruins of Sacsayhuamán, a hilltop fortress with three ramparts of zigzag walls that run for nearly 300 meters on its north side. The largest stones—nearly 8.5 meters high and 361 tons, according to historian John Hemming—were placed at the apex of the walls to strengthen them. Every Inca citizen had to spend a few months of the year working on public works, and the Incas used this tremendous reserve of labor to move the stones, using log sleds and levers. But even engineers have a hard time understanding how the Incas fitted these huges stones so perfectly together.

Only the largest stones of Sacsayhuamán remain. Up until 1930s, builders arrive at Sacsayhuamán to cart away the pre-cut stone of this apparently limitless quarry, so it is difficult to appreciate how impregnable Sacsayhuamán must have been. Three towers once crowned the top of Sacsayhuamán, and two of their foundations are visible. During Manco Inca's great rebellion, the Spaniards managed to establish a base on the opposing hill and spent two days charging across the plain on horseback and attempting to scale the defensive walls. On the first day, one of the stones fired by the Inca slingshots struck Juan Pizarro, Francisco's younger brother, who died that night. On the evening of the second day, the Spaniards launched a surprise attack with ladders and successfully forced the Incas into the three stone towers. As the Spaniards massacred the estimated 1,500 soldiers trapped inside, many Incas preferred to leap to their deaths from the high tower. The next morning, condors feasted on the dead bodies, and this grisly image is emblazoned on Cusco's coat-of-arms.

These days the flat fields outside of Sacsayhuamán, where the Inti Raymi culminates each June, is a peaceful place to stroll. In the mornings, Cusco residents come here to jog or do yoga on the grassy lawn, which is considerable larger than a soccer field. A huge trapezoidal door leads up a walkway to the top of the ruins, which is a marvellous place to bring wine and watch the sun setting over Cusco. Because many tourists come here in the evening, guards are posted to put visitors at ease as dusk falls. If you have time, visit the top of Rodadero hill, where the Spaniards based themselves during their assault on Sacsayhuamán. There is a rock outcrop on top, beautifully carved with sacred steps. Sacsayhuamán is a steep, 2-km walk from Cusco or a 10-minute taxi ride ($2). Taxis wait in the parking lot for the return trip to Cusco.

Q'enqo

One kilometer past Sacsayhuamán is the shrine of Q'enqo (the word means "zigzag" in Quechua). It is a large limestone outcrop carved with enigmatic steps leading nowhere, a sacred motif that is found on nearly every *huaca,* the sacred stone revered by the Incas. On the top of the rock are faint carvings of a puma and a condor. Carved into the rock are perfect zigzag channels, which probably flowed with *chicha* or llama blood during ceremonial rituals, much like the Saywite Stone between Cusco and Abancay (see *The Saywite Stone* in the *Ayacucho and the Central Highlands* chapter.) Below the rock is a series of caves carved with niches where mummies of lesser nobility may once have been kept. Nearby is an amphitheater with niches centered framing an upright stone, which was probably defaced long ago by Spanish extirpators of idolatry. Between Q'enqo and Sacsayhuamán are a series of soccer fields, where rather pitiful horses can be rented for quick rides in the area ($3 per half hour, price negotiable).

Puca Pucara

The least significant of the ruins outside Cusco, Puca Pucara (meaning "red fort" in Quechua) was probably not a fort at all, but rather a storage facility or an Inca *tambo,* or lodge. Perhaps when the Inca emperor came to visit the baths of Tambomachay, his court waited here. There are several chambers below and a platform on top with excellent views. The distance between Puca Pucara and Q'enqo is 6 km along the road.

Tambomachay

Called the Inca's Bath, Tambomachay lies about 300 meters off the Pisac road, though it is well-marked with a sign. It is a well-preserved example of the sacred water fountains found at nearly every important Inca temple, including Pisac,

Ollantaytambo, and Machu Picchu. The Incas took a natural spring and painstakingly channeled the water through three waterfalls, which continue to work perfectly today. There is a fine Inca wall above with ceremonial niches. The Incas worshiped water as a vital life element, and this site no doubt formed part of a water cult. From here, you can see the nearby site of Puca Pucara, on the other side of the road.

ENTERTAINMENT AND EVENTS
Festivals

Celebrated continuously since the devastating quake of 1650, Cusco's procession of the **Señor de los Temblores** (Lord of the Earthquakes) traditionally begins at Cusco's cathedral on the Monday before Easter.

One of Peru's most enigmatic festivals is **Qoyllur R'itti,** which takes place in May or June before Corpus Christi on the slopes of Nevado Ausangate at 4,800 meters. During the three-day festival, elaborately costumed men climb in the middle of the night to hew huge blocks of ice, which they carry on their backs down the mountain at dawn. Thousands of *campesinos* from neighboring communities come to this spot to bring ice down from the mountain or participate in the elaborate masked dances. This festival, Christian only on the surface, grew out of the Andean tradition of worshipping mountains, or *apus,* to ensure rains and good harvests. The pilgrims trek toward the mountain from the town of Tinki, which is several hours away from Cusco on the rough road to Puerto Maldonado. If you are in Cusco during this time, you can find agencies along Plateros in Cusco that sell packages for transport and camping.

During Cusco's **Corpus Christi,** which usually happens in early June, elaborate processions fill the streets of Cusco as all the bells in the city ring. Each procession carries a different saint, which is treated as if it were a living person, in the same way the Incas paraded their ancestors' mummies around these same streets five centuries ago.

A country festival that is straightforward for travelers to attend is the June 15–17 festival of the **Virgen del Carmen** in Paucartambo, a pleasant colonial town that is a four-hour bus ride from Cusco on the way to the Manu. The festival includes an extraordinary range of dances and costumes. Many Cusco agencies offer inexpensive

Inti Raymi, the Inca Sun Festival, is held each year during the the June 24th winter solstice in Cusco.

Cusco and the Sacred Valley

lodge-and-transport packages to the festival, which include a dawn trip to Tres Cruces, a fabulous place to watch the sun rise over the Amazon basin.

Cusco's biggest festival is **Inti Raymi**, the Inca celebration of the June 24 winter solstice. The festival, which last ten days on either side of the solstice, was banned by the Spaniards in 1535. But in 1944, a group of Cusco intellectuals re-created the sacred ceremony by studying chronicles and historical documents. Each year, hundreds dress up as Inca priests, nobles, and chosen women, and one man, chosen by audition, gets to be Inca Pachacútec. The main day, June 24, begins at 10 A.M. at the Coricancha (the Temple of the Sun) and ends around 2 P.M. at Sacsayhuamán, where thousands of tourists sit on the fort's walls for a good view as Pachacútec speaks with a sun god through a microphone. It is a highly staged, touristy production, and completely unlike the more down-to-earth countryside festivals.

Santuranticuy Festival, on December 24, is one of the largest arts-and-crafts fairs in Peru. Nativity figures, miniature altars and ceramics are laid out on blankets in the Plaza de Armas by hundreds of artists.

Peñas and Folkloric Music

The **Centro Qosqo de Arte Nativo** (Sol 604, next to the Center for Traditional Textiles, tel. 084/22-7901, $3.50), founded in 1924, has a highly recommended music and dance show 7–8:30 P.M. on most evenings. The Centro was founded in 1924 as the first organized music and dance center in Cusco. Most of the Peruvian restaurants in the Plaza de Armas have live music during dinner. In San Blas, the Peña Restaurante Kayllapi, at the corner of Tandapta behind the Iglesia San Blas, gets going with live *música criolla* most evenings.

Café-Bars

Two of the hippest, most relaxed places to hang out night or day are **⋈ Los Perros Couch & Wine Bar** (Tecsecocha 426, tel. 084/24-1447, los_perros@yahoo.com, 11 A.M.–midnight daily, $4 entrées) and **Blueberry Lounge** (Portal de Carnes 236, tel. 084/22-1397, 8:30 A.M.–1 A.M. daily, $4–7 entrées).

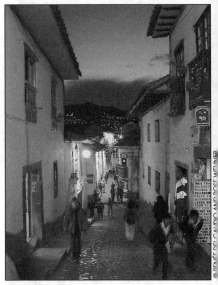

the street of San Blas at night

The **Tangible Myth** (San Juan de Dios 260, tel. 084/26-0519, 8 P.M.–1 A.M. Wed.–Mon.) is a classy jazz bar that doubles as a gallery for contemporary Latin America. Jazz from 10 P.M. onwards.

There is always a fresh, eclectic array of music at **⋈ The Muse** (Tandapata 684, Plaza San Blas, tel. 084/24-6332, themusecusco@yahoo.com, 8 A.M.–1 A.M., $2 entrees, no cover). The café serves English-style breakfasts with espresso and fresh orange juice, and a variety of innovative sandwiches and salads. Live music, ranging from American folk to Argentine tango, starts after 9:30 P.M. Musicians often play in front of the café on Sunday, where the café has a number of tables with good views over the Plaza San Blas. The owners are musicians themselves and have an in-house studio.

The new, family-owned **⋈ The Film Movies & Lounge** (Procuradores 389, 2nd flr., tel. 084/962-5898, $4) isn't kidding when it says, "Sorry, but we have the best movies, crepes, salads, and pies in town." The best films from Mexico, Spain, and Italy, and cult classics from the United States are shown daily at 11:30 A.M., 5 P.M. and 9 P.M. Classics from directors such as

Roman Polanski, Stanley Kubrick, Woody Allen, Quentin Tarantino, and Guy Ritchie are projected on a medium-sized screen. The café serves incredible chocolate-banana crepes, Greek salads, and lúcuma-flavored cheesecake.

Pubs and Live Music

Ŋ Cross Keys Pub (Portal Confiturias 233, 2nd flr., tel. 084/22-9227, 10 A.M.–1 A.M. daily) is a Cusco classic, an English pub with view over the Plaza de Armas that has been around for years and is owned by Barry Walker, British consul and owner of Manu Expeditions. The pub menu includes chili con carne and hamburgers, and there is a dusty pool table and darts on the rickety second level. Happy hour runs 6:30–7:30 P.M. and 9:30–10 P.M.

The atmosphere at **Paddy Flaherty's Irish Pub** (Triunfo 124, 11 A.M.–2 A.M.) is a taste of home, at least for those of us who hang out at Irish pubs. It serves Guinness, among other beers, and has a two-for-one happy hour from 7–8 P.M. The kitchen offers shepherd's pie, Philly cheesesteak sandwiches, and stuffed potato skins.

The other Irish pub in town is the friendlier, laid back **Rosie O'Gradys** (Santa Catalina Ancha 360, tel. 084/24-3514), with great happy hours at 1–2 P.M. and 8:30–9:30 P.M. It serves all kinds of bar food, including Caesar salads, garlic steak, chicken curry, and beef stroganoff.

Mandela's (Palacio 121, 3rd flr., tel. 084/22-2424, 6 P.M.–1 A.M.) is a classy place for drinks and light food on a rooftop terrace behind the cathedral. The dimly lit interior has a huge portrait of Nelson Mandela and a range of music from electronic to jungle rhythms. This place may have changed names by the time you read this.

If you still have energy after a pub or café warmup, there are plenty of places to dance until 5 A.M. in Cusco—and a good range of music. Locals and foreigners head to **Ŋ Ukuko's** (Plateros 316, tel. 084/24-2951, 8 P.M.–5 A.M. daily, $3 cover on weekends), a live music venue and bar that has been leading Cusco's nightlife scene since it was founded a decade ago. Shows start at 10:30 P.M. and range from Afro-Peruvian to cool hippie drumming, with affordable drinks and free movies daily at 5:30 P.M. An-

other Cusco classic for live music is **Kamikase** (Plaza Regocijo, 8 P.M.–5 A.M.), with live salsa and Afro-Peruvian shows from 10:30 P.M. most nights. Happy hour is 8–10 P.M.

Garabato's (10–3 A.M.) is a locals' hangout that serves pricey cocktails and wines by the glass. Videos play until 10 P.M., when live criollo music bands, often from Lima, perform. There are also free movies here around 2 P.M.

Nightclubs

The newly opened **Ŋ Spoon** (Plateros 334, 2nd flr., 10 P.M.–6 A.M., $3–5) is decidedly the most fashionable disco in Cusco. The space is industrial, yet somehow swanky, with steel lattice work, aluminum tread stairs, and loft sitting areas. Drinks here are a bit more expensive than elsewhere but there is an interesting blend of electronic and techno music that plays until the last person goes home. Happy hour is midnight–1 A.M., and free drinks are doled out 1–2 A.M.

The multilevel **Loft** (Waynapata 194, tel. 084/24-6442, 6 P.M.–2 A.M.) is a fashionable club with techno music and the occasional rave or battle-of-the-bands. The space is swanky with a dance floor on the first level. Two-for-one happy hour is 7–8 P.M. Perhaps the most frequented dance spot is **Mama África** (Portal de Harinas 191, 2nd flr., 8–2 A.M. daily), which caters to 20-something backpackers, blasts reggae, and is often packed on the weekends. Happy hour runs 8–9:30 P.M. and a daily movie plays at 6 P.M. The scene is similar at Mama África's lesser spinoff, Mama América.

The best salsa spot in Cusco, frequented mainly by Peruvians, is **El Muki** (Santa Catalina 114, 10 P.M.–late).

SHOPPING

Crafts shops are wall-to-wall along Triunfo, which leads from the Plaza de Armas and becomes Rumiyoc and Cuesta San Blas before dead-ending into Plaza San Blas, the center of Cusco's bohemian/art district. Several families who have been producing crafts for decades have their workshops here and can often be seen at work.

The streets between the Plaza de Armas and

Plaza Regocijo are lined with both inexpensive crafts stalls and high-end jewelry and alpaca boutiques.

Ceramics and Weavings

The family workshop **Artesania Mendivil** (Hatun Rumiyoc 486, tel. 084/23-3234, 8 A.M.–8 P.M. Mon.–Sat.) is known worldwide for its religious sculptures with long mannerist necks made of plaster cloth, rice paste, and wood. Hilario Mendivil began working as a craftsman at the age of 10 in 1939 and, though he has recently passed away, his sons continue the tradition. The figurines range from $35 to $350. At the nearby **Galeria Olave** (Plaza San Blas 651, tel. 084/23-1835, 9 A.M.–noon and 2–6 P.M. Mon.–Sat.), Sr. Olave can often be seen making religious ceramic sculptures.

On the hike up to San Blas, **Galeria Latina Cusco** (Triunfo 350, 2nd flr., tel. 084/24-6588, 9:30 A.M.–9 P.M. Mon.–Sat., 4:30–8:30 P.M. Sun.) has been selling natural dye weavings, alpaca clothing, pottery, and jewelry for 15 years. Near the Plazoleta Las Nazarenas, **Inca Wasi** (Palacio 104, tel. 084/24-1953, 8:30 A.M.–8:30 P.M. daily) sells good replicas of pre-Columbian artifacts and textiles.

There are a variety of crafts market in Cusco where bargaining is standard procedure. One is located right on the Plaza de Armas next to Iglesia de la Compañía (10:30 A.M.–1 P.M. and 3:30–9 P.M. Mon.–Sat., 4–9 P.M. Sun.) and has a decent selection of textiles, carved gourds, paintings and jewelry. A 10-minute walk from the Plaza de Armas, **Centro Artesanal Cusco** (Sol and Tullumayo, 8 A.M.–9 P.M. daily) has a range of affordable textiles. The **Mercado San Pedro** (6 A.M.–7 P.M.) is a good place to buy fruit and just about any other product imaginable and also has a few crafts vendors. This market is notorious for ingenious thefts, including backpack slashers, so leave valuables at home and walk with caution.

The highest-quality textiles for sale in all of Cusco are at **The Center for Traditional Textiles of Cusco** (El Sol 603, tel. 084/22-8117, 8 A.M.–8 P.M. Mon.–Fri., 8 A.M.–6 P.M. Sat.), which has been set up with the admirable goal of recovering ancient technologies, showcasing high-quality weaving, and sending revenue straight back to the remote, neglected villages that produce them. Local weavers give daily demonstrations, and there are displays that explain all the plants, minerals, and berries used for natural dyes. The textiles here are far better than those found elsewhere in Cusco and only slightly more expensive.

Alpaca Clothing and Jewelry

For the finest clothing in alpaca, head to the expensive **Alpaca 111** shop (Plaza Regocijo 202, tel. 084/24-3233), or **Alpaca Mon Repos** (Portal de Panes 139, tel. 084/25-1600). **Werner and Ana** (Plaza San Francisco 295, tel. 084/23-1076) is a hip clothing boutique with styles in alpaca and other fine materials.

There are exclusive jewelry shops all around the Plaza de Armas and up Cuesta San Blas, which mostly sell works of silver. Juana Flores Encalada sells inexpensive beads at her shop **Buhos** (Portal de Panes 123, 9 A.M.–1 P.M. and 3–8 P.M. Mon.–Sat.) on the Plaza de Armas.

Contemporary Art

Contemporary art can be found in several shops along Triunfo, between the Plaza de Armas and San Blas. **Primitiva** (Hatun Rumiyoc 495, tel. 084/26-0152, 10 A.M.–9 P.M. Mon.–Sat., 3–9 P.M. Sun.) features the art of Argentine painter Frederico Coscio, who has spent more than a decade capturing the landscapes and people around Cusco. **Taller de Manuel** (Suyt'uqhato 700) exhibits charcoal drawings and other modern work. **Fototeca del Sur Andino** (Choquechaca 152, 3–9 P.M. Mon.–Sat.) is a cool gallery with black-and-white photos of the Cusco area, including postcards made from the work of world-famous Martín Chambi, who documented the first half of the 20th century in Cusco.

Bookstores

SBS Bookshop (El Sol 781, tel. 084/24-8106, 8 A.M.–1 P.M. and 3:30–7 P.M. Mon.–Fri., 8 A.M.–1 P.M. Sat.) is Peru's foremost importer of English books and has a good collection at its small Cusco shop. **Jerusalén** (Heladeros 143, tel. 084/23-5428, 9 A.M.–9 P.M. Mon.–Sat.) has a good selection of imported books and music. A final option is **Los**

Andes (Portal Comercio 125, tel. 084/23-4231, 10 A.M.–2 P.M. and 5–9 P.M. Mon.–Sat.).

Music Stores
Director Kike Pinto has collected more than 400 instruments for the *Taki* **Andean Music Museum** (Hatunrumiyoq 487-5, tel. 084/22-6897, killincho@yahoo.com, sporadic hours), some of which are for sale along with CDs, books, and music lessons. Kike offers music demonstration on Inca and pre-Inca instruments on Monday, Wednesday, and Friday evenings from 7 to 8 P.M. Call ahead of time to ensure Kike shows up.

Outdoor and Travel Gear
Tatoo (Plazoleta Las Nazarenas 211, tel. 084/26-3099) sells high-end Gore-Tex and fleece goods at a significant markup, along with Nalgene bottles and other camping gear. Many of the travel agencies along Plateros, Triunfo, and Garcilaso sell rain ponchos and other more reasonably priced camping gear.

© RENÉE DEL GAUDIO AND ROSS WEHNER

Cloud Forest Cliffs on day three of the Inca Trail

TREKKING
The Inca Trail is by far the most popular trekking route in the Cusco area because of its spectacular route of ruins and varied ecosystems. But there are a variety of other excellent treks in the Cusco area worth considering. Though they do not have the Inca Trail's variety of ruins nor the cachet of leading to Machu Picchu, they are less crowded and plunge into remote areas of Andean villages, tumbling jungle, and out-of-the-way archaeological sites. While all hikers on the Inca Trail must go with an agency, the other routes described here can be done independently by those with enough Spanish to ask directions. The best time to trek in the Cusco area is during the dry winter months from May to September, though the most crowded months on the Inca Trail are from June to August.

Inca Trail
These days the Inca Trail can only be hiked with a licensed operator, which has jacked the price up from $90 in 2000 to over $200 today. It is no longer as easy to find cheap, last-minute Inca Trail spots because the trail's 130 licensed operators now have to confirm all reservations five days in advance. The government has also begun limiting the number of trekkers on the Inca Trail each day. We recommend making an Inca Trail reservation at least one month ahead of time, especially during the high months between June and August.

To avoid getting ripped off, check to make sure your agency is one of those licensed by IN-RENA, the government conservation agency, which lists all Inca Trail agencies on its web page (www.inrenashm.gob.pe). Before paying, ask a lot of questions: what type of tents the outfitters use, how many people maximum in a group, and whether the price includes train and entry fees. Most important, ensure that your operator is bringing a bathroom tent because, trust us, you will not want to use the public bathrooms. If you don't think you are up to carrying a backpack over the Inca Trail's first 4,200-meter pass, porters can be hired for $10–15 per day to carry your pack for you. There is a legal limit of 25 kg (55 pounds) per porter, which is checked at the beginning of the trail.

Salcantay

Nevado Salcantay, at 6,271 meters, is the sacred mountain that towers above the Inca Trail and eventually drops to Machu Picchu itself. Many agencies offer a four-day trek starting from Mollepata, a town 3.5 hours from Cusco in the Limatambo Valley that can be reached by any bus heading from Cusco to Abancay. From Mollepata, you walk 3 km to the village of Parobamba, where mules and guides can be hired. The route traverses the Cordillera Vilcabamba, including spectacular views of several snow-covered peaks, and crests the 5,000-meter Incachillasca Pass before descending alongside the glaciers of Salcantay. The last day is spent walking from a campsite at Acobamba to the Inca ruins of Patallacta, the traditional starting point of the Inca Trail. From here you can take a train from Km 88 of the train line to either Macchu Picchu or Cusco.

Choquequirao

Choquequirao is a huge Inca complex perched on a ridgetop in the Vilcabamba area that includes many fine Inca walls and double recessed doorways. It was probably built as a winter palace by Inca Túpac Yupanqui, in the same way that his father, Pachacútec, probably built Machu Picchu. It too was discovered by Hiram Bingham in 1911, though it was lost again until the 1980s, when a series of explorers trudged through this rugged territory to find this and other ruins in the area. The Peruvian government, backed by UNESCO, is launching a campaign to restore the ruins and build a road to them, so get there before it changes forever.

The most common approach is from Cachora, reached by taking a bus to Abancay and getting off at a dirt road past the Saywite Stone. Hitchhike the final stretch to Cachora, where mules and guides can be rented. The first day is spent hiking down to the Río Apurímac, and the second continues straight up the other side, a long six-hour slog uphill onto the cloud forest ridge where the city is. Some agencies offer a combined 10-day trek that leads from Choquequirao all the way to Machu Picchu. Another option is to reach Choquequirao from Huancacalle, near the Inca ruins of Vitcos, a spectacular eight-day traverse of the Cordillera Vilcabamba.

Ausangate and the Cordillera Vilcanota

There are a variety of trekking routes through the **Cordillera Vilcanota,** the range east of Cusco that is dominated by the sacred Nevado Ausangate (6,384 meters). Trekking guides say that this is one of the more untouched, spectacular areas of Peru.

The classic route is a seven-day loop around the peak of Ausangate, which begins at the town of Tinki in the high *puna* grasslands and crosses four passes between 1,300 and 1,500 meters. The views include the fluted faces and rolling glaciers of all the mountains of the range, including Colquecruz and Jampa, and the route visits the remote hamlets of llama herders and weavers. This area is famous for its **Qoyllur R'itti** festival in May or June, when thousands of *campesinos* converge on the slopes of Ausangate.

Vilcabamba

The truly adventurous may want to try reaching **Espírítu Pampa,** the true *Lost City of the Incas* that served as the base for the Incas' 35-year rebellion against the Spanish. Gene Savoy's discovery of the ruins in 1964 made world news, and various subsequent expeditions have tried, in vain, to keep the jungle from growing over the immense site.

The trip starts from the village of Huancacalle, which can be reached by taking a truck or bus from Cusco over the Abra Málaga to Quillabamba and hopping off at the Huancacalle turnoff. Hitchhiking is easy along this winding road, which is traveled by trucks several times a day. The Cobos family, which has guided all the Vilcabamba explorers since Gene Savoy, operates a small hostel in Huancacalle and can rent mules for $7 a day. From Huancacalle, a path leads to the Inca emperor's original exile at Vitcos, where Manco Inca was murdered by the Spanish, and the exquisite sacred rock of Chuquipalta (the subject, among others, of Hugh Thomson's *White Rock*). The path heads to New Vilcabamba, a colonial-era mining town, and then crests a 3,800-meter pass before plunging into the jungle

view of the Cordillera Vilcanota from the Sacred Valley

below. The path includes sections of fine Inca staircases along a steep and tortuous valley to the ruins, which are in mosquito-ridden jungle at 1,000 meters. Instead of walking back all the way to Huancacalle, it is possible to walk for a day or two alongside the river on good paths until you reach the town of Kiteni on the Río Urubamba. From here, a bus goes back to Quillabamba. This trip takes between 7 and 10 days, depending on how fast you walk.

Trekking Agencies

When traveling with an agency, follow Leave No Trace principles and encourage your fellow trekkers to do the same. If you notice an agency that does not follow basic LNT practices, please write to us so that we can remove them from this book. To avoid sanitation problems, ask the cooks to wash their hands before cooking. Also ask them to boil enough drinking water for the next day—Inca Trail hikers commonly buy expensive bottled water and generate needless plastic trash in the process.

The prices listed below in parentheses are for the standard four-day, three-night Inca Trail trek,

usually including entry fees and your train ticket back to the starting point.

You will have an excellent trek with the following three agencies, which are the only ones to consistently recycle their trash, pack out all human waste, and filter water before cooking. Clients use comfortable bathroom tents, have their backpack carried as part of the cost, and, on the return from the Inca Trail, take Vistadome trains. Over the last few decades, these operators have developed ties with a number of Quechua communities in the Cusco area, where they are embarking on a new brand of participatory cultural activities that blend in with their treks—harvesting potatoes, building adobe homes, and even herding llamas.

Peruvian Andean Treks (Pardo 705, tel. 084/22-5701; in U.S. 800/683-8148; postmast@patc.usco.com.pe, www.andeantreks.com, $400, 10 percent SAE discount) is owned by American and long-time Cusco resident Tom Hendrickson. It operates on the Inca Trail and runs treks through jungle areas and the Lares Valley in the Cordillera. It is also the best option for climbing the snow-covered peaks around

Cusco. This company was voted Cusco's best tour operator in 2003 and employs (and compensates fairly) many of Cusco's best trekking guides and porters.

ExplorAndes (Garcilaso 316, tel. 084/23-8380 or in Lima 01/445-0532, postmast@exploran.com.pe, www.explorandes.com) is Peru's best-established adventure sports agency. It offers the traditional Inca Trail hike ($389), as well as variations that combine it with treks above the Sacred Valley or past Nevado Salcantay. A six-day trek around Nevado Ausangate is another possibility. Kayaking on Lake Titicaca, rafting down the Tambopata or Apurímac Rivers, and llama-supported treks around the Cordillera Blanca and Huayhuash near Huaraz are other options. Recently it has rolled out a variety of special-interest tours around Peru, focusing on orchids, potatoes and maize, camelids, ceramics, cactus, textiles, or coca and other medicinal plants. ExplorAndes was voted Peru's best overall tour operator by the Ministry of Tourism in 2003.

Trek Peru (Ricardo Palma N-9, tel. 084/25-2899, trekperu@terra.com.pe, www.trekperu.com, $380) was voted best Inca Trail operator in 2003 by the Ministry of Tourism. It also runs trips to Choquequirao, Lares Valley, and Cordillera Blanca and cultural tours all over Peru.

The following agencies carry the vast majority of Inca Trail travelers, and they are listed below because they are generally good about respecting porters and the environment.

Enigma (Garcilaso 132, tel. 084/22-2155, info@enigmaperu.com, www.enigmaperu.com, $290) is a newer agency with excellent guides and gourmet cooks. More expensive treks combine the Inca Trail with Nevado Salkantay, Vilcabamba, and the ruins of Choquequirao. It also offers alternative adventures such as horseback riding, ayahuasca therapy, and bird-watching.

SAS Travel (Portal de Panes 143, Plaza de Armas, tel. 084/23-7292, info@sastravelperu .com.pe, www.sastravelperu.com, $260, 7 percent SAE discount) is a very reputable company with 12 years' experience. It also does tours in the Sacred Valley, Parque Nacional Manu, and Reserva Tambopata. They move the most people along the Inca Trail, and are licensed to operate in the

Parque Nacional Manu as well. You could get a deep discount if you do both the Manu and the Inca Trail with SAS.

Inca Explorers (Suecia 339, tel. 084/24-1070, explorer@amauta.rcp.net.pe., www.incaexplorers.com, 8 percent SAE discount, email for current prices) is a highly profession agency with a reputation for paying porters well. It also does a range of longer trips to Vilcabamba, Choquequirao, and the Cordillera Vilcanota.

Q'ente (Garcilaso 210, tel. 084/23-8245, qente@terra.com.pe, www.qente.com, $300, 5–8 percent SAE discount) is highly recommended for its good service and trained staff.

The following Inca Trail operators are at the bottom of the price range but have been reported to be environmentally responsible.

United Mice (Triunfo 392, tel. 084/24-6041, unitedmi@terra.com.pe, www.unitedmice.com, $250, 7 percent SAE discount) is probably the most recommended backpacker's choice. It also offers a seven-day Salcantay trek for $500. Trekkers use brand-new North Face tents.

Mayuc (Portal Confituras 211, Plaza de Armas, tel. 084/23-2666, chando@mayuc.com, www .mayuc.com, $260, 10 percent SAE discount) has been in business for more than 20 years and also runs rafting trips on the Apurímac.

Andean Life (Plateros 372, Plaza de Armas, tel. 084/22-1491, andeanlife01@terra.com.pe, www.andeanlife.com, $265 adults, $245 students) offers daily departures for the Inca Trail. It also runs trips to Salcantay, Lares Valley, and around Nevado Ausangate.

SPORTS AND RECREATION

Along with Huaraz in the Cordillera Blanca, Cusco is Peru's main adventure sport center. The variety of intriguing options, and high-quality agencies, spur adventurers into Herculean feats of back-to-pack sports. One 21-year-old Israeli we met had trekked to Choquequirao, Salcantay, and the Inca Trail, rafted four days down the Class IV Río Apurímac, and mountain-biked around Maras and Moray above the Sacred Valley. He had just returned from a guided trip down the Río Chilive, just outside the Manu park, where his group floated down for 10 days on a homemade balsa raft. He wanted to ride in a hot-air balloon, paraglide over the Sacred Valley, and ride a Peruvian *paso* horse in Urubamba, but at that point he was broke.

For your safety, and for the environment, choose your agency carefully. If you choose to raft a serious river, like the Class IV Apurímac, go with one of the agencies listed in this book—if they are not listed here, they are *not* recommended. An average of two tourists a year die on the Apurímac alone, and though not even the best agency can take away all the risk, a new raft and an experienced guide make a big difference.

Fly-by-night agencies, with which Cusco is crawling, offer incredibly cheap prices (four-day Río Apurímac trip: $80!) but usually at the expense of your comfort and safety—and, worst of all, at the expense of the environment. This is especially true on the Inca Trail, where trash and human waste is becoming a serious problem. These low-budget agencies also do not pay their porters and cooks enough, and of course they do not invest in their training either.

Dozens of these agencies are closed down each year once the rangers in the Machu Picchu sanctuary catch on. One month later, however, the same agency opens again under a new name, which often mimics the high-quality leaders. The excellent Trek Peru, for instance, is often confused with Peru Trek, Peruvian Trek, Trekking Peru, etc. The courts are so backlogged with copyright cases that rarely do agencies defend their name. So the confusion lingers. Travelers who spend a bit more money to go with reputable agencies are helping to push up the bar of quality for all of Cusco's agencies.

Most of the agencies offer a variety of activities, ranging from mountain biking to rafting, but we have organized them according to their main focus. Amazonas Explorer, for instance, is most famous for its rafting trips but does a good range of trekking, mountain-bike trips, and cultural tours as well.

Rafting and Kayaking

There are many excellent rafting and kayaking options around Cusco. The easiest, and most common, are day trips along the Class III rapids of the Río Urubamba in the Sacred Valley ($25–50) and often include one night of camping near Ollantaytambo, mountain biking, and a chance to see ruins the next day. From December to May, when the river is swollen, agencies tend to raft the upper section above Pisac. When the water drops after June, they run the section of the river lower down near Ollantaytambo up until Chilca. Further downstream, the water rushes onward to Machu Picchu in great cataracts of un-navigable, Class VI water.

Another day option is the easier stretch of the Río Apurímac below the Cusco-Abancay highway, a gentle stretch that passes the foundations of an Inca hanging bridge made famous by Thornton Wilder in his classic *The Bridge of San Luis Rey.* The Apurímac here is generally sunny and subtropical, so bring sunscreen, hat, and mosquito repellent. After a quick dip in local hot springs, the agencies return to Cusco the same day.

A popular three-day rafting trip is on the upper Apurímac ($200–600), which can only be run between June and October. The Apurímac plunges through a steep and wild gorge and an endless series of Class III-V rapids. Agencies that operate this section of the river usually also offer trips on Cotahuasi ($1,850 approximately), a similar though more committing canyon near Arequipa that takes 10 days to navigate and a full-scale, supported expedition.

Our vote for most spectacular rafting expedition, though, goes to the Río Tambopata ($1,500–2,500), which is a great way to combine a mountain rafting adventure with world-class Amazon biodiversity. This 10- to 12-day trip begins in cloud forest north of Lake Titicaca with a few days of Class III-V rapids and ends floating on torpid jungle waters through the pristine Parque Nacional Bahuajua Sonene. Participants usually stay at the Tambopata Research Center, a rustic lodge operated by Rainforest Expeditions (see the section *Lodges on the Río Tambopata* in *The Amazon* chapter) that is minutes from the world's largest macaw clay lick. Floating silently through this untouched rainforest gives you good odds for seeing jaguar or tapir, not to mention a huge range of birds and more common animals such as capybara, turtles, and giant otters. The trip includes a flight back to Cusco from the jungle city of Puerto Maldonado.

If you want to kayak instead of raft, agencies will often loan you a kayak on the easier rivers such as the Urubamba and lower Apurímac. Other agencies, such as Erik's Adventures, offer kayaking schools.

The most professional rafting company in Peru, hands down, is **Amazonas Explorer** (José Gabriel Cosio 400, 1st flr., Urbanización Magisterial, tel. 084/22-7137, or cell tel. 084/976-0840, sales@amazonas-explorer.com, www.amazonas-explorer .com). It runs a variety of innovative trips in Peru, Chile, and Bolivia, including canoeing, mountain biking, trekking, and rafting. Some combine a few of these adventure sports with sightseeing. Many trips include a three-day descent of the upper Apurímac, and it offers a 16-day expedition that begins with sightseeing in Cusco and Lake Titicaca and ends in rafting down the Río Tambopata for two nights at the Tambopata Research Center ($2,300).

ExplorAndes offers high-end rafting trips similar in quality to Amazonas Explorer.

The following, less expensive agencies are recommended for the easy stretches of the Río Urubamba only, not the Aporímac. **Apumayo** (Garcilaso 265, #3, tel. 084/24-6018, contact@apumayo.com, www.apumayo.com, SAE discount) is run by Pepe López, a 30-something kayaker with a lot of experience on Peru's rivers. He started Apumayo in 1994 and has recently built an adventure center on the banks of the Río Urubamba, downstream of Ollantaytambo. The center, which shares profits with the nearby community of Cachiccata, offers hikes and mountain biking for the rafters who arrive here after descending the Río Urubamba. Apumayo's Urubamba trips are $25/day, and it also runs four-day trips down the Apurímac ($345), Tambopata ($1,895), and Cotahuasi ($1,850). It also rents mountain bikes ($60 full day) and offers llama treks and a four-day Inca Trail trek with bathroom tents ($495).

Eric Adventures (Plateros 324, tel. 084/22-8475, cusco@ericadventures.com, www.ericadventures.com, 10 percent SAE discount) operates an excellent day trip on Río Urubamba that includes a visit to Moray and the Salinas salt mines. The agency has recently gotten into the Inca Trail and mountain biking as well. Namesake Eric Arenas kayaked for Peru at the 1992 Barcelona Olympics, and the company offers a three-day kayaking course on the lower Apurímac.

Instinct (Procuradores 50, tel. 084/23-3451, instinct@chavin.rcp.net.pe, www.instinct-travel .com, 10 percent SAE discount) is a tour operator with more than 10 years' experience that has a three-day rafting trip on the Apurímac for $200. It also runs Inca Trail trips and four-day horseback rides past Nevado Salcantay ($500).

Loreto Tours (Calle del Medio 111, tel. 084/22-8264, loretotours@planet.com.pe) provides new wetsuits and Tevas for its cheap one-day river trips. It rents mountain bikes as well.

Mountain Climbing

Cusco is surrounded by snow-covered peaks that offer outstanding mountaineering possibilities, though none should be tried by people without mountaineering experience—even with a good guide. Unlike many of the mountains in the Cordillera Blanca, these routes are steep, icy, and complicated. Avalanches are common, for instance, on Salcantay. Several international climbing agencies operate in Peru. The best local mountaineering agency is Peruvian Andean Treks, owned by climber Tom Hendrickson (see *Trekking Agencies*). A highly recommended guide in Cusco is **Américo Serrano** (tel. 084/23-7064 or 24/7299). Serrano has all the international climbing certifications and in fact is one of the instructors who spend six weeks each year qualifying the new promotion of Peruvian guides in the Cordillera Blanca. In 2003, he assisted Lonnie Thompson, an internationally known glaciologist from Ohio State University, in an expedition to measure glacial recession in Peru's southern Andes.

In addition to Américo Serrano, there are six other internationally certified guides working in Peru. The best way to reach them is through **Camp Expedition** (Triunfo 392, of. 202, tel. 084/43-1468, info@campexpedition.net, www.campexpedition.net), which leads rappelling, climbing and canyoneering adventures in the Cusco area.

Biking

Nearly all of the agencies listed in the *Rafting and Kayaking* section now rent mountain bikes starting from $20 per day and up. Another highly recommended company for bike and motorbike tours is Loreto Tours (Calle del Medio 111, tel. 084/22-8264, loretotours@planet.com.pe). Peru's best-known mountain biker, Omar Zarzar Casis (omarzarzar@aventurarse.com), has written a book available in many Peruvian bookstores describing routes in Cusco and across the country. He is a good English-speaking contact for those planning a major ride in the area.

Many of the Manu tour operators (see *The Amazon* chapter) now allow clients during the drive into Manu to bike partway down the magnificent dirt-road descent from Acanaju Pass at 3,800 meters into the jungle. This whole route, which passes through Pisac and Paucartambo and continues into Manu, is a spectacular blur of more than a dozen ecosystems.

Many of the agencies also offer mountain biking in the Sacred Valley, especially on the Chinchero plateau around Moray and Maras, with a final descent past the salt mines to Urubamba. The Abra Málaga (4,600 meters), which lies along the highway between Ollantaytambo and Quillabamba, is another of Peru's spectacular mountain-to-jungle descents.

Bird-Watching

The Cusco area has one of the world's highest areas of bird biodiversity, particularly where the high Andes drops into the Amazon. Two good spots are the Abra Málaga (4,200 meters) area, en route to Quillabamba, and the Acanaju Pass (3,800 meters) area, en route to Parque Nacional Manu. Barry Walker, owner of Manu Expeditions and author of *A Field Guide to the Birds of Machu Picchu, Peru,* leads excellent birding expeditions and is a good contact for questions. Barry can be reached through Manu Expeditions (Pardo 895, tel. 084/22-6671, birding@manu-expeditions.com, www.birdinginperu.com).

Ballooning and Paragliding

Balloon expeditions with **Globos de los Andes** (Q'apchik'ijllu 271, tel. 084/23-2352, info@glo-bosperu.com, www.globosperu.com, 10 percent SAE discount) range from $55 for floating 200 meters over Moray or $300 for a complete tour over the Sacred Valley. The flights can be quite extravagant, with champagne on landing. The European owners of Sol y Luna Hotel, who claim to be the only internationally certified paragliding instructors in Cusco, offer $100 tandem paragliding flights over the Sacred Valley. Another option is Richard at **Cloudwalker** (tel. 084/993-7333, cloudwalker@another.com).

Horseback Riding

The best horse packer in Cusco is **Manu Expeditions** (Pardo 895, tel. 084/22-6671, adventure@manuexpeditions.com, www.manu-expeditions.com), an extremely professional company run by English ornithologist Barry Walker. The company has a range of trips, described on its web page, that explore areas of the Vilcabamba and Choquequirao ($17 days, $2,785), Machu Picchu and the surrounding cloud forest (15 days, $2,785), and one that heads from the Andes to the Amazon (14 days, $3,500). It also offers one- and two-day rides around Cusco for $70.

The best option for riding Peruvian *paso* horses is Perol Chico in Urubamba, in the Sacred Valley. Also in Urubamba, the Sol y Luna Hotel does Peruvian *paso* rides, and Incaland works in conjunction with Colorado horse packer Gary Ziegler to lead longer horse trips through the Lares Valley and other surrounding areas.

Catapults and Bungee Jumping

A wacky adventure opportunity—and we have no idea how safe it will be, as it has just opened—is Action Valley (office at Portal de Panes 123, ofc. 102, tel. 084/24-0835 or cell 084/9942449, info@actionvalley.com). This park, 11 km away from Cusco on the road to Chinchero, offers the following tantalizing adventures: a 107-meter bungee drop, a catapult that throws people 120 meters into the air with 3.2 g's of force, a 36-meter climbing pole nicknamed *The Peak,* a 124-meter rappel wall, and a 10-meter climbing wall. At the very least this park would make for interesting spectating.

Esoteric Experiences

The Sacred Valley is a hotbed for a range of spiritual and esoteric activities, though unfortunately the main operators seem to change constantly. A good touchstone and longtime expert is José (Pepe) Altamirano, the owner of the excellent agency Gatur (Puluchapata 140, tel. 084/22-3496 or 084/22-7829, gatur@terra.com.pe) and a hostel in San Salvador in the Sacred Valley. Another good contact is Lilo Ccooyllor, an American woman with several years' experience with different kinds of spiritual therapies in Cusco. She now operates the Casa de la Serenidad (www.shamanspirit.net, tel. 073/85-8180) near Mancora on Peru's north coast but returns to Cusco frequently.

Many Cusco agencies, including Enigma, offer sessions with the ayahuasca hallucinogen. Lesley Myburgh at Another Planet (Triunfo 120, tel. 084/22-9379, another.planet@terra.com.pe) is another good contact for both ayahuasca and San Pedro.

ACCOMMODATIONS

Our favorite neighborhood in all of Cusco is San Blas, the bohemian district above the Plaza de Armas that is crisscrossed with narrow alleys and teeming with cozy hostels, artisan galleries, and some of Cusco's best bars and restaurants. San Blas has a relaxing, artsy vibe, and its narrow streets keep out the traffic and smog of central Cusco.

Traffic has made parts of Cusco unpleasant. These areas include the extension of Plateros and Avenida El Sol, where even the back rooms of hotels hum with the noise of taxis and amplified advertisements. Outside of San Blas, Cusco's nicest lodging is along out-of-the-way streets like Suecia, Choquechaca, or Siete Cuartones/Nueva Alta, where classy bed-and-breakfasts are lined up along charming cobblestone streets. Always make a reservation ahead of time in Cusco, and ask for the kind of room you want (e.g., with a view or double bed). Despite a steady increase in Cusco hotels, the best ones are increasingly booked solid from May until November. If you arrive and don't like your room, you can usually wriggle out of your reservation after your first night and head elsewhere—there are lots of good options, especially among the newer, lesser-known hostels.

Under $10

The best choice in this category, although a 15-minute walk from the Plaza de Armas, is **Hostal Tahuantinsuyo** (Tupac Yupanqui 204, tel. 084/26-1410, suya@chaski.unsaac.edu.pe, $6 s, $9 d) with 24-hour hot water, a great atmosphere, laundry service, and a friendly staff that can help arrange tours. Prices include breakfast.

Ask for a room with a view at **Hostal Resbalosa** (Resbalosa 494, tel. 084/22-4839, $4.50 s, $9 d) with bright courtyard and sweeping views over town. The front rooms are older and noisier than the others, but all have hot water. Equally close to the Plaza de Armas, **Hostal Horeb** (San Juan de Dios 260, tel. 084/23-6775, $6 s, $9 d) has hot showers, clean and simple rooms, and a friendly atmosphere. Prices include breakfast.

Youth Hostal Albergue Municipal (Quiscapata 240, San Cristóbal, tel. 084/25-2506, $5 pp dorm) is on the way to Sacsayhuamán and has great views from the balcony, clean bunk rooms, a bar, and a cafeteria. A discount is given to youth hostel members, and groups of budget travelers check in here often.

In San Blas, check out the clean and friendly **El Arcano** (Carmen Alto 288, tel. 084/23-2703, $4 s, $8 d) in the San Blas neighborhood, with hot water from 6 A.M.–6 P.M., good beds, and simple rooms.

$10–25

The best place in town for longer stays, or the chance to have apartment-like digs in Cusco, is the new **M Kamilah Lodge** (Calle Pera 440-A, tel. 084/24-0368, kami-lodge@hotmail.com, $10 s, $15 d). There are three apartments, with four bedrooms each, several bathrooms, cable TV in the rooms, and shared areas including laundry, kitchen, and living area with fireplace. The apartments are totally modern, and bedrooms are on different floors for more privacy. Kamilah's location, five blocks from the Plaza de Armas and smack in the center of the market, has its pros and cons. Yes, it is a bit of a walk to the Plaza, but we found the area safe at night and were fascinated by the experience of being surrounded by a market.

N Niños Hotel (Meloq 442, tel. 084/23-1424, ninos@correo.dnet.com.pe, www.target-found.nl/ninos, $15s, $24 d, includes breakfast) is a remarkable place with a cause. Its Dutch owner uses hotel revenue to house, clothe, and feed twelve street boys. Niños Hotel is a restored colonial house, four blocks from the Plaza de Armas, with large, stylish rooms, hardwood floors, and a lovely courtyard for taking breakfast. There is also a hip café, book exchange, and several apartments for longer stays.

Hostal Rickch'airy (Tambo de Montero 219, tel. 084/23-6606, $12 s, $24 d) has hot water in the morning, laundry service, a nice garden with good views, and tourist information. About a five-minute cab ride east of town is **Casa de la Gringa** (Calle Pensamiento E-3, in the Miravalle neighborhood near Qollasuyo, tel. 084/24-1168, another.planet@terra.com.pe). This American-owned place is recommended for its garden, outside fireplace, hammocks, sweat lodge, and a dedication to spiritual matters that includes the imbibing of San Pedro and ayahuasca.

Just one block from the Plaza de Armas, **N Hostal San Isidro Labrador** (Saphy 440, tel. 084/22-6241, labrador@qnet.com.pe, $35 s, $45 d, includes breakfast) is a simple and elegant place with a handful of rooms, each with their own charm. It is right next to the police station and thus is one of the safer locations in Cusco. This hotel is operated by the Lambarri family, which also runs the best restaurant in the Cusco area, the Huayocarri Hacienda Restaurant in Yucay.

For a location one block from the Plaza de Armas, try **Rojas** (Tigre 129, tel. 084/22-8184, $6 s, $10.50 d shared bath, $10.50 s, $15 d private bath) with clean, carpeted rooms around a sunny courtyard. To stay directly on the Plaza de Armas, there is **Hostal Incawasi** (Portal de Panes 145, tel. 084/22-3992, $15 s, $23 d) with carpeted rooms in an unattractive modern building. Beds are comfortable and there is 24-hour hot water.

In lower San Blas, a hotel with one of the highest charm-for-price quotients in all of Cusco is **N Amaru Hostal** (Cuesta San Blas 541, tel. 084/22-5933, amaru@telser.com.pe, www.cusco.net/amaru, $17 s, $25 d). The 23 rooms, with balconies, are spread around two sun-filled patios overflowing with geraniums and roses. The rooms have comfy beds, wood floors, exposed beams, and small but nice bathrooms with their own water heater. Rooms here vary dramatically—ask for the corner rooms with sun porches, wicker furniture, and vistas on both sides. For those on a budget there are cheaper rooms with shared bathrooms. Other services include affordable laundry ($1/kilo), book exchange, library, and bottled oxygen for altitude sickness. This is a great option for those who want to be in San Blas but don't want to climb uphill every day.

There are several other options along Choquechaca, including the French-owned **Casa Elena** (Choquechaca 162, tel. 084/24-1202, chemin@terra.com.pe, www.geocities.com/casa_elena, $15 s, $25 d, includes breakfast). Rooms are comfortable, with carpet, heaters, cable TV, and private baths. Well-decorated sitting areas along the balcony are great places to relax. A solarium, with a library and two fireplaces, is under construction. Oddly, there is no sign out front—ring the door bell next to the Chocolate shop. **El Balcón Colonial** (Choquechaca 350, tel. 084/23-6738, balcon1@terra.com.pe, www.el-lbalcon-hostal-cusco.com, $4.50 s, $12 d, or $5 per room for SAE members) is a bed-and-breakfast with four clean rooms with firm beds, one with private bath, and a small kitchen with breakfast tables. The newly opened **Hospedaje Familiar Moon** (Canchipata 555, tel. 084/43-1956, hospedajemoon555@hotmail.com, $6 s, $12 d), on one of the alleyways above Choquechaca, offers seven rooms arranged on one side of a garden patio and the chance to hang out with a generous and kind family, including several energetic children. The rooms are plain, with concrete walls, but have hot water.

Smack in the center of San Blas, **Hospedaje San Blas** (Plaza San Blas 630, tel. 084/23-5358, psanblas@corihuasi.com, $7 s, $15 d, includes breakfast, 10 percent SAE discount) is owned by one of the daughters of the family that operates the excellent Hostal Corihuasi. Opened in

2003 and just a few paces away from some of the best restaurants and cafés in Cusco, this charming place offers eight rooms with rough wooden floors, sun windows, and walls painted in crimsons and tans. Everything is in miniature underneath a tiny glass-covered patio, including a cozy sitting area, bar, and dining room.

Heading left down Tandapata from Plaza San Blas, the next good place is **M Hospedaje El Alba** (Tandapata 172, tel. 084/241121, $7.50 s, $15 d). This quirky place has 15 rooms, some with whitewashed walls and exposed beams, and others with massive old stone walls. We especially liked the rooms with upstairs sleeping loft, skylights, and a cool nook downstairs for hanging out. Bathrooms are smallish, with hot water heated either by electric showerhead or hot water tank (ask for the latter). Other services include hand-washed laundry, barbecue and a shared kitchen. There are a few cheaper rooms with shared bath, but all are arranged around a bare, but pleasant, stone courtyard. **Hospedaje Sumaq T'ikaq** (Tandapata 114, tel. 084/23-4569) is a quiet house set back along a garden-lined alleyway off Tandapata with comfortable, quiet rooms.

Farther along Tandapata is **Sihuar** (Tandapata 251, tel. 084/22-7435, $10 s, $17 d), a two-level wood building that looks out over a patio. The rooms are pleasant with wood floors and woven rug, gas-heated hot water, and several queen-sized beds. Even farther along is the tree-house-like **Posada del Sol** (Atoqsaykuchi 296, Barrio San Blas, tel. 084/25-3725, $15 s, $25 d), a new hostel with friendly owners and great views over Cusco. The rooms, unadorned and without heaters, have wooden floors and are comfortable.

$25–50

The elegant and unpretentious **M Hostal Corihuasi** (Suecia 561, tel. 084/23-2233, corihuasi@amauta.rcp.net.pe, www.corihuasi.com, $30 s, $40 d, includes breakfast) is a quick, steep walk up from the Plaza de Armas and has old-world charm that befits Cusco. The rooms of this rambling, eclectic colonial house are outfitted with a blend of rugs, antiques, photographs, and furniture from the 1930s. Verandas and walkways connect the different rooms, which vary considerably.

Some of the rooms are the nicest in all of Cusco, with views over the city and outdoor reading nooks; others are dark, with porthole windows. Ask ahead of time for a better view.

In San Blas, the charming, Swiss-owned **M Pensión Alemana Bed and Breakfast** (Tandapata 260, Barrio San Blas, tel. 084/22-6861, info@cuzco-stay.de, www.cuzco-stay.de, $33 s, $45 d, includes breakfast) is the closest thing to a European pension in Cusco. There are 12 rooms, many with incredible views over the city, that are open, airy, with white walls and lights. This place is clean, safe, and cozy, with extremely comfortable beds, portable heaters, and great showers. There is a pleasant garden to sit in that looks out over the red-tiled roofs of the city, a hearty breakfast, laundry service, and a nightly fire in the dining room.

Another San Blas option is **Tik'a Wasi Hostal** (Tandapata 491, Barrio San Blas, tel. 084/23-1609, tikawasi@hotmail.com, $35 s, $45 d, includes breakfast), which is a good place for a large group, with garden, breakfast nooks, and dining area. This interesting, modern building with lots of glass and exposed beams rises several stories above the garden—ask for the rooms on the top floor with skylights and great views over Cusco.

Further down the street (and up the hill) is **Casa de Campo** (Tandapata 296-B, tel. 084/24-4404, paula96@terra.com.pe, $25 s, $45 d, 10 percent SAE discount). There are two tiled look-out terraces, with the city sprawling below, plus a mostly-glass-walled dining room surrounded by series of whitewashed rooms. Unfortunately it is an extreme hike to get here—even by San Blas standards—but taxis do reach here after much alley navigating. The rooms are a bit cramped, with unfortunate decorations and a small bathroom, but if you want views, this is your place.

The massive portal to the **Hostal Rumi Punku** (Choquechaca 339, tel. 084/22-1102, hostal@rumipunku.com, www.rumipunku.com, $25 s, $35 d, includes breakfast) is original Inca construction—you can't miss it. Charming, wood-floored rooms surround a quaint, flower-filled courtyard with a small chapel. There is also original Inca stonework in the garden.

If you must be on the Plaza de Armas, the

Hostal Virrey (Portal Comercio 165, tel. 084/22-1771, hvirrey@amauta.rep.net.pe, $30 s, $45 d, includes breakfast) has small, dark rooms, hard beds, old furniture, and cable TV.

$50–100

On the lively Plaza Regocijo, just a block from the Plaza de Armas, **Royal Inka I** (Plaza Regocijo 299, tel. 084/26-3276, www.royalinkahotel.com, $64 s, $78 d, includes breakfast, 15 percent SAE discount) occupies a historic 19th-century house. The smaller of the two Royal Inkas, it has loads of character with exposed wood beam ceilings. The more upscale and modern of the pair, the **Royal Inka II** (Santa Teresa 335, tel. 084/23-1067, www.royalinkahotel.com, $89 s, $95 d, includes breakfast, 15 percent SAE discount) also occupies a 19th-century building. The rooms here are more standard, lacking the charm of its sister hotel. There is a piano bar/restaurant on the top floor. Amenities include a Jacuzzi, sauna, and massage.

With about as good a location on the Plaza de Armas as you can get, **Sonesta Posada del Inca** (Portal Espinar 142, tel. 084/22-7061, posada@sonestaperu.com, www.sonesta.com, $90 s, $100 d, includes breakfast) is a homey, cheery place decorated with its signature plaid bedspreads and a fireplace in the lounge. Large, comfortable rooms have all the amenities with hairdryers, mini bars, and cable TV. Discounts are often available, especially if you're also staying at their hotel in the Urubamba Valley. The small, simple **Hostal Cusco Plaza** (Plazoleta Nazarenas 181, tel. 084/24-6161, $50 s, $65 d, includes breakfast) has a great location two blocks from the Plaza de Armas. There is a sunny central courtyard for taking breakfast, and cable TV in the rooms, some of which have nice views.

In San Blas, guests are greeted by tuxedo-wearing doormen at the upscale, Swiss-managed **Los Apus** (Atocsaycuchi 515, info@losapushotel.com, www.losapushotel.com, contact hotel for prices). The rooms have wood floors, heat, comfortable beds, and cable TV. Ask for the double loft room with two levels, stone walls, and a bathtub. Breakfast is served in the glass-roofed courtyard and $1.50/hour Internet is available. The unpretentious **Plaza de Armas Cusco** (Portal Comercio 114, tel. 084/22-2351, hostal_plaza@terra.com.pe, www.peruhotel.com.pe, $55 s, $55 d, includes breakfast) is rather bland but has great views over the Plaza de Armas. Rooms have comfortable beds, cable TV, and heaters. There is a nice lookout from the café, on the top floor.

Over $100

The most memorable place to stay in all of Cusco is **𝕄 Hotel Monasterio** (Calle Palacio 136, Plazoleta Nazarenas, tel. 084/24-1777, reservas@peruorientexpress.com.pe, www.monasterio.orient-express.com, $292 s, $303 d, includes breakfast, 10 percent SAE discount), a 400-year-old monastery that has recently been converted into Peru's most elegant five-star hotel. The stone lobby leads to a dramatic stone courtyard, graced with an ancient cedar tree and lined with two stories of stone archways. Colonial paintings line up along hallways, which wrap around two other fabulous stone patios. The rooms are decked out in old-style Spanish decor, including carved wooden headboards and colonial paintings, and include all the plush five-star comforts. They can even be pumped with oxygen for an additional $25 per night, simulating an altitude 900 meters lower that allows guests to sleep more soundly.

The hotel occupies the former Seminario San Antonio Abad, which was built in 1595 on top of the Inca Amaru Qhala Palace but badly damaged in the 1650 earthquake. During the restoration, a colonial Baroque chapel was added, which remains open to guests and has one of the most ornate altars in Cusco. After yet another damaging earthquake in 1950, the building was condemned and auctioned by the Peruvian government in 1995. It eventually landed in the hands of Orient-Express Hotels, which carefully restored the stonework, planted fabulous gardens, and converted the former cells into 126 plush rooms. These days, guests take lunch in the main square, which is shaded by a giant cedar, scented by a rose garden, and filled with the gurgling of a 17th-century stone fountain. The hotel hosts one of Cusco's two gourmet restaurants, and also includes a small spa where massages are available ($25 per day). It's a few minutes' walk from the Plaza de Armas.

The five-star ꓠ **Hotel Libertador Cusco** (Plazoleta Santo Domingo 259, tel. 084/23-1961, hotel@libertador.com.pe, www.libertador.com.pe, $194 s, $194 d, includes breakfast, 20 percent SAE discount) has a great location next to Coricancha, the Inca Temple of the Sun. It occupies the Casa de los Cuatro Bustos, Francisco Pizarro's last home. It is built on the foundation of the Aclla Huasi, "the house of the chosen ones," where virgins picked by the Incas lived in seclusion from society.

The entrance to the Hotel Libertador is spectacular. A stone portal leads into a glass-roofed lobby, lined on one side by Spanish stone arches and on the other by exposed portions of Inca stone walls. There is an excellent buffet breakfast served alongside another large square, ringed with two stories of stone arcades. The comfortable rooms, with all the amenities, are decorated with colonial paintings and often have good views over the Sun Temple and other areas of the city. Hotel Libertador also has a nice restaurant, bar, and fireplace lounge.

The four-star **Novotel** (San Agustín 239, tel. 084/22-8282, reservations@novotelcusco.com.pe, www.novotel.com, $180 s and d colonial room, $140 s and d modern room, includes breakfast) is a new option for colonial ambience in Cusco center. This restored colonial manor has a sun-filled patio lined with stone arches, lamps, and wicker furniture for evening drinks. There are 16 beautiful rooms on the second floor around the stone courtyard with wood floors, king-sized beds, window sitting areas, and all creature comforts (security box, mini-bar, cable TV, AC). The other 83 rooms are comfortable but bland in an unfortunate five-story modern addition. The colonial rooms seem a good value; the modern ones do not.

A more affordable upscale alternative is the **Picoaga Hotel** (Santa Teresa 344, tel. 084/22-1269, www.picoagahotel.com, $100 s, $120 d, includes breakfast), which occupies a 17th-century mansion just minutes from the Plaza de Armas. Rooms with high ceilings wrap around an arcade courtyard. Again, the modern addition lacks charm, so book a colonial room in advance.

FOOD

Cafés and Desserts

A breakfast favorites for gringos is ꓠ **Jack's Café Bar** (Choquechaca/Cuesta San Blas, tel. 084/80-6960, 6 A.M.–11 P.M. daily, $3), serving up heaping plates of eggs scrambled with roasted tomatoes, basil, and parmesan or smoked trout with fresh herbs. There are big lunch salads (like the Mediterranean, with grilled veggies, avocado, and honey-and-balsamic vinaigrette) and a range of milkshakes, smoothies, and espresso drinks. There are plenty of American magazines to peruse and a full bar, making this a good place to hang out day or night.

If you head up Choquechaca and hang a right on a narrow alleyway, you will discover one of San Blas' truly hidden gems: ꓠ **El Centro Pi** (Atoqsayk'uchi 599, no phone, piorana@yahoo.es, 9 A.M.–9 P.M. Tues–Fri., 10 A.M.–10 P.M. Sat.–Sun.). This simple place, decorated with hip art and staffed by friendly people, is one of the best places to unwind, read a book, or hang out and talk. They have some of the better coffee drinks in Cusco, along with grilled sandwiches and (of course) a few scrumptious pies. Funky music is always in the air, and there is nook for viewing DVDs, a library of cult classics and high-brow literature, and even a darkroom for serious photographers. There is one Internet station and, if you have a laptop, you can connect free (needless to say, that is very high tech for Cusco).

Centro Pi is not so much a café, though, as it is a community center built by a generation of artsy, hip young Cusqueños who are seriously involved in improving their corner of the world. One of the owners, Joaquín Randall, is the son of El Albergue owner Wendy Weeks and has launched a campaign to ban plastics in the Cusco area.

Besides Jack's and Centro Pi, Choquechaca is loaded with quality cafés and dessert options. To satisfy a chocolate craving, stop in the tiny ꓠ **Chocolate** (Choquechaca 162, tel. 084/974-9343, noon–7 P.M. Mon.–Fri., 2–8 P.M. Sat.), a shop serving steaming mugs of hot chocolate and chocolates by the piece. The tiny **Yampi's Café** (Choquechaca 320, tel. 084/22-3602, 7 A.M.–8 P.M., Mon.–Sat., $3) has a country feel, with checker-clothed tables, pancakes, omelets, and sandwiches. **Café Cultural Ritual** (Choquechaca 140, www.caferitual.com.pe, tel. 084/68-2223, 8:30 A.M.–11 P.M., 10 percent SAE discount) serves a range of pancakes, fruit salads, vegetarian lunch menus, and "the biggest sandwiches ever tried," according to their cook. They also show movies and have a second location in Plaza San Blas, though the food seems better in Choquechaca. Finally, a new artsy café with lots of promise, **Inka Fe** (Choquechaca 131-A, tel. 084/968-2112) serves up a mixture of pizzas, gourmet sandwiches, crepes, and Italian espresso.

Around the corner, **Granja Heidi** (Cuesta San Blas 525, tel. 084/23-8383, 8:30 A.M.–9:30 P.M. Mon.–Sat.) is brimming with wholesome Swiss charm, including delicious natural yogurt and homemade granola, bracing coffee, a range of interesting juices, and a sun-filled second-floor café. The best place for ice cream and mind-rocking espresso is **I Due Mondi** (Santa Catalina Ancha 366, tel. 084/24-7677, 8 A.M.–midnight), a gelateria with the slogan *Italian Style, Peruvian Feeling.*

On the Plaza de Armas, the laid-back **Trotamundos** (Portal Comercio 177, 2nd flr., tel. 084/23-2387, 8:30 A.M.–11 P.M. daily, $2) has balcony seating over the Plaza de Armas and is a great place to wile the day away. This artsy café serves good sandwiches, salads, burgers, and a dozen kinds of pancakes, and there is an Internet station. Over in the Plaza Regocijo, the small **Varayoc Café** (Espaderos 142, tel. 084/23-2404, $5–10) is a quiet place to have a crepe, salad, cheese fondue, or cappuccino. The low lights and background jazz music make a great atmosphere for postcard writing.

Peruvian

The area around the Plaza de Armas is overflowing with Peruvian restaurants. Here are the ones we think offer the best quality and are not overpriced. **Mesón Los Portales** (Portal de Panes 163, tel. 084/23-5604, 10 A.M.–10 P.M. daily, $9) serves up *anticuchos, cebiche,* alpaca, or trout in a formal, old-world atmosphere. **La Estancia Imperial** (Portal de Panes 137, tel. 084/25-4005, noon–11 P.M. daily, $7) offers a mesmerizing view of the cathedral, quiet atmosphere, and an exten-

sive, though meat-heavy, Peruvian menu. Though expensive, **Tunupa** (Portal Confituría 233, tel. 084/25-2936, noon–11 P.M. daily, $15, 20 percent SAE discount) is known for great service and an excellent range of Peruvian food, including *aji de gallina, brochetas mixta,* and *lomo a la parilla.* It offers romantic balcony seating overlooking the plaza, wide-ranging dinner buffet and á la carte choices, and live folkloric music daily from 6:30 P.M. onwards. **La Retama** (Portal de Panes 123, 2nd floor, tel. 084/22-6372, laretama@terra .com.pe, www.cuscoperu.com/laretama, $9, 15 percent SAE discount) has a great kitchen and wide-ranging Peruvian menu that draws a lot of locals. There is live jazz on Fridays after 10:30 P.M., folkloric music-and-dance shows during the rest of the week, and good lunch menus. A cheaper alternative to the above restaurants is **Restaurant Los Candiles** (Plateros 323, tel. 084/23-5430), which serves *cebiche,* seafood soups, and a variety of novo-andina plates. The $6 lunch menu here is highly recommended.

A local's favorite for huge plates of pork is **Los Andenes de Andrea** (Clorinda Matto de Turner 56 in San Jerónimo neighborhood, tel. 084/22-4277, 9 A.M.–7 P.M.). A massive plate of *lechón* is $5, and *chicharrón* is $3—the best bang for the Andean buck in all of Cusco, with a nice garden atmosphere popular with Cusqueña families on the weekends. This restaurant is also a good place to try *adobo,* a classic hangover cure served all over Cusco. This soupy concoction of pork, potatoes, and onion is eaten in the morning or at lunchtime and is washed down with a shot of licorice-flavor *anisado* liquor. Then to bed. Los Andenes is 10 minutes from Cusco's Plaza de Armas on the road toward Cusco. Most taxi drivers will take you there for $1.50.

In San Blas, roasted guinea pig and alpaca *anticucho* (roasted heart) can be ordered at **Pacha-Pacha** (Plaza San Blas 120, tel. 084/24-1318, 11 A.M.–9 P.M. daily, $5), which occupies a sunny courtyard across the street from the Iglesia San Blas. Peruvian specialties such as tamales, quinoa soup, *aji de gallina,* and *lomo saltado* are also served. A local's favorite in San Blas is **Quinta Zarate** (Tothora Paccha 763, tel. 084/24-5114, noon–4 P.M., $5), which has a reasonably priced menu of Andean food including grilled meat, cuy, *chicharrón,* and *rocoto relleno* (stuffed pepper). Besides the excellent food, this place has a nice country feel that draws a loyal crowd of locals. From the Plaza San Blas, head right down Tandapata and veer to the left at the fork.

For *cebiche,* try **Emperador** (San Francisco 172, tel. 084/24-3489, 9 A.M.–11 P.M. daily, $3) on Plaza San Francisco. The best *pollo a la brasa* in town is at **Los Toldos Chicken** (Almagro 171, tel. 084/22-9829, 11 A.M.–11 P.M., $3), serving huge portions of juicy spit-roasted chicken with french fries and salad. This place is packed with locals at all hours.

International

The Australian-owned **Ⱳ Los Perros Wine & Couch Bar** (Tecsecocha 426, tel. 084/24-1447, los_perros@yahoo.com, 11 A.M.–midnight daily, $4) is one of Cusco's hipper hangouts. The music is funky, the decor is artsy, and the food is incredible. The tiny kitchen here produces a stream of beautifully presented Asian salads (soy, avocado, and spinach), Mediterranean salads (chicken, sweet potato, cilantro, and parmesan), Indian curries, smoothies, and homemade mint lemonade. This place is delicious for lunch, dinner, or simply an espresso. They have a revolving art exhibit, magazines, and a good international wine list.

The tiny **Blueberry Lounge** (Portal de Carnes 236, tel. 084/22-1397, 8:30 A.M.–1 A.M. daily, $4–7) is another great place to relax that is tucked away on the Plaza de Armas. The menu is Thai/Asian-influenced, with items such as trout sushi, Thai chicken wings, Vietnamese rolls, and massaman chicken curry. While you wait for food, you can enjoy great music, comfy couches, magazines, games, and a book exchange. The tables that spill out into a small courtyard are a fun place to have drinks and hang out in the evenings. The friendly British owner, Tanya Miller, also runs **The Deli,** with Mediterranean food, in the same courtyard. The deli has patés (hummus and baba ganoush), smoked meats, baguette sandwiches, divine chocolate chip cookies, and hard-to-find international goodies like Vegamite. Gourmet box lunches can be bought for $6 or $9.

As if two restaurants were not enough, she and

local gourmet superstar Rafael Casabonne also own the excellent **Ⱳ Greens** (Tandapata 700, tel. 084/24-3820, noon–midnight daily, $5) in the heart of San Blas. This stylish place has a cool, artsy feel, intimate candlelit tables, and a menu that includes gourmet pastas and tender roasted lamb. Make reservations, as this place is often full, especially for the Sundays-only British roast.

Fallen Angel (Plazoleta Nazarenas 221, tel. 084/25-8184, $10) feels like New York's East Village and has a decor that is not for the timid. There are glass tables set over bathtub fishtanks, sofas with rubber pillows, and multicolored daquiris. We were a bit disappointed with the food here and at sister restaurant **Macondo** (Cuesta San Blas 571, tel. 084/22-9415, $8, 10 percent SAE discount). However, the funky setting at both places is a feast for the eyes and makes each one an excellent place to have a pre-dinner drink.

For creative food and excellent coffee, **Al Grano** (Santa Catalina Ancha 398, tel. 084/22-8032, 10 A.M.–9 P.M. daily, 10 percent SAE discount) serves Thai, Chinese, Indian, Vietnamese, and Indonesian food in a small café. This is a treat for travelers looking for a change of pace. Though a bit removed from things, good organic coffee and food prepared by a Cordon Bleu chef can be had at **Manu Café and Restaurant** (Pardo 1046, tel. 084/25-2521, info@manu-peru.com, www.manupero.com, 9 A.M.–10 P.M., $6–7). Specialties here include raclette, a range of organic coffee, gourmet Peruvian dishes, and both cheese and chocolate fondues. This restaurant is operated by Manu Nature Tours, the most upscale Manu operator.

Pizza

Ⱳ Babieca Trattoría (Tecsecocha 418, tel. 084/22-1122, 10–2 A.M., $4 pp) has excellent dough, gourmet toppings, and gigantic pizzas for a mere $13.

Yacana Pizzeria (Choquechaca 216, tel. 084/22-9862, 10 A.M.–10 P.M. Mon.–Sat., $3.50) is a cute, two-level place decorated with Chinese lanterns. Besides pizza, they also serve trout, cuy, and pastas and they deliver to your hotel. **Chez Maggy** (Procuradores 374, tel. 084/23-4861,

6 P.M.–midnight daily, $4, 5 percent SAE discount) has four locations in Cusco, all of which are known for loud live music and good pizzas. They also serve Mexican and Italian food and will deliver.

Mexican

Mexican is nearly impossible to find in Peru, so **El Cuate** (Procuradores 386, tel. 084/22-7003, 11 A.M.–11 P.M., $3) is a real treat. If you are a Mexican-food connoisseur you are likely to be underwhelmed (Mexican ingredients are surprisingly hard to find in Peru), but the chicken in mole sauce, enchiladas, and tortilla soup are worth sampling. In the evenings, they serve margaritas and jars of sangria on an upstairs balcony overlooking Cusco's tourist alley.

Health Food

Halfway between the Plaza de Armas and Qoricancha is the best-priced gourmet café in town— **Moni** (San Augustín 311, tel. 084/23-1029, 8 A.M.–3 P.M. and 6–9 P.M. Mon.–Fri., 10 A.M.– 3 P.M. and 6–9 P.M. Sat., $3.50). This unpretentious place serves inventive vegetarian dishes such as spinach and ricotta lasagna, zucchini madras curry, and scrambled eggs with garlic and mushrooms. The owners are a Peruvian-English couple who are on the ball, and the café is stocked with current magazines. Another vegetarian restaurant is **Govinda** (Espaderos 128, tel. 084/62-4588, 8 A.M.–10 P.M. daily, $3), half a block from the Plaza de Armas. Especially good are the fixed-price lunch menu, as well as the fruit milkshakes, Spanish paella, curry rice, and empanadas at great prices. **Naturaleza** (El Sol 765-A, tel. 084/976-0187, closed Sundays, $1.50) is a bit out of the way from the center but is a long-established vegetarian restaurant with a cheap and good $1.50 lunch menu. A final option is Café Cultural Ritual (see *Cafés and Desserts*).

Fine Dining

The best gourmet restaurant in town is **MAP Café** (Plaza de las Nazarenas 231, tel. 084/24-2476, $6–12), the latest production of passionate restaurateur Rafael Casabonne. Before we even get to the food, a word about the architecture: dinner guests sit in a perfectly proportioned glass box, reminiscent of architect Philip Johnson's glass house, that seemingly floats in the stone courtyard of the Museo de Arte Precolombino. At night the glass box glows, illuminating the Spanish colonial arcades, and guests can combine an evening here with a stroll around this highly recommended museum, which is open until 11 P.M.

Now for the food. There is seared, sesame-crusted tuna served with a potato purée flavored with chili peppers, roasted beef tenderloin with mushroom sauce and red wine *quinotto,* Andean pesto-stuffed chicken with *botija* black olive sauce. The desserts are just too complex to describe.

A comparable gourmet restaurant, though twice as expensive, is inside the **Hotel Monasterio** (Calle Palacio 136, Plazoleta Nazarenas, tel. 084/24-1777, www.monasterio.orient-express.com, $14–21). Candlelit dinners are served in an elegant hallway, decorated with antique gold walls and colonial paintings, which overlooks a colonial courtyard. The menu ranges from poached king fish rolls with a shrimp mousse to rack of lamb with black pepper crust and tomato marmalade.

Markets

The **Mercado San Pedro** (Tupac Amaru, 6 A.M.– 7 P.M.), near the San Pedro train station, has amazing fruits and vegetables. Come here to try the unique and delicious granadilla and chirimoya fruits—but keep your eyes out for pickpockets and those who silently slice backpacks with razors to steal the goodies within. Go in the morning, when the market is busiest, and leave your passport and cash in your hotel. The largest **supermarket** is Dimart (Matará 271) between Q'era and Ayacucho. **Gato's Market** (Portal Belen 115, Plaza de Armas) is more central, but small and pricey.

INFORMATION AND SERVICES

Sightseeing Tours

There is a huge competition, and frequent price wars, between Cusco's agencies for general sightseeing tours, which are clustered around the Plaza de Armas and up along Procuradores and Plateros. If you are interested in seeing as many sights as possible in the most efficient manner, these tours are your best bet. Unless you walk, you are unlikely to do better than their rock-bottom prices.

The most popular tours include a half-day city tour ($5–10) and the full-day tour to the Sacred Valley, which includes Pisac market, lunch in Urubamba, Ollantaytambo, and sometimes Chincheros as well ($10–20). There is also a half-day tour of the ruins outside of Cusco, which include Sacsayhuamán, Q'enqo, Puca Pucara, and Tambomachay ($6–10). Finally there is a half-day tour of the ruins heading toward Puno, including the magnificent church in Andahuaylillas, Pikillacta, and Tipón ($7–10).

There are several excellent agencies in Cusco that cater to large groups. Local agencies that also do a good job with tickets and tours for independent travelers are:

Condor Travel (tel. 084/24-8181, Saphy 848, condorcusco@condortravel.com.pe, www.condortravel.com) is good for ticket issues and also for booking tours.

Dasatour (Pardo 589, tel. 084/22-3341, cusco@dasatriq.com, www.dasatariq.com) is a high-end operator, owned by Dasatriq, which has been around for a half century and handles tours for Hotel Libertador.

Gatur (Puluchapata 140, tel. 084/22-3496 or 084/22-7829, gatur@terra.com.pe) is operated by José Altamirano, one of the most respected authorities on local history and esoteric matters.

Destinos Turísticos (Portal de Panes 123, Office 101, destinos@telser.com.pe) is an inexpensive, Dutch-owned agency with a good reputation.

Naty's Travel Agency (Triunfo 338, tel. 084/26-1811, natystravel@terra.com.pe, www.natystravel.com) is a good budget option and offers Sacred Valley day tours for $10 and a half-day Cusco city tour for $5.

Jungle Trips

Many people who visit Cusco do not realize how close the Amazon jungle is. A half-hour, $50 plane ride and a few hours in a boat lands you in a comfy lodge in Puerto Maldonado, with outstanding opportunities for seeing birds, a few mammals, and monkeys and getting a solid intro to rainforest ecology at the Reserva Nacional Tambopata.

For those with more money and time, a seven-day trip to Parque Nacional Manu ($500–1,600) offers a chance to see a greater variety of birds and monkeys, as well megapredators such as the black caiman and the jaguar. See *The Amazon* chapter for more information.

Tourist Information

The **South American Explorer's Club (SAE)** (Choquechacq 188 No.4, tel. 084/24-5485, cuscoclub@saexplorers.org, www.samexplo.org, 9:30 A.M.–5 P.M. Mon.–Fri., 10 A.M.–1 P.M. Sat.) is a gold mine of information on just about anything regarding Peru. It costs $50 to join as an individual, $80 for a couple, though nonmembers are allowed to look around as well. This is definitely worth the cost if you will be in Peru for any length of time, and is a recommended first stop in Cusco—no matter how much research you have done, you will always learn something here and, at the very least, meet some interesting people. Club members can peruse trip reports for all over the Cusco area, use the well-stocked library, and receive discounts at a wide range of restaurants, language schools, hotels, and agencies (the hardest part is remembering to ask for it!). There are lectures and slide shows most Wednesdays. The club also has offices in Lima and Quito, Ecuador. In this book, establishments that give SAE discounts are indicated in parentheses along with their telephone number, etc.

If all you need is some basic tourist information and a map, services are free at the friendly **i Peru** (Portal de Carrizos 250, tel. 084/25-2974, 8:30 A.M.–7:30 P.M. daily), where tourist complaints can also be filed. More detailed information on Cusco, including information on cultural events, can be found at the **Office of Tourist Information** (Mantas 117-A, tel. 084/22-3701, 9 A.M.–noon and 3–6 P.M. Mon.–Sat.).

Police

Travelers can contact the tourist police through the **i Peru office** on the Plaza de Armas (Portal de Carrizos 250, tel. 084/25-2974, 8:30 A.M.–7:30 P.M. daily) or at the airport (tel. 084/23-7364). A larger, **24-hour tourist police office** is on Saphi 510 (tel. 084/24-9654), where officers speak some English.

Health Care

The major hospitals of Cusco are the **Hospital Regional** (Avenida de la Cultura, tel. 084/24-3240 or 084/23-1131) and the **Hospital Lorena** (Plazoleta Belén 1358 in the Santiago neighborhood, tel. 084/22-1581 or 084/22-6511). A little more expensive, but usually faster and higher quality, is the private **Clínica Pardo** (Av. De la Cultura 710, tel. 084/24-0387 or 084/24-0997 for emergencies, clinicapardo@terra.com.pe, 24 hours).

The best pharmacies are **Pharmacy Popular** (Puputi s/n, tel. 084/22-8787), **InkaFarma** (El Sol 210, tel. 084/24-2631), **Multifarma** (San Andres 330, tel. 084/22-1421), and **Farmacia Humanitaria Beatriz** (Santa Catalina Ancha 390, tel. 084/22-8301) for a more personal and efficient experience. The only good pharmacy in San Blas is at Choquechaca 207A (8 A.M.–10 P.M.). A recommended dental clinic is **Centro Odontológico** (Centro Comercial Cusco, 3rd flr., #7, tel. 084/22-8074 or cell tel. 084/995-6749). Ask for Dr. Gilbert Espejo.

Language Schools

Cusco has more Spanish schools than any other city in Peru, though it is hard to be truly immersed in Spanish unless you can somehow isolate yourself from English speakers. Considering what they include, the packages are extraordinarily cheap: prearranged hostel or home stay with local family, breakfast, airline reservations, volunteer work options, city tour, dance and cooking classes, lectures and movies. An intensive group class with all these perks runs around $200 per week with 20 hours of classes, while a private package is around $300. A private teacher, without lodging or food, is $6 per hour. All prices quoted below are for a week with 20 hours of classes.

Amigos Spanish School (Zaguan del Cielo B-23, tel. 084/24-2292, amigos@spanishcusco.com, www.spanishcusco.com) gives half of its income to disabled children and has highly recommended teachers.

Amauta Spanish School (Suecia 480, tel. 084/26-2345, info@amautaspanish.com, www

.amautaspanish.com, $136 group, $222 private, SAEC discount) offers classes in Cusco, Urubamba and even Manu.

The program at **Cusco Spanish School** (Garcilaso 265, 2nd flr., tel. 084/22-6928, info@cuscospanishschool.com, www.cuscospanishschool.com, 8 A.M.–8 P.M., $205 group, $255 private) offers classes in Cusco, Urubamba, and on Amantaní Island in Lake Titicaca. Prices given include three meals a day.

A larger organization, with schools all over South America, is **Casa de Lenguas** (info@casadelenguas.com, www.casadelenguas.com, $285 group, $360 private). Prices given include a home stay and three meals a day. An intensive option offers six hours of lessons a day for $385/week.

Other options include **Cervantes Spanish School** (Suecia 368, tel. 084/80-6066, cervantesspanishschool@yahoo.es), **Spanish School San Blas** (Tandapata 688, tel. 084/24-7898, spanish_lesson@hotmail.com, www.spanishschoolperu.com, $180 group, $240 private), and **Academia Latinoamericana de Español** (Av. Sol 580, tel. 084/24-3364, info@latinoschools.com, www.latinoschools.com).

Banks and Money Exchange

Getting money out of an ATM usually means a stroll down the first few blocks of Av. El Sol, where **Banco de Crédito** and **Banco de Trabajo** are on the first block and **Banco Continental** and **Interbank** are on the third. For wire transfers, there is a **Western Union** further down (El Sol 627-A, tel. 084/24-4167, 8:30 A.M.–1 P.M. and 3–7 P.M. Mon.–Fri.). The Banco de Crédito is the only bank to be open all day from 10 A.M.–6 P.M. (the others close 1–3 P.M.), with Saturday hours from 9 A.M.–noon. All the banks are closed on Sunday.

Communications

Cusco's main **post office** is the Serpost (El Sol 800, tel. 084/22-4212, 8 A.M.–8 P.M. Mon.–Sat.). The city is crawling with different email places, all of which have cable connections and are generally good. In San Blas, a good place is **Virtu@l.com** (Carmen Alto 274, San Blas, tel. 084/22-1088,

9 A.M.–10 P.M., $0.40/hour before 4 P.M.). If you have a laptop with a cable toggle, plug in for free at **Centro Pi** (Atoqsayk'uchi 599, no phone, matacuy@yahoo.es, 9 A.M.–9 P.M. Tues–Fri., 10 A.M.–10 P.M. Sat.–Sun.). They have one laptop for public use here, though it is often busy. On Choquechaca, head to **killa@net** (Choquechaca 124, 8 A.M.–midnight, $0.50/hour).

Near the Plaza de Armas, check out the fast, nameless place at Procuradores 340, 8 A.M.–midnight, $0.60/hour). Near Corichanca there is **Sokabon** (Plaza Santo Domingo 220-A, 9 A.M.–10:30 P.M., $0.50/hour), which is planning to serve pizza in future.

Long distance and international calls can be made at the **Telefónica office** (El Sol 382-6, tel. 084/24-1114, 8 A.M.–10 P.M. Mon.–Sat.) or slightly cheaper at **Perusat** (San Agustín 403, tel. 084/25-8502). Calls are made via a satellite connection and cost $0.30 per minute for North America, $0.50 for South America, $0.40 for Europe, and $0.75 for Asia.

Immigration

Tourist visas can be extended for 30 days at the **Immigration Office** (El Sol 314, tel. 084/22-2741, 8 A.M.–noon Mon.–Fri.) for $27, though at that cost it is worth heading to Bolivia for a day and getting a fresh 90-day visa.

Car and Motorcycle Rental

An Avis rental car office is located in the airport and is sporadically staffed. A better option is **4x4 Cusco** (Urb. San Borja K-1 in the Wanchaq neighborhood, tel. 084/22-7730 or cell tel. 094/93-2538, erlic32@hotmail.com, www.4x4cusco.com). With insurance included, a car with front-wheel drive costs $35 per day, a 4x4 pickup $65 per day, and a Land Cruiser $80. These costs do not include taxes, and there is a whopping $0.30 charge per kilometer.

Harley-Davidson motorcycles can be rented at **Cuzco Rent A Harley** (Garcilaso 265, tel. 084/24-9348, customer_service@cuzcorentaharley.com, www.cuzcorentaharley.com) for $79 per day and up, including unlimited mileage, helmets for driver and passenger, and locks and saddlebags. You must be 28 years or older and have a credit card.

Laundry

Most Cusco hostels offer laundry service for the going rate of $1/kilo. This is the best way to go in terms of ease and also because laundry places are more careful about not losing clothes for a regular client. Otherwise the best place for washing clothes is **Laundry Service** (Tecsecocha 450, near Café Los Perros, tel. 084/24-3698, 7 A.M.–8 P.M., daily, $1 per kilo). They return clothes within four hours and rarely lose anything. Another highly recommended place is **Lavanderia Inka** on Ruinas 493, with similar reputation, hours, and prices. There are several Laundromats along this street, as well as on Choquechaca and Carmen El Alto in San Blas.

Photography

Digital photographers can download their full media cards to a CD-ROM in 20 minutes at many camera shops in Cusco. The catch is that you usually need the USB cord that works with your camera. An exception is **Foto Panorama** (Portal Comercio 149, in front of the cathedral, tel. 084/23-9800, 8:30 A.M.–10 P.M.), which accepts most different media cards. They will download as much as you have in a half hour for $5, including the CD they give you. Other recommended places for developing or digital services and products include **Foto Nishiyama** (Triunfo 346, tel. 084/24-2922), which has a hotel delivery service, and **Laboratorio César** (Portal Comercio, tel. 084/22-9142).

Massage and Spa

There is no shortage of masseuses in Cusco on the prowl for tired feet or sore backs. Call Sra. Ramirez (tel. 084/962-1281) for massage, acupressure, or aromatherapy. Olga Huaman at **Yin Yang Therapeutic Massage** (Portal Espinar 144, tel. 084/93-9717, 6 A.M.–10 P.M.) offers room service or a session at her office, as does **Angel Hands** (Heladeros 157, tel. 084/22-5159, 6 A.M.–10 P.M.). **Hands of Light** (tel. 084/974-7600) offers shiatsu and reflexology massages. The **Siluet Sauna and Spa** (Quera 253, Interior 4, tel. 084/23-1504, 10 A.M.–10 P.M.) offers massages along with Jacuzzi and hot and dry sauna.

GETTING THERE AND AROUND

Planes

Cusco's airport is 10 minutes south of town and the taxi ride costs $2. Flight schedules for the airport are posted on www.vuelos.com.pe/cusco and you can also call the airport at tel. 084/22-2611. Taxes for domestic flights are $5 pp.

All Cusco-bound travelers must first arrive in Lima and then board another plane in Cusco, for which there are currently three operators. To approach Cusco's airport, planes must fly at considerable altitude and down a narrow valley, passing ice-covered Nevado Salcantay en route. Because of the tricky approach, flights are frequently cancelled because of afternoon winds. Fly in and out of Cusco in the morning if at all possible.

LanPeru (in Lima 01/213-8200, www.lanperu.com, $150–160) has four flights a day in the same stretch. **Taca** (in Lima 01/213-7000, ventaslima@taca.com, $140) has a few flights each week. The cheapeast is **TANS Peru** (in Lima 01/213-6000, ventaslima@tans.com.pe, www .tansperu.com.pe, $120), with two daily flights.

In addition, LanPeru has a daily flight from Lima that picks up passengers in Juliaca every day before continuing on to Cusco (it is not, however, possible to fly from Cusco to Lima). LanPeru has daily flights between Cusco and Arequipa. And Lan and TANS have daily flights between Cusco and Puerto Maldonado.

Buses

There is a new long-distance bus terminal, the **Terminal Terrestre**, on the way to the airport (Via de Evitamiento 429, tel. 084/22-4471). This huge building is busy, safe, and crammed with all of the long-distance bus companies, bathrooms, and a few stores selling snacks. Companies generally open from 6 A.M.–9 P.M. and accept reservations over the phone, with payment on the day of departure (you have to speak Spanish, though). As of this writing, all the bus routes were safe to travel at night except for Abancay-Ayacucho.

The following bus companies are recommended:

A recommended way to get to **Puno** is with one of the tourist buses that visit the ruins on the way. These buses include a huge buffet lunch, English-speaking guide, and stops at most of the major ruins on the way. **Inka Express** (tel. 051/36-5654, inkaexpresspuno@terra.com.pe, $20) makes stops in the exquisite colonial church of Andahuaylillas, the Inca ruins of Wari, and a lunch stop in Sicuani. In the afternoon the bus stops at La Raya pass and the ruins of Pukará before arriving in Puno. The buses generally leave Cusco at 8 A.M. and arrive at 5 P.M. in Puno, include hotel pickup and drop-off, and even have oxygen tanks onboard for altitude problems. A similar service is offered by **First Class** (Sol 930 in Cusco, tel. 084/22-3102, firstclass@terra.com.pe, $20).

For direct service to Puno, **Ormeño** (tel. 084/22-7501) has a daily bus leaving at 9 A.M., which arrives in Juliaca at 1:30 P.M. and Puno at 2 P.M. ($7 for Royal Class, which has on-board food service and plusher seats than even the Imperial buses). **Imexso** (tel. 084/22-9126, imexso@ terra.com.pe) is under new management that has so far upheld this company's rep for good service and has new buses, with English-language videos, that leave at 9 A.M. and 9 P.M. for Puno. **San Luis** (tel. 084/22-3647) has two-story buses with food service leaving at 8 A.M., 11:30 A.M., and 10 P.M. for $6. **Pony Express** (tel. 084/24-3540) offers similar high-quality service, also three times a day, $6.

Many of the above companies offer transfer buses leaving for **Bolivia**, though some go through Desaguadero and others through Copacabana (launching point for Isla del Sol). Ormeño (tel. 084/22-7501) has a direct business-class bus (no meals) through Desaguadero to La Paz, leaving daily at 9 P.M. ($21). To head through Copacabana, try Imexco's (tel. 084/22-9126) 9 P.M. departure that arrives in Puno at 3:30 A.M. From there, another bus leaves at 6 A.M., arriving in Copacabana at 10:30 A.M. and La Paz at 2 P.M. Another recommended company for getting to Bolivia is Litoral, though there are many more options in Puno's excellent and new Terminal Terrestre. The border crossing, which is open between 8 A.M. and 3 P.M., is quick and easy: passengers need only get off the bus for a few minutes on each side of the border to have their passports stamped—remember to ask for the maximum number of days (usually 90).

Buses for the 20-hour haul to **Lima** now head to Abancay before crossing the mountains to the coast at Nazca and then heading north for Lima. Ormeño is planning to soon offer the extra-plush Royal Class service, which leaves at 10 A.M. and arrives in Lima the following day at 6 A.M. For the moment the service is operated with plain, one-story buses for $18 with a stop in Abancay ($5). Palomino (tel. 084/22-2694) has an Imperial class bus leaving for Lima at 5 P.M., which arrives in Abancay at 9 P.M., and in Lima the following day at noon ($27, including food and on-board service). Another recommended company is Expresso Wari.

The only company with tranfer service through Abancay onto **Ayacucho** is **Expreso Los Chankas** (tel. 084/24-2249), with buses leaving every day at 6:30 P.M. and arriving in Abancay at 11:30 P.M. ($3) and Andahuaylas at 5:30 A.M. ($6). From here, passengers board a bus that leaves a half hour later and arrives in Ayacucho at 5:30 P.M. ($12). A bus with a nearly identical schedule leaves at 6 A.M. from Cusco, though this is not recommended because it means traveling at night between Abancay and Ayacucho, where early-morning bus assaults happened in 2003.

The journey to **Arequipa** via Juliaca takes 8.5 hours. **Cruz del Sur** (tel. 084/24-8255) has Imperial buses that include dinner and bingo leaving at 8:30 P.M. for $11, and Ormeño offers a similar quality service. Enlaces (tel. 084/25-5333) has Imperial buses leaving at 5 A.M. and 8 P.M. for $11. **Cial** (0tel. 804/22-1201) has Imperial buses leaving at 7:30 A.M. and 8 P.M. for $11.

Most people who visit Colca head to Arequipa first and then take the three-hour drive to Chivay, the Colca gateway, from there. There is an alternate, spectacular route on rocky roads that branches off from Sicuani and heads past Laguna Languilayo, the Tintaya copper and gold mine, and Condorama Dam on the Río Colca. This Cusco-Chivay route takes at least 11 hours, though more in rainy season, and it is best to do it on Saturday when buses are frequent. First head to Sicuani and scout for a Chivay direct bus or truck.

If none are available, take local buses to El Descanso, Yauri, Chichas, and on to Chivay. (This 250-km route between Sicuani and Chivay would also make an excellent mountain bike journey.) Another option from Colca is provided by the company Colca (tel. 084/26-3254), which has daily buses for Arequipa leaving at 7 P.M. for $8, arriving at 5 A.M. This bus takes the traditional route through Juliaca and then stops at Pampa Cañaguas en route to Arequipa at 3 A.M., where it is possible to transfer onto a 5 A.M. bus to Chivay ($11 total). The only direct option for Tacna, the border town for Chile, is Cruz del Sur (tel. 084/24-8255), which leaves at 3:15 P.M. and arrives at 7 A.M. the following day ($20).

If you are a glutton for punishment you might want to consider the two-day, bumpy, but spectacular bus journey through Ocongate to **Puerto Maldonado**, the hardest of Cusco's three jungle destinations. The best way to do this is to head to Urcos and take a bus or truck onward from there. Atalaya, the gateway to the Parque Nacional Manu, is similarly hard to reach but the journey can generally be made in a long day. Travelers must first head to Paucartambo. For Quillabamba, Ampay (tel. 084/24-9977) has buses leaving for the 8.5-hour journey at 8:30 A.M. and 7 P.M. ($4).

Another option for **Quillabamba**, and all other destinations in the Cusco region, are the informal *terminales* where buses, *combis*, and *colectivos* leave when full. These are often located in places that are unsafe at night or early in the morning. They generally operate from 5 A.M. until as late as 7 P.M. Here is a list of *terminales* for destinations around Cusco. Most taxi drivers know where they are:

For Quillabamba, there is a roadside pick-up spot, called a *terminal de paso,* at the last block of Av. Antoñia Lorena, the principal exit road for the route that goes through the Sacred Valley before heading over Abra Málaga into the jungle (seven hours, $4).

For **Urubamba**, there are two options. Buses for the shorter, 1.5-hour route, through Chincheros, leave from the first block of Grau near the bridge (45 minutes, $0.75 for Chincheros, 1.5 hours, $1.25 for Urubamba).

Buses for **Pisac** and **Calca** leave from Puputi

and Cultura (one hour, $0.75 for Pisac). These buses end their route in Urubamba (2 hours, $1,25).

For **Andahuaylillas** and **Urcos**, on the way to Puno, buses leave from Av. de la Cultura in front of the regional hospital (1.5 hours, $1).

For **Sicuani**, farther along this same route, buses also leave from Cultura but near Manuel Prado (3 hours, $3).

For **Paucartambo**, buses leave from Cultura and Diagonal Angamos (three hours, $3).

Buses for **Paruro** leave from Belen and Grau (three hours, $3).

Trains

The only way to get to Machu Picchu, and a highly interesting way to reach Puno, is via train. **ENAFER**, the former state-owned railroad company, was privatized in the mid-1990s and has been operated since 1999 by **PeruRail** (www.perurail.com, reservas@perurail.com), a division of Orient-Express Hotels. As a result, both the quality and the price have gone way up. A major problem with trains from Cusco, especially during high season, is availability. It is possible to make online reservations, and PeruRail is hoping to introduce online credit card payment in the future. Many Cusco hotels and agencies will also purchase Cusco train tickets with a credit card number and hold them in custody until travelers reach Cusco. Otherwise, the travelers themselves must head down to the train station, a process that can take an hour or two. During high season, make train reservations ahead of time.

Cusco has two train stations. The one for Machu Picchu is San Pedro (Cascaparo and Santa Clara, at the top of the market, tel. 084/22-1291). The train zigzags up the hillside above Cusco and then runs across the high plains through Poroy and Ollantaytambo, where it enters the steep and narrow Urubamba gorge. Even with snow-capped Verónica (5,710 meters or 18,865ft) occasionally appearing on the right (eastern) side of the train, the landscape transforms into the lush and humid *ceja de selva,* or "eyebrow of the jungle." By the time the train reaches Aguas Calientes, the ramshackle town closest to Machu Picchu, travelers have gone from the high plains around Cusco to mountainous cloud forest.

PeruRail offers three train services to Machu Picchu; the **Backpacker** ($60 round trip, $42 one-way), the **Vistadome** ($89 round trip, $60 one-way) and the new, luxury Hiram Bingham service ($417 round trip only). For descriptions and times of these trains see *Getting There* in the *Machu Picchu* section. The Vistadome train leaves the San Pedro station at 6 A.M. and arrives in Aguas Calientes at 9:A.M. In the afternoon this train leaves Aguas Calientes at 3:30 P.M. and arrives back in Cusco by 7:20 A.M. A Backpacker train leaves Cusco at 6:15 A.M. and, in high season, at 6:35 A.M., arriving in Aguas Calientes at 10:10 and 10:40 A.M. They leave Machu Picchu at 3:55 and 4:20 P.M., arriving in Cusco four hours later. The most up-to-date timetable is at www.perurail.com.

Trains for Puno leave from the Wanchaq Station (El Sol s/n, tel. 084/23-3592), from which trains—both a Backpacker ($14 one-way) and a deluxe Andean Explorer ($89 one-way)—depart daily at 8 A.M. and arrive at 5 P.M. in Puno This is a gorgeous, nine-hour way to reach Puno that winds past snow-capped mountains and onto the *altiplano.*

Taxis

A taxi anywhere in Cusco's center costs $0.75 or $1 at night. Take the proper precautions as explained in the sidebar *Taxi Safety.* Because Cusco's center is so compact (and congested) few travelers find the need to take buses or *combis*—though the ones that head down Av. El Sol toward the Terminal Terrestre and airport are useful.

Lake Titicaca and Canyon Country

Nowhere are Peru's people more colorful, or its landscapes more dramatic, than southern Peru, the country's second travel destination behind Cusco and Machu Picchu. At the top of the list is Lake Titicaca, a limitless expanse of water plunked down in the middle of Peru's high plateau. Traveling by boat across the lake's sapphire waters, with the snow-capped mountains of Bolivia in the distance, it is easy to understand why the Incas considered this their sacred, foun-

dational landscape. Lake Titicaca is one of Peru's cradles of civilization, and staying with families on the islands or peninsulas is a good way to experience ways of life that extend back thousands of years. It is also the best way to see the lake's bucolic scenery of winding country lanes, transparent waters, and Mediterranean-like sunlight.

A brand-new highway connects the high grasslands around Lake Titicaca to Arequipa, Peru's most elegant city. Laid back and sunny, Arequipa

is constructed entirely of white volcanic stone and stands out for its sophisticated Spanish charm. Colonial churches and *casonas* line the street leading to the elegant Plaza de Armas, with a stately cathedral that is flanked by palm trees and framed by volcanoes. But the city's architectural highlight is the Santa Catalina Monastery, a city-within-a-city of churches, plazas, and homes where nuns have lived cloistered since 1579.

Arequipa is surrounded by some of the country's most bizarre and remote landscapes: snow-capped volcanoes, lava fields, high-altitude deserts, and the celebrated Colca Canyon, which is twice as deep as Arizona's Grand Canyon. Stone villages, graced with colonial churches and elaborately carved altars, dot the canyon's rim, where life continues as it has for centuries. At one spot, where the canyon drops more than 300 meters, a hundred visitors or more from around the world gather each morning to witness the canyon's most awesome spectacle. Each morning like clockwork, after the rising sun has heated the air, giant Andean condors begin soaring over this spot, sometimes just meters away from those gathered. No other spot in the world offers such intimate, reliable views of the largest flying bird in the world.

PLANNING YOUR TIME

Traveling through southern Peru by bus became much easier after the 2001 completion of the Arequipa–Juliaca highway, which reduced what was once an 18-hour trip to only five hours. An increasing number of travelers can now travel by bus from Lima and stop along the coast at Paracas, Ica, Nasca, and Arequipa before heading up to Lake Titicaca and Cusco. Assaults no longer occur on these routes as they did in the 1990s, but traveling during the day is still recommended. If you are interested in climbing one of Arequipa's volcanoes, a great way to acclimatize is by doing this circuit in reverse, from Cusco to Lima.

Travel options between Puno and Cusco include a revamped train service with excellent views and a high-quality tourist bus that allows budding archaeologists to see the string of ruins on the way to Cusco. Travelers with less time can also jet between Arequipa, Juliaca (the closest airport to Lake Titicaca), and Cusco.

Lake Titicaca has its fair share of tourist traps these days, and Puno, the gateway city, is unpleasant and grimy. For those on a tight budget, Lake Titicaca is a good place to spend a bit more money to get off the beaten tourist path—such as kayaking to **Isla Amantaní** or arranging homestays at the lesser-known Anapia and Yuspique. Traveling by bus along either shore of Lake Titicaca, and stopping in towns along the way, is another interesting option.

Travelers should acclimatize for a few days in Cusco or Arequipa before arriving at Lake Titicaca, a heady 3,810 meters (12,500 feet) above sea level. The best time to visit is between March and November, the sunny winter months—but bring lots of warm clothing for the freezing nights and a wide-brimmed hat and sunscreen for the intense sun.

The so-called Gringo Trail, the main backpacker route, breezes through Puno, detours for a sojourn on the islands, and continues around the south shores of the lake to Copacabana and La Paz, Bolivia. The ancient capital of **Tiwanaku** and the **Islas del Sol y de la Luna,** all on the Bolivia side, are Lake Titicaca's most spectacular ruins. For travelers who can manage to fly into La Paz and out of Peru, traveling around the lake and visiting these ruins makes for an interesting circuit. Another option for getting between La Paz and Puno are two luxury boats, which visit the islands en route.

Must-Sees

Puno

M Folklore festivals: Lake Titicaca is known as the Folklore Capital of Peru, so you shouldn't miss a chance to take in one of the local festivals. Puno's best-known, **Virgen de la Candelaria,** reaches a fever pitch on February 2, when an image of the Virgin Mary is paraded through the streets amid hundreds of dancing devils, angels, and other extravagantly costumed characters (page 106).

cruising the shores of Isla Taquile

M Kayaking on Lake Titicaca: The only way to see the emerald waters and snow-covered mountains of the world's highest navigable lake is by boat—kayaking gives you the view from the water's edge (page 108).

Lake Titicaca

M Islas Taquile and Amantaní: Staying with a family on one of Lake Titicaca's islands is a great way to immerse yourself in the lake's natural beauty and the ancient lifestyles of its villagers (page 117).

Arequipa

M Plaza de Armas: Any tour of Arequipa should begin in Peru's most elegant urban square, with its neoclassical cathedral, arcades, palm trees, flowers, and fountains (page 131).

M Monasterio de Santa Catalina: Since the 16th century, nuns have lived cloistered amid the timeless archways and chapels of this miniature city, built entirely of white volcanic stone (page 134).

Colca

M La Cruz del Cóndor: Nowhere can the Andean condor, the world's largest flying bird, be seen so reliably as from this spot perched on the rim of the Colca Canyon (page 157).

LAKE TITICACA AND CANYON COUNTRY

PACIFIC OCEAN

Islas Taquile and Amantaní **M**

Lake Titicaca

Folklore Festivals **M**

La Cruz del Cóndor **M**

Kayaking on Lake Titicaca

Monasterio de Santa Catalina **M**

Plaza de Armas

PACIFIC OCEAN

CHILE

© RENÉE DEL GAUDIO AND ROSS WEHNER

Lake Titicaca

LAKE TITICACA AND CANYON COUNTRY

CHOQUEQUIRAO

MACHU PICCHU
Ollantaytambo
Urubamba   Pisac   Puacartambo   Quincemil
Limatambo

THE SAYWITE STONE
Abancay   Andahuaylillas   Urcos
CUSCO
Ocongate
Nevado de Ausangate

Antabamba

Santo Tomás   Sicuani   RAQCHI
Abra La Raya

Río Cotahuasi   Suycutambo   Ayaviri
Cotahuasi   PUCARÁ
Valle de los Volcanes   Lampa   Juliaca
Nevado Coropuna   Andagua   COLCA LODGE THERMAL SPRINGS
Cabanaconde   Colca Cyn   Chivay   Deústua   Llachón
Yanaquihua   Yanque   SILLUSTANI
LA CRUZ DEL CÓNDOR   Islas de Uros   Puno   Chuchito
Cañahuas   Abra Toroya
TORO MUERTO   MONASTERIO DE SANTA CATALINA   Reserva Nacional Salinas y Aguada Blanca   Ilave   Juli
Camaña   Volcán Misti   Abra Loripongo   FOLKLORE FESTIVALS   Pomata
Arequipa   Abra Gallatini   KAYAKING ON LAKE TITICACA   Zepita   Yunguyo
PLAZA DE ARMAS   Abra Chocajinani   Desaguadero

Mollendo   Zona Reservada Aymara-Lupaca
La Curva   Moquegua

PACIFIC OCEAN
Ilo

Punta Colorada   Tacna

Arica   CHILE

Río Madre de Dios   Puerto Maldonado

Parque Nacional Manu

Cordillera Vilcanota

Zona Reservada Tambopata   Parque Nacional Bahuaja-Sonene
Guarayos
Madidi

Macusani   San Juan del Oro

PERU

BOLIVIA

Huancané   Moho
Isla Amantaní   I Suasi
I del Sol   Lake Titicaca
ISLAS TAQUILE AND AMANTANÍ   Cordillera Real
I Taquile   I del Sol
I de la Luna
Copacabana
Islas Anapia and Yuspique   La Paz

Desaguadero   Río Desaguadero

0   50 mi
0   50 km

© AVALON TRAVEL PUBLISHING, INC.

Lake Titicaca

Puno

Puno is a sprawling, somewhat unappealing city with a few colonial churches and an incredible number of religious festivals. Because it is Peru's only major city on the shores of Lake Titicaca, most travelers must pass through here toward more interesting destinations. As a result, there is a good range of hotels, restaurants, and agencies.

Great efforts have been made to improve Puno's attractiveness to outsiders. The wooden lake boats, powered by converted car engines from the 1950s, are much safer now that they are equipped with life jackets, fire extinguishers, and cell phones. They also float higher out of the water with an enforced limit on passengers. A new terminal on the edge of town brings all of the major bus companies together and is just a few minutes' walk from the port, where boats leave for Amantaní and Taquile Islands.

During the early days of the Peruvian viceroyalty, Puno was a stopover for those traveling between Arequipa and the Potosí mine, in present-day Bolivia. But in 1688, a silver mine was discovered at nearby Laicota and the town was renamed San Carlos de Puno. During this time, important churches were built in Puno and around the shores of Lake Titicaca, with mestizo facades similar to those in Arequipa.

SIGHTS

Puno's most interesting sight, just outside of town, is the **Yavari** (behind Sonesta Posada Hotel, tel. 051/36-9329, www.yavari.org, 8 A.M.–5 P.M. daily, free), one of the world's great antique ships. The story of how it got here is also one of the great Herculean efforts in Latin American history.

If you have the time and the energy, start your tour three blocks from the Plaza de Armas at **Parque Huajsapata,** the *mirador* overlooking Puno with a huge sculpture of Manco Cápac, the first Inca. Take extra precaution here, as there have been recent reports of robbery assaults on single tourists while visiting this *mirador.*

Otherwise, begin in the Plaza de Armas at the city's **cathedral** (8 A.M.–noon and 3–5 P.M. daily),

which was built in the 17th century by Peruvian master stonemason Simon de Asto. The interior is rather Spartan in contrast to the carved facade, but contains an interesting silver-plated altar. Next to the cathedral is the 17th-century **Casa del Corregidor,** built by Father Silvestre de Valdés, who was in charge of the cathedral construction. It has a pleasant courtyard, now occupied by Puno's most charming café.

Up the street, at the corner of Conde de Lemos and Deústua, is the Balcony of the Conde de Lemos, where Peru's viceroy lived when he first stopped in the city. It is now the headquarters of the Cultural Institute of Peru. Across the street is the **Museo Dreyer Municipal** (Conde de Lemos 289, next to Plaza de Armas, 7:30 A.M.–3:30 P.M. Mon.–Fri., $1) which has a collection of pre-Inca and Inca ceramics, gold, weavings, and stone sculptures, as well as stamps and documents on the history of the Spanish foundation of Puno.

Now head downhill two blocks to Puno's **pedestrian street,** Lima, which connects the Plaza de Armas to **Parque Pino** and has the city's best restaurants and cafés. The 18th-century church gracing Parque Pino is dedicated to San Juan Bautista and contains the Virgen de Candelaria, Puno's patroness and center of its most important festival. If you still have energy, continue past Parque Pino in the same direction. The street, which switches names to Independencia, leads to Arco Deústua, a huge stone arch dedicated to those killed in the battles for independence in Junín and Ayacucho. Another option from Parque Pino is to head a few blocks downhill, toward the lake, to Puno's huge central market, which is especially busy in the mornings.

▶ FOLKLORE FESTIVALS

A highlight of any visit to Lake Titicaca is seeing one of 300 traditional festivals that happen in this area each year. Lake Titicaca has the richest and most vibrant dances and celebrations in all of Peru and it is worth timing your trip to see one. Entire towns participate in the festivals of orchestras,

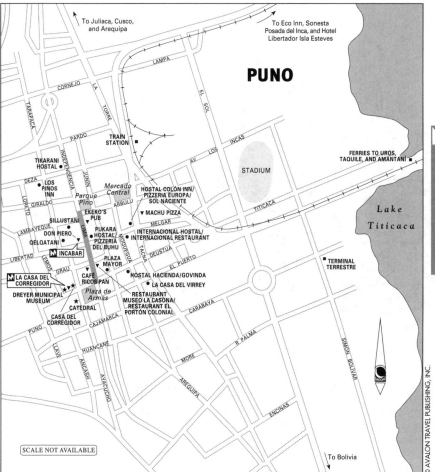

© AVALON TRAVEL PUBLISHING, INC.

musical groups, and elaborately costumed dancers move with precision and endurance. Though performed on Catholic holidays, most of the dances in Puno are rooted in pre-Columbian rituals of harvest, planting, herding, and magic.

The most famous dance is **La Diablada,** performed each year on February 2 during Puno's **Fiesta de la Virgen de la Candelaria.** The dance is essentially a struggle between dozens of elaborately costumed angels and bug-eyed, horned devils, along with an ever-growing cast of new characters: the Widow, the Skeleton, the Old Man, the Mexican, the Redskin, Batman, etc. Other dances include *Choq'elas,* which is performed before the roundup of the vicuñas, and *Q'ajelo,* which ends when the gun-toting shepherds steal the dancing maidens before them and carry them off over their shoulders.

A good example of the intermingling of Spanish with Inca and Aymara are the **musical instruments** themselves. The trumpets, tubas, saxophones, and string instruments are recent European contributions, but the flutes, panpipes, and drums have evolved over thousands of years.

Lake Titicaca

Puno's Virgen de la Candelaria celebration in early February is a whirlwind of dances, costumes, and religious processions.

The flutes range from the tiny *quena,* which looks like a pennywhistle, to the huge *pincullo,* made out of a chunk of algarrobo wood. The panpipes range from the handheld *zampoñas* or *antaras* to the *sicus,* which are almost as tall as their players themselves. There are also a huge range of drums, rattles, and bells.

Other interesting cultural events can be found online at www.casadelcorregidor.com.pe.

NIGHTLIFE

The best pub in Puno is **Kamikaze** (Grau 148, 5 P.M.–midnight Tues.–Sun.) Another top spot for rock, reggae, and blues is **Ekeko's Pub** (Lima 355), which ladles out free drinks from 7:30 to 9:30 P.M. The best disco in Puno is the salsa-influenced **Domino** (Libertad 437, 7 P.M.–3 A.M. Tues.–Sun.). **El Palacio del Folklore** (Lima 723, 7 P.M.–2 A.M.) is a peña that opens on Friday and Saturday nights with a wide range of regional dances, although the schedule is a bit unreliable. Amazing but true, there are no other peñas in Puno, despite its distinguished title as the *Capital of Folklore.*

SHOPPING

Puno is a good place to buy alpaca wool clothing and weavings. Good spots include the **Casa del Artesano** at Lima 549 and the **Arts & Crafts Center** across the street, on the pedestrian mall near the main square, and the market on the railway between Los Incas and Lampa. The highest quality is found at **Alpaka's** (Lima 394, tel. 051/36-3551, 9 A.M.–noon and 4–10 P.M. Mon.–Sat., 4–8 P.M. Sun.) and the expensive **Alpaca 111** (Lima 343), which both sell nice sweaters, scarves, and shawls.

SPORTS AND RECREATION
Kayaking on Lake Titicaca
There is no better way to see the beauty of Lake Titicaca than by sea kayak. We began our kayaking trip far from the hustle and bustle of Puno, where most travelers arrive, at **Llachón**, a Quechuan village on the lake's shore. At dawn, with Bolivia's snow-covered mountains aglow in the morning sun, we launched brand-new sea kayaks onto black waters. I had been to Lake Titicaca several times before but never had I experienced it like this.

Instead of chugging across the lake on a dieselpowered boat, we glided on glassy waters past boulders covered with bright-green algae. We breathed in the musty, seaside air and watched waves fold onto the white sand beaches. I would have sworn we were on an ocean were it not for the impossibly thin air—and the fact that our guide kept drinking the crystal-clear lake water from his cupped hands. We left the shoreline and began to paddle across the lake, as deep as 900 feet in some places, toward the rising hulk of **Isla Amantaní.** By evening, the lake was glassy calm and stained red by the setting sun.

Two of Peru's top adventure agencies are now offing sea kayaking trips on Lake Titicaca. A

IRON BOATS UP AND OVER THE ANDES

Peru is filled with stories about large iron boats lugged to improbable places. In 1890, rubber baron Carlos Fermín Fitzcarrald and an army of 1,000 Piro Indians lugged an entire steamship up and over a ridge, nearly 10 km, to connect two river basins. This hairball scheme became the subject of *Fitzcarraldo,* the 1982 movie directed by Werner Herzog.

An even crazier but less well-known scheme was concocted by the Peruvian Navy in 1861, when it ordered not one but two huge iron gunboats—the *Yavari* and the *Yapuro*—for patrolling the waters of Lake Titicaca. Within two years, the Thames Iron Works and Ship Building in London had the gunboats shipped, in crates, around Cape Horn to Arica, the Peruvian port that would later be snatched by Chile in the War of the Pacific.

This is where the story becomes unbelievable. From the desert coast, with the Andes looming before them, porters hefted the crankshafts to their shoulders, while mules stood, knees quivering, under the weight of hull sections and crates containing more than 2,766 ship parts. The 290-mile journey, up and over the Andes, wound up steep and treacherous trails and included a final 4,700-meter pass. Not surprisingly, getting everything to the shores of Lake Titicaca took more than six years. With much fanfare, the *Yavari* was launched on Christmas Day 1870 and the *Yapura* three years after.

Because of a lack of coal, the Navy—what else could it do—began shoveling a more abundant local fuel source in the ship's boilers: dried llama dung. But more space was needed to accommodate the manure piles. The *Yavari* was cut in half in order to add 12 meters to her hold, bringing her to a total length of 50 meters. Finally, in 1914, her steam engine was replaced by a Swedish-made Bolinder, a four-cylinder diesel. Half a century later, the boats were decommissioned. The *Yapura* was sold for scrap metal, and the *Yavari* was abandoned on the lake's shores, its instruments carted off to Arequipa's municipal museum.

The sight of the forgotten ship, whose hull had rusted little in the lake's fresh waters, moved Englishwoman Meriel Larken to action in the early 1980s. She launched the Yavari Association to save the old ship and attracted the financial support of Britain's Prince Philip, who had visited Lake Titicaca in 1962. In 1999, more than 40 years after her last voyage, the *Yavari* once again slipped her moors and began plying the waters of Lake Titicaca.

The *Yavari* is, without a doubt, the most interesting thing to see in Puno. The bunk, engine, and map rooms have been meticulously restored, and the bridge has all the ship's original navigation equipment, including an old-fashioned sextant and compass. The Bolinder engine, lovingly restored by Volvo engineers, is considered the oldest working ship engine in the world. When the association has more funds, it plans to build 10 cabins and offer what will surely be unforgettable overnight lake cruises.

---

new company called **Titikayak** (Bolognesi 334, tel. 051/36-7747, postmast@titikayak.com, www.titikayak.com), part-owned by the reputable ExplorAndes agency, offers a variety of safe, well-planned trips that leave from Llachón. Half-day trips ($45) tour the shores of the peninsula, a full-day trip ($95) goes back and forth to Taquile in one day, and a three-day trip ($190) explores the island in detail. Longer 10-day trips to out-of-the-way places can be arranged. The company has excellent equipment and provides everything needed. Lodging in Lachón is in the quaint cabins operated by Valentín Quispe. Another reputable agency, the Cusco-based **Ama-**zonas Explorer** (400 Jose Gabriel Cosio, Cusco, tel. 084/22-7137, sales@amazonas-explorer.com, www.amazonas-explorer.com), plans to offer Lake Titicaca trips in the near future.

Island Tours

Tours to the islands range dramatically in quality. At the top end is the socially conscientious **All Ways Travel** (Tacna 234, tel. 051/35-5552, allwaystravel@titicacaperu.com, www.titicacaperu.com), managed by Victor Pauca and his young and entrepreneurial daughter, Eliana, who graduated from Duke University's grad school for International Development Policy in 2002.

The agency's trips are slightly more expensive but worth it for their quality and the benefits received by the community. A two-day trip to Uros, Amantaní, and Taquile, with an overnight on Amantaní, cost $14 pp including meals. The exciting trip, however, is the two- or three-day trip to Anapia and Yuspique, seldom-visited islands in southern Lake Titicaca.

There are dozens of agencies in Puno that offer trips to Taquile, Amantaní, and surrounding sites like Sillustani and Chucuito but some do not deliver what they promise. As always, never purchase a trip or contract a guide in the street, and remember: you get what you pay for. One reliable agency is **Cusi Travel** (Teodoro Valcarcel 126, tel. 051/36-9072). It offers trips to Uros ($4, half-day); Uros and Taquile ($7, full day); Uros, Amantaní, and Taquile ($14, two days, departs 8:10 A.M.); and to Sillustani ($6, departs 2:15 P.M., three hours). **Edgar Adventures** (Lima 328, tel. 051/35-3444, edgaradventures@terra.com.pe, www.edgaradventures.com), run by a Peruvian husband-wife team, has the same schedule with slightly higher prices. A final recommended agency is **Inka Adventure** (Alfonso Ugarte 156, tel. 051/36-5020, reservaspuno@yahoo.com), which apart from city tours offers trips to all the islands with similar departure times. An even cheaper way to get to the islands is via boats that leave every morning from Puno's public dock.

A handful of Puno agencies have fast boats that can cut the 3.5-hour trip to Taquile in less than half. These agencies include **Solmartour** (Libertad 231, tel. 051/35-2901, solmartour@ventanavirtual.com) and **Kolla Tour** (Moguegua 679, tel. 051/36-9863, titikakakolla@terra.com.pe). All Ways Travel has a daily, round-trip fast boat to Taquile for $32 that will cut total boat time to two hours, as opposed to six on a normal boat.

Horseback Riding

Horseback riding can be done at the recommended **Fundo Chincheros,** a country hacienda in the valley just north of Puno operated by the owners of the café La Casa del Corregidor. Apart from trail rides, the day is spent hiking through cactus forest, seeing vicuña, and having a garden picnic next to a rare 17th-century *capilla abierta,* or open chapel. The controversial constructions, which were banned after 1680, allowed Spanish priests to baptize Indians without having to let them in the church.

ACCOMODATIONS
Under $10
A safe place for backpackers is the **Albergue Juvenil Virgen de Copacabana** (Llave 228, tel. 051/36-3766, $3.50 s, $7 d). This family-run hostel is clean and friendly, and has 24-hour hot water. Guests have full use of the kitchen, and laundry can be done for a good price. There are several cheap hostels by the train station, but they are noisy and do not seem safe. Always check the hot water supply before you hand over your money.

$10–25
A decent backpackers' place is **La Casa del Virrey** (Tacna 510, tel. 051/36-9931, $7 s, $10 d). It's not the cleanest, there are no shower curtains, and

sea kayaking along the shores of Isla Taquile

beds are lumpy, but some rooms have a view of the lake. Prices include breakfast. One of the best deals in town is **Los Pinos Inn** (Tarapacá 182, tel. 051/36-7398, hostalpinos@hotmail.com, $10 s, $15 d) with large, light-filled rooms, new private baths, and electric hot water showers. Budget travelers can request rooms with shared bathroom for $5 pp. Another safe, comfortable choice is the **Internacional Hostal** (Libertad 161, tel. 051/51-35-2109, h_internacional@latinmail.com, $13 s, $20 d) with lots of water and cable TV. Prices include breakfast, and Internet is $0.50/hour.

$25–50

The upscale **Pukara Hostal** (Libertad 328, tel. 051/36-8448, pukara@terra.com.pe, $25 s, $40 d) is a tall, narrow building with three rooms and a sitting room on each floor. This hostel has a bohemian air, with pillows on the floor, books for trade, and lots of art. The rooms are charming and have cable TV. The owner, Sonia Cossio, also has the similarly priced **Tikarani Hostal** (Independencia 143, tel. 051/36-5501, pukara@terra.com.pe, $25, $40 d), further north of the Plaza de Armas. For a more traditional hotel, the quiet **Sillustani** (Lambayeque 195, tel. 051/35-1881, sillustani@punonet.com, www.punonet.com/sillustani, $34 s, $46 d, includes breakfast) has comfortable, carpeted rooms with bathtubs and cable TV. Buffet breakfast is served in a formal dining room. One of the most tasteful places in town is the elegant, Belgian-owned **Colón Inn** (Tacna 290, tel. 051/35/1432, coloninn@titicaca-peru, www.titicaca-peru.com, $40 s, $46, includes breakfast), a colonial building with a marble-floored lobby and sun-filled sitting rooms. Large rooms, with wood floors or red carpets, are arranged around an atrium and have cable TV and writing desks. There is Internet ($1.50/hour) and two restaurants in the hotel, both of which are very good.

$50–100

The most comfortable night's sleep in the center of town is at the impeccably clean **Plaza Mayor** (Deustua 342, tel. 051/36-6089, reservas@plazamayorhostal.com, www.plazamayorhostal.com, $43 s, $56 d, includes breakfast), with king-size mattresses, real box springs (a rarity in Peru), feather pillows, bathtub, and cable TV. The hotel manager, also an M.D., is on call around the clock, and breakfasts are served in a sunny dining room. The rooms at the **Qelqatani** (Tarapacá 355, tel. 051/36-6172, hotel@qelqatani.com, www.qelqatani.com, $43 s, $56 d, includes breakfast) are a bit dark, but are large and comfortable with carpet, heaters, cable TV, bathtubs, and a thoroughly Peruvian decor. Internet is available for $1.50/hour, and there is a restaurant in the lobby. The **Hostal Hacienda** (Deustua 297, tel. 051/35-6109, hacienda@latinmail.com, $40 s, $53 d) offers dark, carpeted rooms with cable TV, set around a colonial courtyard. The rooms are bit run down, but this place may improve in the future; 36 new rooms with bathtubs are in the works. The **Eco Inn** (Chulluni 195, tel. 051/36-5525, ecoinn@terra.com.pe, www.ecoinnpuno .com, $60 s, $65 d, includes breakfast), outside of town near the Hotel Isla Estevez, is an unpretentious alternative with lakeside views. Situated on lagoon backwaters, this hotel offers large rooms with bay windows and cable TV, and some of the rooms have bathtubs.

$100–150

The more affordable luxury option, also on the lake near Hotel Libertador Isla Esteves, is the comfortable **Sonesta Posada del Inca** (Sesquicentenario 610, tel. 051/36-4112, posada@sonestaperu.com, www.sonesta.com, $77 s, $90 d). Rooms are cheerful with plaid bedspreads, warm colors, heaters, and all the amenities. An exquisite breakfast buffet ($7) is served on a lakeside dining room, or outdoors on an open porch. The hotel also has oxygen, ATM, and Internet ($4/hour), and the Cusco-Puno train stops at the door for large groups. The *Yavari*, Puno's most interesting attraction, is docked a few meters away, and the reed marsh teems with dozens of different ducks and birds.

Over $150

Of all the former state-owned hotels, the five-star **⛰ Hotel Libertador Isla Esteves** (Isla Esteves s/n, tel. 051/36-7780 or in Lima tel. 01/442-1995, hotel@libertador.com.pe, www.libertador.com.pe, $157 s, $157 d, includes breakfast) is one of the more stunning. It is like a huge alabaster cruise ship, perched on its own island jutting into Lake Titicaca, with stunning aerial views of Puno and the lake. From the marble lobby, the rooms rise on both sides over a huge glass courtyard and an expansive, elegant area with a bar and elegant couches. Lying in the king-size beds, surrounded by five-star amenities, with the sun rising over Lake Titicaca is truly deluxe—especially when you consider the spa, Jacuzzi, and huge buffet breakfast awaiting you. The hotel even has its own dock, where tours leave for the islands. If you can afford it, this is the place to stay.

FOOD

Most of Puno's best restaurants are along Lima, the upscale pedestrian street off the Plaza de Armas. A good local dish to try is *chairo,* a soup of beef or lamb, potatoes, beans, squash, cabbage, *chuño* (potato flour), wheat, and *chalona* (dried mutton). *Trucha* (trout), *pejerrey, ishpi,* and other local fish are excellent, as is the *sajta de pollo,* a chicken stew mixed with potatoes and peanuts.

Cafés and Desserts

The most charming place to hang out is **La Casa Del Corregidor** (Deustua 576, tel. 051/35-1921, www.casadelcorregidor.com.pe, 10 A.M.–10 P.M. Tues.–Fri., 10 A.M.–2:30 P.M. and 5–11 P.M. Sat.–Sun., $1), set in the historic 17th-century home of the same name, next to the cathedral. This charming café, with a cozy interior decorated with contemporary photography and a flower-filled colonial patio, serves up delicious Greek salads and gourmet appetizers in addition to coffee drinks and a range of teas. Cultural exhibits revolve through this extraordinary café, which also includes six fast Internet stations, a multimedia center, and a very interesting library. **Café Ricos Pan** (Lima 424 and Moquegua 330, tel. 051/35-1024, 6 A.M.–10 P.M. Mon.–Sat., $1) serves good yogurt milkshakes, quiche, desserts, and espresso drinks at incredibly cheap prices. Standouts include the apple pie, Black Forest cake, cheesecake, tiramisu and $1.50 Pisco sours.

International

Though pricy, the funky **IncaBar** (Lima 348, tel. 051/36-8031, 8 A.M.–10 P.M. Sun.–Fri., 4–10 P.M. Sat., $6) has really good food. Greek salads, guacamole, pomadoro pasta with plum tomatoes, basil, and garlic, and chicken curry are just a few of the tempting dishes. There is a separate creative menu offering crazy dishes such as curry chicken with a sauce made of papaya, green beans, coconut, and peppers. There is a dimly lit couch room in the back, a great place to hang out and have a coffee or a cocktail. Located inside the charming Colón Inn is the tiny **Sol Naciente** (Tacna 290, tel. 051/35-1432, 10 A.M.–2 P.M. and 6–10 P.M., $5), with a wide-ranging and tantalizing menu of Peruvian, Belgian, French, Italian, and Hungarian cooking.

Peruvian

The long-standing **Restaurant Internacional** (Libertad 161, tel. 051/35-2502, 6:30 A.M.–10 P.M. daily, $2), open now for 25 years, serves *comida tipica* in a diner-like atmosphere. This is the place to try Peruvian specialties like *lomo saltado* and garlic trout. Next door is **La Estancia** (Libertad 137, tel. 051/36-5469) with excellent *parrilas* (grilled meats) and trout. Another recommended old-timey place, around for 20 years, is **Don Piero** (Lima 364, tel. 051/36-5943, 7:30 A.M.–10 P.M. daily, $3), which has good trout for dinner and banana-honey pancakes for breakfast. The elegant **Restaurant Museo La Casona** (Lima 517, tel. 051/35-1108, 9 A.M.–10 P.M. daily, $5), with wood floors, a whitewashed interior, and antiques lining the walls, serves traditional Peruvian food in several small dining rooms. This is your chance to try guinea pig, garlic alpaca meat, and *anticuchos*—though vegetarian pastas and soups are also part of the menu. For a more laid-back experience, **Restaurant El Portón Colonial** (Lima 345, tel. 051/33-7987, 7 A.M.–9 P.M., $3.50) has an extensive menu offering all of the Peruvian specialties, such as *ceviche de pejerrey, papas a la huancaina, pollo a la brasa,* and *chupe de pescado.* Service is excellent.

Pizza

Pizzería Del Buho (Libertad 386, 5–10:30 P.M. daily), just off the pedestrian street, serves some of the best pizza in town and becomes lively at night. Others say the cozy **Machu Pizza** (Tacna 279, tel. 051/992-1838, 8 A.M.–3 P.M. and 5 P.M.–midnight daily, $2) holds the honor for best pizza; it delivers and has a $1 set menu served from 8 A.M.–3 P.M. More expensive than the others, but worth it for the atmosphere, **Pizzeria Europa** (Tacna 290, tel. 051/35-1432, 6–10 P.M. daily, $5) serves espresso drinks and wood-fired pizzas from inside the charming Colón Inn.

Health Food

The reliable **Govinda** (Deustua 312, tel. 051/35-1283, 8 A.M.–8 P.M. Mon.–Sat., $2), found in nearly every Peruvian city, serves vegetarian dishes such as Spanish paella, spinach pizza, and *saltado de broccoli* to four tables in a tiny café. It also sells natural yogurt and has a $1 set menu.

INFORMATION AND SERVICES

Free tourist information and maps are available at **i Peru** (Deustua with Lima, tel. 051/36-5088, 8:30 A.M.–7:30 P.M. daily). For more detailed information, visit the **Regional Tourism Office** (Ayacucho 682, tel. 051/36-4976, 7:30 A.M.–5:15 P.M. Mon.–Fri.). A concise and interesting pamphlet that explains life on the islands and shore is Juan Palao Berastain's *Titikaka Lake: Children of the Sacred Lake,* available in bookstores and tour agencies.

Historical information on Puno can be found in the library at **La Casa Del Corregidor** (Deustua 576, tel. 051/35-1921,10 A.M.–10 P.M. Tues.–Sun.).

The **National Police** (Ayacucho 298, 24 hours) are located on the Plaza de Armas, and the **Tourist Police** (Deustua 538, tel. 051/36-4806, 051/35-7100, or 051/35-3988, 24 hours) are also in the center of town.

For health care, there is **Hospital Manuel Nuñez Butrón** (El Sol, 1022, tel. 051/35-1021, 24 hrs.), **Clínica Los Pinos** (Los Alamos B-2, tel. 051/35-1071) and **Clínica Puno** (Ramón Castilla 178, tel. 051/36-8835). **Santa Cruz Botica** is the best pharmacy at the corner of Lima and Libertad.

For money matters, head to Lima, the pedestrian street for **Interbank** (Lima 485) and **Banco Continental** (Lima 470), with **Banco Weise** on the Plaza de Armas. All have ATMs.

The post office is **Serpost** (Moquegua 269, tel. 051/35-1141, 8 A.M.–8 P.M. Mon.–Sat.).

The best place for Internet in town is upstairs at **La Casa Del Corregidor** (Deustua 576, tel. 051/35-1921, 10 A.M.–10 P.M. daily, $0.50/hour) though there are other fast, cheap connections at Mogequa 371, Libertad 215, and along Lima.

International calls to the U.S. and Europe can be made for $1/min. at the **Telefónica del Peru** (Lima 439, tel. 051/36-9180, 7:30 A.M.–9:30 P.M. daily).

North Americans, Britains, New Zealanders, and Australians do not need visas to enter Bolivia but may want to ask for information at the **Bolivian Consulate** (Arequipa 270, tel. 051/35-1251, 8 A.M.–2 P.M. Mon.–Fri.)—the border was closed, because of political unrest, for weeks during 2003. **Peruvian Immigrations** (Ayacucho 240, tel. 051/35-2801) can extend tourist visas, though expect a wait. Laundry can be done at **Don Marcelo** (Lima 433, tel. 051/35-2444) or **América** (Moquegua 175, tel. 051/35-1642).

GETTING THERE

Plane

Unfortunately, Puno does not have an airport. The closest is **Aeropuerto Manco Cápac** (tel. 051/32-2905) in Juliaca, about 45 minutes north of Puno. **LanPeru** (Tacna 299, tel. 051/36-7227 in Puno, tel. 01/213-8200 for reservations, www.lanperu.com) flies back and forth several times a day between Lima and Juliaca and Arequipa and Juliaca. LanPeru has one flight per day from Cusco to Juliaca, but none in the other direction.

Train

One of the highest passenger trains in the world runs between Cusco and Puno and has been recently overhauled by **PeruRail**, which took over the state-owned ENAFER rail company in 1999. The views along this route are fantastic, though the train rolls right by a series of interesting ruins. It does stop briefly, however, at the high pass of La

Raya, 4,314 meters, where a colonial chapel stands alone in the middle of the high plateau. One train per day leaves Cusco daily at 8 A.M., stops in La Raya at 12:15 P.M. and Juliaca at 3:50 P.M., and arrives in Puno at 5 P.M. Another train leaves each day from Puno at 8 A.M., stops in Juliaca at 9:05 P.M. and La Raya at 12:45 P.M., and arrives in Cusco at 5 P.M. The Backpacker train, which has comfortable seats but includes no snacks, costs $14 one-way, and the deluxe Andean Explorer is $89 one-way, including lunch. This first-class service has elegant dining cars, an open-air bar car, and luxurious coaches (designed by James Parks and Associates, the same company that designed the first-class cabins for Singapore Airlines). Tickets can be bought at the station in Puno (La Torre 224, tel. 051/36-9179) or reserved online (www.perurail.com, reservas@perurail.com).

Bus

Puno's sparkling new **Terminal Terrestre** (1 de Mayo 703, intersection with Bolivar, tel. 051/36-4733 for schedule questions, $0.30 entry), opened in 2001, has greatly improved the pleasure of busing into Puno. It is safe, with restaurants, snack bars, and even a clean, though noisy, hostel ($5 s, $9 d). From here buses arrive from and depart for Juliaca, Arequipa, Tacna, Cusco, Lima, and La Paz, Bolivia (through both Desaguadero and Copacabana). The travel times written below are correct; if a bus company promises you a dramatically shorter ride, as even a reputable bus company like Ormeño does once in a while, do not believe it.

If you're going to spend a day riding to **Cusco,** why not make a day of it? There are two excellent tourist buses that include a huge buffet lunch, English-speaking guide, and stops at most of the major ruins on the way. **Inka Express** (Tacna 255, near mercado, tel. 051/36-5654, inkaexpresspuno@terra.com.pe, $20) makes stops in Pukará and La Raya before having a buffet lunch in Sicuani. The bus then continues to see the extraordinary Inca ruins at Raqchi and the exquisite colonial church at Andahuaylillas. The buses generally leave Puno at 8 A.M. and arrive at 5 P.M., include hotel pick-up and drop-off, and even have oxygen tanks onboard for altitude problems. A similar service is offered by First Class (Lima 177, tel. 051/36-5192, or Sol 930 in Cusco, tel. 084/22-3102, firstclass@terra.com.pe, $20).

Direct, seven-hour options to Cusco include **Cruz del Sur** with an Imperial bus leaving daily at 8:30 P.M. ($9) and **Ormeño** with a similar bus at 2:30 P.M. ($8). Another recommended company is Imexo (tel. 051/36-9514), which has nice buses with TVs and bathrooms leaving at 8 A.M. ($6, with snack) or 8 P.M. ($4, without snack), and Tour Peru (Tacna 282, tel. 051/35-2991).

There are many options for the five-hour trip to **Arequipa.** Ormeño leaves at 8 A.M. ($6) or 8 P.M. ($5, no snack), and Cruz del Sur (tel. 051/36-8524) has an Imperial bus ($8) leaving at 2 P.M. Other buses stop briefly in Arequipa during the brutal, 20-hour push to **Lima**. Cruz del Sur has a Lima bus leaving at 7:30 A.M. ($25), and Ormeño has one at 3 P.M. and a direct bus at 8 P.M. ($14 for a semi-bed upstairs, $31 for luxury beds downstairs). Cruz del Sur also has a Imperial bus for the 9–10-hour drive to **Tacna,** through Moguegua, leaving at 9:30 P.M. ($11). Another option is San Martin (05/36-3631), which has a $6 bus at 7:30 A.M. and 7:30 P.M.

For **Bolivia** routes, see *Crossing into Bolivia.*

Boat

Two luxury boat companies offer interesting, though expensive, options for traveling between Puno and La Paz in a single day—though discounted fares sometimes become available 24 hours before departure. The trips include a bus to **Copacabana,** boat rides and tours of **Islas del Sol y de la Luna** and a final bus journey to **La Paz** (about 13 hours). It can also be done in the opposite direction for those who, for example, want to fly into La Paz and out of Cusco.

Crillon Tours (in Puno at Hotel Qelqatani, Tarapacá 355, or through any travel agent) takes passengers from Puno to Copacabana by bus, from Copacabana to Isla del Sol to Huatajata, Bolivia, by high-speed hydrofoil, and then on to La Paz ($189, a total of 13 hours). At Huatajata, Crillon also operates the five-star Inca Utama

Hotel & Spa and La Posada del Inca, a restored colonial hacienda on Isla del Sol. Crillon Tours offers a variety of all-inclusive tours, including ones that begin in La Paz, cross Lake Titicaca, and end in Cusco. Crillon has offices in the United States (1450 S. Bayshore Dr., Suite 815, Miami, Fla., 33131, 888/TITICACA, or 888/848-4222, daruis@titicaca.com) or in La Paz (Camacho 1223, 591/233-7533, titicaca@gaoba.entelnet.bo) and an informative Web page at www.titicaca.com.

Transturin has buses and slightly slower mini cruise ships, or catamarans, working the same basic route though docking at Chúa, Bolivia. This can either be a day tour or include a night aboard a catamaran docked at Isla del Sol. It has offices in Puno (Libertad 176, tel. 051/35-2771, leontours@terra.com.pe), Copacabana (6 de Agosto s/n, 08/62-2284), and La Paz (Mariscal Santa Cruz 1295, 3rd floor, 5tel. 912/31-0647, sales@turismo-bolivia.com); its Web page is www.turismo-bolivia.com. Trans-turin also offers day trips from Puno to La Paz, visiting Isla del Sol ($145), and a variety of all-inclusive package tours.

GETTING AROUND

The recommended taxi company is **Radio Taxi Seguro** (tel. 051/35-3134).

Inexpensive, safe boats leave from Puno's public dock, at the end of Av. Titicaca, for most surrounding islands. The dock facilities include police, clinic, bathrooms, and stalls that sell food, sweaters, hats, etc. Boats leave for a 2.5-hour tour of Uros between 7 A.M. and 4 P.M. ($3). There are *colectivo* boats that leave for the 3.5-hour trip to Taquile at 7:30 A.M. ($6) Those who want to overnight on Amantaní can take an 8:30 A.M. boat ($9) that visits Uros en route to Amantaní. To travel from Amantaní onto Taquile the next day, you need to arrange transport with a travel agency. A private boat for a one-day trip to Taquile and back costs around $70.

Lake Titicaca

Lake Titicaca seems more like an ocean than a lake. Bright-green algae blankets beach boulders and fills the air with a musty, seaside smell. Waves lap sand beaches. The intense blue waters, as deep as 270 meters, stretch endlessly in all directions. The only reminders, in fact, that Lake Titicaca is a lake are the impossibly thin air and a backdrop of snow-covered mountains—and the sight of islanders drinking the lake's clear waters out of their cupped hands.

The best way to experience Lake Titicaca is to leave behind the bustle of Puno and escape to the lake's placid shores and islands. Here you will find paths bordered by stone walls, a crystal-clear sky, and sweeping views of arid, sun-baked terraces. The land, shaded in places by groves of eucalyptus, plunges into waters below. On sunny days, the air is perfectly still and the sky blends with the water to form a single expanse of blue. The mood changes quickly, however, when squalls swoop in from the high plateaus, plunging temperatures and whipping the lake into a froth of gray waters.

By evening, when the lake is calm again, the sunset appears as a line of fire around a half moon, the curvature of the earth plainly visible.

It is no coincidence that the Incas decided first to conquer this lake, nor that they formed a creation myth around it. The Incas contend that the sun sent his son, Manco Cápac, and the moon sent her daughter, Mamo Ocllo, to emerge from the waters of Lake Titicaca and found the Inca empire. It is also no coincidence that the Spaniards decided to bequeath this lake and its people directly to the king, and not to a *conquistador* as was usually the case. For despite its altitude and barren appearance, Lake Titicaca has been a cradle of civilization and a center of wealth. The dense populations of Quechua- and Aymara-speaking people around this lake have a unique place in Peruvian culture because their ways of life go back at least 3,000 years.

By 600 B.C., the Chiripa and Pukara populations were already building temples around the lake, which offered a perfect combination of

Lake Titicaca

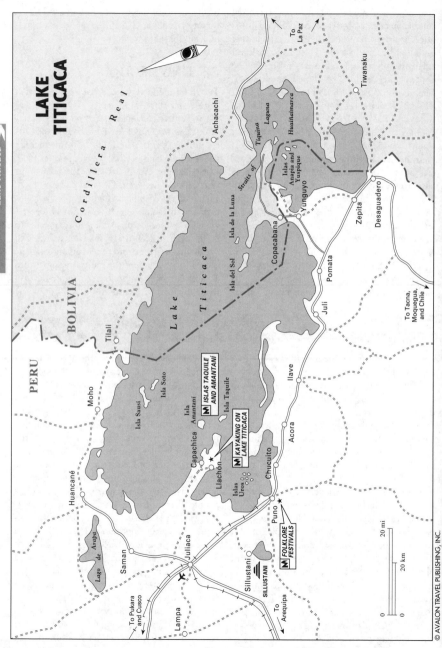

LAKE TITICACA

Cordillera Real

PERU

BOLIVIA

To La Paz

Tiwanaku

Achacachi

Straits of Tiquina

Laguna

Islas Anapia and Yuspique

Huatatamarca

Tilali

Moho

Isla Soto

Isla Sausi

Lake   Titicaca

Isla del Sol

Isla de la Luna

Copacabana

Yunguyo

Zepita

Desaguadero

Pomata

Juli

To Tacna, Moquegua, and Chile

Huancané

Isla Capachica

Isla Amantani

Isla Taquile

ISLAS TAQUILE AND AMANTANÍ

KAYAKING ON LAKE TITICACA

Llachón

Islas Uros

Chucuito

Ilave

Acora

Lago de Arapa

Saman

Juliaca

Sillustani

SILLUSTANI

Puno

FOLKLORE FESTIVALS

To Pukara and Cusco

Lampa

To Arequipa

20 mi

20 km

© AVALON TRAVEL PUBLISHING, INC.

grasslands for llama and alpaca, an ample supply of fish, and good growing conditions for potatoes and quinoa. By 200 A.D. the carved, gold-covered stone blocks were being raised on the shores of Lake Titicaca to build Tiwanaku, a city in present-day Bolivia that lasted a thousand years. The Tiwanaku empire, along with the Ayacucho-based Wari, would later spread its deities and urban ways of life across Peru, laying the foundation for the Inca empire. The Tiwanaku empire collapsed around 1000 A.D., perhaps because of a drought, and the Lupaca and Colla emerged to build the tombs at Sillustani and other monuments. These proud cultures would become famous for their bloody rebellions against both the Incas and the Spanish.

ISLAS UROS

A bizarre sight, which visitors tend to find either depressing or highly interesting, are the floating Islas Uros, about a 20-minute boat ride from Puno. The Uros, an ancient lake civilization who were harassed by the Spanish to near-extinction, probably fled to these islands to escape forced labor in Spanish silver mines, though they may have come here earlier to isolate themselves from the Collas or Incas. Their way of life revolves around the *tótora*, or reed, which they cut and pile to form giant floating islands that are anchored to the shallow lake bottom.

The true Uros people, whom legends say were protected from cold by their thick, black blood, have long since intermingled with the Aymara, whose language they now speak. Nevertheless, the islanders preserve a way of life that is probably based on Uros traditions. They live in family units governed by a grandfather, and they prearrange marriages—sometimes right after the births of the future bride and groom. They fish, hunt birds, and move about the lake in huge tótora rafts that look almost like Viking ships with their huge dragonheads.

Many visitors find it disconcerting to walk upon the springy, waterlogged reeds, which have to be continually replenished as the bottom layers rot, creating the fermented odor that is peculiar to the islands. But the scenery is spectacular and the

islands are unique—the largest even has a clinic, school, and Seventh Day Adventist church on it!

Tourism to the islands, which began in the late 1960s, has helped pull the Uros out of grinding poverty and maintain their population of several hundred. But it has also brought problems. Thousands of tourists each year arrive here with camcorders, creating a generation of begging children and adults who aggressively push miniature reed boats and other trinkets. Do not give money to begging children—give them fruit or buy something from them instead. The islanders also offer $1 boat rides in their reed boats to neighboring islands. Most Puno agencies offer guided tours for the Uros islands, and cheap public boats to the islands leave frequently from the Puno public pier.

ISLAS TAQUILE AND AMANTANÍ

Staying for a night or two with a family on Isla Taquile, about a 35 km boat ride from Puno, has become a signature Lake Titicaca experience. Visitors are picked up at the dock by a family member and led home to clean but rustic accommodations: a simple adobe room next to the family house, lumpy mattress, and an outhouse with no running water. With luck, visitors are invited to help herd the sheep or work on the far western side of the island, which is steeper and terraced entirely with potatoes and quinoa; or perhaps they learn how to weave with backstrap looms. Everyone speaks Quechua, some speak Spanish, and almost no one speaks English. Because Taquile is just 6 km long and 1 km wide, it is possible to walk around the island in two hours on walled paths carved into the hillside that bob up and down along its contours. There are a few beaches, which can be nice on sunny days and conducive to a plunge in the lake's icy waters. There are pre-Inca ruins, though not very elaborate, on the tops of the hills, and an elegant stone arch at the high pass separating the two sides of the island.

During the time we spent on Taquile, our host family on the island taught us how to weave blankets and farm potatoes at high altitude. We joined

men knitting on Taquile's main square

them for family meals, with guinea pig as the main course. We also walked on dirt lanes through hillsides covered with eucalyptus groves and sun-baked terraces, and watched an afternoon squall whip the lake into a froth of gray. By evening, the lake was glassy calm and stained red by the setting sun. Sitting on the stone steps, with a bottle of wine, watching the sunset, we were convinced there was nowhere else we would rather be.

Tourism has become an increasingly important source of income for Taquile over the last decade, and the island elders, or *varayocs,* have struggled to find a system to spread the new wealth evenly throughout the island or, as they say, assure that *todos comemos el mismo pan* ("all of us eat the same bread"). Their solution, based on the communal *ayllu* system, is run by the *varayocs* who meet boats at the docks and rotate visitors to nearly a hundred families. This equitable system has faltered somewhat in recent years because tourist agencies are allowed to do direct deals

with certain families, which end up getting a disproportionate share of guests. These family homes, usually clustered around Taquile's main square, have as many as four guest homes, which seems to water down the homestay experience. As of 2004, the island has its first lodge, TikaWasi (House of Flowers, in Quechua), which has been built by former *varayoc* Alejandro Flores. It clearly raises the bar of quality with wood floors, reed ceilings, comfortable foam beds, clean white-washed walls, and a spectacular terrace with lake views. Because of its privileged access to one of the island's only springs, it is also the only home on the entire island with running water and solar-heated showers. Though comfortable, TikaWasi represents a critical challenge to Taquile's communal way of life.

If you go on a prepaid tour to Isla Taquile, go with a socially responsible agency and ask a few questions beforehand. Ensure, for instance, that the agency pays the islanders the going rate—

THE FABULOUS FASHIONS OF TAQUILE

Partly because of tourism, and partly because of tradition, the islanders on Taquile wear their beautiful traditional clothing all the time, something the men on nearby Amantaní have stopped doing. Women wear a white or red blouse, or *bayeta,* made of sheep wool, a black shawl or *chuco* over their head, a red waist wrap called a *chumpi,* and a dark-colored *pollera,* or skirt, that bulges from the waist. Contrary to appearances, they do not have big hips. In an imitation of the petticoats worn by Spanish women in colonial times, Taquile women wear three to five *polleras* at a time—and during festivals, as many as 20. Apart from defying the slim ideal of western fashion, these bulky skirts also invert traditional gender roles, because they are woven by the men.

The women, however, do make the white *chumpis,* or waist bands, worn by their husbands. The men also wear a white shirt with wide sleeves and black pants and vest. But the most distinctive feature of men's dress on Taquile is the *chuyo,* or hat, which boys must learn to knit at an early age. The hats vary depending on a man's marital status and public authority. Single men were a *chuyo de soltero,* the "bachelor's hat," with red on the bottom and white on the top. Married men, on the other hand, wear a solid-red hat with a repeated geometric design of a man and a woman holding hands. They are also allowed to wear a *chuspa,* or coca bag, at their waist. But the most interesting hats are worn by the town elders (*varayocs*): rainbow-colored with ear flaps!

$5 pp per night of lodging, $2 for breakfasts and $3 for lunch and dinners. Ensure also that no more than two people will stay with each family and preferably away from the touristy area away near the town square. Otherwise, arrange your own homestay by simply hopping aboard the $6 boat that leaves from Puno's public pier every morning between 7:30 and 8 A.M.—you will be assigned a family upon arrival, and will need to pay a $1 arrival fee. There are a dozen rustic restaurants on the island, clustered around the high pass and the main square, which all serve the same basic fare: quinoa soup, steamed or fried *pejerrey,* and egg omelette, or *tortilla,* mixed with potatoes and vegetables. The families also serve meals, though quality and hygiene varies. There is a small but interesting museum on the main square, along with a few stores that sell the island's *chullos,* or hats, and expensive cookies and soft drinks. Travelers are advised to bring their own snacks and beverages—even a small bottle of beer can coast $2 on Taquile. It is also a good idea to bring a sleeping bag to stay warm, a water bottle, soap, and toilet paper.

Though less picturesque, nearby Isla Amantaní is an increasingly popular option for tourists (it is also cheaper, at about $5 per day for room and three meals) looking for a cultural exchange. The people receive far fewer tourists, and the island, which lacks restaurants and stores, has a more peaceful feel.

ISLAS ANAPIA AND YUSPIQUE

All Ways Travel, managed by a father-and-daughter team in Puno, runs a socially responsible homestay program on Islas Anapia and Yuspique, in southern Lake Titicaca. What is interesting about the project is that it could change the reputation Puno's agencies have for low-quality, shoestring tours. By elevating the quality, and the prices, All Ways Travel is introducing a new brand of sustainable tourism that gives back to, and helps preserve, the communities they work with. As a mark of its success, All Ways Traval recently won an award from the Ford Foundation for the *Best Community-Based Project in Peru.*

The trip to these islands begins with a two-hour drive along the Lake Titicaca's south shores, visiting the towns of Juli and Pomata, before passing through Yunguyo to the port of Punta Hermosa. Visitors than hop aboard a sailboat for a two-hour ride to Anapia's beach, where the father of each family leads each visitor to their new home. That afternoon families and guests go hiking on nearby Isla Yuspique, which has a large herd of vicuña, and have a beach picnic to try

Lake Titicaca

© RENÉE DEL GAUDIO AND ROSS WEHNER

learning to weave on Amantaní Island

huatia, which are potatoes cooked in a natural oven with pieces of hot soil.

The trips are not staged or overly planned, which seems like a good thing, so the activities vary: there is usually an evening meeting of neighbors, with conversation and music, or a chance to herd animals, fish, or help build a house. Depending on the time of the year, visitors also help plant or harvest crops. Since the project began in 1997, All Ways participants have helped build a library and a puppet theater and paint the local school. For a group of four, costs are $65 pp for one night and $75 pp for two nights (the latter is recommended). This trip also works well for travelers either coming from, or continuing on to, Bolivia and can be combined with a visit to Tiwanaku or the Islas del Sol y de la Luna. For budget travelers, Eliana at All Ways is also glad to explain how to do this trip independently, for about $43 for two days, using public transportation and boats, which only run on Thursdays and Sundays.

ISLA SUASI

The lake's most elegant lodge is the three-star **Albergue Suasi** (tel. 051/962-2709, www.isla-suasi.com, call for latest prices), with environmentally conscious features. This charming stone and eucalyptus house is set amid gardens and terraces on the lovely Isla Suasi, about 80 km by boat from Puno. There are only 12 rooms, the whole place is solar-powered, the kitchen produces a fabulous range of all-organic food, and the owners of the lodge have converted the entire 43-hectare island into an environmental preserve. A trout farm provides fresh fish to the lodge as well as the chance to fish for your own dinner. Native flowers, herbs, trees, and plants in danger of extinction are being cultivated in the greenhouse. With its rapid boat, All Ways Travel can get passengers here in about two hours.

LLACHÓN

Villagers in Llachón, a charming village on a peninsula near Puno and Juliaca, may not wear traditional clothing anymore, but staying with families is every bit as interesting, and less touristy, than visiting Isla Taquile. Valentín Quispe, who lives outside of town near a cemetery, runs a rustic lodge with fabulous views over the lakes for $10 pp, room and board. The little cabins, with whitewashed walls and thatched roofs, are at the top of a hill and seem like stone huts in the sky. Nearby, an adobe arch supports nothing and leads nowhere—but it beautifully frames a piece of the lake itself. At night a billion stars come out, including the Southern Cross, pointing the way to Isla Amantaní.

LAKE TITICACA: FOLKLORE CAPITAL OF PERU

Lake Titicaca has the richest and most vibrant dances and celebrations in all of Peru. One of the best is the **Fiesta de la Virgen de la Candelaria** on Feb. 2. But there are 299 other possibilities. Whenever your trip is scheduled, you should be able to find some ongoing festivities. The i Peru office in Puno has a full list of festivals, or check online at www.titicacaalmundo.com.

The principal parties are:

- January, third Thursday, **Pacha Mama ceremony** on Isla Amantaní
- Feb. 2–19, **Virgen de Candelaria** in Puno
- February, second Thursday, *Ispalla dance* to Pacha Mama at hilltop pre-Inca temple in Llachón
- All February, **Carnaval** in Puno and surroundings
- May 2–3, **Alasitas,** a festival featuring good luck charms to be hung on the Aymara Ekeko doll, in Puno
- May 3–8, **Fiesta de la Cruz y de San Martin de Porras** in Ilave
- May, first week, **Fiesta de San Bartolomé** in Chucuito
- May 5–17, **Pentecostal celebration of San Isidro Labrador** on Isla Taquile
- May, fourth week: **roundup (*chacu*) of vicuña** on Isla Umayo, near Sillustani. Visitors are invited to join.
- June 10–14, **Founders' Day** celebration in Llachón with dances and bullfights
- June 23–25, **Festival de San Juan** in Puno
- July 2, **Founders' Day** celebration in Capachica, en route to Llachón
- July 25 onwards, **Fiesta de Santiago Apóstol** on Isla Taquile, Chucuito, and Lampa
- Aug. 1–3, **Fiesta de la Octava de Santiago,** in Isla Taquile
- Aug. 6, **Fiesta *Niño de Praga*** in Capachica, en route to Llachón
- Aug. 10–17, **Fiesta de San Simon** on Isla Amantaní
- Aug. 15, **Festividad de la Virgen de Cancharani** in Puno
- Aug. 15–18, **Festivdad de la Virgen de Asunción** in Chucuito
- Sept. 15, **Fiesta de la Virgen de la Natividad** in Acora
- Sept. 24, **Festividad de Nuestra Señora de las Mercedes** in Juliaca
- Sept. 29, **Fiesta de San Migel Arcangel** in Ilave
- Oct. 2, **Fiesta de Nuestra Señora del Rosario** in Acora
- Oct. 12–19, **Fiesta de Nuestra Señora del Rosario** in Chucuito
- October, third week: **national road rally** around Lake Titicaca, with dances in Puno
- Nov. 1–7, **Puno week,** including the arrival by raft of the legendary founders of the Inca empire, Mamo Ocllo and Manco Cápac, on Nov. 5
- Nov. 1–2, **Fiesta de Todos los Santos** throughout area
- Dec. 5, **Fiesta de Santa Bárbara** in Chucuito, Ilave, and Puno
- Dec. 6–8, **Fiesta de la Inmaculada Concepción** in Puno, Lampa, and other villages

Lake Titicaca

Valentín also arranges homestays with other Llachón families, and his lodge serves as the point of departure for Titikayak's sea-kayak trips to the islands. The kayaks can also be rented from Valentín for the day for a reasonable price and there are the ruins of a pre-Inca temple at the top of a nearby hill.

Llachón can be reached by private boat from Puno in the Mercado Bellavista or by bus from Juliaca's Talara Street. Buses leave here every half hour for the village of Capachica (1.5 hours, $1.50), from which the half-hour taxi ride to Llachón should be $7–8. There is a nice beach at Llachón with free camping and a French-owned campground at one end that can rent tents or provide meals. Fishermen are glad to take travelers to nearby Islas Taquile and Amantaní, only 11 km away from here, by sailboat for $6 or private motorboat for $36.

SOUTH SHORES OF LAKE TITICACA

Travelers make a mistake when they breeze between Puno and the Bolivian border without stopping. The road passes through a string of quaint towns, with interesting colonial churches and a seemingly continuous schedule of festivities.

The south shores of Lake Titicaca are the center of Peru's Aymara population, a distinct language and cultural group. They have a historical reputation for repelling domination, whether it be the Incas 500 years ago or the Shining Path in the 1980s and 1990s. In 2004, several towns in this area rose in protests against allegedly corrupt leaders. In the worst instance, the major of the town of Ilave was dragged from a house and lynched by a mob of Aymara Indians. Before visiting these towns, inquire in Puno beforehand about the present situation.

Fertility Temple of Chucuito

Located 18 km south of Puno, Chucuito is one of the oldest towns in the area and is surrounded by farming fields that slope gently down to Lake Titicaca. The town was at one time a capital of the whole province and has colonial churches on its two main squares. **Nuestra Señora de la Asunción** has a Renaissance facade from 1601 and sits near the upper Plaza de Armas. The second church, **Santo Domingo**, is L-shaped with beautifully painted stone arches, a carved wooden altar carved in *pan de oro,* and a single ancient stone tower.

Chucuito's lead attraction, however, is **Inca Uyo** (7 A.M.–dark, free), a walled enclosure next to Santo Domingo that looks, at first glance, like a garden of giant mushrooms. But upon closer inspection, the mushrooms are carved stone penises, some pointing up at the sky (presumable toward Inti, the Inca sun god) and others rammed into the ground (toward Pachamama, Mother Earth goddess). At the center of this obvious fertility temple is the largest phallus of all, placed atop a platform carved with the outlines of a human figure. Village children, who work as the temple's very charming and dead-serious guides, claim that women still sneak into the temple at night, with coca leaves and *chicha,* to perform a ceremony designed to help them get pregnant. The essence of the ceremony, they contend, is that the women sit atop the head of the giant phallus for several hours. The origin of this temple is hotly debated; some say it was built by the Aymaras or the Incas. Others contend that cannot be possible, because the priests, who built the church next door, had a fondness for destroying idols that surely would have included phallus-shaped rocks. Whatever you believe, the site is still interesting.

The best place to stay in town is **Albergue Las Cabañas** (near Plaza de Armas at Tarapaca 538; or Bolognesi 334, in Puno; tel. 051/35-1276, lodgecabanas@ghucuito.com, www.chucuito.com, $22 s, $34 d, includes breakfast). Inside high adobe walls is a charming garden of yellow *retama* and *queñua* flowers surrounding charming bungalows with wood floors, hearths, exposed beams, and new bathrooms. The owner, Juan Palao Berastain, has authored the highly informative pamphlet to the area, *Titikaka Lake: Children of the Sacred Lake,* on sale at the hotel. Members of Hostelling International are charged $7 pp, lodging only. The three-star **Chucuito Resort Hotel** (tel. 051/35-2108) on the highway in front of town has nice views of the lake but seems overpriced. On the lower square, **Tío Juan** (10 A.M.–4 P.M., Mon.–Sat., $2) is a local's hole-in-the-wall that serves up trout, roasted pork, and *chairo*.

Juli

The road from Chucuito to Juli, 84 km. from Puno, heads off from the meandering shores of Lake Titicaca through the town of Platería, a village once known for its silver work, to Acora, and finally to Ilave, a crossroads town that has more commerce than colonial architecture. The road returns to the lake at Juli, which was once a stopping point for silver caravans between the coast and the Potosí mine in present-day Bolivia. This was also an important center for the Jesuits and Dominicans, who trained missionaries here to work with the native Guaraní in Paraguay. The town's principal attractions today are four churches from the 16th and 17th centuries: **San Pedro Mártir** is on the plaza and has an interesting Renaissance facade, Baroque altar, and paintings by Italian master Bernardo Bitti. Beautiful windows made of a translucent stone called *Piedra de Huamanga* can be found at **San Juan Bautista,** down the street, along with a carved altar, 80 paintings from the Cusco School, and beautiful carved sacristy door. **Santa Cruz de Jerusalén** has magnificent doors and excellent views of Lake Titicaca. **Nuestra Señora de la Asunción** offers an eerie glimpse at a church in ruins with a fine remaining door, tower, and arch outside in the atrium. There is a colorful fair in Juli every Thursday.

Pomata

The road continues to Pomata, 104 km from Puno and the crossroads for the roads to Desaguadero and Copacabana. The town's 18th-century church, **Santiago Apóstol de Nuestra Señora del Rosario,** is built of pink granite with a huge gold-covered altar and paintings from the Cusco School. Toward Desaguadero there is another fine colonial church, **San Pedro,** in the town of Zepita.

CROSSING INTO BOLIVIA

From Puno, there are a few ways to make the **border crossing to Bolivia.** The first, and most

popular, is to go from Puno to Yunguyo to Copacabana to La Paz, Bolivia, a route that leads through a series of interesting villages on the lake's south shore before a scenic ferry ride across the **Straits of Tiquina.** From Copacabana, it is easy to visit the **Isla del Sol** (Island of the Sun), a 20-km boat ride from Copacabana. This island, covered in Inca ruins and graced by a sacred stone, was revered by the Incas as the place from where Manco Capác emerged to found the empire. Nearby is the smaller, but interesting **Isla del la Luna** (Island of the Moon), birthplace of Mama Ocllo. **Panamericano** (Tacna 245, tel. 051/35-4001, tourpanamericano@hotmail.com) leaves Puno daily for this seven-hour route at 7:30 A.M. **Tour Peru** (Tacna, tel. 051/35-2191, tourperu@mixmail.com) also has good buses going to Copacabana daily. Or explore the towns along the way by hopping on and off a local bus from Puno to Yunguyo (2.5 hours, $2). These *colectivo* buses leave from the local bus station, two blocks from the main Terminal Terrestre (1 de Mayo 703, intersection with Bolivar) From Yunguyo, take a *colectivo* from the border to Copacabana (30 minutes, $0.50). There are several buses daily from Copacabana to La Paz (five hours, $2.50).

A more direct, but less scenic, five-hour route to La Paz goes through **Desaguadero,** an ugly duckling of a town that straddles the border. Buses along this route pass **Tiwanaku,** the capital city of an empire whose deities and monumental architecture spread throughout Peru nearly a millennium before the Incas. Though ravaged by grave robbers and modern-day reconstructions, the ruins here were once so impressive that even the Incas thought them constructed by giants. What stands out today is the **Kalasasaya temple**, a rectangular temple surrounded by pillars, monolithic figures, and the renowned Gateway of the Sun, chipped from a single piece of andesite and adorned with a carved deity. Ormeño (tel. 051/36-8176) leaves from Puno at 5:45 A.M. ($15), and Panamericana (tel. 051/35-4001) leaves at 8 A.M. Cheaper, slower buses run from Puno to Desaguadero (2.5 hours, $2) frequently, and the last bus from Desaguadero to La Paz (4 hours, $3) is at 5 P.M. Bolivia time (4 P.M. Peru time). This border is open from 8 A.M. to noon, and 2 P.M. to 7:30 P.M.

Crossing is usually a 20-minute, hassle-free process at either place—as long as you have your passport and a valid tourist visa, and the border is open (Bolivia's border shut down for several weeks because of political unrest in 2001 and 2003). Peru gives tourists a 90-day tourist visa, while Bolivia only gives 30 days—always ask for more before having your passport stamped. Border officials occasionally try to charge unsuspecting travelers an *embarcation tax,* which is illegal. North Americans, Britons, New Zealanders, and Australians do not need visas to enter Bolivia at this time, while French travelers do. There is a Bo-

livian consulate in Yunguyo (8:30 A.M.–3 P.M.), although it is best to check updated requirements before you travel.

A longer way to Bolivia leads along the seldom-visited north shore of Lake Titicaca, a string of interesting towns that include Huancané and Moho. As there is no immigrations post at the border of Tilali, travelers must get their exit stamp a day before they depart in Puno at Peruvian Immigrations (Ayacucho 270, tel. 051/35-7103, 8 A.M.–2). For this route travelers must hopscotch on frequent local buses from Juliaca onwards. If you catch a 7 A.M. bus from Juliaca, it is possible to arrive by 3 P.M. that afternoon.

Between Puno and Cusco

SILLUSTANI

The most interesting ruins on the Peruvian end of Lake Titicaca are surely Sillustani (6 A.M.–dark, $3), which are halfway between Puno and Juliaca at the end of a 14-km detour off the highway. The site consists of more than a dozen stone tombs, or *chulpas,* up on a bluff over Lago Umayo. They were mostly built by the Colla, a highland people conquered by the Incas in the 15th century and for whom this quarter of the Inca empire (Collasuyo) was named. The Colla were fine stone craftsmen and built gravity-defying towers that widen as they go up, similar to the Tintero tower at the Chachapoyan citadel of Kuélap, which is also shaped like an upside-down inkwell. Whether they built the towers this way to show off their masonry virtuosity, or to stymie grave robbers, the Incas continued the tradition—in a typical display of superiority—and one-upped the Colla. But even the perfectly fitted granite stones of the Incas have over time spilled onto the surrounding ground, exposing the tower's adobe-filled interior that was long ago ransacked by looters

The drive in passes the stone homes of llama herders, which are decorated with arches and decorated stone bands—another odd link to Chachapoyan architecture. Near the *chulpas,*

don't miss the *waru waru,* an ingenious farming technology that was developed around Lake Titicaca during the Tiwanaku empire. These raised earth platforms are surrounded by a thin pool of water that absorbs the sun's energy during the day and re-radiates it at night, protecting the potatoes and other crops from frost. To arrive, take any bus heading north from Juliaca (many leave from Simón Bolivar) and asked to be dropped off at the Sillustani turnoff (20 km, $0.30). Taxis wait at the turnoff and charge $0.50 to take travelers the remaining 14 km to the ruins.

JULIACA

Juliaca, 45 km north of Puno and the teeming hub of Peru's southern highlands, is a unfortunate collection of ramshackle buildings. Travelers pass through here mainly because of the airport—the closest to Lake Titicaca—and the rail and highway connections to Puno, Arequipa, and Cusco. It is also the launching pad for the quaint towns of Llachón and Lampa and the backroads route into Bolivia along the north shores of Lake Titicaca. The slogan of this working man's paradise is *Mientra Puno danza, Juliaca avanza* ("while Puno dances, Juliaca advances").

The best hotels, restaurants, and services—as

well as the train station—are near Plaza Bolognesi, which is graced by a colonial church, **Iglesia La Merced.** The Plaza de Armas, a few blocks to the northwest, has another colonial church, **Iglesia Santa Catalina.** There is a large **Sunday market** in the Plaza Melgar, several blocks from the center, where you can buy cheap alpaca wool sweaters. A more tourist-oriented daily market is held in the plaza outside the railway station. Beware of pickpockets in this area.

Accommodations

Hostal Luquini (Braceso 409 on Plaza Bolognesi, tel. 051/32-1510, $5 s, $8 d, shared bathroom) formerly Hostal Peru, is the best budget place to stay in Juliaca. The rooms are quiet, arranged around an open communal space, and are fairly clean with good beds. You can get a cable-less TV if you are lucky, and there are some more expensive rooms ($8 s, $13 d) with private bathrooms. **La Maison Hotel** (7 de Junio 535, tel. 051/32-1763, maisonhotel@hotmail.com, $17 s, $27 d, includes breakfast) is a quiet, friendly place with 30 comfortable rooms. Though the orange walls and red plastic furniture are a bit much, the rooms are comfortable with good beds, skylights, cable TV, and spotless bathrooms. At the **Royal Inn** (San Ramón 158, tel. 051/32-1561, hotel_royal_inn@latinmail.com, $23 s, $31 d, includes breakfast), ask for the interior rooms, which are quieter and face a small courtyard. Rooms are decked out with cable TV, refrigerators, and heaters, and some even have Jacuzzis for $3 extra.

Food

Good restaurants are few and far between in Juliaca and most are in the city's best hotels. **La Fonda del Royal Inn** (inside Hotel Royal Inn, San Ramón 158, tel. 051/32-1561, 6:30 A.M.–10 P.M., $3–4) has an excellent selection of entrées that range from ceviche (made from both local *pejerrey* and coastal sea bass), pepper steak, gnocchi with alfredo sauce, and *lomo al vino* (steak in wine sauce). The restaurant itself is a welcome respite from the street, and the waiters hustle. Across the street, **Trujillo Restaurant** (San Ramón 163, tel. 051/32-1945, $4–8) has an endless menu of Andean and Creole food along with a full drink list that includes daiquiris. **Confitería Meli Melo** (Braceso 403) has good-looking pies and cakes.

Information and Services

Most services are within a block or two of the Plaza Bolognesi. The **Tourism Office** (Junín 638, tel. 051/32-1839, 7:30 A.M.–5:30 P.M. Mon.–Fri.), however, is not very conveniently located. The **police station** is at Ramón Castilla 722 (tel. 051/32-1591, 24 hours), and the best health care is at **Clínica Adventista** (Loreto 315, tel. 051/32-1001, emergency tel. 051/32-1071), run by the Seventh Day Adventists. For money matters, there is a **Banco de Crédito** on the plaza itself, and a **Banco Continental** on San Román and 2 de Mayo. The **post office** is on the corner of Salaverry and Sandía. For email, try **Internet Clic** (San Ramon 216, 7:30 A.M.–11:30 P.M. daily). For international calling, there is a **Telefónica office** on San Martín and Tumbes, but there are some closer private phone booths half a block from Plaza Bolognesi on Pasaje Santa Elisa.

Suri Tours Service (Jorge Chavez 133, tel. 051/32-1572, suritour@hotmail.com, www.suritour.com) offers a half-day trip to Lampa for $10 pp as well as a two-day trip in the high jungle around Sandia.

Getting There and Around

Buses for the 45-minute ride to **Puno** leave from a terminal in the Plaza Bolognesi ($0.50, 45 minutes) when full. A private taxi to Puno is about $15. A range of buses for **Cusco** ($3–7, six hours) and to **Arequipa** ($3–5, five hours) leave from a terminal on the 10th block of San Martín. Buses leave for **Lampa** daily from 2 de Mayo, near the Mercado Santa Bárbara ($0.70, one hour).

The best way to get to Cusco, however, is aboard the tourist buses that leave Puno each morning and pick up passengers in Juliaca around 9 A.M. For more information on these companies, **Inka Express** and **First Class**, see Puno's *Getting There* section.

Juliaca has the only airport for Lake Titicaca, **Aeropuerto Internacional Inca Manco Cápac** (Aviación s/n, Santa Adriana, tel. 051/32-8974). A taxi for the 10-minute drive between Juliaca and the aiport is $2; cheap buses and *colectivos* leave from the Plaza Bolognesi. Buses leave the airport regularly for the one-hour drive to Puno ($1.50). The office of LanPeru (San Ramon 125, 8:30 A.M.–7 P.M. Mon.–Sat., 9 A.M.–1 P.M. Saturday) is a block from the Plaza Bolognesi.

Passenger service on the rail line between Juliaca and Arequipa has been suspended as of 2003. PeruRail has revamped the Cusco-Puno train service that makes daily stops in Juliaca for either direction of travel— see Puno's *Getting There* section, above. The rail station is across from the Plaza Bolognesi.

Because the lake-bottom land is so flat, Juliaca is overflowing with bicycle taxis that charge $0.30 for anywhere in town.

LAMPA

Though a bit stranded, the charming village of Lampa was probably fortunate to have been bypassed by both the Cusco-Puno highway and the train line. Otherwise it would have become another Juliaca, a tangle of congestion and ramshackle buildings. Instead Lampa, at 3,910 meters, is a clean-swept, hushed town with two large squares, a huge church from the 17th century, and *casonas* splashed in hues of ochre, maroon, and salmon—hence the town's nickname, La Ciudad Rosada. This entire village, an oasis of red tiles amid the yellow grass of the high plains, feels like a colonial time warp.

Sights

Lampa's huge church in the shape of a Latin cross reflects the fact that Lampa had many more inhabitants—as much as 50 times its current population, some historians say—when a dozen silver mines operated in the area. Construction on the Iglesia Santiago Apóstol began in 1675, the same year Lampa was founded. Like the Republican bridge to the south of town, the church was built of *calicanto,* a combination of lime mortar *(cal)* with river stones *(canto rodado).* The church was immaculately restored in the 1950s by a mining engineer and the town's fa-

Lampa's colonial church is an exquisite work in local stone.

vorite son, Enrigue Torres Belón (1887–1969), who even went to the Vatican to get a rare copy of Michelangelo's *Pietà*.

What is interesting about this church are its huge colonial paintings, a pulpit every bit as elaborate as that of San Blas in Cusco, and extensive catacombs that are crisscrossed with mysterious Inca tunnels from an earlier temple. In a side area of the church, the **Torres Belón mausoleum** offers an interesting comment on mortality and is proof of the slogan "He who lives longest laughs last." While Torres Belón and his wife rest comfortably beneath thick slabs of marble, the skeletons of hundreds of priests, hacienda owners, and Spanish miners hang on the walls of the round chamber above. The bones were transferred here after Torres Belón ordered the catacombs filled with cement to shore up the church's foundations. In this way, the last remains of generations of colonial nobility became mere adornment for the tomb of a modern-day mining engineer.

There are half a dozen homes worth visiting, including the **Casona Chukiwanka** in the Plaza Grau, from which Simón Bolivar addressed the town during the independence wars. A few homes have patios paved with the white and black stones from Lake Titicaca's Isla Amantaní, which are laid out to form huge game boards. One house features a chessboard, while others have popular colonial gambling games, including *juego de la oca,* a sort of craps table with odd animal figures. The rules have long since been forgotten.

A highly recommended bike or drive from Lampa leads south on good dirt roads for 76 km before joining the road to Cusco at Ayavari. From Lampa, the attractions packed along this route include a forest of queña (*Polylepis incana*)—the tree known as *lampaya* in Aymara and the probable origin of Lampa's name. Next along this route come three rough tombs, or *chullpas,* from the Colla culture, the well-preserved remains of two colonial mines, a huge forest of *puya raimondi,* and bizarre geological formations at the **Tinajani Canyon.** Buses do not run this route, unfortunately. Another road leads 6 km west of town to *Cueva de los Toros,*

a cave with animal carvings and funerary towers similar to those at Sillustani.

Entertainment and Events

Lampa erupts into dance and colonial-style bullfights from July 29–31 during the **Fiesta de Santiago Apóstol.** There are also a series of masses and elaborate religious processions Dec. 6–8 centering around **La Virgen de la Immaculada,** which was brought to Lampa from Barcelona in the 17th century.

Accommodations

Hospedaje Milan (Juan José 513, $3 s, $5 d) has queen-size foam beds and plain, clean rooms with shared bathrooms. The owner is the hospitable, and extremely courteous, Edgardo Méndez. On the main square is a red colonial home (Plaza Grau, $10 s, $20 d) that has been well restored by owner Oscar Frisancho and converted into a charming two-star hostel. The rooms have high ceilings, brick floors, and loads of colonial charm.

Food

The best restaurant is **Las Delicias,** on the Plaza de Armas and operated by the charming Señora Delia. Lunch or dinner menu is $1. The other good restaurant in the plaza, **El Pollón,** serves spit-roasted chicken and other food and is also open for breakfast.

Information and Services

The best source for information is the affable Edgardo Méndez at **Hospedaje Milan,** which also offers laundry service. The **police station** is two blocks north of the plaza, along with a nearby **Banco de la Nación** that does not have an ATM. There is a **phone center** on the plaza, and the **IPSS** clinic is one block west of the plaza.

Getting There and Around

The only way to reach Lampa with public transport is from Juliaca, where *combis* leave when full from 2 de Mayo near the Mercado Santa Bárbara (one hour, $0.70). From Lampa, cars leave for Juliaca from the intersection of Juan José and Cuzco, four blocks south of square, when full starting at 5 A.M.

Lake Titicaca

PUCARÁ

This ceremonial center, 107 km north of Puno, was built by the Pucará, one of Titicaca's earliest cultures (300 B.C.–300 A.D.). Though a bit difficult to visualize, the ruins (daylight hours, free admission) offer a glimpse into the shadowy origins of Lake Titicaca's civilized life and show clear links to the Chavín culture, which was flourishing at the same time in Peru's central mountains. The first temple is U-shaped and was originally decorated with stelae, or carved stone slabs, showing a deity similar to the *degollador*, or decapitator deity, of the Chavín. The second, known as the Kalasaya Temple, is rectangular and has eight large niches along the main remaining wall. The stelae recovered from the site are interesting and are housed in a small INC museum near the plaza. Across the street is an exquisite colonial church, **Iglesia Piñon de Pucará,** which the museum caretaker can open upon request.

LA RAYA

At 4,321 meters, La Raya is the highest pass on the route, marks the divide between the Urubamba and Lake Titicaca watersheds, and is roughly the halfway point on the Puno-Cusco journey. Snow-capped mountains stretch out over a plateau that is barren except for one colonial chapel.

SICUANI

There are several nice lunch spots in Sicuani, 138 km south of Cusco. At the **Casa Hacienda Las Tunas** (J.C. Tello 100, tel. 084/35-2480, $4) Sofia Vásquez serves up a huge, scrumptious buffet of Peruvian food from 11:30 A.M. onwards, when the Inka Express bus pulls in. Her sister, Edith, has good trout and meat dishes at the **Cevichería Acuarios** (Garcilazo de la Vega 141, 2nd story, tel. 084/80-9531, $3) on the plaza.

The great hall at Raqchi, five stories high and as long as a football field, is the best preserved example of Inca adobe architecture.

RAQCHI

Raqchi (119 km south of Cusco, 8 A.M.–6 P.M., $3) is a ceremonial center built by **Inca Pachacútec** that offers a fascinating glimpse into the ambition and organization skills of his budding empire. Rising above the humble village of Raqchi, a wall of adobe nearly 15 meters high and 90 meters long sits on a carved Inca wall. This was once the center of a huge hall, the roof of which was supported by adobe columns—one of which has been restored—on either side. On the side are six identical squares, each with six stone buildings, which probably served as a soldiers' barracks. But the most impressive part of Raqchi are line after line of round stone houses-200 in all—that once were filled with a gargantuan amount of quinoa, freeze-dried potatoes, and corn.

URCOS

Driving through the main square of this small village, 47 km south of Cusco, it is hard not to notice Urcos' tidy colonial church with a public balcony on the second floor and stone steps in front. On the outskirts of town, there is the beautifully decorated chapel at Huaro, which is on a hilltop overlooking a small lake. According to legend, Inca Huáscar threw a huge gold necklace into these waters to protect the treasure from the Spaniards. The story seemed probable enough that *National Geographic* recently funded an exploration of the lake's bottom by scuba divers—though thick mud prevented them from finding anything.

ANDAHUAYLILLAS

The colonial village of Andahuaylillas, 37 km south of Cusco, has a charming plaza shaded with red-flowered *pisonay* trees and an adobe church, **San Pedro** (8:30 A.M.–noon and 2–5 P.M., Mon.–Sat., 1–10 A.M., 3–5 P.M., free), which is built on the foundations from the early Inca empire. Though it's unremarkable on the outside, the doors open to a dazzling painted ceiling, frescos, and wall-to-wall colonial paintings. This is the most finely decorated church in all of Cusco, probably in all of Peru, though calling it the *Sistine Chapel of the Americas,* as some do, is going a bit far. One highlight is a mural by Luis de Riaño depicting the road to heaven and the road to hell, with a full-blown display of all the respective rewards and punishments. There is a well-known natural healing center just off the square, **Centro de Medicina Integral** (Garcilaso 514, tel. 084/25-1999, 9 A.M.–7 P.M., medintegral@hotmail.com) with a charming stone courtyard with gardens and plain rooms for $8 pp. The center attracts a considerable number of overseas visitors for massages, meditation, harmonizing energy therapy, and other treatments.

RUMICOLCA AND PIKILLACTA

Though the Incas refused to admit it, much of their highway network and organizational know-how was based on the **Wari Empire,** which spread across Peru like a wildfire from 500 to 1000 A.D. An example of Wari engineering is **Rumicolca,** a huge aqueduct that sits on a valley pass on the side of the highway about 32 km from Cusco. The Incas altered the construction, added a few stones, and converted it into a giant gateway to Cusco, though the remains of the old water channels can still be seen.

Nearby is **Pikillacta** (6 A.M.–6 P.M., $2), the largest provincial outpost ever built by the Ayacucho-based Wari. This curious walled compound, with nearly 47 hectares (116 acres) of repetitive two-story square buildings, sprawls across the rolling grasslands with little regard to topography. The floors and walls, which are made of mud and stacked stone, were plastered with white gypsum and must have gleamed in the sun. But the Incas so thoroughly erased evidence of the Wari that little about their empire is known today. For many years Pikillacta was thought to be a huge granary, like the Inca site of Raqchi. But excavations have revealed evidence of a large population that left behind refuse layers as deep as three meters. Part of the city caught fire between 850 and 900 A.D., and the Wari withdrew from the city around the same time,

Lake Titicaca

The Incas converted the Wari aqueduct of Rumicolca into a gateway to Cusco.

information is available at the new museum at the entrance. In the valley below is Lago Sucre and, even further on, Lago Huacarpay. On the far shores of this lake are the ruins of **Inca Huáscar's summer palace**, much of which continues to be enjoyed today by locals as the Centro Recreacional Urpicanca, the local country club. From the shoulder of the highway, it is possible to see ceremonial staircases the Incas built into the landscape above the lake.

Tipón

One of the most elaborate and well-preserved examples of Inca agricultural terracing is **Tipón** (7 A.M.–5 P.M., $1.50), which lies 22 km south of Cusco and then another 4 km up a valley via a switchbacking gravel road. The terraces, finely fitted and impossibly tall, run in straight lines to the head of a narrow valley. They are irrigated by an elaborate aqueduct that still runs from Pachatusan, the sacred mountain that looms over the site, whose name in Quechua means "cross beam of the universe." There are remains of a two-story house on the site and other ruins, possibly a fort, near the top of the aqueduct.

bricking up the doors as they went. Whether they abandoned the city because of the fire, or burnt it as they left, is unclear. Some historical

Arequipa

Arequipa, the commercial hub of southern Peru, may well be the country's most elegant and romantic city. Like the other great coastal cities of Trujillo and Lima, Arequipa was founded shortly after the Spanish conquest and has a wealth of convents, churches, homes, and fine art to prove it. But Arequipa is more relaxed and genteel, and constructed entirely of white *sillar,* a white and porous volcanic stone that gleams under the bright desert sun. Arequipa has the most stunning Plaza de Armas in all of Peru, teeming with palm trees, framed by volcanoes, and graced by the huge neoclassical cathedral. Down the street, light shifts delicately across the arches, streets, and homes inside of the 400-year-old **Santa Catalina Monastery,** a city-within-a-city that could have been lifted right out of southern Spain.

Arequipa is for lovers, but it is also for adventurers. One of the three volcanoes that tower above the city, **Chachani,** is probably the most attainable 6,000-meter mountain. A bit further away lie some of the country's most extraordinary landscapes, including high-altitude deserts, a magical place called the **Valley of the Volcanoes,** and two of the world's deepest canyons—the **Cotahuasi** and the **Colca.** The better known of these, the Colca, is only four hours away and is an unforgettable experience. Though best known for its condors, what is most remarkable about Colca is a string of villages perched on both sides of the canyon rim. The canyon was only connected to the modern world in the late 1970s, and villagers adhere to their centuries-old ways of life. This is one of the most spectacular, and safe, places in Peru for trekking and mountain biking—rafting is also possible, especially lower down on the Río Majes.

Lake Titicaca

Arequipa's cathedral and Plaza de Armas

The Collagua people occupied the Arequipa area for millennia, as evidenced by the extensive terracing improved by the Incas. But the name for Arequipa apparently comes from Inca Mayta Cápac, who arrived at present-day Arequipa with his army and uttered the Quechua phrase *arique-pay,* meaning "yes, stay here." After conquering the area in the 15th century, the Incas began the practice of sacrificing children atop the area's highest volcanoes. **Juanita,** the mummy of a 13-year-old girl, captured worldwide attention in 1995 when she was discovered atop Volcano Ampato at 6,380 meters. Her mummy can now be seen in Arequipa's Museo Santuarios Andinos.

The city of Arequipa was founded on Aug. 15, 1540, by Captain Garcí Manuel de Carbajal after disease forced the Spaniards from an earlier settlement near Camaná, near the coast. Arequipa blossomed as a go-between for trade between Lima and all of south Peru, including Cusco, Puno, and the rich silver mine of Potosi in present-day Bolivia.

The city has repeatedly been pounded by a series of devastating earthquakes. More than 300 buildings collapsed after a devastating earthquake in 1588, which prompted King Carlos V to issue a royal order limiting building height. The city was covered with ash by erupting Huaynaputina a few decades later and leveled by earthquakes roughly once per century—in 1687, 1788, 1869, 1958, and 1960. The latest earthquake, in 2001, measured 8.1 on the Richter scale and knocked down one of the towers of the cathedral, which has since been repaired.

SIGHTS

Plaza de Armas

Most city tours begin at the lookout and church in Yanahuara, the neighborhood on the other side of the Río Chili. We recommend, however, starting at Arequipa's elegant **Plaza de Armas.** The horizontal, white facade of the neoclassical cathedral stretches almost as long as a football field,

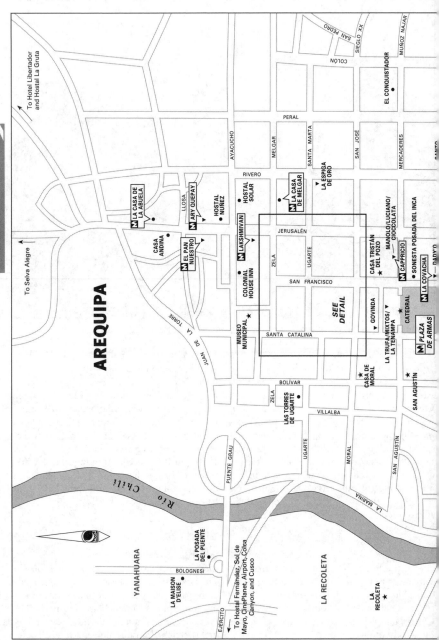

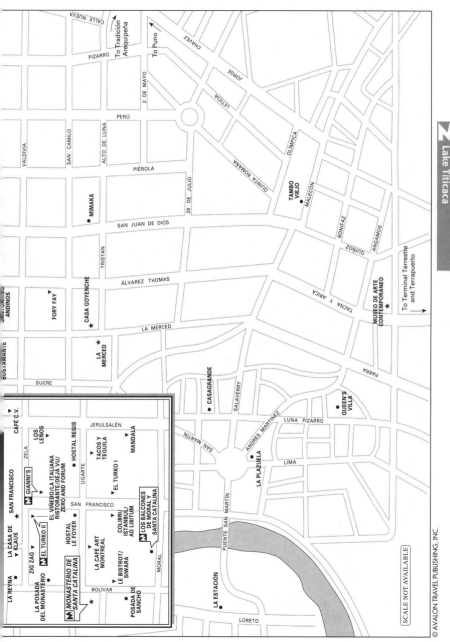

Lake Titicaca

To Terminal Terrestre
and Terrapuerto

SCALE NOT AVAILABLE

© AVALON TRAVEL PUBLISHING, INC.

with a pair of pointed bell towers, ornate square windows, and huge columns. *Portales,* or arcades, take up the other three sides of the square, which overflows with palm trees, flowers, and fountains. **La Catedral** (tel. 054/23-2635, 7–11:30 A.M. and 4:30–7:30 P.M. Mon.–Sat., 6:30 A.M.–1:30 P.M. and 4:30–7:30 P.M. Sun., free, guides work for a tip) is framed on both sides by volcanoes—Misti to the right, Chachani to the left—and is most beautiful in the afternoon when its front is stained orange by the setting sun. It was begun in 1544, partially destroyed in the 17th century by earthquakes and then completely burnt in an 1844 fire. Then it was built in its present neoclassical style and outfitted with one of the largest organs in South American (imported from Belgium) and a carved wooden pulpit that is supported by a swimming, serpent-tailed devil.

On an opposite corner of the plaza is the **La Compañia** (Thomas Álvarez and General Moral, tel. 054/21-2141, 9 A.M.–12:30 P.M. and 3–6 P.M. Mon.–Fri., 11:30 A.M.–12:30 P.M. and 3–6 P.M. Sat., 9 A.M.–12:30 P.M. and 5–6 P.M. Sun., $2 for chapel), which was founded by the Jesuits in 1573, though the present building dates from 1650. The large church, with threes naves and a

cupola, is best known for its mestizo facade and its Chapel of San Ignacio de Loyola, decorated with works from the Mannerist master Bernardo Bitti (1550–1610). The nearby sacristy contains vivid murals of jungle plants and animals, a sort of visual introduction for missionaries being prepared for the Amazon. The Jesuits' minor cloisters—now a crafts market—lie a few doors down General Moran Street. There are gargoyles depicting figures from pre-Inca cultures and, in the adjacent major cloisters, elaborately carved columns with *mudéjar* designs.

 Monasterio de Santa Catalina

The architectural highlight of Arequipa is without a doubt the 425-year-old **Monasterio de Santa Catalina** (Santa Catalina 301, tel. 054/22-9798, 9 A.M.–4 P.M. daily, $7.50, guides work for a tip). The convent is a small city built entirely of *sillar* with a hundred houses, 60 streets, three cloisters, main square, church, cemetery, and painting gallery. As many as 175 nuns lived here during the 17th and 18th centuries, including the daughters of wealthy families who lived in private houses with up to four servants. More than 400 colonial paintings, mostly from the Cusco School, hang in a gallery that was once a homeless shelter for widows, single mothers, and homeless women. Today, there are 29 nuns (oldest 96, youngest 21) living in modern quarters in the convent who subsist on tourist entry fees. The nuns were shut off from the rest of the city until 1985, when they became *half-cloistered*—meaning they can now leave and shop for food or visit relatives (up until that year, they only spoke with families through screened windows). Photographers should visit late in the afternoon, when the light falls across the buildings at interesting angles.

Other Churches

Farther up Santa Catalina lies the Church of **San Francisco** (Zela 103, tel. 054/22-3048, 7–9 A.M. and 4–8 P.M. Mon.–Sat., 10 A.M.–noon Sun.), a 16th-century Franciscan church with a Latin cross shape and an unusual brick entranceway. The next-door convent, also designed in 1569 by Gaspar Báez, is worth visiting if it's open, as is the adjacent **Chapel of the Third**

© RENÉE DEL GAUDIO AND ROSS WEHNER

carved sillar arcade at La Compañia in Arequipa

THE ICE MAIDEN OF AMPATO

Juanita was only 12 or 13 years old when she walked up a wooden staircase and onto the snowy summit of Ampato (6,380 m), accompanied by Inca priests intent on making a sacrifice to the *apu,* or mountain spirit, of Ampato. She wore a feathered headdress and an elaborately woven shawl and skirt, decorated with pieces of gold jewelry. An Inca priest gave her a narcotic potion, which probably put her to sleep after days of fasting—and then killed her with a single, precise blow to her forehead. Juanita was wrapped in a fetal position and surrounded by ceramic pots containing food, figurines made of gold and carved wood, textiles, and other objects needed for the afterlife. Then the tomb was sealed with carved rocks—and, over time, by snow as well.

After being frozen in ice for five centuries, Juanita's concealment came to an end when a neighboring volcano, Sabancaya, began showering ash onto Ampato's summit. The gray ash absorbed the sun's warmth and gradually melted snow, uncovering a trail of curious objects that would eventually lead archaeologists to Juanita's tomb. First there was a round ceremonial square, made of stones, that climber Miguel Zarate discovered in 1989 on a ridge at 5,000 meters. In a subsequent trip, Miguel discovered ceramics and bones at 5,800 meters, along with the remains of wooden stairs. Miguel knew that there was probably a tomb atop Ampato because his father, Carlos Zarate Sandoval, had run into similar evidence before discovering the tomb of an Inca princess atop Picchu volcano in 1964. Miguel went to see high-altitude archaeologist Johan Reinhard, of Chicago's Field Museum of Natural History, who had spent more than two decades uncovering Inca tombs atop Peru's highest peaks without ever finding a well-preserved mummy.

Zarate and Reinhard returned to Ampato in September 1995, accompanied only by a burro driver, and they retraced the path the Inca priests probably took on their way to the summit. They knew they were on the right track when they discovered bits of rope, ceramics, and wood. But the real breakthrough came in the thin air near the summit, when Miguel spotted a fan made of red feathers poking out of the snow. Juanita's stone tomb had melted out of the snow on the summit ridge and slid downhill toward the crater, scattering the fan, gold plates, and three figurines made of silver, gold, and spondyllus shell. But the mummy was nowhere to be seen.

To locate Juanita, the climbers wrapped rocks in yellow plastic and rolled them downhill. Near where the rocks came to rest, they found Juanita, who was still wrapped in her Inca shawl even after her 60-meter roll down a snow slope into the crater. After a few days of work, Miguel and Johan carried the 36-kg mummy to the base of Ampato and then on to the village of Cabanaconde, where she was driven to Arequipa and eventually flown to Johns Hopkins University in Baltimore, Maryland. The fact that the Incas climbed to 6,380 meters, sacrificed children in the snow, and then buried them in bizarre and elaborate tombs made front-page news around the world. Juanita's mummy has allowed scientists to understand what she ate, what her health was like, and who her living relatives are. After much travel, and public ceremonies presided over by the likes of Alberto Fujimori and Hillary Clinton, Juanita is now back in Arequipa at the new Museo Santuarios Andinos.

Reinhard discovered three other mummies, though less well preserved, in subsequent trips to Ampato's summit (it turns out the stone platforms discovered by Miguel Zarate on the summit were the ceilings of tombs). Based on archaeological evidence and Spanish chronicles, Reinhard and other archaeologists believe the Incas sacrificed children as part of *capac-cocha,* a ceremony meant to appease the *apus,* or mountain gods. The purpose of *capac-cocha* was to ensure good rains, but it was also used during earthquakes, volcanic eruptions, droughts, floods, or other times of crisis. Each child was carefully chosen on the basis of beauty, innocence, and intelligence, taken to Cusco for a ritual, and then paraded through towns on the way to the mountain. Participation in *capac-cocha* was an honor for the families because the child, after death, became a spiritual go-between for the people and their *apus. Apus* are still venerated across Peru, though offerings these days consist mainly of coca leaves and *chicha.*

Order, built in 1777. Other convents and churches worth visiting in Arequipa include **Santo Domingo** (corner of Santo Domingo and Piérola, tel. 054/21-3511, 7 A.M.–noon and 3–7:30 P.M. Mon.–Fri., 7–9:30 A.M. and 3–7:30 P.M. Sat., 5:30 A.M.–12:30 P.M. and 6:30–7:30 P.M. Sun.), which was built around 1680 and has the oldest, mestizo-style facade in the city. Another fine mestizo facade is to be found at **San Agustín** (corner of San Agustín and Sucre, tel. 054/20-0066, 7–9 A.M. and 4–8 P.M. Mon.–Sat., 7 A.M.–12:30 P.M. and 6–8 P.M. Sun.), for which construction began in 1576. **La Merced** (third block of La Merced, tel. 054/21-3233, 6:30–9:30 A.M. and 4–8 P.M. Mon.–Sat., 6:30 A.M.–8 P.M. Sun.) has fine carved wooden sculptures and a colonial library. **La Recoleta** (Recoleta 117, tel. 054/27-0966, 9 A.M.–noon and 3–5 P.M. Mon.–Sat., $0.50) is a Franciscan convent built in 1648 with beautiful cloisters, a library, and a museum of Amazon artifacts collected by missionaries. It is located across the Río Chili, about a 10-minute walk east from the Plaza de Armas.

Museums

One of Peru's most interesting museums, dedicated to the high-altitude archaeology pioneered by Johan Reinhard, is the new **Museo Santuarios Andinos** (La Merced 110, tel. 054/21-5013, 9 A.M.–6 P.M. Mon.–Sat., 9 A.M.–3 P.M. Sun., $4, $1.50 students). The museum contains 13-year-old Juanita and the 18 other mummies discovered on top of volcanoes in Peru, Chile, and Argentina, along with the textiles, gold, wood carvings, and ceramics found in their tombs—a rare chance to see Inca art overlooked by both the Spaniards and modern-day grave robbers. Included in the entry fee is an obligatory, excellent one-hour tour that includes a documentary made by *National Geographic.*

Near San Francisco Church is the **Museo Municipal** (Plaza San Francisco, 8 A.M.–5 P.M. Mon.–Fri., $0.75), with a naval museum, portrait gallery of Arequipa's elites, historical photographs of the city, and, perhaps most interesting of all, a series of caricatures and paintings by local artist Jorge Vinatea Reynoso (1900–31). The

Museo de Arte Contemporáneo (Arica 201, near Arequipa, tel. 054/22-1068, mac_arequipa@ yahoo.es, 10 A.M.–5 P.M. Tues.–Fri., 10 A.M.–2 P.M. Sat.–Sun., $1) is a five-minute cab ride from the center but worth the trip. The museum, across from the old train station, is housed in a 1900s mansion built for the manager of the Peruvian Corp., the English train company that built most of Peru's rail lines from the 1870s onward. The museum has an interesting collection of 20th-century art, including a room dedicated to the photography of Miguel and Carlos Vargas. These brothers mentored Martín Chambi, the famed Cusco photographer, and recorded early 20th-century Arequipa in fascinating detail: baptisms, nightlife, and portraits for the city's aristocrats. The museum, with about 180 pieces from 150 artists, showcases an interesting range of young local artists, heavily influenced by the horrors of Shining Path, and a few paintings from Peru's most famous painters—Fernando de Szyszlo and Enrique Polanco, among others. Out back, there are gardens and a restored dining car that now functions as a café.

Colonial Mansions

Arequipa, like Trujillo and Lima, has several colonial mansions, or *casonas,* worth visiting. Many of them were expropriated by President Juan Velasco in the late 1960s and have subsequently been converted into banks. The best of the houses is the **Casa del Moral** (Moral 318, tel. 054/21-4907, 9 A.M.–5:30 P.M. Mon.–Sat., $1.50, $1 students), which was built around 1700 and receives its names from a graceful *mora* (mulberry tree) in a courtyard paved with *canto rodado* (river stones) and lined with beautiful ochre walls. The elaborate and dense mestizo carving over the front door includes pumas spitting out serpents, and the rooms are restored and decorated with period art and furniture. Next, stroll through the **Casona Iriberry** (San Agustin on the Plaza de Armas, tel. 054/20-4482, 9 A.M.–1 P.M. and 4–8 P.M., free), which is a series of graceful stone patios and spacious rooms built in 1793 and recently converted into the Centro Cultural Chávez de la Rosa. Try to read the messages carved above the doorways—one says, in old Spanish, *This house was made in*

THE STONE BEHIND LA CIUDAD BLANCA

Arequipa is nicknamed *La Ciudad Blanca* for its *sillar*, a sparkling white volcanic stone. Light and porous, *sillar* proved ideal for the city's elaborate doorways and baroque church facades. A few decades after Arequipa was founded, builders stopped working with adobe and began making entire buildings out of *sillar* blocks, which were joined together by a mortar made of lime and sand.

The soft, porous quality of Arequipa's *sillar* lent itself to elaborate and intricate baroque facades, which combined western motifs of mermaids, grapevines, and shells with New World elements such as parrots, papayas, and jungle vegetation. The hectic blending of elements from the late 17th century onwards came to be known as mestizo style and, though it spread all over southern Peru, it reached its maximum expression on the church facades of Arequipa. It is considered one of the major architectural innovations of colonial Latin America. The best example of this style is the facade of the Iglesia de la Compañía de Jesus near the Plaza de Armas.

The problem with *sillar*, however, is that it is weak and vulnerable to Arequipa's frequent earthquakes. So Arequipa's buildings, like the cathedral, tend to be long and close to the ground. *Sillar* walls are also as thick as two meters, creating deeply recessed windows and cool, shady interior spaces. Arequipa's signature architectural elements are undoubtedly its *bóvedas,* or elegant vaulted ceilings of *sillar.*

the year 1743. I ask God that he who would live in it, recite an Our Father. The **Casa Tristán del Pozo** (San Francisco 108, tel. 054/21-5060, 9 A.M.–1 P.M. and 3:45–6 P.M. Mon.–Fri., 9 A.M.–1 P.M. Sat.) receives its name from the general who commissioned it in 1738. The house has been converted into a cultural center and offices for the Banco Continental and includes a stately portico, entryway, and double patios. Two other homes worth visiting are on Merced near the Plaza de Armas. The simple and elegant **Casa Bustamante** (Merced 1), presently not open for visitors, was built in 1760. Over the door of **Casa**

Goyenche (La Merced 201, tel. 054/21-2251, 9:15 A.M.–3:15 P.M. Mon.–Fri.) there is an ecclesiastical coat-of-arms of Arequipa's bishop José Sebastián Goyeneche (1784–1872). This home, with a large and graceful patio, is occupied by the Central Bank and contains a good collection of paintings from the Cusco School.

Yanahuara

A jaunt across the Río Chili for lunch at Sol de Mayo—can easily be combined with a digestive stroll, a few blocks north, to the charming square of the Yanahuara neighborhood. It is graced with stone archways, views of Misti, and the 18th-century Iglesia San Juan Bautista (9 A.M.–noon and 4–8 P.M. Mon.–Fri., 7 A.M.–1 P.M. and 3–8 P.M. Sat.–Sun). The church's walls are nearly two meters thick, and the roof's arch was built with a flat shape to accommodate the relative weakness of *sillar* (this shape was found to be stronger than the perfect arch). The elaborately carved facade is considered to be one of Peru's masterpieces of mestizo art and includes cherubim with feathered crowns—a pre-Hispanic symbol of power outlawed in Peru during colonial times. About five minutes away by taxi ($1.50) is the **Mirador de Carmen Alto,** which offers views of all the volcanoes, the city of Arequipa, and a *sillar* quarry used by the Spaniards. There is Collagua terracing nearby, a few resident alpaca and llama, and a small snack bar.

COUNTRYSIDE TOUR

Arequipa is surrounded by pleasant countryside that is best seen in a three-hour *tour campiña,* or country tour, offered by one of Arequipa's agencies—public transportation is confusing, time-consuming, and about the same price.

La Mansion del Fundador

This restored church and home (Huasacache, 6.5 km from Arequipa, tel. 054/44-2460, 9 A.M.–5 P.M., daily, $3) was first owned by Garcí Manuel de Carbajal, who founded Arequipa in 1540. The house later became a Jesuit retreat before being bought, and restored by, the city's illustrious Archbishop José Sebastian de Goyeneche in the early 1800s. The church is plain with an arching stone ceiling, and the home has a large patio flanked with rooms filled with original paintings and furniture. A taxi costs around $4 for the 20-minute drive.

Sabandia

This pleasant country town has a 17th-century *molino,* or flour mill (8 km southeast of Arequipa, 9 A.M.–6 P.M. daily, $2), which still turns with the force of water. The hamlet of Paucartapa, surrounded by Collagua terracing, is a favorite weekend lunch spot with locals and is a bit farther down the road. *Combis* head frequently to Sabandia from Jorge Chávez and Victor Lira ($0.35), or a taxi charges around $3 for the 15-minute trip.

ENTERTAINMENT AND EVENTS

Arequipeños are crazy about the new, American-style mall on the outskirts of town with a state-of-the-art, eight-theater CinePlanet (Ejército 793, 2 km west of center over Puente Grau, Mall Sagafalabella, tel. 054/27-1945, www.cineplanet.com.pe, $4). The food court next door would appear lifted right out of the United States were it not for a *chifa* restaurant (next to Pizza Hut) and *chicha morada* in the soft drink lineup. Movie times and options can be found in *El Pueblo,* the local newspaper, or on CinePlanet's website.

Arequipa has great nightlife, ground zero for which is San Francisco and Zela Streets near Plaza San Francisco. Walk down these streets to survey the options, as bars open and close constantly and vary depending on the night of the week. **Déjà Vu** (San Francisco 319-B, 054/934-7809, 9 A.M.–5 A.M. daily) is normally packed with people, lured by its chic atmosphere of tables under *sillar* arches, live music from Wednesday to Saturday nights, and great pizzas (large is $7, huge is $8). Movies are shown every evening at 7:30 P.M., and a more modern, larger Déjà Vu II will be located nearby at Melgar 119. Next door is **Zero** (San Francisco 317, tel. 054/20-4294, 6 P.M.–3 A.M. daily), a glitzy rock and roll pub with two pool tables and live music on Thursdays. Downstairs from Zero is the sister **Forum** (9:30 P.M.–6 A.M. Tues.–Sat.),

Arequipa's best discotheque, that gets going after 11:30 P.M. The interesting space, with different levels and even a waterfall, has live concerts on Fridays and Saturdays. The other main discotheque, a bit run-down and on the plaza, is **Dady'O** (El Portal de Flores 112, 10 P.M.–5 A.M. Thurs.–Sat.). There are several other pubs nearby, including **Istanbul** (San Francisco 231A, tel. 054/937-2264, 6 P.M.–4 A.M. daily), with charming sofas on the first floor and a romantic nook upstairs (the perfect place for an early-evening drink). **La Casa de Klaus** (Zela 207, tel. 054/25-9830, 10 A.M.–3 A.M. Mon.–Sat., 5 P.M.–3 A.M. Sun.) is a German-owned pub that is a good place to watch sports on the TV, drink German beer and eat authentic *kasespätzle* or frankfurters with sauerkraut. Locals hang out at **Ad Libitum** (San Francisco 233, tel. 054/993-1034, 6 P.M.–4 A.M.), a dimly lit, laidback place with a wide range of affordable cocktails (tumbler of Johnny Walker Black, $3.50).

There are a few more pubs nearby, including **La Café Art Montréal** (Ugarte 210, tel. 054/931-2796, 3 P.M.–2 A.M. Mon.–Fri., 3 P.M.–4 A.M. Thurs.–Fri., 5 P.M.–4 A.M. Sat.). This swanky colonial space, built of *sillar* in the 19th century and divided up into rooms with vaulted ceilings, swings with Cuban protest, Latin rock, and other live music from Wednesdays to Saturdays. There is a light menu including burritos ($3), guacamole, pizza and pastas, and crepes. Nearby is **Siwara** (Santa Catalina 210, tel. 054/20-6051), another popular place with pool table, darts, live music, and yard-long beers.

Arequipa has a lean, but worthwhile, cultural calendar that is promoted in the newspaper, *El Pueblo,* and in posters around town. Teatro Municipal (second block of Mercaderes, 7 P.M., free admission) has weekly concert listings at the door, with live string orchestras, big bands, guitar ensembles, and other Latin groups. Other exhibits and performances are held at Instituto Cultural Peruano Alemán (Ugarte 207, tel. 054/21-8567), Centro Cultural Peruano Norteamericano (Melgar 109, tel. 054/89-1020), and Alianza Francesa (Santa Catalina 208, tel. 054/21-5579).

Arequipa's main festival is founder's day, August 15, which includes a week of fireworks, parades, dancing, and bullfights. One of Peru's more famous pilgrimages is the Virgen de Chapi on May 1. Pilgrims trek 45 km, or about 15 hours, from Arequipa to the small town of Chapi, which is blanketed with flowers by day and lit by fireworks at night. Other local festivals include Virgen de la Candelaria in Cayma on February 2, the bullfighting festival in Characato on June 24, and the Virgen del Rosario in Yanahuara on October 8.

SHOPPING

Arequipa continues to thrive, as it has for centuries, as the center of Peru's wool industry. Wools and fine clothing shops are all over town and, for the real aficionados, the main wool producers can arrange visits to factories and highland ranches with alpaca and vicuña. A good place to start shopping is Pasaje Catedral, a charming street behind the cathedral. **Millma's Baby Alpaca** (Psje. Catedral 117, tel. 054/20-5134, 9 A.M.–9 P.M. daily) is one of the nicer shops, with a wide selection of men's and women's sweaters ($35–95), coats, and scarves. Baby alpaca sweaters ($45), scarves ($6–15), and pashminas can be found at **Links Fashions** (Psje. Catedral 105-B, tel. 054/22-9979, 9:30 A.M.–1:30 P.M. and 4–8 P.M. Mon.–Sat.). The outlet store of **Michell** (Juan de la Torre 101, 054-20-2525, 9:30 A.M.–1 P.M. and 2:30–7 P.M. Mon.–Fri., 11 A.M.–1:30 P.M. Sat.), one of the city's main wool exporters, sells sweaters, scarves, and coats and has people on hand to demonstrate the hand-sorting of alpaca fiber and loom weaving. A tour of the factory, located in Parque Industrial, can be arranged here at the shop.

Incalpaca (Juan Bustamente s/n, Tahuaycani neighborhood, tel. 054/25-1025 or 054/25-9188, 9:30 A.M.–7 P.M. Mon–Fri., 11 A.M.–4 P.M. Sat.), about 10 minutes from the city center, is the only store in Peru licensed to sell vicuña wool, which is sorted into such minute levels of fineness that only Arequipa's top wool merchants can tell the difference. About two vicuñas can produce one kilo, which costs a staggering

Arequipa street life

DON'T LOOK A CAMELID IN THE MOUTH

The most honored gift, and most common form of tribute, among the Incas was not gold—it was finely woven garments of alpaca or, even better, vicuña wool. A relative of the camel, the llama was also the Incas' only beast of burden and their primary source of meat. These high-altitude camelids made the Inca Empire possible.

Arequipa, surrounded by high-altitude grasslands, has been the center of Peru's lucrative wool industry since colonial times and even before. Now that alpaca ranches are spreading across the United States like wildfire, some of Arequipa's main wool exporters—such as Grupo Inca and Michell—occasionally lead tours up to highland alpaca ranches. Participants help round up and shear wild vicuñas and learn how to spin wool and loom-weave.

The finest fiber of any wool-producing animal comes from the **vicuña** (*Vicugna vicugna*), which was brought back from the verge of extinction in the 1960s. Each vicuña is sheared every three or four years, and only yields a mere 250 grams of wool. Shearing vicuña was only made legal again in 1995, and the wool remains highly regulated. Clothing made from vicuña wool, considered the world's most luxurious animal fiber, can cost several thousand dollars. The Incas would have been pleased—they only let nobles wear vicuña clothing. Vicuña herds typically consist of one male who walks in front of a harem of up to six females, though it is not uncommon to see mixed herds of up to 50 vicuña. A good place to see vicuña herds is Pampa Cañahua, en route to Colca Canyon from Arequipa.

The largest camelid, with fiber nearly as fine as the vicuña (around 16 microns), is the **Guanaco** (*Lama guanicoe*). Like the vicuña, it is difficult to domesticate and has a thin, orange-brown wool of incredible fineness. There are only 500,000 guanacos, mostly in the highlands of Chile and Argentina, and their wool is highly regulated on the international market.

The **alpaca** is a whole other animal. For starters, there are more than 10 million alpacas in the world—more than three quarters of which are in Peru—and the wool has a delightful range of browns, blacks, whites, and grays. The wool fiber also has a dramatic range of fineness, which is carefully measured by merchants in determining the value of the wool. All over Peru's highlands, women can be seen weaving in fields as they tend a flock of grazing alpaca, which have a sheep-like abundance of wool that fluffs up even around their eyes. The **Suris**, or long-haired alpacas, can produce over 3 kg of wool every two years! Grilled alpaca meat has been popping up in restaurants around Peru, overtaking llama as the meat of choice.

Because llamas have much coarser wool than alpacas, they are generally used for their meat and as pack animals. Llamas and alpacas can intermingle—the result is called a *huarizo*—and can be difficult to tell apart. But llamas generally are larger, have much less hair, and have a small tail that sticks out in the back. Dried llama meat, a traditional Andean food, is called *charqui*—perhaps the only Quechuan word to make its way into the English lexicon (as beef *jerky*).

A final word of caution: Llamas and alpacas, even the ones with pink tassles tied on their ears, are not friendly creatures. They have a well-deserved reputation for spitting grass loogies at anyone who comes too close. If the cheeks puff out, and the ears flatten, back off!

$900. Even a scarf costs $400. There is a small camelid zoo in the back, along with a museum. It is sometimes possible to visit the factory as well. The largest factory in town is that of **Grupo Inca** (Juan Bustamente s/n, tel. 054/25-1025, free admission)—call ahead to arrange a visit—and there is also **Inca Tops** (Francisco Velasco 126, tel. 054/22-9998, 8 A.M.–12:30 P.M. and 2–6 P.M. Mon.–Fri.).

For ecological textile products, **Baby Alpaca Boutique** (Santa Catalina 208-A, tel. 054/20-

6716, 9 A.M.–1:30 P.M. and 3–8 P.M. daily) sells all-organic material with natural dyes, including purples and greens. It also sells organic brown jungle cotton, part of a project to give coca farmers another option. Organic products are also available at **Colca Trading Company** (Santa Catalina 300-B, tel. 054/24-2088, 9 A.M.–12:30 P.M. and 1:30–8 P.M. Mon.–Sat.), including cotton garments, organic alpaca sweaters, silver jewelry, rugs, and scarves.

Patio de Ekeko (Mercaderes 141, tel. 054/21-

5861, 10 A.M.–9 P.M. Mon.–Sat., 10 A.M.–8 P.M. Sun.) is a touristy complex near the square. Several floors are filled with classy crafts and alpaca shops, a high-end jewelry store, an Internet café, a restaurant, and even a big-screen cinema showing documentaries on Arequipa. La Ibérica, Arequipa's century-old chocolate company, has a shop here, at the Sagafalabella mall, and at the airport.

For jewelery, **Aqlla** (Pasaje Catedral 112, tel. 054/20-5088, 9 A.M.–8:30 P.M. daily) is a stylish shop and showroom of handmade silver jewelry. It also has artistic and modern scarves, sweaters, wool coats, and ceramics. **L. Paulet** (General Morán 118, Claustros de la Compañia, tel. 054/28-7786, 10 A.M.–1 P.M. and 4–8 P.M. daily) specializes in gold and silver handmade jewelry, as well as hand-knit and hand-woven baby alpaca textiles.

There are several antique shops clustered on Santa Catalina. **Antiguedades y Objetos de Arte** (Santa Catalina 204, tel. 054/22-9103, 9 A.M.–1 P.M. and 3–8 P.M. daily), **El Anticuario** (Santa Catalina 300, tel. 054/23-4474, 9 A.M.–1 P.M. and 3–7 P.M. daily), and **Arte Colonial** (Santa Catalina 312, tel. 054/21-4887, 10 A.M.–8 P.M. daily) all sell antiques and crafts. A wide range of inexpensive crafts can be found at the Fundo de Fierro handicraft market, on the corner of the Plaza San Francisco.

Along with Lima, Arequipa has the most bookstores in Peru, the best of which is **Librería el Lector** (San Francisco 221, tel. 054/28-8677, 9 A.M.–9 P.M. daily), with European charm. Owner Fernando Rosas has a great collection of books on Peruvian culture—including many in English—and on archaeology, politics, cooking, music, flowers, photography, and travel. The shop also has an English-language fiction section and a two-for-one book exchange (how fair is that?). There are several other bookshops along San Francisco near the plaza.

SPORTS AND RECREATION

Colca Canyon, and other stunning areas near Arequipa, are one big adventure playground. There are a huge range of adventure options, including rafting, mountain biking, trekking, and climbing, and good agencies to make it happen. Before you go, remember the altitude: acclimatize in Arequipa if you have not already visited Cusco and Lake Titicaca.

Climbing

The closest volcano to Arequipa is **Misti** (5,830 m). Climbers should, however, avoid the route that begins from the outskirts of town—assaults were reported here in 2001. There are a few routes, but the easiest begins from a new road that reaches 3,400 meters. From here climbers ascend six or seven hours to make base camp around 4,700 meters before climbing at dawn up Misti's snowy south side. It is possible to be back in Arequipa by the afternoon.

The easiest 6,000-meter peak—perhaps in all of Latin America, maybe in the whole world—is **Chachani** (6,095 m). Three hours of driving from Arequipa brings climbers to 5,100 meters, from which climbers ascend two more hours to base camp. The summit is another five to six hours away the following morning, though a new road may put future climbers within four hours of the summit. Though it's possible to climb Chachani in a single day from Arequipa, it seems safer (and more enjoyable) to plan on at least two, and more for the un-acclimatized.

Another popular mountain, which can be combined with a trekking circuit through Colca Canyon, is **Ampato** (6,380 m). A car can be driven to 4,900 meters, from which climbers ascend two hours for base camp at 5,200 meters. Summit is then another six hours. Another route from Cabanaconde, in the Colca Canyon, begins at an Inca ceremonial center at 5,000 m near the northeast side of the volcano. The summit is about seven hours away from here, and the neighboring volcanoes of **Sabancaya** (5,995 m) and **Hualca Hualca** (6,095 m) can also be climbed from this same camp. Colca is also the launching point for **Mismi** (5,597 m), the source of the Amazon.

Coropuna (6,425 meters), Peru's second-highest peak, is rarely climbed because it is 10 hours from Arequipa. But its slopes are gentler than many of the other volcanoes, and it is sandwiched by and on the way to both Cotahuasi and Valley of the Volcanoes.

Lake Titicaca

Most of Arequipa's volcanoes are gentle and relatively free of ice, so few climbers rope up, though crampons might be required for the summit push. Although not as technical as the mountains around Huaraz, any mountain near 6,000 meters demands caution and experience. Go without a guide only if you have climbing experience and have done your homework ahead of time.

The most experienced guide in Arequipa, without a doubt, is Carlos Zarate Sandoval. At 83, he is the oldest working mountain guide in the world. Where most mountain guides are tall and stocky, Carlos is small and spry—less than 1.5 meters (five feet) tall. His deeply tanned, wrinkled face, and broad smile are hard to miss. He operates **Carlos Zarate Aventuras** (Santa Catalina 115A, Window B, tel. 054/20-6314 or 054/997-1535) with three of his sons, including Miguel "Miki" Zarate, who discovered the Juanita mummy atop Ampato in 1995. Zarate Aventuras guides all the local volcanoes, along with a range of treks, and its services include food and transport. Prices are $120 pp for Misti, $170 for Chachani, and $450 for the Colca/Ampato trek and climb. Carlos Zarate (the elder) can also be reached at his house at Alfonso Ugarte 305, in the Jesus Maria–Paucarpata neighborhood.

To make things confusing, his son Carlos Zarate operates **Carlos Zarate Aventuras** (Santa Catalina 204, office 3, tel. 054/26-3107, czarate@rh.com.pe, www.rh.com.pe/zarate), which offers similar treks and climbs. A final recommended guide is Vlado Soto at **The Adventure Center** (Jerusalén 401B, colcatrek@hotmail.com). His shop has the best range of camping gear for sale and rent in the area, and he usually has white gas. Tourists can contact another two dozen certified guides, many English-speaking, through **Casa de Guias** (Desaguadero 126, tel. 054/26-3107, 9:30 A.M.–1 P.M. Mon.–Fri.) There are lots of other adventure agencies on the fourth block of Jerusalén, but choose carefully. Before paying, make sure you inspect the equipment, confirm the schedule, and ask to see your guide's certificate. There are also several good and affordable guides in Chivay, contactable through Chivay's tourism police (Plaza de Armas, tel. 054/48-8623).

Trekking

The areas around Arequipa offer fabulous trekking for those who like views of canyons and volcanoes and a hot, sunny climate. Unlike the more popular Cordillera Blanca, trekkers have no problem getting off the beaten path and need not worry much about robbery or other safety issues. The views range from immense canyon rims to wide valleys studded with volcanoes. The villages, isolated during centuries, are friendly and unforgettable.

The agencies listed in the climbing sections offer the best-organized treks, and are glad to answer questions for those going on their own. Topographical maps can be bought at the South American Explorers clubhouses in Cusco and Lima, or the Instituto Geográfico Militar (or, in a pinch, copied in Arequipa). Ask for detailed information—especially concerning the availability of water—at each village you pass. Apart from running out of water, the main things to watch for are sunburn and getting cold at night. Bring a wide-brimmed hat, sunscreen for the day, a warm sleeping bag, and a jacket. Specific route information can be found in the sections on Colca, Cotahuasi, and Valley of the Volcanoes.

Horseback Riding

Rancho de los Amigos (Predio Salterio, Callapa, tel. 054/25-1816, atagamarra@star.com.pe), in Sabandia, is a 15-minute drive from the center of Arequipa and offers half- to two-day tours on Peruvian *paso* horses. Several of the lodges in Colca rent horses as well.

Rafting and Kayaking

The best rafting operator in Arequipa is **Cusipata** (Jerusalén 408A, tel. 054/20-3966 or 084/937-2585, gvellutino@terra.com.pe, www.cusipata.com), run by Gian Marco Vellutino. Gian Marco is an expert kayaker, and his father, Antonio, accompanied a team of Polish adventurers in the first rafting descent of Colca Canyon in the early 1980s. From April to December, Cusipata has daily half-day trips down the Río Chile, which tumbles through Arequipa and includes one Class IV chute ($25 pp). Another excellent option is a three-day kayaking school, the last two days of which include time on the Class III waters of the Río Majes ($120, including food), the large downstream section of the Río Colca.

Cusipata's more serious endeavors include descents of the Cotahuasi Canyon twice a year in conjunction with Bio Bio Expeditions in the United States. Expert boaters rank Cotahuasi up with Cusco's Río Apurimac, another extraordinarily beautiful wilderness river with a steady stream of Class IV rapids. Colca, on the other hand, is a steeper and more closed canyon with unavoidable Class V rapids. Rafting guides prefer Cotahuasi over Colca because there are portages around all the Class V rapids, the hillsides offer more ruins and terracing, and the river is doable even for first-time rafters—that doesn't mean, however, that it's not hard. See the *Cusco and the Sacred Valley* chapter for other agencies.

Mountain Biking

Cusipata rents mountain bikes for $15 a day, $8 half-day, and can suggest routes around Arequipa (at the base of Misti, for instance). They also lead two- and three-day trips through Colca Canyon, as does **Colca Adventure** (Jerusalén 412 B, tel. 054/69-2139, joselucho31@hotmail.com, www.geocities.com/aventuras_colca). The standard Colca mountain bike route begins at Patapampa, at 4,950 meters, and drops into the Colca Canyon at Chivay at 3,650 meters. Bikers follow dirt roads along the north side of the river and cross the bridge to Yanque. The third day would include the Cruz del Condór and Maca, and end in Cabanaconde. Cusipata can also design extraordinary routes in Cotahuasi and the Valley of the Volcanoes.

Sightseeing Tours

There is not enough tourist traffic through Arequipa for the daily, inexpensive pool tours that exist in Cusco and Lima. So prices for the two main tours—one of the city, the other of the country, both about three hours—can be quite expensive for only one or two people. The city tour includes Yanahuara church and lookout, the Compañia church, and the Santa Catalina Monastery—ask for your guide to visit colonial homes as well. The country tour includes the

THE REPUBLIC OF AREQUIPA AND THE STATE OF AREQUIPEÑISMO

Arequipeños stick out in Peru, much in the same way that it is hard not to miss a Texan in the United States. Arequipeños seem more Spanish, more confident, and have a fierce regional pride that manifests itself in passports for the *Republic of Arequipa*. No one jokes, however, about the several revolutions that have been plotted here over the last two centuries. Nor that the mayor of Arequipa, as recently as 2001, publicly discussed secession and that two of Peru's most notorious recent historical figures—Shining Path head Abimael Guzmán and Fujimori henchman Vladimir Montesino—both hail from here.

One theory behind *Arequipeñismo*—as the local braggadocio is called—is population-based. There have always been more Spaniards in Arequipa. In the mid-18th century, for instance, there were 22,000 Spaniards out of a total population of 37,000 (Lima, at the same time, had only 18,000 Spanish out of a total population of 62,000). Arequipa received even more European immigrants after Independence, when numerous English families settled in Arequipa and set up trading houses for the area's alpaca wool.

Probably the main reason for Arequipa's distinct feel is its geographic and economic isolation from the rest of the country. It is far closer to Bolivia and Chile than to Lima, for instance, and Arequipeños have long complained that they are neglected by the centralized powers that be in Lima. The huge *haciendas*, which dominated other parts of Peru, have always been balanced by small landowners and merchants who have depended an internal, southern economy between Tacna, Moguegua, Mollendo, and Puno—not to mention La Paz, Bolivia, and Arica, Chile.

mill at Sabandia and the Mansion de Fundador. The most reputable agency is **Giardino Tours** (Jerusalén 604A, tel. 054/22-1345, giardino@terra.com.pe, www.giardinotours.com), run by the same owners as La Casa de la Abuela in Arequipa and Mama Yacchi in Colca Canyon. The company's city and country tours run $15–40 each, depending on number of people, and its Colca trips lodge at Mama Yacchi ($49 for two days, $87 for three days). Another agency with a good reputation is **Colonial Tours** (Santa Catalina 106, tel. 054/28-6868, colonialtours02@hotmail.com, www.colonialtours.net), which offers county and city tours starting at $15 along with a variety of two- and three-day trips to Colca Canyon. A small and recommended Arequipa agency is **Reisebüro** (Jerusalén 524B, tel. 054/20-1222, perureisen@star.com.pe, www.peruurlaub.com), run by German expat Manfred Miedl. It offers a $25 city tour, similarly priced country tour, and a two-day Colca Canyon tour ranging from $30 (staying at Casa de Lucila in Chivay) to $85 (staying at Colca Lodge).

ACCOMMODATIONS

As one of Peru's top business centers, Arequipa has dozens of hotels, including many charming options under $50 for a double. Above that, however, options become quite meager outside of several 1970s-style homes and the excellent, five-star Hotel Libertador.

Under $10

The walls are thin at the **Hostal Le Foyer** (Ugarte 114, tel. 054/28-6473, hostallefoyer@yahoo.com, $5 dorm, $9 d), and there's some street noise, but it's still one of the better, well-located budget options. Amenities include clean rooms with shared bath, TV with cable, and a nice rooftop terrace; rooms with private bath are another $4. Also well located, **La Reyna** (Zela 209, tel. 054/28-6578, $4 s, $8 d) has small rooms with tile floors and shared baths spread through a crumbling 1813 mansion. Rooms are a bit dirty, though with plenty of character, and range from shared dormitories to two very nice rooms with private baths overlooking Santa Catalina for $11.

$10–25

The best budget option is **Colonial House Inn** (Puente Grau 114, tel. 054/22-3533, colonialhouseinn@hotmail.com, $6 s, $12 d), with seven rooms with shared bathroom around a courtyard and a nice rooftop terrace with mountain views. Breakfast is said to be well above the standard bread-and-butter fare at most hostels. Though the inn is located on a busy, unpleasant street, the thick colonial walls keep out the noise. The owner is friendly and speaks English. Call ahead of time, as this place is often full. **Posada de Sancho** (Santa Catalina 213-A, tel. 054/28-7797, $12 s, $20 d) is a simple colonial home with 15 large rooms and two tiled patios with sitting tables and potted geraniums. Rooms have wooden floors, high ceilings, and windows facing either the street or the patio. As hostels go, this is plain but pleasant. Rooms with private bath cost $6 more. **Hostal Regis** (Ugarte 202, tel. 054/22-6111, Regis@qunet.com.pe, $5 s, $10 d) occupies a late-19th-century building with high ceilings and a sunny rooftop terrace with small pool, funky bar, and fabulous city panorama. Rooms are up four flights of stairs, have parquet floors, and clean, shared bathrooms; private baths cost another $4. Breakfast costs $1 and laundry service is available for $1.50/kilo. This place is often full, so call ahead.

One of the more interesting places to stay the night is in a 1920s train cabin at **La Estación** (Loreto 410, tel. 054/27-3852, laestacion@backpackerperu.com, www.backpackerperu.com, $10 s, $20 d, including breakfast). This creative adaptive-reuse project has restored two luxury trains, manufactured locally in 1929 and 1955, into backpacker sleeping cars. Compartments are somewhat cramped, with small bunkbeds, but have all-original decor with wood paneling and brass washbasins. Group showers are outside the train, as well as a communal area in the main lodge with a TV and bar. There is a kitchen, laundry service, and Internet. La Estación is a five-minute taxi ride across the river from the Plaza de Armas. The location of **Tambo Viejo** (Malecón Socabaya 107, tel. 054/28-8195, room@tamboviejo.com, www.tamboviejo.com, $9 s, $14 d) is not central, but this funky old house has a quiet atmosphere and a lot of character. Most rooms have shared baths; private baths are an additional $4. The grassy garden has sitting tables and a bar, the sitting rooms have chess tables, and there is free Internet.

$25–50

We applaud the simplicity of **M** **Los Balcones de Moral y Santa Catalina** (Moral 217, tel. 054/20-1291, rafael@losbalconeshotel.com, www.losbalconeshotel.com, $19 s, $26 d, including breakfast), with a quiet reception room, simple breakfast area, and a row of huge, comfortable rooms overlooking the cathedral bell towers. Apart from being large, the rooms have gorgeous wood floors, nice beds, furniture, and cable TV. More rooms, around an interior courtyard, will be restored in the future.

For a fascinating glimpse into 18th-century Arequipa, book a room at the beautiful colonial house known as **M** **La Casa de Melgar** (Melgar 108, tel. 054/22-2459, lacasademelgar@terra .com.pe, www.lared.net.pe/lacasademelgar/, $25 s, $35 d, including breakfast). The house has 1.5-meter-thick *sillar* walls, vaulted ceilings, wood floors and shutters, and three interior patios. Each room is unique, with antique rocking chairs and armoires, vaulted stone showers, rotary phones, and funky stained-glass skylights. Room 104 is huge with a fireplace.

M **La Casa de la Abuela** (Jerusalén 606, tel. 054/24-1206, lacasa@terra.com.pe, www.lacasademiabuela.com, $26 s, $33 d) is a delightful oasis of gardens and lawns, six blocks from the Plaza de Armas, that offers every conceivable traveler's service. Though not too big, the rooms have excellent beds, cable TV, phones, good bathrooms, and nice views over gardens. Breakfast is served in the garden ($3), and other services include laundry ($2/kilo), library, game room, Internet, pool, and one of the best tour agencies in Arequipa—Giardino Tours. La Boveda (10 A.M.–10 P.M.), the restaurant in the back of the compound, has live music and a varied menu. Some of the backpacker rooms, which are smaller with shared bathrooms, are almost as nice and have garden views as well (13 s, $17 d).

Hostal El Solar (Ayacucho 108, tel. 054/24-

1793, solar@star.com.pe, www.rh.com.pe/solar, $18 s, $28 d, including breakfast) is a charming colonial house in the center of town, with a small library, sitting room, and rooftop terraces. Eight rooms have wood floors, *sillar* walls, high ceilings, and TV. The kitchen is available for guest use.

The entry to the **El Conquistador** (Mercaderes 409, tel. 054/21-2916, elconquistador@hotmail.com, $27 s, $35 d) is quite stunning, crossing an elegant colonial patio and entering into the reception and dining area with vaulted *sillar* construction built in the 1770s. The actual rooms, however, are an unfortunate 1980s modern addition lacking charm. Rooms are a bit dark, but are comfortable with carpet, cable TV, and telephones. The original building is worth a visit even if you don't plan to stay here.

For those who prefer to be out of the city center, Vallecito is a quiet, relaxed neighborhood with homes built in the early 20th century, about a five-minute taxi ride south of town. **La Plazuela** (Plaza Huan Manuel Polar 105, Vallecito, tel. 054/22-2624, laplazuela@terra.com.pe, $36 s, $44 d) is a large home from the early 1900s that has been converted into a bed-and-breakfast with a nice lawn, sitting area, and dining area. The rooms, however, are rather drab. Also in this area is **Queen's Villa** (Luna Pizarro 512, tel. 054/23-5233, $25 s, $32 d), with rooms and a handful of bungalows surrounded by pleasant gardens, sitting tables, palm trees, and a nice pool. The rooms vary in quality and have either parquet, tile, or carpeted floors. The rooms are in need of an update but the tranquil setting and amenities—Internet, inexpensive laundry, cable TV, and kitchenettes in some bungalows—make this a good value.

$50–100

Casa Andina (Jerusalén 601, tel. 054/24-4481, ventas@nexushoteles.com, www.casaandina.com .pe, $45 s, $55 d) is a completely remodeled modern hotel that stands out for the startling, red-and-orange blocks adorning its facade. Though completely un-colonial, Casa Andina is comfortable. Its 94 rooms have security boxes, cable TV, and comfy beds, and many have tubs. The **Sonesta Posada del Inca** (Portal de Flores

Lake Titicaca

116, tel. 054/21-5530, reservasarequipa@son-estaperu.com, www.sonesta.com, $78 s, $90 d) has a stunning location right on the Plaza de Armas, though its rooms are in the midst of a badly needed update. There is a rooftop terrace with a small pool, lunch served on a terrace overlooking the square, and a handful of rooms with private terrace over the square itself (the remaining rooms look into a modern, interior courtyard). Rooms have AC, fridge, and cable TV.

The more charming options in this price category are outside the city center, starting with the upscale neighborhood of Selva Alegre just north of the city center. **Hostal La Gruta** (La Gruta, tel. 054/22-4631, lagruta@terra.com.pe, www.lagrutahotel.com, $45 s, $55 d, including breakfast) offers 12 rooms in a discreet 1970s house. Each room is different, one with an interior garden, another with a fireplace. All have carpet, fridges, and cable TV, and open up to a small garden. It doesn't really feel like a hotel here, more like staying in a guest room.

West of town is **La Posada del Puente** (Puente Grau w/ Bolognesi 101, tel. 054/25-3132, hotel@posadadelpuente.com, www.posadadelpuente.com, $60 s, $70 d), located underneath Puente Grau. The location is an odd place to build a new hotel, with the traffic noise from the bridge above, but the landscaping is well done and the modern rooms with vaulted ceilings nod toward the local historic architecture. The elegant dining room has a view of the river, and two alpaca graze in the garden. Across the street is the quiet, modern **Hotel La Maison D'Elise** (Bolognesi 104, tel. 054/25-6185, mdelisehotel@terra.com.pe, www.hotelmaisondelise.com.pe, $57 s, $74 d, including breakfast). The modern, blocky exterior doesn't jibe with the architecture of the rooms, which attempt to mimic the local colonial construction. However, the sheer size of the 43 rooms and their amenities make up for it: each room has a small patio, cable TV, phones, large bathrooms, and easy access to a grassy lawn with a small pool and good views of Misti.

South of the center in Vallecito, **Casagrande** (Luna Pizarrro 202, Vallecito, tel. 054/22-2031, casagrande@star.com.pe, $45 s, $55 d) is an imposing stone building, rising like a castle out of

the quiet suburb. The rooms are modern and big, with tall windows, cable TV, fridges, and nice bathrooms. The marble-floored reception looks out over a small, manicured lawn, as does the restaurant downstairs that serves cocktails and a light menu of international food. The stately suites, at only $10 more, are a good value.

$100–150

The grand **Hotel Libertador** (Plaza Bolivar s/n, Selva Alegre, tel. 054/21-5110, arequipa@libertador.com.pe, www.libertador.com.pe, $148 s, $148 d, including breakfast) sits next to one of the city's largest and prettiest parks, yet is still only a 15-minute walk to the Plaza de Armas. The rose-colored, colonial-style building has a grand lobby with elegant details carried throughout the building. Large rooms are decorated in colonial style with dark wood furniture, deep red carpets, and huge bathrooms with tubs. The big outdoor pool is surrounded by gardens and a playground. The Sunday buffet is served poolside and is excellent.

Long-Term Stays

A recommended agent for rental homes and property is **Mónica Tejada** (Urb. León XIII A-6, Cayma, tel. 054/25-4835, monica_aqp@mixmail.com).

FOOD

Arequipeños are proud of their cuisine, and rightly so because there are more good restaurants per capita here than anywhere else in the country—not only Peruvian but Turkish, French, and Italian as well. Chefs whip up choice local ingredients, such as local river prawns, into creative, tantalizing combinations. Probably the most famous local dish is the appetizer *ocopa a la arequipeña,* which are boiled potatoes smothered in a cheese and peanut sauce.

Cafés and Desserts

Arequipeños take their desserts very seriously, as is evident by the colorful window displays of cakes and pies along the first block of Mercaderes or on Portal de Flores on the Plaza de Armas. The lineup on Mercaderes starts with **Manolo** (Mercaderes 107, tel. 054/21-9009, 7 A.M.–1 A.M. daily, $1.50), a relaxed diner where locals come to indulge in inexpensive Peruvian meals and decadent desserts. Next door is **Luciano** (Mercaderes 115, tel. 054/20-6075, 8 A.M.–10 P.M. Mon.–Sat., 9 A.M.–9 P.M. Sun., $1), where the neighborhood comes to get their daily empanadas and breads. The cake and pie selection is pretty good too, and breakfast for $1.50 is a great deal including an empanada. For a light lunch, dessert, or milkshake, **Cioccolata** (Mercaderes 120, tel. 054/24-7180, 10 A.M.–11 P.M., $2–4) has a rather gourmet menu including spinach and prosciutto salads. The best cakes and pies on the block, however, are at ⊠ **Cappricio** (Mercaderes 121, tel. 054/89-1000, 10 A.M.–10 P.M. Mon.–Fri., 10 A.M.–11 P.M. Sat., 11 A.M.–10 P.M. Sun., $4), serving espresso, Italian food, and desserts in a diner-like atmosphere. The menu includes *tequeños* and chicken brochettes for starters, with lasagnas and pastas for the main course.

Cafés on the Plaza de Armas are similar but with tourist prices. The exception is the fabulous ⊠ **La Covacha** (Portal de Flores 130, tel. 054/20-4991, $1), serving espresso and desserts including tiramisu, chocolate mousse, and cheesecake. It also makes natural yogurt, crepes, and empanadas. Near the Santa Catalina Monastery is **Le Bistrot** (Sta. Catalina 208, 9 A.M.–midnight Mon.–Sat., $3), a chic café with Caesar salads, crepes, quiches, and 30 different espresso drinks. Next door to the best bookstore in town, Librería el Lector, is the charming **Colibri** (San Francisco 225, tel. 054/21-1120, 8 A.M.–11 P.M. Mon.–Thurs., 6–11 P.M. Fri.–Sun., $1), with vaulted *sillar* ceilings, wood floors, and great espresso. It serves crepes, pies, salads, and brochettes. Simply the best empanadas in all of Peru are at the tiny ⊠ **El Pan Nuestro** (Jerusalén block 5), where all breads, cakes, and pies cost $0.30 each. For a coffee with a cause, head to **Café C.V.** (Jerusalén 406, tel. 054/48-5542, 7 A.M.–8 P.M., $1), with cheap empanadas, lemon pie, cheesecake, and espresso drinks. The house is an orphanage for street kids and sells their baked goods, as well as handmade purses and backpacks to support the children.

Peruvian

The best Peruvian food in the historic center is ⊠ **Ary Quepay** (Jerusalén 502, tel. 054/20-4583, 11 A.M.–11 P.M., $5), owned by the hardworking husband-and-wife team Marcos and Gloria Verapinto. The food tastes like it's out of your grandmother's kitchen, prepared with love by Gloria and her daughter. The family recipes of *pastel de papas* and *soltero de queso* are highly recommended for starters. Main courses concentrate on traditional Arequipeño plates such as *cuy chactado* (grilled guinea pig), *adobo* (pork in its broth), and *rocoto vegetariano* (pepper stuffed with veggies). Service is great, there are 25 different Pisco drinks, and live folkloric music starts every night at 6:30 P.M.

A good place for *cebiche* is **Fory Fay** (Álvarez Tomás 221, tel. 054/24-2400, 9:30 A.M.–4:30 P.M. daily, $4), where ceviche is served in bowls of *leche de tigre* (the lime juice and ají used to soak the fish) in under five minutes. Carnivores should

---

PASS THE STUFFED ROCOTO PEPPERS

Arequipa has some of the most developed cuisine in all of Peru, and the quality and range of its restaurants is second only to Lima. When in Arequipa, plan on spending a lazy afternoon at a country restaurant. If you are too squeamish for the local specialty, roasted *cuy* (guinea pig), other plates to try include:

- *Pastel de papas:* evaporated cream, olive oil, and cheese over fried potato slices.
- *Soltero de queso:* fresh salad of cheese, broad beans, peas, corn, onions, olive, and rocoto pepper in a vinegar dressing.
- *Ocopa Arequipeña:* boiled potatoes in a sauce made of yellow chiles, cheese, peanuts, and *huacatay* herbs.
- *Rocoto relleno:* red rocoto pepper stuffed with chopped beef, cheese, milk, and potato.
- *Adobo Arequipeño:* chunks of pork marinated and then stewed in a clay pot with *chicha,* vinegar, red chiles, onions, and spices.
- *Camarones:* A variety of dishes made with river shrimp.

head to **El Viñedo** (San Franciso 319, tel. 054/20-5053, noon–11 P.M., $5–8). This Argentine grill serves prime rib, ostrich, pork ribs, and *anticuchos*.

International

Middle Eastern food is not easy to find in Peru, thus **El Turko II** (San Francisco 311, tel. 054/tel. 054/21-5729, 8 A.M.–12 A.M., daily, $5–7) is a real gem. Hummous, falafel, eggplant dishes, and succulent lamb kabobs (the most tender meat we have eaten in Peru) are just a few items on this delicious Turkish menu. Guests soak in the *sillar* ceilings, wood floors, and modern art before knocking the meal back with a complimentary, but obligatory, shot of anise. The sister restaurant, **El Turko I** (San Francisco block 2, tel. 054/20-3862, $3–5), is a smaller, more affordable café down the street serving Turkish pita sandwiches with raita, a sauce of yogurt, cucumber, and garlic.

There are several restaurants with rooftop and sidewalk seating on Pasaje La Catedral, the charming pedestrian alley behind the cathedral. The best views, of both the cathedral and volcanoes, are from the rooftop at **Mixto's** (Psj. La Catedral 115, tel. 054/20-5343, $4–7). The menu offers just everything from *cebiches* to pastas to pizzas. Next door, **La Trufa** (Psj. La Catedral 111, tel. 054/40-5290, 9 A.M.–11 P.M. daily, $3–7) has good pasta, chicken curry, seafood, and great service. Try the *ocopa arequipeña.* Live folkloric music is Mon.–Sat. from 7 P.M.

Pizza

The best pizza in town is at **Gianni's** (San Franciso 304, 6 P.M.–1 A.M. Mon.–Sat., $5–6), an Italian-owned restaurant with the freshest of ingredients (the mushrooms aren't canned here, always the true test). Dinners are served with generous glasses of Chilean or Argentinean wine or liters of sangria. The gnocchi and fettucini are handmade, but the pizzas are the highlight. Right across the street is **La Italiana Ristorante** (San Francisco 303, tel. 054/20-2080, 11 A.M.–midnight daily, $4), which could have been lifted right out of New York's Little Italy district. Tuxedo-wearing waiters attend candle-lit tables and a blind, smiling accordion player can knock

out any tune requested. The most laid-back of all the pizzerias is the cavelike **Los Leños** (Jerusalén 407, tel. 054/28-9197, 3–11 P.M. daily, $6), serving great wood-fired pizzas for over a decade. The dim lighting and graffiti on the *sillar* walls give it a college pub atmosphere.

Mexican

Behind the cathedral is **Tenampa** (Psj. La Catedral 108, tel. 054/93-2722, 9 A.M.–9 P.M. Mon.–Sat., 3–9 P.M. Sun., $1–5), a hole-in-the-wall serving tacos, burritos, and guacamole and $1 Corona beers. For a more elaborate Mexican menu, try **Tacos y Tequila** (Ugarte 112, tel. 054/49-6249, 9 A.M.–2 A.M. Mon.–Sat., 6 P.M.–midnight Sun., $2), with burritos, tamales, *chile con carne,* tacos, Mexican beer, and margaritas. There is live music on Friday nights.

Health Food

The strictly vegetarian **Lakshmivan** (Jerusalén 402, tel. 054/22-8768, 7 A.M.–10 P.M. daily, $2.50) serves incredibly well-priced, creative dishes in a pleasant garden patio. The menu includes seven different soy meat dishes, vegetarian paella, spinach lasagna, tofu and soy hamburgers, pumpkin soup, and 16 different salads under under $2 (including the hard-to-find Greek salad). This is also the best place around for a healthy breakfast of muesli, yogurt, and homemade bread. The tried-and-true **Govinda** (Santa Catalina 120, tel. 054/28-5540, 7 A.M.–9:30 P.M. daily, $2) has one of its largest restaurants here, a half block from the Plaza de Armas, with both indoor and courtyard seating. The menu is a range of vegetarian, Italian, Hindu, and Peruvian plates. Natural yogurt can be bought by the liter or quaffed in the form of a mango shake along with the $2 lunch menu. A simpler vegetarian restaurant is **Mandala** (Jerusalén 207, no phone, 8:30 A.M.–9:30 P.M., $2), with a $2 menu and pizzas, omelettes, and mango ice cream.

Fine Dining

A trip to Arequipa is not complete without having lunch in one of several *quintas,* or country restaurants, outside of town, with garden seating, huge menus of traditional food, and live music.

One of the best is 🍴 **Tradición Arequipeña** (Dolores 111, tel. 054/42/6467, noon–7 P.M. Sun.–Thurs., noon–8:30 P.M. Fri., noon–midnight Sat., $5–10). The menu includes *adobo,* 11 versions of *camarones* (river shrimps), and a range of *chupes,* or seafood soups. Food is served either indoors under bamboo ceilings or in an outdoor garden of fountains and cactus. There is always a live band playing, including an orchestra on Saturdays at 5 P.M. Also recommended, with a similar menu, is 🍴 **Sol de Mayo** (Jerusalén 207, Yanahuara, tel. 054/25-4148, 11 A.M.–10 P.M. Mon.–Sat., 11 A.M.–6 P.M. Sun., $5–9). Sophistication is taken up a notch here with cloth umbrellas and tablecloths, and seating under stone arches or in the garden. Highly recommended dishes are the *ocopa con queso frito* ($3), *rocoto relleno* ($4), and anything with *camarones.* The service here is excellent, with the waiters literally running from table to table!

Set in a colonial house with *sillar* domes and a hip, modern addition is the romantic **Zig Zag** (Zela 210, tel. 054/20-6020, 6 P.M.–midnight, $4). The house specialities include fondues and alpaca, ostrich, and lamb grilled on a stone slab at your table or served carpaccio style. Its claim to fame is an iron spiral staircase built, they say, by Gustav Eiffel. For a varied menu of Swiss, Arequipeño, and Novo Andino cuisine, try **Grill** (San Francisco 317, tel. 054/20-4294), with cathedral views from its upstairs dining room. Fondue, filet mignon, and sea bass in shrimp sauce are some specialties. Both these restaurants are in the heart of Arequipa's San Francisco–Zela nightlife district.

There is a good produce market on the corner of Catalina and Puente Grau and a better fruit market on the corner of Consuelo and Tomás Álvarez.

INFORMATION AND SERVICES

Tourist Information and Police

The **i Peru** (Portal de la Municipalidad 110, tel. 054/22-1228, 8:30 A.M.–7:30 P.M. daily) tourist information office on the Plaza de Armas is fairly helpful. There is a second **tourist information office** at the airport (tel. 054/44-4564). The **Tourism Police** is at Jerusalén 315

(tel. 054/20-1258). A good new website on Arequipa is www.patiodelekeko.com.

Health Care

For health care, **Clínica Monte Carmelo** (Gómez de la Torre 119, La Victoria, tel. 054/23-1444, 24 hours) is a fully equipped hospital and pharmacy with some of the better doctors in town. **PAZ-Holandesa** (Jorge Chávez 527, tel. 054/20-6720, 24 hours) is another well-equipped medical practice founded by a Dutch neurosurgeon from Rotterdam. It began as a children's hospital that is now seeing tourists and providing dental care as well. A specialized dental clinic in town is **Dental Care San José** (Quiñones B-5, Yanahuara, 9 A.M.–1 P.M. and 4–9 P.M. Mon.–Fri., 9 A.M.–7 P.M. Sat.).

The friendly **Botica Bellido** (Moral 121, tel. 054/21-5551, 7 A.M.–9 P.M. daily) pharmacy has not changed either its location or its name in 150 years. The two largest pharmacies are **Boticas Fasa** on the corner of Mercaders and San-Juan de Dios, and **Inka Farma** on the second block of Mercaderes.

Language Schools

There are many language schools in Arequipa. The **Centro de Intercambio Cultural** (Cercado, Urb. Universiteria, tel. 054/22-1165, ceica@terra .com.pe, www.ceicaperu.com) offers individual lessons for $6/hour or 20 hours of group classes for $90. Course schedules are flexible, and homestays are available for $40/week or $70/week including meals. Contact Carmen Cornejo de Balbuena. **UNSA** (Paucarpata 327, 54/28-6929, info@spanish-peru.com, www.spanish-peru.com/) charges $6/hour for individual lessons or $65 for 25 hours a week of group lessons. It also offers a weeklong crash course of five hours a day with groups of no more than four people.

Inexpensive options include the **Spanish Center** (Raimondi 40, tel. 054/22-4248, cecilft@hotmail.com, $2.50/hr), teaching all levels and offering conversation hours with special workshops on the geography, history, and food of Peru. **Cepesma Idioma's** (La Marina 141, tel. 054/40-5927, cepesma.idiomas@peru.com, www.geocities.com/cepesmaidiomas) multilingual teachers charge $3/hour and **Centro de Idiomas** (San

Agustín 106, tel. 054/24-7524, 8 A.M.–noon Mon.–Fri.) has similar prices.

Banks and Money Exchange

There are many money-change offices around the first block of San Francisco, and most of the banks with ATMS are near the Plaza de Armas, including **Banco Wiese** (Mercaderes 410) and **Banco de Credito** (Jerusalén 125). Money wires can be received at **Western Union** (Santa Catalina 115, 8:30 A.M.–7:30 P.M. Mon.–Sat., 9 A.M.–1 P.M. Sun.).

Communications

Serpost is at Moral 118 (8 A.M.–8 P.M. Mon.–Sat., 9 A.M.–2 P.M. Sun.). The quietest café with the fastest Internet is **CiberMarket** (Santa Catalina 115-B). For late-night Internet, try **Online** (Jerusalén 412, 9 A.M.–midnight). International Internet calls can be made at **Catedral Internet** (Psj. La Catedral 101, tel. 054/22-0622, 8 A.M.–11 P.M. daily) and at the café at Jerusalén 301. In Vallecito, Internet is available at San Martin 222. There are private phone booths at the **Telefonica office** (Santa Catalina 118), and **AQP Comunicaciones** in the Terminal Terrestre offers cheap long-distance telephone calls. **DHL** is located at Santa Catalina 115 (tel. 054/23-4288).

Immigration Office

Tourist visas can be extended at the **Immigration office** (J.L. Bustamente and Rivero, Urb. Quinta Tristan, tel. 054/42-1759, 8 A.M.–1 P.M. Mon.–Sat.).

Laundry

The best laundromat in town is the **Fairy Laundry** (Jerusalén 528, tel. 054/21-8648, 24 hours, $1.50/kilo); it does an expert job in five hours or less. Also good is **Quick Laundry** (Jerusalén 520, tel. 054/20-5503, 7 A.M.–8 P.M. Mon.–Sat., 7 A.M.–1 P.M. Sun., $1.50/kilo) and **Magic Laundry** (Jerusalén 404).

Car Rental

You don't need a four-wheel drive for the bumpy, but beautiful drive to Colca Canyon. Compa-

nies include **Genesis Rent A Car** (Alcides Carrión 701, tel. 054/20-2356, no credit cards), **Avis** (Palacio Viejo 214, 24 hours, tel. 054/28-2519, must be 24 or older), and **CARISA** (Pampita Zevallos 325, Yanahuara, tel. 054/25-5474, carisarent@terra.com).

GETTING THERE

LanPeru (tel. 01/213-8200, www.lanperu.com) flies back and forth several times a day between Lima, Cusco, Juliaca, and Arequipa. El Aeropuerto Rodríguez Ballón (Aviación s/n, tel. 054/44-3464) is 7 km northwest of the city, or about a $3 cab ride. The airline has offices near Arequipa's Plaza de Armas—Santa Catalina 118-C.

A new highway between Arequipa and Juliaca, completed in 2002, transformed what was once a miserable 19-hour journey on potholed roads to a five-hour cruise on perfect pavement. Because more people are traveling between Arequipa and Lake Titicaca/Cusco by bus, passenger trains have been cancelled along the historic line between Juliaca and Arequipa, though cargo cars continue to rumble along the track. PeruRail, who took the line over from state-owned ENAFER in 1999, does, however, have two antique coaches, the *Misty* and the *Ampato,* that can be chartered along this route for large groups.

All long-distance Puno buses leave from two terminals—the rather empty **Terrapuerto** and the bustling **Terminal Terrestre**—right next to each other on Jacinto Ibañez, a five-minute, $1 taxi ride outside of town. Most companies have offices in the Terminal Terrestre that are open from 7 A.M.–9 P.M. As of this time, all the bus trips from Lima are safe to do at night.

Most bus companies make the 14-hour direct trip to Lima overnight, with more economic buses stopping along the way in Nasca and Ica. **Ormeño** (Terrapuerto, tel. 054/42-4187, 6 A.M.–10 P.M.) has $26 direct Royal Class buses leaving at 4 P.M., 6 P.M., and on Sundays only at 10 P.M. The $14 business-class bus, with video and bathroom, leaves at 9:30 P.M., while the $9 economy bus leaves at 7 A.M., 5:30 P.M., and 9:30 P.M.

Lake Titicaca

Laguna Languilayo on the off-road Colca–Cusco route

Cial, also in the Terrapuerto terminal, has Royal Class buses similar to Ormeño's leaving every evening at 5 P.M. and 6:45 P.M., with a $14 bus leaving at 9 P.M. **Cruz del Sur** (Terminal Terrestre, tel. 054/42-7728, www.cruzdelsur.com.pe) has direct, deluxe service at 5:30 P.M. and 7 P.M. with nearly full beds on the first floor for $36 and reclining seats on the second floor for $25. They also have five economic buses per day for $10 each. Other Lima options offered in the Terminal Terrestre include **Tepsa** (tel. 054/23-9188, $7, leaves 4:30 P.M. and 8:45 P.M.), **Transportes Flores** (tel. 054/23-8741, $10–20), and **Enlaces** (tel. 054/43-0333, $18 for economic, $26 for direct, leaves in afternoon.)

Direct buses also leave Arequipa for the five-hour journey to Tacna, Peru's border town with a duty-free port but few tourist attractions besides the heaps of imported, almost-new Toyota station wagons ($3,000 each). From here a $3 half-hour taxi can be taken across the border to Arica, Chile, where most travelers continue south in Chile by bus or by domestic flight. Ormeño buses leaves for Tacna three times a day for $5, and Cruz del Sur offers an $8 Imperial service at 7 A.M. daily. Transportes Flores has buses that head south daily to Moguegue

(3.5 hours, $4), Ilo (five hours, $6), and onto Tacna (six hours, $7).

For the Colca Canyon, **Turismo Milagros** (Terminal Terrestre, tel. 054/42-3260) has buses leaving daily at 4 A.M. and 2:30 P.M. for the three-hour journey to Chivay. The buses wait there a half hour and then continue two hours onto Cabanaconde, arriving at 9:30 A.M. and 8 P.M. The morning bus drops travelers off at the Cruz del Cóndor, about 20 minutes before Cabanaconde. Return buses leave Cabanaconde at 11 A.M. and 10 P.M., and from Chivay at 1:30 A.M. and 2:30 P.M. To travelers looking for the wild overland route to Cusco, **Carhuamayo** (tel. 054/42-6835) has buses leaving for Arequipa that pass by Pampa de Cañaguas, Condorama Dam, Espinar, and Sicuani en route to Cusco, a 10-hour journey through beautiful, rugged highlands. The $8 bus leaves at 7 A.M. and 7:30 P.M. daily.

GETTING AROUND

Though Arequipa is a safe city by Peruvian standards, it is always better to call a taxi rather than flagging one on the street. Recommended companies are **Taxi Tourism** (tel. 054/45-8888) and **Taxi Seguro** (tel. 054/45-0250).

Colca Canyon and Vicinity

Road engineers could hardly believe their eyes when they visited the Colca Canyon in the late 1970s to build the area's first road. Condors cruised through the brilliant blue skies. A river lay thousands of feet below at the bottom of an impenetrable canyon. Potatoes and corn overflowed from thousands of stone terraces. A line of stone-and-adobe villages, each with a small but elegant colonial church, were strung like pearls along the canyon rim. Woman herded alpacas in fantastically embroidered skirts and waistcoats, their hats decorated with bizarre ribbons and sequins.

Even with a spate of new roads and tourist hotels, Colca Canyon is still an odd combination of historical time warp and geological freak of nature. The Collagua and Cabana peoples lived here for at least 2,000 years and, from 800 A.D. onwards, built an ingenious terracing system on the canyon walls that collects snowmelt from nearby volcanoes. Inca Mayta Cápac arrived here with his army in the 15th century and, according to Spanish chronicler Francisco Jerónimo de Oré, sealed the conquest by marrying Mama Tancaray Yacchi, daughter of a local Collagua chief. The Inca built for her a house of copper that, according to legend, was melted to make the gigantic bells that still hang in Coporaque's towers.

The Spaniards, a century after the Incas, were less kind: they herded villagers into *reducciones,* or new settlements, and put them to work in plantations or the nearby Caylloma silver mine. All the while, the Collaguas absorbed Catholic imagery into their festivals. The women even copied the petticoats of the Spanish women, adding their natural indigos and bright blues and their fine, paisley-like embroidery. And then Colca, with neither roads nor communications, was forgotten.

In 1981, shortly after the road was built for the Condorama Dam, a motley crew of six Polish adventurers and local rafter Antonio Vellutino discovered another side of Colca: extreme adventure. In a grueling five-week journey, they navigated the Class V waters of the canyon and confirmed that the Colca Canyon is as deep as 3,400 meters—more than twice as deep as Arizona's Grand Canyon. Since that expedition, Colca Canyon has become, along with Cusco and Huaraz, a center for adventure sports. From Cabanaconde, near the end of the canyon road, climbers begin a trek to climb Ampato, the 6,300-meter volcano where the Juanita mummy was discovered. Numerous other hikes and mountain bike routes lead throughout the canyon and its spectacular villages.

EXPLORING COLCA

The shortest way into Colca is a four-hour journey on bumpy, dusty roads from Arequipa. After the first hour of smooth pavement outside Arequipa, the route veers into a lunar landscape, decorated only with rocks, ichu grass, and the blob-like yareta plant. (The fluorescent green **yareta** appears to be a moss-covered boulder but is actually a plant that lives for centuries but only grows to less than one meter tall. The yareta requires a very specific climate: the dry, desolate tundra over 4,200 meters where even ichu grass struggles to live. The plant survives because of its hundreds of tightly bunched waxy leaves, which trap moisture inside and allow the plant to withstand temperatures down to -50°F.)

This whole area is part of the **Reserva Nacional Salinas y Aguada Blanca,** which is devoid of humans but teems with animals: flamingos, geese, and black-faced Andean gulls congregate at salty lakes, vicuñas graze the grasslands, and rabbit-like *vizcachas* (actually a rodent) dart among the stony fields. The route climbs as high as 4,700 meters, passing the **Sumbay cave** with petroglyphs and a lonely plain called **Patapampa** where the Collagua built hundreds of mysterious stone piles. Then the road drops to **Chivay,** the gateway to Colca Canyon, at 3,650 meters.

From Chivay, there are roads that lead down both sides of the canyon, which gradually becomes deeper and more pronounced as it works its way down from Chivay. The villages on the right (north) side are less visited by tourists but have

Colca Canyon is lined on both sides with ancient terraces still in use today.

nice colonial churches. Starting from Chivay, a dirt road crosses the Río Colca and passes through Coporaque, Ichupampa, and Lari, and dead-ends in Madrigal. Cars can return to the other side of the canyon via a bridge near Coporaque but, apart from that, there are only footbridges. The more often visited side of the canyon is the left (south) side, leading to **Cruz del Cóndor,** where a 60-km dirt road leads from Chivay to Yanque, Achoma, Maca, Pinchollo, and Cabanaconde.

Colca is spread out, and churches keep odd hours, so travelers who want to see a lot of Colca in just two days should consider going with an agency (the one-day tour is simply too exhausting). Unless you are staying in backpacker hostels, the agency deals are usually cheaper anyway. The standard two-day tour, offered by many agencies in Arequipa, varies in price from $35 to $65 depending on the hotel. Apart from lodging, the price usually includes transportation, guide, tourist ticket, and breakfast. The better agencies, such as Giardino and Colonial Tours, have new buses and more informed guides. Groups are often just a few people.

Most two-day tours leave Arequipa and stop to see vicuñas and other archaeological remains in the Reserva Nacional Salinas y Aguada Blanca before exploring the Inca ruins and churches around Chivay. But the highlight is a starlit evening soak in thermal hot springs, either near Chivay or, better yet, at the Colca Lodge. Groups rise early the next morning to drive an hour or two down the canyon to the Cruz del Cóndor. Afterwards, groups visit the churches in Maca, Pinchollo, or Yanque and then head back to Arequipa the same way. Because of road conditions, few agencies are unfortunately taking the longer *Pulpera* return route, which takes a few more hours but passes through the interesting villages of Callali, Sibayo, and Tuti, and the petroglyphs at Mollepunko Cave. Until the road improves, this last route is only recommended for diehard Colca fans with another day to spare.

If you are traveling on your own, it is easy to take a bus to Chivay or Cabanaconde and travel around on foot or by *colectivo*. The National Institute of Culture is now selling a $2 tourist ticket (soon to be $6) to the Cruz del Cóndor and surrounding churches. Proceeds are used for maintenance of the canyon's historical sights, though locals complain that not enough of the money returns to their communities.

Colca's skies are sunny and navy blue from April to October, making a wide-brimmed hat and sunscreen essential. Make sure, too, to bring plenty of warm clothing, as temperatures can get below freezing at nights. If you are not coming from Cusco, stay in Arequipa for a few days to avoid *soroche,* or altitude sickness, at the 4,700-meter pass during the drive in. Chivay itself is at 3,652 meters (11,970 feet—higher than Cusco).

CHIVAY

The village of Chivay, at 3,652 meters, lies at the junction where the main road to Arequipa meets the Colca Canyon. It is the traditional base for exploring Colca Canyon, though it has become a bit rundown and touristy in recent years. Many backpackers are now heading to Cabanaconde, closer to the Cruz del Cóndor, or to excellent new lodges near Coporaque or Yanque. Chivay has the best-equipped clinic (and the only one with a laboratory), the only Internet in all of Colca—and it's the police and mountain rescue headquarters.

Sights

Chivay has an interesting 18th-century church, **Nuestra Señora de la Asunción,** and a bridge with Inca foundations right outside of town that once supported a hanging bridge made of plant fibers. Immediately on the other side of the bridge is the Inca road to Cusco, marked by a path leading up stone grain stores. On the hillside above are several round Inca storehouses.

Chivay's main draw, however, are the **thermal baths** (4:30 A.M.–7 P.M., $3 for foreigners) that lie 2 km outside of town. There are five hot pools, including two new ones designed for tourists. The first is an outdoor pool at river's edge and the second is round and enclosed with a domed ceiling. Both are clean and kept at a temperature of 40°C, though they can become quite packed with travelers during the evenings. The best hot baths in the area—in all of Peru

for that matter—are the riverside tubs at **Colca Lodge.** They are a half-hour drive away ($5–10 for roundtrip taxi) and are the same price.

The 17th-century **San Sebastián** church in **Pinchollo,** 27 km west of Chivay, is another church worth visiting, with a baroque altar and a baptistry with elaborately painted entrance.

Accommodations

The best choice in town for those on a budget is the friendly **La Casa de Lucila** (Grau 131, tel. 054/53-1109, $7 s, $14 d, including continental breakfast), with very clean, comfortable, carpeted rooms and hot showers. Another option, near the market, is **Colca Wasi Kolping** (Siglo XX s/n, tel. 054/53-1076, $10 s, $20 d). The **Colca Inn** (Salaverry 307, tel. 054/53-1088, reservas@hotelcolcainn.com, www.hotelcolcainn.com, $25 s, $35 d, including breakfast) is a good midrange choice with large, comfortable rooms with great beds and writing tables. The bathrooms and carpet are in need of an update, but the tradeoff is that the attached bar downstairs has a pool table. **Casa Andina** (Huayna Cápac s/n, tel. 054/53-1020, ventas@casa-andina.com, www.casa-andina.com, $48 s, $58 d, including buffet breakfast), part of a well-run national chain, is a charming complex of 30-odd bungalows with stone walls and thatch roofs. The rooms are tastefully decorated, with nice bathrooms and comfortable beds with down comforters and heaters. The large dining room serves buffet dinners with a nightly folkloric show. A better option, because of its location, is the picturesque **Pozo del Cielo** (Apurímac 113, tel. 054/53-1041, reservas@pozodelcielo.com.pe, www.pozodelcielo.com.pe, $40 s, $50 d, including breakfast). The hotel is right across the Inca bridge from Chivay, perched up on a bluff that is an easy walk to the nearby Inca ruins. The lodge is laid out like a small stone and adobe village, with rooms of whitewashed walls, exposed beams, and excellent canyon views. The cozy dining room has a wood stove and serves typical Andean food.

Food

There are a few pizzerias of dubious quality on the

main square. **Lobo's Bar Pizzeria** (Plaza de Armas 101, tel. 054/53-1081, 9 A.M.–10 P.M., $4) is the trendiest of the group, with hip music, pizzas from a wood-fired oven, and three drinks for $3 at happy hour, 6–10 P.M. The locals' favorite lunch spot is the clean and well-run **Yavari** (Plaza de Armas, tel. 054/80-3351, 7 A.M.–9 P.M., $3), serving spit-roasted chicken or a delicious daily $3 menu with lots of options. Also on the Plaza de Armas is **El Balcón de Don Lacarias** (22 de Agosto 102, tel. 054/53-1108, 10 A.M.–3 P.M. and 6–11 P.M. daily, $5), serving a lunch and dinner buffet mainly to tourist groups. The third-floor mountain views make up for an otherwise drab interior. The buffet spread includes vegetarian, international, and Andean food. Cocktails are well priced and a peña starts most nights at 7:30 P.M. Three blocks beyond the plaza is **Calamarcitos** (José Gálvez 232, tel. 054/53-1102, 11 A.M.–4 P.M. and 7:30–10 P.M. daily, $4), which has vegetarian options, a range of local food, and even alpaca and ostrich. There is a nightly peña show and a large patio for outdoor seating. For dinner, **El Nido** (Zarumilla 216, tel. 054/53-1010, 6–11 P.M., $6) is probably the classiest choice in town. It serves alpaca seven different ways and have a good wine list and intriguing cocktails such as El Inca Rabioso (The Pissed-Off Inca), a concoction of maté de coca and pisco. It also has a nightly peña at 8 P.M.

For drinks try **McElroy's Irish Bar** (General Moran, Plaza de Armas, 6 P.M.–midnight), with a pool table, Guinness, and a menu that includes pizzas. Chivay's best peña, for hearing local music and seeing a variety of local dances, is **Yllalkuy** (22 de Agosto 330, tel. 054/80-3353, 9 A.M.–11 P.M. daily, $6). This odd sunken chamber is in need of a good scrubbing and, like most peñas, is best known for its drinks and dancing—not its food. The dances start at 8 P.M. most evenings, but call or stop by ahead of time to confirm.

Information and Services

The office of Colca's main **Tourism Police** (tel. 054/48-8623, 24 hours) and mountain rescue are on the main plaza. There is a 24-hour **health center** (Puente Inca s/n, tel. 054/53-1074), and the best pharmacy is **Cueva y Yllañez**, one block

above the plaza. There is a **Banco de la Nación** on the plaza, but no ATM. The post office, **Serpost**, is also on the plaza.

Getting There and Around

Chivay's new bus station, with good bathrooms and snack shops, is a five-minute walk on the outskirts of town. **Empresa de Transportes Reyna** (tel. 054/53-1090) has $4 buses leaving for Arequipa in the afternoon at 12:30, 3, and 4:30 P.M. With the last two buses, it is also possible to disembark at Pampa de Cañahuas and board an evening bus headed for Cusco. **Turismo Milagros** (tel. 054/53-1115) also has $4 buses for Arequipa, leaving at 12:30 A.M. and 2:30 P.M.

Once in Chivay, *colectivos* for the thermal baths leave when full from the main square ($0.15, 15 minutes)—or a taxi costs $0.75. *Colectivos* also leave from the main square for the Cruz del Cóndor ($15 round trip); a private taxi for up to four people is $30. From Chivay, *colectivos* also leave frequently for villages on both sides of the canyon.

YANQUE

Yanque, 10 km west of Chivay, is a simple town with dirt streets and a baroque church, **Inmaculada Concepción**, which was rebuilt in 1702 and has a mestizo facade carved with various saints, including Santa Rosa de Lima. From the east side of the Plaza de Armas, a path leads about 1 km to an ancient stone bridge over the Río Colca. From the bridge, the adobe walls of Inca hanging tombs are perched on the cliff face. Those with energy and four hours of daylight can cross the Colca and climb up to the ruins at **Uyu Uyu**, above Coporaque, where the Collagua lived before the Spanish forced them to settle in present-day Coporaque. Return by walking over the car bridge just downstream of Yanque, where there are public hot springs (4 A.M.–7 P.M., $0.50). A better hot tub option is nearby Colca Lodge.

Accommodations

There are a handful of backpacker hostels but the best is the basic and clean **Hospedaje Don Manuel** (Ampato, two blocks from plaza, $5 pp). Though a bit isolated on the road at the outskirts

Lake Titicaca

Lake Titicaca

The Río Colca, like Cusco's Urubamba, has different names per section. Up high it's the Colca, then the Majes, and finally the Camaná—but it all dumps into the Pacific Ocean. On its way to the ocean, the Colca slices past several volcanoes, including Ampato (6,380 m) and Mismi (5,597 m). But not all of the rain and snow that falls on Mismi ends up in the Colca. Some of it collects in two lakes on the north side, which are often frozen and shrouded in fog. After months of studying aerial photographs and making precise measures, a National Geographic expedition tromped up to these lonely lakes in 1975 and declared them the official source of the Amazon. Incredibly, water from these lakes drains into a small stream that eventually, after hundreds of kilometers, ends up in Cusco's Río Urubamba. So depending on its position, a snowflake that falls on Mismi's summit can either have a brief but bumpy 75 km trip to the Pacific Ocean—or it can have a meandering journey of more than 7,000 km, passing first through endless stretches of high-altitude desert, then down the Sacred Valley and past Machu Picchu and into brown rivers that laze their way to Brazil.

of town, **Tradicion Colca** (Colca s/n, tel. 054/42-4926, www.geocities.com/tradicioncolca, $40 s, $48 d) has a charming feel, with comfortable rooms with large beds in a stone building with thatched roof and a fireplace sitting area. **El Mirador de los Collaguas** (0tel. 01/242-9984 in Lima, miradorcollaguas@infonegocio.net.pe, www.miradordeloscollaguas.com, $55 s, $65 d) is four blocks from Yanque's square and has views over the canyon. Owned by the Vellutino family, this thatched lodge is built of adobe and stone and has nice carpeted rooms with bay windows and lofts. There is a plan in the works to build a spring-fed hot tub on the property.

The most charming lodge in all of Colca Canyon is **N El Parador del Colca** (Curiña s/n, tel. 084/24-1777, colca@peruorientexpress.com, www.peruorientexpress.com.pe, $70 s, $70 d, including buffet breakast), which was built by Colca pioneer Mauricio de Romaña but recently bought by Orient-Express Hotels Ltd. This hotel, perched on a secluded bench above the Río Colca, is a rustic country lodge with touches of elegance in spectacular natural surroundings. The rooms have tile floors, stone doorways, sculpted adobe walls, dark wooden lofts, and private porches with outdoor fireplaces. Meals are served in a tiny but elegant cellar or outside on a stone patio overlooking the canyon.

But the best part of El Parador is the surrounding gardens. An unimaginable range of organic vegetables, spices, and fruits are grown here, from arugula and rhubarb chard to gooseberries and Andean squash. Guinea pigs, geese, trout, and rabbits are also raised here organically and listed on the kitchen's home-style menu. Travelers in need of relaxation could easily spend a few days here, walking through the gardens, sipping Colca Sours (made from the fruit of the Sancayo cactus), or reading books and playing games in the cozy loft above the dining room. César Torres, surely one of the friendliest and most professional hotel managers in Peru, can help arrange transport and other logistics for passengers traveling independently. Orient-Express, which owns top-rate hotels such as Cusco's Monasterio and the Machu Picchu Sanctuary Lodge, is holding off on promoting El Parador until it is renovated into a five-star health spa in 2005—with luck the upgrade will not ruin the charm.

MACA AND THE CHOQUETICO STONE

Maca, 23 km west of Chivay, was nearly destroyed by repeated eruptions of nearby Volcano Sabancaya in the late 1980s and a devastating earthquake in 2001. The village's charming church, Santa Ana, is damaged but still standing. The church has a facade decorated with miniature false pillars, carved flowers, and a curious balcony that was used by missionaries to preach and present images to the native populace. On the way outside of town, the Choquetico Stone is a carved scale model of nearly 10,000 hectares of Collagua terracing in the Colca Canyon. Like the similar Saywite Rock near Abancay, this rock was perhaps used for prophetic or rainmaking rituals, perhaps in conjunction with *chicha* or llama blood. On the surrounding hills are a series of ancient *colcas,* adobe-and-stone granaries for which the canyon is named. On the road outside of town there is a large, charmless compound of thatched bungalows known as **Pachamarka Real** (22 km west of Chivay, tel. 054/20-6565, pacamankareal@terra.com, $45 s, $60 d).

Ν LA CRUZ DEL CÓNDOR

Colca's main draw, the condor lookout, has become touristy beyond belief and teems most mornings with trinket vendors and tour buses. Still this spot, perched 360 meters above the Colca Canyon and about 60 km (1.5 hours) from Chivay, commands a spectacular view over the canyon and is, hands down, the best spot in

the world to see the Andean condor. This enormous vulture, with a silver collar and a wingspan of nearly 3.3 meters (11 feet), zooms past the lookout nearly every morning—usually around 8 A.M., again at 10 A.M., and sometimes in the later afternoon as well. At least a pair, but sometimes as many as a dozen, show up nearly every morning during the non-rainy months between April and December, though fewer show up during the September–October mating season. The birds sleep on the canyon walls at night and, after the sun heats the air, ride thermals up into the sky until they are nearly out of sight. Further up the road there is the less mobbed Tapay lookout, where condors fly but less frequently. Any bus headed to Cabanaconde will let travelers out at either of these spots.

CABANACONDE

Cabanaconde, at 3,287 meters and 65 km west of Chivay, is the last of the five villages strung out along the southern edge of the Colca Canyon. The road doesn't end here, but it does become rougher and heads away from the canyon, which becomes much deeper and more serpentine from this point onwards (buses do, however, travel the 12 hours to Arequipa along this road). Cabanaconde is a great place to stay because it is quiet, has a few inexpensive hostels, is only 15 minutes from the Cruz del Cóndor, and is the best launching point for a variety of adventures. The town's church, **San Pedro Alcántara,** was rebuilt after a 1784 earthquake and has sun, moon, and stars carved onto an imposing stone front.

Accommodations

There are two good hostels in Cabanaconde with double rooms under $10. The best-known is **Valle del Fuego** (Grau, one block from plaza, tel. 054/28-0367), which is basic and clean with solar-powered showers. The owner, Pablo Junco, is a great source of information, and he also operates the recommended and inexpensive restaurant Ranch del Sol. The other place is **La Posada del Conde** (San Pedro and Bolognesi, tel. 054/44-0197, pdelconde@yahoo.com), with private bathrooms. The nicest and most upscale place to stay in

THE SACRED CONDOR

Watching Andean condor *(Vultur gryphus)* soar over Colca Canyon, it is easy to see why the Incas and other highland peoples considered it a sacred bird. It flies for hours without flapping its wings using only thermals to spiral so high into the sky that it can disappear from sight. The Andean condor is the largest flying bird in the world, with a weight of more than 10 kg and a wingspan of over 3 meters. But apart from its size, the condor is easy to spot because of the white ruff around its neck, the finger-like feathers at the end of its wings, and a wide band of white at the top of its wings. Juvenile condors are a solid, soot-brown color and take about four years to reach adult plumage. Though the condor's habitat extends from the Venezuelan Andes to Tierra del Fuego in Chile, most of the world's condors are concentrated in Chile, Bolivia, and Peru. The condor's main food source is carrion, which it is able to detect thousands of feet up in the air because of its extraordinary eyesight and sense of smell.

Lake Titicaca

Cabanaconde is **Kuntur Wassi** (Cruz Blanca s/n, tel. 054/28-0212, reservaciones@kunturwassi.com, www.kunturwassi.com, $25 s, $35 d, $6 dorm, including continental breakfast). This friendly and well-run hotel, which opened in 2003 and is one block uphill from the plaza, has adobe-and-stone rooms (that are built around boulders) and nice bathrooms. The bathtubs feel great after a long walk out of the canyon. The restaurant here, open from 7 A.M.–10 P.M., is recommended.

Getting There and Around

From Arequipa, **Turismo Milagros** (Terminal Terrestre, tel. 054/42-3260) buses leave daily at 4 A.M. and 2:30 P.M. for the three-hour journey to Chivay. The buses then wait a half hour in Chivay and continue two hours on to Cabanaconde, arriving at 9:30 A.M. and 8 P.M. The morning buses from Chivay to Cabanaconde drop travelers off at the Cruz del Cóndor, about 20 minutes before Cabanaconde. Buses leave Cabanaconde for Arequipa at 11 A.M. and 10 P.M. Buses for Arequipa leave from Chivay at 1:30 A.M. and 2:30 P.M. For more information on buses see the section on Chivay.

COPORAQUE

Across the river from Chivay and about 8 km west is the tiny village of Coporaque. There are no services here, and the only phone in the area is the plaza's pay phone (the two hotels listed below have radios only). Coporaque's church, **Santiago Apóstol,** was built in 1569 and is the oldest in the valley. Its square bell towers and false balconies seems almost medieval and contain the bells said to be melted from Mama Yacchi's house. Inside there is a fascinating and primitive altar and a variety of 16th-century images. Around the corner is the interesting facade of **La Capilla de San Sebastián**. Coporaque is building a hot springs similar to those at Chivay, but no word yet on completion date.

Accommodations and Food

Some of the best food in Colca Canyon is cooked at **La Casa de Mama Yacchi** (tel. 054/24-1206 in Arequipa, reservas@lacasademamayacchi.com, www.lacasademamayacchi.com). This hotel, small and intimate, is walking distance from Coporaque's main square and is a great base for day hikes around the Colca Canyon. The whitewashed rooms are comfortable and clean, with plenty of hot water and great valley views. The hotel is exceptionally well run and the kitchen churns out a variety of fresh salads, well-cooked meat dishes, and homemade sauces—the $5 lunch buffet is an excellent value. An unlikely staff member is Juanita, the pet llama who waits for guests at the front door.

Colca Lodge (tel. 054/20-2587 in Arequipa, info@golca-lodge.com., www.colca-lodge .com, $53 s, $60 d, including buffet breakfast) has the distinct advantage of being the only place in Colca—and in all of Peru except Hotel Laguna Seca in Cajamarca—to have world-class thermal baths. The hotel, owned by Grupo Inca, has a fabulous riverside location and even hands out trout fishing poles and floatable duckies for guests who want to play in the river, which is a short stroll through fields of corn and quinoa. The rooms feature wood floors, lofts, and excellent river views, and there are suites with fireplaces and family cottages as well. The food is excellent, and even the buffet breakfast includes local sausages, Andean and Edam cheeses, boiled quinoa, granola, and a variety of fruits. There is a lounge with fireplace and a cozy bar, and the hotel can arrange horseback and walking rides to the ruins of Uyu Uyu, the Inca bridge and Yanque. But the best part is down a stone trail, where boiling hot springs bubble into stone pools and steam into the cool river air. At night, with an inky-black sky full of stars, the setting is magical. Nonguests can use the baths, open 24 hours a day, for a mere $3—or free for those who buy the $7 lunch buffet.

ENTERTAINMENT AND EVENTS

Outside of the peñas in Chivay, evenings in the Colca Canyon are spent enjoying hot tubs. Colca, like Huancayo and the shores of Lake Titicaca, has a well-deserved reputation for beautiful festivals. **La Virgen de Candelaria** is celebrated in Chivay, Acoma, and Maca on Feb. 2–3. Both

Carnival, in late February, and **Easter Week**, in April, are lively in Colca. **La Fiesta de San Juan** is celebrated in Yanque and several other Colca towns on June 13.

The celebration of the **Virgen del Carmen** around July 16 is a huge event in Cabanaconde and Chivay, along with that of **Santiago Apóstol** in Coporaque and Madrigal on July 25. An interesting eight-day festival takes place in Chivay from Aug. 15 on, in honor of the town's patron saint, **La Virgen de la Asunción**, with simultaneous celebrations taking place in Coporaque, Maca, and Yanque.

Yanque's **Spring Festival** takes place on Sept. 23. **La Fiesta de la Virgen del Rosario** takes place Oct. 7 in Chivay, Achoma, Ichupampa, Maca, and Yanque. **Todos Santos** (All Saints' Day) **y Los Fieles Difuntos** (All Souls' Day) take place throughout Colca Canyon on Nov. 1–2. The final big event is a celebration for **La Virgen Imaculada** in Chivay and Yanque, during which time the five-day Wititi dance is performed. The Wititi is also performed in Yanque from Dec. 25 onwards.

SPORTS AND RECREATION

Those who enjoy hiking in Arizona's Grand Canyon will love Colca Canyon, which has the added beauty of volcanoes and untouched villages. Information on rafting, biking, climbing, and trekking is given in the *Arequipa* section, above. Here is specific information on trekking routes.

A popular short trek drops 1,200 meters down into Colca Canyon from the village of Cabanaconde to Sangalle, a riverside oasis where three campgrounds with pools have sprung up since 2000. Their names—Paradise, Oasis, and Eden—play off the same themes and are easy to confuse. Sangalle, which feels subtropical even when Chivay is chilly, is a great place to read books and lounge by the pool. But don't expect any cross-cultural encounters. You can camp for a few dollars a night ($2 pp) or rent cane huts ($3 pp) with rickety beds, and they also sell beer ($2.50 for a big bottle) and food—but it's probably safer to bring a stove and do your own cooking. As they are close to one another, check out each campsite before you choose. Give your organic trash to the campsite manager, but pack out cans, glass, and plastic—a look at the riverbanks will show the area's trash management problems. Hiking down takes two or three hours but returning to Cabanaconde, which most people do the second day, can take twice as long.

A longer, more interesting, option is to cross a footbridge at Sangalle and hike up the other side of the Colca Canyon to the charming village of Tapay. Another path leads from here back to a good camping spot further upstream on the Río Colca. From here the path winds uphill, approximately 1,200 meters, to the Cruz del Cóndor. This trip could be done in two or three days, though getting to the Cruz del Cóndor by 8 A.M. would mean breaking camp by 4 A.M.

Other interesting treks involve hiking along the canyon rim between various towns. Despite what your maps say, there are ancient Collagua paths connecting most villages together. Because most of the tourists travel along the Cruz del Cóndor side, the best trekking is on the north side of the

© RENÉE DEL GAUDIO AND ROSS WEHNER

sub-tropical Sangalle, at the bottom of Colca Canyon

canyon—though it is easy to cross back and forth at the bridges near Maca and Yangue. Colca is a safe and easy place to improvise a route, as long as you have a few liters of water, a bit of Spanish, and a wide-brimmed hat.

A truly adventurous four- or five-day route leads from Cabanaconde to the Valley of the Volcanoes and retraces the steps of Robert Shippee and George Johnson, who flew over and mapped the entire area in 1929. They were so intrigued by the Valley of the Volcanoes that they forged out from Cabanaconde to find it. Their route drops west (downstream) into the Colca Canyon and then back up the other side to the village of Choco, at 2,473 meters. After camping here, hike up and over a 4,500-meter pass and then on to the village of Chacas, 3,100 meters. A road, with sparse traffic, leads from here to Andagua, at the head of the Valley of the Volcanoes, one day's hike away.

COTAHUASI CANYON

Cotahuasi Canyon, the deepest in the world at 3,354 meters, is more rugged than Colca to the south and was overlooked by the Spanish, who built few churches here. The Incas, however, built a highway along much of the canyon for transporting dried fish from Puerto Inca on the coast all the way to Cusco. Today the ruins of these roads, and other precarious paths, connect several villages perched above the river that grow citrus fruits on thousand-year-old terraces.

The main town is Cotahuasi, which is a 12-hour bus ride from Arequipa at 2,680 meters. There are a few simple places to eat, sleep, and buy groceries here. The best is **Alojamiento Chavez** (Cabildo 125, tel. 054/21-0222), with a pleasant courtyard and an owner who is friendly and knows the walking routes well.

The road continues up the canyon to the villages of Tomepampa, Lucha, and Alca, the end-of-the-road town with the recommended Hostal Alcala (no phone). One good trek heads down the canyon from Cotahuasi along a path that crosses the river several times and leads, after a few hours, to the village of **Sipia**. Nearby is the thunderous 60-meter-high Cataratas de Sipia. Trekkers

can continue downstream to more isolated villages and ruins—and, with enough time, all the way to the Pacific, as the Incas did. A variety of agencies in Arequipa, such as Colonial Tours, offer four-day treks to these areas for around $120, including transport. Arequipa-based Cusipata and other Cusco-based rafting agencies lead eight-day trips down the Cotahuasi Canyon downstream of here.

Buses for Cotahuasi leave around 5 P.M. from Arequipa's bus terminal (12 hours, $9) and arrive at dawn. Return buses to Arequipa also leave Cotahuasi daily around 5 P.M. Travel this spectacular route during the day if at all possible. The road passes over a 4,650-meter pass between Coropuna (6,425 m) and Solimana (6,093 m) before dropping into Cotahuasi.

VALLEY OF THE VOLCANOES

Partway along the Arequipa–Cotahuasi Canyon route, the road branches off for Andagua, a small village at the head of the Valley of the Volcanoes. The small valley, sandwiched between Colca and Cotahuasi and only 65 km long, is a bizarre and seemingly endless lava field, lorded over by the snow-capped Coropuna and Escribano and punctuated by more than 80 perfect volcanic cones, some only 24 meters high. In the middle of it all is a lake and the gentle Río Andagua, which runs underground through much of the valley. Few people travel here, and those who trek along this valley need to carry a tremendous amount of water. A few days' trek away from Andagua, the valley leads to Lago Mamacocha, near the Village of Ayo. There is also an adventurous five-day route through Chacas to Cabanaconde in Colca Canyon, which retraces the 1929 route of Shippee and Johnson. Andagua-bound buses leave several times a week from Arequipa's bus station.

For those with a four-wheel-drive vehicle, a fascinating circuit connects Cotahuasi and Andagua and then heads to the Colca Canyon via Cailloma. Apart from Chivay, there is probably no gasoline along this route and not even the best maps are completely accurate, but the scenery is legendary.

The Amazon

If there were an international poll on what image comes to mind when people think of Peru, a sweeping panorama of Machu Picchu would surely win. Running second would be a highland *campesino* in a broad, colorfully woven dress and, in distant third, the white hat and poncho of a rider atop a coastal *paso* horse. Fewer people would think of an Amazon native paddling down a river in a dugout canoe, or a flock of scarlet macaws flying over rainforest.

Surprisingly, nearly two-thirds of Peru is jungle, and there are few places in the world where the Amazon Basin is as accessible, biodiverse, and comfortable as it is in Peru. In as little as three hours after boarding a flight in Lima or Cusco, travelers can be boating down a chocolate-brown river with the jungle rising on both sides like a canyon of green. Guaranteed animals to see, on nearly any jungle trip, are monkeys, pig-sized aquatic rodents known as capybara, alligator-like caimans, pirañas, and hundreds of kinds of birds. Large mammals, like anteaters and jaguars and tapirs, require at least a day's travel into more remote areas, and even then are a long bet. Seeing these animals through all the greenness of the rainforest is a serious challenge, but being on a river or lake with good binoculars and an experienced guide greatly increases the odds.

First-time jungle visitors usually worry about suffocating heat, malaria, mosquitoes, and a host of other discomforts. But Peru's Amazon is surprisingly cool, requiring a light jacket at nights,

Must-Sees

M **Strange animal sighting:** Whether it's the giant otter (page 192), the pink river dolphin (page 205), the taricaya turtle (page 197), the prehistoric hoatzin (page 182), or the German shepherd–sized capybara rodent (page 202), you are likely to encounter something odd.

M **World's best birding:** The Amazon attracts serious birders hoping to catch a glimpse of a laughing falcon or yellow-ridged toucan. But you won't even need binoculars to witness dozens of brightly colored macaws, parrots, and parakeets—they swarm about clay licks, or *collpas,* early each morning (page 186).

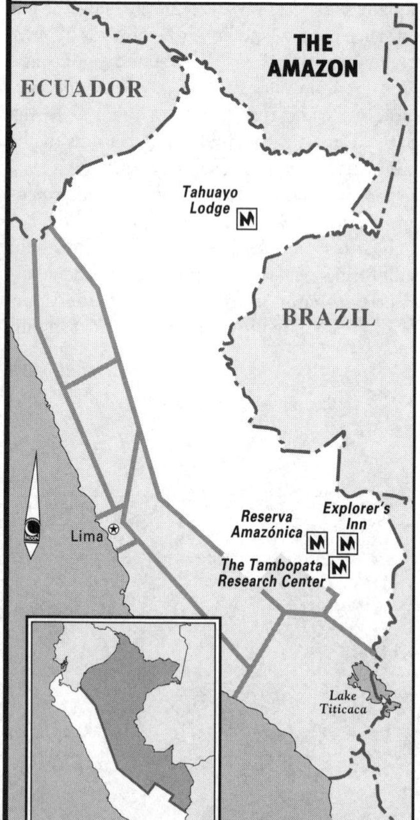

M **Fishing for piraña:** Dunk a hook and a piece of meat into even the most recommended swimming hole and you are likely to feel the aggressive tug of a palm-sized, knife-toothed piraña (page 189).

M **Nighttime caiman search:** It's simple: Shine your flashlight along the shores of the river until you see two red dots, which are the eyes of the alligator-like caiman lying in the mud and wondering if you could be dinner (page 198).

M **Canopy walk:** Getting high into the canopy, whether by ladder or ropes, is the only way to understand that most everything in the jungle happens a hundred feet off the ground (page 210).

The Best Amazon Lodges

M **Explorer's Inn:** With a comfortable, worn-in feel, the oldest eco-lodge in Puerto Maldonado offers the best combination of convenience, price, and biodiverse rainforest (page 184).

M **The Tambopata Research Center:** Located on the Rio Tambopata, this is the only lodge near the Parque Nacional Bahuaja Sonene. It's also just 500 meters away from the world's largest macaw clay lick (page 185).

M **Reserva Amazónica:** This most luxurious, and most romantic, lodge in the Peruvian Amazon is on the Río Madre de Dios (page 188).

M **Tahuayo Lodge:** The most acclaimed lodge of Peru's Northern Amazon offers access to the extraordinary Reserva Nacional Tamshiyacu Tahuayo, the habitat of the rare red uakari monkey (page 213).

The Amazon

THE AMAZON

ECUADOR

BRAZIL

Tahuayo Lodge **M**

Lima

Reserva Amazónica **M** Explorer's Inn **M**

The Tambopata Research Center **M**

Lake Titicaca

PACIFIC OCEAN

CHILE

and most of it is malaria-free (most travelers choose to take malaria pills anyway, however). The mosquito issue can be solved by wearing long clothing and a head net, especially in the evenings. With the new generation of well-out-fitted eco-lodges, the experience of visiting Peru's Amazon can also be very comfortable. There are dozens of well-run lodges that operate in Peru's Amazon ranging, from stylish bungalows with electricity, hot water, and tile floors to simple wood rooms with cold water and a mosquito net over the bed.

Most of the lodges are clustered around Iquitos in the north and around Cusco further south—though there are important differences between these areas. The lodges arrange all transport and often use a combination of converted four-wheel-drive trucks and huge canoes rigged with shade canopies and powerful outboard motors. Food is included in the package prices and tends to be a simple and nutritious combination of beans, rice, fish, and local foods such as manioc root or heart of palm. Common features of most lodge programs include early-morning bird-watching, a visit to an oxbow lake and/or macaw clay lick, day hikes through the forest, piraña fishing, and evening boat rides to spot caiman. Some lodges also have canopy walks or observation towers, which is an exhilarating way to see birds and the jungle canopy up close. A visit to a shaman for a talk about medicinal plants, or to a local farm, can be an added bonus to a jungle trip—though some village visits around Iquitos are awkward, staged affairs. A key component of any jungle trip is a knowledgeable, English-speaking guide, whose job is to spot wildlife and introduce the extraordinary web of connections among plants, trees, animals, and insects.

Peru's Amazon, though under siege from oil and gas drilling and illegal logging, continues to host the world's greatest biodiversity—1,700 species of birds, thousands of trees, millions of (mostly undocumented) insects, and rare, endangered mega fauna like the black caiman, giant otter, pink river dolphin, and harpy eagle. Humans have been part of the web of life for at least a thousand years, and small pockets of isolated, *no-contact* groups continue to live in areas of the Manu Biosphere Reserve and the Lower Urubamba Basin. Other native cultures, such as the Piro, Machiguenga, and Esa Eja near Cusco, the Ashininka near Chanchamayo, and the Yaguas, Cocamas, and Huitotos near Iquitos are now running lodges, hosting village visits, and marketing their crafts.

Tourism does bring change, but there is little doubt that responsible eco-tourism is immensely better for the Amazon than the more traditional industries of gold mining, illegal hardwood logging, bush meat hunting, and exotic animal commerce. The integration of native peoples into Peru's eco-tourism is a positive and necessary development that has come about largely because of win-win deals struck between lodges and native communities. The communities agree to stop hunting and cutting down trees and, in exchange, the lodge uses the land and provides funding for health care and education. Some lodges share profits or transfer ownership back to the community after a certain number of years. The net result of all this wheeling and dealing is that peoples' minds are turning to conservation and more and more rainforest is being preserved. By visiting, you are helping to preserve the Amazon as well.

PLANNING YOUR TIME

Where you go in Peru's Amazon largely depends on how much money and time you have, and also what time of the year you are traveling. If you only have three to five days, and a few hundred dollars, look into lodges around **Puerto Maldonado** or **Iquitos.** If you have a week or more, and a bigger budget, go to **Manu Biosphere Reserve,** the crown jewel of the Amazon. There are exceptions to this rule, however. There are world-class lodges with Manu-like levels of wildlife outside of Iquitos and Puerto Maldonado, places that normally take up to seven hours to reach by boat. The best time to visit Peru's jungle is during the dry months from May through October, though Iquitos can be visited year-round.

To figure out where to go, it helps to understand Peru's different jungle zones. The jet stream in the southern hemisphere moves west, not east as in the northern hemisphere, so Amazon humidity

COLOMBIA

ECUADOR

BRAZIL

Río Putumayo

Rio Napo

Río

Rio Pastaza

Andoas

Anatico

Tambo

Río Marañón

Río Mayo

Moyobamba

Yurimaguas

Lamas

Tarapoto

Sauce

Bellavista

Juanjui

Pampa Hermosa

Contamana

Orellana

Río Huallaga

Santa Cruz

Lagunas

Concordia

Marañón

Río Samiria

Río Pacaya

Reserva Nacional Pacaya-Samiria

Río

Rio Tigre

Miraflores

Nauta

Santa Elena

Nueva Alejandria

Requena

Río Tahuayo

Reserva Comunal Tamshiyacu-Tahuayo

★ TAHUAYO LODGE

Iquitos

Mazán

Francisco de Orellana

Amazon River

Pebas

Pijuayal

Chambira

Caballococha

Leticia

Tabatinga

THE AMAZON

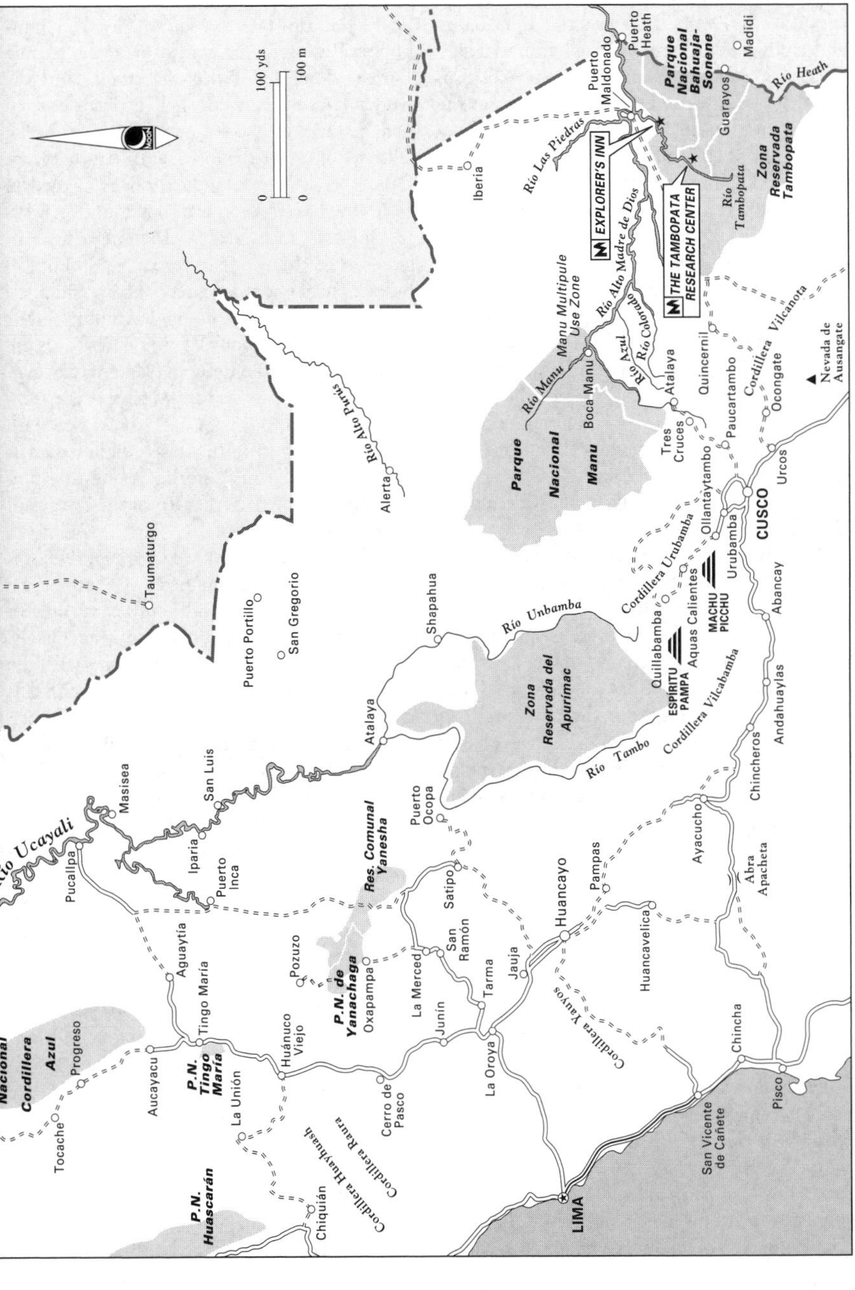

Map labels:

100 yds
100 m

Puerto Heath
Parque Nacional Bahuaja-Sonene
Madidi
Rio Heath
Puerto Maldonado
Guarayos
Zona Reservada Tambopata
EXPLORER'S INN
Rio Las Piedras
Iberia
Rio Alto Madre de Dios
Rio Tambopata
THE TAMBOPATA RESEARCH CENTER
Rio Azul
Rio Colorado
Atalaya
Quincemil
Cordillera Vilcanota
Nevada de Ausangate
Manu Multiple Use Zone
Rio Manu
Boca Manu
Quincemil
Paucartambo
Ocongate
Urcos
Parque Nacional Manu
Tres Cruces
Alerta
Rio Alto Purús
Taumaturgo
Puerto Portillo
San Gregorio
Shapahua
Rio Urubamba
Cordillera Urubamba
Ollantaytambo
Urubamba
CUSCO
Abancay
Zona Reservada del Apurímac
Quillabamba
ESPIRITU PAMPA
Aguas Calientes
MACHU PICCHU
Cordillera Vilcabamba
Rio Tambo
Andahuaylas
Chincheros
Ayacucho
Abancay
Atalaya
San Luis
Masisea
Iparia
Puerto Inca
Rio Ucayali
Pucallpa
Aguaytia
Res. Comunal Yanesha
Puerto Ocopa
Satipo
San Ramón
La Merced
Pampas
Huancayo
Huancavelica
P.N. de Yanachaga
Oxapampa
Pozuzo
Junín
Tarma
Jauja
La Oroya
Abra Apacheta
Chincha
Tingo María
P.N. Tingo María
Huánuco Viejo
Cerro de Pasco
Cordillera Raura
Cordillera Huayhuash
Chiquián
La Unión
P.N. Huascarán
Cordillera Azul
P.N. Cordillera Azul
Progreso
Aucayacu
Tocache
San Vicente de Cañete
Cordillera Yauyos
Pisco
LIMA

The Amazon

© AVALON TRAVEL PUBLISHING, INC.

cools and condenses as it is forced over the eastern edge of Peru's Andes. This gives rise to the damp and chilly cloud forests perched around 1,500 meters elevation on the mountain slopes. This is the preferred habitat of the **Andean cock of the rock,** a crimson, chicken-shaped bird, as well as a huge range of colorful orchids, bromeliads, epiphytes, and hummingbirds. Peru's most accessible cloud forests are around Tarapoto and the drive into Manu Biosphere Reserve.

Lower down into the jungle, clear mountain streams cascade through steep mountain forests. Eventually the crystalline streams give way to broader, progressively muddier rivers that weave in serpentine shapes through the increasingly flat landscape and leave stranded oxbow lakes behind. This type of lowland rainforest occurs in Manu and Puerto Maldonado but reaches its greatest expression all the way downriver near Iquitos—here, the Amazon is a mile wide and the forest is perfectly flat.

The **Manu Biosphere Reserve,** which ranges in elevation from 4,100 to 5,000 meters, is one of the most pristine swaths of Peruvian Amazon and is the best place in Peru to see a wide range of birds, monkeys, and mammals. The best time to visit here is during the dry season from May to October, though only sporadic rains occur in November and December. During the coldest and sunniest months of May and June, as many as 30 percent of Manu visitors see jaguars sunning on river logs (as opposed to 10 percent during the rest of the year). There are only eight licensed tour operators in Manu, which charge between $600 and $2,000 for five- to nine-day tours ranging from beach camping to comfortable lodges. The Manu, like Puerto Maldonado, is in Peru's southern jungle and is easily reached from Cusco.

The advantage of the lodges around **Puerto Maldonado,** downriver from Manu Biosphere Reserve, are cost and access: travelers arrive at lodges within a few hours of flying from Cusco, and a two-night stay costs anywhere from $60 to $200. This area, on the edge of the **Reserva Nacional Tambopata,** has a good variety of monkeys, birds, caiman, and small mammals. Like Manu, the best time to visit here is May–October. There are levels of wildlife comparable to Manu

at the Tambopata Research Center, a seven-hour boat ride from Puerto Maldonado. The Tambopata Research Center is next to the remote **Parque Nacional Bahuaja Sonene** and the world's largest macaw clay lick, which is covered with macaws, parakeets, and parrots year-round. The city of **Iquitos,** in Peru's northern Amazon, forged Peru's tourism industry back in the late 1970s but has grown so large that tourists have to go a long ways these days to find interesting jungle—at least four hours by boat, or 80 km (50 miles). There is a wide variety of cost, and quality, in the Iquitos area. If you don't mind traveling a bit longer, some of Peru's best lodges are upriver and near the **Reserva Nacional Pacaya-Samiria,** Peru's largest protected piece of Amazon. Like the Manu, this park has oxbow lakes with world-class opportunities to see wildlife such as giant otter and tapir. Another interesting preserve in the area is the **Reserva Comunal Tamshiyacu-Tahuayo.**

Unlike Manu or Puerto Maldonado, Iquitos is just as fun to visit during the rainy season. Even in April, the wettest month, rains come only in the afternoons and then clear up immediately. Although the weather is relatively constant, the level of the river is anything but. When rain falls in the Andes between November and May, much of the jungle surrounding Iquitos is flooded. Animals can most often be spotted on the mud banks after the river drops, between June and September. The cost of Iquitos lodges range from $15 to $150 per night, depending on the distance from Iquitos.

There are other access points to Peruvian jungle, including **Chanchamayho,** in Peru's central jungle, and **Tarapoto,** which is upriver from Iquitos. There are few operators in these areas, however, so travelers need to choose carefully, and an ability to speak Spanish is a definite advantage. Other areas, such as **Pucallpa** or **Apurimac,** are not covered in this book because they are near centers of cocaine production and have limited tourist infrastructure.

Lodges in this book are recommended based on the following criteria. First, we looked at each lodge's environmental ethic, sustainable design, and the relationships forged with surrounding communities. Second, we tried to sort out which lodges have greater amounts of wildlife and less disturbed forest. Third, we evaluated food and lodging. And fourth, we recommend lodges that are fully licensed and work with professional guides, who are essential for spotting wildlife and getting a basic sense of how the rainforest works. A good guide should give the English and scientific name for all birds, talk about a wide range of trees and medicinal plants, and boil down the complexity of symbiotic relationships and rainforest ecology.

Avoid private guides, who will often promise trips down remote rivers for an unbelievably low price. We have heard of at least one case of a supposed guide in Iquitos who robbed his clients at gunpoint and left them stranded on a riverbank. But more common experiences include mediocre food, faulty equipment, and unfulfilled promises. If you must, use only private guides that come recommended from a trusted source. A better option is to use the agencies recommended in this book, which are professional, safe, and, in some cases, quite affordable.

Packing for the Jungle

Yes, there are biting insects in the jungle, so bring plenty of repellent (20 percent+ DEET). The best defense, however, is to cover the body with light, drip-dry clothing and, for the evenings, a mosquito head net. Apart from two or three pairs of long pants and shirts, other items include T-shirts, lots of socks, swimsuit, one pair of shorts, sweater or fleece for chilly evenings, hiking or rubber boots, tennis shoes, rain suit or poncho, toiletries, sunglasses, sunscreen, binoculars, headlamp, water bottle, photocopy of passport, camera, and plenty of film. Most agencies require that you keep your luggage to a minimum because of tight space on the planes and boats.

HISTORY

Of the 68 officially recognized ethnic groups in Peru, 65 of them live in the Amazon Basin. Still, it is largely a mystery as to when, and exactly how, human civilization fanned out through the waterways of the Amazon. The **Incas** were re-

spectful of the difficulties of Amazon travel, as well as the archery skills of its inhabitants. Inca Pachacútec built the fortress of Pisac, near Cusco, to guard against attacks from Antisuyo, the eastern corner of the empire dominated by the Anti, a now-vanished jungle people from the Madre de Dios area. From Pisac, an Inca road led to Paucartambo and onto coca plantations maintained by the Incas in the high jungle at Pilcopata (this is still the main route to reach the Manu Biosphere Reserve). Inca Garcilaso de la Vega, a mestizo chronicler of the 16th century, records the legend that it was also Pachacútec who attempted to conquer the **Río Madre de Dios,** reaching perhaps as far as the Bolivian border. There are Inca ruins in **Manu Biosphere Reserve,** though none that have been found so far are very large.

Apart from Pilcopata, the Incas conquered other jungle fringe areas, including present-day **Chachapoyas** and **Moyobamba,** in some of the more difficult campaigns they waged. The Incas clearly used jungle archers as an important part of their army, as the Spanish learned the hard way at the battle of Ollantaytambo. Even before the Incas, trade routes were established from the jungle to the coast to export exotic woods, monkeys, parrots, jaguar pelts, otter grease, cacao, natural dyes, medicinal plants, and even turtle oil for lamps.

The Spanish were much less respectful of the jungle and paid a heavy cost in their search for fabled gold cities. One of the first expeditions was led by Pedro de Anzures in 1538, soon after the Spaniards' arrival in Peru. He ventured into the Madre de Dios jungle near Cusco but his army was quickly decimated by disease and poison arrows. The death tally was 143 Spanish, as many as 4,000 Quechuan-speaking Indians, and 100 horses.

Based on news of a gold-rich kingdom east of Quito, Ecuador, known as El Dorado, Gonzalo Pizarro ordered his brother, Francisco, to undertake an exploratory expedition the following year in Peru's northern jungle that would rival the conquest itself in audacity. **Francisco Pizarro** left Cusco in 1539, followed the Inca highway to Quito, and then spent months marching through jungle until arriving at a navigable stretch of the Río Napo. On the banks of the river they built a ship and, after two months of hunger and tropical fevers, found an Indian tribe that told them of a river with huge riches. Pizarro sent **Francisco de Orellano** further downstream to find food and materials to repair the ship but Orellano—for reasons that have never been fully explained—kept going. Orellano met a series of tribes along the way until, on Feb. 12, 1542, he arrived at the junction of the Napo and the Amazon, just downriver from present-day **Iquitos.**

Pizarro meanwhile came searching for Orellano but found only Hernan Sánchez, a Spaniard who opposed Orellano's decision to continue downstream and was left abandoned on the banks of the Napo. Pizarro returned to Cusco, retracing his journey up the Napo and back over the Andes. By that time, Orellana was long gone: floating downstream on the muddy waters of the Amazon, the lush canopy of the jungle moving by in an epic odyssey of more than 2,000 miles before reaching the Atlantic Ocean. Orellana sailed up the coast of Brazil to the Caribbean and then to Spain, where he told King Charles V of the things he had seen. Orellana's report of vast uncivilized territory triggered what is perhaps the largest missionary effort ever. Long after Spanish conquistadores had given up their search of gold in the Amazon, Jesuit and Franciscan missionaries hacked their way down into nearly all of the Amazon's important tributaries. The cities of Cajamarca, Moyobamba, Huancayo, and Cusco were important bases for these evangelical missions.

The expulsion of the **Jesuits** from Latin America in 1767 left not only an intellectual abyss but also large tracts of the Amazon nearly abandoned. At one point, much of what is now the Peruvian Amazon was attached to the Viceroyalty of Santa Fe (present-day Argentina). But because access to the Amazon is easiest from Peru, a royal dictate of 1802 transferred much of the Amazon basin to the Viceroyalty of Peru—without this document, signed on the eve of the independence movement, Peru would have far less Amazon territory than it does today. Even so, pieces of Peru's Amazon have been chipped away by Brazilian settlers and slave

traders in the 18th century, a Columbian border dispute in the 1920s, and an Ecuadorian border war in the mid-1990s.

A big chapter in Amazon development came in 1839, when **Charles Goodyear** mixed sulphur with rubber to create an elastic, durable substance that could be fused into objects for real use. Suddenly the gooey, white latex from the rubber tree, known as *caucho,* became a valuable commodity. First Brazil, and later Peru, became the center of the **rubber boom** that began in 1880 and peaked in the years before World War I. The rubber boom caused a massive immigration to Iquitos, which exploded in size and suddenly became the richest city in Latin America. The city boasted the Iron House designed by **Gustav Eiffel,** and elaborate mansions decorated with tiles imported from Seville. There are tales, probably true, of families who sent their laundry to Paris, and rubber barons who ordered entire shipments of beaver top hats, discarding hundreds into the river before finding the one perfect fit. This was also a time of abysmal slavery, and the Indians who were forced to collect *caucho* in the forest were some of the most abused, wretched workers in Peru's history. Enslaved by debt, malnourished, and diseased, *caucho* workers often faced the choice of perishing or attempting an escape through the jungle.

For the most part, the rubber boom was centered in the Iquitos area though an extravagant entrepreneur named **Fermín Fitzcarrald** successfully extended it to Peru's more remote southern Amazon. Fitzcarrald—the subject of Werner Herzog's 1982 movie *Fitcarraldo*—discovered an isthmus linking what he thought was the headwaters of the Ucayali and the Purus Rivers. Using a force of a thousand Indians, Fitzcarrald dragged an entire steamship up and over a 500-meter ridge. Although Fitzcarrald's plan did not work, the city of Puerto Maldonado in Peru's southern Amazon did swell with an immigration of Indian, mestizo, and even Japanese immigrants. The *caucho* industry in Peru's southern jungle took off after the construction of a road from the Río Tambopata to the coast in 1903, boosting production from 12,569 kilos in 1902 to 293,212 kilos in 1909. But the rubber boom collapsed in 1912 as rapidly as it had begun. Dutch and English plantations in Malaysia began producing *caucho* at a far cheaper cost, thanks to a railroad network and orderly rows of trees, where collecting latex was far easier than among the wild trees of the Amazon forest.

After the collapse of *caucho* prices, a former rubber magnate discovered oil on the Amazon river in the 1920s. Engineers from international oil companies were among the first outsiders, along with Mormon missionaries, to explore many remote headwaters of the Amazon. Huge pipeline projects such as the **North Peruvian Oil Pipeline,** completed in 1996, and the **Camisea Pipeline,** currently under construc-tion, have brought foreign revenue to Peru but have also affected huge areas of virgin Amazon. Whenever a large pipe has to be filled with fossil fuel, a network of roads, platforms, testing paths, helicopter pads, and pumping stations springs up in front of it. Besides the thousands of people who come to work on the project, the new roads are used by colonists and poachers in search of il-legal game or timber. The other principal indus-tries of the Amazon basin include gold mining, lumber, exportation of exotic animals, cocaine, and fishing. **Chanchamayo** and **Tarapoto,** on the fringe of the Amazon, export fruit and other agriculture but struggle against the high cost of transport on jungle roads.

Manu Biosphere Reserve

Sprawling across the eastern slope of the Andes, this chunk of wilderness is one of the most bio-diverse corners of the planet. Roughly the size of New Hampshire, the park begins at high-alti-tude grasslands at 4,100 meters, drops through cloud forest and mountainous rainforest, and then fans across a huge swath of rainforest at around 350 meters. There are 13 species of mon-keys here (more than anywhere else in the coun-try), 15,000 plants, 1,300 butterflies, and more than a million insects that have not been even close to documented. In May and June, the be-ginning of the colder and dry season, the odds in-crease of seeing jaguars, which come out to sun themselves on river logs. From August to No-vember, near the end of the dry season, macaws, parrots, and parakeets are especially abundant around the riverside clay licks. Other frequently seen mega fauna include giant otter, black caiman, tapirs, armadillos, anteaters, sloths, wild pigs, and the endangered harpy eagle. If that was not enough, Manu is one of world's top birding spots, with more than 1,000 confirmed species—almost 15 percent of the world's total!

The **Parque Nacional Manu** was created in 1973, but the area was deemed so biodiverse that UNESCO incorporated the whole sur-rounding area into a biosphere in 1977. Then Manu won the ultimate accolade when the In-ternational Union for the Conservation of Na-ture declared it a **World Heritage Site,** one of only 200 in the world.

These days the biosphere is classified into sev-eral areas. The section along the Río Alto Madre de Dios is the Multiple Use Zone (commonly referred to as the **Cultural Zone**), where there are a few villages and a variety of eco-lodges. The more pristine section up the Río Manu is the Parque Nacional Manu, to which access is strictly controlled. To enter the area, travelers must be with one of Manu's eight licensed operators who have built comfortable safari camps (and one lodge) alongside oxbow lakes. The lower part of the Río Manu, formerly known as the Reserved Zone, is used for sustainable eco-tourism and research.

The vast majority of the 1.5-million-hectare Parque Nacional Manu is closed off to everyone but licensed biologists and anthropologists. This chunk of rainforest shelters at least two ethnic groups who have had almost no contact with western civilization, the Kogapacori and the Mashco Piro. Other groups have only limited contact with the modern world.

Only eight companies are allowed to operate in Parque Nacional Manu. They offer trips from five to 10 days that range from $500 for camping to $2,000 for more comfortable, high-end tours

The Amazon

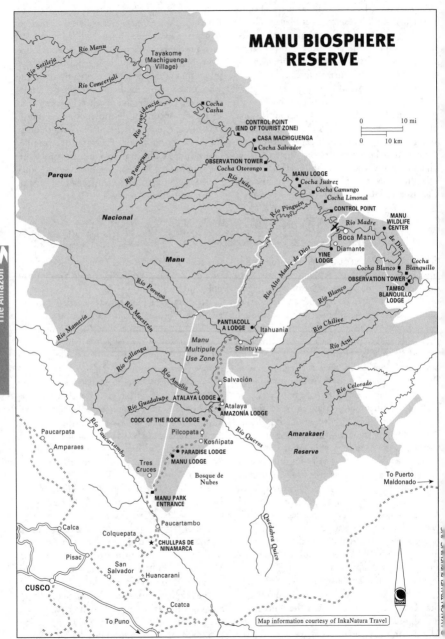

MANU BIOSPHERE RESERVE

Rio Sotileja

Rio Manu

Tayakome (Machiguenga Village)

Rio Comeerjali

Rio Providencia

Cocha Cashu

0   10 mi

0   10 km

CONTROL POINT (END OF TOURIST ZONE)

CASA MACHIGUENGA

Cocha Salvador

Rio Panagua

OBSERVATION TOWER
Cocha Otorongo

MANU LODGE
Cocha Juárez

Parque

Rio Juárez

Cocha Camungo

Cocha Limonal

Rio Pinguén

CONTROL POINT

MANU WILDLIFE CENTER

Nacional

Rio Madre

Boca Manu

Manu

Diamante

YINE LODGE

Cocha Blanco

Cocha Blanquillo

Rio Porotoa

Rio Alto Madre de Dios

OBSERVATION TOWER

TAMBO BLANQUILLO LODGE

Rio Maestrón

Rio Blanco

Rio Mameria

Rio Chilive

Rio Azul

PANTIACOLLA LODGE

Itahuania

Rio Callanga

Manu Multipule Use Zone

Shintuya

Rio Colorado

Rio Amalia

Salvación

Rio Guadalupe

ATALAYA LODGE

Atalaya

AMAZONÍA LODGE

COCK OF THE ROCK LODGE

Pilcopata

Rio Queros

Amarakaeri

Rio Paucartambo

Paucarpata

Amparaes

Kosñipata

PARADISE LODGE

Reserve

MANU LODGE

Tres Cruces

Bosque de Nubes

To Puerto Maldonado

MANU PARK ENTRANCE

Calca

Paucartambo

Quebrada Quico

Colquepata

CHULLPAS DE NINAMARCA

Pisac

San Salvador

Huancarani

CUSCO

Ccatca

To Puno

Map information courtesy of InkaNatura Travel

Jaguar are occasionally spotted sunning on riverside logs in the Manu Biosphere Reserve.

The Amazon

that include lodges with cotton sheets, electricity, and hot water. Some of the agencies are offering new adventure options, from rafting and trekking to extreme mountain biking and even llama-cart touring.

One of the best parts of Manu is getting there and dropping through the dizzying sequence of ecosystems along the way. The first day is spent driving seven hours through the *altiplano* near Cusco to one of a handful of new lodges, perched in the cloud forest and surrounded with orchids, hummingbirds, butterflies, and the crimson cock of the rock. Visitors descend to the lower jungle that same morning and take a several-hour boat ride down the Río Alto Madre de Dios.

The small town of **Boca Manu** and a small airport known as the **Aerodrome** lie at the junction of the Madre de Dios and Manu Rivers. There are two lodges here, but the highlight for most people is heading up the slow-moving Río Manu into the park itself, where guests commonly stay in safari camps and spend their days exploring oxbow lakes with floating platforms and spotting scopes.

The return to Cusco has been complicated by unreliable plane service from Boca Manu, a bumpy grass strip from which light aircraft return to Cusco in a mere half hour. Air taxi companies suspended flights after the Aerodrome was deemed unsafe in late 2003. The landing strip has since undergone some maintenance, and small planes are once again flying into the area. Because pilots fly into here entirely by sight, the flights can be cancelled because of rain or ground mist.

To avoid the potential complications of flying and to reduce costs, some operators are backtracking all the way up the Río Madre de Dios to return to Cusco by road. Other agencies are continuing down the Río Madre de Dios to the gold rush town of Colorado, which is an eight-hour drive to Puerto Maldonado's airport. Either of these overland options is a grueling one-day combination of boats and trucks. A shorter option, offered by the Manu Wildlife Center, is a trip further down the Río Madre de Dios with a 75-horsepower outboard to Laberinto and then on to Puerto Maldonado via car. This latter option can take as little as eight hours.

A WEEK IN THE LIFE OF MANU

The Manu has become one of the finest spots in the world in which to observe wildlife. Today you don't have to sit, as in the good old days, in a damp, slow canoe and camp on a sandbank. Instead you sit in airline comfort in a built-up, roofed dugout with a 55 or 75 hp Evinrude, humming you and eight or so others up or down the swirling Río Alto Madre de Dios and the more torpid but equally exciting Río Manu. The guide will call out "Snowy egret at 10 o'clock, that big branch between us and the beach," or "Capybara family, mum, dad, and three kids in that muddy bit up ahead on the right." After a day or two of this, including expeditions into the forest, you begin to get the idea: you are in a zoo without bars. A fresh jaguar's paw-mark or a troop of army ants becomes a personal experience. Q: Who are howler monkeys howling at? A: Other howler monkeys, to warn them off their turf.

A trip to the Manu will start typically in one of two ways. You either catch a small plane from Cusco airport and in half an hour you're at the airstrip in Boca Manu within another half-hour's trip of a lodge. Or you catch a specially constructed bus to take you on a seven-hour trip across the highland and down into the cloud forest.

Most Manu visitors choose the latter—not only because it is less expensive, but because the journey itself offers a good introduction to the amazing, profuse world of the Western Amazon jungles and the complexities of its interrelated worlds of weather, insects, plants, birds, and mammals. The journey begins in the barren, pea-green plains outside of Cusco and crests at Acanaju Pass at 3,800 meters (12,500 ft.) elevation. From here the road plunges 3,100 meters (10,300 ft.) to the jungle below, passing a series of climates that make the western slope of the Andes some of the most biodiverse terrain on the planet.

The first night is spent in a simple but comfortable lodge in the damp cloud forest at 1,500 meters. You rise before five o'clock, with the raucous sounds of the forest around, and walk along a path to a bird blind. As daylight filters into the forest, several hen-shaped, deep crimson birds appear in the foliage, bobbing up and down as part of their elaborate and bizarre courtship. This is the rare Andean cock of the rock, an almost guaranteed sight in Manu's cloud forest.

Later in the morning you arrive at Atalaya, a muddy, riverside village where you and your travel companions clamber into your main transport for the next week or so—a 10-meter, outboard-powered dugout where from a comfy seat you watch the jun-

---

Apart from the eight operators listed here, many other Cusco agencies sell Manu trips. Some of these agencies simply *endorse* their clients over to a licensed Manu operator at an additional cost. Others only take passengers through the Cultural Zone of the park, which is cheaper because there is no $45 park fee and less gas is used. You will have better guides, see more wildlife, and be more comfortable if you stick with one of the eight operators listed below, who also offer budget options. It is not recommended to visit Manu on your own or with a private guide. Boat traffic is highly sporadic and, without one of the licensed agencies, the rangers absolutely will not allow you into the Parque Nacional Manu.

The best time to visit Manu is during the dry season from May to October, though rains only become unbearably heavy during January and

February. Considering how hard Manu is to reach, it does not make sense to go for less than six days—except for those who fly in and out of Boca Manu and choose to bypass the cloud forest.

MANU AGENCIES AND LODGES

All the prices quoted below are all-inclusive, covering food, lodging, $45 park entrance, and airfare between Cusco and Boca Manu.

Manu Nature Tours

Manu Nature Tours (Pardo 1046, Cusco, tel. 084/25-2721, info@manuperu.com, www.manuperu.com, $1,725 for six-day trip) has the most comfortable and expensive trips and the only lodge inside the Parque Nacional Manu (except for the rustic Casa Machiguenga at the Cocha

gle slide by as your guide calls out the names of different birds. Among the dozens we saw was a laughing falcon winging across the river with a snake twisting in its claws. Before nightfall you are at Boca Manu and at a simple wooden lodge with a cold beer and supper before a cooling shower and bed. You are now around 350 meters above sea level and 2,500 miles from the mouth of the Amazon.

The next several days consist of a fascinatingly agreeable sequence of simple but comfortable eating and sleeping, sitting in the canoe or, most frequent of all, walking along simple paths in the forest. We were up early one morning—indeed, every morning—to walk through the forest to an oxbow lake, where a platform floated atop a couple of dugouts. Locals paddled us gently away from shore until we reached the hunting grounds of an extended family of giant otters. The mother had just caught a fine fish, must have been two feet long, but refused for some reason to share it with her three hungry cubs who kicked up an almighty fuss demanding their breakfast as they played in a complex of logs with older members of the family.

Every day would have these dramatically pleasant encounters. An anteater—covered in fleas, poor thing—saunters across the path a couple of yards in front and climbs steadily up into the canopy. An emperor tamarin monkey is suddenly just a few feet above and ahead looking us steadily in the eye—and then suddenly it's not there anymore.

Over the next week we climbed up to observation platforms and sat spellbound in floating blinds watching macaws at a massive cliffside lick, where they came to eat bits of mud to counter the toxins in most Amazonian leaves, one of many hundreds of examples of the complexities of staying alive in the jungle. Everything, we discovered, had its uses and defenses. A leaf would have enough poison to defend itself from being instantly ravaged by insects. A butterfly enough camouflage to confuse an enemy but not enough to be missed by a potential mate. This kind of thing, repeated in an endless sequence of encounters with everything from tapirs to monkey, tiny frogs to great alligators, gave us—myself, my wife, and a couple of early-teen children—food for thought and conversation as we walked throughout the forest, sat in the dugout, or relaxed listening to the throaty sounds of the jungle, the sounds that are worth, just in themselves, coming to the jungle.

(Contributed by Nicholas Asheshov, a British journalist who has covered Peru for four decades. Asheshov heads the Planning Division of the Incaland Hotel and the Sacred Valley Railway, in Urubamba.)

Salvador). The company was launched in 1985 by Boris Gomez with funding from American biologist Charlie Munn, who has been a key force behind preservation of the Manu and other rainforests. It was voted the best Manu operator by Peru's Ministry of Tourism in 2002 and 2003.

The company was the first to build a lodge in the cloud forest, and all the other Manu agencies followed suit. **The Manu Cloud Forest Lodge** is a magnificent thatched structure with a glass atrium and view over a whitewater creek. Guests can try a half- or one-day **rafting trip** down two rivers in the area, the Kosñipata and Tono, which are Class III or IV depending on the season.

In 1987 Manu Nature Tours also built the first lodge inside the Parque Nacional Manu. **Manu Lodge** is built of salvaged mahogany next to a lake where guests can see black caiman, brown capuchin, and giant otters. For the more adventurous, there is a tented camp at Lago Salvador and a 30-meter-high treehouse, which guests can either climb up to or be pulled to by pulley.

Manu Nature Tours' latest innovation is the **Llama Taxi** project with the Jajahuana community, in the high grasslands on the way to Manu. For the moment, guests take a 15-minute ride on a cart pulled by a llama, after which the villagers explain their medicinal plants, weaving, and natural dyes. The goal is to empower the Jajahuana people over the next several years to lead their own treks from the grasslands into the edge of the Manu rainforest.

In addition Manu Nature Trips also offers **trekking** and **mountain biking trips** from the grasslands into the Manu, a brain-spinning descent of thousands of feet through the cloud forest.

The Amazon

Manu Expeditions

Manu Expeditions (Pardo 895, Cusco, tel. 084/22-6671, adventure@manuexpeditions.com, www.manuexpeditions.com, manuwildlifecenter.com, $1,235 for six-day trip) is run by English ornithologist Barry Walker and has a solid reputation for high-quality tours and world-class bird guides. On their way to Manu, guests first stay at the **Cock of the Rock Lodge,** a wood building in the cloud forest with cozy, simple rooms lit by candles and kerosene lamps. Once in the rainforest, guests typically stay nights at Madre de Dios lodge near Boca Manu and the company's own safari camp near Cocha Salvador in the Parque Nacional Manu. Some trips also stay at the Casa Machiguenga Lodge on the Cocha Salvador.

Manu Expeditions also sends guests to the **Manu Wildlife Center** (www.manuwildlifecenter.com), which it owns along with Peru Verde, a nonprofit Peruvian conservation group. The 44-bed wooden lodge is 90 minutes downriver from Boca Manu in a section of rainforest adjacent to the Manu Biosphere Reserve. There are 35 km of trails through mature forest, two 35-meter-tall canopy platforms, and oxbow lakes with giant otters and floating observation platforms. A natural salt lick near the lodge offers the best chances in Manu for seeing the tapir, a 250-kg cousin of the hippopotamus. Because tapirs mainly forage at night, guests camp out overnight in a comfortable nearby blind, which is outfitted with mosquito netting, snacks, and mattresses. The lodge is also 20 minutes from Manu's largest macaw lick. The cost of a nine-day Manu trip, which includes the center, is $1,595. Or guests can fly in and out of Boca Manu for four days at the center only for $940.

Barry personally leads private birding tours to Manu and all over Peru and Bolivia, which are described in a home page (www.birdinginperu.com). An 18-day odyssey around the Marañon Valley, including Chiclayo, JaÉn, Bagua Chica, Abra Patricia, and Celendín, costs $3,800.

Manu Expeditions also leads excellent **trekking** and **horse trips** all over the Cusco area, including innovative journeys to Machu Picchu and even to the lost Inca city of Choquequirao. No previous riding experience is necessary, and an effort is made to find routes off the beaten path—there is even one trip each year in search of genuine lost cities. Prices range from $1,566 for eight days to $3,500 for two weeks.

InkaNatura

The other high-end Manu operator is InkaNatura Travel (in Lima tel. 01/440-0022, www.postmaster@inkanatura.com.pe, www.inkanatura.com, $1,190 for six-day trip), which is one of Peru's leading eco-operators, with programs in Chachapoyas, Puerto Maldonado, and the jungle around Quillabamba as well.

InkaNatura is the profit-making arm of the Peru Verde conservation organization that owns Manu Wildlife Center. It offers a four-day trip to a tented camp at Cocha Salvador, with a round-trip flight between Cusco and Boca Manu and an optional two-day extension to the Manu Wildlife Center.

InkaNatura is also involved with an innovative community-based lodge on the other side of the Manu Biosphere Reserve in the lower Urubamba Basin. **The Machiguenga Center** is reached via a 50-minute flight from Cusco to a landing strip at Timpia, which is downstream from the jungle city of Quillabamba. Another option for getting there is a 10-hour bus ride to Quillabamba and another three hours to Kiteni on the Río Urubamba. From here a boat is taken downstream to Timpia.

The lodge is owned and operated by a local Machiguenga community and includes ten screened rooms, flush toilets, and hot-water showers. There are 125 Machiguenga families in Timpia and they cooperate in showing guests the biodiverse jungle in the area, which includes a half-dozen clay licks and a chance to see a wide range of wildlife. Only one hour down the Río Urubamba is the famous Pongo de Mainique, a two-mile-long whitewater gorge that is festooned with orchids and swarming with military macaws. For a group of four people the cost is $200 pp for five nights, not including transportation. This is a wonderful opportunity to get off the beaten path and get a good sense of how people live in the Amazon.

InkaNatura is represented in the United States

by Tropical Nature Travel (in the U.S. 877/827-8350, www.tropicalnaturetravel.com).

Pantiacolla Tours

Pantiacolla Tours (Plateros 360, Cusco, tel. 084/23-8323, pantiac@terra.com.pe, www.pantiacolla.com, $850 for seven-day trip) was started in 1991 by conservationist Gustavo Moscoso, who was born in Boca Manu, and his wife, biologist Marianne van Vlaardingen.

Pantiacolla offer a series of highly recommended camping trips into Parque Nacional Manu, which are broken up with stays in rustic lodges. Pantiacolla operates a wooden lodge with shared bunkrooms in the cloud forest and a similarly rustic tented camp near Cocha Salvador.

The couple has recently launched the nearby **Yine Project,** one of Peru's more successful community-based tourism efforts. Working with the Yine Indians in the community of Diamante, Pantiacolla has built an attractive and rustic wooden lodge that is four hours' walk from Diamante. Guests spend time with villagers, participate in traditional art workshops, and learn how to canoe with the expert Yine boatsmen. Far from the staged village visits offered by Iquitos lodges, the Yine Project projects a realistic view of a people who are caught between their traditional ways and the encroachments of modern society. Pantiacolla also offers seven-day trips ($815) and nine-day trips ($785), with an option to visit the large macaw clay lick downriver from Boca Manu.

Caiman Tours

Caiman Tours (Plateros 359, Cusco, tel. 084/25-4042 or cell 084/965-0879, explorcaiman@terra.com.pe, www.manucaiman.com, $850 for six-day trip) is run by Manu pioneer Hugo Pepper and is best known for custom-designed, creative adventure trips in and around the Manu. Hugo took the first tourists to the Manu, in the early 1980s; they camped on beaches and boiled water from the river.

Caiman is famous for its five-day Cusco-Manu **mountain biking trips,** which pass through Pisac and include a 3,100-meter descent from Tres Cruces, which overlooks the Amazon, to the edge of the Río Madre de Dios at Atalaya. These trips include a cook and a support vehicle that follows the bikers.

Upon request, Hugo can dream up an extraordinary range of Manu adventures. A recent brainstorm, covered by *Outside* magazine, included a two-day hike from Salvacíon, on the banks of Río Madre de Dios, over the jungle into the headwaters of the remote Río Chilive. From here, a crew of expert native guides helped the adventurers assemble a flotilla of **balsa wood rafts,** held together with hardwood nails and tethered with bark fiber. The descent of the river ended up taking only eight days, thanks to a series of storms that dramatically quickened the river current! After reaching the Río Manu, the crew took a *peke-peke* boat to the gold-mining town of Colorado and a truck onward to Puerto Maldonado. Hugo is planning on offering these trips in the future, which can easily be combined with a night's stay at the Tambo Blanquillo lodge and a visit to the large macaw clay lick.

Hugo has not lost sight of the original Manu experience—his most successful ventures are rugged camping trips throughout the Manu. Before venturing into the wild, however, groups stay at the brand-new and highly comfortable **Manu Paradise Lodge** (reserv@manuparadise.com, www.manuparadiselodge.com). The lodge has screened rooms, spring beds, full bathrooms, a gorgeous dining area and a rooftop library with views over the jungle. Once in Manu's Reserved Zone, Caiman's groups stay at a safari camp on Cocha Salvador.

Other Budget Agencies

There are three other budget operators to Manu that can be booked at the last minute, often at sharply discounted prices, for travelers who don't mind waiting in Cusco for a few days. The prices quoted below include trips into the Parque Nacional Manu but not airfare, and they can often be combined with Inca Trail trips at very little additional cost.

Manu Ecological Adventures (Plateros 356, Cusco, tel. 084/26-1640, www.cbc.org.pe/manu, $650 for eight-day trip) has worked in Manu for nearly two decades and leads the greatest

The Amazon

MANU'S GIPSY MOTH BIPLANE

Abel Muñiz's hacienda in the jungles of the lower Cosñipata Valley, near Pilcopata on the road to Manu Park, has been stitched together over the past six or seven centuries. Today the buildings are a homey mixture of wood, clapboard, stone, cement, palm thatch, and corrugated iron.

He's just putting in two more balconied rooms for tourists and has already added a nice stone-sided, sand-floored swimming pool. "We check it every morning. We've only had a snake in it once so far," says Grete, Muñiz's wife.

The hacienda features the same sounds and smells as farmyards the world over—ducks, sheep, cows, horses, pigs, chickens, geese, dogs, cats, mice, bats. In addition, the pets include a small caiman, four tapirs, river tortoises, an armadillo family, monkeys, macaws, and parrots.

A pack of women and children swirls vaguely around the kitchen patio. The warm air is sliced by a thousand full-color and full-throated tropical birds. The distant rush of water over a set of rapids in the Río Tono is a gray-noise background to the scritch and hum of a million insects and amphibians.

Today Muñiz, a portly 60-year-old agronomist who tells a good story, is a director of a European Union program aimed at keeping poachers and loggers out of the Manu Park by encouraging tourism and agriculture around the edges as a kind of *cordon sanitaire.* The borders of the Park, one of the world's great wildlife reservations, are just a few miles upriver.

Muñiz says that the farm, Villa Carmen, belonged to Isabel Chimpuoccllo, a daughter of Inca Huayna Capac and the mother of Garcilaso de la Vega, the most famous of the post-Conquest chroniclers.

Farms in the jungle in those days, as they frequently still do, produced coca that, then as now, was a big money-spinner. On the dirt road that joins this charming, isolated valley with the sierras of Cusco, our family pickup was stopped twice, once by a small truck whose driver asked us politely if we'd seen the drugs authorities and who looked relieved when we said no, and later by the drugs authorities themselves, in an unmarked truck, who were equally polite but who rightly wasted no time on us.

Muñiz keeps cows, has some ponds of carp, and takes tourists up the Río Piñipiñi, the lowest reaches of which flow through his property after running down a section of the Pantiacolla hills in the Manu National Park.

Lost City mavens will instantly have perked up at the name Pantiacolla. This is a favourite haunt of planners of expeditions to discover Paititi, the last refuge of the Incas. Paititi is protected, legend says, by fierce Indians, great bushmaster snakes, and

---

number of trips a year. It leads camping-and-lodge trips to Manu as well as esoteric trips for taking ayahuasca.

The largest Inca Trail operator, **SAS Travel** (Portal de Panes 143, Plaza de Armas, Cusco, tel. 084/23-7292, info@sastravelperu.com.pe, www.sastravelperu.com, $650 for eight-day trip) is a reputable company with more than a decade of experience that has recently been licensed to operate in the Parque Nacional Manu. It operates nearly every tour imaginable in the Cusco area.

The final licensed Manu operator is **Expediciones Vilca** (Plateros 363, Cusco, tel. 084/25-1872, manuvilca@terra.com.pe, www.cbc.org.pe/manuvilca/, $720 for eight-day trip), which offers Manu trips at the Casa Machiguenga and Tambo

Blanquillo Lodge. It also offers Inca Trail and other adventure trips.

Independent Manu Lodges

There are a few independent lodges that the above Manu operators often use in their packages. **Casa Machiguenga** is a lodge built and operated by Machiguenga natives in the communities near Yombebato and Tayakome, with financial assistance from a German nonprofit organization. Manu Expeditions is sending its first fixed departure every month to the lodge, and other agencies may be using it in the future. The wooden lodge, with adequate bathrooms, is more rustic than other Manu lodges but offers a good change to glimpse the lifestyles of Manu's true people.

giant pumas, and the Pantiacolla fills the bill by containing all of the above.

Not much was heard of the Cosñipata Valley till the 1960s, when Alliance-for-Progress President Belaunde drew a line on the map between Cusco and Río Branco in Brazil and called it an Intercontinental Highway. This, thank goodness, was never built, partly because the people of Lake Titicaca want it to go their way while the people of Cusco want it to go to them and both are prepared to go to war about it.

In a field a couple of hundred yards from the hacienda buildings is a remarkable, evocative sight. Here, in a clearing in the jungle, stands a large biplane—yes, a giant Gipsy Moth, quite new-looking. A tatter here, a bird's nest there, but the tires are full of air.

Against a backdrop of warm, misty, menacing jungle hills and a powerful river nearby, this is an impossibly romantic sight. Like most piston aircraft of the old school, the nose is way in the air, with a four-blade propeller. Inside, the fuselage slopes steeply backwards. One climbs up toward the cockpit, keeping an eye and an ear open for snakes.

There are some Cyrillic signs in the cockpit, and it takes no imagination to picture the pilot and co-pilot in those tight leather helmets and threatening oval goggles familiar from movies involving the Russian air force.

The plane is, Abel Muñiz tells me over a warm beer on his kerosene-lamp-lit veranda, an Antonov Two. They're apparently still in production in Poland at US$300,000 apiece, and in service there and in Cuba today. Its single nine-cylinder engine produces 1,000 hp. It takes 15 passengers at a top speed of 170 mph, and a stall speed of 55 mph. Unloaded, it can land in 55 meters, and take off with up to 500 kilos in just over 70 meters. With a full 1,500-kilo load, it can take off in 450 meters.

Abel's initial idea was to fly tourists over the jungle: "Started off pretty well. But what with devaluations and recessions, terrorists and drug people and no tourists, it flopped," he said. "My friends and relations thought I'd become a drug baron and insisted that I lend them hundreds of thousands. Of course the police and the tax people were the same. It's hard to make anything work in Peru, let alone in the jungle."

Abel Muñiz can be reached at tel. 084/22-4262. More information on Villa Carmen, which charges $50 per night, can be found at www.edym.com/tourism/villacarmen/eng/home.html.

(Contributed by Nicholas Asheshov, a British journalist who has covered Peru for four decades. Asheshov heads the Planning Division of the Incaland Hotel and the Sacred Valley Railway, in Urubamba.)

The Madre de Dios Lodge is a simple wooden lodge near the town of Boca Manu that is owned by town mayor Juan de Dios de Carpio.

Tambo Blanquillo Lodge is owned by one of the owners of the reputable ExplorAndes agency. It includes an observation tower and is a 10-minute boat ride to the largest of Manu's macaw clay licks.

Puerto Maldonado and Vicinity

For the quality of the lodging, and the amount of wildlife that visitors see, the jungle lodges around Puerto Maldonado represent an excellent Amazon value. Just a half-hour plane ride from Cusco, Puerto Maldonado is the place for people with a limited budget and time. In an action-packed stay of two or three nights, visitors are likely to see a few types of monkeys (there are seven species in the area), capybara and other jungle rodents, a wide variety of water and forest birds, caiman, and turtles. Large mammals such as tapir and jaguar are seldom seen, though chances become better farther into the jungle at the Tambopata Research Center, which is inside the **Parque Nacional Bahuaja Sonene.**

Though there are fewer species here than in Manu, getting to the Puerto Maldonado's jungle is a heck of a lot easier. Visitors arrive at the airport, where they are picked up by their lodge and taken up a river in motorboat. In as little as three hours after leaving Cusco, visitors can be in a comfortable jungle lodge surrounded by miles of Amazon rainforest. Standard features of most trips include early-morning bird-watching followed by a nature walk, piraña fishing, and a visit to a local community and/or medicinal plant talk by a local shamán. If guests have energy, guides lead night jungle walks or boat rides to spot baby caiman, a close relative of the alligator, along the river bank. Prices include airport transfer, boat transport, lodging, and food.

There are two main protected areas near Puerto Maldonado. The **Reserva Nacional Tambopata** (275,000 hectares) stretches east from Puerto Maldonado all the way to the Río Heath on the Bolivian border. It serves as a buffer zone around the **Parque Nacional Bahuaja Sonene** (1.1 million hectares). The whole area of 1.4 million hectares is across the Río Heath from the **Parque Nacional Maidídi** in Bolivia, forming the largest patch of protected rainforest in South America.

The jungle lodges are clustered in two areas on the edge of the Reserva Nacional Tambopata. The first group is an hour's boat ride down the Río Madre de Dios. The lodges here include

some of the most comfortable in the Amazon, including Reserva Amazónica and Lake Sandoval Lodge. There are also lower-budget options in this area as well.

The other main group is three to four hours up the Río Tambopata, on the way to the Parque Nacional Bahuaja Sonene. In general, wildlife-spotting opportunities are about equal between these two groups of lodges—all of them are near the reserve's buffer zone and are mostly surrounded by secondary forest.

An exception is **Explorer's Inn,** built in 1976, which is the only lodge inside the Reserva Nacional Tambopata and seems to have more bird and animal species than the other lodges—including frequent sightings of the giant otter and world-record levels of birds and butterflies. The reserve also includes areas of virgin forest, unlike the other lodges, whose large mahogany and cedar trees were cut down years ago.

The world's largest macaw clay lick, which attracts nearly all the area's species of macaws, parrots, and parakeets, is seven hours up the Río Tambopata near the **Tambopata Research Center.** Most Puerto Maldonado lodges offer two-day trips to the lick, which include a night of camping on a sandy beach, a guided hike through the forest, meals, and a morning visit to the lick.

PUERTO MALDONADO

Puerto Maldonado began as a rubber boomtown in 1902 after a mule road was built from the coast to the headwaters of the Río Tambopata. After the rubber craze ended, gold mining and lumber took its place and continues today, though fortunately tourism and Brazil nuts are increasingly important. The wide avenues of *Puerto,* as locals call the city, quickly peter out into mud lanes and ramshackle rows of wooden buildings. Instead of cars, mostly scooters and three-wheeled *motocars* buzz the streets. Puerto Maldonado is smaller and infinitely more relaxed than the Amazon megalopolis of Iquitos. Most travelers fly into Puerto Maldonado and transfer immediately to one of

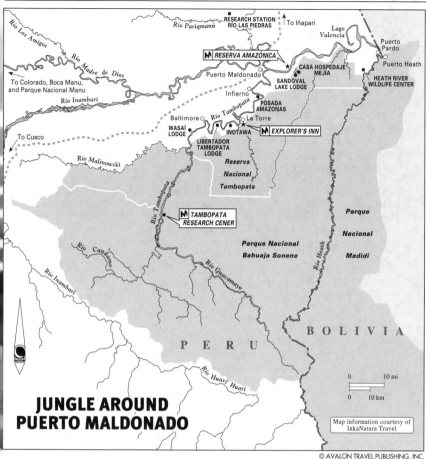

**JUNGLE AROUND
PUERTO MALDONADO**

Map information courtesy of
InkaNatura Travel

© AVALON TRAVEL PUBLISHING, INC.

The Amazon

two dozen lodges in the area. Avoid staying the night in Puerto, as the jungle is more interesting.

There were two explorers with the last name of Maldonado who explored the Madre de Dios. The first, Juan Álvarez Maldonado, was a Spanish explorer who came here in 1567 in search of gold. He was the first to make it all the way to the Río Heath, the present-day Bolivian border, but he lost 250 Spaniards from disease and Indian attacks in the process. He returned to Cusco months later, half-crazed and in rags, and claimed to have found a sophisticated, wealthy jungle city known as Paititi.

Though the legend of Paititi grew, the memory of Maldonado's hardships prevented the Spaniards from returning to the area for nearly three centuries. In the mid-19th century Col. Faustino Maldonado returned to make the first map of the area. But he perished, along with his valuable journals, in a rapid on the Río Madre de Dios. He carved his name on a tree trunk at the junction of the Tambopata and Río Madre de Dios rivers, where the town named in his honor is located today.

Puerto Maldonado is also the location of the Peruvian Amazon's best language school, **Tambopata**

GOLD AND MAHOGANY: PROFIT AND LOSS

The number one and two industries in Puerto Maldonado—gold mining and lumber, respectively—may be at critical turning points after two decades of wreaking havoc in the surrounding jungle. Though prospectors had worked its rivers for years, Puerto Maldonado's **gold mining** industry took off after the gold rush in the nearby Brazilian Madeira in the late 1980s. Production in the Madre de Dios watershed peaked in 1997 at 12,600 kg and is now at 10,000 kg per year and dropping.

The gold is found in river silt, but there is not enough of it to support corporate, large-scale operations. Instead, thousands of small teams of two to eight gold miners work riverbanks and flood plains, especially along the Inambari, Colorado, and Kalinowski tributaries of the Río Madre de Dios. Though many are lured, few get rich. A team of five people average about two grams per day—about the size of four rice kernels, and worth about $20.

Where there is gravel there is often gold, and miners have a variety of techniques to separate the two. Some use wheelbarrows and wash boxes, others divert creek channels over coarse sifting rugs, and then there is always the old-fashioned technique of gold panning. Up to this point in the process, gold miners have caused little damage to the environment. Though they create hills and canals on the flood plains, swollen rivers during flood season wipe away their work in a day or two.

The problem with gold mining is that **mercury**—and lots of it—is mixed with the final sediment in order to separate the gold dust, which gloms onto the mercury in silvery clumps. Later the mercury and gold are roasted over an open fire to evaporate the mercury and leave the pure white gold, like tooth fillings in a frying pan.

The heated mercury evaporates into the sky and returns to the jungle as rain, but mercury is also dumped straight into the river along with the leftover water. This mercury then enters the food chain and poses the threat of poisoning local native peoples, who rely on fish as their main food source. Though there have been several studies on the mercury problem in the Río Madre de Dios, there's been no conclusive evidence to date that there are dangerous levels of mercury in local fish. Even so, lodges such as the Explorer's Inn have chosen not to serve local fish to their visitors. Besides the mercury, miners cruise up into pristine mountain streams to

Education Centre (Madre de Dios at the obelisk, tel. 082/57-4016 or 082/57-3935, tinasmith@ terra.com.pe, www.tambopata-language.com). The school was founded by Tina Smith, an English naturalist who came to the area in the mid-1990s as a guide for Explorer's Inn. The school employs excellent Spanish teachers and offers packages ($195/week) that include 20 hours of Spanish a week, home stay and food with a local family, discount air tickets, and a variety of excursions to learn about Amazon cooking, gold panning, and medicinal plants. Tina Smith is an expert on the area and helps students set up interesting, affordable trips into the jungle.

There are also a variety of interesting volunteer opportunities that range from serving as a field assistant at a biological research station, reforesting

with park rangers, improving conditions at the local zoo, or working at a local farm to learn about medicinal plants. For $20 a day, volunteers receive full board and lodging,

ENTERTAINMENT

There are two nice pubs with games and dart boards that are next to each other on the Plaza de Armas. **Boulevard** (Daniel Carrión 271, tel. 082/57-2082, 6 P.M.–midnight daily) is right behind Hornito's, the pizza spot. The similar **Amnesis** is next door.

For a more rowdy atmosphere, head across the plaza to **Anaconda Disco Pub** (Loreto, on Plaza de Armas, 8:30 P.M.–2 A.M. Tues.–Sat., no cover charge). If it's a weekend night, head later to

scope out new mining grounds. Because they survive by hunting whatever they see, resident capybara, peccary, tapir, and monkey are quickly eliminated by the miners.

Recently the government has required miners to have a license to buy mercury, and also to purchase an $80 box-like device that minimizes the amount of mercury that leaks into the environment. There are a handful of people in charge of enforcing this new rule and thousands of miners. Not much progress has been made.

Second to gold mining, **logging** is the second main industry that took off when roads were completed to Shintuya, near Manu, and Puerto Maldonado in the 1960s. By 2003, there were an estimated 20,000 loggers in the Río Madre de Dios. The industry has more than doubled since 1990 and exported a whopping 23 million board feet in 2003.

Loggers cruise the rivers and floodplains searching for three trees in the mahogany family that are used in furniture making, including cedro *(Cedrela odorata)*, coaba *(Swietenia macrophylla)*, and tornillo *(Cedrelinga catenaeformis)*. Very few of these trees, which can grow to up to 60 meters high, are left, except in remote headwaters or inside one of the parks. As a result, the focus is being shifted now to new, less-valuabe species such as *lupuna*, which is used for plywood, *kapok*, and ironwood. After cutting a tree, loggers use chain saws to make thick planks that are tied together into a raft and floated into Puerto Maldonado.

The government's effort to control logging in the region has generated considerable resentment. Loggers have reached the borders of Parque Nacional Manu and other protected areas and are clamoring for the right to selectively cut trees inside. INRENA, the Peruvian natural resources authority, has rejected the request and gone further by handing out concessions only to large timber companies that are easier to monitor. These concessions are the result of a forestry law passed in 2003, but small loggers see it as another example of big business and government trading money back and forth for their own benefit. In May 2003, thousands of small loggers, led by union activist Rafael Río López, rose up in anger in May 2003 and burnt offices belonging to INRENA and other conservation groups in Puerto Maldonado. Río Lopez eventually turned himself in and was jailed but, in a highly unusual example of popular sentiment, was elected president of the Madre de Dios region from his cell.

The Amazon

Waititi Disco (León Velarde 141, no cover charge, 7 P.M.–3 A.M.Fri.–Sat.), a better dance spot that gets swinging after 11 P.M.

Cine **Madre de Dios** (Carrión 385, $1.50), shows a movie daily at 7:15 P.M. and 9:15 P.M.

ACCOMMODATIONS

Under $10

The best of the budget options is **Royal Inn** (Dos de Mayo 333, tel. 082/57-1048, $7 s, $10 d), with shared baths and cold water. It can get noisy here, so ask for a room away from the street and the central courtyard. The other budget option is the rather crummy **Hotel Wilson** (Gonzáles Prada 355, tel. 082/57-1086, $7 s, $10 d).

$10–25

Even for budget travelers, Puerto seems like a good place to upgrade to **Cabaña Quinta** (Cusco 535, tel. 082/57-1045, $13 s, $20 d, including breakfast) with smallish, tile-floored rooms and nice gardens. Rooms have hot water, cable TV, and optional air-conditioning for twice the price. The setting is quiet and the hotel restaurant is one of the better ones in town.

$25–50

Don Carlos Hotel (León Velarde 1271, tel. 082/57-1029, www.hotelesdoncarlos.com, $20 s, $26 d, including breakfast) is a pleasant hotel perched on a hilltop on the edge of town. There is a nice wood porch for having a drink, and a decent restaurant. The rooms have wood floors,

THE "PREHISTORIC" HOATZIN—CLAWS AND ALL

In Madre de Dios, few birds are more common and bizarre than the hoatzin, a chicken-like bird with a spiky crest that can often be seen flapping noisily around bushes at water's edge. Hoatzins stand out from other birds because they are clumsy fliers and make a creepy grunting sound. They also eat only leaves and, like cows, have three stomachs—called crops—for digesting the organic material. The leaves ferment inside their crops, give these birds a bad odor and the local nickname of "stinky bird." The hoatzin doesn't mind being smelly, however, because that is its main protection from predators.

Hoatzin chicks have an even more interesting defense. The chicks are born with claws on their wings—like the flying pterodactyl. When an anaconda or other predator comes to the nest to eat the chicks, they dive into the water. When the danger is past, they use their claws to climb back into their nest. Many Amazon guides say these claws are proof that the hoatzin is a prehistoric bird that has changed little since the Mesozoic era. Recent DNA analysis, however, indicates the hoatzin is a strange member of the cuckoo family and its claws are probably a relatively recent adaptation.

nice beds, optional air conditioning, and clean bathrooms with a limited hot water supply.

A better value is **Brombu's Lodge** (Carretera Maldonado Km 4.5, tel. 082/57-3230, brombuslodge@yahoo.es, $15 s, $20 d, including breakfast), a 10-minute taxi ride outside of town on the way to the airport. The bungalows are large, sparsely decorated, but pleasant, and surrounded by plants and trees. There is a restaurant, probably Puerto's finest, with river views and a full bar. Avoid this place on weekends because of a next-door *peña* that cranks loud music all night.

The most charming and expensive place in town is **Wasaí Maldonado Lodge** (Guillermo Billinghurst, tel. 082/57-2290, www.wasai.com, $36 s, $48 d, including breakfast), a mini jungle lodge overlooking the Río Madre de Dios. Stilts and wooden ramps support and connect 16 wooden bungalows and rooms, which include minibar, cable TV, hot water, and a choice of air conditioning or fan. There is a tiny pool with a waterfall, Puerto's fanciest restaurant, and a gazebo bar with great views. This hotel is operated by Wasaí Lodge on the Río Tambopata.

FOOD

A good place for breakfast, hamburgers, or a light lunch is **La Casa Nostra** (León Velarde 515, tel. 082/57-3833, 7 A.M.–1 P.M. and 5–11 P.M. Mon.–Sat., $2), a small café with good service.

The best food in town is at **Brombu's Lodge** (Carretera Maldonado Km 4.5, tel. 082/57-3230, 7 A.M.–10 P.M. daily, $4) near the airport, though other hotels like Wasaí, Don Carlos, and Cabaña Quinta also have good restaurants. Brombu's dining room looks over the river in a forest that is a surprisingly good place to bird-watch. The wide-ranging menu includes local dishes llike *patarashka de pollo,* and the chicken brochettes with Brazil nut sauce are scrumptious.

Another good option, and a local favorite, is **El Califa** (Piura 266, tel. 082/57-1119), which serves local jungle cuisine and good Peruvian menus. Also for typical jungle food, try the *no-frills* **El Majas** (Tambopata with Dos de Mayo, 6–11 P.M. daily, $2) where meats are barbequed in front of you.

The best bet for pizza is **Hornito** (Daniel Carrión 271, Plaza de Armas, tel. 082/57-2082, 6 P.M.–midnight), with good music and cozy, pub-like interior.

The best spit-roasted chicken is La Estrella (León Velarde 474, tel. 082/57-3107, 5–10 P.M., $3 for half-chicken and fries).

INFORMATION AND SERVICES

The **Tourism Ministry** has an office in Puerto Maldonado at Fitzcarrald 252 (tel. 082/57-1164, 7 A.M.–3:30 P.M. Mon.–Fri.) and a small booth at the airport, but visitors should do their research before arriving in Puerto Maldonado. For questions and advice, contact Tina Smith of the **Tambopata Education Centre** (Madre de Dios at the obelisk, tel. 082/57-4016 or 082/57-3935, tinasmith@terra.com.pe, www.tambopata-language.com) who is helpful and knowledgeable.

The **police** are located on Carrión 410 (tel. 082/57-1022) and can be called by dialing 105. Puerto's best medical care is at **Hospital Santa Rosa** (Cajamarca 171, at Velarde, tel. 082/57-1046, 24 hours). For medical emergencies, dial 117. **Es Salud** (Dos de Mayo block 17, tel. 082/57-1230) is a new hospital open 24 hours a day. A recommended private clinic is **Clinica Madre de Dios** (28 de Julio 702, tel. 082/57-1440).

The **Banco de la Nación** (Carrión 233, tel. 082/57-1064) and **Banco de Crédito** (Arequipa 334, tel. 082/57-1001) both have ATMs. Only Banco de Crédito lets you withdraw using a credit card and only accepts AmEx or Visa. There are several exchange houses on Puno. Few places in Puerto Maldonado accept credit cards, so bring cash.

The **post office** is located on León Velarde 675 (tel. 082/57-1088, 8 A.M.–9 P.M. Mon.–Sat., 8 A.M.–3 P.M. Sun.) and there are pay phones on the main square. Internet in Puerto Maldonado is slow but available at **León Velarde 718** (8 A.M.–midnight, $0.80/hour).

Internet is available around the plaza and on León Velarde, but the most comfortable place is Unamad, with air-conditioning, on the corner of León Velarde and Dos de Mayo.

There are a few places in town to rent **scooters** for $1/hour, including Gonzales Prada 321 and the intersection of Prada and Puno.

Laundry is available at **Lavandería Silán** on León Velarde 930 (closed Sundays) and several other places down the street.

GETTING THERE AND AROUND

The road between Cusco and Puerto Maldonado is a bumpy, grueling two-day journey that passes through the village of Ocongate and the peak of Ausangate before plunging off the eastern edge of the Andes. During rainy season, trucks can take as long as seven days. From Cusco, those up to the challenge should head first to Urcos and catch a truck on from there.

Given the road, nearly all travelers arrive by plane. Puerto Maldonado's airport (tel. 082/57-1531) is 8 km from town, or about $2 per taxi. Airlines fly Lima-Cusco-Puerto. **LanPeru** (in Lima tel. 01/213-8200, www.lanperu.com, $76 one-way from Lima, $39 from Cusco) has three flights a week and a local office at León Velarde 503 (tel. 082/57-3677, 8 A.M.–8 P.M. Mon.–Sat.). The cheapest option is **TANS** (tel. 082/57-3141, ventaslima.com.pe, www.tansperu.com.pe, $60 from Lima, $35 from Cusco), with daily flights.

The Bolivian border is six hours downstream from Puerto Maldonado, and boats sporadically leave from the Puerto's port of Capitanía. Before you leave, however, you must get your passport stamped with an exit stamp at **Peruvian Immigrations** (Ica at Plaza Bolognesi, tel. 082/57-1069, 9 A.M.–1 P.M. Mon.–Fri.). The **Bolivian consulate** is located on the main square on Loreto, though visas are not required at this time for travelers from North America, Britain, New Zealand, and Australia.

Motocars are everywhere and cost $0.75 for a jaunt across town. *Colectivo* boats ferry passengers across the Tambopata and Río Madre de Dios and can be hired at the Capitania port for local tours ($20–25 per day).

The Amazon

Río Tambopata

LIBERTADOR TAMBOPATA LODGE

This lodge has recently affiliated itself with the exclusive Libertador hotel chain and as a result is being transformed into one of Peru's more luxurious jungle lodges. The older wooden bungalows are charming with porch, hammock, and thatched roof—plus the new comforts of hot water, tiled bathrooms, and electric lighting (though candles are still provided).

Tambopata Lodge is also building a new generation of larger, luxurious bungalows made from cement, the new material of choice for eco-lodges because it lasts longer than wood and does not require the felling of trees. These cement bungalows have the same comforts but with larger, newer rooms and queen-size beds (the only downside is that there are two units per bungalow, so you hear your neighbor through the open-air ceiling). The bungalows are spread out in a jungle clearing, with the cozy bar and dining room a short walk away along a wooden ramp.

The lodge is surrounded by 100 hectares of secondary forest, in which a few old trees remain. Highlights of a visit are the slide show, bird-watching at Lago Condenado, a medicinal plant talk at a local farm, and a bird-watching platform that is 24 meters high. An excursion to the macaw clay lick, several hours further upstream, costs between $400–500 pp extra. The lodge is three hours upstream from Puerto Maldonado (in Cusco tel. 084/24-5695, tplcus@terra.com.pe, www.tambopatalodge.com, $214 pp for two-night stay).

⛰ EXPLORER'S INN

Built in 1975, Explorer's Inn is the oldest eco-lodge in Puerto Maldonado and has a comfortable, worn-in feel. The thatched wood bungalows have foam mattresses, bamboo walls, simple bathrooms, and no hot water, and are lit by candles at night. They are comfortable but not luxurious. The central dining room is made entirely of wood and has an upstairs library with a number of exhibits and animal samples left behind by biologists who have worked here over the decades.

Compared to other Amazon lodges, Explorer's Inn has the best combination of convenience, prices, and biodiverse rainforest. It is the only lodge within the Reserva Nacional Tambopata, and it has exclusive rights to 5,500 hectares of pristine rainforest that began as a private reserve and has since been incorporated into the new Reserva Nacional Tambopata (the private property of the lodge is 105 hectares). The owner, Max Gunther, speaks flawless English and has been a leading figure in Peruvian conservation for three decades.

Biologists have proclaimed the 5,500 hectares surrounding the lodge to be "the most biodiverse place on the planet" because of a number of Guiness World Records that have been set there for animal species, including 500 bird species and 1,235 types of butterflies. Though the lodge is not a research station per se, many biologists come here to do research and lead visitors on guided walks in exchange for their room and board.

There are 37 km of well-marked trails that lead to huge tracts of virgin forest, a small macaw clay lick, and two lakes where giant otters live. In one two-hour walk, we saw 20 bird species, including macaws and toucans, howler monkeys, otters, and a meter-long coral snake. The guides are extremely knowledgeable, and most tours include a visit to a farm in the nearby community of La Torre. The lodge also arranges other trips, including a mystic adventure with an ayahuasca session, a trip to the macaw clay lick on the Río Tambopata, a six-night birdwatchers program, and a variety of camping trips with the chance of waiting at a tapir salt lick at night. The lodge is 3.5 hours upstream from Puerto Maldonado (in Lima tel. 01/447-8888, safaris@amauta.rcp.net.pe, www.peruviansafaris.com, $180 for normal two-night stay).

INOTAWA

A good budget option, about 15 minutes past Explorer's Inn, is Inotawa, which has a main thatched building with open-air rooms and single beds with mosquito net covering. Bathrooms are shared, with flush toilets but no hot water. There is a small bar, restaurant with vegetarian food, and option to visit the clay lick near the Tambopata Research Center. Inotawa is 3.5 hours upstream from Puerto Maldonado (in Lima tel. 01/467-4560, inotawa@hotmail.com, www.inotawaexpeditions.com, $120 two nights).

WASAÍ LODGE AND EXPEDITIONS

This well-equipped lodge is a five-hour motorboat ride upstream. Packages typically include lodging at the excellent lodge in Puerto Maldonado and a visit to Lago Sandoval on the Río Madre de Dios. It also operates a variety of adventure trips, including a 500-kilometer mountain-bike-and-raft journey between Cusco and Puerto Maldonado and camping trips into the Río Las Piedras (in Cusco tel. 084/22-1826, wasai@wasai.com, www.wasai.com, $155 two nights).

POSADA AMAZONAS

Operated by Rainforest Expeditions, this lodge is a ground-breaking experiment in cooperation with the community of Infierno two hours upstream of Puerto Maldonado. The people of Infierno, mestizo descendents of Ese Eja Indians, receive training, jobs, and a share of the profits, while the lodge gets use of the land. The goal of the project is to integrate the community into ecotourism and the overall preservation of rainforest.

The lodge has 24 thatched rooms, with the outside wall completely open to keep guests in contact with nature. They have private bathrooms (no hot water), beds with mosquito canopies, and candlelight only. There is a hammock lounge, library, and open-air dining room. Tours include visits to oxbow lake to see otters, an ethno-botanical center at Infierno, and a canopy tower 35 meters off the ground.

Rainforest Expeditions is a well-managed outfit with biologist guides, excellent boats, and reliable service. It has won a series of sustainable development awards and also operates the more rustic and remote Tambopata Research Center. Contact information for both lodges is the same (in Lima tel. 01/421-8347, postmast@rainforest.com.pe, www.perunature.com, $780 five nights).

◪ THE TAMBOPATA RESEARCH CENTER

Also operated by Rainforest Expeditions, the Tambopata Research Center offers five- to seven-day packages where guests will experience a huge range of biodiversity that is comparable to the Parque Nacional Manu or Reserva Nacional Pacaya-Samiria. Compared to those areas, the seven-hour journey up the Río Tambopata is a relatively short trip. It is the only lodge near the Parque Nacional Bahuaja Sonene, a rainforest wilderness the size of Connecticut. The lodge is also 500 meters away from the world's largest clay lick, where dozens of species of macaws, parrots, and parakeets come to ingest detoxifying mud.

The lodge has 13 double bedrooms with shared bathrooms (no hot water) and, like Posada Amazonas, one wall is completely open to the forest. Programs often include a night at Posada Amazonas, along with visits to a 35-meter canopy tower, oxbow lake with giant otters, the macaw lick, and platforms and observation points in different habitats (in Lima tel. 01/421-8347, postmast@rainforest.com.pe, www.perunature.com).

MACAW CLAY LICKS

There are few natural sights more remarkable than a macaw clay lick, or *collpa*, covered early in the morning with dozens of brightly colored macaws, parrots, and parakeets who come to eat the mineral-rich mud. The world's largest *collpa* is located near the Tambopata Research Center on the Río Tambopata, about a seven-hour boat ride upstream from Puerto Maldonado. At dawn, there may be as many as 600 birds—including all six species of macaws—that perch on surrounding trees before their cautious descent to the riverbank, where they squawk and jostle with each other for access to the mineral-rich clay. By 7 A.M. the show is over though a few birds may return in the late afternoon. There are similar, but smaller, *collpas* spread throughout the Parque Nacional Manu and the Reserva Tambopata.

Scientists have only recently understood why these birds need the minerals in the clay. Because of monkeys, bats, insects, birds, and the incredible variety of fruit-eating animals in the jungle, most fruits are eaten before they ripen fully. To prevent the fruit from being eaten before the seeds are fully developed, plants have evolved toxins that give unripe fruit that sour, bitter taste. The macaws, parrots, and parakeets have somehow learned they can eat green fruit as long as they eat clay from the riverbank that neutralizes the toxins (much in the same way humans eat kaolin). In this way, these birds have a competitive advantage over most other fruit-eating animals. Here are some of the more common macaws found in Madre de Dios:

- **The red-bellied macaw** is mostly green, with a dullish yellow color on the underside of its wings and tail.
- **The chestnut-fronted macaw** is also mostly green, but the underside of its wings and tail are a dull red color.
- **The scarlet macaw** is mainly scarlet with yellow median upper wing coverts. They have bare white skin on the sides of their heads and a very loud voice.
- **The red-and-green macaw** is mainly deep scarlet with green median upper wing coverts and distinctive narrow lines of red feathers on the sides of its head.
- **The blue-and-yellow macaw** is bright blue on top and yellow underneath. When not at the clay lick, these birds can typically be found feeding in the high canopy near water, or flying in pairs or groups of three.
- **The red-bellied macaw** is typically found sitting on Mauritia palms.

© PROMPERÚ

The blue-and-yellow macaw and other parrots and parakeets feed on mineral-rich mud in order to digest green fruit.

Río Madre de Dios

SANDOVAL LAKE LODGE

This comfortable lodge has a privileged location on Lago Sandoval, a crystal-clear lake fringed with Mauritia palms and teeming with aquatic birds. The lodge's operator, InkaNatura, often combines a trip to this lodge with a sister operation near the Bolivia border, the Heath River Wildlife Center.

The Sandoval Lake Lodge has clean rooms made of recycled cedar, with electricity and hot water. The lake itself is an enchanting place, especially when waters turn pink and orange with the sun's rising and setting, forming a perfect mirror for the elongated palms at the water's edge. About 30 bird species, mostly aquatic, can be seen on a typical boat ride, including several species of kingfisher, herons, and egrets. There are giant otters on the lake, but they are hard to see. Trails from the hotel's backyard lead into the Reserva Nacional Tambopata, which backs up against the property.

Reaching the lodge is the best part. Boats drop guests off at a dock, from where they walk 3 km through a jungle lane flitting with butterflies. Then guests board a canoe, which is paddled across the lake to the lodge. Each leg of the journey, motorboat, walking, and canoe, takes about 45 minutes.

The lodge is the result of a deal struck in 1996 with the Mejía family, who homesteaded around the lake in the 1950s and now operate their own lodging nearby, Casa Hospedaje Mejía. A two-night program costs $190 and can be booked through InkaNatura Travel (in Lima tel. 01/440-2022, www.postmaster@inkanatura.com.pe, www.inkanatura.com) or in the United States through Tropical Nature Travel (877/827-8350, www.tropicalnaturetravel.com).

The Amazon

Bird guides on Lago Sandoval and elsewhere in the Amazon will identify birds before you even see them.

CASA HOSPEDAJE MEJÍA

This option is extremely rustic, bordering on untidy, but we challenge you to find a cheaper Amazon alternative ($8 s, $10 d). It is run by the Mejía family, who settled here in the 1950s. There are a dozen rough huts with rusting screens and bamboo walls in a yard teeming with hens and dogs. Its main advantage is being on Lago Sandoval.

The Mejía family members lead canoe-and-walking walking tours, though they speak only Spanish and are not trained biologists. They do know this jungle better than anyone, however, and seem friendly.

The only way to contact this lodge is via a sporadically functioning cell phone (082/961-2346) or their address in Puerto Maldonado (León Velarde 471, tel. 082/57-3567). To reach the lodge, head to the port of Capitanía in Puerto Maldonado and hire a boat for the 45-minute trip to Lago Sandoval's dock ($10 one way). From there it is a 45-minute walk to the lake, plus a canoe ride, if they know you are coming. It is also possible to walk all the way to the lodge, about 1.5 hours.

M RESERVA AMAZÓNICA

This fabulous lodge is the most luxurious, and most romantic, in the Peruvian Amazon. It was founded in 1975 and, along with the Explorer's Inn, is the oldest lodge in the area. It is yet another production from José and Denise Koechlin, Peru's ecopioneers who also own the elegant Machu Picchu Pueblo Hotel.

Near the riverbank, a sophisticated round dining building sets the tone for this lodge. This is not the kind of place where guests sit around in mud-spattered rubbers. After long walks or boat rides, guests take hot showers, get cleaned up, and take cocktails in the dining loft with hip lounge music. The elegant dinner buffet, served downstairs, features organic salads and gourmet jungle entréea like *paca,* which is *doncella* fish, tomatoes, and onions cooked inside a bamboo tube over an open fire. There are 41 private wooden bungalows, including three luxury suites, with wood porches and hammocks,

beds with mosquito netting, hot showers, kerosene lamps, and interesting touches like wooden sinks and the hotel's own line of organic shampoo and conditioner.

The lodge has several unique attractions. First, it is surrounded by 200 hectares of private lands plus an endless 10,000-hectare reserve. A 500-meter hanging canopy walk is in the works, and an island in front of the lodge has been converted into a refuge for rescued monkeys—including brown capuchin, squirrel, and the tiny, nectar-eating saddleback tamarin. There are long hikes to different habitats, canoe trips up the nearby Río Gamitana, an eco-center with a glass box for viewing the inside of a leaf cutter ant colony, and a butterfly cage. A number of animals have been rescued from various predicaments and now live on the property, including a Cuvier's toucan, razor-billed curassau, pale-winged trumpeter, and scarlet macaw. Even a tapir pops in once in a while (in Lima tel. 01/610-0404 or in the U.S. 800/442-5042, central@inkaterra.com, www.inkaterra.com, $157 for two nights).

Just downstream from the lodge, InkaTerra has launched **Fundo Concepción,** an environmental research and education center run jointly with the U.S.-based ACER. The main building is the restored home of Dr. Arturo Gonzáles del Rio, a beloved local doctor who bought a steamship from the Bolivia Navy in the 1930s and used it as an ambulance for local native people. The rusty girders and boilers of the boat can be seen during the walk into the center, which also has the area's largest garden of medicinal plants.

RESEARCH STATION RÍO LAS PIEDRAS

This rustic backpacker lodge is on the Río Las Piedras, a tributary of the Río Madre de Dios, which is a two-day boat ride from Puerto Maldonado. Surrounded by 4,000 hectares of rainforest, the station is owned by an English-Peruvian couple, Emma and J.J., trained biologists who also operate the Tambopata Expeditions agency. Travelers who have come here recommend it for biodiversity, good guiding, simple but clean wooden rooms, and a family-like atmosphere. Volunteers come here for weeks at a time, paying $15 per day for room and food, to work on trail maintenance, construction, mapping, or biology fieldwork. Because of its distance from Puerto Maldonado, most visitors come for at least three nights. Highlights include a small clay lick, an oxbow lake, and overnight camping at a clay lick visited by tapirs.

Tambopata Expeditions also offers six-day camping trips on the Río Las Piedras for $300, and a five-day trip that includes a visit to Río Tambopata's large macaw clay lick for $420 pp (cell phone 086/960-0109, info@tambopataexpeditions.com, www.tambopataexpeditions.com).

HEATH RIVER WILDLIFE CENTER

Off the beaten path and in a seldom-visited part of the Amazon, the Heath River Wildlife Center has recently been transferred to a local community of Ese Eja Indians, though InkaNatura Travel continues to guide its management. The lodge is a 4.5-hour boat journey from Puerto Maldonado and is sandwiched between Bolivia and Peru and in the middle of South America's largest patch of protected rainforest. The lodge has six bungalows with hot showers and a rustic communal space. A three-night stay costs $490, and longer programs often include the related Lake Sandoval Lodge. Trips can be booked through InkaNatura Travel (in Lima tel. 01/440-2022,

The Amazon

FISHING FOR PIRAÑA

A must-do activity at nearly any jungle lodge in the Peruvian Amazon is **piraña fishing**. The only equipment you'll need is a string, a hook, and a chunk of red meat (the bloodier, the better). Just plunk the baited hook into the still waters of nearly any Amazon backwater and—presto!—you will feel the aggressive tug of a piraña as it zigzags your line beneath the water's surface. Before you grab hold of your fish, however, check out the fingertips of your jungle guide. Chances are they are scarred by fumbled attempts at handling this palm-sized fish, which has a bulldog face, powerful lower jaw, and a set of razor-sharp teeth that grow back when broken, like those of a shark. The fish will snip at anything in reach and cause a nasty bite, so leave the fish handling to someone who knows what they are doing.

Piraña prefer the still backwaters of the Amazon basin, but they also thrive in Hawaii and parts of Central America, where they have been introduced. There are 20 species in a rainbow of colors, though the most common in Peru is the **red-belly piraña**, which is crimson on the bottom and silvery-green on the sides. Like its cousins around the Amazon basin, the red-belly pirañ hunts in schools and eats whatever it can. This includes mollusks, crustaceans, insects, birds, lizards, amphibians, rodents, baby caiman, and other piraña. During the Amazon's high-water months, the piraña is also known to eat submerged fruit.

Contrary to the pop-culture image of pirañas devouring people instantly in a bloody maul of frothy water, these fanged fish rarely bother humans—as the troops of children playing in rivers prove. There is, in fact, no recorded case of a human being killed by piraña, although plenty have been nipped. If you swim in a jungle river, avoid the warm, still waters favored by these fish—a spot with current is better. And remember that piraña, like sharks, are attracted by blood and splashing in the water. The fish are especially aggressive when food is scarce, such as when trapped in a drying lake. They are most active at dawn and dusk and sleep at night.

Though small and bony, piraña is a tasty fish that is occasionally served in restaurants, either fried or steamed. Many lodges will cook the fish you catch, though most encourage you to release the fish back into the water. Amazon natives rarely eat piraña because there are so many larger fish to choose from, such as *paiche*, which has succulent white meat.

www.postmaster@inkanatura.com.pe, www.ink-anatura.com) or in the United States through Tropical Nature Travel (877/827-8350, www.tropicalnaturetravel.com).

CHANCHAMAYO: SAN RAMÓN AND LA MERCED

From Lima the closest shot of jungle warmth is Chanchamayo, an area that includes the towns of **San Ramón** and **La Merced** on the Río Chanchamayo. The newly paved highway has shortened the drive from Lima to five to seven hours, and there are nice bungalows on the road between the two towns. San Ramón is a sleepy town with a good restaurant and hostel. The bigger and much dirtier La Merced has more restaurants and agencies, and a collection of drab hostels.

There are lots of interesting things to see and do around Chanchamayo. There are 100-meter waterfalls in the nearby **Perene Valley,** virgin forest with colossal cedars two hours away, and visitor-friendly Ashininka villages. There are Class III–IV rafting rivers, great mountain biking, and a bizarre Austrian-German colony from the mid-19th century, where villagers still speak German and hold onto their Tyrolean customs. Via a network of roads and rivers, truly wild jungle on the Río Tambo can be reached in a day or two. The best time to visit is during the dry months from April to October.

The **Franciscans** who came here in 1635 had to leave after Spaniards entered the area looking for gold and were slaughtered by local Indians. Other missionaries who entered the area were killed by Indians, but by 1750 a few plantations in the valley were growing sugar cane, cocoa, coffee, and coca leaves. But the settlers were massacred during the indigenous rebellion led by Juan Santos Atahualpa, a local Indian who claimed kinship with Inca Atahualpa. Colonists entered the area for good after 1850—after more than two centuries of trying—when a rough road from Tarma down into the valley was constructed. The area today is famous for its tropical fruits, avocado, *rocoto,* and high-octane coffee.

Perene Valley

Impala Tours and other agencies have put together one-day tours into the valley below Chanchamayo that pack an extraordinary number of activities into one day. These include crossing a river on a wire trolley, sun-bathing on a sandy beach, traveling by boat from the river port of Pichanaki to an Ashaninka community, and swimming—or even rappelling—off a set of extraordinary, 120-meter-high waterfalls known as Bayoz and Velo de la Novia (Brides's Veil). The closest waterfall is the 35-meter Cascada El Tirol, just outside San Ramón.

San Miguel

This interesting Asháninka village in the Perene Valley has a lodge that has been recommended by Norwegian anthropologist Ole Steinert as an excellent way to understand the daily life of the **Asháninka,** the largest ethnic group of Peru's central jungle with 30,000 to 50,000 members. The Asháninka Ñapirori Lodge (which means "strong man" in the Asháninka language of Arawak) consists of three houses in native style, each with a double bed and a balcony out front. Around the lodges are mango trees, coffee plants, tropical flowers, and spectacular views of the Perene Valley. The 40 families that live in San Miguel are very friendly and proud of their un-commercialized settlement. Men still hunt with bows and arrows and, during communal meetings, show up in traditional dress. This is a great place to stay for a week or so and be enriched with the Asháninka way of life.

Colectivos leave frequently from La Merced to Santa Ana (also called Villa Perené) the capital of the Asháninka, which is the largest ethnic group in Peru's central jungle. *Colectivos* and trucks head from Santa Ana in front of the Grifo San Jacinto to San Miguel throughout the afternoon. The dirt road to San Miguel is about 5 or 6 km up in the hills, or about 20 minutes. From here it is a 500-meter walk further to the village, where guests should ask for lodge owners Mercedes and Luis Samaniego.

Pozuzo-Oxapampa

After a formal invitation from the Peruvian government, a group of German and Austrian immigrants from Prussia and Tyrol hacked their way into a remote jungle enclave north of the Chanchamayo Valley in 1857. They survived despite the odds, were largely forgotten, and over time developed a charming, and somewhat bizarre, Bavarian village in the Amazon that they christened **Pozuzo.**

Where else in the Amazon can you find three-story Tyrolean homes with carved wooden rafters, blonde-haired damsels who speak German, and huge wheels of cheese? The blue-eyed villagers have built comfortable, Alps-style guesthouses that charge as little as $6 pp, including breakfast. There are also caves, ox-driven sugarcane mills, waterfalls, and German dancing contests during holidays. **Oxapampa,** founded by Pozuzo settlers in 1891, is a 2.5-hour (80 km) journey from Chanchamayo on rough dirt roads and Pozuzo is another four hours (80 km.) further on spectacular, bumpy roads that cross several streams. Recommended establishments in Oxapampa include **Restaurant El Trapiche** (first block of Mullembruck, tel. 064/76-2551, trapicheoxa@hotmail.com) and **Hospedaje Loechle Sinty** (12th block of San Martín, tel. 064/76-2180, silkels@yahoo.es).

Pampa Hermosa

A two-hour drive (24 km) along a rough road from San Ramón's Victoria Bridge, followed by a steep two-hour walk, leads to a stunning patch of high cloud forest known as Pampa Hermosa. This 80-hectare forest contains primeval cedar, walnut, and strangler fig trees. It is oddly flat, like an island of jungle perched 1,600 meters in the air. Steep access has kept loggers away, and nearby communities are now protecting this last patch of virgin Chanchamayo forest, which is filled with the noises of monkeys and the musky odor of the white-collared peccary. On the hike up is a *lek,* a sort of sexual playground where up to a dozen male Andean cock of the rocks flit up and down every dawn and dusk to attract their mates. At the roadhead, a local family has built a beautiful collection of wooden bungalows with thatched roofs, solar-heated water, and river-generated electricity. Make reservations ahead of time with **Pampa Hermosa Lodge** (in Lima tel. 01/225-

1776, signori@terra.com.pe, www.pampahermosalodge.com, $40 pp with full pension).

Deep Jungle and High Mountains

Undisturbed jungle areas can be found within the **Parque Nacional Yanachaga-Chemillén,** three to four hours from Chanchamayo. More remote jungle is a day's journey from Chanchamayo. A seven-hour *combi* ride leads to Puerto Bermudez, a lazy settlement on the Río Pachitea. Both the river and the dirt road (not passable in rainy season from November to March) lead all the way to Pucallpa, an adventurous journey that runs through the town of Puerto Inca. Another option is to head to the ramshackle town of **Satipo,** two hours along paved road from Chanchamayo, and then travel further by *combi* to the riverside town of Puerto Ocopa. From here, boats can be hired to descend the Río Tambo, a remote corner of Peru's Amazon.

If you are driving, or not shy about hitchhiking, there is a spectacular dirt road to Huancayo from Satipo, which leads up and over a 4,320-meter pass, Abra Tortuga, in the Huaytapallana range. No regular transport follows this route, a 10-hour journey between Satipo and Huancayo.

Entertainment and Events

San Ramón has a lively **Founder's Day** celebration in late August, with burro races and cooking contests. Oxapampa, another four hours into the jungle, has a similar celebration that includes Asháninka archery competition. The two main German colonies have fascinating, beer-soaked celebrations that also include cockfighting championships and *torneo de cinta,* a jousting contest on fast horses where men lunge for bits of suspended embroidery—Pozuzo's is in late July, and Oxapampa's is in late August. If you plan to overnight on these dates, make reservations well ahead of time.

La Merced's discotheques are on the road west of La Merced: **El Bosque** (Manuel Pinto 597, tel. 064/53-1805, Thurs.–Sat.) and **Paradise** (Peru 571, tel. 064/53-2322, Sat.). San Ramón's best discotheque is **Lostic,** on the southern end of town.

The Amazon

THE ENDANGERED GIANT OTTER

River otters were once found throughout thousands of miles of Amazon waters but now have been reduced to two species found mainly in remote Amazon headwaters and out-of-the-way oxbow lakes. The larger species, the giant otter, is most commonly seen in lakes, both in the lakes in Parque Nacional Manu and around Puerto Maldonado. With a length of up to 1.8 meters (six feet) and weight of 30 kg (66 pounds), the giant otter is considerably larger than the sea otters found along the West Coast of North America.

A family consists of a pair of adults plus a few juveniles, and their home is a mud cave in an oxbow lake bank, which is marked by trampled vegetation and carefully placed boundaries of feces and urine. The otters typically maintain a few campsites, which they head to during the day to sun and fish. The giant otter has stubby feet, making it an awkward land traveler, but a powerful, flattened tail for acrobatic, fast swimming. The otters eat up to 4 kg of fish a day, which they can be seen (and heard) noisily chomping from their log perches. When the opportunity presents, they will also eat baby caiman, snakes, and young turtles. Though extremely inquisitive animals, they avoid the aquatic megapredators, including the adult black caimans and anaconda that can be up to 8 meters (26 feet). In combat, a group of otters would probably prevail over these animals, with their powerful jaws and swimming abilities. A lone otter, however, is more vulnerable.

After being raised with their family, juvenile otters eventually go off on their own, staying close at first before eventually crawling overland to homestead new, empty waters. Biologists believe that less than a third of the juvenile otters survive the experience of heading out on their own, an ingrained part of otter life that does not seem to be helping the species recover from the edge of extinction.

Because of intense hunting between the 1940s and 1970s, otter populations have plummeted to the point where they have become officially endangered. Even though it is illegal to hunt otters and sell their pelts, river otter populations continue to decline in some areas. Because they are at the top of the food chain, many biologists consider their decline to be a worrisome sign of watershed contamination from the mercury used in gold mining.

For more information, see the web page of the Giant Otter Research and Conservation Project, which was launched by the Frankfurt Zoological Society in 1990: www.giantotters.com.

Sports and Recreation

Gustavo de Madariago at **Impala Tours** (Tarma 290, Plaza de Armas, tel. 064/53-2476 or 064/53-2219, info@impalaperu.com, www.impalaperu.com) is an excellent source of information on the area. He is a rafting guide who can arrange mountain biking, remote river trips, rappelling, and bird watching in the area. He has developed some very creative routes through the area—such as his one-day romp through the Perene Valley, and multi-day trips into the wilds around Pozuzo—that are highly recommended.

Another option is **Roger Tours** (Tarma 381, Plaza de Armas, tel. 064/53-1844, rogertoursperu@hotmail.com).

Lucho Hurtado, the energetic owner of **Incas del Peru** in Huancayo (Giráldez 652, tel. 064/22-3303, incas_peru@hotmail.com, www.incasdelperu.org, 9 A.M.–1 P.M. and 4–7 P.M. Mon.–Sat., 10 A.M.–1 P.M. Sunday), takes groups into the Chanchamayo area for a five-day, action-packed stay at his father's farm near Pozuzo.

Shopping

Asháninka and Shipibo Indians sell a variety of trinkets, including bead jewelry and woven cloth, on La Merced's main square most evenings. There are a few *artesania* shops scattered around town, including El Chunchito (Tarma 202, tel. 064/53-1234, 10 A.M.–10 P.M.). There is a bustling, all-day market near Ayacucho and Arequipa, with plenty of the therapeutic *uña de gato* herb for sale.

Accommodations

La Merced is a rather unappealing town, and its lodging options are lackluster. San Ramón is cleaner but has few services. If at all possible, spring for the charming bungalows between the two towns.

Under $10: La Merced has a few plain but clean hostels in this range—the trick is avoiding street noise. **Hospedaje Cristina** (Tarma 582, tel. 064/531276, $7 s $9 d) has parquet floors and peeling walls but the bathrooms are clean. **Hospedaje Los Victor** (Tarma 376 interior, tel. 064/80-9550, $7 s $10 d), in the small passageway off the main square leading to Los Koquis Restaurant, has clean, small rooms and one with a great view of the plaza. The newest rooms are to be had at **Hostal Kankun** (Tarma 578, tel. 064/53-1576), which has simple rooms with tile floors and almost no noise in the back. All these options include cable TV.

$10–25: In La Merced, **Hostal El Rey** (Junín 103, tel. 064/53-1185, $17 s $20 d) has been in business 25 years and has a reputation for excellent service. It has retiled all of its rooms, which are clean, spacious, though a bit sterile (we also found many of the rooms quite noisy). The same owner recently opened the drab but somewhat better **Hotel Reyna** (Palca 259, tel. 064/53-1780, rchareyna@hotmail.com, $17 s $23 d), which offers clean, safe rooms with huge showers a half-block from the main plaza.

In San Ramón, a highly recommended option is the peaceful, quiet, and friendly **Hospedaje El Parral** (Uriarte 355, tel. 064/33-1128, $10 s, $14 d). Just east of San Ramón, cheap bungalows are to be had at **Hospedaje El Rancho** (road to waterfall El Tirol, tel. 064/33-1076, elranchoperu@yahoo .com, www.geocities.com/elranchoperu, $10 s, $20 d, including breakfast). There are no luxuries here, but the river is nearby and the bungalows are nice and out of earshot from the road.

$25–50: The oldest, and still the best, bungalow option in Chanchamayo is ⊠ **Golden Gate** (just west of Herreria Bridge outside La Merced, tel. 064/53-1483, divnafly@latinmail.com, $22 s, $31 d, including cable TV and breakfast). Golden Gate—named after a nearby bridge that resembles the San Franciscan original—was opened in 1983 by longtime Chanchamayo residents Rudolf and Divna May. This amicable German-Yugoslav couple love to explain local history from their front door, which also doubles as the reception of this cozy, down-home establishment. Service is friendly and informal, rooms are comfortable, and there

are several family bungalows lined with beautiful dark wood and nestled between gardens against the hillside (single beds only). Other services include a nice pool and ping-pong tables, bar, communal kitchen, and swimming pool.

Another set of nice bungalows, recently opened, is **Gad Gha Kum** (3 km east of San Ramón, tel. 064/33-1580, gadghakum@terra.com.pe, $23 s, $31 d, including cable TV and breakfast). These brand-new bungalows, with intricate bamboo ceilings and mosquito net windows, have real spring mattresses, fridges, and hammocks. There are also a few romantic round bungalows with queen beds and thatched roofs, a restaurant that serves vegetarian food, and waterfalls nearby.

Next door to Golden Gate is **Cocos Hospedaje** (tel. 064/53-1793, or in Lima tel. 01/344-0035, santari@terra.com.pe, $28). This has a nice pool, beautiful bungalows, and a bar but its slick, overly polished atmosphere appeals mainly to young Limeños.

In San Ramón, **El Refugio** (El Ejército 490, tel. 064/33-1082, $23 s, $29 d) has a set of 21 rather bland concrete bungalows, with spectacular gardens and a nice pool.

Food

La Merced has three safe and well-known restaurants, all lined up near the main square and specializing in jungle cooking, including *cebiche* made from *doncella* fish (ordering the deer or wild pig only encourages commercial hunters). The first, **Los Koquis** (Tarma 376 interior, tel. 064/53-1536, $3–6, 11 A.M.–11 P.M.) has excellent *cebiche* and *pachamanca*-style chicken. The second, **Shambari-Campa** (Tarma 389, tel. 064/53-2842, $3–6), has an even more extensive menu and an interesting series of old historical photos on the wall—along with more recent portraiture of Carol and Darlene Bernaola, blonde twins from the nearby town of Villarica that were Playboy Playmates in 2000! The third, **El Sabroso,** is next door with a similar menu but a cleaner, less cluttered interior. For dessert, head to **Dulceria La Encantada** (Tarma 252, tel. 064/33-5237), a new establishment that serves delicious apple pie.

The quieter San Ramón also has two excellent options. If you are leery of the sketchy sanitary habits of most *chifas*, you can dive in head-first at **Felipe Siu** (Progresso 440, tel. 064/33-1078, elsi465@hotmail.com, 11:30 A.M.–3 P.M. and 6–11 P.M.). This charming, decades-old establishment with sun-filled garden is known for *pollo chijokay*, fried chicken with ginger sauce, and *limon kay*, strips of chicken in lemon sauce. Meat eaters can find everything grilled to perfection at **El Parral** (Uriarte 355, tel. 064/33-1128, noon–4 P.M. and 6–11 P.M.), which also has a bar and the recommended Hospedaje El Parral next door.

Information and Services

There is a **phone center** at 158 Junín and also on the Plaza de Armas. Internet is offered by **Selvanet** (Arica 131, with Ayacucho, 9 A.M.–10:30 P.M., $0.75 per hour) and **Delvi Net** (Tarma 381 on Plaza de Armas). For tourist information, see Gustavo de Madariago at **Impala Tours.**

Getting There and Around

La Merced's main bus station is on the eastern end of town, at the triangular intersection of Fitzgerald and Carmen. From here, *combis* can be taken nearly anywhere: to Satipo ($3, two hours, leave throughout day), Oxapampa ($3, four hours, leave between 4–6 A.M.), Puerto Bermudez ($7, seven hours, leave between 3–5 A.M.), or Huancayo ($3, three hours). Double-decked buses from **Empresa de Transportes Junin** also leave from here to Lima for $7 per seat, a seven-hour drive. Across the street is **Transmar** (Fitzgerald 572), which offers buses

along the paved highway to Pucallpa on Sundays, a 18-hour journey with stops in Huáunuco and Tingo Maria that costs $13. Two other high-quality companies, with double-deck buses and good safety records, are **Nuestra Señora de la Merced** and **Chanchamayo.** These are both located west of the main drag and have several buses to Lima daily.

There is an airport just west of San Ramón that is a hub for small planes flying in and out of the jungle. These three-passenger planes can be contracted to fly anywhere in the area for $220 per hour. **AMSA** (tel. 064/33-1254, rfmamsa@viabcp.com) flies to Puerto Inca (one hour), Puerto Bermudez (42 minutes), or Pucallpa (1.5 hours). Unless you return the same day, however, you also have to pay the plane's return flight.

Another option is to hang around the airport and hitch a ride on a private plane with an extra seat. Though drug trafficking has been largely eradicated from this area, choose planes with caution. No matter what the pilot says, be prepared to take a *combi* on the way back (trust us on this one). Even getting back from Puerto Bermudez is a grueling, seven-hour *combi* ride and much more during rainy season.

Motocars are everywhere in La Merced but are not really needed unless you want to take the $1 ride to the hilltop cross, a fabulous lookout over the Chanchamayo Valley that is not safe at night. *Combis* are also frequent between La Merced and San Ramón and leave when full from Junin and Arica in La Merced (every 15 minutes).

Iquitos

Though commonly viewed as a launching pad for exploring Peru's north Amazon, Iquitos is swanky and interesting enough to detain travelers for a day or two. It is Peru's quintessential jungle town and, at nearly half a million inhabitants, is probably the largest city in the world that cannot be reached by road. Hemmed in by muddy rivers and flooded rainforest on all sides, Iquitos' only bridge to the outside world are planes and cargo boats.

Because of its isolation, terrorism never reached

here in the 1980s and 1990s. Perhaps as a result, Iquitos has a relaxed, laid-back vibe that seems much closer to Bangkok than, say, Cusco. The air is thick and steamy, and life revolves around the mile-wide Amazon River, lazy and torpid after collecting water from all of Peru's major rivers. People here look Asian, because they are descendants of a dozen different Indian groups, along with waves of Italian and Chinese immigrants. The women have beautiful dark hair and limit their clothing to flip-flops, shorts,

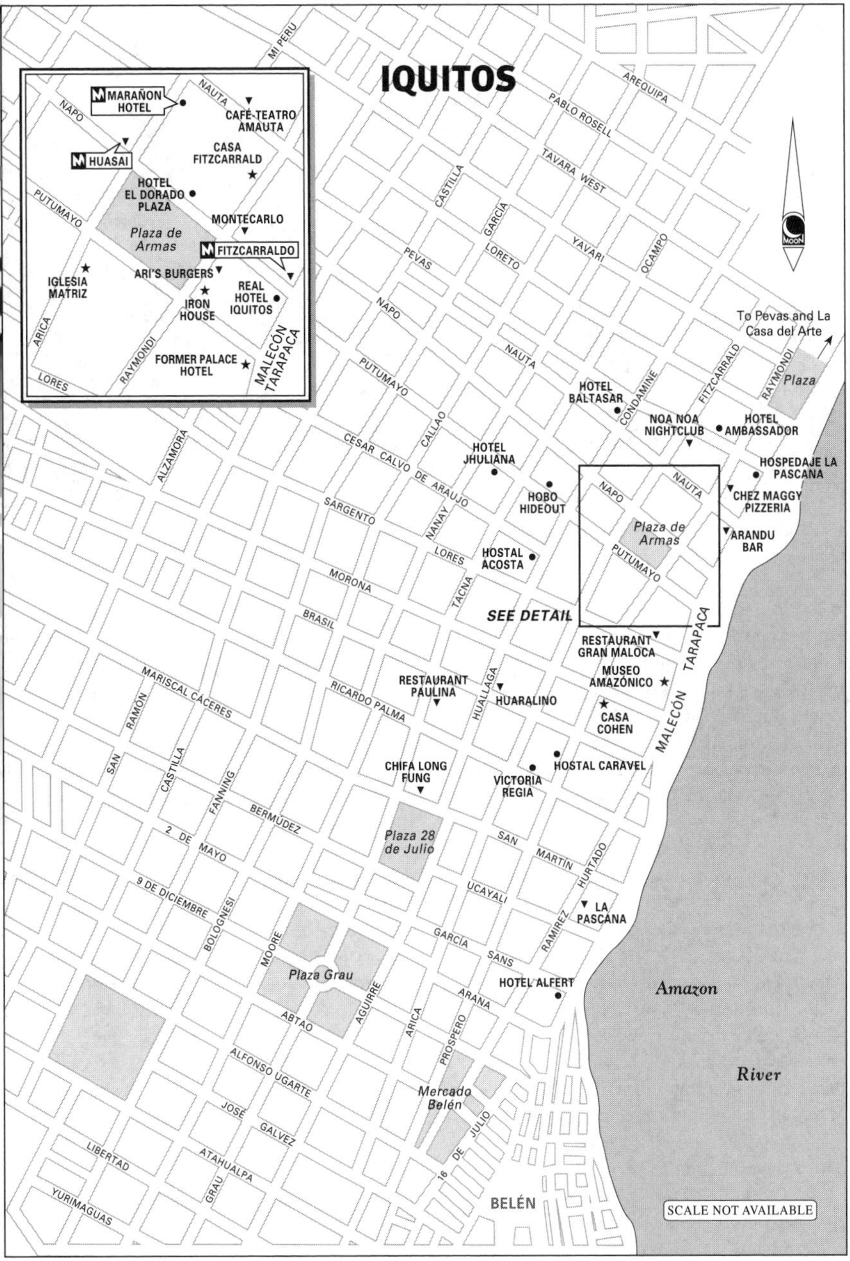

IQUITOS

Detail map:

MARAÑÓN HOTEL
CAFÉ-TEATRO AMAUTA
CASA FITZCARRALD
HUASAI
HOTEL EL DORADO PLAZA
MONTECARLO
Plaza de Armas
FITZCARRALDO
IGLESIA MATRIZ
ARI'S BURGERS
IRON HOUSE
REAL HOTEL IQUITOS
FORMER PALACE HOTEL
MALECÓN TARAPACÁ

Streets (detail): MI PERU, NAUTA, NAPO, PUTUMAYO, ARICA, LORES, RAYMONDI, CASTILLA, GARCIA

Main map streets: MI PERU, NAUTA, NAPO, PUTUMAYO, ARICA, LORES, CASTILLA, GARCIA, PEVAS, LORETO, YAVARI, OCAMPO, AREQUIPA, PABLO ROSELL, TAVARA WEST, CONDAMINE, FITZCARRALD, RAYMONDI, CESAR CALVO DE ARAUJO, CALLAO, SARGENTO, ALZAMORA, NANAY, LORES, TACNA, MORONA, BRASIL, HUALLAGA, RICARDO PALMA, MARISCAL CACERES, RAMON, SAN, CASTILLA, FANNING, BERMÚDEZ, 2 DE MAYO, 9 DE DICIEMBRE, BOLOGNESI, MOORE, AGUIRRE, ABTAO, ALFONSO UGARTE, JOSE GALVEZ, LIBERTAD, ATAHUALPA, GRAU, YURIMAGUAS, SAN MARTIN, UCAYALI, GARCIA, SANS, RAMIREZ, HURTADO, ARANA, PROSPERO, ARICA, 16 DE JULIO, MALECÓN TARAPACÁ

Labeled places (main map):

Tø Pevas and La Casa del Arte
Plaza
HOTEL BALTASAR
NOA NOA NIGHTCLUB
HOTEL AMBASSADOR
HOSPEDAJE LA PASCANA
CHEZ MAGGY PIZZERIA
ARANDU BAR
HOTEL JHULIANA
HOBO HIDEOUT
Plaza de Armas
HOSTAL ACOSTA
SEE DETAIL
RESTAURANT GRAN MALOCA
MUSEO AMAZÓNICO
CASA COHEN
RESTAURANT PAULINA
HUARALINO
CHIFA LONG FUNG
VICTORIA REGIA
HOSTAL CARAVEL
Plaza 28 de Julio
LA PASCANA
Plaza Grau
HOTEL ALFERT
Amazon River
ALFONSO UGARTE
Mercado Belén
BELÉN

SCALE NOT AVAILABLE

The Amazon

© AVALON TRAVEL PUBLISHING, INC.

An Amazonian native from the Loreto Department, which includes Iquitos, wears a headdress made of macaw feathers.

and tank tops. The men dress much the same, but forego shirts altogether.

The weather in Iquitos, even during the October–May rainy season, is predictable. The sky dawns blue most days but by late afternoon fills with the clouds of convection storms, which release sheets of cool rain. Between January and June, the Amazon rises a staggering 15 meters (50 feet), carrying silt and fallen trees brought down from the Andes. The river floods hundreds of miles of forest around Iquitos. Oceangoing tankers of up to 13,000 tons make the 3,600-kilometer odyssey from the Atlantic.

The floods enrich the surrounding fields, which are planted with rice, peanuts, watermelon, and pumpkin as soon as the water begins to recede in July. Fish leave the oxygen-poor oxbow lakes in the low season and concentrate in the river, prompting huge harvests of bass *(corvina)*, catfish *(dorado)*, and *paiche*, a prehistoric-looking fish that outsizes most NBA players.

The first outsider to see this area was Spanish explorer **Francisco de Orellana,** who made an epic descent down the Amazon River in 1542 and contacted the area's ethic groups, which included the Iquitos, Cocamas, Huitotos, Boras, Ticunas, and Orejones. Eventually the Spaniards left the area to the Jesuits, who founded a settlement here in the 1750s but were expelled from Latin America shortly thereafter. Iquitos had shrunk to only 100 inhabitants when Italian explorer **Antonio Raimondi** visited in the mid-19th century and described it as a *small Indians' quarters.*

The ramshackle settlement, however, exploded into one of Peru's richest cities thanks to the 1880–1912 rubber boom. Monuments to this time, now badly faded, include an iron house designed by Gustav Eiffel in the Plaza de Armas and various Italianate mansions with lavish mahogany interiors and outer walls decorated with Sevillean tiles. A small locomotive, which now sits abandoned in Iquitos' Plaza 28 de Julio, chugged around town hauling loads of *caucho,* or rubber latex, during the week. Old photos show men with top hats and women with parasols boarding this train on Sundays with picnic baskets.

The flip side of the opulence was the oppression and abject poverty of the Indian and mestizo rubber tappers, who lived in virtual enslavement and frequently died of malaria and other diseases. The floating city of **Belén,** which some call the "Venice of South America" and others a slum, is also a leftover from that era.

By World War I the rubber boom ended as quickly as it began, when plantations in Malaysia used seeds smuggled from Peru to produce *caucho* at a far lower cost. Though the rubber boom revived briefly during the Japanese occupation of Asia in World War II, Iquitos sunk into a bust cycle until 1960, when oil began to be pumped from rich fields near Nauta. Companies like PetroPeru, Texas-based Occidental, and the Brazilian PetroPlus continue to pump oil and process it at a refinery 14 km downriver from Iquitos, which is next door to another sign of the times. From a discreet military base on the banks of the Amazon, the Peruvian Navy and U.S. Drug Enforcement Agency patrol the waters and air for signs of cocaine trafficking. No one, however, can stop the native smugglers who pack the unprocessed coca paste, or *pasta básica,* north through rainforest paths toward laboratories in Colombia.

Iquitos is the pioneer of Amazonian tourism, which began here in the 1960s, and is the base for a variety of lodges, cruise ships, and adventure agencies. Other industries include lumber, agriculture, the export of exotic fish and birds, and *barbasco,* a poisonous plant used by the natives to kill fish that is now being used as an insecticide.

SIGHTS

In the center of the **Plaza de Armas** you will find the Obelisk, a monument to the Iquitos military heroes who fought in the War of the Pacific against Chile in 1879. The south side of the plaza is marked by the most important Catholic church of the city, **Iglesia Matriz,** built in 1919. Inside you will find religious paintings by Américo Pinasco and César Calvo de Araujo. Also on the plaza, on the corner of Putumayo and Próspero, is the **Casa de Fierro,** or Iron House, designed by Gustav Eiffel for the 1889 Paris Exhibition. It was bought by wealthy rubber businessman Anselmo del Aguila and shipped in pieces down the Amazon to Iquitos, where it was reassembled on its current site. The Iron House is beautiful when lit at night and con-

THE SIDE-NECKED TARICAYA TURTLE

Fossils indicate that earth's first turtles could not withdraw their heads into their shells. Instead they tucked their heads to one side, as the side-necked taricaya turtle still does. Reaching a maximum of 45 cm (about a foot and half) in length, the taricaya turtle eats meat but also chomps on fruits and seeds, which it can reach during the high waters of rainy season. They are solitary nesters and lay approximately 30–50 eggs, which have been an important source of protein for Peru's Amazon natives. Thanks to programs in Reserva Nacional Pacaya-Samiria, they have been brought back from the edge of extinction in some parts of Peru though they remain fairly common along the Madre de Dios and Manu rivers. Look for groups of this aquatic turtle, all stacked on top of each other like fallen dominos, on logs jutting from the water. They sun themselves in order to increase body temperature and probably also to eliminate the buildup of algae on their shells, or *carapaces.*

tains a café and upstairs English pub. Around the corner at Napo and Raymondi is the **Casa de Barro,** the mud-and-wood house that was used as a warehouse by rubber baron Fermín Fitzcarrald. Inside is a central patio with arches.

A block from the plaza along the Amazon River, the pedestrian Malecón Tarapacá, or Boulevard, is the other focus of activity in Iquitos and a prime viewpoint from which to view the river's landscape. The construction of this walkway began during the rubber boom in the late 19th century, and uit has been recently improved with fountains, benches, and street lamps. The promenade is lined with 19th-century mansions built by rubber barons and decorated with azulejos, or tiles imported from Spain and Portugal. The most spectacular of these is the Former Palace Hotel at Malecón Tarapacá 208. Built in 1908 in an art nouveau style, this three-story building was the most luxurious in Peru's Amazon. Its iron balconies were imported from Hamburg, the marble from Carrera, and the multicolored mosaics from Seville. The building currently

THE CAIMAN: NEITHER CROC NOR GATOR

A caiman is first a reptile, and second a crocodilian, which can reach up to six meters (20 feet) long and prefers the warm, still waters of oxbow lakes and lower rivers. They are very good swimmers, with long, slender bodies and powerful tails that drive them through the water. They can crush anything with their powerful jaws and, though their main food source is fish, they will eat anything they can get their jaws on, including capybara, juvenile otters, birds, insects, and mollusks.

There are four species of caiman in Peru: the dwarf (one to five meters), the smooth-fronted (two meters), the spectacled (five meters), and the black (up to six meters). This last has black marks, a spiky tail, and a short snout and is second in size in the Upper Amazon to the eight-meter-long anaconda snake. After being hunted relentlessly for their skins in the first half of the 20th century, the Amazon's caiman population is a fraction of what it was in 1900.

Caimans mate in October and lay 20–60 eggs in January. The black caiman nest is a compound of tree leaves 1.5 meters in diameter with eggs arranged in two layers that are separated and apparently warmed by rotting leaves.

Perhaps caimans are such fierce predators because they have such a hard time growing up. The eggs are eaten by snakes, fish, and hawks. After hatching, baby caimans hide in the water grass, coming out only at night, to avoid being eaten by a turtle, otter, or wading bird. Only 5 percent of caimans survive the ordeal.

Caimans can be easily spotted by their eyes' red reflection in a flashlight beam, a common night activity at many jungle lodges. With a fast jab into the water with their hands, most Amazon guides are capable of pulling a juvenile caiman up to a half meter out of the water for inspection. Though interesting, this practice no doubt makes life a bit harder for the baby caiman and should be discouraged.

The black caiman can reach up to six meters in length and is the largest of Peru's four caiman species.

serves as the Cuartel General, or Army House.

Further along the Malecón Tarapacá is the **Biblioteca Amazónica** (Malecón Tarapacá 354, 9 A.M.–5 P.M. Mon.–Sat.), an excellent library containing a range of books, maps, old photographs and newspapers, films, and a map archive that specializes in regional issues in the Americas. Next door is the **Museo Amazónico** (Malecón Tarapacá 386, 9 A.M.–1 P.M. and 3–7 P.M. Mon.–Fri., 9 A.M.–1 P.M. Sat., $0.85), which houses the "Sons of our Land" exhibit created by Fellipe Lettersten in 1987. The artist formed 76 fiberglass statues of indigenous Indians from various tribes of Peru, Brazil, and Venezuela to preserve the memory of these rapidly vanishing cultures. He covered live natives in an emulsion of mud and plaster to create the molds for the statues. Like Madame Tussaud's wax figures, the statues have an eerie, lifelike quality. The museum also displays photographs of early-20th-century Iquitos. The museum itself was built in 1863 as the governor's house and then restored in 1996 and converted into a museum. It contains wall panels, doors, and ceilings of intricately carved old-growth mahogany.

There are a scattering of elegant old rubber baron homes near the city center, including the **Casa Cohen** at Próspero 401. The Cohen family brought tiles from Morocco and grates from Paris to build this spectacular house in 1905, which now houses a supermarket. Down the street is the neoclassic **Casa Morey** at Próspero 502.

BELÉN

During the 1980-82 filming of *Fitzcarraldo,* Werner Herzog did not have to look far to re-create the poverty of the rubber worker slums. He simply shot the film at Belén, a gigantic floating shantytown of homes built atop rafts of balsa wood that rise and fall with the river. It is an exotic sight, with children jumping into the water from their front porch and entire families paddling along the waterways in dugout canoes. Closer to the riverbank, other families live in thatched homes lifted above the water on rickety stilts. Because of the recent meandering of the Amazon away from Iquitos, the whole area be-

comes a gigantic mud flat during the dry months from July to December. Although the municipality does a good job with trash collecting, there are serious health problems during the dry months because of the open sewers.

To visit the floating city, head down Próspero south from the Plaza de Armas to Belén's raucous and colorful market, which begins around García Sanz. Along with plastic kitchen items and cheap clothing imported from Brazil, vendors sell every imaginable jungle fruit and vegetable, dried fish, medicinal herbs, chickens, and contraband meat of *sajino,* the wild pig, and *venado,* or deer. If you are tall, you will be ducking frequently under the plastic awnings. The smells of garbage, mud, and all of these foods baking in the sun can become overpowering at times, so visit in the morning when the market is cleanest and most active. The area is safe by day but it is still best to leave your watch and most of your money at your hotel.

Once in the market, head left toward the waterfront along 9 de Diciembre and walk out on wooden walkways toward the water. Here there are people with canoes who will paddle you around Belén for $3 a half hour. Make sure to

Amazon boats with floating city of Belén in the background

children at play in the floating city of Belén

bring sunscreen, glasses, and a hat because the sun on the river is poweful. For your walk home, return up Próspero and hang a right at García Sanz toward Hostal Alfert, where there is an excellent view over the thatched homes along the riverbank. From here, skirt the waterfront until Malecón Tarapacá. A recommended *cebiche* lunch stop is Restaurant La Pascana.

PILPINTUWASI BUTTERFLY FARM

There are a number of places to visit outside Iquitos, though frankly the surrounding jungle is far more interesting. About 15 minutes west of the city is the **Quistococha Tourist Center,** which has a lake with rowboats, a fish farm, and a rather pitiful zoo. Iquiteños head here and to **Lago Moronacocha,** 3 km east of the city, on the weekends to swim, sunbathe, and water-ski. The best day trip, however, is **Pilpintuwasi** (tel. 065/23-2665, pilpintuwasi@ hotmail.com, www.pilpintuwasi.com, 9 A.M.– 5 P.M. Tues.–Sun., $5 adults, $3 students), which means "butterfly's home" in Quechua.

Huge mesh tents contain 42 species of butterflies, which flutter above the stone paths that lead through exotic gardens maintained by owner Gudrun Sperrer. She has designed the garden to contain all the fruits, flowers, and leaves that the caterpillars and butterflies need for survival.

Notable species include the brilliant blue morpho and the *buho,* or owl buttefly, that reveals two giant black spots when spread on a tree in mimicry of an owl. Apart from butterflies, the farm also contains a young jaguar, a tapir, and the large *agouti* rodent, all of which Sperrer reluctantly adopted to save them from Iquitos' zoo. To reach Pilpintuwasi, first head to the port and swimming beach of Bella Vista–Nanay, which is 15 minutes outside of town and can be reached by *colectivos* along Próspero that say *Bella Vista–Nanay.* It is about a 20-minute boat ride to Pilpintuwasi from here, passing Bora and Yagua villages along the way, though in low-water months passengers have to disembark early and walk along a path for 15 minutes.

ENTERTAINMENT AND EVENTS

Iquitos' nightlife is clustered around the first block of Malecón Tarapacá. **Arandu Bar** (Malecon Tarapacá 113, tel. 065/24-3434, 4 P.M.–2 A.M.) plays hip music and serves pricey drinks. Next door are less classy bars but drinks are about half the price. Toward the plaza, **Café-Teatro Amauta** (Nauta 250, tel. 065/23-3366, 8 P.M.–2 A.M.) is an artsy place; its sidewalk tables and bohemian atmosphere would fit in well on the streets of Paris. It is a good place to eat and drink and has Iquitos' best-known *peña* after 10 P.M. most nights, featuring live Amazon and Latin music. For a night of dancing try **Noa Noa Nightclub** (Pevas 292, tel. 065/23-2902). This trendy disco near the Plaza de Armas plays salsa and Latin rock over a two-level dance floor.

Late-night drinks can always be found at **The Yellow Rose of Texas** (Putumayo 180, tel. 065/24-1010, 24 hours, $4–8). The best place for late-night munchies is **Ari's Burgers** on the Plaza de Armas. (see *Food*).

The Festival of San Juan

The Amazon can be very cold, as is clear to anyone in Iquitos for the Festival of San Juan, which is celebrated from June 23–25. During this time, cold winds that originate in Patagonia sweep across the Amazon basin and plunge temperatures to as low as 8°C (46°F). These cold spells, or *friajes,* can happen anytime from May to August but are most common around San Juan's birthday in late June. Don't expect to see many animals during a *friaje*—the monkeys huddle up together in balls to stay warm and the birds roost until it's all over.

The religious and meteorological coincidence has merged over the centuries into Iquitos' biggest party, celebrated these days at the Mercado Artesanal San Juan on the way to the airport with dance competitions from indigenous groups and rock concerts. During the festival, everyone in Iquitos makes and eats *juanes,* tamale-like bundles of chicken, tomato, and onion that are wrapped in a leaf from the bijao palm, which imparts a delicious flavor to the concoction. And don't forget to bring a sweater or a windbreaker, because *Los Vientos de San Juan* ("The Winds of San Juan") make the place feel more like Seattle or London than Iquitos.

Iquitos also has a Founder's Day celebration on Jan. 5 and a carnival in late February or early March. Santo Tomás, a lakeside village 15 km northeast of Iquitos that is known for carved root and ceramics handicrafts, has a handicraft fair on Aug. 21 and festival in honor of its patron saint Sept. 23–25.

SHOPPING

A series of market stalls on stilts hovering above the Amazon make up the **Centro Artesanal Anaconda** (Malecón Tarapacá, 8 A.M.–10 P.M. daily). Vendors sell jewelery, sandals, paintings, beaded curtains, shoulder bags, and other souvenirs. There are also a line of crafts stores along Próspero south of the Plaza de Armas, though Iquitos' largest handicraft market is the **Mercado Artesenal de San Juan** (Av. Quiñones Km 4.5, 9 A.M.–10 P.M. daily), on the road to the airport. A notable find here are the colorful native jungle seeds sold by the kilo. These can be used to make your own jewelry or other artistic endeavors. For books and drawing and writing materials, go to **Libreria Tamara** (Próspero 268, tel. 065/22-1711, 8 A.M.–1 P.M. and 3:30–9 P.M.). Rubber boots, binoculars, and other jungle equipment can be found at **Mad Mick's Trading Post** (Putumayo 180-B) near the Iron House. Locals do their food shopping at the colorful **Belen Market,** which is liveliest in the mornings. Much of Iquitos slows down, or shuts down, in this area during the afternoon siesta, 1–3 P.M. Nearby there is also a cluster of handicraft stores on the sixth block of Arica, which are generally open all day, 8 A.M.–9 P.M.

ACCOMMODATIONS

Most hotels in Iquitos will pick you up at the airport and save you the hassle of dealing with taxi drivers. In the budget category, many of the inexpensive hotels make false claims about water, so it is a good idea to hold your hand under the faucet before paying. In general the area north of

CAPYBARA: MASTER OF THE GRASSES

The cuddly shape and peaceful demeanor of the capybara seems profoundly out of sync with the brutal, anaconda-eat-jaguar world of the Amazon rainforest. Troops of capybara can be seen munching on the lush grasses and aquatic vegetation at the banks of most Amazon rivers (their name in Guarani means "master of grasses"). At the first whiff of danger, these timid animals scurry into the muddy water and sink like submarines out of sight. Though they are mammals, they can hold their breath underwater for up to five minutes and can even sleep underwater, their snouts barely protruding above the surface.

The Capybara (scientific name: *Hydrochaerus hydrochaeris*) is the largest of the world's nearly 1,800 rodents and looks like a cross between a guinea pig and a hippopotamus. It grows to about the size of a pig (roughly 100 pounds and four feet long) and is covered with a thin layer of reddish-brown hair. It has small ears and nose, and eyes that are perched at the top of its barrel-shaped snout for easy use while swimming. Though clumsy on land, capybaras are agile swimmers with their slightly webbed toes and feet that are longer in the front than in the back.

Capybara is a prized bush meat among Amazon natives and is an important prey for Amazon megafauna such as anaconda, jaguar, puma, ocelot, harpy eagle, and caiman. Despite all the hunting, capybara remains common in Peru's Amazon, thanks to its rapid reproduction: females begin mating in the water a year after they are born and have between two to eight babies at a time. Both male and females live to be about 10 years old.

Certain aspects of capybara life continue to perplex biologists. For one thing, the animals have a strange bump at the end of their snout that may be a scent gland for marking territory. As rodents go, capybaras are extremely vocal. They emit a bewildering series of chatters, whistles, grunts, clicks, and purrs. When danger is present, the dominant male will bark to alert the troop, much like the marmot's shriek.

---

the Plaza de Armas is safer and more attractive. There are dozens of hostels clustered around the Belén Market, south of the Plaza de Armas, but they are mostly grimy and filled with the drone of passing *motocars*.

Under $10

A night at the **Hobo Hideout** (Putumayo 437, tel. 065/23-4099, mail@safarisrus.net, www.safarisrus.net, $8 s, $10 d) is the closest you can come to sleeping in the jungle without actually getting on a boat. This tiny place, overflowing with jungle plants, rates high on the charm scale despite its unfortunate collection of animal skins. Inside is a group room with six bunks, two private double rooms (one with private bath), and a big kitchen for backpackers. Out back is a treehouse that sleeps up to four and rents for $15/night.

Another good value is **Hospedaje La Pascana** (Pevas 133, tel. 065/23-3466, pascana@tsi.com.pe, $9 s, $12 d, including breakfast), located next to Iquitos' spectacular malecón. Simple, unadorned

rooms with clean bathrooms and tile floors are lined up along a central, plant-filled courtyard. There is also a book exchange and a related travel agency. **Hotel Baltasar** (Condamine 265, tel. 065/23-2240, $7 s, $10 d) is an excellent value for a more traditional hotel, with clean rooms, cable TV, and hot water. Rooms with air-conditioning are an additional $5.

There are a few decent options south of the Plaza de Armas. The best of these, with stunning views over Belén and the Amazon River, is **Hostal Alfert** (García Sanz, tel. 065/23-4105, reservacionalfert@yahoo.es, $5 s, $8 d). This 17-room establishment has been operated for two decades by former riverboat captain Alfonso Fernández, who has staked out a prime stretch of riverbank. The nine upstairs rooms look out over the river toward Belén and a vast complex of thatched homes propped up off the water on stilts. We spent hours marveling at the sight, and the rooms are simple and clean with spongy beds and a bit of hot water. **Hospedaje Manu**

(Próspero 1017, tel. 065/23-5391, $6 s, $9 d) has an odd collection of rooms painted with fluorescent teddy bears. The rooms have private baths, no hot water, and TV with cable and tend to be quieter away from the street.

$10–25

You've come all this way to Iquitos, why not rent a room overlooking the Amazon at **Real Hotel Iquitos** (Malecón Tarapacá with Napo, tel. 065/23-1011, $15 s, $20 d)? This grand dame of a hotel, though somewhat abandoned, is a great choice for those willing to sacrifice some modern comfort for quirky, historic charm. This 50-year-old historic hotel has a grand, though somewhat rundown interior, and the rooms have wood or black-and-white tile floors. Rooms of the same price vary from small and cozy to absolutely enormous (especially Room 218). This location on the pedestrian waterfront is wonderfully quiet. Amenities include private bath, TV, and refrigerator.

For a more standard hotel and a good value, try **Hostal Jhuliana** (Putumayo 521, tel. 065/23-3154, hostaljhuliana@e-milio.com, $20 s, $25 d, including breakfast). Carpeted rooms have comfortable beds, air-conditioning, refrigerators, and hot water. There is a full-service restaurant and bar.

Hostal Caravel (Próspero 568, tel. 065/23-2176, iquitos@backpacker.com, $6 pp, includes breakfast) is under new management and has a few backpacker bunk rooms with cable TV, breakfast, and access to a kitchen at dinnertime. It is a safe, well-managed place and only four blocks from the main square.

Hospedaje Mi Selvita (Qui onez Km 3.5, Distrito San Juan Bautista, tel. 065/26-0165, llaida@terra.com, $6 pp, including breakfast) is near the airport and the zoo and is a quick *motocar* ride into Iquitos. As its name suggests, this bed-and-breakfast is set amid a little jungle, with a tropical garden and a pond for the huge *paiche* fish and turtles. The rooms are clean with cool water showers, fans, and televisions upon request. The owner, Aydee Rios Cardenas, speaks passable English and can arrange tours and plane tickets.

$25–50

The price seems too good to be true at the [N] **Marañon Hotel** (285 Nauta, tel. 065/24-2673, hmaranon@ec_red.com, $25 s, $30 d, including breakfast) Opened in 2002, this new hotel is somewhat of an oasis in this hot, sticky town. Large rooms are kept cool with tile floors, air-conditioning, and walls painted cool shades of blues and purples. Amenities include refrigerators, comfortable beds (hard to find in Iquitos), a large tub, 24-hour hot water, a nice outdoor pool, and a Peruvian restaurant. Make reservations ahead of time, as this hotel fills up frequently.

Hotel Acosta (Araujo and Huallaga, tel. 065/23-5974, info@hotelacosta.com, www.hotelacosta.com, $25 s, $30 d) is another comfortable hotel with all the amenities, including AC, hot water, cable TV, phones, refrigerators, and safe boxes. Internet is available in the air-conditioned lobby. There is no pool here, but you are welcome to use the pool at its sister hotel, the comfortable but overpriced **Victoria Regia** (Ricardo Palma 252, tel. 065/23-1983, info@victoriaregiahotel.com, $40 s, $50 d). Prices at both hotels include a continental breakfast and airport transportation and are frequently linked to the Heliconia Lodge, 80 km downriver from Iquitos. **Hostal Ambassador** (Pevas 260, tel. 065/23-3110, $20 s, $30 d) has hot water and is clean but rooms are dark and musty. This hotel, affiliated with Paseos Amazonicos, makes sense if you are a member of Hosteling International and qualify for a $10 discount.

Over $50

The five-star hotel of Iquitos is **El Dorado Plaza Hotel** (Napo 258, Plaza de Armas, tel. 065/22-2555, iquitos@eldoradoplazahotel.com, $88 s, $88 d). The 65 rooms are plush business fare, decked out with all the amenities, and some on the upper floors have nice views toward the Amazon River. Additional services include gym with sauna, boutique, business center, a huge sun-filled atrium in the lobby, and an outdoor pool with bar and jacuzzi. There is also a good though pricey restaurant, Mitos.

FOOD

Iquitos' most famous dish is *juanes,* and restaurants serve a variety of exotic jungle juices made from the *cocona, ungurahui,* and *camu camu* fruits. Main plates include *paiche con chonta* (fish with palm heart salad) and *tacacho con cecina* (fried banana mixed with jerky). *Inchicapi de gallina,* chicken soup with peanut, cilantro, and manioc root is also quite good.

Apart from these typical foods, many restaurants serve bush meat, including alligator, deer, the *agouti* rodent, turtle stew, and even grilled monkey. Eating these plates only encourages illegal hunting. There is a ban on fishing or serving *paiche* during its reproductive season from October to February. If you eat *paiche* during this time, ensure that it comes from one of the fish farms near Pucallpa—not from the river.

Cafés and Desserts

For a change of pace from traditional Peruvian food, try **The Yellow Rose of Texas** (Putumayo 180, tel. 065/24-1010, 24 hours, $4–8), an eclectic restaurant and bar owned by Texan Gerald Mayeaux, the former director of tourism of Iquitos, who did such a good job that he was eventually forced to step down. Waitresses in cowgirl-cheerleader outfits serve up everything from banana pancakes to BBQ ribs to burritos. Sit on a horse saddle bar stool for a cold beer or Pisco sour, or try out one of the romantic nooks out back. There is also an extensive selection of games and books. Gerald is an excellent source of information on the Iquitos area.

A block off the Plaza de Armas is **☒ Huasai** (Napo 326, tel. 065/24-2222, 7 A.M.–4:30 P.M., $4), a tiny, charming café with six tables that fill up very quickly at the lunch hour. Most people come for the $2 lunch menu with fish, chicken, beef, or vegetarian options. It also serves tamales, *cebiche,* sandwiches, and juices. Another great place for a $2 menu is **Papa Dan's Gringo Bar** (Putumayo Block 100, 7 A.M.–midnight, $2–7). Despite the name, this sidewalk café is often full of locals. It serves Peruvian dishes, hamburgers, and pastas, and has a book exchange.

A main Iquitos hangout for both locals and gringos is **Ari's Burgers** (Próspero and Napo, tel. 065/23-1470, 7:30 A.M.–3 A.M., $1–7). This open-air establishment, which resembles an American diner, is on the Plaza de Armas and impossible to miss with its fluorescent signage. The huge menu includes burgers and fries, milk shakes, vegatarian dishes, grilled meats, and a huge range of desserts.

Excellent wood-fired pizzas, lasagnas, and raviolis are served in a cozy atmosphere at **Chez Maggy Pizzeria** (Raymondi 177, tel. 065/24-1816, 6 P.M.–midnight, $3.50) Colorful art and a full bar make this a great place to have a leisurely dinner.

Chifa

The best place for Peruvian-Chinese food is **Chifa Long Fung** (San Martin 454, in front of Plaza 28 de Julio, tel. 065/23-3649, noon–3 P.M. and 6:30–11 P.M., $4–6), formerly known as Chifa Way Ming.

Peruvian

There are two excellent places for Peruvian food on the south end of town. **Restaurant Paulina** (Tacna 591, tel. 065/23-1298, $4–6) has a rather noisy streetfront but manages to serve up a mouth-watering array of local food, including *cebiche* and *paiche a la loretana,* served with fried *yucca* and palm heart salad. The owner, Paulina Angulo, has operated here for more than a decade, attracting locals with a good-value $2 lunch menu. **Huaralino** (Huallaga 490, tel. 065/22-3300, 11 A.M.–3 P.M. and 6–11 P.M.) serves up *cebiche de pato* (duck *cebiche*) and a range of local fish dishes.

Some of the best grilled meats we tried in Peru were at a hole-in-the-wall called **☒ Lidias** (Bolognesi 1142, 7 A.M.–9 P.M. daily), which serves up heaps of grilled pork, sausage, chicken, fish, and even *juanes.*

Locals say the best *cebiche* in Iquitos is to be found at Restaurant **La Pascana** (Hurtado 735, 8 A.M.–5 P.M., $2–7), an unassuming place near the riverfront that specializes in fish and has been in business for three decades. Another locals' favorite is *Don Diego* (Moore 467, near Brazil, 11 A.M.–2 P.M.), an extremely busy hole-in-the-wall that serves up *cebiche de dorado* for a mere $2.

PINK RIVER DOLPHINS

One of the Amazon's most flabbergasting sights, seen only in the Iquitos area, is the hot-pink body of the pink river dolphin as its rises above the muddy waters of lakes or rivers. Sometimes these enchanting creatures even swim alongside motorboats or poke their curious eyes and long, narrow snouts out of the water.

Though they look like traditional bottlenose dolphins from the water's surface, underwater photography reveals a bizarre shape. As if hot pink was not extravagant enough, their body has a strange S-shape, with a dorsal hump instead of a fin and a huge set of flippers. Once considered prehistoric, these unusual features are now regarded by biologists as adaptations to their specialized environment. Their unfused vertebrae, for instance, allow them to contort their bodies nearly 180 degrees in search of crustaceans and fish in the grassy waters and flooded forests of the Amazon.

Biologists have not studied the dolphin enough to understand its strange color, much of which is due to capillaries near the surface of the skin. Nor has their intelligence been measured, though their brains are 40 percent larger than humans'. Like most dolphins, they communicate through underwater whistles, chirps, and clicking noises. But unlike their oceangoing cousins, they have no known predators and thus no need to swim in large pods. Large groups of both pink and gray river dolphins can sometimes be seen, however, herding and banking fish at the mouths of rivers.

It is no wonder that the pink river dolphin occupies a special place in the mythology of Amazon tribes. Some tribes consider it a sacred animal that is credited with pushing drowning humans to shore, while others say it is an evil spirit that seduces young women and leads them to a watery death. Regardless of its exact reputation, the pink river dolphin has never been hunted by Amazon tribespeople and was as a result extremely common in the lower waterways of the Amazon up until about three decades ago.

The biggest enemy of the dolphin these days is deforestation, which has damaged the dolphin's aquatic home, and gill nets, which ensnare and drown the dolphin. The California-based International Society for the Preservation of the Tropical Rainforest (info@isptr-pard.org, www.isptr-pard.org) has launched a major campaign on the Río Yarapa near Iquitos to protect the pink river dolphin. After a decade of working with local villages and the Peruvian police, the organization reports that the number of pink river dolphins in the river has increased over the last two decades from eight to about 30 specimens. They gladly accept donations and operate a small lodge on the Yarapa known as Dolphin Corners.

International

The best restaurant in town, with a stunning view of the Amazon to boot, is ⋈ **Fitzcarraldo** (Napo 100, on the Malecón Tarapacá, tel. 065/24-3434, 11 A.M.–1 A.M. daily, $5–7), a stylish restaurant owned by a Peruvian-Italian family left over from the rubber boom days. The restored colonial house has a pleasant, open-air atmosphere, and there are also tables outside on the malecón, though guests tend to be pestered here by roving street vendors. The creative menu includes brochettes of meat, fish, and chicken and *pescado en salsa de maracuya* (Amazonian fish with passion fruit sauce). The pizzas, which they also deliver, are the best we had in Peru, and the salads are big enough to be a meal in themselves.

Located in a grand, tile-covered 19th-century house, **Restaurant Gran Maloca** (Lores 170, tel. 065/23-3126, maloca@tvs.com.pe, noon–10 P.M. daily, $4–10) serves a wide variety of jungle dishes, including alligator and butterfly. If bush meat does not appeal to you, there is also a full range of pastas. The restored house has a front café with French windows opening to the street or a more formal (air-conditioned!) dining room in the back. It has a recommended and affordable three-course menu at lunchtime and also sells homemade homemade wine, rum, whiskey, and coffee.

Restaurant Regal (Putumayo 182, tel. 065/22-2732, 8 A.M.–midnight daily, $5–10) has a great location on the second floor of the Casa de Fierro and feels like a British pub with its wooden bar, old photographs and antique furniture. *Paiche* here is served in ten different ways thought this is probably a better place for having a drink on a balcony overlooking the Plaza de Armas.

Fine Dining

Despite the casino downstairs and the neon lights outside, the most elegant restaurant in Iquitos is surely **Montecarlo** (Napo 140, second flr., tel. 065/23-2246, montecarlo5t@hotmail .com, noon–3:30 P.M. and 6 P.M.–midnight daily, $5–10). Dine on exquisite seafood, jungle dishes, or steak at a table set with linens, silver, and wine and water glasses.

Markets

The largest supermarket is at Próspero 401, located in a 19th-century mansion called Los Portales that is covered in Portuguese tiles. Another option is Mini Market Marthita (Arica and Ucayali, tel. 065/23-5734, 6:30 A.M.–1 A.M.).

INFORMATION AND SERVICES

The **tourist information office** on the Plazas de Armas (Napo 232, tel. 065/23-6144, iperuiquitos@promperu.gob.pe, 8 A.M.–8 P.M. daily) is helpful, but more up-to-date information is available at the **Ministry of Tourism** (Palma and Malecón Tarapacá, fourth flr., tel. 065/23-4609, 8:30 A.M.–12:30 P.M. and 2:30–4:30 P.M.). Neither place, however, can be relied upon for good recommendations on agencies or lodges.

Gerald Mayeaux, the proprietor of the **Yellow Rose of Texas,** is a former director of tourism who gives frank, honest advice on different Iquitos options.

Most of the travel agencies and airline offices are found along Próspero, south of the Plaza de Armas.

Another good resource written in English is the *Iquitos Monthly,* a free newspaper available at many cafés that provides up-to-date information and news.

In an emergency, call the **Tourist Police of Iquitos** (Lores 834, tel. 065/23-1852, or 065/24-2081).

For health care, the **Hospital Regional de Iquitos** (28 de Julio s/n, tel. 065/25-1882 or

065/25-2743) is open 24 hours. A good pharmacy is **InkaFarma Pharmacy** at Próspero 383.

Banco Wiese and **Banco de Crédito** both have ATMs and are located on the Plaza de Armas. Further south are the **Banco Continental** at Lores 171 and **Interbank** at Próspero 336. During the week banks close after 1 P.M. and sometimes do not open again until 4:30 P.M. Banks are open only in the morning on Saturdays and closed on Sundays.

Iquitos' **post office** is located at Arica 402 (tel. 065/23-1915, 8 A.M.–7 P.M. Mon.–Sat., 9 A.M.–1 P.M. Sun.).

There are plenty of Internet cafés around town. **Snack-Bar Internet** (Fitzcarrald 131, 8 A.M.– 1 A.M. daily) is a social place serving hamburgers and beers, while **Jungle Net** (Putumayo 388) has a quieter atmosphere.

The cheapest place to make international calls in Iquitos is **Gamma.Com** (Huallaga 359, 7 A.M.–11 P.M.), where calls to the U.S. can be made for $0.30 per minute.

The **Peruvian Immigrations** office, where tourist visas can be extended, is at Mariscal Cáceres 18 (tel. 065/23-5371).

For a choice of full-service or coin-operated laundry go to **Lavandería Imperial** (Putumayo 150, tel. 065/231-768, 8 A.M.–7 P.M. Mon.–Sat.) or **Lavandería Popular** (Loreto 640, tel. 065/22-3514, 8 A.M.–8 P.M., $0.60/kilo). South of the Plaza de Armas there is laundry at Próspero 459 (tel. 065/24-2136).

To rent a motorcycle or a four-wheel-drive vehicle, head to **Warmi Alquiler** (Pevas 252, tel. 065/24-2029). A popular motocross challenge is the muddy road that was recently built to Nauta.

GETTING THERE AND AROUND

Because Iquitos is water-locked, nearly all visitors arrive by plane. Iquitos' airport is 7 km outside of town or a $5, 20-minute cab ride. Have a plan ahead of time for where you want to stay, because taxi drivers will insist on driving you to second-rate hotels that give them commissions.

From Lima, try **TANS** (in Lima tel. 01/213-6000, ventaslima.com.pe, www.tansperu.com.pe, $120 round trip). **Star Up** (in Lima, tel. 01/446-

LAND AND WATER ODYSSEY TO IQUITOS

If you want to save money on a plane ticket to Iquitos, and get a unique perspective on the jungle in the process, hop aboard a cargo boat from either **Pucallpa** or **Yurimaguas.** As you lounge in a hammock on the boat's deck, the Amazon jungle passes by in vivid color, sandwiched between muddy waters and a bright blue sky. Just when it begins to get hot, an afternoon rain falls to reveal a spectacular nighttime sky dominated by the Southern Cross. With a little preparation, and the right attitude, a journey aboard an Amazon cargo boat can be comfortable, safe, and exhilarating.

Pucallpa is three to four days upstream of Iquitos along the Río Ucayali, which is a long time to be on a cargo boat. A better option is Yurimaguas, which is only a day and a half away from Iquitos and reached via an eight-hour rough drive from Tarapoto. Although trucks and buses travel this route, the *colectivo* cars are comfortable and arrive in plenty of time to do some last-minute shopping before hopping aboard the afternoon cargo boats. Avoid this road during the rainy season from December and March when it becomes a muddy quagmire.

Cargo boats push off from Yurimaguas most afternoons around 4 P.M., with accommodations ranging from covered decks for slinging hammocks to cabins with private bathrooms. The best boat service, by far, is Transportes Eduardo (in Yurimaguas, tel. 065/35-1270 or 065/35-2991 or in Iquitos tel. 065/967-3477), which has five boats, the best of which are the *Eduardo IV,* with a private third deck, and the *Eduardo V,* with cabins that apparently have queen-sized beds and tiled bathrooms. The best bet is to call a day ahead of time from Tarapoto and find out whether an Eduardo boat is leaving for the next day. Prices range from $15 for hammock space to $50 for a cabin. Be warned, however, that boats wait until their cargo deck is full, and sometimes even confirmed departures get delayed. There are several basic hostels in Yurimaguas, but the best place is Puerto Patos, a jungle lodge operated by the Puerto Palmeras resort in Tarapoto (in Lima tel. 01/242-5550, ctareps@puerto-palmeras.com, www.puertopalmeras.com, $30 pp, including breakfast).

The boat ticket includes three hot meals a day, served up by the boat cooks and announced by a bell—though passengers must bring their own spoon, bowl, and mug. We found the food surprisingly good, mostly meaty stews and fish and rice, and we did not get sick. Buy several liters of bottled water per person, fruit, and whatever food you think you may want beforehand in Tarapoto, because the Yurimaguas port can be a madhouse. Freelance ticket salesman, contracted by competing boat companies, swarm around cars carrying passengers and scream at the top of their lungs. Once on board the boat it is possible to buy a hammock ($6–10, depending on your bargaining skills).

We preferred the upper, open-air deck to the lower deck, which was musty and crammed wall-to-wall with hammocks. The upper deck does, however, get chilly and damp at night, so bring a sleeping bag and hat. In order to guard backpacks at night, most hammock travelers post a night guard, so larger groups mean more sleep for everyone. For that reason, couples or solo travelers might want to consider the security of a locked cabin—you can always lock your things in the cabin and sleep on the deck.

Amazon houses at Yurimaguas, on the Río Huallaga

The Amazon

2485, ventas@starup.com.pe, www.starup.com.pe, $120 round trip) has a single flight arriving on Monday and leaving on Saturday.

From Iquitos, Star Up also flies back and forth to Chiclayo, Caballococha, Leticia, and Yurimaguas. TANS flies back and forth a few times a week between Tarapoto and also Pucallpa. Unfortuately flights to and from Miami and Cusco are no longer operating.

The only other way to enter or leave Iquitos is by boat. From Puerto Masusa, on the north end of Iquitos, boats leave sporadically on the weekends for Puerto de Coca in Ecuador up the Río Napo, a 15-day trip that costs around $25. Public *colectivo* boats head upstream to Nauta from the Puerto Bella Vista–Nanay, 15 minutes outside of town and reachable from buses that run along Próspero.

Covered passenger boats also go down the Amazon from here to Pevas and the border towns of Leticia, Colombia, and Tabatinga, Brazil. Most of these companies have their offices in the third block of Raymondi. The most recommended is **Transtur** (Raymondi 344, tel. 065/22-1356, transtur@terra.com.pe), which charges $40 for the nine-hour boat ride to Leticia. Its boats leave from a small dock on Marina Avenue across from the San Carlos gas station. Another option is **Mi Reyna** (Raymondi 390, tel. 065/22-3097).

There are virtually no cars in this island town but hundreds upon hundreds of noisy, stinky *motocars*, which provide cheap and quick transportation. A ride anywhere in the city costs a mere $0.50.

Jungle Around Iquitos

The jungle around Iquitos can be explored in a number of ways: by visiting a jungle lodge, cruising on a river boat, or going on a camping trip. What you see depends in large part on how far you travel from Iquitos. The riverbanks near Iquitos that were mostly wilderness in the 1960s are now wall-to-wall farms and cow pastures. Most of the jungle within 80 km of Iquitos is secondary forest, but dolphins, monkeys, and a variety of birds can still be seen. The jungle gets more interesting the farther away from Iquitos you travel. **Reserva Nacional Pacaya-Samiria** (12 hours upstream) or the **Reserva Comunal Tamshiyacu-Tahuayo** (four to six hours) have wildlife and pristine jungle comparable to Parque Nacional Manu in Peru's southern Amazon.

One advantage that Iquitos has over Peru's southern Amazon is that even during the rainy season, it typically only rains in the afternoon, so lodges can be visited year-round. It's also the only place in Peru where pink river dolphins live. There is a high-water season, however, between January and June, when the Amazon rises 15 meters and floods much of the surrounding forest. Guides say there are more birds during these months, though mammals are easiest to see dur-

ing the low-water months from July to December when they hang out on the muddy riverbanks. The numbers of monkeys seems to hold steady year-round.

The land that does not become flooded is called *terra firme* and has a different variety of animals and birds. Typical birds in a flooded forest include flycatchers, tanagers, woodcreepers, kingfishers, finches, woodpeckers, parrots, macaws, and all species of cotingas. Because there is more food in a non-flooded forest, there are a greater variety of mammals and reptiles and a different variety of birds, including antbirds, manakins, curassows, guans, foliage cleaners, and all species of woodcreepers and woodpeckers. To see the greatest range of wildlife and birds, choose lodges that have access to both flooded forest and *terra firme*.

Competition is intense among the jungle outfits in Iquitos, and discounts are sometimes handed out to those who make their reservation in town, as opposed to over the Internet. Iquitos is teeming with con artists, thieves, and other disreputable types who do most of their business with unsuspecting travelers at the airport. *If you come into town without a reservation, avoid*

© RENÉE DEL GAUDIO AND ROSS WEHNER

red howler monkeys in flooded rain forest near Iquitos

them at all costs. Use the agencies, lodges, and guides recommended in this book and, when in doubt, consult the tourist office or the Ministry of Tourism. We recommend steering clear of private guides, who rarely seem to deliver what they promise in the Iquitos area.

JUNGLE LODGES AND AGENCIES

Though more expensive than Peru hotels of the same category, jungle lodges are an excellent deal when you consider that transport, English-speaking guide, food, lodging, and a full range of activities are included in the price. These activities include boat rides to fish for pirañas and see the giant *Victoria regia* lily pads, night-time caiman spotting, early-morning bird-watching, forest walks, and a visit to a shaman for a talk about medicinal plants. Some of the lodges also offer visits to Indian villages, which are usually awkward, staged affairs and can be given a miss in exchange for downtime back at the lodge.

In general, you get what you pay for, and the

better guides tend to work at the more expensive lodges. Because the main cost of any lodge is gasoline for the outboard motor, the lodges farther away from Iquitos become progressively more expensive but offer the chance to see a wider array of animals.

Explorama

Founded by Wisconsin native Peter Jensen in 1964, Explorama (tel. 065/25-2533 or 800/707-5275, La Marina 340, amazon@explorama.com, www.explorama.com) is the original eco-pioneer of the Peruvian Amazon. Explorama has grown into a large, highly professional organization, with five lodges, great cooking, huge boats, and some of the Amazon's best guides. As a bonus, all of the lodges offer access to both flooded and *terra firme* forest. Explorama's claim to fame is the longest canopy walkway in the world, a half kilometer of continuous hanging bridges suspended between more than a dozen giant trees. At 35 meters (115 feet) off the ground, the walkway is an excellent way to spot birds and see tremendous jungle vistas.

Explorama's **Ceiba Tops Luxury Lodge** (two days/one night: $225/one, $400/two, additional night $85) is a mere 40 km downriver from Iquitos and right on the banks of the Amazon. With modern, air-conditioned bungalows, hammock house, a beautiful swimming pool with slide, and a huge dining room and full bar, it qualifies as the only resort in Peru's Amazon. Activities include nature walks through the lodge's large private reserve that contains nearly 40 hectares of old-growth forest, bird-watching by canoe, village visits, and a tour of a nearby lake with *Victoria regia*. A visit to the canopy walkway, 75 miles by river from Ceiba Tops, is possible on a longer visit. This lodge is a good option for people who don't really want to rough it. With Explorama's fast boat, it can be reached in 45 minutes from Iquitos.

Explorama Lodge (three days/two nights: $325/one, $570/two, additional night $85) is 80 km downriver (about 1.5 hours) from Iquitos near the Amazon's junction with the Río Napo and is surrounded by 1,700 hectares of a private reserve that consists of large portions of primary

CANOPY WALKS

Visitors to the Amazon are often surprised by how dark, gloomy, and colorless the floor of a rainforest can be. The situation is completely different a hundred feet or more up in the air, where a dazzling array of orchids, cacti, bromeliads, and mosses hang out on the treetops and soak in the scorching sunlight. The fragrant scents of these epiphytes and the succulent fruit of the ubiquitous *matapalo*, or strangler fig, lure monkeys and a huge range of pollinators, including birds, bats, and insects.

Most of the Amazon's biodiversity is in fact in the canopy, which American biologist Bruce Rinker describes as a "leafy aerial continent, elevated on stilts, called the treetops." No longer content with studying fallen trees, biologists have come up with ingenious ways to explore this airy world with a combination of suspended cable walkways, treehouse-like platforms, and rope-climbing techniques adapted from rock climbing.

In the early 1990s the nonprofit ACEER organization funded the Amazon's longest canopy walkway, which was built 80 km south of Iquitos at the **Explorama Lodge.** It is a cable bridge, suspended between a series of giant rainforest trees, that runs for nearly half a kilometer and reaches a dizzying 35 meters above the ground. Visitors hang out for hours on the walkway, peering down the sides of trees to the jungle floor below or scanning over the treetops for hundreds of different birds. The bridge is completely safe, even for children.

There are safety cables at shoulder height to grab onto, a wooden floor, and thick mesh stretched between. The whole thing is like a giant channel of mesh out of which it would be hard to climb, much less fall. Visitors climb up a wooden tower with wide staircase to access the bridge, and no harnesses or other safety precautions are necessary. Guides usually let visitors wander wherever they want on the bridge.

Reserva Amazónica in the Puerto Maldonado area is building a similar canopy walkway and a dozen other lodges in Peru's rainforest offer observation platforms. These platforms, such as the one at the **Manu Wildlife Center,** are up to 35 meters off the ground and are usually reached via a circular staircase that is made of steel and held upright via a series of steel cables. Again no safety harnesses are required and, as long as you are not terrified of heights, getting to the platform is easy.

There are plenty of more-adventurous canopy options in Peru's rainforest, including the wooden platforms at **Cocha Salvador** in the Parque Nacional Manu. To reach these airy treehouses, you must don a rock-climbing harness and climb the rope via a set of jumars, or cammed ascending devices. It is a completely safe, though strenuous, experience that allows you to appreciate how high 35 meters off the ground really is. For those uncomfortable with climbing the rope, another option is to be pulled up into the treehouse by a geared contraption that is cranked by the guide (the device is similar to that on trailers for hauling boats out of the water).

The **Tahuayo Lodge,** 145 km upstream of Iquitos, has what it calls a zipline, which is essentially a harness that slides along a set of steel cables about 30 meters above the ground. From a wooden platform, visitors launch into space and can either zing through the canopy or stop and hang quietly in order to observe wildlife. Obviously this is for those extremely comfortable with heights! Many other lodges in Peru's Amazon offer canopy walks; see the individual descriptions for more information.

sunset on Explorama's canopy walkway

bromeliads and birds next to Explorama's
suspended cable footbridge

rainforest. It was one of the first lodges constructed in the Iquitos area, in 1964, and has recently been renovated. A series of palm-thatched
buildings have up to 17 sleeping rooms with
shared, cold-water bathrooms and covered walkways lit by kerosene lamps. The dining room
serves a huge variety of food, buffet style, and
has a bar with an excellent Pisco sour.

The largest of Explorama's private rainforest reserves can be visited from **▼ ExplorNapo Lodge**
(five days/four nights: $1,135/one, $1,760/two,
additional night $85), which is 160 km (about
three hours) from Iquitos on a tributary of the
Río Napo. Accommodations are similar to those
at Explorama Lodge with wooden rooms with
shared bathrooms and a long thatched corridor
that leads to a dining room; it's illuminated at
night by kerosene lamps. The lodge also maintains an extensive botanical garden, carefully designed by Peru's leading ethno-biologist, Dr. Jim
Duke. Erlin, Explorama's highly experienced
shaman, gives presentations to groups anad can
arrange ayahuasca sessions.

Most important, the ExplorNapo is a 45-minute
walk from the **ACTS Field Station,** where both
scientists and travelers can stay, and Explorama's
world-famous canopy walkway that looks over
nearly 100,000 hectares of mostly primary forest. More than 85 species of birds can be spotted
from here. We saw a few extraordinarily beautiful
and hard-to-see species, such as the black-necked
red cotinga and the ivory-billed aracari.

Explorama's fifth, and most remote lodge, is
ExplorTambos Camp (five days/four nights:
$1,160/one, $1,804/two, additional night $120),
a primitive camp for a maximum of 16 people.
Guests sleep on open-sided platforms in beds
covered with mosquito nets. It's a two-hour hike
into the rainforest from ExplorNapo Lodge, and
due to its isolation offers the best possibilities
for spotting wildlife. Prices given are for one
night at ExplorTambos and three nights at other
Explorama Lodges.

Paseo Amazónicos

Another well-managed outfit that has been around
for nearly three decades is **Paseos Amazónicos**
(Pevas 246, tel. 065/23-1618, p-amazon@amauta
.rcp.net.pe, www.paseosamazonicos.com). It has
excellent guides and three lodges, which have been
built in native style and purposefully left rustic
with simple rooms and kerosene lamps. The lodges
are listed below in order from most comfortable to
most adventurous.

Amazonas Sinchicuy Lodge (two days/one
night: $96/person; four days/three nights: $217/
person) is one of the older lodges in the Iquitos
area and is Paseo Amazónico's most comfortable. Located on the Río Sinchicuy, about 30
km from Iquitos, the lodge consists of 32 pleasant wooden rooms with mosquito screens,
thatched verandas, private bathrooms, and
kerosene lamps.

The lodge organizes a highly interesting visit to
a local shaman, who gives a talk on medicinal
plants and is recommended for those interested in
ayahuasca experiences. There are also visits to
Yagua villages, which are so close to the lodge
that there is not much wildlife in the area other
than dolphins and birds.

Sinchicuy Lodge can easily be combined with
a visit to the more remote **Tambo Yanayacu,**

The Amazon

which is on the shores of the Río Yanayacu about 60 km from Iquitos in a patch of flooded rainforest. The lodge is absolutely silent in the middle of a huge flooded forest and contains 10 wooden rooms with private bathrooms, kerosene lamps, and a simple dining room where all food is cooked over an open hearth. There is an excellent number of birds here, and at night the stars are reflected in the black, still waters alongside the lodge. It is a magical place that can be visited as part of the three-night package with Sinchicuy Lodge.

Unlike Paseo Amazónico's other lodges, **Tambo Amazónico** (four days/three nights: $383/person) is upriver from Iquitos in flooded rainforest along the pristine Río Yarapa. It is a rustic campsite used as a way stop for backpacker excursions into Reserva Nacional Pacaya-Samiria. There are two bunkrooms, each with 10 beds covered with mosquito netting. The services are basic: cold-water showers, kerosene lamps, and outhouses.

Cumaceba Lodge

A good option for a one-night stay is **Cumaceba** (Putumayo 184, tel. 065/22-1456, info@Gumaceba.com, www.cumaceba.com, two days/one night: $114/person), which is 35 km downstream of Iquitos. The thatched lodge has nice rooms with private bathrooms, cold water, and kerosene lamps, along with a dining area and a

© PROMPERÚ

Tourist visits to Amazonian villages can benefit both sides if handled properly.

AMAZON VILLAGE VISITS

If your Iquitos tour operator says the package may include a visit to a native community, you should know what you're getting into. *Native* these days means a highly staged experience, where Yagua or Bora Indians emerge in grass skirts, explain a few aspects of village life, do a quick song and dance, and then emerge with handicrafts to sell. Some foreigners feel uncomfortable with the situation, which has its pros and cons.

On one hand, there are few remote tribes left in the Amazon, and tourists, missionaries, and maybe even anthropologists should leave them alone. The Indians who have chosen to have contact are extremely glad to have the dollars—for them it is an important means of acquiring the cash to buy city items such as sugar, salt, gasoline, and medicine.

The benefit of tourist visits is even clearer with the visits to the *mestizo,* or mixed-blood, towns that continue to sprout up along tributaries of the Amazon. These towns begin with a few thatched huts and can grow up to 30 families, with soccer fields and a sidewalk, within two decades (as is the case with Pueblo San Juan near Muyuna Lodge near Iquitos). With each town comes the rapid clearing of land for yucca, frijol, and maíz and a rapid decimation of local wildlife. If clearing and hunting go too far, it is unlikely the area will ever recover. But if controlled in time, the area begins to repopulate with both wildlife and important tree species (remember that Amazon trees rarely live more than 130 years before being toppled by winds).

Under signed contract, Muyuna Lodge gives money to the villages to help them pay for school supplies, sanitation, and medicine. Because Amazon tourism depends in large part on wildlife, these villagers quickly change their attitudes about hunting. "If I see anyone hunting, I'll turn them in," remarked one San Juan villager during a recent visit.

hammock hall. The lodge's packed one-night, two-day tour includes a walk through a patch of primary rainforest, caiman spotting, bird-watching, piraña fishing, and a visit to a Yagua village. To make up for a general lack of wildlife, guests visit a nearby family that keeps monkeys, turtles, sloths, parrots, and a pet anaconda.

Heliconia Amazon River Lodge

Heliconia Amazon River Lodge(Próspero 574, tel. 065/23-5132, ventas@heliconialodge.com.pe, www.heliconialodge.com.pe, three days/two nights: $240/one, $440/two, additional night $70) is owned by the same group that operates the Acosta and Victoria Regia hotels in Iquitos. Heliconia, 80 km downriver from Iquitos, is a good midrange resort with a comfortable lodge, rooms with private bath, and well-guided tours.

Muyuna Amazon Lodge

Muyuna Amazon Lodge (Putumayo 163, tel. 065/24-2858, amazonas@muyuna.com, www.muyuna.com, three days/two nights $330 pp) was founded in 1999 as a labor of love of Analía and Percy Sanchez, a young couple from Lima. It has already developed a solid reputation among backpackers for excellent guides, simple but comfortable rooms, and very affordable rates. At 140 km upriver from Iquitos on the Río Yanayacu, it is nestled in an interesting swath of flooded forest that has several types of monkeys, a large variety of birds, caimans, sloths, pink dolphins, and a good chance of seeing a giant otter, armadillo, or porcupine. The rooms are simple with private bathrooms and the guides are energetic and well-spoken, willing to make late-night forays into the jungle or spend time visiting the local community of San Juan, with which Muyuna has forged an excellent relationship. Muyuna works with a local shaman for visitors wishing to try ayahuasca, and also has equipment for listening to the whistles that mother dolphins use to communicate with their young.

Yarapa River Lodge

One of the best new Amazon options is the **Ⓝ Yarapa River Lodge** (800/771-3100, yarapariverlodge@hotmail.com, www.yarapariverlodge.com, four days/three nights: $600/one or two). This lodge, around the corner from the Reserva Nacional Pacaya-Samiria on the pristine Río Yarapa, is surrounded by world-class jungle and oxbow lakes teeming with exotic birds, pink dolphins, sloths, and a large variety of monkeys.

Along with Explorama, Yarapa River Lodge probably has the most experienced and eloquent guides in the Amazon, and they are absolutely relentless in their efforts to pinpoint as many species as possible. In a single morning we saw 30 bird species, including the rare Amazonian umbrella bird, which has a crest of black hair that earns it the nickname "the Elvis bird."

The lodge itself is a magnificent structure with huge wooden rooms with private bathrooms and solar power for both electricity and hot showers (there are also less-expensive rooms with shared baths). The food is excellent, consisting of fresh fish and a large range of salads, and there are nice small details—like icy towels after each jungle outing. The lodge has a good relationship with villages in the vicinity and has a green system for everything from local building materials to flush compost toilets.

As a sign of its success, the lodge has partnered with Cornell University, which has built an adjacent research station for the professors and students who visit here each year, along with groups from The Nature Conservancy. The lodge is entirely surrounded by flooded rainforest, but guests who stay a few days often make trips to remote areas of *terra firme* upstream. The lodge organizes recommended tours into the nearby Reserva Nacional Pacaya-Samiria.

Ⓝ Tahuayo Lodge

The most acclaimed lodge of Peru's Northern Amazon is unquestionably **Tahuayo Lodge** (10305 Riverburn Dr., Tampa, FL 33647, 800/262-9669, paul.beaver@gte.net, www.perujungle.com, seven days/six nights, $1,295), which is operated by Amazonia Expeditions. The lodge has been listed as one of the top ten travel finds by *Outside* magazine, and its survival school was the subject of a January 2001 *Outside* feature and an award-winning documentary.

What sets this lodge apart is that it is the only

Ⓜ The Amazon

one near the extraordinary Reserva Nacional Tamshiyacu Tahuayo, which was designated a reserve by the Peruvian government in 1991 to protect the rare Uakari monkey. Biologists have since recorded 500 bird species and exceptional levels of biodiversity. The whole area has so many endemic species that biologists believe that it was a Pleistocene refuge, or a zone that remained forested in the last Ice Age.

The wooden lodge has 15 cozy rooms, some with larger beds, and all with flush toilets. There is a dining room, hammock hall, library, free laundry, and a laboratory with a terrarium that contains tarantulas and other creepy-crawlies. There is access to both flooded and *terra firme* forest in the area, a controlled zipline that allows guests to cruise through the canopy at a hundred feet off the ground, and nearly fifty different activities listed on its excellent web page. The lodge is 145 km away from Iquitos on the Río Tahuayo, or four hours by speedboat.

The lodge tailors itineraries to individual interests. There are honeymoon programs, for instance, that include swimming with pink dolphins, bathing in a secluded waterfall glen filled with orchids, and a ceremony in which a shaman blesses the union. But the program that has caught most attention is the survival school, a weeklong baptism-by-fire where jungle master Moises Chavez takes neophytes into the jungle with nothing but a machete and teaches them how to survive. Topics covered include how to build a lean-to, use poisonous sap to stun fish, make natural medicines, fashion a bow and arrow, collect edible nuts and berries, and build a raft. Many of these techniques are described by Paul Beaver, the owner of Tahuayo Lodge, in his excellent new autobiography *Diary of an Amazon Jungle Guide*.

RIVER CRUISES

Cruises on the Amazon are a great option for those who are lured to the romance of traveling by boat on the world's largest river and want to travel in relative comfort. The boats bear an uncanny resemblance to Mississippi paddleboats without the paddle, and come in varying degrees of luxury and price. The most popular trips are upriver to the Reserva Nacional Pacaya-Samiria, where passengers disembark for walks into the jungle and village visits. The smaller boats can enter shallow rivers where more wildlife can be

Homes along the Amazon River are built on stilts to survive the high-water months.

seen. It is hard to see much wildlife from a boat deck, apart from dolphins and birds.

Amazon Tours & Cruises

Amazon Tours & Cruises (Requena 336, tel. 065/23-1611, in U.S. and Canada 800/423-2791, info@amazontours.net, www.amazon-tours.net) is a well-run and conscientious company found more then three decades ago by American Paul Wright. It offers midlevel air-conditioned cruises, though its boats are not as luxurious as Jungle Expedtions. All-inclusive tours begin and end with an airport pick-up and include good food, cabin, excellent guides, and a full program of activities. It offers a five-night cruise into Pacaya Samiria aboard the smaller *Delfin* boat or an option aboard the larger *ARCA* that heads up the Río Marañon with stops in the reserve before arriving at Yurimaguas, where passengers can connect with a related land tour to Chachapoyas and other parts of north Peru.

The most intriguing product offered by Amazon Tours is a *Cross the Continent* package, in which the company arranges all the logistics for an odyssey between Peru's Pacific and Brazil's Atlantic (or vice versa). Clients travel with an Amazon Tours guide and use Amazon Tours boats for Yurimaguas to Iquitos and then on to Tabatinga on the Brazil border. From there travelers board a series of Brazilian passenger boats, disembarking in Manaus and Belem before reaching the Atlantic. The trips are reasonably priced, and travelers can choose any of the segments individually.

Check the website for specials. The Iquitos-Yurimaguas trip sells for as little as $300 pp, and Iquitos to Tabatinga drops to $900. There are special trips for birders, sport fishers, and even esoteric tours with ayahuasca sessions. A recent offering, for instance, was an 11-day birding cruise through Pacaya Samiria with a Green Tracks guide for $1,675.

Jungle Expeditions

Jungle Expeditions (Quiñones 1980, tel. 065/26-1583, www.junglex.com) cruises the Amazon with six elegant, five-star boats that look as if they were transported right out of the 19th century. Nine-day tours of the Pacaya Samiria reserve start at $2,800

pp and include deluxe air-conditioned cabins, professional guides, and gourmet meals served in a grand dining room. During the evening, drinks are served on the upper canopy deck. The trips spend a night or two at La Posada Lodge, the company's upscale rest stop on Río Marañon, with the opportunity to visit both flooded and *terra firme* forest. The company offers a range of other trips as well to the south of Iquitos. Jungle Expeditions only accepts passengers through its Lima booking office (tel. 01/241-3232) or the U.S.-based International Expeditions (800/643-4734, www.internationalexpeditions.com).

THE RESERVA NACIONAL PACAYA-SAMIRIA

One of the most pristine areas of Peru's northern Amazon is the Reserva Nacional Pacaya-Samiria, an immense wedge of flooded rainforest between the Ucayali and Marañon Rivers. At just over two million hectares, it is Peru's largest nature reserve, and its vast network of lakes, lagoons, swamps, and wetlands harbor many endangered animals. Opportunities for spotting wildlife here rival Parque Nacional Manu, though there are no lodges in the reserve.

Commonly seen animals in the reserve include the huge charapa turtle, the Amazon manatee, tapir, gray and pink river dolphin, black and white caiman, giant otter, twelve types of monkeys, the monstruous *paiche* fish, and hundreds of aquatic birds. The best times to visit the park are the low-water months between July and December, when animals can often be spotted on the riverbanks. The reserve began in the 1940s in an effort to save the endangered *paiche*. After biologists realized its world-class biodiversity, the present reserve was established in 1982. The reserve includes a large number of colonists and indigenous inhabitants—more than 30,000 at last count, including Cocamas, Huitotos, Boras, and Yaguas Indians.

Visitors to this park require a guide, a $33 entrance fee, and at least five days, whether you motor the 300 km upriver from Iquitos (15–18 hours) or downriver from Yurimaguas (10 hours). Because there are no lodges in the reserve itself,

giant lily pads (*Victoria regia*) near Reserva Nacional Pacaya-Samiria

options range from deluxe cruises to rustic camping trips, though a few native lodges have recently opened. Trips usually travel up the Río Ucayali to the town of Requena, and then enter the heart of the reserve through the Canal de Puinahua and the Río Pacaya. Generally speaking this southern side of the reserve has more wildlife than the northern area along the Río Samiria.

A fast access point for the reserve is Yurimaguas, which lies six hours on rough road from Tarapoto. The cargo boats that leave here most afternoons chug down the northern border of the park for nearly two days (see box *Land and Water Odyssey to Iquitos*). The fringes of the park, however, have been heavily impacted by colonists, and the more pristine areas can now only be reached by a two- to three-day canoe journey inside the reserve. Sometime in the middle of the first night after leaving Yurimaguas, cargo boats stop in the small village of Lagunas. From here it is possible to contract a local guide and a canoe for about $20 per day, though there are no guarantees on the quality of service. A surer bet is to set up a guide and transport in Tarapoto through either Puerto Palmeras resort or adventure guide César Reategui. From Lagunas,

a half-hour *motocar* ride will take you to the headwaters of the Río Samiria. From here, it is a three-day paddle to Laguna Pastacocha, a huge oxbow lake teeming with wildlife. Fewer tourists enter the park via this route, so this is more of a wilderness experience. The further you go, the more you are likely to see.

Agencies from either destination usually take care of the official permission that is required from the parks authority INRENA in Iquitos (Pevas 350, tel. 065/23-1230) or in Lima (Los Petirrojos 355, Urb. El Palomar, tel. 01/224-3298). If you are going with an independent guide, inquire about this paperwork beforehand.

Camping and canoeing through the Reserva Nacional Pacaya-Samiria is an amazing experience with the right equipment and a good operator. When combined with a stay at a community-based lodge, it is one of the best ways to understand the rhythms of life in a flooded forest.

Pacaya Samiria Amazon Lodge

The most comfortable of the roughing-it options is the new **Pacaya Samiria Amazon Lodge** (Raimondi 378, tel. 065/23-4128, lodge@pacayasamiria.com.pe, www.pacayasamiria.com.pe, six days/five nights: $685). This lodge is four hours upriver from Iquitos on the banks of the Río Marañon just past the village of Requena, on the ouskirts of the Pacaya-Samiria reserve. Rooms have a private bathroom, shower, and hammocks, and there is electricity in the evenings. The lodge is clean and well-run and offers recommended camping trips into the reserve. The six-day program, for instance, includes an ascent of the Río Yanayacu and two nights camping near the native village of Yarina.

Paseo Amazónicos

Paseo Amazónicos (Pevas 246, tel. 065/23-1618, p-amazon@amauta.rcp.net.pe, www.paseosama-zonicos.com) offers well-priced four- and five-night backpacker trips to Reserva Nacional Pacaya Samiria. Groups spend their first night at the rustic Tambo Amazónico Lodge on the Río Yarapa before heading into the reserve to camp on the beach and ascend the Río Yanayacu toward the village of Yarina.

ProNaturaleza

ProNaturaleza (in Lima Alberto del Campo 417, Magdalena, tel. 01/264-2736, agarfias@pronat-uraleza.org, www.pronaturaleza.org) is one of Peru's leading environmental organizations and is in the process of coordinating three community-based lodges in the Reserva Nacional Pacaya-Samiria. Information will be posted on its web page.

Pascana Amazon Tours

An exciting new option, offered by Pascana Amazon Tours, the agency of Hospedaje Pascana, allows travelers to stay inside the reserve at San Martín de Tipishca, a Cocamas community. Trips last five to ten days and begin by taking one of the Eduardo passenger boats from Iquitos overnight to Leoncio Prado, a town upriver from Nauta on the Río Marañon. From Nauta, San Martín de Tipishca is a half hour away by boat. Travelers spend their time working and living with the Cocamas Indians and exploring the reserve by canoe. Longer-term stays are also possible but subject to approval by local authorities. Costs are $50 per day, including everything except for

$20 round-trip fee on the Eduardo boat and $33 park entrance. For more information contact Virginia Blum (virginiablum@yahoo.com) or Pascana Amazon Tours (Pevas 133, tel. 065/23-3466, pascana@tsi.com.pe).

INDEPENDENT GUIDES

The Ministry of Tourism used to keep track of registered guides, but received so many complaints from travelers that it no longer keeps any track at all. A private association of guides, organized by Jorge Lache of the Amazon Lodge, now keeps a list of guides who are supposedly reputable—though we have no independent confirmation of this. For more information, see **Jorge Lache** at his office (tel. 065/25-1078, Marina 592A). In general, guides charge $20–30 per day and use *colectivos* and canoes as transport.

The one guide we can recommend is **Juan Tejada** (Pasaje Benavides 133, tel. 065/25-0956), a former Explorama guide who is the single most experienced birder we met while in Iquitos. He has an encyclopedic knowledge of the birds, their calls, and their habits and speaks flawless English and German. He charges $20 per day, not including transport, food, lodging, and other trip expenses.

SHAMANIC EXPERIENCES

Most of the jungle lodges are quite happy to arrange a hallucinogenic ayahuasca experience. Recommended shamans include **Don Lizardo** (tel. 065/967-8108, Ejército 1350 in Morona-cocha), who works with **Muyuna Lodge.** An older and reliable shaman, who conducts ayahuasca sessions in his home, is **Don Solón** (tel. 065/23-2861). Both charge around $25 for a one-night experience.

PEVAS AND LA CASA DEL ARTE

The best place to stop for a night or two for those traveling downstream to Brazil is Pevas, a laid-back village 145 km downstream of Iquitos that was founded by missionaries in 1735. Pevas' main attraction is La Casa del Arte, a huge thatched

THE WRONG WAY TO TAKE AYAHUASCA

There are right and wrong ways to take the jungle hallucinogen ayahuasca, and this story unfortunately is an example of the latter. It happened near Iquitos in 1992, when some friends and I hopped a boat up the Río Nanay to a budget jungle lodge. A group of backpackers were headed out into the jungle to take ayahuasca with the lodge's *curandero*, or healer. So we went along.

There were a few telltale signs that we were headed for trouble. During a log crossing over a creek, the shaman fell into the water, and then he instructed us to erect our group tent over what later turned out to be a giant anthill.

As night fell, we all sat quietly in a circle as he drank a cupful of the fearsome brew in front of us. He then retired some distance into the woods and began to vomit in a way I had never heard before. It was a throaty, continuous retching, like the bellow of a frog. Just when we thought he was finished, he would begin again. Around the circle, we looked at each other and gulped in fear. After an hour, he returned, red-eyed, and began chanting a song, or *ícaro*, while he administered to each one of us a cup. Those who vomited were given another cup immediately. For some reason I did not vomit—at first.

The rest of the night is a bit blurry. Fat drops of rain plunked through the forest canopy, forcing us inside the group tent. The rain began to fall in continuous sheets, producing a deafening roar against the tent, but the *curandero* sat unconcerned, chanted his *ícaro* and shook a bunch of leaves. We all sat dazed and silent, periodically attempting to avoid the encroachments of water and ants. While none of us had truly hallucinogenic visions, I remember seeing for quite some time the intricate patterns of an Inca textile. When the *curandero* finally stopped chanting at dawn, we all scrambled out the door into the forest to vomit and relieve ourselves.

My first ayahuasca experience was not a disaster, but it could have been much more meaningful. It was the typical ceremony that many Amazon lodges put on for tourist—for as little as $15 per person. Those who get the most out of ayahuasca are true spiritual seekers, not just those looking for a frivolous drug trip. They are willing to spend more time and make personal sacrifices, such as embarking on the rigorous diet necessary beforehand. They also do their research, and take the time to find a *maestro curandero*, who not only has an encyclopedic knowledge of Amazon medicinal plants and rituals, but is also pure of spirit and heart.

structure on the banks of the Amazon that serves as studio and home of Francisco Grippa, one of Peru's better-known painters. Grippa was born in Tumbes in the 1940s, attended art school in Los Angeles, and somehow ended up in Pevas, where he paints the extreme beauty and destruction of the Amazon on canvases he makes himself from tree bark. His work ranges from the mystical to the abstract, though his best-known works portray Amazon natives, animals, or landscapes with explosions of color reminiscent of Jackson Pollock. A sampling of Grippa's work can be seen in the lobby of the El Dorado Plaza Hotel or at Camu-Camu, an Amazon art gallery at Trujillo 438 (tel. 065/25-3120). For more information about Grippa, see his website at www.art-and-soul.com.

There are a few lodging options in Pevas, but the best is **Casa de la Loma,** a rustic lodge run by Americans Judy Balser and Scott Humfeld. Contact Amazon Tours & Cruises for more information or call tel. 065/23-1265.

MOYOBAMBA

For travelers coming over the Andes from Peru's northern coast, Moyobamba is the first city with an unmistakable jungle feel. The air is warm and humid, cooled by rains that fall heaviest between January and March. People here wear less clothing (men in shorts, women in tank tops) and speak in fluid, melodious dialects. Travelers also encounter a variety of exotic new fruits and an ex-

footbridge over Río Mayo near Moyobamba

plosion in animal and plant life. In the cloud forest surrounding Moyobamba, for instance, there are more than 2,500 recorded types of orchids. The long river boats common to the lower Amazon also navigate the lazy meanderings of the Río Mayo, fringed by alternating patches of fields and high jungle.

Moyobamba is one of the few jungle areas conquered by the Incas—Tupac Yupanqui conquered the local tribes of the Motilones, Chachapuyas, and Muyupampas in the mid-15th century. The city of Moyobamba was founded by the Spanish captain Juan Pérez de Guevara in 1540. In Quechua, Moyobamba means "circular plain," which makes sense because the city is situated on a flat area perched above the Río Mayo. Various streets dead-end into spectacular views of the muddy, snaking river, which offers a good range of whitewater rafting and kayaking. There are also thermal baths, caves, and waterfalls in the area, with relatively pristine patches of cloud forest that harbor orchids and mammal species such as the yellow-tailed monkey.

Around Moyobamba

The best of Moyobamba lies outside the city. In the town there is little to see besides a modern cathedral, on the Plaza de Armas, and a municipal museum with sporadic hours on Benavides 380.

The **Gera Waterfalls,** about 12 km south of the city near Del Gera hydroelectric project, fall more than 120 meters in three stages before reaching the electric dam. At the falls themselves, there is good swimming reached via a pleasant jaunt through the forest. To get there, take a $4 *motocar* or catch a bus at Moyobamba's Calle Grau toward the village of Jepelacio. After showing your ID to the guard, walk about 800 meters, or 20 minutes, along a forest path to reach the falls. From Jepelacio it is also possible to visit Cataratas de Pacchua, about a 20-minute walk from the village.

No matter where you are in Moyobamba, you can always see **Morro de Calzada,** an isolated, hump-backed mountain that rises above the landscape about 12 km from Moyobamba. There is a pleasant, two-hour walk through cloud forest to the top, past a few small waterfalls and a variety of orchids. There are caves at both the top and bottom of the hill and an incredible panoramic view from the summit. This overlook is also a launching point for hang-gliders and parapenters.

For a pleasant view of the Río Mayo, and the tiny river port of Puerto Tahuishco, head to **Punta de Tahuishco,** 20 minutes northeast of the Plaza de Armas ($1 by *motocar*). The municipality has built a variety of gardens and pleasant overlooks in this neighborhood known as Zaragoza. Nearby are the Tullpa de Mamá restaurant and Agroriente Viveros (Reyes Guerra 900, tel. 042/56-2539, agroriente@terra.com.pe), a commercial greenhouse featuring a wide range of local orchids.

Entertainment and Events

Discos in Moyobamba come and go quickly, but a reliable bet is **La Oveja Negra Video Pub** (Grau 284, second flr., tel. 042/56-2975).

The town erupts into a week of parties, local dances, beauty pageants, and processions that spans both the town's birthday (July 25) and Peru's independence celebration (July 28). Orchid lovers descend on Moyobamba in the first week of November for the annual Orchid Festival.

Sports and Recreation

Hotel Puerto Mirador offers tours to all the above-described sites outside Moyobamba, as does the Marcoantonio Hotel. In nearby Rioja, a recommended operator is **Bombonaje Tours** (Faustino Maldonado 517, tel. 042/55-8600, bombonajetours@peru.com).

Accommodations

The budget hotels are all pretty similar in Moyabamba. **Hostal Albricias** (Alvarado 1066, tel. 042/56-1092, $6 s, $7 d) is a good value, with hot water and gardens between quiet rooms. Another safe, clean choice is **Country Club Hostal** (Manuel del Aguila 667, tel. 042/56-2110, countryclub@moyobamba.net, www.moyobamba.net/countryclub, $7 s, $10 d), with quiet rooms laid out around a courtyard and a nice staff. Rooms have cable TV and hot water, and breakfast costs $1. **Hostal Atlanta** (Alonso de Alvarado 865, tel. 042/56-2063, $7 s, $11 d) is also safe, clean, and quiet; however it charges an additional $1.50 for hot water. Rooms have cable TV. For better beds and more all-around comfort, there is **Hotel Marcoantonio** (Pedro Canga 488, tel. 042/56-2045, hotel_marcoantonio@hotmail.com, $22 s, $28 d), which has both casino and restaurant. Unfortunately, rooms here are so unbearably noisy that you are better off at one of the cheaper hostels for a decent night's sleep.

The resort option in Moyobamba is **Hotel Puerto Mirador** (Sucre s/n, tel. 042/56-2050, pmiradorhotel@terra.com.pe, $30 s, $40 d, including breakfast). Located in a peaceful setting on the outskirts of town, this hotel offers brick bungalows and a swimming pool overlooking the Río Mayo. Rooms are large with cable TV and private terraces, though they're a bit dark and musty. The soaring main lodge has a good, though often empty, restaurant and a full bar. The hotel offers tours to various lakes, waterfalls, and thermal baths, as well as boat tours on the Río Mayo.

Food

Three restaurants that stand out in Moyobamba all happen to have the same owner: local entrepreneur Marta Weninger. **La Olla de Barro** (intersectiom of Canga and Filomenco, tel. 042/56-1034, 8 A.M.–11 P.M., $2–5) serves traditional food as well as pizzas and pastas in a charming, jungle themed atmosphere. Further toward the plaza is the tiny **Chico's Burger Club** (Canga and the main square, tel. 042/56-1222, 3 P.M.–2:30 A.M., $2–4) serving burgers, milkshakes, and the same delicious pizzas as La Olla de Barro, though slightly cheaper and not as touristy.

Weninger's third production, and by far the most interesting, is **La Tullpa de Mamá** (Boulevar Puente de Tahuishco, tel. 042/69-3567, 9 A.M.–6 P.M. daily, $2–4.50) that can be reached by taxi for $0.30. This treehouse-like restaurant has spectacular views of the jungle and the Río Mayo below. The extensive menu focuses on local dishes such as *cecina con tacacho* (pork with mashed bananas), *asado de majaz* (roast wild pig), and the local tilapia fish.

If you're interested in dining outside of the Weninger monopoly, we highly recommend having a light dinner at **N Antojitos al Paso** (Alvarado 788, 4–11 P.M., $0.30). It serves some of the best *humitas* (ground green corn stuffed with olives and meat) and *tamales* (ground red maize stuffed with peanuts and meat) we have tasted in Peru yet. For a special meal prepared by a true chef, visit the restaurant at **Hotel Puerto Mirador** (Sucre s/n, tel. 042/56-2050, $3–7). It serves Peruvian and international food in a peaceful, jungle setting. The brochettes are excellent.

Services
The **Tourism Police** is located at Canga 298 (tel. 042/56-2508).

Both **Banco de la Nación** on the Plaza de Armas and **Banco de Credito** on Alvarado 903 have an ATM.

For medical issues, **Essalud** is located in the first block of Grau (tel. 042/56-1396).

The **post office** is at Filomeno 501 at Canga. For a super-high-speed Internet connection, go to the corner of Alvarado and Benavides (9:30 A.M.–midnight, $0.75/hour). Another good place for Internet is on Canga, across from Hotel Marcoantonio.

La Popular Lavanderia (Alvarado 874, tel. 042/56-2440) does wash for $1/kilo.

If you are in need of long pants or shirts for the jungle, try the **street market** around 25 de Mayo and Callao.

Getting There and Around
The nearest large airport that handles jets is at Tarapoto, 105 km or 2.5 hours away by bus. All the buses between Chiclayo and Tarapoto pass through Moyobamba after a 10-hour journey. See the *Tarapoto* section for recommended bus companies.

Moyobamba is teeming with cheap *motocars* that costs $0.75 for a local trip.

TARAPOTO

Tarapoto lies further down in the Río Mayo watershed from Moyobamba and is surrounded by mountainous cloud forest that tumbles into the flat, steamy lowlands of the Amazon basin. This is an area of impossibly steep cloud forest, known for waterfalls, orchids, and unusual birds.

Tarapoto was founded in 1782, at the base of Cumbaza and Shilcayo Rivers, and named after the endemic palm tree, *Taraputus,* that grows there. It has always been famous for its rich agricultural lands, which yield corn, banana, manioc, cocoa, tobacco, tea, coffee, palm oil, and a variety of tropical fruits. Its role as a center of commerce between the Amazon and the upper regions was cemented by the construction of the Margin Highway to the coast in the 1960s.

During the 1970s, however, coca cultivation began in the nearby upper Huallaga Valley and much of the area's valuable lands were destroyed by slash-and-burn agriculture. Tarapoto became the place where all narco-traffickers built their lavish homes and washed their money in all kinds of lavish real estate projects that dot the city. During the 1980s, Tarapoto was at the center of the territory belonging to the MRTA, or Movimento Revolucionario Tupac Amaru, which briefly occupied every city in the area except for Tarapoto. Over time, the organization developed ties to the area's drug dealers.

During the Fujimori presidency, Tarapoto's prominent drug traffickers were jailed and the MRTA was completely defeated—most of the guerillas surrendered under Peru's amnesty law, and a small remaining faction was wiped out after taking over the Japanese Embassy in Lima in 1996.

Tarapoto is now a safe place to visit and is making a dramatic comeback as a tourist destination, especially for those who fly in from Lima with just a few days on their hands. The leader of the tourist comeback in Tarapoto is the **Puerto Palmeras** resort, which operates several lodges in the area. Though pricey, its accommodations and tours are worth it.

Sights
If you want to see the elusive cock of the rock, head at dawn or dusk to **Aguashiyaku Waterfalls** ($1 admission at trailhead hut), about 14 km or 45 minutes outside Tarapoto on the rough road to Yurimaguas. If you are quiet, you have a good chance of spotting these crimson birds as they fly in and out of their nests on the rock wall below the waterfall. During the heat of the day the waterfall converts into a swimming hole and, along with admiring the cloud forest, there is not much more to do, because the path dead-ends

KICKING ADDICTIONS WITH AYAHUASCA

The Takiwasi Center in Tarapoto is the only center in the world that treats drug addiction with ayahuasca, the jungle hallucinogen that has been used by Amazon healers for centuries. The Center claims that more than two-thirds of its clients are permanently cured of their addictions.

The clinic's innovative and controversial approach was forged by French physician Jacques Mabit, who came to the Peru's northeastern Amazon in the 1980s with the organization Doctors Without Borders. During his work, he became intrigued with Amazon healers, or *curanderos,* and their mastery of a huge range of medicinal plants.

At that time cocaine processing was ramping up in the nearby Huallaga Valley just outside Tarapoto, and local kids were coming to the *curanderos* with a deadly new disease: addiction to smoking *pasta básica,* the unrefined paste used to make cocaine. Without a second thought, *curanderos* began treating these patients as they always had—with the full arsenal of Amazon medicine, including purgative plants and hallucinogens such as ayahuasca.

Mabit himself tried ayahuasca, and in one of his sessions he saw himself using the plant to treat drug addicts. He began working with *curanderos* in 1986 to put together a full rehabilitation program and, six years later, opened the Takiwasi Center. His doctors are *curanderos,* and the only medicines they use are those provided by the Amazon.

Takiwasi has some simple rules. First, patients can leave whenever they want. Second, no one is ever turned away for lack of funds. Though the cost of the nine-month rehab program is $500 per month, Takiwasi has always found a way to pay for anyone who is motivated to get better.

The Takiwasi program gets off to a fast start. On the first day, a patient drinks a solution made from Yawar Panga, a purgative plant that provokes two or three hours of vomiting followed by a deep sleep. The plant is taken again on the third day, to help the body rid itself of toxins and prepare for the upcoming regime of psychotropic medicines.

During the first two weeks, patients must stay confined to a bungalow so that the smells of chemicals leaching from their bodies do not cause other patients at the center to relapse into addiction. Their isolation ends with an ayahuasca session, which begins the process of unlocking dreams and fears that are buried in the subconscious and that Mabit believes are at the root of addiction.

The patient is then integrated with the rest of the group, which averages between 15 and 20 patients at a time, and enters into the daily rhythm of Takiwasi's 2.5-hectare complex of gardens and bungalows outside Tarapoto. After early-morning exercises and a meal, group members follow a routine that includes working in the garden, cooking, baking bread, playing soccer, and participating in workshops that range from woodworking to improvisational pantomime. During the first three months, patient take ayahuasca weekly, along with other cleansing and purgative plants. They are not allowed to have any contact with their families or friends.

After two months of physical cleaning, the patient is ready to begin what Mabit describes as psychic cleansing and the exploration of emotions. "We want to get to the root cause," he says. "Why did they start taking drugs in the first place?"

The new stage begins when a *curandero* leads the patient to a secluded hut in the rainforest for the *dieta,* an eight-day regime of isolation and a grueling diet of plantains, rice, and oatmeal. Each morning the patient drinks a brew of purgative herbs and pyschotropics (though not ayahuasca), which causes the person to re-live emotions, have visions, and open mental doors.

"This is where you start realizing how wrong you've been," explains Gustavo, a clean-cut 26-year-old who first smoked *pasta básica* in a Tarapoto discotheque two years earlier. He was addicted within a week, and soon after the only job he could hold down was working as a *caficho,* or street hustler for prostitutes.

Gustavo and his fellow patients are between *dietas,* which Takiwasi patients generally undergo every two months. Now they are locked together in a daily routine that is designed to give new structure to their lives: communal labor, shared meals, and workshops like dancing and acting that help them to re-establish a withered connection to their own body. They also take ayahuasca every week as a group and discuss their visions afterwards among themselves.

Another patient, Lucas, is a sales supervisor in his early 30s who says he spent years addicted to alcohol and sex. He tried a range of treatments before finally ending up at Takiwasi. "Drugs are a symptom," he says. "The problem dwells in the person."

Lucas has recently had a life-changing experience during the group's weekly ayahuasca session. During these sessions, the *curandero* takes ayahuasca along with the other patients, whom he guides through the experience by chanting a song, known as an *ícaro,* and shaking a bundle of *shacapa* leaves.

At some point, the *curandero* envisioned Lucas' belly as a balloon ready to burst from all the alcohol he had consumed in his life. Lucas meanwhile was locked in a vision of a huge multicolored cross that came rushing toward him and implanted itself in his forehead.

Suddenly he leapt to his feet and began to dance. "I felt the most incredible tranquility and peace," says Lucas, who believes the root of his addiction were traumas he suffered when he was an infant. "I had to return to the age of three years old to reach the age I have now."

Both Gustavo and Lucas are in the final and third stage of the Takiwasi program, which involves re-connecting with family and putting together a new life plan. For most patients it also involves developing a set of religious and spiritual beliefs that will get them through the hard moments ahead.

About 500 patients have passed through Takiwasi since it opened more than a decade ago, and more than two-thirds of the patients who completed the program are still off drugs, according to Mabit. The remaining third have either relapsed or fallen out of contact with the center.

About three-quarters of Mabit's patients are from Peru, and the rest are from Europe, where some doctors have criticized him for using cutting-edge hallucinogenic therapies that have yet to be tested and approved by modern medicine.

But Mabit remains unapologetic. The wisdom of *curanderos* is centuries old, he argues, and every Takiwasi patient gets a full health screening for conditions like schizophrenia that would be exacerbated by taking ayahuasca.

Mabit also draws a clear line between what he is doing and what Timothy Leary, Allen Ginsberg, and the other psychedelic pioneers did during their time in the Amazon. "They were playing neurochemists like apprentice sorcerers," Mabit scoffs. "They divorced the ancient medicine from its cultural contexts and used it as a mere drug."

Ayahuasca, unlike cocaine and alcohol, is not addictive. "It has a terrible taste, and people throw up at the beginning of every session," Mabit smiles. "It's hard to get addicted to something so horrible."

The Amazon

© PROMPERÚ

The Andean cock of the rock bobs its crimson breast during its elaborate and poorly understood courtship rituals.

into an escarpment. If you have a bird guide (available at Puerto Palmeras), there is excellent birding on nearby ridges. There is also a restaurant and swimming hole down the road at Lago Venecia, a popular weekend spot for renting canoes.

There are plenty of other options for those looking for more wilderness. The **Huacamaillo Waterfalls** are reached after a two-hour walk from the village of San Antonio de Cumbaza, 18 km north of Tarapoto. This waterfall jets forth from a stunning rock gorge and is well worth the walk.

Another recommended day trip is to **Laguna Sauce**, a two-hour trip from Tarapoto that involves crossing the Río Huallaga by steel barge. There are several hotels and restaurants around the town of Sauce, and canoe rental is available. At the far end, accessible via narrow channel, is the more remote **Lago Lindo**, a 1,000-hectare private reserve with the beautiful bungalows of Puerto Patos. There are a number of rafting opportunities on the nearby Río Huallaga and Río Mayo.

Tarapoto is also home to two unusual sites. The first is the village of **Lamas**, 21 km north of Tarapoto, an isolated village of people known as the *lamistas* who speak a mixture of Quechua and jungle dialects. They are grouped together in

one half of the town, have their own museum, and have a sense of community and identity that never fail to impress visitors.

The second is the **Takiwasi Center** (Alerta 466, tel. 042/522-818, takiwasi@terra.com.pe, www.takiwasi.com, call before visiting), a drug rehabilitation center that uses ayahuasca and other hallucinogenic jungle medicines as a central part of its treatment. The center also caters to the growing number of travelers interested in taking ayahuasca. Because of its decade of experience, staff of authentic jungle *curanderos* (healers), and serious philosophy that includes post-experience debriefing with a psychoanalyst, participants almost invariably have a safe, meaningful experience. Takiwasi, no doubt, is the best place to sample ayahuasca in all of Peru.

Along with Iquitos, Tarapoto is an excellent launching point for visiting the immense and biodiverse Reserva Nacional Pacaya-Samiria. To the south lies the brand-new and largely unexplored Cordillera Azul, 1.3 million hectares of mountainous cloud forest and high-altitude marshlands that were only declared a national park in 2001. During a three-week ecological inventory in 2000, biologists estimated the park contained 6,000 plant species, 500 types of birds, 100 types of fish, and 45 types of palm. They also discovered 30 new species of plants and animals, including a new species of woodpecker *(Capito wallacei)*.

Entertainment and Events

Tarapoto's most frequented discotheque is **Papillón**, 5 km outside of Tarapoto in the Morales district, which is near the Río Cumbaza bridge on the highway to Moyobamba. There are several discotheques in the neighborhood, including **Tropicana, Ovni,** and **Las Rocas.** To start off an evening's activities, head toward a clump of pubs and karaoke bars on the second block of Lamas, near the Plaza Mayor.

Tarapoto's most festive day is its birthday, July 16, which comes in the middle of **Tourist Week.** Lama's **Fiesta de Santa Rosa** at the end of August is said to be spectacular.

Shopping

Few people associate Tarapoto with 21st-century art, but the truth is that there is a growing community of exceptionally talented painters and sculptors in and around the city. Information about these artists is posted on Puerto Palmeras' web page (www.puertopalmeras.com).

Of the six most prominent painters, Juan Echenique stands out for his Picasso-like paintings (ranging from political satire to nudes), and Savrín with his well-known series of Dalí-esque ayahuasca hallucinations. The paintings are exhibited at Puerto Palmeras and at Hostal La Patarashca, where contact information for the artists can be obtained, as well as gallery **Rupay** (San Martín 499, tel. 042/52-8173). There are some handicraft stores at the corner of Delgado and Pimentel and at **Artesenía Riojas** (Rioja 357, tel. 042/522616). If you need inexpensive though high-quality clothing, the city is teeming with stores hawking jeans, surfing shorts, and shirts imported up the Amazon from Brazil. The best place to go bargain shopping is Jimenez Pimentel, near the southwest corner of the Plaza Mayor.

Sports and Recreation

There are a handful of agencies in Tarapoto that offer excellent, reasonably priced tours to the area, which include lunch and have a three-passenger minimum. The following prices quoted are pp. **Puerto Palmeras** (Carretera Marginal Sur Km 3, tel. 042/52-3978, ctareps@puertopalmeras.com, www.puertopalmeras.com) has well-maintained Land Rovers that head to Lama ($10), Huacamaillo waterfalls ($25), the Jacuzzi-like Baños de la Unión ($10), and the Ahuashiyaku Waterfall ($20). It can also arrange rafting trips down an 8-km section of the Río Mayo, downstream of the town of San Miguel ($20). From Puerto Perico, its lodge in Yurimaguas, this company also offers trips to Reserva Nacional Pacaya-Samiria for $50/day with a minimum of two people. An eight-day trip allows one full day at remote Lake Pastococha, and the $400 pp cost includes all meals, camping, and shaded canoe. The other recommended agency in Tarapoto, which also visits all the local sites, is **Martín Zamora** (San Martin 213, tel. 042/52-5148, martinzamora@mixmail.com).

Adventure options include guide César Reategui, owner of hostel and restaurant **La**

Patarashca (Lamas 261, tel. 042/52-3899, lapatarashca@hotmail.com). He is willing to go anywhere, including out-of-the-way river spots and treks into the remote Cordillera Azul and camping trips into a little-known freshwater mangrove swamp near Moyobamba, where monkeys and river otters can be spotted. He also leads backpacker treks to Pacaya-Samiria. The best rafting outfitter in town is **Los Chancas Expeditions** (Rioja 357, tel. 042/52-2616), which organizes day trips on the Río Mayo, which gets up to Class III during the rainy months of November to March. This agency also organizes trips into the Pacaya Samiria and longer, six-day trips down the Class IV waters of the lower Río Huallaga between July and October. This section of the river is not near the Upper Huallaga, the well-known center of cocaine production.

For up-to-date information on ways to visit the unexplored **Parque Nacional Cordillera Azul**, contact the headquarters in Lima (San Fernando 537, Miraflores, tel. 01/444-3441, cima@telefonica.net.pe, www.fmnh.org/cordilleraazul) or Tarapoto (Santa Inés 269, tel. 042/52-5379). Another contact is Luis Benites, Tarapoto representative of INRENA, the Peruvian parks authority, at tel. 042/52-6732.

Accommodations

Under $10: Tarapoto is a jungle city, so don't expect any budget lodging to have hot water. **Hostal Residencial Juan Alfonso** (Urzua 309, tel. 042/52-6526, hostalresidencialjuanalfonso@hotmail.com, $7 s, $9 d, shared bathrooms cheaper) is a clean, tranquil option with whitewashed walls, iron frame beds, and a few squawking parakeets. Ask the hospitable owner, Rita Gardini, for one of the seven windowless rooms in the back that are the quietest.

Hostal Misti (Prado 341, tel. 042/52-2439, $4.50 s, $6 d) is another clean, quiet backpacker choice with a friendly staff, amenable front room, and rooms that have both shower and fan. This hostel also has a tiny *pichico* monkey to play with. Neither of these places caters toward prostitutes, as most of Tarapoto's hostels do in this price category.

$10–25: ⩗ La Patarashca (Lamas 261, tel.

042/52-3899, lapatarashca@hotmail.com, $10 s, $13 d, including breakfast) is a funky backpackers' hangout with clean rooms painted in colorful and interesting jungle tones. Each room is decorated with plants, paintings from local artists, and interesting gourd lamps—did we mention it has hot water? Owner César Reategui operates a restaurant next door and, in his spare time, works as a wilderness guide. Though a bit more expensive, this is the nicest backpackers' hostel in Tarapoto and well worth the money—especially if you plan on contracting César for tours. Groups of two or more will enjoy the room with a loft.

N **La Posada Inn** (San Martín 146, tel. 042/52-2234, laposada@terra.com.pe, $25 s, $35 d, including breakfast) is a renovated colonial house that is a few yards from the Plaza de Armas. Off the busy street, guests enter a hushed atmosphere of orchids, stained wood floors, and comfortable rooms with hot water, refrigerators, TV, phone, and either AC or fans. The landings outside the rooms are a great place to relax and chat, and the inn includes a clean well-managed restaurant that serves breakfast. The inn's manager, Claudia, is extremely helpful and a great source of information on sights, transport, etc. Make reservations in advance here. and ask Claudia for the preferable second-story rooms.

About 17 km outside of Tarapoto, in the village of San Roque de Cumbaza, is the spiritual retreat known as **Casa Hunab-Ku** (tel. 042/52-0310 or 042/69-6454, contact annicksyrius@yahoo.es for prices). The center includes a rustic collection of buildings established by an American healer, who offers vegetarian cooking, sweat lodge, medicinal baths, massages and Reiki, and meditation and shamanic sessions.

$25–50: Hotel Nilas (Moyobamba 173, tel. 042/52-7331, hotelnilas@hotmail.com, inkaweb .tripod.com/nilas.html, $38 s, $49.50 d, including breakfast), a modern business hotel, has all the services but none of the charm of La Posada. The five-story building includes room service, pool with a bar and great view, jacuzzi, large gym, AC in all rooms, refrigerators, cable TV, and room terraces with views of surrounding hills.

$50–100: If you are going to spend the money, head for **N** **Puerto Palmeras** (Carretera Marginal Sur Km 3, tel. 042/52-3978, ctareps@puertopalmeras.com, www.puertopalmeras.com, $60 s, $88 d). This tasteful and relaxed resort is tucked into a river bend far from the hustle and bustle of Tarapoto. It is a perfect getaway for both couples in search of solitude and families looking for a range of well-organized activities. Everything—riverside restaurant, poolside bar, elegant rooms, local tours—is done with the highest level of quality that makes this one of Peru's better resorts. Rooms are spacious, with beautiful bathrooms, refrigerators, TV, loads of hot water, and private terraces that look out either over the pool or the river.

For moments of peace and quiet, there are stone courtyards and open-air sitting areas decorated with a mind-blowing collection of paintings from local artists. The sprawling grounds around the resort also include playing fields and a lake with canoes and an island population of monkeys. This resort, constructed during the strife-ridden 1990s by the determined Dr. Carlos Gonzalez, is the crown jewel in a network of hotels that includes Puerto Patos, 2.5 hours away at Laguna Azul; Puerto Perico, eight hours by rough road to Yurimaguas; and Puerto Pumas, seven hours toward the coast at Lago Pomacocha.

A cheaper, though not as charming, option outside the city is **Hotel Río Shilcayo** (2 km outside Tarapoto, Pasaje las Flores 234, Banda de Shilcayo, tel. 042/52-2225, hotelrsh@terra.com.pe, www.geocities.com/hotelrioshilcayo, $45 s, $55 d). Brick buildings surround a round pool with bar, thatch-shaded tables, and well-maintained palm groves and lawn. Rooms have all the modern services, but brick walls chip away at their charm. Another option is more private bungalows, which sleep up to three and cost $65. This company also offers three-day packages for as low as $90, which include food, lodging, and tours (see http://members.spree.com/sip/rioshilcayo/hotel.htm).

Food

For a budget meal try **Las Terrazas** on the Plaza Mayor, a small café serving *lomo saltado, cecina* (smoked pork), and other meat dishes. Though somewhat overpriced, **Real Grill** (Plaza Mayor, Moyobamba 131, tel. 042/52-2714, 8 A.M.–

11 P.M., $3.50–8) has a great variety of food, including meats, seafood, salads, pastas, and excellent milkshakes and yogurt drinks. You can get just about anything here—even the elusive martini—though the meat was a bit tough.

A better option for meat eaters is **El Callejon de las Parillas** (one block of Plaza Mayor, San Martín 158, tel. 042/52-8408), which serves Peruvian food and grilled meats. **Chifa Tai Pai** (Rioja 252, tel. 042/52-4393) is clean, and **La Pizzeria** (corner of Lamas and Pablo de la Cruz) is Tarapoto's best pizza joint.

La Patarashca (Lamas 261, tel. 042/52-3899,10 A.M.–11 P.M., $6–8), next to the hostel of the same name, has an upstairs treehouse-like space, decorated with paintings, that serves up delicious local food. The specialty of the house is La Patarashca, a delicious seafood stew of fish and local river shrimp in a broth of cilantro and local *bijao* leaves. This is also a good place to try *paiche* (from a fish farm in Pucallpa) with *chonta*, freshwater prawns and a white sauce. Another good spot for seafood and a locals' favorite is **El Camaron** (San Pedro de la Cruz 232).

Hotel Puerto Palmeras (Carretera Marginal Sur Km 3, tel. 042/52-3978), which has an excellent restaurant and, if you are not staying there, can be reached via a 10-minute, $2 *motocar* ride from downtown. The spinach salad is tasty and safe to eat, and a resident chef whips up a range of meats, seafood, and pastas. The best deal is the hotel menu, which starts with a Greek salad, followed by roasted chicken over Spanish rice, and a chocolate pudding for dessert. The open-air restaurant is filled with the chirping of birds and the gurgle of a nearby river.

Information and Services

The best sources for tourist information in Tarapoto are the agencies or Claudia at the **Posada Inn**.

Police are located on the Ramirez, block 1 (tel. 042/52-6112).

The health care options are either the **state hospital** (third block of Delgado, tel. 042/52-2071) or the private **Clínica San Marcos** (Leguía 604, tel. 042/52-3838).

Good places to buy medicine include **Pharmacy San Pedro** (Pedro de Ursúa 163, tel. 042/52-2652) or **Pharmacy Guadalupe** (Maynas 300, tel. 042/52-8154).

The best supermarket is **La Inmaculada** (Martinez de Compagñon 126, tel. 042/52-3216).

The **Banco de Crédito** with an ATM machine is on San Martín 156 and next to the post office (San Martín 153, tel. 042/52-6668).

The best places for email are **Ciber Nautas** (San Pablo de la Cruz 110, $0.60/hr) or **Cabinas Internet** on Pimentel 134. The **post office** is on San Martín 482 (tel. 042/52-2021, 8 A.M.–10 P.M. Mon.–Sat., 9 A.M.–1 P.M. Sun.).

Cheap international calls can be made from **Gama.Com** (Plaza Mayor, Pablo de la Cruz 182).

Laundry is available at **El Churre** (San Pablo de la Cruz 140, tel. 042/52-7133), and a second location is at **Delgado 184** (tel. 042/52-6258).

Getting There

Tarapoto is connected by air to Lima, Iquitos, Yurimaguas, and Chachapoyas, and the airport is a $3 *motocar* ride from town. **TANS Peru** (in Lima tel. 01/213-6000, ventaslima.com.pe, www.tansperu.com.pe) also has daily flights to Tarapoto. Other companies that fly into Tarapoto a few times a week include **Magenta Air** (in Lima tel. 01/241-7777, reservas@magentaair.com, www.magentaair.com) and **Star Up** (in Lima, tel. 01/446-2485, ventas@starup.com.pe, www.starup.com.pe). All these companies are in the same price range. Star Up also flies from here to Yurimaguas a few times a week. Tans Peru flies between here and Iquitos five times a week.

Tarapoto has been an important jungle crossroads ever since completion of the Carretera Marginal in the mid-1960. The highway east toward Moyobamba and the coast is in excellent shape; the muddy road west to Yurimaguas is a spectacular, potholed mess; and the highway south to Juanjui, Tocache, and the other drug-producing towns of the Upper Huallaga Valley has been all but abandoned and is not safe at this time for travelers. Though it seems a convenient, direct route to the center of this country, stay away from this route— the danger is not so much drug runners as opportunistic bandits, and the road is a continuous stretch of jagged rocks, mud, and potholes.

The Amazon

Most of the bus companies are lined up along block 6 and 7 of Salaverry. The best place to buy bus and plane tickets and get up-to-date travel information is **Quiquiriqui Tours** (Jiménez Pimentel 309, tel. 042/52-4016, quiquiriqui@terra.com.pe). The best and safest bus service to Chiclayo (12–15 hours) is **Paredes Estrella** (Próspero 1212, tel. 042/52-3681, $10). These buses also stop in Moyobamba (2.5 hours), as do frequent *combis* from downtown.

The bumpy journey to Yurimaguas can take eight hours by car or up to 12 hours by truck, and the prices are in proportion to the amount of jolts and bumping a passenger will have to endure on the muddy road. Cars leave early each morning and arrive in Yurimaguas before cargo boats depart in the afternoon for Iquitos. For tickets, have Quiquiriqui Tours or Claudia at La Posada call and reserve a ticket for the following day, as the terminals are hard to find.

The Amazon

Nasca and the Desert Coast

The deserts of Peru's south coast, sucked dry by the frigid air of the Humboldt Current, are even drier and less populated than the north coast. Rivers here often simply disappear into the sand before reaching the Pacific Ocean. To solve their water problem, ancient cultures such as the Paracas, Nasca, and Chincha moved inland and built aqueducts from the mountains.

The Panamericana Highway follows the ancient inland migration, veering away from the coast toward the towns of Ica and Nasca, and in the process isolates a huge chunk of spectacular, wild desert wedged against the Pacific. A handful of qualified guides with 4x4 trucks are now leading travelers into this ocher lunar land. What do they seek? Dunes for sand-boarding, star-filled nights, the spiritual stillness of the desert, and the world's greatest collection of marine fossils—including

Must-Sees

Look for **M** to find the sights and activities you can't miss and **N** for the best dining and lodging.

Nasca

M Nasca Lines: There are certain mysteries, like huge astronauts and hummingbirds etched onto the desert plain, that you have to see to believe (page 234).

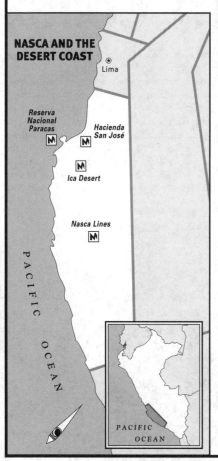

NASCA AND THE DESERT COAST

the rock formation known as La Catedral in the Reserva Nacional Paracas

Ica

M Ica Desert: This ancient ocean floor, heaved upward by tectonic activity, is littered with marine fossils, sculpted hills, and towering dunes. Those who venture into this remote sandscape return dazzled by the experience (page 242).

The Paracas Peninsula

M Reserva Nacional Paracas: This coastline of rugged cliffs and islands is a good place to see a wide array of birds and marine mammals and, in the process, camp or hike amid the spectacular surroundings (page 254).

El Carmen and Chincha

M Hacienda San José: With its whitewashed chapel, long wooden veranda, and creole cooking, San José recalls the day when more than 1,000 African slaves worked and lived here. The descendants of the slaves now live in nearby El Carmen, a village that has blossomed into the heartbeat of Afro-Peruvian dance and music (page 261).

Nasca and the Desert Coast

Frisbee-sized teeth from a gigantic extinct shark known as megalodon.

On the northern edge of this desert is the **Reserva Nacional Paracas,** a series of cliff bluffs that drop to long desert beaches teeming with 200 bird species, sea lions, seals, and the endangered Humboldt penguin. Camping, hiking, or mountain biking here is an unforgettable and safe experience.

Just up the coast at **El Carmen,** thousands of slaves from Africa stumbled off boats in the 17th and 18th centuries to work in the sugarcane plantations of El Carmen. These days El Carmen, which seems lifted right out of the Cuban countryside, is a center of Afro-Peruvian dance and music. Down the road is Hacienda San José, the best-preserved hacienda in all of Peru.

The highlight of the south coast, however, are the **Nasca Lines,** giant enigmatic drawings of hummingbirds, whales, and mythical beings etched onto the desert floor and surrounded by a maze of lines and triangles. Though theories range from E.T. landing strips to sacred water symbols, the riddle of the Nasca Lines remains unsolved. The Nasca people who made the lines also produced some of the finest ceramics and textiles in pre-Columbian Peru, which are on display in excellent museums in Paracas, Ica, and Nasca.

PLANNING YOUR TIME

Since the highland highways to Cusco (from both Nasca and Arequipa) have been fixed up and repaved, more travelers are hopping aboard a bus for at least one leg of this entertaining jour-

PUERTO INCA

The nicest place to stop on the seven-hour drive between Nasca and Arequipa is the half-moon beach of Puerto Inca, at Km. 603, 10 kilometers south of Chala. The Incas had a settlement here, thus the beach's name, where fish was caught for the Inca and run up to Cusco along Inca roads that can still be seen receding into the mountains. Today what's left is an area of ruins with other smaller ruins nearby—including a strange carved seat on a rocky cliff to the south. Located scandalously close to the ruins, **Hotel Puerto Inka** (Panamericana Sur Km. 603, tel. 054/27-2663, $24 s, $36 d) has the beach all to itself, and all 31 rooms have ocean views. There is a video library, pool table, discotheque with karaoke, swimming pool, and playground, and camping with showers costs $2 pp. The hotel rents kayaks for $3 an hour and jet-skis for $42 an hour.

ney to and from Lima. If you have the time, and are interested by what you read here, points at the south coast can make for quick, easy visits—with the exception of a 4x4 desert safari in the Ica desert, for which you need between three and five days.

Nasca is roughly the halfway point in the 20-hour journey between Lima and Nasca and is well worth the stop—there is no way to really comprehend the lines in the desert without flying over them. If you are short on time and prefer to fly, the Nasca Lines can also be seen in a one-day, round-trip package from Lima.

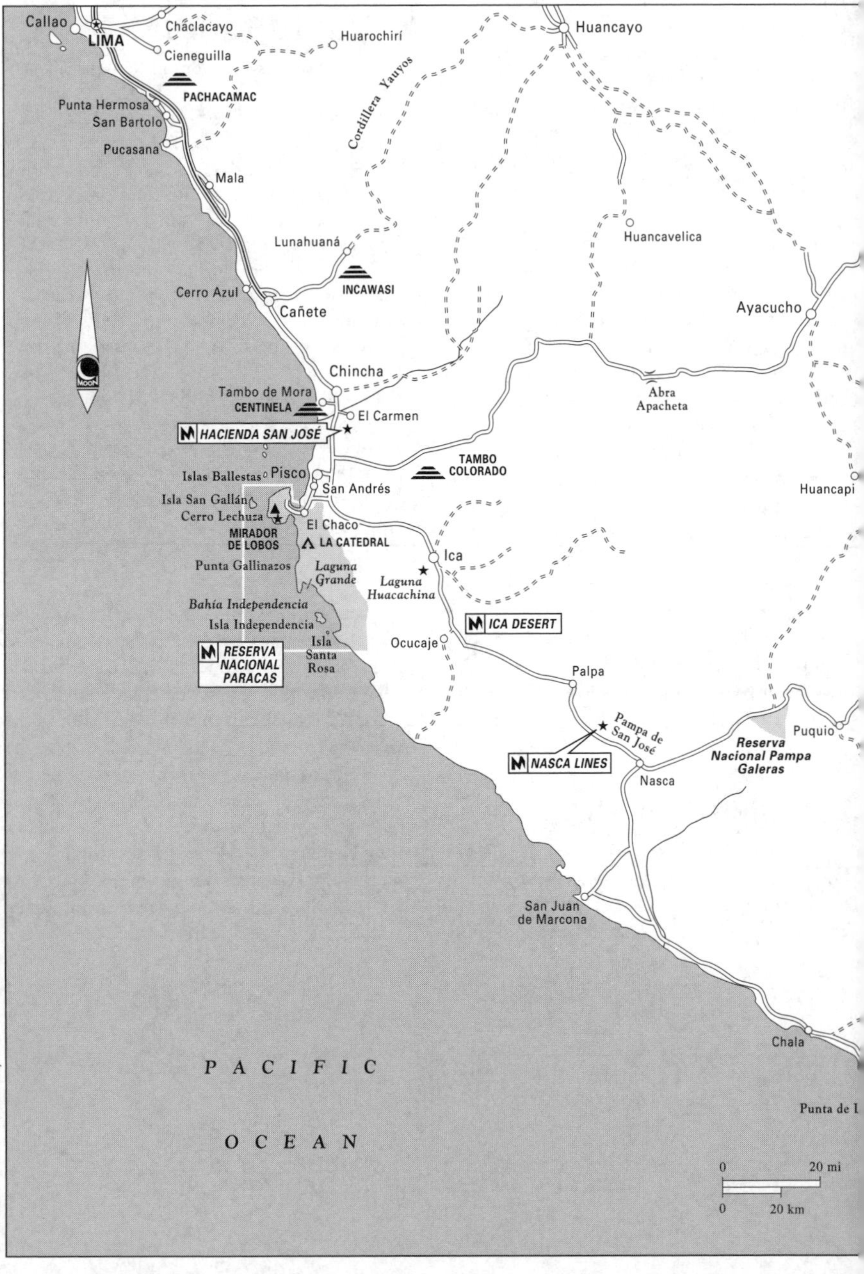

Callao
LIMA
Chaclacayo
Huarochirí
Huancayo
Cieneguilla
Cordillera Yauyos
PACHACAMAC
Punta Hermosa
San Bartolo
Pucasana
Mala
Lunahuaná
Huancavelica
INCAWASI
Cerro Azul
Cañete
Ayacucho
Chincha
Tambo de Mora
CENTINELA
El Carmen
Abra Apacheta
HACIENDA SAN JOSÉ
TAMBO COLORADO
Islas Ballestas
Pisco
San Andrés
Huancapi
Isla San Gallán
Cerro Lechuza
MIRADOR DE LOBOS
El Chaco
LA CATEDRAL
Ica
Punta Gallinazos
Laguna Grande
Laguna Huacachina
Bahía Independencia
Isla Independencia
ICA DESERT
RESERVA NACIONAL PARACAS
Isla Santa Rosa
Ocucaje
Palpa
Pampa de San José
Puquio
NASCA LINES
Nasca
Reserva Nacional Pampa Galeras
San Juan de Marcona
Chala
PACIFIC
OCEAN
Punta de l
0
20 mi
0
20 km

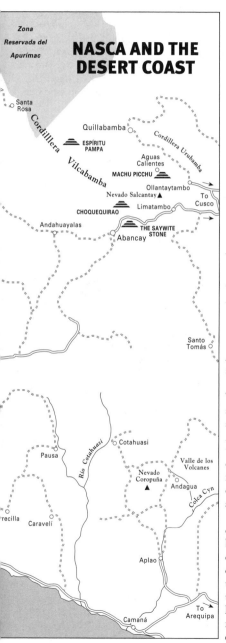

NASCA AND THE DESERT COAST

Nasca

Nasca would be just another dusty highway town were it not for its enigmatic lines in the San José desert, which have tormented scientists ever since they were spotted by the first planes to pass over the area in the 1920s. When seen from above, the stylized forms of hummingbirds, a killer whale, monkey, and other animals sprawl across the desert floor, surrounded by a maze of trapezoids and geometric figures and lines that recede to the horizon. The lines are so bizarre that many believe they are landing strips for extraterrestrials, as claimed by the book and movie *The Chariots of the Gods.* That theory has somewhat faded, along with a dozen others, but the mystery of the Nasca Lines remains. They are one of South America's greatest enigmas.

Despite the desolate surroundings, a series of advanced cultures have occupied the Río Nasca Valley since the Paracas culture (800–200 B.C.), which probably made the area's first hillside etchings around 400 B.C. They also began work on Cahuachi, a huge complex of pyramids 28 km northwest of Nasca. The Nasca culture (100–600 A.D.) continued building Cahuiche and also built an ingenious aqueduct that pipes water under the desert floor and is still used by farmers today. The Nasca are world-famous for ceramics and, along with the Paracas, weavings, and excellent examples of both can be seen at the town's new Museo Antonini. After the Nasca, the area fell under the successive influences of the Wari, Chincha, and Inca. A small Spanish settlement was founded here in 1591 but has been destroyed so often by earthquakes—most recently in 1942 and 1996—that no colonial architecture remains.

Nasca today is a noisy hodgepodge of concrete buildings. The best places to stay, both budget and high-end, are in the surrounding countryside. Nasca has a particularly aggressive culture of *jaladores,* or salespeople, that swarm tourists when they get off the bus. The city's tourism commission has passed laws making it illegal to sell tourist services on the street, because many travelers have become ripped off, or pissed off, by this town's informal tourism racket. Pay a bit more money and go to one of the agencies listed below (see *Sports and Recreation*).

NASCA LINES

The Spanish chronicler Pedro Cieza de León was the first European to comment on the hillside drawings that can be seen from ground level near Nasca and Paracas. Archaeologists had also studied similar hill drawings in Arequipa, Lima, Trujillo, and the mountains of Bolivia and Chile. But the profusion of lines etched onto the perfectly flat San José desert are the continent's fullest expression of this cryptic practice, and were not fully appreciated until the first planes flew over the area in the 1920s. When viewed from above, more than 70 giant plant and animal figures pop into view, etched impermeably onto the desert floor, along with hundreds of straight lines, trapezoids, and other figures as long as 10 km. The shapes cover an astonishing 1,000 square kilometers (386 square miles), including a cluster of drawings further north near Palpa.

The shapes were made thanks to the area's peculiar geography. A thin layer of manganese and iron oxides, called desert varnish, covers the rocky surface of the San José desert. The Nasca removed the dark rocks to expose the lighter-colored rocks beneath, in canals that average about 20 cm deep. They piled the rocks into walls about a meter high to enhance the canal's edge. The Nasca probably made the drawings in small scale and then used ropes and stakes to reproduce them larger on the desert floor.

The best way to see them is by airplane, which costs anywhere from $35 to $75. There are a dozen or so companies, and all seem to have professional pilots and well-maintained light aircraft—there has been only one accident over the last 25 years. Pilots bank sharply so that people on both sides of the plane can see the lines, but many people end up clutching barf bags as a result. Even those with a stomach of steel should avoid breakfast before flying and consider taking Dramamine or other motion sickness meds beforehand. The best time to fly is in the morning before winds pick up, decreasing visibility and making the flight bumpier.

Another option for viewing the lines is a three-story observation tower 19 km north of Nasca and on the way to the Museo Maria Reiche. Three small lines can be seen from here, including a set of hands, a lizard, and a tree. A few hillsides offer good views during the clearest light of the morning, especially the giant sand dune of Cerro Blanco.

MUSEO ANTONINI

This museum (Av. de la Cultura 600, tel. 056/52-3444, 9 A.M.–7 P.M. daily, $3) is the labor of love of Giuseppe Orefici, whose excavations at Cahuachi continue to be funded by the Italian government. This museum has a small but exquisite collection that sheds light on the Nasca's profoundly religious way of thinking, including a ceremonial fishing net with embroidered crimson edges and a cotton coat fringed with supernatural dolls that look like tiny, cactus-like beings.

Other Nasca ceramics here portray a pantheon of seafaring creatures, pelicans, cats, birds, lizards, and snakes. These deities often have serpentine shapes emerging from their mouths, which archaeologists believe reflect the Nasca belief that blessings come from the nose and mouth. There are also elongated skulls, and others with trepination holes, and a few well-preserved mummies. Out back there is a replication of a Nasca tomb, a Nasca irrigation canal, and a scale model of the Nasca Lines. Orefici has a spectacular collection of painted textiles that he hopes to put on display in the future.

CASA-MUSEO MARIA REICHE

During much of her six decades living in Nasca, German mathematician Maria Reiche, the "dame of the desert," lived in a simple room in the village of Pascana, about 27 km south of Nasca. When she died in 1998 at the age of 95, she was buried here and her home converted into the Casa-Museo Maria Reiche (Panamericana Km. 420, tel. 056/23-4383, 9 A.M.–7 P.M. Mon.–Fri., 8:30 A.M.–6:30 P.M. Saturday, 9 A.M.–1 P.M. Sunday). The place now pays tribute to Reiche's life and her theories about the Nasca Lines through

FROM UFO LANDING STRIPS TO RAIN CEREMONIES

The Nasca Lines first caught the world's attention in 1939, when American archaeologist Paul Kosok splashed their pictures across world newspapers. His translator, the German mathematician Maria Reiche, was so intrigued by Kosok's research that she moved to Nasca a year later. She spent the next six decades of her life living in austerity and spending her days measuring the lines under the broiling desert sun. By the time she died in 1998, she had developed an elaborate theory to support Kosok's original claim that the lines were "the biggest astronomy book in the world." In the process she had become a much-loved and venerated personality in Nasca, where her birthday remains the town's biggest celebration.

Many other researchers have wandered the deserts of Nasca and come up with theories that range from clever to crackpot. In 1947 Hans Horkheimer said they were tribal symbols, while George Von Breunig likened them to a giant running track in 1980 and Henri Stirlin claimed a few years later they represented huge weavings and strands of yarn. The International Explorers Club claimed that the Nasca people could in fact see the lines from the air. He attempted, unsuccessfully, to build a balloon from reed and cloth. The theory that struck the public imagination, however, was that proposed by Erich von Daniken in his book and movie *Chariots of the Gods*. He claimed the whole pampa was a giant landing strip for extraterrestrials and that one of the drawings, which shows a snowman-looking figure with large round eyes, was an astronaut (that name stuck, by the way).

But a broad consensus is emerging among Nasca experts that the lines are mainly about water. Unlike the broad coastal valleys of the north that supported huge cities of the Moche and Sicán, the valleys of the south are narrow and run with water only during the rainy season in the mountains. During a dry year, the Río Nasca may never even reach the town, much less the Pacific Ocean. In a valley where drought meant death, much of Nasca cosmography—as evidenced by their ceramics, textiles, and ceremonial architecture—is shaped by religious or magical practices to ensure a steady supply of water.

Researchers point out that the first drawings, made around 400 B.C., were of spirals, a water symbol that recurs throughout South America. These later morphed into other marine creatures such as sharks, orcas, and whales. Giuseppe Orefici, who has led excavations around Nasca since the early 1980s, says the subsequent phase of bird images is also water-related. The hummingbirds that suck life-giving nectar from flowers are fertility symbols, he says, and their fluttering wings are sacred dispensers of water. After studying lines in Chile and Bolivia, Dr. Johan Reinhard came to a similar conclusion—that the Nasca Lines are part of a pan-Andean fertility tradition.

After decades of gathering dust, the theory of the first-ever Nasca researcher, a Peruvian named Toribio Mejía Xesspe, is being picked up by modern-day researchers. Mejía Xesspe argued that the lines were sacred paths upon which hundreds of people walked during magical ceremonies. On close inspection, the lines that form the drawings do have an entrance and an exit, as if they were in fact made for walking. A recent documentary made by the Discovery Channel showed what these ceremonies may have looked like. The swarm of humans tracing the drawings' edges seem to make these fertility symbols come alive, converting them into living icons for the gods above.

The last phase of the lines, perhaps done as late as the Wari (600–1000 A.D.) or even the Chincha (1000–1400 A.D.) cultures, are the huge lines and intersecting plazas. There is evidence that huge masses of people also gathered here for ceremonies. There are stone constructions that appear to have been altars, and a number of clay flutes and arrowheads were found nearby and were probably used in ceremonial dances.

There are aspects of the lines that have not been fully understood, though they all seem to involve water-producing, cosmic forces. Many of lines point at sacred mountains, or *apus,* or at points on the horizon that mark important lunar or solar events. One leads to Cahuichi, the ceremonial complex of pyramids that faces the pyramids and is located on a sacred spot along the Río Nasca. Whatever relationship the pyramids had with the lines, archaeologists believe it too probably had to do with water.

photographs, maps, and models. Another good way to understand Reiche's theories is at the Hotel Nasca's evening planetarium show.

CANTAYOC AQUEDUCT AND PAREDONES

Faced with droughts and famine, the Nasca culture came up with a brilliant engineering solution around 300–500 A.D. to guarantee a year-round water supply. They went to the mountains where water gurgles out of the rock and built underground aqueducts, or *puquios*, to carry this water under the desert floor. These aqueducts, similar to *qanats* in Iraq, are one of the engineering marvels of pre-Columbian America and are still used today.

Some archaeologists believe the canals were originally exposed but became buried after a series of *aluviones*, or muddy flash floods. The canals can be accessed by periodic *respidores*, or spiral ramps that lead down to an exposed section of the canal. During the dry months from September to December, local farmers crawl through the tunnels between *respidores* to clean the canals, which are S-shaped to slow the flow of water during the rainy months. There are 36 of these ancient aqueducts that irrigate Nasca's fields today, though archaeologists believe that many others have been forgotten under the desert floor.

The aqueducts are 4 km southwest of town near the Hotel Cantayo and reachable via taxi ($2) or transport that runs along the nearby Abancay highway. Guards are now charging a $3 entrance fee, which includes two other nearby sites. The Inca ruins of Paredones are a badly deteriorated *tambo*, or resting place, made of adobe walls atop stone foundations. Two lines, known as El Telar and Las Agujas ("the weaving" and "the needles"), can also be seen from a nearby hill. This area is safe to walk around until 4:30 P.M., when the guards go home.

CAHUICHI

Excavations at Cahuichi, an area of low-lying hills 28 km northwest of Nasca, are gradually

a recently unearthed skull and backdrop of bones from a Nasca cemetery recently looted near Lomas

revealing a city of walls, staircases, and plazas that, at 24 square kilometers, was even bigger than the Chimú city of Chan Chan, near present-day Trujillo. Unlike Chan Chan, however, there is no evidence of homes or food production nearby. Giuseppe Orefici, who has been excavating Cahuichi since 1985, believes the area's 40-odd pyramids were used exclusively for public ceremonies to thank the gods for water. The whole complex faces the Nasca Lines and is built on a sacred spot, where the Río Nasca re-emerges from under the desert floor.

Like the adobe pyramids of the Moche and Sicán in Peru's north, the Nasca pyramids are huge—the Great Pyramid is 25 meters high and 100 meters long, and Orefici's team is working to restore its elaborate north facade by 2011. These pyramids are not solid adobe, but rather a cap of adobe bricks over the existing hill. Cahuichi was built in five main phases between 400 B.C. and 400 A.D., when it was abandoned because of flooding. The site has been badly looted by grave robbers but Orefici's teams have found tombs in the past, including a series of painted Nasca textiles. There is no public transport to the site, though more and more agencies are including this site in their day tours. A round-trip taxi, including the wait, from Nasca costs $15 and the trip takes 40 minutes each way.

Cementerios de Chauchilla

Nasca agencies frequently visit this graveyard from the Chincha period (1000–1460), though more than anything it is a bleak reminder of the destructive force of grave robbers. Thousands of scraps of textiles, bones, and patches of human hair lay spread across the sands, though a few of the clay tombs have been restored and have bleached skeletons, with huge dreadlocks, on display inside. At other cemeteries, like the one near Lomas, locals have even used bulldozers to unearth the cemeteries of their ancestors, leaving skulls strewn across the sand. "Every day information is being lost here," shrugs local archaeologist Giuseppe Orefici. "It is a race against thieves and the ravages of time." The cemetery is about 8 km off the Panamerican Highway south of Nasca, or about a half-hour drive from Nasca. There is no public transport to the site, though agencies visit here frequently and a round-trip taxi from Nasca costs $15.

ENTERTAINMENT AND EVENTS

Discos get cranked up in Nasca only on the weekends. The most popular place is the artsy **Etnia Pub** (Santa Teresita and Prolongación Callao, 8 P.M.–3 A.M. Thurs.–Sat.), with bronze armored guards and wooden cross out front. **Las Cañas** (Bolognesi 279, tel. 056/80-6891, 8 A.M.–8 P.M.) is a hip restaurant that transforms into a discotheque after 9 P.M. on weekends.

The biggest party in Nasca is **Fiesta Jacu Raymi,** which kicks off with Maria Reiche's birthday on May 15 and includes dances, *pachamancas,* and other celebrations. Religious holidays include the **Virgen del Carmen** on Sept. 19 and the **Virgen de Guadalupe,** patroness of Nasca, on Oct. 8. During the low-water months between September and December, communities gather in the fields to clean the ancient aqueducts.

SPORTS AND RECREATION

Nasca Overflights and Sightseeing Tours

Nearly a dozen companies offer Nasca overflights, which range in price from $35 to $75 depending on the time of year and length of flight. Make advance reservations from June to August, when entire days can be booked by gigantic package tours. Otherwise, travelers get the best price by negotiating directly at the overflight companies, which are lined up along the Panamericana alongside the airport and south of Nasca's center. This is a few kilometers south of town, about a five-minute taxi ride. This is especially true between September and May, when even the top companies charge the low price of $40.

AeroCondor and its agency **NC Travel** (Lima 199, tel. 056/52-1168, contanas@terra.com.pe, www.nctravelnasca.com) offers two basic tours with its five-passenger Cessna 206: a 30-minute flight over the Nasca Lines for $50, or a 45-minute flight over the lines of Nasca and Palpa for $72. The reputable **Alegría Tours** (Lima 168, tel. 056/52-2444, alegriatours@hotmail.com, www.nazcaperu.com) offers the same flights and prices, as does **AeroIca,** (tel. 056/52-2434 or in Lima tel. 01/446-3026, aeroica@terra.com.pe, www.aeroica.net). These are the three largest agencies in Nasca, and they all offer package deals with hotels. Of the three, we recommend AeroCondor's NC Travel, because it has the best reputation for service and its hotel, Nido del Condor, is the most pleasant. The $75 price includes 30-minute flight, breakfast, a day tour of Nasca, and a buffet lunch at a local restaurant. The price does not include a $2 airport tax or the $3 tourist ticket. For people who want to see the lines but are short on time, AeroCondor offers a one-day round-trip package from Lima for around $140 pp (minimum two people). Smaller but reputable airplane companies include **AeroParacas** (tel. 056/52-2688, www.aeroparacas.com, aeroparacas@wayna.rcp.net.pe) and **Alas Peruanas** (tel. 056/52-3400, info@alasperuanas.com, www.nazcalinesperu.net).

Nanasca Tours (Lima 160, tel. 056/52-2531, www.nanasca.com, info@nanasca.com), run by the Benavides family, is recommended for its one-day tours that include an overflight and visit to Paredones and the Museo Antonini. Nanasca and the other agencies in town offer affordable tours to the Cemetery of Chauchilla, Cahuachi, Pampas Galeras, and even the Reserva Nacional Paracas.

Trekking

Local trekking guide **Alan Watkin** (also the town's youngest-ever president of the local tourism board) is a nice guy, has lived in Nasca all of his life, and speaks good English. He has put together a range of interesting hikes, including a 12-hour jaunt from the altiplano to the summit of Cerro Blanco, one of the world's largest sand dunes, which rises 2,000 meters over the valley floor and offers good views of the Nasca Lines (all day, $40, includes lunch). He also has an interesting three-day package that includes an overflight of the Nasca Lines, a walking tour around the the Cementerio de Chauchilla, and a full day of cultural tourism in a farming community near the former hacienda of the Benavides family.

Four-Wheel Safaris

Enzo Destro, the Italian owner and manager of **Hotel Cantayo** (tel. 056/52-2264, info@hotel-cantayo.com, www.hotelcantayo.com), offers a series of deluxe four-wheel-drive tours of the area for up to four people for $250 per day, including guide and elegant picnic lunch. Destinations include Pampa Galera, the high-altitude national reserve above Nasca with herds of wild vicuña; Punta San Fernando, a remote Pacific point that offers reliable sightings of Humboldt penguins, sea lions, and the Andean condors trying to eat them; and a descent along the rugged coastline between Nasca and Puerto Inca, including the quaint port of Lomas and a dozen wild, unforgettable beaches.

Sandboarding and Biking

Alegría Tours (Lima 168, tel. 056/52-2444, alegriatours@hotmail.com, www.nazcaperu.com) offers sandboarding on Cerro Blanco (six hours, $30) or a four-hour biking trip ($35) that drops 2,000 meters in 45 km and whizzes past Cerro Blanco.

ACCOMMODATIONS

Under $10

The best budget place is **Estrella del Sur** (Callao 568, tel. 056/52-2764, $6 s, $9 d, including breakfast), on quiet street three blocks from the Plaza and across from the hospital. We liked this place because it was clean, fresh-smelling, and friendly and had big rooms with closet, TV cable, fair bathrooms—and some even have a porch. Next door is the **Hostel Nasca** (Lima 438, tel. 056/52-2085, $3 s, $6 d), which offers depressing rooms with concrete floors and shared baths. The tiled rooms with private baths ($9 s, $12 d) are somewhat nicer. There is great camping with showers at **Wasipunko** ($5 pp, see below).

$10–25

The small and charming **Oro Viejo** (Callao 483, tel. 056/52-2284, $20 s, $25 d includes breakfast), is a family-run place a few blocks from the plaza but away from the noise. There are nine rooms, arranged around a lovely flower garden, with nice furniture, big bathrooms, and fans. There is an outdoor bar and tables in the garden, and an indoor dining room with candlelit tables.

The new, modern **Paredones Inn** (Lima 600, tel. 056/52-2181, paredoneshotel@terra.com, $15 s, $20 d, including breakfast) is one of the best deals in town, with impeccable rooms, comfy beds, large bathrooms, cable TV, and 24-hour hot water. Breakfast can be taken on a rooftop terrace.

Hotel Las Lineas (Arica 299, tel. 056/52-2488, laslineashotel@hotmail.com, $15 s, $20 d) is on the plaza and right above its recommended sister restaurant. The location is noisy, but the red-carpeted rooms are cozy with cable TV, fans, and decent art. **Hostal Internacional** (Maria Reiche 112, tel. 056/52-2744, hostalinternacional@hotmail.com, $13 s, $18 d) has seven quiet rooms with bamboo ceilings, nice bathrooms, and cable TV.

$25–50

The family-run **N Wasipunko** (Panamericana Km. 457, tel. 056/52-3212, wasipunko@hotmail.com, $15 s, $30 d, including breakfast), owned by Olivia Sejuro Watkin, is a rustic country hostel 12 km south of Nasca. Out of the surrounding scrub, her family has eked out a paradise of palms, acacia, and *huarango* trees, scented by bougainvillea and jacaranda blooms and filled with the songs of 16 different bird species. The nine simple rooms have whitewashed adobe walls, bamboo roofs, antique furniture, beds covered with handmade quilts, clean bathrooms, and Olivia's own watercolors of local plants. The dining room is an adobe structure with large *huarango* beams, stained glass, and a telescope for star gazing. Because there is no electricity here, everything is illuminated with kerosene lamps at night and phone calls are possible, but expensive. This is a great place to hang out for a day or two, hop aboard a horse ($4 per hour), and relax. There is a good $7 lunch menu, a camping area with showers and dining tables ($5 pp), and Olivia's son, Alan Watkin, speaks English and French and offers excellent local treks.

All the major agencies own hotels that are typically bundled together in the overflight packages. Owned by Alegría Tours, **Hotel Alegria** (Lima 166, tel. 056/52-2444, awww.nazcaperu.com, alegriatours@hotmail.com, $20f s, $30 d) is a modern building in the center of town with lots of light and air and a nice pool. The rooms are large and nice and there is also laundry service, a book exchange, and a cafeteria in a quiet, grassy backyard.

The other two agency hotels are located right across from the airport and a five-minute taxi ride from the center. Owned by Aerocondor, **Nido del Condor** (Panamericana Sur Km. 447, tel. 056/52-1168, contanas@terra.com.pe, $25 s, $35 d) is the better of the two. The rooms have flowery bedspreads and tacky decorations, but they have TV, fans, phone, and clean bathroom. There are nice gardens outside with a small pool and a bamboo hut bar. Camping is possible for $3 pp. Owned by AeroIca, **La Maison Suisse** (Panamericana Sur Km. 447, tel. 056/52-2434, aeroica@terra.com.pe, www.aeroica.net, $47 s, $55 d) has funny-smelling rooms, tacky furniture, wood paneling, ceiling fans, and fair bathrooms. There is a small terrace with a pool and lawn areas for camping.

Hotel de la Borda (tel. 056/52-2750, turmajoro@yahoo.com, $40 s, $50 d, including breakfast) is a country hotel that is charming but in need of renovation. There are 40 comfortable, cool rooms with high ceilings and country views. There are two nice pools, which have bougainvillea-covered rock islands shaded by fruit trees and gardens. Camping here is $5 pp, or $6.50 with breakfast.

$50–100

Our highest recommendation goes to **N Hotel Cantayo Spa & Resort** (tel. 056/52-2264, info@hotelcantayo.com, www.hotelcantayo.com). Every last detail of this place, which opened in 2001 as a sort of spiritual retreat, was thought through by owner and manager Enzo Destro, from Padua, Italy. From the ruins of a hacienda, Enzo managed to save original archways, floor tiles, a well, and a centuries-old ficus tree. Around these elements, he built a spacious and light-filled lobby graced with the old well and the contemporary art and Tibetan tapestries he collects.

The hotel succeeds in its goal of being a complete refuge from stress. Songbirds flit around the lawn out back, where the huge ficus tree rises alongside two elegantly shaped pools, which glint in the desert sun and are landscaped with sunflowers and palms. There are grassy areas for yoga and meditation, a walkway with river stones for foot relaxation, and a *dojo* for Kyudo (an archery range for Japanese meditation). There is also a gym, Jacuzzi, and, in the near future, a spa with sauna, hydro-massages, and both Turkish and herbal baths. For those who want to leave the hotel, there are Peruvian *paso* horses for country rides, and Enzo enjoys taking guests on four-wheel-drive safaris to his favorite remote spots in the area. For a midafternoon nap, guests stroll down shaded archways to the rooms, which have huge white walls, all the five-star amenities, fridge, luxurious bathrooms with tubs, queen-sized beds with hypoallergenic alpaca wool blankets, fans, remote controlled AC, and heat—but, of course, not television.

The best hotel in the city itself is **Nazca Lines** (Bolognesi s/n, tel. 056/52-2293 or in Lima 01/261-0240, reservas@derramajae.org.pe, $69 s, $88 d), a hacienda that was completely remodeled in 1983. Whitewashed arcades wrap around a luxurious patio with two pools, fountains, and tables shaded with palm trees and bougainvillea. The rooms are tastefully decorated with *sautillo* tile floors, cable TV, and bathrooms with tubs, while the suites have fridges and Jacuzzis. The excellent restaurant (6 A.M.–10 P.M., $6–9) serves *cebiche,* scallops, sea bass, and chicken brochettes in a breezy dining room. The hotel's **Maria Reiche Planetarium** (7 P.M. daily, $6, $3 students) gives an excellent explanation every evening of the Nasca Lines and Reiche's theory of their relation to the stars.

FOOD

Peruvian

Locals flock to the tasty and affordable **Don Hono** (Arica 254, tel. 056/52-3066, $2 lunch menu, closed Saturday) which serves up a range of great local food prepared by an internationally trained cook. **La Kañada** (Lima 160 tel. 056/52-2917, $5–6) has been operated by the Benavides family for 40 years and serves excellent ostrich (raised locally), vegetarian, and seafood dishes such as sea bass with prawns from the Río Palpa. There is live folkloric music at 8 P.M. most nights, a good bar, and four Internet stations.

The very clean **Las Lineas** (Arica 299, tel. 056/52-2066, 6 A.M.–10 P.M. daily, $4) serves appetizers such as avacado salad, *papas a la huancaina,* and entrées of meat, fish, and seafood. Located on a quiet street, **La Encantada** (Callao 592, tel. 056/52-2930, 8 A.M.–11 P.M. Mon.–Sat., 11 A.M.–4 P.M. and 6–11 P.M. Sunday, $3–8) also serves up Peruvian fare like *cebiches, salpicon de pollo,* and *camarones.* They can prepare vegetarian meals upon request, and have a daily menú.

International

The new **Las Cañas** (Bolognesi 279, tel. 056/80-6891, $4) has good atmosphere, with well-designed bamboo construction and nice natural lighting. The wide-ranging menu includes salads, burgers, pastas, garlic steak, *cebiche,* and seafood— and this place becomes a discotheque after 9 P.M. on weekends. It's easy to believe that La Taberna (Lima 321, tel. 056/80-6783) has been around

for more than 20 years, judging from the walls covered in Nasca's best collection of wall graffiti. The clean kitchen dishes up a wide-ranging menu that includes salads, pastas, *cebiche,* and local favorites such as *lomo saltado* and *arroz con mariscos.*

The two best pizzerias in town are **La Pua** (Lima 169, tel. 056/52-2990, 6–11 P.M. daily, $4) and **Puquio** (Bolognesi 481, evenings only).

Nasca's best pastas are available at **El Portón** (Morsesky 120, tel. 056/52-3490, 11 A.M.–midnight daily, $3–7), which also serves up local dishes like *aji de gallina* and *seco de cabrito* along with *ensalada caprese,* seafood lasagna, and excellent pizzas. Stepping up a bit, the **Nazca Lines Hotel** (Bolognesi s/n, tel. 056/52-2293, 6 A.M.–10 P.M., $6–9) has an excellent restaurant, serving both in a patio and in a breezy dining room, which specializes in seafood dishes such as *cebiche,* scallops, sea bass, and *brochetas.*

Fine Dining

The best restaurant **Hotel Cantayo** (tel. 056/52-2264, info@hotelcantayo.com, www.hotelcantayo.com, , 7 A.M.–10 P.M. daily) serves, without question, the best food in Nasca—and all of it is organic. Breakfast begins with fruit, toast, and eight types of gourmet marmalades, ranging from *membrillo* to *guanábana* fruits. Lunch is tender chunks of lamb, chicken, veggies, and potatoes cooked in an underground *pachamanca* pit. For dinner, there are a variety of homemade pastas or lighter entrées, such as sea bass steamed in a bamboo tube, along with organic salad and a bottle from the hotel's vast wine cellar. Much of the food here is imported from Italy, including large wheels of Parmesan cheese (cut with four separate Parmesan knives, of course).

Markets

The **mercado central** is between Arica and Tacna. There are excellent fruit markets all up and down Lima, the best of which is a nameless stand at Lima 504.

INFORMATION AND SERVICES

Maps are available at the **tourist office** inside the municipality building (Plaza de Armas, tel.

056/52-2418, 8 A.M.–2 P.M.). Good tourist information is also available at **www.nanasca.com.**

Police are on the highway just outside of the center (Los Incas block 1, tel. 056/52-2442).

The best healthcare is available from the **Red Cross clinic** on the Plaza de Armas (8 A.M.–1 P.M. and 4–8 P.M. Mon.–Fri., 8 A.M.–1 P.M. Saturday), which has good doctors, pharmacy, and laboratory, and a dentist works next door. They will also respond to 24-hour emergencies at tel. 056/52-2607. Another 24-hour option that is around the corner is Nasca's **Hospital de Apoyo** on the fifth block of Callao. The largest pharmacy is **Inkafarma** (Lima 596, tel. 056/52-3065, 7:30 A.M.–11 P.M. daily), and a smaller option is **Boticas Universitarias** (Bolognesi and Grau).

For money matters, **Banco de la Nación** (Lima 431) and **Banco de Credito** (Lima and Grau) both have ATMs.

The **post office** is at Fermín del Castillo 379, between Bolognesi and Lima (9 A.M.–5 P.M. Mon.–Fri.). There are several Internet cafés with speedy connections, including **CyberCafé** (Lima 103, tel. 056/52-3500, 24 hours, $1/hr), **Planet Net** (Plaza de Armas, 9 A.M.–11 P.M. daily, $0.50/hour) though the fastest is at the corner of Arica and Lima.

For overseas phone calls, the **Telefonica office** (Lima 525, tel. 056/52-3758, 7:30 A.M.–11 P.M. daily) has private phone booths. Using a 147 or Hola Peru card will be cheaper than their rates of $0.90 for North America and Europe.

GETTING THERE

AeroCondor used to offer regular flights to Nasca, but that service has recently been suspended. Several agencies in Lima, including **AeroIca,** fly in tourists from Lima to have lunch and see the lines before returning the same day.

All of Nasca's bus companies are congregated around the roundabout at the end of Lima, where the Panamericana skirts around town. The bus trip between Lima and Nasca is seven or eight hours, and **Ormeño** is the only one with deluxe (or Royal Class, as they say) bus, which leaves Lima at 1:30 P.M. and gets in around 8 P.M. Cheaper, less direct, Ormeño buses pass through Nasca every hour on their way to Arequipa. **Flores** has about six buses daily between Lima and Nasca, and other recommended companies include Civa and Tepsa.

Because of highway improvements, buses now travel between Lima and Cusco in 20 hours and turn toward the mountains at Nasca. The highway that leads uphill from Nasca passes the Reserva Nacional Pampa, crests over the Andes at 4,400 meters, and reaches Abancay before heading on to Cusco. Ormeño travels this route, but the company with the most buses is Expreso Wari-Palomino.

GETTING AROUND

There are unfortunately no large taxi companies in Nasca. Recommended taxi drivers include Bali (tel.056/969-9464) and Roberto (tel. 056/962-6677).

A good option for staying on the coast is **Hotel Puerto Inka** (Panamericana Sur Km. 603, Atiquipa, $24 s, $36 d), with 31 simple rooms on a private beach, all with ocean views. The hotel is located next to a fairly interesting archaeological complex of Inca ruins. Many tombs were found here with the remains of cotton textiles and wood vessels. What can be seen are the remains of several stone rooms where the Incas are speculated to have cleaned and stored seafood. The hotel game room has a video library and pool table and turns into a disco with karaoke at night. Camping, including showers, are available for $2 pp, kayaks for $3 hour, and jet-skis for $42 hour. There is a swimming pool and playground for kids.

Ica

At 420 meters above sea level, sunny Ica is an oasis of palm trees and sand dunes that lies just above the line of fog, or *garua,* that blankets Lima much of the year. To the west there is the Ica desert, a moonscape of sand dunes and eroded dirt formations that stretches all the way to the Pacific Ocean. This wilderness is known only to a select group of paleontologists who come here to search for the fossilized bones of long-gone sea lions and gigantic sharks. But recently the local guides of these paleontologists have begun taking travelers into this remote landscape for two- to five-day desert safaris. Activities include hunting for gigantic fossilized teeth, four-wheeling up and down humongous dunes, examining the bones of marine animals scattered in the sand, and sleeping under a brilliant star-filled sky. No one who has gone on one of these trips has ever been disappointed—this desert, which includes the coastline from Paracas down to Nasca, is one of the most wild and spectacular in the world.

What Ica is most known for, though, is its **vineyards,** which were first planted by the Spaniards in the 16th century. Ica is surrounded by more than 80 *bodegas,* which produce the world's best pisco, or white grape brandy, and a variety of ports and wines. Touring these operations is the highlight of an Ica trip and a great way to understand a tradition that has changed little over five centuries. There is a huge range of *bodegas,* from the haciendas that have been outfitted with state-of-the-art technology, such as Tacama and Ocucaje, to more rustic mom-and-pop operations where grapes are still crushed underfoot and pressed with the weight of a huge *huarango* trunk. Most visitors like to see one of each.

The city of Ica changed dramatically after a wave of highland settlers came here to escape terrorism in the 1990s. The city is more crowded now, and assaults on tourists have become common. Areas that were recommended by guidebooks just five years ago should now be avoided. When in Ica, walk in groups, stay near the plaza at night, and avoid the whole east side of the city between the plaza and and the Río Ica. The best lodging options are now outside the city, including Hotel Hacienda Ocucaje, Lago Huacachina, or the quiet Angostura neighborhood on the edge of town.

Lago Huacachina, 6 km outside of town, is a magical and incongruous sight, a lake of green waters fringed with palm trees and reed swamps and surrounded on all sides by huge sand dunes. There are a number of excellent lodging options around the lake, which is just far enough from Ica's light pollution to make for perfect star-gazing. During the day, the dunes are the best place in Peru to try sandboarding and dune buggy riding. What both sports have in common is traveling at high speeds down 50-degree sand slopes. For those who don't want to stay in Nasca, overflights of the nearby lines leave frequently from Ica, though at a slightly higher cost than from Nasca itself.

Ica has endured a series of natural disasters, from an earthquake that killed 500 people way back in 1664 to an El Niño flood in 1998. As a result, there are few colonial buildings or well-preserved ruins in the area, even though the valley has been home to a series of ancient cultures: the Paracas, Nasca, Wari, and Chincha. Inca Pachacutec conquered and integrated this valley into the Inca Empire in the 15th century. A century later Luis Jerónimo de Cabrera founded the first city, Villa de Valverde, in 1563. The Spaniards, no doubt missing the *riojas* and *ribieros* of their homeland, had already planted the first grapes in all of South America here by the 1540s.

ICA DESERT

Ica is the best launching point for tours through the desert, which apart from being beautiful also happens to be one of the world's richest hunting grounds for marine fossils. You need at least three days, preferably a week, to get there and back from truly remote, wild desert, and make sure you have a hat, plenty of sunscreen, a gallon of water per day pp, and a desert-worthy vehicle with plenty of spare tires (protection against razor-sharp volcanic rocks). The three desert guides recommended below are intellectual but all self-taught, absolutely passionate about the desert, and safe. They make a living by guiding foreign paleontologists, and they know all the local *huaqeros,* or grave robbers, who tip them off about new fossil areas.

The guide with the best transport, and most experience, is Roberto Penny Cabrera, alias **Desert Man** (tel. 056/23-3921 or 056/962-4868, icaderttrip@yahoo.es). It is hard to miss Roberto, who hangs out most evenings in Ica's El Otro Peñoncito Restaurant. He is the one with the desert hat, camo military khakis, and huge bowie knife strapped to the waist. A former prospector for mining companies, he can show you detailed satellite imagery and geology maps

of the whole area, and a quick glimpse of his truck is the best proof that you will not end up dying of thirst or crawling out of the desert on your hands and knees. His powerful diesel pickup has mattresses for three, a 22-gallon shower, and even an air pump for inflating his three spare tires. He speaks impeccable English, is a descendant of the town's founder, and lives to this day on the Plaza de Armas. He is intense, well-organized, and endlessly entertaining. One evening at El Otro Peñoncito, for instance, Roberto was showing us maps when he suddenly held up his forearm for us to inspect. "You see this?" he shouted. "That's chicken skin. That's passion. I love this stuff!" His 300-km round trip desert excursions combine geology, archaeology, anthropology, and paleontology. He charges $100 a day and can take up to three or four people.

THE SANDS OF AN ANCIENT BREEDING GROUND

Looking out over the endless sand dunes west of Ica, it is impossible to visualize the area as a huge ocean, with giant sharks, sea lions, penguins, dolphins, and whales all mating with each other. But that is what was going on here before the shifting of tectonic plates two million years ago heaved the ocean floor up into the hot, dry air where it is today.

After a paleontologist discovered a new dolphin species here in the 1980s, the Ica Desert has produced dozens more and become known as the best place in the world to hunt for marine fossils. There are so many, in fact, that bumpy points on the top of sand dunes are not usually rocks, but rather the perfect vertebrae of some long-extinct swimming animal. Experienced guides know where the most interesting fossils are, whether it's a sea sloth (oddly similar to a jungle sloth but with a beaver-like tail and hook hands for excavating soils), the delicate baleen of huge, plankton-eating whales, or a prehistoric pelican with a nine-meter wingspan.

Paleontologists believe that the whole area was once a shallow breeding ground for a variety of marine life, like the bays of Mexico's Baja California. The animals died, perhaps naturally or because of storms, and floated to the bottom where their carcasses were quickly covered with mud.

One of the more spectacular animals is the *Carcharocles megalodon,* the *Tyrannosauruus rex* of the sea. This gigantic, whale-eating shark was up to 14 meters (46 feet) long. Like sharks today, the megalodon had more than a hundred teeth, arranged in seven lines, which were constantly falling out and being replaced. These gigantic teeth, up to 20 cm long, are now fossils that can be picked right out of the dried mud.

Geological maps show the different formations around Ica and to which epoch they belong. The Pisco formation, a huge area of marine sediment that stretches from Arequipa to Pisco, contains mostly fossils from the Upper Miocene to the Lower Pliocene, or from about 16 to 2 million years ago. The huge bluff closer to the coast, which forces the Río Ica south on its way to the Pacific, is the Caballo Formation. It is far older, with fossils from the Triassic (145 to 230 million years ago) and even the Precambrian that goes back three billion years to the beginning of life on earth.

Other recommended guides include ℕ **Marco León Villarán**—see Punta Hermosa for a complete description—who leads trips in the Ica desert and works as a professional bone hunter throughout Peru's coast. He is a genuinely nice person who leads very professional expeditions and speaks Spanish only.

Mario Urbina (mariourbina01@hotmail.com or contact Hotel Hacienda Ocucaje) is assembling a fossil museum at Hacienda Ocucaje, speaks English, and is probably the most academic of the bunch. He does not have his own vehicle, but can rent a Land Rover for $50/day.

A final option is Marc Romain, a young Frenchman who has several brand-new dune buggies at the Hostal La Rocha at Lago Huacachina. He has started a company called **Desert Adventures** (tel. 056/21-2314, Nextel 98169352, desert_adventures@hotmail.com). He offers six-hour desert tours ($30 pp), a 10-hour wilderness beach tour ($35 pp), and two-day expeditions ($50 pp) that explore wild beach scenery and fossil grounds and include a barbecue with cocktails. Unlike the others, Marc does not work as a paleontologist guide and does not have the fossil knowledge. But he is young and friendly, and man does he have fast dune buggies.

SIGHTS

There are a few churches to see in Ica along with two recommended museums. The **Plaza de Armas** is lined with ancient trees and has been rebuilt with an obelisk and fountain since a 1998 flood sent a meter of water running through town. The 19th-century **cathedral** on the corner has a neoclassical facade and beautiful, though spooky, wood carvings inside. The biggest church in the city, **San Francisco,** is a block to the west and has a number of stained-glass windows illustrating the life of the patron saint. The most beautiful church, however, is **Señor de Luren,** which is reached by walking south on Lima for eight blocks and turning right on Cutervo. The church has a beautiful interior graced with an image that brings pilgrims each October. There are a few colonial and Republican *casonas* around town, including **Casa de las Cornucopias** (Dos de Mayo 158), **Casa del Valle** (San Martín 159), **Edificio del Estanco** (Lima 390) and **Casa Colonial El Porton** (Loreto 233).

The **Museo Cabrera** (Bolívar 170, on Plaza de Armas, tel. 056/23-1933 or 056/21-3026, call for appt) is a wildly imaginative collection of thousands of stones and boulders collected by the late Dr. Javier Cabrera, a descendant of the town's founder. Carved on these enigmatic stones are depictions of ancient hunts, brain surgery and even dinosaurs. Archaeologists doubt the authenticity of the stones though no one has been able to explain exactly who carved the nearly 11,000 stones that Dr. Cabrera claimed to have found in tombs around Ica. Dr. Cabrera, who died in 2002, never revealed the exact origin of the stones. If nothing else, this idiosyncratic museum is a monument to one man's obsession.

El Museo Regional de Ica (8th block of Ayabaca, near intersection with J.J. Elias, 084/234-4383, 8 A.M.–7 P.M., Mon.–Fri., 9 A.M.–6 P.M., Sat.–Sun., $3) is 1.5 km from the Plaza de Armas but definitely worth the visit. It is one of Peru's best small museums and offers a fascinating glimpse into the Paracas, Nazca, Wari, Chincha and Inca cultures. There are a range of textiles, ceramics, trepanned skulls, mummies and *quipas,* or bundles of knotted strings that served as memory devices. The museum presents a good historical overview of the area, along with photos and furniture from the 19th century and a full model of the Nasca Lines. To get there take a $0.50 taxi or hop aboard any *combi* ($0.15) that says *universidad* at the cathedral in the Plaza de Armas.

LARGE PISCO BODEGAS

Most of Ica's *bodegas* welcome visitors with free tours and then wine and dine them with their own wines and piscos and heaps of home-cooked food. Ica's *bodegas* have a charming, down-home feel, and most visitors end up staying longer, and drinking more, than they had planned. The larger wineries are the best place to understand how pisco is made, though the smaller *bodegas* have a more charming atmosphere for eating and tasting. Tours can be arranged, though taxis from Ica are cheap and easy to hire, even for non-Spanish

THE FORGOTTEN CHINCHAS

During the time of the Inca conquest, the most flourishing culture on the coast, apart from the Chimú in the north, was the Chincha. This kingdom rose out of two millennia of cultures that included the Paracas, Nasca, and Wari. The Chincha Kingdom spread from Río Cañete at least as far south as Nasca, but its center was Tambo de Mora and Centinela, near present-day Chincha. These ceremonial centers were once painted dazzling white and covered with friezes of stylized birds, fish, and geometric designs. Though badly deteriorated, the huge adobe mounds still offer commanding views over the Pacific Ocean on one side and Inca roads that wind up the valley on the other.

There is an interesting legend, which seems to have some truth in it, about the Inca conquest of the Ica Valley, just south of Chincha. After peaceful overtures had been rejected by Chincha leader Aranvilca, Inca Pachacutec sent his son Inca Tupac Yupanqui to take the valley by force. Marching at the head of his troops, however, the young Inca was struck by the beauty of a daughter of Aravilca's, named Chumbillalla. Tupac Yupanqui called off the invasion and began courting the princess, who explained her people's lack of water for farming. The Inca immediately threw his 40,000 soldiers at an ambitious scheme to build an aqueduct from the mountains through the desert, which, legend says, was completed in ten days. This aqueduct, known as the Achirina del Inca, still serves as Ica's lifeline. It runs 30 km through the desert from Molinos to Tate and irrigates 11,000 hectares of fields planted in asparagus, cotton, pecans, and grapes.

Though building a major canal in ten days seems like a stretch, there is well-documented evidence of the grandeur of the Chincha. In his *Crónica* of 1533, Pedro de Cieza de León comments that "as soon as the Incas had finished their conquest, they took from [the Chincha] many customs and copied their clothing and imitated them in other things." The famous map made by Diego Rivero of Peru in 1529, three years before the conquest, marked the location of the Chincha Kingdom but made no mention of the Incas. There were at least two litters carried into the square of Cajamarca on Nov. 16, 1532, the date of the fateful first meeting between the Incas and the Spaniards. One litter held Inca Atahualpa and the other the lord of Chincha. The two litters were so luxurious that the Spaniards became momentarily confused as to who was the real Inca. In the ensuing slaughter, the lord of Chincha was killed, something which caused Atahualpa deep sadness.

The end of the Chincha Kingdom is heartbreaking. By 1550, after Hernando Pizarro had been given Chincha as his *repartimiento,* the valley's population had plummeted five to one, according to Cieza de León. Because of the ravages of European diseases, enslavement by the Spaniards, and profound culture shock, the citizens of the Chincha Kingdom, like coastal Indians across Peru, appear to have simply lost the will to live, as English historian John Hemming asserts in his *Conquest of the Incas.* When Bartolomé de Vega made his famous complaint to the Spanish king in the 1560s, he estimated that the population in the Chincha Valley, estimated at 40,0000 when the Spanish arrived, had dropped to a mere 1,000. By that time, the famous centers of Centinela and Tambo de Mora were already in ruins.

speakers. For the return home, taxis are usually lined up outside and can be called in a moment's notice. The most interesting time to visit is during harvest, or *vendimia,* between January and March. Only Ocucaje and Tacama have English-speaking guides on hand always, but the others can arrange for one with advance notice.

Hotel Hacienda Ocucaje (Panamericana Sur km.335.5, Ocucaje, tel. 056/40-8001, reservas@hotelocucaje.com., www.hotelocucaje.com)

is a charming resort winery 36 km south of Ica in the dusty village of Ocucaje. Unlike other large wineries, Ocucaje retains a look and feel that has changed little since the Jesuits produced wine here in the 16th century: hundreds of huge oak barrels stretch through cellars kept cool and musty via a combination of dirt floors, thick adobe walls, and cane-and-mud ceilings. A highlight of the Ocucaje winery tour is the 19th-century *alambique,* the bronze distillery where the pisco is made. Nearly 2,300 liters of fermented grape juice are heated in each boiler, and the evaporated pisco is cooled and collected in a series of tubes submerged in water. Wine tasting is offered at the end of the tour—try the Moscatel port, sold under the Juana María label.

The Rubini family bought the 1,200-hectare hacienda in 1898 but was stripped of the property during the Agrarian Reform in the late 1960s. The family was able to buy back some of the land and the building later, but the colonial aqueduct leading from the mountains had fallen into disrepair. As a result, grapes are no longer grown at the hacienda itself. The family has converted the 1920s hacienda into a relaxed, hospitable resort with comfortable rooms, romantic dinners in the cellar, sauna made from a wine barrel, Jacuzzi, horses, bikes, pools with slide, a *piscoteca,* sandboarding, dune buggy riding, fossil tours—you name it! Taxi costs $5 from Ica, and the hotel also picks guests up from Ica bus stations.

Just 11 km northeast of Ica, **Tacama Winery** (Camino a La Tinguiña s/n, tel. 056/22-8395, 8:30 A.M.–noon and 3–4:30 P.M. daily) produces Peru's best (and only) dry wines and, along with Ocucaje, is a leading producer of pisco. There is a modern warehouse with state-of-the-art facilities, which backs up to the ochre walls of a colonial hacienda, a plaza of river stones, and a driveway lined with ancient trees. An old bell still rings every day from a tower, from which visitors can look out over 180 hectares planted with 20 different grape varieties.

The Olachea family bought the hacienda in 1898, lost much of the original 750 hectares in the Agrarian Reform, and is now producing about 1.5 million liters of wine and pisco per year—which is only half of the installed capacity. A tour of the winery includes a visit to an old grape press made from a *huarango* tree, a 19th-century *alambique,* and a full tour of the modern warehouse. There is an interesting museum of wine technology from the past few centuries and a wine-tasting room. The blended white wines—especially the Blanco de Blancos and the lighter Gran Blanco—are very good and sold at a 50 percent discount off retail. Taxi costs $3 from Ica.

Another large winery even closer to Ica is **Vista**

Alegre (Caminio a La Tinguiña Km. 2.5, tel. 056/23-2919, 9 A.M.–5 P.M. daily), which is only 3 km from Ica across the Río Ica. Vista Alegra, like Ocucaje, was operated by the Jesuits in the 18th century. It was then purchased by the Picasso family in 1875, which continues to operate it today. Unfortunately the half-hour walk to Vista Alegra—down Grau and across the Río Ica—takes you through the unsafe side of the city. Take a $1 taxi instead.

SMALL PISCO BODEGAS

Ica's best small *bodegas*—Lazo and El Catador—are just 2 km apart along the dirt road that leads to Tacama. The more authentic of the two is **Bodega Lazo** (Camino de Reyes s/n, tel. 056/970-5979 or 056/403-430, 7 A.M.–10 P.M.). Locals come here to drink port and eat under the bougainvillea-covered bowers or inside the *bodega* itself, which is a charming and elegant space filled with wine barrels, presses, and other objects from the bodega's history, which began in 1809. There is a good tour here of the vines and winery, though you need to speak Spanish.

El Catador (Fundo Tres Esquinas 102 Subtanjalla, tel. 056/40-3295 or 056/962, josecarrasco50@hotmail.com, www.go.to/elcatador) is a more established spot on the *bodega* circuit, run by the Carrasco family, which has large spaces for visitors to drink, eat, and dance. But first go on the excellent tour of the colonial wine and pisco process: The grapes are crushed underfoot and then pressed in a huge adobe platform with a 150-year-old *huarango* trunk as a weight. Then the juice is poured into clay containers, known as *botijas de barro,* which were used in this area long before the Incas. The pisco is distilled in huge brick boilers with copper basins known as *falcas.* In March, the height of the grape crushing, visitors are asked to roll up their pants and lend a foot. In the evenings, a disco even cranks. The food is good and reasonably priced, with entrées around $4 and a full lunch menu for $5. An alternate way to arrive at these wineries is via the *Collazos* buses ($0.50) that leave from the first block of Loreto or third block of Moguegua from 3 P.M. onwards.

El Catador, a small winery outside of Ica, still uses clay jugs known as *botijas de barro* for storing pisco, a brandy distilled from grapes.

ENTERTAINMENT AND EVENTS

Nightlife in Ica is a weekend affair. At Lago Huacachina, head to the bar at Hostal La Roche. On the Panamericana and near the entrance to the Angostura neighborhood is **La Peña de Alamo**, which gets hopping Friday and Saturday nights around 11 P.M. with live Creole music.

Otherwise most nightlife options are in the city of Ica itself. Pisco tasting can be done any time at **La Villa de Ica** (Lima 139, Plaza de Armas, tel. 056/970-7550, 7 A.M.–3 A.M.)—try a sip of Castañeda or Bohorquez, the best local brands, and hang out afterwards in the café-pub. **Restaurant Chalán** (Callo 179, tel. 056/21-3722, 7:30 P.M.–11 P.M. daily) is a Republican patio with crumbling adobe walls that makes for a good place to have a shot of pisco and move on. A locals' favorite for beers and cocktails is the dark and swanky **Pekados** (Lima 261). A more tranquil place for a beer and a game of pool ($0.75/hr) is **El Poll** (Salaverry 224, 10 A.M.–11 P.M. daily). The best disco is **La Who,** inside the Hotel Real Ica on Maestros. A new cinema-mall complex, **Ica Sur,** is opening near the Museo Regional.

The best Ica festival is the **International Grape Harvest Festival,** which takes place during the height of the harvest in the first half of March. There are concerts, cockfighting, and beauty pageants. The girl chosen as the Queen of the festival ends up wallowing in a vat of grapes.

Ica has been a center for **Peruvian *paso* horses** for centuries, and the **Sol de Oro horse competition** is held here every June, though the exact date varies. Peru's national day of pisco is July 25 and Iqueños celebrate with raucous parties. Our Lord of Luren takes place the third Sunday in October, and includes processions of hundreds of people and streets covered with carpets of flowers. For more information on Ica festivals, visit www.flyperu.com, and www.larutadelpisco.com.

SPORTS AND RECREATION

Ica is the best place in Peru to try sandboarding and **dune buggy riding.** Dune buggies are available through Mario Vera, the dune buggy pioneer of Ica, inside the Paracas, Las Dunas, and Ocucaje hotels. Las Dunas and many of the Angostura hotels provide sandboards free of charge, though

sand-boarding on dunes above Lago Huacachina

make sure they are waxed or they will not go very fast. The best place for these sports, however, are the huge, perfect dunes around Lago Huacachina. At the green control entrance to the lake there are dune buggies for rent—the best are available through Marc Romain at Hostal la Rocha, or Eduardo Barco, who is opening another hostel around the corner. The going rate is about $12 pp for a two-hour ride. Dune buggy riding is like a roller coaster without a track, because the machines zip down 50-degree slopes at up to 80 km per hour. Accidents do happen, so make sure you have seatbelts with chest harness and good roll bars—and don't hesitate to get out if your driver is reckless. The best times for both of these sports are early morning or late afternoon, to avoid heat and winds that pick up around midday.

ACCOMMODATIONS

The best place to stay near Ica is Lago Huacachina (southwest of town, $1 taxi). The best place for families and a completely relaxing spot is Hotel Hacienda Ocucaje, a half hour drive south from Ica. Finally, Ica's Angostura neigh-borhood is quiet and safe and only a few minutes from town.

Under $10

The main backpacker place on Lago Huacachina is **Hostal Rocha** (Balnerio Huacachina s/n, $4 s, $8 d), with a friendly, family feel and an open-door policy even the rowdiest of backpackers. The rooms have yellow tile or polished concrete floors and some have balconies, private baths, and hot water. A breakfast of fruit and eggs is served for $2. The owner, Lucho Rocha, rents sandboards for $1.50 per day and the hostel has an excellent fleet of buggies operated by French driver Marc Romain. There are a few other hostels around the lake but the best, for the moment, is this one.

In Ica itself, the best budget lodging is **Hospedaje Callao** (Callao 128, tel. 056/22-7741, $6 s, $7 d), a half block from the Plaza de Armas and run by the kind Huamani family. Rooms are quiet, safe, and pleasant with 4.5-meter ceilings, pastel purple walls, red polished cement floors, and a few odd pieces of furniture. Private bathrooms have hot water and the Huamani family runs a good Internet place next door. A basic

LAGO HUACACHINA: LAKE OF TEARS

The name Huacachina is Quechua: *wakay* means to cry and *china* means young woman. According to local legend, a young woman and her lover strolled most afternoons in the countryside around Ica. But just when the couple was to be married, he dropped dead. The woman was wracked with sorrow and spent the days afterwards wandering through the countryside and retracing her walks with her lover. As she walked, her tears formed a lake.

As she sat by the lake one day, an evil spirit in a man's form tried to rape her. She jumped into her lake's waters, imploring the water gods to protect her from evil spirits by covering her with a cloak of snow. Though she escaped the man, she drowned in the lake. Now, every full moon, she floats over Lago Huacachina, cloaked in sparkling white light. Locals say she drowns nighttime swimmers as a sacrifice to the lake gods who protect her.

place that's not too noisy is **Hostal Antonio's** (Castrovirreyna 136, tel. 056/21-5565, $6 s, $9 d), sandwiched between the market and plaza but still on a safe street. Rooms have foam mattresses, TV, and hot water. The front of **Hostal Oasis** (Tacna 216, tel. 056/23-4767, $6 s, $10 d) is a colonial home a block from the plaza and close to most of the bus terminals. Rooms are plain, but some have queen-size beds with private bathrooms, TV, and hot water.

$10–25

In the Angostura neighborhood, **Hostal El Huarango** (El Medano Y-5, tel. 056/25-6257, el huarango@terra.com.pe, $17 s, $23 d including breakfast) offers large rooms with parquet floors, TV, big bathrooms, and antique furniture. Deep roof eaves make the rooms a bit dark, but great for sleeping. There is a restaurant next to the pool that serves excellent Peruvian food, and there are sandboards for surfing the dunes right next to the hotel. The owner, Antonio Carrión, can also arrange dune buggy rides ($13 for two hours) and *bodega* tours ($10 pp). Nearby is **Hotel Austria** (La Angostura 367, tel. 056/25-

6106, $35 s, $35 d), a pleasant compound with red tile floors, large rooms with TV, and a nice pool run by an Austrian-Peruvian couple. Criolla food is served for a reasonable price. This is one of the cleanest hotels in Peru, though a bit rigid in its Austrian impeccability. You will not find a speck of dust here.

In Ica, a rather ugly modern option is **Sol de Ica** (Lima 265, tel. 056/21-8931, soldeica_ hotel@peru.com, www.soldeicahotel.com, $20 s, $24 d), a huge building a block from the Plaza de Armas that has a pool and restaurant. The rooms are small and plain, with cable TV, clean bathrooms, and thin stucco walls that let in the street noise.

$25–50

A new option on Lago Huacachina is **M Hostería Suiza** (Balneario de Huacachina 264, tel. 056/23-8762, www.hostesuiza.5u.com, hostesuiza@yahoo.com, $20 s, $30 d). The Baumgartner family, which ran the Hotel Mossone in the heydays of the 1940s, bought this house two years ago and converted it into a peaceful, friendly family hotel. The 14 rooms have comfortable beds, fans, and big bathrooms and some have views over the lake. Though the rooms aren't particularly luxurious, the pool outside is very nice and this hostel runs like a fine-tuned Swiss watch.

$50–100

The old-world ambience of **M Hotel Mossone** (Balneario de Huacachina, tel. 056/21-3630, $52 s, $71 d) is the pride and joy of every Iqueña and, after years of neglect, is undergoing somewhat of a Renaissance. This grand hotel was one of the country's most famous resorts from the 1920s to 1950s, when politicians and diplomats came here to relax on the elegant colonial porch overlooking the lake and sand dunes. Present management is restoring the hotel's fabulous grounds, which include a stone patio with huge ficus and huarango trees, a dining room and porch overlooking the lake, and an elegant pool across the street. The colonial rooms are simple with high ceilings, AC, TV, fridge, and bathtubs. Guests can use bikes and sandboards free of charge.

Just north of Ica, the luxury hotel **Las Dunas**

RENÉE DEL GAUDIO AND ROSS WEHNER

Desert guide Mario Rubina from the Hotel Hacienda Ocucaje examines a huge whale fossil in the nearby Ica desert.

(La Angostura 400, tel. 056/25-6224, or in Lima tel. 01/241-8000, dunas@invertur.com.pe, www.lasdunashotel.com, $94 s, $114 d, prices are lower on weekends) could easily be in Marrakech, with its sparkling white buildings and looming sand dunes overhead. Rooms are shaded and cool, with red tile floors and all the comforts of a three-star hotel, including TV, fridge, phone, and fans. Las Dunas feels at times like an American theme park, with tennis, golf, volleyball, sandboarding, horseback riding, three pools with a 37-meter water slide and poolside bar, playground, bicycles, bocce ball, discotheque, game room, and even a small golf course. An extraordinary buffet of international and regional cuisine is served on an outdoor dining terrace. Horseback riding in the desert ($11 per hour with guide), sauna with massage ($18), and the planetarium ($5) all cost extra. The hotel offers a variety of packages that include lodging and tours to Paracas, Tambo Colorado, Ica wineries and churches, and overflights over the Nasca Lines.

 **Hotel Hacienda Ocucaje** (Panamericana Sur Km. 336, Ocucaje, tel. 056/40-8001, reservas@hotelocucaje.com, www.hotelocucaje.com, $64 s, $64 d, more expensive on weekends) is a unique *bodega* resort a half hour south of Ica. This spacious hacienda from the 1920s is less expensive and fancy than Las Dunas and has a more down-home, relaxed feel. Amenities include a nice pool with a slide, bar and restaurant with excellent food, plain but comfortable rooms, sauna, Jacuzzi, horses, bikes, and sandboards, all included in the price. Resident paleontologist Mario Urbina leads fossil hunting trips in the area. Three-day packages include lodging, elaborate meals served in the wine cellar, wine tour and tasting, horseback riding, and sandboarding for $100 during the week, and $130 for weekends. Not surprisingly, this is a popular weekend getaway for families from Lima. The winery next door, Ocucaje, is one of Ica's most charming and historic large operations.

FOOD
Cafés and Desserts
Most of the area's better restaurants are in Ica. For breakfast, natural yogurt and health drinks are available at **Nueva Vida** (Tacna 212, 8:30–9 P.M. daily). A locals' favorite for pies and empanadas is **Dulcería Pastelería Vela** (Grau 199, tel. 056/23-2831, 8 A.M.–9 P.M. daily), which was founded in 1930 and serves up a staggering away of local sweets. The best-known sweet maker in Ica is **Helena Chocolates & Tejas** (Nicolas de Ribera 227, Urb. Luren, tel. 056/23-3308), which offers tours of its factory 11 blocks south of the Plaza de Armas. There is also a store near the plaza, at Cajamarca 139, which sells the local specialty *tejas*, which are pecans and candied fruits—figs, lemons, grapes, oranges—filled with *manjar blanco*, a milk caramel, and bathed in sugar. The chocolate-covered version is called *chocotejas*.

Peruvian
Founded in 1968 by the Hernández family,  **El Otro Peñoncito** (Bolivar 255, tel. 056/23-3921, 7 A.M.–midnight, $5–7) has a huge, classy menu of Peruvian concoctions including a dozen different salads, meats, pastas, fish, and vegetarian

WHEN IN PERU, DRINK PISCO

Peruvians have a lot of national pride about pisco, a grape brandy distilled from sweet grapes cultivated in Peru's desert near Ica. Peruvians got all up in arms during the 1980s when Chile tried to patent the name pisco—in the same way the French laid sole claim to Champagne, leaving the rest of the world to make sparkling wine.

Experts agree that Peru makes a more delicate, aromatic pisco—though the Chileans might beg to differ. The key difference between the countries is that Peru's hot climate allows it to produce sweeter grapes. With sweeter grapes, Peruvian *bodegas* can distill pisco from grape juice that has been fermented for 45 days. The less-sweet Chilean grapes, on the other hand, have to be made into wine first, distilled, and then cut with water to lower their alcohol content. The difference is noticeable. Fine Peruvian pisco, such as Biondi from Moguegua, or Castañeda or Bohorquez from Ica, has a delicate range of flavors that experienced pisco sippers recognize immediately.

Peru's pride in pisco goes back several centuries. The Spaniards first planted red grapes in the Ica Valley around 1547 and, within a decade, began exporting wine to Spain and its colonies. Sometime thereafter, someone came up with the idea of distilling the fermented juice of the dark-red Quebranta grape and pisco was born. Peru's climate is too hot to compete with the fine, dry wines of Chile and Argentina, but its pisco was an immediate success around the world. Pisco became an important drink in Spanish salons and even in the saloons of 1849 gold rushers in San Francisco—after all, it was much cheaper to ship pisco up the Pacific Coast than to lug whisky across the Panama Strait from the East Coast of the United States.

No one knows for sure how pisco got its name. The word means *bird* in Quechua, and apparently the Nasca and Paracas cultures used the word to describe the huge clay jugs they used for fermenting *chicha*. The Spaniards later used these same jugs for fermenting pisco. The port through which the brandy was exported to the world was also called, surprise, Pisco, and its first reference comes in a 1574 map made by Diego Méndez.

There are five different types of pisco: *Pisco Puro* is made from nonaromatic grapes such as Mollar, Quebranta and the black grape; *Pisco Promático* is made from Albilla, Torontel, Italian, and Moscatel grapes; *Pisco Aromatizado* gets its fruit bouquet from limes or cherries added during the distillation process; *Pisco Acholado* is a blend of many different grapes; and *Pisco Mosto Verde* is made from impartially fermented grapes.

Although fine pisco is chilled and sipped by itself, Peruvians have invented many pisco-based cocktails: they range from the Algorrobina, a caramel-colored sweet drink prepared with the honey of the *algarroba* tree, to the *Cuba Libre,* a simple mix of Coca-Cola and pisco. No doubt the favorite, however, is the Pisco Sour, which was invented in the early 20th century in the Maury Hotel's *Rojo Bar* in downtown Lima. The preparation is simple: fresh-squeezed lime juice, sugarcane syrup, egg white, and water are blended together, topped with Angostura bitters and served in a tumbler. Drink as many as possible while in Peru. The small, bitter limes essential for *Pisco Sour*—known as *limón de pica*-are impossible to find outside of Peru.

Pisco Sour—the national drink of Peru

3 oz. pisco (white grape brandy)
1 oz. fresh-squeezed lime juice
1/2 oz. sugarcane syrup
1 egg white
4 ice cubes
Blend for 20 seconds. Drop 2 drops of Angostura bitters on top before serving in cocktail glass or, in the case of a double, in a short but wide tumbler.

Algarrobina

1.5 oz. pisco
1 tsp. sugar
3/4 oz. *algarrobina* syrup
2 oz. evaporated milk
1 egg yolk
4 ice cubes
Blend for 1 minute. Serve in a champagne glass and garnish with nutmeg or cinnamon and two short straws.

Nasca and the Desert Coast

cuisine. Try *pollo a la Iquerías:* grilled chicken with spinach covered in a pecan sauce. The Hernández family makes their own pisco, and bartender Hary is one of Peru's better-known bartenders. A larger branch of this restaurant is opening down the street, though Bolivar 255 will probably be more charming.

Anita's (Libertad 133, on Plaza de Armas, tel. 056/21-8582, 8 A.M.–midnight daily, $3–8) is an upscale, rather expensive café and restaurant with great service. The huge menu is good for breakfast and includes a wide range of Peruvian dishes and desserts. **Plaza 125** (Lima 125, Plaza de Armas, tel. 056/21-1816, 7 A.M.–2 A.M., $3) serves salads, *adobos,* steaks, and $2 pisco sours. The same owner runs the new **Caine y Pescao** (Elias 417) serving fish, shellfish, and creole food.

International

The best place for homemade lasagna, ravioli, and canelloni is **Novaro** (J.J. Elias, Urb. Santa Elena C-15, five-minute taxi from center, tel. 056/22-8986). **Restaurant Venezia** (Lima 230, tel. 056/23-2241, 10 A.M.–3 P.M. and 6–11 P.M., $4) is the best place for pizza, and serves gnocci, homemade pasta, and ice cream. The best place for fish is **La Candela** (Tupac Amaru F-5, Urb. San Jose, around corner from Museo Regional, tel. 056/21-3182, $3–6). The menu includes a range of mouth-watering *cebiches, tiraditos,* and other seafood plates.

Health Food

For vegetarian food, try **Food Light** (Ayabaca 184, tel. 056/21-6929, 8 A.M.–8 P.M. Sun.–Thurs., 8 A.M.–5 P.M. Fri., $1.50), which has a cheap lunch menu and is across from the hospital on the way to Lago Huacachina. Another good vegetarian restaurant, near Ica Center, is **Mana** (San Martín 248, tel. 056/80-8366, 8 A.M.–8 P.M. Sun.–Fri.). The best supermarket is Ica Market (Municipalidad 260).

INFORMATION AND SERVICES

The **Tourist Office** (Grau 150, 8 A.M.–2:30 P.M. Mon.–Fri.) is helpful, and the **Tourism Police** (tel. 056/22-7673) is located on the Plaza de Armas next to **Banco Continental** and also on the fourth block of Elias. The best hospital is **Felix Torre Alba** (Cutervo s/n, tel. 056/23-4798), and there is also a clinic in the Angostura neighborhood. There are several pharmacies on the second block of Grau, and one natural medicine pharmacy, **FarmaNatur** (Grau 138, 8 A.M.–9 P.M.). *La Opinion* is a great regional newspaper run by the enterprising Isabel Tueros, who is a good source of information and available most evenings (Municipalidad 132, office #16). **Banco Weise, Continental,** and **Crédito** are all on Plaza de Armas. Most are open 8 A.M.–5 P.M. Mon.–Fri., mornings only on Saturdays, and travelers' checks can be exchanged at the Banco de Crédito. The **post office** is on San Martín 156 (tel. 056/23-4549, 8 A.M.–6:30 P.M. Mon.–Sat.), and the best **Internet** places are Internet (Municipalidad 247, 9 A.M.–11 P.M. daily, $0.75/hr), Cabin@sClub (Grau 175, 9 A.M.–11 P.M. daily, $0.50/hr), and the quiet **Internet Callao** (Callao 128, 8 A.M.–11 P.M. daily). The best option for international calls is **Datel** (Municipalidad 132, Plaza de Armas), which has private phone booths and crystal-clear, $0.15/min service to the U.S. There are private phone booths in the Telefónica office on Lima, in the Plaza de Armas. There are several laundromats along San Martin, but the best is **Laundry** (Chiclayo Block 5, 8 A.M.–1 P.M. and 4–8 P.M., tel. 056/21-5684).

GETTING THERE

There is no main bus station in Ica, but all the main bus companies are clustered on the east end of town, a few blocks from the Plaza de Armas near the corner of Lambayeque and Salaverry. The best option to and from Lima is **Soyuz** (Matias Manzanilla 130, near Lambayeque, tel. 056/22-4138), which has comfortable buses leaving every 15 minutes for as little as $4–6, though nicer buses cost more. The four-hour trip includes stops outside of Pisco (with a shuttle to the town center), Chincha, and Cañete. **Ormeño** (Lambayeque 180, tel. 056/21-5600) has nicer, $9 Royal buses that leave for Lima every day at 7 A.M. and 1 P.M. (four hours) and a similar $23 bus that leaves for Arequipa at 1 P.M. and 7:30 P.M., or a $29 semi-bed bus at 9:30 P.M. (10 hours). It also has a service between Ica, Nasca, and Hotel Paracas. A more affordable, but recommended option for Arequipa and Nasca is **Flores** (Lambayeque and Salaverry, tel. 056/21-2266 or 056/21-2266). The only bus that goes directly to Pisco, the launching pad for exploring the Reserva Paracas, is **SAKI** (Lambayeque 217, tel. 056/21-3143). Buses leave every half hour from 6:15 A.M. TO 8 P.M. for the one-hour trip.

GETTING AROUND

Ica is swimming with taxis but, for trips to the wineries or Lago Huachachina, it is probably best to go with a driver recommended by your hotel. Reliable taxi companies are Taxi Ya (tel. 056/23-5361) or Taxi a Uno.

Several agencies on the Plaza de Armas offer a variety of tours, including **Desert Travel** (Lima 171, tel. 056/23-4127 or 056/601576, desert_

travel@hotmail.com), **Colibri Tours** (Lima 121, tel. 056/21-4406 or 056/960-1576), and **A Dolphin Travel** (Municipalidad 132, tel. 056/21-8920 or 056/966-9193, av_dolphintravel@hotmail.com). Local tours cost $8 and include Museo Regional, Lago Huacachina, Cachiche (a town known for its now-disappeared tradition of witchcraft), Luren Church, and a *bodega* or two. One option would be to take this tour and then stay at the wineries and take a taxi home.

If you are short on time, Ica can be a good base for seeing the Nasca Lines, and 35-minute overflights from here coast around $40 pp. Because the flight is longer from Ica, pilots occasionally try to save gas by skipping some of the lines. So have the agency write down a list of lines beforehand, and pay extra if necessary to get more flight minutes. These agencies also offer $20 tours to the Reserva Nacional Paracas that includes a trip to the Islas Ballestas. This seems, however, like a very rushed way to see such a spectacular reserve.

The Paracas Peninsula

The frigid waters of the Humboldt Current cause a rich upwelling of mineral waters near the Paracas Peninsula, a sledgehammer-shaped chunk of desert coastline that juts into the Pacific Ocean. The rich waters feed phytoplankton, which in turn feed huge schools of anchovy, which in turn feed one of the world's largest collection of sea birds (about 200 species, including the Andean condor), two types of sea lions, a rare otter known in Spanish as *chungungo,* and the endangered Humboldt penguin.

From 1,000 B.C. onwards the area's rich waters also sustained the Paracas culture, which inhabited the surrounding coastline before being subsumed by the the Nasca culture in 200 A.D. In 1925, Peruvian archaeologist Julio Tello discovered 400 mummy bundles in the Paracas Necropolis, an ancient cemetery on the peninsula that had been preserved in the bone-dry climate and hidden by wind-blown sands. What was extraordinary were the textiles, woven from cotton or camelid fiber and decorated with birds, fish, and

other designs, that wrapped each mummy. They remain today the finest, and most richly decorated, textiles produced in pre-Columbian Peru.

The Reserva Nacional Paracas was set up in 1975 to protect 335,000 hectares of this spectacular area from the peninsula south to Independence Bay. It is Peru's largest chunk of protected coastline, and its attractions include the Museo Julio Tello, which contains Paracas textiles, and El Candelabro, a huge hillside etching of a candelabra that has a mysterious origin.

But the reserve's number-one attraction is its desolation and rugged beauty, extraordinary even by Peruvian standards. It's like the coast of Oregon or Northern California, but with no trees, no people, and ten times the marine life. Southwesterly ocean winds blast the Paracas coastline each afternoon and, together with the surf, have sculpted promontories with tunnels and odd shapes. Cooled by the ocean, these winds are warmed when they hit the sun-baked land and their capacity to hold water rises. This is why no

The cliffs drop 200 feet to the Pacific Ocean at the southern end of the Reserva Nacional Paracas.

rain falls on Paracas and much of the Peruvian coastline, even though fog blankets the area between July and October because of a winter temperature inversion.

Although the late-afternoon winds can be a challenge, camping or mountain biking along this coastline is a highly recommended experience. It is not difficult at all to find a deserted beach, and the controlled access to the reserve make this a safe place to camp overnight on a beach.

RESERVA NACIONAL PARACAS

There is a road junction right after the control booth of the Reserva Nacional Paracas ($1.50, 7 A.M.–6 P.M.). The left road leads to the remote south coast beaches, which are anywhere from 30 minutes to three hours away on bumpy dirt roads. This road first passes a turnoff for the sculpted seaside formation known as **La Catedral** (The Cathedral) and then heads to Playón, the salt flats of Otuma, Mendieta, and Independence Bay. These are some of the more beautiful, less-visited beaches in the reserve and can be visited during a four-wheel expedition through the desert to Ica.

The paved road that leads straight from the control booth heads onto the peninsula. First stop is the museum, after a few kilometers, and, further on, **Playa Atenas,** which is often crowded and has a good restaurant known as El Griego. The beach is a combination of rocks and sand and is a favorite windsurfing spot with its flat waters and strong afternoon winds. From Atenas a road leads to a huge etching in the hillsides, similar at first glance to the lines of Nasca. Because it is of a candelabra, a rather European invention, archaeologists think pirates may have dug it into the hillside as a navigation aid. Visitors are prohibited from getting closer than 20 meters, and its huge shape, difficult to discern close up, can best be seen during a boat tour to Islas Ballestas.

At the museum an alternate dirt road leads to **Lagunillas Bay,** which has a handful of restaurants (the best of which is **Tía Fela**) and two of Paracas' most beautiful (and, in the summer, crowded) beaches, **El Raspón** and **La Mina.** The road ends at **Arquillo,** where there is a lookout over a rocky area crowded with sea lions, especially during mating season from December to March.

rock formation at El Playón in the south end of the Reserva Nacional Paracas

MUSEO JULIO C. TELLO

The finest textiles produced in pre-Columbian Peru are on display at the **Museo Julio C. Tello** (7 A.M.–4 P.M., daily, $2 in addition to park entrance). There are also ceramics, mummies, and an exhibit on how the Paracas people used boards and weights to change the shape of the skull according to a person's social status. The Paracas practiced trepanation, an early form of brain surgery whereby a disk was cut from the front of the cranium. Because of scar tissue, the trepanned skulls in the museum prove that patients survived this technique, which may have been used to treat mental disorders. Nearby are Cabezas Largas and Cerro Colorado, Paracas cemeteries that were excavated by Julio Tello and are now covered with dirt to prevent looting.

ISLAS BALLESTAS

Though sea lions can be seen from the Arquillo lookout and other places around the reserve, visitors have a good chance of seeing dozens of sea lions, seals, and even a penguin or two during a four-hour boat tour of Islas Ballestas, the islands just to the north of the peninsula.

Hundreds of thousands of birds also roost on the islands, covering them with guano (which is another Quechuan word that's become commonly used by English speakers). Guano contains 20 times more nitrogen than cow manure and is a highly coveted fertilizer that sparked Peru's 1850–70 guano rush. Nearly 10 million tons of the stuff was dug off the Islas Ballestas, along with the Islas Chincha 7 km to the north, lowering the islands' height by as much as 30 meters. These days the guano is removed in a sustainable fashion by the Peruvian government.

EL CHACO AND EL PISCO

El Chaco is a small beach town right at the reserve entrance that wins our vote for the best place to stay while visiting Paracas. Two of the area's better high-end hotels are here, along with a few budget options and a restaurant or two. There are no services here, but the town has a relaxed, safe feel. During the day, Peruvian families stroll along the rocky beach against a backdrop of fishing boats and grounded cargo

Nasca and the Desert Coast

THE WHO'S WHO OF PARACAS BIRDS

Birdwatchers rightly flock to Peru's Amazon, home to 1,000 species of birds, or about 10 percent of the world total. Often overlooked though is Paracas' anchovy-rich waters, which attract nearly 200 species from around the world. Populations of these birds decline, or migrate south, during El Niño years, when coastal waters warm and anchovy move offshore. Here's a who's who:

• **Cormorants:** These long-billed diving birds are found throughout the world but are so abundant in Paracas that up to four birds can nest in a single square meter. Along with the boobies and pelicans, they are Peru's main guano-producing birds. They are recognizable for the sleek bodies and long necks. They dive underwater, guiding themselves with their wings in order to catch anchovy, crabs or whatever else is available. The two main species around Paracas both have red legs. But the guanay is black and white, whereas the red-legged, *chuita* in Spanish, is more grayish.

• **Boobies:** Peru has six of the world's ten booby species, including the blue-legged booby, but the most common in Paracas is the Peruvian booby. These chicken-sized birds have compact bodies and almost look like pelicans with smaller bills when they are sitting around. They are dramatic divers, like the cormorants, but eat only fish, so suffer huge declines in El Niño years.

• **Frigatebirds:** These large birds with forked tails, hooked bills, and long slightly V-shaped wings are superb gliders. They are known as aerial pirates for harassing boobies, gulls or terns until they drop their fish. The two species in Paracas, the magnificent and great frigatebirds, are hard to distinguish: both males have red necks and black bodies, while females have black bodies and white necks.

• **Peruvian Pelican:** One of the larger flying birds, the Peruvian pelican has a wingspan of up to 2.7 meters, a gray body, and streaks of light yellow on the neck. It is a superb glider, traveling up to 80 km in a single day and just centimeters above rolling water. It scoops fish out of the water and stores them temporarily in its large pouch.

• **Flamingo:** This wading bird, with pink body, long neck and baby-blue legs, uses its strangely bent bill to filter minute mollusks, algae and di-

atoms found in Peru's brackish salt lakes. They summer in the *altiplano* near Ayacucho and winter in Paracas.

• **Andean Condor:** Sightings of the world's largest bird around Paracas are increasing, after *guano* workers nearly wiped the local population out for harassing local bird chicks. These massive vultures, with wing spans of up to 3.3 meters, descend from the highlands and feed mainly on sea lion carcasses.

• **Inca Tern:** Terns, or *zarcillos* in Spanish, are known for migrating all over the world. They look like gulls, though they have smaller bodies, pointed wings, and a pointed bill and dive after shrimps and minnow. Out of the half-dozen tern species at Paracas, the Inca tern is unmistakable: red feet and bill, dark-gray body, and odd white feathers that curl downward from its eyes.

• **Oystercatchers:** These seagull-sized birds usually wade around rocky coastlines, where they use their long red bill to open oysters and clams with amazing speed. Paracas has two species, the blackish (all black) and the American (white chest, common in the United States).

• **Whimbrel:** This sandpiper scurries in an erect posture along sandy beaches in search of mollusks. It has a mottled brown body, horizontal black stripes near its eyes, and light blue feet. It spends October through April along the South American coast before migrating back to North America for the rest of the year. It has a high-pitched scream when frightened, thus its name in Spanish, *Zarapito Trinador* (the whistling sandpiper).

• **Seagulls:** Paracas has more than a half dozen gull species, but the most common is the band-tailed gull, which has a black band at the end of its white tail feathers. These birds cruise the beaches for fish, though they are not above eating other birds' chicks.

• **Humboldt Penguin:** One of the best places in the world to see this endangered penguin is at the Islas Ballestas. It is less than knee-high, and wobbles along on its two webbed feet with its shrunken wings that allow it to swim with amazing speeds underwater. It has a black body and face, with a white belly speckled with black dots. It nest in holes it digs in the guano.

ships. All the boats for Islas Ballestas leave from El Chacho.

Because of bus schedules and outdated guidebooks, most visitors still end up staying in Pisco, a pushy little town near the highway that has grown up along with the nearby fishmeal plants. Most of the Paracas agencies are based here, along with a full range of services and inexpensive hostels. Pisco's busiest evening spot is Comercio, a pedestrian street that leads from the plaza and is lined with pizzerias and other restaurants. Pisco is 22 km or 20 minutes' drive from the reserve entrance.

Entertainment and Events

At El Chaco, the only things happening at night are the lapping of waves and a few drinks being served at Brisa Marino, one of the beach restaurants. If you want wine or alcohol, pack in a bottle.

In Pisco, **As de Oro's** (San Martín 472, 3.5 blocks from the plaza, tel. 056/53-2010, 11:30 A.M.–midnight) is a restaurant with a pool by day but transforms into Pisco's best discotheque on weekend nights. Catch a taxi at the door when you leave, because the surrounding neighborhood, though only four blocks from the plaza, is not safe at night.

On **June 17,** fishermen in Pisco float the images of Saint Paul and Saint Peter into the Cove of San Andrés, as musicians perform on shore and cooks battle in a cooking contest of shellfish and fish dishes. Pisco's tourism week is the last week of September and includes **Peruvian paso horse shows, wine contests,** and an **international sandboarding contest.**

SPORTS AND RECREATION

Camping at Paracas is an extraordinary and safe experience and can be combined with a four-wheel-drive safari through the Ica deserts. To camp at Paracas, buy all your groceries ahead of time in Lima or Pisco and make sure you pack plenty of water (three or four liters pp per day), sunscreen, clothes to protect from the wind and sun, and a camping stove—there is little driftwood on the beach. Contract a taxi in El Chaco to leave you at a beach and return the next day at a pre-arranged time ($8 each way). The more remote beaches are on the south coast, past La Catedral, though if it is not a weekend La Mina is a beautiful, close beach that could be empty too.

The waters of the Paracas Bay, especially around Playa Atenas, remain flat even during stiff (over 30 knot) afternoon winds. This makes for ideal Hobie Cat and windsurfing conditions. We were unable to find any rentals, except for local Pedro Ramos (reachable through the Paracas Explorer agency in El Chaco) who rents his windsurfer for $7 per hour. There is a good surfing break off San Gallán, the large island south of Islas Ballestas Islands that can only be reached via a private boat from El Chaco ($30).

The standard four-hour agency tour of the Reserva Paracas includes stops at the museum, La Catedral, Lagunillas, La Mina, and the sea lion lookout at Arquillo. The best way to see the reserve, however, is to contract a car with a driver. This often ends up being cheaper for a group of two or more anyway and allows for unscheduled stops such as lounging on the beach. For four hours, El Chaco taxis cost $15 while drivers from Pisco charge $25. El Chacho taxis can also leave you at a beach and return for you later in the afternoon for an additional $8.

The Islas Ballestas tours all leave from El Chaco. Before you buy your tour, inquire beforehand whether the agency has its own fast boat, or you are likely to chug out of port on someone else's slow boat. Private tours are expensive and should not be done in the afternoon, when winds and seas pick up.

Most of the agencies are based in Pisco. The exception is Zarcillo Connections has an office at the entrance to El Chaco on the left side of the road. It offers half-day tours to Islas Ballestas ($10) and the reserve ($6), as well as full-day excursions to the Inca ruins at Tambo Colorado ($15). Nearby Hotel Paracas also offers tours that are open for nonguests. Boats leave every day from the hotel's pier at 8 A.M. for Islas Ballestas ($18 pp). The hotel also offers a three-hour tour to the Reserva Paracas for $15, a three-hour tour to Tambo Colorado for $20, water-skiing for $70/hour, and dune buggies for $25/hour. A new El Chaco agency is **Paracas Explorer** (Av. Paracas L9, El Chaco, tel. 056/54-5141, sealiontours@latinmail.com), which tours

Islas Ballestas ($10) and the reserve via dune buggy ($15). In El Chacho, the cheapest Islas Ballestas boats leave from the town pier every morning at 8 A.M. ($8), and when there is demand, also at 10 A.M. Tickets should be bought the day before at a green control booth near the pier. The El Chaco taxi drivers cooperative sells tickets in another booth nearby for a four-hour driving tour of the reserve ($6).

In Pisco, all the agencies are lined up on San Francisco near the Plaza de Amras. The most reputable is **Ballestas Travel** (San Francisco 249, tel. 056/53-3095 or in Lima tel. 01/257-0756, www.barrioperu.terra.com.pe/ballest, jpachecot@ terra.com.pe), which charges $16 for a full day including Islas Ballestas via speedboat plus a tour through the reserve. Also highly recommended is **Zarcillo Connections** (San Francisco 111, tel. 056/53-6543, www.barrioperu.terra.com.pe/ zarcillo, zarcillo@terra.com.pe). New Pisco agencies include **Las Amigas** (Progreso 167, second flr., tel. 056/31-1984) and **Paracas Reservas Tours** (San Francisco 257, tel. 056/53-4993). Most of these agencies offer trips to Tambo Colorado and overflights of the Nasca Lines for between $35–50 depending on the time of the year. Ask a lot of questions beforehand: what type of airplane, where is the airport, how long is the flight, and which lines will you see.

ACCOMMODATIONS

As with any Peruvian beach town, prices can be negotiated down during weekdays and in the off-season (April 1–Dec. 15). The upper-end hotels have lower published fares during these times and also occasionally offer packages on their web pages.

Under $10

There are no budget hostels in El Chaco, but Pisco has the funky old **Hotel Pisco** (San Francisco 120, tel. 056/53-6669, www.geocities/hotel_pisco, hotelpisco@terra.com, $7 s, $ 10 d), with small, quiet rooms set far back from the street. Rooms are a bit old but have good beds and hot water, and the bunk rooms cost $3 pp. Boris, the friendly English-speaking owner, can help plan trips. There's free In-

ternet, and breakfast is served in a room with stained-glass windows that transforms into a bar at night. Another recommended budget hotel in Pisco is **San Isidro** (San Clemente 103, five blocks from the plaza, tel. 056/53-6471, $5 s, $8 d). **Hostal Colonial** (Comercio and Plaza Belén, $4 s, $7 d) also has clean second-story rooms with wood floors and OK shared bathrooms. Rooms in the back are quieter and have balconies with nice views over Plaza Belén.

$10–25

In El Chacho, the budget hotels are within a block or so of the small square and offer private baths, hot water, and TV without cable. The best value is **Hostal Los Frayles** (Paracas Mz D5, tel. 056/54-5141, $12 s, $12 d), which has clean rooms with great beds (some queen-size), private bathrooms, TVs, and several rooms with ocean views. **Hostal El Amigo** (Balneario El Chaco s/n, tel. 056/54-5042, $12 s, $15 d, including breakfast) is clean and well-run, and rooms have tile floors and pressed sheets (TV is $3 extra). The rooftop terrace has hammocks and ocean views. **Hospedaje El Chorito** (El Chaco s/n, tel. 056/54-5054, $20 s, $20 d, including breakfast) has seven large, rooms with tile floors and ocean views over crumbly rooftops.

$25–50

At El Chacho's entrance is the traditional Paracas getaway **Hotel Mirador** (Carretera Paracas km.20, tel. 056/54-5086, reserva@elmiradorhotel .com, www.elmiradorhotel.com, $45 s, $60 d, including breakfast). This place oozes 1970s decor but is clean and absolutely quiet, with simple rooms and nice views over the bay. It also has one of the area's better restaurants (lunch menu, with *cebiche,* $8).

In Pisco, the ⋈ **Posada Hispana Hostal** (Bolognesi 236, 1.5 blocks from the plaza, tel. 056/53-6363, posadahispana@terra.com.pe, www.posadahispana.com, $15 s, $25 d, including breakfast) was opened in 1996 by Milagros and Joan, a Peruvian-Spanish couple who have developed a reputation for friendly, reliable service. Their 23 rooms have cable TV, private bathrooms, and hot water. There is a good restaurant with a cozy bistro atmosphere, free Internet, laundry area, and even a barbecue pit. Apart from Spanish, the couple speak Italian, French, and Catalan (Joan is from Barcelona) and are one of the best sources for information on the area. Make reservations in advance, because the place is often crowded.

The most elegant hotel in Pisco is the brand-new, underpriced (for the moment anyway) **N** **Villa Manuelita Hostal** (San Francisco 227, half block from plaza, tel. 056/53-5218, $20 s, $24 d, including breakfast). This restored colonial house has a tangerine-color entryway that leads into an upscale, yet relaxed atmosphere. The large rooms have cable TV and nice baths and are decorated with wooden tables and cabinets, bright reds, and fresh flowers. Reserve a room with window—the others only have skylights. There is a small patio with a fountain, elegant sitting areas, and a pizzeria is on its way.

$50–100

Two of the area's best high-end resorts are in El Chaco. **El Condor Hostal Club** (Panamericana Sur, Km.249, tel. 056/54-5080, elcondorhostal@ yahoo.com, $80 s, $80 d) has ten spacious rooms with excellent beds, sitting area with a sofa, TV, and a private terrace—it's nicer, in fact, than the more expensive Hotel Paracas. The five rooms that look onto the hotel's private beach are $10 extra, while the other rooms look over gardens with a nice pool. There is a bunk room for backpackers ($10 pp) that rarely gets used. VHS and videos are available to rent for $4. The restaurant here is one of the better in town, serving fresh salads, fish, and meat.

Over $100

Also in El Chaco, the four-star **Hotel Paracas** (Paracas 173, tel. 056/54-5100, hparacas@terra .com.pe, www.hotelparacas.com, $112 s, $112 d, including breakfast) is a world unto itself, a compound of 117 rooms and bungalows connected with lush gardens, palm trees, a pool with sunbathing island in the middle of it, and walkways lined with white columns. Given the elegant surroundings, the rooms are surprisingly plain, with vinyl-cushioned chairs and white tile floors,

though the firm king-size beds and private cocktail porches ain't too shabby. This is an excellent place for families, with a strip of lawn in front of the beach that has a playground. Guests rarely leave once they enter, because the buffet lunch is the best in town and the hotel operates a range of excellent tours.

FOOD

In El Chaco, there are several inexpensive seafood restaurants along the waterfront that have a reputation for causing traveler's diarrhea (*cebiche*, with all of its bacteria-killing lime juice, is usually safe). **El Chorito** (El Chaco s/n, tel. 016/54-5054, 7 A.M.–9 P.M. daily, $7), one block back from the beach, has great grilled fish and good but expensive *cebichería.* **El Condor Hostal Club** (Panamericana Sur, Km.249, tel. 056/54-5080, $8) has good salads and meats, though if you're going to splurge, set aside a few hours for the buffet at the Hotel Paracas.

In Pisco, Panadería San Francisco (San Francisco 111, Plaza de Armas, 6 A.M.–10 P.M., daily) is the best place for fresh bread, empanadas, espresso, fruit salads, or lemon pie and has $1–2 breakfast menus. It has a second location with the same hours at San Francisco 111. Pisco's best restaurant is **Don Manuel** (Comercio 179, tel. 056/53-2035, 6 A.M.–3 P.M. and 6–11 P.M. daily, $3–5), which serves up a range of grilled fish, shellfish, and *cebiches* and has an excellent $5 lunch menu. On the Plaza de Armas is **La Catedral** (San Juan de Dios 108, tel. 056/53-5611, 6 A.M.–9:30 P.M.), with a good Peruvian buffet on Sundays, breakfast and lunch menus, and a range of chicken, beef, and seafood plates. **Restaurante Catamaran** (Comercio 166, tel. 056/53-3547, 8 A.M.–midnight) serves up good-looking large pizzas ($9), and there is another pizzería across the street.

INFORMATION AND SERVICES

There is a medical post near the Hotel Paracas. Internet, post office, and a public phone are all within a block of the small main square.

Tourist information is available from Pisco's

municipality on the main square (tel. 056/53-2525), though nearby agencies on San Francisco are a better bet. Candid advice is always available from Joan and Milagros at the **Posada Hispana Hostal** (Bolognesi 236, tel. 056/53-6363, posadahispana@terra.com.pe).

Pisco's **police station** is on the plaza (San Francisco, tel. 056/53-2165).

For medical issues in Pisco, go to **Clínica San Jorge** (Juan Osores 440, tel. 056/53-6100).

All the banks with ATMs are on Pisco's square, including **Banco Continental, Banco de Comercio, Interbank,** and **Banco Wiese.**

The **post office** is on Pisco's main square (Bolognesi 173, 8 A.M.–6 P.M. Mon.–Sat.), there are private phone booths opposite the cathedral (Progreso 123A), and **email** places are located a half block away on Comercio.

In Pisco, laundry is available at **El Pacífico** (Callao 274, tel. 056/53-2443) for $1.50/kilo.

GETTING THERE AND AROUND

To get to the Reserva Nacional Paracas get off at Km. 234 of the Panamericana and drive 5 km to Pisco and then another 3 km to the gate of the reserve itself. The town of El Chaco is on the right a few kilometers before the reserve gate.

The best bus company for getting to and from Pisco is **Ormeño** (San Francisco 259, one block from the plaza, tel. 056/53-2764). It has three buses a day between Pisco and Lima that range from $4 (with stops in Chincha and Cañete) to $10 for direct Royal Class. Ormeño also operates a Royal Class bus that heads south daily at 4:30 P.M. for Ica and Nasca ($13).

A cheaper option, with frequent buses to and from Lima, is **San Martín** (San Martín 199, one block from plaza). The other bus companies leave passengers at the entrance to Pisco, which is 13 km away on the Panamericana. Soyuz has an office next to the cathedral on Pisco's plaza from which passengers are shuttled out to the highway to meet buses that are constantly rumbling north and south.

From Pisco, taxis charge $3 for the 20-minute drive to El Chaco. Buses marked *El Chaco-Paracas* leave every half hour from the market near Nicolas Piérola and takie about 30 minutes (6 A.M.–6 P.M., $0.30). Buses return to Pisco every half hour from El Chaco's main, and only, entrance. For transportation into the reserve, see *Sports and Recreation.*

El Carmen and Chincha

Most travelers blow right by El Carmen, and its larger, not-so-appealing sister city of Chincha, on their way south to Nasca and Paracas. But El Carmen, 10 minutes off the highway at Km. 200, is worth a stop, because it is the center of Afro-Peruvian dance and music and has the best-preserved colonial hacienda in Peru. This laidback village would not seem out of place in the Cuban countryside and is the home of 70-year-old Amador Ballumbrosio, who sparked a renaissance in Afro-Peruvian music in the 1970s with the help with Spanish guitarist Miguel Gonzalez.

Many of Ballumbrosio's 12 children continue the tradition today with a variety of dancing including *zapateo* (tap dancing) and a percussive music that involves seven instruments: *bongo* and *tumba* (two types of drums), *caracacha* (a burro's jaw with rattling teeth), *cajón* (a box that is sat upon and drummed with the hands), *cincero* (a large bell), *castanuela* (castanets), and *cabaza* (a hand-held sheet metal drum with chains that rattle when twisted).

El Carmen, along with Chincha 15 km away, erupts into all-night celebrations of music and dance several times a year, attracting Limeños for 24-hour partying and dancing. Lodging prices double or even triple during these parties—make reservations well in advance or, as many do, dance all night and take a bus onwards in the morning. Outside the festivals in Chincha and El Carmen, the Ballumbrosio family puts on recommended shows of music and Afro-Peruvian dance, called *baile de los negritos,* on most weekends ($60 per group, plus home-cooked lunch for $9). You can also just stop by the home of this warm, generous family. Something is always going on, and the

© PROMPERU

Peru's tiny Afro-Peruvian community, centered in El Carmen and Chincha, has indelibly marked the country's cuisine, dance, and music.

family even offers lodging to music students and inquisitive souls who simply want to linger longer.

There are plenty of other things to see in the area. At the top of the list is the Hacienda San José, one of several plantations in the area that imported black slaves from Guinea to work in the cotton and sugarcane fields. Near the coast there are the ruins of Huaca Centinela and Tambo de Mora, which formed the capital of the Ica-Chincha culture, which was incorporated into the Inca empire in the late 14th century. The adobe ruins, once painted a dazzling white and covered with friezes of fish and birds, are badly deteriorated but offer commanding views over the Pacific Ocean on one side and Inca roads that wind up the valley on the other. Grocio Prado, a small village just north from Chincha along the Panamericana, is a good place to see traditional basket weaving, and further along there is the long wide beach at Jahuay. Finally, there are sev-

eral pisco *bodegas* near Chincha, including Tabernero, right off the highway at Chincha, and Naldo Navarro, in Sunampe. All these places can be reached through inexpensive taxis from Chincha ($20 for one day) or through tours offered by the Hacienda San José.

HACIENDA SAN JOSÉ

Built on the backs of imported African slaves and local Indians, Peru's vast network of haciendas was systematically dismantled by the agrarian reform of President Juan Velasco from 1968 through 1972. Most of Peru's haciendas—some more than four centuries old—were abandoned after the owners were forced out and their land sold to newly formed worker cooperatives. Some haciendas were looted and burned, but most were simply neglected. Without upkeep, mud-and-cane roofs deteriorate quickly, allowing humidity to rot wood beams and plaster walls.

A notable exception is Hacienda San José, which looks much as it did when it began as a sugarcane plantation in 1688 with 87 slaves. After the Jesuits were expelled from Latin America in 1767, San Jose's owners also bought San Regis, one of several Jesuit haciendas in the area. This made Hacienda San José the largest in the Chincha Valley, with more than 1,000 slaves.

But the independence wars of the 1820s, the abolition of slavery in 1854, and the Pacific War with Chile (1878–82) took its toll on the hacienda. When the liberation troops of Don José de San Martin arrived in Pisco in 1821, the Spanish *hacendado,* or owner of the hacienda, fled to Spain as most of his slaves defected for San Martin's army. The hacienda limped along until the chaos caused by the Pacific War, when slaves rebelled and murdered the family's last heir on the front steps of the hacienda. After a period of turbulence, the Hacienda San José was sold in 1913 to the Cillóniz family, which continues to operate it today.

How Hacienda San José escaped from the agrarian reform is an interesting story. Ángela Benavides de Cillóniz struggled for years—and even met with President Velasco—to prevent the government from taking the hacienda. A deal

Nasca and the Desert Coast

The veranda at Hacienda San José has not changed since it was built in 1688.

was eventually struck in which the Cillóniz family gave up the Hacienda San Regis in exchange for keeping San José and 100 surrounding hectares. In the middle of it all, Ángela Cillóniz's husband died and left her with 12 children to support, from the age of 3 on up. She started the restaurant and the hotel soon after and began buying the hacienda back little by little from her brothers and sisters.

Except for one new building, the hacienda looks the same as it did on a certain Sunday in 1839, when a slave painted the hacienda's main square. In the painting, which now hangs in the hacienda, slaves sing and dance in a circle, a troop of soldiers marches, *hacendados* barter over supplies, and a crowd bets on a cockfight. The same wide steps lead from the square onto the hacienda's airy veranda and front room, where portraits hang of the plantation's founders. Further along is a stone patio, decorated with old plows, brands, mule yokes, and other relics of the past, including an 18th-century billiard table, two huge leather bellows used in the iron foundry, and a three-meter bronze bathtub imported from Spain in the 17th century.

Beneath the hacienda are an intricate maze of catacombs, which connect to the chapel where the owners were buried (their bones are now scattered on the floor). The dark tunnels were probably used to store food and hide gold from the periodic incursions of pirates. Because of tunnels found near the coast, there is evidence that all the area's haciendas may have been connected via an underground network used to smuggle slaves and avoid the head tax.

Adjacent to the hacienda is the **Capilla San José,** an exquisite and unrestored chapel built in 1700. It is a whitewashed adobe building, shaped like a shoebox and sparsely decorated, with a carved Baroque altar made of Nicaraguan cedar. All slaves were baptized here, but only those who worked inside the house were allowed to sit on seats against the wall and hear Mass.

A chilling reminder of plantation brutality is a room just paces away from the chapel entrance, where runaway slaves were tortured after being recognized by the brands on their shoulders. There is a device in the room to which slaves were shackled in excruciating positions after receiving 20 lashes in the main square. They remained in the room, in total dark, for up to two weeks.

ENTERTAINMENT AND EVENTS

The biggest festivals in the Chincha–El Carmen area are Verano Negro at the end of February, the festival of Virgen del Carmen in the middle of July, El Carmen's festival in late August, and an elaborate Christmas celebration that begins in mid-December and ends Jan. 6. For more information, see www.perutravels.net.

ACCOMMODATIONS

Chincha has dozens of hotels, but none of them seem a very good value for what they offer, especially considering the noise and confusion of the city itself. Instead, head to El Carmen, to stay at Casa Hacienda San José or inquire about a homestay with the Ballumbrosio family (San José 325, tel. 056/27-4014).

Under $10

The only other lodging option in El Carmen is the rather dingy **Parador Turístico** on the main square. In Chincha, **Hotel Leo's Inn** (Callao 228, tel. 056/26-6745, $6 s, $10 d) is a block from the Plaza de Armas and is one of the better budget options. Rooms are basic but clean and have private bathrooms with hot water and cable TV. There are many other budget options nearby.

$10–25

In Chincha, **Hostal Condado** (Santo Domingo 188, tel. 056/26-1216, $20 s, $21 d, including breakfast) is a good value for those who don't mind the sparkling white tiles running from floor to ceiling. The rooms, remodeled in 2003, include porches with skylights, cable TV, and new bathrooms with plenty of hot water. Some even have a Jacuzzi, and guests are allowed to use the pool at a sister hostel near Sunampe, at Km. 195 of the Panamericana (tel. 056/26-1424).

$25–50

The rooms at  **Casa Hacienda San José** (3 km before El Carmen, tel. 056/22-1458 or 056/817-9749, or in Lima 01/444-5242, www.haciendasanjose.com.pe, hsanjose@terra.com.pe) are impossibly large: a sitting room with lúcuma-col-

Afro-Peruvian dance at the Hacienda San José in El Carmen

© RENÉE DEL GAUDIO AND ROSS WEHNER

ored walls and cane ceiling, a spacious bedroom *and* a living-room–sized bathroom with red floor tiles and cast-iron tubs—and the suites, just a bit more expensive, are even bigger! The rooms have pleasant skylights, no telephone nor TV, and are decorated with 19th-century etchings of hacienda life. Included in the price are horseback rides, pool with hammocks and bar, tennis courts, sitting areas on the veranda or on the back porch, tractor-and-wagon tours through the fields, and tours of hacienda's catacombs, which were built to hide treasure from pirates. The hacienda also has a Lima reservations office (Juan Fanning 328, #202, Miraflores, tel. 01/44-5242) that offers a variety of packages and tours.

In Chincha, one of the more pleasant lodging options is **Lega's Hostal** (Benavides 826, tel. 056/26-1984), a miniature walled compound with modern rooms, terrace, gardens, cozy bar, and small pool. The rooms are large, decorated with pastels and flowers, and include cable TV, tables, and nice bathrooms. It is on the Panamericana, next door to the Soyuz bus station and a five-minute walk from the center.

Nasca and the Desert Coast

In the center of Chincha, **Hotel Princess** (Lima 109, tel. 056/26-1031, $23 s, $31 d) has a pleasant brick interior with polished wood floors and prints of French Impressionist paintings on the walls. Rooms have comfy beds, cable TV, and nice furniture, and the bathrooms are fair.

FOOD

Apart from the Ballumbrosio family, there are few eating options in El Carmen outside of festival times. There is an extraordinary Sunday lunch buffet at **M Hacienda San José** ($20, 1–3 P.M. Sunday), which features a full range of *comida criolla—tamales, ají de gallina,* stewed lamb, you name it—and a highly entertaining show of Afro-Peruvian music and dancing. Even the waiters are stand-up comedians, adding spice to the dances, which range from erotic to comic and everything in between.

In Chincha, good *cebiche* and seafood is available at **La Costa Marina** (Plaza de Armas 148, tel. 056/26-2700) on the main square. Good creole food is available at **La Casona,** on Grau two blocks from the main square. **Don Uho,** on the main square, serves pastries and cakes.

INFORMATION AND SERVICES

There is no Internet and no services of any kind apart from a medical post in El Carmen. Chincha's Plaza de Armas has a bank with **ATM, post office, pharmacy, phone center,** and **police station.** Chincha has several fast Internet places, including **Santo Domingo** 192 (9 A.M.–1 A.M., daily), which converts into a disco in the evenings. The hospital is south of the center on the Panamericana.

GETTING THERE

Most of the major bus companies stop in Chincha en route to Ica and Nasca, though **Soyuz** and **Ormeños** have the best and most frequent service. *Combis* leave the Panamericana in Chincha frequently for the 30-minute drive to El Carmen ($0.50).

LUNAHUANÁ

This relaxed town at the edge of the Río Cañete is an adventure sports center two hours (184 km) from Lima. It's high enough up a desert canyon to enjoy fog-free, sunny days. Lunahuaná's claim to fame is its rafting and kayaking, which push Class III–IV during the high-water months from December to April, and are mellower but still fun the rest of the year. There are good trails for hiking and mountain-biking in the area, and paragliders zip through the air during the town's annual sports festival, held the first week of March.

About 10 km downriver from Cañete is **Incawasi,** a well-preserved Inca compound with two squares, storage spaces, and fine stone buildings that were probably elite residences. Archaeologists believe the compound was a military base for conquering Cañete, one of Peru's last coastal valleys to fall to the Incas. There are also about ten wineries in the area that make pisco and *cachina,* a fortified wine. The best time to visit these is during the *vendimia,* or harvest, between January and March.

Sports and Recreation

Agencies charge $10–25 for a full day of rafting, including lunch, on the Río Cañete. There are some real hairball agencies operating on the river, so make sure that the rafts are in good shape and the guides experienced. A recommended local agency is **HemiRiver Rafting Co.** (Grau 255, tel. 01/534-2339, or cell tel. 01/9965-8635, www.geocities.com/hemiriver, hemiriver@hotmail.com), run by Michael Torres.

Accommodations

There are about ten hostels in town, the best of which are **Hostal Casuarinas** (Grau 295, tel. 01/284-1045), **Hostal Los Andes** (Los Andes, tel. 01/284-1041), and **Garden Hotel** (a few km before Lunahuaná on main road, tel. 01/284-1308), which has a nice country setting. There are a few three-star hotels with pools in Lunahuaná that all cost around $40 for a double, including **Rio Alto** (Canete-Lunahuana Highway Km. 38.5, in Lima tel. 01/463-5490, $42 s, $42 d),

Embassy (in Lima tel. 01/472-3525), and **Fortaleza del Inca** (Anexo de Paullo Km 31.5, www.peru-hotels.com/canforta).

Food

The best restaurants in town are **El Pueblo** (Grau 408, tel. 01/284-1085) and **Incawasi** (in Hotel Embassy, tel. 01/472-3525). In Cañete, recommended restaurants are **Muelle 56** (Bolognesi 156) and **El Piloto** (Panamericana km 138, tel. 01/581-3184, $5–7).

Getting There

Lunahuaná is 42 km off the Panamericana via a road that branches inland at the village Cañete (Km. 142 of the Panamericana), which sits at the foot of a valley famous for its surrounding fields of asparagus, cotton, and tangerines. *Colectivos* leave frequently from Cañete for the one-hour drive to Lunahuaná. The dirt road continues inland up and over the Andes, passing the snow-covered Cordillera Yauyos and spectacular emerald lakes en route to Huancayo. An **ETAS** bus leaves Cañete every morning for this 12- or 13-hour drive and picks up in Lunahuaná.

Most major bus companies headed south drop passengers in Cañete, from which *colectivos* run to Imperial, 5 km up the dirt road. **ETTUSA** (Montevideo 752 in Lima, tel. 01/428-0025) has direct daily buses to Imperial, from which *colectivos* leave frequently for Lunahuaná ($0.75, 45 minutes).

Lima

Lima's taxi drivers tend to be educated, perceptive, and opinionated. When asked what they think about Lima, they will tick off a litany of complaints: the highways are congested with buses and swerving *combis* and the air is full of exhaust and noise. Slums have sprawled willy-nilly across all the desert hills around Lima and residents there lack plumbing, water, and sometimes even electricity. The city's politicians and business leaders create a daily circus of corruption, and there is a huge, and growing, seperation between the rich and the poor. And then, if that weren't enough, there's the *garúa*. This blanket of fog rolls in from the ocean and blankets everything from May to November, deposting a patina of grime that lends the city its gray, dismal appearance.

But, in the same breath, the taxi driver will extol the virtues of this once-opulent capital of the Spanish viceroyalty that stretched from present-day Ecuador to Chile. Limeños are an exotic cocktail, a bit of coast, sierra, and jungle blended with African, Chinese, and European to create an eclectic, never-before-seen blend. Heaps of tangy *cebiche* and succulent shellfish can be had for a few dollars, along with shredded chicken served in a creamy concotion of milk, mountain cheese,

Must-Sees

Look for **M** to find the sights and activities you can't miss and **Y** for the best dining and lodging.

© RENÉE DEL GAUDIO AND ROSS WEHNER

Lima's Cathedral

M Catedral: After two decades of turbulence, the center of Lima is roaring back, and at the center of it all is a refurbished main square and the 16th-century cathedral, with elegantly carved choir stalls and a huge painting gallery (page 274).

M Casa de Aliaga: This colonial mansion in the heart of Lima's old town is in pristine condition and offers a fascinating glimpse into domestic life during the opulent days of the viceroyalty (page 275).

M San Francisco: This 16th-century convent has a brightly decorated patio and painting gallery upstairs, and labyrinthian catacombs downstairs that served for centuries as Lima's general cemetery (page 276).

M Museo Larco: With a huge collection of gold, textiles, and more than 40,000 ceramics, this museum offers a complete survey of all of Peru's archaeological treasures (page 280).

M Museo Nacional de Arqueología: The best way to wrap your mind around Peru's complex succession of ancient cultures is by visiting this compact and concise museum that is a 15 minutes' walk from the Museo Larco (page 281).

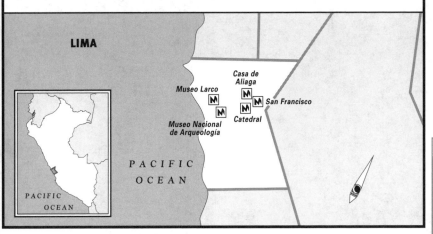

LIMA

Museo Larco M

Casa de Aliaga M M San Francisco

M
Museo Nacional M Catedral
de Arqueología

PACIFIC
OCEAN

PACIFIC
OCEAN

Lima

LIMA

SAN JUAN DE LURIGANCHO

INDEPENDENCIA

Río Rímac

LAS PALMERAS

PANAMERICANA

TÚPAC AMARU

NORTE

Cerro San Cristóbal ▲

RÍMAC

EVITAMIENTO

M SAN FRANCISCO

M CASA DE ALIAGA

CENTRAL LIMA

BARRIOS ALTOS

★ ★

PLAZA MAYOR

M CATEDRAL

TACNA

ABANCAY

GRAU

UNIVERSITARIA

SAN MARTÍN DE PORRES

EMANCIPACIÓN

UGARTE

PIÉROLA

MANCO CAPAC

GARCILASO DE LA VEGA

JOSÉ GRANDA

MORALES DUÁREZ

ARGENTINA

ARICA

SEE "CENTRAL LIMA" MAP

BREÑA

JESÚS MARIA

BRASIL

PERU

FAUCETT

Río Rímac

TINGO MARIA

M MUSEO NACIONAL DE ARQUEOLOGÍA

★

AEROPUERTO JORGE CHÁVEZ

COLONIAL

PUEBLO LIBRE

BOLIVAR

M MUSEO LARCO ★

LA MAR

SUCRE

SALAVERRY

GAMBETTA

VENEZUELA

UNIVERSIDAD CATÓLICA

Parque de las Leyendas

MAGDALENA

ARGENTINA

FAUCETT

BELLAVISTA

SAN MIGUEL

CIRCUITO

Play Mar B

CALLAO

LA MARINA

LA PAZ

SAENZ PEÑA

GRAU

LA PERLA

■ FUERTE REAL FELIPE

PACIFIC

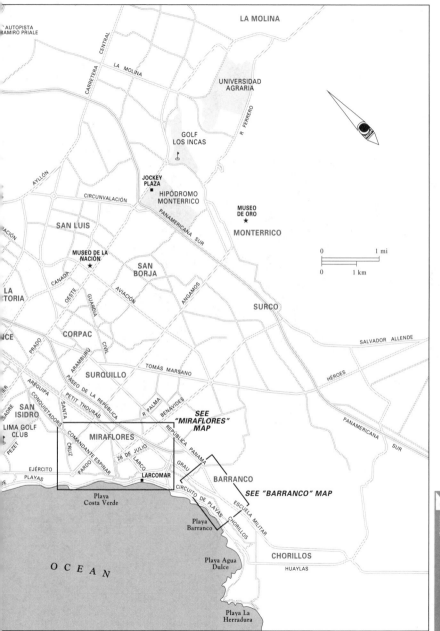

AUTOPISTA
RAMIRO PRIALE

LA MOLINA

CARRETERA CENTRAL

LA MOLINA

UNIVERSIDAD
AGRARIA

R. FERRERO

GOLF
LOS INCAS

AYLLÓN

JOCKEY
PLAZA

HIPÓDROMO
MONTERRICO

CIRCUNVALACIÓN

MUSEO
DE ORO
★

PANAMERICANA SUR

MONTERRICO

SAN LUIS

MUSEO DE LA
NACIÓN
★

SAN
BORJA

CANADA

ÁCIÓN

OESTE

GUARDIA

AVIACIÓN

ANGAMOS

SURCO

LA
TORIA

SALVADOR ALLENDE

CORPAC

ARAMBURU

CIVIL

NCE

PRADO

TOMÁS MARSANO

HÉROES

SURQUILLO

PASEO DE LA REPÚBLICA

AREQUIPA

CONQUISTADORES

PETIT THOURAS

R PALMA

BENAVIDES

SEE
"MIRAFLORES"
MAP

PANAMERICANA SUR

SAN
ISIDRO

SANTA

COMANDANTE ESPINAR

REPÚBLICA PANAMÁ

LIMA GOLF
CLUB

PEZET

MIRAFLORES

CRUZ

PARDO

28 DE JULIO

LARCO

GRAU

BARRANCO

SEE "BARRANCO" MAP

EJÉRCITO

LARCOMAR

PLAYAS

CIRCUITO DE PLAYAS

ESCUELA MILITAR

Playa
Costa Verde

Playa
Barranco

CHORILLOS

Playa Agua
Dulce

HUAYLAS

CHORILLOS

OCEAN

Playa La
Herradura

Lima

0   1 mi

0   1 km

© AVALON TRAVEL PUBLISHING, INC.

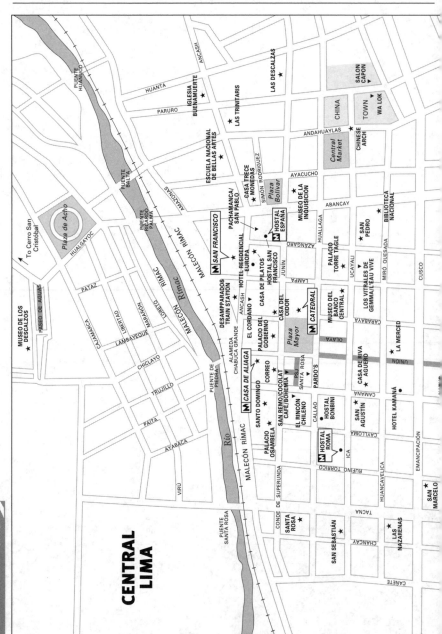

CENTRAL LIMA

Lima

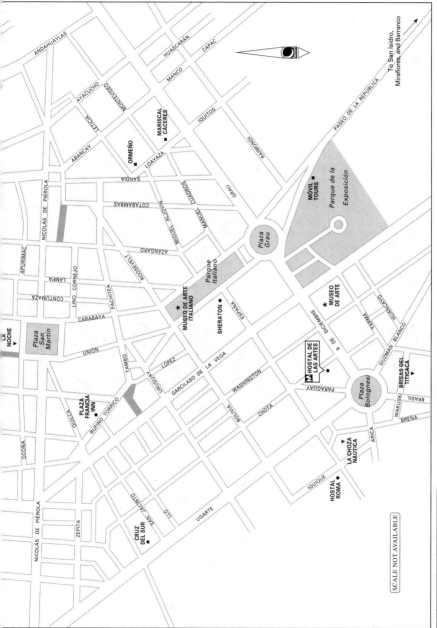

SCALE NOT AVAILABLE

nuts, and *ají* pepper. Bars, clubs and local music venues, called *peñas,* explode most nights with dance and the rhythms of *cumbia,* salsa, Afro-Peruvian pop, and a dozen forms of creole music. There are sandy beaches just a half hour south of the city. And despite all its griminess, the center of Lima shines forth with a wealth of colonial art and architecture, rivaled perhaps only by Mexico City, the other great center of Spanish power in the New World.

The bottom line: Lima is an extraordinary city, but it takes a little getting used to. The country's leading museums, churches, and restaurants are here, along with nearly eight million people, almost a third of Peru's population. It is the maximum expression of Peru's cultural diversity (and chaos). Whether you like it or not, you will come to Lima, because nearly all international flights land at this gateway. But do yourelf a favor and see Lima at the end of your trip, not at the beginning. That way you have a better chance of understanding what you see and not becoming overwhelmed in the process.

PLANNING YOUR TIME

Depending on your interests, Lima can be seen in a day's dash or several days to take in most of the museums, churches, and surrounding sights. As noted in the introduction above, Peru travelers tend to enjoy Lima more at the end of a trip than at the beginning. After visiting Puno, Cusco, and other Peruvian cities, travelers are more prepared to deal with the logistics of getting around this huge city. They have also seen enough of the country to make better sense of the the vast, and often poorly explained, collections in Peru's museums. Things start making sense.

If you are short on time and are visiting Cusco, one headache-free option is to fly from Cusco to Lima early in the morning and spend the day touring Lima on an organized tour (if you are planning on seeing Lima on your own, plan on one day for just acclimatizing). There are a variety of good day tours, which include lunch at one of the better restaurants in the city. In the evening, you can head to the airport for your flight home.

This is also a good way to avoid a long layover at Lima's unpleasant airport. Because of afternoon winds, most flights leave Cusco in the morning. But from Lima, international flights tend to leave in the evenings. So travelers coming from Cusco often end up spending several hours at Lima's airport on their way home.

HISTORY

Present-day Lima was never the center of any great empire but rather a verdant valley where a series of cultures flourished alongside the shrine of **Pachacámac,** which by the Incas' time housed one of the most respected, and feared, oracles in the Andes. Huaca Pucllana, in Lima's upscale Miraflores neighborhood, was a ceremonial center built out of adobe bricks by the seafaring **Lima culture** from around 200 A.D. onwards. The valley later fell under the influence of the Ayacucho-based **Wari culture** and was integrated by 1300 into the **Ychma kingdom,** which built most of the monumental architecture at Pachacámac. **Inca Tupac Yupanqui** conquered the area in the mid-15th century and built an enclosure for holy women alongside Pachacámac's stepped pyramid.

The first Spaniard to arrive in the area was **Hernando Pizarro,** who rode with a group of soldiers from Cajamarca in 1533 to investigate reports of gold at Pachacámac. They found nothing, but his brother, Francisco, returned two years later to move the capital here from Cusco. **Francisco Pizarro** was drawn to the spot because of its fertile plains and the natural port of Callao. (Both Pizarros had come here in January, in the middle of Lima's brief summer, and must have thought it was a sunny place!)

Pizarro laid the city out in typical checkerboard pattern, with the main square butting up against the **Río Rímac** (meaning "talking river" in Quechua), a natural defensive line. He christened the city **Los Reyes** (City of the Kings), and a decade later it was designated the capital of the Spanish viceroyalty in South America and eventually seat of the continent's archbishop. **Universidad San Marcos,** America's first university, was founded here in 1511, and the city was completely walled by the 17th century.

Most of the Catholic orders established themselves in Lima and built more than a dozen baroque churches and convents. Even the Spanish Inquisition for South America was based here (its headquarters is now an interesting museum). By royal decree all the commerce of the entire viceroyalty—essentially the entire west side of South America—had to pass through Lima, fueling a construction boom of elegant homes and promenades, such as the Paseo de Aguas on the far side of the Río Rímac (these days a downtrodden neighborhood).

The city was quickly rebuilt after a devastating 1746 earthquake that destroyed 80 percent of the city and slammed the port of **Callao** with a 12-meter tsunami. Lima's prominence began to fade after the Independence Wars of the 1820s, when it lost its monopoly over South American commerce.

Even in the early days of Lima, neighborhoods of black, mulatto, Indian, and mestizo workers began to crop up around the city, and the expansion continued after the city's walls were torn down by **President José Balta** (1868–72). During the **War of the Pacific** (1879–83), Lima was sacked by an invading Chilean army, which carted off church gold and most of the national library's books to Santiago de Chile.

There had always been a main avenue leading through the countryside to the port of Callao but, as the city expanded, other principal avenues were built outside the center, and the city's first electric train was inaugurated in 1906. For four centuries Lima had been a small city and even in 1919 only had 173,000 inhabitants. Over the rest of the 20th century, Lima's population would swell 44-fold to its current population of nearly 8 million.

Like La Paz, Bolivia, and other South American capitals, Lima's population exploded as the country transitioned from a rural economy to one based on large industry. Impoverished *campesinos* immigrated here from the countryside and built ramshackle slams, called *pueblos jóvenes,* which today are sprawling faster than ever over the desert hills around Lima. These neighborhoods often lack water and sewerage, though many now have electricity. Tele2000, an enterprising telecom company, installed wireless phone booths in many of them in the 1990s.

Lima's poverty became intense during the 1980s and 1990s, when a series of countryside massacres committed by both the **Shining Path** and the Peruvian Army sparked a crushing migration to Lima. The new immigrants worked at whatever they could find, and many ended up becoming street vendors *(ambulantes),* causing the center's main streets to become completely congested. After being elected in 1990, **President Alberto Fujimori** put an end to the rampant inflation, rolling blackouts, and car bombings that were terrorizing Lima residents by capturing Shining Path leader **Abimael Guzmán** in 1992. **Túpac Amaru,** the country's other main guerilla group, staged a final stand in Lima in 1996 by taking 490 hostages during a gala at the Japanese Embassy. The standoff ended four months later after a Peruvian special forces team freed the hostages, killing the 14 guerillas in the process (only one hostage died—of a heart attack).

Even before the terrorism years, much of the commerce and most of the wealthy families had abandoned the center of Lima and established the upscale neighborhoods and corporate centers of Monterrico, Miraflores, and San Isidro, where nearly all of the city's best hotels and restaurants are now located.

Though still a bit grimy and unsafe to walk around in at night, the center of Lima is making a comeback. Fujimori banned street vendors in the mid-1990s, and now the Plaza de Armas has been renovated with new riverside promenades and a spate of nice restaurants. Businesses like *Caretas,* the country's leading newsmagazine, are moving back to the center. Compared to the mid-1990s, the center of Lima feels pleasant and safe.

Lima

Sights

Lima can be thought of as a triangle, with the center at the apex. The base begins with the port of **Callao** and the nearby airport and runs along the coast through the neighborhoods of **Miraflores, Barranco,** and **Chorillos.** Other neighborhoods, such as **Pueblo Libre** and **San Isidro,** are in the middle of the triangle.

Lima is jam-packed with sights, but what is most interesting to many people are the colonial churches, convents, and homes in Lima's center, which is safe but warrants precautions nonetheless: leave your passport and money in the hotel, and guard your camera.

Lima's best museums are spread out, set in neighborhoods that are sandwiched between the coast and the center. Excellent collections of pre-Columbian gold, textiles, and ceramics can be found at the **Museo Larco** in Pueblo Libre, **Museo de la Nación** in San Borja, and **Museo de Oro** in Monterrico. English- and sometimes French-speaking guides are usually available at these museums.

Most Lima visitors stay in San Isidro, Miraflores, and Barranco, neighborhoods near the coast with the best selection of hotels, restaurants, and nightlife. There is little to see here, however, except for giant adobe platforms that were built by the Lima culture (200–700 A.D.) and now rise above the upscale neighborhoods.

There are so many sights to see in downtown Lima that you would need a few days to see them all. The best idea is to start early with the big sights, be selective, and work your way down the list as energy allows. The old town is bordered by the Río Rímac to the north, Avenida Tacna to the west, and Avenida Abancay to the east. The center of Lima is perfectly safe, but it is a good idea not to stray too far oustide these main streets—except for a lunchtime foray to Chinatown or a taxi ride to Museo de los Descalzos, on the other side of the river. Mornings are best reserved for visits to Lima's main churches, which are all open from 8 A.M.–1 P.M. and 5–8 P.M. daily and have English-speaking guides who request tip only. Taxis into the center from Miraflores cost $3 (15–30 minutes), or on Arequipa Avenue catch a *Todo Arequipa* bus that runs to within walking distance of the center ($0.30, 20–50 minutes).

CATEDRAL

Start on the **Plaza Mayor,** which is graced with a bronze fountain from 1650 and flanked on one side by the **Catedral,** which was built in the late 16th century. It contains the carved wooden sepulcher of Francisco Pizarro, who was murdered in 1541 by mob of Almagristas, a rival political faction. As you enter, the first chapel on the right is dedicated to St. John the Baptist and contains a carving of Jesus that is considered to be among the most beautiful in the Americas. But the highlight of the cathedral are the choir stalls carved in the early 17th century by Pedro Noguera, and the museum (9 A.M.–4:30 P.M. Mon.–Fri., 10 A.M.–4:30 P.M. Saturday, $1.50). Paintings here include a 1724 work by Alonso de la Cueva that paints the faces of the 13 Inca rulers alongside a lineup of Spanish kings from Carlos V to Felipe V. There is no clearer example of how art was used to put order on a turbulent, violent succession of kings. There are also a series of allegorical paintings painted in the 17th century by the Bassano brothers in Northern Italy (no one knows how or when this priceless art was imported) and a series of chest altars, one from Ayacucho and the other from Cusco, with an astounding number of miniature painted figures made of potato flour.

Head right out of the cathedral and pass the magnificent **Archbishop's Palace** (not open to the public) and, on the corner, the **Casa del Oidor.** This 16th-century house is closed to the public but has Lima's signature wooden balconies on the outside, with carvings inspired by Moorish designs and wood slats from behind which women viewed the activity on the square. Next door is the **Palacio del Gobierno,** the president's palace, which forms the other side of the Plaza Mayor and was built by the Spanish on top of the home of Taulichusco, the ruler of the Rímac Valley at that time. It was at this spot that liberator Jose de San Martín proclaimed the symbolic in-

the Catedral on the Plaza Mayor

dependence of Peru on July 28, 1821. There is an interesting change of the guard at 11:45 A.M. and a change of the flag at 5:45 P.M. Mon.–Sat.

From the palace, continue away from the cathedral and toward the side of the Plaza de Armas that is flanked with the **Municipality** and the **Club de la Unión,** a business club formed in 1868 that is a bit empty these days. Between these buildings are the pedestrian streets of Pasaje Santa Rosa and Escribanos, which are lined with upscale restaurants, cafés, and bookstores. At the corner of the palace and the municipality is Lima's antique post office, the **Casa de Correos y Telegrafos** (176 Conde de Superunda, 8 A.M.–8 P.M. Mon.–Sat., 8 A.M.–4 P.M. Sunday), which has a small stamps museum. Behind the post office is the pedestrian Pasaje de Correos, which had a glass roof until a 1940 earthquake and is now lined with vendors selling postcards, teddy bears, and other miscellaneous items.

CASA DE ALIAGA

From Plaza de Armas head right a half block down Unión to **Casa de Aliaga** (Unión 224),

which was built in 1535 and is the oldest home on the continent still family-owned after 17 generations. It is one of the best-preserved colonial homes in Peru, with a series of salons representing decor from the 16th, 17th, and 18th centuries. The land for the home was first deeded to Jerónimo de Aliaga, one of the 13 men who remained with Francisco Pizarro during his grueling exploration of Peru's coast in 1527. All visits must be arranged in advance through Lima Tours (tel. 01/424-9066 or 7560).

SANTO DOMINGO AND LIMA RIVERFRONT

Backtrack and head down the Pasaje de Correos to **Santo Domingo,** which is on the corner of Camaná and Conde de Superunda. This church was built in 1537 by the Dominicans and was remodeled in neoclassic style in the 19th century. At the end of the right nave is the Retablo de las Reliquias (Altar of the Relics), with the skulls of Peru's three Dominicans to reach sainthood. From left to right, they are San Martín de Porras, Santa Rosa, and San Juan Macias. Next door is

Lima

Church courtyards offer a welcome respite from bustling downtown Lima.

the attached convent (9 A.M.–12:30 P.M. and 3–6 P.M. Mon.–Sat., 9 A.M.–1 P.M. Sunday, $1), with carved balconies around a patio, fountains covered with Seville tiles, and a library with colossal 17th-century choir books. This convent was the first location of America's first university, **San Marcos,** and the balcony where students read their theses can still be seen in the Sala Capitular.

A half block down Conde de Superunda is **Palacio Osamblea** (Superunda 298, 9:30 A.M.–5 P.M. Mon.–Fri.), a neoclassic, rose-colored home with five elegant balconies. It has been converted into a space for revolving exhibitions hosted by the Centro Cultural Garcilaso de la Vega. Returning to Santo Domingo, head left on Camaná for one block to the **Alameda Chabuca Grande,** a new public space dedicated to one of Peru's best-known musicians, whose creole music is famous worldwide. This used to be the sprawling Polvos Azules market, which was shut down by the government in 2000 and moved to its present location along the Vía Expresa. The space

is now used by musicians and artists and is generally safe to walk around until 9 P.M., when the security guards go home.

The Río Rímac, brown with mud and clogged with plastic, tumbles by here. Across the river, the Rímac neighborhood was populated by mestizos and mulattos during colonial times. The large hill on the other side is **Cerro San Cristóbal**. Walk upriver along Ancash to **Desamparados,** Lima's beautiful old station that is being converted into a cultural center with revolving exhibits.

SAN FRANCISCO

A block further on Ancash is **San Francisco** (Ancash and Lampa, 9:30 A.M.–5:45 P.M. daily, $1.50, $0.75 students). This 16th-century convent has a patio lined with centuries-old *azulejos* (Sevillean tiles) and roofed with *machimbrado,* perfectly fitted puzzle pieces of Nicaraguan mahogany. There are frescoes from the life of Saint

Azulejos, or Sevillean tiles, line the courtyard of the 16th-century convent San Francisco in central Lima.

Francis of Assisi, a 1656 painting of the Last Supper with the disciples eating guinea pig and drinking from gold Inca cups *(qeros),* and a series of paintings from Peter Paul Rubens' workshop depicting the passion of Christ. But the highlight is the catacombs, or public cemetery, where slaves, servants, and others without money were buried until 1821 (rich citizens were usually buried in their home chapels). The underground labyrinth is a series of wells, some 20 meters deep, where bodies were stacked and covered with lime to reduce odor and disease. After they decomposed, the bones were stacked elsewhere. Across the street from San Francisco is Casa de Pilatos (Ancash 390, closed to the public), a colonial home that is occupied by Lima's Constitutional Tribunal.

MUSEO DE LA INQUISICIÓN

Continue down Ancash and cross the busy Avenida Abancay to **Casa de las Trece Monedas** (Ancash 536, closed to the public), which was built in 1787 and gets its name from the thirteen coins in the coat of arms on its facade. On the next block is the **Plaza Bolívar,** flanked by Peru's congress building and graced with a bronze statue in honor of liberator Simón Bolívar. On the far side of the plaza is the interesting **Museo de la Inquisición** (www.congreso.gob.pe/museo.htm, 9 A.M.–5 P.M. daily, free), which served as the headquarters of the Spanish Inquisition from 1570 until it was abolished in 1820. The museum explains the harsh and bizarre punishments that the church doled out for crimes ranging from heresy and blasphemy to seduction and reading banned books. There are creepy dungeon-like spaces in the back where the punished were given 50 lashes and jailed while others were sent to work on slave ships or in public hospitals. This was also where auto-da-fés were ordered, public condemnation ceremonies in the Plaza de Armas where witches, bigamists, and heretics were hung to death or burned at the stake.

CHINA TOWN

Now it's time for lunch, so hold on to your wallet and head farther down Junín for a block and a half and then take a right on Andahuaylas. Lima's **central market** is to your right and in front a **Chinese arch,** entryway to **China Town.** This is an excellent place to have lunch or late-afternoon tea, in the midst of a neighborhood founded by Chinese indentured workers, or coolies, who came here after finishing their contract on the train lines or coastal haciendas. The main street is Capón, which has three Asian temples and a variety of stores.

WALKING TOUR EXTENSION

If you still have energy after lunching in China Town, there is plenty more to see in central Lima. From the end of Capón, head right on Miró Quesada and cross Abancay once again to Peru's **Biblioteca Nacional,** a beautiful old library that is open to the public.

Head right on Azángaro to the 16th-century **San Pedro** (Azángaro and Ucayali), which has a

COLONIAL VS. REPUBLICAN HOMES

The differences between colonial (1534–1822) and Republican homes (1820–1900) are clear in theory but muddled in practice. Most of Peru's old homes were built by Spaniards in colonial times who received the prized plots on or near the Plaza de Armas. These houses, passed down from generation to generation, were often restored in the 19th or early 20th century with Republican elements. So most houses, or *casonas*, are somewhat of a blend.

But all share in common the basic Spanish layout: a tunnel-like entry, or *zaguán*, leads into a central courtyard, or *traspatio*. The rooms are built with high ceilings and a second-story wood balcony around the courtyard. Rich homes have stone, instead of wooden columns, and additional patios.

During the nearly three centuries of the Peruvian Viceroyalty, homes went from the solid, fortified, construction of medieval times to the more intricate decorations of the baroque, which were often based on *mudéjar*, or Arabic, patterns brought from Spain. After Independence, however, homes demonstrate neoclassic elegance and a more confident use of colors favored in the New World, such as bright blues, greens, and yellow.

Colonial Homes

- *Traspatios* paved with *canto rodado*, river stones
- Sparse interiors
- Heavy brown and green colors
- Simple ceilings, often made of plaster, cane, and tile
- Baroque or rococo decorations with *mudéjar*, or Arabic, patterns
- Forged iron windows with intricate lace patterns
- *Celosia* balconies where women could observe, but not be observed

Republican Homes

- *Traspatios* paved with polished stone slabs
- Elegant interior decorations and furniture
- Light yellow, white, and blue colors
- Elaborate, often carved, wooden ceilings
- Neoclassic decorations with ornate columns

drab mannerist facade but one of the most spectacular church interiors in Peru. Huge white arching ceilings lead to a magnificent altar covered in gold leaf and designed by Matías Maestro, who is credited for bringing the neoclassic style to Peru. At the end of the right nave, ask permission to see the mind-blowing sacristy, decorated with tiles and graced with a magificent painting of the coronation of the Virgin Mary by Peru's most famous painter, Bernardo Bitti. Painted on the ceiling boards above are scenes of the life from San Ignacio. If you come in the morning, it is possible to ask permission to see the cloisters and two interior chapels as well.

A half block down Ucayali is the **Palacio Torre Tagle** (Ucayali 363), a mansion built in 1735 that is, like Casa de Aliaga, in pristine condition. Visits can be arranged by popping into the Ministry of Foreign Affairs next door at Ucayali 318. Another half block down the street at the intersection of Ucayali and Lampa is the **Museo del Banco Central** (tel. 01/427-6250, 10 A.M.–4 P.M. Mon.–Fri., 10 A.M.–1 P.M. Sat.–

Sun., free). The ground floor holds a colonial money exhibit, one flight up is a 19th- and 20th-century painting gallery, and the basement shines with pre-Columbian ceramics and textiles (including a range of intriguing Chancay pieces). The paintings include a good selection of watercolors from Pancho Fierro (1807–79), paintings from 20th-century artist Enrique Polanco, and etchings by Cajamarca's indigenous artist José Sabogal (1888-1956).

Keep heading down Ucayali and cross Jirón Unión, the pedestrian street that runs five blocks from the Plaza Mayor to the Plaza San Martín, and continue to the church of **San Agustín** (corner of Ica and Camaná).This 18th-century baroque facade is one of the most intricate in the Americas and looks almost as if it were carved from wood, not stone. Upon exiting the church, head right on Camaná a half block until the **Casa Riva Agüero** (Camaná 459, 10 A.M.–1 P.M. and 2–8 P.M. Mon.–Sat., $5, or museum only $0.75). This 18th-century home, with all original furniture, has an interesting museum of colo-

Palacio Torre Tagle

which was built in the 19th century and is still thriving today. The park is ringed with a high fence and is best entered at the corner of 28 de Julio and Inca Garcilaso de la Vega. Nearby is an artifical lake with paddleboats and the Kusi Kusi Puppet Theatre (basement of German-style gingerbread house, tel. 01/477-4249), which has Sunday performances listed in the cultural section of the *Comercio* newspaper. Here too is the **Museo de Arte** (9 de Diciembre 125, tel. 01/423-4732, www.museoarte.perucultural.org.pe, 10 A.M.–5 P.M. Thurs.–Tues., $3.50 adult, $1.75 students), which houses the best range of Peruvian paintings in the country, an espresso bar, and a cinema. The museum contains colonial furniture, some pre-Columbian ceramics, and a huge collection of paintings from the viceroyalty to the present. Another nearby park is the **Parque Italiano,** which contains the **Museo de Arte Italiano** (tel. 01/423-9932, Paseo de la República 250, 10 A.M.–5 P.M. Mon.–Fri., $1) with a collection of European art mainly from the early 20th century.

nial handicrafts as well as ceramics and textiles from the Lima culture.

Other interesting churches, which are clustered together, are **La Merced** (Unión and Miró Quesada), which was built in 1754 and holds a baroque retablo carved by San Pedro de Nolasco, and San Marcelo (Rufino Torrico and Emancipación). Nearby there is a string of three 17th-century churches within four blocks of each other on the busy Avenida Tacna: **Las Nazarenas** (6 A.M.–noon and 5–8:30 P.M.), which holds the image of El Señor de los Milagros, the city's patron saint whose October festival draws as many as a half million celebrants; **San Sebastián,** and **Santa Rosa** (9:30 A.M.–noon and 3:30–7 P.M. daily).

ART MUSEUMS NEAR CENTRAL LIMA

If you are taking a taxi from San Isidro or Miraflores into the center, you will travel along a sunken highway known as the **Vía Expresa** (also nicknamed *El Zanjón,* or The Ditch). The highway emerges on ground level and passes along a series of public parks before entering old town. One of these is the **Parque de la Exposición,**

MUSEO DE LOS DESCALZOS

Right across the Río Rímac from Lima is the downtrodden **Rímac** neighborhood, which began as a mestizo and mulatto barrio during the viceroyalty and was refurbished in the 18th century by the Lima aristocracy. All the sights here are close to the Plaza de Armas—and take a taxi, as assaults are common in this area.

The **Museo de los Descalzos** (end of Alameda Los Descalzos, tel. 01/482-3360, 10 A.M.–1 P.M. and 3–6 P.M. Tue.–Sat., 11:30 A.M.–6 P.M. Sunday) was a convent and spiritual retreat for the Franciscans, and today contains interesting and elegant cloisters, a chapel with a gold-covered baroque altar, an elegant refectory, and a gallery with more than 300 paintings from the 17th and 18th century—including a masterpiece by Esteban de Murillo. On the taxi ride home, ask your taxi driver to pass the nearby **Paseo de Aguas,** an 18th-century French-style promenade where Lima's elites strolled along its artificial waterways. All that remains today is a neoclassic arch, hidden next to a towering Cristal Beer factory. Nearby is the giant **Plaza de Acho,** Lima's bullring, where bullfights are held from early October to early December. Inside is the **Museo Taurino** (Hualgayoc 332, tel. 01/481-1467, 9 A.M.–6 P.M. Mon.–Sat., $1.50), which contains a wide range of bullfighting relics.

Towering above Rímac is **Cerro San Cristóbal,** where Francisco Pizarro placed a cross in thanks that Quizo Yupanqui and his Inca army did not succeed in crossing the Río Rímac into Lima during the Inca rebellion of 1536. Today the hill is encrusted with a dusty *pueblo jóven* named Barrios Altos. There is a lookout over Lima at the top, a small museum, and a giant cross that is illuminated at night. To reach the top, take a taxi from the Plaza de Armas ($5) or wait for buses with English-speaking guides that leave from the Municipality ($1.50).

MUSEO DE ORO

Monterrico, an upscale suburb in eastern Lima that is often sunny when the rest of the city is covered in fog, is known for its **Museo de Oro** (Gold Museum, Molina 1110, Monterico, tel. 01/345-1292, 11:30 A.M.–7 P.M. Mon.–Sun., $9). This fabulous collection of gold pieces was one of Lima's must-see tourist attractions until 2001, when a scandal broke alleging that many of the prize pieces were fakes. Newspapers pointed the finger at the sons of museum founder Sr. Miguel Mujica Gallo, whom the newspapers accused of selling the originals and replacing them with imitations. The family countered, saying false pieces were bought by mistake and Sr. Mujica Gallo died of sadness in the process. Only true gold pieces are on display now at the museum, but the museum continues to suffer from a credibility problem. Gold pieces include spectacular funerary masks, ceremonial knives *(tumis),* a huge set of golden arms, exquisite figurines, and crowns studded with turquoise. It is a huge potpourri of gold, with little explication in English, bought over decades from tomb raiders who work over Moche, Nasca, Sicán, and Chimú sites. Other objects of interest include a Nasca poncho made of parrot feathers and a Moche skull that was fitted, postmortem, with purple quartz teeth.

Almost as impressive is the **Arms Museum** upstairs, which is a terrifying assemblage of thousands of weapons ranging from samurai swords and medieval arquebuses to Hitler paraphernalia.

MUSEO DE LA NACIÓN

Peru's largest museum, and cheaper to see than the private collections, is **Museo de la Nación** (Javier Prado Este 2466, tel. 01/476-9878, 9 A.M.–5 P.M. Tue.–Sun., $2, $1 students), in the east Lima suburb of San Borja. Though criticized for a rambling organization, this museum has a new and improved chronological layout following a recent renovation. There are three levels of exhibits showcasing Peru's entire archaeological history, from Chavín stone carvings and Paracas weavings all the way to the Incas. There are good models of Machu Picchu, the Nasca Lines, and the Lords of Sipán tomb excavated near Chiclayo in 1987, one of the great finds of Latin American archaeology. This is a full-blown version of Peru's culture for the history-hungry. A more condensed alternative is the **Museo Nacional de Arqueología.**

M MUSEO LARCO

The charming neighborhood of Pueblo Libre is just south of central Lima and has a relaxed, small-town vibe. Its best-known sight is the **Museo Larco** (Bolívar 1515, tel. 01/461-1312, www.museolarco.perucultura.org.pe, 9 A.M.–6 P.M. daily, $6, $3 student), which rivals the Museo de Oro in terms of gold pieces and has far more ceramics and textiles. Found in 1926 in an 18th-century mansion built atop a pre-Hispanic ruin, this museum has more than 40,000 ceramics and 5,000 pieces of gold and textiles. There are huge Mochica earrings and funerary masks, a Paracas textile with a world-record 398 threads per inch, and a jewelry vault filled with gold and silver objects. A back storage room holds thousands of pre-Hispanic ceramic vessels, including a Moche erotic collection that will cause even the most liberated to blush. To reach this museum from Miraflores, catch a bus at Arequipa Avenue that says *Todo Bolívar* and get off at the 15th block.

ⓂMUSEO NACIONAL DE ARQUEOLOGÍA

A 15-minute walk away from Museo Larco, and linked to it with a blue line drawn on the sidewalk, is Pueblo Libre's laid-back Plaza Bolívar, and the **Museo Nacional de Arqueología, Antropología, e Historia** (Vivanco block 7, tel. 01/463-5070, 9 A.M.–5 P.M. Tues.–Sat., 9 A.M.–4 P.M. Sunday, $3 including tour). Though smaller than the Museo de la Nación, this museum presents a clearer, certainly more condensed, view of Peruvian history. Exhibits include Moche ceramics, Paracas tapestries, Chimú gold, and scale models for understanding sights of hard-to-see Chavín and Wari sites.

The museum's most important piece is the Estela Raimondi, a giant stone obelisk that once graced one of Peru's first ceremonial centers, Chavín de Huantár (1300–200 B.C.), near present-day Huaraz. It is carved with snakes, pumas, and the first appearance of the Dios de los Báculos (the Staff-Bearing God), which would reverberate throughout Peru's ancient history. The tour includes a walk through the adjacent colonial home where Independence leaders José de San Martín and Simón Bolívar stayed.

Lima by night

Around the corner is the 16th-century **Iglesia Magdalena** (San Martín and Vivanco, 6:30–8 P.M. Fri.–Tues., 8 A.M.–8 P.M. Thursday), which has attractive carved altars and a gold painting of Señor de los Tremblores (Lord of the Earthquakes). An excellent restaurant, café, and pisco-tasting bodega, all steeped in tradition, are down the street.

MIRAFLORES AND SAN ISIDRO

What appears to be a clay hill plunked down in the middle of Miraflores is actually a huge adobe pyramid from the Lima culture, which built a dozen major structures in and around what is now Lima between 200 and 700 A.D. **Huaca Pucllana** (General Bolognesi 800, Miraflores, tel. 01/445-8695, 9 A.M.1 P.M. and 1:30–5 P.M. Wed.–Mon., free) has a small but excellent museum, which includes ceramics, textiles, reconstructed tombs, and artifacts from this culture that depended almost entirely on the sea for sur-

vival. A recently discovered pot shows a man carrying a shark on his back—proof that this culture somehow hunted 455-kilo sharks. No free wandering is allowed, but guides lead tours every half hour around the ceremonial plazas and a few inner rooms. This is a good option for those who cannot see the larger Pachacámac, 31 km south of Lima.

A similar, though completely restored, stepped pyramid in San Isidro is **Huaca Huallamarca** (Nicólas de Piérola 201, tel. 01/222-4124, 9 A.M.–5 P.M. Tues.–Sun., $1.50), which offers a chance to understand what these temples once looked like. From the top, there is an interesting view over Lima's most upscale district.

Museo de Historia Natural (one block west of the 12th block of Arequipa, Arenales 1256, Lince, tel. 01/471-0117 9 A.M.–3 P.M. Mon.–Fri., 9 A.M.–5 P.M. Saturday, 9 A.M.–1 P.M. Sunday, $1) is a severely underfunded museum with an aging taxidermy collection that nevertheless offers a good introduction to the fauna of Peru. Many

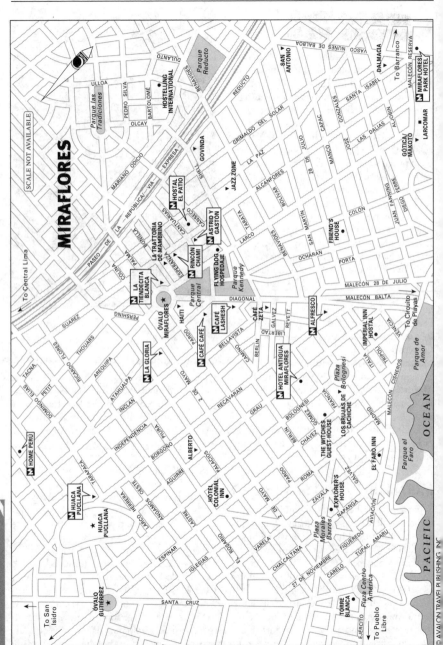

MIRAFLORES

SCALE NOT AVAILABLE

Lima

of Peru's top biologists work from here. Ask for permission to see the storage area in the back, where thousands of stuffed birds are archived.

Museo Amano (Retiro 160 near 11th block of Angamos Oeste, tel. 01/441-2909, tours at 3, 4, and 5 P.M. Mon.–Fri., donations appreciated) has a small but interesting collection of 200 pre-Columbian ceramics, including a Nasca piece with a scene of human sacrifice, and a range of textiles.

Museo Enrico Poli (Lord Cochrane 466, tel. 01/422-2437 or 440/7100, 4–6 P.M., by appointment only, $10) is one of Lima's more intriguing private collections with a huge range of textiles, gold and silver objects, and other artifacts. The owner, Enrico Poli, gives the tours personally and speaks Spanish only. Agencies often visit here with their own interpreters.

BARRANCO

This bohemian barrio has a few small museums, the best of which is **Museo Pedro de Osma** (San Pedro de Osma 423, tel. 01/467-0141, 9 A.M.– 7 P.M. Tues.–Sun., $3), which holds an exquisite private collection of colonial art and furniture. The museum itself is one of Barranco's oldest mansions and is worth a peek just for that reason. Down the street is a small exhibit on electricity in Lima at the **Museo de la Electricidad** (San Pedro de Osma 105, tel. 01/477-6577, 9 A.M.–1 P.M. and 2–5 P.M. Tue.–Sun., free). A restored electric tram, which used to connect Barranco to Miraflores and Lima, runs down the street on Sundays ($0.75).

PACHACÁMAC

This extensive complex of adobe pyramids, 31 km south of Lima in the Lurín Valley, was the leading pilgrimage center on the central coast and home to the most feared, and respected, oracle in the Andes. The name of Pachacámac in Quechua translates to "Lord of the World." Both the Wari and local Inca empires respected the oracle, adding to its prestige with additional buildings and consulting it for important decisions.

During his imprisonment at Cajamarca, Inca Atahualpa complained bitterly because the oracle had falsely predicted he would be victorious against the Spaniards. But Hernando Pizarro was so intrigued by Atahualpa's reports of gold at the oracle that he and a troop of Spanish soldiers rode here from Cajamarca in three weeks. Pushing aside the priests, Pizarro strode to the upmost level of the stepped pyramid. He describes a cane-and-mud house at the top, with a door strangely decorated with turqoise, crystals, and corals. Inside the dark space was a roughly shaped wooden idol. "Seeing the filth and mockery of the idol," Pizarro wrote, "we went out to ask why they thought highly of something so dirty and ugly."

What can be seen today is the idol itself (probably a replica) in the on-site museum and excavations of the main temples and huge pyramids, which have revealed ramps and entranceways. From the top of the Temple of the Sun there is an impressive view of Lima's well-organized shantytown, Villa El Salvador, and the Pacific Coast. The Palacio de Las Mamacuña, the enclosure for holy women built by the Incas, can be seen with a guide only ($4 for English-speaking tour of entire site). On the way to the ruins, you will pass **Reserva Pantanos de Villa** at Km 18 of the Panamericana Sur. There is a surprisingly good range of ducks and other migratory aquatic birds here that lures bird watchers.

The easiest way to see the ruins is with an agency tour from Lima. Buses marked *Pachacámac* leave from Montevideo and Ayacucho in central Lima and can be picked up at the Primavera Bridge along the Panamericana Sur ($2 taxi ride to bridge from Miraflores). Ask to be dropped off at *las ruinas,* as the town of Pachacámac is further along.

SAN PEDRO DE CASTA AND MARCAHUASI

Marcahuasi, a strange set of rock formations on the high plains above Lima, have attracted a range of theories ranging from simple wind erosion to the work of UFOs or ancient cultures. The rocks are shaped like people and animals, inspiring names like the Frog, Indian, Three Virgins, and Turtle. Marcahuasi is set amid attractive country scenery

BARRANCO

SÁENZ PEÑA

MIRAFLORES

KITSCH ▼

SARGENTO
PIMIENTA ▼

EL LEJANO
OESTE
▼

SAN ANTONIO

SANTA ROSA

Plaza San
Francisco

MARTINEZ

● LA VILLA
BARRANQUINA

GRAU

COLÓN

SAN FRANCISCO

BOLOGNESI

DÁVALOS

LAS
GUITARRAS
▼

SAN MARTIN

BATALLA DE JUNIN

COLINA

GENOVA

LA UNIÓN

MANUEL SEGURA

SALAVERRY

Plaza
Raymondi

Ⓜ THE POINT ●

UGARTE

PARRO

ESPINOZA

LA CANTA
RANA
▼

HOSTEL
DOMEYER ●

PACIFIC
OCEAN

DOMEYER

SUCRE

PEDRO OSMA

LA MESITAS ▼

LA NOCHE ▼

JUAN E PASOS

BOULEVARD

PUENTE DE LOS
SUSPIROS ★

AYACUCHO

ABREGU

ZEPITA

LA ERMITA ▼

Circuito de la Playa

LA ESTACIÓN DE
BARRANCO
▼

EL EKEKO/
DEJA VU BAR ▼

JUANITOS ▼

BARRANCO MUSEO-
GALERÍA ARTE DE ★
AYACUCHO

Plaza de
Barranco

GRAU

CASTILLA

★
MUSEO DE
ELECTRICIDAD

MELGAR

●
Ⓜ MOCHILERO'S
BACKPACKERS
HOSTEL

28 DE JULIO

PEDRO OSMA

2 DE MAYO

BOLOGNESI

MALECÓN

BRESCIANA

SOLARI

NAYLAMP ▼

MANOS
MORENAS ▼

TARAPACA

LIBERTAD

LAVALLE

MUSEO PEDRO
DE OSMA ★

SCALE NOT AVAILABLE

and, along with the nearby charming town of **San Pedro,** makes for a great weekend outing from Lima. To arrive, catch a bus from Av. Grau in Lima (near Plaza Grau in the center) and travel an hour and a half to **Chosica,** a resort town 860 meters above sea level that is popular with those trying to escape Lima's fog belt. There are plenty of budget and nicer lodging options here. From Chosica's Parque Echenique, buses leave at 9 A.M. and 3 P.M. to San Pedro, a beautiful four- or five-hour trip that climbs to 3,750 meters above sea level. There is a hostel ($3 pp) in the main square, along with two restaurants and a tourist information office. Marcahuasi, at 4,100 meters over sea level, is a 3-km, 1.5-hour hike; donkeys can be rented for $6. Entry fee is $3.

Entertainment and Events

NIGHTLIFE AND PEÑAS

Barranco

The most happening neighborhood for nightlife in Lima is Barranco. **La Noche** (Bolognesi 307, tel. 01/477-4154, 7 P.M.–3 A.M., $2–4) is Barranco's best live music bar, with tables set on different levels to look down on a range of (mostly jazz) performances. Monday nights, when there is no cover charge, are especially crowded. Live Cuban salsa plays at **El Ekeko** (Grau 266, tel. 01/247-3148, 10 A.M.–midnight Mon.–Wed., 10 A.M.–3 A.M. Thurs.–Sat., $3–6) Wednesday through Saturday nights and artsy events like poetry readings often take place on other nights. **Mochileros** (San Pedro de Osma 135, see *Accommodations* in Barranco) is best known as a backpacker's hostel but has a raucous bar as well, with live rock bands and mind-blowing cocktails.

Located in one of Barranco's oldest colonial homes, **Deja Vu Bar** (Grau 294, tel. 01/247-3742, 6:30 P.M.–4 A.M. Mon.–Sat.) is a dance club for the young and wild, with a selection of techno and rock. To begin your evening, or end it, head to **Juanito's** (Grau 274), a hole-in-the-wall bar that has been a gathering spot for intellectuals since the 1960s. The traditional fare at Juanito's, right on the main square, is malt beer and smoked ham sandwiches.

Barranco is full of *peñas* (live *criollo* music clubs) that make for a rowdy night out among locals. A local favorite is **Las Guitarras** (Manuel Segura 295, tel. 01/247-3924, Fri.–Sat.) with live Latin weekend shows. **La Candelaría** (Bolognesi 292, tel. 01/247-2941, www.lacandelaria-peru.com, 9:30 P.M.–2 A.M. Fri.–Sat., $7) is a new and comfortable *peña* where spectators do not stay seated for long. With a slightly older crowd, **La Estación de Barranco** (Pedro de Osma 112, tel. 01/247-0344) is a nice place to hear *música criolla* in the digs of an old train station. The most upscale *peña* in Lima, and a good restaurant, is **Manos Morenas** (Pedro de Osma 409, Barranco, tel. 01/467-0421, $12). Shows start at 9 P.M. Tuesday through Thursday, and at 10:30 P.M. Friday and Saturday. See *Food* in Barranco for more details.

Miraflores

The nightlife in Miraflores is more spread out and harder to find than Barranco's. And that is precisely why many a traveler ends up at **Calle de las Pizzas** (The Street of the Pizzas), a seedy row of pizza-and-sangria joints right in front of Parque Kennedy. If you are in the area, and looking for a place to start your evening, head instead around the corner to **Café Haiti** (Diagonal 160, tel. 01/446-3816, 7 A.M.–2 A.M. Sun.–Thurs., 7 A.M.–3 A.M. Fri.–Sat., $7), a sidewalk café that is still serving excellent pisco sours after a half century in business.

Jazz Zone (La Paz 656, tel. 01/241-8139, 10 P.M.–2 A.M. Mon.–Sat., free Mon.–Wed., $4 Thurs., $9 Fri.–Sat.) rivals Barranco's La Noche as the place to see live jazz. Come on Monday for Afro-Peruvian, Tuesdays and Wednesdays for Latin jazz, Thursdays for bossa nova, and weekends for all of the above.

There are several British-style pubs in Miraflores, good for drinking draft ales, playing darts, and eating meat-heavy bar food. **Benchley Arms** (Atahualpa 176, tel. 01/445-9680, closed

Lima

GAY AND LESBIAN LIMA

Though smaller than that in other Latin American capitals, Lima's gay scene is growing with a few great new discos and bars. There are a number of websites on gay Peru, but the best and most up-to-date information is http://gaylimape.tripod.com. This site, written in English, gives travel tips, chat room, links, and an opinionated listing of gay and lesbian bars, discos, saunas, cruising spots, and even retirement options.

Two gay-friendly bars to start off the evening are **La Sede** in Miraflores (28 de Julio 441, 01/242-2462, www.publasede.com, 10 P.M.–late Wed.–Sat.) and **Kafe Kitsch** in Barranco (Bolognesi 743, 10 P.M.–late, Wed.–Sat.).

Gay-and-lesbian discos do not start swinging until 1 A.M. and continue until the wee hours of the morning. Entry is typically free on non-weekend nights and goes up after midnight on weekends.

Miraflores' hippest, classiest gay-and-lesbian disco is **Legendaris** (Berlin 363, www.gayperu .com/legendaris, 11 P.M.–late Wed.–Sun., $4.50 before midnight, $6 after), which opened in January 2004 with an extravagant decor, great sound system, and room for 350.

The flamboyant **Downtown Vale Todo** (Pasaje Los Pinos, Miraflores, 01/444-6433, www.peruesgay.com/downtownvaletodo, 10 P.M.–late Wed.–Sun., $4 Fri.–Sat.) is still open despite some citizens' efforts to shut it down. This disco attracts a younger crowd, with drag queen performances and cruising bar on upper deck. The smaller gay disco **Splash** (Pasaje Los Pinos 181, Miraflores, 10:30 P.M. onwards Thurs.–Sat.) is on the same street.

A late-2003 addition to San Isidro is **Mercury** (2 de Mayo 1545, 01/592-2340, www.peruesgay.com/mercury, 11 P.M.–late Fri.–Sat., $4.50, $6 for couples). This disco has two levels, good music-and-light show, and is in the middle of one of Lima's most fashionable districts.

The only option in central Lima is **Sagitario** (Wilson 869, 01/424-4383, www.gayperu .com/sagitariodisco, daily, free except after midnight on weekends), one of Lima's original gay-only bars. The neighborhood is sketchy at night, so travel by taxi.

Avenida 13 (Manuel Segura 270, off block 15 of Arequipa, 01/265-3694) is a gay-and-lesbian dance club that is **women-only** on Fridays.

Gay-friendly hotels include **Hostal de las Artes** in the center, **Hostel Domeyer** in Barranco, **Aparthotel San Martín** in Miraflores, and **Loft** in San Isidro.

Sundays) has a good selection of imported ales and beers, not to mention British newspapers and good bar food. **O'Murphy's Irish Pub** (Schell 627, tel. 01/445-1444) is Miraflores' classic Irish bar with Guinness on tap, darts, and pool table.

There is always something happening at Larcomar (Malecón de la Reserva 610), the oceanfront mall at the end of Avenida Larco. Even those who dislike malls are impressed with this public space, buried in the cliffside and overlooking the Pacific. Lima's hottest, and most expensive, new disco is the exclusive **Gótica** (Larcomar, Malecón de la Reserva 610, 4 A.M. or later Thurs.–Sat., $12), with multilevel dance floors, dance shows, and a great range of fast

dance music. There are two other clubs in Larcomar that appeal to older and younger age groups and are open Monday to Saturday.

Near the Parque Kennedy, there are a number of bars and discos along Calle Berlin.

San Isidro

If you have come to Avenida Conquistadores for dinner, there are a few night options along this strip. The best is the swanky sushi restaurant **Asia de Cuba** (Conquistadores 780, San Isidro, tel. 01/222-4940), which has an upscale bar and an eclectic after-dinner nighlife scene, including a hookah and blackberry-flavored tobacco in the plush loft. Another good option is **Antica Taverna** (Conquistadores 605, tel. 01/422-8429,

6:30 A.M.–1 A.M. daily), with a second-story couch area for beer or cocktails. See *Food* in San Isidro for more details on both options.

Central Lima

There are a few night options in the center of Lima, though partakers should take a taxi to and from each one. The same owners of La Noche in Barranco have opened **La Noche** (corner of Camaná and Quilca, tel. 01/423-0299, www.barlanoche.com, Mon.–Sat.) on a pedestrian street adjacent to Plaza San Martín. This live music bar has a great atmosphere, an adjacent art gallery, and a nonstop schedule of events that includes poetry readings, comedy shows, and a range of live music. Nearby on the Plaza San Martín is **El Estadio Futbol Club** (Nícolas de Piérola 926, tel. 01/428-8866, until 2 A.M. Mon.–Sat.), which is a soccer-lover's pardise bedecked from floor to wall with *fútbol* paraphernalia.

One of the largest and best *peñas* in Lima is **Brisas del Titicaca** (Wakulski 168, near Block 1 of Brasil and Plaza Bolognesi, tel. 01/332-1901, Thurs.–Sat., $7) Foreigners come here on Thursday nights for an extraordinary exhibition of dance and music from around Peru that runs from 9:30 P.M. to midnight. Those who want to see the same dances, and do a lot of it themselves, should come on weekend nights when mainly Peruvians party from 10 P.M. to 4 A.M. This is a safe neighborhood and is an easy taxi ride from Miraflores.

CINEMAS

Lima has more cinemas than the rest of the country combined. Most foreign movies are shown in their original language with subtitles, except for children's movies, which are always dubbed. In Miraflores alone there are three multiplexes showing both Hollywood and Latin American movies, **Cineplanet Alcázar** (Santa Cruz 814, Óvalo Gutierrez, Miraflores, tel. 01/421-8208, $4), **El Pacífico 12** (Jose Pardo 121, Miraflores, tel. 01/445-6990, $3.50), and **Multicines Larcomar** (in Larcomar mall at end of Larco, tel. 01/446-7336, $3). A smaller recommended theater is **Cine Club Miraflores** (Larco 770, Mi-

raflores, tel. 01/446-2649). In central Lima there is **Cineplanet Centro** (Jr. de la Union 819, tel. 01/428-8460, $2, $1.50 Mon.–Wed.).

For art and classic films, check out **El Cinematógrafo** (Pérez Roca 196, Barranco, tel. 01/477-1961, $3.50) or **Museo de Arte's Filmoteca** (9 de Diciembre 125, tel. 01/423-4732, www.museoarte.perucultural.org.pe).

Check **El Comercio** for film listings, or the web page www.elcomercioperu.com.pe/.

PERFORMING ARTS

For the most up-to-date listing of cultural events, pick up the monthly *Guía del Arte de Lima*, available free in most museums and cultural centers, or view its web page (http://guiadelarte.perucultural.org.pe). **El Comercio** newspaper also has complete listings (www.elcomercioperu.com.pe).

Lima's performing arts received a body blow when the **Teatro Municipal,** the main venue for ballet, symphony, and opera, burnt to the ground in 1998. Some of these events have been transferred to the Museo de la Nación (Javier Prado Este 2466, San Borja, tel. 01/476-9878) or the Teatro Segura (Huancavelica 265, central Lima, tel. 01/426-7189).

Theater productions, always in Spanish, can be seen at **Teatro Canout** (Petit Thouars 4550, Miraflores, tel. 01/422-5373), **Teatro Marsano** (General Suárez 409, Miraflores), **Centro Cultural PUCP** (Av. Camino Real 1075, tel. 01/222-6899, San Isidro), **Teatro La Plaza Usil** in Larcomar (tel. 01/242-9266), **Alianza Francesa** (Arequipa 4595, tel. 01/241-7014), **Centro Cultural de España** (Natalio Sánchez 181, Sta. Beatriz), and **Teatro Británico** (Bellavista 531, tel. 01/447-1135, Miraflores), which occasionally has plays in English. Tickets are normally purchased at the box office only for $3 to $8.

Other frequent cultural events such as films, concerts, and expositions are held at the **Centro Cultural Ricardo Palma** (Larco Herrera 770, San Isidro, tel. 01/446-3959), **Associación Cultural Peruano Británica** (Bellavista 531, Miraflores, tel. 01/447-1135), and **Instituto Cultural Peruano Norteamericano,** with a location in Miraflores (corner of Angamos and

Arequipa, tel. 01/446-0831) and in central Lima (Cusco 446, tel. 01/428-353).

CASINOS

Lima is overflowing with casinos, though the most reputable ones tend to be in the major hotels. Wherever you go, do not play the slot machines, as they tend to be rigged. Casinos open in the evenings and usually close around dawn and offer free drinks and cigarettes to those who are betting. Better casinos include the **Stellaris Casino** at the Marriott (Malecón de la Reserva 615, across the street from Larcomar, tel. 01/217-7000), which has minimum $3 bets at the blackjack tables; the upscale **Country Club Lima Hotel** (Los Eucaliptos 590, San Isidro, tel. 01/440-4060) with minimum $5 blackjack bets; **Casino la Hacienda** (28 de Julio 511, tel. 01/445-3980), minimum $3 bet; and **Hotel Sheraton** (Paseo de la República 170, tel. 01/315-5000).

SPECTATOR SPORTS

Lima is a great place to catch a **soccer game,** either at the Estadio Nacional along the Vía Expresa and 28 de Julio or at the more modern Estadio Monumental Lolo Fernández in the Molina neighborhood. Games happen mostly on Wednesdays, Saturday, and Sundays, and prices and locations are published two days beforehand in the newspaper. Tickets run $3–7 and can usually be bought the same day for non-championship matches. Tickets are bought at the stadium, at Farmacia Deza (Conquistadores 1140, San Isidro, tel. 01/222-3195), and at TeleTicket counters at Wong and Metro supermarkets.

Bullfighting takes place at the Plaza de Acho (Hualgayoc 332, tel. 01/481-1467) near the center of Lima from the first week of October to the first week of December, a centuries-old tradition that coincides with Lima's biggest festival, El Señor de los Milagros. Tickets for the Sunday afternoon events range from $30–100 for a two-hour contest featuring world-class bullfighters from Spain and Peru. Tickets are also sold at Farmacio Deza and at TeleTicket counters in Wong and Metro supermarkets.

Horse races can be seen at the **Jockey Club of Peru** (Hipódromo de Monterrico, Panamericana Sur and Javier Prado, tel. 01/435-1035), where betting races are held Tuesdays, Thursdays, and weekends.

FESTIVALS

Lima's biggest festival is **El Señor de los Milagros** (The Lord of Miracles), which draws as many as a half million people on its main days of October 18 and 28 and is accompanied by bullfights at Plaza de Acho. The processions begin in central Lima at **Iglesia Las Nazarenas** (Tacna and Huancavelica), which was built atop a wall where a black slave painted an image of Christ in the 17th century. The wall was the only thing left standing after a 1755 earthquake, prompting this annual festival in October, the month when Lima's worst earthquakes have traditionally struck. To this day a brotherhood of priests of mainly African descent care for the image, which some anthropologists say is related to the pre-Hispanic cult of Pachacámac.

Other good festivals include **Lima's anniversary** on Jan. 18, the **Feast of the Crosses up San Cristóbal** on May 3, the **Feast of Santa Rosa de Lima** on Aug. 30, and **Día de la Canción Criolla** (Creole Music Day) on Oct. 30, when *peñas* hold a variety of concerts around the city.

There are a number of **Peruvian paso horse competitions** held in the Lurín Valley south of Lima that are highly recommended. These include the Peruvian Paso Horse Competition in February, a national competition in Mamacona in April, and the Amancaes competition, also in Mamacona, in July. For more information see the Spanish-only web page www.yachay.com.pe/especiales/caballos/.

Shopping

Lima is the clearinghouse for handicrafts produced in places like Huancayo and Ayacucho and sold with a considerable markup. There is a huge range, from cheap tourist-oriented items to boutique shops, but bargaining is always an option. Several American-style malls have been built in Lima, most notably the cliffside Larcomar at the end of Av. Larco and under the Parque Salazar. The largest malls in Peru, however, are Jockey Plaza (tel. 01/435-9122) on Javier Prado in Monterrico and on Avenida Marina on the way to the airport.

HANDICRAFTS

The most sophisticated range of handicrafts in Lima can found in Barranco. **Las Pallas** (Cajamarca 212, tel. 01/477-4629, 9 A.M.–7 P.M. Mon.–Sat.) is a high-end gallery with exquisite Amazon textiles, tapestries, and carved gourds from Huancayo, and colonial ceramics from Cusco. Prices run $20–600. Another good option for high-end crafts and art is **Dédalo** (Saenz Pena 295, Barranco, 477-0562, 11 A.M.–9 P.M. Tues.–Sun.). Unique art and antiques from all over the world can be found at **San Francisco Gallery of Art** (Plaza San Francisco 208, tel. 01/477-0537, 10:30 A.M.–1:30 P.M. and 3:30–7 P.M. Mon.–Sat.). Expensive gifts, including jewelery and purses, are sold in the courtyard. For Ayacucho crafts, try **Museo-Galería Popular de Ayacucho** (Pedro de Osma 116, tel. 01/246-0599). Lima's top art gallery, with works from Peru's leading painters, is **Praxis** (San Martin 689, Barranco, tel. 01/477-2822 or 01/930-130, www.praxis-art.com/Lima, 5–8 P.M. Mon.–Fri.).

The largest crafts markets are in Miraflores on blocks 52 and 54 on Petit Thouars. Market after market is filled with alpaca clothing, silver jewelery, ceramics, and textiles from all over the country. **Mercado Indio** (Petit Thouars 5245) and **Indian Market** (Petit Thouars 5321) are the best of the lot, with nicely presented stalls and wide selections. Nearby is a **Manos Peruanas** (Plaza Artesanal, Petit Thouars 5411, tel. 01/242-9726, 10:30 A.M.–7:30 P.M. daily) with a contemporary

IS YOUR ALPACA SHINY?

Few travelers to Peru return home without a fuzzy alpaca wool sweater. Because of its hollow fibers, alpaca wool is light, silky smooth, and warm. It also sheds water better than a plastic poncho, which is why Quechuan-speaking highlanders stand nonchalantly in even the most bone-chilling rainstorms.

But travelers who buy these sweaters in Lima or Cusco (for as cheap as $6 per sweater!) often don't realize what they are getting. These days most alpaca wool sweaters are commonly mixed with itchier wool from llama or even sheep. Even worse, a growing number of alpaca sweaters are made in large factories and mixed with acrylic fibers. Because the sweaters are dyed, demand for pure white alpaca fiber has soared. The amazing hues of South America's alpacas, which include shades of auburn, cinnamon, mustard and steel gray, are slowly dying out in favor of the white version.

A few tips on buying an alpaca sweater: it should feel silky between the fingertips. If it stinks when wet, then it's mixed with llama wool. If it's shiny, it's acrylic. The best test is to pinch off a few fibers and burn them. (It's worth noting, however, that it's probably not wise to be pinching and burning sweater fibers in the marketplace before you make a purchase.) If it burns and releases a pungent odor, it's the real deal. If it shrinks into a tight plastic ball, it's acrylic.

The best way to purchase an alpaca sweater is to buy them directly from highland villagers throughout Peru, who are rarely seen without a spindle, known as a *pushka*, bobbing up and down from their hands. In the United States, the most responsible merchant is Global Marketplace (www.globalmarketplace.org), a California-based organization based on fair trade principles.

Miraflores street market

line of handcrafted silver earrings, necklaces, and bracelets. Other huge, cheap crafts markets are **Feria Artesanal** on Avenida Marina on the way to the airport (every taxi knows it) or in central Lima across from Iglesia Santo Domingo, at the intersection of Camaná and Superunda.

Miraflores' other main shopping strips are the area next to Parque Kennedy that includes La Paz, Schell, and Diez Canseco streets. One of our favorite spots for unique crafts is La Floristería (La Paz 646, #20, tel. 01/444-22-88). The reasonably priced **Hecho a Mano** (Diez Canseco 298) has a high-quality selection of crafts from all parts of Peru, especially Ayacucho. Another plaza at Diez Canseco 380 is filled with jewelry shops, and a wide selection of baby alpaca sweaters can be found at Diez Canseco 378.

For a more upmarket shopping experience, visit the hugely popular **Larcomar** (Malecón de la Reserva 610, Miraflores), an elegant open-air mall dug under Miraflores' Parque Salazar and perched over the ocean. Upscale alpaca clothing stores (the finest of which is Alpaca 111), cafés, a sushi restaurant, bars, a disco, and a 12-screen cinema are just a few of the businesses here. An excellent place for high-quality jewelry, alpaca clothing, textiles, and creative gifts is **Peru Art-Crafts** (Malecón de la Reserva 610, Larcomar).

An excellent crafts markets with a cause is **La Casa de la Mujer Artesana Manuela Ramos** (Juan Pablo Fernandini 1550, 15th block of Brasil, Pueblo Libre, tel. 01/423-8840, 9 A.M.–5P.M. Mon.–Fri.). Proceeds from this market benefit women's programs across Peru.

CAMPING EQUIPMENT

If you need to buy outdoor gear, you will pay a premium in Peru and your only options are Lima, Huaraz, and Cusco. Varying qualities of white gas, or *bencina blanca,* can be bought at hardware stores across Peru, so test your stove before you depart. Gas canisters are available only at specialty outdoor stores.

Miraflores has several stores: **Alpamayo** (Larco 345, tel. 01/445-1671, 10 A.M.–8 P.M. Mon.–Sat., 50 percent SAE discount) sells tents, backpacks, sleeping mats, boots, rock shoes, climbing gear, water filters, MSR stoves, and more. Similar items are found at **Camping Center** (Benavides 1620 Miraflores, tel. 01/242-1779, 10 A.M.–7 P.M. Mon.–Fri., 10 A.M.–1 P.M. Saturday), and **Moun-**

tain **Worker** (Centro Comercial Camino Real, A-17 in basement, tel. 01/421-2175). **Todo Camping E.I.R.L.** (Angamos Oeste 350, 242-1318, 10 A.M.–8 P.M. Mon.–Sat.) also sells more technical equipment like crampons and higher-end fuel stoves.

BOOKSTORES

There are several bookstores, or *librerías*, in Miraflores with good English and other foreign language sections. **Época** (Pardo 399, tel. 01/447-2149, 10 A.M.–2 P.M. and 3–8 P.M. Mon.–Sat., 11 A.M.–2 P.M. Sunday) has a whole floor dedicated to books in English and French, and there is another location at Óvalo Guierrez. Despite its humble door, **SBS** (Angamos Oeste 301, tel. 01/241-8490, 8 A.M.–7 P.M. Mon.–Sat.) has the best collection of English-language guidebooks. **Crisol** (Santa Cruz 816, Óvalo Gutierrez, tel. 01/221-1010) is a huge, glassy bookshop in the same mall as the Cineplant Alcázar. Other options are **Zeta** (Comandante Espinar 219, tel. 01/446-5139, 10 A.M.–9 P.M. Mon.–Sat., also at Lima airport) and **Delta Bookstore Librería** (Larco 970, tel. 01/445-8825, 10 A.M.–9 P.M. Mon.–Sat., 11 A.M.–6 P.M. Sunday). International newspapers are available from Miraflores street vendors in front of Café Haiti by Parque Kennedy. The best bookstore in central Lima is **El Virrey** (Paseo los Escribanos 115, tel. 01/427-5080, 10 A.M.–1 P.M. and 1:30–7 P.M. Mon.–Sat.), which also has a store in Larcomar in Miraflores (tel. 01/445-6883, noon–9 P.M. daily) and in San Isidro (Miguel Dasso 141, tel. 01/440-0607).

Sports and Recreation

BIKING

There are great places to go mountain-biking within a few hours of Lima, including Pachacámac and the Reserva Nacional Paracas. Good bike shops include **Best Mountainbikes** (Comandante Espinar 320, Miraflores, tel. 01/263-0964, bestint@terra.com.pe). **BiciCentro** (Paseo de la República 4986, Miraflores, tel. 01/475-2645) is good for repair and services. **BikeMavil** (Aviación 4021, Surco, tel. 01/449-8435, bikemavil@terra.com.pe) rents bikes and leads excursions.

BIRD-WATCHING

Swedish ornithologist Gunnar Engblom (tel. 01/476-5016 or 01/900-7886) of the Associación ProAve Peru leads bird-watching trips to **San Pedro de Casta** and **Lomas de Lochay,** a national reserve 105 km north of Lima that protects a rare patch of Pacific coastal fog forest.

BOWLING

There are plenty of lanes at **Cosmic Bowling** (Larcomar, Malecón de la Reserva 610, Miraflores, 445-7776, 10 A.M.–1 A.M., $12/hour), which turns out the light so patrons have to use the "cosmic light" to guide their aim.

COOKING

For those familiar with Lima's culinary delights, it should come as no surprise that it hosts a cooking school licensed by Cordon Bleu (Nuñez de Balboa, Miraflores, tel. 01/242-8222, adalamau@cordonbleu.edu.pe, www.cordonbleu-peru.edu.pe). There are a variety of classes, including short-term seminars.

CRICKET

Those who play cricket or want to try should visit the Lima Cricket and Football Club (Justo Vigil 200, Magdalena del Mar, tel. 01/264-0027, cricket@terra.com.pe). You can walk in, borrow everything you need, and be of just about any caliber (including low or none) to play. Games are Sunday afternoons from January to May, and players retire afterwards to the club's English pub, which was shipped from Cornwall.

Lima

HORSEBACK RIDING

Check out **Cabalgatas** (tel. 01/221-4591, www.cabalgatas.com.pe), an option for riding Peruvian *paso* horses near Mamacona, the town where the *paso* horse competitions are held each year. They lead interesting excursions around the ceremonial center of Pachacámac.

PARAGLIDING

First-time visitors to Miraflores are shocked to see paragliders doing laps back and forth along the oceanfront bluffs, sometimes just meters above the heads of those promenading on the *malecón*. There's a professional company that takes people on tandem flights off the Miraflores cliffs, as well as the nearby towns of Lunahuaná and Paracas. Peru Fly (Jorge Chávez 658, Miraflores, tel. 01/444-5004, jose@perufly.com, www.perufly.com) also offers six-day courses.

ROCK-CLIMBING WALLS

Millennium Gym (Jr. Independencia 145, Miraflores, tel. 01/242-8557) has good rock-climbing walls, but you must become a member to climb. **Youth Hostal Malka** in San Isidro also has a rock wall.

SCUBA

There are no coral reefs on Peru's Pacific coast, but a number of agencies offer interesting dives anyway. **Peru Divers** (Huaylas 205, Chorrillos, tel. 01/251-6231, perudivers@terra.com.pe) has packages starting at $25 pp led by PADI-certified instructor Luis Rodriguez. **AguaSport** (Conquistadores 645, San Isidro, tel. 01/221-1548, aquasport1@terra.com.pe, www.divereru.com) rents all equipment for snorkeling and scuba diving. Standard scuba day trips from Lima include a 30-meter wall dive at Pucusana, an 18-meter dive to a nearby sunken ship, or diving with sea lions at Islas Palomino off Lima. Two dives are $80 or $35 if you have your own equipment.

SURFING

Lima is at the center of world-class surfing, and the best source of information is www.peruazul.com, which details the better breaks such as La Herradura in Chorrillos, Punta Hermosa, and Punta Rocas. Though the swells in front of Lima are dotted with dozens of surfers, we do not recommend surfing in these polluted waters. Head south instead to the beaches south of Lima.

For surfing classes, call Rocio Larrañaga at **Surf School** (tel. 01/264-5100 or celular tel. 01/9710-7345), who will pick you up at your hotel and lend you a wetsuit and board. If you're just looking to rent, **Centro Comercial** (Caminos del Inca Tienda 158, Surco, tel. 01/372-5106) has both surfboards and skate boards. **Big Head** (Larcomar, Malecón de la Reserva 610, 242-8123) sells new surf/body boards and wetsuits. One of the better surf shops in Peru is **Focus** (Leonardo DaVinci 208, San Borja, tel. 01/475-8459, 9 A.M.–1 P.M., 3–7 P.M. Mon.–Fri., 9 A.M.–1 P.M. Sat.). The staff is knowledgable about local suring spots and rents boards at a good price.

OFF-THE-WALL FUN

Quazer pick-up battles are available at the **Jockey Club's Daytona Park** (El Derby, Puerto 4, Hipódromo de Monterrico, Surco, tel. 01/435-6130, dp_daytona@terra.com.pe) and cost $3 for 30 minutes. Here too it is possible to go-kart around a racetrack ($1.50 for two rounds).

There is a company in Lima that operates an air-conditioned **party bus**, where people hop get on a board, drink as much as they want, and listen to live performers—all for $20. The bus travels from Miraflores to Plaza Mayor in central Lima and then takes passengers to the popular Barranco peña La Candelaria (entry included). The company is **Bus Parrandero** (330 Benavides, Suite 1, Miraflores, tel. 01/445-4655, informaciones@busparrandero.com, www.busparrandero.com).

SIGHTSEEING TOURS

Do not get hustled by agency reps at Lima's airport or bus stations. They will arrange travel packages that tend to be as expensive as, or more expensive than, if you were to do it on your own.

Many of the recommended agencies below sell tours run by **Lima Vision** (Chiclayo 444, Miraflores, tel. 01/810-2110, 24 hours, limavisi@limavision.com, www.limavision.com), the city's standard pool service that offers three- to four-hour daily tours of Lima's center ($20), museums ($30), Pachacámac ($35), Museo de Oro ($25), or a full-day city tour with lunch ($70). Whether you buy from Lima Vision or from an agency, the cost is the same. All of Peru's main agencies are based in Lima. For a complete list, see the *Know Peru* section.

Our favorite travel agency in Lima is **Fertur Peru,** run by the enterprising Siduith Ferrer with offices in Miraflores (Schell 485, tel. 01/445-1974, 8:30 A.M.–8 P.M. Mon.–Sat.) and central Lima at the Plaza Mayor (Junin 211, tel. 01/426-0188, same hours). It can buy a variety of bus and plane tickets and set up tours around Lima and day tours to see Paracas or the Nasca Lines.

Peru's most reputable agency, with decades in business, is **Lima Tours,** with offices in central Lima (Belén 1040, tel. 01/424-5110, www.limatours.com.pe) and San Isidro (Pardo y Aliaga 698). Its city tours have exclusive access to the pristine 17th-century mansion Casa de Aliaga.

A good agency for booking flights and other logistics is **Nuevo Mundo,** with offices in the center (Camaná 782, tel. 01/427-0635), Miraflores (Jorge Chavez 225), and San Isidro (28 de Julio 1120, tel. 01/610-8080).

Reputable agencies in Miraflores include **Exprinter** (Pardo 384, tel. 01/444-5350) and **Carlson Wagonlit Travel** (Ricardo Palma 355, tel. 01/242-0080 or 01/447-5520).

Another good agency in central Lima for tours and tickets is **Roma Tours** (Ica 326, tel. 01/427-7576, resroma@terra.com.pe, www.hostalroma.8m.com) run by Dante Reyes, the owner of the excellent Hostal Roma.

A final option for day tours in Lima is **Peru Smile** (tel. 01/997-1349, perusmile@yahoo.com), which is run by Jorge Fernández and has tours and prices similar to Lima Vision (but without the large groups).

Lone Wolf Adventures (José Santos Chocano 128, #201, San Borja, tel. 01/970-46849, tours@lonewolfadventure.com, www.lonewolfadventure.com) offers two-day camping trips to Marcahuasi. **Alta Ruta 4x4** (Javier Prado Este block 54, at Los Frutales, tel. 01/436-6740) charges $50 pp per day for four-wheel-drive trips around Lima. It also has maps and routes for those with their own vehicle.

For those who can't make it to Paracas, **Ecocruceros** (Arequipa 4960, tel. 01/910-8396, ecocruceros@infonegocio.com.pe) offers half-day boat tours from the port of Callao to see sea lions at the Islas Palomino.

A range of creating walking and bicycle tours around Miraflores, including haunted houses of Lima, will be offered by Ramiro Garay at **Home Peru** (see *Accommodations,* Arequipa 4501, tel. 01/241-9898, www.homeperu.com). Another option for walking tours around Miraflores is the language school **El Sol** (Grimaldo del Solar 469, tel. 01/242-7763).

Private guides for day tours of Lima are also available for those with special interests or with an aversion to groups. Recommended and certified private tour guides are **Tino Guzmán Khan** (tel. 01/429-5779, tinogpc@yahoo.com), who speaks English, Chinese, and French, and **Cecilia Paredes** (tel. 01/475-3829), who speaks English, Spanish, and Italian. If you are just looking for a driver, see *Getting Around.*

Accommodations

You should stay in the center of Lima if you are comfortable in rough cities and interested in understanding the city's colonial center. Considering their charm, central Lima's best backpacker hostels are excellent values and can be perfectly safe for travelers who take reasonable precautions. The neighborhood of Breña is a more peaceful alternative to the center that is close to the Museo de Arte and a 10-minute walk to the edge of old town. Pueblo Libre, only a 10-minute taxi ride to the center, has a charming small-town feel for those who are uncomfortable with city life and want to get off the beaten track.

Perched on the oceanside and teeming with good restaurants and bars, Miraflores draws the lion's share of travelers with its excellent hotels and restaurants in all categories. San Isidro, Lima's aristocratic business district, has most of the city's five-star hotels and is worlds away (though only 10 minutes by taxi) from funky and bohemian Barranco. There are excellent budget options in oceanside Barranco, along with the city's best nightlife and shopping.

CENTRAL LIMA
Under $10

The best budget option in downtown Lima is **M Hostal España** (Azángaro 105, tel. 01/428-5546, hotel_espana@hotmail.com, www.hotelespanaperu.com, $6 s, $9 d, rooms with private baths $4 extra) This backpacker's classic of a hostel is a labyrinth of tight halls and patios, decorated with hanging ivy, marble busts, and reproductions of colonial paintings. The rooms are small and basic with clean, shared bathrooms and hot water. The strength of this place is that it is a peaceful compound disconnected from the hustle and bustle of the center. It has a safe feel and charming upstairs restaurant and Internet station. Make reservations early. A lesser option next door is **Hostal San Francisco** (Azángaro 127, tel. 01/426-2735, hostal_san_francisco@terramail.com.pe, tel. 01/426-2735), which has large and undecorated rooms with tile floors,

quirky bedspreads, and foam beds. All rooms have shared baths.

In Breña, the friendly **Hostal Iquique** (Iquique 758, tel. 01/433-4724, hiquique@terra.com.pe, $7 s, $9 d, rooms with private baths $4 extra) is a longtime backpackers' favorite with good service, shared bathrooms, kitchen, rooftop terrace, and hot water. Rooms with red-tiled floors are not too noisy and some even have TVs.

$10–25

The charming **M Hostal Roma** (Ica 326, tel. 01/427-7576, resroma@terra.com.pe, www.hostalroma.8m.com, $16 s, $25 d, including breakfast) is a charming, elegant place catering to backpackers. Huge ceilings, wood floors, and 10 different types of breakfast make it stand out from the rest. Internet, safety boxes, and airport transfers are available. A small café is attached that serves espresso, beer, and cocktails. The 36 rooms here fill up fast, so make reservations early.

The **Plaza Francia Inn** (Rufino Torrico 1117, Center, tel. 01/330-6080, franciasquareinn@yahoo.com, www.incacountry.com.pe, $11 s, $14 d) is a friendly place with clean rooms run by the owners of Posada del Parque. Dorm rooms are available for $7 pp and airport pickup is available.

In Breña, **M Hostal de Las Artes** (Chota 1460, tel. 01/433-0031, artes@terra.com.pe, http://arteswelcom.tripod.com/, $8 s, $14 d) is a clean, well-managed, gay-friendly place with Dutch owners. Sevillean tiles line the entrance off a quiet street that is a 10-minutes walk from Plaza San Martín. Rooms are simple with white-washed walls, dark wood, comfy beds, and near silence, which is hard to find in the center. There are a number of good restaurants down the street.

$25–50

The two hotels in this price category in old town have more comforts but lack the charm of the backpacker hostels. The new **Hostal Bonbini** (Cailloma 209, tel. 01/427-6492, $30 s, $40 d) has large rooms with blackout curtains, cable TV, radio, and new bathrooms. Avoid noisy rooms on street front. **Hotel Kamaná** (Camaná 547, tel. 01/427-7106, reservas@hotelkamana.com, www.hotelkamana.com, $37 s, $46 d, including breakfast) is safe, well-operated, includes a 24-hour snack bar, and has quiet back rooms.

South of central Lima but near the Museo de Arte is the recommended **Posada del Parque** (Parque Hernán Velarde 60, tel. 01/433-2412, posada@incacountry.com.pe, www.incacountry.com.pe, $27 s, $33 d). The English-speaking couple also run the Plaza Francia Inn and have created here a quiet escape from the city with clean rooms with cable TV, nice art, and airport transfer.

$50–100

The only five-star hotel in central Lima is the **Hotel Sheraton** (Paseo de la República 170, tel. 01/315-5000, www.sheraton.com, reservas@sheraton.com.pe, $170 s, $185 d), a square tower that rises at the entrance to old town. This dated busines hotel has a huge open atrium rising 19 floors. The normal rooms have older furniture and feel four-star-ish. If you stay here, upgrade to the tower rooms on the upper floors, which have easy chair, California king–sized beds, elegant wood floors and paneling, all the other five-star comforts, and astounding views over Lima. Other services include Jacuzzi, sauna, gym, and ground-floor casino. Prices at this hotel get as low as $83 if you bargain, making this Lima's cheapest five-star by far.

Keep your eyes peeled for the re-opening of the **Hotel Gran Bolívar** (Unión 958, tel. 01/428-7672, bolivar@terra.com.pe), Lima's classic 1920s hotel on the Plaza San Martín. Poor managment and lack of capital recently led this hotel to close down. But it was, and probably will be in the future, a lodging option for those who want to stay in antique suites and sip Lima's best pisco sour under a stained-glass atrium.

MIRAFLORES

Along with San Isidro, Miraflores is one of Lima's upscale districts, with the city's best range of shopping and restaurants. You are also a 10-minute cab ride to nightlife action further down the coast at Barranco. The closer you are to Miraflores' center, the less walking and cabbing you will do.

Under $10

A great place for budget travelers is **Explorer's House** (Alfredo León 158, tel. 01/241-5002, explorers_house@yahoo.es, $5 dorm includes breakfast) with shared dormitory rooms, a common kitchen, and TV room with a video library. Communal baths are clean, and laundry is $1/kilo.

Casa del Mochilero (Cesareo Chacaltana 130A, second flr., tel. 01/444-9089, pilaryv@hotmail.com, $4 pp) is a clean and plain backpackers' hangout, about 10 minutes' walk from Parque Kennedy, with bunk rooms, shared bathrooms, and group kitchen. Mochilero's Inn is a lesser, though similarly priced, knockoff down the street.

Shared bunk rooms are also available at **Friend's House** (Manco Capac 368, tel. 01/446-6248, $5 dorm), which has a small TV room and a shared kitchen. Rooms are a bit dull and communal baths are small, but the central location is ideal.

$10–25

One of the best places in town to meet other travelers is **⋈ Home Peru** (Arequipa 4501, tel. 01/241-9898, mail@homeperu.com, www.homeperu.com, $11 dorm, includes breakfast), a restored colonial mansion five blocks from Miraflores' Parque Kennedy. Spacious, sunny wood-floored rooms have comfortable bunk beds and new shared baths with hot water. There is a nice room on the ground floor with cable TV, free Internet, inexpensive laundry, shared kitchen, and a charming open-air dining area where breakfasts are served in the mornings, The owner, Ramiro Garay, is a gold mine of information about Peru's restaurants and nightlife and leads a variety of interesting walks around Lima.

It doesn't get more secure than at **The Witches' Guest House** (Bolognesi 364, tel. 01/446-7722, gizik@hotmail.com, $5 dorm, $11 d), an old house tucked away behind fortress-like walls. As the name implies, the atmosphere here is slightly spooky, with huge, high-ceilinged bunk rooms with clean, shared baths.

Flying Dog Hospedaje (Diez Canseco 117,

tel. 01/445-0940, flyingdog@mixmail.com, $9 dorm, $20 d, including breakfast) offers tight dormitory rooms as well as private rooms with or without private baths. The atmosphere here is cheerful, with casual sitting rooms and clean bathrooms and lots of hot water.

The upside of **Imperial Inn Hostal** (Bolognesi 641, tel. 01/445-2504, imperialinn@terra.com, $12 s, $15 d, plus $5 with cable TV) is value: two blocks from the oceanfront and private rooms with bathrooms. The downside is the dated decor.

Hostelling International (Casmiro Ulloa 328, tel. 01/446-5488, hostell@terra.com.pe, www.limahostell.com.pe, $10.50 s, $21 d) has a variety of rooms spread out in an old home with sunny courtyard that is a 10-minute walk to Parque Kennedy. There is a travel agency in the lobby.

$25–50

The charming **ⴹ Hostal El Patio** (Diez Canseco 341, tel. 01/444-2107, hostalelpatio@qnet.com.pe, www.andix.com/hostalelpatio/espanol, $30 s, $35 d, including breakfast) is a memorable colonial building overflowing with plants and flowers and cheerfully painted walls. Large rooms have sautillo-tiled floors, nice furnishings, and wood balconies. Ask for a mini-suite for an additional $5—you'll get your money's worth with a mini-kitchen. Rooms are interspersed with terraces, which are great places for reading or sun-bathing.

The brand-new **El Faro Inn** (Francia 857, tel. 01/242-0339, $32 s, $34 d, including breakfast) is a modern hotel one block from the oceanfront. Small rooms are carpeted, with cable TV, OK furnishings, and other amenities, include cheap Internet and laundry and a rooftop terrace. Also one block from the oceanfront is **Hostal Torre Blanca** (José Pardo 1453, tel. 01/242-1876, hostal@torreblancaperu.com, www.torreblancaperu.com, $35 s, $45 d, including breakfast), which offers large carpeted rooms with cable TV and mini-fridge. There is free Internet and airport transfer.

$50–100

Our favorite upscale hotel in Lima is the charming **ⴹ Hotel Antigua Miraflores** (Grau 350, tel. 01/241-6166, hantigua@amauta.rcp.net.pe,

www.antiguamiraflores.com, $64 s, $74 d, including breakfast). This turn-of-the-century mansion has all the comforts of a fine hotel and the warmth and charm of a bed-and-breakfast. The rooms are large, cozy, and handsomely decorated with hand-carved furniture, local art, and warm colors (did we mention the new bathrooms with huge tubs?). There are plush couches in the downstairs sitting room, and breakfast is served in a sunny, black-and-white-tiled café decorated with iron furniture. It is worth paying another $10 for a room in the old part of the house, and suites are also available with kitchens and Jacuzzis.

Hotel Colonial Inn (Espinar 310, tel. 01/241-7471, coloinn@terra.com.pe, www.hotelcolonialinn.com, $59 s, $70 d) is a mix of old and new, with antique furnishings and a modern restaurant addition. Rooms have writing tables, cable TV, mini-fridges, and large bathrooms. The hotel seems slightly overpriced with a less-than-ideal location on a busy street. The new, upscale **Casa Andina** (28 de Julio 1088, tel. 01/241-4050, ventas@casa-andina.com, www.casa-andina.com, $50 s, $60 d, including breakfast) is also on a busy street but is a good value. The carpeted rooms are comfortable, with huge bathrooms with large tubs, cable TV, mini-fridges, A/C, and comfortable beds.

Over $100

Most of the five-star hotels are in San Isidro, but Lima's best is **ⴹ Miraflores Park Hotel** (Malecón de la Reserva 1035, tel. 01/610-4000, mirapark@peruorientexpress.com.pe, www.mirapark.com, $295 s, $295 d). This elegant glass highrise, located on a park overlooking the ocean, offers the best in service, comfort, and views in Lima. The grand marble entry is decorated with antique furnishings that are complemented by modern art. The luxurious rooms offer ocean views, elegant furnishings, cable TV with VHS, fax machines, and cable Internet connection. Other amenities include video library, massage ($40), swimming pool, and squash court.

The brand-new **Marriott** (Malecón de la Reserva 615, tel. 01/217-7000, www.marriotthotels.com/limdt, $175 s, $190 d) occupies prime real estate overlooking the Pacific Ocean and just across the street from the deluxe, full-service Larcomar mall. The rooms live up to five-star Marriott quality and are nearly silent despite the street below. For the best view, ask for a room on one of the upper floors with ocean view. Perks include glassy bars and restaurants, casino, pool, and tennis court.

SAN ISIDRO

$10–25

The bulk of San Isidro's hotels are oriented toward high-class business travelers, but there are some exceptions to this rule. **Youth Hostal Malka** (Los Lirios 165, San Isidro, tel. 01/442-0162, hostelmalka@terra.com.pe, www.youthhostelperu.com, $6 s, $12 d) is a rare find with its own rock climbing wall. This converted home has simple, clean bunk rooms, Internet, laundry service, a grassy yard with a ping-pong table, and a common room with cable TV. There are a few private rooms available for an extra $3, and a supermarket and a few restaurants are down the street.

Samay Wasi (Conquistadores 1054, San Isidro, tel. 01/422-7059, info@samaywasiperu.com, $10 s, $20 d) is a converted home on the busy Conquistadores street that is at the foot of San Isidro's restaurant alley. Rooms are slightly dark and noisy, but the place is safe, the owner speaks flawless English, and each room has its own lockers.

$50–100

Aparthotel San Martín (San Martín 598, tel. 01/242-0500, antonio@sanmartinaparthotel.com.pe, www.sanmartinhotel.com, $70 a night, $60 if more than three nights) is an excellent value. It offers a spacious suites with living room, double bedroom, closet, bathroom, kitchen, cable TV, and phone. There are beds for two people and a pull-out couch for two more, and the establishment is gay-friendly.

Another apartment option in San Isidro, with a minimum stay of 15 days, is **Loft** (Jorge Basadre 255, of. 202, tel. 01/222-8983, loftapar@terra.com.pe, www.loftapar.com). Rates start at $400 a month for these luxurious, fully equipped one-, two-, and three-bedroom apartments.

Over $100

At the top of El Olívar, a park shaded by ancient olive trees, **Sonesta Posadas del Inca** (Pancho Fierro 194, San Isidro, tel. 01/221-2121, www.sonesta.com, $138 s, $138 d, including breakfast) has spacious though quite ordinary rooms, a beautiful sitting area with bar, and a rooftop pool. Ask for the rooms with views over the olive grove.

Built in 1927, the elegant **Country Club Lima Hotel** (Los Eucaliptos 590, San Isidro, country@hotelcountry.com, www.hotelcountry.com, $150 s, $165 d, including breakfast) has an elegant, turn-of-the-century charm. Couches fill a marble lobby decorated with Oriental rugs, dark wood, and high windows. Perks include an elegant restaurant, English-style pub, gymnasium,, and pool. Ask for a room with a balcony or view over the golf course, which is near-impossible to play on unless you know a member.

Los Delfines (Los Eucaliptos 555, San Isidro, tel. 01/215-7000, reservas@losdelfineshotel.com.pe, www.losdelfineshotel.com, $145 s, $145 d) with a pool full of leaping dolphins, was an extravagant concept from the go-go Fujimori years. But guests eating breakfast or having a drink at the bar seem to love the dolphins, which by the way seem well cared for. The comfortable rooms feel completely brand-new and are decked out with dark green carpets, elegant tables, and huge bathrooms. There is a casino, luxurious outdoor pool, spa with massages, aerobics room, sauna, and Jacuzzi, and the restaurant serves first-class Mediterranean food. Now that's luxury.

Like its sister hotels around the country, **M Hotel Libertador Lima** (Los Eucaliptos 550, San Isidro, tel. 01/421-6666 or in North America 800/537-8483, hotel@libertador.com.pe, www.libertador.com.pe, $166 s, $166 d, including breakfast) is an elegant, classy act. These five-star rooms are a great value, with dark-stained furniture, elegant carpets, golf course views, and all the creature comforts, including luxurious bathrooms with tubs. There is a elegant pub downstairs with lots of wood and an excellent restaurant, the Ostrich House, that serves up ostrich and other types of delicious steaks. There is also a sauna and gymnasium.

Sandwiched between the Camino Real Mall and a glassy office park, **Swissôtel** (Via Central 150, San Isidro, tel. 01/421-4400, in North America 800/637-9477, reservations.lima@swissotel.com, www.swissotel-lima.com, $261 s, $261 d, including breakfast) is one of Peru's leading business hotels, owned by Raffles International. All rooms have king-sized beds, down comforters, large bathrooms with tubs, ISDN lines, and ocean views. Each floor has its own security card. There are also both Swiss and Italian restaurants, an elegant swimming pool surrounded by grassy lawn, a tennis court, a Jacuzzi, a sauna, and a gym.

BARRANCO
$10–25
Ν The Point (Malecón Junin 300, tel. 01/247-7997, the_point_barranco@hotmail.com, www.thepointhostel.com, $7 pp, includes breakfast) is a fun-loving, new backpacker option with everything a traveler needs: Internet, long-distance calling, sitting room with cable TV, nice bunk beds with shared bathrooms, cheap lunches, pool table, sauna, book exchange, travel agency, a grassy lawn, and an outdoor bar. This restored Republican-era house is just paces away from Barranco's best bars and sweeping ocean views. There are frequent barbecues and Monday night outings to the local jazz bar, La Noche.

Ν Mochilero's Backpackers Hostel (Pedro de Osma 135, tel. 01/477-4506, backpacker@amauta.rcp.net.pe, www.backpackersperu.com, $10 pp, $25 d, including breakfast) is also a restored Republican home with large dormitory rooms. Considering the six-meter ceilings, the bunk beds have plenty of headroom, though there are also private double rooms. The shared bathrooms are large and clean, and the sitting rooms have cheerful, brightly painted walls. Other amenities include safety lockers and boxes for each guest, and a group kitchen. The hostel has a loud, but good, bar.

Backpackers Inn (Malecón Castilla 260, tel. 01/247-3709, backpackersinnperu@hotmail.com, $9 pp, includes breakfast) is a newly reovated old

home with views over the ocean. There are a range of rooms, including some with only two beds.

Another great option in this price range is the student special at **La Villa Barranquina** (Martinez de Pinillos 129, tel. 01/477-0772, luersa@ascinsa.com.pe, $10 students, $50 s, $60 d, including breakfast).

D'Osma Alojamiento (Pedro de Osma 135, tel. 01/251-4178, deosma@ec-red.com, $10 pp, including breakfast, SAE discount) is a great option if you are looking for a tranquil, family-oriented environment.

$25–50
On a quiet, tree-lined street by the water, **Hostel Domeyer** (Domeyer 296, tel. 01/247-1413, domeyerhostel@peru.com, www.page.to/domeyerhostel, $25 s, $35 d, including breakfast, 15 percent SAE discount) has an enchanting entrance with bright colors, fish tanks, and Japanese decorations. The rooms are a bit of a let-down, with musty carpet and cheap furnishing, though there is cable TV and 24-hour beverage service. It's gay friendly.

$50–100
La Villa Barranquina (Martinez de Pinillos 129, tel. 01/477-0772, luersa@ascinsa.com.pe, $10 students, $50 s, $60 d, including breakfast) is a 1906 home with two-floor mini-apartments featuring queen-sized beds, two pull-out couches, kitchenette, cable TV, and sound system. There is a large bar and restaurant in the basement, and laundry service is available. These apartments, which are big enough for four people, are a great deal for groups. Discounts are available for week stays.

PUEBLO LIBRE
The artist-owned **Guest House Marfil** (Parque Ayacucho 126, Pueblo Libre, tel. 01/463-3161, casamarfil@yahoo.com, $6 s, $12 d) is a converted house with splashes of color, lots of paintings on the walls, and three resident cats. The bohemian rooms are private (instead of bunks), making this a great value, and the shared baths are clean and gushing with hot water. There are two

Internet stations, group kitchen, and banks and supermarkets nearby. This place is a good bet for discounted, longer-term stays.

Smack dab on the tranquil and refined Plaza Bolívar, **El Museo Inn** (Plaza Bolívar 137, Pueblo Libre, tel. 01/460-3117, elmuseo@starmedia.com,

$12 s, $20 d, including breakfast) is a small converted home. The private rooms have their own bathrooms, yellow-tiled floors, and foam beds and are quiet. There are several café and restaurant options nearby, not to mention two of the city's better museums.

Food

Peruvian cuisine has an extraordinary palate of flavors and ingredients, and nowhere is that more evident in all of Peru than Lima. The range of high-quality, and surprisingly affordable, restaurants is extraordinary, from sumptuous seafood prepared as only Peruvians know how to all the flavors of European and Asian cuisine with a creole twist. The best lunch deal is always the fixed-price lunch meals, *menús,* which typically include three well-prepared courses. Upscale restaurants tack on a 10 percent service charge and an 18 percent value-added tax.

The center has good budget eateries, including some of the best *chifa* (Chinese-Peruvian) in town. But the best restaurants are in Miraflores and San Isidro, where dozens of Cordon Bleu chefs are kept busy catering to their refined Lima clientele.

CENTRAL LIMA

Central Lima's restaurants are spread around the center, except for a cluster around the pleasant pedestrian streets of Los Escribanos and Pasaje Santa Rosa, which are just off the Plaza Mayor. Be safe and take a taxi after 9 P.M.

Cafés and Desserts

Sandwiches and salads, as well as truffles, cakes, and mousses, are available at **Cocolat Café** (Los Escribanos 121, tel. 01/427-4471, $4), located in the pedestrian restaurant row just off the Plaza Mayor. Nearby is the historic **El Cordano** (Ancash 202, tel. 01/427-0181, 8 A.M.–9 P.M.), a century-old establishment that was a favored haunt of writers and intellectuals. Though a bit tattered, this is an excellent place to come for a $2 pisco sour.

Peruvian

OK, it is a chain, but **Pardo's** (Psj. Santa Rosa 153, tel. 01/427-2278, $3.50) still serves the best spit-roasted chicken, with affordable lunch menus and open-air tables right off the Plaza Mayor. It also serves *anticuchos,* brochettes, and *chicharrón.*

For budget travelers, **Pachamanca** (Ancash 400, tel. 01/428-7920, 8:30 A.M.–11 P.M., $2) is a classy, well-run, gay-friendly place with a cheap three-course menú and good cocktails in the evening. Another good place to sample creole cooking down the street is **San Pablo** (Ancash 454, tel. 01/427-5681, 6 P.M.–midnight), which also serves pastas, pizzas, fish, and seafood.

A brand-new and more upscale spot is **Los Virtrales de Gemma** (Ucayali 332, tel. 01/426-7796, $5), in a restored colonial home one block from the Plaza Mayor. The hard-working owners have created an excellent and varied Peruvian menu.

Though a bit faded from its past glory, **L'Eau Vive** (Ucayali 370, tel. 01/427-5612, 12:30–3 P.M. and 7:30–9:30 P.M. Mon.–Sat, $5) still serves up wholesome and delicious lunch *menús* prepared by a French order of nuns. Dinners feature cocktails, large wine list, and an eclectic selection of international entrées.

In Breña, **La Choza Náutica** (Breña 204, off first block of Arica, tel. 01/423-8087, 11 A.M.–1 A.M., $5), is a former hole-in-the-wall *cebichería* that has become more upscale and successful over the years. It serves a variety of special *cebiches* (including an *erotic* version) and *tiraditos* in huge portions. Around the corner are two Peruvian restaurants, though Azato is not as good as **Likos** (Arica 284, 10 A.M.–11 P.M. daily, $3–6), a 1950s-era joint with a $2 lunch menu and generous portions of *lomo saltado.*

International

The pedestrian alley that runs from the Plaza Mayor opposite the cathedral is lined with good restaurants. **San Remo** (Los Escribanos 137, tel. 01/427-9102, 9 A.M.–9 P.M. Mon.–Sat., 9 A.M.–4 P.M. Sunday, $6) is an upscale place serving good pasta, meats, and fish. It also has a daily lunch menú. Across the street is **Bohemia** (Los Escribanos 148, tel. 01/427-5537, $7), the twin of the San Isidro restaurant, with an upscale ambience and a large menu of local and international foods.

Chileans are not normally known for their haute cuisine, but **El Rincón Chileno** (Camaná 228, tel. 01/428-8640, 10 A.M.–3 P.M. Mon.–Sat., 9 A.M.–4 P.M. Sunday, $2) makes up for lost cooking with an excellent menu of Chilean empanadas, *pastel de choclo* (a delicious blend of meat, chicken, and corn), and a good selection of the country's famous wines. There is a highly recommended and affordable $2 lunch *menú*.

Chifa

When in central Lima, do not miss the opportunity to sample *chifa* (Chinese-Peruvian cuisine) at one of the largest China Towns in South America. There are at least a dozen places spread along the town's two main streets, Capón and Paruro. The best of Lima's China Town is **Wa Lok** (Jiron Paruro 864, tel. 01/427-2656, 9 A.M.–11 P.M. daily, $10) serving more than 20 types of dim sum. Try *Ja Kao dim sum,* a mixture of pork and shrimp with rice, or *Siu Mai de Chanco,* shredded pork with mushroom and egg pasta. A good, less expensive alternative to Wa Loc is **Salon Capon** (Paruro 819, tel. 01/426-9286, 9 A.M.–11 P.M. Mon.–Sat., 9 A.M.–8 P.M. Sunday, $5–8), serving Peking duck, *Langostinos Szechuan* (sauteed shrimps with *ají*), and *Chuleta Kin Tou* (grilled sweet pork).

Health Food

A small but popular vegetarian restaurant, **Natur** (Moquegua 132, tel. 01/427-8281, 8 A.M.–9 P.M. Mon.–Sat., 10 A.M.–5 P.M. Sunday) is also a health food store with local herbs and remedies. Fresh vegetables, salads, yogurts, veggie burgers, and soy meats are on the menu, which also caters to vegans.

The Hare Krishna–operated **Govinda** (Callao 480, tel. 01/426-1956, 9:30 A.M.–9 P.M. Mon.–Sat.), the country's tried-and-true vegetarian chain, has a varied, inventive menu with pizzas, sandwiches, yogurts, and veggie Chinese food.

MIRAFLORES

Even if you are on a limited budget, splurging on one of Miraflores' top restaurants will be memorable experience you will not regret.

Cafés and Desserts

One of Lima's classic cafés is surely **Haiti** (Diagonal 160, tel. 01/446-3816, 7 A.M.–2 A.M. Sun.–Thurs., 7 A.M.–3 A.M. Fri.–Sat., $7), in operation for half a century on Parque Kennedy. Indoor and sidewalk tables are overflowing with Peruvians day and night, and catered to by hustling, tuxedo-wearing waiters. Haiti is less known for its food than as a hub of intellectual conversation with good coffee and, most important, pisco sour. Right across the street is **M La Tiendecita Blanca** (Larco 111, tel. 01/445-1412, 7 A.M.–midnight daily, $9), an elegant Swiss-style café and deli that has been in business since 1937. Anything you eat here will be excellent. This is Miraflores' most happening business breakfast spot, and steamy fondues emerge from the kitchen in the evenings.

Nearby is more youthful, trendy **M Café Café** (Mártir Olaya 250, tel. 01/445-1165, 8:30 A.M.–1 A.M. Sun.–Thurs., 8:30 A.M.–3 A.M. Fri.–Sat., $4–8), an American-style coffeehouse with a huge menu of well-prepared salads, sandwiches, and desserts. Dinner options range from chicken curry to the *lomo saltado,* though many people come here to lounge at the coffee bar or read in this thoroughly relaxed atmosphere.

Dalmacia (San Fernando 401, tel. 01/445-7917, 8 A.M.–2 A.M. Mon.–Sat., 9 A.M.–9 P.M. Sunday) is an elegant café serving affordable Mediterranean and Peruvian food as well as a range of quiches, empanadas, and Spanish tortillas. For dessert, try an espresso and a tiramisu, cheesecake, or apple pie.

Dove Vai (Ovalo Benavides 228, tel. 01/241-8763, 8:30 A.M.–1 A.M. daily) serves up scoops of delicious gelato on the Parque Kennedy, though Limenos say **4D** (Angamos Oeste 408, tel. 01/447-1523) has the best ice cream and gelato in Lima.

San Antonio (Vasco Núñez de Balboa 762, tel. 01/241-3001, 7 A.M.–11 P.M. daily) is a bakery/café/deli with 35 gourmet sandwiches (including smoked salmon and Italian salami), huge salads with organic lettuce, and an extensive dessert case with an out-of-this-world *tortaleta de lúcuma.*

Peruvian Seafood

Budget eaters flock to **Ñ Rincón Chami** (Esperanza 154, tel. 01/444-4511, 8 A.M.–9 P.M. Mon.–Sat., noon–5 P.M. Sunday, $4) for *cebiche,* tamales, *brochetas,* and **lomo saltados,** dished up in a diner-like atmosphere. Each day there is a different special of the house (Sunday, for instance, is *chupe de camarones,* a cream-based soup with sea shrimp).

An upscale *cebicheria,* **Ñ Alfresco** (Malecón Balta 790, tel. 01/444-7962, 9 A.M.–5 P.M. daily, $8) serves grilled shrimp, clams, and a special *cebiche alfresco* with three sauces. This stylish place also serves tempting desserts such as *crocante de lúcuma* and *suspiro de Limeña* and international wines. With an upscale menu and refined atmosphere, **Franceso** (Malecón de la Marina 526, tel. 01/442-8255, noon–5 P.M., $7–15), caters to an expat and business lunch crowd with grilled *lenguado, cebiche,* and steamed *camarones.*

International

La Trattoria di Mambrino (Manuel Bonilla 106, tel. 01/446-1192, 1–3:30 P.M. and 8:30–11:30 P.M. Mon.–Sat., 1–3:30 P.M. Sunday, $8–12) is owned by a Roman and may be Peru's best Italian restaurant. This cozy place serves authentic Italian dishes like gnocchi with pesto genovese, risotto with wild mushrooms, pan-fried shrimp with wine sauce, and porcini mushroom pizza.

For Middle Eastern food found nowhere else in Peru, stop in at the new **Ñ Café Lashesh** (Benavides 358, tel. 01/242-5394, 9 A.M.–noon Mon.–Fri., 9 A.M.–1 A.M. Sat.–Sun., $2) with sidewalk tables across from Parque Kennedy. Lamb kababs, Greek salads, tabouli, and falafel are prepared fresh for incredibly cheap prices. Don't miss the lúcuma juice.

Located at Larcomar mall, **Makoto** (Malecón de la Reserva 610, tel. 01/444-5030, 11 A.M.–7 P.M. Mon.–Sat., 11 A.M.–3 P.M. Sunday, $15) is an excellent sushi restaurant with high prices. The chef here owns his own lunch-only restaurant on Alejandro Iglesias 580 where sushi is half the price.

Near Plaza Bolognesi, **La Carbonara** (Grau 400, tel. 01/241-7210, 12:45–4 P.M. and 7:45 P.M.–midnight, $5) serves excellent pizzas, calzones, lasagnas, pastas, and salads in a charming, cozy trattoria.

No country does steaks like Argentina does, and that is why **La Tranquera** (Pardo 285, tel. 01/447-5111, $8–13) has been in business for three decades. There are a range of other meats on the menu as well, including rabbit, lamb, and *cuy.*

Mexican

Tex-Mex is near-impossible to find in Peru but there is plenty of it at **Sí Señor** (Bolognesi 706, tel. 01/445-3789, evenings only, $6–10), which also has a good selection of Mexican beers and tequilas.

Health Food

Miraflores' best vegetarian restaurant is **Govinda** (Schell 634, tel. 01/444-2871, 10:30 A.M.–8 P.M. Mon.–Sat., 11 A.M.–4:30 P.M. Sunday, $2.50). The creative dishes of this Hare Krishna–operated restaurant include pad thai, Asian tofu salad, and *lomo saltado* with soy meat.

Fine Dining

Our vote for best restaurant in Peru is **Ñ Astrid y Gastón** (Cantuarias 175, tel. 01/444-1496, 1–3 P.M. and 7:30–11:30 P.M. Mon.–Sat., $13–20). This adventurous gourmet restaurant, set in an elegant Republican home, is the labor of love of a Peruvian-German couple who met at the Cordon Bleu in Paris. The evening begins with creative pisco drinks such as the aguaymanto sour, made with *pisco puro* and juice of the tangy aguaymanto fruit. Then, as diners watch through a glass wall, chefs concoct never-before-sampled entrées such as kid goat basted in algorroba honey and marinated in *chica de jorra,* or river prawns served with red curry, coconut milk, and jasmine rice. Save room because the desserts are the best part: *blanco mousse* with a sauce of *sauco* and blackberries, *crocante de crème broulée,* or light mango ravioli flavored with maracuya creme and topped with homemade crunchy praline ice cream. The menu changes constantly, based on the new experiments of Gastón and the vivacious Astrid, who makes a point of visiting everyone's table mid-way through the meal.

You will not regret the cab ride to ℕ **Pescados Capitales** (La Mar 1337, tel. 01/421-8808, 12:30–5 P.M. Tues.–Sun., $8), a witty play on words (*pescados* means fish but rhymes with *pecados,* or sins) that makes sense when you see the menu. Each dish is named for a virtue or sin; *Diligence* will bring you a *cebiche* of tuna and *conchas negras,* while *Patience* will bring you a *cebiche* of shrimps with curry and mango chutney, and *Vanity* fortunately will bring you grilled salmon with a meunière sauce over risotto. If you're not done sinning, you might get a cheescake smothered in a delicate *sauco* sauce.

The elegant ℕ **Huaca Pucllana** (General Borgoño block 8, tel. 01/445-4042, noon–4 P.M. and 7 P.M.–midnight Mon.–Sat., $7–22) has a magical feel when the ruins of the same name, only six meters away, are lit up at night. Guests sit at linen-covered tables on an open-air patio next to the ruins and enjoy dishes such as grilled portobello mushroom salad with goat cheese, rabbit stewed in a red wine, mushroom sauce over polenta, and grilled lambchops.

If you're in the mood for Mediterranean, head to ℕ **La Gloria** (Atahualpa 201, tel. 01/446-6504, 1–4 P.M. and 8 P.M.–midnight Mon.–Sat., $11). Especially good are the *carpaccio de pescado* with ginger and the seared tuna steaks.

Two restaurants are locked in battle for Lima's best place for *comida criolla.* **Los Brujas de Cachiche** (Bolognesi 460, noon–2 A.M. Mon.–Sat., 12:30–5 P.M. Sunday, $20) has an extraordinary buffet every day of the week except Monday and Saturday that includes a *tour de force* of centuries of indigenous Peruvian cooking, from traditional favorites like *aji de gallina* to fresh fish cooked with a creative combination of creole herbs. The restaurant is an old, rambling home in the middle of Miraflo-

res with warmly decorated rooms reverberating with the song of live creole music.

El Señorio de Sulco (Malecón Cisneros 1470, tel. 01/441-0389, noon–midnight Mon.–Sat., noon–5 P.M. Sunday, $8–16) also has an extravagant daily lunch buffet and a range of seafood-oriented plates that are often served in earthenware pots. Try the *chupe de camarones,* a cream-based soup full of sea shrimp, yellow potatoes, and *ají* pepper.

We think Lima's time-honored seaside gourmet restaurant, Rosa Naútica, is a bit faded. A new contender, **Costanera 700** (El Ejército 421, tel. 01/421-4635, $20), is gaining ground and has been repeatedly voted one of the best restaurants in Lima. This is a good place to come for an elegant array of both Peruvian and international cuisine.

Markets

There are no shortage of supermarkets in Miraflores; Plaza Vea (Arequipa 4651, tel. 01/437-9889), Santa Isabel (Pardo and Comandante Espinar, and also Benavides 487) and Wong (Santa Cruz 771, tel. 01/422-3300) and Metro (Arequipa, block 46 near Angamos) have large selections of international and domestic foods.

SAN ISIDRO

The restaurant and nightlife row of San Isidro begins at the busy Óvalo Gutierrez, which is ringed with movie theaters, restaurants, supermarkets, bookstores, and a range of American franchises (T.G.I. Friday's, Chili's, Starbucks, and McDonalds). From here Avenida Conquistadores leads into the heart of Lima's upscale corporate district with restaurants lining both sides. San Isidro is much more spread out than Miraflores, so be prepared to hike or taxi-hop.

Cafés and Desserts

With a lot of glass and exposed wood beams, ℕ **News Café** (Santa Luisa 110, near interesection with Manuel Bañon, San Isidro, tel. 01/421-6278, 10 A.M.–1 A.M., $7) has a sophisticated coffeehouse ambience and recommended salads, pastas, desserts, and a full bar.

For budget travelers, **Botica Francesca** (Jorge Basadre 485, San Isidro, tel. 01/440-7631) has an excellent $2 lunch menu (very cheap for San Isidro) and a good range of cakes and ice creams. **The Ice Cream Factory** (Conquistadores 395, tel. 01/222-2633, 11 A.M.–11 P.M. daily) has a good range of ice creams and affordable sandwiches. For those with a sweet tooth, **Don Mamino** (Los Conquistadores 790, tel. 01/316-1016, 7 A.M.–10 P.M. daily) has gourmet desserts.

Peruvian

Punta Sal (Conquistadores 948, tel. 01/441-7431, 11 A.M.–5 P.M. daily, $8–12) is a large, casual place for great seafood and *cebiche*. The lunch-only **Segundo Muelle** (Conquistadores 490, tel. 01/421-1206, noon–5 P.M. daily, $6–10) sucessfully combines pastas with seafood and has great *cebiche*. Try the ravioli stuffed with crab meat or lasagna with shrimp and artichoke.

On Óvalo Gutierrez, **Bohemia** (Santa Cruz 805, San Isidro, tel. 01/446-5240, noon–1 A.M. daily, $9) serves sandwiches, pasta, pizzas, and, some say, the best *lomo saltado* in Lima.

International

Asia de Cuba (Conquistadores 780, San Isidro, tel. 01/222-4940, $13) is a swanky sushi house with over-the-top decor that includes a doorway fashioned from huge red-velvet curtains. There are more than 30 types of martinis, a range of buttery sushi, and other Asian fusion cuisine. Lima's most fashionable come here, and after dinner, guests stay for late-night antics. The two other leading such places in San Isidro are **Matsuei** (Manuel Bañon 260, 12:30–3:30 P.M. and 7:30–11 P.M. Mon.–Sat.) and the new **Sentori Sushi** (Miguel Dasso 110, tel. 01/440-0766).

Divina Comedia (Conquistadores 928, San Isidro, tel. 01/221-2962, 12:30–4 P.M. and 7:30 P.M.–midnight Mon.–Sat., 12:30–4 P.M. Sunday, $9–11) is a charming Italian restaurant with a brick entrance and stone courtyard that looks and feels like an Italian plazuela. Owned and run by Northern Italians who import many of the ingredients, this is one of the better Italian restaurants around. A recommended main plate is ravioli stuffed with porcini mushrooms.

Lima's best steak tartare is made by **Le Bistrot de mi Fils** (Conquistadores 510, San Isidro, tel. 01/422-6308, 9 A.M.–6 P.M. Mon.–Fri., 9:30 A.M.–12:30 A.M. Sat.), which has a casual interior with blue-checkered drapes and warmly painted walls decorated with photographs from 1920s Paris. If you are in the mood for an Argentine grill, head to **La Carreta** (Rivera Navarrete 740, tel. 01/442-2690).

Pizza

The cheapest pizza and hot sandwiches are at **Meter** (Camino Real 1215, tel. 01/422-5095, $4). Truly gourmet, thin-crust pizzas are served at **Antica Taverna** (Conquistadores 605, tel. 01/422-8429, 6:30 A.M.–1 A.M. daily, $10), a contemporary bar with candlelit tables and couches arranged around the upstairs loft. Martinis are served for happy hour, 6:30–8:30 P.M.

Mexican

A casual place for great Mexican and margaritas is **Como Agua Para Chocolate** (Pancho Fierro 108, San Isidro, tel. 01/222-0297, noon–midnight Mon.–Sat., noon–10 P.M. Sunday, $6), with brightly colored walls and friendly service.

Markets

A **Wong** supermarket is at Óvalo Gutierrez and also 2 de Mayo 1099 (tel. 01/422-2222).

BARRANCO AND CHORRILLOS

There are a number of romantic eateries and cafés under Puente de los Suspiros (Bridge of Sighs), which hangs over a cobblestone walkway that leads to views of the ocean. There are always *señoras* here grilling *anticuchos,* bits of roasted cow heart on a stick, which are addictive once you get over the intial apprehension. The best place here is **La Ermita** (Bajada de Baños 340, tel. 01/247-0069, $7), which serves traditional Peruvian cuisine in a romantic, candlelit setting.

On Barranco's nearby main square, **El Hornito** (Grau 209, tel. 01/477-2465, $5–7) serves backpacker-priced pizzas. The best pizzas, however, are at the new **Antica Trattoria** (San Martín 201, tel.

Lima

01/247-3443, $7–10), a charming Italian eatery with stucco walls, exposed beams, and rustic furniture. The lasagna here is excellent, as are the array of homemade pastas.

Right around the corner from Antica Trattoria is **La Canta Rana** (Génova 101, tel. 01/477-8934, $7–10), a no-frills lunch place with loads of history that serves up great *cebiche* and a range of seafood. **El Lejano Oeste** (Grau 709, tel. 01/247-5675, 12:30 P.M.–midnight daily) is a good choice for inexpensive grilled meats, *anticuchos,* and *cebiches.*

With bow-tied waiters and an old piano, **La Mesitas** (Grau 341, tel. 01/477-4199, noon–1 A.M. daily, $3–6) has an old-timey feel. For those on a budget, this is a great place to sample Peruvian food, including *humitas, tamales, sopa criolla, ocopa arequipeña,* and *lomo saltado.*

At the southern end of Barranco is **Naylamp** (2 de Mayo 239, tel. 01/467-5011), Barranco's new hot spot for *chupe de camarón* (shrimp stew) and a variety of *cebiches.* Around the corner is the excellent *peña* and eating spot **Manos Morenas** (Pedro de Osma 409, Barranco, 467-0421, $12), whose name (Brown Hands) makes reference to its Afro-Peruvian food and dance shows. The rustic wooden tables are arranged around an open courtyard with warm yellow walls and a performance stage. The menu features excellent versions of Peruvian classics such as *ají de gallina, lomo saltado,* and *tamalitos verdes* (green tamales). Guest who stay for the music-and-dance show pay the $12 cover.

The next barrio down the coast from Barranco is Chorrillos, a more tranquil neighborhood with leafy streets and a few hidden culinary gems. One of the most memorable meals we had in Peru was at **Ⅶ Puntarenas** (Santa Teresa 455, just off the Malecón de Chorillos and at the intersection of Huaylas, puntaarenas@terra.com.pe, tel. 01/467-0053, $5–8). This unpretentious place with canvas awnings and rough cement floor offers an extraordinary array of reasonably priced seafood: heaping portions of *arroz con mariscos* (rice and assorted shellfish), *sudado de camarone* (a tomato-based stew with shrimp), and large portions of *cebiche.*

Pueblo Libre

If you are staying in Pueblo Libre, or visiting the Museo Larco, there are a few good restaurants nearby. **El Bolivariano** (Pasaje Santa Rosa, fifth block of Sucre, tel. 01/261-9565, elbolivariano_yahoo.com, $8) is a time-honored Lima restaurant in an elegant Republican home that is visited mainly by Peruvians. The menu includes Peruvian classics such as *seco de cabrito* (stewed goat) and *arroz con pato* (rice with duck). There is a huge Sunday buffet for $9, which includes pisco sour or wine (2–4 P.M.).

Identical to its sister restaurant in Breña, **La Choza Náutica** (La Mar 635, tel. 01/261-5537) has excellent *cebiche* and seafood. **Antigua Taberna Queirolo** (San Martín 1090, tel. 01/460-0441) is a charming Spanish-style café that has been open since 1880. This is a good place to come in the afternoon or evenings to sample pisco or fortified wine made in the winery next door. There is a slim but good menu, that includes salted ham sandwiches, plates of sausage, and steamed fish.

Information and Services

Tourist Information

The best traveling information in Peru, along with maps, advice, trip reports, restaurant and hotel discounts, and all-around friendly people is the amazing **South American Explorer's Club** (Piura 135, Miraflores, tel. 01/445-3306, limaclub@saexplorers.org, www .saexplorers.org, 9:30 A.M.–5 P.M. Mon.–Fri., 9:30 A.M.–1 P.M. Saturday).

Free maps and tourist information are available at **i Peru** (Jorge Chávez Airport, main hall, tel. 01/574-8000, daily, 24 hours). There are other branches in San Isidro (Jorge Basadre 610, tel. 01/421-1627, iperulima@promperu .gob.pe, 8:30 A.M.–6:30 P.M. Mon.–Fri.) and Miraflores (Larcomar, tel. 01/445-9400, noon– 8 P.M. daily).

Near the Plaza Mayor in the center, try the privately owned **InfoPeru** (Escribanos 145, tel. 01/427-4848, 9 A.M.–6 P.M. daily).

In Barranco, **Intej** (San Martín 240, tel. 01/247-3230, www.intej.org, intej@intej.org) is the Lima base for all student travel organizations. Student travel cards can be aquired here with a letter on the appropriate stationery, and student flights can be changed.

Maps

The easiest place to buy maps is the **South American Explorer's Club,** which has good maps of Lima, the Huaraz area, and Peru in general. It also sells the more popular of Peru's military topographic maps.

If you are planning on driving or biking through Peru, excellent driving maps and information are contained in *Inca Guide to Peru* (Peisa, 2002), which is available in most bookshops. Another recommended series is published by Lima 2000 and also available in bookshops.

For hard-to-find topo maps, head to the **Instituto Geográfico Nacional** (Aramburu 1180, Surquillo, 475-3085, 8 A.M.–6 P.M. Mon.–Fri.), which also sells digital, geological, and departmental maps.

Police

The 24-hour tourist police is in the main hall of the airport with a 24-hour English-speaking attendant (tel. 01/574-8000). There are also police stations in the center near Plaza San Martín (Pasaje Tambo de Belén 104, tel. 01/ 424-2053), in San Isidro (Jorge Basadre 610), and in the neighborhood of Magdalena (Moore 268, tel. 01/460-1060 or 0965). Dialing 105 also reaches police from a private phone or 116 for the fire department.

Health Care

Lima has Peru's best hospitals, and it is easy, and quite inexpensive, to get parasite tests and yellow fever or tetanus shots. All of the places listed below have English-speaking doctors. The best (and most expensive) medical care in Peru is at San Isidro's **Clínica Anglo-Americana** (Alfredo Salazar, block 3 s/n, tel. 01/2213656, 8 A.M.– 8 P.M. Mon.–Fri., 9 A.M.–noon Sat.), which charges $60 for a doctor's visit.

Other cheaper, high-quality options include **Clinica Adventisa de Miraflores** (Malecón Balta 956, Miraflores, tel. 01/241-3256, 9 A.M.–midnight) and in central Lima **Clínica International** (Washington 1471, 8 A.M.–8 P.M. Mon.–Fri., 8 A.M.–2 P.M. Saturday). Doctor's visits at both places cost around $30.

The easiest option is to call **Doctor Más** (tel. 01/444-9377), a company that will send an English-speaking doctor to your hotel to check on you and write a prescription for $20. Doctor Más doctors can also be reached directly on their cell phones, including **Dr. Ana del Aguila** (tel. 01/9818-2561) and **Dr. Jorge Garmendia** (tel. 01/9818-2554). You can even pay with a credit card if you notify them while setting up the visit.

For lab testing and shots, **Suiza Lab** (Atahualpa 308, Miraflores, tel. 01/444-2288, 9 A.M.–midnight) is very professional, clean, and reasonably priced.

Two English-speaking dentists are **Dr. Victor Melly** (Conquistadores 965, San Isidro, 422-5757, 9:30 A.M.–6 P.M. Mon.–Fri.) and **Dr. Flavio**

Larrain (Psje. Sucre 154, Miraflores, tel. 01/445-2586, 8 A.M.–7 P.M. Mon.–Fri.). Both charge $30 for a checkup and cleaning.

Most pharmacies are willing to deliver to your hotel. In Miraflores, try **IncaFarma** (tel. 01/314-2020, will deliver), **Farmacias 24 Horas** (tel. 01/444-0568), **Superfarma** (Benavides 2849, tel. 01/222-1575, or Armendariz 215, tel. 01/440-9000). In San Isidro, try Deza (Conquistadores 1144, San Isidro, tel. 01/442-9196, 24 hours). Near the center, the Metro supermarket in Breña (corner of Venezuela and Alfonso Ugarte) has a good pharmacy.

Language Schools

There are many Spanish schools in Lima, though getting away from all the English speakers is a challenge. In Miraflores, **Instituto Cultural Peruano-Norteamericano** (Angamos Oeste 160, Miraflores, tel. 01/241-1940, postmaster@icpna.edu.pe, www.icpna.edu.pe) charges $54 for 40 hours of lessons plus $82 in materials.

For a well-rounded Spanish school, try **El Sol** (Grimaldo de Solar 469, Miraflores, tel. 01/242-7763, elsol@idiomasperu.com, www.idiomasperu.com), which has a "Survival Spanish" program for travelers that includes cooking and dancing classes, city walks, volunteer opportunities, conversation partners, and family homestays. El Sol charges $15 per hour for small group lessons or $110 for 10 hours of semi-intensive classes. Their one-week program for beginners is $50.

San Isidro language schools include **Instituto de Idiomas** (Camino Real 1037, San Isidro, tel. 01/442-8761, idiomas@pucp.edu.pe, www.pucp.edu.pe, 11 A.M.–1 P.M. daily), which charges $105 for 36 hours of lessons. **Asociación Cultural Peruano-Británico** (Arequipa 3495, San Isidro, tel. 01/221-7550, informes@acpb.edu.pe, www.britanico.edu.pe) charges $66 for 36 hours of lessons.

For one-on-one lessons, some recommended private tutors are Lourdes Galvez (tel. 01/435-3910, $5/hour), Llorgelina Savastaizagal (tel. 01/275-6460, $5/hour), and Alex Boris (tel. 01/423-0697, $5/hour).

Film and Cameras

Lima's best developing and camera repair shop is **Taller de Fotografía Profesional** (Benavides 1171, tel. 01/241-1015). Other top-quality developing with one-day service is available from **Laboratorio Color Profesional** (Benavides 1171, tel. 01/214-8430, 9 A.M.–7 P.M. Mon.–Fri., 9:30 A.M.–1 P.M. Saturday). A cheaper option is **Kodak Express,** which is open 9 A.M.–9 P.M. Mon.–Sat. with offices in Miraflores (Larco 1005), San Isidro (Las Begonias), and central Lima (Unión 790, Centro). For camera repairs in the center, try **Reparación** (Cusco 592, central Lima, fourth flr., tel. 01/426-7920, 10 A.M.–2 P.M. Mon.–Fri.). For digital technical glitches contact **Jorge Li Pun** (General Silva 496, Miraflores, tel. 01/447-7302, 10:30 A.M.–8 P.M. Mon.–Fri.).

Newspapers

Lima's largest newspaper is *El Comercio,* but we personally prefer the tabloid-format *La Répública* for its daily **Mirko Lauer** political column and a more straightforward approach to news. Lima's best magazine for news, humor, and cultural information is, hands down, *Caretas.*

Banks and Money Exchange

For those just arriving in Peru, there are several banks inside the Lima airport, typically open from 9 A.M.–6 P.M., that exchange travelers checks for a 2.5 percent commission. In general, the best place to cash travelers checks is at any Banco de Crédito, which charges the lowest commission—1.8 percent. ATMs are now ubiquitous across Lima (and most of Peru) and work with Visa, MasterCard, Cirrus, etc.—but not American Express. Take care getting money at night (a good trick is to have a taxi waiting).

Money-change houses (*casa de cambio*) offer slightly better rates than banks and are mercifully free of the hour-long lines that snake inside most banks. There are many change houses on Larco in Miraflores and on Ocoña in central Lima. Be careful changing money with people on the steet, even if they do have the requisite badge and bright-yellow vest. Safe places for money-changing on the street are Parque Kennedy or Pardo and Comandante Espinar in Miraflores.

Here is an alphabetical listing of banks, which are generally open 9 A.M.–6 P.M. Mon.–Fri.,

9 A.M.–12:30 P.M. Saturday. All banks are closed on Sunday.

American Express (Santa Cruz 621, Miraflores, tel. 01/221-8204, 9 A.M.–5:30 P.M. Mon.–Fri., 9 A.M.–1 P.M. Saturday) will replace its traveler checks.

Banco de Crédito, or BCP, is Peru's biggest bank, with offices in Miraflores (Pardo 425 or Parque Kennedy on Larco), Barranco (Grau 599), San Isidro (Jorge Basadre and Camino Real), and central Lima (Lampa and Ucayali).

Banco Continental has offices in Miraflores (Larco and Benavides and in Larcomar) and San Isidro (1152 Conquistadores).

Banco de la Nación, which handles all government payments, has offices in Miraflores (Pardo y Olaya) and central Lima (Abancay 491).

Banco Wiese Sudameris has offices in Miraflores (291 Angamos Oeste or Larco 1123), San Isidro (1098 Conquistadores), and central Lima (245 Cuzco).

Interbank has offices in Miraflores (Larco 690) and central Lima (Unión 600).

A recommended change house is **Lac Dolar** with locations in the center (Camaná 779, tel. 01/428-8127) and Miraflores (La Paz 211, tel. 01/242-4069). It will change travelers checks for a 2 percent commision and are open 9:30 A.M.–6 P.M. Mon.–Sat.

For money wiring, there are two **Western Unions** in Miraflores (Petit Thouars 5135, tel. 01/422-0014, and Block eight of Larco, tel. 01/422-0014).

Communications

The main **post office** is on the corner of Lima's Plaza Mayor (Psj. Piura, s/n, 8 A.M.–8 P.M. Mon.–Sat., 8 A.M.–3 P.M. Sunday). The Miraflores branch (Petit Thouars 5201, tel. 01/511-5018, 8 A.M.–8:45 P.M. Mon.–Sat., 8:45 A.M.–2 P.M. Sunday) has slightly different hours. There is also FedEx (Pasaje Olaya 260, tel. 01/242-2280, Surco) and DHL (Los Castaños 225, tel. 01/422-5232, San Isidro).

High-speed Internet is ubiquitous in Lima. Recommended places in Miraflores are **@lf.net** (Manuel Bonilla 126, 9 A.M.–10 P.M. Mon.–Fri., 11 A.M.–8 P.M. Sat.–Sun., $0.50/hour) and **Refu-**

gio Internet (Larco 1185, tel. 01/242-5910, 8:30 A.M.–11 P.M. Mon.–Fri., 9:30 A.M.–11 P.M. Saturday, 10:30 A.M.–11 P.M. Sunday, $0.75/hour), or the helpful and cheap **Via Planet** (Diez Canseco 339, 9 A.M.–midnight daily, $0.30/hour) In central Lima, try **Internet** (Psj. Santa Rosa 165, Center, 7:30 A.M.–9 P.M. daily, $0.75/hr). Both these places do Internet calls as well.

For local calls or national calls, buy a 147 card and dial away from Telefónica booths on nearly every corner.

For international calls, put away those phone cards, because a new generation of cable or satellite shops are crystal-clear and as low as $0.15 per minute to the U.S. **Call Center USA** (Junín 410, four blocks toward Vía Expresa from Arequipa and near the Home Peru hostel, 9 A.M.–midnight daily) offers cable calls to the U.S. ($0.15/min), Europe ($0.20), or Asia ($0.25). This place also has high-speed Internet.

Immigrations Office

Lima's **Migraciones** (immigrations office) is located near the center (España 734, Breña, tel. 01/330-4144, 8 A.M.–1 P.M. Mon.–Fri.). Arrive early and with $20 if you want to receive a new visa the same day.

Laundry

Recommended places in Miraflores are **Servirap** (Schell 601, Miraflores, 241-0759, 8 A.M.–10 P.M. Mon.–Sat., 10 A.M.–6 P.M. Sunday, $2.50/kg), which offers drop-off and self-service. Another good option is **Miraflores Express** (28 de Julio, Miraflores, 445-8182, 9 A.M.–7 P.M. Mon.–Sat., $1).

In San Isidro, **Lava Center** (Victor Maurtua 140, San Isidro, 440-3600, 9 A.M.–7 P.M. Mon.–Fri., 9 A.M.–3 P.M. Saturday, $1/kg) and **Lavandería Cristalina** (Conquistadores 820, San Isidro, tel. 01/222-2396, 9 A.M.–7 P.M. Mon.–Sat.) are reliable.

In Barranco, **Neptuno** (Grau 912, 477-4472, $2/kg) is good.

In Breña try **Lavanderia KTO** (España 481, tel. 01/332-9035, 7 A.M.–8 P.M. daily, $1/kg) or in the central Lima at Callao 158 (second flr., tel. 01/428-2776, will deliver).

Car Rental

The major rental car agencies are **Avis** (Javier Pardo Este 5235, La Molina tel. 01/434-1111, 24 hours,, $60/day, $350/week), **Budget** (La Paz 522, Miraflores, tel. 01/444-4546, $25–30/day, $178/week), and **Hertz** (Centuarias 160, Miraflores, tel. 01/445-5716, $41/day, $265/week). These three also have offices at the airport. There

are many more options under *Automóviles-alquiler* in the yellow pages.

Luggage Storage

Besides your hotel, you can also store bags at the aiport for $6/day. **SAE** members can store luggage at the clubhouse (Piura 135, Miraflores) free of charge.

Getting There and Around

GETTING THERE

Plane

Lima's international airport is **Jorge Chávez** (tel. 01/595-0606), 16 km west of the city center at Callao. The airport contains banks, post office, phones, trinket shops, rental car agencies, a few upstairs restaurants, and, outside, a recommended 4D ice cream shop with playground. There is a $28 departure tax for international flights and $4.50 for domestic flights, payable in dollars or soles.

For those arriving, there is a bank for money changing in the luggage claim area. Pushy taxi drivers will be waiting for you outside the airport. Have your address written down and be prepared to bargain. Taxi prices from the airport to the center should be around $6, and to Miraflores about $10. Or you can book a taxi for slightly more money inside the luggage claim.

The best way to check on flight schedules is through one of the agencies listed in the *Sports and Recreation* section. But any Lima agency will have a copy of the *Guía Aérea,* a monthly booklet with updates on the constantly changing flight schedules.

Leading airlines include **LanPeru** (Pardo 513, Miraflores, tel. 01/213-8200, www.lanperu.com) and the budget **TANS Peru** (Arequipa 5200, Miraflores, tel. 01/213-6000, ventaslima@tans.com.pe, www.tansperu.com.pe).

Useful for specific routes are **Magenta Air** (Arica 628, seventh flr., central Lima, tel. 01/241-7777, reservas@magentaair.com, www.magentaair.com) for Tarapoto and Cajamarca; **Star Up** (Pardo 269, Miraflores, tel. 01/446-2485, ventas@starup

.com.pe, www.starup.com.pe) for Chiclayo, Iquitos, Yurimaguas, and Tarapoto; and **Aerocondor** (Juan de Aroma 781, San Isidro, tel. 01/614-6014, reservas@aerocondor.com.pe, www.aerocondor.com.pe) for Cajamarca, Huánuco, Huaraz, and Nasca lines.

All of the international airlines that fly into Peru also have offices in Lima, including Aerolineas Argentinas (Bolognesi 291, Miraflores, tel. 01/444-0810, www.aeroargentinas.com); AeroMexico (Victor Andrés Belaúnde 147, of. 701, tel. 01/421-3500, www.aeromexico.com); Air France (José Pardo 501, of. 8701, tel. 01/444-9285, www.airfrance.com); Alaska Airlines/Horizon Air (Miguel Dasso 126, of. 205, San Isidro, tel. 01/221-7446, www.alaskaair.com); Avianca (José Pardo 14, Miraflores, tel. 01/445-9902, www.avianca.com); Continental Airlines (Victor Andrés Belaúnde 147, of. 101, San isidro, tel. 011/221-4340, www.continental.com); Copa Airlines (Dos de Mayo 741, Miraflores, tel. 01/610-0808, www.copaair.com); Delta Air Lines (Victor Andrés Belaúnde 147, of. 701, San Isidro, tel. 01/211-9211, www.delta.com); Lloyd Aero Boliviano (José Pardo 231, Miraflores, 01/241-5513, www.labairlines.com); Taca Peru (Comandante Espinar 331, Miraflores, tel. 01/231-7000, www.taca.com); Varig (Camino Real 456, Ofs. 803-804, San Isidro, tel. 01/221-0628, www.varig.com).

Bus

Highways in Peru have improved immensely over the last decade, making in-country bus travel not only cheap but efficient. From Lima, buses head to every major city in Peru except water-locked Iquitos. The South American Explorers Club has an excellent Lima folder with a detailed rundown of bus companies and the schedules. Unfortunately, there is no main bus station in Lima. Instead, companies have their own terminals in the center and sometimes also on Javier Prado or Paseo de la República near San Isidro. All these neighborhoods are rough, so take a taxi to and from the terminal and keep a hand on all your belongings.

The two reputable bus companies in Lima are Cruz del Sur and Ormeño, and a third, Movil Tours, gets consistently strong reviews. **Cruz del Sur** has a terminal in the center (Quilca 531, tel. 01/424-1005) and near San Isidro (corner of Javier Prado and Nicolas Ariola, tel. 01/225-6163). Though it does not go as many places as Ormeño, Cruz del Sur's Royal Class is the most luxurious bus service in Peru and the company gives a 10 percent discount to students with an ISIC card. Best of all, tickets can be bought instantly from any agency in Lima or at the TeleTicket counters at Wong and Metro supermarkets (in Miraflores there is a Wong at Óvalo Gutierrez and a Metro at the 46th block of Arequipa, near Angamos). Spanish speakers can even call the Cruz del Sur call center (tel. 01/225-6163, have passport number ready) and

LIMA BUS SCHEDULE

The following is a thumbnail of times and prices with a range from economical to luxury service. At the bottom end, buses stop frequently, are crowded, and lack bathrooms. The top-end buses are decked out with reclining semi-beds, clean bathrooms, on-board food and beverage service, video, and a second story with great views. Prices increase 50 percent around holidays including Christmas, Easter, and the July 28 *Fiestas Patrias* weekend.

City	Price	Time
Arequipa	$11–31	13–15 hours
Ayacucho	$9–17	8–9 hours
Cajamarca	$11–29	14 hours
Chachapoyas	$6–17	25 hours
Chanchamayo	$7–11	8 hours
Chiclayo	$10–27	10 hours
Cusco	$17–43	25–30 hours
Huancayo	$5–10	7 hours
Huaraz	$6–11	8 hours
Máncora	$11–37	16–17 hours
Nasca	$7–9	8 hours
Piura	$9–31	14–15 hours
Pisco	$5–11	4 hours
Piura	$9–31	14–15 hours
Puno	$16–43	21–24 hours
Tacna (Chile border)	$17–20	18–20 hours
Trujillo	$6–24	8 hours
Tumbes (Ecuador border)	$13–37	18 hours

have their tickets delivered free of charge. Payment is in cash upon receipt of tickets. Buses leave first from the central Lima terminal and pick up passengers a half hour later at the Javier Prado terminal. For complete route information see the web page www.cruzdelsur.com.pe/.

Ormeño also has a terminal in the center (Carlos Zavala 177, tel. 01/427-5679, www .grupo-ormeno.com) and an international terminal near San Isidro (Javier Prado Este 1059, La Victoria, tel. 01/472-1710). Ormeño has better coverage and is slightly cheaper than Cruz del Sur. To buy an Ormeño ticket, visit a terminal, go through an agency (the agency will get the tickets a few hours later), or call the Spanish-only call center: tel. 01/472-5000. Again, have passport number when calling and cash in hand when the ticket is delivered.

The highly recommended **Movil Tours** (Paseo de la Republica 749, La Victoria, tel. 01/332-0024) has a station near San Isidro and runs mainly to the northern cities, including Huaraz, Chachapoyas, and Chiclayo and is about the same price as Ormeño. Phone reservations accepted for payment at terminal.

Phone reservations do not work well at the other companies. Your best bet is to buy tickets at the terminal.

Expreso Wari (Montevideo 809, central Lima, tel. 01/428-8591) goes to Nasca, Ayacucho, and Cusco.

Empresa Molina (Ayacucho 1141, central Lima, tel. 01/428-4852) goes to Huancayo, Ayacucho, and Cusco.

Enlaces (Paseo de la República 749, La Victoria, tel. 01/433-3311) runs north and south along the coast and also to Cusco.

Flores has the best coverage of the small bus companies, lower prices, and a terminal in both central Lima (Montevideo 523, tel. 01/426-3523, perubus@terra.com.pe) and near San Isidro (Paseo de la República 627, La Victoria, tel. 01/424-3278). It has cheap buses for Arequipa, Cajamarca, Chiclayo, Máncora, Nasca, Piura, Puno, Tacna, Trujillo, and Tumbes.

Mariscal Cáceres has offices both in central Lima (Carlos Zavala 211, tel. 01/427-2844) and near San Isidro (28 de Julio 2195, La Victoria, tel. 01/474-7850) and heads primarily to Huncayo.

Soyuz (Carlos Zavala 217, tel. 01/436-2943, www.soyuz.com.pe) has good frequency on the south coast.

Companies where travelers report frequent delays, breakdowns, or other problems include **Tepsa** and **Civa.**

Recommended international companies include:

Caracol (Brasil 425, Jesus María, tel. 01/431-1400, caracol@perucaracol.com, www.peru-caracol.com) receives the best reviews and covers the entire continent. It partners with Cruz del Sur so you can buy tickets from either company's terminals. Among other places, Caracol travels to Santiago, Chile; Santa Cruz and La Paz, Bolivia; Asunción, Paraguay; Córdoba and Buenos Aires, Argentina; Montevideo, Uruguay; São Paulo and Rio de Janeiro, Brazil; and Quito and Guayaquil, Ecuador. Check the web page for what must be grueling trips: Travelers plunk down $235 for a one-way ticket to Rio and spend five days and 11 hours on a bus.

Ormeño (Javier Prado Este 1059, tel. 01/472-1710) no longer travels to Colombia nor Brazil, but does go to Santiago, Chile; Buenos Aires, Argentina; and Guayaquil, Ecuador.

El Rápido (Rivera Navarrete 2650, Lince, tel. 01/422-9508) has cheaper fares to Santiago, Chile; and Buenos Aires, Argentina.

Train

Between May and October, a passenger train still departs once a month or so from Lima's antique Desamparados train station downtown. After climbing the steep valley above Lima it crests the Andes at 4,751 meters (nearly 15,700 feet!) and continues to Huancayo.

During these months Sunday excursion trains also leave the station for San Bartolomé, a country hamlet 1.5 hours by train outside Lima that is often sunny when the city is fogged in. These trains leave at 6 A.M. and return at 6 P.M. For tickets and exact departure information, contact the **Desamparados train station** (Ancash 201, tel. 01/361-2828, ext. 222).

GETTING AROUND

Taxi

If you want to make a spare buck in Lima, buy a taxi sticker from the market for $0.50, plop it on your windshield, and start picking up passengers. Understandably, the vast majority of taxis in Lima are unofficial and unregulated, and assaults on passengers picked up at the airport occur occasionally.

The best way to take a taxi is to call a registered company and pay an additional 30 to 50 percent more. Recommended taxi companies include **Taxi Lima** (tel. 01/271-0974, daily 24 hours), **Taxi Miraflores** (tel. 01/446-4336, daily 24 hours), **Taxi VIP** (tel. 01/960-7657, San Isidro, daily 24 hours), and **Taxi Móvil** (tel. 01/422-6890 or 01/422-6899, San Isidro, daily 24 hours).

If you feel comfortable, and have a smidgen of Spanish, stand on the street until a safe-looking, registered taxi passes by. These should be painted yellow and have the taxi sign on the hood of the car and a registration sticker on the windshield. Older taxi drivers tend to be safer than young ones. Of course, avoid old cars with tinted windows and broken door handles. Bargain before you get in a taxi or you will get fleeced. Fares from the airport to Miraflores should be $6–8, airport-to-center about $6, Miraflores-center about $3, and Miraflores-Barranco about $2. Prices go up during rush hour and at night. Taxis can also be rented by the hour for $8 (registered taxi) or $6 (street taxi).

Bus and Colectivo

Buses and *colectivos,* or minibuses, are an interesting, economical way to travel around Lima. Bus fares are $0.30 on weekdays and a fraction more on Sundays. *Colectivos* cost $0.50 on weekdays and $0.60 on Sundays. You can tell where buses and *combis* are going by the sticker on the front windshield (not by what's painted on the side). There are also slightly more expensive *colectivo* cars, which can take up to five passengers and are a bit faster than the van-style *colectivos,* which in turn are faster than buses. To get off a bus or *colectivo* simply say *baja* ("getting off") or *esquina* ("at the corner"). Have your change ready, as money is collected right before you get off.

To reach Miraflores from the center, head to Garcilaso de la Vega (formerly Wilson) and take one of the buses or *colectivos* marked *Miraflores* or *Todo Arequipa,* which go all the way to Parque Kennedy. To reach Barranco, take a bus from the same place marked *Barranco/Chorrillos.* Or head to Miraflores and change buses there.

From Miraflores, most buses and *colectivos* can be taken from Larco along Parque Kennedy. To reach central Lima, take the bus marked *Tacna/Wilson* and ask to be dropped off at the central street of Ica or Callao. To reach Barranco, take the bus marked *Barranco/Chorrillos,* and the aiport is *Faucett/Aeropuerto.* However, buses for the airport aren't very reliable and at times only come within five blocks of the airport. Take a taxi and keep your luggage safe.

Private Car

Private drivers can also be hired for the hour, day, or for a trip like the Nasca Lines. A highly recommended driver for a city day tour or Nasca Lines trip is **Miguel Vásquez Díaz** (Carlos Izaguirre 1353, central Lima, tel. 01/9809-23321, sumisein@latinmail.com). Others include **Mónica Velasquez** (tel. 01/9943-0796 or 01/224-8608, vc_monica@hotmail.com, www.monicatourism.da.ru) and **Fidel Loayza Paredes** (tel. 01/533-1609, armandoloayza280671@hotmail.com).

Southern Beaches

We notice with some dismay that many guide-books write badly about the beaches just south of Lima. The general thought is that they are dirty, crowded, treacherous, and, in general, not worth visiting. Though it is true that the white sands and subtropical climate of Peru's north beaches are more alluring, they are also a 20-hour bus ride to the north of Lima. If you are in Lima and in need of a beach fix, head south for a half hour to Punta Hermosa or San Bartolo. You will find sandy beaches, world-class surfing waves, protected beaches for safe swimming, rocking nightlife, a few good hostels, and lots of *cebicherias*. The only time to visit these beaches is during the summer months from mid-December to the end of April—they are cloudy during the rest of the year. Make reservations well in advance, especially from January to mid-March, when surfers from around the world flock here along with Peruvian students on summer break. The best time to go is from Sunday to Thursday night, when beaches are empty and hotel prices are often 30 percent lower than listed below.

There are other options besides Punta Hermosa and San Bartolo—check out the *Guia Inca de las Playas,* for sale at Lima bookstores, for more details. A basic hit list includes Santa María, at Km 48 of the Panamericana, an upscale beach with a control point that admits only residents and respectable-looking day-trippers. If you want a fancier, clean, but fairly snobby beach experience, this is your place, though there are few or no lodging options here. Pucusana is a picturesque fishing town at Km 58 picturesque fishing town at Km 58 of the Panamericana. Puerto Viejo, at Km 72 of the Panamericana, is a long beach good for beginning surfers—including a left point break that ranges between one and two meters. Leon Dormido (*Sleeping Lion*) at Km 80 has a calm beach that is often crowded. The best parties, however, are at Asia, Km 97, which becomes an explosion of discos, condos, private clubs, and even car dealerships in the summer. Teenagers here for the parties pack the beach and the discos at night. Near Asia's beaches, and close to shore, there are several islands with great sea-kayaking and possibilities to see Humboldt penguins and sea lions. Finally, Cerro Azul at Km 128 is a forgotten port, with a small fishing community and pleasant beach with both pipeline and beginner waves for all levels of surfers.

PUNTA HERMOSA

A half hour south of Lima at Km 40 of the Panamericana, Punta Hermosa is a big-time surfing destination with a great range of beaches and services. It is here that **Pico Alto,** the largest wave in South America, forms in May and reaches heights of up to 12 meters. The town itself is on a rocky peninsula, called La Isla, which is surrounded by seven beaches. From north to south, these are El Silencio, Caballeros, Señoritas, Pico Alto, Playa Norte, La Isla, and Kontiki. When covered in rocks and not sand, Playa Norte is a good place to get away from crowds, along with Kontiki. But wherever you stay in Punta Hermosa, any of these beaches are no more than a half-hour walk away.

Entertainment and Events

Every May or June, during the first big swell of the year, Punta Hermosa comes alive with Peru's annual big-wave competition. There is no fixed date for the competition and it is usually organized within a week or two—check out www.buoy-weather.com (you have to pay) or www.storm-surf.com (free) for the right ocean conditions, or stayed tuned to www.peruazul.com, the country's premier surf page.

Otherwise nightlife is clustered around the entry to Punta Hermosa and the few pubs on the waterfront.

Sports and Recreation

Punta Hermosa has several places to rent a board and wetsuit, get an instructor, and surf a variety of waves from gentle to suicidal. The best beginner beaches in Punta Hermosa are Caballeros, Pracas, and La Isla. Taxis and surfing camps can

arrange transportation to beginner beaches further south, such as Puerto Viejo and Cerro Azul.

The honest and straightforward **Marco León Villarán** (see Accommodations below) can arrange a variety of fabulous adventures in the area. His main passion is **spear fishing,** and if you have the snorkel, fins, and mask he can lead you to just about any fish you have ever dreamed of seeing—or spearing—including 1.2-meter yellowtail or gigantic flounder near Punta Hermosa. In his Zodiac with outboard motor, he also leads trips to nearby Isla Pachacamac ($25 pp) for the rare opportunity to see Humboldt penguins, sea lions, and the occasional sea otter (known in Spanish as *gato de mar,* because of its cat-like appearance).

Marco is also a professional bone-and-fossil hunter who knows Peru's desert coastline very well—from the fossil-rich deserts of Ica to the pristine and remote surfing beaches north of Chiclayo. He owns a reliable 4x4 van and is an excellent, affordable, and trustworthy option for getting into remote areas of the Ica desert. Like all fossil hunters, Marco keeps in touch with all the local *huaqeros,* or grave robbers, and can even arrange an opportunity to witness their ceremonies. Before they begin digging at midnight, they read coca leaves and drink *aguardiente* to

protect themselves from evil spirits. He charges a $50 daily guiding fee and then bills travelers for gas, food, and other expenses, probably another $50 per day for a group of up to four people. He speaks Spanish only.

Accommodations

Punta Hermosa's better places are in La Planicie, a quiet neighborhood to the north of town that offers a nice respite from the rowdy surfer scene in town, a 10-minute walk away. There is a good restaurant and Internet nearby along with Señoritas and Caballeros beaches. There are more hotels and nightlife, and the monster Pico Alto wave itself, near the center of Punta Hermosa—along with crowds of rowdy Brazilian and Argentinean surfers who are in town to test their mettle on waves that have made Punta Hermosa known as the Hawaii of South America. Nearly all of the hotels below offer full pension—for another $10–15 per day, you can take all your meals at your hostel. This is an excellent deal and a good way to avoid stomach issues.

Finding a room for under $10 a night is possible, but not easy in Punta Hermosa's high season. The best bet is to simply walk around town and look for signs that say *Se Alguilan Cuartos*

(Rooms are rented here)—these can often be clean and as cheap as $5 pp per night. Surfer hostels spring up in Punta Hermosa in the summer and are listed at www.peruazul.com. We found many of these to be noisy, so choose carefully. For a mere $9, Cebichería Carmencita will set up a tent on the beach for up to seven people and make a campfire!

In the Planicie neighborhood, long-time Punta Hermosa resident Marco León Villarán offers something for everyone at the **M Peru Adventure Lodge** (Block Ñ, Lote 1, La Planicie, tel. 01/230-8316 or 01/230-8351, marsub@terra.com.pe, www.peruadventure.com, $10 s, $20 d). His rooms are quiet, large, and comfortable, with tons of hot water and two black labs who can lick you awake every morning for a bit extra. He and his wife, Gloria, prepare excellent meals and his son, Daniel, is an excellent, English-speaking surfing instructor ($10 for two hours). The family owns a huge, ancient longboard that is almost a sure bet for novice surfers looking to stand up for the first time.

A good friend of Marco's, right around the corner, is Flavio Solari, a surfboard shaper and international surfing judge who runs **Señoritas Surf Camp** (Block N, Lote 4, tel. 01/734-8968, srtsurfcamp@yahoo.com, $10 s, $20 d). "What I offer is a lifestyle," explains Flavio. "A surfer's pension." The wooden rooms are smaller and simpler than Marco's, with tapestries from Bali and nice lighting. Rooms range from simple bunks to a private room with queen-size beds. Flavio also sells his extraordinary boards ($250 for short, $400 for long) and rents both boards ($10/day) and wetsuits ($5/day). He gives a two-hour surfing intro class for $10.

A final surf camp in Planicie is the **Punta Hermosa Surf Camp** (Block R, Lote 19, tel. 01/230-8357, puntasurfcamp@hotmail.com).

In Punta Hermosa, **Hostal La Isla** (Malecón Central 943, tel. 01/230-7146, info@surfcamp-peru.com, www.surfcampperu.com, $15 s, $25 d, including breakfast) is a relaxed guesthouse run by the family of longtime Punta Hermosa resident and surfer Sandro Testino. Though a bit more expensive than the rest, Hostal La Isla is on Punta Hermosa's beach promenade, has nice ocean views, and is close to town but still quiet at night. The rooms are simple but comfortable with nice shared terraces. Services include laundry, surfboard rental, transport to surfing areas, and Internet. Another camp is run by Oscar Morante, a surf guide who leads trips all around Peru for several surfing international surfing agencies. His **Pico Alto International Surf Camp** (www.surfcampperu@terra.com.pe, $35 pp per day, all food included) is good, but pricey.

If you value high-quality art, you might want to consider a $12 bunk with shared bathroom at the Casa Barco (Punta Hermosa 340, tel. 01/230-7081, tel. 01/944-3000, info@casabarco.com, www.casabarco.com). The room is simple, but the pool and general charm of this place makes it an excellent value. A final good hostel, also near the center, is **Hospedaje Nylamp Wasi** (Pacasmayo 167, tel. 01/230-8401, tel. 01/931-4360, pateurquiaga@hotmail.com, $10 s, $20 d, including breakfast).

Hotel La Rotunda (Bolognesi 580, above the restaurant of the same name, tel. 01/230-7390, tel. 01/9668-7311, larotondasurfcamp@hotmail.com, $20 s, $40 d) has eight nice rooms with ocean views and cable TV. These are right near the bars, however, and probably get noisy at night.

One of the nicest places to stay on the Peruvian coast, and one of the better values, must be **M Casa Barco** (Punta Hermosa 340, tel. 01/230-7081, tel. 01/944-3000, info@casabarco.com, www.casabarco.com, $56 d, including breakfast). A five-minute walk from the center, this small and friendly hostel has a great pool with Jacuzzi, a beautiful flower garden, and a classy bar/restaurant with a full, reasonably priced menu of sushi, sashimi, and *cebiche*. The rooms have black-and-white floor tiles, luxurious beds, cable TV, wraparound porches with ocean views, and huge, beautiful showers. The best part, however, is the art. The owners, ceramic artist Teresa Carvallo and writer Felix Portocarrera, have assembled a mind-blowing collection of contemporary art from Peru's best painters and sculptors.

Food

There are many seafood restaurants but probably the safest is **La Rotonda** (Bolognesi 592,

084/230-7266, 8 A.M.–11 P.M. daily, $5). Apart from *cebiche,* the restaurant also does *chicharrón* and grilled fish, serving on a second-story deck with good views of surfers on Pico Alto. Another option is **Cebichería Carmencita** (Malecón de Punta Hermosa 821, tel. 01/9976-4792, 7 A.M.–10 P.M. daily, $5), which serves a range of fish dishes and will even set up a tent and campfire for you. At Señoritas beach, ask around for the *cebiche* stall run by Paco and Cecilia, which has a good reputation among locals.

For Italian check out **Donde Luis** on the Punta Hermosa waterfront or, in La Planicie, **Trattoria Don Ángelo** (near control gate, tel. 01/230-7104, tel. 01/9740-9982, trattoria_donangelo@hotmail.com, 7 A.M.–midnight daily, $5). This is a family-run store and restaurant that serves pizzas and a variety of homemade pastas, including lasagna, ravioli, canneloni, and gnocchi.

Getting There

Probably the easiest way to get to **Punta Hermosa** from Lima is to hire a taxi ($10) or arrange a pickup through your hotel. **Flavio Solaria** (see *Accommodations*) picks up groups from the Lima airport for $25. Buses for Mala—which stop outside of Punta Hermosa, San Bartolo, and Santa María—pick up passengers at the circle, or *trébol,* where Av. Javier Prado intersects with the Panamericana in Monterrico. These buses, called *Maleños,* take 45 minutes to reach Punta Hermosa and charge $0.75.

Getting Around

Three-wheeled *motocars* abound in Punta Hermosa and are a $0.50 option for getting between La Planicie and the town center.

SAN BARTOLO

Further down the Panamerican, past an exclusive area of homes perched on a seaside cliff and an exclusive beach club known as La Quebrada, lies the laid-back beach town of San Bartolo. The town itself is perched on a bluff above an attractive horseshoe-shaped beach, lined with hotels, condos, and a *malecón,* known as Playa Norte. San Bartolo is less of a surfer party spot than the cen-

ter of Punta Hermosa even with Peñascal, a right reef break that gets as high as four meters on the south end of the Playa Norte. There are gentler waves, and a good place for swimming, on the north end of Playa Norte, along with a few nice beachfront hotels. After entering from Km 48 of the Panamericana, the main drag into town is Av. San Bartolo. Most of hotels are along Mar Pacífico, a street that runs to the left (south). To the right, another road leads around to Kahuana Hostel and Playa Norte.

Entertainment and Events

San Bártolo's only disco, **Huaico,** is near the town's highway entrance and is only open during the summers.

Accommodations

On the bluff above town, **Playa Mar Hostal** (San Bartolo 211, tel. 01/430-7247, $10 s, $12 d) is a surfer's hangout with brick walls, bamboo ceilings, tile floors, and private bathrooms with electric showerheads. Another good option, and much cleaner than a few other hostels nearby, is **Hostal La Marina** (San Martín 351, tel. 01/430-7601, $15 s, $23 d). About half the 20 rooms have ocean views with cable TV, restaurant, and all-you-can-drink potable water.

For what it is, **M Hostal 800** (Malecón 800, tel. 01/430-7514, tel. 01/430-7307, $40 d, cheaper by week) is a great value. This hotel, like the others on the beach, is built up onto the hillside, so all the rooms have great ocean views. But these apartments are huge and luxurious, with private porch, commodious bedroom, and a separate kitchen with fridge and microwave. There are also slighter cheaper rooms without terrace for $15 a night. The owners of Hostal 800 also have **Hostal 110** (Malecón 110, tel. 01/430-7514, $50, cheaper by week) on the south end of the beach, a similar setup with even larger two- or three-bedroom apartments.

Great service and plush surroundings can be found at **Sol y Mar** (Malecón 930, tel. 01/892-1999, $25 s, $40 d), with white leather couches, huge tiled rooms, and great bathrooms, cable TV, fridges, and full kitchens in a few rooms, and terraces with great ocean rooms. The other nice, though not too friendly, place on Playa Norte is **La Posada del Mirador** (Malecón 105, tel. 01/430-7822, tel. 01/948-0688, fernandoferraro@hotmail.com, www.lanzadera.com/ferraro).

Peruvian surfing champion Makki Block rents surfboards and offers lessons from his **Kahunas Hostal** (tel. 01/430-7407, kahunasurf28@hotmail.com, $35 s, $50 d, including breakfast). The hostel is perched on a bluff at the north end of Playa Norte and overlooks the Penascal surfing break. Perks include a secluded terrace, pool, hydro-massage and TVs in all the rooms, which are decorated with surf decor.

Food

Most of the eating options—except for the spit-roasted chicken at Mar Pacífico 495—revolve around seafood. **Restaurant Curazao** (San Bartolo 231, tel. 01/430-7787, 8 A.M.–8 P.M., $3–5) is known for both Chilean and Peruvian seafood plates. There's a line of restaurants down Mar Pacífico. The best of these include **El Arador del Mar** (Mar Pacífico, tel. 01/430-8215, $3–5), with a good seafood lunch menu for $3. But the next-door **El Rincón de Chelulo** (Mar Pacífico, tel. 01/430-7170) wins out for a greater variety of fish and shellfish, unbelievable friendly service,

and a larger $3 lunch menu. These restaurants are in front of the plaza where the town's market opens up every morning. On this square are also a few ice cream shops and pizzerias, open in summers only.

Information and Services

The best place for local info is **www.sanbartoloperu.com,** and the town's chamber of commerce can respond to questions in Spanish at **sanbartoloperu@yahoo.es.** Or check the surfers' page **www.peruazul.com.** Both the **police** and the **local clinic** are located on Av. San Bartolo near the highway entrance. There is Internet at **Mar Pacífico 495** (tel. 01/430-7137, $0.60 per hour), which is also a surf shop.

Getting There

Probably the easiest way to get to San Bartolo from Lima is to hire a taxi ($15) or take the Cruz del Sur bus, which stops at the town entrance. Local buses for Mala—which stop outside of Punta Hermosa, San Bartolo, and Santa María—pick up passengers at the circle, or *trébol,* where Av. Javier Prado intersects with the Panamericana in Barranco. These buses, called *Maleños,* take 50 minutes to reach San Bartolo and charge $0.75.

Ayacucho
and the
Central Highlands

The villagers of Peru's Central Highlands were already hard-hit in the 1980s by bad roads, little or no phone communication, and a life that revolved around subsistence agriculture. Then came the **Shining Path** *(Sendero Luminoso),* a movement based on Maoist ideals that tried to spark a nationwide revolution by destroying whatever villagers had left.

During the 1980s and early 1990s, a staggering 69,000 people were killed in the crossfire between the Shining Path and the army. Shining Path was a countryside movement and, from its roots in Ayacucho, wreaked most havoc in the Central Highlands—more than 75 percent of those killed were Quechua-speaking villagers.

These days terrorism has disappeared and the

Must-Sees

Look for **M** to find the sights and activities you can't miss and **N** for the best dining and lodging.

Huancayo

M Festival de Apóstol Santiago: This July 25 festival features dancing and a ritualistic branding of cattle that blurs Christian and pre-Hispanic religious beliefs. It is but one of hundreds of traditional celebrations throughout the year in Huancayo and the surrounding Mantaro Valley (page 325).

The Mantaro Valley

M Hualhuas: The authentic tapestries and rugs

AYACUCHO AND THE CENTRAL HIGHLANDS

Hualhuas
Cochas Grande
Lima
Festival de Apóstol Santiago
Wari
Ayacucho Walking Tour
Barrio Santa Ana

PACIFIC OCEAN

PACIFIC OCEAN

weaving in Hualhuas

© RENEE DEL GAUDIO AND ROSS WEHNER

found in the Ayacucho Market are produced here (page 330).

M Cochas Grande: Here artisans practicing gourd carving—which dates to pre-Incan times—are glad to invite visitors into their homes (page 331).

Ayacucho

M Ayacucho Walking Tour: The streets of this hidden jewel include Renaissance and baroque churches and the friendliest and most interesting market in Peru, where bubbling pots of corn stews, dozens of *chichas,* and huge rocks of black salt are on display alongside a staggering array of countryside produce (page 337).

M Wari: Exploring the countryside around Ayacucho leads to the ruins of Wari, the empire that made the Incas possible. Just 15 km up the road, you'll find **Quinua,** a charming adobe village known for its red-clay ceramics (page 339).

M Barrio Santa Ana: The winding streets of this charming Ayacucho neighborhood are lined with stone carvers and rug weavers and graced with **Santa Ana de los Indios,** a simple baroque church with an embossed silver altar (page 342).

highways are in fantastic shape—thanks to the national government, which is doing everything it can to connect this forgotten part of Peru to the rest of Peru. The area is safe for travel—even the conservative U.S. Embassy says so. Families have moved back to their towns, and there is a sense of recovery, of wounds slowly healing.

But still fewer than 500 travelers a month end up in **Ayacucho,** which is without question the most spectacular of Peru's Andean cities. There are 27 colonial churches in Ayacucho, a huge amount of colonial art, colorful markets, artisan studios on every corner, and one of Latin America's most famous Easter Week celebrations.

Huancayo, further north, is equally as interesting but for its countryside, not its city. There are a dozen or more quaint adobe villages in the surrounding Mantaro Valley where artisans make a living by carving gourds or making weavings from alpaca wool and natural dyes. There are more traditional festivals here than anywhere else in Peru and outsiders are welcome. After such bitter years, they are overjoyed to have guests.

PLANNING YOUR TIME

Most travelers arrive to Huancayo via bus from Lima, a comfortable six-hour journey on 300 km of paved roads. The Lima-Huancayo railroad, billed as the highest train in the world, is once again running, though its schedule is much-reduced and sporadic.

After visiting Huancayo, most travelers return to Lima but a growing number continue to Ayacucho (8–10 hours), and on to Andahuaylas (10 hours) and then Abancay and Cusco (10 hours). This is a fascinating bus journey, well off the Gringo Trail, and on steadily improving roads. If traveled by day, it is completely safe.

The most interesting town in the Central Highlands—in the whole of Peru's Andes—is Ayacucho but, for those short on time, it does not make sense to spend 20 hours on a bus to Cusco. Right now the quickest way on is to return to Lima and fly to Cusco, but watch for Ayacucho-Cusco flights in the future. Plan on spending at least three days in Ayacucho.

Over the Andes from Lima

If you want a crash course in Peruvian geography, take a bus up the Carretera Central, the well-paved highway that connects Lima with the interior of the country. Even on the foggiest of Lima's winter days, blue skies and sun can usually be found after less than an hour's drive inland to the towns of Chaclacayo, Chosica, and Santa Eulalia. From here the Carretera Central follows the Río Rímac through the subtropical valleys outside Lima, sheer rock canyons, desolate expanses of *puna,* or high plains, and down into the jungle on the other side.

This trip is not for the fainthearted: in two hours, or 126 km, travelers head from sea level to the town of Ticlio and the Anticona Pass at 4,820 meters (15,080 feet)! One of Peru's greatest engineering achievements was building a railroad over this pass in the 19th century. When traveling this route, bring warm clothing and water, and travel quickly to avoid headaches, nausea, crabbiness, and the other effects of altitude sickness.

After passing snow-capped Nevado Anticona and Lago Huacracocha, the route drops through striking, pea-green *puna* and a string of grimy mountain towns that end with La Oroya, an industrial rust heap hemmed in by bare hillsides. The river that runs through it is choked with foundry runoff and crossed by a series of concrete bridges, over which miners with plastic helmets and sooty faces trudge to and from their shifts.

At La Oroya the highway branches toward two Lima weekend spots, both of which are about a two-hour drive away: to the south lies the highland countryside around Huancayo; to the east lie the towns of La Merced and San Ramón, or Chanchamayo as they are collectively known.

The Chanchamayo road winds gently to **Tarma,** a colonial city at 925 meters that is famous in Peru for its Easter celebration. Past Tarma the road plunges another 2,300 meters to Chanchamayo, a fertile region for growing coffee, yucca, and banana.

Central Highlands

A third route to the north leads past Junín, a battlefield from the Peru's war for independence, Tingo María, and the low-jungle city of Pucallpa. Tingo Maria and Upper Huallaga Valley north of it is Peru's prime cocaine-producing region and is not safe for travel. For that reason, this route is not included in this book.

TARMA

Tarma is the first decent lodging option on the long haul between Lima and Chanchamayo, and strolling townspeople crowd the streets in the evening, a warming sight after the barren landscape of the *puna* above. Because of its chilly weather and altitude (925 meters or 3,053 feet), people coming from Lima occasionally feel altitude sickness here.

Tarma was founded by the Spanish soon after the conquest, though narrow streets and a handful of old homes are the only clues to its colonial pedigree. There are two churches worth a visit on the main square. **La Capilla del Señor de la Cárcel** (Chapel of the Lord of the Prison) was built in 1800 and remodeled in 1954 by General Manuel Odria, Tarma's most famous son and a Peruvian dictator during the 1930s. The church receives its name from the Christ image painted on its left wall and the fact that it was built atop the town's prison. Across the plaza is **Catedral Santa Ana** (6–10 A.M. and 5–8 P.M. daily), which was also built by Odria.

What Tarma is most know for, however, are incredible festivals, starting with elaborate processions, singing contests, and water balloon–throwing during February's *carnaval*. During Tarma's Easter Week, millions of flowers and seeds are carefully arranged on and around Plaza de Armas. The resulting flower carpet—depicting everything from landscapes to religious images—sets a new world record every year, covering every inch of street in an eight-block area around the main square, an estimated 3,400 square meters. At 5 A.M. on Easter Sunday, a religious procession walks over the carpet and through a number of decorated wooden arches on its way to and from the cathedral.

Other nearby attractions include **Tarmatambo,**

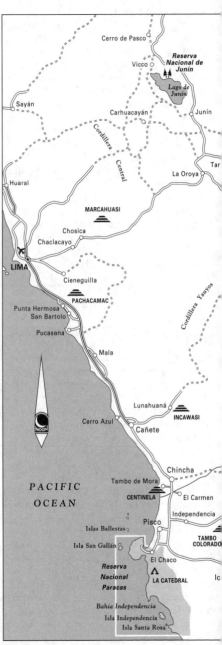

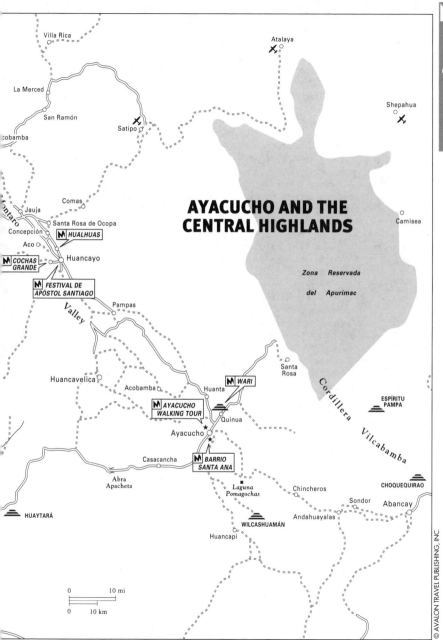

AYACUCHO AND THE
CENTRAL HIGHLANDS

Zona   Reservada

del   Apurímac

Villa Rica

Atalaya

Shepahua

La Merced

San Ramón

Satipo

Camisea

cobamba

Comas

Jauja

Santa Rosa de Ocopa

Concepción

HUALHUAS

Aco

COCHAS
GRANDE

Huancayo

FESTIVAL DE
APÓSTOL SANTIAGO

Valley

Pampas

Santa
Rosa

Huancavelica

Acobamba

Huanta

WARI

Cordillera

AYACUCHO
WALKING TOUR

Quinua

ESPÍRITU
PAMPA

Ayacucho

Vilcabamba

Casacancha

BARRIO
SANTA ANA

CHOQUEQUIRAO

Abra
Apacheta

Laguna
Pomagochas

Chincheros

Sondor

Abancay

HUAYTARÁ

Andahuaylas

WILCASHUAMÁN

Huancapi

0   10 mi

0   10 km

OVER THE ANDES BY TRAIN

One of Latin America's great engineering achievements of the 19th century was the completion of a train line across the Andes between Lima and Huancayo. The 12-hour journey begins in the desert coast around Lima and climbs through a subtropical river valley, dozens of rock tunnels, onto the *puna,* and finally up and over the snow-covered Cordillera. Needless to say, the 12-hour ride is a memorable experience, though the train only runs every month or so.

The train was built between 1870 and 1908 and was the brainchild of American entrepreneur Henry Meiggs, who bragged that he could "get a train wherever a llama can walk." Polish engineer Ernest Malinowski designed most of the 61 bridges, 65 tunnels, and 21 switchbacks, built over four decades by 10,000 workers—more than half of whom were indentured workers, or coolies, from China.

The train, considered to serve the highest passenger station in the world, climbs nearly nine meters per minute until reaching Ticlio at 4,758 meters. Shortly afterwards it climbs to its highest point at La Galera, a tunnel through the Andes at 4,781 meters. Depending on the season, the snow line hovers a few hundred meters above.

The service was shut down in 1991, following attacks by *Sendero Luminoso.* It began again briefly in the late 1990s but once again fell out of service. Hotel and restaurant owners are pushing hard so that the service, which greatly increases Huancayo's tourism cachet, will continue this time.

If you're coming from Lima, there's really no way to acclimatize for this journey except by sipping plenty of water (or even better, *maté de coca*) and being well-rested. Symptoms of altitude sickness include headaches and sometimes nausea—which usually pass once the train descends, though some passengers continue to suffer from *soroche,* or altitude sickness, even in Huancayo (3,240 meters).

Mountain guides swear the best medicine to take for altitude headaches is Excedrin. While adjusting to a higher altitude, it is always a good idea to avoid alcohol, heavy foods, and physical exertion. As the Bolivians say, *Come poco, tome poco, y duerme solo.* ("Eat little, drink little, and sleep alone").

---

a collection of Inca ruins 9 km to the south of Tarma. The **Santuario del Señor de Muruhuay** is a huge white modern church with an electric bell tower, visible from the highway 9 km east of Tarma at Acobamba. This is only the latest building to cover a rock carving of Christ reputed to have miraculous properties. Tradition maintains that it was etched on a boulder from a survivor of the Junín independence battle of Aug. 6, 1824.

There is world-class **caving** near Palcamayo, 23 km north of Acobamba along a dirt road. This town is the launching point for exploring one of Latin America's largest caves, the **Gruta de Huagapo.** Cavers using scuba equipment and oxygen tanks have descended as far as 2,800 meters into the cave. Guides can be contracted locally to help descend some distance into the cave,

but unguided visitors with headlamps can enter to about 300 meters.

Accommodations

The best budget option in Tarma is **Hostal Dorado** (Huanuco 488, tel. 064/32-1914, $4 s, $7 d, $3 extra for cable TV), a colonial home with a plant-filled courtyard and wooden second-story balcony. Rooms are simple, clean, and quiet, and cheaper rooms with shared bathrooms are available. **Hostal Central** (Huánuco 614, tel. 064/32-1198, $6 s, $10 d) is a bit run-down but has a high-powered telescope for viewing the stars. **Hotel Galaxia** (Lima 262, tel. 064/32-1449, $12 s, $15 d, with cable TV) is clean and quiet, despite its location on the main square, but lacks charm.

The luxury option in Tarma is **Los Portales** (Ramón Castilla 512, tel. 064/32-1411, $44 s, $62 d), which was built (of course) by General Odria in the 1950s on the main road just west of town. For the price, we found the rooms musty, unimpressive, and in need of an update. A German-Swiss couple are running **Ⓜ La Florida** (6 km outside Tarma, tel. 064/34-1041 or 064/34-1358, Kreida@terra.com.pe), a colonial hacienda that once belonged to Peruvian painter José Otero. There are 12 tastefully decorated rooms, some decorated with antiques, and courtyards and gardens for strolling.

Food

For spit-fired chicken, trout, meats, and meal-sized soups, head to **Restaurant Señorial** (Huánuco 140, 8 A.M.–3:30 P.M. and 6–11 P.M., $2–5). Lo Mejorcito de Tarma (Arequipa and Huaraz, tel. 064/32-3500, 10 A.M.–11 P.M.) has an excellent Peruvian buffet on Tuesday, Friday, and Sunday. **Restaurante Midamar's** (Plaza de Armas, Arequipa 221, 7 A.M.–11 P.M.) serves breakfast and has a good lunch menu.

Information and Services

There is some tourist information, and guides for surrounding sights, at the **information office** on the main square next to the municipality. A good local guide, who speaks only Spanish, is **Carlos Torres** (tel. 064/32-3483, carlos-tours@latinmail.com) who is often found at the Librería XXI on the corner of Lima and Moguegua. The town's fastest Internet is **Infomedia,** on the corner of Paucartambo and Lima.

Getting There

The two main transport companies, with terminals in Lima, have daily buses down to Chanchamayo and to Huancayo. **Empresa de Transporte Nuestra Señora de la Merced** (Vienrich 420, tel. 064/32-2937) has $4 buses to Lima three times a day, including a semi-bed version for $6 at 11:30 P.M., and transfers to Huancayo from Tarma. The company also offers $2 buses to Chanchamayo three times a day between noon and 5 P.M. **Empresa de Transportes Chanchamayo** (Callao 1002, tel. 064/32-1882) is another reputable bus company for the Lima-Chanchamayo journey.

Huancayo

The Mantaro Valley in Peru's central highlands is one of the country's most productive agricultural areas, a giant swath of flat land famous for its potatoes, corn, barley, quinoa, artichokes, and many vegetables. The charming adobe villages of this valley are the best places in all of Peru to see a wide range of craftspeople at work (and acquire the highest quality artwork at a fair price that benefits the artist, not the merchant).

Artisans here produce the ceramics, weavings, carved gourds *(mates burilados),* and silver filigree that is sold, at a considerable markup, in the crafts markets of Cusco and Lima. Many of the artisans are national champions in their disciplines and produce works of staggering beauty that are impossible to find elsewhere in the country. The artisans are glad to work and chat at the same time and gladly invite in visitors who knock on their unmarked, wooden doors.

More so than other more touristy areas of Peru, Mantaro Valley villagers do not behave differently in front of foreigners and go about their lives much as they have for centuries. They are proud and prosperous people. Depending on the time of the year, villagers are out in the fields planting or harvesting, threshing wheat with horses and donkeys, herding cows with colorful tassels tied to their ears, or building rammed-earth homes that are the same chocolate color as the surrounding fields. There is a festival nearly every day somewhere in the valley.

A good way to experience local culture is through one of the walking or mountain bike routes mapped out by the energetic and affable Lucho Hurtado at Incas del Peru, the best source of information on the area (see *Sports and Recreation* below). He has good contacts among local craftspeople and leads treks to the Cordillera Huaytapallana, a small but spectacular range 50 km east of Huancayo that includes a number of

uncarved gourds on market day at Cochas Grande

glaciated peaks, including Mount Lasuntay (5,780 meters).

There are many local ruins from the Xauxa and later Huanca culture, which ran a lively coast-jungle trade from 900 A.D. onwards until being conquered by the Incas in the 15th century. Like the Chachapoyans further north, the Huancas resented Inca rule and sided with the Spanish, who followed the Inca Roads through the Mantaro Valley en route to Cusco in 1533. The following year, Francisco Pizarro returned to the area to found Jauja, Peru's first, though short-lived capital, and the land was divided up among the Spaniards (a source of dismay, no doubt, to Huancas elders).

During the independence struggle three centuries later, the Spanish troops based themselves in Huancayo for three years until they were defeated at nearby Junín and Ayacucho in 1824. During the War of the Pacific (1879–83), several bloody battles were again fought in the Mantaro Valley between Chilean soldiers and the Peruvian army led by General Andrés Cáceres, who was dubbed

the Wizard of the Andes for his ability to attack and quickly disappear into the mountains. During the 1980s and 1990s, Mantaro Valley villages were caught in the crossfire between the Shining Path and the Peruvian army. The area is recovering strongly, thanks in part to good farming lands, crafts production, and tourism.

The best base for touring the valley is Huancayo (3,240 meters), an unfortunate sprawl of cement buildings topped off by the exhaust of far too many old buses. The city's biggest attraction is the Sunday market, where fresh food is sold side by side with handicrafts. There are not many other sights, nor good lodging options, in the city itself—the best options are on the edge of town or in the nearby village of Concepción.

SIGHTS

The best way to enjoy Huancayo is to take a taxi to the east end of Giráldez and walk up Cerrito de la Libertad, which offers nice views over the city and a few stands with *comida típica*. From there continue another 2 km to an odd formation of sandstone towers known as **Torre Torre** and then traverse the hillside above the city for another few kilometers. The end point is the **Parque de la Identidad Huanca,** an interesting Gaudí-esque park with curving stone walls, sculptures, and native plants. It is a great evening hangout spot near a range of affordable Peruvian restaurants. A map of this walk, which takes a few hours, is available through Lucho Hurtado (see *Sports and Recreation,* below).

There is not much to see in Huancayo itself. The Plaza de Armas is nondescript, and Huancayo's churches are all modern, except for **La Merced,** on the first block of Real, where Peru's constitution was signed in 1839. **El Museo Salesiano de Ciencias Naturales** (Santa Rosa, El Tambo, tel. 064/24-7763, 9 A.M.–1 P.M.) has an amazing collection of more than 13,000 Amazon insects, jungle birds, butterflies, fossils, and archaeological artifacts.

▼ FESTIVAL DE APÓSTOL SANTIAGO

Some of Peru's most interesting (and most frequent) festivals are found in the Mantaro Valley, which has more traditional festivals than there are days in the year. During the Festival de Apóstol Santiago on July 25, villagers throughout the Mantaro Valley brand their livestock amid much dancing and drinking of *chicha,* or fermented corn beer. Though Christian on the surface, this pre-Hispanic ritual invokes the protection of Andean deities.

Other festival highlights include Fiesta del Niño in January, Carnaval in February, Cruz del Mayo in May, Fiesta de San Pedro and San Pablo on June 28 and 29, la Fiesta de Santiago on July 25, and Todos los Santos (Day of the Dead) on Nov. 1. In Jauja there is Jala Pato (Pull the Duck) in late January, when horsemen compete to yank off the head of a suspended duck. The village of Sapallanga is known for the colorful processions of the the Virgen de Cocharcas Sept. 7–9. For a complete list of Mantaro Valley festivals, see www.incasdelperu.org.

ENTERTAINMENT

La Cabaña (Giráldez 652, tel. 064/22-3303, 7 P.M.–midnight) is an excellent drinking and dancing spot that is popular with both locals and travelers. Local bands crank out folkloric music Thurs.–Sat. from 9 P.M. onwards. **Antojitos** (Puno 599, tel. 064/23-7950, 5 P.M.–2 A.M.), on the corner of Arequipa and Puno, serves up light food in an atmosphere of classic rock and salsa, as does **Galileo** (Paseo La Breña 378, 6 P.M.–midnight Mon.–Sat.).

The three best discotheques of Huancayo are **Taj Mahal** (Huancavelica 1056, 7 P.M.–2 A.M. Mon.–Sat.), **La Noche** (San Antonio 241, 9 P.M.–3 A.M. Fri.–Sat.), and **El Molino** (Ugarte 503, 7 P.M.–2 A.M. Thurs.–Sat.). Cover charges hover around $3, including a drink, and things get going around 11 P.M. There is a good karaoke spot on Plaza de Armas called **Torre Torre** (Giráldez 137, 7 P.M.–2 A.M. Mon.–Sat.).

Cine Mantaro (Real 950, tel. 064/25-3157, 4 P.M.–midnight daily) shows Hollywood movies daily.

SHOPPING

Huancayo is famous for its Sunday market on Huancavelica Street, where fresh food is sold alongside handicrafts on three blocks from Puno to Loreto. The best time to go is around 4 to 5 P.M., when vendors are packing up and are eager to bargain. There are several small markets in Huancayo that sell mostly tourist items—the best place is **Casa de Artesano** on the Plaza de Armas (Real 495, closed Thurs.). However, you will receive better prices and have a memorable experience if you buy directly from the artists in their homes.

Villages around the Mantaro Valley have markets where crafts are sold on different days of the week, including Wednesday in San Jerónimo de Tunán, Saturday in Chupaca, and Sunday in Concepción and Jauja.

SPORTS AND RECREATION

Lucho Hurtado at **Incas del Peru** (Giráldez 652, tel. 064/22-3303, incas_peru@hotmail.com, www.incasdelperu.org, 9 A.M.–1 P.M. and 4–7 P.M. Mon.–Sat., 10 A.M.–1 P.M. Sun.) speaks flawless English and is full of adventurous options for the Huancayo area.

He rents mountain bikes ($8 half-day, $15 full day) and hands out free walking and biking maps to those who rent bikes or stay in the Casa de la Abuela, the hostel across the street, run by his mom. The walks include the lake-to-lake circuit near Jauja and loop above Huancayo; ruins and hot mineral baths at Matachico, north of Jauja; a ridge walk between the villages of Ahuac and Chupaca that passes through a line of Huanca granaries and offers views of the snow-covered Cordillera Huaytapallana and Lago Ñahuimpuquio; a walk from the village of San Jerónimo to the Ingenio trout farm and then back to Concepción; and a walk between the artisan towns of Hualhuas and San Jerónimo.

Lucho is well-connected among the artisans in the valley and offers a great crafts tour to shops in several villages for $35 pp, including lunch and guide. He also offers archaeology tours of the valley and leads three- to five-day treks to out-of-the-way places, including a trek along an old llama trail that threads 4,400-meter passes in the Cordillera Huaytapallana. He knows the jungle around Chanchamayo well and takes travelers out to his father's ranch on the way to Pozuzo, a great chance to see how locals live and do some rough-and-tumble exploring. Lucho is a gifted teacher who helps people understand their surroundings.

The best private guide in Huancayo is Jorge Sanabria, the son of Juana Sanabria at **Peru Andino Lodging** (Pasaje San Antonio 113, San Carlos, tel. 064/22-3956, peruandino_1@yahoo.com). Jorge has an incredible passion for both the Andes and the Amazon and is always out exploring new routes in the surrounding area. He charges $30 per day as a guide along with $4 per mule and $6 per muleteer.

The other tour agencies in Huancayo include cheaper tours that do not include food, entry fees, or truly bilingual guides. They are, however, much cheaper, about $10 a day. Recommended agencies include **Peruvian Tours** (Plaza de Armas on the side of the cathedral, tel. 064/21-3069, sheboperu@terra.com) and **Dar-**qui Tours** (Ancash 367, Plaza de Armas, tel. 064/23-3705).

ACCOMMODATIONS
Under $10

La Casa de la Abuela (Giráldez 691, tel. 064/22-3303, casa_abuela@yahoo.com, www.incasdelperu.org, $6 pp, 10 percent SAEC discount) is a charming 1930s house stuffed with art objects, maps, magazines, games, and books. There are a few double rooms with private bath for $9, though most guests sleep in the bunk rooms. La Casa de la Abuela is more like a forgetful household than an efficient hotel, but that is precisely its charm. The second floor's sporadic water, an early-rising, squawking parrot, and whatever other blemishes there may be are wiped away by Margarita Hurtado, the quintessential grandma with curly gray hair and a mischievous smile who lives on the first floor. Prices include a yummy breakfast of coffee, bread, fruit, and juice plus a welcoming *Calentito,* a hot pisco drink. Casa de la Abuela is a backpacker's beehive and is a 10-minute walk from downtown, just enough on the edge of things to enjoy quiet, clean air.

Peru Andino Lodging (Pasaje San Antonio 113, tel. 064/22-3956, peruandino@mixmail .com, www.geocities.com/peruandino_1, $6 pp, shared bath) is a modern home in a quiet neighborhood run by Juana and Luis Sanabria. The beds are firm, bathrooms are clean, and the surrounding San Carlos neighborhood is absolutely quiet. Rooms with private bathrooms are $7 pp and there are two nice rooftop rooms with a bit more privacy.

If you value a creative atmosphere over reliable service, peek into **Casa Alojamiento Bonilla** (Huánuco 332, tel. 064/23-2103, $7 s $12). Bizarre, beautiful sculptures tower over a garden of native plants, surrounded by rooms with high ceilings, wood floors, and wildly creative paintings. One of the shared bathrooms is a bit crummy, but the other has a huge, ceramic tub—a rare find in Peru. Service is spotty, things are a bit dishevelled, but the ambience is powerful—exactly as an artists' studio should be.

$10–25

For those willing to forgo charm for a firm bed, plenty of hot water, and a central location, try the modern **El Marquéz** (Puno 294, tel. 064/21-9026, elmarquez@elmarquezhuancayo.com, www.elmarquezhuancayo.com, $26 s, $35 d). Rooms are large, carpeted, and quiet and have cable TV. **Susan's Hotel** (Real 851, tel. 064/20-2251, $17 s, $29 d) is another modern hotel on the main street with clean bathrooms, firm beds (with kitschy lion bedspreads), and quiet back rooms.

$25–50

Hotel Turismo Huancayo (Ancash 729, tel. 064/23-1072, $34 s, $48 d) is an elegant 1930s colonial-style hotel, smack in the center of town, with good views over the Plaza Huamanmarca. There is a rather empty feeling to its long tile hallways, but the rooms are genuinely comfortable: king-size beds, heater, cable TV, and immaculate bathrooms and not too noisy. If you need to be in the city and want some comfort, this is your place.

$50–100

Located 20 minutes north of Huancayo, the new **M Hotel Loma Verde** (Leopoldo Peña, Concepción, tel. 064/58-1569, or in Lima 01/242-7599, lomaverdeperu@lomaverdeperu.com, www.lomaverdeperu.com, $50 s, $60 d, including breakfast) has plenty of country charm. The main lodge has sitting areas with fabulous views over the Mantaro Valley. Rooms are crafted from stone, plaster, and exposed beams and feature feather comforters, fireplaces, cable TV, and private porches with sunset views. The restaurant serves a wide variety of food on a veranda, and food is often cooked in the *pachamanca* pit or over open fire. There are horses and mountain bikes for rent. The only drawback is audible truck traffic on the highway below.

Derrama Magisterial (Oriente s/n, Concepción, tel. 064/58-1001, cpijno@derramaje.org.pe, $27 s, $35 d) is another country retreat nearby with pleasant walks and good reading rooms—but not as charming as Loma

Verde. Bedrooms are simple and clean with mediocre bathrooms.

FOOD

Huancayo has some excellent places for *comida típica*, all of which are a taxi ride from the center. The region's most famous dish is *papas a la huancaína*, yellow potatoes smothered with a yellow sauce made from fresh cheese, oil, ground yellow chili pepper, lemon, and egg yolk—and topped off witih black olives.

Cafés and Desserts

An interesting place for coffee or wine is the **Plaza Jugería** (Puno 412, tel. 064/21-9534, 10 A.M.–3 A.M.), which is decorated in a jungle theme. The best place for a rich cappuccino, light snack, or dessert is **Pastelería Koky** (Puno 298, tel. 064/23-4707, 7 A.M.–10 P.M., $1). It also makes homemade bread and sells deli meats and cheeses, good for picnics.

A good place for hamburgers, pizzas, cake, or ice cream is **La Moderna** (Paseo la Breña 165), though the best chocolate cake is at the tiny **Berisso** (Giráldez 258, tel. 064/22-5634). Cafetería Loredo (Loreto 632, tel. 064/21-2853, 7:30 A.M.–noon and 3:30–10 P.M.) has been around for 40 years and is a cheap, unpretentious place to have coffee, oatmeal and milk, *biscocho,* and empanadas. The family produces *turrones de Doña Pepe* (a toffee-like sweet) around September and *panetones* (a puffy Christmas cake laden with candied fruit) in December.

Peruvian

Huancahuasi (Mariscal Castilla 2222, El Tambo tel. 064/24-4826, 8 A.M.–8 P.M.) is a great place for Sunday lunch, with live folkloric music and steaming chunks of pork, beef, and lamb from the *pachamanca* pit, accompanied by corn and roasted beans. **La Tullpa** is also highly recommended and has one of the town's only chefs certified in Peruvian food.

La Chacra del Abuelo (behind the cemetery and near the corner of Daniel Carrión and Ica Nueva, tel. 064/23-7143, $3–6) has the town's best *tiradito de trucha* (strips of trout cooked in lemon juice), *cuy chactado* (pan-fried cuy with corn), and excellent cuts of meats.

Locals say the best *pachamanca* is to be had at **Doña Teófila,** a hole-in-the-wall hidden among a whole line of restaurants stretched along the road to Puno in the southern suburb of Asapampa.

After an evening's stroll around the Parque de la Identidad, wander over to **Restaurant Comida Wanka** (next to the park, 10 A.M.–9 P.M. daily), where 10 food stalls each sell yummy, safe local dishes, including *chicharrón colorado, picante de cuy,* and *pachamanca.*

El Viejo Madero (Paseo a la Brena 125, tel. 064/21-7788, noon–11 P.M., $2) serves only one thing: huge chunks of juicy, spit-roasted chicken, topped off with french fries and a salad that is safe for foreigners.

A recommended place for fried pork ribs is **Chicharronería Cuzco** (Cuzco 173).

Pizza

The stylish **La Cabaña** (Giráldez 652, tel. 064/22-3303, 5–11 P.M. daily, $7) is a cozy place with a fireplace, art, and great pizza. Live folk music plays Thurs.–Sat. from 8 P.M. It also serves grilled meats, sandwiches, and pitchers of sangria. Good pizza, sandwiches, and inexpensive lunch menus can be found at **Antojitos** (Puno 599, tel. 064/23-7950, 6–11 P.M.Mon.–Sat.), which has live rock music on the weekends.

In the San Carlos neighborhood, try **Italia** (Leandra Torres 441, at Parque Tupac Amaru, tel. 064/23-3145, 5:30–11:30 P.M.), which delivers and has lasagna and a range of other pasta.

Health Food

Nuevo Horizonte (Ica 578, tel. 064/21-3817, 7 A.M.–10 P.M. Sun.–Fri.) has good $1 vegetarian lunch *menús* and a relaxing atmosphere.

Markets

The best small market is **Comercial Huaychulo** (Paseo a la Brena 174) with fruits, vegetables, deli meats, and cheeses. Grocery stores include **Supermercado Dia** on Giráldez 271 and **Supermercado Casa Sueldo** (Real 696, corner of Loreto, 8:30 A.M.–10 P.M. daily).

INFORMATION AND SERVICES

The **tourist office** (corner of Breña and Real, tel. 064/23-8480) is located inside the Casa de Artesano; its hours change constantly. The best source of travel information in Huancayo is Lucho Hurtado at **Incas del Peru** (see *Sports and Recreation*).

The **tourist police** are located on Ferrocarril 555 (tel. 064/21-9851).

The pharmacy with the widest selection is **Botica Arcangel** (Real 467, tel. 064/20-2200, 24 hours) on the Plaza de Armas, or try **Bristol** (Giráldez 267, tel. 064/21-9995).

For health care, try the English-speaking Dr. Felix Ortega at **Clínica Ortega** (Daniel Carrión 1552, tel. 064/23-5430) or the hospital down the street (Daniel Carrión 1552, tel. 064/23-2222).

Incas del Peru (Giráldez 652, travelinfo@incasdelperu.org, www.incasdelperu.org, tel. 064/22-3303) offers a Spanish for Travelers class with courses starting every Monday. The budget course for $110 includes three hours of daily lessons, five days lodging at La Casa de la Abuela, and three meals a day. Additional options include homestays, weekend excursions, and field trips around town. The agency can also arrange classes for Quechua, weaving and natural dyes, Peruvian cooking, dancing, Andean music, jewelry design, and gourd carving.

Most banks are located on blocks 5 and 6 of Real, including **Banco de Crédito, Interbanc, Banco Continental,** and **Banco Wiese.** There is a **Western Union** (365 Ancash, tel. 064/23-3705) on the Plaza de Armas. Rigged calculators are a problem in Huancayo, so change bills in a bank or in a money exchange.

The **post office** is located in the Plaza Huamanmarca, near intersection of Real and Huamanmarca.

The Internet places around the Plaza de Armas are slightly more expensive, and there are several faster places along Giráldez, including **Cibercentro** (Giráldez 275, $0.50/hour, also does international calls), a 24-hour place at Giráldez 288, and another good place across from La Casa de la Abuela at Giráldez 692.

Telephone cabins located at Real and Lima are open 7 A.M.–10 P.M.

The best place to take your dirty laundry is **Chic** (Breña 154, tel. 064/23-1107, 8 A.M.–10 P.M. Mon.–Sat., 10 A.M.–6 P.M. Sunday).

There is a **sauna and massage center** at Ica 578, next to the vegetarian restaurant Nuevo Horizonte. The sauna, both dry and steam, operates Sundays 6 A.M.–10 P.M. and costs $1.50. Massages and reflex therapy sessions can be arranged a day or two ahead of time. Call Ivan Bustamante at tel. 064/36-7401.

GETTING THERE

There are no flights to Huancayo, though the Trans-Andean railroad has once again resumed service between Lima and Huancayo. The ride takes about 12 hours and schedules change often—contact Incas del Peru agency for more information. Currently the train runs only once a month.

There are lots of options for bus service to and from Huancayo. The best include **Ormeño** (Mariscal Castilla 1379, tel. 064/25-1199), which has a Royal Class bus ($13) leaving for Lima at 11 P.M. and normal class ($7) leaving at 1:30 P.M. and 10:30 P.M. Other options included **Cruz del Sur** (Ayacucho 281, tel. 064/22-3367), running buses at 8 A.M., 1:30 P.M., 11 P.M., and 11:45 P.M., **Mariscal Cáceres** (Real 1247, tel. 064/21-6633), and **ETUCSA** (Puno 220, tel. 064/23-2638).

For Tarma and the jungle around Chanchamayo, try **Empresa Transporte San Juan** (Omaryali 159). Buses leave hourly for Tarma between 5 A.M. and 8 P.M. ($3), with connections on to Merced ($4) and Satipo ($5).

For the rough and beautiful ride to Cañete Valley on the coast, try **ETAS** (Loreto 744, tel. 064/21-5424), which has buses leaving at 6 A.M. for the 13-hour journey on dirt road through Yauricocha and past the Yauyos range ($9).

For Ayacucho, try **Empresa Transporte Molina** at Angaraes and Real. The road has been improved and the trip now takes around 8–10 hours. Buses leave in the morning and evening and cost $9.

There are several options for reaching Huancavelica, the best and most comfortable of which is the train. The station is located at 1766 Leoncio Prado (no telephone), where an express train ($3) leaves at 6:30 A.M. Mon.–Sat. and arrives—assuming there are no breakdowns—five hours later. Offering basic seating compartments, the cargo train ($2.50) leaves the same days at 1 P.M. and arrives at 7 P.M. On Sundays, there is a train with buffet lunch service ($4) that leaves at 2 P.M. and arrives at 7 P.M. Buy tickets a day ahead as the trains are sometimes full.

There are bus companies that head to Huancavelica, but the roads are rough and the going is more comfortable in *colectivos,* which leave from Real between Tarapacá and Angaraes Streets. The 3.5-hour trip costs $6. **Empresa Huáscar,** at Ancash and Angaraes, has several buses ($4) a day for the 4.5-hour ride to Huancavelica.

GETTING AROUND

With the Carretera Central running through Huancayo, finding transport around the Mantary Valley is easy. All transportation to the north (Hualhuas, San Jerónimo, Concepción, Jauja, Sicaya) passes the corner of Giráldez and Huancas. Transportation to the south passes the nearby corner of Ferrocarril and Giráldez.

The Mantaro Valley

The Mantaro Valley is filled with ruins, churches, and, most important, entire villages that specialize in one type of handicraft. With an early start, it is easy to take public transportation and visit these towns on your own—many of the better artisans are now marked by yellow signs.

A spectacular way to walk between towns, and have a picnic lunch on the way, are the out-of-the-way paths that have been mapped out by Lucho Hurtado. If you go on your own, get recommendations ahead of time and avoid the *artesanía* stores in the entrance of the towns. The easiest way to tour workshops is with an organized tour.

◪ HUALHUAS

This weaving town 20 minutes north of Huancayo produces tapestries, rugs, and clothing—mostly from hand-spun wool and natural dyes.

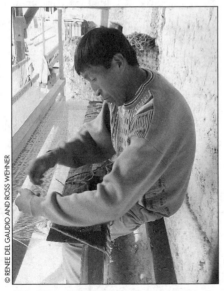

© RENEE DEL GAUDIO AND ROSS WEHNER

Victor Hugo Ingaroca Tupac Yupanqui at work in Hualhuas

THE ART OF NATURAL DYES

Weavers in Hualhuas are keeping alive a tradition of making the unmistakably vibrant natural dyes that were pioneered by pre-Inca cultures such as Nasca and Paracas. The dyes are made by grinding up roots, leaves, flowers, fruits, vegetables, minerals, and even bugs. Some of these are seasonal, so certain dyes are only available during certain times of the year. After the dye is made, handspun wool is soaked in the color, then fixed with minerals and hung to dry. Here are a few of the sources for the natural dyes:

- **Yellow:** crushed lichen
- **Reds and pinks:** extracted from cochinilla, a parasite that lives in the prickly pear cactus
- **Green:** chilca plant
- **Brown:** walnuts
- **Copper:** onion

The highest quality is found at **Victor Hugo Ingaroca Tupac Yupanqui** (Huancayo 315, Hualhuas, tel. 064/967-0462). His weavings, based on pre-Columbian techniques used by the Nasca and Paracas cultures, are stunning. His rugs sell for close to $400 at www.novica.com, but can be bought for a better price at his home.

Antonio Cáceres (28 de Julio 888, Hualhuas) produces more affordable weavings and is an expert on the natural plants, bugs, and minerals used to make his bright, natural dyes.

To see a busy workshop of weavers at their looms, stop at **Taller Ecotextil** (Alfonso Ugarte 1175, Hualhuas, tel. 064/67-0353, ecotextil@hotmail.com). Production here is high volume and of a wide variety, with purses, ponchos, and rugs of various sizes and styles.

A mother-and-daughter team sell their weavings at affordable prices at **Artesenia El Inca** (Parque Principal 1046, Hualhuas).

To reach Hualhuas, catch a *combi* at the corner of Giráldez and Huancas ($0.50, 20 minutes).

COCHAS GRANDE

Carved gourds *(mates burilados)* are an art form from pre-Inca times that continues to thrive in **Cochas Grande** and **Cochas Chico,** a pair of towns tucked behind the hills a half hour east of Huancayo. These gourds are carved in mind-boggling detail and usually tell a story about country life. Common stories include courtship, marriage, and childbirth; or planting, harvest, and celebration; or the process of building a home. Some even include current political commentary, and gourds carved during the 1980s are rife with images of the Shining Path.

Delia Poma (Huancayo 797, Cochas Grande, tel. 064/993-7722, deliapoma58@latinmail.com) is a national champ and is one of Cocha's most talented carvers. Her gourds are considered collectors' pieces and range in price from $25 to $100, though less expensive ones are made by her husband.

Alejandro Hurtado and Victoria Janampa, another award-winning couple, operate **Artesania Hurtado** (Loreto 326, Cochas Chico, tel.

Alejandro Hurtado and Victoria Janampa carve gourds at Cochas Grande.

064/24-5045). They have a series of fine gourds but also less expensive Christmas ornaments, boxes, and bowls. This is an excellent place to learn about the various engraving techniques, and to watch Alejandro and Victoria at work.

Teodosio Poma (Huancayo 504, tel. 064/993-0170) specializes in large gourds, ranging in price from $80 to $500.

To reach Cochas, take a bus from the corner of Giráldez and Huancas ($0.50, 30 minutes).

SAN JERÓNIMO DE TUNÁN

This village 13 km north of Huancayo is known for silver filigree. It is fascinating to watch **Jesús Suarez Vasquez** and his sister **Nelly Vasquez** (Arequipa 496, three blocks east of Plaza de Armas) make their delicate silver jewelry. A necklace that sells for $16 in Lima can be bought here for $6. Wednesday mornings are a good day to visit San Jeronimo, to catch the weekly market. There are many stores down the road and, on the main square, a beautiful 17th-century church with a baroque altar.

Other lesser crafts centers in the valley include **San Augustin de Cajas,** known for its wool hats; **Molinos,** near Jauja, which makes wood carvings including masks and stools decorated with animal shapes; and **Aco,** a center of ceramics. The best time to visit Aco is during its early Friday morning market, when ceramics wholesalers from all over the country snatch up pots and other goods for cheap.

SANTA ROSA DE OCOPA AND INGENIO TROUT FARM

There is a lot to see at **Santa Rosa de Ocopa** (9 A.M.–noon and 3–6 P.M. Wed.–Mon., $1.25), a San Francisco convent founded in 1723 that is near Concepción, or about 25 km northwest of Huancayo. As evangelical churches have grown, Santa Rosa has withered, and now only six monks are left. But the story behind Santa Rosa is fascinating. Franciscan missionaries embarked from here to proselytize in the Amazon jungle, and 86 were killed in the process, according to a commemorative plaque inside.

a potter at Aco

Baroque altars adorn the chapel and it is usually possible to descend into the catacombs. The newer convent building has a museum with stuffed jungle animals, paintings from the Cusco school, and gruesome paintings of missionaries being tortured by Amazon natives. The highlight of the convent, however, is a library that contains more than 25,000 volumes from the 15th century onwards. The oldest book in the library, published in 1497, is St. Agustine's reflections on the Bible (the convent used to have a 1454 catechism in Aymara, Quechua, and Spanish, but it was stolen in a 2002 armed robbery, along with a painting from the Flemish School). The original adobe cloisters include a stone courtyard, a metal shop, and other rooms.

The best lunch spot nearby is Ingenio, home to Peru's largest fish farms that produce approximately 50,000 kilos of trout per year. Most visitors tour the state-owned trout farm before sitting down to lunch at either Ávila or Llao Llao, small restaurants that serve trout heaped with local artichokes. Afterwards there is a pleasant, hour-long walk up a dirt road alongside the river to a set of waterfalls.

Most Huancayo agencies visit Ingenio and Santa Rosa as part of a Mantaro Valley tour, though it is easy to arrive at both places via public transport. *Combis* for Concepción leave every 30–40 minutes ($0.80) from Pachitea in Huancayo. In Concepcion, there are nearby *colectivos* and *combis* that head to both Ingenio and Santa Rosa de Ocopa.

JAUJA AND LAGUNA PACA

Peru's first capital is located 45 minutes, or 40 km, northwest of Huancayo on the highway from Lima. It is an alternate base for exploring the valley but has few services. Few travelers come to this bustling, friendly town of old adobe homes and colonial churches. The main church, **Iglesia de Jauja,** was the first church Francisco Pizarro ordered to be built. Inside are a few finely carved wooden altars. Built in the 1920s, **La Iglesia del Cristo Pobre** is based on the chapel of France's

© RENEE DEL GAUDIO AND ROSS WEHNER

Santa Rosa de Ocopa

Notre Dame. This church was the first building constructed of cement in the Mantaro Valley. Lodging options include a small pension run by Niegemann Ilse Mancho on Manco Capac 575 (tel. 064/36-1620) and **Cabezon's Hostal** (Ayacucho 1027, tel. 064/36-2206, $5 s), with shared bathrooms.

From Jauja there are $0.50 *motocars* to Laguna Paca, the shores of which have been unfortunately marred by a line of cheap restaurants. A quick boat ride to the Isla de Amor, a tiny island in the middle of the lake, offers good views of Xauxa ruins on a nearby ridge and the mountains to the west. A good walk leads up from the lake to these and other Inca ruins in the area and passes through the villages of Acolla, Marco, and Tragadero. This is a good walk for those who want to spend the day walking through country and tracking down rarely visited ruins. The walk ends at a smaller, upper lake near a road where *combis* return to Jauja. A shorter hike is possible to Tunanmarca, the old city near Jauja. The trail starts in the town of Concho and takes about 2.5 hours. Maps of these walks are available from Lucho Hurtado. Cars to Jauja ($0.90), and many other places, leave from Calixto Street in Huancayo.

WARIWILCA

These ruins from the Huanca and Wari cultures are 6 km south of Huancayo. The ruins are located below the plaza of the village of Huari, which is next to Río Chancas. The ceremonial center includes a high wall, staircase, interior passageways, and two huge *molle* trees. The name means "sacred place of the Wari," the Ayacucho-based culture that spread throughout Peru's highlands between 600 and 1000 A.D. The nearby museum (8 A.M.–1 P.M. and 3–6 P.M. Tues.–Sun., $0.50) includes many pre-Inca artifacts found at the site, including *spondyllus* shells imported from Ecuador, ceramics, metalworks, and a female mummy, found at the site, known as *The Maiden of Wariwilca*. To get to the ruins, near the town of Huari, take a blue-and-white bus to Huari from the corner of Giráldez and Ferrocarril.

HUANCAVELICA

Huancavelica, at 3,680 meters, was a rich and world-famous mining town during colonial times. It withered into a ghost town during the last few centuries and was badly battered by the war against *Sendero Luminoso.* Though the town is trying to make a comeback, the chief reason for coming here these days is to wander around colonial churches and homes and get away from tourists.

The city was founded shortly after the nearby Santa Barbara mercury mine was opened in 1563. Mercury was invaluable for extracting purer grades of silver from the ore extracted at Potosí, Bolivia. As a result, Huancavelica and Ayacucho—where the owners of the Santa Barbara mine lived—exploded into the Viceroyalty's richest mining towns. From here, caravans of mules and llamas carried the mercury in leather pouches to the Peruvian coast, where it was shipped to Arica, Chile, and transported into Bolivia.

Sights

There are eight colonial churches in tiny Huancavelica. The **Plaza de Armas,** bordered by the cathedral, town hall, and some colonial homes, features a granite fountain installed in the mid-19th century. The cathedral itself has a good collection of colonial paintings and a magnificent baroque altar and pulpit. The churches of **San Sebastían** (1662) and **San Francisco** (1774), in Plaza Bolognesi, are worth seeing for their collections of baroque art. The best time to find these churches open is during early-morning Mass or on Sundays, when there is an excellent market along Torre Tagle that draws villagers from all over the surrounding countryside.

The **San Cristóbal Mineral Springs** (5 A.M.–5 P.M. $0.30), 10 minutes northwest of the city, have a great reputation for curing skin diseases, although they are more on the lukewarm side than hot. Ask at hotels for directions and hours.

There are also good walks in the surrounding area, including the area around the Santa Barbara mine, which closed in the early 19th century.

Accommodations

Huancavelica's best hotel is **Hotel Presidente**

(Plaza de Armas s/n, tel. 067/75-2760, $26 s, $34 d), in a historic building on the Plaza de Armas. Prices quoted are for the executive rooms which have been recently updated, have lots of hot water and cable TV. There are also slightly cheaper tourist rooms ($23 s, $29 d), which are a bit older but have the same services. The hotel also has one of the city's better restaurants, Cheaper options include **Hotel Camacho** (Carabaya 481, tel. 067/75-3298, $5 s, $7 d) is the town's best budget choice, with clean rooms, decent mattresses and lots of blankets. There is hot water in the morning only. Another budget option is right on the Plaza de Armas: **Hotel Asención** (Manco Capac 481, tel. 067/75-3103, $5 s, $7 d). Check on hot water before paying for the room.

Food

Good restaurants are hard to find in Huancavelica. The best is probably in the **Hotel Presidente** (Plaza de Armas, tel. 067/75-2760, 7 A.M.–3 P.M., 6–10 P.M. daily, $3–5), which serves up chifa, trout and a few chicken and beef dishes.

The best regional food is served at **Los Portales** (Virrey Toledo 158) and **Paquirri** (Arequipa 137). For Chifa, head to **Restaurant Joy** (Virrey Toledo 216, tel. 067/75-2826, $3-$6), which also offers a good lunch menu for $2.

Information and Services

Tourist information is available at **Turismo Andino** (Manchego Muñoz 391, second floor, tel. 067/69-2383). The **National Police** (tel. 067/75-2729) are located at Huayna Capac s/n. For health emergencies, **Hospital Essalud** (Teresa Jornet s/n, tel. 064/75-1143 or 064/75-3155) is located in Barrio de Yananaco. The best pharmacies are **Salud** (Arequipa 145) and **Imaculada** (Virrey Toledo 276). For money matters, there is **Banco de la Nación** (Escalonada 127) and **Banco de Crédito** (Virrey Toledo 383). The post office, Serpost, is located at Ferrúa 105, in Barrio Santa Ana. Internet is available at **Ccoyllor** (Manchego Muñoz 488) and **Yomax** (Manchego Muñoz s/n). There are phone booths at Carabaya and Virrey Toledo.

Getting There

Cargo trains travel daily between Huancavelica

and Huancayo at 6:30 A.M. and sometimes at 12:30 P.M. as well. The five-hour ride is only $4 and offers breathtaking views. Most locals travel the rough road to Huancayo via *colectivos* ($6, 3.5 hours), which leave from the Plaza de Armas throughout the day. The best bus company for the route is **Empresa Ticllas** ($4, 4.5 hours).

From Huancavelica buses from Empresa Ticllas and other companies also head west on dirt roads over the 4,800-meter Chonta pass, past a series of beautiful lakes and down to Pisco and the Paracas marine reserve on the Pacific coast.

Empresa Ticllas also runs buses on the complicated, rough route toward Ayacucho. An easier option is to take local transport to the town of Santa Inés, which is on the paved Pisco-Ayacucho highway. From there, wait for an Ayacucho-bound bus.

Ayacucho

It is easy to understand why Peruvians are so fond of Ayacucho. This hidden jewel of Peru's southern Andes has Renaissance and baroque churches around every corner (33 in all!), the country's most elaborate Easter Week celebration, and one-of-a-kind Wari and Inca ruins in the surrounding countryside. Ayacucho is colonial enough to seem like a time warp. At dawn, townsfolk stream into churches to listen to mass. In the nearby market, *campesinas* in big straw hats and colorful hand-knit skirts serve up breakfast: *puca picante* (a spicy red stew of chili, pork cracklings, crushed peanuts, and potatoes), goat's head soup, and 10 varieties of *chicha*. Quechua is spoken everywhere in the soft, swishing sounds of the local dialect.

Ayacucho is known as one of Peru's most artistic towns. Some of the country's best *huayno* singers come from here, along with world-famous harp player Florencio Coronado and the guitarist Raúl García Zárate. Nearly every man knows how to play guitar—an essential skill for evening serenades—and artisans around the city produce ceramics, weavings, miniature altars, and stone carvings in alabaster, the local stone known as *piedra de huamanga*. At 2,761 meters above sea level, the city has one of the best climates in all of the country—the dry landscape, scattered with cactus and *agave,* receives only drizzle in the rainy season from January to March. There are sunny skies and warm temperatures the rest of the year.

Ayacucho was a dangerous place to visit in the 1980s and early 1990s. The Shining Path, or *Sendero Luminoso,* was founded here by Abi-

mael Guzmán, a philosophy professor from Arequipa who came to work at the local university. His movement, based on Maoist philosophy, fought an 11-year civil war that claimed the lives of 69,000 people across the country. The fighting was most intense around Ayacucho, where both guerillas and army soldiers terrorized local villages and caused a widespread migration to cities.

Ayacucho has been a safe place to visit since Guzmán's arrest in 1992 and the subsequent disintegration of the Shining Path. The U.S. Embassy has taken Ayacucho off its travel advisory. But only 500 foreign travelers arrive in Ayacucho each month—as opposed to 45,000 per month in Cusco—mostly because Ayacucho is isolated by rough highways and lack of a plane connection to Cusco.

HISTORY

Ayacucho was the seat of the Wari Empire, which spread across Peru from 500 to 1000 A.D. and built many of the highways, cities, and fine stone buildings that made the Inca Empire possible. Their capital, also named Wari, is 550 hectares of stone ruins that continue to yield clues about this mysterious empire. Between 900 and 1000 A.D. the Wari Empire was probably conquered by the Chancas, who in turn yielded to the Incas in the mid-15th century.

After the Spaniards arrived, Inca forces retreated to the nearby jungle of Vilcabamba and would sporadically attack passengers on the main road that linked Lima, Cusco, and Potosí, in present-day Bolivia. Ayacucho was founded in

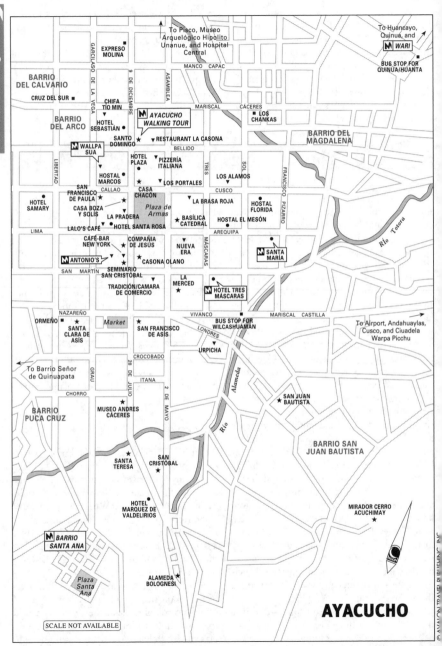

To Pisco, Museo Arqueológico Hipolito Unanue, and Hospital Central

To Huancayo, Quinua, and

M WARI

BUS STOP FOR QUINUA/HUANTA

MANCO CAPAC

BARRIO DEL CALVARIO

CRUZ DEL SUR

EXPRESO MOLINA

CHIFA TIO MIN

BARRIO DEL ARCO

HOTEL SEBASTIÁN

SANTO DOMINGO

MARISCAL CÁCERES

M AYACUCHO WALKING TOUR

★ RESTAURANT LA CASONA

LOS CHANKAS

BARRIO DEL MAGDALENA

M WALLPA SUA

HOSTAL MARCOS

HOTEL PLAZA

PIZZERÍA ITALIANA

BELLIDO

LOS PORTALES

LOS ALAMOS

SAN FRANCISCO DE PAULA

CASA CHACÓN

CUSCO

HOTEL SAMARY

CASA BOZA Y SOLIS

LA PRADERA

LALO'S CAFÉ

HOTEL SANTA ROSA

Plaza de Armas

LA BRASA ROJA

BASÍLICA CATEDRAL

HOSTAL FLORIDA

HOSTAL EL MESÓN

LIMA

AREQUIPA

CAFÉ-BAR NEW YORK

COMPAÑIA DE JESÚS

M ANTONIO'S

NUEVA ERA

CASONA OLANO

M SANTA MARÍA

Río Totora

SEMINARIO SAN CRISTÓBAL

SAN MARTÍN

TRADICIÓN/CAMARA DE COMERCIO

LA MERCED

M HOTEL TRES MÁSCARAS

NAZAREÑO

ORMEÑO

SANTA CLARA DE ASÍS

Market

SAN FRANCISCO DE ASÍS

VIVANCO

BUS STOP FOR WILCASHUAMAN

MARISCAL CASTILLA

LONDRES

To Airport, Andahuaylas, Cusco, and Ciuadela Warpa Picchu

To Barrio Señor de Quinuapata

CROCOBADO

ITANA

URPICHA

CHORRO

BARRIO PUCA CRUZ

MUSEO ANDRES CÁCERES

28 DE JULIO

GRAU

2 DE MAYO

Alameda

Río

SAN JUAN BAUTISTA

BARRIO SAN JUAN BAUTISTA

SANTA TERESA

SAN CRISTÓBAL

HOTEL MARQUEZ DE VALDELIRIOS

MIRADOR CERRO ACUCHIMAY

M BARRIO SANTA ANA

Plaza Santa Ana

ALAMEDA BOLOGNESI

AYACUCHO

SCALE NOT AVAILABLE

1539 (only three years after Lima) as a base for defending travelers on this route and soon thereafter became the home of Spanish families involved with the Santa Barbara mercury mine in Huancavelica. Money from this mine—which supplied the mercury critical for extracting silver in the mines of Potosí—financed a huge building campaign in the city, with rich families building entire churches and often competing for the most lavish altars.

Ayacucho, still referred to today by its more ancient name of Huamanga, is also known for a series of bloody battles in Spanish times—its name in Quechua means "Place of the Soul." It was here that Peru's new viceroy, Cristobal Vaca de Castro, brought peace to the colony by defeating the rebel Almagrista forces at the Battle of Chupas in 1542. The bodies of the slain officers were probably buried at the tiny Templo de San Cristobal, one of the city's first churches after the Temple of La Merced. During the Independence Wars, the plains above Ayacucho were the site of the final, decisive battle between the Spanish and the patriot forces led by José Antonio Sucre. The independence treaty was signed in the nearby village of Quinua, which today is a Quechuan town known for producing the clay houses—called *casas de quinua*—that adorn the roofs of homes in the area. Recent studies have proven that Huamán Poma de Ayala, one of America's first Indian writers, was from Ayacucho. He is most known for *Nueva Crónica y Buen Gobierno,* a compilation of letters written by Huaman Poma over several years toward the end of 17th century that form a scathing critique of repression under the Toledo viceroyalty, 1569–81.

Ⓝ AYACUCHO WALKING TOUR

An Ayacucho walking tour begins with an early-morning visit to churches—most of which open for mass at 6:30 A.M. and close an hour or two later. Get up at dawn and start two blocks from the Plaza de Armas at **Santo Domingo** (corner of Bellido and 9 de Diciembre, 6:30–7 A.M. daily), which has a simple Renaissance facade covered with a bizarre column-and-balcony addition. According to local tradition, Spanish Inquisition judges held public trials, and hung their victims, from this balcony. Inside are several examples of Andean-Catholic syncretism: profiles of Incas with headdresses abound on the altars and, on the main altar, the eagle of San Juan is replaced with a local hummingbird.

Next stop is **San Francisco de Paula** (corner of Garcilaso de la Vega and Cusco, 6:15 A.M.–7:30 A.M. and 6:15–7:30 P.M. daily), which competes with San Blas in Cusco for Peru's finest carved pulpit. The altar is brimming with angels and is one of the few in the city that is not covered with gold plating—but the Nicaraguan cedar is just as pretty. **La Merced** (corner of 2 de Mayo and San Martin, 6:15–7:30 A.M. daily) was constructed in 1541 and is the second oldest church in town. A mark of its antiquity is its simple Renaissance facade—as opposed to the later, more effusive baroque style. **Santa Clara de Asís** (corner of Libertad and Nazareño, 6:30–8 A.M. daily) holds the revered Jesus of Nazareth image that is the center of Ayacucho's most important procession during Easter Week. The ceiling above the altar is an intricate wood filigree of *mudéjar,* or Spanish-Arabic, design.

On the way to the next church, cross Grau and head into the **market,** which is clean, relaxed, and full of local foods. *Pan chapla,* a local favorite, is a round bread with hollow center, and from August to October there is also *Wawa* (*baby* in Quechua), an infant-shaped bread that is meant to be consolation for women who became pregnant during Carnaval in February. There are also large rocks of black salt, a variety of *chichas* made from corn and grains, and huge pots of *puca picante.*

Emerge on the other side to a huge, rust-colored arch next to **San Francisco de Asís** (corner of 28 de Julio and Vivanco, 6:30 A.M.–8:30 A.M. Mon.–Sat., 6:30 A.M.–10:30 A.M. Sunday), a Renaissance church built in 1552. Next door is the related convent, open to visitors only via prior arrangement, which contains one of the country's finest collections of colonial paintings.

The final stop is the **Compañia de Jesús** (28 de Julio between Lima and San Martin, 9:30 A.M.–12:30 P.M.), the Jesuit church built in 1605 with a facade of sculped flowers. Next door is the Jesuit College, now known as the Seminario San Cristobal, where Indian children were taught music, Latin, painting, and wood carving until the Jesuits were kicked out of Latin America in 1767. A large international grant, interestingly, once again trained local kids to carve stones and restore the building. Stop here to have breakfast at one of the cafés and shop at the stores, which are slowly paying back the costs of the restoration.

After breakfast, head down 28 de Julio to the **colonial home and museum of Andres Cáceres** (28 de Julio 508, tel. 066/83-6166, 8 A.M.–1 P.M. and 2–6 P.M. Mon.–Sat., $0.75), Peru's top general during the War of the Pacific, who moved troops so quickly through the mountains that he was known as *The Wizard of the Andes.* The home contains his letters, photos, travel desk, weapons, etc., and has an excellent (and unrelated) collection of baroque paintings, alabaster stone carvings, and *petacas,* the elaborate burro satchels used by missionaries

Next go to **Santa Teresa** (one block further down 28 de Julio, 6:30–7:30 A.M.), the church and Carmelite monastery where nuns remain cloistered today. The nuns make *mazapan, turrones,* and *agua de agráas* (a *chicha* made from local flowers), sold in the church's foyer. By knocking on the door, visitors often gain admission here during the day to see the baroque altar and a painting of the *Last Supper* where Jesus is seated before a roasted guinea pig. If admitted after hours, visitors should leave a small donation as a courtesy.

Further down the street is **San Cristóbal** (1540), the city's oldest chapel, which is rarely open, and the pleasant promenade known as **Alameda Bolognesi.** From here, walk uphill on steep streets to **Barrio Santa Ana,** a neighborhood with a small-town feel, and the **Iglesia Santa Ana,** referred to commonly as the Iglesia de los Indios because of the various ethnicities the Spanish brought here in the 16th century to serve as a buffer against the attacking Incas. Working in the streets around the plaza are some of Peru's most famous weavers, who have exhibited their work all over the world—see the section *Barrio Santa Ana* below for more details.

Ayacucho's elegant **Plaza de Armas** is bordered by the cathedral and university on one side and continuous stone arcades on the others. The best time to visit the cathedral, which was completed in 1672, is in the evening from 5:30 to 7 P.M. when its huge interior is illuminated. There are two interesting examples of Andean-Spanish fusion: San Juan's eagle is replaced by a condor on top of the dome's columns, and the sacred half moon of Andean cosmology is at the foot of the Virgin Mary.

Next to the cathedral is **La Universidad San Cristobal de Huamanga,** which opened in 1677 but went bankrupt and closed two centuries later during the Pacific War with Chile. The university was reopened in 1958 and now has a charming café that is open 7 A.M.–9 P.M.

Around 1969 the Velasco government expropriated many of the colonial mansions around the main square, forcing their families to vacate, and resold them to banks. **Casa Boza y Solís** (Portal Constitución, Plaza de Armas, 8 A.M.–8 P.M. Mon.–Fri., free) today houses government offices and stands out for its massive stone arcade and Seville tiles decorating an original stone fountain, staircase, and second floor. The Banco de Crédito occupies the **Casa Chacón** (Plaza de Armas, 10 A.M.–6 P.M. Mon.–Sat.). The rooms of this colonial mansion have been converted into the highly worthwhile **Museo de Arte Popular** (10:15 A.M.–5:30 P.M. Tues.–Fri., 9:45 A.M.–12:15 P.M. Saturday, free), a showcase for the extraordinary range of art produced locally. The Banco de la Nación occupies the **Casona Olano** (28 de Julio, a half block from Plaza de Armas, 9 A.M.–3 P.M. Mon.–Sat.).

The Museo Arqueológico Hipólito Unanue (Independencia, 1 km outside town, 8:30 A.M.–1 P.M. and 3–5 P.M. Mon.–Sat.) has a range of objects from the Warpa, Wari, and Chanka pre-Inca cultures: ceramics, weavings, turquoise jewelry, and seven priest monoliths carved out of volcanic stone. Plus, there is a botanical garden next door with more than 120 kinds of regional cacti.

A beautiful view of Ayachucho can be had from the top of **Cerro Acuchimay,** which can be reached by taxi ($2.50) and then descended via a long staircase that ends at the Plaza San Juan

Bautista, near Londres Street. Do this walk during the day only.

N WARI

There are three worthwhile sites to the north of Ayacucho that can be seen in one (very full) day. **Wari** (22 km from Ayacucho, 8 A.M.–6 P.M., $0.75) is the sprawling capital of the same-named empire. Much of the city, which sprawled over 300 hectares (740 acres), has been buried by drifting sands. Additional buildings at the periphery of the city spread over an additional 250 hectares (620 acres). The ruins are badly deteriorated and largely unexcavated, but what can be

seen today includes huge complexes of walls up to 12 meters high.

The best place to start a visit is at the on-site museum, which lies on the road between Ayacucho and Quinua and contains a stone monolith, ceramics, and a few useful historical charts. A short walk away lies the ceremonial center of Monqachayoc, which has an enigmatic half-moon shape. It appears to be a calendar, because it faces exactly north and contains 18 niches, which is a strange link to Mayan calendars in the Yucatan Peninsula of present-day Mexico. Stone cylinders were found nearby and were probably once used for casting shadows onto the niches. Nearby are a few unexcavated pyramids,

THE WARI: PERU'S FIRST EMPIRE BUILDERS

Partly because the Incas (and the Spanish) consolidated power by erasing past history, the Wari's role in Peruvian history has until recently been vastly underestimated. Archaeologists are still trying to explain the rise of the Wari, whose complex, polychromatic ceramics began to replace the simple, two-color pots of Ayacucho's Huarpa culture around 500 A.D. The Huarpa were one of south Peru's early cultures, along with the Nasca on the coast and the Tiahuanaco at Lake Titicaca. The Wari appear to have grown out of all three, combining their different technologies and religious beliefs into a more powerful combination. But many Wari beliefs stretch even farther back in time—Wari ceramics repeatedly portray a staff-wielding warrior deity, apparently the same worshipped by the much earlier Chavín culture (1,200–300 B.C.) in Peru's northern mountains.

Jokingly referred to as the *Mormons of the Andes,* the Wari built their empire by persistent evangelization, not by force. By 700 A.D. the Wari had spread as far north as the Moche capital near present-day Trujillo, and images of the Moche decapitator god, Ai-Apaek, begin to appear on Wari ceramics. At the height of the Wari Empire, around 900 A.D., the capital near present-day Ayacucho (also named Wari) covered 300 hectares (740 acres) and sustained a population of anywhere from 10,000 to 70,000. The empire was connected by good roads and stretched from Arequipa in the

south to Chiclayo in the north. The Wari did beautiful work in bronze, silver, lapis lazuli, and gold, made architectural models for all of their new buildings, and produced weavings with as many as 250 threads per square inch.

The Wari literally paved the way for the Incas. They were the first to base their empire on large cities—and not just ceremonial centers used during festival times. Their transnational roads and advanced stone-carving techniques formed the foundation upon which the Inca Empire was built. Other traditions passed on to the Incas include mummy worship and the use of quipus, which were bundles of brightly colored strings with elaborate knots tied in them. Ethnohistorians will probably never decipher exactly what information was catalogued by the elaborate knots and different colors of thread.

Like the Huns invading Rome, a weakening Wari state was invaded by less civilized rebel groups, probably the fierce Chancas from the Huancavelica area. Sometime between 900 and 1,000 A.D. the empire collapsed—perhaps overnight. At the capital city of Wari, some of the tunnels leading into the underground funerary chambers appear to have been hastily blocked—an effort perhaps to protect the sacred mummies. Today the city of Wari, 22 km outside of Ayacucho, remains largely unexcavated—most of the ruins have been literally covered by the sands of time.

Central Highlands

covered with prickly pear cactus, and a huge stone table where sacrifices were probably made. Archaeologists believe the umbrella-shaped *Paty* trees were used in a potion that prevented blood from coagulating during sacrifice ceremonies—a trick the Wari may have learned from the Moche in Peru's north.

A tunnel, closed to visitors, leads underground 200 meters from the ceremonial area to a labyrinth of funerary chambers that was excavated in 1997 and leads an astonishing 19 meters below ground—the hidden level underground is apparently built in the shape of a llama.

Another interesting area, called Cheqo Wasi, lies a half kilometer further up the road and includes more funerary chambers, some of which join 1.5-ton rock slabs with bronze joints. The joints between the rocks are perfectly smooth and rival later Inca stonework. One theory holds that the Wari used these fortified chambers to store, and guard, both their own mummies and those of the cultures they conquered. Like the Incas, the Wari worshipped their ancestors' mummies as a source of power and displayed them in public during sacred festivals, much the same way Catholic images are paraded during Ayacucho's Easter Week festivities.

QUINUA

Another 15 km up the road lies **Quinua,** a pleasant Quechuan village 37 km outside Ayacucho, which is known for its *Iglesias de Quinua,* miniature clay churches that are placed on the roofs of homes to bring good luck. There is a variety of other hand-shaped ceramics as well, all in the region's red clay and bright mineral paint, ranging from religious images to more humorous depictions of musicians and drunken men. This remarkable town of cobblestone streets, adobe houses, and colonial church has a few good restaurants and a few basic rooms for rent at the Hotel Qenwa. The owner is Quinua's longtime, and somewhat controversial, mayor, who headed up the town's militia against the Shining Path—an 11-year battle that forced much of the town's population to flee for Ayacucho or Lima.

PERU'S CAVEMAN HISTORY

Archaeologists know a great deal about Ayacucho's Paleolithic history thanks to the Pikimachay Cave, 25 km from Ayacucho, which has yielded the oldest evidence of human presence in all of Peru and South America. As glaciers advanced and retreated to shape the local valleys in the Ice Age from 23,000 to 10,000 B.C., a series of nomadic groups sheltered in this cave starting around 15,000 B.C. During excavations in the 1970s, archaeologists discovered stone tools and animal bones, which were then, unfortunately, shipped to the United States. The cave's inhabitants were nomadic, probably lived in groups of 15 top 20 people, collected a variety of plants and roots, and hunted now-extinct animals such as mastodons, giant sloths, sabertooth tigers, and miniature horses. As the climate warmed and dried up between 11,000 and 8,000 B.C., the glaciers retreated and the large herds of animals left the area. Inca priests and modern-day mystics claim the cave is a center for cosmic energy. Though it is a standard stop for most of the agencies visiting Wari and Quinua, there is not much to see. The cave itself—about 12 meters high and 24 meters wide—lacks painting and has been thoroughly excavated.

PAMPA DE AYACUCHO

A short walk uphill from Quinua is the **Pampa de Ayacucho,** the broad plain where Spanish and patriot troops clashed on December 9, 1824, in the final battle of South America's independence. This is one of Peru's three historical sanctuaries, along with Machu Picchu and the other independence battlefield at Junín. Above the plain rises Cerro Condorccuncca, where the Spanish force of 9,300 soldiers were led by the Viceroy José de la Serna. On the plain below, 5,800 patriot soldiers from all over South America and Europe were led by General Antonio José de Sucre—not Simón Bolívar as is commonly believed (Bolívar was in Lima at the time). The battle began at 10 A.M. after relatives and friends on opposing sides were allowed to greet each other. After a series of tactical mistakes by the Spanish, the patriots pushed downhill and won the battle after six hours of grueling, mostly hand-to-hand fighting. By 4 P.M., the patriots had lost 300 men and the Spanish 1,800.

The wounded Viceroy de la Serna signed a peace treaty in a room on Quinua's plaza—now glassed off for public viewing—while the wounded were being treated in the town's church. Today the battlefield is marked with a stone obelisk, 44 meters tall in recognition of the 44 years between this battle and Tupac Amaru II's indigenous rebellion against the Spanish in 1780. There is a recommended two- to four-hour walk between Quinua and Wari that includes good views and interesting countryside. Ask in Quinua for the start of the well-marked path.

An agency day tour to Wari and Quinua usually includes the Pikimachay Cave, a few kilometers past the turnoff to Quinua on the road to Huanta. Some agencies also continue on through a striking desert valley, known for its production of avocados and lúcuma fruit, to visit villagers and take a hike up the nearby *mirador* of Huatuscalla.

Buses from Ayacucho to Quinua can be taken at Salvadar Cavero 124, next to El Nino Restaurant on the northeast edge of town. *Combis* leave when full ($1, 1.5 hours). If taking public transport, visit Wari on your trip out and then continue on to Quinua—*combis* passing Wari in the afternoon on their way to Ayacucho are usually full, making it hard to get home.

WILCASHUAMÁN AND LAGUNA PUMAQOCHA

After Cusco, Peru's most important Inca city is **Wilcashuamán,** the administrative center founded by Inca Pachacútec after the defeat of the Chanca. The present village of Wilcashuamán, site of horrific massacres during the Shining Path revolution, is built entirely on Inca ruins. There are the ruins of a fine sun temple, on top of which is the colonial church of San Juan Bautista with its carvings of serpents, monkeys, and pumas. According to the chronicler Pedro Cieza de León, this three-level sun temple was decorated inside with sheets of silver and gold, along with another, now disappeared, moon temple.

A block away is an *ushno,* a four-level Inca pyramid that can be found nowhere else in Peru and is the main reason for making the Wilcashuamán trek. A trapezoidal doorway and stairs lead to the upper platform, where the throne with two seats was probably used by the Inca administrator and his wife, or *colla.* This *ushno* originally had a clear view of the temples through a single, gigantic plaza and is surrounded by three sacred mountains, or *apus.* The shadows from tubes placed on the corner of the platform reach the center during equinoxes and solstices, and it is not surprising perhaps that President Fujimori often brought TV cameras to this place to make important announcements. The festival of the sun, or Vilcas Raymi, is celebrated here during the July 28th weekend but lodging is almost nonexistent.

On the way to Wilcashuamán, it is possible to see Laguna Pumaqocha, a spectacular lake located up a side road 4 km before the town of Vishongo. The detour from the main road takes about 10 minutes by car or half an hour walking. There are different semi-buried Inca constructions around this sacred lake, a huge variety of fine walls, and a bath that features a 13-sided rock with twin water chutes.

Puya raimondii, a gigantic agave-like plant that shoots up a 15-meter flower stalk only once at the end of its life, can be seen on the high plains toward Wilcashuamán. Titankayoq, the largest forest of these plants in the world, sprawls across 440 hectares, a two-hour uphill walk from the village of Vishongo. Between May and September there is always a *Puya raimondii* in bloom—a rare and beautiful sight. Hugo Zaga, who works in the Vishongo municipality, is a great guide and charges $6.

Combis to Wilcashuamán leave from 5:30 A.M. onwards from the third block of Vivanco in Ayacucho (a sketchy neighborhood at dark) for the bumpy five-hour ride. There is no lodging in Vishongo, but Wilcashuamán has several options, the best of which is Willka Waman ($4 s, $6 d, with private bath). A private car and driver to Wilcashuamán can be rented for $43 for a one-day round trip, but the best, and easiest, way is to go with an agency. This way you can visit Lago

Pumaqocha and Wilcashuamán, along with the *Puya raimondii* along the way, in a single day.

ENTERTAINMENT AND EVENTS

Discotheques come and go quickly in Ayacucho, but **Puka's** (Cusco 246, evenings only) is for the moment packed on weekends. The best *peña* is **Los Balcones** (Asamblea 187, second flr.), which is a disco from Tuesday to Thursday and a peña on Fridays and Saturdays. **Warpas** (Mariscal Cáceres 1033, tel. 066/81-5559) has a good *peña* on Friday and Saturday night (don't eat here, though). A good bar is **Magia Negra** (9 de Diciembre 293, tel. 066/960-5644, 7 P.M. onwards Tues.–Sun.), and an evenings-only pool hall operates on the corner of Bellido and Garcilazo. A small cinema on the Plaza de Armas, near the corner of Cusco and Asamblea, shows movies and documentaries sporadically.

Ayacucho's **Easter Week** is Peru's best known religious festival. Other important festivals in Ayacucho include **Carnaval** (usually the last day of February), **Inti Raymi** in late June at Lago Pumaqocha, the **Virgin de Cocharcas** in Quinua Sept. 8–11, the feast of **El Señor de Maynay** in Huanta in mid-September, and **Vilcas Raymi** at Wilcashuamán during the July 28th weekend.

⊠ BARRIO SANTA ANA

A short walk above Ayacucho is the Barrio Santa Ana, a quirky neighborhood with cobblestone streets that is filled with an amazing variety of crafts workshops. At the center of it all is the Plazuela Santa Ana, which is graced with the colonial **Iglesia Santa Ana de los Indios** and lined with artisan studios.

At **Galería Latina** (Plazuela de Santa Ana 105, tel. 066/52-8315, wari39@hotmail.com), Alejandro and Alexander Gallardo are the third and fourth generation of weavers in their family and produce exquisite tapestries based on Wari designs. The Gallardo family makes its own natural dyes and produces only a few dozen rugs per year, which are mostly sold to galleries in Europe and the U.S. Even if you are not buying (a 1.2-by-1.6-meter rug costs between

$250–350 here, three times that overseas), the weaving demonstration is fascinating.

Locals also highly recommend the weavings of **Chrisantino Montes.** His production is small, and exclusively of naturally dyed pure alpaca wool. Prices are similar to Gallardos. Ask around Barrio Santa Ana for directions to his workshop.

Alfonso Sulca Chavez (Plazuela de Santa Ana 83, tel. 066/81-2990) is another highly skilled weaver whose designs are a free interpretation of pre-Inca motifs in brilliant natural dyes. Next door is the Huaranca family, which focuses on animal and nature themes. Though hard to transport, carvings in the local *piedra de huamanga,* or alabaster, are made by **Julio Gálvez** (Jerusalén 12, Plazuela de Santa Ana, tel. 066/81-4278, edgard_galvez@yahoo.es).

For a good introduction of what crafts are produced in the Ayacucho area, visit the Museo Popular in the Banco de Crédito on Ayacucho's Plaza de Armas. Other crafts stores outside the Barrio Santa Ana including **Guitarras Flores** (Graud 676, Plaza Santa Teresa, 6 A.M.–8 P.M.), where the Lago family sells handmade guitars for $70–115. Brightly painted metal crosses, candelabras, and masks can be bought from Ignacio and Victor Bautista, a father-son team, at their store on Londres 235.

Especially beautiful are the brightly colored *retablos,* portable altars made of wood and plaster, which were once used by mule drivers to pray for a safe journey. The *retablos* usually have two opening doors that reveal a religious scene on top and a secular one on the bottom. Good places to buy these and other crafts are **Seminario San Cristobal** as well as **Galeria Union** (Portal Union 25), **Galerias Artesanales Pascual** (corner of Cusco and Asamblea in Plazoleta San Agustin), and **Mercado Artesanal Shosaku Nagase** (Plazoleta Maria Parado de Bellido, Bellido and 9 de Diciembre).

The best place to buy ceramics is the town of Quinua, which is famous for miniature clay chapels known as *Iglesias de Quinua* that are placed on the roofs of homes for good luck. Recommended ceramics workshops in Quinua include the Sánchez and Lima families and Galerias Limaco, all on the main street of Sucre.

EASTER WEEK IN AYACUCHO

Peruvians regard Ayacucho's Semana Santa, or Easter Week, as Peru's most beautiful and intense religious festival. For the 10 days leading up to Easter Sunday, Ayacucho becomes a city of flower-carpeted streets, solemn processions, fireworks, and wild partying. Religious processions throughout the week depict the various passions of Christ, and there are also art shows, folk dancing, music concerts, sporting events, livestock fairs, and traditional food contests. During the festival, lodging and bus tickets triple in price and are often sold out, so book in advance. The tourist office publishes an annual brochure and information may be available at www.ayacuchocompetitivo.org.pe The principal events are as follows:

• On the Friday before Palm Sunday, the first religious procession starts from the Iglesia Magdalena.

• Palm Sunday itself has two important celebrations. At noon there is a huge caravan of mules and llamas carrying dried *retama* (broom) flowers and accompanied by several orchestras. After processing around the plaza twice, the *retama* is unloaded to be burned during all important religious ceremonies. At 4 P.M., Christ on a white mule leaves from the Carmelite monastery of Santa Teresa, along with crowds of people carrying golden palm fronds, and proceeds around the plaza to the cathedral.

• The most sacred, and intense, ceremony of the week occurs on Wednesday, when the Plaza de Armas becomes a stage for the allegorical meeting of Jesus of Nazareth and the Virgin Mary. During this mystic ceremony, the images are carried on their thrones as townspeople, many in tears, watch. Because most visitors arrive the following day, there are mostly *Ayacuchanos* at this event.

• Friday night is a candlelit procession of the deceased Jesus and the Virgin Mary, during which all the lights in the city are turned off.

• On Saturday morning, a bull is released every half hour from 11 A.M. onwards from the Alameda Bolognesi. Surrounded by shouting kids, some of whom are injured each year, a total of six bulls run through a cordoned-off area of town. People party in the Plaza de Armas until late in the night with dancing and orchestras.

• At 5 A.M. on Sunday, before dawn, El Señor de la Resurrección (the crucified Christ) is carried out of the cathedral atop a huge white pyramid adorned with 3,000 candles. As many as 250 people carry the pyramid, which goes around the plaza until 7 A.M., amid ringing bells, fireworks, and smoke from the last bit of buring *retama*.

The highlight of Ayacucho's Semana Santa comes before dawn on Easter Sunday, when a huge pyramid bedecked with over 3,000 candles is carried around the main square in complete silence.

SPORTS AND RECREATION

Ayacucho has a variety of **mountain biking** routes in the area, mapped out by Peruvian mountain bike champion George Scoffield and available from Warpa Picchu Eco-Aventura. There are also rafting opportunities on the Río Pampa as well as treks to waterfalls near Cangallo, a village reached by a branch highway on the Wilcashuamán route.

The best agency in Ayacucho is **Warpa Picchu Eco-Aventura** (Portal Independencia 65, Plaza de Armas, tel. 066/81-5191, verbist@terra.com.pe, www.warpapicchu.com, 8 A.M.–8 P.M.). Belgian owner Pierre Verbist conducts tours in French, English, and Dutch, and partner Carlos Altamirano is probably Ayacucho's most knowledgeable guide; he speaks Spanish and Quechua and has a good knowledge of English. For a group of two, the agency charges $10 pp for a city tour, $15 for Wari-Quinua, $30 for Wari-Quinua plus Huanta hike, $33 for the waterfalls around Cangallo, and $34 for Wilcashuamán. Verbist has also mapped out a series of interesting walks and mountain biking routes in the area. Contact him for more information and about bike availability.

Other recommended agencies include **Central Tours** (Portal Constitución 17, Plaza de Armas, tel. 066/81-1546, centraltours@hotmail.com) and **Urpillay Tours** (Portal Unión 33-D, Plaza de Armas, tel. 066/81-5074, urpillaytours@terra.com). Urpillay's owner is an archaeologist and an extremely knowledgeable source of information on the area.

ACCOMMODATIONS

There are great hotel options in Ayacucho, both for the budget and upscale traveler—even the best hotels are relatively inexpensive. Rates triple for Easter Week and rooms are booked months in advance.

Under $10

The new **Hostal Sebastian** (Passageway near 9 de Diciembre 247, tel. 066/81-1742, $4 s, $7 d) is a quiet hostel set off the street with single beds only. Rooms are large, with unfinished wood floors and cable TV, and the shared bathrooms have electric showerheads to heat water. Rooms vary, so ask to see several. Another excellent budget option is **Hostal El Mesón** (Arequipa 273, tel.

plowing fields in the Mantaro Valley

066/81-2938, hselmeson@hotmail.com, $6 s, $9 d). Clean rooms with tile floors front a sunny courtyard and include cable TV. Some rooms have private bathrooms, and there is 24-hour hot water. If this place is full, the next best choice is **Hotel Samary** (Callao 329, tel. 066/81-2442, $6 s, $7 d), with communal and private bathrooms, bedrooms with tile floors, and hot water in mornings only.

With clean bunkrooms, **Hostería Caribe** (Libertad 675, tel. 066/81-4421, vickyedhu@hotmail.com, $3 pp), run by Vicky Pizarro Acosta, is a cheap but basic option.

$10–25

The best deal in town is **Hotel Tres Máscaras** (Tres Máscaras 194, tel. 066/81-4107, hoteltresmascaras@yahoo.com, www.ayacuchoperu.com, $9 s, $14 d). The gardens and cool sitting areas have great views of the surrounding hills. Large, carpeted rooms have good beds, cable TV ($1 extra), and lots of hot water. Another great deal is the quiet, comfortable **Hostal Florida** (Cuzco 310, tel. 066/81-2565, $10 s, $14 d), with comfortable beds, hot water, and cable TV. The second-floor sunny terrace has great views over the city. **Hotel Marquez de Valdelirios** (28 de Julio 720, tel. 066/81-8944, $14 s, $18 d) is a restored old home with large, carpeted rooms and a sunny courtyard. The hotel is in front of a nice park and near the crafts workshops of Santa Ana.

The new **Santa Maria** (Arequipa 320, tel. 066/81-4988, $18 s, $23 d) stands out for its modern architecture, exquisite art, and luxurious furniture. The huge rooms are decorated with beautiful armoires and luxurious beds. Cocktails are served at a hip bar with leather couches. A tip for budget travelers looking for a little luxury: Two people are welcome to stay in the large single rooms at no additional charge.

A lesser option, but only a half block from the Plaza de Armas, is **Hostal Marcos** (9 de Diciembre 143, tel. 066/81-6867, $14 s, $18 d) with large, clean, though plain rooms and parquet floors.

$25–50

Ciuadela Warpa Picchu (Km. 5 Carretera al Cusco, tel. 066/81-9462, verbist@terra.com.pe, www.warpapicchu.com, $25 s, $35 d, buffet breakfast included) is a country retreat with large rooms, big pool, sauna (both dry and steam), jacuzzi, horse stables, bar, and a restaurant that puts an international twist on local dishes. Camping, which includes showers and use of the pool, is $3 per person. The owners, a Belgian-Peruvian couple, also operate the excellent Warpa Picchu Ecco-Aventura agency and can arrange a variety of trips.

The elegant courtyard of **Hotel Santa Rosa** (Lima 166, tel. 066/81-4614, $16 s, $26 d) is a beautifully restored colonial building, but the rooms don't match up. The overpriced **Hotel Plaza** (9 de Diciembre 184, tel. 066/81-2202, hplaza@derramajae.org.pe, $40 s, $50 d) is Ayacucho's most luxurious hotel from the outside, but the rooms need an update. The best bet is a $75 suite—two large rooms, queen-size bed, bathtub, and a balcony overlooking the Plaza de Armas.

FOOD

Ayacucho has an excellent range of restaurants. One of the few options for an early breakfast is Hotel Santa Rosa, which opens at 6:30 A.M. Do not miss the local specialty *qapchi,* a delicious sauce of *queso fresco* and chives over boiled yellow potatoes.

Cafés and Desserts

For breakfast or a light snack, **Cafe-Bar New York** (28 de Julio 178, tel. 066/80-2851, 8 A.M.–10:30 P.M. Mon.–Sat., $1) has a peaceful, sunfilled colonial patio. **Lalo's Cafe** (Lima 169, tel. 066/81-9012, 7 A.M.–1 P.M. and 4–10 P.M., Mon.–Sat.) is a charming place with balcony seating and good espresso, cakes, and pies. Try the cherimoya mousse, *pie de lúcuma,* and *empanadas.* **Café La Miel** (Portal Constitución 12-11, Plaza de Armas, tel. 066/81-7183, 9:30 A.M.–10:30 P.M. daily) has good service and desserts. La Universidad de Huamanga, next to the cathedral, has converted one of its stone patios into a student café.

Peruvian

Past its humble door, **Wallpa Sua** (Garcilaso de las Vega 240, tel. 066/965-0809, wallpasua@hotmail.com, 6–11:30 P.M. Mon.–Sat.,

$3–6) is a warmly lit Republican house with great food ranging from spit-roasted chicken to tender steaks smothered in basil and garlic. Locals are met at the door by owner Mario Chahud, who joins them for a long, slow dinner.

The best place for *comida típica* in town is **Urpicha** (Londres 272, $3–6), which serves the sectioned and pan-fried guinea pig that is much easier to eat than the roasted, fuller-bodied version. **Los Álamos** (Cuzco 215, tel. 066/81-2782, 7:15 A.M.–10 P.M. daily, $3) has a good $2.50 menu, tasty grilled trout, and a pleasant colonial courtyard. **La Brasa Roja** (Cusco 130, tel. 066/81-2388, daily, $2–4) is another locals' favorite that serves *puca picante* and *qapchi*.

Tradición (San Martin 406, tel. 066/81-2695, 8 A.M.–10 P.M. Mon.–Sat., $2.50) has a good lunch menu. **Cámara de Comercio** (San Martin 432, tel. 066/52-8464, 9 A.M.–10 P.M. daily, $2–3.50) serves spit-roasted chicken after 4 P.M., as well as fried trout, *cebiche,* and salads in a colonial courtyard. **Restaurant La Casona** (Bellido 463, tel. 066/81-2733, 9 A.M.–11:30 P.M. daily, $2–5) serves up huge portions of *comida típica* at reasonable prices. **Café Restaurant 4 en 1** (Callao 219, tel. 066/81-6822, 7:30 A.M.–9:30 P.M. Mon.–Sat.) is a clean, rather plain place with a good reputation and a range of food from all over Peru.

Italian

The town's best pizzeria is **Ⓜ Antonino's** (5 P.M.–midnight daily, $7 for big pizza), on the second-floor balcony of Seminario San Cristobal, the 17th-century Jesuit college. This is the best hangout spot in the whole city, where locals come to drink beer and watch soccer games. **Pizzeria Italiana** (Bellido 486, 6 P.M.–midnight, $6) serves pizzas from a wood-fired oven in a cozy atmosphere.

Chifa

The best, and safest, Chinese food in town is **Chifa Tio Min** (Mariscal Cáceres 1179, 5–11 P.M., $2–4).

Cebiche

The sunny courtyard at **Los Portales** (next to Urpillay, Portal Unión, Plaza de Armas) is a great place to relax and have some fresh *cebiche* (fish is brought in daily from the coast).

Vegetarian

The best vegetarian restaurant is **Nueva Era** (Arequipa 170, 7 A.M.–3 P.M. Mon.–Sat.), with a delicious set menu. There is also *La Pradera* (Portal Constitución 9, in a basement space next to Café La Miel, 7 A.M.–9 P.M. Mon.–Sat.).

Markets

The two best minimarkets are at Independencia 60 on the plaza and at 28 de Julio 100. The biggest supermarket is **Top Market** (Asamblea 151, 8 A.M.–10 P.M.).

INFORMATION AND SERVICES

A new web page chock-full of information about Ayacucho is at www.ayacuchocompetitivo.org.

Tourist Information is available at the **iPeru** office (Portal Municipal 48, tel. 066/81-8305, 8:30 A.M.–7:30 P.M. Mon.–Sat., 8:30 A.M.–2:30 P.M. Sunday) on the Plaza de Armas and also at the airport.

The **Tourism Police** is at 2 de Mayo 103, near the intersection with Arequipa (tel. 066/81-2055).

Health care is available at Central's **Clinica de la Esperanza** (tel. 066/81-7436, 8 A.M.–8 P.M.) or **Clínica el Nazareno** (Quinua 428, tel. 066/81-4517, 7 A.M.–9 P.M.). The pharmacy with the widest selection is **Inka Farma** (28 de Julio 262, tel. 066/81-8240).

The **Banco de Crédito** (Portal Union 27 on the Plaza) and **Banco de la Nación** (half block from plaza on 28 de Julio) both have ATMs.

The **post office** is on Asamblea 293 (tel. 066/81-2224, 8 A.M.–7 P.M. Mon.–Sat.).

Fast **Internet cafés** are at Cusco 136 ($0.50/hr) and Bellido 532. There are private **telephone booths** for international calling at Bellido 364 and also on the plaza.

The **laundries** at Bellido 295 (8 A.M.–12:30 P.M. and 2:30–7 P.M.) and Bellido 316 charge by the piece and are quite expensive. There are no other public laundromats at press time.

GETTING THERE AND AROUND

Flights between Cusco and Ayacucho may be available in the near future. For the moment, most visitors fly back and forth from Lima with **LC BUSRE** (tel. 066/81-6012 www.lcbusre. com.pe), or **Aerocondor** (in Lima 01/614-6-14, www.aerocondor.com.pe, $60 one way). The airport is 4 km outside of town or a $2.50 taxi ride.

With a new paved highway connecting Ayacucho to Pisco on the coast, bus times to Lima have shortened to as little as nine hours. The bus route from the coast crosses a 4,480-meter pass along the Ruta de los Libertadores, which José de San Martín traveled before proclaiming the independence of Peru in 1821 (the battles, and official independence, came over the next three years). The best companies on this route are **Cruz del Sur** (Mariscal Cáceres 1264, tel. 066/81-2813), the only company with direct buses; **Ormeño** (Libertad 257, tel. 066/91-2495); and **Expreso Molina** (9 de Diciembre 458, tel. 066/81-2984). There are both day and night buses to and from Lima with reclining seats that cost approximately $16.

Before the 1980s' terrorism, many travelers went from Lima to Huancayo and then on to Ayacucho and Cusco. This route is once again becoming popular. The best Huancayo-Ayacucho company is Molina, with both day and night buses for $8 ($10). As of 2004, this route was safe for night travel. There are actually two routes: the faster one goes low through the towns of Huacrapuquio, Imperial, Acostambo, Izcuchaca, and Mayocc, where it meets up with the high route before continuing to Huanta and Ayacucho. The higher route is 12 hours of dusty, bumpy driving, but is used by some buses because it goes through more populated areas. Avoid this route if possible.

The best company for traveling south to Andahuaylas, Abancay, and Cusco is **Los Chancas** (Mariscal Cáceres 921, tel. 066/81-2391). Buses leave at 6:30 A.M. and 7 P.M. from Ayacucho, arriving in Andahuaylas at 5 P.M. and 5:30 A.M. Another Chancas bus leaves Andahuaylas at 6 P.M. for Abancay, where it arrives at midnight. A private car and driver from Ayacucho to Andahuaylas can be rented for $115, or $330 for the one-way trip to Cusco.

The rough dirt roads between Ayacucho and Andahuaylas are the most spectacular part of the journey to Cusco. The route first heads up and over the frigid *puno* before descending to the Pampa Valley, a cobalt-blue river meandering through subtropical desert. On the other side lies the Apurimac Department and the Quechuan town of Chincheros. The road then climbs to a series of stunning views and switchbacks along precipices that drop thousands of feet before arriving in the pleasant Andahuaylas valley.

After the dark years of terrorism, all the highways in and out of Ayacucho are safe now, though night assaults have occurred recently on the road to Andahuaylas. It is always better, anywhere in Peru, not to take night buses. By no means should travelers continue on the dirt road past Quinua into the Apurimac Valley, which is a fast-growing center of drug production.

Ayacucho is teeming with $0.75 *motocars*.

ANDAHUAYLAS

Tourism has not yet reached Andahuaylas, a city of steep, narrow alleys that has one of the poorest demographics of the Peruvian *sierra*. The city sits on the banks of the Río Chumbau and is sandwiched between the smaller towns of San Gerónimo and Talavera. Most travelers stop here for the night only because Andahuaylas is midway in the Ayacucho-to-Cusco odyssey—it's roughly 10 hours by bus to either place. This is a good place to stretch the legs and walk through pleasant countryside and friendly villages.

Andahuaylas was once the region of the Chancas, a warrior tribe that may have toppled the Wari around 1000 A.D. and almost extinguished the Inca Empire before it started. Despite overwhelming odds and panic in Cusco, the young Inca Yupanqui managed to rally the troops and turn back the Chancas. The event was so important in the Inca's mythological history that the young Inca afterwards changed his name to Pachacútec, meaning "He Who Moves the World." The Inca Empire grew relentlessly from that point forward.

Andahuaylas' main colonial building is the cathedral, built of huge granite blocks in the 17th century. The best time to visit the cathedral is during early-morning mass, usually around 7 A.M.

Fortress of Sondor and Lago Pacucha

The city's biggest attraction is the Chanca fortress of Sondor, 21 km outside Andahuaylas on the way to Cusco. The fort itself is a rather unimpressive series of hilltop terraces, with a reconstructed garrison nearby, but the view is fabulous. The fort was obviously built to protect the rich valley-bottom land around Lago Pacucha. On the other side of the fort, the valley drops thousands of feet toward the Pampa and Apurímac drainages. Lago Pacucha itself, 17 km from Andahuaylas via a short cut off the main highway, has attractive marshlands, a few species of ducks, and dirt roads for walking. On the far side of the lake, *combis* from Andahuaylas arrive at the town of Pacucha, which has a few restaurants. The town is best known for its annual Yawar festival.

Entertainment and Events

The discotheques **Kusi Kusun** at Cáceres 361 and **Choza Inn,** next door, are open most nights after 9 P.M. **Ciné Antoon Spinoy** in the Plaza de Armas shows nightly movies.

Andahuaylas' best-known festival is **Fiesta de Yawar,** or the Festival of Blood, which takes place at the end of July in Pacucha. A week before the event, men from the village head into the high *sierra* and capture several condors, using horsemeat as bait. During the festival, the condors are tied, one by one, onto the back of a bull. Anthropologists theorize that the ensuing struggle may represent a symbolic confrontation between the Incas (condor) and the Spanish (bull). The contest ends before either animal is killed and the condor is always released back into the wild.

El Niño Jesús de Praga takes place in Andahuaylas in late January. The **Virgen de la Candelaria** is celebrated in San Jerónimo in early February, and **Nuestra Señora de Cocharcas** is feted in Cocharcas on Sept. 8.

Accommodations

Our favorite lodging in the whole city is **Hostal Delicias** (Juan Francisco Ramos 525, tel. 083/72-1104, $6 s, $10 d), a simple but clean place with pleasant lúcuma-colored walls, hot water, tile floors, and nice furniture. Considerably further down on the food chain is **Hostal Cusco** (Pedro

Casafranca 520, tel. 083/72-2148, $4 s, $7 d), offering simple, small rooms with electric shower heads. Rooms without private baths are even cheaper. Other lesser budget options, such as **Hostal Los Libertadores Wari** and **Hostal Las Americas,** are down the street.

The most luxurious hotel is **El Encanto de Oro** (Pedro Casafranca 424, tel. 083/72-3066, $13 s, $17.50 d, including breakfast), with great beds, tons of hot water, and cable TV. A generous breakfast is served in a fourth-story restaurant overlooking the city. Similar in quality is **Sol de Oro Hotel** (Juan Antonio Trelles 164, tel. 083/72-1152, $13 s, $17.50 d), with large, comfortable rooms and parquet floors.

Food

The best restaurant in town is **Pico Rico** (corner of Constitution and Andahuaylas, 5 P.M.–midnight, $2.50), which serves one thing and does it well: *pollo a la brasa,* with soup, French fries, and salad. A recommended *chifa* is **Chun Yion** (corner of Antonio Trelles and Constitution, 3–11 P.M.). **Pizzería Napolitana** (Ramón Castilla 431, tel. 083/72-2196, 7 A.M.–10:30 P.M.) serves decent pizzas and juices, and is one of the few places in town that sells ice cream. Another locals' favorite for *comida típica* is **Club Social** (Juan Antonio Trelles 251, tel. 083/80-1781, 7 A.M.–10 P.M., $2). House specialties are huge dishes of *caldo de gallina* and *adobo* stewed in corn *chicha*—best washed down with a shot of *Anisado.* Basic cafés for breakfast, bread, desserts, or coffee are **El Don Nuestro** (Ramón Castillo 559, tel. 083/72-1644, 6 A.M.–10 P.M.) and **Las Delicias** at Ramón Castillo 468.

Information and Services

There is no permanent source of tourism information, though an agency sporadically operates in front of the cathedral. **Police** are located on Av. Peru.

Banco de la Nación on the Plaza de Armas and the **Banco de Crédito** on the second block of Peru both have ATMs.

The best **Internet cafés** are located at Tres Sierra 322 (8 A.M.–11 P.M.) and at Andahuaylas 328 (9 A.M.–11 P.M.). There are private **phone**

booths at Juan Francisco Ramos 317 (7 A.M.– 9:30 P.M.).

The local laundromat is **Lavandería Di-Li** (Cáceres 352, tel. 083/72-1978, 9 A.M.–7 P.M.).

Getting There

From Andahuaylas, **Expreso Los Chankas** (Malecón Grau 248, tel. 083/72-2441, $6) has buses to Cusco at 6:30 A.M. and 6 P.M. (10–11 hours), and north to Ayacucho at 6:30 A.M. and 6:30 P.M. (10–11 hours). **Aero Condor** (Guillermo Cáceres Tresierra 326, tel. 083/72-2877) has flights leaving for Ayacucho ($30 one way) and Lima ($60 one way) Tues.–Thurs. and Sunday.

The route between Andahuaylas and Abancay takes around five hours and includes a climb to the Andean *puna* around Kishuara (3,450 meters) and a descent to the balmy climate of the Río Pachachaca Valley (2,000 meters), where sugarcane is cultivated. During the drive, Abancay appears far in the distance with snow-covered Nevado Ampay looming overhead. From Abancay, there is another five hours of paved road to Cusco, passing through the balmy Apurímac Valley.

ABANCAY

Along with Andahuaylas, Abancay is mostly a resting stop for travelers along the Ayacucho-Cusco route. Most of the services are grouped along the busy streets of Arenas Arequipa. The Plaza de Armas, one block away, is quiet and graced by a colonial cathedral. El Señor de la Caída, en la Plazoleta la Victoria, is a very simple colonial church that has fine paintings from the Cusco School. These churches are mostly open during early-morning mass, with longer hours on Sunday.

Abancay is at the center of one of the purest Quechua-speaking zones in Peru, and even urbanites rant in a Quechua-Spanish hodgepodge. The road between Abancay and Cusco was paved in 2002, cutting travel time between the two cities down to four hours.

There is good trekking around the snow-covered **Ampay** (5,240 meters), center of a 364-hectare national sanctuary that preserves one of the last highland forests of *itimpa,* Peru's only indigenous conifer. Though rarely visited, this wilderness contains small lakes up high near the snowline. The entrance to the park is a mere 6 km from Abancay itself.

Some trekkers also use Abancay as a launching point for reaching the ruins of Choquequirao, though nearly all of the trekking agencies are based in Cusco.

Entertainment

Carnaval is a colorful tradition during February and March in Abancay and apparently includes a contest in which young men spar with whips. The **Yawar Fiesta** is celebrated in Antabamba on Oct. 8. **Abancay Day,** a large town party, is Nov. 3.

The main strip in Abancay is first called Arenas and then becomes Arequipa, and it's where all the discos, bus stations, cheap restaurants, and hostels are. A popular evening hangout is the **Parque Micaela Bastidas,** on the second block of Arenas. *The* pub to hang out in is **Garabato** (Arenas 164, tel. 083/968-4256, 7 P.M.–1 A.M.), with furry benches, full bar, and nice atmosphere. It has a sister pub in Cusco. There are several other pubs in this vicinity. The best disco is the nearby **Choza Inn** (third block of Arequipa, weekends only).

Accommodations

A great budget option is **Hostal El Dorado** (Arenas 131-C, tel. 083/32-2005, $7 s, $10 d) with private baths, cable TV, and telephones in the rooms. The rooms are a bit musty, but there are banana and lemon trees in the patio, a swing set, and humorous stalactite formations in the eaves of the rooms.

The best place for a comfortable night's sleep is the quiet **Hostal El Imperial** (Díaz Bárcenas 517, tel. 083/32-1578, $12 s, $16 d), with great beds, cable TV, hot water, parking, and good service. Across the street at **Hoteles y Turismo Abancay** (Díaz Bárcenas 500, tel. 083/32-1017, hoturs@terra.com.pe), the rooms are a bit stuffy and overpriced, but there is a backpacker's special ($9 s, $14 d, no TV), and the restaurant is probably the best in town. On the main drag near the bus stations is **Hostal Residencial Victoria**

THE SAYWITE STONE

On the road to Cusco 47 km outside of Abancay lies the **Saywite Stone** (7 A.M.–dark, $1.50), an immensely interesting half-egg-shaped boulder that was dragged down from the fields above and carved with what appears to be the Inca kingdom in miniature. Among other things, there are obvious architectural models of Machu Picchu, Choquequirao, Ollantaytambo, Pisac, and Tipón, all roughly geographically oriented. The four corners *(suyos)* of the Inca empire *(Tawantinsuyo)* are represented by four square indentations, or windows, on the blank side of the rock. A variety of animals represent the three realms of Inca cosmology: a monkey and condor represent the heavens; puma and deer represent the earth; and frog and snake the area beneath the ground.

Perhaps most interesting, the different climates of the Inca kingdom are spread around the rock and conjured by their corresponding animals—octopus and lobster for the coast, llama for the mountains, and jaguar, wild pig, and tapir for the jungle. Finger-width channels lead from above to all these areas before draining off the rock through miniature tunnels. One theory is that priests poured llama blood, or *chicha,* on the rock in order to control or predict rainfall. Crops would be good in whatever region of the rock was reached by the liquid. Unfortunately, some of the figures have been chipped away—by the Spanish, locals say—and are hard to distinguish. Ask the person collecting tickets for some of the harder-to-see details.

The rock was the center of a religious complex. A labyrinth of stone walls next to the rock was probably once a granary and home for the priests. A staircase leads down a ridge past a series of restored pools. At the bottom of the hill, a huge boulder has been split in half and is carved with steps leading nowhere, another set of four square windows, carved circles, and other mysterious geometric figures. In the fields above and on the other side of the Abancay-Cusco road, there is a boulder field with another half-carved stone that is similar in appearance. The Saywite Stone is about an hour outside of Abancay and three hours from Cusco. Bus drivers between the two cities can drop travelers at the site, which is well known and marked with signs. From Cusco, the trip to the Saywite Stone leads through the spectacular Apurimac Canyon.

(Arequipa 305, tel. 083/32-1301, $8 s, $11 d) has small rooms with tile floors, lots of hot water, and cable TV. The beds are quite squishy, unfortunately. It has cheaper rooms without private bathrooms. **Hotel Flor de Amancaes** (Lima 840, tel. 083/32-2038, $9 s, $12 d) has simple, clean, tile-floored rooms.

Food

The Health Ministry did a sanitary inspection of all of Abancay's restaurants in 2003, and only the following three passed: The state-owned **Hoteles y Turismo Abancay** (Díaz Bárcenas 500, tel. 083/32-1017, $3–5) serves good salads and grilled meats in its dining room. **Mauri's** (Arenas 170, tel. 083/32-3042, 5 P.M.–12:30 A.M., $2–4) is easily identifiable by its familiar golden arches sign and is popular for grilled meat and *pollo a la*

brasa. It offers delivery. Finally, **Wachi** (Lima 862, 8 A.M.–3 P.M.) has the best *comida típica* in town.

Other safe places that were not evaluated because they are somehow not considered restaurants include these spots: **Focarela Pizza's** (Díaz Bárcenas 521, next to Hostal El Imperial tel. 083/32-2036, $3) serves above-average pizzas out of a wood-burning oven, and the owner's 12-year-old son is the head waiter. Rumor has it that **Pizza Napolitana,** two blocks further down the street, has better crust.

The best places for breakfast, cakes, and pies is **Café Heladería Dulce y Salado** (Arequipa 400, 8 A.M.–10 P.M.) and **Café Heladería Mundial** (Arequipa 301, 8 A.M.–9:30 P.M.).

The best supermarket is **Comercial Karina** (Arenas 156, 9 A.M.–11 P.M.).

Information and Services

The **state hospital** is on Venezuela, tel. 083/32-1165. The best pharmacies are **El Olivo** (Arequipa 401, 8 A.M.–1 P.M. and 3–10 P.M.) and **Luren** at Diaz Bárcenas 519.

The **Banco de Crédito** on the third block of Arequipa changes money, with exchange houses along the street and private phone booths across the street.

The **post office** is located at Arequipa 217.

Good **Internet cafés** are at Diaz Barrenas 539 (9 A.M.–11 P.M.), Cusco 377 (9 A.M.–1:30 P.M. and 3–11 P.M.), and Arenas 169 (8 A.M.–midnight, also private phone booths).

Getting There and Around

The route to Cusco is entirely paved and only takes four or five hours, including incredible scenery in the Apurímac Valley and a long ascent into the high plains around Anta before entering Cusco.

The best bus company is **Expreso Wari-Palomino** (Arenas 200, tel. 083/32-2932), which runs buses to Cusco ($3.50, $4.50 with reclining seats) at 4 A.M., 7 A.M., 10:30 A.M., and noon.

The company also runs buses over the dirt road that passes Puquio (and a 4,400-meter pasas) to Nasca ($13, $23 with bed), where a different bus can be taken to Lima. These buses leave six times a day, around the clock, for this beautiful drive.

Turismo Ampay (corner of Arenas and Nuñez) runs buses for the five-hour trip to Cusco at 6 A.M., 1 P.M., and 11 P.M., and to Quillabamba in the jungle at 7 A.M., 1 P.M., 4 P.M., and 7 P.M. Expreso Los Chankas (Diaz Barcena 1033) has two buses a day leaving for Cusco and Andahuaylas-Ayacucho.

The only recommended guide in Abancay is Carlos Poacheco with **Karlup Andean Trek** (tel. 083/32-1070, karlupandeantrek@terra.com).

Huaraz and the Cordillera Blanca

The jagged peaks and crystalline glaciers of Peru's Andes sprout magically out of the pea-green high plains, a remarkable sight considering the country's subtropical latitude and the sunny, dry months from May to August. Glaciers sprawl across more than a dozen ranges in south and central Peru, where the Andes rise above 5,000 meters (16,500 feet) and freeze Amazon humidity carried west by the jet stream. Most of these ranges are rarely visited because they are very remote (such as the Cordillera Yauyos east of Lima), very small (the snow-capped volcanoes around Arequipa), or very technical (the Urubamba and Vilcanota ranges around Cusco).

The exception is the Cordillera Blanca, the highest mountain range in the world outside of

Must-Sees

Look for **M** to find the sights and activities you can't miss and **M** for the best dining and lodging.

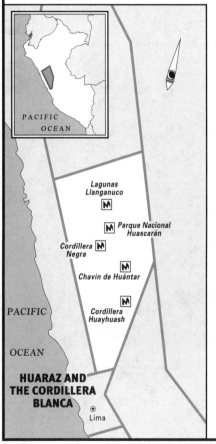

the turquoise waters of Lake Llanganuco

Huaraz and Vicinity

M **Chavín de Huántar:** Built nearly 2,000 years before the Incas, this center of the Chavín Culture includes underground tunnels that lead to the Lanzón, a carved rock pillar that was the center of a cult that spread across the Andes (page 360).

M **Lagunas Llanganuco:** These turquoise-blue, high-altitude lakes glow in the midday sun beneath the Cordillera Blanca snow pyramids (page 376).

Trekking

M **Parque Nacional Huascarán:** Two days is enough time for a quick jaunt through this park, which includes Peru's tallest peak (page 386).

M **Cordillera Huayhuash:** Spend two weeks circumnavigating this stunning range, with some of the finest mountain scenery on earth (page 389).

M **Cordillera Negra:** This often-overlooked range, just west of the Cordillera Blanca, offers challenging mountain-bike routes with panoramas of glaciers and snow peaks (page 390).

© RENÉE DEL GAUDIO AND ROSS WEHNER

Cordillera Blanca

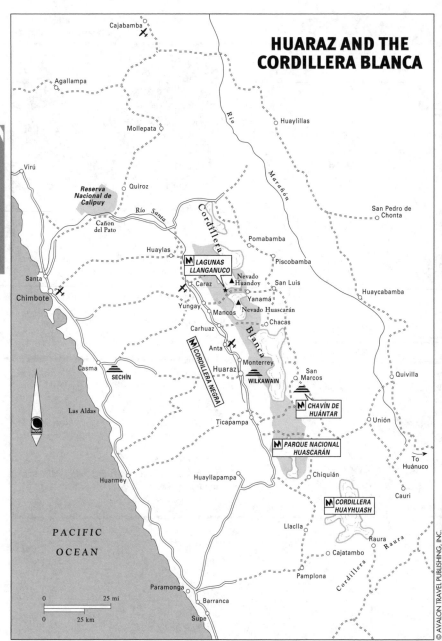

HUARAZ AND THE CORDILLERA BLANCA

Cordillera Blanca

Cajabamba

Agallampa

Mollepata

Huaylillas

Virú

Quiroz

Reserva Nacional de Cálipuy

Río Santa

Cañon del Pato

San Pedro de Chonta

Cordillera

Huaylas

Pomabamba

LAGUNAS LLANGANUCO

Piscobamba

Caraz

Nevado Huandoy

San Luis

Santa

Yungay

Yanamá

Huaycabamba

Chimbote

Mancos

Nevado Huascarán

Carhuaz

Chacas

Casma

Anta

Huaraz

Monterrey

San Marcos

Quivilla

SECHÍN

CORDILLERA NEGRA

WILKAWAIN

Las Aldas

CHAVÍN DE HUÁNTAR

Unión

To Huánuco

Ticapampa

PARQUE NACIONAL HUASCARÁN

Huarmey

Huayllapampa

Chiquián

Cauri

CORDILLERA HUAYHUASH

Llaclla

PACIFIC OCEAN

Raura

Raura

Cajatambo

Paramonga

Pamplona

Cordillera

Barranca

Supe

0   25 mi

0   25 km

MOON

Blanca

© AVALON TRAVEL PUBLISHING, INC.

the Himalaya. This extravagant collection of jagged pyramids, glacier domes, and knife-edge ridges runs north-south for 180 km but is only 20 km wide. To the west lies the **Cordillera Negra,** a humble, snowless range that reaches 5,200 meters before petering out on the other side to the coast. Between the two valleys runs the **Río Santa Valley,** also known as the **Callejón de Huaylas.** The highway from the coast drops into this valley toward **Huaraz,** near the top of the valley, and leads through a string of villages before reaching the city of **Caraz.** At this point the Río Santa jags toward the coast, and the road somehow follows it, through a spectacularly steep canyon known as the **Cañon de Pato.**

The Cordillera Blanca contains 22 peaks over 6,000 meters (19,850 feet), including the world-famous snow pyramids of **Artesonraju, Chopicalqui,** and **Tocllaraju.** Some of the surrounding peaks such as **Pisco** and **Ishinca** are accessible to first-time climbers with experienced guides, and there are even a few gentler *trekker* peaks such as **Urus** and **Maparaju.** The area's most postcard-perfect peak is **Alpamayo,** a peak at 5,747 meters that lures climbers to its 70-degree face.

The mountain that dominates the entire valley, however, is **Huascarán,** the third-highest mountain in South America at 6,768 meters (22,204 feet). Huascarán looms over Huaraz much like Mt. Blanc towers over Chamonix, France, a fact that may explain why so many French people live in Huaraz. Huaraz's streets are flooded with rough-shaven adventurers in fluorescent parkas and trekking boots during the climbing season from May to August, when the weather is dry and sunny. The whole area is a world-class mountain destination, in the league with the Himalaya or the Alaska Range.

Farther south is the **Cordillera Huayhuash,** a stunning range that is an increasingly popular option for treks ranging from five days to two weeks. Whereas the gradual, glaciated valleys of the Cordillera Blanca allow trekkers to walk over the range, the Huayhuash is an odd island range fortified with jagged peaks and serrated ridges— your only choice is to circle. One of mountain climbing's most famous dramas was acted out on Siulá Grande (6,356 meters) and is recounted

by Joe Simpson in his memoir *Touching the Void,* which was made into a docudrama for the big screen in 2003.

Besides trekking and climbing, there are plenty of other adventure sports around Huaraz. There are excellent mountain bike circuits in the Cordillera Blanca, including multi-day adventures up and over the mountains, and rafting down the Río Santa's stretches of Class III–IV whitewater. In the **Cordillera Negra** there are hikes, rides, and treks with the best views of the glaciers and snow peaks on the other side of the valley. There are horses to be rented, and at least one agency is now offering paragliding as well. There is excellent rock climbing, ranging from sport routes to 1,000-meter granite walls.

This area of Peru gave birth to one to the Andes' first advanced cultures, the Chavín. Their carved stone capital of this 3,000-year-old empire, **Chavín de Huántar,** can be visited from Huaraz in a day and is worth a look. Right outside Huaraz there are also the Wari ruins of **Wilcawaín.**

Huaraz is an unappealing city, but it offers the best range of hostels, restaurants, guides, and equipment rental shops. An increasing number of travelers, especially those who have done their research and reservations ahead of time, are basing themselves out of the more pleasant small towns farther down the valley, including **Monterrey, Carhuaz,** and especially **Caraz.**

PLANNING YOUR TIME

The Cordillera Blanca is unfortunately on the way to nowhere and is not easily integrated into Peru's other major travel circuits. But that is just fine with a good number of trekkers and climbers who spend their entire Peru trip right here. There are two rugged dirt roads on either end of the range, one of which leads to **Huánuco** in Peru's central highlands and the other to **Cajamarca,** but these take a few days to travel and require hopping a few buses.

There are no regular flights to Huaraz, but newly paved roads have cut the journey from Lima to a comfortable seven hours. Most travelers who plan on visiting Cusco come here from Lima, where they return before flying to Cusco.

Cordillera Blanca

The twin peaks of Huascarán frequently are covered by clouds in the afternoon.

Those who want to see North Peru can come here from Lima on the main highway and then, to continue their journey, can take a more adventurous route back to the coast over the Cordillera Negra (see the sidebar *Adventure Routes to Huaraz*).

The traditional climbing and trekking season runs from May to September, but the best weather and snow are in June and July. For most visitors, there is little to do in Huaraz between October and April because of the almost daily rains.

Huaraz and Vicinity

Huaraz is a ramshackle sprawl of cement-and-rebar buildings, muddy rivers, and sprawling produce markets at 3,028 meters (9,934 feet). Despite its ragged appearance, Hauraz has a range of quaint hostels and coffeehouses, and quite a few French restaurants. This is the heart of the adventure sports scene in the Cordillera Blanca—indeed in all of Peru—and has the best range of guides, agencies, and equipment shops, though hustlers, con artists, and phony guides abound. With a bit of common sense, hustle, and moolah, it is possible to arrive in Huaraz with no equipment whatsoever and leave almost

immediately on a trek, climb, mountain-bike trip, or day of rafting.

People in Huaraz are friendly, gregarious, and uncommonly festive. The Plaza de Armas is often blocked off by a stream of children's parades, *marinera* contests, and military formations. **Luzuriaga,** the town's main drag, is an eyesore jumble of restaurants, gear shops, and agencies. Farther to the north, the market sprawls on both sides of the **Río Quilcay.**

Prices for transport and lodging double, and sometimes triple, when Limeños flood to Huaraz during holidays. Some final words of advice for

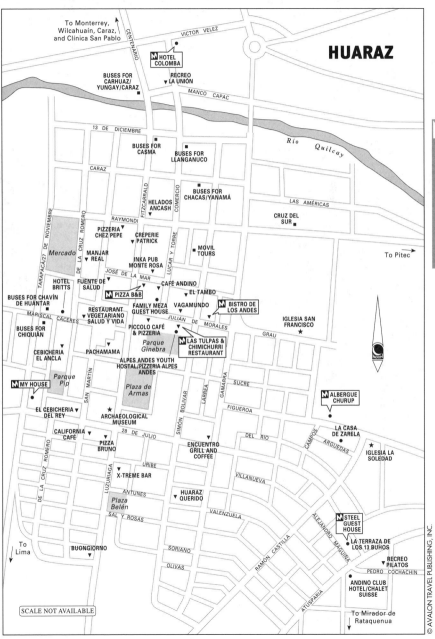

Cordillera Blanca

ALUVIONES:
MUDSLIDES IN THE CORDILLERA BLANCA

Huaraz's ramshackle appearance is due to a series of natural disasters that have, over the millennia, wrought havoc not only on this city but in the villages along the valley, which is known as the Callejón de Huaylas. The trouble is the hundreds of turquoise-colored lakes, which are perched thousands of feet above the valley. The lakes form behind "push moraines, the huge hills of rock and dirt that an advancing glacier pushes like a bulldozer. When the glaciers retreat, as they have been doing for half a century, water collects behind these moraines to form lakes. After the lake fills, water trickles slowly over the top of the moraine and creates picturesque mountain streams. But trouble lies above, where the huge lakes are time bombs waiting to be sparked by the next earthquake, avalanche, or landslide—or sometimes a combination of all three.

Imagine holding a bucket filled with water and shaking it from side to side. Waves reverberate back and forth against the surface, banging and spilling over the sides of the bucket. When this happens to a glacial lake, the waves crash over the moraine again and again until it begins to erode. Then it goes altogether.

The result is a maul of boulders and mud that crashes and careens down the narrow mountain valleys at speeds over 100 miles per hour. Scientists believe the debris moves this quickly because it travels over a cushion of air, like a puck on an air hockey table. These mudslides, or *aluviones,* have carved the steep sides of the Cordillera Blanca's valleys for millions of years and leveled the plains with silt. Within the last few decades, they have also killed tens of thousands of people in the Huaraz area.

In 1941, an *aluvión* from Lago Palcacocha wiped out the northern third of Huaraz, killing more than 5,000 people. Similar *aluviones* struck the village of Chavín in 1945, Cañon de Pato in 1950, and the village of Ranrahirca in 1962. In 1970, an earthquake that measured 7.8 on the Richter scale leveled Huaraz and killed more than 70,000 people throughout the surrounding Ancash Department. During the earthquake a huge avalanche fell from Huascarán, which plunged into a lake above Yunqay, just north of Huaraz along the highway. Within minutes the village was obliterated

by a 10-meter-high wall of mud and boulders, which destroyed buildings and crushed schoolbuses into balls of steel. When it was over, the only thing left of Yunqay was the tops of a few palm trees sticking above the mud. The only survivors of the *aluvión* were children who had gone to a nearby circus and a few hundred villagers who managed to clamber in time up to a hilltop cemetary. The rest of the town, an estimated 18,000 people, were buried alive.

After 1970 the Peruvian government got serious about reducing the risk of mudslides in the area and launched an effort to build control dams in the high mountains. More than 35 control dams, large cement blocks that prevent the moraines from eroding, have been built since then. Most important, these dams include a pipe that drains the lake and prevents it from becoming full.

In early 2003 a satellite operated by the NASA, the U.S. space agency, detected a major crack in the glacier above Lago Palcacocha, the same lake that wiped out a third of Huaraz in 1941. Huaraz became world news for a moment as the Associated Press and other world media jumped on the threat of an imminent mudslide that could, according to NASA, reach Huaraz in 12 minutes. But when local glaciologists arrived at the scene, they realized that the *crack* NASA saw was not a crevasse in the glacier at all. Rather it was a band of rock that had melted through the glacier, which was only a few feet thick in some places. Far from being a menace, the glacier had receded to the extent that it was a pitiful reminder of what it was just two decades ago, another victim of what many feel is human-induced global warming.

Local glaciologists are, however, worried about Quebrada Shallap, another valley that feeds into Huaraz. Here a controversial dam has been built that some glaciologists say puts this city of 60,000 in danger. The dam was built by Duke Energy of Charlotte, North Carolina, which purchased the Cañon de Pato hydroelectric station from the Peruvian government during a 1995 privatization auction. Duke Energy has long complained of low water flows through the canyon, which drains the Cordillera Blanca, during the dry months from

June to October. Its solution was to create a huge summertime reservoir above Huaraz by plugging up the control dam that drains a lake at the top of Quebrada Shallap. Then it built another dam on top of it to form a huge reservoir to supplement the low-water months. The company conducted a survey of the surrounding glaciers, which have receded out of sight up the mountainside in recent years, and concluded there is no danger.

Many of Peru's archaeologists are not so sure. Benjamin Morales, the glaciologist who led Peru's drive to build the control dams in the Callejón de Huaylas, sharply criticized the project. "Avalanches are not a danger in Quebrada Shallap," agrees local glaciologist Alcides Ames. "But what about landslides?" If they are big enough, landslides can, like avalanches, cause a lake to wash over a dam. In 2003 such a landslide dumped into Huaraz's main reservoir, muddying water and shutting off the water supply for several days. Glaciologists are concerned the same could happen in Quebrada Shallap, but on a larger scale.

The problems that Duke Energy faces in getting year-round water to make electricity are probably going to get worse in the coming decades. Bernard Francou, a glaciologist with the French government's Institute of Research and Development, has spent the last two decades studying the retreat of tropical glaciers in Ecuador, Bolivia, and Peru. He predicts that all of South America's small glaciers—about 80 percent of the continent's total—will disappear in the next 15 years. Many of Peru's glaciers are retreating uphill by as fast as 35 yards a year and one glacier Francou studies in Bolivia has lost two-thirds of its volume in the mid-1990s alone. "The trend is so clear that you can't argue with the numbers," he says.

Retreating glaciers do not affect only hydro-electric companies. One of Francou's main backers is the city of Quito, Ecuador, which is worried about its water supply from the fast-disappearing Antizana Glacier. Farmers along Peru's desert coast, who supply a big chunk of Peru's gross domestic product, rely on mountain runoff to irrigate their fields. Even climbers and trekkers in the Huaraz area are affected, when ice routes disappear or gentle, snow-covered passes melt away to reveal loose scree and impassable cliffs.

a bus destroyed by the 1970 Yungay mudslide

© RENÉE DEL GAUDIO AND ROSS WEHNER

Huaraz travelers: Keep an eye on your backpack, be careful where you eat, and take at least two days to acclimatize before heading up into the mountains.

SIGHTS

Huaraz's chief attraction is the **Museo Arqueológico de Ancash** (Luzuriaga 762 on the Plaza de Armas, tel. 043/72-1551, 9 A.M.–1 P.M. and 2:30–5 P.M. Mon.–Sat., 9 A.M.–2 P.M. Sunday, $1.50). It contains a well-organized collection of stone sculptures from the local Chavín (800–200 B.C.) and Recuay (200–700 A.D.) cultures. Upstairs are displays of pottery, textiles, and metal objects from the later Wari, Chimu, and Inca cultures, which also left their mark on this valley.

The Plaza de Armas is a sprawl of concrete and tile that spills onto Luzuriaga. Directly uphill from the plaza is the **Iglesia Soledad,** which survived the 1970 earthquake and is today surrounded by a pleasant plaza. There are a few good hotels in the surrounding neighborhood and some of the best views of both the Cordillera Blanca and sunsets over the Cordillera Negra.

A popular acclimatization hike leads through this neighborhood to the **Mirador Rataquena,** the hilltop above town marked with a giant cross. To get there, head up Villón or Confraternidad Este to the cemetery and then head right, up a switchbacking gravel road. Travel in groups and during the day, as assaults have been reported in this area.

WILCAWAÍN

Monumento Arqueológico de Wilcawaín (7 km north of Huaraz, 7 A.M.–6 P.M., $1.50) consists of two imposing stone buildings built around 600–900 A.D., when the Wari empire expanded north from the Ayacucho area and took over the local Recuay civilization. The main building has a gravity-defying roof of thick stone slabs and three floors of finely wrought, spooky stone chambers. These rooms once held the mummified bodies of prominent leaders, kept dry by ventilation ducts running throughout the complex. The outer walls were decorated with sculpted heads, one of which remains today in the shape of a mountain lion.

Wilcawaín stands out from other ruins in Peru because it is an intact building that requires no imagination to understand. Bring your flashlight in case the electricity goes out, as it did when we were there. The guides here are some of the most articulate, charming 8-year-olds we have ever met! *Combis* marked *Wilcahuaín* cost $0.60 and leave frequently from the bridge over the Río Quilcay in Huaraz for the half-hour journey. Or take a cab ($2). The two ruins are a few hundred meters apart along a dirt road. This makes for a pleasant two-hour walk back to town through pleasant countryside and villages. Walk in a group and visit during the day.

Cooperativa Artesanal Don Bosco

Catholic priest Padre Ugo de Censi began this nonprofit organization (Palestra de Roca *Los Pinos 3A,* Marcará, tel. 043/74-3061, andesdbosco@virgilio.it) in 1970 as a way to give people working skills and a way out of their poverty. The organization has blossomed from its roots in Chacas, a small town on the other side of the Cordillera Blanca, into a large workshop in Marcará, just north of Huaraz. Here teenagers learn how to make world-class furniture, ceramics, blown glass, weavings, and stone sculptures. The furniture includes beds, cabinets, and chairs in a range of attractive contemporary designs. Visitors tour through all the workshops and have a chance to see an interesting video. The organization also has offices in Lima (Av. Alejandro Tirado, 158, Sta. Beatriz, tel. 01/471-0515) and Cusco (Primavera, 100 S. Jerónimo, tel. 084/277-316).

◼ CHAVÍN DE HUÁNTAR

Chavín de Huántar (tel. 043/72-4042, 8 A.M.–4 P.M., $1), four hours east of Huaraz, was the capital of the Chavín culture, which spread across Peru's northern highlands from 900–200 B.C., nearly 2,000 years before the Incas. The site includes a sunken plaza ringed with stylized carvings of pumas and priests holding the hallucinogenic San Pedro cactus. A broad stairway leads to a U-shaped stone temple, called the **Castillo,** which rises 13 meters off the ground in three levels of stone. Much of the site was covered by a 1945 mudslide, which also wiped away a Chavín bridge that was still in use.

This site was visited by Italian explorer **Antonio Raymondi** in the 19th century and later excavated in the early 20th century by **Julio Tello.** Both men brought back elaborately carved pillars from here, now on display in Lima's museums. Tello developed an elaborate theory that Chavín de Huántar was the launching pad for all of Peru's advanced cultures. Recent excavations have revealed that the city was preceded by Caral and other important centers on the coast, but Chavín's importance is still irrefutable. During its peak from 400–200 B.C., the Chavín culture spread across Peru as far as Ayacucho in the south and Cajamarca in the north. Its exotic deities, which included the puma and a mythical deity with a staff in its hand, became central icons in Peru's ancient art and iconography from the Moche to the Incas. Chavín was Peru's first pan-Andean culture and set the stage for the Tiahuanaco, Wari, and Inca states.

The highlight of Chavín de Huántar are the underground chambers that lead beneath the main temple and are now illuminated by electric light. Three of these passages converge underground at an extraordinary stone carving, known as the **Lanzón.** This granite pillar is carved with a frightening mythical being, which has thick, snarling lips and a pair of menacing canines that arch upward. Heavy earrings hang from the ears and snakes appear to grow from the head. The notched top of the pillar extends upward into an upper gallery, where priests may once have performed rituals.

There is a spectacular trek that crosses the southern end of the Cordillera Blanca from **Olleros,** a village just south of Huaraz, to Chavín de Huántar. The trek, which is not crowded, heads along an ancient trade route up and over Yanashallash Pass at 4,700 meters (see *Routes* in the *Parque Nacional Huascarán* section).

Many of Huaraz's agencies offer a day tour to Chavín de Huántar, which leaves Huaraz at 8 A.M. and returns 12 hours later. If you go on your own, contract one of the Spanish-speaking guides at the entrance to better understand the place. Buses head to the town of Chavín, about 1 km north of the ruins; for details see *Getting There* for Huaraz. There are a few restaurants and hostels in Chavín, but your best bet for hot water is **Hotel Chavín Arqueológico** (Inca Roca 141, tel. 043/75-4055, $8 s, $14 d).

Pastoruri Glacier

The easiest way to touch ice in the Cordillera Blanca is by making the day trip to the flat, road-accessible Pastoruri Glacier, 70 km south of Huaraz. Though not spectacular by Cordillera Blanca standards, the ice caves and walls of this glacier are an alternative for those not able to climb or trek. Catching *combis* into the area is complicated and time-consuming. so the best way to go is with an agency tour from Huaraz, which generally costs around $8 per person and last nine hours. Tours spend about two hours walking up and around the glacier to about 5,240 meters (17,190 feet), so prior acclimatization in Huaraz is necessary. As a bonus, tours also stop along the way and see the gargantuan *Puya raimondii* plant.

ONE BIG PINEAPPLE

The *Puya raimondii*, common to Peru's high-altitude grasslands, is considered the largest bromeliad in the world and a cousin to the pineapple. In an adaptation aimed at casting its seeds as far as possible, this agave-looking plant with spiky, waxy leaves shoots up a 12-meter-high stalk only once during its 100-year life. When in bloom around May, the stalk erupts into as many as 20,000 flowers in the last three months before dispersing six million seeds. Even when not in bloom, these giant plants stand out on Peru's high-altitude grasslands and are worth seeing. In the Huaraz area, these plants can be seen on the way to the Pastoruri Glacier. Peru's biggest forest of these monsters, however, is outside Ayacucho.

ENTERTAINMENT AND EVENTS

The coolest bar in town is **Vagamundos Travelbar & Maps** (Julian de Morales 753, tel. 043/75-6818, vagamundo@comic.com, 5:30 P.M.–2 A.M. daily), with acid jazz, funk, and Latin music, appetizers, and couches, in a cozy, swanky atmosphere. There is often a nightly fire burning in the courtyard, and happy hour is 6–7 P.M. A popular backpacker spot playing Latin rock is **X-Treme Bar** (Luzuriaga and Gabino Uribe, tel. 043/72-3150, 7 P.M.–late), a relaxed place to hang out, with couches and dartboards. The hot spot for dancing is the **El Tambo** (José de la Mar 776, tel. 043/72-3417, 8 P.M.–dawn, cover $3), with Top 40 pop, salsa, and techno spun by the DJ. It also has live *peña* bands on weekends. Several other nightlife options are nearby, including the new and popular **Makondos** (José de la Mar 812, cover varies), which blasts disco and Latin pop until the wee hours of the morning. For a beer with the best view in all of Huaraz, go to **La Terraza de Los 13 Buhos** (Alejandro Maguiña 1467, tel. 043/72-9709, 7 A.M.–midnight), on the rooftop of the Steele Guest House in the Soledad neighborhood. Come before sundown to be mesmerized by the Cordillera Blanca and stick around for the sunset (this bar is undergoing a management change, so its name is likely to change in the future).

Huaraz's biggest celebration is **Semana Santa,** when Huaraz natives return home from Lima along with a lot of their friends in the week before Easter. There are important religious processions on Good Friday and Easter Sunday, along with a lot of partying and a carnival-like spirit that includes plenty of water balloons. During the **Fiesta de Mayo** (May 2–9) there are ski races, processions, and dance festivals for Huaraz's earthquake-controlling patron saint, El Señor de la Soledad (*Our Lord of Solitude*). **Semana de Andinisimo,** which shifts between May and June, includes adventure-sport events such as rock climbing, biking, kayaking, and paragliding competitions. Transportation and lodging prices can rise significantly during these festivals.

SHOPPING

The finest Peruvian handicrafts can be found at **Shumaq Maki,** which in Quechua means "Beautiful Hands" (Lucar y Torres 560, tel. 043/72-8886, shumaqmaki2002@yahoo.com, 10 A.M.–1 P.M. and 4–8 P.M. Mon.–Sat.). This upscale gallery sells Peruvian textiles, silver jewelry, ceramics, carved wood, and paper crafts made in cities around Peru. Another high-quality souvenir shop is **Andes Souvenirs** (Parque Ginebra, 9 A.M.–8:30 P.M. Mon.–Sat., 11 A.M.–5 P.M. Sunday), selling textiles, silver jewelry, T-shirts, and Andean music CDs. For cheaper prices, and goods made by the local Huaraz community, browse the two crafts markets off the Plaza de Armas and at a number of shops along Luzuriaga south of Raymondi. Beautiful Andean rugs, sweaters, bags, and blankets are sold here for affordable prices. **Andean Expressions** (Julio Arguedas 1246, 10 A.M.–8 P.M. Mon.–Sat.) sells hand-printed T-shirts with traditional Andean and contemporary designs.

SPORTS AND RECREATION

Before you hop on a bike or put on your backpack, remember that Huaraz is at 3,050 meters (10,000 feet) and the mountains above are much, much higher. Do yourself a favor and take a day or two to acclimatize properly.

Trekking and Climbing

Many fly-by-night agencies in Huaraz offer guides who lack sufficient training and experience. There are also plenty of shops that sell gear stolen from base camps during the season. Patronizing reputable and high-quality establishments, like those listed here, helps push the bar up for everyone.

Many of these companies also offer rock-climbing lessons at the local crags around Huaraz. They also head to the ice caves and walls of Glacier Pastorouri for a day of near-vertical ice climbing. For tips on hiring mountain guides, equipment, and organizing a climb or trek, see the section at the end of this chapter: *Planning Your Trek.* Good routes are listed by the Lima-based Trekking and

Backpacking Club (tebac@yahoo.com, www.angelfire.com/mi2/tebac/).

Casa de Guias (Parque Ginebra 28-G, tel. 043/72-1811, agmp@terra.com.pe, 9 A.M.–1 P.M. and 4–8 P.M. Mon.–Fri., 9 A.M.–1 P.M. Saturday) represents the Mountain Guide Association of Peru and has a complete list of internationally certified guides in Huaraz. The president of the association is Koky Castaneda (kokyperumg@yahoo.com), who charges $100 per day for guiding any mountain in the area and speaks English, French, and Spanish. The Casa de Guias also has a list of less expensive guides-in-training *(aspirantes),* who can be a good choice on nontechnical routes. Before you sign up for a climb, come here to ensure your guide is certified. Casa de Guias has maps, route information, weather forecasts, snow condition reports, and a bulletin board for climbers looking for partners. It is a good all-around source of information and keeps a good list of porters, *arrieros* (muleteers), and cooks.

Montañero (Parque Ginebra 30-B, tel. 043/72-6386, andeway@terra.com.pe, www.trekking-peru.com) is a good rental shop next door, where Selio is another excellent source of information. He rents everything from crampons to parkas and also runs recommended trekking and climbing expeditions. Celio is a certified mountain guide who runs treks and climbs and also provides logistical support. French, German, and English is spoken.

MountClimb (Mariscal Caceres 421, near Parque Pip and the market, tel. 043/72-6060, mountclimb@yahoo.com, www.mountclimb.com, 9 A.M.–1 P.M. and 5–10 P.M.) is an equally good place to buy maps and rent high-quality, cutting-edge gear. The owner, Alfredo Quintana, speaks English and is a fully certified mountain guide who organizes highly recommended climbs, treks, ice-climbing courses, and even guided ski descents in the area. Even if you don't hire his services, he doles out free advice on *arrieros,* out-of-the-way trekking routes, and the best local spots for rock climbing and bouldering.

Eduardo Figueroa at Edwards Inn (tel. 043/72-2692, edwardsinn@yahoo.com) is a fully certified mountaineer who organizes excellent treks and climbs. He is a great source of information for those planning a trip on their own.

Monttrek (Luzuriaga 646, second flr., tel. 043/72-1124, monttrek@terra.com.pe) sells and rents a range of gear and covers the gamut of Huaraz adventure options.

A recommended, fully certified mountain and trekking guide, who spends a third of her year in Huraz, is **Val Pitkethly** (133 Rundle Crescent, Canmore, Alberta, Canada, Tlw 2L6, tel. 403/678-6834, valpk@hotmail.com). Val leads a few trips in the Cordillera Huayhuash each year.

Our favorite local guide, who is certified and speaks excellent English, is **Richard Hidalgo** (richard_hidalgo@yahoo.com, tel. 01/9964-6427). Richard is extremely safe and is one of Peru's most talented climbers. He charges the going rate of $70–90 depending on the difficulty of the mountain.

A recommended trekking contact, who has spent a lot of time in the Cordillera Huayhuash and runs logistical support for expeditions, is **Chris Benway** at Café Andino.

Rock and Ice Climbing

If you're coming to Huaraz to mountaineer, don't forget your quick draws and rock shoes. Heading to local crags is a great way to acclimatize or take a day off. The best crag near Huaraz is Chancos, which offers eight bolted routes on sedimentary rock with big, chunky holds ranging from 5.6 to 5.9. To reach Chancos from Huaraz, head to the bridge area near Centenario and take a Carhuas *combi* north for 11 km to Marcará. From here the crags are on the left side, about a 30-minute walk up the road. There is a nice river for bathing, and the hot springs of Chancos are nearby.

A closer spot, though not as good, is Monterrey, which is only 7 km north of Huaraz. There are a handful of sport routes here, also about 40 feet long, that are a short walk from town. In the town itself you will also find hot springs and an artificial climbing wall. There are bouldering problems at Huanchac near Huaraz.

There is an artificial climbing wall behind the municipality in Huaraz and a bouldering cave at **Andean Kingdom** (Luzuriaga 522). This climbing agency, however, has had a series of accidents and is not recommended.

Advanced climbers will have plenty to keep

ice climbing in the Cordillera Blanca

them busy in the polished granite walls that line many of the valleys leading into the Cordillera Blanca. Over the ppast several years, teams of climbers have put up a series of both free and aid routes on the cliffs of Quebrada Llaca and Ishinca. The best known hard-core areas are in the Rurec Valley and the Torre de Parón, also known as the Sphinx. Ask **Montrek** or one of the climbing agencies for more info.

Mountain Biking

At least two agencies in Huaraz have well-maintained mountain bikes, usually Trek or better, with front suspension. The other agencies along Luzuriaga have cheaper bikes and sometimes do not even supply helmets. The best day trips and views are to be had in the Cordillera Negra, which has single-tracks that lead a thousand meters back to Huaraz. There are also long trips up and over the Cordillera Negra along single-track all the way to the Pacific Ocean. A few agencies offer a weeklong loop through the Cordillera Blanca, including loads of valley single-track and a few passes over 4,500 meters. These longer trips involve support vehicles to carry gear.

Julio Olaza at **Mountain Bike Adventures** (Lucar y Torre 530, tel. 043/72-4259, julio.olaza@ terra.com.pe, www.chakinaniperu.com) offers a range of guided mountain-bike trips and bike repairs. Julio is a long-time Huaraz resident who speaks perfect English. Rates start at $20/day for renting a bike.

John Lockwood is an American mountain spends half his year in Colorado and the other half in Huaraz. He offers good bikes and trips through his company **Pedal Peru** (P.O. Box 1921, Fraser, Colorado, 80442, tel. 970/726-7202 or 800/708-8604 in the U.S., pedalperu@ hotmail.com, www.pedalperu.com).

Rafting and Kayaking

The Río Santa can be anywhere from Class II to IV+ rapids depending on the section. Water levels are highest November to May.

The best agency in town for rafting is **Monttrek.**

Ario Ferri (info@yurakyaku.com, www.yurakyaku.com) is a good rafting guide and kayak instructor who works in the area part of the year. He's based at Casa de Pocha in Carhuaz.

Bird-Watching

For information on bird-watching in Peru, see Michael at **Pachamama** (San Martín 687, tel. 043/72-1834, pachamama@hotmail.com, www .huaraz.net/pachamama). Michael is a Swiss citizen who speaks English, French, German, and Spanish. He is a good source of information on birding spots and what species can be seen.

Fishing

There are opportunities for fishing around Huaraz, especially at stocked lakes such as Lago Querococha in the Cordillera Blanca. According to the regulations of Parque Nacional Huascarán, it is illegal to keep fish below 25 cm (about 10 inches). Michel, the French co-owner of Bistro de los Andes, is an authority on local fishing. His company **Pérou Voyages** (Frederico Sal y Rosas 831, tel. 043/72-6249, b_michel@hotmail.com, www.perouvoyages.com) leads fishing and trekking trips.

Horseback Riding

Horseback riding is easy to set up in Huaraz and includes beautiful routes through the Cordillera Negra. A recommended outfit in Yungar, a village

20 minutes north of Huaraz along the highway, is **La Posada de Yungar,** which offers excellent day trips in the Cordillera Negra. It also offers longer rides into the Quebrada Ishinca in the Cordillera Blanca or up and over the Cordillera Negra all the way to the coast at Huarmey. Another outfit in nearby Marcará named **Las Cordilleras** offers horseback trips from Huaraz to Chavín de Huántar (nine days) or Huaraz to Cajamarca (two weeks). The only way to contact these places is by heading to the towns and asking around.

Paragliding

Though the sport is common in the Cordillera Blanca, nearly all paragliders bring their own equipment. The most common launching spots are Pan de Azúcar, a round hill near Yungay, and the Cordillera Negra, though European daredevils can often be seen hucking themselves off snow peaks as well. **Monttrek** (Luzuriaga 646, second flr., tel. 043/72-1124, monttrek@terra.com.pe) may offer tandem flights in the future.

Skiing

The Cordillera Blanca is not an ideal place for ski mountaineering. Finding good snow often means heading well above 5,000 meters. Because of rapid glacier retreat, even the most experienced guides cannot keep track of new crevasses from year to year. The most frequented skiing spot is Glacier Pastoruri, though other good options include moderate mountains such as Huálcan and Copa. A good contact is Alfredo Quintana at **MountClimb.** Skis can be rented here or at **Montrek** or **Inka Pub Monte Rosa** (José de la Mar 661, tel. 043/72-1447, 11 A.M.–midnight), Huaraz's official distributor of Swiss Army knives.

Sightseeing Tours

The standard day tour from Huaraz costs around $10 pp and includes transport and guide. Bring plenty of warm clothes, bag lunch, sunglasses, hat, and sunscreen and make sure your guide speaks English well. The three most popular day tours are Chavín de Huántar, Glacier Pastorouri and the *Puya raimondii* plant, and Lagunas Llanganuco.

The best tour operator is **Pablo Tours** (Luzuriaga 501, tel. 043/72-1145, pablotours@ terra.com.pe). There are many options along the street, including **Chavín Tours** (Luzuriaga 502, tel. 043/72-1578, hct@chavintours.com.pe, www.chavintours.com.pe) and **Sechín Tours** (Luzuriaga 772, tel. 043/72-1577, sechintours@ huaraz.org, www.huaraz.org/sechintours).

Albergue Churup (see below) arranges tours as well.

ACCOMMODATIONS

A top destination for international trekkers and climbers, Huaraz is crawling with high-quality hostels.

Under $10

The best budget accommodation is the family-run **M Albergue Churup** (Figueroa 1257, tel. 043/72-2584, churup@hotmail.com, www.churup.com, $8 d, $10 d). This popular establishment has well-furnished sitting areas with a fireplace and a spacious back garden that are a great place to read a book and relax. It has a book exchange, laundry service, shared kitchen, equipment rental, even Spanish classes. A fortifying breakfast ($3) is served by owners Nelly and Juan Quiros, and their son, Juan Manuel, is a trekking guide who leads great one-day trips to Chavín de Huántar. There are also cheaper bunk rooms downstairs ($4 s, $6 d). This place is the perfect one-stop shop for the weary budget traveler and is full in high season—make reservations well in advance.

The very simple and secure **Alpes Andes Youth Hostel** (Parque Ginebra 28-G, tel. 043/ 72-1811, casa_de_guias@hotmail.com, $4 s, $9 d) is located above the Casa de Guias, the city's best source for trekking and climbing info. There is a bunk room with 11 beds and a shared kitchen. The excellent Pizzeria Alpes Andes downstairs serves granola and pancakes in the morning, pizzas in the evening. This is a good place to meet fellow climbers.

Familia Meza Lodging (Lucar y Torre 538, familiameza_lodging@hotmail.com, $5 s, $10 d) has private rooms with shared bath in a safe and

Cordillera Blanca

© RENÉE DEL GAUDIO AND ROSS WEHNER

camping in the Cordillera Blanca

pleasant building just a block from Luzuriaga. There is also a terrace with views, the next-door Café Andino, laundry, and shared kitchen. This is one of Huaraz's most friendly families, which operates a plethora of recommended businesses out of an office downstairs: the Sierra Verde Spanish School, Mountain Bike Adventures, and a store with maps and books.

The Way Inn (Buenaventura Mendoza 821, near Parque Fap, tel. 043/72-8714, thewayinn@ hotmail.com) is an innovative concept in hostels: You pay whatever you want! A friendly English couple has launched this eccentric, charming place a few blocks from town, and is also building an acclimatization lodge near Pitec for trekkers. The Way Inn features orthopedic mattresses, shared kitchen, living space with videos and board games, and rooftop bar with views.

Jo's Place (Daniel Villaizan 276, tel. 043/72-5505, josplacehuaraz@hotmail.com, www .huaraz.com/josplace, $5 s, $10 d) is north of the Río Quilcay and about a 15-minute walk from city center. There are pretty mountain views, a garden with hammocks, shared kitchen, friendly management, and cheaper rooms with shared bathrooms.

$10–25

The best Cordillera Blanca view in all of Huaraz (as well as the best place to watch the sunset), is from the new, Israeli-owned 🄼 **Steel Guest House** (Psj. Alejandro Maguiña 1467, tel. 043/72-9709, steelguehouse@yahoo.com, $15 s, $20, 15 percent SAE discount, 10 percent student discount). Sunny, large rooms have comfortable beds with feather comforters (!) and modern bathrooms. The distractions are endless; rooftop bar, pool table, table tennis, Foosball, sauna, video library, book exchange, Internet. A large kitchen is available for the use of all guests.

🄼 **My House** (27 de Noviembre 773, tel. 043/72-3375, bmark@ddm.com.pe, www.andeanexplorer.com/micasa/, $10 s, $20 d) is a charming home tucked away in a central, but tranquil, neighborhood with six rooms spiraling up around a sunny courtyard. Beds are very comfortable, rooms have writing desk and private bath, and breakfast is served in a sun-filled dining room. The hostel is the home of longtime Huaraz residents Francisca and Alcides Ames, who both speak French and a smattering of English. Alcides is one of Huaraz's foremost glaciologists and has climbed up, around, and down nearly every peak in the Cordillera Blanca.

A solid favorite among climbers is **La Casa de Zarela** (Julio Arguedas 1263, tel. 043/72-1694, zarelaz@hotmail.com, www.zarelaz.cjb.net, $6 s, $12). Zarela's house-turned-hostel grows taller every year, with a fifth-floor terrace under construction recently. Spiral stairs lead up from a sunny courtyard to rooms and terraces with spectacular Cordillera Blanca views. Rooms are simple but a good value. Breakfast is served in the homey downstairs area, where there is also a bar and a center for trekking and climbing information and logistics. A kitchen is available for the use of all guests.

The six story, modern **Hostal Brit's** (Mariscal Cáceres 399, tel. 043/72-6720, hotelbrits@hotmail.com, www.huarazinfo.net/brits, $12 s, $21 d), located on the Parque Pip, offers carpeted rooms with cable TV, very comfortable beds, and views of the Cordillera Blanca if you ask. The restaurant here is not recommended.

The main upside to **Edward's Inn** (Bolognesi 121, tel. 043/72-2692, near the stadium, www.huaraz.com/edwards, edwardsinn@yahoo.com, $10 s, $20 d) is the owner himself. Eduardo Figueroa is a certified guide and is one of the top resources for information on treks, climbs, *arrieros,* you name it. His little hotel has gardens, a small café, and simple rooms with private bathrooms and lots of solar-heated hot water. There are also cheap dorm rooms ($3 s, $5 d).

Olaza's Guest House (Julio Arguedas 1242, tel. 043/72-2529, info@andeanexplorer.com, $10 s, $15 d) is a new guest house run by mountain bike guide Julio Olaza a few blocks above the center on a quiet street. The rooms are comfortable and have plenty of hot water and private bathrooms, and there are nice views of the mountain from a rooftop deck.

$50–100

All the rooms in this price category offer laundry service and have phones in the room for making calling-card calls.

Our vote for most elegant hotel in Huaraz goes to **N Hotel Colomba** (Francisco de Zela 278, tel. 043/72-1501, colomba@terra.com.pe,

www.bed42.com/hotelcolomba, $33 s, $45 d). This original hacienda has been converted into a series of large rooms spread out through a labyrinth of gardens and grassy lawns. Lucho and Sylvana Maguiña, the Peruvian-Argentine owners, are extremely generous and kind. With all the birds, and the peace and quiet, it's almost as if you were in a ranch in the middle of the countryside. This hotel is north of the Río Quilcay and a few minutes' taxi ride into the center.

San Sebastian Hotel (Italia 1124, tel. 043/72-6960, andeway@terra.com.pe, www.hotelhuaraz.com, $45 s, $53 d) is owned by the same owners as the excellent Montañero agency and Campo Base Restaurant and Pizzería. It is a large, white-washed building with comfortable, three-star rooms and views overlooking the mountains. Though a bit out of town, this is a very relaxed, safe option.

The distinctively Swiss **Andino Club Hotel** (Pedro Cochachín 357, tel. 043/72-1662, andino1@wayna.rcp.net.pe, www.hotelandino.com, $60 s, $68 d) is the luxury hotel of Huaraz, with an elegant lobby, great views, and an expensive but very good Swiss restaurant. The rooms are upscale, though we found them unadorned and a bit dark. More expensive rooms include terrace with views and bathtubs. This three-star hotel has all the perks, including laundry, mail service, and free Internet. It also has a travel agency that rents four-wheel-drive vehicles and organizes horseback riding, canoeing, and fishing adventures. Most of the international climbing and trekking agencies stay here with their groups, so make reservations ahead of time.

FOOD

Food poisoning is a major problem in Huaraz, more so than other areas of Peru. Be careful what and where you eat.

Cafés

Café Andino (Lucar y Torre 530, third flr., tel. 084/72-1203, cafeandino@hotmail.com, www.cafeandino.com, 8 A.M.–10 P.M. daily) is a great meeting spot for Huaraz trekkers and climbers. American owner Chris Benway works as a trekking guide in the Cordillera Huayhuash and is a gold mine about that area. Chris knows the value of a strong cup of joe, which he makes from his own roasted beans. There are also a range of yummy desserts and food, a great library, board games, bulletin board; in short, everything required to while away the day. Café Andino always has a good supply of the area's latest maps, Brad Johnson's must-have *Classic Climbs of the Cordillera Blanca,* and Val Pitkethly's *Trekking and Climbing in the Andes.*

The American-owned **California Café** (28 de Julio 562, tel. 043/72-8354, http://huaylas .com/californiacafe/, tibben@ocf.berkeley.edu, 7:30 A.M.–11 P.M. Mon.–Sat., 8 A.M.–10 P.M. Sun.) feels like a café lifted out of Berkeley, California, with strong espressos and lattes, tempting desserts, board games, magazines, a big book exchange, and couches that will keep you seated for hours. It serves breakfast and light meals.

Encuentro Grill and Coffee (Gamarra 790, Parque del Periodista, tel. 043/72-6865, 7:30 A.M.–10:30 P.M. daily, $3.50–5) has tables set in a sunny square and is a good place to sit and have a beer, lemonade, or coffee. It serves Peruvian food such as tamales, *trucha,* and roasted guinea pig as well as sandwiches and grilled meats.

Piccolo Café and Pizzeria (Julian de Morales 632, tel. 043/962-6342, 6:45 A.M.–midnight daily, $3.50–8) has outdoor tables on the park and an extensive menu including milkshakes, pastas, and local trout.

The cozy **Pizzeria Alpes Andes** (Parque Ginebra 28-G, tel. 043/72-1811, 6–11 A.M. and 5–11 P.M.) is next to the Casa de Guias and serves seriously strong coffee, yogurt, and muesli in the mornings, as well as great pizzas in the evening.

Desserts

A walk to the south end of Luzuriaga is worth the trip for the apple pie at **Buongiorno** (Luzuriaga 1190, tel. 043/72-7145, $0.50). **Manjar Real** (Juan de la Cruz Romero 523, near the market) will cure your sweet tooth with tempting ice creams, cakes, and pastries. The town's favorite ice cream shop is **Helados Ancash** (Raymondi 729, tel. 043/72-1955, 8 A.M.–9 P.M.), with a wide array of local flavors, including lúcuma and cherimoya.

International

The French-owned 🏔 **Bistro de los Andes** (Julián de Morales 823, tel. 043/72-6249, 7 A.M.–10 P.M. Tue.–Sun., 6–10 P.M. Monday, $5–9) is an elegant taste of Europe and a great spot for a special meal. The menu includes red curry chicken, grilled trout, pesto pasta, a vegetable stir-fry, and beef bourguignon. As you wait, there are fresh-baked French baguettes and an extensive wine list to enjoy.

The Swiss-owned **Pachamama** (San Martín 687, tel. 043/72-1834, pachamama@hotmail .com, www.huaraz.net/pachamama, $4–6) serves a variety of Italian and Peruvian dishes, as well as the house specialty, *raclette.* The owners, Michael and Katya, serve great cocktails and have created a maximum number of distractions: fireplace, pool and ping-pong tables, giant chess board, occasional live music, and intriguing paintings for sale. The indoor, glass-covered garden is great for star-gazing.

The French-owned 🏔 **Pizza B&B** (José de la Mar 674, tel. 043/72-1719, 11 A.M.–midnight, $3–5) serves lasagnas, Argentine cuts of meats, flambé, and pizzas cooked in a wood-burning oven in a stylish, Andean atmosphere.With advance notice, it can throw together a Peruvian feast for large groups.

A great place for any meal of the day is the French-owned **Creperie Patrick** (Luzuriaga 422, tel. 043/72-3364, 8 A.M.–10:30 P.M. daily, closed 2:30–6 P.M. in low season, $2–8). The sunny rooftop patio is fun for breakfast, with excellent coffee and espresso. The specialty of the house is, of course, crepes, which can either be dessert or a main meal. Also on the menu are meats, fish, lasagnas, and quiches and a good selection of wines.

There is a nice pub atmosphere at **Inka Pub Monte Rosa** (José de la Mar 661, tel. 043/72-1447, 11 A.M.–midnight, $4–9). This is a good place to have a beer and try the good menu, which includes excellent pizzas, grilled meats, pastas, Peruvian food, fondue, and imported wines. There's a good gear shop here too.

Campo Base (Luzuriaga 407, above Ortiz supermarket, tel. 043/72-5772, evenings only) has a good range of Italian and international foods, along with fresh trout and alpaca. There is often live music.

Peruvian

For great Peruvian food, head to **M Las Tulpas & Chimichurri Restaurant** (Julian de Morales 660, tel. 043/72-2206, www.huaraz.com/tulpas, 7 A.M.–11 P.M., $3–9). The new and stylish place serves gourmet Peruvian food, including *lomo al pesto, brochetas, pachamamas* (weekends only), and *arroz con pato.* An Internet station is available free for customers, and it will deliver within Huaraz.

For country-style Peruvian fare in a relaxed countryside setting, head to one of the many *recreos* spread out along the highway that runs through the Callejón de Huaylas. One we especially like in Huaras is the **Recreo Pilatos** (Pedro Cochachin 146, tel. 043/72-2444, noon–6 P.M., $1–2). It serves steaming white-corn tamales, roasted guinea pig, and huge piles of chicharrón. Also recommended is **Recreo La Union,** at Luzuriaga and Manco Capac just on the north side of the Río Quilcay.

Italian

The French-owned **Pizza Bruno** (Luzuriaga 834, tel. 043/72-5689, 6 A.M.–midnight daily, $5) has a highly recommended *pizza caprese,* along with a variety of steaks, salads, pastas, and crepes.

The charming **Pizzeria Chez Pepe** (Raymondi 624, tel. 043/72-6482, 4–11 P.M. daily, $3–5) serves pizzas as well as raviolis, lasagnas, trout, and their specialty of the house, pepper steak. It has a great list of wines and cocktails, including *algorrobina,* a sweet, creamy concoction made from a desert tree that tastes like a White Russian with a Peruvian kick.

Cebiche

Huaraz may be in the mountains, but it's only a few hours from the coast, and fresh fish arrrives in the city each morning. A good *cebiche* spot is **Huaraz Querido** (Simón Bolívar 981, tel. 043/72-2592, 9 A.M.–5 P.M., $4–7), which also serves Peruvian chicken, meat, and trout dishes. Don't pass up a glass of *leche de tigre,* the marinated lime-and-fish juice, to start.

El Cebicheria del Rey (San Martín 492, tel.

043/75-6099, 7 A.M.–10 P.M. daily, $2–5) is like being on the coast where the *cebiche* is *muy picante.* This place is packed with locals eating *sudados* (a substantial seafood soup) and *chicharrón.*

Cebichería El Ancla (Mariscal Cáceres 418, Parque Pip, tel. 043/72-8300, 9 A.M.–5 P.M. daily, $3–6) serves heaping plates of *cebiche, sudados,* and *chicharron.* Try the *jaela mixta,* a specialty of the house.

Vegetarian

Fuente de Salud (De la Mar 562, tel. 043/978-0641, 7:30 A.M.–11 P.M. daily, $1–6) serves natural yogurts, muesli, and fruit salads for breakfast, as well as steaks, pastas, and vegetarian food throughout the day. It has an excellent set-price vegetarian menu. Specialty drinks include espressos, cappuccinos, hot chocolate, and pitchers of sangria. The tiny **Restaurant Vegetariano Salud y Vida** (Mariscal Caceres 491, 8 A.M.–9 P.M., $1) has an excellent and economical vegetarian fixed menu, as well as juices, fruit salads, and rice dishes à la carte.

Markets

Huaraz's market runs along Raymondi from Luzuriaga down to Cruz Romero and is generally open from dawn to dusk. The best selection is in a market building at the corner of San Martín and Raymondi. Inside are a few booths that supply a wide range of food for trekkers, including some imported products (although no freeze-dried food, thank goodness). The market round about is overflowing with fruits, vegetables, big blocks of mountain cheese, and freshly slaughtered chickens. Anything you cannot find here, like fresh bread, will be in the mini-markets on San Martín.

The best range of imported products, though with quite a markup, is at **Market Ortiz** (Luzuriaga 401). In the south end of town, good grocery stores are at Luzuriaga 882 and across the street at **Minimarket Gianrafo** (Luzuriaga 867).

INFORMATION AND SERVICES

The best spot for trekking and climbing info is **Casa de Guias** (Parque Ginebra 28-G, tel.

043/72-1811, agmp@terra.com.pe, 9 A.M.–1 P.M. and 4–8 P.M. Mon.–Fri., 9 A.M.–1 P.M. Saturday). All the agencies listed above in *Trekking* also sell maps, along with **Vagamundo Travelbar & Maps** (Julian de Morales 753, tel. 043/75-6818, vagamundo@comic.com, 5:30 P.M.–2 A.M. daily) and **Café Andino** (Lucar y Torre 530, third flr., tel. 084/72-1203, cafeandino@hotmail.com, 8 A.M.–10 P.M. daily). Not much information is available at the government's **tourist information office** on Plaza de Armas (Luzuriaga 734, second flr., Psj. Atusparía, tel. 043/72-8812, 8 A.M.–1 P.M. and 5–8 P.M. Mon.–Fri.).

Parque Nacional Huascarán (Sal y Rosas 555, Huaraz, tel. 084/72-2086, 8:30 A.M.–1 P.M. and 2:30–6 P.M. Mon.–Fri.) sells entry tickets to the park ($20 for climbing and trekking, $2 for day) and has some information.

The best web page on Huaraz is www.huaraz.com. Other good pages include www.andean-explorer.com, www.huaraz.org, and www.huaylas.com. The outfits that maintain these web pages put out very helpful brochures with surprisingly good maps of the areas. Weather information can be found at www.senamhi.gob.pe.

Police and Emergency

The **24-hour Tourism Police** is in a small passageway on the west side of the Plaza de Armas (Luzuriaga 734, second flr., Psj. Atusparía, tel. 043/72-6343.) There is also **24-hour national police** (tel. 043/72-1021, 28 de Julio 701). For mountain emergencies call the **Casa de Guias** (Parque Ginebra 28-G, tel. 043/72-1811, agmp@terra.com.pe, 9 A.M.–1 P.M. and 4–8 P.M. Mon.–Fri., 9 A.M.–1 P.M. Saturday). For 24-hour help contact Yungay's **High Mountain Rescue Unit** (tel. 043/79-3333, tel. 043/79-3327, or 043/79-3291, usam@pnp.gob.pe, www.huaraz.info/usam, 24 hours Mon.–Fri.).

Health Care

Dr. Rafaél Pais Hurtado (cell phone 043/961-2002) is an excellent doctor who makes house calls at a very reasonable price. The most upscale clinic in town, where Dr. Pais works, is **Clínica San Pablo** (Huaylas 172, tel. 043/72-8805 or 043/72-8811, 24 hours).

For non-emergencies the public hospitals are much cheaper. The best is **Hospital Huaraz** (Luzuriaga, 13th block, tel. 043/72-1861 or 043/72-4146, 24 hours). The widest variety of medicines is available at **Inka Farma** (Luzuriaga 435, tel. 043/72-1092, 24 hours).

Language Schools

The best language school in Huaraz is **Sierra Verde** (Lucar y Torres 538, tel. 043/72-1203, sierraverde_sp@hotmail.com), which offers individual classes for $6/hour or cheaper group classes. One of the teachers, Ethel, will get you speaking in no time. Another option is **Langway** (Luzuriaga 975, #203, tel. 043/72-4286, langwayhuaraz@hotmail.com, www.huaraz.org/langway).

Banks and Money Exchange

Banks are open 9:30–1 P.M. and 4:30–6:30 P.M. Mon.–Fri. and 9:30 A.M.–noon Saturday. There are many banks with ATMs clustered around the Plaza de Armas. **Banco Wiese Sudameris,** on the east side of the plaza, accepts most bank cards. There are money-change places all along Luzuriaga.

Communications

The **post office** (702 Luzuriaga, tel. 043/72-1030, 8 A.M.–8 P.M. Mon.–Sat.), is on the main plaza.

There are many fast Internet cafés around town, including **Speedy** (San Martín 1102, 9 A.M.–noon daily, $0.60/hr) and **Portalnet** (Plaza Belén 1035, 9 A.M.–11 P.M.), both at the south end of town, **Andean Services** (Gamarra 872, $0.60/hr) to the east of Luzuriaga, and the centrally located **Cabinas Internet** (Parque Ginebra 630, $0.60/hr), which also offers international phone calls ($0.15/min to the U.S.)

Laundry

The best laundries are **Lavanderia Denny's** (José de la Mar 561, tel. 043/72-9232, 8 A.M.–9 P.M. Mon.–Sat., 9 A.M.–noon and 6–8 P.M. Sunday, $0.90/kilo) and **Lavanderia Tintorería** (José de La Mar 674, tel. 043/72-1719, 9 A.M.–1 P.M. and 3–8 P.M. Mon.–Sat., $0.90/kilo).

Massage and Spa

A recommended massage therapist is **Flor**

Figueroa (28 de Julio 1341, tel. 043/72-1049, $10/90 minutes), who also does reflexology and Shiatzu therapies at her office.

There are wet and dry saunas at **Baños a Vapor** (Raymondi 904, tel. 043/72-2092, 2–9 P.M. Mon.–Fri., 9 A.M.–6 P.M. Sat.–Sun.). **En Forma** (José de Sucre 1225, tel. 043/75-6420) has saunas and a pool and offers aromatherapy, reflexology, and Reiki therapies.

GETTING THERE

Only chartered flights arrive at the area's airport, which is 32 km north of Huaraz in Anta.

With the recently paved highway through the coastal town of Pativilca, Huaraz is a comfortable seven-hour bus ride from Lima. The highway runs up to Lago Conocha at 4,000 meters before dropping into the Callejón de Huaylas and Huaraz. Buses going back and forth to Lima often start and end in Caraz, passing Huaraz en route and stopping at the corner of Fitzcarrald and Raymondi.

At least one night bus between Lima and Huaraz was robbed at gunpoint in 2003. To reduce the chances that robbers board the bus, many companies now videotape all passengers before departure. When in Peru's mountains, travel by day only.

There are many bus options in Huaraz for traveling to Lima. The best company for Lima-Huaraz travel is **Movil Tours** (Simón Bolívar 452, tel. 043/72-2555, $13), which has a range of buses to Lima from $7–14. The buses leave throughout the day at 9:30 A.M., 1 P.M., 10 P.M., and 11 P.M. They are double-decker buses with reclining seats. A similar service is provided by **Ormeño** (Antonio Raymondi 242, tel. 043/72-8726, $12) and **Cruz del Sur** (Raymondi 242, tel. 043/72-8726, $12), which has an 11 A.M. bus and Imperial nonstop service at 10 P.M. **Bus Ancash** (Raymondi 821, tel. 043/427-7536) is a cheaper option, with Lima-bound buses at 1:30 P.M. and 8:45 P.M.

Several companies head to Chimbote via three different routes. Movil Tours operates night buses that take the highway down to Pativilca and then head back up the coast to Chimbote, continuing on to Trujillo. **Yungay Express** (Fitzcarrald 237, tel. 043/72-4377) has day buses that travel to Chimbote via the dirt road to Casma and also along a gravel road through the Cañon de Pato (see the sidebar *Adventure Routes to Huaraz*). Another option for the Casma route is **Transporte Huandaoy** (tel. 043/711633, $9). The company's old, 30-seater Mercedes buses make the six-hour journey between the two cities a few times each day starting at 7 A.M. from either end.

For reaching Chavín de Huántar and the cities east of the Cordillera Blanca in the Callejón de Conchucos, **Chavín Express** (Mariscal Cáceres 338, tel. 043/72-4652) has three buses per day to Chavín, San Marcos, and Huari.

For making the interesting journey across the high plains east of Huaraz to Huánuco, **Transportes El Rápido** (Mariscal Cáceres and Tarapacá, tel. 043/72-2887) will get you as far as the midway point of La Unión. The company also travels to Huallanca and Chiquián, two starting point for treks in the Cordillera Huayhuash. The company has a bus at 6 A.M. and 1 P.M. to Chiquián ($3, three hours), and 6 A.M. and 12:30 P.M. to Huallanca ($4, four hours), continuing on to La Unión (10 hours).

For heading north to **Monterrey,** catch the green-and-white buses from the corner of Luzuriaga and 28 de Julio ($0.30, half hour). Or hop one of the *combis* at the bridge near Centenario that run as far as **Caraz.** For reaching **Recauy** and points along the highway south of Huaraz, head to the Transportes Zona Sur terminal at Gridilla and Tarapacá.

Bus companies and schedules change frequently, so inquire locally before heading to the bus station.

GETTING AROUND

Taxis are cheap and ubiquitous in Huaraz and cost $1 for in-town travel.

John Lockwood of **Pedal Peru** (pedalperu @hotmail.com, www.pedalperu.com) has a private *combi*, with a CD player and lots of leg room. He drives trekkers to trailheads and will even pick up a group in Lima.

Romero Córdova (Gridilla s/n, Rosas Pampa, tel. 043/72-3950) is a reliable driver with a new 20-passenger Coaster bus. He will drive or pick up in Lima for $300. The Andino Club Hotel and the Inka Pub Monte Rosa rent four-wheel-drive vehicles and motorcycles.

MONTERREY

Monterrey is an easygoing village 6 km north of Huaraz (about 10 minutes in a *combi*) that is mostly visited for its hot springs. There are a few hotels and restaurants as well. The **hot springs** (7 A.M.–6 P.M., $1) include two large pools, of varying temperatures, along with a number of private bathing rooms for one or two people. Don't be put off by the water, which is stained brown by minerals. Though far from pristine, these baths are the most hygienic and best maintained in the area. The best time to go is early in the morning, because the baths are cleaned each day at closing.

Accommodations

There are no good budget options in Monterrey. The best lodging choice is the three-star **El Patio de Monterrey** (tel. 043/72-4965, elpatio@ terra.com.pe, $40 s, $55 d), a colonial-style place with tile roofs, a stone terrace, and water fountain. The rooms have nice furniture, tubs, phones, and TV (only local channels). Many of the rooms look out over gardens, and meals are served in a dining area with fireplace.

Right next to the hot baths is the former state-owned **Real Hotel Baños Termales Monterrey** (tel. 043/72-1717, $58 s, $58 d). This rather austere hotel has rooms with hot showers, a handful of more expensive bungalows, and free access to the hot baths.

Food

Monterrey Café Bar (10 A.M.–5 P.M. daily) is right next to the baths, has its own bouldering wall, and is a good place for lunch or beers. There are several small *recreos,* or countryside restaurants, near Monterrey. The best is **El Ollón de Barro** (Km 7 of highway, tel. 043/72-3364, $3–8), which serves up huge portions of *chichar-*

rón, huge red *rocoto* peppers stuffed with spiced meat, local trout, and grilled meats. Tables are spread around a grassy lawn, and there is a playground nearby for kids.

Getting There

From the south end of Huaraz, catch the green-and-white buses to Monterrey from the corner of Luzuriaga and 28 de Julio ($0.30, half hour). Or from the north end, hop on any north-bound transport from the bridge near Centenario. A taxi costs $2 from Huaraz to Carhuaz. From the main road through Monterrey, *combis* pass frequently in either direction.

CARHUAZ

Carhuaz is a quiet, peaceful town with stunning views of **Hualcán** and a sunny climate. At 2,650 meters above sea level, it is about 400 meters lower than Huaraz and about 32 km farther down the valley. Carhuaz has just the right amount of tourist infrastructure to make it a comfortable place to stay, and remains a pleasant relief from the go-go atmosphere of Huaraz. The stunning Plaza de Armas, with its fragrant rose gardens and palm trees, is a relaxing place. The **Sunday market** here is spectacular, with a range of both Andean and tropical foods, dried herbs, crafts, and colorfully dressed *campesinos* selling livestock.

The views of the Cordillera Blanca here are arguably more beautiful than around Huaraz, and the town is certainly more pleasant. For $3 you can hire a taxi to take you to **Mirador Ataquero** in the Cordillera Negra, which offers stunning mountain views and an easy walk back down to Carhuaz. There are rustic hot baths above town at the rustic **Baños de la Merced** ($0.30). The **Cueva de Guitarros,** a cave that was inhabited 12,000 years ago, is an hour's walk west of Tingua, which is just north of Carhuaz along the highway.

A highly recommended day excursion from here is to take one of the early-morning *combis* that head east up the *Quebrada Ulta* to Chacas, on the other side of the Cordillera Blanca. There are starting points for two excellent day hikes before the *combis* wind the final switchbacks to the high pass of **Punta Olímpica** (4,890 meters). The first leads to **Laguna Auquiscocha** (4,320 meters), where there is a granite waterfall reminiscent of Yosemite Falls in the Unites States. The second leads to the stunning alping cirque around **Lago Yanayacu** (4,600 meters).

An extraordinary source of information, and an all-around nice guy, is local resident **Felipe Díaz,** who authored the Cordillera Blanca's most-used trekking map. If you speak Spanish, he will talk your ears off about all the exciting trekking options in the area. Ask for him at the Café El Abuelo. Carhuaz also has a small tourist office (Comercio 530, tel. 043/79-4294, 7:30 A.M.–12:30 P.M. and 1:30–4:P.M. Mon.–Fri.).

Accommodations

The best budget option is the friendly **Las Bromelias Guesthouse** (Brasil 208, tel. 043/79-4033, $6 s, $9 d), with nice rooms surrounding a garden with a *chirimoya* tree, a beautiful cat, and some interesting cactus plants. Rooms are clean with good beds, tile floors, and hot water.

Our favorite country retreat in all of Peru is **M Casa de Pocha** (1.5 km east of town, tel. 043/96-3058, lacasadepocha@yahoo.com, $30 pp, including dinner and breakfast), perched in lovely forests and hills above Carhuaz with stunning views of Hualcán. This hand-built hacienda, surrounded by eucalyptus forest and a working organic farm, is completely self-sufficient, with vegetable gardens and solar-powered energy. Everything here is made by hand, including cheese, marmalades, soaps, and even furniture.

The adobe rooms are simple and rustic and decorated with an artist's touch. Dinner is served either outdoors or in a charming dining room with stained glass windows. Nearby is a dry or wet sauna below the rooms, and there are great walks and horseback rides into the nearby mountains. Pocha's son, Ario Ferri (info@yurakyaku.com, www.yurakyaku.com), is an English-speaking international river expert who runs rafting and kayaking trips all over Peru. He takes groups out on the Río Santa in up to Class IV rapids. He also runs a whitewater kayak school, and there is a pool on the property for kayak rolling lessons. The lodge is 1.5 km east out of town on a dirt road heading up the valley. Call or email ahead for reservations and directions.

A more modern choice is the sparkling new **Hostal El Abuelo** (9 de Diciembre 257, tel. 043/79-4456, hostalelabuelo@terra.com.pe, www.barrioperu.terra.com.pe/hostalelabuelo, $30 s, $40 d, including breakfast), around the corner from the Plaza de Armas. Meals are served on a sunny patio in a citrus grove. The rooms upstairs are decorated with beautiful Andean rugs and have comfortable beds and modern bathrooms with plenty of hot water. The sunny upstairs terrace has great views of the Cordillera Negra.

Food

Café Heladería Restaurant El Abuelo (Plaza de Armas, tel. 043/79-4149, 8 A.M.–9 P.M. daily) is clean but pricey, with a great selection of natural ice creams and milkshakes (including beer- and pisco sour–flavored varieties!). It serves espressos, sandwiches, pastas, meats, and cocktails, and sells homemade marmalades made from the local *sachatomate* (Andean tomato) and *sauco* berries. It also sells exquisite local sheep wool weavings, which range from $4 to $38 and are colored with natural dyes.

For a cheaper meal, **La Punta Olímpica** (La Merced, Plaza de Armas, tel. 043/79-4022, 8 A.M.–10 P.M., $1.50) serves *comida tipica* such as *lomo saltado,* roasted guinea pig, and a good fixed menu.

Getting There

Carhuaz is a half hour north of Huaraz. From Huaraz, hop a Caraz-bound *combi* from the bridge near Centenario and get off halfway, in Carhuaz. From Carhuaz's Plaza de Armas, *combis* leave every 15 minutes heading south to Huaraz and north to Caraz. From here, *combis* head west toward the Mirador Ataquero and farther into the Cordillera Negra from the market on Wednesday and Sunday at 10 A.M.

Cordillera Blanca

Cordillera Blanca

ADVENTURE ROUTES TO HUARAZ

To travel back in time, and have an adventure in the process, hop off the highway along the coast and follow a dirt road into the mountains. If there is a village at the end of the road, a *colectivo* or *combi* is sure to take you there. The fastest route from the coast to Huaraz is along the smooth highway that branches off from the Panamericana at *Pativilca*, 200 km north of Lima. But if you are in the mood for fabulous scenery and a rush of adventure, there are three wild rides to Huaraz—one from **Casma** over the Cordillera Negra, another from **Chimbote** through the famous **Cañon de Pato**, and a completely hairball, multi-day overland route from **Cajamarca.**

The Casma route begins in a large flood plain before beginning the endless switchbacks up a 2,800-meter pass over the Cordillera Negra, at which point a full view of the snow-covered Cordillera Blanca swings into view. From here the road drops directly into Huaraz, nestled in the valley below. The road is dirt, surprisingly smooth, and only takes six hours—though much longer in the rainy season. Leave for this journey early in the morning to enjoy spectacular views, as clouds tend to form in the afternoon. The best time to take this route is April or May, at the end of the rainy season, when roads are somewhat dry and mountain fields are brimming with flowers.

The most popular backpackers' route—though far bumpier, dustier, and longer than the Casma route—is the Cañon de Pato route, which begins in **Santa,** just north of Chimbote. This 10-hour journey follows the old highway, built by a mining company in the 1930s, along the Río Santa from the dry desert near its mouth up into the sheer walls of Cañon de Pato. Dozens of tunnels were drilled through the canyon walls to make this route along

the river, which has been reduced to a trickle because of the hydroelectric dam operated by **Duke Energy,** the Charlotte, North Carolina–based energy company. Because it is mostly gravel, this road can be taken during the rainy season, and it becomes fully paved at **Huancacalle,** at the northern end of the Callejón de Huaylas, where there is the recommended **Hostal-Restaurant Kokis** (tel. 043/80-4425, on the main road). For bus companies that travel these routes, see *Getting There* for each city.

The third route to Huaraz, from Cajamarca, is the most rugged and time-consuming but rewards with extraordinarily wild mountain scenery. This route requires perseverance, several days, and a certain amount of faith because most of the people you talk to will say the route is not even possible. Locals know how to get to the next town, but rarely beyond, so the journey becomes a connect-the-dots exercise. If you are driving your own vehicle, expect to have to make repairs afterwards, as we did, and to use your spare tire. By all means, bring plenty of food and water.

From Cajamarca, head first to the pleasant country town of **Llacanora** along the highway that begins at Baños de Inca. The route climbs through beautiful *altiplano* and passes through the towns of Namora, Matara, and San Marcos before crossing the Río Cisneros near La Grama. The first major city along this route is **Cajabamba,** a small town with the simple Restaurante La Casona (Plaza de Armas, $5–7) and a few *hospedajes*. If at all possible, pass through Cajabamba and head toward the better services of **Huamachuco,** which has good hostels and important Inca ruins outside of town. The smooth, rolling dirt road between Cajabamba and Huamachuco offers stunning vistas of green fields

YUNGAY

Yunkay, 54 km north of Huaraz, is a quiet town with minimal services but is the closest launching point for Lagunas Llanganuco and classic peaks such as Pisco and Huascarán. The original village was the site of a horrific tragedy on May 31, 1970, when an earthquake dislodged an immense chunk of mud and ice from Huascarán. The resulting *aluvión* destroyed the town

in minutes and killed 18,000 people, nearly the entire village.

The few hundred survivors of the tragedy built a new settlement on a nearby, more protected, site. New Yungay is a mix of modern buildings and a hundred or so prefab wooden cabins that were donated by the former Soviet Union. The silt plain above the old village has been converted into the **Campo Santo Cemetery** (8 A.M.–6 P.M., $0.60) and remains a solemn place today. The

and rolling mountains and is an excellent mountain-bike route. On the way, you will pass Laguna Sausayocha, a high-altitude lake famous for its trout, and the hot springs of Yanasara, a two-hour detour along a dead-end road. Several bus companies in Cajamarca, spread along Grau, go to Cajabamba. But only one, Emp. Transportes Anita (Grau 1170), has bus service to Cajabamba and beyond to Huamachuco. The $2.50 Cajabamba bus leaves every day at 8:30 A.M. and 12 P.M., arriving five hours later at Cajambamba, from where another four-hour bus can be taken to **Huamachuco.**

From Huamachuco, most buses head down for the smooth, six-hour trip to Trujillo, passing near the pleasant town of **Santiago de Chuco,** birthplace of Peruvian poet Cesar Vallejo. This makes for a wonderful, and not too jarring, route between Cajamarca and Trujillo. For those headed to Huaraz, however, the tougher and more remote terrain, with the least public transport, lies ahead. Huaraz travelers should ask directions for the Carretera Florida, which branches off from the road to Trujillo a few kilometers southwest of town shortly before a bridge. There are occasional *combis* leaving Huamachuco along this route for the village of **Cachicadán** and, from there, onward to **Mollepata.** This road quickly becomes a rocky road suitable only for four-wheel-drive vehicles or trashed *combis* until you reach **Mina Simón.**

This fast-growing gold mine, along with the nearby Mina Comarsa, is owned by Wilmer Paredes Sánchez, originally from the nearby hamlet of Mollepata. This mine, like Newmont's Yanacocha mine and those operated by Barrick Corp. in the Cordillera Huayhuash, extracts gold by filtering a cyanide solution through piled-up dirt terraces.

The mine has built a well-groomed, high-altitude shortcut to Mina Comarsa and, beyond, to Mollepata. Mining trucks seem happy to pick up walkers along this route, which branches off to the left at a cemetery several kilometers past Mina Simón. Otherwise, *combis* continue right, along a lower route that passes through a more populated route that includes Cachicadán, which has hostels and hot baths, **Mollebamba,** and the larger town of Mollepata. Plan on anywhere from seven to nine hours between Huamachuco and Mollepata, depending on which route you take.

Mollepata has only one rather dirty hostel being built on the Plaza de Armas, which is undergoing a major construction campaign funded by Mr. Paredes Sánchez. (He is also the patron of the town's annual San José Festival, which runs July 14–23 and features bullfights, cockfights, and all the beer, *aguardiente,* and beef you can consume.) From Mollepata, the road winds down an impossibly steep river valley before climbing, in a series of endless hairpin turns, on the other side to **Conchucos** and the pleasant town of **Pallasca,** two hours past Mollepata and a good option for a second night's lodging if you can get here before dark. *Combis* along the rough road to Pallasca are infrequent, but mining trucks rumble by every hour. This charming town, with narrow cobblestone streets and a colonial church, has a home on the main square that rents rooms to visitors ($3 per night). Buses leave from Conchucos and Pallasca every Monday night to Chimbote, descending the four-hour route to Chuquicara in the Santa Valley. Huaraz-bound travelers can wait here for a bus to take them through the spectacular Cañon de Pato to Huaraz (six hours).

only evidence of the village are the tops of a few palm trees, which once ringed the town's square and now just barely stick out of the hardened mud. Miraculously, one of these trees is still alive.

A re-creation of the church's old facade has been built above the old square. In the flood plains nearby, huge boulders and a crumpled bus attest to the power of the mudslide. A huge white statue of Christ with outspread arms now stands above the town's hilltop cemetery, where a few

hundred people clambered to safety during the mudslide. From here, there are views over the entire valley up to the flanks of Huascarán, where the path of the mudslide can still be seen. There are two festivals here in October, including Virgen del Rosario in the first week of October and the town's anniversary, Oct. 25–28.

Accommodations

The best place to stay in Yungay is **Hostal Gledel**

The facade of Yungay's church was the only building left standing after the 1970 mudslide.

(tel. 043/79-3048, $3 s, $6 d), where the gregarious Señora Gamboa will spoil you with puddings, cakes, and fresh bread. This spotless hostel has solar-powered electricity and rooms with shared baths; the nicest rooms are upstairs. The shared bathrooms have both electric showerheads and a hot-water heater, so guests are guaranteed a hot shower. Excellent food is served in the dining room, and the Señora even makes Huascarán-shaped cakes for expeditions after climbs.

Information and Services
Yungay is headquarters of the national police **High Mountain Rescue Unit** (tel. 043/79-3333, tel. 043/79-3327 or 043/79-3291, usam@pnp.gob.pe, www.huaraz.info/usam/, www.pnp.gob.pe/direcciones/altamontana.asp, 24 hours Mon.–Fri.).

Getting There
Tourist mini-buses for the 26-km journey to Lagunas Llanganuco leave from Yungay during the high tourist months from June to August. Buses for Yanama, on the other side of the Callejón de Huaylas, also leave from Yungay early most mornings from the intersection of Graziani and 28 de Julio. You can ask to be dropped off at the lakes.

Combi transport heading north to Caraz or south to Huaraz is frequent.

◪ LAGUNAS LLANGANUCO
This pair of pristine lakes, surrounded by rare *polylepis* trees, are perched high in the glacial valley above Yungay at 3,850 meters, between the tumbling glaciers of Huascarán's north summit (6,655 meters) on one side and Huandoy (6,160 meters) on the other. The lakes' turquoise waters, a result of glacial silt, glow in the midday sun. The first lake is Chinacocha, and rowboats can be rented here 8 A.M.–3:30 P.M. The second lake is called OrconCocha, and the best views of the mountains are a little further on.

The highway from Yungay passes these lakes en route to Portachuelo Llanganuco, a high pass at 4,767 meters, and leads to the towns of Vaquería, Colcabamba, and Yanama in the Callejón de Conchucos. Shortly before the lakes, there is a control booth of the Parque Nacional Huascarán, which charges day visitors $2 and longer-term visitors $20.

These lakes are one of the starting points for the popular Santa Cruz trek. The base camp for climbing Pisco and the newly built Refugio Peru in a four-hour hike from the Lagunas Llanganuco at 3,865 meters up to 4,665 meters. The best time to visit the Lagunas Llanganuco is at midday when the sun is brightest. The lakes fall into shade in the afternoon, when chill winds whip their waters.

Getting There
Many agencies in Huaraz offer day tours to these lakes for $8 to $10 pp. See the *Yungay* section for details on public transport to the lakes.

CARAZ
Caraz, at the north end of the Callejón de Huaylas, is the valley's best option for those who are looking for a peaceful, less touristy option to Huaraz. It is a pretty town with a graceful plaza and a colonial air that comes from never having been destroyed by an *aluvión*. A market comes alive each day here with fresh food, colorful bas-

The waters of Lake Llaganuco are turquoise in the midday sun.

ketry, gourd bowls, votive candles, and woven hats. The city sprawls across a grassy plan beneath the tumbling glaciers of Huandoy, where the Río Santo begins to tumble toward the Pacific.

Though much smaller than Huaraz, Caraz offers a good range of hotels and one of the valley's best climbing and trekking agencies. At 2,285 meters, it is 800 meters lower than Huaraz and enjoys much warmer weather. Its nickname, *Caraz Dulzura* (Sweet Caraz) belies its reputation as a land of milk and *manjar blanco,* the gooey caramel made from cow's milk.

Caraz is well-positioned for the valley's major climbing and trekking endeavors. It is near the endpoint of the popular Santa Cruz trek and is close to Alpamayo, Pisco, and Huascarán. This is also the starting point for explorations into the rugged northern regions of the Cordillera Blanca.

Sights

There are a few excellent day excursions from Caraz. Just north of town, a road leads 31 km up past towering granite walls to the spectacular Lago Parón, the largest lake in the Cordillera Blanca. A dozen snow pyramids hem the lake in on all sides, including the perfect towers of Pirámide (5,885 meters) and Chacraraju (6,185 meters), which rise from its farthest end. This is a good spot for camping, even more spectacular than Lagunas Llanganuco.

Just a few kilometers north of Caraz is **Tumshukaiko,** a huge area of stone walls that looks like a fort and may have been built by the Chavín Culture (1,000–200 B.C.). To walk here from Caraz's main square, follow San Martín uphill, take a left on 28 de Julio, and continue to the bridge over the Río Llullan. The ruins are another 300 meters from here and before the road for Lago Parón. There is also an interesting one- or two-day hike south along the foothills of the Cordillera Blanca to Ranrahirca, from where *combis* return to Caraz.

The 67 km between Huaraz and Caraz can be driven in one hour by a direct bus or two hours by a stop-and-go *combi.* Caraz has access to the coast through the rough and spectacular Cañon de Pato (see the sidebar *Adventure Routes to Huaraz*), along which buses travel daily to the sea port of Chimbote. There is also a rough dirt road that heads west over the Cordillera Negra toward a gigantic stand of *Puya raimondii* plants at **Paso de Huinchus** (4,300 meters). This road leads to the coast and, in the dry season, makes for a spectacular and fast mountain bike descent.

Sports and Recreation

The two tour agencies in town are both on the Plaza de Armas. **Pony Expeditions** (Jr. Sucre 1266, tel. 043/79-1642, ponyexp@terra.com.pe, www.ponyexpeditions.com) was founded a decade ago by longtime guide Alberto Cafferata and is one of the better adventure outfits in the whole valley. It has top-rate equipment and offers a range of climbing, trekking, mountain-biking, and fishing trips in the Blanca, Huayhuash, and Cusco area. Cafferata speaks English, French, and German and is the best source of information in Caraz.

The prices for the five-day Santa Cruz trek run from $75 for just an *arriero* and burro, $175 with food added, $240 with guide added, and $300 for a full-service, private trek with tables, bathroom tents, the works. Pony Expeditions also runs a 12-day loop around Alpamayo's north side and offers guided climbs on nearly all of the technical peaks around Lago Parón, including world-famous Artesonraju. There is also a good gear shop here that sells white gas, maps, and books.

Another good agency is **Summit Peru** (Sucre 1106, inside Café Terraza, tel. 043/79-1958, summitperu@terra.com.pe, www.summitperu.50megs.com), run by Carlos Tinoco and Haren Montes.

Accommodations

The backpackers' choice is **Los Pinos Lodge & Camping** (Parque San Martin 103, tel. 043/79-2159, lospinos@apuaventura.com, www.apuaventura.com, $10 s, $20 d, includes breakfast) with tourist information, gear and bike rental, book exchange, and nightly movies. Spacious rooms have high ceilings and decent beds. The restaurant serves pizzas, pastas, local trout, and lots of cocktails. There is a small grassy area for camping ($2.50 pp).

For good service and a location on the main square, try **Hostal Perla de los Andes** (Plaza de Armas, tel. 043/79-2007, $10 s, $16 d). Simple, unadorned rooms are clean, with cable TV and private baths, and there is a café downstairs.

Tucked away in a neighborhood above town is **Grand Hostal Caraz Dulzura** (Sáenz Peña 212,

tel. 043/79-1523, carloshuaman@hotmail.com, $7 s, $13 d), a new hotel with a more modern feel and a friendly staff. Three large rooms are carpeted and impeccably clean, and have comfortable beds, TV, and electric showerheads. For backpackers there are $5 bunk beds.

The nicest hotel in Caraz is the **M Hostal Chamanna** (Nueva Victoria 185, near the end of 28 de Julio, tel. 043/978-1094, chamanna@terramail.com.pe, www.chamanna.com, $6 s, $20 d), a German-owned hostel above town with five handsome bungalows and an excellent Alsatian restaurant. The large, well-decorated rooms are interspersed with bougainvillea gardens, streams, and patios offering views of the Huandoy glacier. Full breakfast is $6.

Food

Many of the best options in Caraz are cafés. For homemade ice cream head to **Heladería Caraz Dulzura** (Plaza de Armas, next to Perla Los Andes). **Café la Terraza** (Jr. Sucre 1106, $2) serves flavorful espresso and omelettes, sandwiches, quiches, and pastas in a charming little patio. It also makes box lunches to go for day hikers.

Upstairs from Pony's Expeditions is the charming **Café de Rat** (Jr. Sucre 1266, tel. 043/79-1642, 8 A.M.–10 A.M. and 4–9 P.M.) serving pasta, pizzas, and beers in a pub-like atmosphere. This cozy place turns into a bar at night with good music.

The best Peruvian restaurant is **Restaurant Punta Grande** (Daniel Villar 595, tel. 043/79-1320, 8 A.M.–8 P.M. daily, $3), on the highway leading out of town. This pleasant garden restaurant serves fresh trout roasted over an open fire, grilled meats, and good corn tamales. **Restaurant Alpamayo** (Km 255 of the highway, tel. 043/79-3090, 8 A.M.–7 P.M. daily, $2–4) serves fortifying breakfasts of *chicharrón* and *tamal* and serves a range of Peruvian food throughout the day, such as local trout and *pachamanca*-style meats.

At **M Hostal Chamanna** (Av. Nueva Victoria 185, tel. 043/978-1094, $7–18), an Alsatian chef whips up a smorgasbord of European cuisine with crisp mountain views. Call for a reservation, or it may not be open.

Information and Services

The **tourist office** (San Martín, tel. 043/79-1029, 8 A.M.–1 P.M. and 2:30–5 P.M.) has city maps, though the best information is available from the agences on the plaza.

There is a **Banco de la Nación** near the plaza at Raymondi and a **Banco de Crédito** at Daniel Villar 217, but neither have an ATM. **Pony Expeditions** will change U.S. dollars and euros.

There is a place to make **international calls** at Raymondi 408, and a few places around the plaza for fast satellite **Internet.**

Laundry is available at **Lavandería Marshall** (San Martín, 11th block, 8 A.M.–2 P.M. and 4–8 P.M.).

Getting There

Combis leave frequently along the highway south toward Yungay and Huaraz. Cars leave when full from the corner of Ramón Castilla and Santa Cruz at 5 A.M. and 1 P.M. for the 90-minute drive to Pueblo Parón, the small village that lies 9 km before Lago Parón. Cars from Pueblo Parón return to Caraz at 6 A.M. and 2 P.M. From Ramón Castilla and Santa Cruz, cars also leave when full for Cashapampa, the traditional endpoint of the Santa Cruz trek. Trekkers can use these cars on their return trip to Caraz.

Several bus companies travel to Lima from Caraz and pick up passengers in Huaraz along the way. **Movil Tours** (tel. 043/79-1922) is the best among a handful of Lima-bound bus companies in the first block of Córdoba. **Yungay Express** (Villar 316, tel. 043/79-1693) has an 8:30 A.M. bus down the Cañon del Pato ($6, nine hours) to Chimbote, from where buses can be taken to Trujillo the same evening.

HUAMACHUCO

This charming mountain town lies in the middle of the Cajamarca-Trujillo route, and from here a bumpy dirt track also leads on to the Cañon de Pato and Huaraz. A bell tower in the main square is all that remains of the church where Simón Bolívar delivered a rousing speech about independence to the city populace. Nearby, and set back from the main square, is the colonial church of San José (6:30–8:30 A.M. and 6:30–8 P.M.

Mon.–Fri.). On another corner of the square, next to the Caja NorPeru, is the house of Sanchez Carrión, Bolívar's secretary general, who returned to this town after the revolution. There is a colorful market on this plaza on Sundays.

A worthwhile walk from Huamachuco leads to the impressive Inca ruins of **Marca Huamachuco,** a rambling military and ceremonial center perched on a mountaintop about 9 km, or a three-hour walk, outside of town. From the main square, cross Puente Grande, the bridge for the highway heading south out of town. Take an immediate right on a gravel road heading along the river. After 200 yards take the first left on a dirt lane that eventually heads above town until you reach a concrete arch, marking the entrance to the ruins 2.8 km later. Proceed up the steep, switchbacked jeep trail for another 6.3 km until you see several acres of stone structures, including two-story buildings with strange curved walls that seem to be a blend of Chachapoyan and Inca building techniques.

Accommodations

The best place to stay is **Hostal Huamachuco** (Castilla 354, tel. 044/44-1393, $9 d, $6 s) on the Plaza de Armas. This restored, though still rickety, wooden house has balconies over a central courtyard where cars can be parked and large rooms, new mattresses, lukewarm water, a trustworthy staff, and TVs for an extra $2. The second option, a block from the Plaza de Armas, is **Hotel Colonial** (Ramón Castilla 537, tel. 044/44-1334, $13 d, $8 s), which has comfortable rooms, TV, a quiet atmosphere, and plenty of hot water.

Food

The best place to eat is **La Casona,** Balta 252, with an excellent three-course menú. There is also **Turco,** a mini-market at 664 Balta near the Plaza, that serves scrumptious natural yogurt in lucúma, vanilla, strawberry, and peach flavors.

Information and Services

Most everything in Huamachuco is clustered around the main square, starting with the **police station** at the corner of San Ramón and San Martín. Also on the square is a **cinema,** which hosts an

Cordillera Blanca

eclectic variety of reruns and the occasional concert, and a good Internet spot named **Yogur** (Castilla 366, 9 A.M.–2 A.M., $1/hour). The municipality, where maps and reliable directions can be obtained, is a few blocks from the square and is easy to find. **Laundry** is available at 532 Castilla, two blocks from the square. **Hospital Leoncio Prado** is located at Diez de Julio 209 (tel. 044/44-1210).

Getting There

Buses run daily between Trujillo and Huamachuco. From Huamachuco, check with bus companies located on Balta, near the main square. One company, Negreyos, charges $4.50 for the six-hour trip to Trujillo on good dirt roads in a large bus, departing every day at 8:30 P.M. Horna, in the pedestrian street of Pasaje San Martín, has another bus leaving at 8:45 P.M. There are also smaller cars leaving every day at 1 P.M. and arriving in Trujilo by 7 P.M. For the trip to Cajabamba and on to Cajamarca, ask for Empresa Transportes Anita.

Trekking

The sparkling blue skies and dazzling white peaks of the Huaraz area make for unforgettable trekking and climbing experiences, in the same league with the European Alps, the Alaska Range, or the Himalaya. The Cordillera Blanca, the second-highest mountain range in the world, lures the lion's share of visitors with its easy access and huge range of options for both trekkers and climbers. Nearly every peak in the range is encompassed by Peru's most important alpine park, Parque Nacional Huascarán. Though more difficult to reach, the Cordillera Huayhuash has a more remote, wilderness feel and a handful of climbs for advanced climbers only.

PLANNING YOUR TREK

The easiest way to trek or climb in the Huaraz area is to sign up for a trip with a reputable agency and let it take care of all the details. Or you can get together a group, custom-design a trip, and then hire one of these agencies to take care of all the logistics for the expedition, including transport, food, lodging, porters, *arrieros,* cooks, and local guides. Sometimes a private trekking or climbing guide, available for $35–40 per day from the Casa de Guias in Huaraz, can take care of trip logistics. Or you can do it all on your own, which is really not that hard if you speak a smidgen of Spanish.

When to Go

The traditional climbing and trekking season for the Huaraz area is May to August, but the best weather and snow conditions are in June and July. Most of Huaraz's best hostels are booked solid during these months, a problem that reaches crisis proportions during the Fiestas Patrias weekend around July 28, Peru's biggest national holiday. If you are gunning for a main peak or trekking route, you will encounter fewer people during the tail ends of the season in May or August. The weather is often just as good in these months, and you can call a Huaraz guide agency in April to know what snow conditions are like. A heavy snow year will rule out certain routes in May, while a light snow year exposes crevasses early and makes certain summits more technical or altogether impossible by late August. But there are always loads of options in the Cordillera Blanca, and it is easy to switch from one route to another at the last minute.

Trekking Agencies and Guides

The most hassle-free way to go on a trek in the Huaraz area is to sign up for a pre-arranged trek through an agency in Huaraz or Caraz. You will usually get a better price if you sign up for a trek once you arrive in the area, and there are usually daily departures for the most popular routes during the high season.

If you have a group of two or more people you will have a more intimate experience by hiring your own trekking guide from the Casa de Guias in Huaraz for $35–40 per day. The

sunset at Camp II on Tocllaraju

trekking guide can set up transport and lodging and will arrange food and gear rental for an extra fee.

Before you pay, make sure that your agency or guide understands and abides by the principles of **Leave No Trace** (www.lnt.org), which has pioneered a set of ecotourism principles that are slowly being adopted by protected areas around the world.

Climbing Agencies and Guides

The motto "you get what you pay for" is especially true when it comes to hiring a climbing agency or guide. You will be safer with a guide who is properly certified by the Casa de Guias in Huaraz, which represents the Mountain Guide Association of Peru. Accidents, and sometimes fatalities, happen each year in the Cordillera Blanca because of guides with insufficient training and experience. Though guides can also be contracted for the Cordillera Huayhuash, the peaks there tend to be extremely technical, with the exception of Nevado Diablo Mundo.

You also have a much better chance of summit success with a certified guide. He or she will know the latest routes, the condition of the snow

pack, and the right acclimatization schedules. No matter how well you climb, you are never going to know a route better than someone who has already climbed it a few times *that season.* The going day rates are $60–70 for a mountain guide for moderate peaks like Pisco, Urus, and Ishinca, and $90 for technical peaks such as Tocllaraju, Huascarán, Chopicalqui, Artesonraju, and Alpamayo.

Huaraz is filled with fly-by-night agencies and gear shops that sell stolen gear. Recommended local agencies are listed in the Huaraz and Caraz sections. International agencies are listed in the *know Peru* section under *Tours.*

On Your Own

When planning your own self-supported trek or climb in the Huaraz area, you have to keep in mind altitude, which makes it difficult for many people to carry a backpack. A trek around the Cordillera Huayhuash, for instance, includes a series of grueling 4,500- to 5,000-meter passes. Unless you are Reinhold Messner, you will definitely not enjoy this with a pack on your back.

Even the Cordillera Blanca's most popular trek, the four- or five-day trek through the Santa

approaching summit of Tocllaraju (6,304 meters, 19,792 feet)

Cruz Valley, involves at least one high pass, Punta Unión, at 4,760 meters. Fit, acclimatized trekkers can do this with a backpack, but many choose to hire burros and an *arriero*. There are other reasons to hire an *arriero* as well. It is a great cultural experience, makes your trip safer, and is the best single thing you can do to help the local economy.

Groups often hire a cook too. Forget about freeze-dried food and powdered soups; Peru's cooks pack in fruit, vegetables, sacks of rice, and often even a live chicken or two. People who hire a cook can end up eating better on the trail than they do in the city.

Most climbers simply head into an area and hire an *arriero* once they get there. Make sure the terms are very clear before departing, though. Many *arrieros* will try to squeeze an extra day of wages by saying, for instance, that they have arrived at base camp too late to return that night. Make sure the deal is very clear from the beginning.

Your best bet is to get a recommendation for an *arriero*, and certainly a cook, ahead of time. The **Casa de Guias** in Huaraz keeps a list of *arrieros*, cooks, and porters, and all of the agencies listed in the Huaraz *Trekking* section can give you suggestions as well. Our favorite cook in

the Huaraz area is **Melky Bedon** (around the corner from Ormeño bus station, Prolongación Cajamarca y Pasaje Ranrapalca #6, tel. 043/72-7731). Melky will arrange your *arrieros* and transport and buy all the food in the market, getting a much better deal than you would—all for an extra day's wage. He can also organize trips into the Huayhuash area including tents, stoves, and transport.

Pay the people you hire fairly and treat them with respect. You are their employer, so you are ultimately responsible for their health and safety. It is also your responsibility to provide them with a tent and food during the trip. These are some standard daily wages: $10 for an *arriero* and $5 for every mule, $15 for camp guardian, $25 for a porter, and $25–30 for a cook.

Before you go, check out the **Inka Porter Project** (porters@peruweb.org, www.peruweb.org/porters), an innovative nonprofit that invests in equipment, education, and the overall quality of life of Peru's porters. It has an equipment loan center in Cusco, and will soon have one in Huaraz, where porters can borrow a backpack or parka if they do not have one. Inka Porter Project welcomes donations.

Ocshapalca Glacier near Huaraz

Entry Fees

By Peruvian standards, visiting Parque Nacional Huascarán is not cheap. Climbers and trekkers pay $20 for a pass that lasts one month, and day-trippers ante up $2. This fee can be paid at the park's headquarters in Huaraz (Sal y Rosas 555, tel. 084/72-2086, 8:30 A.M.–1 P.M. and 2:30–6 P.M. Mon.–Fri.) or at ticket booths at Laguna Llanganuco, Pastoruri Glacier, the village of Musho on the way to Huascarán, and a new booth in Quebrada Ishinca. Like most parks in Peru, this one is badly underfunded and needs all the money it can get for basic infrastructure like trail maintenance, trash removal, park rangers, rescue infrastructure, endangered species protection, and community-based programs. For foreigners, $20 is a small price to pay for traveling through this spectacular alpine area. There are rumors that the park may require travelers to use guides in certain areas in the near future.

Local communities throughout the Huaraz area have recently begun charging informal fees in an attempt to get their fair share of local trekking traffic. Collón, for instance, charges $5 to groups that enter the Quebrada Ishinca. In other areas,

such as Quebrada Quilcayhuanca, there is a gate that climbers need to pay in order to pass through the territory (though trekkers without pack animals can just climb over).

There is as of yet no entry fee for trekking in the Cordillera Huayhuash, though the area may soon be incorporated into a government-run national reserve. Villagers in the area do, however, frequently charge a $1.50 grazing fee per campsite and sometimes a per-person fee as well. New fee areas in the Huayhuash include Laguna Viconga, Cajatambo, and Huayllapa.

Maps, Guidebooks, and Information

Detailed Peruvian military topos and other maps can be bought from the South American Explorers Club in Lima. Most of the agencies listed under *Trekking*, above, sell maps and guidebooks, as does the Café Andino.

For the Cordillera Blanca, the 1:100,000 map published by Felipe Díaz and Alcides Ames gives a good overview for the basic trekking routes but does not give enough detail for climbers. The Austrian Alpine Club has published an excellent 1:100,000 topo map for the north end of the Cordillera Blanca and is working on one for the south end as well. For the Cordillera Huayhuash, the Alpine Mapping Guild published an excellent 1:65,000 in 2002 that rapidly sold out in Huaraz. A new version of this map in 1:50,000 scale is now on sale in Huaraz for around $12.

The best climbing guide for the Cordillera Blanca is Brad Johnson's recent *Classic Climbs of the Cordillera Blanca*, which has up-to-date information on the area's rapidly changing snow and ice routes. Our favorite trekking guide for the Huaraz area is the Globetrotter guide *Trekking and Climbing in the Andes,* co-authored by Val Pitkethly. It has a good description of the 12- to 14-day Huayhuash circuit as well as the Llanganuco–Santa Cruz trek, a two-week loop around Alpamayo's remote north side and an exploratory circuit through the less-crowded valleys near Huaraz.

The best source of up-to-date information are climbers and guides returning from the areas you are headed to. Casa de Guias in Huaraz is the area's number-one information center.

Gear

Most people who are trekking or climbing on their own in the Huaraz area bring all their own gear, though high-quality equipment can be rented for affordable prices in Huaraz. You can request prices and make reservations ahead of time by emailing the agencies listed in the Huaraz section. Agencies also sell carabiners, headlamps, etc., though at a huge markup. If you are climbing, it is always safer to bring your own ropes and slings.

Most U.S. airlines are no longer allowing passengers to fly with stoves that have been used, even in checked luggage. One option is to bring a new stove (in the box) and then sell it in Huaraz. It is easy to sell used gear in Huaraz, either to a gear shop or other climbers. MSR Whisperlites can also be rented in Huaraz, along with other models.

Peru's tropical sun is intense, so bring strong sunscreen, sun hat, dark glacier glasses, and long-sleeved shirt. Most trekkers use trekking poles for descending the scree slopes and steep trails. The weather is cold but not as extreme as the Himalaya or Alaska. We had no problems using sleeping bags rated for 0 degrees Fahrenheit and did not need fleece pants, even on early-morning summit days.

Pretty much everything but freeze-dried food is available in markets in Huaraz and Caraz, including pasta, powdered soup, cheese, powdered milk, beef jerky, dried fruit, etc. White gas *(bencina blanca)* is sold at hardware stores and along Luzuriaga in Huaraz, though it is best to get a recommendation from a gear shop to ensure the highest quality. Fire up your stove before you go to make sure it works well with the gas you have bought.

Acclimatization

No matter what you want to do in the mountains, you will have more success at it if you acclimatize gradually. Even the first camps of many of the major climbs and trekking routes are high enough to make people seriously ill. As an example, if you are going to climb in the popular Quebrada Ishinca—launching pad for Ishinca, Urus, and Tocllaraju—the first day's walk to the lodge leads to 4,350 meters. The other major climbs are even worse: Pisco's refuge is at 4,665 meters and Huascarán's is at 4,700 meters! Most of the passes in the Cordillera Huayhuash are between 4,500 and 5,000 meters, and the second day of the popular Santa Cruz trek is at 4,700 meters too.

Instead of getting ill and losing time, spend your first day in town walking slowly up to the Mirador Rataquena above Huaraz. Another option from Huaraz is to hop aboard a *combi* heading east up over the Cordillera Negra and get off at Callán Pass (4,225 meters). If you have a group, a taxi will only cost around $15. From here you can walk or mountain-bike back down to Huaraz on a network of dirt trails in the area (see Julio Olaza at Mountain Bike Adventures in Huaraz for rental bikes and more information about these routes). That night, sleep in Huaraz.

For the second night, many trekkers simply camp at their trailhead. Most climbers, however, take advantage of the excellent acclimatization possibilities near Huaraz. A good second-day walk is **Laguna Churup** (4,485 meters) and a flat nearby option is **Quebrada Quilcayhuanca**. There is a place to camp at Pitec, the village near the Churup trailhead, at 3,850 meters. Another good lodging option just below Pitec will be a charming stone lodge being built by the owners of The Way Inn.

Another second-day option, if you have your own transport, is a slightly longer drive up to the refuge in Quebrada Llaca ($15 pp lodging, $5 admission pp into the area). There is a lodge here and excellent camping spots. There is a knife-edge moraine trail with mind-blowing views of Ranrapalca (6,162 meters) and the near-vertical south face of Ocshapalca (5,888 meters).

Hazards and Precautions

There has been a spate of recent crimes in the Huaraz area. Base camp robberies, ranging from minor pilfering to well-organized robbery, have become commonplace at major climbing base camps in the Cordillera Blanca. In one of the bigger heists, thousands of dollars of gear, including climbing boots and sleeping bags, were stolen from the base camp in Quebrada Ishinca in July 2003. Smaller-scale robberies have happened in most of the area's other popular base camps. This problem can be taken care of by hiring a camp guardian to look after your base camp while you are away for $15 a day.

A more serious problem has been robberies, sometimes at gun- or knife-point. These have occurred in areas frequented by tourists, such as the Mirador Rataquena, the bouldering area at Huanchac, Laguna Churup, and the ruins at Wilcawaín.

As the Cordillera Huayhuash opens to the outside world, villagers have begun to treat foreign trekkers differently. Assaults against small groups are on the rise, and a Peruvian-American couple was murdered near Nevado Diablo Mundo in 2002 in what appeared to be a robbery. These two trekkers were traveling on their own and without an *arriero*. Another series of assaults at gunpoint occurred in July, 2004. Fortunately, no one was seriously injured.

The vast majority of trekkers to the Huaraz area have no problem whatsoever. But still we recommend trekking in a group of four or five people and, especially, trekking with a local *arriero*. Mountain bandits rarely mess with local *arrieros*, for fear of being recognized. *Arrieros* know the lay of the land and will keep you out of trouble. They can also help negotiate a confusing array of new grazing and other fees being charged by villagers throughout the area.

The good news is there are loads of less-crowded places where it is possible to trek by

Fallen seracs like these on Tocllaraju must be negotiated carefully.

Cordillera Blanca

yourself and have a perfectly safe time. We recommend the valleys above Huaraz.

In the Cordillera Huayhuash, trekkers should be entirely self-sufficient. Common items like cheese, potatoes, and beer can be bought in the range's larger villages, such as Llamac, Pocpa, and Huayllapa. But there are few medicines and other supplies, and medical evacuation can take several days.

In any major climbing area there are accidents, but the Cordillera Blanca seems to be particularly prone to them because the glaciers are retreating rapidly. This has become a big problem in Huascarán's ice fall, which has become noticeably more unstable in recent years. Some international guiding agencies have stopped guiding this route. On July 21, 2003, at 9 A.M. huge blocks of ice fell down the 350-meter face of Alpamayo, killing eight climbers ascending in the vicinity of the Ferrari chute. *Rock and Ice,* a U.S. climber's magazine, raised the question as to whether this accident, and others like it around the world, are linked to human-induced climate change and increasingly unstable ice conditions. Huascarán and Alpamayo are the two most popular, and well-known, peaks in the Cordillera Blanca, but plenty of other mountains exist of equal difficulty that do not involve their level of objective danger.

In case of an accident, climbers should contact the **Casa de Guias** (Parque Ginebra 28-G, tel. 043/72-1811, agmp@terra.com.pe, 9 A.M.–1 P.M. and 4–8 P.M. Mon.–Fri., 9 A.M.–1 P.M. Saturday) or Yungay's **High Mountain Rescue Unit** (tel. 043/79-3333, tel. 043/79-3327, or 043/79-3291, usam@pnp.gob.pe, www.huaraz.info/usam/, www.pnp.gob.pe/direcciones/altamontana.asp, 24 hours Mon.–Fri.). Any rescue will cost hundreds of dollars; if a helicopter is involved, it will be in the thousands. Consider buying an international insurance policy that covers high-risk sports.

ⓜ PARQUE NACIONAL HUASCARÁN

The spectacular wilderness of the Parque Nacional Huascarán includes Peru's tallest peak, Huascarán, and every bit of the Cordillera Blanca

above 4,000 meters (except for Nevado Champará at the extreme northern end). The land drops away on all sides of this long but narrow range, creating an interesting island habitat containing several endangered species. Among the park's 340,000 hectares (840,140 acres), there are odd plants such as the *Puya raimondii,* the largest bromeliad in the world, and forests of endangered *polylepis,* the highest-altitude trees in the world. Andean condor can be seen here, and there are populations of vicuña, white-tailed deer, Andean dwarf deer, Andean lynx, fox, puma, and more than 100 species of birds.

From the Cordillera Negra, the Blanca looks like a huge wall of glaciated peaks rising from the Río Santa Valley. Nevertheless, the range dips low enough in places to allow trekking routes, and a few roads, to cross it. The road to Chavín de Huántar, one of Peru's most enigmatic ancient ruins, tunnels through the lowest pass at 4,450 meters (14,596 feet). The valley on the far side of the range, known as the Callejón de Conchucos, is an isolated and remote area of small towns linked only by rough dirt roads. Glaciers spread over much of the terrain, along with more than 300 lakes. Unlike national parks in Europe and the U.S., thousands of people continue their traditional ways of life inside the Parque Nacional Huascarán. For the most part, the range's inhabitants live below the poverty line, subsisting on maize, quinoa, and *kiwicha* grains, and a variety of potatoes and tubers. Their latest source of income, and one that is fast-growing, is providing burros for the foreigners who pass through this world-class trekking and climbing paradise.

The roads that lead up and over the Cordillera Blanca provide good access for day hikes. To hike here, stay in any of the villages along the Callejón de Huaylas, including Huaraz, Carhuaz, and Caraz. Then contract a taxi or horse or hop aboard a *combi*—but make sure to plan for your return ride in the afternoon. Many agencies in Huaraz offer cheap day excursions to Lagunas Llanganuco or Pastoruri Glacier for $8–10 and can pick you up at any of the towns along the way. Another option is to hike in to one of the refuges and use them as launching pads for day hikes.

Laguna Cuchillacocha, a day's walk above Huaraz in Quebrada Quilcayhuanca

Routes

The most spectacular, and crowded, trekking route in the park is the four- to five-day, 40-km **Santa Cruz trek,** which traditionally begins from the small settlements of **Vaquerí** or **Colcabamba** and ends at **Cashapampa** near Caraz. The high point of the pass is **Punta Unión,** at 4,760 meters, and the rest of the trek is all downhill along the Quebrada Santa Cruz, which offers a series of emerald lakes and mesmerizing views of Taulliraju, Alpamayo, Quitaraju, Artesonraju, and other snow peaks. Two days can be added to the beginning of the trek by starting at Lagunas Llanganuco and heading over the **Portachuelo Llanganuco** pass at 4,767 meters. Acclimatized and fit trekkers can hike this route with a light backpack, and burros can be contracted at Vaquerí or Colcabamba.

A two-week, 150-km option starts in Cashapampa and involves a huge **northern circuit around Alpamayo.** The trek takes in pristine mountain scenery and a roller coaster ride of high passes on Alpamayo's remote northern side, including Paso los Cedros at 4,900 meters. If you start from Cashapampa, the final days of

the trek leads down the Quebrada Santa Cruz along the traditional route. This trek is operated by Pony Expeditions in Caraz and is almost always done with burros.

Just above Huaraz, we recommend a two- or three-day hike up the **Quebrada Quilcayhuanca,** with a longer option to climb over a high pass and descend **Quebrada Cojup** on the return. Another option is a hike into **Quebrada Rajucolta,** the next valley to the south. All of these are pleasant two- or three-day hikes up into the valleys to lakes. Because few tourists walk these routes, they are safe to do alone or with another person. No burros are required.

There are at least two highly recommend routes that cross the Cordillera Blanca south of Huaraz and end at the ruins of **Chavín de Huántar.** The best-known version starts from **Olleros,** a village just south of Huaraz, and heads up and over **Punta Yanashallash** at 4,700 meters along an ancient trade route. If you get a ride up the dirt road above Olleros, this 35 km-route should take anywhere from three to four days and can be done with or without a burro.

CLASSIC PEAKS OF THE CORDILLERA BLANCA

Peaks	Altitude (meters)	Altitude (feet)	Time	Alpine Grade
Huascarán	6,786	22,264	6–8 days	PD/AD
Chopicalqui	6,354	20,847	4–6 days	AD
Tocllaraju	6,034	19,792	4–5 days	AD
Artesonraju	6,025	19,762	4–5 days	AD+
Alpamayo	5,947	19,512	6–8 days	AD+/D
Pisco	5,752	18,872	3–4 days	PD
Ishinca	5,534	18,151	3 days	PD
Urus	5,420	17,778	3 days	PD

Note: The alpine grading system is a French method for rating climbs according to their technical difficulty, number of belays, quality of rock, exposure to heights, objective dangers, etc. F=Easy *(Facile)*, PD=Moderately difficult *(Peu difficile)*, AD=Fairly difficult *(Assez difficile)*, D=Difficult *(Difficile)*, TD=Very difficult *(Très difficile)*, ED=Extremely difficult *(Extrêmement difficile)*, ABO=Horrible *(Abominable)*.

The other 40-km, four- or five-day route, which includes a bit of mountaineering, starts above the village of Pitec above Huaraz and climbs the Quebrada Quilcayhuanca and then forks south into the **Quebrada Cayesh.** At the end of the valley, a rough trail leads up and over a snowy pass next to **Nevado Maparaju** (5,326 meters). This peak can be climbed from the saddle before continuing down the pass on the other side to the village of **San Marcos,** 8 km from Chavín de Huántar. Or you can simply cut across country on a rough patchwork of trails and head directly to Chavín de Huántar. Ask around about conditions before you try this route, as we have received reports that the far side of the pass is badly melted out and difficult to descend. If you are doing this route, you should bring crampons and an ice axe for the snowy portion, and inquire beforehand if there are snow-covered crevasses or other conditions that might merit a rope as well.

Accommodations

Recently three lodges have been built inside the park to accommodate visitors in the three most popular climbing areas. If you have been to Ecuador and Mexico, you'll appreciate that these lodges are much nicer—very similar to, or even better than, what you might find in the French Alps. They were built by Operación Mato Grosso (tel. 043/074-3061, andesbosco@virgilia.it, www.huaraz.org/omg), an Italian relief organization based in Marcará that is affiliated with Don Bosco en los Andes. All profits go to aid projects.

Each lodge had 60 bunks in different rooms. There is a large dining area downstairs and an amiable kitchen staff that whips up huge pitchers of sweet coca tea or pizzas on request. The prices are pretty reasonable as well: $30, including lodging, breakfast, and dinner, and hot teas and other drinks average from $1.50 to $3. Anyone is welcome to stay.

Refugio Ishinca (4,350 meters) is in the Quebrada Ishinca, a four-hour walk from the village of Collón and the launching point for Urus, Ishinca, and Tocllaraju. **Refugio Peru** (4,665 meters) is a three-hour walk from Llanganuco and at the base of Pisco. **Regugio Giordano Longoni** is a four-hour walk from the village of Musho and at the base of Huascarán. All these peaks except for Huascarán and Tocllaraju could be climbed directly from these *refugios,* eliminating the need for a tent, though climbers usually bring one anyway to bivouac in. There's a refuge in Quebrad Llaca ($15 pp lodging, $5 pp admission into the area) owned by the Mountain Guide Association of Peru, but it is run down and most people prefer to camp.

Getting There

There are a variety of transport options for accessing different areas of the park, ranging from public *combis* to private cars. See the *Getting There* sections in this chapter for Huaraz, Carhuaz, Yungay, and Caraz.

▶ CORDILLERA HUAYHUASH

Though only 30 km long, the Cordillera Huayhuash packs in some of the most dramatic mountain scenery on earth. It is one continuous serrated ridge that falls away into fluted snow faces and glaciers. Seven peaks here top 6,000 meters, and another seven are over 5,500 meters. The highest peak, Yerupajá (6,634 meters), is the second-highest peak in Peru and is followed by Siulá Grande (6,356 meters), where Joe Simpson fell into a crevasse and lived to tell the story in *Touching the Void.*

The Huayhuash is 50 km southeast of the Cordillera Blanca yet utterly different. First, there are no broad, U-shaped valleys in the Huayhuash that lead over high passes to the other side. Instead trekkers must walk around the outer edges or the range, climbing up and over passes between 4,500 and 5,000 meters. To manage these heights, nearly all trekkers use *arrieros* and burros, which can be contracted easily at the range's trailheads (a recommended *arriero* in Chiquián is Natividad Bedón).

The other main difference with the Cordillera Blanca is its remoteness. Even with a rash of new roads, getting into the Huayhuash still takes one or two days. The range has a raw, wilderness feel, especially along its pristine eastern side, where rocky ridges cede to turquoise lakes and wide-open rolling grasslands that drain into the Amazon basin. Condors are seen here frequently, along with a range of migratory birds, and small herds of vicuña live up in the narrow valleys.

Unfortunately, the Huayhuash is changing quickly as new roads approach from all sides. Mit-

sui Mining and Smelting has converted once-pristine wetlands on the range's west edge into industrial wastes. Local residents say that a local mine explosion has contaminated their water supply. The Peruvian government declared the range a protected area in 2002, the first step toward making the area a park or national reserve. Villagers are in large part opposed to the area's new protected status, because they fear they will lose grazing rights on what has always been their communal land. A great new website, www.huayhuash.org, focuses on the responsible use of the Huayhuash area following Leave No Trace principles.

Routes

The time-honored trek in the Cordillera Huayhuash is a 12-day loop around the entire range that begins and ends in the village of Chiquián. This route has become somewhat shorter these days because new roads have been built onwards from Chiquián, which for years was the range's closest launching point. From Chiquián, *combis* now travel to Llamac via a new mining road, which shortens the route by a day. This trek continues clockwise around the entire range and crosses eight passes between 4,600 and 5,000 meters before completing the circle at Pacllón, where a new road returns to Chiquián.

Many groups are now entering through Huallanca, a village at 3,400 meters that lies along the dirt road between Huaraz and Huánuco. Huallanca was rarely used as an entry point in the past because it was a long one- or two-day slog to get to the Huayhuash. But *combis* now travel along a new road that goes as far as the village of Matacancha. Trekkers usually get off beforehand at the tiny village of Ishpac and head over the 4,700-meter Cacanpunta Pass en route to their first campsite at Lago Mitacocha. This trek essentially does half of the full circuit and skirts the range's eastern side. After a campsite at Lago Carhuacocha, the trail diverges, and trekkers have to decide between a 4,600-meter pass or a pass 200 meters higher with better views of the glaciers. The next camps are at the village of Huayhuash and then on to Laguna Viconga, where hot springs lie a mile to the southwest. The final day is a long walk over rolling hills out to Cajatambo, where a good road leads to Pativilca on the coast.

Because of the new Huallanca access, trekkers can now see a good bit of the Cordillera Huayhuash in five days. But there is a downside. Huallanca, at 3,400 meters, is the same altitude as Cusco and takes some getting used to. Those who come from the coast usually have to spend a day or two in Huaraz before trekking. Another issue is that each day of this five-day route includes a pass over 4,600 meters, which is a feat even for the acclimatized. The full circuit, on the other hand, has three days of acclimatization on rolling hills before hitting this string of knockout passes. Another problem is luggage: Five-day trekkers come in from the Huaraz side of the range and exit at the coast, so they have to carry everything with them. And of course this route misses the mountain views on the west side of the range. Val Pitkethly guides in the Huayhuash each year and has written the Globetrotter guide *Trekking and Climbing in the Andes.* She highly recommends the full circuit for all the above reasons, but also because "it's just too beautiful of a place to rush through."

Accommodations

There are hostels and restaurants in all the main access towns of the Cordillera Huayhuash. In **Chiquián,** try the Hostal Nogales (Comercio 1301, three blocks from main square, tel. 043/74-7121, hotel_nogales_chiquian@yahoo.com.p, s $6, d $12, cheaper rooms have shared bath). In **Cajatambo,** try Tambomachay (Bolognesi 140, 01/244-2046, $10 s, $15 d) or the upscale International Inn (Benavides, fourth block, 01/244-2071, international.inn@hostal.net, $40 s, $50 d, prices negotiable). There are a few basic hostels in **Huallanca,** from where public transport leaves to Matacancha and Ishpac (90 minutes).

Getting There

Transportes El Rápido (Mariscal Cáceres and Tarapacá, tel. 043/72-2887) in Huaraz has a bus at 6 A.M. and 1 P.M. to Chiquián ($3, three hours) and at 6 A.M. and 12:30 P.M. to Huallanca ($4, four hours), continuing on to La Unión (10 hours). Empresa Andia in the main square of

Cajatambo has buses every morning at 6 A.M. to Lima ($8, nine hours).

CORDILLERA NEGRA

Though overshadowed by the snowy summits of the Cordillera Blanca, the brown mountains of the Cordillera Negra on the other side of the valley offer some of the area's best hiking and biking. Routes often begin up in high-altitude grasslands and follow trails that have been used for centuries, passing Andean villages, old bridges, creeks, and fields along the way. There is a range of difficulty for bikers, ranging from broad traverses to dodgy, downslope single-track, and the views of the glaciers and snowy peaks are like something out of a fairy tale.

There are dirt roads leading into the Cordillera Negra from **Huaraz** and throughout the Río Santa Valley from **Yungar, Carhuaz, Caraz, and Huallanca.** Private transport can always be hired to ascend these roads and, because most trails lead downhill, it is almost impossible to get lost. Here are some hiking and biking routes in the Huaraz area used by mountain bike guides Julio Olaza (www.chakinaniperu.com) and John Lockwood (www.pedalperu.com):

Callán Pass to Huaraz

This pure downhill route begins with a *combi* ride to the high pass above Huaraz at 4,225 meters and makes for a good acclimatization day for climbers and trekkers. If you don't mind improvising your route a bit, this route can even be done without a guide.

A network of foot paths and mule tracks leads downhill through russet fields of grains and potatoes, though the best route takes you through the villages of Culcururi and Atipallán. The bizarre rock formations along the way have earned the area the moniker of "Little Moab," and the route finishes down steep, hair-raising shortcuts through the hillside suburbs above Huaraz.

Shecta to Huaraz

This route begins at 4,050 meters in the village of Shecta near Huaraz and follows a long traverse to the settlement of Huáscar before plunging 1,000 meters on dodgy single-track back to Huaraz. This strenuous, daylong route is best for the well-acclimatized.

Summit to Sea

This phenomenal route leads not west to the Río Santa but east toward the Pacific Ocean and includes a mind-boggling descent through remote countryside. A truck from Catac, a village north of Huaraz, takes you up to the start of the route at Huancapeti Pass (4,680 meters). From here nearly 40 km of stone paths and steep single-track lead to the mountain village of Aija, where transport awaits for the ride back to Huaraz. The adventurous can continue another 80 km all the way to the town of Huarmey on the coast.

Trujillo and the North Coast

Depending on your perspective, it is either a terrible injustice or happy circumstance that most visitors never see the North Coast, which holds much of Peru's best ruins, untrammeled wilderness, and world-class surf breaks. Because 9 out of 10 foreign tourists begin in Machu Picchu in the south, the average visitor simply runs out of time.

Peru's north coast, however, is one of the richest and most diverse archaeological zones in all of the Americas. An ocean teeming with fish and desert coastline punctuated by verdant river valleys formed a cradle of civilization comparable to Egypt or Babylon. The most important cultures were the **Moche, Chimú,** and **Sicán** empires, who built elaborate adobe cities over a millennia and a half before being conquered by the Incas around 1470.

Little was known about these cultures because the Incas carefully erased memory of them in order to consolidate their own power. But in the late 1980s, the world glimpsed the splendor of these forgotten civilizations when archaeologists

Must-Sees

Trujillo

M **Old Trujillo:** After a tour of Trujillo's Spanish homes and churches, there is no better way to soak in colonial elegance than having a drink on the Plaza de Armas at the bar of the stately Hotel Libertador (page 402).

M **Museo Cassinelli:** The best collection of ceramics in Peru, including a range of erotic Moche

© AMBER PIRKER

Museo Tumbas Reales de Sipán

pieces, are housed in this odd but worthwhile museum in the basement of a Mobil gas station in Trujillo (page 405).

M **Huaca de la Luna:** This 10-story adobe pyramid is an impressive monument to the Moche culture with recently uncovered murals of *Ai-Aepek,* the decapitator god, and commanding views of Trujillo and the surrounding valley (page 406).

Chiclayo

M **Museo Tumbas Reales de Sipán:** This recently opened museum outside of Chiclayo is dedicated to the dazzling objects found in 1987 inside of a series of royal Moche tombs, which recall the splendor of King Tut's tombs in Egypt (page 420).

M **Museo Sicán:** Chiclayo's other must-see, modern museum contains an elaborate reconstruction of a royal Sicán tomb excavated in 1991, which contained 20 sacrificed women, two huge golden arms, and nearly a ton of metal objects (page 422).

Máncora, Las Pocitas and Vichayito

M **Máncora:** What was once a small fishing town has become a surfing mecca, with a stunning coastline that attracts waveriders from around the world (page 441).

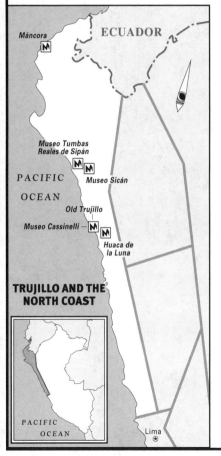

Máncora
M

ECUADOR

Museo Tumbas
Reales de Sipán
M **M**
Museo Sicán

PACIFIC

OCEAN
Old Trujillo

Museo Cassinelli — **M**

Huaca de
la Luna

**TRUJILLO AND THE
NORTH COAST**

PACIFIC
OCEAN
Lima

M Trujillo and the North Coast

TRUJILLO AND THE NORTH COAST

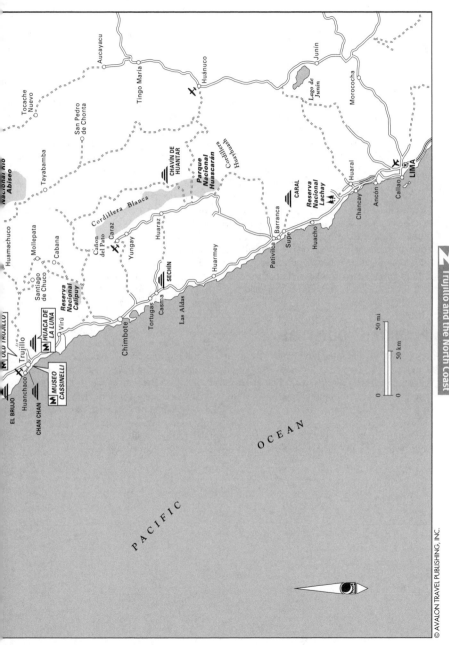

unearthed royal tombs from the Moche and Sicán cultures. The tombs, somehow overlooked by 500 years of diligent grave robbers, were filled with exquisite works in gold and silver, including gigantic earrings, breastplates, and delicately worked spiders perched on webs of gold. The tombs gave archaeologists their first clear understanding of the complex social and religious structure of these northern empires. The objects found in the tombs are now on display in two fabulous new museums outside of Chiclayo: Museo Tumbas Reales de Sipán and Museo Sicán.

The great cities of the north collapsed after being conquered by the Incas in the 1470s. By the time the Spaniards rode into the area six decades later, the Chimú city of Chan Chan had been reduced to ruins. The Huaca de la Luna, abandoned in 800 A.D. by the Moche, looked much as it does today—an eroding mountain of adobe bricks. Near this spot Gonzalo Pizarro founded Trujillo, an important colonial city that today contains Peru's best collection of colonial homes.

PLANNING YOUR TIME

It's a common dilemma: How can I see Machu Picchu, Cusco, *and* the ruins of the North Coast? Even though Peru's two richest archaeological regions are at opposite ends of the country, it is possible to see both within two weeks. The logical start is to fly to colonial Trujillo, see Chan Chan and the Moche *haucas,* and then take a bus to Chiclayo for the Lords of

Sipán treasures, Túcume, and the Museo Sicán. After this immersion in pre-Inca history, travelers can fly from Chiclayo to Lima, and then Lima to Cusco, to continue on with Inca and Spanish history.

For those with more time, the principal attractions of the north can be thought of as a sideways U, starting in Trujillo. The first leg of the journey is to Cajamarca, which serves as a launching point for the journey through the Marañon Valley to Chachapoyas. Whereas Cajamarca, Trujillo, and Chiclayo can be visited in as little as two days each, the remote and spread-out ruins of Chachapoyas require several days at the minimum—especially considering the effort it takes to get there. IncaNatura in Lima and Gran Vilaya Tours in Chachapoyas offer extremely well-organized tours that follow this basic sequence.

For most, Peru's northern beaches are an inessential side trip. But surfers and beach lovers jet from Lima to Peru's northernmost city of Tumbes, then take public transport an hour or two south to Máncora. After just a morning's travels, they are walking on white sand and eating *cebiche,* having left the ruins to the archaeologists.

Still another option is to head east after visiting Chachapoyas and travel the dramatic route into the Amazon Basin to Tarapoto and Yurimaguas, from where cargo boats leave daily for a three-day journey to Iquitos. Getting from Chachapoyas to Iquitos is a stunning journey of a week or more, taking in nearly all of Peru's climates, with an easy escape flight back to Lima.

Caral and Sechín

Most visitors to Peru's northern coast make the trip from Lima to Trujillo in a straight eight hours, a journey that begins in the dusty sprawl of the capital's shantytowns and cuts through a string of grimy towns best known for stinky fish-meal factories and a bustling trade with mountain towns of the Ancash province. But if you have the time, there are a few oft-overlooked ruins that warrant a visit.

CARAL

Six pyramids arranged around a central courtyard form what archaeologists have recently hailed as the oldest city of the Americas. Caral is in fact the largest of a series of 18 city sites that stretches up into the Río Supe Valley, beginning with the Aspero pyramid (near the town of **Supe** on the coast). Although Caral's pyramids were discovered in the 1950s, excavations did not begin until 1996, when a puzzling lack of ceramics tipped archaeologists off to the site's antiquity. Subsequent digs atop one of the oldest pyramids unearthed a 10-year-old boy wrapped in a cane mat, which scientists carbon-dated to 2,900 B.C. The University of San Marcos in Lima continues to fund a team of about a dozen archaeologists at the site, who unearth new findings nearly every month. Visitors are few, as the site is well off the highway and few people know about it. For the moment, student archaeologists pause from their labors to guide visitors around the complex, which include elaborate courtyards, an amphitheater, and 12-meter-high pyramids with commanding views over the valley. The site serves as an excellent introduction to later, but related, cities such as Sechín, Chan Chan, and Sipán further up the coast.

Accommodations and Food

With an early start from Lima, it should be possible to visit Caral and continue northward to Casma or even Trujillo. If you overnight in the area, however, Huacho is preferable to Supe. In Huacho, head 30 minutes west to the beach for **Fundo Centinela** (tel. 01/994-5813, cell phone, tatodebemardis@hotmail.com, www.surfsurvival.com/fundocentinela, $45 s, $55 d), a quaint farm nestled among sugarcane fields within walking distance of Playa Paraíso, one of the 10 most beautiful beaches in Peru (according to the *Guia Inca de Playas*). The owners, Americo and Ursula Debernardi, serve heaping plates of delicious Italian food.

In Supe, a safe though somewhat noisy option is **Hostel Las Palmeras** (tel. 01/236-4037, $6 s, $12 d), on the highway 1 km north of town on the left side. Major bus companies stop here when asked. Get coffee and breakfast at Doña Lobatón's on the main square. Right around the corner, Charito serves traditional *ceviche de pato,* a stew of duck, potatoes, and onions.

There is a wider selection of hotels and restaurants in Barranca, 5 km north along the Panamericana from Supe but still within taxi distance of Caral. **Hostel Emilio** (Gálvez 651, tel. 01/235-5224, $8 s, $12 d) offers huge, comfortable rooms with TVs on the main drag. The rooms in the back are quieter, and Jacuzzis are available for about twice the price. Slightly fancier, but considerably more expensive, is **Hotel El Chavín** (Gálvez 222, tel. 01/235-2358, $12 s, $19 d), which is newly carpeted and has a pool. Recommended restaurants include **Restaurant Gitana** (near the intersection of Bolognesi and the Pan Americana, $4–6), known for its *ceviche mixto.* Also cheap and clean are **Los Tronkitos** (Gálvez 787, $3–5) and **El Alaska** (Galvéz 564), which serves espresso and scrumptious desserts until midnight.

Getting There

Caral is most easily reached via a dirt road that begins on the Panamericana about 3 km north of Huacho. There is another bumpier though more scenic road up the Río Supe Valley that begins about 3 km south of Supe. The latter road crosses the Río Supe at one point and becomes impassible during the mountain rainy season between October and May.

CARAL: THE OLDEST CITY IN THE AMERICAS

The deeper and farther afield archaeologists dig on the coast of Peru, the farther back they push the estimates of when city life began in the Americas. Dated at 2900 B.C., Caral smashed the long-held theory of Peruvian archaeologist J. C. Tello that Peru's first city was Chavín de Huántar, which was built near Huaraz from 900 B.C. onwards.

Caral is in fact contemporary with the Egypt's Old Kingdom pyramids-and a thousand years older than the Olmec pyramids in Mexico, which were once considered the oldest ceremonial structures in the America. The finds at Caral have been trumpeted in a BBC documentary and a *National Geographic* feature, which proclaimed Caral the "oldest city of the Americas."

The main reason Caral qualifies as a city, and not just a ceremonial center, is that a range of people, from priests to commoners, lived nearby.

Six pyramids, each about 6 to 12 yards high, are arranged around a central courtyard. Priests lived in elaborate dwellings alongside each pyramid, while townspeople lived in two areas nearby under excavation. Burnt offerings were made at hearths atop each pyramid.

Residents cultivated large quantities of cotton, peanuts and beans and had ample supply of anchovies, sardines and shellfish from the coast. Because ceramics had not yet been invented, Caral's early residents cooked their foods with hot rocks, much like the *pachamanca* technique still used by highlanders. The central courtyard of Caral may have functioned as a large amphitheater with terraced seats. Nearby archaeologists found a remarkable stash of over 30 bone flutes carved with monkey designs - an indication that Caral not only had musical performances, but also trade routes extending as far as the Amazon.

The best way to reach Caral is to contract a round-trip taxi in Huacho or Supe for $14, though cheaper *colectivos* also run from Huacho. It is about 45 minutes on either route. Allow one or two hours to see the ruins.

Fortaleza de Paramonga

Traveling north through Barranca and the nearby town of Pativilca, you'll find the **Fortaleza de Paramonga** (Km 210 of the Panamericana, 8 A.M.–5 P.M., $1.50), a fascinating introduction to the Chimú empire. The massive adobe fortress, which may have had both religious and military functions, is composed of seven defensive walls constructed on a hill next to the highway. It is still possible to see remnants of the murals admired by Hernando Pizarro when he passed by the fortress in 1533, less than half a century after an invading Inca army overran the fort in its conquest of the Chimú Empire. The top of the yellow fortress offers panoramic views of the surrounding sugarcane fields. The on-site museum is worth a visit. The fort will become visible after passing a hill about 4 km north of the Huaraz turnoff on the Panamericana, or 7 km north of Barranca. If traveling from Barranca, go to the north end of

town and take a *colectivo* or *combi* to travel 4 km north to the village of Pativilca, where you can either walk the remaining 3 km or take a taxi for $2.

SECHÍN

While some of Peru's adobe ruins require a little imagination to understand, no such effort is required for **Sechín** (5 km southeast of Casma, 8 A.M.–5 P.M., $1.50), a temple complex built around 1500 B.C. Along the temple's base, hundreds of warriors with their mutilated prisoners are carved into the granite with startling and gruesome detail. Soldiers carved into stone columns march on both sides toward the temple entrance with decapitated heads of the defeated hanging from their bodies. The range of human cruelty exhibited at Sechín is a prelude to the rituals of human sacrifice during the Moche and Chimú empires. The adjacent Museo Max Uhle contains reconstructed murals along with models of Sechín and other nearby ruins. Bilingual guides are available for the museum and the temple for $4.

For archaeology buffs, Sechín is only one of several sites in the Casma area that can be visited in a day-long circuit. Nearby lies **Sechín Alto, a**

carvings of mutilated war prisoners at Sechín

deteriorated U-shaped complex. Further south at Km 361 of the Panamericana is the fortress of **Chanquillo,** a watchtower surrounded by three concentric walls. Also of interest is the **Moxeque Complex,** which lies along a dirt road off the highway between Casma and Huaraz. The best way to see these is to contract a guide with a *motocar* in Casma.

Accommodations

Under $10: Las Aldas is a long beach separated by a rocky point that lies at Km 345 of the Panamericana, 30 km south of Casma at the fishing village of La Gramita. A set of clean, simple Scottish-owned bungalows at the northern end of the beach, named **Las Aldas** (01/440-3241, $6 s, $8 d), serve as a good base for exploring the nearby, deserted beaches. There are a few ruins in the hills above the bungalows.

$10–25: Casma has two good budget options. **Hostel Ernesto's,** (Garcilazo de la Vega, tel. 043/711-475, $7 s, $12 d) has basic, clean and quiet rooms and a restaurant that cranks out good breads and desserts. **Hostel Gregory** (Luis

Ormeño 530, tel. 043/712-019, $4–10 s, $7–14 d) is a friendly place with quiet rooms.

The best value in Casma is the **Hostel El Farol** (Tupac Amaru 450, tel. 043/712-183, hostel-farol@terra.com.pe, $12 s, $18 d), a spacious hotel laid out on landscaped grounds complete with caged monkeys and tropical birds. The bungalow rooms surround a courtyard with a pool and have cable TV and plenty of hot water. On the north edge of town is **Hotel Las Poncianas** (Km 376 of Panamericana, tel. 043/711599, ponciana@terra.com.pe, $20 s, $25 d), a large hotel with nice views from the second floor and similar amenities, plus a sauna, pool table, playground, restaurant, and a very friendly owner. Larger, more comfortable rooms are also available ($30 s, $35 d).

The best lodging option around Casma, however, is El Farol's sister hostel at Tortugas, a beach town 22 km north of Casma that is marked by a huge blue arch at Km 391 of the Panamericana. **⋈ El Farol** (tel. 043/991-1693, $20 s, $26 d) is perched on the hills at the southern end of Tortugas' stone-and-sand beach

© RENÉE DEL GAUDIO AND ROSS WEHNER

carving of decapitated head at Sechín

and offers breathtaking views of the surrounding desert hills and the clear blue waters. There is good snorkeling, safe swimming, a fine assortment of seafood restaurants, and a secluded beach that is a short walk over the hills to the south. Make reservations during summer and holidays. There are also several basic budget hostels in Tortugas, including **Hospedaje Pedro Pablo** (tel. 043/487-593, $6 s, $9 d) near the road entrance to Tortugas.

Food

It's a long walk or a five-minute *motocar* ride through the fields to **Recreo Campestre Los Pacaes** (Prolongación Bolivar, tel. 043/711505, $3–7), the place most recommended by locals. Musicians play while guests lunch under a flower-covered trellis. Local specialties include *chicharrón de pato* (deep-fried duck), *pepián de pavo* (rice and turkey casserole), and *cuy* (guinea pig). The best in-town option is **Restaurant Tío Sam** (Huarmey 138, $3–4), with excellent Creole food, including a delectable *sopa criolla*.

In Tortugas, the best food is at **El Farol** (tel. 043/71-1064, $5–9), where chefs prepare fresh *lenguado* (sole) with a mouthwatering garlic/tomato sauce. Huber, the manager, can prepare you a stiff *cuba libre* as you admire the extraordinary views. For less expensive food, there are several good restaurants near the road entrance to Tortuga, the best of which is 30-year-old **Restaurant Costa Azul** (corner of road entrance to Tortuga, $3–6).

Getting There

All the major bus companies stop at Casma, which is a five- or six-hour drive from Lima. Recommended companies include **Cruz del Sur, Ormeño,** and **Flores,** which head to Trujillo and beyond. Casma, along with Chimbote further north, is also the starting point for the dramatic, though bumpy, ride over the 2,800-meter Callan Pass to Huaraz, which offers excellent views of snow-covered mountains. Taxis charge $5 for the 15-minute drive north to Tortugas. The cheaper three-wheeled canopied motorcycles are not recommended for the exposed highway drive.

Getting Around

Sechín is 3 km south from Casma along the highway, and then another 2 km east along a well-marked dirt road. Taxis from Casma will take you there and back for $3–4. Another option is to hire a guide at **Renato Tours** (Nepeña 370, tel. 043/712-528, renatotours@yahoo.com) to take you on a full day tour of the surrounding ruins for about $3 per hour. If you do not speak Spanish, make sure to engage your guide in conversation before you go to ensure he or she speaks English—there is a wide range of quality among guides.

Trujillo

Modern-day Trujillo has one of Peru's greatest collections of colonial homes, but it is only the latest city over the last few millennia in the Moche Valley. A few kilometers on the other side of town is the **Huaca de la Luna,** where archaeologists continue to unearth pristine murals from the Moche empire (1–700 A.D.). Then there is **Chan Chan,** a vast city of elaborately painted and sculpted walls that served as the capital of the Chimú, the largest pre-Inca empire in Peru (900–1471 A.D.). When Inca Pachacutec and his son Tupac Yupanqui conquered the city in the 1470s, they were dazzled by the grandeur of the largest adobe city in the world. At the coastal village of **Huanchaco,** 14 km west of Trujillo, fishermen launch their reed rafts into the surf as they have for thousands of years.

Trujillo thrived after the arrival of the Spaniards, who, like the Moche and Chimú before them, reaped tremendous wealth from fertile Moche Valley and the nearby ocean. Shortly after conquering Peru, Pizarro came to Trujillo in 1535 and helped found the city named after his hometown in Spain, Trujillo de Extramadura. Large sugarcane haciendas flourished here and financed large homes, churches, and a way of life that included two icons of *criollo* culture, the Peruvian *paso* horse and the *marinera* dance.

Trujillo became a center of Peru's war of independence from Spain. It was the first Peruvian city to declare itself independent of Spain, in December 1820. Liberator Simón Bolívar later established himself here after moving his way down the coast from Ecuador. From the Casa Urquiaga on the Plaza de Armas, Bolivar planned the campaign that culminated in the battle of Ayacucho, where Spanish forces were turned back for good on December 9, 1824.

A century later, a bohemian movement flourished in Trujillo that produced Peru's best poet, César Vallejo, painter and musician Macedonio de la Torre, and one of Peru's most controversial political leaders, Victor Raúl Haya de la Torre. Vallejo eventually emigrated to France but Haya de la Torre launched what would become one of Peru's most influential political parties: APRA, the Alianza Popular Revolucionaria Americana. With its call for worker rights, APRA was banned by the military governments of the time. As repression against the party continued, a crowd of angry Apristas attacked an army outpost in 1932 and killed 10 soldiers. In retaliation, the government rounded up nearly 1,000 Apristas, trucked them out to the sands near Chan Chan, and executed them by firing squad. Torre was exiled to Mexico but returned and was elected president in 1962—only to have the victory voided as a fraud by the military government.

Trujillo is in the middle of a campaign to gain recognition from the United Nations as a World Heritage Site, which would help raise funds for historic preservation. Great effort has been made to preserve the center's colonial feel, including the burial of electrical and power lines. But at least one well-intentioned effort has backfired. The city government banned buses and *micros* from entering the city center in 1990, causing an explosion in the taxi pool. These days the air pollution and constant honking of *taxistas* as they troll for passengers is unbearable. If you prefer quiet and clean air, we suggest that you consider staying in nearby Huanchaco. Remember, in Trujillo and much of the north, people take their siesta seriously and most sights are closed 1–4 P.M.

Trujillo and the North Coast

N OLD TRUJILLO

Allow at least a half day on foot for seeing Trujillo's colonial core, which offers a dense cluster of well-preserved homes and churches to the north of Plaza de Armas. Start at the northern edge of town at Avenida España, the congested beltway that was once a six-meter wall built between 1680 and 1685 to ward off pirate attacks. The crumbling military wall was knocked down in 1942, but a section has been preserved at the intersection of España and Estete. The waterworks for colonial Trujillo can be seen a few blocks away at Plazuela El Recreo (Estete and Pizarro), where the Spaniards extended Moche and Chimú irrigation channels in order to deliver river water to the aristocratic households of the city. The *plazuela* is graced with an elegant fountain, carved from local marble in 1750, and then relocated from the Plaza de Armas in 1828.

Iglesia y Monasterio El Carmen (Colón y Bolivar, 7 A.M.–8 P.M. daily, free), a Carmelite monastery founded in 1724, is home to a small group of nuns and Trujillo's best collection of colonial art. It has somehow withstood the earthquakes that have rocked Trujillo and houses the city's best-preserved gilded baroque altar. Its *pinacoteca,* or painting gallery, contains 150 colonial works, including *The Last Supper* by Otto Van Veen (Peter Paul Rubens' mentor).

If you have extra time, the **Museo Arqueológico** (Junin 682, 9:30 A.M.–2 P.M. Monday, 9:15 A.M.–1 P.M. and 3:30–7 P.M. Tues.–Fri, and 9:30 A.M.–4 P.M. weekends, $2) is nearby and traces Peruvian history from 12,000 B.C. to the arrival of the Spaniards. Because the University of Trujillo is directing the excavations at the Huaca de la Luna, the museum contains excellent artifacts from that site, including gold objects found there in 1996. A peek inside the courtyard will give you a sense of the grandeur of the **Palacio Itúrregui** (Pizarro 688), which houses the Club Central and is not open to the public. The house was built in 1855 in the Italian Neo-Renaissance style by General Juan Manuel Itúrregui and has three plazas ringed with ornate columns.

Nearby is the headquarters of the APRA political party (Pizarro 672). Another nearby center

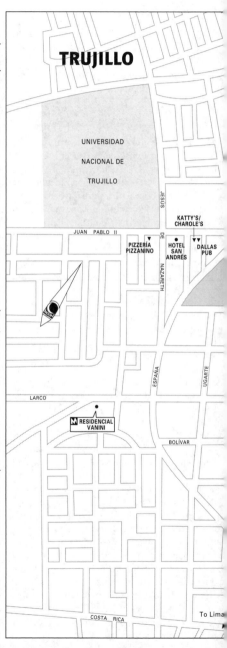

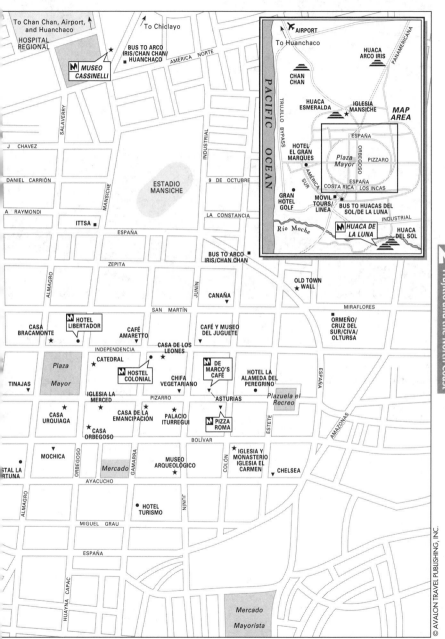

To Chan Chan, Airport, and Huanchaco
To Chiclayo
HOSPITAL REGIONAL
BUS TO ARCO IRIS/CHAN CHAN/ HUANCHACO
AMÉRICA NORTE
MUSEO CASSINELLI
SALAVERRY
J CHAVEZ
INDUSTRIAL
DANIEL CARRIÓN
A RAYMONDI
MANSICHE
9 DE OCTUBRE
ESTADIO MANSICHE
LA CONSTANCIA
ITTSA
ESPAÑA
ZEPITA
BUS TO ARCO IRIS/CHAN CHAN
ALMAGRO
JUNÍN
CANAÑA
OLD TOWN WALL
MIRAFLORES
SAN MARTÍN
HOTEL LIBERTADOR
CAFÉ AMARETTO
CAFÉ Y MUSEO DEL JUGUETE
ORMEÑO/ CRUZ DEL SUR/CIVA/ OLTURSA
CASA BRACAMONTE
INDEPENDENCIA
CASA DE LOS LEONES
CATEDRAL
DE MARCO'S CAFÉ
HOTEL LA ALAMEDA DEL PEREGRINO
ESPAÑA
TINAJAS
Plaza Mayor
HOSTEL COLONIAL
CHIFA VEGETARIANO
Plazuela el Recreo
IGLESIA LA MERCED
PIZARRO
ASTURIAS
CASA URQUIAGA
CASA DE LA EMANCIPACIÓN
PALACIO ITURREGUI
PIZZA ROMA
ESTETE
AMAZONAS
CASA ORBEGOSO
BOLÍVAR
STAL LA RTUNA
MOCHICA
ORBEGOSO
Mercado
GAMARRA
MUSEO ARQUEOLÓGICO
COLÓN
IGLESIA Y MONASTERIO IGLESIA EL CARMEN
CHELSEA
ALMAGRO
AYACUCHO
HOTEL TURISMO
JUNÍN
MIGUEL GRAU
HUAYNA CAPAC
ESPAÑA
Mercado Mayorista

AIRPORT
To Huanchaco
HUACA ARCO IRIS
PANAMERICANA
CHAN CHAN
HUACA ESMERALDA
IGLESIA MANSICHE
MAP AREA
TRUJILLO BYPASS
ESPAÑA
HOTEL EL GRAN MARQUES
ORBEGOSO
PIZARRO
Plaza Mayor
AMÉRICA SUR
ESPAÑA
COSTA RICA
LOS INCAS
GRAN HOTEL GOLF
MÓVIL TOURS/ LÍNEA
BUS TO HUACAS DEL SOL/DE LA LUNA
INDUSTRIAL
Río Moche
HUACA DE LA LUNA
HUACA DEL SOL
PACIFIC OCEAN

Trujillo and the North Coast

© AVALON TRAVEL PUBLISHING, INC.

© AMBER DIRKER

Trujillo's Plaza de Armas at Christmastime

of dissent is the **Casa de la Emancipación** (Pizarro 610, 9:15 A.M.–1 P.M. and 4–6:30 P.M. Mon.–Fri., 9:30 A.M.–1 P.M. Saturday, free), a beautifully restored republican home where Marquis Torre Tagle signed a document declaring Trujillo's independence from Spain in 1820—long before the *libertadores* arrived. The house also contains a small exhibit on César Vallejo, Peru's most famed poet, who was born in the nearby mountain town of Santiago de Chuco. Another block south on Pizarro is the **Iglesia La Merced** (Pizarro 550, 8 A.M.–noon and 5–8 P.M. Mon.–Sat.). This 17th-century church was built by Portuguese artist Alonso de las Nieves and has an impressive rococo organ and cupola. When the order lacked the money for a traditional wood and gold-plated altar, they instead opted to paint one onto the wall in 1755—the only painted altar in the city. Near the altar is an interesting juxtaposition of the virgins that most embody the old and new worlds: Mexico's brown-skinned and dark-haired Virgen de Guadalupe and Spain's blue-eyed and blond Virgen Fátima.

The 17th-century **Casa del Mariscal de Orbegoso** (Orbegoso 503, 9 A.M.–1 P.M. and 4–8 P.M. Mon.–Sat.) is a showcase for the features of colonial homes: a plaza of *canto rodado* (river stones), brick and lime floors, simple ceilings, and enormous, sparsely decorated rooms. This was the home of José Luis Orbegoso, who led troops during the War of Independence and served as president of Peru from 1833 to 1838.

The **Plaza de Armas** is where Martin de Estete began to lay out the city grid in December 1534, in preparation for Francisco Pizarro's arrival the next year. At the center of the plaza is the Monumento de La Libertad, and the face of the winged figure holding a torch closely resembles that of Simón Bolívar. On the other side of the plaza is the Casa Bracamonte, occupied by the Ministerio de Salud and not open for tours. Its most famous features are a *balcón de celosia* (a wooden balcony from which women could see but not be seen) and finely wrought iron windows, an art form that flourished in 18th-century Trujillo.

Compare the colonial style of Casa Orbegoso

Catedral de Trujillo

with the more elegant Republican design of **La Casa Urquiaga** (Pizarro 446, 9 A.M.–3 P.M. Mon.–Fri,, 10 A.M.–1:30 P.M. weekends, free with guide). This house is one of the best-preserved and most elegant republican houses in Trujillo. The original house was destroyed in the 1619 earthquake and was remodeled at least twice, mostly recently in the mid-19th century. Simón Bolívar lived here during his military campaign against Spain, and many of his personal possessions remain in the house, including his mahogany writing desk and personal china.

Construction of Trujillo's **Catedral** (Plaza de Armas, 7:50–9:30 A.M. and 5:30–8:30 P.M. daily, free) began in 1610 but had to begin anew after the devastating earthquake on February 14, 1619, which destroyed the city and prompted townspeople to adopt Saint Valentine as their patron. A more recent earthquake, in 1970, partially destroyed the main altar, which contains an image of Saint Valentine, among other saints. The cathedral's **museum** (9 A.M.–1 P.M. and 4–7 P.M. Mon.–Fri., 9 A.M.–1 P.M. Saturday,

$1.25 admission) contains the shadowy paintings of the baroque Quito School as well as access to catacombs.

MUSEO CASSINELLI

Buried deep within the basement of a grimy Mobil station on the edge of town is the **Museo Cassinelli** (Nicolas de Pierola 601, 9 A.M.–1 P.M. and 3–6:30 P.M. daily, $2). This fabulous collection of ancient ceramics was assembled, piece by piece, over four decades of haggling between Sr. Cassinelli and the local community of *huaqeros* (grave robbers). There are pieces here you won't see anywhere else in Peru: an enigmatic Moche pot of a bearded man (a Viking?) and a ceramic partridge from the Huari civilization that doubles as a bird whistle. Make sure to have the museum keeper open the locked erotic collection, which depicts masturbation, anal intercourse, necrophilia, and nearly every conceivable sexual practice from Moche and earlier cultures. There is even a penis-shaped *chicha* vase from which brides reportedly drank during Moche weddings!

HUACA DE LA LUNA

To see the latest discoveries of Peruvian archaeology, head 8 km south of Trujillo toward two massive, crumbling adobe mounds that rise from the desert. These were built during the Moche Empire (1–700 A.D.). The farthest, Huaca del Sol (Temple of the Moon), was an administrative center, and the other, Huaca de La Luna, was a religious complex. This last *hauca* has been the focus of a well-funded archaeological campaign since 1991 and has produced some of the most dazzling and best-preserved murals in all of Peru.

The *hauca's* shape mirrors that of **Cerro Blanco,** an adjacent mountain that has a curious arching dike of black rock near its summit. The Moche probably believed this arch represented the rainbow serpent, a fertility symbol that appears alongside Ai-Apaek. Archaeologists believe the *hauca's* first single, compact platform was built around 100 A.D. But every century, the Moche apparently sealed the bodies of deceased rulers into the *hauca* and then completely covered the platform with a new, stepped platform above it. In this way, over 700 years, the L-shaped temple evolved into a 100-yard-long stepped pyramid with as many as eight stepped levels. The overall shape is oddly similar to temples of the Maya, a culture that some say influenced the Moche.

Because of the gold buried here, the temple has been the target of relentless plundering by *huaqueros* since at least colonial times. A dozen caves penetrate the base of the *hauca* and a massive house-sized hole is found up top, with an alley cut through the sides of the pyramid where the grave robbers cleared debris. Although much treasure and murals have been lost, the *huaquero* holes have helped archaeologists examine cross-sections of the temple's various platforms. On the *hauca's* north face, archaeologists have discovered a stairwell and a horizontal mural of soldiers performing a victory dance. Elaborate designs of Ai-Apaek in the form of a snake, crab, octopus, spider, and even a potato and a corn

cob have also been found. In 1997, just a few inches from a *huaqero's* hole, archaeologists discovered a cane basket filled with gold disks, textiles, and characteristic feline images, an indication that tombs remain hidden nearby and below, hidden in hundreds of feet of adobe bricks.

The top of Huaca de la Luna, nearly 10 stories high, offers an impressive view of Huaca del Sol, which was built with an estimated 100 million adobe bricks and is considered one of the largest adobe structures in the world. Few excavations have been done at Huaca del Sol, however, and there is little for visitors to see. Much of the *hauca* was eroded in the 17th century when the Spaniards diverted the Río Moche in a failed attempt to uncover hidden treasure. A Moche city with irrigation channels between the two

HUMAN SACRIFICE AT HUACA DE LA LUNA

Archaeologists believe Huaca de la Luna was a center for human sacrifice because murals often show Ai-Apaek, the fearsome Moche deity with a crescent-shaped ceremonial knife (called a *tumi*) in one hand and a severed human head in the other. Additional proof came in 1996, when archaeologists discovered the skeletons of more than 40 men, aged 15 to 32, buried in thick sediment near the back of the *huaca*. The men—many with their throats, hands, and legs cult or pelvis bones ripped out—were apparently sacrificed to stop the El Niño rains that partially destroyed the temple and forced the Moche to relocate further north. Above the skeletons, there is the pyramid's upper throne, which appears in Moche ceramics depicting human sacrifice, and a sacred rock from which the victims were apparently thrown into the mud below. In a famous scene known as the *Presentation,* often painted on ceramic copies around Trujillo, a priest appears to cut open a prisoner's chest to either remove his heart or drain out blood. A cup of blood is then presented to the ruler, possibly to be drunk. High levels of uric acid found in the bones of Moche rulers in the Sipán tombs could, scientists say, indicate they drank blood—or that they ate a lot of shellfish.

haucas is being excavated and will be open for tours in the future.

The **Huaca de la Luna** (9 A.M.–4 P.M. daily, $3, including guide) can be reached via $6 round-trip taxi or via the *combis* at Suárez and Los Incas near the Mercado Mayorista that say *Campiña de Moche*. Get off near Huaca del Sol and walk the half kilometer toward Huaca de la Luna.

HUACA ARCO IRIS AND ESMERALDA

As a warmup for Chan Chan, head first to the restored Huaca Arco Iris (Rainbow Temple), which was built by the Chimú around 1200 A.D. before being covered, and partially preserved, by desert sands. The temple is guarded by thick, six-meter clay walls, and there are two main platforms inside connected by a ramp. The first platform contains seven restored adobe panels that are carved with the *hauca's* namesake motif, two lizard-like beings with an arching rainbow or serpent overhead. The ends of the rainbow/serpent connect to two human figures dancing below, and the relief is fringed with sea otter figures. The exact meaning of the mural has been lost, but many archaeologists believe the mural represents a kind of rain dance or fertility ritual. The rainbow/serpent and the sea otter are associated with rain and are a recurring fertility symbol of both Moche and Chimú art. The sea otter, repeated endlessly at Chan Chan, is also a fertility symbol.

The second platform contains 14 niches that were probably used to store ritual objects such as textiles, shells, seed necklaces, and gold objects. Local legend has it that Huaca Arco Iris was also the home of Tacaynamo, the mythical, bearded man who arrived by raft to found the city of Chan Chan. At the top of the *hauca,* there was probably a small temple where priests communicated with the gods. Nowadays there is a panoramic view of La Esperanza, a neighborhood of Trujillo founded in the 1960s by *campesinos* looking for work in a now-defunct industrial park. Because of combined effects of the 1970 earthquake, terrorism, and Peru's ongoing economic crisis, La Esperanza has ex-

ploded to its present population of 700,000, more than half of Trujillo's total population.

To get to Huaca Arco Iris, take a one-way taxi for $1 and have it drop you off (there are plenty of taxis in the area). Or from in front of the Museo Cassinelli, take a blue-and-white *combi* that says *La Esperanza* and get off at the *quinto paradero* (fifth stop). You will see the *hauca* on the side of the highway, surrounded by walls.

Another *hauca* that is often mentioned in tourist literature but only worth visiting if you have extra time is Huaca Esmeralda. This partially restored *hauca* consists of two superimposed platforms with areas for storing foods and stylized carvings of nets with birds and fish. Unfortunately this *hauca* used to be a favorite hangout for drug addicts and has been mostly destroyed. To get there, take a *combi* toward Huanchaco and get off at Iglesia Mansiche and then walk four blocks. The best option, however, is to go with a guided tour from Trujillo or take a round-trip taxi for $3, as the neighborhood is not safe. Make sure to buy a pass beforehand at Chan Chan or Huaca Arco Iris, because they are not sold at Huaca Esmeralda.

CHAN CHAN

The highly evolved Chimú civilization emerged in 900 A.D. after the decline of the Moche culture and stretched 1,300 km from Chancay, near present-day Lima, to Tumbes. It was Peru's largest pre-Inca empire, and its capital was Chan Chan, now reduced to 20 square kilometers (4,940 acres) of eroded adobe. The city was abandoned in the 1470s, when Chan Chan was overrun by the army of Inca general Tupac Yupanqui.

In its heyday, Chan Chan was an elaborately sculpted and painted adobe city with nine-meter-high walls and an intricate complex of ramps, courtyards, passages, terraces, towers, gardens, palaces, and homes for an estimated 30,000 to 60,000 people. One of the most important archaeological sites in Peru, it was declared a UNESCO World Heritage site in 1986, which has helped protect it somewhat from looting and the El Niño rains of 1983 and 1998.

At the center of the ruined city are 10 royal compounds, or *ciudadelas,* built by successive

cermonial Chan Chan figure with stylized sea otters in background

Chimú dynasties, that cover 6 square km (2.3 square miles). Only the upper strata of Chimú society was allowed to enter these palaces, through a single north entrance that breached massive walls. The palaces were used during the life of the king and then sealed and converted into a mausoleum upon his death, a custom also followed by the Incas in Cusco. The most often visited of these is Ciudadela Tschudi, which some say has been restored too much, but the signed pathway helps visitors make sense of it all.

From the entrance, the pathway leads into a vast walled plaza, where religious ceremonies were once held. The king sat on a throne near a ramp at the front of the square and was flanked by hundreds of priests and other court attendants, while human sacrifices were made on an altar in the center of the square. The walls are decorated with reliefs of sea otters—a fertility symbol passed down from Moche times—and cormorants. The acoustics of the plaza are stunning: the ocean, more than a kilometer away, roars on a windless day. From the plaza, the cir-

cuit continues down a corridor decorated with pelicans and zigzagging fish designs that probably represented the ocean tide and currents. On the opposite wall are diamond-shaped designs of fishing nets, a motif throughout Chan Chan. This passageway leads to a more intimate square with a ceremonial altar (now covered in adobe to preserve it) and U-shaped audience chamber.

One of the more surprising sights of Tschudi, given the desert surroundings, is a pool with a marsh reed at one end that was probably once a pleasure garden for Chimú royalty and a place for worshipping the moon. Unlike the Incas, the Chimú apparently valued the moon over the sun because it comes out both during day and night and controls the oceans. It was here that El Niño rains in 1983 uncovered two adolescent sacrifice victims, one with a mask of gold and another with a collar of jungle seeds used in shamanic rituals. At the back of the palace complex is the royal tomb surrounded by niches where human sacrifices were probably placed. Most of Chan Chan's tombs, once laden with

THE HAIRLESS PERUVIAN POOCH

When at the ruins in Chiclayo and Trujillo, don't be alarmed if you see mudbrown, bald dogs lying prostrate in the afternoon sun. They are neither diseased nor street muts, but rather fine specimens of the Peruvian Hairless, declared a distinct breed by Kennel Club International in 1986 and a national treasure by the Peruvian government in 2001. These declarations capped a modern-day struggle of legitimacy for an ancient dog known commonly in Peru as *perro biringo* or *perro calato* (both are a rather insulting way of saying *naked dog*).

Archaeologists know that the Peruvian Hairless has been around Peru for at least 4,000 years because the dogs are pictured in Vicus and Chavín ceramics and their skeletons have been found in the tombs of the Moche, who considered them both guardians and guides of the dead. They were also favored by Inca nobles, who kept them as pets.

Though they make excellent sight dogs for the blind, Peruvian Hairless are legendary for their healing properties. They have an unusually high body temperature and, after being bathed, are often tucked into the bed of sick people suffering from rheumatism. The dog also brings positive energy into a household and contact with its skin is said to cure asthma in children.

Peruvian Hairless often have odd sprinklings of hair on their bodies (*called powder puff*), which occurs commonly in litters that produce hairless pups. But the most prized version of these dogs, worth as much as $400, is medium-sized with a gray tail and a solitary patch of black hair on its head.

gold and silver objects, were ransacked as early as Inca times, according to colonial documents. Near the end of the circuit, there are warehouses and a ceremonial hall with 24 niches that were probably used for idols. The nearby Museo Chan Chan does not have much of interest except for a collection of *tumi* knives and a display showing the evolution of Chimú pottery.

The $3 admission to **Chan Chan** (9 A.M.–4:30 P.M. daily) includes Huaca Arco Iris, Huaca Esmerelda, and the museum. For $10, a taxi will make the round-trip from Trujillo and wait while you are in the ruins. Or take the *Huanchaco combi* or *colectivo* along España or, even safer, from the main stop at óvalo Grau where the Museo Cassinelli is. Ask the driver to let you off at the *Cruce de Chan Chan* (7 km) and walk a few hundred yards along a safe dirt road that leads to the ruins. Excellent guides wait daily in the Chan Chan parking lot, included the highly recommended Oscar Loyola (tel. 044/273-351). Guides generally charge $6 for Chan Chan, or $17, including transport, for the four Chimú sites covered in the ticket.

Wandering through the endless maze of ruins outside of Chan Chan's Tschudi Palace is not advised, as assaults on tourists have been reported—especially during the daily change of

© PROMPERÚ

The Peruvian Hairless, favorite companion of the Moche and Inca, was finally recognized as a distinct breed in 1986.

police guard between noon and 2 P.M. The neighborhood around Huaca Arco Iris and especially Huaca Esmeralda can also be dangerous. We recommend a guided tour that includes all of these sites plus the museum—you'll learn more and will be relaxed and safe.

ENTERTAINMENT AND EVENTS
Nightlife

Trujillo has a well-hidden but interesting nightlife. If you are looking for something before midnight, shoot pool and mingle with university students at **Billas Pub** (Jesus de Nazareth 311) or **Dallas Pub** (Juan Pablo II 135). The best pub in town is **Chelsea** (Estete 675, tel. 044/257-032, open until 4 A.M.), which has a restaurant and different kinds of live music depending on the night. **Cañana** (San Martín 788, tel. 044/232-503) is a good restaurant with an elegant courtyard that becomes a nightclub around midnight. For dancing, try **Tinajas** (Almagro and Pizarro), the once-separate pub and disco will soon be adjoined via

a tunnel. For a little bit wilder, younger scene on the edge of town, try **Luna Rota** (América Sur 2119, tel. 044/221-488). Luna Rota also offers a Thursday-night *peña* from midnight on with traditional Creole instruments such as *cajón, maracas,* and *guitarra típica.* If you have the late-night munchies, head to **Jano's Pub,** Trujillo's well-frequented, 24-hour hamburger shop near the Plaza de Armas.

Festivals

Marinera dancers from up and down Peru's coast flock to Trujillo in the last week of January for the **National Marinera** Contest. In between rounds of judged dancing, the city comes to life with cockfights, horse-riding championships, a multitude of parties, and even surfing contests at Huanchaco. The partying is especially intense during the last weekend when the dancing finals take place.

Trujillo has a similar fiesta called **Festival de la Primavera,** a celebration of the beginning of spring in the last week of September. The event is best known as a showcase for Trujillo's other icon

schoolgirls on parade, Trujillo

of Peruvian Creole culture, the *caballo de paso.* These graceful horses with tripping gait allow riders to float even during a full trot and are highly prized around the world. Because the best *caballos de paso* are bred in ranches around Trujillo, buyers from California, Texas, and other areas flock to this event. Visit www.perutravels.net or www.welcometoperu.com for more information on these and other festivals.

SHOPPING

Libreria Peruana (Pizarro 505) and **Adriatica Libros** (Junin 565) are two good bookstores. There are two camera shops for supplies and developing on the 300 block of Jesus de Nazareth and at Pizarro 523, near the Plaza de Armas. Peruse the art of **Los Tallanes** (San Martin 455), a group of artists who sell unique paintings, ceramics, textiles, and antiques out of a pretty courtyard. For anything from beef to shoes, try the **Mercado Central de Trujillo** at Ayacucho and San Augustín.

SPORTS AND RECREATION

Several tour companies in Trujillo cover the city, Huaca de la Luna y Sol, Chan Chan, and even El Brujo. The best of these is **Guia Tours** (Independencia 580, tel. 044/234-856, guiatour@amauta.rcp.net.pe). Also recommended is **Trujillo Tours** (Diego de Almagro 301, tel. 044/25-7518).

ACCOMMODATIONS
Under $10
The best budget option in Trujillo is **Ⓜ Residencial Vanini** (Larco 237, tel. 044/200-878, enriqueva@hotmail.com, http://kikevanini.8m.com, $6 s, $9 d), operated by the gregarious Señora Marcela Vanini. After her seven children grew up and married, she converted her family home into a hostel. There are half a dozen wood cabins ($4 pp) on the roof, with shared showers and a little terrace with potted geraniums for beers and sunsets. The more expensive rooms with private bath-

rooms are inside the house, where the single phone and TV are located. Two blocks from the plaza, **Hostel La Fortuna** (Almagro 126, tel. 044/251-536, $6 s, $10 d) offers 40 clean rooms with cable TV, hot water, laundry, and a restaurant.

$10–25
The charming **Ⓜ Hostel Colonial** (Independencia 618, tel. 044/258-261, hostolonialtruji@hotmail.com, $12 s, $18 d) has simple and tasteful rooms arranged above a courtyard that is adorned with Huanchaco's reed boats. There are nice reading areas downstairs and a café/bar that offers room service. Ask for the quieter rooms away from the street. For more amenities, try the modern **Hotel Turismo** (Gamarra 747, tel. 044/244-181, $14 s, $21 d). All rooms include big private bathrooms, cable TV, and refrigerators. The building is not much on charm, and a bit noisy and dark, but it works. The hotel has laundry service and a restaurant, and prices include breakfast.

$25–50
Hotel San Andrés (Juan Pablo II 155, tel. 044/258-236, reservas@hotelsanandres.com, www.hotelsanandres.com, $23 s, $31 d) is a clean and comfortable modern hotel with a restaurant, rooftop pool, and all the amenities. Rooms have telephones, cable TV, and room service. Located on the car-free pedestrian block of Pizarro, **Hotel La Alameda del Peregrino** (Pizarro 879, tel. 044/470-512, alamedaperegrino@viabcp.com, www.perunorte.com/alamedaperegrino, $30 s, $40d) is one of the few places in all of Trujillo sheltered from the din of honking taxis. It's well managed by the hospitable English-speaking owner. Rooms are clean and pretty, and some have good views of the city. Rooms include phones, cable TV, and refrigerators. The hotel has Internet and laundry service, tour agency, and a restaurant serving pasta and Peruvian plates ($2–6).

$50–100
Gran Hotel El Golf (Los Cocoteros 500, Urb. El Golf, tel. 044/282-515, $55 s, $65 d) offers a collection of small but comfortable rooms arranged around gardens and a central pool. It is

a 10-minute drive outside of town, but the relaxed setting and clean air are worth it. The facilities, which include two saunas and an indoor pool, are a bit outdated. Visits can be arranged to the club's golf course across the street. The best option for this price is **Hotel Gran Marqués** (Díaz de Cienfuegos 145, Urb. La Merced, tel. 044/223-990, $56 s, $65 d), on a quiet side street about a five-minute drive from the city center. The hotel offers a modern spa, well-equipped rooms, excellent service, and a good breakfast buffet. Transport to and from airport is included.

Over $100

With its colonial facade and a sun-filled atrium, **N Hotel Libertador** (Independencia 485, Plaza de Armas, tel. 044/232-741, www.libertador.com.pe, $115 d, $230 suite) is *the* five-star hotel of Trujillo. This newly refurbished hotel is located directly on the Plaza de Armas but its large elegant rooms, with tall ceilings and tasteful colonial decor, are sheltered from the noise. All the usual services are available and there is also a sauna, buffet breakfast, and jewelry shop. A restaurant off the lobby serves Creole and international cuisine. The elegant Malabrigo Bar, with dark wood, leather chairs, and windows looking over the square, is the best place in town for a drink.

FOOD
Cafés

Try **Café Amaretto** (Gamarra 368, tel. 044/221-451, $2–5) for delicious salads, sandwiches, and fruit drinks. The *ensalada de atún* is superb with grilled potatoes, tuna, Spanish olives, and fresh tomatoes. Stop back in the evening for a cappuccino and homemade lúcuma cake. **Asturias** (Pizarro 739, tel. 044/258-100) is a busy café with a little bit of everything, including great fruit juices. Owned by Peruvian painter Gerardo Chávez Lopez, **N Café y Museo del Juguete** (Jr. Independencia 701, tel. 044/297-200, 9 A.M.–11 P.M.) is Trujillo's classiest café. The ambience is old-world Paris with an antique cash register, wood bar, and a piano in the back room. The walls are covered with photographs of Mario

Vargas Llosa and Peruvian intellectuals who have stopped in for a drink. Try a Mistela, the house drink, or one of their sandwiches, tamales, or soups. Part of the proceeds go to the upstairs **Museo del Juguete** (Independencia 705, 10 A.M.–6 P.M. Mon.–Sat., $1.50), which has a small but intriguing collection of rattlers, whistles, figurines, and other Chancay, Moche, and Chimú toys from as far back as 1000 B.C. Gerado Chavez's paintings, and those of his lesser-known brother, are on display in a gallery next door.

Local Favorites

For a delicious Italian or *criolla* meal, go to **N De Marco's Café** (Pizarro 725, tel. 044/234-251, $3–9). Try the perfectly spiced *lomo saltado,* an ingenious Peruvian concoction of grilled steak, peppers, tomatoes, french fries, and onions. There's also a full bar and coffee menu. If you can't afford to stay at the **Hotel Libertador** (Independencia 485), have breakfast or lunch there in the refined dining room with small windows that look over the Plaza de Armas. Reliable **Mochica** (Bolivar 462, tel. 044/224-247, $4–10) serves heaping plates of *criolla* cooking in this and other locations in Huanchaco and Moche. For inexpensive lunchtime fixed menus, try **Katty's** (Juan Pablo II 139) or **Charole's** (Jaun Pablo II 137).

Pizza

The best place for pizza in Trujillo is the tiny **N Pizza Roma** (Colón 500, $3–5). The chef is Italian and he lets you know it—you may find him expertly flipping pizza dough as he dances to Italian opera and serves his potent, and delicious, sangria. Besides pizza, the crowded **Pizzería Pizzanino** (Juan Pablo II 183, tel. 044/263-105, 6 P.M.–midnight) offers desserts and a full bar.

Health Food

Start your morning off with a heaping portion of fresh homemade yogurt and exotic fruits for around $0.50 from one of the many yogurt shops around town, including a few on Pizarro northeast of the Plaza de Armas. Vegetarians can find *chifa* food, yogurts, and fruits at **Chifa Vegetariano** (Pizarro 687).

Markets

There's a good but small **fruit market** on Espana 584, **el mercado central** is at Ayacucho and San Augustín, and the modern **Merpisa supermarket** is at Pizarro and Junín.

INFORMATION AND SERVICES

The **iPeru** tourist information office (Pizarro 412, iperutrujillo@promperu.gob.pe, 8:30 A.M.–7:30 P.M. daily) is on the Plaza de Armas.

The **Tourist Police** are located on the Plaza de Armas near i Peru and also at Independencia 630 (tel. 044/29-1705).

The best medical service in town is at **Clínica Peruano-Americana** (Mansiche 702-810, tel. 044/23-1261).

Banks, often in beautifully restored colonial buildings, are scattered around the center of town; **Agrobanco** (Independencia 246), **Banco Nuevo Mundo** (De Almagro 545), and **Banco Continental** (Gamarra 547) between Bolivar and Pizarro.

The **post office,** Serpost, is located at Independencia 286, and there is a cluster of **Internet cafés** on Larco south of the Plaza Mayor. However, for a quiet experience and a speedy connection, go to Gamarra 713.

Laundry is available at Pizarro 683 or Bolivar 355. The **American Dry Cleaners** (Bolognesi 782) are the best but expensive.

Rental cars are available for $60 per day, at **C.M. Rent a Car** (Prolong. Buenos Aires 293, tel. 044/42-0059).

GETTING THERE AND AROUND

All the following bus companies are recommended and have daily service, usually in the evenings, for the eight-hour haul to or from Lima: **Oltursa** (Ejército 342, tel. 044/263055), **Cruz del Sur** (Amazonas 438, tel. 044/261802), **Ormeño** (Ejército 233, tel. 044/259782), **Linea** (América Sur 2855, tel. 044/286538), **ITTSA Sur** (Mansiche 145, tel. 044/224248, also has a 1 P.M. departure to Lima).

The recommended **Movil Tours** (América Sur 3959, tel. 044/286538) has comfortable buses to Huaraz and Chachapoyas, and Linea covers the same destinations plus Cajamarca. Most of the above bus companies head north as well, and Ormeño offers direct service to Ecuador.

Taxis within the center of the city cost $0.75, and *combis* and *colectivos,* which only operate outside the center, are frequent. The best place to pick up public transport headed north, including Chicama, Chan Chan, and Huanchaco, is Ovalo Grau opposite the Museo Cassinelli.

HUANCHACO

A considerably more laid-back base from which to visit the ruins around Trujillo is Huanchaco, an ancient fishing village that has exploded over the last few decades into a favorite resort for Peruvians and a well-worn destination on the Gringo Trail. Even as new adobe homes fill the 14-km gap between Huanchaco and Trujillo, this beach town still maintains a good bit of its village charm. Huanchaco has an excellent assortment of inexpensive and well-run hostels and restaurants for a range of travelers.

Huanchaco is the mythical landing spot of Takaynamo, the bearded founder of the Chimú Empire who reputedly ordered the construction of Chan Chan around 1200 A.D. Even before Takaynamo's arrival, however, Huanchaco's fishermen were using their exquisitely crafted *caballitos de tórtora,* reed rafts with gracefully curved bows that are depicted on 2,000-year-old Mochica ceramics. About 80 full-time fishermen straddle their *caballitos* each morning, legs dangling into the water on each side as they fish with line and hook or drop weighted gill nets. The anglers surf in on the waves in the afternoon and then stand their boats upright to dry. Called *patacho* in the native tongue spoken first by the Moche and later by Chimú, the boats are made of tied bundles of reeds, which are cut from the marsh, or *wachaque,* at the north end of town. A few residents still speak the nearly extinct native tongue, including one 90-year-old woman who is known for singing Moche ballads.

Most visitors to Huanchaco come for a rest from the rigors of travel and enjoy a relaxed nightlife that includes occasional bonfires on the beach, roving musicians, and a few pubs.

© AMBER PIRKER

Laid-back Huanchaco is becoming a surfing mecca.

Brazilians cram into the hostels along the beach, sure proof of good surfing. This is a great place to learn how to surf with gentle waves, with surfboards for rent and quality instructors.

There is an important historical site on the hill above the town: **Santuario de la Virgen del Socorro,** reputed to be the second-oldest church in Peru. The yellow church with colonial facade and large bell tower has served as a landmark for sailors ever since the Spaniards built it atop a Chimú temple in 1540. After a Spanish caravel sunk one late night in a storm off the coast, legend has it that a box floated to shore containing the *Virgen del Socorro* (Virgin of Rescue). It sparked the conversion of Huanchaco's natives, so the story goes, and has been venerated ever since.

A word of caution: Any beach spot popular with foreigners will have its share of *bricheros,* delinquents who specialize in ripping off tourists. They will often befriend travelers by offering free surfing lessons, only to end up in a bar later that night where the *gringo* is left with the bill. Travelers who wander the streets of Huanchaco—or most other cities in Peru for that matter—late at night either drunk or on drugs are asking to be robbed.

Sports and Recreation

For **surfing lessons,** go to Chicho, a Huanchaco native who traces his ancestry to a famous Chimú warrior and whose real name is Henry Huamanchumo. Chicho offers a two-hour group surfing lesson that comes with surfboard and wetsuit ($9) or just a day rental of surfboard and wetsuit ($6). A recent group of eight first-time surfers all stood up on their boards, thanks to Chicho's excellent instruction and the area's perfect learning waves. He runs his lessons out of his house (Las Horencias 497, tel. 044/461-721, chicho@huanchaco.zzn .com), but he can also be found at Sabes Pub (Larco 920), where he is a bartender. Casa Suiza also rents surfboards and wetsuits for $6 a day or $7.50 for a longboard.

Entertainment and Events

One of Huanchaco's more famous celebrations happens in the last days of June when a flotilla of *caballitos de tótora,* including a gigantic one made especially for carrying the religious image of San Pedro, arrives on the beach in Huanchaco atop breaking waves. The two-day **festival of San**

Pedro, patron saint of fishermen, also includes a religious procession and celebrations.

There are occasional beach bonfires, but there is always something happening at the two main pubs in town: **La Tribú** on the town's tiny plaza and **Sabes Pub** (Larco 920, tel. 044/461-555, 8 P.M.–3 A.M.). Sabes Pub has a pool table and lots of happy hour specials from 10 to 11 P.M. More pubs are on the way.

Accommodations

Most Huanchaco hotels and lodges offer discounts outside holidays and the summer months from Christmas to March.

Under $10: The Swiss-owned ⚑ **Casa Suiza** (Los Pinos 451, tel. 044/46-1285, www.casasuiza .com, albergue@casasuiza.com) is a few blocks from the beach, but it runs like a Rolex with small but neat rooms that are integrated into a hip decor. Services include laundry, kitchen, free bodyboards, and the fastest Internet in town. Even non-budget travelers will enjoy ⚑ **Naylamp** (Victor Larco 1420, tel. 044/46-1022, naylamp@terra.com.pe, $9 s, $12 d). This oceanfront hostel offers a safe, relaxed atmosphere of hammocks, gardens, open kitchen, and simple but clean rooms with a camping area for $2–3 pp (depending if you have your own tent or not). Both hostels are often full, so make reservations beforehand. **Hostel Los Tumbos,** at the south end of the beach, and **Mami Mia** (Larco 562, tel. 044/960-8223, $4.50 pp) are next in line among Huanchaco's dozen or so backpacker hostels.

$10–25: For wonderful oceanfront views, rooms leading onto terraces, and a lookout tower over the whole beach, try **Caballito de Tótora** (La Rivera 219, tel. 044/461-154, caballito@trujillovirtual.com, $18 s, $27 d). **Hostel El Malecón** (La Rivera 225, tel. 044/461-275, hostel_elmalecon@yahoo.com, $8 s, $15 d) is a converted house with nicely decorated rooms and ocean views. TV sets are available for an additional cost. Once you walk through the doors, **Huanchaco Hostel** (Victor Larco 287, tel. 044/461-688, huanchaco_hostel@terra.com.pe, www.solui.com/Huanchaco_Hostel, $20 s, $23 d) stands out for its circular staircase, antique furniture, and lots of dark wood. The rooms aren't anything special, but the refined atmosphere (plus a game room with pool, billiards, and Foosball) make this a reasonable value if you value peace and quiet.

$25–50: Hostal Bracamonte (Jr. Los Olivos 503, tel. 044/461-266, hostelbracamonte@yahoo .com, http://welcome.to/hostelbracamonte, $55 s, $87 d) is a tasteful spread of bungalows on the north entrance to town with a dazzlingly clear pool, restaurant and bar, game room, and Internet. The Belgian-owned **Huanchaco International Hotel** (on the main road before town, tel. 044/46-1754, hotel@huanchacointernational.com, www.huanchachointernational .com) offers comfortable rooms, sunny restaurant, and dazzling, heart-shaped pool.

Food

Huanchaco offers many great budget eateries. **Don Pepe** (Larco 502, $3–5) offers the *cangrejo reventado,* a somewhat messy local dish that includes a crab shell stuffed with a blend of crab meat, sea algae, scrambled eggs, and ají. For homemade pasta and ice cream, find Fernando Ferrer at **Mama Mía** (Larco 538, tel. 044/960-8223). A little more upscale, **Restaurant Huanchaco Beach** (Larco 602, tel. 044/461-484, huanchacobeach@hotmail.com, $5–8) has pioneered a secret *cebiche* sauce called *crema huanchaco* where chili peppers are peeled, liquefied, and then cooked into a rosy, creamy concoction that is poured over raw fish "cooked" in lime juice. The waterfront restaurant **El Mochica** has reliable seafood at each of its locations—here, in Moche, and in Trujillo. The best place to get a cocktail is the elegant and tastefully decorated **Club Colonial** (Grau 272, tel. 044/461-015, ccolonial@yahoo.com, http://clubcolonial.hypermart.net, 11 A.M.–11:30 P.M.), set in a colonial home on Huanchaco's main square. Inside, 5.5-meter-tall plaster walls are covered with paintings for sale from some of Peru's leading contemporary painters. The charming pub with antique wood is covered in black-and-white photographs from the town's past, while Humboldt penguins, an endangered species on Peru's coast, splash around in a pool outside. Unfortunately, the quality of the food ($6–10) is hit-or-miss.

Delicious *palta rellana* (stuffed avocado) and *cebiche* are found in Huanchaco restaurants.

The Belgian owner of Club Colonial also operates a charming café on Huanchaco's decrepit pier that serves pizza, cocktails, and desserts.

Getting There
From Trujillo, $0.75 *colectivos* run along Av. España before heading to Huanchaco. A taxi for the 10-minute drive will cost $4–5.

CHICAMA VALLEY

This valley, just north of Trujillo and the Moche Valley, is a worthwhile location for those in search of the world's longest left-breaking wave in the world, or who want to explore further afield in Moche archaeology.

El Brujo
About 60 km north of Trujillo, reachable only via unmarked dirt roads, is **El Brujo** (tel. 044/29-1894, 9 A.M.–4 P.M. daily, $1.50). Out-of-the-way and unexplored, El Brujo is difficult to explore without a guide but is considered one

of the more important ceremonial centers of the north coast, used from 3000 B.C. through colonial times. If you enjoyed seeing Chan Chan and the *haucas* outside of Trujillo, El Brujo is the logical next step: a complex blend of the ancient cultures of the Chicama Valley, but above all the Moche. The site is essentially three *huacas*. Huaca Cortada contains reliefs of Moche warriors, *tumi* in one hand and decapitated head in the other. There is also Huaca Prieta, but the most interesting is Huaca Cao, a huge platform with murals on five levels depicting figures of priests, sacrificial victims, and dancing warriors—similar to those recently unearthed at Huaca de la Luna.

Visits to El Brujo should be arranged beforehand by telephone or by stopping by the **National Institute of Culture in Trujillo** on Independencia in Trujillo. Because the nearest public transport goes only to Magdalena de Cao, about 5 km away on unmarked roads, it is best to go with a guide from one of the Trujillo agencies. From Trujillo's Av. America Sur, buses leave for Chocope, from which it is possible to take a *colectivo* to Magdalena de Cao, and a final taxi (or hot walk) to the ruins.

Chicama

Puerto Chicama is a plain beach near an ugly town with only a few rundown places to stay and eat. As Chicho, the Huanchaco surfing pro, explains, "the only good thing Chicama has are the waves." The only reason travelers come here at all is to surf the longest-breaking wave in the world, which forms most often between March and June. The wave ranges in height from 1 to 2.5 meters and runs a reputed 2.5 km, the apparent result of a flat, sandy beach, steady cross-winds, and ocean currents from the south and west. It's actually formed by four separate waves that connect only on magical days: the point, cape, *el hombre,* and *el muelle* (pier). Surfers need a spare set of legs to surf it, as locals joke, and a *combi* ride to travel back up the beach afterwards.

Long before surfing was in vogue, Chicama was a major port for the sugar and cotton brought by railroad from the nearby Hacienda Chicama. As a result the town has an old pier with railroad tracks and a group of old, wooden *casonas* along the waterfront. Most surfers pitch in and rent a group car to visit here for the day from bases further north, such as órganos or Máncora. If you plan to stay, check out **Hostal El Hombre** (tel. 044/640-504, Arica 803, $5 s, $7 d). One of the area's top surfers, known only as *El Hombre,* owns this hostel and may give surfing lessons. Another potential surfing instructor is named *El Zorro* ("the fox"), well known around town. Chicama is reached via a dirt road from the town of Paiján, at Km 614 of the Panamericana. From Trujillo, take a bus from óvalo Grau near the Museo Cassinelli that says either *Puerto Chicama* or *Paiján.* Collectivos run to Puerto Chicama often from Paiján.

Pacasmayo

This early-20th-century port, 105 km north of Trujillo, has a famous old pier where tobacco, cotton, and sugar were loaded onto large sailing ships and, later, steamers. Boat traffic is still concentrated on the northern side of the pier, while sunbathers and swimmers congregate on the south. Precisely because so few people ever visit here, Pacasmayo is imbued with memories of a time gone by, a nostalgia augmented by a large and interesting railroad museum outside of town.

the charming, all but forgotten seaside town of Pacasmayo

Just before the village of Guadalupe are the ruins of Pacatnamú. This complex of pyramids, cemeteries, and homes, occupied before Moche times, is rarely visited even though it is comparable in size to Chan Chan. There are several hostels but the best lodging is **Hotel Pakatnamú** (Malecon Grau 103, tel. 044/52-2368, hotelpakatnamu@hotmail.com), which offers nice rooms, televisions, and a waterfront view. The best restaurant in town is **El Encuentro de Ignacio** on the Plaza de Armas, though the unpretentious Silvana's is also recommended. All the major north-south buses stop in Pacasmayo, from which buses depart regularly for Cajamarca. The turnoff for Cajamarca is just 15 km north of Pacasmayo, a road junction famous among Peruvians for a cluster of seafood restaurants. The best is El Gordo, which serves heaping plates of local shrimp and other seafood.

Chiclayo

Among Peru's large cities, Chiclayo stands out as an underdog with a curiously humble beginning. The city began as a mule watering spot between the opulent cities of Ferreñafe, Lambayeque, and Zaña, which were founded by the Spanish between 1550 and 1565. But in a twist of history, these once-proud Spanish towns have withered while mestizo Chiclayo has boomed in recent years as the commercial hub of northern Peru. There is not much colonial architecture in Chiclayo, but there are a few things you will not find elsewhere: a crooked street layout based on winding farmer's lanes and a witch's market that sells potions and amulets.

Chiclayo is northern Peru's number-one travel destination because of the **Moche** and **Sicán** cultures, which built elaborate cities and tombs in the surrounding desert from 100 A.D. until the arrival of the Incas in 1470. Royal tombs from both cultures were unearthed in 1987 and 1991, stunning archaeologists with their complexity and beauty. They were finds as important in Latin American history as the unearthing of King Tutankhamun's tomb in Egypt. After several world tours, the gold objects from this and 11 other royal tombs unearthed by Walter Alva are on display at a new, state-of-the-art museum in Lambayeque.

The Moche empire declined around 750 A.D. and a new culture known as the Sicán (or Lambayeque) emerged to build **Batán Grande,** a complex of pyramids 57 km outside Chiclayo. In 1991 Japanese archaeologist Izumi Shimada discovered two royal Sicán tombs, filled with beautiful gold masks, jewelry, and solid-gold disk earrings that rival those of the Lords of Sipán. The objects are now on display at Museo Sicán in Ferreñafe, another fascinating, well-designed museum that is a must-see. Around 1050 A.D., the Sicán mysteriously abandoned Batán Grande and built the even more elaborate city of **Túcume**, which is 33 km north of present-day Chiclayo. Túcume's 26 adobe pyramids, reduced by time to dirt mountains, are spread through a dramatic desert at the base of Cerro Purgatorio.

Other sites of interest around Chiclayo include **Zaña,** an affluent colonial city that is now a ghost town of stone arches, columns, and church facades; **Huaca Rajada** (Cracked Pyramid), the twin adobe pyramids where the Lords of Sipán were found; **Monsefú,** a market town known for its woven straw and cotton goods; and **Santa Rosa,** a beach and fishing village with *caballitos de tótora* and a few good *cebicherias.*

It is possible, but not recommended, to see both the Sipán and Sicán museums in a single exhausting day. A better option is to see Museo Sicán and Gran Batán in one day, Museo Tumbas Reales, Bruning, and possibly Túcume in another day, and a third, optional, day devoted to seeing Zaña, Huaca Rajada, Monsefú, and Santa Rosa.

DOWNTOWN CHICLAYO

The first inhabitants of present-day Chiclayo were Indians forced to settle here as part of a Spanish *reducción.* Religious conversion began here in 1559 when Franciscan friars from Trujillo founded El Convenio San María. The remains of this convent, all but ruined by El Niño rains, can be seen

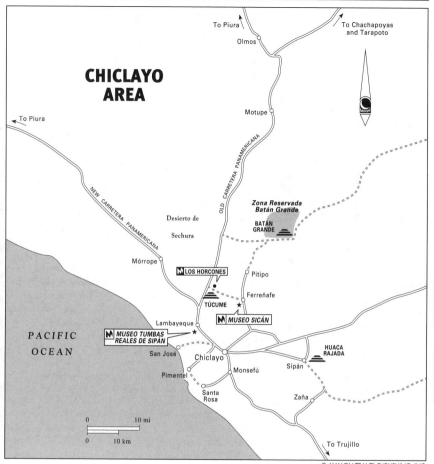

on Calle San José at the Plaza de Armas. Most of Chiclayo's streets were once dirt lanes that led to the convent and are named after saints.

Chiclayo does not have a Plaza de Armas but rather a Parque Principal, which was inaugurated in 1916. Historians believe this park once served as a goat corral for José Domingo Chiclayo, the town's namesake, who came here after Zaña was destroyed in a 1720 flood. (The city may have been named for him, though the word also means *place where there are green branches* in the all-but-lost Mochica language). Also on the main park is **La Catedral,** built in 1869 by

José Balta, Chiclayo's most famous citizen, who launched a coup in the 1830s and briefly served as president of Peru. The other main churches in town are even more recent: **Iglesia La Verónica,** at Torres Paz and Alfonso Ugarte, was built in the late 19th century, and **Basílica San Antonio,** at the intersection of Luis Gonzales and Torre Paz, was built in 1946.

Chiclayo has a highly interesting *mercado de brujos* (Arica, inside the Mercado Modelo, 7 A.M.–5 P.M.). Here are piles of all the materials used by Peru's *curanderos*—shark jaws, deer legs, snakeskins, potions, scents, amulets, and *huayruro*

herb vendor at Chiclayo's Mercado de Brujos

jungle beads for warding off a hex. There are heaps of dried mountain herbs and San Pedro cactuses, which, when sliced and reduced in boiling water, form a hallucinogenic drink used by shamans—and an increasing number of travelers. Shamans can be contracted here for fortune-telling or healing sessions. But beware of sham artists or shamans who dabble in the dark side—they are everywhere and can pose a real threat to your psychic health. It is always best to make *curandero* contacts through a trusted source.

If you have spare time in the evening, head to **Paseo Las Musas** (José Balta and Garcilazo de la Vega), an odd promenade with Greco-Roman statues and a triumphal arch sustained by armless Egyptian beauties. It is a charming Chiclayan invention, often filled with wedding parties emerging from the cathedral, five blocks away.

LAMBAYEQUE
MUSEO TUMBAS REALES DE SIPÁN

Give yourself at least two hours to see this extraordinary museum (Juan P. Vizcardo y Guzmán s/n, tel. 074/28-3977, 9 A.M.–5 P.M. Tues.–Sun.,

$2), 11 km north of Chiclayo in Lambayeque. The museum, shaped like a Moche pyramid, contains the gold masks, scepters, jewelry, and other objects of the royal Moche tomb discovered by Walter Alva in 1987. This museum succeeds in evoking the full grandeur and sophistication of the ancient Moche civilization (100–750 A.D.) in a way that adobe pyramids, now reduced to mud mountains, often do not. After nearly 500 years of continuous looting up and down the coast of Peru, it is nothing short of a miracle that these tombs remained undisturbed. Their meticulous excavation has unlocked many of the mysteries of Moche society, built around a hierarchy of kings, priests, and military leaders. Come with a guide (or hire one at the museum for $4) who can explain Moche cosmography and point out things a first-timer would miss: the king and priest found in these tombs, for instance, are the actual people depicted on ceramics and murals found throughout the empire, which stretched 600 km along Peru's north coast to present-day Piura.

To reach Museo Tumbas Reales, hire a taxi in Chiclayo for $4 or take a $0.30 *combi* ride from Vicente de la Vega and Leonardo Ortiz, in front of the Otursa bus terminal. Slightly cheaper combo tickets are available at the Museo Tumbas Reales for those who plan on also visiting Huaca Rajada and Túcume.

Museo Bruning
Lambayeque is also home to the **Museo Arqueológico Nacional Bruning** (Block 7 of Huamachuco, tel. 074/28-2110, 9 A.M.–5 P.M. daily, $2), an interesting museum founded in 1925 that has been nearly forgotten since the Sipán treasures were moved from here to the new Museo Tumbas Reales. Nevertheless, Museo Bruning has an interesting collection: Sicán gold masks found at Batán Grande, with the famous winged eyes and red patina of mercury ore; a variety of weapons and musical instruments found at Túcume; and a Moche ceramic collection that includes a variety of marine animals, an enigmatic vase of a man straddling what appears to be a torpedo, and other Moche vases depicting a range of human disease and sexual practices. This ceramic collection alone is

KING TUT'S GOT NOTHING ON THE LORDS OF SIPÁN

Peruvian archaeologist Walter Alva knew he had found something big at Huaca Rajada in 1987 when he unearthed more than a thousand ceramic pots—with the food, apparently, for an afterlife journey. A bit deeper Alva found the skeleton of a sentry with the feet cut off—symbolizing eternal vigil—and the remains of wood beams that once supported a tomb. Below was a disintegrated sarcophagus with heavy copper fastenings, an array of gold covers and decorations, and, at the bottom, a Moche king in all his splendor. Around and on top of him, were huge earrings of turquoise and gold, breastplates of delicately threaded shell beads, a necklace of gold spheres and another of huge peanut shells-ten of which were in silver, ten in gold. By his hand lay a scepter with an inverted gold pyramid decorated with scenes of human sacrifice. Gold balls were found in the king's mouth, abdomen, and right hand, and a silver ball was found in his left. There were seven sacrificial victims buried along with the king—the sentry, a general, a standard bearer, three young women, and a child—along with two llamas and a spotted dog.

After carbon-dating the tomb at 300 A.D., Alva's team found an earlier tomb nearby that may have belonged to the grandfather, referred to as El Viejo Señor de Sipán (*The Old Lord of Sipan*). This ruler was buried along with a woman and a decapitated llama and, although the tomb is smaller, the 53 gold objects found here show the highest level of craftsmanship. There are exquisite gold balls of spiders straddling their webs, necklaces with minute gold and silver filigree, and jewelry with the same octopus and crab motifs found in the recently uncovered murals at the Huaca de la Luna near Trujillo.

Alva's team discovered a total of 10 other tombs, including that of a Moche priest-the mythical *bird man* who appears alongside the king in the human sacrifice ceremonies depicted on Moche ceramics and murals. The priest was found with a gold scepter capped with an Ulluchu—this sacred fruit, now extinct, is believed to have prevented blood from coagulating during ceremonies of human sacrifice. (It may also have had hallucinogenic properties as well, judging by the dazed look on the faces of several flying priests.)

The excavation of these tombs began with a midnight call that local police made to Alva's home in 1987. Grave robbers digging at midnight near Huaca Rajada, the Moche Pyramid near the village of Sipán, had found a royal tomb and begun lugging rice sacks filled with gold objects. At one point, the robbers quarreled and one of them was killed in the ensuing fight. When police found out they called Alva and launched an international search for objects that had already been smuggled overseas. Police recovered a few objects, including a gold mask and a gold plate, called a *taparabos,* which the Moche elite hung behind their bodies. This last piece was recovered by the U.S. FBI, which arrested a Panamanian diplomat in Philadelphia in 1997 trying to sell the piece for $1.5 million. For a fascinating account of the Sipán heist and the worldwide network of antiquities smugglers, read American novelist Sidney Kirkpatrick's *Lords of Sipán.*

worth the visit, especially if you missed Museo Cassinelli in Trujillo.

After the colonial center of Zaña was destroyed in a flood in 1720, Lambayeque flourished and several important colonial homes and churches were built. Now Lambayeque is a sleepy town with one new hotel and a handful of restaurants. Worth seeing if you have the time is **Iglesia San Pedro,** a large, yellow-and-white church on the main square that was completed by 1739. Inside are large murals and ten altars, the oldest being the baroque Virgen de las Mercedes. One block away, at the intersection of Dos de Mayo and San Martín, is the **La Casa Montjoy,** with the largest balcony in Peru—over 65 meters long! It was from here that Liberator San Martín gave the first shout of independence in 1820. To reach Lambayeque from Chiclayo, take a combi from Vicente de la Vega and Leonardo Ortiz, in front of the Otursa bus terminal.

Food

No food is available inside the Museo Tumbas Reales, so you may want to eat beforehand down the street at **Los Penachos.** The café has limited choices but offers a good $2 menú in a breezy, plant-filled bamboo tent. There are a good variety of restaurants in Lambayeque that have sprung up to service the hungry lunchtime crowds spilling out of the museums. Try **Mis Algarrobos** (Ramón Castilla 840, tel. 074/58-1669), in front of the Mercado Modelo, for a wider variety of *cebiche,* duck, fish, and seafood dishes. For *cebiche,* try **El Pacifico** (Huamachuco 970, tel. 074/28-3135, $3–5), and for *comida típica,* try **El Rincón del Pato** (Leguia 270, tel. 074/28-2751, $4–5) for *criollo* food including duck, *cebiche,* and seafood.

M MUSEO SICÁN

This museum (Block 9 of Av. Batán Grande, tel. 074/28-6469, 9 A.M.–5 P.M. Tues.–Sun., $2) is located 18 km outside of Chiclayo in Ferreñafe. Though unfairly overshadowed by the Museo Tumbas Reales, this modern museum has a fabulous collection of gold objects of the Sicán Culture, which succeeded the Moche in 750 A.D. and succumbed to the Chimú in 1375. The Sicán, also called the Lambayeque, were the first culture in Peru's north to discover bronze, which they made by mixing arsenic with copper—a technique learned from the Tiahuanaco and Wari cultures in southern Peru. The Sicán were at the hub of a great commercial network that moved emeralds and shells from Ecuador, gold nuggets from the Amazon, and mercury ore for their metallurgy from Peru's southern sierra.

The Sicán buried their kings in a unique way: deep within vertical shafts, sometimes accompanied by more than 20 sacrificed attendants and more than a ton of metal and other objects. Archaeologists believe that up to 90 percent of all gold plundered from tombs in Peru comes from Sicán sites in the Lambayeque Valley. Indeed, Sicán masks, with their characteristic *ojos alados* (winged eyes), are found in private collections all over their world. In 1936, renowned Peruvian archaeologist Julio Tello managed to track down a huge collection of gold artifacts looted from Huaca La Ventana en Batán Grande, including a gold *tumi* (ceremonial knife) weighing 992 grams. Fortunately Tello was able to save many of these objects for Lima's Museo de Oro

(sadly, the *tumi* was later stolen by delinquents and melted down).

Yet little was known about the Sicán civilization until 1991, the year that Japanese archaeologist Izumi Shimada was able to carefully excavate two royal Sicán tombs at the first Sicán capital of Batán Grande. In the east tomb, the king was surrounded by sacrificed women and buried upside down, his decapitated head placed in front of him. The mass of objects in the tomb included two huge golden arms, sacred spondylus shells from Ecuador, a square copper-gold mask stained red with mercury ore and several *cuentas,* or massive heaps of shell beads. The west tomb is even larger, with similar gold masks and *cuentas* surrounding the king, along with niches containing women, sacrificed in pairs. DNA and dental tests have revealed that the two kings, and many of the women in both tombs, were close relatives. Guides are available for $3 outside of the museum. *Colectivos* to Ferreñafe can be taken from the Terminal de Epsel at the corner of Av. Oriente and Nicolás de Pierola in Chiclayo.

BATÁN GRANDE

This sprawling pyramid complex, set amid a dry-forest nature reserve, was the first Sicán capital and the source for the majority of the plundered gold that was either sold to private collections or—before collecting became popular in the 1940s—simply melted down. **Batán Grande** (57 km northeast of Chiclayo, tel. 074/20-1470, 7 A.M.–6 P.M., free) is about a half hour drive further along the same road that leads to Museo Sicán. The royal tombs were discovered in front of Huaca de Oro (Pyramid of Gold), one of 34 adobe pyramids in the 300-hectare Reserva Bosque Pómac. The excavated tombs have been covered up to deter grave robbers, and there is little to see except for the pyramids, which look like huge dirt hills. They were badly eroded by the El Niño rains of 1982 and 1998, which did however boost the surrounding dry forest of algarobbo, ficus, zapote, and vichayo trees (one algarobbo tree, forced to the ground by its own weight, is reputed to be 800 years old and is the center of shamanic rituals). There is a range of in-

THE MYTH OF NAYMLAP

The deepest mystery of the Sicán culture is the identity of a man, with beak-shaped nose and *ojos alados* (*winged* or almond-shaped eyes), who is depicted everywhere on Sicán masks, ceramics, and images. Like the Chimú's mythical Takaynamo who landed at Huanchaco, the Sicán culture has a well-recorded legend of a mythical king who arrived by sea around 750 A.D. with a wife and full royal court. This king, named Naymlap, founded a temple and installed an idol known as Yampallec—the origin of the name Lambayeque. Upon his death, the relatives of Naymlap spread the rumor that the kind grew wings and flew away, leaving his son to rule. The dynasty founded by Naymlap included 12 kings, according to historical evidence. According to legend, the last Naymlap king, Fempellec, committed a series of sins that caused a devastating flood and a period of crisis for the Sicán people. This is certainly possible: nearly 1.5 meters of water coursed through Batán Grande during the El Niño floods of 1982 and a similar even might have caused the Sicán to abandon and burn the city in 1050 A.D. The Sicán then moved their capital to Túcume, where even larger pyramids were built.

teresting wildlife in the reserve: 41 species of birds, numerous reptiles (iguanas, snakes, lizards), as well as fox, deer, anteaters, and ferrets—though the spectacled bear and puma long ago disappeared from this forest.

More than anything, the reserve is a depressing case study of how Peruvians, driven by necessity, continue to plunder their cultural and natural treasures. Villagers frequently venture into the park at night to cut down trees for lumber or dig around the pyramids, though *huaqeros* are no longer finding the treasures they used to here. The punishments for these crimes are ridiculously low—$60 for the first offense and $120 for the second, with no jail time nor confiscation of vehicles. The four guards in charge of patrolling the 5,800-hectare nature reserve have one motorcycle and one pickup truck between them. During a recent visit, the motorcycle had broken down and the pickup truck was out of gas. Park rangers act as guides and appreciate tips. To reach Batán Grande, take a *colectivo* from the Terminal de Epsel at the corner of Av. Oriente and Nicolás de Pierola in Chiclayo. Because the site is large, spread out, and hard to find, it is best to see it on an organized tour.

HUACA RAJADA

After seeing the Sipán treasures, many people want to see where it was all found, at **Huaca Ra-**jada (Cracked Pyramid, tel. 074/800048, 9 A.M.– 5 P.M. daily, $2), about 28 km east of Chiclayo. The only thing to see here are the two clay pyramids, built by the Moche around 300 A.D. that today are clay mountains about as high as a 10-story building and as long as a football field. Nearby is the lower platform, about 120 yards long, where *huaqeros* plundered a first tomb before they were caught. Immediately afterwards, Walter Alva and his team of archaeologists found 12 Moche tombs here, including two kings and a priest. Nearby is a small museum with photos from the 1987–89 excavations.

The pyramids are composed of *argamasa,* an adobe mixture that includes water, earth, seashells, ceramic fragments, llama dung, small stones, and *algarrobo* branches. This mixture sat for 20 days before being put in cane molds and baked in the sun. The pyramid itself was built in huge, separate blocks of bricks in order to allow shifting, and prevent cracking, during an earthquake.

It is possible to climb to the top of the largest pyramid for a good view of the surrounding fields and the village of Sipán, a community of sugarcane workers who protested Alva's excavations and continue to feel resentful that their town has received so little financial benefit from all of Sipán's riches. The town only received electricity in 2001, and there is a long-delayed proposal to install running water and sewerage. Five police and an archaeologist are stationed full-time to protect the pyramids, which have not yet been excavated, and the platform, which is 75 percent excavated, according to archaeologist Julio Chero. Buses to Sipán leave from the Terminal de Epsel at the corner of Av. Oriente and Nicolás de Pierola in Chiclayo. From there it is a short walk to the ruins, where guides can be contracted. Because of problems with the town, guided three-hour tours from Chiclayo seem the better option. If taking public transport, start early in the day, as there are no places to stay in Sipán.

ZAÑA

Connected to Sipán by dirt road, Zaña was an opulent town during the viceroyalty that might have been the capital of Peru if not for English pirate Edward Davis, who sacked the city in 1686. Many believed the subsequent decline of Zaña was due to the libertine ways of its inhabitants, earning it the moniker of *la ciudad malita* (the naughty city). That suspicion was confirmed in 1720 when an El Niño flood, of biblical proportions, destroyed what remained of the city and forced the citizens to move to Lambayeque. Today what is left is a fascinating ghost town of archways and columns. Most local tours include Zaña, which is 47 km from Chiclayo. Buses also go there from Terminal de Epsel at the corner of Av. Oriente and Nicolás de Pierola in Chiclayo.

MONSEFÚ AND SANTA ROSA

Woven straw goods and embroidered cotton cloth are made by hand and sold in a daily market at Monsefú, 8 km from Chiclayo. Another 5 km toward the coast is Santa Rosa, a fishing village of brightly painted boats where fishermen return from the sea late in the morning to mend their nets in the afternoon. Although though not as beautiful as the beaches further north of Piura, this is the best of several beaches around Chiclayo and a good place to relax and have a leisurely *cebiche* lunch. This circuit could be done with a tour agency, hired private car ($30 per day), or via *combis* leaving Terminal de Epsel at the corner of Av. Oriente and Nicolás de Pierola in Chiclayo.

TÚCUME

Túcume, the final capital of the Sicán culture, is 35 km along the the old Panamericana from Chiclayo. Archaeologists believe that Túcume was built after the Sicán burnt and abandoned their former capital of Batán Grande around 1050 A.D. The most stunning thing about Túcume is the landscape, which can be best seen from a lookout on Cerro Purgatorio: A huge desert mountain, Cerro Purgatorio, rises in the midst of 26 eroded adobe pyramids scattered throughout 200 hectares of surrounding *bosque seco*. There is a powerful energy to the place, especially at dawn and dusk, which is probably why the Sicán chose it in the first place and why many shamanic rituals continue here today (notice all the makeshift hearths for ceremonies).

Like Bátan Grande, there is not much here in the way of murals or reliefs, though many have been found here. The last major excavation was undertaken here between 1989 and 1994 by the Norwegian adventurer **Thor Heyerdahl,** who spent much of his life in this area. What excavations continue are closed to the public. Walking around these huge pyramids can make for interesting viewing—the Huaca Larga is an astonishing 700 meters long, 270 meters wide, and 30 meters tall. The area is commonly referred to as the **Valle de las Pirámides,** which is easy to understand from the lookout on Cerro Purgatorio, which offers a view over the entire complex.

Archaeologists believe the pyramids, like the Huacas de la Luna y Sol outside Trujillo, are superimposed structures built in phases. These pyramids were probably inhabited by priests and rulers even after waves of conquest (and new construction) by the Chimú in 1375 and the Incas in 1470. Atop Huaca Larga, for instance, archaeologists have uncovered a Chimú **Temple of the Mythical Bird** from around 1375 with an even newer Inca tomb, built of stone from Cerro Purgatorio, on top. The heavily adorned, and scarred, body inside the tomb was apparently a warrior who was buried with two other men and 19 women between the ages of 10 and 30. There is a small **site museum** (9 A.M.–4:30 P.M., tel. 074/80-0052, $2) that is uninteresting except for a series of

At Túcume, 26 eroded pyramids sprawl throughout the desert.

outlandish, wall-sized cartoons that which trace Western history, somehow combining the medieval Crusades and the Gutenberg press with the winged disappearance of Naymlap. For those who want to linger and soak in the place—or use it as a base for visiting Chiclayo's surrounding ruins—there is an excellent hotel neaby, Los Horcones.

To get local transport to Túcume, you have to get to Lambayeque first by taking a *combi* at Vicente de la Vega and Leonardo Ortiz, in front of the Otursa bus terminal in Chiclayo. Frequent *combis* run to Túcume from in front of Lambayeque's market, two and a half blocks from Museo Tumbas Reales. From the town of Túcume, it is another 3.5 km to the ruins, either a 15-minute walk or a $0.75 *motocar* ride.

ENTERTAINMENT AND EVENTS
Nightlife
For an early-evening beer, go to **Restaurant Chopperia Le Boulevard** (627 Colon, intersection with María Izaga, open until 1 A.M.), a friendly little pub on a back street. The most popular pub, however, is **Premium** (Balta 323, intersection with Tacna, 074-228850, 9 P.M.–5 A.M.). The two best

discos in town are **Dreams** (Luis Gonzales and Torres Paz, tel. 074/2303030, $4) and **Music World** (Grau and Dallorso, $3). These places tend to start filling up at 1 A.M. and do not empty until 4 A.M. Places to see movies include **Cine Primavera,** at Luis Gonzales and Pedro Luis, and **Cine Tropical** on the Plaza de Armas.

Festivals
Monsefú, a town known for embroidered cotton and woven straw goods, is also famous for the procession of **El Señor Cautivo de Monsefú.** According to legend, this effigy of Christ floated ashore one day and is chained inside the church because it has escaped before to perform miracles in other towns. The festival includes fireworks, dances, and music throughout the month of September, with the biggest day being Sept. 14. Other important festivals include the **Purísima Concepción** in Túcume in February and the **Señor de la Justicia** in Ferreñae in April.

ACCOMMODATIONS
Chiclayo's lack of colonial history has resulted in a glut of modern, concrete hotels that are efficient

and utterly drab. Notable exceptions include Hostal Royal on the Plaza de Armas and Los Horcones in Túcume, 33 km outside of Chiclayo.

Under $10

⚜ The **Hostal Royal** (San José 787, tel. 074/23-3421, $7 s, $10 d) is one of the few colonial buildings in town, plus it's right on the Parque Principal. Rumor has it that the building's historic status has prevented the owners from restoring it. The result is big, unadorned rooms with original wood floors, high colonial ceilings, and private baths with sporadic hot water. Choose from big rooms with spectacular views of the cathedral and avoid the more dingy rooms in the back. Very friendly staff.

$10–25

Hostal Sol Radiante (Izaga 392, tel. 074/23-7858, hsolradiante@terra.com.pe, $7 s, $12 d) is a superb value with big, clean, bright rooms with wood floors and cable TV—avoid noisy rooms near the street. Located near the cathedral and market, **Hotel Paraiso** (Pedro Ruiz 1064, tel. 074/22-8161, hotelparaiso@terra.com.pe, $12 s, $15 d) is a cozy place with all the modern conveniences. Comfortable rooms have private baths and cable TV. There is a tiny workout room and a 24-hour restaurant that offers room service and an excellent $1.50 lunch menu. The neighborhood is a bit noisy, so get a room away from street.

The 90-year-old, renovated **Hotel Europa** (Aguirre 466, tel. 074/23-7919, hoteleuropachiclayo@terra.com, lapaginaweb.de/hoteleuropachiclayo, $10 s, $13 d) boasts that it's the oldest hotel in Chiclayo. Clean, basic rooms have private bath, phones, and cable TV. Located two blocks from Parque Principal.

For a new hotel on a quiet side street, try **Eras Hotel** (Vincent de la Vega 851, tel. 074/23-6333, negoturh@terra.com.pe, www.erashotel.cjb.net, $16 s, $20 d, including breakfast). Clean rooms painted in light colors have cable TV and phones. The hotel has laundry service and a restaurant.

The only hotel in Lambayeque, right across the street from Museo Bruning, is **Hotel Real Sipán** (Huamachuco 664, tel. 074/28-3967, alvitezcompaq@peru.com, $11 s, $14 d). This concrete hotel opened in 2002 with a septic aqua-green interior and thick window plates looking onto a quiet street. Rooms are clean, with TV.

$25–50

If you are mostly interested in the Lords of Sipán, and are interested in the energy that certain natural places have, we urge you to stay at the beautiful **⚜** **Los Horcones de Túcume** (Lima reservations only, tel. 01/477-4534, jbrc@terra.com.pe, www.infoperu.org/loshorconesdetucume/, $15 s, $30 d). This hotel is in the backyard of the 26 massive pyramids of Túcume, which are 33 km from Chiclayo and 22 km from the Lambayeque and the Museo Tumbas Reales. Six airy rooms, made of adobe with *algarrobo* beams, open up to covered terraces with views od the surrounding fields. Bamboo trellises drip with purple ponciana flowers that shade outdoor spaces from the hot sun. This whole place, built by its architect-owner, has a pleasant harmony that appeals to people from around the world who come here to be close to Túcume and enjoy starry nights free of light pollution. Los Horcones has horseback riding and a nice, affordable restaurant with vegetarian food, meat cooked in a *pachamanca* pit, and pizzas.

Close to Chiclayo's main square, **Inca Hotel** (Gonzales 622, tel. 074/23-5931, incahotel@cpi.udep.edu.pe, $30 s, $40 d, including continental breakfast) is a comfortable though not very exciting modern hotel with clean rooms, refrigerators, phones, and cable TV. There is a restaurant and casino.

In front of the Paseo Las Musas, and six blocks from the Parque Principal, is the comfortable **Las Musas Hotel & Casino** (Los Faiques 101 Urb. Santa Victoria, tel. 074/23-9884, lasmusas@terra.com.pe, www.lasmusashotel.com, $37 s, $50 d, including breakfast). Rooms have refrigerators, cable TV, and telephones. The upscale hotel offers laundry service, Internet, and a restaurant serving Peruvian and Lebanese cuisine.

$50–100

⚜ **Costa del Sol** (Balta 399, tel. 074/22-7272, ventaschiclayo1@costadelsolperu.com, www.costadelsolperu.com, $55 s, $65 d) is a more intimate version of the other hotels in this price category.

Rooms are curiously decorated in a Valentine's Day color scheme, but have refrigerators, phones, cable TV, and big bathrooms. This well-equipped hotel has a nice rooftop pool, Jacuzzi, dry sauna, a small gym, and Internet. There is a cozy restaurant and bar on the second floor.

Garza Hotel (Bolognesi 756, tel. 074/23-8968, garzahot@chiclayo.net, chiclayo.net/garza-hotel, $49 s, $69 d) is your standard corporate high-rise hotel on a busy street, four blocks from the Parque Principal. The rooms are comfortable, however unexciting, with refrigerators, telephones, and cable TV. The value is in the offerings—excellent service, a pool and gym, a restaurant with room service, bar, casino, and Internet in the lobby.

Chiclayo's largest and most luxurious hotel is **Gran Hotel Chiclayo** (Villarreal 115, tel. 074/23-4911, reservas@granhotelchiclayo.com.pe, www.granhotelchiclayo.com.pe, $ 66 s, $80 d) a concrete building several blocks from downtown. Large rooms have baths, cable TV, and telephones. There is an excellent, expensive restaurant offering room service; a café serving capuccinos, pizzas, pastas, and salads; a lively casino; and a pool. Prices include a welcome pisco sour, an excellent breakfast buffet, a newspaper each morning, Internet, and transportation. Service is top-notch.

FOOD

You won't find many upscale restaurants teeming with character in Chiclayo, but rather excellent food in nondescript establishments that have been around for years. Typical dishes of Chiclayo include *seco de cabrito* (casserole of tender kid marinated in *chicha de jora* and vinegar) and *arroz con pato a la chiclayana* (tender duck meat cooked in dark beer, mint, and cilantro). Chiclayo also has excellent *cebiche*.

Local Favorites

Parrillada Hebrón (Balta 605, tel. 074/22-2709, 7:30 A.M.–midnight, delivery available, $2–5) and **El Rancho** (Balta 1115, tel. 074/27-3687, 7:30 A.M.–12:30 A.M., delivery available, $2–5) are two sister restaurants with excellent, inexpensive food and good service. Both serve *pollos*

a la brasas (spit-roasted chicken) and have extensive *criollo* and à la carte menus. Hebrón has a big playground for kids upstairs.

For generous portions of basic *criolla* fare, try **Las Américas** (Elias Aguirre 824, tel. 074/23-7294, 7 A.M.–11 P.M., $3), right on the Parque Principal. Classic dishes include *arroz con pato, seco de cabrito,* and *chicharrón de pollo en salsa verde* (chicken nuggets in a green sauce). An excellent place used by locals on a daily basis for fixed menus and *pollo a la brasa* is the lively **El Boom** (San José 677, tel. 074/27-0549, 7 A.M.–10 P.M., menú $1). Sit upstairs for a quieter meal.

Meat lovers should head to **M Restaurant La Parra** (Maria Izaga 752, tel. 076/22-7471, 5 P.M.–1 A.M., $3–7, menú $2). The open grill serves up huge portions of top-quality grilled meats, roasted chicken, and *cebiches* in a relaxed atmosphere. The *brochetes de lomo* (beef skewers) served with fries and salad is an excellent choice. Come also for pitchers of sangria. Next door is a *chifa* restaurant with the same owner.

Pizza

If you need a break from *criolla* cuisine, grab some pizza at either **Chez Maggy** (Balta 413, tel. 074/20-9453, evenings only) or **Pizzeria Venecia** (Balta 365).

Chifa

The best chifa in town is **Chifa China** (Bolognesi 773, tel. 074/20-4201, 12:30–3 P.M. and 6:30–11:30 P.M., $6). But try **Chifa La Parra** (Izaga 752, 5 P.M.–1 A.M.) if you're cruising for chicken.

Cebiche

Lunch at **Jhon** (Colon 282, 10 A.M.–5 P.M., $4) will bring you huge portions of *cebiche,* but we found the fish to be rather salty. We recommend trying one of the other *cebicherias* along this same 200 block of Colon, which are typically open 11 A.M.–4 P.M.; try **El Puerteño, El Púlpito,** or the old-timey **Chechar** on the corner of Bolognesi and Colon.

Health Food

Vegetarians will be happy to find **Govinda** (Balta 1029, tel. 074/22-7331, 8 A.M.–9:30 P.M., $1–2).

This Hare Krishna café serves bean soup, potato dishes, spinach lasagna, and salads. A variety of herbal remedies are also sold here. **Ben Hur** (Vicente de la Vega 159, tel. 074/27-2152, 8 A.M.–10 P.M., $1, delivery available) is highly recommended for natural yogurt, fruit, and fresh juices, near a peaceful, quiet park. Another good yogurt shop can be found at San José 577.

Cafés and Desserts

Stop into the busy **Romana** (Balta 512, tel. 074/22-3598, 7 A.M.–1 A.M., $2), a big café popular with locals, for fresh juices, sandwiches, and local dishes. Around the corner is **Roma** (Maria Izaga 710, tel. 074/20-4556, 7 A.M.–noon, $2), a café that has been serving breakfast, hamburgers, sandwiches, and milkshakes here since 1944.

Chiclayo has its share of ice cream shops, including **Grayce** (Elias Aguirre 600, tel. 074/23-3118), **Don Benny** (Balta 465, tel. 074/46-5499), and **Heladeria Africa** (San José 473). Venture out and try some local fruit flavors like lúcuma or guanábana.

Fine Dining

The two restaurants with the best gourmet reps in town are oddly devoid of charm: **Restaurant Tipico La Fiesta** (Salaverry 1820, tel. 074/20-1970, 9:30 A.M.–11 P.M. daily, $8–13), 2 km west of the Gran Hotel Chiclayo, and **Restaurant El Hauralino** (La Libertad 155, Urb. Santa Victoria, tel. 074/27-0330, $10) have wide-ranging menus with excellent food that include the standard meat, poultry, and seafood options along with *langosta* (lobster).

Finally a Chiclayo restaurant with charm! **M Pueblo Viejo** (Maria Izaga 900, tel. 074/22-9863, noon–5 P.M. daily) serves a creative *criolla* lunch menu in an elegantly rustic atmosphere. Sit upstairs under colored skylights and among plants and wooden walkways. Fish and shellfish dishes are especially good here.

Markets

The **Mercado Modelo** (961 Balta) is a huge and friendly produce market. The best supermarket is **El Super** on Gonzáles 883, or try **El Centro** at Elias Aguirre and Gonzáles. A smaller market good for ice cream and snacks is **Don Benny** at Balta 465.

INFORMATION AND SERVICES

The regional **tourism office** is located at Sáenz Peña 838 (tel. 074/23-3132), and there are tourism booths outside the Hebrón Restaurants and at Balta and Izaga, Balta and Prado, and San José and Colón on the Parque Principal.

The **Tourism Police** (Saenz Peña 830, tel. 074/23-6700, ext. 311) is open 24 hours a day.

The two recommended clinics for travelers are **Clínica Chiclayo** (La Florida 225, urb. Santa Victoria, tel. 074/20-9095) and **Clínica del Pacífico** (Ortiz 420, tel. 074/23-3705). The main hospital is **Hospital Las Mercedes** (González 635, tel. 074/237-021).

Many **bookstores** are clustered around the intersection of Alfredo La Point and San José, but they stock few books in English.

Most **banks, ATMs,** and **exchange** places are clustered near Balta and Elias Aguirre on the Parque Principal. If you're cashing travelers checks, rates vary, so shop around.

The **Chiclayo Post Office** (Elias Aguirre 140, tel. 074/23-7031, 8 A.M.–8 P.M. Mon.–Sat., 8 A.M.–1 P.M. Sunday) is about 6 blocks from the Parque Principal at the intersection with Grau. Internet is widely available around town. Recommended places are **Aronet** (San José 545, tel. 074/20-9651, 24 hours), **Cybercafé** (San Jose 604), **@eronet** (Izaga 651, tel. 074/20-4473) for fast connections, scanners, and international calling, and **Cibert Café Internet** (Izaga 716, tel. 074/22-8729) for fast connections and cheap international calls.

GETTING THERE

Flights arrive at **Aeropuerto José Abelardo Quiñones Gonzales** (Bolognesi s/n, tel. 074/23-3192), which is 2 km east of downtown. Taxis should not cost more than $3.

Buses pour into Chiclayo from all directions, though many only travel at night. Bus terminals are spread out along Bolognesi, five blocks or more from the main park. For traveling to and from

Lima, we recommend **Ormeño** (Victor Raul Haya de la Torre 250, tel. 074/23-4206), **Cruz del Sur** (Bolognesi 888, tel. 074/22-5508), and **Linea** (tel. 074/24-5181). Linea also has comfortable buses every hour to and from Trujillo for $3. Movil Tours (Bolognesi 195, tel. 074/72-2555) has two buses a day to and from Chachapoyas ($9, 10 hours) or Tarapoto ($11, 13 hours).

GETTING AROUND

Chiclayo is a nice city to walk around in, but if you're in a hurry, taxis cost $0.75 for anywhere around town. Even longer trips, as far afield as Túcume, can be negotiated for surprisingly cheap. A good option for seeing Chiclayo's far-flung sights is to rent a car for about $40 a day at Chiclayo Rent a Car (lobby of Gran Hotel Chiclayo, Villareal 115, tel. 074/23-7512). A recommended, honest taxi driver is Polo Custodio Moreno (Pedro Ruiz 1058, Dpt. 10, tel. 074/49-6842).

Guided tours are a good option for getting to Chiclayo's far-flung sites and having them explained by an informed guide. The best operator in Peru's north is **InkaNatura Travel,** which has a Chiclayo office in the lobby of the Gran Hotel (Federico Villareal 115, tel. 074/20-9948, pvargas@inkanatura.com.pe, www.inkanatura.com). InkaNatura runs a range of cultural tours in the area that link with Trujillo and Chachapoyas. InkaNatura can be contacted through its main Lima office (Manuel Bañon 461, San Isidro, tel. 01/440-2022, postmaster@inkanatura.com.pe, www.inkanatura.com) or through its U.S. agent, **Tropical Nature** (www.tropicalnature.org).

Other recommended local agencies include **Tumi Tours** (Elias Aguirre 532, tel. 074/22-5371, tumitours@terra.com.pe); **Turismo Ideal** (Balta 901, tel. 074/27-2656); and **Indiana Tours** (Colón 556, tel. 074/22-2991, indianatours@terr.com.pe). Good local guides include **Juan Manuel Acuña** (tel. 074/215481), who speaks English, and Ana María Paz (tel. 074/20-3446), who speaks Spanish only.

Piura and the Northern Beaches

There is a secret about Peru that is jealously guarded by surfers around the world: Peru has fabulous beaches, especially in the north, where the frigid Humboldt Current veers off into the Pacific and leaves behind a subtropical coastline bathed in balmy waters. If you're imaging the clear waters of the Caribbean, or the rainforests of Costa Rica, you've got the wrong idea. Picture instead desert hills that ease into a winding, varied coastline of white sand and a smattering of palm trees. There are plenty of half-moon bays, and other beaches where odd volcanic formations break up the surf. These are perfectly safe for swimming: no currents and no sharks. But there are also thundering point breaks and some of the best lefts in the world for surfers, who flock here when the surf is highest between January to March.

There is a lot of new development here, but the result, so far at least, is a pleasingly eclectic blend of mom-and-pop options—especially in the 25-km stretch of spectacular coastline that includes the beaches of Órganos, Vichayito, Máncora,

and Punta Sal. You can find excellent value for food and lodging, ranging from $5 surfer bungalows to exquisite B&Bs for honeymooners. Unless you love huge parties, do not dream of coming here during the major Peruvian holidays (New Year, Easter week, July 28 Independence Day weekend), when rates triple and beaches overfill with *Limeños.* If you value empty beaches and deep discounts on lodging, try the off-season between April and mid-December (whales pass here on their way to southern Chile in October). The sun still shines, even through the occasional overcast day, and the temperatures are plenty hot (80–90°F, or 27–32°C). For surfers, there is always a wave at Máncora, which ranges from gentle beginner waves to six-footers when the swell is up.

The two gateways for the northern beaches are Piura and Tumbes, from where the Spanish launched their conquest of Peru. Piura's main attractions are the market town of Catacaos; the remote *brujería* (witchcraft) center of

Fishermen along Peru's coast still rely mostly upon sail power to reach their fishing grounds.

Huancabamba (a two-day journey into the mountains); and the nearby beach resort of Colán. Tumbes has spectacular nature reserves of mangrove swamps and coastal tropical jungle. Between the two, Piura is probably more interesting and certainly more relaxing than Tumbes. Those whose only interest is the beach can arrive in these cities and easily get on the beach the same day with an early start. Up-to-date information on all the north's best beaches is available at www.vivamancora.com.

Piura was magically described in *Casa Verde,* Mario Vargas Llosa's masterful novel that divides this city into two main *barrios:* the Mangachería, a sprawling den of iniquity to the north of the city known for beautiful women, gambling, and the novel's namesake brothel. And the Gallinacera, south of present-day Sánchez Cerro Street, the respectable, urbane side of the city known for singers, *guitaristas,* and players of the *cajón.* That boundary remains today: the further south you walk toward Piura's laid-back and pleasant Plaza de Armas, the gentler Piura becomes. Narrow colonial streets and old, unrenovated homes

conjure up what life was like in the 19th century when this town's population was only 5,000. Outside the city is Catacaos, one of Peru's major arts and crafts markets, and the pleasant beach of Colán. Among Peruvians, Piura is famous as a center for *brujería,* or witchcraft. The heart and soul of this tradition is centered around a series of lakes up in the mountains near Huancabamba, a seven-hour journey from Piura.

SIGHTS

Piura's cathedral dates to 1588, the year the city was relocated to this spot on the Río Piura. It had been a long, rocky ride for Piurans thanks to the vagaries of pirate attacks and torrential flooding, which had made life until then all but impossible. The first city, named San Miguel de Piura, was founded by Francisco Pizarro in 1532 before the conquest of the Incas. But that site, on the Río Chira near the present-day site of Sullana, was so hot and disease-ridden that the settlers had to move. But the second place did not work either, so they shifted to Paita, which remains

AN EL NIÑO WARNING

El Niño rains and floods along Peru's coast have been severe enough to spark the downfall of the Moche and Sicán empires, archaeologists say. But the El Niño cycles have become even more intense over the last half century, according to a recent United Nations report, because of global warming.

The warm, equatorial current is named after *El Niño Jesús*, or baby Jesus, because it arrives on the coast of Ecuador and Peru every year around Christmas. Some years, however, it extends far into the south Pacific and disrupts the Humboldt Current. The warm waters prevents the upwelling of deep, nutrient-rich waters, which causes anchovies to go elsewhere and ruins what is usually a world-class fishery. Winds across South America generally blow west to Asia, but during El Niño years they reverse and blow towards the continent, pushing up sea levels and sending huge systems of humid air toward Peru's desert coast.

The worse El Niño of the century was 1983, when torrential rains began in Peru's north on January 4th and did not stop until the middle of July—the flooding alone destroyed 36 bridges and 1,685 kilometers of roads. Nine years later, in 1992, there was a similar El Niño. But both of these were dwarfed by the El Niño of 1998, which destroyed as much as 90 percent of the banana, rice and cotton crops grown along Peru's north coast. The floods killed several people in Piura when a bridge was swept away and created a huge, temporary lake in the middle of the Sechura desert between Chiclayo and Piura. The lake, known as *Lago La Niña*, forms after most El Niño years but had never been this big-300 km, stretching as far as the eye could see. While it lasted, fisherman even began working on the lake and charter boats offered tourist excursion.

Travel becomes difficult and dangerous, or even impossible, during El Niño years. In early 1998, the 20-hour trip from Lima to the Ecuadorian border took over four days. Buses would drive until a washed-out bridge, where passengers would then wade through water, slog through mud or board a boat toward buses waiting on the other side. Many people were became trapped for days on end, waiting for waters in both the south and north to subside before continuing their journey.

today a pleasant, breezy fishing port. But in 1577—a decade before the English Navy delivered a body blow to the Spanish Empire by wiping out its Armada—an English pirate by the name of Sir Thomas Cavendish pillaged and burned the city, including the convent of La Merced. That was the last straw for Piurans, who packed up their things and headed inland to the city's present-day location. Piura is safe, but being so far inland it is also hot, in fact the hottest of Peru's coastal cities, and assuaged only occasionally by evening breezes. Though the pirates never returned, Piura has been hit hard by El Niño floods, most recently in 1983, 1992, and 1998.

Inside the **cathedral** (7 A.M.–noon and 4–7 P.M. daily, free) is a gold-covered altar and paintings by **Ignacio Merino** (1817–76), one of Peru's leading painters who was born in Piura but spent most of his life in France. Inside there is also an image of baby Jesus, often surrounded by teddy bears, which is known as the Jesús de Praga and is much loved by Piurans. The image is a copy of a Jesus figure made in the Andalucia province of Spain by a Carmelite nun who prayed every night to see baby Jesus' face and then be allowed to die. During her dreams one night her wish was fulfilled, and she awoke to make this beautiful image, dying shortly thereafter. The image then made its way to Czechoslovakia, with a princess who married the Prince of Prague, and became world-famous for the miracles it produced. This rendition is now one of the more venerated of the cathedral's images.

The relaxing **Plaza de Armas** is ringed with tamarind trees and presided over by a marble liberty statue given to the city by then-president José

THE WAR OF THE PACIFIC

With his British-built destroyer *Huascar*, Peruvian admiral Miguel Grau managed to elude a larger, and more modern, Chilean fleet during the War of the Pacific (1879–80). He repeatedly broke the Chilean blockade, disrupted the enemy's communications, and even managed to bombard the Chilean city of Antofagasta. In the battle of Iquique, on March 21, 1879, Grau sunk the Chilean destroyer *Esmeralda* and killed Chile's top naval officers, Arturo Prat. In a show of magnanimity—not returned by Chileans when they later sacked and burned most of the country—Grau picked the surviving sailors out of the water and returned them to a Chilean beach. He even sent the objects he found alongside Prat's body, along with a consolatory letter he penned, to Prat's widow. Grau's end came in October of that same year when the entire Chilean fleet chased the *Huascar* down, exploding its control tower and killing Grau instantly. That battle marked a critical turning point in the war, allowing Chile to invade Peru and seize the port of Arica and nearby valuable nitrate fields.

Balta in 1870. A half block away is the home of **Admiral Miguel Grau** (Tacna 662, erratic daytime hours, free), Peru's foremast naval hero. Grau's brilliant military maneuverings during Peru's disastrous War of the Pacific (1879–80) continues to be a source of consolation for Peruvians.

Follow Tacna past the cathedral on your right before coming to Grau, the city's main commercial street. Further north along Tacna—and the parallel streets of Arequipa, Libertad, and Lima—there are narrow streets with colonial buildings made of cane and adobe and fringed with fine woodworking. These are some of Peru's most untouched colonial neighborhoods. Where Tacna hits Sánchez Cerro, you will find the 18th-century **Iglesia del Carmen,** which now houses a religious museum (8 A.M.–noon daily, $0.75). It has a golden baroque altar and some painting in the style of the Cusco School, but its pulpit was robbed of its carvings of angels and the four evangelists. Crimes like this caused church leaders to close down the Benedictine convent that had been here up until the 1980s.

Now the National Institute of Culture operates the building as a museum.

Other lesser sites in Piura include **Iglesia San Francisco,** near Lima and Ica, where Piurans announced their independence from Spain in 1821; and the **Museo Municipal** (Huánuco and Sullana, 8 A.M.–1 P.M. and 5–7 P.M. Mon.–Sat., $1), with a variety of ceramics and gold objects from the Vicus culture, which thrived around the time of Jesus Christ and was centered at Cerro Vicus, 27 km east of Piura. Objects found there, and on display at the museum, include a gold feline head with sharp teeth and extended tongue.

ENTERTAINMENT AND EVENTS

Piura is a peaceful town where nightlife is often nothing more than a stroll through the plaza with an ice cream. But if you're hell-bent on finding some action, try block 5 of Ayacucho, where you'll find **Bloom Moon** and **Alex Chopp,** a popular nightspot with good beers and seafood. There is also the friendly **Iguana Pub** (324 Loreto), and the best discos are **JJ** (Arequipa 654, near Ica, 8 P.M.–4 A.M. Mon.–Sat.), and **JL** (Óvalo Grau, same hours). **Cine Municipal** shows movies daily at Arequipa and Sánchez Cerro for $1. **Cine Manuel Vegas Castillo,** a more modern theater north of the city, shows current films for $1.

The **Easter week** celebration of Catacaos is famous around Peru—especially its Palm Sunday procession, a recreation of Jesus' entry into Jerusalem that features a locally famous white *burro.* One of North Peru's most sacred shrines is that of *El Señor Cautivo* in the small mountain town of Ayabaca, where pilgrims from Ecuador and Peru converge Oct. 12–13. During the first week of October there is a festival of *tondero,* a livelier version of the *marinera,* at the Club Grau in Piura.

ACCOMMODATIONS

The choices for accommodations in Piura range from basic to luxury with not a lot to recommend in between. So we suggest you either go big or tuck your money away for another time.

Under $10

Hostal California (Junin 835, tel. 073/32-8789, $5 s, $8 d) is a popular choice with backpackers who don't mind a fusion of floral bedspreads and tablecloths topped off with hanging plastic flowers. It's safe and clean and has a nice, sunny feel. If this is full, spend a few more dollars for the Hostal San Jorge—the dozen other backpacker options we surveyed in Piura, including the oft-recommended Hostal Oriental at Callao 446, tend to be loud, with dirty bathrooms and dirty bedsheets.

$10–25

The safe, well-managed **Hostal San Jorge** (Loreto 960, tel. 073/32-7514, $7, $10) has 33 large, unadorned rooms with private bath and cable TV available for another $1.50. But the best choice in this price range is **Hotel San Miguel** (Apurimac 1007, tel. 073/30-5122, $12 s, $15 d), in the pleasant southern end of town on the Plaza las Tres Culturas. This is one of the few inexpensive hotels in Piura on a quiet street, and it has all the modern conveniences; telephones and cable TV in rooms, laundry service, a café, and a tour agency. The **Hotel Peru** (Arequipa 476, tel. 073/33-3421, $12 s, $18 d) is a find for the price, with a nice lobby and restaurant just up the street from the Plaza de Armas. Rooms are quiet, if a bit dark, and have cable TV, telephone, and a fan

$50–100

The four-star **Río Verde Hotel** (Ranón Mujica, Urb. San Eduardo el Chipe, tel. 073/32-8486, hotel@rioverde.com.pe, www.rioverde.com.pe, $68 s, $87 d) could easily be confused for a Caribbean beach resort, with its coconut palms, shaded poolside dining areas, extensive gardens, and tasteful gift shop. Rooms include phones, cable TV, air-conditioning, and room service. Prices include a buffet breakfast. Golfing can be arranged through the hotel's connections with Piura's nearby country club. The hotel is a five-minute taxi ride from the center, but the absolutely peaceful, quiet neighborhood makes it worth the distance. This is the best luxury option in Piura.

Hotel Los Portales (Libertad 875, tel. 073/32-3072, losportales@cpi.udep.edu.pe, www.ac-ceso.peru.com/countryclub, $65 s, $85 d) is the other luxury hotel of Piura—smack-dab on the Plaza de Armas. This restored colonial home has rooms off balconies wrapped around an elegant, sun-filled courtyard. Large rooms, with impossibly high ceilings, have cool tile floors and large bathrooms and all the modern goodies: AC, fridge, cable TV, dial-out phones, and room service. There is a bar and restaurant by the pool, as well as an indoor dining room. Prices include buffet breakfast and a welcome drink upon your arrival.

FOOD

Given the dry, hot climate of Piura, many restaurants close for several hours each day during siesta (1–4 P.M.), while others are open only in the afternoons.

Cafés and Deserts

Heladeria Italia (Grau 172, 7 A.M.–noon daily) makes homemade ice cream. So does **Heladeria Venecia** (Libertad 1007, 8 P.M.–noon, $0.50), where the delightful Doña Luz give liberal samples of gelato made from local fruits, including lúcuma, maracuya, tamarindo, and guanábana. Make a dessert stop at the charming **d'Pauli** (Lima 541, 9 A.M.–1 P.M. and 4–10 P.M.). This tiny café in a colonial building serves good coffee and tempting treats such as lúcuma cheescake and apple or pecan pie. The smell of fresh bread will lead you straight to **La Predilecta** (Huancavalica and Euguigeren).

Peruvian

El Arrecife (Ica 610, tel. 073/58-4107, 8 A.M.–5 P.M. daily, $2–5) is an intimate place loved by locals for its fish, art, and great selection of Latin music. It is also a good, safe place to try the local specialty of *conchas negras*. For exquisite *criollo* food in a relaxed, intimate atmosphere, go to **Picanteria La Santitos** (Libertad 1014, tel. 073/33-2380, 10:30 A.M.–4 P.M. daily, $3–7). This quirky little restaurant has wood floors, bamboo ceilings, and seashell curtains in the doorways. Start with an *algarrobina* (a creamy-brown, sweet cocktail made from the fruit of the *algarrobo*, or carob, tree) and roasted *conchas negras* sprinkled with parmesan.

Las Tradiciones (Ayacucho 579, tel. 073/32-2683, 11 A.M.–3:30 P.M. and 6:30–10 P.M. Mon.–Sat., 11 A.M.–3:30 P.M. Sat.–Sun.) has an excellent lunch menú for only $2. Another good deal is at **Don Matias** (Junín 790, tel. 073/30-4051, 6 P.M.–1 A.M. Mon.–Sat., noon–midnight Sunday), where you can share a full spit-roasted chicken and 1.5 liter of Coke for $7. The best chifa is **Chifa Kin Tou** (Callao 828, tel. 073/30-5988, Mon.–Sat.)

Pizza and Burgers

The best pizza place is **Pizzeria la Cabaña** (Ayacucho 598). **Carburmer** (Libertad 1014, tel. 073/33-2380, 6:30 P.M.–1 A.M.), the Italian sister restaurant to Picanteria La Santitos, opens at night to offer pizzas, lasagnas, fettuccini, canneloni, and meats. A last resort is **Dominos** (Sánchez Cerro, tel. 073/34-4949). The place to go for a burger, fries, and a milkshake is the busy, bright **El Chalán** (Tacna 520, on Plaza de Armas, tel. 073/30-6483, 7:30 A.M.–10:30 P.M., $1.50–4). The burgers are huge.

Health Food

There is a cluster of health food cafés around the corner of Lima and Sánchez Cerro. **Santa Natura** and **Vita Jugos** (211 Sánchez Cerro) are small cafés with fruit salads and yogurts. The best place, however, is **Ganimedes** (Lima 440, 7 A.M.–10 P.M. Mon.–Sat., 11 A.M.–8 P.M. Sunday, $3), which serves exquisite juices, yogurt-and-fruit shakes (try lúcuma-strawberry), fruit salads, and vegetarian sandwiches. It also sells natural products: shampoos, skin creams, vitamins, olive oils, honeys, soy protein, and fresh-baked organic bread, which arrives every afternoon at 4 P.M.

Markets

Shop for specialties such as chocolate, nuts, wines, and liquors at **Cabo Blanco** (Sánchez 293). The big supermarkets in town are **Tusol** at Óvalo and Grau, and **Cossito** (Sánchez 525).

INFORMATION AND SERVICES

The best sightseeing agency in town is **Delta Reps** (Libertad 640, tel. 073/32-1784, deltareps @terra.com.pe), which offers Catacaos and city tours and has free maps.

The **Tourist Office** (Ayacucho on the Plaza de Armas, 8 A.M.–1 P.M. and 5–8 P.M.) is helpful with maps and city brochures. Other maps may be available at **Touring y Automóvil Club de Peru,** Sánchez Cerro 1237. There is no tourism police station in Piura, but in an emergency call **Piura Police** (Sánchez Cerro block 12, tel. 073/30-7641, 24 hours). Find healthcare at **Hospital Reátegui** (Gra 1150, tel. 073/33-1157, 24 hours) or **Hospital Cayetano Heredia** (Independencia and Castilla, 073-34-2648, 24 hours). There are many banks near the Plaza de Armas, including **Banco Continental,** corner of Ayacucho and Tacna, and **Banco de Crédito.** *Cambistas* cluster around Grau and Arequipa. The **post office** is at Libertad and Ayacucho (tel. 073/32-7031, 8 A.M.–4 P.M. Mon.–Sat.). A good place for Internet is at **Sánchez and Arequipa,** where you can also make international Internet calls. Take your laundry to **Lavas** (tel. 073/58-4135, Mon.–Sat.) at the corner of Cusco and Callao.

Getting There and Around

Most major carriers have daily flights into Piura's airport (tel. 073/32-7733), which is 2 km out of town. A taxi costs $2–3.

Most bus companies are located on Sánchez Cerro, blocks 11–13. The best bus lines for getting back and forth to Lima are **Oltursa** (Bolognesi 801, tel. 073/33-5303) and **Cruz del Sur** (Libertad 1176, tel. 073/33-7094). **El Dorado** (1119 Sánchez Cerro) has daily buses to Tumbes for $4.50, or you can take a faster, $6 *colectivo.* El Dorado (1119 Sánchez Cerro) has direct buses to Loja, Ecuador, an excellent option for making the crossing (see the sidebar *Hassle-Free Routes into Ecuador* in the *Cajamarca and the Northern Highlands* chapter).

Unless you are going to a bus station or one of the outlying luxury hotels, Piura's colonial center is compact and best done on foot. Local *motocars,* however, cost $0.75.

CATACAOS

The village of Catacaos, a friendly, dusty little

town 12 km southwest of Piura, is the best arts and crafts market in northern Peru. The town is famous for a variety of handicrafts sold along four blocks of the old Calle Comercio, including Panama hats, placemats, and other finely woven goods made of *toquilla* straw imported from Ecuador. Also watch for earrings and other jewelry wrought in gold and silver filigree, an art form that has flourished here since colonial times when gold was imported from the Amazon and Cajamarca. There are also painted ceramics in the shape of rotund *campesinos,* wood carvings and kitchen utensils made of *zapote* wood, colorful hammocks, wicker lampshades and baskets, and some leather goods.

As a bonus, this bustling town has some excellent restaurants, or *picanterías,* for northern cuisine: here you can find *seco de chabelo, tamalitos verdes, el majao de yucca,* and other dishes that combine local foods like plantain, chile, and cassava with beef and pork. The market is biggest on the weekends, and stalls are set up around 10 A.M. and taken down as late as 7 P.M.

The town was first inhabited by the Tallan culture, which was eventually conquered by the Moche and later Chimú empires. The Tallan built some early pyramids at Narihualá, about 5 km south of Catacaos. To reach Catacaos, hire a taxi for $4 or take a $0.30 *colectivo* at terminals on the third block of Sánchez Cerro or the intersection of Román Castilla and Tacna.

COLÁN

At 65 km from Piura, this is the favorite local beach destination, a pleasant stretch of white sand with gentle waves perfect for swimming. The beach is fringed with stilted beach homes built during the 1950s, classic old wooden structures with long balconies facing west. There are few services (Internet, restaurants, etc.) outside of several resorts, which are all but dead in the off-season from late March to early December. The beach is presided over by **Iglesia San Lucás de Colán,** the first church the Spanish built in Peru, near the small town of Esmeralda. This magnificent and unique stone church, recently restored to its original thatch-and-mud roof, has ancient

wood columns and, with typical Spanish shrewdness, is built atop a Chimú *huaca*—inside you will find the coats of arms for the royal Spanish Hapsburg line.

Another 10 km south along the coast is the picturesque fishing town of Paita, founded in the 16th century by the Spanish and the place where Manuela Saenz, Simón Bolívar's mistress, spent her final days ostracized from Lima society. This area's clear, starry skies at night and pastel clouds at sunset have given rise to the oft-repeated Peruvian saying: *Nada como la luna de Paita y el sol de Colán* (There is nothing like the moon of Paita and the sun of Colán).

The **Colan Lodge** (tel. 073/32-6778, piura-tours@mail.udep.edu.pe, www.pagina.de/colan-lodge, $55 d, $75 for five-person bungalow) has seven wooden bungalows (painted an odd choice of pink and blue) strung out along the best section of beach in Colan. The deep, sandy beach offers shaded hammocks, volleyball, and dining tables covered with individual thatched roofs. The main lodge feels like the mess hall at summer camp, except it has a well-stocked bar and serves great food. There's also an oceanside pool and tennis court. A good, cheaper option is **Sol de Colan** (tel. 073/32-1784, deltareps@terra.com.pe, www.elsoldecolan.piuranet.com, $20 d, $50 for six-person bungalow). Nine brick bungalows and six rooms run back from the water along a stone walkway. Each tile-floored bungalow has a kitchen, separate sitting room, and covered terrace. The poolside restaurant serves excellent fish. Ocean water comes right up to the hotel, so no sandy beach here. Transportes Dora, third block of Sánchez Cerro in Piura, has frequent $0.75 taxis to Paita, where you can take another $0.50 *combi* further north to Colán. If these are full, try the other two resorts: **Hotel Playa Colán** (south beach near Las Palmeras, tel. 073/64-1449) or **Bocatoma Resort** (north beach, Av. Costanera s/n, tel. 073/97-0100).

HUANCABAMBA

A truly adventurous journey that requires a minimum of four days and a lot of stamina leads to Huancabamba, a picturesque mountain town that is the center of *brujería* (witchcraft and healing) for Peru's coast. The powers of the area's *brujos* (shamans) and *curanderos* (healers) are legendary and attract Peruvians from all over the country. *Brujería* is part of an ancient spiritual tradition in Peru that mixes natural medicine with spiritual beliefs and plays a major role in a country that lacks even basic medical services. People come here for a variety of problems, such as infertility or psychological ailments that *curanderos* call *susto* (fear), which resembles depression or post–traumatic stress syndrome in that patients suffer from loss of appetite and insomnia. But probably the single largest group of seekers come for affairs of the heart: jilted lovers place hexes on a competing suitor or bring a piece of clothing to lure back a departed lover. Others come to have a hex removed or because they want to see into the future and know how a difficult situation will be resolved.

The center of all this work is **Huaringas,** a collection of 14 lakes over 3,900 meters (13,000 feet) where healing ceremonies, or *mesas,* typically include dunkings in the icy-cold water along with herbs and hallucinogenic substances such as the San Pedro cactus. The most famous of these lakes is Shimbe, which can be reached after a daylong mule ride, but there are closer lakes as well. The trip from Piura is a 215-km, five- to seven-hour bus ride that passes through the scenic town of Chanchaque and a bumpy mountain pass before arriving at Huancabamba, around 1,950 meters (6,500 feet), where there are several hostels and cheap restaurants. ETIPSA (first block of Av. Guardia Civil, near Primavera bridge) has buses leaving daily at 7 A.M. and 3:30 P.M. Once in Huancabamba, the lakes are another few hours by *combi,* and most people make the final trek upwards on foot or on mule.

Huancabamba was inhabited by people who maintained a jaguar cult until Inca Túpac Yupanqui conquered the area around 1480. Then it became a crossroads for the royal Inca highway and later, after the first conquistadores marched through it, an important Spanish colonial center. It is known as *Resbalabamba* or "the city that walks," because a stratified, water-soaked foundation is causing the town to slide inexorably downhill. There are excellent mountain bike circuits and walks to Inca ruins in the area, and guides are available in town.

A word of caution on Huaringas: If you come for healing, get a referral ahead of time from a recommended source. There is real energy to this place, and its people, and it can be used either for

fishermen-to-be on beach at Cabo Blanco

THE TRUTH BEHIND HEMINGWAY'S CABO BLANCO

The rocky, dusty coastline around Cabo Blanco was rarely visited until the 1940s, when the English-owned International Petroleum Corp., IPC, established itself in Talara and started setting up oil wells along the coast. That was the beginning of Peru's oil industry, which spread from here into the Amazon.

As far as Cabo Blanco is concerned, the story begins to get interesting around in 1945 when foreign oil executives founded the Cabo Blanco Fishing Club, a simple building with a pool and a dozen rooms built atop a spectacular, and remote, white sand beach at Cabo Blanco. The club was not built to take advantage of the beach, however, but rather the world's richest marlin fishing ground, which lies off the coast here.

The size of the marlin caught here quickly attracted worldwide attention, beginning with a 465-kilo (1,025-pound) black marlin caught by oil executive Alfred Glassell Jr. in 1952—Glassell still holds the world record for a 709-kilo (1,560-pound) marlin he caught here. Over the next two decades, American companies took over IPC, and sport fishermen from around the world flocked to the humble digs of the Fishing Club. Among these were a range of luminaries and movie stars who arrived in Talara via direct flights from the United States. The list includes Ernest Hemingway, Bob Hope, Nelson Rockefeller, and Prince Philip of Edinburgh.

But the golden age of what became known as *Marlin Boulevard* ended in 1968 when the military government of Juan Velasco expropriated the oil wells. The hotel shut down soon after and is now a

spectacularly sordid and peeling building that serves as home to a few hard-drinking local workers, along with a collection of chickens and dead seagulls. The beach in front of the Fishing Club would still be spectacular were it not crisscrossed by pipes from nearby oil wells.

The stories from the Fishing Club are nonetheless still spectacular and fondly recounted by Pablo Córdoba, who owns Restaurant Cabo Blanco in town. John Wayne came here and met a woman from Paita whom he married and lived with until the end of his life. Many believe that Ernest Hemingway was inspired to write his *Old Man and the Sea* here, but the truth is he got the idea in Cuba. (He did, however, spend 45 days here in 1956, drinking whisky and pisco sours, as he and director John Sturges filmed the movie with the same name.)

The best-known story perhaps is that of the "million-dollar marlin." A wealthy New York City businessman arrived at the club in 1954 with his secretary. After a week of fishing, however, the fish weren't biting and, on the final day, the man had such a bad hangover that he decided to stay in bed. The secretary, however, ended up catching a 702-kilo (1,545-pound) marlin, the woman's world record, which still stands. The catch was front-page news in the United States, which was unfortunate for the married man because his wife met him at the airport with divorce papers. The settlement, of course, was $1 million. "That was an expensive trip for that gentleman," chuckled one of the current residents of the Fishing Club.

good or bad purposes. There are sham artists here, but there are also people who know what they are doing but work, as Peruvians say, *en el lado oscuro* (on the dark side). It is also not a good idea to come if you are skeptical or merely curious: *curanderos* sense that attitude immediately and often say it disrupts their work. Recommended, and well-known, *brujos* in Piura include Estela Coronado (La Alborada H-8, tel. 073/35-0367) and Marino Aponte (La Primavera, Manzana E1, Lote 4, tel. 073/34-2006). They can perform ceremonies locally and provide current contacts in the Huancabamba area.

CABO BLANCO

Cabo Blanco is the point where the frigid Humboldt Current rushes headlong into the lukewarm El Niño current from the equator. The result is a dazzling fishing ground and, for surfers at least, a welcome break from the wetsuits that are obligatory in Peru's chilly coastal water. From Cabo Blanco northward lie the stunning beaches of Órganos, Máncora, and Punta Sal, and the water only becomes progressively warmer. There are some beautiful, lonely beaches around Cabo Blanco, but the scenery is unfortunately marred

Trujillo and the North Coast

Cabo Blanco's pipeline wave

by hundreds of pumping iron horses spread around the hills. Cabo Blanco was once known internationally for its Fishing Club, which attracted a range of stars through the 1950s and 1960s, include Ernest Hemingway and Nelson Rockefeller. Now it is known by surfers around the world for a monstrous, and dangerous, pipeline wave that forms here in June and then again between October and January. This wave reaches up to 3.5 meters (12 feet) high and travels nearly 70 meters (240 feet) before closing out, expulsing a giant plume of air and spray as it does. The wave forms over sand but crashes in front of large rocks, which has been the cause of many badly scraped and broken surfers.

The only place to stay is **Hotel El Merlin** (tel. 073/85-6188, $30 d with ocean view, $20 d without), a clean, white building on the oceanfront with stone floors and a cool, dark interior. The bathrooms have not been renovated since the hotel was built in the early 1980s, but the atmosphere is pleasant enough. The best restaurant in this one-street village is **Restaurant Cabo Blanco,** and there is no Internet and few services. To get there, take a *colectivo* from Tumbes to El Alto, a highway town where you can catch a

$3 *motocar* or cheaper *colectivo* for the 3-km, 10-minute drive on dirt roads to Cabo Blanco. Most visitors to Cabo Blanco, however, come for the day and make the 31-km drive (about 30 minutes) from Máncora. To get to the Fishing Club, pass the dirt turnoff for the town of Cabo Blanco and look for a run-down, whitewashed building on the left.

ÓRGANOS

Órganos is an up-and-coming beach spot that gets its names from the organ-like sound the wind makes against the eroded rock walls of **Punta Veleros** (Sailboat Point), a cliffy point to the south of town that is named for the fishing boats that sail past every afternoon. The town itself was developed but then forgotten by the petroleum industry and does not have the same charm as the beach-and-fishing towns of Máncora and Punta Sal to the north. The beach between Punta Veleros and the town is quite nice, but not as clean and empty as its northern cousins. But Órganos is a great place to find affordable and nice lodging, especially for families, and it is a laid-back playground for surfers.

STINGRAY WARNING

Swimmers are not the only ones who love the warm, shallow waters of Peru's northern beaches. Stingrays occasionally bury themselves under a thin layer of sand and, when stepped on, will sting with a vengeance. Fresh-water stingrays are also surprisingly common in many jungle areas in Peru, especially in areas with sandy or silty bottoms. Like their saltwater relatives, they have a poison-producing organ and a painful tail stinger. They can grow up to 70 cm, or over two feet, in length and weigh up to 15 kg, or 33 pounds. Peru's stingray is not nearly as painful as those in Baja Mexico or other parts of Latin America, but still a few words of caution are in order.

When arriving at the beach, ask the locals if stingrays are around. They come and go for a variety of reasons and do not appear at all in certain places. If you suspect there are stingrays, shuffle and bang your feet against the sandy bottom as you enter in order to scare them away. Even surer bets are to wear running shoes—Tevas or sandals are not sufficient protection—or tap the sand in front of you with a stick. If you get stung, a Sawyer extractor can remove much of the venom and reduce pain. The best treatment, however, is to place your foot in a pot of hot water for 10–20 minutes. Like boiling an egg, hot water coagulates the protein in the stingray poison, reducing the swelling and the fierce, radiating pain that can make even the most stoic jungle explorer burst into tears. If you are nowhere near hot water, you can always ask a friend to pee on your foot! (As unappealing as this particular pain reliever may sound, it really works.)

There is a three- to eight-meter (10- to 27-foot) pipeline that forms off Punta Veleros, just to the south of the main beach, from November to March and a beginner's wave a bit north that forms from July to February.

Sports and Recreation

Órganos has one of the few deep-water **fishing** boats in the area, the *Cristina,* a 10-meter (33-foot) wooden fishing boat. The boat can handle up to four passengers and charges $350 for six hours, $450 for eight hours, and $550 for 10–12 hours, though price is negotiable. All drinks and food included, and *cebiche* is made on the spot. The best fishing is about 42 kilometers off the coast, and recent catches of black and striped marlin weighing a few hundred pounds have been reported. Reservations can be made by calling tel. 073/85-7103 in Órganos, tel. 01/368-1844 in Lima, or email prodexco@infonegocios.com. The best fishing is from December to April and again in July and August.

Accommodations

Órganos' hippest lodging is ℕ **Las Pirámides Surf Point** (Km 1153 of the Panamericana, cell 073/996-8166 or 073/961-8397, laspiramides_1999@yahoo.com, www.vivamancora.com/laspi-ramides). The owners are Peruvian national champion surfer Cesar Aspíllaga and his wife, María Eugenia Vargas. Together with their daughter, Mohana, the couple is slowly building a series of bamboo, pyramid-shaped bungalows high above the ocean on Punta Veleros. The bungalows feature an upstairs love nest for two with views of the stars. Downstairs there are beds for three more, along with kitchen and funky sitting area. There is of course no hot water, no TV, and precious little electricity, but these things aren't missed in the spacious, rustic surroundings. Each bungalow costs $10 pp though prices vary. Rooms, with interesting adobe bathrooms and cloth curtains, are also available for $10. Food is served only during high season on a thatched patio in front of the ocean. Perhaps the best part is that César, who is a competitive surfer on the world circuit, offers lessons for $10 per hour plus all-day board rentals for $3. Of his famous point break, César says, "It's like Hawaii because it's a good reef base with a good tube that sucks air."

Hardcore surfers also congregate around **Bungalows Playa Blanca** (200 meters north of Punta Veleros on beachfront road, $10 pp). This recommended place has charming stone bungalows, cane-and-palm roofs, wicker furniture, and hammocks. Unless you like to party, avoid the rooms

the beach in Órganos

here, because you are likely to be up all night listening to reggae music whether you like it or not. The restaurant is open only during the summer.

Another good option, especially for families, in Órganos is **La Perla** (tel. 073/85-7389, wwwelaperla.com.pe, $25 pp with pension, $15 without), a hotel constructed by a Russian family that features many odd touches from their motherland—such as bright red colors from the Baltic Coast and miniature paintings of windswept Russian landscapes. The rooms are immaculately clean, with sparkling tile floors, TV with cable, and perfectly made beds in fair-sized rooms. The owners are blue-eyed, affable Russians, and they speak more Spanish and German than they do English. There are a few other lodging options, with more on the way, that are available if these are full on the beachfront just north of Punta Veleros. There are also some tourist restaurants here, but cheaper (and sometimes better) food in town.

Getting There and Around

The easiest way to arrive at Órganos is from Tumbes, either via airport taxi (1.5 hours, 127 km, $25) or via the frequent *colectivos* from Transportes Carrucho, at the intersection of Tumbes and Piura. The ride costs around $3 and takes two hours with stops along the way. Once dropped off in town, take a $0.75 *motocar* to the beaches on the south end of town.

Máncora, Las Pocitas, and Vichayito

Over the last decade Máncora has gone from a small fishing town with a few beach hotels to Peru's main surfer's mecca. During the summer from late December to March, and during vacations such as Easter week and July 28, the town of Máncora overflows with surfers, hippies, Rastafarians, and young sun worshippers from Lima and around the world. Máncora has become such a summer scene that it is hard to say what is the bigger attraction at this point, the waves during the day or the parties at night. In response to the crowds, quite a few low-budget hostels have sprung up in a concentrated area on the south end of Máncora, accompanied by a variety of surf schools, restaurants, and bars, some of which are open only during the summer. During the offseason, Máncora is one of the few Peruvian beach towns that still receives a good flow of visitors and has a variety of restaurants to choose from—unless you like crowds, this is the best time to visit.

The scene is completely different south of town, past the bridge and fishing wharf, where there is a long stretch of white sand known as Las Pocitas and, even further south, Vichayito (both these beaches are described after Máncora). Here families, couples, and gray-haired surfers come to enjoy quiet, laid-back walks on the beach, lounging by pools, excellent seafood, and a beautiful, tranquil atmosphere. In the mornings, fishermen pull rafts made of lashed bamboo and balsa wood into the ocean, where they drop weighted nets for fish and dive for *langosta* (lobster), a local specialty. The surf here is gentle, and the beach is fringed with palm trees around the resorts, which are wall-to-wall near Máncora and more spread out near Vichayito. This area has been the center of an intense campaign of beachfront development that shows no signs of slowing down. Generally speaking, the resorts in Las Pocitas are compact hotel complexes, whereas Vichayito is mostly bungalows.

Important considerations when staying in this area include the quality of the food and the beach. Though the restaurants of Máncora are only 5–10 minutes away by *motocars* that wait patiently outside the hotels, chances are you will be eating quite often at your hotel's restaurant—quality ranges dramatically, and prices tend to be quite a bit more expensive than in town. The beach is also important because, in Máncora especially, the white sand is often interrupted by rock formations that make swimming and body surfing impossible. This whole area has a fantastic website, www.vivamancora.com.

ⓜ MÁNCORA

Máncora's big claim to fame is that there is always *something* to surf. From January to March, a Pacific swell creates large, relatively safe waves. But its long stretch of white sand enjoys some kind of surfable break year-round.

Entertainment

Bars come and go in Máncora, and many are closed down outside summer. A reliable bet, however, is the upscale **Punto G** (Piura 344, tel. 073/85-8386, 7 P.M.–2 A.M. Tues.–Sun., $7), which serves cocktails and gourmet appetizers like *ensalada caprese* and tuna tartare in a sleek atmosphere. Artsy pornography hangs on the walls of this bar.

Accommodations

$10–25: Our first budget recommendation is **Kimbas Bungalows** (Panamericana Km. 1164, tel. 073/96-1273, kimbas00@hotmail.com, $10 s, $15 d). Though it's on the wrong side of the highway, and about a five-minute walk to the beach, the setting here is so peaceful that guests do not seem to mind. There are six bungalows along a stone walkway shaded with palm trees. Each bungalow has a private, open-air bathroom (cold water only) filled with tropical plants, and a private terrace with hammock. Decorations come from Indonesia and South Africa, where Lucho, the mellow Peruvian owner, has traveled widely. If Kimbas is full, but you like the idea of budget bungalows, there are a few other

sunset on Máncora Beach

cheaper, but less charming, options next door including El Pirata, Quebrada, and Media Luna.

On the beach there is **Hostal Sol y Mar** (no tel., $10 s, $20 d), the epicenter of the local party and surf scene. There are 50 rooms with private baths and cold water, and some even have ocean views. There is a restaurant, small pool, round-the-clock partying, and a few reports of thefts at this hotel. Apart from these recommended options, there are also a variety of rooms for rent, along with smaller hostels across the road in the south end of town. These change frequently but are easy to investigate on foot.

$25–50: For a more peaceful option, try the tasteful **Del Wa Wa** (tel. 073/85-8289, mancora@hotmail.com, www.delwawa.com, $13.50 s, $27 d) next door. It has five simple oceanside rooms and four in the back, some with hot-water baths. The restaurant has excellent food and is also popular with surfers. **Hostal Las Olas** (tel. 073/85-8109, lasolasmancora@terra.com.pe, www.vivamancora.com/lasolas, $10 s, $25 d) has a similar setup with 11 rooms with private terraces, including three cabins on the beach. The bright pink paint is less pleasant than Del Wa Wa, but the friendly staff gets high marks and there's a

good restaurant. Surfboards are for rent at all of these places, and lessons can easily be arranged.

Another option in town, but on the pricier end of the spectrum, is **Hotel Punta Ballenas** (entrance just south of bridge, tel. 073/85-8136, harryschuler@hotmail.com, $40 d, $50 suite), named after the pods of whales that head south along Peru's coastline from August to October. The hotel has been run since the mid-1980s by Harry Schuler, whose Swiss father was a well-known hotelier and entrepreneur in Lima. Harry, who has self-published a book of bawdy jokes (titled *¡Harry! A mí que Chuler!*), probably has more Peruvian than Swiss in him though his quirky collection of 10 large rooms are nicely decorated and some even have glassed displays of ancient ceramics. He operates a charming bar that looks over a rocky beach. Sandy beaches are a few minutes' walk away.

Food

Inexpensive cafés line the Panamerican, which becomes Calle Piura when it passes through Máncora. There are a variety of eateries here, but the most elegant and elaborate are in Las Pocitas. The best and most inexpensive seafood

view from Máncora Beach Bungalows

can be had at locals' favorite **M** **Cebichería Las Gemelitas** (past market and in front of school on Micaela Bastidas, $3–5). Here you can safely gorge on heaping plates of *cebiche* made from everything pulled from the ocean around here: *mero* and *róbalo* fish, *conchas negras* (black clams), *pulpo* (octopus), or *mixto,* a combination of all the shellfish. Unless you are an *ajiero* (chile lover), you should ask them to tone down the *ají,* however. Other suggestions here include *langosta* (lobster) and *majarisco,* a plate of mashed green bananas topped off with a shellfish sauce, all washed down with a pitcher of *chicha morada.* The other good seafood restaurant, more oriented toward tourists, is **La Espada** (Piura 501, tel. 073/85-8304, $3.50–7), where you can get two fresh lobsters for $13. **Iguana's Place** (Piura 245, tel. 073/9-926-8093, 8 A.M.–11 P.M., $1.50–3.50) is great for fruit salad with yogurt, vegetarian sandwiches, and *tequeños rellenos* (crispy and stuffed like wontons). Many places open only in the evening during the offseason, like **Las Velas** (Piura 372, 7–11 P.M.,$6), a candlelit restaurant serving brochettes and seafood, and the nearby **Chan Chan** (7–11 P.M., $6), serving delicious pizzas in a cozy, Polynesian atmosphere. **Café La Bajadita** (Piura 424, $6) has excellent international food and

serves capuccinos, gooey chocolate cake, and brownies (hard to find in Peru).

For groceries, the best selection is **Roviluz** (Piura 509) or the open market that is just north of the touristy area of Máncora and two blocks to the right on Micaela Bastidas (right before Cebichería Las Gemelitas).

Information and Services

The most up-to-date information on virtually any service can be found at the bulletin board at **grocery store Roviluz** (Piura 509), or the website www.vivamancora.com. Stop by the **Escuela de Surf** (Piura 202) for surfing lessons in Spanish or English. We recommend surfing instructor Roberto (073/983-0425, robbymunoz@hotmail.com). **Botica San José** (Piura 520, tel. 073/85-8009, 24 hours) has a good collection of medicine and will deliver. Travelers can change money at **Banco de la Nación** (Piura 527, 8 A.M.–2:30 P.M. Mon.–Fri.), and the best **ATM** is at Piura 518. Internet is slow in Máncora but available at **Cibernet** (Paita 149, 9:30 A.M.–11 P.M. Mon.–Fri., 10 A.M.–11:30 P.M. Sat.–Sun.) and at a few other places on the main drag. There is an excellent next-day laundry service at Piura 263, which charges $1 per kilo.

Getting There

The best buses from Lima to Máncora are operated by **Cruz del Sur,** which leaves Lima at 4:30 P.M. and arrives the next morning after a 17-hour journey. These buses cost $29 for normal, or $37 for VIP, but buy the former because the attendants don't mind if you sneak yourself an upgrade along the way. Other Lima companies that have buses to Máncora include **Cial, Civa,** and **Flores.**

The closest airport to Máncora is Tumbes, reachable by a $138 flight that leaves Lima every day at 6:45 A.M. and arrives in Piura at 9 A.M. Taxis can then be rented for $29 for the 1.5-hour, 127 km-journey to Máncora. Or you can take a $2 taxi into Tumbes to Transportes Carrucho, at the intersection of Tumbes and Piura, where $2 buses leave every half hour for Máncora and nearby beaches. Once dropped in Máncora, it is a short walk or *motocar* ride to the cluster of hotels at the south end of town.

LAS POCITAS

Just south of the bridge that leads into Máncora, a dirt road branches and runs south along the beach for a few kilometers past Las Pocitas before ending in Vichayito. This was the old Panamericana, but its once-paved surface has been completely battered and, in some places, washed away by El Niño rains.

Accommodations

The first set of hotels encountered along the first 3 kilometers of the dirt road, are pleasant, though compact, hotels with pools. All have direct access to the beach, which is rockier in some areas than in others (*las pocitas* means "little pools" and refers to the sand pools that form around the rocks after the tide goes out). The best of this first group of hotels is **Los Corales** (tel. 073/85-8309 or 073/69-9170, sandrapqr@yahoo.com, www.vivamancora.com/loscorales, $20 pp, includes breakfast), which offers beautiful and large, clean rooms with tile floors and thatched cane roofs. The rooms have private porches, and the ones upstairs are larger. There is also a playground, a nice open sitting area with coconut trees, and a mostly sandy beach. Despite its ugly entryway, **Casa de Playa** (tel. 073/85-8085, casadeplayamancora@yahoo.com, www.vivamancora.com/casadeplaya, $25 s, $50 d, including breakfast) has a nice pool, terrace, and restaurant and some excellent second-story rooms with private porches and hammocks. The other rooms here, however, are smaller and the beach has quite a few rocks. For a bit more space, and a sandy beach, try **Las Pocitas** (tel. 073/961-6070, in Lima tel. 01/874-3636, laspocitas@hotmail.com, www.laspocitasmancora.com, $20 pp, including breakfast). This is the first hotel constructed in Las Pocitas, and it seems somewhat trapped by 1980s poolside decor, but the rooms are large, with stucco walls, polished cement floors, and with excellent beach views. Other options, that don't seem as good a value for their tight quarters, are **Puerto Palos** (tel. 073/85-8198, puertopalos@terra.com.pe, www.puertopalos.com, $35 s, $50 d, including breakfast) and **Playa Bonita** (tel. 073/85-8113, in Lima tel.

01/326-1262, playabonita@terra.com.pe, www.vivamancora.com/playabonita.htm, $40 pp).

For honeymooners and couples looking for a romantic break, try **Ⓜ Sunset** (tel. 073/85-8111, info@hotelsunset.com.pe, www.hotelsunset.com.pe, $58 s, $66 d, $90 t), which rightly describes itself as a "seafront boutique hotel." The five rooms are unique and each intensely private, with stunning second-story balconies with hammocks and comfortable furniture. Inside, the large rooms are elegantly decorated with framed tapestries, elegant lighting, brush-painted walls, and vaulted bamboo ceilings. This hotel is filled with elegant touches and also has an excellent, though relatively expensive, Italian restaurant. There are a variety of excursions: a $120-per-person evening mud bath with wine, guided walks to nearby secluded beaches, horseback riding on the beach, and sport fishing on the *Cristina*, a yacht based in nearby Órganos.

About 3 km down the dirt road, on the southern extreme of Máncora, are two excellent beach resorts. **Ⓜ Máncora Beach Bungalows** (tel. 073/85-8125, or in Lima tel. 01/241-6116, mancora@peru-hotels-inns.com, www.hotelmancorabeach.com, $50 d, $30 s) is American-owned and offers large, comfortable rooms in a pleasant two-story building. Each room has solar-heated water, large and modern tiled bathroom, telephone, TV with cable, and a private porch with hammock and sweeping views of the ocean and sandy beach. There are two pools, a local fishing boat that has been converted into an outside bar, and a restaurant. The staff here is a friendly and fun-loving family.

Next door is the more formal **Hotel Las Arenas de Máncora** (tel. 073/85-8240, or in Lima 01/441-1542, lasarenas_demancora@terra.com.pe, www.lasarenasdemancora.com, $25 pp, including breakfast), a spread of bungalows in an oceanfront palm forest. The spacious bungalows have the normal resort amenities, plus air-conditioning, refrigerator, and the most privacy in all of Las Pocitas. Rooms are $40 with lunch and $50 with full pension. The excellent restaurant is a good place to watch the numerous semitropical birds that flit around the property. This resort is a favorite among Peruvian families and has a large pool and sandy beach.

A third resort in this area should open in 2005.

Further south in Máncora is a spiritual beach retreat known as **Casa de la Serenidad** (tel. 073/85-8180, liloselven@yahoo.com, www .shamanspirit.net, $25 s, $40 d), operated by a Swiss-American woman named Lilo Ccoyllor ("morning star" in Quechua). Though originally from Saratoga, California, the owner lived for several years in the Cusco area and offers a range of New Age therapies. These include Reiki healing sessions ($30), shamanic cleansing, vision quest with ayahuasca and San Pedro, crystal and sound therapy, and power animal card readings.

Food

The resorts at Las Pocitas have the most elegant restaurants in the area, including **Hotel Las Arenas** (tel. 073/85-8240, $5–8), which offers an extensive seafood menu on a palm-shaded terrace. Máncora Beach Bungalows (tel. 073/85-8125, $4–7) has an open-air restaurant overlooking the ocean with fish and Mexican entries. The most romantic option is **Sunset Residenza & Ristorante** (tel. 073/85-8111, $10), where gnocchi, ravioli, lasagna, and a variety of homemade pastas are made daily by an Italian chef and smothered in creative sauces. The candlelit dinner is served oceanside, with a wine list of Italian and Chilean wines and espresso for after dinner.

VICHAYITO

Continuing down the dirt road from Máncora, the landscape opens onto the exposed point of Vichayito, where complexes of bungalows, some better than others, are springing up left and right. The best of these is the American-owned **Hotel Vichayito** (tel. 073/975-0990, info@vichayito.com, www.vichayito.com, $30 pp, or $15 for kids up to 12, including breakfast). The spectacular bungalows have five-meter-high thatched roofs, wood floors, and soft muslin drapes with view to the ocean. Amenities include a huge and expansive sandy beach, nice pool, restaurant, and bar. The best other option is **Peña Linda Bungalows** (tel. 073/85-8435, penalinda@yahoo.com, www.vivamancora.com/penalinda), a collection of pleasant bungalows near a sandy beach. There

are several other bungalow places in the area, but they either do not have beachfront or seem overpriced considering the cramped, rustic bungalows they offer. Some of them do, however, offer camping with access to bathrooms and showers. For large families or groups, there are plenty of huge homes for rent in the area, which would be good options for large families who want privacy. Check www.vivamancora.com for more listings.

PUNTA SAL

Like Cabo Blanco, Punta Sal was once a beach favored by the foreign execs at the International Petroleum Company. This long, half-moon beach of pure sand has a laid-back atmosphere and quiet, lapping waves better for bathing than surfing. There are a few affordable hotels and large resorts, visited mainly by Peruvians. There is only one restaurant outside of these resorts, which is closed during low season, and few services of any kind.

Accommodations

$10–25: The best value in Punta Sal is **Hotel Caballito de Mar** (tel. 072/54-0058, or in Lima tel. 01/241-4455, caballito@amauta.rcp.net.pe, www.hotelcaballito.com.pe, $25 pp, including breakfast, or $35 for all meals). The rooms are fresh and spacious, with terraces, bamboo closets, and big bathrooms. The hotel rents jet-skis and dune buggies (both $25 per hour) and can arrange other activities—horseback riding, surfing lessons, massages, mud bath tours, you name it. This hotel offers a $30 Tumbes airport shuttle, Internet, and an incredible cheap, two-day, $80 honeymoon special with lots of frills.

The original resort for petroleum execs is now the pleasant **Hospedaje Hua Punta Sal** (tel. 072/54-0023 or 072/54-0043, huapuntasal@ yahoo.com, $20 s, $25 d). This backpackers' hostel has only seven rooms, so make reservations ahead—especially if you are interested in the more expensive rooms with a view ($25 s, $40 d). Though there is no pool, this hostel does offer two kayaks, restaurant, bar that serves *cuba libres* year-round, and the only Internet in town. Across the street (i.e., not on the beach) is **El Bucanero** (tel. 072/54-0118, hotelbucaneroptasal@hot-mail.com, www.geocities.com/el_bucanero_punta_sal, $25 pp). This two-story hotel has a small pool, rooms with new mattresses, and a reasonably priced bar and restaurant.

If you are looking to go fishing, you need only see Carlos Testino, the owner of **Sunset Punta Sal** (tel. 072/54-0041, puntasunset@hot-mail.com, www.sunsetpuntasal.com, $25 pp, including breakfast, or $35 for all meals). The gregarious Sr. Testino can easily charter a yacht for **deepwater fishing** ($400–500 for a full day, owned by Club Hotel Punta Sal). He has rods for surf fishing, or snorkel equipment and spear gun for $10 per hour—the clearest waters of the year are between January and April. This hotel offers a pool, large rooms, nice view, and access to a sandy beach.

$50 and Up: There are a few other resorts in this area, visited mainly by Peruvians. The best of these, 4 km further north along the beach, is **Club Hotel Punta Sal** (Km 1192 Panamericana, in Lima tel. 01/442-5992, pun-tasal@terra.com.pe, www.puntasal.com.pe, $62 pp with all meals included). This resort offers a full array of water sports, including water-skiing and kayaking, tennis courts, two pools, and a replica pirate ship with an authentic masthead left behind by English pirates in nearby Paita. The food is reputed to be excellent and plentiful, though the bungalows are a bit cramped and in need of an update.

Getting There

Punta Sal is several kilometers off a lonely stretch of Panamericana between Máncora and Tumbes. Buses from Lima to Tumbes can drop you off at the main turnoff to Punta Sal, at Km 1187 and well-marked with signs, where several *motocars* are usually waiting (do not do this, however, at night). Club Hotel Punta Sal has a separate entrance further north at Km 1192. From the Tumbes airport you can also take a $2 taxi to Transportes Carrucho, at the intersection of Tumbes and Piura, where $2 buses leave every half hour for the beaches. Have them drop you at Punta Sal and take a *motocar* to the beach.

TUMBES

The desert Peruvian coast goes awry when reaching Tumbes, a riot of palm trees and *motocars* with leopardskin seats where the tropical takes hold and continues all the way up to Central America. There are a lot of other things that makes Tumbes unlike any other Peruvian coastal city: everyone wears shorts, bananas are piled all over the place, and there is green everywhere—not just where it's been irrigated.

Don't stay long in Tumbes, a rough-and-tumble coastal town that has a history of hassling foreigners ever since Pizarro arrived here for the third and final time, in 1532. With their knowledge of the surrounding mangrove swamps, the resident Tumpis Indians managed to turn back the Spanish army that later defeated the Incas. Pizarro left only a cross on the beach (at present-day Caleta La Cruz, Bay of the Cross) before moving his troops further south, where he founded the city of San Miguel de Piura. Little has changed for foreigners in Tumbes, who complain of scamming money changers with rigged calculators, pick-pocketing youths, and lousy service at local restaurants.

Tumbes, however, is the main gateway for the cluster of excellent beaches near Máncora, one hour south (these beaches are, by comparison, 2.5 hours north of Piura). Tumbes is also the best spot for visiting an astounding, north-south ecological corridor of nature reserves, which includes ecosystems unique to Peru and a good variety of both mammals and birds. There are interesting mangrove swamps to visit, with the only crocodiles in Peru, from the small fishing town of Puerto Pizarro.

One startling embodiment of how Tumbes is different from other coastal towns is the Cámara de Comercio (Chamber of Commerce), a space-ship-like structure covered completely in florid mosaics and electric blues and greens, which spans Piura Avenue. This building lies near two of the city's many pedestrian streets, Bolívar and San Martín, which are good places to walk in the evenings, with a cluster of useful services. The Plaza de Armas is dominated by leafy trees known as *matacojudos* ("fool-killers" would be a polite translation), whose large fruit has knocked more than one person on the head. At the other end, there is a giant stage with a conch-shaped mosaic titled *Encuentro de Dos Mundos* (Meeting of Two Worlds). The mural depicts local flora and fauna and the enraged face of Chilimaza, the Tumpi leader who led the Battle of the Mangroves against Pizarro in 1532. Also on the plaza is the **Iglesia San Nicolás de Tolentino,** a church built in the 17th century by Augustine monks. It has been completely rebuilt in Republican style, however, and renovated again in 1985. Heading a few blocks along Grau you will come across dilapidated buildings that demonstrate colonial construction: *caña de Guayaquil* (Guayaquil cane and mud) walls, with high second stories supported by wooden columns and walled entirely in shutters, which are propped open for ventilation. Above the shutters there are often intricate wood designs.

Nature Reserves

Tumbes' out-of-the-way location has kept visitors away from the country's only **mangrove swamps** and a fascinating chain of inland nature reserves—which all comprise the **Reserva de Biosfera del Noroeste** (Northwestern Biosphere Reserve).

The mangrove swamps can be seen during an easy, two- to three-hour boat tour from **Puerto Pizarro,** a fishing port 13 km north of Tumbes. Things to see include Peru's only crocodiles, endangered because of hunting but now slowly reproducing in a nearby nursery. There are also interesting sediment islands in the area, including Isla de los Pájaros, a good birding ground, Isla Hueso de Ballena, and Isla de Amor, which has a good swimming beach. All the agencies in town arrange visits to this area and the more pristine mangroves at the **Santuario Nacional Los Manglares de Tumbes,** a nearly 3,000-hectare reserve that is an hour's drive from Tumbes and includes canoe, not motorboat, tours. Though there is no crocodile nursery at the Santuario, you are likely to see a greater variety of birds. The mangroves can easily be visited without an agency by taking a $0.75 *colectivo* along Tumbes Avenue to Puerto Pizarro, where you can barter with boat drivers (the going rate is about $30 for the two- to three-hour trip). They can also take you for a longer trip to the Santuario, or you can walk several kilometers northeast along the coast on a dirt road from Puerto Pizarro to reach the small town of El Bendito, where fishermen sometimes take out visitors in canoes.

Trujillo and the North Coast

SHRIMP FARMING

The biggest industry in Tumbes is shrimp farming, which has meant the destruction of 1,500 hectares of local mangroves around Puerto Pizarro to make room for the shrimp pools. The shrimp craze began in the 1980s in Ecuador, where shrimp farms spread across 200,000 hectares of mangrove swamps to become one of the country's most profitable, and important, exports. Peru's production began soon thereafter but peaked at about 5,000 has. because of limited production areas. The industry has experienced severe ups and downs because of El Niño rains, which raise the water temperatures of the shrimp pens and cause die-offs, and a disease called la *mancha blanca* ("white stain"). The virus spread from Asia to Central America in early 1999 and spread to Peru a few months later, where it devastated local production. From 1998 to 2001, Peru's shrimp exports dove from $50 billion to less than $4 billion. This has meant a huge economic loss for Tumbes, including the loss of 4,500 direct jobs. There is no known cure for the virus, which is named after white calcium deposits that form on the heads of infected shrimp. Scientists have developed strategies for living with the virus, however, which include using *bio-safe* shrimp larvae and sticking to a strict production schedule. Many of Peru's shrimp farmers tend tiny, unregulated pools and have neither the access to, interest in or cash for this new technology. (Information cited from *Tumbes: y los Bosques del Noroeste,* by Walter Wust, 1998.)

Tumbes is also the starting point for four inland reserves, which form a south-north biological corridor critical for the conservation of the area's endangered species. Because roads into these parks are lousy, government permission is needed, and there is no visitor infrastructure whatsoever, the easiest way to visit is with one of Tumbes tour agencies. Make sure to bring bug repellent, and don't go during the rainy season of January through March, when roads become nearly impassable. If you have a four-wheel drive, camping equipment, and a sense of adventure, you could also explore these parks on your own. Permits and up-to-date information can be arranged through INRENA, which administers the area and is located at new offices on the Panamericana north of the soccer stadium.

Your best bet for seeing a range of wild animals, and the park we most recommend, is **Zona Reservada de Tumbes,** a 75,100-hectare reserve at the northern end of the corridor that butts up against Ecuador. The reserve encompasses one of Peru's only chunks of Pacific tropical forest and contains endangered species such as the Tumbes crocodile, a local howler monkey called the *mono coto,* and a local sea otter, *nutria del noroeste.* The park is filled with orchids and gigantic trees such as the *ceibo*—a tree with bright-green bark and umbrella-shaped crown—and *pretino,* a related tree with gray bark that drops seed pods the size of soccer balls. Anteaters, cats (well, just their prints), and a wide variety of birds can be seen in the reserve. The heart of the reserve, the guardpoint at **El Caucho,** is 45 km from Tumbes on a rough dirt road. The journey from Tumbes presently takes 2.5 hours in a four-wheel-drive vehicle, plus one hour of walking, but there are plans to improve the road soon. Most agencies that visit this park offer overnight trips with camping near El Caucho, which is a good idea so you can get up early in the morning to see wildlife. The hikes include swimming in rivers and spectacular scenery.

To the south and divided by the Río Tumbes lies the drier, mountain climate of **Parque Nacional Cerros de Amotape,** which sprawls across 91,300 hectares of equatorial dry forest. The landscape here is more open, and hotter, as it is exposed more to the sun. Resident animals include puma, gray and red deer, anteater, and the Andean condor. A royal Inca highway ran along the ridge of the Amotape hills, and there are a few interesting ruins that can be visited along the way into the park. For those who prefer to ride through the park, burros can be rented for $6 per day, including the guide.

Farther south is a hunting reserve called the **Coto de Caza el Angola,** a 65,000-hectare chunk to the southwest of the Amotape Mountains. Finally there is Peru's first private nature reserve, founded in 2001, **Area de Conservación Privada Chaparrí** (tel. 072/221-4092). The 34,000-hectare reserve of dry forest is administered by the local *campesina* community and funded by several Peruvian corporations and large environmental organizations. The park's goal is to conserve, and re-introduce, endangered species such as the *pava aliblanca* (white-winged turkey), *el oso de anteojos* (the spectacled bear), the guanaco (a camelid), and the Andean condor, the world's largest flying bird. Visits to these two reserves are difficult but can be arranged.

Sports and Recreation

The best, and sometimes only, way to visit the natural attractions around Tumbes is with the travel agencies, which charge a per-person rate based on groups of two or more. The main tours include the mangrove swamps ($25–35 pp), day trips to Amotape or the Zona Reservada ($50–70 pp), and a day tour that includes nearby mud baths, beaches, and archaeology sites ($25–35 pp). The best agencies are **Cocodrilos Tours** (Huáscar 309, tel. 072/52-4133, amgonzales@viabcp.com, cocodrilostours@terramail.com.pe), which also operates the next-door Hotel César, and **Tumbes Tours** (Tumbes 341, tel. 072/52-6086, tumbestours@terra.com.pe), which also operates a lookout tower with an excellent view of the geography around Tumbes.

Accommodations

There are loads of cheap hotels in Tumbes to

accommodate the border traffic to and from Ecuador, but most do not have hot water and none have charm. **Hospedaje Franco** (San Martín 105, tel. 072/52-5295, $6 s, $9) or **Hospedaje Tumbes** (Grau 614, tel. 072/52-2203, $5.50 s, $8.50 d) are your best bets for a reasonably clean, quiet room with a private bath. **Hostal César** (Huascar 353, tel. 072/52-2883, $12 s, $15 d) is the best value in town, with hot water, cable TV, pleasant rooms, and big, clean bathrooms. If this place is full, try **Hotel Lourdes** (Bodero 118, tel. 072/52-2126, $12 s, $17.50 d), offering the same amenities but less comfortable beds.

The more expensive option is **Hotel Costa del Sol** (San Martín 275, tel. 072/52-3991, costadelsol@mail.udep.edu.pe, $55 s, $65 d, including breakfast) on the pleasant and quiet Plaza Bolognesi. The hotel itself is an oasis in this hot, dusty city, with a nice pool, excellent restaurant, and fully equipped rooms with AC. However, the rooms have less charm than they should, thanks to their brown wall tones. About 4 km north on the Panamericana, outside the city center, is **Hotel Chilimasa** (tel. 072/52-4555, $23 s, $35 d, including breakfast). This is a fairly upscale hotel, with a nice pool for sunbathing and large rooms with cable TV, fridge, and AC. The isolated location is a bit lonely, but it is a good option for corporate travelers and those who want to avoid Tumbes altogether.

Food

Tumbes is a good place to try *conchas negras*—black clams with an aphrodisiac kick that local fishermen harvest from among the roots in the mangrove swamps. **Los Gustitos** (Bolivar 149, tel. 072/52-2878, 6:30 A.M.–11 P.M., $3.50) and **Restaurant Latino** (Bolivar 163, tel. 072/52-3198, $3.50) are recommended for this delicacy, and Latino has a pet monkey to keep you entertained as you wait. For a finer dining experience and an international menu, try **El Manglar** (San Martin 275, tel. 072/52-3991, 7 A.M.–11 P.M., $4.50) inside the Hotel Cosa del Sol. It offers *cebiches,* fajitas, pizzas, grilled meats, and an excellent fixed menu for $4.

Information and Services

The **Tourist Information Office** (Bolognesi 194, tel. 072/52-3699, tumbes@mitinci.gob.pe, 7 A.M.–noon, 1 P.M.–4:30 P.M. Mon.–Fri.) on the second floor of the civic center—the ugly government complex on the Plaza de Armas—is friendly and helpful. The **Ecuadorian Consulate** is across the plaza next to Restaurant Gustitos (Bolivar, 123, 9 A.M.–1 P.M. and 4–6 P.M. Mon.–Fri.). The two local police stations are **San José District Police** (corner of Novoa and Zarumilia, tel. 072/52-2525, 24 hours) and **Tablazo Police Station** (Carrasco 515, tel. 072/52-4823).

Jamo Hospital (24 de Julio 565, tel. 072/52-4775, 24 hours) or **Zorritos Medical Post** (Grau S/N, tel. 072/54-4158, 8 A.M.–8 P.M. Mon.–Sat.) can be called in an emergency. Most necessary services can be found on the two pedestrian streets heading north from the Plaza de Armas, Bolivar and San Martín. There is a **24-hour pharmacy** on Bolognesi near the plaza, or try **Farmacia San Vicente** on Grau 461.

Travelers can exchange money at **Banco de la Nación** on the corner of Grau and Bolivar at the Plaza de Armas. *Cambistas* hang out on the corner of Bolivar and Piura, but ripoffs and rigged calculators have been reported. **ATMs** are located at Bolivar 123 or 209. The **Tumbes Post Office** is at San Martín 208 (tel. 072/52-3868, 8 A.M.–8 P.M. Mon.–Sat.) and the main **Telefónica office** is right up the street. The cheapest international calling, however—including $0.30 per minute to the U.S.—is available at Los Libertadores 209. Check **email** at Bolognesi 122 and take your laundry to **Flash** at the corner of Piura and Barete. A good collection of highbrow literature (in Spanish only) can be found at **Feria de Libros** (tel. 072/52-6173) at San Martín and Piura.

Getting There and Around

For Máncora, taxis can be rented at the airport ($29, 1.5 hours). Or take a $2 taxi into Tumbes to Transportes Carrucho, at the intersection of Tumbes and Piura, where $2 buses leave every half hour for Máncora and nearby beaches.

For travel on to Ecuador, **Ormeño** (Piura

499, tel. 072/52-2288) has Royal Class buses leaving at 7 A.M. and arriving at noon. **CIFA** (Tumbes Norte, tel. 072/52-7120) also has excellent direct bus service nine times a day to Guayaquil for $6.

Cruz del Sur and **Ormeño** each have a few daily buses to Lima that run $23–37. Less ex-pensive service is also provided by **Civa, Cial,** and **Flores.** The direct trip is about 16 hours, 18 hours for economy class.

Tumbes is absolutely filled with *motocars,* which charge $0.50 for an in-town trip, and *colectivos* that run north and south along the Panamericana.

Cajamarca and the Northern Highlands

Though cartographers have penciled in the names of rivers and towns, much of Peru's northern highlands remains largely unexplored—and filled with extraordinary adventures. The Andes are lower here and sliced down the middle by the mighty Marañón Canyon, which ranges from subtropical at the river's edge to high-altitude *altiplano* at the canyon rim. To the east the land tumbles away into rugged rainforest, where explorers continue to

find lost cities and tombs built by the Chachapoya culture. An amazing road journey, described in the *Discover Peru* section, slices through this entire area en route to the jungle.

The first stop from the coast is **Cajamarca,** one of the hidden gems of Peru's Andes. Though growing rapidly because of a nearby gold mine, Cajamarca retains its charm with cobblestone streets, Inca ruins, and a collection of baroque

Must-Sees

Look for **M** to find the sights and activities you can't miss and **N** for the best dining and lodging.

Cajamarca

M Complejo Belén: This 17th-century religious order in Cajamarca is an eerie glimpse into how the Bethlemites combined medieval medicine with Catholicism, including one of the most awe-inspiring baroque church facades in Peru (page 459).

M Cuarto de Rescate: A single stone room, with the perfect blocks and water channels of Inca

© RENÉE DEL GAUDIO AND ROSS WEHNER

Only one person at a time can enter through Kuélap's defense walls.

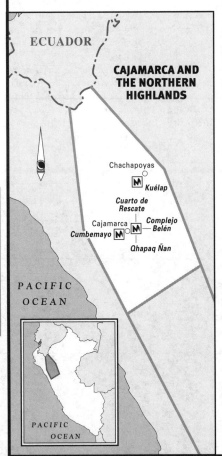

stonework, is all that is left of the huge stone buildings that once graced the city's square. Historians believe this dark and solemn space was where Inca Atahualpa waited for eight months—only to be executed in the end (page 459).

M Cumbemayo: Up in the magical *ichú* grasslands above Cajamarca, crystal-clear water flows along perfectly sculpted stone canals, which were built thousands of years ago and continue to befuddle archaeologists (page 461).

M Qhapaq Ñan: A main reason to come to Cajamarca is to experience its wide-open, majestic countryside, and the best way to see it is by choosing from a handful of one- to seven-day hiking routes along the area's rediscovered Inca highways (page 462).

Ruins in the Chachapoyas Area

M Kuélap: This stone citadel, perched on a limestone ridge thousands of feet above the Río Tingo, is the most accessible and dramatic of the Chachapoya ruins. With 420 round houses and a variety of bizarre buildings, many visitors find it as impressive as Machu Picchu (page 479).

Northern Highlands

churches. Villagers roam the streets selling huge blocks of local cheese and herding cattle. Cajamarca is Cusco without the fanfare.

The city's main square is the precise spot where **Francisco Pizarro's** men captured **Inca Atahualpa** in 1532 and brought the Inca Empire to its knees. It is also where the main Inca highways crossed, which today are fabulous trekking routes through remote villages and sprawling, majestic countryside. A two- or three-day trek in the Cajamarca area is one of the best, and cheapest, ways to experience Peru's highland culture.

From Cajamarca, a bumpy dirt road heads east toward the country hamlet of Celendín before seemingly falling off the face of the earth into the **Marañón Canyon,** which at 3,000 meters is deeper than Arizona's Grand Canyon and every bit as spectacular.

On the other side of the canyon is the **Chachapoya cloud forest,** home to a vanished federation of city-states that the Incas, despite a half century of trying, were never able to fully subdue. The grandeur of Kuélap, a stone citadel floating in the air atop a limestone ridge, is often compared to Machu Picchu.

Most of the major ruins in the Chachapoya area can be reached via horseback or day hikes, though we recommend multi-day, mule-supported treks. Chachapoya treks offer an unforgettable combination of forest scenery and lost ruins and are the best alternative for those looking to escape the crowds on Cusco's Inca Trail.

As a final bonus, a visit to Peru's northern highlands can be made into a loop that includes a visit to the ancient pyramids and world-class museums on the coast at Trujillo and Chiclayo. Or continue from Chachapoya east to the Amazon, floating down the Amazon with a hammock and a bunch of bananas.

PLANNING YOUR TIME

The best way to explore northern Peru is via bus. Start in Trujillo, head up to Cajamarca, and then brace for the rough but spectacular journey down and up the Marañón Valley to Chachapoya (see the sidebar *Overland to Chachapoyas*). The return journey, on gentle highways, ends in Chiclayo. Whereas Cajamarca, Trujillo, and Chiclayo can be visited in as little as two days each, the ruins of Chachapoya require several days at the minimum—especially considering the effort it

lush valleys leading to Cajamarca

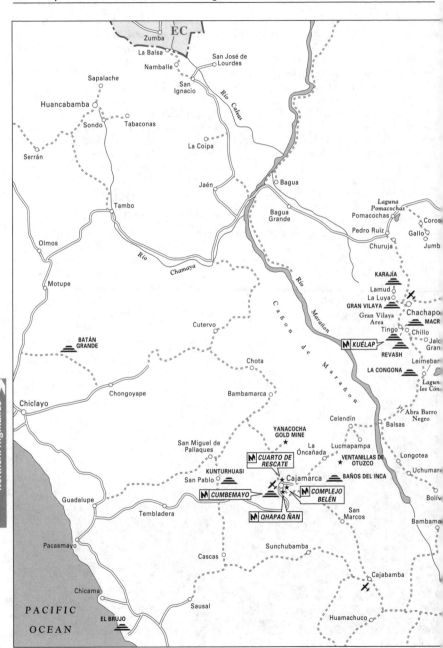

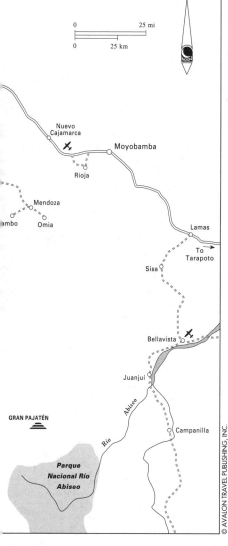

CAJAMARCA AND THE NORTHERN HIGHLANDS

0   25 mi

0   25 km

Nuevo
Cajamarca

Moyobamba

Rioja

Mendoza

ambo   Omia

Lamas

To
Tarapoto

Sisa

Bellavista

Juanjuí

GRAN PAJATÉN

Campanilla

Río   Abiseo

*Parque
Nacional Río
Abiseo*

© AVALON TRAVEL PUBLISHING, INC.

takes to get there. So the whole route could take 10 days to two weeks. InkaNatura in Lima and Gran Vilaya Tours in Chachapoyas offer extremely well-organized tours that follow this basic route, known as the *Northern Circuit.*

This circuit can be shortened by flying into Cajamarca or even Chachapoyas—though flights into the latter city have been cancelled in the past for lack of demand.

Another option after visiting the Chachapoya area is to head east and plunge into the jungle around Tarapoto and Yurimaguas, from where cargo boats leave daily for the three-day chug down the Río Marañón to Iquitos. The total journey takes a least a week—more if you visit the Reserva Nacional Pacaya Samiria—with an easy escape flight back to Lima.

Cajamarca

If you are looking for what Cusco must have been like before the tourism boom, head to Cajamarca, the most charming city of Peru's northern Sierra. Cajamarca is brimming with country charm: *campesinos* with straw hats, bright shawls, and wool spindles scuffle along this city's cobblestone streets. This laid-back city revolves around its Plaza de Armas, flanked by two spectacular colonial churches and brimming with strolling couples and screaming schoolchildren. Cajamarca's charming countryside produces a cornucopia of products including *manjar blanco* (a type of gooey caramel), wheels of edam and gouda, and fresh yogurt. Cajamarca is booming thanks to the **Yanacocha** gold mine, the fifth largest mine in the world.

One of the pivotal moments of Latin American history happened in Cajamarca's Plaza de Armas on Nov. 16, 1532, when a motley army of 160 Spanish *conquistadores* brought the entire Inca Empire to its knees by capturing **Inca Atahualpa**. The Incas themselves had only conquered the local **Caxamarca** culture six decades earlier and used Cajamarca as a staging ground for invading the Chachapoyas, Chimú, and Huamachuco empires. In Cajamarca's square, the Incas built large stone warehouses where tribute from the surrounding territories was stored—these buildings were all destroyed by the Spaniards.

The Caxamarca people probably built the mysterious and perfectly sculpted aqueducts at **Cumbemayo,** 22 km outside of Cajamarca. They were at the center of a busy commerce between the coast and the jungle, and southern Peru and Ecuador, and the Incas later improved these routes by constructing stone highways that crossed in Cajamarca's main square.

An exciting new development for Cajamarca visitors is the possibility of trekking through the Cajamarca countryside via the **Qhapaq Ñan,** the old network of Inca trails that was mostly forgotten until an enterprising nonprofit organization known as **APREC** (Association for the Rescue of Cajamarca's Ecosystem) retraced and mapped them. Detailed maps of these routes are now available, along with more than a dozen guides in English examining history, folklore, birding, and plants along the way. This is the best way to experience the culture and natural beauty of Cajamarca's countryside, far better than an agency car tour.

SIGHTS

Cajamarca's Inca layout can best be appreciated from the top of Cerro Santa Apolonia, the hilltop shrine that towers over Cajamarca to the southwest. It can be reached either by taxi ($1.50) or by a long walk up stone stairs. From the summit, you can see the Spanish Plaza de Armas, surrounded by the cathedral and the Iglesia San Francisco. The plaza was at least twice as long during Inca times and surrounded by three stone warehouses filled with textiles made of cotton, llama, and vicuña wool, the last of which the Incas valued even over gold. The clothing was paid as tribute from all the surrounding empires of the north and also woven by hundreds of women who were hand-picked by the Inca to live in a sort of city convent, known in Quechua as *aclla huasa* (house of the chosen ones). Jirón Inca branches out diagonally from the Plaza de Armas on the right, or east side, of town—this is the Inca highway that Atahualpa traveled along before his fateful meeting with Pizarro. The old highway cuts through the fields to **Baños del Inca** and can be seen switchbacking up between two hills on its way to Cusco. The opposing highway to Quito leads up from the plaza and can still be seen zigzagging into the hills above Cajamarca to the left, or west. Inca highways that ran northeast to the federation of Chachapoya cites, and southwest to the Chimú capital of Chan Chan, crossed in what is now the Plaza de Armas and still exist.

Cerro Santa Apolonia was a shrine used first by the Caxamarcas, then by the Incas (as evidenced by the carved altars near the lookout), and finally by the Spanish, who worshipped at the hilltop Iglesia Santa Apolonia from 1571 until it was

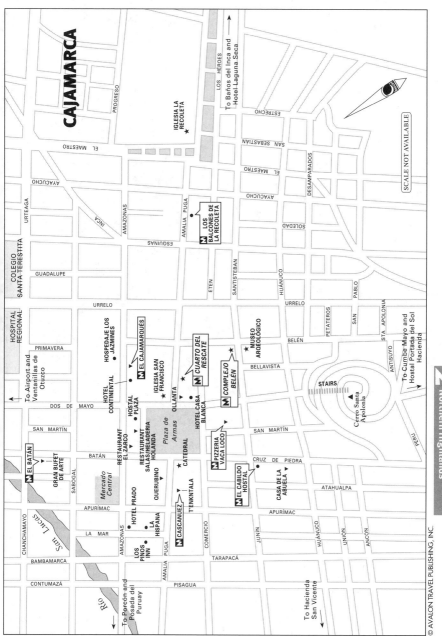

CAJAMARCA

SCALE NOT AVAILABLE

N Northern Highlands

© AVALON TRAVEL PUBLISHING, INC.

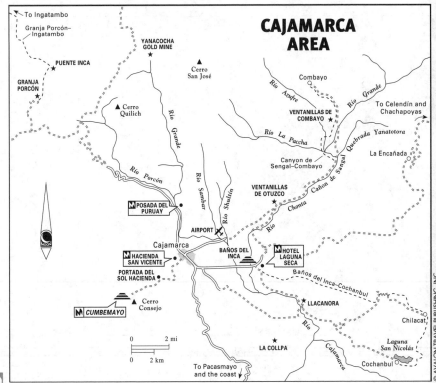

CAJAMARCA AREA

To Ingatambo

Granja Porcón–Ingatambo

PUENTE INCA

GRANJA PORCÓN

YANACOCHA GOLD MINE

▲ Cerro San José

Combayo

Río Azufre

Río Grande

To Celendín and Chachapoyas

▲ Cerro Quilich

Río Grande

VENTANILLAS DE COMBAYO

Río La Paccha

Quebrada Yanatotora

La Encañada

Río Porcón

Canyon de Sengal–Combayo

Cañón de Sengal

Río Sambur

Río Shultín

VENTANILLAS DE OTUZCO

Chonta

Río

M POSADA DEL PURUAY

AIRPORT ✈

Cajamarca

M HACIENDA SAN VICENTE

BAÑOS DEL INCA

M HOTEL LAGUNA SECA

Baños del Inca-Cochanbul

PORTADA DEL SOL HACIENDA

▲ Cerro Consejo

LLACANORA

Río

Chilacat

M CUMBEMAYO

0   2 mi

0   2 km

LA COLLPA ★

Río Cajamarca

Laguna San Nicolás

Cochanbul

To Pacasmayo and the coast ↓

MOON

burnt down by invading Chileans during the War of the Pacific (1879–83). The Santa Apolonia image, forgotten by the Caxamarca devout after more than four centuries, can now be found in the museum at the Iglesia San Francisco. Scanning the horizon on the left, there is a triangular, earth-colored summit poking just above the hills in front of it. This is **Cerro San José,** also known as Cerro Carachugo, a sacred mountain that lies exactly north of the city and has been used as a reference point for thousands of years. Within a decade, if not sooner, it will disappear as it gets eaten away by the Yanacocha gold mine.

In the Plaza de Armas, the **cathedral** (8–11 A.M. and 6–9 P.M. daily, free) contains the only original baroque altar in the city, built in 1780. The construction of the city's seven churches so overwhelmed the city's stonemasons that the construction of the cathedral dragged

on for nearly a century (1682–1780). On the opposite side of the plaza, the **Iglesia San Francisco** (8 A.M.–10 A.M. and 2:30–6 P.M. daily, free) has a baroque facade that features two angels trumpeting the power of the Pope, who is represented only by his papal hat, or *mitra.* Inside are several interesting colonial religious images, including El Señor de la Caña, depicting Jesus in the hours before his crucifixion. The church's **religious museum** (same hours as church, $1, Fridays free) has a fabulous collection of 17th-century paintings that were made in serial fashion by Indian painters in the Franciscan workshop. Because Cajamarca is directly between Cusco and Quito, these paintings show characteristics of both schools of painting. There is also access to the catacombs where the Franciscans were buried, along with the Spaniards and Indians who had enough money for the privileged spot.

© AMBER PIKKER

that the spirit of the devil would leave their bodies. They were bled nearly constantly, usually until they died, and families were not permitted to use either their traditional medicines nor burial rituals. After death, families of the dead often became indebted as they struggled to pay for Masses that would elevate their loved one's status from hell to purgatory and finally to heaven.

Across the street is another hospital built for women, which has a startling sculpture on the facade of a woman with four breasts. As the facade was sculpted by Indian artisans, some say the woman is a fertility symbol, while others claim that multiple nipples (known in medical terms as *polythelia,* or supernumerary nipples!) are a relatively common occurrence in the nearby town of Chilacat. Inside is the **Museo Arqueológico,** which displays an excellent collection of ceramics and implements from Andean life, most of which are still in use today. The guides at the museum's entrance ask for a tip in exchange for explaining the exhibits.

◪ COMPLEJO BELÉN

This sprawling colonial religious compound (9 A.M.–1 P.M. and 3–5:45 P.M. Mon.–Sat., 9 A.M.–1 P.M. Sunday, $1.25) was built between 1627 and 1774 by the Bethlemite religious order, which arrived from Nicaragua with the express purpose of building a hospital for the local Indians. The compound, made of volcanic stone, is now converted into medical and archaeological museums. Though its towers were never finished, **Iglesia Belén** has one of the most stunning baroque facades in all of Peru: four angels float above swirling sculpted forms and guard a central window, through which the souls of the dead entered before traveling down the nave onto the cupola, where more painted angels sustain the weight of heaven on their fingertips. The altar, like most in Cajamarca, is neoclassical, from the late 19th century, and was replaced after the first altar was burnt during the War of the Pacific.

A quick tour around the adjacent men's hospital—which operated until 1965!—gives a sense of how miserable conditions were: patients stretched out in dark niches, watching Mass so

◪ CUARTO DE RESCATE

Though the volcanic rock has not weathered as well as the granite in Cusco, there is no mistaking the perfect Inca stonework at the **Cuarto de Rescate** (8:30 A.M.–12:30 P.M. and 2:15–5 P.M. Mon.–Fri., 8:30 A.M.–noon weekends, admission included with Complejo Belén). The house was probably part of an Inca sun temple, destroyed long ago by the Spaniards, and has a stone canal that once gurgled with water. It was this room, tour guides say, that Atahualpa filled entirely with gold objects for his ransom. But the existing white line, which Atahualpa supposedly drew to mark the level, is almost certainly a fake. One of the chroniclers, Cristobal de Mena, wrote that the line was so tall that even the reach of the tallest of the Spaniards fell about a palm short. By this reckoning, the line must have been about two meters and four centimeters. John Hemming and other historians contend that this room is where Atahualpa was probably held captive—the ransom room was smaller, with a capacity of 88 cubic meters.

There are many artistic renderings of the first

A KING'S RANSOM

When Inca Atahualpa heard the news of a strange group of bearded white men traveling into his empire, his first thoughts were to breed their marvelous horses, sacrifice most of the Spaniards to the sun, and castrate the rest to guard his wives and do household chores. Atahualpa never dreamed of being captured by the Spanish—especially when surrounded by thousands of trained Inca soldiers.

It is hard to imagine Francisco Pizarro's audacity, leading his men in strict formation down into Cajamarca's valley as a sea of Inca soldier tents spread out before them. On Nov. 16, 1532, Atahualpa was resting in hot baths outside of town and celebrating his victory over his half-brother Huáscar and the end of a civil war that had killed thousands and badly damaged the empire's infrastructure. Pizarro had been traveling through the deserts and mountains of South America for nearly two years to find the heart of the Inca Empire. Huáscar had 40,000 to 80,000 soldiers, fresh from battle. Pizarro had 170 men, and only 60 had horses.

Pizarro nevertheless invited Atahualpa to visit him on the main square of Cajamarca, which was flanked by three empty stone warehouses, each about 180 meters long. The Spaniards hid inside these buildings when the Inca arrived the next day, carried atop an elegant litter borne by 80 officials and accompanied by 5,000 elegantly dressed soldiers. Atahualpa was so confident of the encounter that he had come dressed for ceremony, not combat, and his men were armed only with light battle axes, slings, and rocks.

The first Spaniard to approach Atahualpa was Dominican Friar Vicente de Valverde, who walked up to the Inca, explained his mission to spread the Catholic faith, and extended him a small breviary. After looking the book over, the Inca threw it on the ground. Moments later, the Spaniards emerged in full force and created what must have been a terrifying spectacle for the Inca soldiers. Amid the cacophony of trumpets, cannon, and rattles, fully armored Spaniards on horseback charged into the crowd with lances and swords flying. As the Spaniards began their slaughter, the Indians panicked to such an extent that many suffocated in the rush. A wall nearly two meters thick was pushed over by the fleeing crowd.

But the Spaniards chased after them, lancing them down until well after dark, when an estimated 7,000 bodies lay littered across what is today downtown Cajamarca. Accounting for exaggeration and those killed by suffocation, English historian John Hemming estimates that each Spaniard killed an average of 15 Incas in those two gruesome hours. Pizarro, with a group of soldiers, meanwhile had fought his way to Atahualpa's litter and dragged him inside one of the buildings. In just a few minutes, the New World's most powerful and best-organized empire had been brought to its knees.

Shortly thereafter, Atahualpa offered his infamous ransom: in exchange for his liberty, he would fill a large room (nearly 88 cubic meters!) with gold and another two rooms with silver. Pizarro rapidly agreed and, as llama trains loaded with gold began to arrive in Cajamarca, he sent messengers back to the coast to call for reinforcements. Nine furnaces ran continuously between March 16 and July 9 to melt down nearly 10,000 kilos of exquisite gold sculptures, chalices, and other priceless items into gold bars. The eventual result, according to Hemming, was 6,100 kilos (13,420 pounds) of 22-karat gold and 11,820 kilos (26,000 pounds) of good silver.

Though he met his ransom, Atahualpa was far from free. As rumors filtered to the Spaniards of a large army approaching, the Spaniards began to suspect that Atahualpa was plotting against them. Though Francisco Pizarro objected, and no trial was held, a majority of Spanish officers made the hasty decision to execute the Inca. As dusk fell on July 26, 1533, Atahualpa was led onto the main square. Atahualpa allowed himself to be baptized at the last minute, apparently to avoid being burnt at the stake as a heathen. Instead he was hung from a rope. When Emperor Charles V learned of the execution some months later, he condemned the conquistadores for their audacity in killing a sovereign prince.

encounter between Pizarro and Athualpa, though few are accurate. Examples include the paintings hanging near the entrance by local artists Camilo Blas, who painted Inca soldiers deserting Atahualpa at the moment of his capture, and Andres Zevallos, who depicted the Inca being burnt to death. The truth is quite different, according to eyewitness accounts written by Pedro Pizarro. Atahualpa's servants were so loyal, he says, that the Spaniards had to kill them or hack off their arms before they could pull the Inca from the litter. Also Atahualpa was not burned—he was hung from a rope.

◪ CUMBEMAYO

Located 19 km southwest of Cajamarca up a dirt switch back to 3,390 meters is **Cumbemayo** (8 A.M.–5 P.M. daily, $2), a shrine of **carved water canals** that still confounds archaeologists. The canals are at least 2,000 years old, but the exact date—and the reason they were built—is unknown. The lines are so perfect, and the rock ground so smooth, that it is difficult to imagine these works of art being carved with obsidian hammers, the state-of-the-art technology at the time. Because Cajamarca has an abundant water supply, the canals were not necessary, so they may have had a ceremonial or religious function. If you arrive at this spot early in the morning, the religious explanation of Cumbemayo becomes more plausible. The power and energy of the area, which is covered in ichú grass and punctuated by bizarre volcanic formations, is palpable.

There is a marked trail from the parking lot that descends to a rocky formation, through which a cave leads with several mysterious petroglyphs—including one that resembles a wooly mammoth. Follow the path through the cave (a headlamp really helps) until you emerge on the other side. Then head up a hill and down a drainage to a trail junction. Head right and follow the canals until you reach a carved chair-like stone, which obviously served a ceremonial purpose. Return the same way and follow the canals downhill, where the road leads back to the parking lot.

© RENEE DEL GAUDIO AND ROSS WEHNER

Aqueducts at Cumbemayo were cut at right angles to slow water.

The road to Cumbemayo passes through villages where *campesinos* produce everything they need to live except for salt, matches, and kerosene. They live in *casas de tapial,* or rammed earth homes, and are for the most part vegetarian. Their diet consists of *oca* and *ulluco* (two types of tubers), corn, super-grains such as *kiwicha* and quinoa, and lentils—or *chocho,* the seeds of a purple-flowered, lupine-looking plant that are cooked, mixed with tomato and cilantro, and sold on Cajamarca street corners. Despite the climate, there are oddly no llamas or alpacas in this part of Peru, and the sheep and other animals are rarely eaten but sold instead for what little cash their owners seem to need. Before reaching Cumbemayo itself, there is a pyramid-shaped hill on the right named **Cerro Consejo** ("The Hill of Advice"). According to local legend, this *apu,* or sacred hill, gives advice to those who ask.

Sporadic $1.50 *colectivos* that will put you within walking distance of Cumbemayo can be taken from behind Cerro Santo Apolonia—this is the best option, as a guided tour is not necessary to visit Cumbemayo.

BAÑOS DEL INCA

There is no better way to wash away the accumulated dust of overland travels than by soaking in the hot mineral water at the Baños del Inca, 6 km east of Cajamarca. There are two ways to enjoy the baths: either stay at the deluxe Hotel Laguna Seca, or visit the cheaper, but slightly rundown, municipality baths, which also rents bungalows. The municipality baths, known as the *Complejo Turístico Baños del Inca,* can receive more than a thousand visitors a day, so avoid the crowds during weekends and February *carnaval.* There are different price schemes according to the quality of the tub, but the best is the recently restored *pabellón imperial* (royal pavilion), which offers 30-minute private baths for $1.50 pp, from 5 A.M. to 8 P.M. daily. The complex also includes a public pool, sauna, and spa with a $3 massage that lasts 20–30 minutes. Within the complex, and included in admission, are bath ruins from the Caxamarca culture, along with the **Pozo del Inca,** the bath where Inca Atahualpa was bathing with his concubines when the Spaniards first entered Cajamarca. Getting to the Baños del Inca is an easy 10-minute trip, either via a $2 taxi from Cajamarca or via cheaper *colectivos* labeled *Baños del Inca* that leave from Calle Amazonas. The best lunch place in Baños del Inca is **El Salas Campestre** (11 A.M.–5 P.M. Fri.–Sun.), which serves *comida típica* and is four blocks from the town square next to the Nestlé milk plant. For *cebiche* made from fish brought fresh every morning from the coast, try **La Bahía** (518 Manco Capac, main square, 11 A.M.–7 P.M.)

ℕ QHAPAQ ÑAN

Cajamarca's countryside is stunning and ranges from the high-altitude *jalca,* where only the hearty *ichú* grass grows, to lush pastures where farmers leave metal jugs of milk out for roadside pickup after every afternoon's milking. Although there are only a few pockets left where people speak Quechua, the mountain folk of the Cajamarca sierra live as they have for centuries. They live in *casas de tapial,* weave their own clothes, grow native foods, and rely on herbs and natural medicines.

Interesting one- and two-day hiking routes

around Cajamarca are being pioneered in a responsible fashion by **APREC** (Association for the Rescue of Cajamarca's Ecoystem, at Hotel Laguna Seca, tel. 076/89-4600, oper@aprec.org, www.aprec.org), a nonprofit dedicated to saving the natural beauty and culture of Cajamarca's countryside. APREC's strategy involves bringing trekkers together with the *campesinos* living along the Inca highways, which are known in Quechua as *Qhapaq Ñan* (Great Paths). Cajamarca contains an important crossroads of the nearly 30,000-kilometer-long Inca highway system. APREC's hope is that ecotourism will encourage local communities to preserve their way of life and their ecosystem. It is a bold project, but APREC is taking a grassroots approach that seems to be working. For the moment, hikes are led exclusively by APREC guides, though private agencies may begin operating trips in the area as well.

The routes often integrate existing attractions—such as cliff tombs at **Ventanillas de Combayo** or the agricultural cooperative of **Porcón**—along with an astonishing range of new ruins and natural wonders that have been rediscovered in the course of tracing the Inca highways. During the day, trekkers stop at villages to share a meal with hosts and then curl up at night on sheepskins inside local rammed-earth houses, after eating trout, dried potato soup, and other local food.

It goes without saying that trekkers should take special care to follow APREC's strict guidelines and be respectful of the land and people they encounter. This is undoubtedly the best option for seeing the Cajamarca countryside, as opposed to day tours to the different farming cooperatives touted by agencies on the Plaza de Armas. APREC's offices are currently inside the Hotel Laguna Seca, though this might soon change. APREC has published a series of excellent guides on Qhapaq Nan, including flora, fauna, birds, folklore, maps, etc., that sell for around $5 each and include topographic maps. There is no camping equipment for rent in Cajamarca.

At this time, there are four principal routes:
Ingatambo–Granja Porcón. This highly recommended day hike begins in the tiny hamlet of **Ingatambo,** 47 km from Cajamarca, and traces a 16-km section of the Inca highway that led

THE SACKINGS OF CAJAMARCA

Cajamarca has always been the center of gold production for Peru. Consequently, it's been the target of fierce sacking by different armies, first the Incas in 1470, then the Spaniards in 1532—the year that 18,660 kilos of gold were paid by **Inca Atahualpa** for ransom and promptly exported to Spain.

After nearly three centuries of once again accumulating gold, silver, and precious gems, Spanish priests had to hand them over in 1822 as **Simón Bolívar** demanded donations for the independence cause. Because the Spanish controlled southern Peru, Bolívar relied on churches and wealthy families in Trujillo, Cajamarca, and Lambayeque to finance the entire campaign.

But the worst sacking of Cajamarca happened during the **War of the Pacific** (1879–83), when marauding Chilean soldiers demanded that the city pay a certain amount of gold and silver. When the town paid only a portion, the enraged Chileans burned the Santa Apolonia church and the altars of every church in town except for the Cathedral, which was saved by the frantic begging of a priest. Soldiers stripped the cathedral's altar of its gold plating, however, and removed all the precious ornaments from the town's religious images—see the dense clustering of precious religious charms on the Virgin de Dolores in Iglesia San Francisco to get an idea of the wealth this must have represented.

from Cajamarca to Quito. The walk, which usually takes around eight hours, can also be divided into an overnight trip. Start near the ruins of an Inca *tambo,* a resting place for *chasquis* (foot messengers who formed a sort of Pony Express), and visit with *campesino* families along the way. Enter the pine forests of **Granja Porcón** before ending at a fabulous Inca bridge. From here, it is possible to visit or overnight at Granja Porcón.

Combayo–Cañon Sangal. After a two-hour drive from Cajamarca to the colonial town of **Combayo,** set out on the best-preserved section of Inca highway near Cajamarca. First stop is **Ventanillas de Combayo,** a larger and more remote example of the cliff tombs at Ventanillas de Otuzco. The 10-km day hike includes dramatic rock formations, rickety log bridges, and several homestays. But the highlight is **Cañon Sangal,** formed by two thin rock ridges punctured by the Río Chonta. This is one of the few areas of the Cajamarca countryside that has not been altered by the European cows imported into the area in the 1940s, according to APREC director Carlos Díaz. The result is a staggering abundance of native plants, trees, and birds—one recent group spotted up to 60 bird species in a single day, including the endemic grey-bellied comet hummingbird.

Cochambul–Baños del Inca. The 20-km, two-day hike begins in the small hacienda of Cochambul and leads first to Laguna San Nico-

las, where *pejerrey* are fished using handmade nets and reed rafts. Camp is set up here in order to visit the nearby fort of Coyor, the unexcavated site of a battle between the Incas and the Caxamarcans. Next stop is the town of Chilacat, where everyone from 5 years old and up is dedicated to making guitars. Along the way there is an excellent section of paved Inca highway with knee-high walls on each side. End at the Baños del Inca for a well-deserved soaking.

Cajamarca–Cumbemayo and Beyond. When you visit Cumbemayo, why not walk back downhill to Cajamarca instead of being bounced around in the back of a car? The three-hour walk follows the last bit of Inca highway that connected the Chimú capital of Chan Chan with Cajamarca and passes through Andean villages and an Inca *huaca,* or holy stone. The trail was still used by horseback riders as late as 1940 to arrive at the coast within a week.

Another popular and recommended three- or four-day route, well described in the *Bradt Trekking Guide,* keeps going on this route past Cumbemayo to San Pablo, a distance of 85 km along fairly moderate terrain. The route heads up and over a 3,900-meter pass above Cumbemayo and down a spectacular valley to the town of **Chetilla,** one of the few places in the Cajamarca region where Quechua is still spoken. The route ends in the colonial village of **San Pablo,** where there is a hostel and a few restaurants. Nearby are the pre-Inca ruins of Kuntur Wasi, where there are a few stone carvings showing the feline figures typical of the Chavín culture.

Granja Porcón

Of the four farming operations visited by tourists around Cajamarca, **Granja Porcón** (29 km northeast of Cajamarca, tel. 076/825-631, www.geocities.com/porconperu, granjaporcon@yahoo.com) is the only one thriving and worth visiting. Every aspect of local farm life—from milking cows to working with leather and wood—is on display here. The whole farm runs like a well-oiled clock, with a rustic restaurant serving local trout, bungalows, a hostel, and a zoo with vicuña, deer, lynx, eagles, and even monkeys. The farm is surrounded by a 10,000-hectare (24,700 acre) plantation of pine trees, which looks like it was lifted out of the Rocky Mountains.

Avoid visiting Cajamarca's other cooperatives, which were also set up in the agrarian reform of the late 1960s but are now withering. **Hacienda Colpa** used to be famous across Peru because ranchers were able to call individual cows out of the herd at milking time. Now the herd, once in the hundreds, numbers five. The same story goes for **Hacienda Llacanora.** Porcón, on the other hand, seems to have thrived because of its well-organized community, support from the nearby Yanacocha gold mine, a joint venture with the European Union, and a lot of faith-backed hard labor (a series of billboards on the road in tout biblical quotes extolling hard work, prayer, and other values of Porcón's evangelical approach). Brand-new wooden bungalows ($20 s, $30 d) have fireplaces and an upstairs loft. There is also a pleasant hostel ($7 s, $15 d). Porcón's Cajamarca office (Chanchamayo 1355, tel. 076/971-082) can get you here, as can any of Cajamaraca's agencies. But the best way to arrive is on foot, via theQhapaq Ñan route that runs from Ingatambo to Granja Porcón.

ENTERTAINMENT AND EVENTS

Casa Luna (Dos de Mayo 334, tel. 076/333-072, akaeshcafe@yahoo.com, 10 A.M.–10 P.M. Mon.–Thurs., 10 A.M.–3 A.M. Fri.–Sat.) is a bo-hemian hangout started by a Cajamarca native who goes by the name *Colo Luna* and has spent time living overseas and in the Amazon with a Stone Age tribe on the Río Napo. He has largely succeeded in creating a pleasant, well-decorated cultural space with theater, poetry readings, and live music on many nights. Even without these attractions, there is a range of more than 30 coffee drinks (including a surprisingly delicious concoction of coffee mixed with liquefied bananas), a gallery, board games, pool table, and a meditation area upstairs with a fireplace.

Dancing and drinking gets going at midnight and goes on until dawn at the upscale **Los Frailones** (Peru 701, tel. 076/82-5113), six blocks up Santa Apolonia from the plaza. The disco pumps full force, waiters shuffle around in monk habits, and the dance floor offers a fantastic view of the city. The best place for local live music is **Peña Usha Usha** (Amalia Pugia 142, 9P.M.–dawn Mon.–Sat.), where local musicians bang out *criollo* music until the wee hours of the morning. The bar serves liquor only and is liveliest on the weekends. Other nightclubs worth checking out are **Las Vegas Discotec** (5 Esquinas 1037), **Kaos Bar** (San Martín 325), and **La Hacienda** (Av. Via de Evitamiento Norte 300).

International movies can be seen nightly at the **Cine Teatro San Martin** (Junín 829, tel. 076/82-3260, $1.50).

Festivals

Every February or March, serene Cajamarca explodes in a riot of water balloons, paint, elaborate parades, and roaming bands of tipsy youths singing *coplas,* or rhymed couplets that have been sung on the street during *carnaval* since colonial times. If you do not want to get drenched in water, paint, or worse, avoid Cajamarca at this time. This is Peru's wildest *carnaval*—actually, it's called a *carnavalón* (which is even bigger!)—and all the hotels are booked.

Cajamarca also has a beautiful **Corpus Christi** celebration in May or June, which includes parades, live music, dancing, bullfights, and horse shows. The village of Porcón celebrates a colorful **Easter Week** with traditional songs and the carrying of a heavy wooden cross on Palm Sunday. For more information, see www.perutravels.net.

SHOPPING

A few handicraft shops above the Plaza de Armas on Dos de Mayo sell leather goods, ceramics, alpaca wool sweaters, jewelry, and handwoven hats. There is a good store for knit goods and art inside **Casa Luna** (Dos de Mayo 334), where paintings for sale hang on the walls. Handicrafts are sold on the sidewalk of Belén behind the Iglesia San Francisco. Local artists sell paintings and photography in revolving expositions in the upstairs gallery of **Restaurant El Batán** (Batán 369, tel. 076/82-6025). The rare visitor who has a week and $150 to spare can have an alpaca wool suit fitted and tailored out of the wool shop run by **Julio Martos** (Amazonas 531, tel. 076/82-3295, 9 A.M.–1 P.M. and 3–7 P.M.). For all other needs, head to the **Mercado Central** on Amazonas. This bustling market sells everything from women's lingerie to farming equipment, and alpaca wool sweaters and blankets can also be found.

SPORTS AND RECREATION

The best agency for going on treks on the surrounding Inca trails is **APREC** (Association for the Rescue of Cajamarca's Ecoystem, Manco Capac 1098, Baños del Inca, tel. 076/89-4600, oper@aprec.org, www.aprec.org).

Hands down the best city guide in Cajamarca is **Manuel Portales,** a walking encyclopedia who can rattle off direct quotes from obscure Spanish chronicles and has an excellent command of English. He is simply an amazing resource. He can be located at **Cumbe Mayo Tours** (Amalia Puga, on the Plaza de Armas, tel. 076/822938) or at home (tel. 076/821476), and he also offers highly recommended tours to Chachapoyas ($30 per day).

Other agencies include **Inca Baths Tours** (Amalia Puga 635, tel. 076/82-1828, ask for Oscar) or **Cajamarca Tours** (Dos de Mayo 323, tel. 076/82-5674). These companies are clustered around the Plaza de Armas and offer half- and full-day tours to sights around Cajamarca for $3–6, and longer trips to Kuélap in the $150–200 range. Check your guide's English before paying.

ACCOMMODATIONS

Under $10

The backpackers' choice is **Hostal Plaza** (Amalia Puga 669, tel. 076/82-2058, $4 s, $7 d shared bath, $7 s, $12 d private bath), a wooden colonial house on the plaza. Rooms are unadorned, but big, clean, and very historic. Hot water in mornings and evenings only.

$10–25

The German-owned **Hospedaje Los Jazmines** (Amazonas 775, tel. 076/82-1812, assado@hotmail.com, $9 s, $13 d shared bath, $12 s, $18 d private bath) is a converted colonial house with six quiet rooms and a café around a small courtyard. Rooms have cable TV, and all profits go to deaf and developmentally disabled children. If you're looking for peace and quiet, head to **Hotel Prado** (La Mar 582, tel. 076/82-6093, $10 s, $20 d), on a calm side street. The cement building lacks character, but the dark and silent rooms make for a good place to cocoon with cable TV, hot water, and big, clean bathrooms. **Hotel Casa Blanca** (Dos de Mayo 446, tel. 076/82-2141, hotelcasablanca595@hotmail.com, $17.50 s, $26 d, including breakfast) offers 30 rooms in a renovated colonial building on the Plaza de Armas. The rooms are ordinary, the furniture outdated, and the hotel understaffed, but this place has an irresistible feel of old-world Cajamarca. The rooms are surprisingly quiet, given the location, and have cable TV. The hotel also has a tourist agency, laundry service, and a restaurant.

M Los Balcones de la Recoleta (Amalia Puga 1050, tel. 076/82-3302, $12 s, $18 d) is a charming colonial house, with vine-covered balconies and a garden overflowing with colorful plants. Nearby is the charming Iglesia La Recolata and, five minutes in the other direction, the Plaza de Armas. Owners have restored the hardwood floors and painted the walls in tasteful shades of red and yellow. The rooms are quiet, charming, and an excellent value with cable TV, hot water, and refrigerator.

$25–50

M El Cabildo Hostal (Junín 1062, tel. 076/82-

7025, cabildoh@latinmail.com, $20 s, $28 d, including breakfast) is a friendly, small hotel in a colonial building one block from the Plaza de Armas. The stone courtyard, with columns and balconies on all sides and a fountain in the middle, is one of the best places in Cajamarca to sit and relax. Off the courtyard there is a common room with a fireplace and TV, and an outdoor restaurant. Rooms include TV with cable.

M Hacienda San Vicente (Revolución, above Cerro Santa Apolonia, tel. 076/822-644, $35 s, $45 d, including breakfast and transport) is one of the most unusual hotels in all of Peru. The architect took a hillside, built gardens and staircases, sculpted cave-like rooms with adobe, and then covered the whole thing with a massive sloping tile roof. The hotel could well have been designed by Antoni Gaudí: a building that grows organically down the hillside with natural rock outcroppings and the odd root that would have made Bilbo Baggins feel at home. Choose carefully, because each room is unique: one features a round bed with star-viewing skylight, and another has a kids' bed and a cozy sleeping den for mom and dad. Because San Vicente is perched on the hillside above Cajamarca, the views are fabulous from the breakfast nooks and tables spread across the back lawn. The hotel even has its own shaman who provides cleansing and other rituals upon request. The only downsides are the lumpy mattresses and crumbly floors, but it all seems part of the pleasant, if slightly, bohemian experience.

La Hispana (La Mar 542, tel. 076/838-489, $21 s, $29 d) is a newly constructed hotel with a pleasant homey feel. Its lack of a colonial pedigree in no way diminishes its character: Rooms feel more like bedrooms, not hotel rooms, with attention to detail extending from oil paintings all the way down to its hip shower curtains. This tiny place is set back off the street and has quiet rooms equipped with cable TV and phone. **Los Pinos Inn** (La Mar 521, tel. 076/825-991, pinoshostal@yahoo.com, $19 s, $29 d) is an elegant hotel a block and a half from the Plaza de Armas. The ground floor has grand salons with fireplaces and velvet chairs, and a small restaurant. The entry leads you up a light-filled, marble staircase to 21 rooms and two apartments on the top floor. Rooms have cable TV and phones, and the hotel also offers laundry and Internet. **Hotel Continental** (Amazonas 760, tel. 076/822-758, $32 s, $47 d) is a clean, modern hotel with all the conveniences and solid service. The 103 rooms have cable TV, hot water, and phones and some have views of the surrounding hills. The hotel offers laundry service, a parking lot, and restaurant and bar.

Hostal Portada del Sol Hacienda (tel. 076/823345, $26 s, $34 d) is 6 km outside Cajamarca on the road to Cumbemayo and is a great value for a country hacienda. This converted weekend house has 15 large, yet simple rooms, many with views of the surrounding eucalyptus forest. There is also a restaurant and bar, walking trails, horseback riding, and no TVs.

The Complejo Turístico Baños del Inca (6 km east of Cajamarca, tel. 076/83-8249, ctbinca@terra.com, $42 per bungalow) has undergone major renovation and now has eight brand-new bungalows with two bedrooms and its own thermal baths. For another $1 you can add sauna and pool privileges. If you want to hunker down and soak for a few days, this may be your place.

$50–100

A stay at **M Posada del Puruay** (Carretera Porcón Km 4.5, tel. 076/828-318, postmaster@puruayhotel.com.pe, www.puruayhotel.com.pe, $60 s, $75 d) may be your most relaxing experience in Peru. This beautifully restored 1822 hacienda, with elegant rooms spread around a stone courtyard, is plunked down in the middle of a country paradise about 15 minutes outside of Cajamarca. The grounds include horse stables, trout farm, eucalyptus and pine forests, and a botanical garden with hundreds of labeled plants. During the day, you can head out on Peruvian *paso* horses for breathtaking circuits through the countryside, grab a mountain bike, or hike on one of the area's many trails. At night, you snuggle under feather comforters and fall asleep to the sounds of rustling trees and a nearby gurgling brook. The restaurant serves up salads loaded with vegetables from the organic garden, an excellent chicken-and-beef fondue that comes

THE PROBLEM WITH YANACOCHA

Given the fact that the *conquistadores* and Francisco Pizarro, Simón Bolívar and even the Chileans have ransacked Cajamarca for its gold, it is perhaps not surprising that Cajamarca's citizens have mixed feelings about Yanacocha. Over the last decade this Peruvian- and American-owned open-pit mine has spread across 9,720 hectares (24,000 acres) of the mountains outside of Cajamarca to become the fifth largest mine in the world. It is majority-owned by Newmont Corp. of Denver, Colorado, who produced a staggering 218 tons of high-quality gold from Yanacocha between 1992 and 2002 and plowed the profits into new mines in Australia and Indonesia. After a recent merger, the company is now the world's top gold producer.

Trouble is brewing for Newmont, however, because of a controversy over whether to mine **Cerro Quilich,** a pyramid-shaped mountain that promises to be the mine's richest gold deposit yet. Local *campesinos* are opposed to the project because they revere Cerro Quilich as an *apu,* or a mountain with a sacred spirit. To make matters worse, Cerro Quilich drains into the Río Grande, which supplies water to Cajamarca's 50,000 (and growing) residents.

City officials say the mine would destroy the grasslands that serve as a spongy reservoir for the area's drinking and irrigation water. And because the mine uses cyanide to dissolve gold from massive dirt piles, city officials worry about water pollution. But Yanacocha execs say the hill accounts for only 4 percent of the city's water. They also point out that Yanacocha has invested more than $100 million a year in the Cajamarca economy, including the creation of 7,000 new jobs.

The conflict escalated into a court battle when Cajamarca's last mayor declared Cerro Quilich a nature reserve based on a single endangered flower found there. Yanacocha appealed, and the issue went before Peru's Supreme Court in 2003, which asked the mine to return with an environmental impact statement.

This controversy has stirred up the bad feelings that most residents seem to have against the mine. Prostitutes have appeared for the first time on the city's main square, catering to the mineworkers who have come from all over Peru. Violent crime is on the rise, as are hundreds of yellow Tico taxis and mining trucks that clog the city's narrow streets.

Highest on the list of complaints, however, is the health disaster that occurred on June 2, 2001, when a Yanacocha truck leaked mercury, a by-product of the extraction process, along a 30-mile stretch of road outside Cajamarca. Thinking it was silver, villagers rushed out to scoop up the shimmering substance with spoons, bowls, even their bare hands. They stored the mercury in their homes, and some even boiled it. Over the next few days, 800 people were treated for mercury poisoning and a few remain permanently disabled.

Political insiders say Cerro Quilich will go forward because Yanacocha is the country's single largest taxpayer (in 2001 it paid $16.5 billion in taxes) and has tremendous political influence. That likelihood does not sit well with Cajamarca residents, who threaten to block the town's only access road, which runs right through Cajamarca. They did exactly that in 2000 when a mishap with the mine's drainage system polluted Cajamarca's water supply and caused a massive trout die-off. Trucks were backed up for nearly two miles, and the mine was shut down for a week, before villagers finally cleared the road.

Yanacocha, near Cajamarca, is the fifth-largest mine in the world.

with six local sauces, homemade apple pie, and a *Calientito Cajamarquino,* a hot rum drink invented by Lucho the bartender for cold mountain nights. The gregarious owner, Nora Regalado, has built up a staff that works like a family and plays soccer most afternoons (guests invited). Rooms include cable TV, VCR, access to a huge video library, and refrigerator. This resort is an excellent place for kids and offers frequent packages on its web page.

The best spa and thermal baths in Peru is without a doubt ☒ **Hotel Laguna Seca** (Manco Capac 1098, Baños del Inca, tel. 076/89-4600, reserva@lagunaseca.com.pe, www.lagunaseca .com.pe, $76 s, $92 d). The hotel draws from the same hot springs that Atahualpa enjoyed in 1532, which run through the grounds in steaming, open canals before being piped into each room. The rooms are outfitted with all the five-star amenities, including cable TV, king-size beds, video library, fridge, and terrycloth bathrobes—but guests forget all these luxuries as they slip into their room's own huge tile tub, which fills with thermal water in minutes. Outside the rooms are a Turkish sauna, three heated pools, and a professional spa that offers full clay treatment, herbal baths, and full-body massages ($15/3/6). Next door is the hotel's *fundo,* a farm that includes an organic vegetable garden and an area for children to pet alpacas, parrots, rabbits, turkeys, cows, and a pair of monkeys. Rides on Peruvian *paso* horses are also offered, and the hotel includes a travel agency and the offices of APREC, the organization dedicated to the area's Inca trails. The whole place runs like a finely tuned clock thanks to manager John Herdin, a Swedish-Peruvian whose wife's family bought this historic hacienda—once the largest in all of Cajamarca—nearly a decade ago. One of the hotel cooks, Santos Colorado, has worked at Laguna Seca since the 1930s and is storehouse of knowledge about the hacienda's past.

FOOD

Cajamarca's verdant countryside is Peru's dairy center and its finest producer of fresh butter, yogurt, and *manjar blanco* (a gooey caramel made from milk, sugar, and egg whites). Cheese lovers

be warned: The area produces sophisticated, delectable cheeses that rival those of France. Shop for dairy products at **La Feria** (Amalia Puga 802), **Villanueva** (Dos de Mayo 615, tel. 076/82-1807), or one of the many *queserías* (cheese shops) on the 500 block of Amazonas.

The preponderance of farms, and lack of seafood, makes dining out in Cajamarca a meat-heavy experience. Local specialities include *el picante papa con cuy frito* (roasted guinea pig with peanut sauce, with chile and potato) *chicharrón con mote* (deep-fried chunks of pork with corn), and *caldo verde* (a broth prepared with seven different types of herbs). Desserts include *quesillo con miel* (nonfat cheese curd served with cane syrup) and *dulce de higos* (fig preserves).

Cafés and Desserts

Cajamarca's best café is ☒ **Cascanuez** (Amalia Puga 554, tel. 076/82-6089, 8 A.M.–11 P.M., $1.50–6), which serves sweet corn *humitas,* hamburgers, and a huge range of coffee drinks and desserts. Across the street from Iglesia San Francisco, **Ollanta** (Amalia Puga 726, tel. 076/83-0911, 8 A.M.–11 P.M.) also serves soups, hamburgers, fresh pasta, and fish and meat entrées. A Peruvian take on a Midwestern American diner, **La Casa de la Abuela** (Cruz de la Piedra, 671, tel. 076/84-8031, 9 A.M.–11 P.M. daily, $3.50–6) has a fireplace, checkered tablecloths, and a menu that includes hamburgers, pizzas, pastas, and desserts. But the pie is a far cry from Grandma's.

The Dutch-owned **Heladeria Holanda** (Amalia Puga 657, Plaza de Armas, 9 A.M.–7 P.M. daily) serves up homemade ice cream and gelato, with flavors harvested from the surrounding countryside.

Peruvian

Locals tend to congregate at **Restaurant Salas** (Amalia Puga 637, tel. 076/82-2867, 9 A.M.–10 P.M. daily, $1.50–6, menú $2.50), a popular dining hall that has held its spot on the Plaza de Armas since 1947 and has the best *humitas* (sweet corn tamales) in town. It serves monstrous portions of *comida típica* and has good drinks and wines. Around the corner is another less expensive locals' favorite: **Restaurant El Zarco** (Batán 170, $1.50) which serves meaty fare along with trout and vegetarian dishes, which are rare in Cajamarca.

Pizza

The German-owned 🔣 **Pizzeria Vaca Loco** (San Martín 330, tel. 076/82-8230, 6–11 P.M., $2.50–8.50) is a charming little restaurant that celebrates the cows and cheeses of Cajamarca. It's decorated with cow-skin seat covers, cow paintings, and cow ceramics. The comfy cow booths are perfect for sipping sangria and eating pizza, lasagna, or calzone. **Rocco's Pizza Bar** (Cruz de Piedra 653, $5) is less expensive and popular with teenagers. The intimate El Marengo (Junín 1201, tel. 076/828045, 7–11 P.M.) serves up pizza from a wood-fired oven.

Chifa

The best spots for those seeking Peruvian-Chinese cuisine are **Chifa Central** (Amazonas 548, tel. 076/82-1197) and **T'Enkntala** (Amalia Puga 531, tel. 076/828-547).

Fine Dining

🔣 **El Batán** (Batán 369, tel. 076/82-6025, 10 A.M.–midnight daily, $4–6) successfully combines food, music, and art in a relaxed atmosphere that comes alive on weekend nights with a *peña*. The sophisticated menu includes Greek salad, tenderloin steak in cognac sauce, flambé-cooked meat with mashed potatoes, and martinis. The woven placemats, wood bar, and dim lighting create an elegant atmosphere that is complemented by excellent service and an upstairs gallery featuring local artists.

Around the corner from the cathedral you'll find **Querubino** (Amalia Puga 589, tel. 076/83-0900, 9 A.M.–midnight daily, $3.50–7), a classy restaurant with excellent Peruvian foods and international wines. Daily specials often include fish, and an exquisite *sopa criolla* is divine. The full bar offers 20 different pisco cocktails.

🔣 **El Cajamarqués** (Amazonas 770, tel. 076/82-2128, 8 A.M.–11 P.M., $3–6, lunch menú $1.75) is an elegant, peaceful place to dine. The colonial building conjures up Old World Spain with iron chandeliers, carved wood mirrors, and a view of Iglesia San Francisco from the garden.

The Peruvian and international food is excellent and inexpensive.

Markets

Cajamarca's bustling **Mercado Central** stretches along Amazonas and sells everything from dairy products to guinea pig and is open throughout the day. There is a small **supermarket** on the 700 block of Amazonas, a few blocks from Plaza de Armas.

INFORMATION AND SERVICES

Tourist guides and maps are available at the Regional **Tourism Office** (Belén 600, tel. 076/82-2997, 8:30 A.M.–1 P.M. and 2:30–6:30 P.M. Mon.–Fri.), which has Cajamarca guides for sale. The small **Oficina de Información Turística** (Batán 289, tel. 076/82-1546, 8:30 A.M.–1 P.M. Mon.–Fri.) is helpful and gives out free city maps.

The **police station** is located at Plaza Amalia Puga (tel. 076/82-2944 or 076/82-2832).

The best health care is at **Clínica Limatambo** (Puno 265, tel. 076/82-4241).

Money changers congregate around the Plaza de Armas and the large banks with ATMs including **Banco Interbank** (Dos de Mayo, Plaza de Armas), **Banco de Crédito** (Comercio 679), and **Banco Wiese** (Comercio 251). Many of these banks do not exchange travelers checks. For quick money transfers, there is a **Western Union office** (Dos de Mayo 323) within the Cajamarca Tours office.

Cajamarca's **post office** is at Amazonas 443 (tel. 076/82-4065, 8 A.M.–9:30 P.M. Mon.–Sat.).

Internet cafés filled with teenagers are everywhere—the speediest, and quietest, connection we found was at Cruz de la Piedra 657. Other locations include Amalia Puga 976, Amazonas 107, Amazonas 676, Dos de Mayo 693, or Dos de Mayo 568. Atajo (Comercio 716, open until 1 A.M.) is centrally located and offers Internet calls to the U.S. for 30¢ per minute.

The only public laundry service we could find was **Lavanderia Dandy** (Amalia Puga 545, tel. 076/82-8067, 8 A.M.–7:30 P.M. Mon.–Sat., $1.45/kilo), which is good and reasonably priced. Many hotels also offer laundry service for customers at a higher, per-piece price.

🔣 Northern Highlands

GETTING THERE AND AROUND

Jets from **Aerocondor, L.C. Busre, Atsa,** and **Magenta Air** land daily at Cajamarca's airport, 3 km east of the Plaza de Armas. Taxis into town costs $1.50.

Cruz del Sur, Expreso Cia., and **Transportes Línea** have daily bus service to Cajamarca from all major cities on the coast, including Lima (14 hours), Trujillo (seven hours), and Chiclayo (six hours). In Cajamarca, the best bus companies are **Transportes Línea** (Av. Atahualpa 318), charging $28 to Lima, $9 to Trujillo, and $10 to Chiclayo; Cruz del Sur (Av. Atahualpa 600), charging $28 to Lima; **Turismo DIAS** (Jr. Sucre 422, tel. 076/82-8289), charging $9 to Trujillo.

For travel info to Chachapoyas, see the sidebar *Overland to Chachapoyas.* To reach Celendin (four hours), **Transportes Atahualpa** (Av. Atahualpa 299, tel. 076/82-3075) runs daily buses at 1 P.M. for $4. **Transportes Royal Palace** (Av. Atahualpa 339, tel. 076/82-5855) runs buses to Celendin at 8:30 A.M. and 1 P.M. for $4.

Taxis are ubiquitous and cheap in Cajamarca ($0.75), though downtown congestion often makes walking faster.

OVERLAND TO CHACHAPOYAS

Regular flight service has recently begun to Chachapoyas, but most people still arrive via two spectacular routes, which are worth enjoying (and describing) in detail. The first—the 322 km of dirt road between Cajamarca and Chachapoyas—involves a 3,000-meter plunge into the **Marañón Valley** amid some of the most dramatic scenery in all of Peru. It is like a wider, and deeper, version of Arizona's Grand Canyon. This journey has the reputation of being a grueling, 24-hour drive from hell along potholed roads on sheer cliff faces, but it is actually more like 14 hours on mostly sandy (and we thought safe, by Peruvian standards) roads. Broken up in two days, this can be an interesting journey with some of the best scenery Peru has to offer.

The route has another advantage: By getting off a few hours early in **Leimebamba,** travelers can visit the ruins of La Congona and get a great introduction to the area at the new museum. Then they can proceed down the valley, staying and visiting ruins along the way, before taking the 10-hour highway trip back to Chiclayo. Those who travel there and back on the highway, on the other hand, have to backtrack three hours if they want to visit Leimebamba.

From Cajamarca, the route passes through *altiplano* scenery on bumpy rock roads until it reaches **Celendín,** a plain country town with basic services. Past Celendín, the road switchbacks 3,000 meters (9,900 feet) down into the huge expanse of the Marañón Canyon. Over a rickety bridge, and past the small, subtropical town of Balsas, the road climbs steeply up 2,400 meters (7,920 feet) of switchbacks on the other side before entering the drainage of the Río Utcubamba. Shortly thereafter travelers arrive at the village of Leimebamba. Bus travel times are three hours from Cajamarca to Celendín, another eight hours to reach Leimebamba, and another three to the city of **Chachapoyas.**

Travelers should avoid this route in the rainy months from December to March when mud slides, accidents, and delays are more likely, and mountain vistas become smothered in cloudbanks. Even in dry season, skies tend to cloud over in the afternoon, so it is best to do the most spectacular part of the journey—the Marañón Canyon—in the morning. Bring plenty of food and water (and gas and a spare tire, if you are driving) because there are no services along the way.

The other route, along paved, all-weather highways, also threads through fabulous scenery in the 10-hour bus ride from Chiclayo to Chachapoyas. From **Chiclayo,** the route heads toward the sierra just before **Olmos,** a colonial town surrounded on all sides by the Sechura Desert and famous for its limes. The next 38 km climbs up and over Porculla Pass at 2,144 meters is the lowest pass over the Andes and the shortest route from the coast to the Amazon. Around the pass there is a long subtropical zone, with some banana farms, before dropping into the arid Marañón Valley.

CELENDÍN

If you are making the Cajamara-Chachapoyas overland journey, **Celendín** (2,648 meters) is a friendly place to stay for the night—and, with the bus schedules, you probably won't have a choice. Celendín is a clean, tranquil town with a few nice places to stay and eat and many friendly, helpful people. Walking around the large plaza is a relaxing way to shake off dust and prepare for the next leg of the journey.

The inhabitants of this area were once part of the Caxamarca culture, which was conquered by the Incas in 1470. Choctamalque, a center of Caxamarca culture, was located near Celendín. It was an important stopping point in the trade route that interconnected the Chimú, Caxamarca, and Chachapoya cultures, which inhabited this part of present-day Peru from the coast to the cloud forest before the Incas invaded. Legend has it that the city's last prince, **Intihuaquishagua**, fled from the Incas across a natural bridge spanning the Río Marañón, destroying it as he went. Celendín was founded in 1793, carved out of a hacienda that had 485 Spanish and Portuguese shareholders at the time.

There is an interesting market on Sundays and a good *artesanía* shop at 2 de Mayo 319.

Jaén, a good rest stop, is 17 km off the highway and just before the Río Marañón. Sedimentary layers, standing end on end and exposed by erosion, have made this area famous for fossils and dinosaur bones. The highlight of the journey, however, is the **Cañon Urcubamba,** where lush, steep walls of vegetation drop to a thundering river. The canyon widens and reaches **Pedro Ruiz,** where the Chachapoyas road branches right. The highway continues another 31 km up to Lago Pomacochas, a miniature Lake Titicaca, before dropping toward the Amazon, to **Moyabamba** (180 km, four hours), **Tarapotoa** (295 km, six hours), and, on very rough roads, to **Yurimaguas** (469 km, 14 hours).

The best bus company for the Chiclayo-Chachapoyas route is Móvil Tours (Libertad 1084 in Chachapoyas, tel. 041/77-8545, Bolognesi 199 in Chiclayo, tel. 041/27-1940). Buses leave Chiclayo at 8 P.M., arriving in Chachapoyas at 5 A.M., or leave Chachapoyas at 10 A.M., arriving in Chiclayo at 7 P.M.; fare is $9 or $12 from Trujillo. The other transportation in Chachapoyas is Tras Servis Kuelap (Ortiz Arrieta 412 in Chachapoyas, tel. 041/77-8128, Bolognesi 536 in Chiclayo, tel. 074/27-1318). This bus leaves Chachapoyas at 9 P.M. and arrives in Chiclayo at 5 A.M. Most buses to Chiclayo also stop briefly in Olmos, Bagua, and Pedro Ruiz. Bring a lunch for the ride, as not all restaurants on the way to Chachapoyas are recommended.

The only bus company between Celendín and Chachapoyas is La Virgen del Carmen (Caceres 117 in Chacha) The trip to Celendín takes 10–12 hours, costs $8, and leaves Chacha every day at 8 A.M., arriving by 8 P.M. It is necessary to overnight in Celendín to catch the four-hour bus ride to Cajamarca the next morning. From Celendín, buses leave for Chacha Sundays and Thursdays at 11 A.M. from the main plaza.

heading up to Porculla Pass along the Chiclayo–Chachapoyas highway

Like Leimebamba, Celendín celebrates the festival of its patron saint, *La Virgen de Carmen,* in July. The principal day of the celebration is usually July 30, the anniversary of Celendín, with a religous procession, dancing, orchestras, cockfights, and even a bullfight featuring matadors from Mexico and Spain.

Hostal Loyers (José Gálvez 410, tel. 076/85-5210, $3 s, $5 d) is Celendín's best budget option. Basic, quiet rooms surround a large, pleasant courtyard. Prices given are for shared bath; water is lukewarm. Add $3 for private bath. One step up (and as good as it gets) is the family-run **Hostal Celendín** (Unión 305, tel. 076/85-5041, $8 d) on the Plaza de Armas. A friendly staff offers rooms with rickety wood floors, hot showers (if you wait), and TV for an extra $1.50. There is a good restaurant on the ground floor. Another basic choice is **Raymi Wasi** (José Galvez 420, tel. 076/85-5374, $5 s), with hot water, TV, and a restaurant.

The best restaurant in town is the oddly decorated **La Reserve** (Dos de Mayo 549, tel. 076/85-5415, 8 A.M.–11 P.M., $2). Locals watch TV movies in this cozy place while they dine next to a faux fireplace. An excellent choice is the *pollo con vino blanco,* served with *papas fritas. Pollo a la brasa,* brochettes, and *lomo saltado* are also on the menu. The bartender makes a good cuba libre. The other option is **Jalisco** (Union 317, Plaza de Armas), next to Hostal Celendin, serving *comida típica.>@P> This restaurant is popular with locals but may not be entirely hygienic. To cure a sweet tooth,* visit **Heladería El Rosario** (Pardo 426, tel. 076/85-5109, 10 A.M.–11 P.M., $1) on the Plaza de Armas. Here you can find ice cream, flan, puddings, cakes, and hamburgers.

For medical emergencies see Dr. Francisco Caceres (Grau 470, no telephone). There are no ATMs in town, but there are but a few places to use the Internet. For bus info, see the sidebar *Overland to Chachapoyas.*

Chachapoyas

Chachapoyas, a huge area of remote cloud forest, lies between the Marañón and Huallaga Rivers and contains some of Peru's most rugged and least-explored territory. Every decade or so, explorers and archaeologists here discover a major lost city from one of Peru's most mysterious civilizations, a federation of city-states known as the Chachapoya. If the Spanish had arrived in Peru three centuries earlier, they probably would have had their butts kicked by the independent and feisty Chachapoya, whose well-fortified cities were a constant headache to the Incas. This wilderness, ranging from 1,800 to 2,500 meters, hosts endangered species such as the Andean spectacled bear and the marvelous spatule-tail hummingbird and is, unfortunately, rapidly being destroyed by new roads and colonists.

The main fortress of **Kuélap** is built atop a foreboding mountain ridge that rivals Machu Picchu in size and natural beauty. Only one person at a time could enter through the narrow passageways leading into the city, built atop a six-hectare platform created by backfilling huge walls.

Kuélap contains many of the classic Chachapoya architectural elements found at other sites: round homes with intricate stone friezes, a lookout tower, and cliff tombs, or *chullpas.*

Kuélap is only one of dozens of worthwhile sites dispersed throughout this rugged wilderness. The most visited include the human-shaped sarcophagi perched on a cliff at **Karajía;** a settlement of 60 round homes near the Río Utcubamba road known as **Macro;** the brightly painted funerary homes on the cliff at **Revash;** mummies and other artifacts on display at a new, excellent museum outside **Leimebamba;** and the ruins of **Congona,** a sprawling Chachapoyan city that is a short trek into the hills above Leimebamba. Making sense of how to reach these sites, and in what order, is a daunting task. For efficiency's sake, even the most independent of travelers opt for organized, multiday tours through this area.

Chachapoyas is a paradise for those who enjoy trekking in the jungle. There are a number of ruins—such as the **Laguna de los Cóndores** tomb site and the vast area of **Gran Vilaya**—

the Marañon Valley from high pass above Leimebamba

that can only be reached by multiday treks made, most often, with burros and horses. Trekking and camping in villages is the best way to understand the life of the modern-day Chachapoya, whose fair skin and clear eyes have fueled much speculation as to their ancestry. The scenery includes plunging waterfalls, squawking parrots and other colorful birds, and ridgetops blanketed in dense cloud forest.

Considering all there is to see and do, it is surprising how few visitors come to this area. For the year 2002, the Institute of National Culture reported fewer than 1,500 visitors *total* for Kuélap, as compared with up to 1,000 per day for the once-lost Inca city of Machu Picchu. The dearth of visitors is due in large part to accessibility. Flights are unreliable to Chachapoyas, so most visitors were arriving via road from Cajamarca (16 hours), Chiclayo (10 hours), or Tarapoto (10 hours). A road leads straight to Kuélap, but many of the other ruins make for a day hike at least.

Contracting a guide or going with a guided tour seems like a good idea in Chachapoyas. Travelers who forge out on their own can spend hours, even days, looking for ruins that blend perfectly into the hilly, jungle-covered landscape. Most visitors base themselves in the city of Chachapoyas, the capital of the Amazonas Department with a nice collection of hotels, restaurants, and other services. An increasing number of agencies, however, are forgoing the 30-minute detour to Chachapoyas and basing themselves instead in **Choctamal, Tingo,** or **Chillo,** small towns close to the majority of ruins. Avoid the entire area during the intense rainy season from December to March, when roads and trails become awash with mud.

Though a bit out of the way, the city of Chachapoyas is by far the biggest town, with the best services and transport options, in the area. This mountain town is closer to the Andes than to the Amazon at 2,335 meters, with chilly nights and hot, sunny days. Travelers have traditionally used it as a base for exploring Kuélap (two or three hours away by *combi*) and other ruins, though travelers are increasingly turning to convenient new lodges in Choctamal, Tingo, or Chillo. The access road to Chachapoyas, which branches off the main Río Utcubamba road, was asphalted in 2003 and the detour now takes only 30 minutes each way.

© RENÉE DEL GAUDIO AND ROSS WEHNER

Workers pause from making a rammed-earth home.

The nearby village of **Levanto** was the second center of Spanish authority (Jalca Grande was the first, in 1538, and moved to Levanto shortly thereafter), but Chachapoyas was founded soon after, in 1545, by conquistador Alonso de Alvarado. The location of the city has changed several times but present-day Chacha, as it is called by locals, contains quite a few old colonial homes with wooden balconies and large courtyards. It is a friendly and relaxed town with a spacious plaza that is a favorite strolling spot for families and teenagers. In the plaza's center is a monument to **Toribio Rodriguez de Mendoza,** who grew up in a large home on this square and went on to be a priest and one of the intellectual leaders of Peru's independence. Though the cathedral on the plaza is of modern construction, there are a few interesting colonial churches, including **Capilla de la Virgen Asunta,** at Asunción and Puno, and **Iglesia del Señor de Burgos,** at Amazonas and Santa Lucía. Also on the plaza is the INC's **Museo Amazonas Arqueológico** (Ayacucho 908, 8 A.M.–1 P.M. and 2–5 P.M., free), which con-tains a range of Chachapoya artifacts, including mummies, ceramics, and utensils.

ENTERTAINMENT AND EVENTS

Towns around Chachapoyas have a lively **February carnaval,** including the cutting down of *humishas* (gift-covered trees) in Luya. The festival for Chachapoyas' patron saint, *Virgen Asunta,* takes place the second week of August and is recommended, as are the **patron saint festivities** for surrounding villages: Luya (June 24), Jalca Grande (June 28). and Lamud (second week of September).

There is some, though not much, weekend nightlife in Chachapoyas at several bars and clubs along Ayacucho's 800 and 700 blocks. The best discos are **La Noche** (Triunfo 1061, doors open 8 P.M.), and **Non Limit Disco Bar** (Grau 380).

SHOPPING

Artesanias Kuyacc (Amazonas 814, one block from plaza, 8 A.M.–9 P.M.) sells beautiful alpaca sweaters, scarves, and hats along with shoulder bags, ceramics, jewelry, and musical instruments. **Artesanía Ecológica** (Amazonas 371, 7 A.M.–9 P.M.) sells wood sculptures made by a local Chachapoyas family. The town market is located on Libertad between Grau and Ortiz Arrieta, behind the Plaza de Armas.

SPORTS AND RECREATION

Be careful with contracting trekking guides in Chachapoyas. Either use these agencies listed below or get recommendations from traveler reports in the South American Explorers Club. There have been reports of theft with independent guides who work in Chachapoyas.

Vilaya Tours (Ayacucho 624, in Gran Vilaya Hotel, tel. 041/77-7506, info@vilayatours.com, www.vilayatours.com) is managed by Englishman Rob Dover, who is friendly and knowledgeable and has lived in Chachapoyas since 1997. The company offers excellent hotel-based tours, which start at $760 for five days and go up

Northern Highlands

to $1,065 for eight days. Most important, Vilaya Tours offers an extraordinary series of treks to out-of-the-way places, such a two-week trek thoroughly the completely roadless mountains south of Leimebamba along the old Inca Trail to Cusco, including a visit to the ruins of Cochabamba, a remote Imperial Inca site with double-jambed doorways, fountains, and *kancha* enclosures ($1,920). The agency also leads the best treks to Laguna de los Cóndores.

Recommended hotel tours are offered by **InkaNatura** (Manuel Bañon 461, San Isidro, Lima, tel. 01/440-2022, postmaster@inkanatura.com.pe, www.inkanatura.com) or through its U.S. agent, **Tropical Nature Travel** (www.tropicalnaturetravel.com). InkaNatura offers a five-day trip to Chachapoyas from Chiclayo ($840, including transport, lodging and board) or a seven-day loop from Chiclayo to Chachapoyas and onto Cajamarca via the adventurous Marañón Valley road.

Chachapoyas Tours (Grau 534, second flr., Plaza de Armas, tel. 041/77-8078 or in U.S. 800/743-0945, kuelap@msn.com, www.kuelapperu.com) is an agency founded by Charles and Tina Motley, an American-Peruvian couple who live in Orlando, Florida, but summer in Chachapoyas. They have built two excellent lodges, one in Levanto and the other in Choctamal, and offer a range of treks. They offer full-service guided treks to Gran Vilaya ($589, five days) and Laguna de los Cóndores ($300, three days) and even the remote Gran Pajatén. They also offer stripped-down backpacker versions that include guide only and go as low as $160 for five-day trip to Gran Vilaya, three-person minimum.

The other agencies, useful for inexpensive day trips to Kuélap, include **Amazon Tours** (Arrieta 520, Plaza de Armas, tel. 041/77-8294), **Cloudforest Expedition** (Puno 368, tel. 041/77-7610), and **Turismo Explorer** (Arrieta 412, tel. 041/77-8128). The only independent guide we can recommend is **Manuel Portales,** who can be reached at Cajamarca's Cumbe Mayo Tours (Amalia Puga, on the Plaza de Armas, tel. 076/822938) or at home (tel. 076/821476). His Chachapoyas tour runs $30 per day.

ACCOMMODATIONS

Because of Chacha's damp, cold nights, travelers should check for hot—not lukewarm—water before paying for a room.

Under $10

For those on a tight budget, **Hostal Kuélap** (Amazonas 1057, tel. 041/77-7136, $3 s, $4 d) has small, cramped, but quiet rooms. Prices given are for rooms with shared bath. Hot water and TV are each $2 extra.

$10–25

The modern **Hostal Johumaji** (Ayacucho 711, tel. 041/77-7279, $6 s, $12 d), two blocks from the plaza, is a good budget choice offering private baths with hot water and cable TV. Tile-floored rooms vary in size and are quiet and very clean. There is a full-service restaurant that stays open fairly late in the evening.

The most charming budget option is **M Hostal Revash** (Grau 517, tel. 041/77-7391, $9 s, $13 d), a rambling colonial house with huge rooms surrounding a courtyard teeming with plants and birds. The house is much as it must have been two centuries ago, except for the new wood floors, cable TV, and modern bathrooms with hot water. It's amazingly quiet despite being right on the plaza, and there's a restaurant on the ground floor. **Hostal El Tejado** (Grau 534, tel. 041/77-7654, $8 s, $12 d) is another colonial house on the plaza with charming clean rooms that can get noisy because of a second-story restaurant. The office of Chachapoyas Tours is here.

The best-preserved colonial *casona* in Chachapoyas is **La Casona Monsante** (Amazonas 746, tel. 041/77-7702, casona@terramail.com.pe, www.casonamonsante.com, $12 s, $20 d, including breakfast). The rooms are huge and sparsely decorated, with ancient doors and high ceilings, tile floors, comfortable beds, and cable TV. The courtyard garden is filled with orchids and begonias. **Gran Hotel Vilaya** (Ayacucho 755, tel. 041/77-7664, $18 s, $24 d, including breakfast) is a four-story modern hotel with large, dark, carpeted rooms with comfortable beds, phones, cable TV, and hot water. The café-bar is downstairs, along with the office of Vilaya Tours.

$25–50

A charming hostel with a fireplace in each room, **Ⓜ Casa Vieja** (Chincha Alta 569, tel. 041/77-7353, casavieja@viabcp.com, www.casaviejaperu .com, $20 s, $28 d, including breakfast) is worth the money. Carpeted rooms of varying sizes and decor surround a stone courtyard and rose garden. The smell of burnt hickory wafts through the house and into the grand sitting room and dining area. Rooms have telephones and cable TV, and free Internet is available downstairs.

FOOD

Cafés and Desserts

For juices, cakes, and fruit salads, locals converge on **Café Mass Burger** (Ortiz Arrieta, Plaza de Armas, 8 A.M.–10 P.M. Mon.–Sat.). One traveler even claims that this place produces *the best chocolate cake in South America*. **Café de Guias** (Ayacucho 755), inside the Gran Hotel Vilaya, serves organic coffee, sandwiches, desserts, and vegetarian food. It is also a resource for tours, maps, and books on the area. Several bakeries can be found near Union and Triunfo next to the Belén Plaza.

Peruvian

The crowded **Bar Restaurant Mataleche** (Ayacucho 616, tel. 041/77-8325, 7 A.M.–9 P.M. daily) is a favorite among locals, serving beef, chicken, and guinea pig at locals-only prices. Heaping plates of *comida típica* are also served up at **Restaurant Cha Cha** (Grau 545, Plaza Mayor, tel. 041/77-7107, $1–6) underneath the Hostal El Tejado on the Plaza Mayor. A cleaner, though plainer restaurant is upstairs in the Hotel Tejado (Grau 534). For grilled meats and pizzas, the best in town is **La Tushpa** (Ortiz Arrieta 753, tel. 041/77-7198, 1–11 P.M. Mon.–Sat., 6–11 P.M. Sunday, $1–3). Despite a cold, nondescript atmosphere, this place serves mouth-watering *brochetas* (meat and vegetable skewers), *parrillas* (grilled meats), and *anticuchos* (roasted cow heart). The prices are dirt-cheap and the kitchen immaculate.

For typical local food in a friendly atmo-

sphere try **La Chozas de Marlisa** (Ayacucho 1133, tel. 041/77-7118, 10 A.M.–8 P.M., $2–5). It serves *cecina* (dried, smoked pork), *cuy con papas* (guinea pig with potatoes), and *pollo frito*. **Don Chamo** (Libertad 548, tel. 041/77-7619, 7:30 A.M.–5 P.M. Mon.–Sat., 8:30 A.M.–3 P.M. Sunday) serves around a dozen different *cebiches* and *comida criolla*, or coastal food, on the weekends.

Health Food

With two locations and the freshest of ingredients, **Ⓜ Restaurant Vegetariano El Eden** (Grau 432, Plaza Mayor, and Amazonas 1091, tel. 041/77-7136, 7:30 A.M.–9 P.M., $1–2) has the best and cheapest menú in town. It serves excellent yogurts, salads, soups, and large helpings of rice and soy-based dishes. Vegetarian or not, don't miss this place.

Markets

For the best selection of groceries, try **Mini-Market** (Ortiz Arrieta 528, Plaza Mayor, 7 A.M.–11 P.M.), with a café-bar on the second floor, or **Tito and Rojasa** on La Libertad block 6. Another small fruit market selling pineapples, bananas, tomatoes, and other goods is at Ayacucho 716. The **Mercado Central,** full of local fruits and vegetables, is located on Libertad between Grau and Ortiz Arrieta, behind the Plaza de Armas.

INFORMATION AND SERVICES

There is a **Tourist Information Office** at Ortiz Arrieta 1250 (tel. 041/77-8355). Above the **Institute of National Culture Museum** (Ayacucho 904, Plaza de Armas, 8 A.M.–1 P.M. and 2–5 P.M.) there is a library and some tourist information. The office of **Chachapoyas Tours,** in the Hotel Tejado (Plaza de Armas, Grau 534), is a useful source of information with maps and books on the area. A great Chachapoyas web page is www.chachapoyas.com, hosted by Keith Muscutt, author of *Warriors of the Clouds: A Lost Civilization in the Upper Amazon of Peru*. Other recommended pages are www.amazonas-explorer.com and www.kuelap.org.

The **National Police** is at Ayacucho 1040 (tel. 041/77-7176).

For health care, the two options are **Hospital Chachapoyas** (third block of Triunfo, tel. 041/77-7016 or 041/77-7354, 24 hours), and **Centro Médico Virgen del Carmen** (Grau 603, no telephone, 9 A.M.–1 P.M. and 3–9 P.M., $6 per consultation).

Banks with ATMs include **Banco de la Nación** (Ayacucho block 800) and Banco de Crédito (Ortiz Arrieta 580, on the plaza). **Banco de Crédito** also gives cash advances on Visa cards and changes travelers checks.

The **post office** (Grau 553, tel. 041/77-7019, 8 A.M.–8 P.M. Mon.–Sat.) is located on the Plaza de Armas.

Chachapoyas now has speedy **Internet,** with a good place on the plaza (Ortiz Arrieta 520, second flr). Other options are **Ciber Club Internet** (Triunfo 769, tel. 041/77-8419) or an unnamed place at Amazonas 828 (8:30 A.M.–midnight) where international calls cost $0.30. **Telefónica de Peru** (Ayacucho 924, on the plaza) sells international calling cards (7 A.M.–11 P.M. daily, $1/min for most international).

The best place for laundry is **Lavandería Clean** (Amazonas 813, tel. 041/77-7078, 8 A.M.–9 P.M. Mon.–Sat., $1/kilo), offering same-day service, one block from the plaza.

GETTING THERE AND AROUND

Taxis charge $3 to the airport, 4 km out of town. For bus information, see the sidebar *Overland to Chachapoyas.*

Chachapoyas is such a small town that no one ever seems to take a taxi. Check the descriptions of each set of ruins for how to arrive there via public transport. *Combis* leave for Pedro Ruiz, on the Chiclayo-Tarapoto highway, between 4 A.M. and 10 P.M. at *Comite Pedro Ruiz* (Grau 337, $3). *Combis* leave for Leimebamba ($2.50), and all points in between, at noon from Dos de Mayo block 4 and Grau 302, and at 1 P.M. from the corner of Grau and Salamanca. *Colectivos* leave for Tingo ($3.50) and Yerba Buena from Grau 302 (block 3 of Grau) when they have at least four passengers.

TINGO AND CHILLO

Tingo and Chillo, small villages along the Rio Utcubamba, lack the services of Chachapoyas but have the advantage of being a full hour closer to Kuélap, Revash, and Leimebamba. Being in the river valley at 1,800 meters—more than 400 meters below Chacha—they are also a lot warmer at night than chilly Chachapoyas. A string of charming lodges in the area have been convincing travelers to base themselves here.

Tingo has rebounded nicely from the 1993 El Niño flood, with one recommended restaurant, a backpackers' hostel, and a new bungalow complex. Backpackers overnight in Tingo during the Levanto-Kuélap trek before climbing the 10-km path to Kuélap. The climb is over 1,000 meters and takes four to five grueling hours. Get an early start, take plenty of water, and avoid walking alone on this trail—at least one assault has been reported against a traveler hiking alone at dusk. Only 5 km south is the small town of Chillo, with two highly recommended lodges.

Accommodations

In Tingo, **Albergue León** ($6 s, $8 d) is a squat, white building set back from the street. Cramped rooms share clean bathrooms with cold water only. However, the owner is friendly and knowledgeable about the area. Unmistakably modeled after Kuélap itself, **Valle Kuélap Hotel Inn** (Grau 623, tel. 041/77-8433, vallekuelap@hotmail.com, www.vallekuelap.com, $10 s, $20 d) is a brand-new complex of relatively deluxe bungalows that climbs up onto a nearby hillside. Rooms have wood floors, modern baths, comfortable beds, and plenty of hot water.

Just a few kilometers down the road toward Chillo lies **Estancia Chillo** (Km 46 of the main road, tel. 041/77-8438, $9 s, $18 d), a lodge in which nearly every detail—furniture, doors, sculptures, you name it—was hand-built by the owner, Oscar Arce Cáceres. Rustic, stone-floored rooms are strung around a patio and various sitting rooms, and there is even a pool, filled with local creek water, for an afternoon dip. Visitors spend time playing with a humorous pair of hostesses, a Great Dane named Van Damme, and a Pekingese named Jackie Chan. There is also a handmade (of course) chess set next to the fireplace in one of the salons, flanked by fruit trees and bougainvillea. For $30 per day, visitors get lodging with full board (including box lunch). Though he speaks only Spanish, Señor Arce is a good source for information about local ruins and a long-time guide who enjoys taking travelers up to Kuélap (or anywhere else) on horseback.

Peter Lerche, Señor Arce's brother-in-law, has a lodge in Chillo, about 5 km up a dirt road marked by another arched entranceway south of Estancia Chillo. This quaint lodge has small rooms with shared baths. Views across the Utcubamba Valley are very impressive.

Food

The best restaurant in Tingo is **Restaurant Tingo** (no tel., 6 A.M.–10 P.M., $1 menú), a clean place with a range of *comida típica*. The owner, Doña Flor Mendoza Góngora, is cheerful and knowledgeable. Her son operates El Gran Shubit restaurant in El Tambo, near Kuélap. There is a single telephone in Tingo, in a white house on the eastern side of the bridge over the Río Utcubamba. There are no restaurants in Chillo outside of the lodges themselves.

Getting There and Around

These cities are an easy drop-off with any transport headed between Leimebamba and Chachapoyas. From Chachapoyas, *colectivos* leave for Tingo from Grau block 3. There is no direct transport to these towns from Pedro Ruiz. Apart from public transport that passes along the road, options for getting around once you are there include horseback and transportation arranged by your lodging.

CHOCTAMAL AND MARIA

Choctamal is one of the villages on the way to the road to Kuélap and has a wonderful lodging option with the best possible view of Kuélap, a mere half hour's drive away. **N Choctamal Lodge** (tel. 041/77-8078, kuelap@msn.com, www.kuelap.org, $10 pp with breakfast), operated by the community of Choctamal, sits high

on a hilltop with a direct view of Kuélap from the bedroom balconies. The rooms with wooden floors are elegant, though spartan, and there are plenty of blankets for the area's chilly nights. The outdoor hot tub, sunset over the valley, and tamale breakfast are not to be missed. This lodge also has a $3 pp special for backpackers doing the **Gran Vilaya** trek, which ends just up the road. In the nearby town of El Tambo, there is a good restaurant named **El Gran Shubit** (no tel., $3–6), which serves local dishes and fresh trout. The owner, Roberto, is very friendly and knowledgeable about the area.

LEIMEBAMBA

Leimebamba, near the head of the Utcubamba Valley at 2,000 meters, is a quiet, stone town with cobblestone streets and a forgotten feel that befits a town that can only be reached by several hours on dirt roads. Leimebamba is only 80 km (three hours) south of the city of Chachapoyas, but the dirt roads make this journey far longer, and more difficult, during the rainy season. Past Leimebamba, the road climbs out of the Utcubamba watershed and plunges headlong into the Marañón Valley, en route to Celendín and Cajamarca on the far side.

Leimebamba has the excellent **Museo Leimebamba** that displays mummies recovered from Laguna de los Cóndores in 1997. A three-hour walk above the city are the ruins of **La Congona.** Leimebamba, whose original name has been lost, was one of the first Chachapoya towns that **Inca Tupac Yupanqui** encountered when he entered the Utcubamba Valley with his army in 1472. It was here that the Inca celebrated the Festival of Inti-Raymi, a celebration of the summer solstice that marks the beginning of the planting season. Afterwards the town was renamed to Raymi-Pampa, meaning "field of the festival of the sun," which became Leimebamba over the years. The town celebrates its patron saint, *Virgen de Carmen,* in mid-July.

Museo Leimebamba

The brand-new Museo Leimebamba, 5 km southwest of Leimebamba on the highway, is an excellent introduction to Chachapoya culture. More than 225 mummies and 2,000 artifacts recovered from cliff tombs at **Laguna de los Cóndores** in 1997 are housed here. The mummies, housed in funerary homes similar to those at Revash, were perfectly preserved thanks to an odd microclimate caused by a waterfall falling over an overhang. As a result, the mummies, textiles, and other artifacts are in perfect condition, creating an odd time warp as if they were only decades, instead of centuries, old. DNA from the mummies is helping scientists understand migration patterns, diseases, and the genetic origins of the mysteriously fair-skinned Chachapoya. Other artifacts include colorful shawls, feathered headdresses, baskets, sandals, flutes—the best collection of Chachapoya artifacts currently available—and artistic renderings of what Kuélap and other Chachapoya sites may once have looked like. This is a good first stop before visiting ruins.

Accommodations and Food

There are two basic hostels with spotty water and electricity on the road between the plaza and the river. **Laguna de los Cóndores**($4 s, $8 with bath), a block from the plaza, has hot water and helpful, knowledgable owners. Another recommendation with hot water is **La Casona de Leimebamba** (Amazonas 221, tel. 041/77-0261, $13 d). The rooms here are large and have private baths. The best of the simple restaurants is **Celi,** a couple blocks from the main plaza, serving excellent $2 meals. **El Sabor Tropical** and **El Caribe** are also recommended.

Getting There

All buses from Cajamarca to Chachapoyas stop in Leimebamba. From Chachapoyas, Leimebamba *colectivos* leave when full from Grau 302 at noon, and from the corner of Salamanca and Grau at 1 P.M. For more information on travel to Cajamarca see the sidebar *Overland to Chachapoyas.*

Ruins in the Chachapoyas Area

The following is a list of principal Chachapoyas ruins, from north to south, with rough instructions on how to get there. Get prior recommendations when hiring local guides in small towns—theft was a problem recently with guides contracted in Yerba Buena, the town nearest Revash. Tourists should register in the Leimebamba tourist office on the plaza and pay a $1.75 archaeological tax before venturing into the hills.

◪ KUÉLAP

Perched on a limestone ridge above the Utcubamba Valley, Kuélap (8 A.M.–5 P.M. daily, $3) must have been a nearly impenetrable fortress. This imposing stone citadel, 700 meters long and 110 meters at its widest, is surrounded by huge walls and sheer cliff faces. Visitors enter from the east, via one of three narrow passageways that penetrate the massive and remarkably intact walls, which were backfilled with mud and blocks to create Kuélap's six-hectare (15-acre) platform. Above are the ruins of more than 400 round stone homes, some of which were as wide as grain silos. Roofed with a peaked thatch roof, these two-story homes have stones protruding from their sides that were probably gutters to keep rain away from the foundations. Friezes with zigzag, rhomboid, or serpentine shapes wrap around many of the buildings. *Nogal* and other cloud-forest trees grow around the ruins, which are heaped over with moss and bromeliads. Cool mountain breezes flow through the complex, mingling with the buzzing of hummingbirds.

From the east entrance, there is a network of poorly marked paths to the right (northwest) that leads to an area that was once the most fortified part of the citadel. At the top of a stone lookout tower, archaeologists found a cache of 2,500 shaped rocks—ammo for the Chachapoya slings. Glancing down the vertiginous walls, it is easy to understand why Manco Inca wished to use Kuélap as the center of his rebellion from the Spaniards. But the Inca's envoys were slaughtered by the Chachapoya, who were bitter after years of Inca repression and forced relocation.

Canadian anthropologist Morgan Davis has reconstructed a Chachapoyan round house with a mid-level rain gutter to protect the foundation.

The only way into Kuélap is up narrow, steep stone stairs.

After Manco Inca's 1539 rebellion was crushed, he retreated to the jungle of Vilcabamba instead.

Square buildings, which some say were built by the Incas, lay near the center of the platform. Canadian anthropologist Morgan Davis and a team from Levanto have reconstructed a round house nearby, complete with its thatched roof, which gives a good idea of what the city may once have looked like. Kuélap's most famous building, however, is a stone tower whose walls widen as they go up, like an upside-down ink well or *tintero*—its name in Spanish. Animal sacrifices were found inside, so archaeologists believe this building had a religious purpose, though other say it was a solar observatory or a cemetery. It bears an odd resemblance to the similarly shaped tombs at Sillustani, near Lake Titicaca.

Many backpackers arrive via the traditional approach to Kuélap, a five-hour, 10-km hike from the village of **Tingo** that follows a trail of stone slabs laid by the Chachapoyans. The trail, best hiked in the cool of the morning, rises 1,210 meters from Tingo and is marked with red arrows. The National Institute of Culture operates a backpacker's hostel near the ruins ($3 pp), which is pleasant and has electricity though no running water. Ask to stay here and inquire about meals when you sign in for the ruins. There are a few *hospedajes* in Pueblo Maria with basic accommodations and meals. Since the road was completed in 1982, most visitors now arrive at Kuélap via a day tour or *combi* from Chachapoyas, a three-hour drive. After a 15-minute hike to the entrance gate, most visitors meet Gabriel Portocarrero, who sells Kuélap tickets from a small booth. He may be the best living example of what Chachapoya warriors once looked like: fair skin, clear eyes, rugged six-foot frame. After meeting him, theories about the Vikings founding the Chachapoya confederation do not seem far-fetched.

From Chachapoyas, $3 *combis* leave from the corner of Grau and Salamanca at 4 P.M. and 4 A.M. If you book your place on the morning bus the night before, it will pick you up at your hotel. Often the afternoon bus is full, so

A BRIEF HISTORY OF THE CHACHAPOYA

Not much is known about the Chachapoya, who did not have writing and had nearly vanished by the time Pizarro's men invaded Peru. What is clear from archaeological evidence, however, is that the Chachapoya were never so much of an empire as a federation of city-states that stretched over a huge area of cloud forest from 800 to 1500 A.D.

Along trade routes originally established by the Wari culture, the Chachapoya traded coveted jungle merchandise to other parts of Peru, including coca, medicinal and hallucinogenic plants, hardwoods, vegetal dyes, and parrot feathers. But they were never truly *connected* to the rest of the region as other cultures were. They were oddly apart, isolated by the cloud forest, and their culture developed along remarkably independent lines. They produced plain ceramics, but their weavings were intricate and unusual enough to make the Incas green with envy. Their houses meanwhile stand out among Peru's pre-Hispanic cultures for their decorative stone friezes.

Inca Tupac Yupanqui ventured into Chachapoyas before passing off the headache to his son, Topa Inca, in the 1470s. According to Inca Garcilaso de la Vega, the Chachapoya were fiercely independent and rebelled repeatedly against the Incas. Even Inca Atahualpa complained bitterly about their stubbornness when he first met the Spaniards in Cajamarca in 1532, and Manco Inca had his envoys slaughtered when he asked permission to seek refuge in their territory in 1538. But by the 1530s the Chachapoya federation had all but collapsed. During six decades of Inca subjugation, nearly 50 percent of the population had been exported to other areas of the empire, in a forced labor scheme the Incas called *mitimayo.*

Hints of the long-gone Chachapoya language remain in names such as Kuélap and Choctamal. A mystery that intrigues most visitors is the ancestry of the Chachapoya, who are taller than most Peruvians and have startlingly fair hair, pale skin, and clear eyes. Some say the fair features are an adaptation to the area's long months of rain, while others say the Chachapoya are descendants of Vikings. Recent DNA analysis, however, has retraced the blond blood to Spanish ancestry.

arrive ahead of time. The bus passes Tingo, Choctamal, Longuita and Maria en route to Malcapampa, a 15-minute walk from Kuélap. There are no fixed return *combis.* In the case of Kuélap, it seems most sensible to go with a local Kuélap agency for as little as $10. If you have a group, A private *combi* can be rented in Chachapoyas for the round-trip journey to Kuélap for about $30.

KARAJÍA

At Karajía, clay tombs with human forms and eerie, oblong faces peer from cliff ledges over a dramatic river valley. Most of the sarcophagi, made by the **Chipuric** subculture, were sacked and shattered long ago, but at least one group remains of six figures. Binoculars are a must to see the ochre details on the sculptures, and the skulls perched on top of them.

There are two ways to reach Karajía, which is about a 70-km drive northwest of Chachapoyas.

The far shorter, half-hour walk is from **Cruzpata,** a village at the end of a dirt road where villagers are now charging a $1 entrance fee. To reach Cruzpata from Chachapoyas, take a $2 *combi* for the 1.5-hour trip to Luya, departing every hour until 6 P.M. from the Luya *comite de combis,* a block from the Chachapoyas market at Ortiz Arrieta 364. From Luya, take $7 *colectivo* from the main square to Cohechan, then pay the driver a bit more for the additional stretch to Cruzpata. Guides can be hired at Cruzpata for $5, though there are signs indicating the way.

The other route also goes to Luya, but then branches off to Lamud and Trita, starting point for a 1.5-hour walk that crosses an Inca bridge and should be avoided in rainy season (December to March). For this walk, it is best to hire a guide in Trita, Lamud, or Luya for about $12 per day—and perhaps visit Pueblo de los Muertos later in the same day. Public transport to Lamud and Trita leaves from Luya's main square.

flowers near Karajía

Pueblo de los Muertos

The site, which translates to *Village of the Dead*, is a mini-village of funeral houses that were plastered with mud and built onto a cliff ledge. Some of the round houses are decorated with serpents and other more abstract anthropomorphic symbols. This necropolis, which was sacked by treasure hunters after **Gene Savoy** publicized it in the 1960s, once contained hundreds of mummies housed in adobe statues like those found at Karajía. Hire a guide in Lamud for this hike, which is a strenuous one-hour hike from the road outside Lamud. It is important to view the tombs from a distance only. Tourists could put the buildings and themselves in jeopardy by crossing to the main ledge. To reach Lamud, see directions for Karajía.

LEVANTO, YALAPE, AND COLLA CRUZ

The picturesque village of **Levanto** (2,600 meters), and the Inca and Chachapoya ruins around it, make for a pleasant day's outing from Chachapoyas. Levanto is part of the popular two-

to three-day trek that begins in Chachapoyas, passes through Magdalena and Tingo, and ends at Kuélap. Accommodations and food can be obtained along the way—see Levanto, Tingo, and Kuélap sections. This trail follows the Inca highways that ran through this area between Cusco and Quito and the coast and the jungle.

Chachapoyas Tours (Grau 534, second flr., Plaza de Armas, tel. 041/77-8078 or in U.S. 800/743-0945, kuelap@msn.com, www.kuelap-peru.com) has the best directions for this trek. It operates a **backpacker's lodge** in Levanto ($8 pp), a round, thatched building that's like a Chachapoya home with flush toilets, electricity, and hot water. It has also recently donated a ceramic kiln to the community, which is a new source of income for residents. Another lodging option is the **Levanto Lodge** (main square, $6 pp).

Approximate hiking times are four or five hours for Chachapoyas to Levanto, five hours from Levanto to Tingo, and six hours from Tingo to Kuélap. To shorten the hike, *colectivos* from Chachapoyas to Levanto leave at 8 A.M. from the corner of Sosiego and Cuarto Centenario—

confirm beforehand as the service is not reliable. The car leaves Levanto at 2 P.M. to return to Chachapoyas. A private car charges $14 one-way and $17 both ways.

On the road between Chachapoyas and Levanto are the ruins of **Yalape,** a residential complex made of white limestone that sprawls across a hill overlooking Levanto. There are fine defensive walls with diamond-shaped frieze patterns and numerous vine-covered walls and buildings. Nearby is an Inca aqueduct that once provided water to this area.

Morgan Davis has restored an Inca garrison guarding the crossroads at **Colla Cruz,** about a 20 minutes walk outside Levanto. The round Chachapoya-style building, built atop an impeccable Inca stone foundation, has a reconstructed, three-story thatch roof. Ask for directions once in Levanto.

MACRO

Consisting of 60 circular buildings, Macro is built on a hillside along the Río Utcubamba, about 2 km (a 40-minute walk) north of the village of **Magdalena,** or a 30-minute walk from Tingo. Macro is a small site, and thorns and steep terrain make it hard too reach, but it is easy to see from the main road—if you know where it is. Most of the buildings are built on narrow platforms made on the cliff face. These ruins can be seen heading south from Chacha along the main road and can be walked to as a side trip from the Levanto-Kuélap trek.

HUANCAS

Huancas, 10 km north of Chachapoyas, is a picturesque village known for its clay pottery and easygoing, traditional feel. There is a beautiful colonial church, plenty of minor ruins in the area, petroglyphs, and a stunning lookout over the Cañon Sonche. *Colectivos* ($0.50) leave for Huancas hourly from Ortiz Arrieta 364 in Chachapoyas.

PURUMLLACTA

Purumllacta is the closest major ruin to the city of Chachapoyas and may have been one of the seven major cities of the Chachapoya confederation, recorded by Garcilaso de la Vega and Cieza de León. The complex consists of numerous ruins scattered around hills, including white stone houses, agricultural terraces, and large stone buildings that may once have served as temples or palaces. Near the center of the complex are stairways, plazas, and a few two-story buildings. Purumllacta was recently the focus of a renovation effort and excavations that unearthed two tombs.

To reach Purumllacta, take a 3 P.M. bus to Cheto from Hermosura 319 in Chachapoyas. Purumllacta lies just a short distance beyond. If taking public transportation, try to leave Chachapoyas early in the morning to make it back the same day. Accommodation can be found in the Municipalidad.

GRAN VILAYA

More than a city, Gran Vilaya is a vast area of once-populated cloud forest that was *discovered,* and publicized, in 1985 by American swashbuckler **Gene Savoy,** who was probably led to the spot by Tim Cahill's detailed description of it in *Outside* magazine. Starting from the Belén Valley, Savoy walked to the village of Vista Hermoasa with a small army of workers and cleared a trail along the main ridge above town. In ten days of constant work, Savoy found ruins of several large urban settlements, which he somewhat absurdly called **Chacha Picchu.** Locals now call the ruins Pueblo Viejo and accuse Savoy of stealing gold and other objects from the sites—holes were dug all around the ruins, they say, and helicopters flew in and out of the area after Savoy cleared out of Vista Hermosa. Longtime Peru journalist Nicholas Asheshov, who knows Savoy well, says the accusation is absurd and typical of problems that even Peru's most reputable archaeologists run into with locals.

Whatever the truth, Savoy's public claims for Gran Vilaya were clearly exaggerated. He claimed the area consisted of 2,300 sites, whereas Chachapoyas expert Morgan Davis more judiciously put the figure at 150 sites, with about 30 being noteworthy and 15 being exceptional. By anyone's count, there are a lot of ruins in the

© RENÉE DEL GAUDIO AND ROSS WEHNER

Valle Belén on the way to Gran Vilaya

the town of Vista Hermosa in Gran Vilaya

area, and travelers should plan on three days for getting there and back and another few days at least for exploring ruins. Travelers are advised to get a recommended guide ahead of time in Chachapoyas, though Spanish speakers can also, like Savoy, hike in on their own from Belén Valley and hire a local guide in Vista Hermosa. To avoid problems, independent travelers should get a letter from the National Institute of Culture in the main square of Chachapoyas.

Most trekkers start from the village of **Cohechan,** the beginning of a controversial road that may one day reach the remote town of Vista Hermosa. Locals want the road to transport their coffee, but the animals, already threatened by heavy hunting, will vanish with new roads and colonists. The area's fauna includes the marvelous **spatule-tail humingbird,** which has leaf-shaped tail feathers twice the size of its body that are splashed with turquoise and electric green, and the **andean spectacled bear.** For the moment, the road stops in the Belén Valley, which can also be reached by trail from the Quechua-speaking village of Colcamar.

Belén, as its biblical name suggests, is a postcard-perfect valley with a river meandering through green pastures. It makes for a fine campsite but gets frosty in the evenings. The path to **Vista Hermosa** heads up and over a cloud-forest pass and traces the Inca highway that led from Levanto to Cajamarca. On the other side of the pass, there is a stretch of Inca steps, known as **La Escalera,** which have somehow survived centuries of mule hooves. Nearby is **La Pirquilla,** also known as Shukshu-Pirka, an area with dozens of well-made round buildings. Further below is a flat area known as the **Plazuela,** which was once a Kuélap-style settlement before the stones were taken for a nearby hacienda.

The trail leads into the Sesuya Valley, passing through the village of Congón on the other side of the river before climbing up into the village of **Vista Hermosa** on the other side of the river, where the Bardales family welcomes trekkers with food and allows them to pitch tents in their front yard. Vista Hermosa makes an excellent base for exploring ruins in the area. The easiest ruins to visit from here are **Cacahuasha,** a large village perched on top of a mountain, about a two-hour, mostly uphill, walk from Vista Hermosa. The site is owned by an old carpenter, Don José, who maintains the steep trails and asks for a small contribution from visitors. The site is divided into two sections, separated by a saddle, and includes 10-meter walls similar to those found at Kuélap. This was probably a ceremonial center and has extraordinary views over the valley.

Pueblo Viejo, the city "discovered" by Savoy, is more impressive but is a hard day's hike or strenuous horseback ride from Vista Hermosa— and a cantankerous neighbor was blocking this route in 2003. These city is perched on a cloud-forest ridge that stretches all the way to **Abra Yumal,** the high pass at 3,270 meters where the traditional Gran Vilaya trek ends at a newly built road. Some guides are avoiding Vista Hermosa by entering here at Abra Yumal and staying at a new lodge being built along the path. It is also possible to reach Savoy's cities from this area, and there are other large ruins even closer, including **Tulupe** and a new site known as **Lanche.**

Morgan Davis also recommends the sites of **Macchu Llaqta** and **Paxamarca,** which are near villages to the west of Vista Hermosa. The first, an hour to the east of the village Pueblo Nuevo, was an important ceremonial center that includes a ridgetop lookout tower and a large plaza with large circular houses extending in all directions, according to Davis. Paxamarca, 1.5 hours east of the village of Pirca Pampa, covers about 20 hectares atop a ridge and includes ceremonial terraces, numerous circular buildings, and rectangular buildings with trapezoidal doorways—proof of Inca occupation following their invasion circa 1480.

After the grueling uphill hike from Vista Hermosa to Abra Yumal, trekkers can either hike or, if transport is waiting for them, ride down to **Choctamal,** where there is an excellent hostel operated by Chachapoyas Tours. Down the road are more hostels in the nearby village of Maria, the must-see citadel of Kuélap, and a few *combis* daily back to Chachapoyas.

THE UTCUBAMBA VALLEY: JALCA GRANDE AND OLLAPE

Jalca Grande is a Quechuan village with cobblestone streets and thatched roofs that is rapidly modernizing. The older people still speak Quechua, wear colorful wool clothing, and go about their lives much as they have for centuries. But sheet-metal roofs, cement roads, jeans, and Spanish are cropping up. This town has kept the area's best-known anthropologists busy over the years. Peter Lerche, a German ethno-historian who is building a lodge in Chillo and works as a local guide, conducted his thesis research here in the early 1980s. One block west of the main square is a Chachapoya home, known as **La Choza Redonda,** which was lived in continuously until 1964, according to Morgan Davis. The house, with a double zigzag frieze at the top, remains in nearly perfect condition today and served as the model for Davis' reconstruction of Inca and Chachapoya homes in Levanto and Kuélap. The entire village of Jalca Grande, in fact, is built on an old Chachapoyas-style city, and many circular walls peek through more modern constructions today. The town has a beautiful stone church and square.

A half-hour walk to the west of the city is **Ollape,** a Kuélap town that once numbered 150 buildings, where it is now possible to see a number of platforms with rhomboidal and zigzag friezes that are different from friezes at other sites. About 2.5 hours north of Jalca Grande is Moyuk Viejo, a hilltop ruin that Lerche considers the sixth city of the Chachapoya, mentioned by Inca Garcilaso de la Vega in his *Comentarios reales.* It is a larger, though more primitive site than Ollape, with many fallen buildings and a few well-preserved balconies. To reach Jalca, take a *combi* from the city of Chachapoyas down the Utcubamba Valley and get off at the village of Ubilón, where a dirt road leads up to Jalca Grande. This is a three-hour walk where you have a good chance of getting a ride along the way. There are also $2 *colectivos* for Jalca Grande leaving from Salamanca and Libertad in Chachapoyas every afternoon, a 3.5-hour trip. There is a small, very basic hostel near the Plaza de Armas.

REVASH

Revash is a collection of house-like tombs perched on cliff ledges that once contained hundreds of mummies but were looted long ago. What remains are several houses in good condition, along with red-and-white paintings of men, animals, and other abstract designs. Out of respect for the site and its preservation, visitors should not scramble onto the ledges but rather use binoculars to view them from a distance. Apart from the main site, there are 18 lesser sites spread through this Santo Tomás Valley, according to Morgan Davis.

To reach Revash, hop on a Chachapoyas-Leimebamba *combi* and get off at Yerba Buena, which is south of Ubilón and Tingo. At this point, a taxi can take you another half hour west on a dirt road that crosses the bridge. Proceed until you see a house built of sheet metal, where the trail begins. The walk up to the tombs takes three hours, and they are difficult to find without a guide. Guides costs $12 at the Estancia Chillo along the way or $6 in the nearby village of Yerba Buena—only contract recommended guides, however, as assaults have been reported in this area. *Combis* leave regularly from the second block of Grau in Chachapoyas to **Yerba Buena,** from where it is possible to walk or take local transport to the Revash trailhead. *Combis* from Leimebamba to Chachapoyas pass Yerba Buena after 3 P.M. on most days.

CERRO OLÁN

Along with Kuélap and La Congona, **Cerro Olán** was once a prosperous city and is one of the impressive sites in the Chachapoyas region—though of the three it is the hardest to reach. It is spread out for 1 km along a moon-shaped ridge with a beautiful view of the Utcubamba Valley. Davis has identified three main sections: the northernmost consists of ten circular platforms with three or four homes still standing, with walking balconies and intricate diamond-shaped friezes. One of the buildings in the middle section, about eight meters high and six meters wide, is in excellent condition and decorated with a masonry band found only at this site. In the southern section, there are three circular towers in good condition—the largest being about five meters high.

Cerro Olán is approximately 70 km from the city of Chachapoyas along a dirt road that branches east from the main Utcubamba Valley road at

Coshac, which is south of Tingo and Yerba Buena. One way to get there is to take a *combi* from Chachapoyas to Leimebamba and get off at Coshac. From here it is a two-hour walk to **Montevideo,** passing the village of Duraznopampa along the way. Montevideo has a few restaurants and stores, and San Pedro, from which the ruins are visible to the east, is another half-hour walk further. Bring your sleeping bag and ask around town for families with guest rooms, or camp near the ruins. Direct combis to Montevideo leave at noon ($2) from Grau block 3 in Chachapoyas.

LA CONGONA

If you get to Leimebamba, definitely make the three-hour hike up into the hills northwest of the town to see **La Congona,** a small site that has some of the most beautiful ruins in the region. This hilltop, covering around 5 hectares, contains a few circular homes in excellent condition, some of which are built on unusual square platforms. Inside the homes are elaborate stone niches, probably ceremonial, and outside are wide walking balconies and highly decorated, and elaborate, stone friezes. A lookout tower

entering the cloud forest on the Chiclayo–Chachapoyas highway boasts an extraordinary flight of curved switch-back steps, from which it is possible to look across the Utcubamba Valley to the ruins of Cerro Olán. A guide is recommended for this trek; ask at the Museo Leimebamba.

day hike from Leimebamba through remote cloud forest filled with Chachapoya ruins, bromeliads, and birds. The goal is a spectacular lakeside tomb site. Both Chachapoya's Vilaya Tours and Chachapoyas Tours offer treks in this area.

LAGUNA DE LOS CÓNDORES

Along with Gran Vilaya, **Laguna de los Cóndores** is Chachapoyas's other most popular trek. This stunning lake is reached after a one- or two-

FROM CHACHA TO CHICLAYO

Jaén

More than anything, Jaén is a good rest stop on the scenic highway trip from Chachapoyas and

HASSLE-FREE ROUTES INTO ECUADOR

Most travelers heading up the coast for Ecuador make the crossing on the coastal highway at **Aguas Verdes,** a dirty, loud town of vendors, border guards, and ripoff artists. This crossing has become easier as relations between Peru and Ecuador have simmered down since the 1995–98 border war. Passengers still have to disembark at least twice to get passports stamped on each side, but the process now takes less than one hour. The easiest way to cross the border here—and avoid the hassle of Aguas Verdes—is to use a bus line, such as Ormeño or Cruz del Sur. These buses stop at the Peruvian immigration office (9 A.M.–noon and 2–5 P.M. daily), located in the desert 3 km before Aguas Verdes. Then the buses roll through Aguas Verdes and military checkpoints at the bridge before stopping at the Ecuadorian immigrations office (8 A.M.–1 P.M. and 2–6 P.M. daily) in the border town of **Huaquillas.** The process is possible, but complicated, to do by a combination of taxis and walking. Watch your belongings. Remember too that Ecuadorian time is one hour behind Peruvian time.

But for a more scenic and a less hectic crossing, try the **La Tina-Macara** crossing, where Peruvian and Ecuadorian immigration offices have the same hours as those at the Aguas Verdes–Huaquillas crossing. The asphalted, though rough, road winds through carob, kapok, and mango trees, but the journey can be hot, so travel with water. Direct buses leave from Piura in the morning and arrive by evening in the Ecuadorian mountain town of Loja. The best of these companies is Transportes Loja, which has a daily bus leaving for Loja at 9 A.M. for $7. It is also possible to catch *colectivos* to the border from Sullana, a town along the way. There is no good lodging in La Tina so, if you get stuck at the border, try to stay in Macara, Ecuador. The best plaace to stay in this pleasant, laid-back town is the **Hotel Paradero Turístico** (tel. 593-7/694-099, $5 d), which is about 500 meters before the town on the road leading from the border. The international telephone code for Ecuador is 593.

Finally, there is the **Jaén-Loja** crossing, the option for the truly adventurous cross-county traveler who is looking for a break from the gringo trail and a shortcut between Chachapoyas and Ecuador's Vilcabamba. This two- or three-day trip involves lots of mountain scenery, and travelers who have done it say it's not nearly as difficult as it looks. This crossing starts in Jaen, a pleasant town with great lodging and restaurants, where you take a $3 *combi* for the three-hour, 104-km trip to San Ignacio. From there, take another $2.50 *combi* for 44 km to Namballe, where the road dead-ends at the Río Calvas. A bridge is being built, but for now the crossing is done by a $0.25, five-minute ride on an oil drum raft. Once in the Ecuadorian town of La Balsa on the other side, catch a *combis* to nearby Zumba, where lots of buses run to Loja. Travelers say the route is safe, with decent lodging options and very friendly, inquisitive people along the way. With an early start, travelers can go from Jaén to Zumba in one day, and then Zumba to Loja in another.

Chiclayo—and a launch pad for getting to Ecuador (see the sidebar *Hassle-Free Routes into Ecuador*). Few foreigners visit this friendly, off-the-highway town, which has a few tidy hotels thanks to a thriving agricultural economy.

The Montegrande ruins outside of town are from the **Chavín,** who apparently arrived here around 400 A.D. after following the Marañón Valley from Chavín de Huantár, near Huaraz, around 400 A.D. The area's inhabitants maintained strong ties with surrounding cultures such as the Moche, Chimú, Caxamarca, and Chachapoyas and were conquered, like everyone else, by Tupac Inca Yupanqui in the 1470s.

Juan Porcel de Padilla was sent by **Francisco Pizarro** to conquer the area in 1536, and the city of San Leandro de Jaén de Bracamoros was founded a decade later, though it was moved in the early 1800s to its present location on the banks of the Río Amojú. The town grew quickly after the highway from Olmos to the Río Marañón was opened in 1943. The rich countryside produces rice, coffee, cocoa, and a variety of fruits, and there are interesting botanical gardens outside of town.

There are low-prices hostels on Diego Palomino and Bolivar, which is just off Mesones Muro, the main drag. But the best budget option is **Hotel Cesar** (Mesones Muro 168, tel. 076/73-1277, $11 s, $15 d, including breakfast). Don't be alarmed by this building's busy streetfront: interior rooms face a quiet alley and are clean, with new beds, cable TV, and a reasonably priced laundry service. **El Bosque** (Mesones Muro 632, tel. 076/73-1184, $21 s, $24 d, including breakfast) has the most relaxed atmosphere, with nice bungalows, gardens, and a swimming pool. Rooms include cable TV cable, hot water, and fans and some have AC.

For any meal, head to **Lact Bac** (Plaza de Armas, Bolivar and Mariscal Castilla, tel. 076/73-3286, 7 A.M.–midnight, $3–4), which serves natural yogurts, juices, hamburgers, spit-roasted chicken, chifa, local foods, *cebiche,* and Spanish paella. Lact Bac also serves pitchers of sagria ($6)

drying clothes at Lake Pomacochas

Northern Highlands

and a full range of cocktails. Next to Lact Bac is good Internet at Infocenter (8 A.M.–midnight, $0.50 per hour). Police and medical post are just off the main square.

Lago Pomacochas

A good stop on the way to Tarapoto is Lago Pomacochas (2,200 meters), a miniature Lake Titicaca that is 31 km east of Pedro Ruiz, where the road turns off to Chachapoyas. Its blue-green waters and extensive *tótoras* (marshlands) are the last bastion of high ground before the highway rises over the Cordillera Oriental and descends toward the Amazon along the Rio Mayo watershed. There are Chachapoya ruins within walking distance of the lake, which are described in Morgan Davis' *Chachapoyas: The Cloud People,* available from Chachapoyas Tours.

There are a few basic restaurants and hotels, but the best place by far is **Puerto Pumas** (entrance marked by sign on south side of highway, in Lima tel. 01/242-5550, ctareps@puertopalmeras.com, www.puertopalmeras.com, $60 s, $88 d, including breakfast). This former state-owned hotel is now operated by Puerto Palmeras resort in Tarapoto and, though the lumber-and-concrete construction is a bit austere, the hotel has excellent views of the lake itself and has a fabulous collection of paintings from Tarapoto artists. There are usually not many guests at the hotel, so this is the perfect place for a peaceful retreat. Rates are half the price in low season. The highway east of the lake, leading up Abra Patricia (2,270 meters) makes for a great bicycle route and attracts birders from around the world. Just before Pomacochas is one of the best and most accessible places to see the marvelous spatule-tail hummingbird. The whole area east of the lake is gorgeous, wild territory that would make for fascinating exploring.

Know
Peru

The Land

How could such an abundance of life and ancient culture spring from a geography as rugged and desolate as Peru's? Deserts line the entire coast, the Andes spring to well over 6,000 meters, and the Amazon jungle fans out thousands of miles toward the Pacific Ocean.

Peru's foreboding terrain belies its extraordinary fertility. Peru's arid coastal climate is caused by the frigid **Humboldt Current,** which sucks moisture away from the land. But these Antarctic waters also cause a rich upwelling of plankton, which in turn nourishes one of the world's richest fishing grounds. Peru's earliest cultures took root near the ocean and depended on mollusks and fish for their survival.

Peru's snow-covered mountains and high passes would appear to be an impediment for the spread of advanced cultures. But the slow melting of the snow pack provides the desert coast with a vital source of year-round water. Once they developed irrigation technologies, Peru's early cultures could cultivate crops and began to spread up into the fertile coastal valleys and the mountains. The ingenious aqueducts at Nasca, which carry mountain water for miles underneath the desert floor, are still in use today.

In the more moderate topography of North America and Europe, temperature differences and climate zones are largely a question of latitude—Florida produces oranges, while Kansas produces wheat. But in Peru, climate zones are caused by altitude, not latitude. In places Peru's coast rises from sea level to over 6,000 meters (19,700 feet) in only less than 100 km, creating a variety of climates apt for fruits, vegetables, grains, and potatoes. The same phenomenon occurs to an even greater extent where the Andes plunge into the Amazon, a dizzying range of ecosystems that nourish a whole new set of fruits and a huge storehouse of medicinal plants, including the coca leaf.

As a result of Peru's vertical geography, trade routes from the Amazon over the Andes to the desert coast were key to the flourishing of Peru's ancient cultures. The Chavín culture, based in the high grasslands near the Cordillera Blanca, pictured pumas, snakes, caiman, and other Amazon animals in their enigmatic carvings. They traded their high-altitude grains and potatoes for dried fish and vegetables from the coast.

GEOGRAPHY

Peru's total land area is 1.28 million square kilometers (nearly 500,000 square miles), or about three times the size of California. Peru's narrow strip of desert coast runs 2,500 km (1,550 miles) between the borders of present-day Ecuador and Chile. Some 50 rivers cascade from the Andes to the coast, though only about a third of these carry water year-round. In these areas, people are entirely dependent on the seasonal rains in the Andes. In Peru's extreme south, the coast forms part of the **Atacama Desert,** one of the driest places on earth.

The Andes rise so abruptly from the coast that they can be seen from the ocean on a clear day. They represent the highest mountain chain on earth next to the Himalaya, and **Huascarán,** Peru's highest peak at 6,768 meters (22,204 feet), is the second-largest mountain in South America. The Andes are divided into different ranges (called *cordilleras* in Spanish), which often run parallel to each other. In northern Peru, for instance, the Andes rise four separate times to form different *cordilleras* known as the Negra, Blanca, Central, and Oriental.

Between these mountain ranges lie fertile valleys and grasslands between 2,300 and 4,00 meters—the so-called bread basket of Peru, where the majority of its indigenous highlanders live and produce about half the country's food supply. The Incas and other cultures terraced and irrigated this landscape in order to grow a range of crops, including maize, hardy grains such as *kiwicha* and **quinoa,** potatoes and other indigenous tubers such as *olluco* and *oca.*

On the journey between Cusco and Lake Titicaca, travelers can appreciate the most extreme of

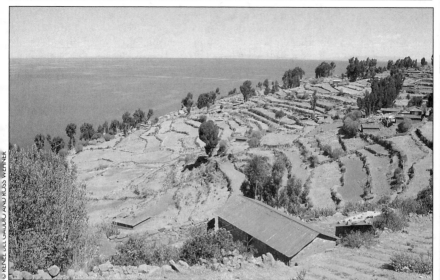

© RENÉE DEL GAUDIO AND ROSS WEHNER

Peru's mountain climates, the **puna** or **altiplano**. These rolling grasslands between 4,000 and 5,000 meters look bleak but form rich pasturelands for Peru's variety of camelids, including the wild **guanacos** and **vicuñas** and the domesticated **llamas** and **alpacas.** These animals continue to provide wool, meat, and transport for Andean highlanders.

Eventually the Andes mountains peter out into a series of ecosystems that cascade into the Amazon basin. Near the top of the eastern edge of the Andes is the cloud forest, a mist-drenched, inhospitable place that is one of Peru's most biodiverse habitats. Here live thousands of types of hummingbirds, orchids, and butterflies. Clear mountain streams cascade down these slopes, eventually merging to form the broad, muddy rivers of the lowland rain forest. This carpet of green is the largest jungle on the planet and stretches thousands of miles through present-day Brazil to the Atlantic Ocean.

CLIMATE

Peru's weather is a complex set of patterns caused by the Humboldt Current, the Andes, and the jet stream, which blows west (not east as in the Northern Hemisphere) and picks up the Amazon's moisture as it travels.

On the coast, the southwesterly trade winds that blow toward Peru are chilled as they pass over the frigid waters of the Humboldt Current. When these cold winds hit Peru's sun-baked coast, they gradually warm and rarely release rain because their ability to hold water increases. Clouds form only when the air begins to rise over the Andes, dropping rain over Peru's mountain valleys and high grasslands.

During much of the year, however, a curious temperature inversion occurs along much of Peru's coast. The rising air from the coast is trapped beneath the warm air pushed westward by the jet stream. Fog, known in Lima as **garúa,** blankets sections of the coast.

The jet stream heads west over the Amazon basin toward the Andes, picking up transpiration from the Amazon basin. As this warm, humid air rises over the Andes it also condenses into a fine mist that nourishes the cloud forest. As it rises even higher over the *puna,* it falls as rain.

The heaviest periods of rain in the Peruvian Amazon and Andes occur between December and April, a time that Peruvians refer to as the *época de lluvia* (the rainy season). The first rains, however, begin in October, which is the beginning of the highland planting season. Soon after, rain from the Andes begins to cascade down in the coast, where deserts farmers use it for irrigation, and into the Amazon, where rivers become swollen and muddy. At Iquitos the Amazon River can rise a staggering 15 meters (50 feet) during the brunt of the rainy season in the Andes, which is why most natives live in stilted homes.

EARTHQUAKES AND EL NIÑO

Peru is prone to a series of natural disasters caused by both its young geological formation and its peculiar climate. On the western edge of South America, the **Nasca Plate** is slowly sliding beneath the continent, and the resulting friction causes periodic earthquakes and volcanic eruptions. The area most affected by this is southern Peru, including **Arequipa,** which was destroyed by an earthquake in 1588 and then covered in ash when the nearby Huaynaputina volcano exploded shortly thereafter. The city averages roughly one major earthquake per century, most recently in 2001, when one of the cathedral towers collapsed across the Plaza de Armas.

The hardest-hit region, however, has been the **Cordillera Blanca,** where earthquakes cause glacial lakes to burst their dams and send huge mudslides, or *aluviones,* to the valley below. In 1970, an earthquake that measured 7.8 on the Richter scale destroyed much of Huaraz and triggered a wall of mud and boulders that swept down the valley above the nearby town of **Yungay.** Within minutes, an estimated 18,000 people were buried alive. Today the only trace of old Yungay are the tops of a few palm trees that once graced the town's square and now poke a few feet out above the silt plain.

El Niño, the periodic fluctuation in the water temperature of the Pacific Ocean, wreaks havoc across Peru and appears to be increasing in frequency—possibly, some scientists think, as a result of climate change. In 1982 and again in 1998 El Niño events dumped torrential rains onto Peru's northern desert, causing floods that washed out bridges and stranded highway motorists for weeks.

These El Niños also caused droughts in the southern Andes and a collapse in Peru's coastal fishery, as the plankton, anchovy, and larger fish move deep into the ocean to follow the colder water.

ENVIRONMENTAL ISSUES

Peru suffers from a range of environmental problems that come from a lack of infrastructure and a series of extractive industries based on fishmeal, mining, oil, natural gas, and lumber. Over the decades, environmental problems with these industries have occurred as a result of shoddy regulation, corruption, and the economic demands of a cash-starved country.

Peru's zinc, copper, mercury, silver, and gold mines continue to pollute water supplies with mine tailings, especially in the areas of La Oroya in central Peru and the Cordillera Huayhuash. The American-owned Yanacocha gold mine near Cajamarca has taken adequate environmental precautions, but has still stirred up public sentiment by profoundly altering the city's sacred landscape of mountains, or *apus.*

Over the last three decades, gas and oil exploration in the Amazon has caused water pollution, deforestation, and a huge impact on native cultures. The most controversial recent project is the Camisea Gas Field, which is exporting 13 trillion cubic feet of natural gas from the lower Urubamba basin, one of the most remote and pristine areas of the Peruvian Amazon. The project includes a pipeline over the biodiverse Cordillera Vilcabamba and a gas refinery next to Paracas, the country's most important marine reserve.

Sewerage treatment is also unheard-of in Peru, and water pollution and algae blooms in rivers are a serious problem. The situation is especially acute around Lima, where local beaches are often declared unfit for swimming. Across the country, trash is dumped in landfills and burned. Because there is no recycling in Peru, much of the plastic garbage ends up blowing across the land and floating down rivers—even in the Sacred Valley near Cusco, plastic bottles can be stacked up to a meter deep along the beaches of the once-sacred Río Urubamba.

ECOTOURISM AND LEAVE NO TRACE

When compared with mining, oil drilling, and the illegal timber industry, ecotourism is Peru's best hope for the long-term preservation of its landscapes and native peoples—and a new generation of eco-friendly agencies and lodges in Peru are making a huge difference. In the Amazon, jungle lodges are working with native communities to preserve huge swaths of rainforest. In the highlands, trekking agencies have come up with innovative programs for bringing travelers to highland villages in a way that raises cultural awareness on both sides of the fence. Some of these agencies have lobbied the government for preservation of remote areas such as the Cordillera Huayhuash, which is now under consideration for Peru's next national reserve.

Travelers to Peru can either help or hurt Peru's long-term survival depending on how they plan their trip and how they behave once in the country. A good ecotourism reference in the United States is **The International Ecotourism Society** or **TIES** (202/347-9203, ecomail@ecotourism.org, www.ecotourism.org), which defines ecotourism as "responsible travel to natural areas that conserves the environment and improves the well-being of local people." A handful of Peru's jungle operators belong to this association. Before paying, find out whether your lodge or agency lives up to these basic principles set forth by TIES:

- Minimize impact.
- Build environmental and cultural awareness and respect.
- Provide positive experiences for both visitors and hosts.
- Provide direct financial benefits for conservation.
- Provide financial benefits and empowerment for local people.
- Raise sensitivity to host countries' political, environmental, and social climate.
- Support international human rights and labor agreements.

A huge concern in Peru's main trekking areas, such as the Inca Trail and the Cordillera Blanca, is environmental degradation as a result of sloppy camping. A wonderful resource for traveling lightly through wilderness is **Leave No Trace** (www.lnt.org),

which has pioneered a set of principles that are slowly being adopted by protected areas around the world. More information on these principles can be found on the LNT web page:

- Plan ahead and prepare.
- Travel and camp on durable surfaces.
- Dispose of waste properly.
- Leave what you find.
- Minimize campfire impacts.
- Respect wildlife.
- Be considerate of others.

Great pains have been made throughout this book to recommend only agencies and lodges that have a solid ethic of ecotourism. But the only way to truly evaluate a company's environmental and cultural practices is by experiencing them firsthand. Your feedback is tremendously valuable to us as we consider which business to recommend in the future. Please send your experiences—both positive and negative—to us at **atpfeedback@avalon-pub.com** (www.moon.com).

bromeliads and birds at Explorama's canopy walkway

Population growth is also exerting tremendous pressure on Peru's resources, especially in the highlands. Overgrazing and the chopping of trees for firewood has caused the area's thin soils to wash away. The loss of vegetation causes mudslides, including one during the El Niño rains of 1998 that swept away the railroad tracks that once led past Machu Picchu to Quillabamba. Much of the eroded silt ends up in Amazon rivers and kills off fish populations.

In the Amazon, recent government efforts to regulate small-time gold panning, timber poaching, and illegal hunting have led to conflict. Riots erupted in Puerto Maldonado in May 2003 when INRENA, Peru's natural resources commission, attempted to institute a concession system that would force small-time loggers to come up with a 20-year management plant. INRENA's offices in Puerto Maldonado were burned to the ground.

The INRENA offices in Iquitos are just a few blocks away from the Belén market, where wild pig, deer, and other illegal bush meat is openly displayed for sale. INRENA wildlife director Viviana Ruiz said that its inspectors are routinely chased out of the market by stick-wielding vendors. "This is deeply rooted in their personality," she said. "They think the jungle is rich and they don't realize it will end."

Protected Areas

There are 53 protected areas in Peru, which total more than 127,000 square kilometers or 15.3 percent of the country. There are eight national parks, three of which have been classified internationally as Natural World Heritage sites. These include the national parks of Huascarán, Manu, and Río Abiseo, a huge swath of remote cloud forest in northern Peru that includes the ruins of Gran Pajatén.

Only tourism and scientific research are allowed inside national parks, which are meagerly funded and policed with a skeleton crew of rangers. The other strict category of protection in Peru are the natural or historic sanctuaries, which is how Machu Picchu and the mangrove swamps around Tumbes are classified.

Lesser designations include national reserves (reservas nacionales), and reserved zones (zonas reservadas), which allow for continued use of resources. Unfortunately these areas can be radically underfunded and woefully neglected. The only infrastructure is a lone station with a few rangers who must patrol on foot.

Environmentalists say that only a third of Peru's protected areas are managed effectively by the state. The rest are being degraded by a variety of illegal and uncontrolled activities, such as livestock grazing, hunting, and timber poaching.

Flora and Fauna

If in case of a planet catastrophe we would have the choice to choose from one country to save and rebuild the planet from, undoubtedly I would choose Peru.

English scientist David Bellamy

As Bellamy suggests, Peru would be an excellent place from which to select the plants and animals for a modern-day Noah's Ark. Peru's tumultuous geography contains 87 ecosystems (out of a world total of 104) and the world's highest levels of biodiversity. There are 1,700 species of birds in Peru alone, nearly 20 percent of the Earth's total, along with 15,000 plants and an estimated 30 million insects.

FLORA

Desert

Few plants can grow in the bone-dry conditions of Peru's southern and central coast, which is dominated by shifting sand dunes. The irrigated valleys, however, are covered in cash crops, including olives, grapes, nuts, and a range of fruits and vegetables. In Peru's northern valleys, the hotter temperatures are ideal for the cultivation of cotton, rice, tobacco, and sugarcane.

As the Humboldt Current eases off Peru's coast at Cabo Blanco, trade winds bring humidity—and even some rain—to the coast. In the Chi-

sunflowers at Lake Pomacochas

clayo area, there are vast tracts of **bosque seco,** a scraggly low-lying forest composed mainly of *algarroba,* or carob, a mesquite-like tree whose sweet pods are the base of the *algarrobina* cocktail. Other trees in these forest include ficus, zapote, and vichayo.

Even farther north, the coast becomes subtropical and occasional patches of palm trees line the coast, along with large **mangrove swamps** near **Tumbes.** The swamps are protected as part of the Zona Reservada de Tumbes, which includes Peru's only chunk of Pacific tropical forest. Here there are orchids and gigantic trees such as ceibo, with its umbrella-shaped crown, and the pretino, which drops seed pods the size of basketballs.

Andes

The high grasslands, or **puna,** is home to a collection of bizarre plants with endless adaptations for coping with the harsh climate. Many of the plants have thick, waxy leaves for surviving high levels of ultraviolet radiation and fine insulating hairs for surviving frequent frosts. They grow close to the ground for protection from wind and temperature variations. In Peru's north, a wetter grassland known as **páramo** stretches along the eastern edge of the Andes into Ecuador. It has a soggy, springy feeling underfoot and serves as a sponge to absorb, and slowly release, the tremendous amounts of rain that fall in the area.

Peru's most famous highland plant, the **Puya raimondii,** grows in the *puna* near Huaraz and Ayacucho. It rosette of spiky, waxy leaves grows to three meters in diameter and looks like a giant agave, even though the plant is in the bromeliad family along with the pineapple. The *Puya raimondii* lives for a century and, before it dies, sends a giant spike three stories into the air that eventually erupts into 20,000 blooms. Once pollinated, the plant's towering spike allows it to broadcast its seed as far as possible in the wind.

The most ubiquitous feature of Peru's high plains are the spiky tussocks of grass known as **ichu.** Highlanders use *ichu* to thatch their roofs, start their fires, and feed their llama and alpaca. Cattle, which were imported from Europe in the

16th century by the Spanish, are unable to digest this hardy grass. That is part of the reason highlanders burn large tracts of hillside every year—the cows can only eat the *ichu* when it sprouts anew as a tender green shoot.

The high deserts of southern Peru, such as those on the way to the Colca Canyon, are so dry that not even *ichu* can survive. Instead green blob-like plants, called **yareta,** spread along the rocky, lunar surface. This plant's waxy surface and tightly bunched leaves allow it to trap condensation and survive freezing temperatures.

A few trees can be found in Peru's montane valleys. **Eucalyptus,** which was imported to Peru from New Zealand, is used by highlanders for firewood and ceiling beams. Its rapid spread has greatly reduced the numbers of Peru's most famous highland tree, **queñual.** This scraggly, high-altitude tree can still be seen in abundance, however, at Lagunas Llanganuco in the Cordillera Blanca.

Amazon

The cloud forests that blanket the eastern escarpments of the Andes are a remarkable tumble of gnarled trees that cling to the steep, rocky soil. These trees have evolved to trap the thick blankets of mist that form when humid jungle air cools as it rises over the Andes. A host of aerial plants, such as ferns, mosses, orchids, cacti, and bromeliads, cover the trees and are collectively known as **epiphytes.** Because they have no roots to the soil, they must gather all of their water and nutrients from the passing mist. This forest has a dark, primeval feel and is seen in Chachapoya, Machu Picchu, and the road to the Parque Nacional Manu. The Peruvians somewhat poetically call it the *ceja de selva,* or the "eyebrow of the jungle."

The forest takes on a whole different feel farther downhill in the lowland tropical rainforest, where steep slopes give way to swampy soil and the rivers become slow and muddy. The trees are huge, often over 60 meters tall, and the understory is dark and curiously free of plants. Huge gray vines, as thick as the human body, descend from the highest branches into the ground. These are the **strangler figs,** called *matapalo* in Spanish, that begin life high in the canopy where birds and bats drop their seeds after gorging on the fig fruit. After dropping their vines to the forest floor, these vines merge together and form a sheath that envelops the tree, slowly choking off its nutrients. When the host tree dies, the parasite strangler fig remains in its place. They are often the largest, noblest trees in the forest, and it is hard to believe they began life as assassins.

Life in the rain forest, as the strangler fig knows, is a battle for sunlight. This becomes readily apparent to those who climb up to the tree platforms or canopy walkways that have been built by Peru's Amazon jungle lodges. Perched high in the canopy are an astounding number of epiphytes, far greater than in the cloud forest. Each of these plants has made adaptations to deal with the intense sunlight and evaporative breezes of the upper canopy. **Tank bromeliads** have long leaves that work as troughs to collect rain, while the orchids store water in their bulbous stems. All the plants, especially the cacti, have tough, waxy skins to retain moisture. These epiphytes are here for the sunlight, but also for the breezes that help disperse seeds and the vast number of bats, birds, and insects that forage in the canopy and serve as pollinators.

The fight for sunlight is evident on the forest floor when a large trees fall over, dragging its vines and smaller trees along with it. The sun-filled clearings created by falling trees are called "light gaps" and form fascinating mini-ecosystems for fast-growing **pioneer** trees, such as the ubiquitous **cecropia.** Its thin gray trunk, often marked with white rings, twists in odd shapes to catch the sunlight with its huge palm-shaped leaves. These clearings are wonderful places to examine the epiphytes, insect nests, and other forms of canopy life.

Large rainforest trees include several species of **mahogany,** including **caoba, cedro,** and **tornillo,** a highly valuable wood for making furniture that can now only be found in Peru's stands of primary forest. You might also see the **Brazil nut tree,** which drops round pods containing

MEDICINE PLANTS OF THE AMAZON

There are very few modern clinics in Peru's Amazon. That is just fine with most natives, who have relied for centuries on village curanderos, or healers, and the abundant pharmacy of plants in the rain forest. Most of the medicines are based on the complex chemical defenses that plants produce to defend themselves from insects and other predators. North American and European pharmaceutical companies spend a lot of time and money to meet with *curanderos* and investigate the efficacy of various plants and herbs.

Here are the top 10 medicinal plants you are likely to see in the rain forest.

1. Uña de gato, also known as Cat's Claw, is a hairy vine named for its cat-like tentacles. The bark of this vine is boiled for tea, or soaked in alcohol, and consumed to treat prostate and lung cancer, rheumatism, and arthritis.

2. Jergón Sacha, also known as the fer-de-lance plant, is an understory herb with bark patterns nearly identical to the fer-de-lance, one of the Amazon's most poisonous snakes. The plant's bulbous root is made into a tea that is an effective remedy against the fer-de-lance bite. The root can also be applied directly to the wound.

3. Hierba Luisa, also known as Lemon Grass, smell like citron and is a prime ingredient in both Inca Cola, the national soft drink, and citronella, the natural insect repellant. When boiled, it makes a stress-reducing tea.

4. Bellaco Caspi, also known in English as himatanthus, exudes a white latex when its bark is cut. The gooey substance can be used to heal cuts, set broken bones, and even suffocate the botfly larvae that burrow beneath the human skin.

5. Shiringa, the rubber tree, brought extreme prosperity and misery to the Amazon during the 1880–1910 rubber boom. Like Bellaco Caspi, this tree exudes a white latex when cut. Ironically, natives have few uses for it besides repairing leaky boats.

6. Pan de Árbol, also known as breadfruit, is a staple food in the Pacific Islands and Southeast Asia, from where it was imported to Peru in the 19th century. In the Amazon basin, its leaves are used for cleaning and sterilizing a woman after she gives birth.

7. Clavo Huasca is a pungent, clove-smelling vine. It is a powerful aphrodisiac and one of the several medicinal substances used in the Solución de Siete Raíces, a tonic taken to improve energy levels, reduce fever, and boost the immune system.

8. Achiote is a shrublike tree with a red, spiky fruit from which the Yagua Indians in the Iquitos area extract a crimson dye for painting their bodies and palm-fiber skirts. It is also used to treat dysentery, venereal diseases, hepatitis, and skin rashes.

9. Sangre de Grado, or Dragon's Blood, is a medium-sized tree that exudes a reddish latex used to stop vaginal hemorrhaging during childbirth. It is also used to decrease scarring and wrinkles. The sap is currently undergoing clinical trials in the United States.

10. Cocana is a tree that yields a tomato-like fruit that is high in vitamin C and often served as a juice in Amazon restaurants. It is also taken to control nausea and to treat snake or insect bites.

—information taken from *A Field Guide to Medicinal and Useful Plants of the Upper Amazon,* James Duke et al, Feline Press, Gainesville, Florida, 1998.

seeds used to make organic oils and lip balms. There is also the **kapok** (also called **ceiba),** which is readily identifiable by its huge red seed pods hanging from branches. When these pods open, they release seeds that are borne by the wind on cotton-like tufts, which Amazon natives use for making hunting darts. At the ground level, the kapok stands out for its huge buttress roots, which fan out in all directions and are often wider than the tree itself.

If you scuff the ground with your foot, you will understand the reason for the roots. Jungle soil is amazingly poor because all the minerals are either sucked up by the voracious competition of plant life or leached away by the constant rains. As a result, even the roots of the largest trees run along the surface in a desperate search for minerals. Because rainforest trees lack the deep taproots of temperate-forest trees, they need buttress roots to help stay upright, especially

THE SUNSTAINABLE BRAZIL NUT

Apart from the depredations of gold mining and the timber industry, Puerto Malonado's third major industry stands out as a hopeful model for rainforest development. Though useful as lumber, the **Brazil nut tree** (*Bertholletiq excelsa,* locally known as *castaño*) is often the largest tree left standing in the forest because its nuts are more valuable than its wood. The tree's round seedpods look like the pod inside of a coconut and fall to the ground in December and January. Each pod contains between 12 and 24 Brazil nuts, and a single tree can produce as many as 500 kg of nuts in a year. The nuts are sold as food or for a burgeoning overseas organic products industry that uses Brazil nut oil in lip balms and skin lotions.

The tough shells prevent birds from eating the seeds before they ripen and are used by natives as candle holders. Only one species of insect, the englossive bee, is physiologically able to pollinate the Brazil nut tree's flowers. Once pollinated, the tree relies on only one animal for the dispersal of its seeds, the brown agouti, a diminutive jungle rodent who collects the seeds and buries them in the ground for later eating. Luckily for the tree, the agouti either forgets where the hole is or returns after the seeds have already germinated. People have often tried to bury and germinate Brazil nut seeds without success. Apparently the mild-mannered agouti has a few well-kept gardening secrets.

The base of a Brazil nut tree is also a good place to find the deadly bushmaster snake, which is perfectly camouflaged among the leaves as it waits for the agouti. For this reason, Brazil nut workers use a forked pole to pick up Brazil nut seeds off the ground.

during the violent windstorms that snap the tops of many trees right off.

Another surprising difference between temperate and rain forests is the age of the trees. In the United States, old-growth forests take centuries to develop. But rainforests are much more dynamic—the average life of a tree here is a mere 80 to 135 years.

For those of us used to the pines and oaks of temperate forests, the sheer variety of trees in the rainforest can be overwhelming. There are more than a thousand different tree species in Peru's Amazon, and even finding the same tree twice can be a challenge. There is no complete guide to rainforest trees and, even if one existed, it would be the size of a telephone book. Instead of trying to keep a mental catalog of the trees you see, it makes more sense to try to understand how different trees use common defenses to survive. The thorns and spikes on many rainforest trees serves as a protection against animals, while peeling bark prevents vines from climbing the trunk. Many leaves have thin hairs or contain a complex array of toxins that serve as protection from the predation of caterpillars and insects.

Some trees have developed symbiotic relationships to survive. The **Palo Santo** (Holy Tree), for instance, has hollow chambers and a gooey nectar that provide both food and lodging to fire ants. These ants are totally dependent on the tree for survival and will chase off any predator who would otherwise eat parts of the tree.

FAUNA
Desert

The rich oceans off Peru's coast support a wide variety of marine mammals and sea birds. At the **Reserva Nacional Paracas,** the country's most important coastal reserve, visitors to the **Islas Ballestas** can see dozens of sea lions, seals, and the endangered **Humboldt penguin,** a diminutive creature with white belly, black flippers, and a spoon-shaped bill. Hundreds of thousands of birds also roost on these islands, which are covered in thick layers of guano, or bird dung. There are more than 200 bird species at Paracas, including a variety of gulls, pelicans, boobies, cormorants, frigate birds, hawks, ospreys, and vultures. If you are lucky you might even see a **pink flamingo** or an **Andean condor.**

The dry forests further north begin to support a variety of mammals, such as gray and red deer, anteaters, foxes, and the extremely rare *oso de anteojos* (spectacled bear) and **puma**. A few dozen unique forest birds also live here, along with a range of iguanas, snakes, and lizards. Peru's small chunk of Pacific coastal forest near the border with Ecuador is home to the only crocodile in Latin America, the endangered **Tumbes crocodile.**

Andes

The most ubiquitous animals of Peru's Andes are the four species of native **camelids** that eat the high-altitude *íchu* grasses and produce wooly coats as protection from the rain and cold. Two of these, the llama and alpaca, were domesticated thousands of years ago by Peru's highlanders, who tie bright tassels of yarn onto the animals' ears. Herds of the much smaller, and finely haired, vicuña can be seen in the sparse grass-

lands above Arequipa. The fourth camelid, the guanaco, is harder to spot because its main range lies south in Chile and Argentina.

Other animals in the Peruvian Andes include white-tailed deer, foxes, and the endangered puma. The only animal you are likely to see, however, is the **vizcacha,** which looks like a strange mix between a rabbit and a squirrel and lives among the rocks.

There is a huge range of birds in the Andes, the most famous of which is the Andean condor, the world's largest flying bird. Its range extends from the high jungle, including Machu Picchu, all the way to the coast. It can easily be seen in Colca Canyon, along with a variety of other raptors including the powerful mountain caracara with a black body, red face, and brilliant yellow feet. There are also aplomado falcons, which have a russet belly and can often be seen hovering over grasslands in search of mice.

A variety of water birds can be seen at Lake Titicaca and in the cold, black lakes of the Andean puna. This is the habitat for the **Andean goose,** a

a curious alpaca

huge, rotund bird with a white belly and black back, and a variety of shimmering ducks including the **puna teal** and **crescent duck.** There are even flamingos and a few wading birds, such as the red-billed **puna ibis.** One of the most interesting birds, which can be seen in the river near Machu Picchu and in the Colca Canyon, is the **torrent duck.** This amazing swimmer floats freely down whitewater that stymies even experienced rafters.

Amazon

The Amazon is a zoo without bars. Exotic birds flit through the air, turtles line up on riverside logs, and pig-sized aquatic rodents called **capybaras** submerge like submarines under the water's surface. Sloths clamber slowly through the trees along with noisy troops of monkeys. Just in the jungle around Puerto Maldonado and Parque Nacional Manu, there are more than 1,000 bird species, 1,300 butterflies, an estimated 30 million insects, and a range of animals including **tapirs, jaguar, armadillos, anteaters, wild pigs, caiman, otter,** and **anaconda** snakes. A slightly different range of birds and animals are seen farther down in the Iquitos basin, including the **pink river dolphin.**

The problem is that the Amazon's lush greenery can make these animals hard to spot. To see much of anything, you need a good pair of binoculars and an experienced guide to spot them for you. The longer you stay in the jungle, and the further you are from cities, the more you will see.

A walk in the rainforest, however, will nearly always produce sightings of monkeys. Among the most common are troops of large **squirrel monkeys,** which shake the branches in search of sugary fruit. Accompanying them are **black-fronted nan birds,** which eat the katydids that jump away from the commotion. You will also see (and hear) **red howler monkeys** and with luck the **pygmy marmoset,** which can survive on a few drops of sap per day and is the smallest monkeys on earth.

There are a variety of snakes, which is the reason jungle guides walk in front of visitors to inspect the path. Near Puerto Maldonado, we saw a meter-long **coral snake,** which stood out among the brown leaves with its brilliant bands of red and

orange. There are also plenty of iridescent **frogs,** some of which have elaborate chemical defenses on their skin that the Amazon natives use for their poison blow-darts. Colorful **butterflies** flit through the forest and, if you're sweating, one might land on your shirt to eat your salt. Most of all you will see **insects,** including long lines of **leaf-cutter ants** carrying bits of leaves on their backs toward their huge ground nests. There are also smaller **army ants** and **termites,** which build tunnels toward their nests of mud built around tree branches. You may not see them but you will hear thousands of **cicadas,** which make a deafening chorus by vibrating a plate under their wings.

One of the jungle's more extraordinary sights are macaw clay licks, which are spread through the Amazon basin. A huge variety of **parrots, parakeets,** and **macaws** congregate here every morning to eat the mineral-rich mud that allows them to digest unripe fruit. The largest birds are the macaws, with the more common species being the chestnut-fronted, scarlet, and the blue-and-green. At the world's largest clay lick, near the Tambopata Research Center, hundreds of these birds can be seen squawking and flying about as visitors use spotting

red howler monkeys in flooded rain forest near Iquitos

THE AMAZING, UBIQUITOUS LEAF CUTTER ANT

If you visit the jungle, there is no way to avoid contact with the tens of thousands of insect species that crawl, fly, hop, and generally dominate the rain forest under story. The most visible of these is the leaf cutter ant, which clears neat paths from its colony to the areas where it collects its leaves. These paths are often littered with discarded leaf fragments and can stretch a kilometer or more.

There are many species of leaf cutters, but all make underground colonies that can reach the size of a living room. The red-colored colonies are made from earth, while black ones are made from partially chewed twig fragments.

Anywhere from one million to 2.5 million workers live inside a leaf cutter colony, divided into five castes:

1. The queen or egg-layer
2. Male reproducers, who fertilize the queen
3. Leaf cutters, who chew and transport the leaves
4. Leaf travellers, who remove the waxy cuticle from the leaf and protect the treasure from parasitic *phoridae* flies.
5. Cultivators, who tend and fertilize a fungus that grows on the leaves.

Biologists believe these leaf cutters are responsible for nearly half of all herbivore consumption in the Neotropics, but the ants do not actually eat the leaves. Instead they pile them up inside their colony to cultivate a fungus, which occurs only in leaf-cutting colonies and is the ants' only food source. The ant and fungus rely on each other for survival, an example of how specific and complex rain forest symbiosis can be.

scopes to watch them from a blind. There are also salt licks that attract mammals, including one at the Manu Wildlife Center that attracts reliable night-time views of tapirs and **Brocket ceer.**

All Amazon jungle lodges offer an early-morning boat cruise to see birds. The **ringed kingfisher** darts above the river with its light blue body, russet belly, and white-ringed neck. Mealy, orange-winged and festive parrots squawk noisily through air. You may see the **Cuvier's toucan,** which uses its huge tri-colored beak for eating

eggs and baby chicks from the nests of other birds. Smaller, colorful birds such as **flycatchers, cotingas,** and **tanagers** can often be seen perched on branches above the river, including the **slate-colored hawk** and **yellow-headed caracara.** Rustling through lakeside bushes is the **hoatzin,** a chicken-like bird with a spiky crest and a grunting call. If you're lucky, you might see an **Amazonian umbrella bird,** nicknamed the "Elvis Bird" for a crown of feathers that flops over its head.

History

Apart from natural diversity, Peru also gave birth to the largest patchwork of human civilizations in the ancient Americas. Its cultures were far more diverse, for example, than the Mesoamerican cultures that spread through present-day Central America and Mexico.

The first Peruvian states were worshipping at stepped adobe platforms on the coast before the Egyptians were building their pyramids at Giza. And as the Roman Empire spread across modern-day Europe, Peru's first empires states were moving like wildfire across the Andes. The

Chavín and **Tiahuanaco** cultures established patterns of religion, commerce, and architecture that remain alive today among Peru's Quechuan-speaking highlanders.

Western notions of conquest and military-backed empires do not fit easily over Peruvian history. Peru's three large **empires**—the Chavín, the Wari, and the Incas—spread across Peru in three stages that historians call *horizons.* Like the Aztecs in Mesoamerica, these cultures spread more through commerce and cultural exchange than through military force. Even the Incas, who were capable of raising vast armies, preferred to subdue neighbors through gifts and offers of public work projects. The Incas used military force only when peaceful solutions had been exhausted.

Following the European arrival in the New World, Peru's history follows the same basic stages as the United States and other areas of Latin America. There was first a colonial period, which lasted longer and ended later than the United States', a war of independence, and then a period of rapid nation building and industrialization in the 19th and 20th centuries.

ORIGINS OF HUMAN CIVILIZATION

Human life in Peru, indeed all over the Americas, is a relatively recent event made possible when the last Ice Age allowed human settlers to cross the Bering land bridge that connected present-day Russia to Alaska between 30,000 and 20,000 B.C. The first evidence of human civilization in Peru is at **Pikimachay Cave** outside of Ayacucho, where arrowheads and carbon remains have been dated to as early as 15,000 B.C. By 2,900 B.C.,

PERU TIMELINE

20,000 B.C.: The first humans arrive in Peru.

15,000 B.C.: First evidence of human life in Peru at Pikimachay Cave outside Ayacucho.

2900 B.C.: The adobe ceremonial center of Caral is built on the coast north of Lima.

900–200 B.C.: Early Horizon: Chavín culture unifies Peru for the first time from its base near present-day Huaraz.

200–600 A.D.: Intermediate Early Horizon: the Moche, Nasca, and Tiwanaku cultures flourish in different areas of Peru.

300 A.D.: Moche Lords of Sipán are buried at Huaca Rajada near present-day Chiclayo.

600 A.D.–900 A.D.: Middle Horizon: the Wari culture spreads across Peru from near present-day Ayacucho.

900–1,450 A.D.: Intermediate Late Horizon: The Wari state is replaced by a range of cultures, including the Sicán near present-day Chiclayo, Chimu near Trujillo, Caxamarca near Cajamarca, Ica-Chincha on the south coast, and the Huanca and Chancas in the central Highlands.

1438–1532: Late Horizon: the Inca empire stretches from southern Chile to northern Ecuador.

1530–1532: Huáscar and Atahualpa, both sons of Huyana Cápac, plunge the Inca empire into civil war.

1532: Francisco Pizarro and an army of 170 *conquistadores* march from Tumbes and capture Atahualpa in Cajamarca.

1533: Athualpa is executed and a puppet leader, Manco Inca, is installed.

1535: After the Inca gold has been melted in Cusco, Pizarro founds Lima.

1536–1537: Manco Inca's rebellion and subsequent retreat to Vilcabamba.

1538: Conquistador Diego de Almagro is executed after rebelling against Francisco Pizarro's authority.

1541: Almagro's son and other *almagristas* assassinate Francisco Pizarro in Lima.

1542: Spanish King Charles I establishes Viceroyalty of Peru, Spain's second colony in the New World apart from Mexico.

1569: The last Inca, Tupac Amaru, is captured by the Spanish in the jungle at Vilcabamba and executed a few years later.

1780–1781: Tupac Amaru II leads a rebellion against the Spaniards and is executed.

1820–1921: Argentine general José de San Martín proclaims the independence of Peru even though Spanish forces remain in the central highlands.

1822: San Martín leaves Peru after a meeting with Venezuelan liberator Simón Bolívar, who takes over the campaign to wrestle Peru from Spanish control.

1824: The last Spanish forces are defeated at the battle of Ayacucho and Peru's independence is formally proclaimed.

1826–1866: After Bolívar leaves Peru, the country

Peru's first advanced cultures were cultivating cotton and peanuts at **Caral,** one of a string of adobe ceremonial centers built along a coastal valley near present-day Supe, north of Lima.

EARLY HORIZON (900–200 B.C.)

The Chavín culture began constructing an elaborate stone temple at Chavín de Huántar, near present-day Huaraz, in about 900 B.C. The stone walls and obelisk inside and around the temple were chiseled with an eclectic range of deities,

including pumas, snakes, and mythical beings. During the height of the Chavín culture from 400 to 200 B.C., the Chavín cult spread across Peru's highlands, bringing together Peru's isolated regions for the first time.

INTERMEDIATE EARLY HORIZON (200–600 A.D.)

After the **Chavín** culture faded from prominence in 200 B.C., a variety of cultures sprang up to take its place. On the North Coast, the **Moche**

Know Peru

enters a period of political turbulence with 35 presidents in 40 years.

1840: Peru signs lucrative contract for exporting guano, or bird dung.

1849–1874: Cotton and sugar plantations on Peru's north coast import 100,000 Chinese coolies to replace freed slaves.

1879–1883: Peru loses the the Pacific War against Chile.

1911: Hiram Bingham discovers Machu Picchu, Vitcos, and portions of Espíritu Pampa.

1927: Raúl Haya de la Torre founds the Alianza Popular revolucionario Americana (APRA) from political exile in France.

1963–1968: President Fernando Belaunde begins land reform but is overthrown by General Juan Velasco.

1968–1975: Velasco reshapes the Peruvian economy by nationalizing foreign-owned companies and transferring all of Peru's hacienda land to worker cooperatives. Economic chaos results.

1970: An earthquake kills 70,000 in the Huaraz area, including 18,000 when a mudslide slams the town of Yungay.

1980–92: Sendero Luminoso, Shining Path, launches its revolution from Ayacucho. Massacres and conflicts with the Peruvian military will claim the lives of 69,000 Peruvians, three-quarters of whom are Quechuan-speaking highlanders.

1982–83: El Niño floods devastate Peru's north.

1985: APRA candidate Alan García is elected president and pushes the country into hyperinflation and a downward economic spiral.

1987: The royal Moche tombs of the Lords of Sipán near present-day Chiclayo are excavated by Peruvian archaeologist Walter Alva.

1990: Dark-horse candidate Alberto Fujimori defeats novelist Mario Vargas Llosa to become president of Peru.

1992: Fujimori dissolves congress in his *auto coup* and Shining Path's leader is captured.

1994: 6,000 Shining Path members surrender under Peru's amnesty law.

1996–1997: Tupac Amaru guerillas take over the Japanese embassy, and are eventually defeated after a four-month standoff with Peruvian military.

1996: American Lori Berenson is convicted of treason by a secret military court for involvement with Tupac Amaru. Her life sentence was reduced to 20 years in 2001 but she remains in prison.

1998: El Niño storms ravage north coast.

2000: Fujimori is re-elected president under allegations of electoral fraud, but leaves the country after a scandal implicates him in extortion, corruption, and arms trafficking.

2001: Alejandro Toledo is elected president.

2003–2004: Calls for Toledo's resignation heighten as Peru's largest union, the General Confederation of Workers, holds nation-wide strikes.

culture began building the Huaca de la Luna, a stepped adobe pyramid near present-day Trujillo. Their empire would spread along the north coast, and their most important rulers, the Lords of Sipán, were buried near present-day Chiclayo around 300 A.D.

On the south coast the **Nasca** culture began making elegant weavings from cotton and camelid fiber that are considered today the most advanced textiles produced in pre-Columbian America. They also developed quipus, a system of communication that used knotted strings and yarns of different colors to relay encoded messages. Their complex cosmography is evident in the Nasca Lines, giant etchings in the desert floor that were probably once used for rain-inducing ceremonies.

Near Lake Titicaca, the **Tiwanaku** culture built an elaborate stone complex on the south shores of Lake Titicaca and developed a system of raised-bed farming that allowed them to cultivate crops despite the area's freezing temperatures. The perfect monumental stonework at the ceremonial center of Tiwanaku, near Lake Titicaca in present-day Bolivia, laid the base for Inca architecture nearly a thousand years later. Tiwanaku architecture and religious ideas spread throughout the Peruvian highlands.

MIDDLE HORIZON (600–900 A.D.)

Though influences from the Chavín and Tiwanaku culture had spread throughout Peru's highlands, **Wari** was the first culture in South America to establish a true empire. They rose out of a potent new combination of the Nasca, Tiwanaku, and local Huarpa cultures that included remarkable weavings, fine stonework, and highways that stretched throughout Peru's highlands. They were also the first culture to build not only ceremonial centers but also well-populated cities. Their capital at Wari, near present-day Ayacucho, covers nearly 300 hectares (740 acres) and includes aqueducts, warehouses, temples, and elaborate mausoleums for storing mummies. Archaeologists say the city's population was at least 10,000 and maybe as high as 70,000.

Around 650 A.D. the Wari spread south toward the Tiwanaku culture near Lake Titicaca and Cusco, where they built the huge walled city of **Pikillacta.** The city spreads across 47 hectares (116 acres) of rolling grasslands and contains a maze of walled stone enclosures of the city and elaborate stone aqueducts. In the south, near Arequipa, the Wari built the remarkable stone fortress of **Cerro Baúi** atop a sheer-sided mesa. The Wari spread as far north as the edge of the Moche capital near present-day Trujillo and built a walled city near Huamachuco, in the highlands above Trujillo. By the time the empire faded around 900 A.D., the Wari had left an indelible pattern of organization over Peru that would be repeated in larger scale by the Incas.

INTERMEDIATE LATE HORIZON (900–1450 A.D.)

Once again, as happened after the Chavín culture, Peru splintered into various independent kingdoms after the fall of the Wari. The most important of these were spread along the coast and included the Chimu, Sicán, and Ica-Chincha cultures.

The **Chimu** built their citadel, Chan Chan, outside present-day Trujillo and a short distance from the adobe stepped platforms built earlier by the Moche. Chan Chan is the largest city ever built by Peru's pre-Hispanic cultures, and its walled plazas, passageways, temples,, and gardens spread over nearly 20 square kilometers (4,940 acres). Over time the kingdom would spread along the coast of Peru from Chancay, a valley north of Lima, to the present-day border with Ecuador.

As the Chimu were flourishing, other descendants of the Moche culture known as the **Sicán** were building adobe pyramids at Batán Grande further north near present-day Chiclayo. Discoveries of royal Sicán tombs there in the early 1991 revealed a wealth of gold masks, scepters, and ceremonial knives, along with elegant jewelry made from spondylus shell imported from Ecuador. After a devastating El Niño flood destroyed the center, the Sicán began building even larger pyramids a bit further north at Túcume, which remains an enigmatic and largely unexcavated site today. By 1350, the Sicán culture was conquered by the Chimu.

Peru's south coast was dominated by the **Ica-Chincha** kingdom, which spread along Peru's southern desert valleys south of Inca. This culture developed elaborate aqueducts for bringing water from the mountains under the desert floor. Their ceremonial center of La Centinela, near present-day Chincha, was an adobe complex painted with sparkling-white gypsum and decorated with ornamental friezes.

During this time, other cultures flourished throughout the highlands. The largest of these were the **Chachapoya,** a mysterious federation of city-states that spread across the cloud forests of northeastern Peru. The Chachapoya's most celebrated city is Kuélap, a stone citadel perched atop a sheer limestone bluff, but there are dozens of other major city sites.

Other cultures included the Caxamarca, near present-day Cajamarca, the **Huanca** and **Chancas** in the central highlands, and the **Colla** and **Lupaca** near Lake Titicaca. One of these groups, almost too small to mention, was a diminutive tribe of highlanders in the Cusco area that called themselves the **Incas.**

LATE HORIZON (1438-1532)

The exact beginnings of the Inca Empire are obscured by myth but historians believe that Manco Cápac, the first Inca leader, began his rule around 1200 A.D. For more than two centuries the Incas developed slowly in the Cusco area, until 1438, when the neighboring Chancas tribe threatened to overrun their city. Though Inca Viracocha fled the city, his son Inca Yupanqui beat back the Chancas, took over from his disgraced father, and changed his name to Pachacútec (Shaker of the Earth). He launched the meteoric rise of the Inca Empire, which within a century would stretch for more than 4,000 kilometers (2,480 miles) from southern Chile to northern Ecuador and include huge chunks of Bolivia and Argentina as well. Pachacútec was also responsible

for much of the Inca's monumental architecture, including the fortress of Sacsayhuamán and, in the Sacred Valley, Pisac and Ollantaytambo. Historians also believe he built Machu Picchu, probably as a winter palace.

Though the Incas are known for their fine stonework, their greatest accomplishment was the organization of their empire. Cusco was actually smaller than other capitals of pre-Hispanic Peru, including Tiwanaku, Wari, and Chan Chan. But the Inca imperial city was at the center of a paved road network that led throughout the empire, which the Incas called Tawantinsuyo (Four Corners, in Quechua). Inca runners, known as *chasquis,* would run along these roads carrying messages recorded in quipus, the knotted bundles of string used both the Nasca and Wari cultures. The *chasqui* would run at near-sprint speed until reaching the *tambo,* or rest house, at which point a new Inca runner would continue. In this way, quipus recording harvests, weather, population data, and numerous other statistics could pass from present-day Quito to Cusco in several days—just a bit slower than buses take to travel the same route today.

As the Incas spread, they built a network of satellite centers that allowed them to support their far-flung conquests. Like most everything in the Inca world, these miniature cities were divided into upper *(hanan)* and lower *(hurin)* parts. The cookie-cutter pattern, which can be seen all over Peru, included one or two plazas, a ceremonial platform for viewing ceremonies *(ushnu),* a compound for the chosen women of the Inca *(acllahuasi),* a large hall *(kallanka),* and grain storehouses *(colca).*

The Incas offered rich economic and cultural benefits to neighboring cultures that submitted peacefully to their rule. When the Ica-Chincha empire was integrated into the empire, the Incas helped build a vast aqueduct that is still used near present-day Chincha. Though the Incas changed the names of places they conquered, and encouraged the spread of their religion and language, they accepted a wide degree of cultural diversity. Spanish chroniclers such as Pedro Cieza de León were impressed with the tremendous variety of languages and native dress in Cusco at the time of the conquest. The Incas also behaved brutally to those who opposed them. After waging a long war against the Chachapoya, the Incas deported half the population to other parts of the empire as part of the forced-labor scheme known as *mita*.

Pachacútec's son and grandson, Tupac Yupanqui and Huanya Capac, spent most of their lives abroad, extending the Inca empire to its farthest limits. Huayna Capac died in 1527 during a smallpox epidemic that devastated Peru's population and was probably spread by the Spaniards, who had set foot on the northernmost fringe of the Inca Empire during a preliminary trip in 1526. His sudden death led to a devastating civil war between his two sons, Huascar and Atahualpa, which had just ended when the Spaniards began their march from Tumbes.

SPANISH CONQUEST

Pizarro and his men rode through desert and into the Andes and found Atahualpa and an army of 40,000 to 80,000 Inca soldiers at Cajamarca. Atahualpa had just crushed the forces of his half-brother Huascar and was returning, jubilant and victorious, to his home city of Quito. The Spaniards invited Atahualpa to a meeting the next day in Cajamarca's square and planned a bold ambush. Firing their arquebuses and charging with their horses and lances, the Spaniards sparked a massive panic, killed at least 7,000 Inca soldiers, and took Atahualpa hostage. The Inca offered to pay a ransom that, when melted down six months later, amounted to an astounding 6,100 kilos of 22-karat gold and 11,820 kilos of good silver. The Spaniards executed Atahualpa anyway.

The Spaniards achieved their successes over far superior Inca forces because of their guns, dynamite, steel, and horses but also because Pizarro understood how to play Inca politics. After Atahualpa's death, the Spaniards befriended Manco Inca, another son of Huayna Capac, and declared him the new leader of the Inca Empire. Manco Inca did not remain a docile puppet for

long, however, after the Spaniards sacked Cusco for all of its gold and raped the wives of Inca nobles. After the gold was gone, Francisco Pizarro left Cusco and headed for the coast to found Lima, which would soon become the capital of the newly declared Spanish Viceroyalty of Peru.

By 1536, Manco Inca had launched a rebellion and laid siege to Cusco with an estimated army of 100,000 soldiers. Against overwhelming odds, the Spaniards routed the Incas from their fortress of Sacsayhuamán during a week of constant fighting. Manco Inca repelled an army of Spaniards at Ollantaytambo in the Sacred Valley before retreating to the jungle of Vilcabamba. For the next 35 years, the Incas would use this jungle stronghold to continue their resistance against the Spaniards until the last Inca leader, Tupac Amaru, was captured and executed in 1572.

Just after the Inca rebellion, the Spaniards themselves erupted into civil war after differences arose between Francisco Pizarro and his junior partner, Diego de Almagro. After a series of bloody clashes, Pizarro's forces won out over the *Almagrista* faction in 1538, and Pizarro shocked the king in Spain by executing Almagro. A few years later, Pizarro himself was murdered by a group of *Almagristas* that included Almagro's son.

VICEROYALTY

Cusco became a center of religious art during the viceroyalty but otherwise fell out of the spotlight after the conquest as the Spaniards turned their attention to mines. In a cynical use of Inca tradition for Spanish ends, Viceroy Francisco de Toledo legalized the Inca's old labor scheme of *mita* in 1574 in order to force huge numbers of Indians to work at the Potosí silver mine, in present-day Bolivia, and the Santa Barbara mercury mine near Huancavelica. Far from home, thousands of Indians perished while working in virtual slavery at these mines.

Indians in other parts of Peru were not being treated much better. Some were forced to relocate to *reducciones,* or new settlements, that allowed the Spaniards to better tax the Indians and convert them to Christianity. Rich farmland was divided into *encomiendas,* and all the Indians living on it became slaves to the Spanish owner, known as the *encomendero.* Other times Indians were herded into sweatshops, called *obrajes,* where they made textiles and other objects for export under prison-like conditions.

One of the best descriptions of this misery was written by a full-blooded Indian, Guamán Poma de Ayala, who penned a 1,200-page letter to the king of Spain and titled it *Nueva Crónica y Buen Gobierno.* The wildly creative document includes a series of careful hand etchings and an exuberant mix of Spanish and Quechua. It was discovered in 1908 in the Royal Library of Copenhagen and is considered Peru's most complete "vision of the vanquished."

Given the abuse, it is not surprising that an Indian uprising spread across Peru in the late 18th century. The leader of the 1780–81 revolt was Túpac Amaru II, who claimed to be a direct descendent of the last Inca, Tupac Amaru. After a year-long rebellion, the Spaniards finished off Túpac Amaru II as they had his ancestor two centuries before: He was garroted in Cusco's main square and then his body was ripped apart by teams of horses pulling in opposite directions.

INDEPENDENCE

After nearly three centuries of being administered from Spain, the native-born people of the Peruvian Viceroyalty began to itch for independence. News of the American revolution in 1776 and French revolution in 1789 filtered to Peru and encouraged a groundswell of reform that was inspired by the European Enlightenment. The descendents of Europeans born in Peru, known as *criollos,* were increasingly resentful of the privileges according to Spaniards, or *españoles,* who held all the powerful positions in the viceroyalty. Colonial society was rigidly classified into a hierarchy that attempted to make sense, and control, the uncontrollable mixing between races in colonial Peru. The main categories include mestizos (European-Indian), *mulato* (European-African), *negro* (African), *zambo* (Indian-African), and *indio* (Indian). Dozens of labels were applied to all the possible combinations and proportions of different ethnic mixtures, and some categories even included bizarre animal names such as *lobo* (wolf), which was used to describe certain types of *mulatos.* Despite the apparent rigidity, recent scholarly work has revealed that racial lines in the viceroyalty were surprisingly fluid and had more to do with wealth than skin color—wealthy mestizos were usually considered *criollos,* for instance.

When Napoleon forced Spain's King Charles IV to abdicate in 1808, independence movements erupted across South America. By 1820, the last bastion of Spanish control was Peru, which for centuries had served as the main Spanish port and administrative center for South America. After liberating Chile, Argentine General José de San Martín routed the royalist forces from Lima in 1821 and proclaimed the symbolic independence of Peru. But he ceded control over the independence struggle to Venezuelan general Simón Bolívar, whose troops won two separate battles in Peru's central highlands in 1824 against the last strongholds of Spanish force.

Bolívar envisioned a grand union of South American states known as Gran Colombia, which was modeled on the United States. After serving as Peru's first president for two years, he returned to Bogotá, Colombia, in a last-ditch attempt to hold the federation together. Bolívar's scheme fell apart as the former colonies bickered among themselves, and Peru plunged into a half century of chaos. During the four decades following Bolívar's departure, more than 35 presidents came and went.

Despite the chaos, Peru's rising class of merchants found new opportunities for making money besides mines. The biggest business was guano, the huge piles of bird droppings that covered the islands off Peru's coast. This natural fertilizer fetched exorbitant prices in Europe. The guano boom helped finance the ambitious project, spearheaded by American entrepreneur Henry Meiggs in 1870, to build a railroad line into the steep valleys above Lima to the La Oroya mine. Following the abolishment of slavery in the mid-19th century, hacienda owners in the

Know Peru

PERU'S WHITE GOLD

The Huallaga Valley in northeastern Peru was once deemed one of the country's great un-developed assets, according to a United Nations report published in 1950. "There are huge areas apt for agriculture that have still not been touched by man," concluded the report. "The area could become an incalculable treasure for Peru the day that an adequate highway system is constructed through the valley." That highway, the Carretera Marginal, was constructed in the following decade by President Fernando Belaunde, who backed the ambitious scheme to build the road from Tarapoto all the way to the village of Tocache.

The road did indeed spur development, but not the kind the United Nations had envisioned. Today the Carretera Marginal is an abandoned, rocky road that leads into the heart of Peru's cocaine industry, a business that rakes in between $300 million and $600 million in under-the-table money and employs in the neighborhood of 200,000 Peruvians. The Peruvian government and the U.S. DEA have been waging a war against Peru's cocaine industry since 1995, shooting down drug planes and burning or spraying 70 percent of Peru's illegal fields of coca, the shrubby plant used to make the drug. But still Peru continues to be the world's second-largest producer of cocaine behind neighboring Colombia.

Coca has not always been a curse for Peruvians. The leaves of the plant have been used for thousands of years by Andean highlanders for its medicinal properties. When chewed, the *coca* gives energy, dulls hunger, and fortifies the body against altitude. The Incas considered the leaf so powerful that they created a monopoly and allowed only nobles to use it.

These days *coca* is more popular than ever in Peru's Andean culture. Men chew leaves as they work in the fields, and women use it to ease the pain while giving birth. When a young man is about to ask a woman to marry him, he first must present a bag of leaves to his future father-in-law. *Curanderos* use the leaves as magic symbols to predict the future, and the leaves are placed carefully inside coffins at burials. When tourists arrive at Cusco's airport, they are greeted with a hot cup of *maté de coca*, an infusion made from the leaf that does wonders for altitude sickness.

The effects of the *coca* leaf were discovered in Europe and the United States during the 19th century, when a Parisian chemist named Angelo Mariani marketed a wine made from the leaf (it contained nearly 0.12 grains of cocaine per fluid ounce!). The success of the product in-spired a number of wine imitations in the United States, including one that was converted into a carbonated soft drink called Coca-Cola after the temperance movement hit Atlanta, Georgia, in 1885. By 1903 a public outcry over the ill effects of cocaine forced the Coca-Cola company to remove cocaine from its beverage. What is not generally known is that Coca-Cola today continues to use flavoring from coca leaves, which have been *decocainized*. (Interest-ingly, New Coke, which flopped in 1985, contained no coca leaf flavoring.) Two new Peruvian beverages—Kdrink and Vortex energy drink—also contain traces of the outlawed stimulant and are trying to overcome vague legal language that prevents them from being imported into the United States.

Shortly after the process for making cocaine was discovered, Sigmund Freud was one of sev-eral European intellectuals who experimented with the drug, which was commonly prescribed in the 19th century as a euphoric. Some scholars even believe he wrote his most famous work,

The Interpretation of Dreams, under the influence of cocaine. Freud's use of cocaine came to a screeching halt when a good friend died of a consuming cocaine addiction.

Taking and making cocaine today remains a nasty business. Villagers in the impoverished Huallaga Valley and other areas of Peru grow the plant because they can get as much as $2 per kilo for the leaves, many times more than they would receive for selling wheat, potatoes, or corn. Cultivating *coca* takes a lot out of the soil, and fields therefore have to be changed constantly. The Huallaga Valley, once covered in cloud forest, is nearly denuded and covered with a patchwork of eroding fields.

The process of making cocaine is even worse. The leaves must first be crushed underfoot and soaked in water to remove their essence. This water is then mixed with kerosene and other toxic chemicals and stirred until a white substance floats to the top. This substance, known as *pasta básica* or *bruta,* is further refined to make pure cocaine, known officially as cocaine hydrocholoride. About 400 kilograms of *coca* leaves produces one kilo of cocaine. The villagers who help stir the *pasta básica* can readily be identified by their scarred arms, which are burned pink by the toxic chemicals.

The cocaine industry has also wreaked havoc on Peru's cities. Though cocaine is widely available in Peru and used often by young Peruvians, the real problem lies in the dusty shantytowns, or *pueblos jóvenes,* on the outskirts of Lima. Because cocaine is too expensive, teenagers smoke cheap cigarettes made from the unrefined *pasta básica,* which is different from crack cocaine but equally as powerful. People become addicted immediately to the $0.30 cigarettes and, like crack smokers in the United States, their lives head downhill fast.

Experts say that the collapse of the Medellín and Calí cartels in the mid-1990s probably boosted Peru's cocaine business by fragmenting the industry and allowing players who were in the shadows to grab new market share. One of the new leaders in the cocaine industry is the FARC, the Revolutionary Armed Forces of Colombia, which began cultivating coca in northern Peru near the Colombian border, according to statements made by Peruvian Defense Minister Roberto Chiabra. Peruvian drug authorities also believe that the FARC is behind a dramatic rise in Peru's cultivation of poppy, which is used to make opium and heroine.

During the boom days of the cocaine industry of the 1980s and early 1990s, Tarapoto's airport was busier than Lima's on certain days, and planes flew back and forth freely to deliver the *pasta básica* to refining laboratories Colombia. But now much of the cocaine is being processed inside Peru and transported by a variety of methods, including boat, truck, and *mulas,* or people that swallow condoms full of cocaine before boarding a plane to Miami. Recently, Amazonian Indians have also begun to carry cocaine through the rainforest toward the Colombian border.

The situation has become so complicated that it appears likely that the U.S. DEA will become even more involved in Peru's drug war. U.S.-backed air patrols, which were suspended in 2001, will probably resume again, according to a 2004 statement posted on the web page of U.S. Embassy in Peru. The DEA has already established a command-control center with the Peruvian military in Pucallpa, a jungle city in the vicinity of the once-promising Huallaga Valley.

ADVICE FROM A REFORMED TERRORIST

Javier Vela, 35, now works as a night security guard in his hometown of Tarapoto. But when he was 19 he entered the Movimiento Revolucionario Tupac Amaru and spent the next six years of his life fighting and hiding in the jungle. After the MRTA leadership divided in 1992, Vela left the MRTA and turned himself in under President Alberto Fujimori's amnesty laws. Under this law, both Shining Path and MRTA members who turned themselves in would serve for up to two years in the military to be "rehabilitated." MRTA's ideology is socialist and re-sembled other guerrilla groups in Central America.

Vela's story follows, in his own words:

As a student in Tarapoto, I was reading Marx and Lenin and began to believe in the armed revolution of Che Guevarra and others. I wanted to fight for the better of my country so I entered the MRTA in September, 1986. It was difficult to live in the *monte* (cloud forest) so far from family. During the day we trained a lot, simulated at-tacks on police posts, and read revolutionary pamphlets. We walked only at night. My first military action was the invasion of Juanjui. We entered at 6 P.M. when the police weren't expected us. About 500 of us attacked four police stations at the same time, causing four police deaths and no MRTA deaths. I was in charge of one of the assault groups. We then took prisoners to the main square for an *asamblea popular,* where we called the young people to rise up in armed conflict and help the poor *campesinada* (rural population). After a half hour, we disappeared again into the *monte* before police reinforcements could arrive. We were always victorious. We had well-prepared mili-tants and we always used the surprise attack. We were also very good at improvising. In this way, we also entered the cities of Yurimaguas, Zapo Soa, Tabalosa, San Jose de Sisa, Picota, Bellavista, Moyobamba, Rioja, Nueva Cajamarca, but never Tarapoto. We never got that objective.

Problems started when I went to an MRTA leadership meeting in Lima in 1989. People had entered the movement who were more interested in revenge, working with drug traffickers, assassinating other militants, and common delinquency. We had got-ten to be more of a military organization than a political one. So the MRTA around Tarapoto formally separated from Nestor Serpa Cartolini's group in Lima on January 11, 1992 and I left the MRTA altogether soon after. On May 23rd, 1993, I turned my-self in under the Law of Repentance and served three months in the military.

At the time, I had been hiding for two years with a reward on my head of $50,000. My wife was pregnant at the time. I realize now it was an error to enter the armed struggle, because we were always hiding and never received official recognition. But things in this country have not changed. If you go to a small town there are people who don't eat and malnourished children. These are forgotten towns, between misery and hunger. The government of Alejandro Toledo is not completing its promises. The *guer-rilla* will take advantage of this to stir up the people. Violence could easily return.

(*Contributed by Nicholas Asheshov, a British journalist who has covered Peru for four decades. Asheshov currently heads the Planning Division of the Incaland Hotel and the Sa-cred Valley Railway, in Urubamba.*)

north began exporting large numbers of Asian indentured workers, or coolies, to work on cotton and sugar plantations.

Despite all the abundance, Peru was devastated by the Pacific War against Chile, 1879–83, during which time Chilean armies sacked most of Peru's major cities. After surrendering, Peru was forced to cede an entire southern province to Chile, which contained valuable fields of nitrate, used to make fertilizer. After the war, Peru plunged into bankruptcy and had to negotiate with its British creditors, who agreed to forgive the debt in exchange for 200 million tons of guano and a 66-year concession over the country's railroads. The British-owned Peruvian Corporation was set up in Arequipa in 1890 and built the present-day railroads that lead to Arequipa and Cusco. British families poured into Arequipa at this time to grab a share of the booming alpaca wool business, and American investors were active as well. Following the completion of the Panama Canal in 1904, U.S. investors set up a series of mines and factories in Peru, including the Cerro de Pasco mine in the highlands above Lima.

THE TWENTIETH CENTURY AND TODAY

As foreign investors increased their grip over Peru's main industries, worker dissent began to simmer following the October Revolution in Russia. In 1924 exiled political leader Raúl Haya de la Torre founded the Alianza Popular Revolucionario Americana, APRA, a workers party that continues to exert a tremendous influence over Peruvian politics. When Haya lost the 1931 elections, his supporters accused the government of fraud and attacked a military outpost in Trujillo, killing 10 soldiers. In revenge the Peruvian military trucked an estimated 1,000 APRA supporters out to the sands of Chan Chan and executed them in mass firing squads.

Peru's economic development in the mid-20th century was hampered by the hacienda system of land ownership inherited from the days of the viceroyalty. The independence movement had passed leadership from the *españoles* to the *criol-los,* but otherwise Peru's economic structure remained the same—a minority of Europeans still controlled the bulk of Peru's land and wealth. As Peru moved from an agricultural economy to an industrial one, *campesinos* flocked to Lima in search of a better life and built sprawling shantytowns, or *pueblos jóvenes,* around the city. Pressure for land reform began to grow.

Fernando Belaunde was president of Peru during much of the 1960s and instituted a few moderate reforms. But he was overthrown in 1968 by General Juan Velasco, who despite being a military man launched a series of radical, left-wing reforms that stunned Peru's white elite and transformed the Peruvian economy. He expropriated nearly all of Peru's haciendas and transferred the land to newly formed worker cooperatives. He kicked foreign investors out of the country and nationalized their fish meal factories, banks, oil companies, and mines. He introduced food subsidies for urban slum dwellers and, in a profound gesture of recognition to Peru's Indians, made Quechua the official second language of Peru.

Velasco's restructuring was so rapid and ill-planned that nearly all of Peru's major industries plunged to new lows and the country entered a severe economic crisis. Velasco was overthrown and replaced by another military leader who attempted to control the economic chaos of the 1970s. Amid widespread strikes in the late 1970s, APRA politician Haya de la Torre headed a constituent assembly that finally secured full suffrage for all Peruvian citizens.

Peru's first full democratic election, in 1980, coincided with the first actions of Sendero Luminoso (Shining Path), a guerilla group based on Maoist ideals that rose out of the country's economic chaos and would terrorize Peru's countryside over the next decade and a half. The Shining Path rose alongside the smaller Tupac Amaru Revolutionary Movement, or MRTA, in northern Peru. Both groups began receiving significant financial support from the cocaine business, which had just begun to grow rapidly in the upper Huallaga Valley. Between 1980 and 1992, Andean villagers were frequently caught in the crossfire between guerillas and the Peruvian army.

The Shining Path would force the villagers to give them food or supply information, and the army in retaliation would massacre the whole village, or vice versa. People in the city were largely protected from the countryside war and were shocked to hear the official results of the government's 2004 human rights report. More than 60,000 people were killed during the terrorism years—and three quarters of them were Quechua highlanders. Half were killed by Shining Path, a third by the government, and the rest are so far unattributed.

The worst massacres of the Shining Path were between 1983 and 1984, the same year that Latin American economies collapsed under a debt crisis and that Peru's north was devastated by El Niño rains. Charismatic APRA candidate Alán García Pérez won the 1985 elections because he offered a jubilant, hopeful future for Peruvians. He promptly shocked the international finance community by announcing that Peru would only be making a small portion of its international debt payments. García's announcement sparked a two-year spending spree followed by Peru's worst economic collapse ever, with hyperinflation so extreme that restaurants were forced to increase their menu prices three times each day. Peru's struggling middle class saw their savings disappear overnight.

Peruvian novelist Mario Vargas Llosa led a series of middle- and upper-class protests, and Vargas Llosa appeared likely to win the 1990 election. He was beat at the last minute however by Alberto Fujimori, a university rector of Japanese descent who appealed to Peru's mestizo and Indian voters precisely because he was not part of Lima's elitist white society. Former president García, meanwhile, fled Peru in 2002 under a cloud of allegations of extortion and corruption.

Soon after winning the elections, Fujimori reversed his campaign promises and implemented an economic austerity program that had been championed by his opponent Vargas Llosa. Fujimori's plan aimed to stimulate foreign investment by slashing trade tariffs and simplifying taxes. Fujimori also began the process of privatizing the state-owned companies that President Velasco had nationalized in the late 1960s. This program, which was nicknamed *Fuji-Shock,* caused widespread misery among Peru's poor populations as food prices shot through the roof. Fortunately, the program achieved immediate results—inflation dropped from 7,650 percent in 1990 to 139 percent in 1991.

After struggling to convince Peru's congress to pass legislation in 1992, Fujimori strained international relations with the United States and other countries after he dissolved the congress in his famous *auto golpe* (self-coup). That same year, Peru's level of terror reached a high point when Shining Path detonated two car bombs in the middle-class Miraflores neighborhood, killing 20 people and injuring 250.

That same year, Fujimori's popularity shot through the roof when the Peruvian military captured both Shining Path leader Abimael Guzmán and the main leaders of the MRTA. The economy began to pick up and, by 1993, was one of the fastest-growing in the world. Fujimori launched a new constitution and recovered international credibility by re-opening Peru's congress.

Having tackled Peru's twin nightmares of terrorism and inflation, Fujimori was riding a wave of public support and easily beat former UN Secretary General Javer Pérez de Cuellar in the 1995 elections. The following year a group of MRTA guerillas took hundreds of prominent hostages after storming a cocktail party at Lima's Japanese Embassy. After releasing most of the hostages, the guerillas held 71 prisoners and maintained a tense standoff with the military for four months, until April. As the situation grew desperate, Fujimori authorized Peruvian commandos to tunnel under the embassy and take it by surprise. The operation was an amazing success. Only one hostage died during the operation—of a heart attack— and Peruvians raised few objections to the fact that all 14 guerillas were shot to death—including the ones who were surrendering.

Fujimori ran for a controversial third term in 2000, even though he himself had changed the constitution to allow presidents to run for only one re-election. Once again, Fujimori fell out of favor with the international community when he strong-armed his way into the elections against economist Alejandro Toledo. After alleging vote fraud in the main election, Toledo refused to run in the May 2000 runoff election, and the international community also threatened sanctions. Fujimori went ahead with the election anyway and was, despite the flawed process, elected president.

A huge scandal broke a month later, however, when hundreds of videos were leaked to the media. The videos showed Fujimori's head of intelligence, Vladimiro Montesinos, bribing a huge cross-section of elite Peruvian society, including generals, journalists, politicians, and business executives. The resulting investigation uncovered more than *$40 million* in bribes paid to subvert the three key institutions of democracy: the judiciary, the legislature, and the media.

A subsequent study by the Stanford Graduate School of Business revealed that Peru's four main TV channels shared some $26 million in bribes, while newspapers received $2.5 million. Montesinos' grip on the media was so tight that he even held daily "news meetings" with national editors to discuss which stories should be emphasized for that day's coverage. In the judiciary, 21 top justices-including members of the supreme court—received bribes ranging from $2,500 to $55,000. Montesinos also bribed a range of politicians—even those within Fujiimori's own party—for as much as $10,000 to $20,000 per month. Others received cars or houses. One congressman's received an all-expenses-paid education in the United States for his daughter.

To make matters worse, Peruvian investigators also concluded that both Fujimori and Mon-tesinos amassed huge personal fortunes through extortion, arms trafficking, and the drug trade.

Fujimori conveniently resigned from the presidency while on a state visit to Japan. These days he lives in a luxury apartment in an exclusive Tokyo neighborhood and stays actively involved in Peruvian politics (see www.fujimorialberto.com). Back in Peru, an international warrant for his arrest was issued because of his involvement in paramilitary massacres of left-wing political activitists in the early 1990s. Montesinos was arrested in Venezuela after being on the run for eight months and is in a high-security prison near Lima—one he helped design to house Peru's most feared criminals. About $250 million in his funds have been recovered from bank accounts in the Cayman Islands, Panama, and Switzerland. Following Fujimori's departure, a caretaker president governed Peru until Alejandro Toledo was elected in 2001.

Toledo's political inexperience and lack of strong leadership caused his popularity to plunge among Peruvian voters, many of whom missed the dramatic results and bold programs of Fujimori. Strikes and civil unrest plagued the country in May 2003, which led Toledo to declare a temporary state of emergency to clear highways of protesters. After allegations of corruption, calls for Toledo to step down reached a fever pitch in early 2004. Peru's largest union, the General Confederation of Workers, held nation-wide strikes in mid-2004, while thousands of coca farmers marched in Lima to demand an end to the U.S.-sponsored eradication of their crops.

Ironically, the two politicians who lead public opinion polls for the next elections are those who have been most implicated in corruption scandals: Alán García and Alberto Fujimori.

Government and Economy

GOVERNMENT

President Alejandro Toledo, though suffering in the polls, has restored a high degree of democracy to Peru's government after the authoritarian Fujimoro. There are 10 major parties in Peru's congress, which has become an effective counterbalance to the executive branch during the Toledo administration.

Fujimori dissolved Peru's two-house legislative system during his *auto coup* in April 1992 and launched a new constitution with a single congress with 120 seats. Fujimori's new constitution also allows the president to run for two consecutive terms. The president appoints a Council of the Ministers, which is presided over by the prime minister. Apart from the president, Peruvian voters also elect two vice presidents. Voting is compulsory between the ages of 18 and 70, and those who do not vote can be fined. Members of the military are not allowed to vote.

The weak point of Peru's democracy is its judicial branch, which is rife with corruption. It is still common for judges to accept bribes in order to free prisoners or make favorable rulings. The country's top courts include a 16-member Supreme Court and a Constitutional Tribunal. Each of Peru's departments also has a superior court that serves as a court of appeals for the lower courts. There is a huge backlog of cases in the Peruvian court system, and temporary courts have been set up during the Toledo administration. Even a matter as simple as a damage dispute over a car accident can take a year or more to work its way through the courts.

During the Fujimori government, terrorist suspects were tried in secret military courts and many were sent to jail without a fair trial. Under the

the capitol in Lima

Toledo government, these suspects will receive new trials in civilian courts. The judicial branch is also currently prosecuting those accused of corruption under the Fujimori government.

ECONOMY

The investment-oriented reforms of the Fujimori years caused Peru to be one of the fastest-growing economies in the world between 1994 and 1997. Much of this growth was easy, however, because in many cases Peru's factories were simply returning to the level of production they had achieved before the chaotic 1980s.

Peru's stock marketed plummeted in early 1995 because of the *Tequila Effect* caused by Mexico's Zapatista revolution and the collapse of its economy. Peru's economy stagnated between 1998 and 2001 because of a variety of other factors as well, including the El Niño floods of 1998, global financial turmoil, and the collapse of the Fujimori government in 2001.

Toledo maintained investment-friendly policies upon taking office in 2001, which caused Peru's economy to bounce back from only 2.2 percent growth in the gross domestic product (GDP) in 2001 to 5.2 percent in 2002. The GDP continued growing in 2003 at 4 percent, and hovers

CAMISEA GAS FIELD: THE LAST PLACE ON EARTH

Up until the last few years, natural barriers had kept outsiders away from Peru's lower Urubamba basin, a vast swath of Amazon rain forest in southern Peru that biologists consider one of the last undisturbed corners of the planet. A treacherous river gorge sank boats that tried to enter upstream from Quillabamba, and the sheer flanks of the **Cordillera Vilcabamba** washed away the roads of would-be colonists.

Thanks to its isolation, the lower Urubamba has one of the world's highest levels of endemic plant and animal species, according to Conservation International, which recently proclaimed the area one of the world's 25 mega-diversity hot spots. The Smithsonian Institute calls the area one of earth's last virgin rainforests, "an intact wilderness with abundant biodiversity."

This swath of mountains and jungles, about 100 km downriver from **Machu Picchu**, is also the last hiding place for a few thousand semi-nomadic Indians who choose to live in complete isolation from the outside world. These tribes fled to these remote headwaters a century ago to escape the disease and slavery of the rubber boom, the last major Amazon bonanza. Their way of life was supposedly protected in the 1970s when the Peruvian government declared the area a cultural reserve for the Yine, Nahua, and Kirineri peoples.

That protection has been crumbling ever since

engineers discovered 13 trillion cubic feet of gas under the jungle floor, known as the **Camisea Gas Field.** After nearly two decades of failed negotiations, the Peruvian government finally signed an agreement with U.S. and Argentine companies to extract the gas. The place has never been the same.

Dynamite explosions now replace the murmur of rivers and shrieking of parrots, as engineers map the contours of the vast gas deposit along a checkerboard of paths spaced a mere 300 yards apart. Chainsaws and bulldozers clear forest to make way for access roads, unloading zones, a processing plant, and four drilling platforms, three of which are inside the cultural reserve. Helicopters buzz the canopy to count pockets of people in the area, the fastest way to produce the census required by international finance organizations. A 25-meter-wide corridor of cleared jungle, with pipelines buried but uncovered in places by erosion, snakes its way up and over the Cordillera Vilcabamba and down into the jungle below.

The Camisea project is divided between two consortia—upstream (gas production) and downstream (gas transportation). The two main players in both consortia are **PlusPetrol** from Argentina and the Texas-based **Hunt Oil,** which are leading the effort to drill the gas and then ship it to the coast via two separate pipelines. Another Texas company, the Kellogg Brown & Root unit of **Halliburton,**

continued on next page

CAMISEA GAS FIELD: THE LAST PLACE ON EARTH (cont'd)

will begin construction by 2004 on a $2 billion gas plant—located next door to **Paracas,** Peru's most important marine reserve on the Pacific Coast. Conservationists are outraged that a single tanker spill could wipe out the reserve's marine life. The project is going ahead regardless.

During the early stages of the project, U.S. media coverage focused on the **Bush administration's** financial ties to Hunt Oil and Halliburton. But President Bush put an end to public controversy, and an intense lobbying campaign, by abstaining from an Inter-American Bank vote in 2003 on whether to provide the last bit of financing for the $1.6 billion project. The bank approved the funding anyway, and cheap natural gas from Camisea should be arriving in California by 2005.

The real story, however, is not the political wrangling in Washington, D.C., but the destruction in the lower Urubamba, which is so remote that it is reached only by helicopter or by several days' journey on trucks and canoes. The service roads and test paths being built by Hunt Oil will soon be highways for colonists, illegal loggers, and wildlife poachers—the same pattern of destruction that has destroyed most of the Amazon in the 20th century.

Despite international laws protecting the isolation of indigenous populations, PlusPetrol workers have contacted tribes to negotiate pipeline right-of-ways, workers camps, and unloading zones. In one case documented by the environmental group Amazon Alliance, lawyers helicoptered into a remote village with reams of technical documents and offered villagers $3,000 in exchange for a 15 km right of way. Village elders declined the offer, even after they were offered a flight that same day to the nearby city of Quillabamba for contract signing and payment.

Because the lower Urubamba is so remote, the specifics of the damage are unclear and remain undocumented. It is believed that unchecked erosion has muddied water supplies and decimated fish, the main food source, in some areas. But there have been no detailed reports of wildlife and ecosystem damage. Nor has there been word of any epidemics like that caused when **Royal Dutch Shell** first explored the area in the 1980s. Shell now acknowledges that diseases spread by its loggers killed more than 40 percent of the Nahua population.

The Peruvian government, for its part, says the Camisea Gas Field will produce valuable foreign revenue and help Lima make its transition to cleaner-burning fuels. The oil companies have promised to minimize impact by using oil platform technology used for deep-sea drilling. "This is a project that is close to finished, is going to benefit everyone, and we should not put stones in its way," concluded Energy Minister Hans Flury during a visit to Reserva Nacional Paracas in 2003. But only time will tell the impact of Camisea.

---

around $61 billion. Toledo has managed to control the fiscal deficit, keep inflation to 2 percent, and create the country's first trade surplus in 11 years with $7.7 billion in exports and $7.5 billion in imports. The key sectors of the Peruvian economy include banking, retail services, agriculture, mining, and manufacturing.

In the near term, foreign investment in mining, oil and gas, and tourism will play an important role in Peru's economy. Major players in the mining arena include the U.S.-owned Yanacocha gold mine in the Cajamarca area and the Canadian-owned Antamina copper-zinc mine north of Huánuco. The Camisea Gas Field Project, a $1.6 billion project led by American and Argentine companies, has recently begun pumping gas from the Amazon basin north of Cusco. A related $2 billion gas refinery is presently being built by the Kellogg Brown & Root unit of U.S.-owned Halliburton on the Peruvian coast near Paracas.

The People

Even before the Spaniards arrived, Peru was covered by a patchwork of diverse cultures created by Peru's extreme geography. Valleys on the coast are separated by long stretches of barren desert. The canyons and peaks of the high Andes created such a degree of isolation that one anthropologist likened them to an archipelago. But the most culturally diverse area of Peru is the Amazon, where at least 53 different ethnic groups live today.

Peru's population, especially on the coast, is an exotic cocktail of world cultures that have been mixing for nearly five centuries. The mixing of Peruvian culture began with the Incas' forced-labor scheme, *mita,* where rebellious tribes were moved to other parts of the empire where they would cause less trouble. The Spaniards continued *mita* and moved highlanders long distances to work in different mines.

The mixing between the Spanish and Peruvian cultures began the moment the *conquistadores* landed on the shores of Peru, giving rise to Peru's first mestizo, or mixed, population. The cocktail of racial mixes got richer when African slaves were imported to Peru during the viceroyalty. After slaves were freed in the mid-19th century, large numbers of Chinese and Japanese coolies were imported to work in plantations and on the railroad lines from 1850 to 1920. There were also waves of Italian and Palestinian immigrants, and a pocket of German and Austrian colonists established themselves in the jungle at Oxapampa, in the Chanchamayo area. From the 1960s onward, huge waves of immigrants from the Andes settled in the shantytowns around Lima, especially during the height of Shining Path terrorism during the 1980s.

DEMOGRAPHICS

Peru's population today is around 29 million and growing about 1.5 percent each year. Nearly half the country, or 45 percent, is of full Indian blood and resides in the Peruvian highlands. Of the remaining population, 37 percent are mestizo

and 15 percent are of pure European descent. The remaining 3 percent of the population is of pure African, Japanese, and Chinese descent and also includes a tiny pocket of 200,000 Amazon natives who are divided into 53 ethnic groups. There remains a cultural and economic divide, passed down from colonial times, between the upper class of European descent and the middle and lower classes of mestizo and Indians. But Peru's racial dividing lines have, even since the colonial times, been based more on economics than skin color. Marriage certificates from the 18th century, for instance, reveal that affluent mestizos were automatically considered *criollos* because of their wealth. In the same way, a full-blooded Indian in today's society goes from being an *indio* to a mestizo the moment he or she abandons native dress and puts on western clothing.

During Peru's economic growth of the mid-1990s the average wages of Peruvians also increased. The Fujimori government built new schools throughout Peru's impoverished regions, and the illiteracy rate dropped for the first time in Peru's history below 10 percent (though it is still 13 percent for women). Medical care also spread, dropping infant mortality rates from 57 per 1,000 births in 1991 to 33 in 2000. An estimated 98 percent of all infants in Peru now receive immunizations.

Despite these advances, Peru remains a crushingly poor country. More than half of Peru's population, or 54 percent, lives beneath the poverty line of $54 per month, and 24 percent live in extreme poverty, earning under $32 per month. Nearly 40 percent of Peru's population live in the informal economy—that is, they live in isolated country hamlets or disenfranchised city slums and eke out a living outside of government taxes and services.

LANGUAGE

Peru's official language is Spanish, though a large proportion of Peru's highland population speaks

a young Amazonian boy with a toy dart gun

Quechua, the language of the Incas. Among Quechua speakers, there is a huge range of dialects, and people from Huancayo, for instance, have a hard time understanding their cousins in Cusco. These mini-dialects have grown as a result of the isolating effects of Peru's extreme geography. In the Lake Titicaca area, there is a smaller group of Peruvians who speak Aymara, the language of an ethnic group that spreads into Bolivia. In the Amazon there are 200,000 native inhabitants divided into 53 ethnic groups and about 12 linguistic families.

FOOD

Peruvians were not surprised one bit when a *New York Times* poll of international chefs voted their country to have one of the most exquisite and varied cuisines in the world, along with China and France. Peru's range of climates—84 out of the world's 104 ecosystems—create a cornucopia of fresh ingredients that would make any chef green with envy. These include ocean catches of shellfish and fish, mountain harvests of sweet corn, chili, and tubers, and a jungle bounty of exotic fruits, succulent *paiche* fish, palm hearts, and wild game. Most of these ingredients are impossible to find outside Peru, which is one reason there are few Peruvian restaurants abroad.

The Spanish conquest of Peru brought together two great culinary cultures of the 16th century—the **Spanish** and the **Andean**—and exploded their possibilities. When Pizarro's men landed in Peru, they had their first taste of corn, tomatoes, avocados, potatoes, cassava root, peanuts, alpaca meat, and blistering *ají* peppers. The Spaniards brought olive oil, lime, and garlic to the table and shortly thereafter created a local supply of lamb, beef, pork, wheat, rice, and sugar.

Things got even more complex with the arrival of **Africans** during the viceroyalty, **Chinese** coolies in the mid-19th century, and successive waves of **Italian** and **Japanese** immigrants. All the different hands in the pot created a bewildering range of dishes and entire subsets of Peruvian cuisine, such as *chifa,* a mixture of Cantonese and local creole cooking.

Peruvian cuisine is very much in evolution (the latest addition are ostrich steaks in Arequipa) and is difficult to classify into pat categories. Because Peruvian cooks work only with ingredients at hand, there do tend to be styles of Peruvian cooking separated by geography. Here are some highlights you should not miss.

Peru's coast is known for creole cuisine, or **comida criolla,** which is based mainly on a huge range of seafood including sea bass *(corvina),* sole *(lenguado), langosta* (lobster), crab *(cangrejo),* shrimp *(camarones),* squid *(calamar), choros* (mussels), and black scallops *(conchitas negras).*

Some of the more famous dishes include *cebiche,* chunks of raw fish marinated for 10 minutes in lime juice, spiced with *ají,* and served with popped maize kernels, or *cancha.* A delicious variation of *cebiche* is *tiradito,* which are long strips of fish also marinated in lime but with a buttery, less spicy taste. Filets of fish can be served in a variety of ways, including steamed *(sudado),* grilled *(a la parilla),* baked *(al horno),* **a la chorillano** (basted with onion, tomato, and white wine), or **a lo macho** (fried with yellow chili or *ají amarillo).*

Chupe de camarones is a cream-based soup spiced with chili and laden with succulent sea shrimp. Another cream-based soup is *sopa a la criolla,* a mildly spicy concoction of noodles, beef, milk, and peppers with a fried egg on top. *Anticuchos* are beef heart brochettes roasted over an open fire and served with a wonderful assortment of spicy sauces. If you are in the mood for *chifa,* try *tallarines saltados,* which are noodles spiced with ginger, green onions, and bok choy. To drink, try a pitcher of *chicha morada,* a delicious juice made from purple corn.

Peru's mountains are known for Andean cuisine, commonly referred to in Peru as *comida típica.* The mountains stand out for a range of meats, sweet corn *(choclo),* high-altitude supergrains such as *kiwicha* and quinoa, and a huge variety of more than 200 edible tubers, including potatoes, freeze-dried *chuño,* and strange-looking tubers like *olluco* and oca.

The high point of mountain cooking is *pachamanca,* which means "earth oven" in Quechua and consists of a variety of meats, tubers, corn, beans, and native herbs roasted underground with red-hot rocks. A specialty of the north is **seco de cabrito,** roasted goat marinated with fermented corn beer *(chichi)* and served with beans and rice. Another popular dish, of Asian influence is **lomo saltado,** which are strips of beef stir-fried with yellow chili, tomatoes, onions, and slices of yellow potato. Andean restaurants often serve **trucha,** which is fried mountain trout, and **cuy,** or roasted guinea pig.

Andean also features a range of fortifiying potato dishes and broths that are good for shaking off the mountain chill. *Papa rellena* is mashed potato stuffed with meat, vegetables, onions, olives, boiled eggs, and raisins. *Papa a la Huancaína* is a cold appetizer of potatoes smothered in a spicy sauce made from Andean cheese *(queso andino).* *Papa ocopa* are boiled potatoes that are sliced and smothered in a spicy peanut sauce and garnished with eggs, olives, and rice. *Sopa de quinua* is a broth made with Andean potatoes and quinoa grains. Lastly, make sure to sample *choclo con queso,* which is an ear of steamed street corn with a strip of Andean cheese, and *chicha,* the fermented corn beer that comes in variety of colors and flavors.

If you head to the jungle, you will have a whole new type of cuisine to sample. At the top of the list are the roasted filets of succulent jungle fish, including *paiche* and **dorado,** and *patarashca,* fish filets wrapped in banana leaves and seasoned with spices before being baked over coals. There is also *paca,* fish steamed inside a bamboo tube. Iquitos is famous for *Juanes,* a rice tamale stuffed with spices, chicken, and rice. Because of problems with illegal hunting in the Amazon, we recommend that travelers avoid wild game dishes including *sopa de motelo,* or turtle soup, and *sajino,* or roasted wild boar. If you tried *chicha* in the highlands, you have to try **masato** in the jungle, which is an alcoholic drink made from fermented yucca. Most of the jungle dishes are garnished with palm heart, which is often cut into piles of paper-thin ribbons, or green plantains *(plátanos verdes).*

palta rellana (stuffed avocado) and *cebiche*

Did we mention dessert? On the coast, you can try **suspiro limeño,** a sweet custard topped with meringue and vanilla, and **mazamorra morada,** a purple pudding made from corn and potato flour mixed with clove and fresh fruit. Peru's exotic fruits make incredible desserts with flavors that can be shocking to a North American or European palate. Lúcuma, a small fruit with a dark peach color and a rich, smoky flavor, is often made into pies or ice creams, as is maracuyá, or passionfruit. Chirimoya, or custard apple, is so exquisitely sweet that it is often served on its own as *chirimoya alegre.* Other delicious fruits such as granadilla (another type of passionfruit), *guayaba* (guava), *tuna* (prickly pear fruit), and *guanábana* are made into delicious juices—or try a few slices of papaya sprinkled with lime juice.

MUSIC AND DANCE

The simplest way to order the mishmash of genres and styles that is Peruvian music is by dividing everything between music from the coast, known as **música criolla,** and music from the mountains, or **música folklórica.** The best-known example of the latter is Paul Simon's 1960s hit "El Cóndor Pasa," which is an adaptation of the ancient, haunting melody of an Andean *huayno.* The *huayno,* like most Peruvian music, grew hand in hand with dance and a rich pre-Columbian tradition of oral poetry. **Felipe Guamán Poma de Ayala,** Peru's first native chronicler, described dozens of poetic forms that were sung by Peru's highlanders on different occasions, such as a victory in war, marriage, planting, or harvesting. The names of the genres are no longer used, but their words and tones have blended into the *huayno,* an ever-changing genre that blares from radios across Peru's highlands. The *huayno* is pop music in the sense that it has an audience of millions of listeners across the Andes and is in constant evolution, though its themes remain the pain of love lost and being far from home. The best collection of traditional *huaynos* is *Mountain Music of Peru,* a collection of songs from remote Andean villages that were recorded by John Cohen and later re-issued by Smithsonian Folkways. To hear the future of the *huayno,* check out the band Belém, which has mixed rock and roll and cumbia with the *huayno* and emerged with a popular new dance music called **chicha.**

Andean music sounds different from much

European music in part because it relies mainly on pentatonic or diatonic scales instead of octaves. The instruments too are different, including a mix of flutes, panpipes, drums, and even conch shells. The flutes range from the tiny *quena,* which is played like a recorder and is made from wood or llama bone, to a variety of handheld panpipes, including *zampoñas* and *antaras.* These panpipes usually have two rows of bamboo pipes, cut in different lengths to achieve different notes. Some panpipes, such as the *sicus,* are almost as tall as their players themselves. There is also a huge range of rattles, bells, and drums, such as the *tambor* and *bombo* that are made from stretched animal skins. These instruments, as excavations at Caral on Peru's central coast prove, are at least 5,000 years old.

In the last five centuries Peru's highlanders have incorporated a range of Spanish instruments into the mix, including trumpets, tubas, French horns, and saxophones. But the most important European contributions were stringed instruments like the guitar, lute, and harp, which were transformed into the *Andean harp* and the ubiquitous *charango.* The Andean harp looks much like a western harp with 36 strings but has a half-conical, boat-like base that gives it a rich, deep sound. The 10-stringed *charango* is about the size of a mandolin and is made from wood or the shell of an armadillo. The fast, high-pitched strumming of the *charango* and the breathy, rapid notes of the panpipes are a perfect evocation of the windswept plains and high passes of Peru's Andes.

Music evolved in a whole new way on Peru's coast, where African slaves were imported for three centuries to work on sugarcane and cotton plantations. Though slavery was less pervasive in Peru than elsewhere in Latin America, Peru's African population continues to exert a huge influence on Peru's music, food, and sense of national identity. The slaves brought with them rhythms from all around and combined them with Spanish and Andean music to create electric music such as the *festejo* and the *resbalosa.* Dance forms sprung up alongside the music, including *zapateo,* a form of tap dancing, and *zamacueca.* In one erotic dance, known as *El Alcatraz,* women shake their hips furiously in order to avoid having their skirts lit on fire by men holding candles behind them.

The center of Afro-Peruvian music is south of Lima in the town of El Carmen, where a renaissance began in the 1970s that made Afro-Peruvian music famous around the world. The best-known Afro-Peruvian performers include Susana Baca, Eva Ayllón, Amador Ballumbrosio, and Chabuca Grande, whose music relies on string instruments but mostly on a huge range of percussive instruments. These include several types of drums, the rattling jawbone of a burro known as a *caracacha,* a box that is drummed with the hands known as a *cajón,* a large bell called the *cincero,* a handheld drum of chains known as the *cabaza,* and the castanets or *castanuela.*

There are other more refined, supposedly European, forms of music and dance on Peru's coast, including the *valse,* which was inspired by the Viennese waltz, and *marinera,* Peru's national dance that is similar to the Argentine tango but with a more refined, stately air. Both of these also have unmistakable origins in Afro-Peruvian music as well. Of course, international pop music is played all over Peru. A walk down nearly any city street in Peru is like a battle of the bands, with competing sound waves of international rock and roll mingling with wildly popular Latin rhythms such as **salsa, cumbia,** and **merengue.**

LITERATURE

Like the Greeks, the ancient Peruvians had a rich tradition of oral poetry that was passed along through song. Because Peru's cultures had no writing and fragmented quickly after the Spanish invasion, most of the verse has been lost, though traces remain in traditional music forms such as the Andean *huayno.*

A variety of 16th-century Spanish chroniclers, most notably **Bernabé Cobo** and **Pedro Cieza de León,** attempted to describe the exotic conditions of the New World through the confining looking glass of the Spanish worldview and lexicon. An entirely different perspective was presented by indigenous writer **Felipe Guamán**

Poma de Ayala, an Inca whose decision to write the king of Spain blossomed into a 1,200-page work titled *Nueva Coónica y Buen Gobierno,* completed in 1615. Apart from a detailed view of Inca customs, what is most fascinating about this work is Poma de Ayala's Joycean blend of Spanish and Quechua juxtaposed with a series of 400 ink drawings that portray the bloodiest moments of the Spanish conquest. His is one of the first voices from the New World and the beginning of what literary historians now refer to as the "vision of the vanquished."

Inca Garcilaso de la Vega (1539?–1616) was educated in Cusco as the son of a Spanish conquistador and an Inca princess. He emigrated as a young man to Spain, where he would spend the rest of his life writing histories and chronicles of his Inca homeland. His best-known work, *Comentarios reales* (1609), is a highly anecdotal and personal view of the Inca empire. Throughout the text Garcilaso employs a variety of rhetorical strategies to ennoble the Inca aristocracy—and in the process, himself—in the eyes of the royal Spanish court. It is the first example of a mestizo author from the New World grappling with the complexities of a torn identity.

During the viceroyalty, **theaters** in Lima and Cusco were at the center of the social life of the Peruvian aristocracy. Most of the productions were imported and written by Spain's Golden Age authors, who had no problem being approved by Peru's Catholic censors. Local playwrights were occasionally approved, and their works, though innocuous on the surface, often contain subtle critiques of the viceroyalty's racial and political power structure. Scathing **poetic satire** was circulated secretly throughout upper-class Peruvian society and reflecting the growing tensions as Peru's creole elite strained against the straitjacket of Spanish rule.

Literary Romanticism took root in Peru following the 1824 Independence but evolved in an entirely different direction from its European counterpart. Instead of a preoccupation with personal identity and freedom, Peru's Romantic writers fell into the task of nation-building and describing what it means to be Peruvian.

Peru's best-known Romantic writer is **Ricardo Palma** (1833–1919), whose most famous work is a picaresque collection of legends and personality sketches known as *Tradiciones.* Like Washington Irving in the United States, Palma created a legendary sense of the colonial past and colored it with humor, wit, and scandalous episodes that helped define how Peruvians view themselves today.

Peru's best-known female writer is **Clorinda Matto de Turner,** who was born in Cusco in 1852 and wrote both in Quechua and Spanish. She edited a series of acclaimed literary journals, including *Peru ilustrado* and wrote a trilogy of novels, the best-known of which is *Torn from the Nest.* The novel was translated into English in 1904 after her home and printing press were burnt in Lima and she was forced into exile in Argentina. She died in 1909 and was forgotten for decades, though she is slowly gathering critical acclaim and recognition as one of the pioneers of Latin American feminism.

Peruvian poet **César Vallejo** (1892–1938) is one of the most acclaimed poets in the Spanish language, whose most famous collections include *Los heraldos negros* (1918) and *Trilce* (1922). Vallejos was born in Santiago de Chuco in Peru's northern highlands, and his poetry reflects the left-leaning political ideology of the APRA political party, which he helped found in Trujillo (after spending three months in jail). He emigrated to Paris in the 1920s, where spent the rest of his life immersed in the vanguard movement and the rise of international communism.

The growing industrialization of Peru in the 20th century, and the continued oppression of the Indian population, gave birth to a new genre of socially conscious literature. **José María Arguedas** (1911–69) was an Indian born in Andahuaylas in Peru's southern Andes who went to Lima to be educated at the University of San Marcos. His works of social realism portray the oppression of Indian communities and helped inspire the liberation theologies that continue to cause conflict in Peru's Catholic church. Two of his most famous novels, *Yawar Fiesta* and *Los* *ríos profundos* (Deep Rivers), have been translated into English and published by the University of Texas Press.

Ciro Alegría (1909–67) was a mestizo born in the Marañón Valley of northern Peru whose lyrical novels, like those of Arguedas, portray the suffering of Peru's Andean peoples. His best-known works are *La serpiente de oro* (The Golden Serpent, 1935) and *El mundo es ancho y ajeno* (Broad and Alien Is the World, 1941), which became widely known outside Peru in the mid-20th century and were translated into several languages. The classic of Peru's socially conscious literature is **Eduardo Galeano's** *Las venas abiertas de América Latina* (The Open Veins of Latin America). Though written three decades ago, this work's critique of U.S. imperialism in Latin American has lost none of its relevance.

Peru's most critically acclaimed novelist is **Mario Vargas Llosa** (born 1936), who was one of the half-dozen authors of the Latin American **Boom** movement. Llosa and the other Boom writers launched Latin American literature onto the world scene by dropping the regionalist, folkloric themes of their predecessors and experimenting wildly with form and content. Llosa uses biting humor to explore the contradictions and taboos in all levels of Peruvian society. Nearly all of his novels have been translated into English and make an excellent introduction for those wishing to explore Peruvian literature. Vargas Llosa led a middle- and upper-class revolt against President Alan García Pérez in the late 1980s and then ran for president in 1990. After being defeated from Alberto Fujimori, Vargas Llosa become so disgusted with his homeland that he emigrated to Spain and become a Spanish citizen. He even sold his oceanside mansion in Barranco, the bohemian Lima neighborhood, with the strict stipulation that the new owner had to first destroy the house. **Alfredo Bryce Echenique** (born 1939) is Peru's other best-known novelist, who has produced a dozen novels and numerous collections of short stories. After spending much of his life in Europe, he now resides in Peru.

Another young Peruvian has recently made waves on the international literary scene. **Sergio Bambarén** (born 1960), was born in Lima, lived much of his life in Australia, and was educated at Texas A&M University in the United States. His self-published novel *The Dolphin-Story of a Dreamer* is a best-selling inspirational novel starring Daniel the Dolphin. It reads much like 21st-century version of Richard Bach's 1970s classic, *Jonathan Livingston Seagull.*

SPORTS

Peruvians are absolutely wild about *fútbol,* which is the main Sunday social activity in small towns across Peru. Hotly contested matches between teams such as **Alianza Lima** and **Universitario** ("La U") fill stadiums throughout the year in major cities across Peru. **Ciencano,** an underfunded team from Cusco, made world news when it somehow defeated huge, internationally acclaimed teams such as River Platte in Argentina and Santos of Brazil—Pele's old team. In December 2003 Ciencano became the first Peruvian team ever to win the coveted **Copa Sudamericana.**

Bullfighting is a long-running tradition from Peru's colonial days and a standard part of many festivals celebrated in Peru's highland towns (though the bulls are skittish and the fighters a bit tipsy). Lima's bullfighting season begins with the Señor de Milagros (Lord of the Miracles) religious festival in August and continues until early December. During these months Limeños pack the city's main bull ring, **Plaza de Acho,** in order to see the Sunday-afternoon contests featuring internationally acclaimed bullfighters.

Kids in Lima and other parts of coastal Peru often grow up **surfing,** and it is no surprise that several Peruvians are among the world's top-ranked international surfers. **Paragliding** has always been popular in Lima, where thermals rise along the ocean cliffs and allow hours of aerial acrobatics. Other adventure sports such as **rafting, kayaking, mountain biking, trekking,** and **mountain climbing** have lured a generation of young Peruvians who often make a living working as guides for foreigners.

Getting There

All overseas flights from Europe and North America arrive in Lima at **Jorge Chávez International Airport** (tel. 01/517-3502 24-hour customer service, tel. 01/595-0666 flight info, www.lap.com.pe for flight info). Many travelers wait in the airport for connecting flights elsewhere, while others head to Miraflores or the center (about 16 km away), where there is a good selection of hotels. The airport has a range of services, including a place to leave luggage for $3 per day. There is a $4.50 tax on all domestic flights leaving Lima and a $28 tax on all departing international flights. On your way home, arrive at the airport two hours in advance. Airlines are notorious for changing flights and bumping passengers, so reconfirm your tickets 72 hours ahead of time and confirm flight time before heading to the airport.

There are a few other obscure international flights into the country outside Lima. **Lloyd Aereo Boliviano** (in Lima José Pardo 231, tel. 01/241-5210, or in U.S. 800/337-0918, www.labairlines.com, $142 including taxes) runs a flight Tuesdays and Thursdays between La Paz, Bolivia, and Cusco. This allows Peru travelers to arrive in La Paz, travel overland to Cusco via Lake Titicaca, and then return to La Paz without having passed through Lima.

There are no longer direct flights from Miami to Iquitos. However, there are flights between Iquitos and the border town of Leticia, Colombia. The flight costs $50 one way and is run by **AviaSelva** (in Iquitos, Próspero 439). From here it is possible to cross the Amazon River to Tabatinga, Brazil, and catch connecting flights throughout Brazil. It is also possible to reach Iquitos from the Brazil/Colombia border via a nine-hour boat ride up the Amazon River.

Overland travelers most commonly enter Peru through the Lake Titicaca area of Bolivia or from buses traveling along the Pan-American Highway (Panamericana) from either northern Chile or southern Ecuador. There are a few interesting way to cross into Ecuador.

PLANE

Because Peru lies in the same time zone as the East Coast of the United States and Canada, North American travelers feel no jet lag after arriving in Peru. Depending on where you are flying from in North America, the flight can be anywhere from six to 10 hours, and many people fly in the evenings in order to catch early-morning flights on to Cusco. The cheapest tickets start around $550 from Miami.

Most Europeans find it cheaper to travel to Peru via flights that stop over in the U.S. or the Caribbean, though there are direct flights from Madrid and Amsterdam. The cheapest flights from major European cities start around $700. Travelers from Asia, Africa, New Zealand, and Australia will also need to make at least one layover en route to Lima.

The most expensive time to fly to Peru are the Christmas vacations and the high tourist months from June to August. Prices begin to drop around May and September and are at their lowest during the shoulder seasons from October to December and January to April.

Cheap Fares

The cheapest tickets can be found through consolidators, which commit to selling huge blocks of tickets for airlines in exchange for preferred bulk rates. Most consolidators do not deal with the public, so the best way to get your hands on consolidated tickets is to call an agency that works with a consolidator. Consolidators sell out their cheap tickets early during the high tourist months, so purchase at least two months in advance. The hardest time to find consolidator tickets is around Christmas and Easter and especially during the high tourist months from May to September. They are easier to find during the shoulder months from January to April and then from October to December.

A variety of web pages also sell cheap tickets (though consolidators often do not allow their cheapest fares to be published online). These include **Travelocity** (www.travelocity.com), **Expedia** (www.expedia.com, **Cheap Tickets** (www.cheaptickets.com), and **Flights.com** (www.eltexpress.com).

The weekend sections of many newspapers contain special fares, and there are also online auctions. To sort out all the options, visit **www.airlineticketsinfo.com.** Remember that nearly all of these budget tickets are nonrefundable.

Travelers often regret using frequent-flyer miles for a Peru trip unless they arrange the tickets far in advance. There are apparently few frequent-flyer seats for most Latin American destinations, so frequent flyers often end up with huge layovers or nonsensical zigzagging routes. Either save your frequent-flyer miles or reserve far in advance.

Even nonstudents can buy discounted airfare from the **Student Travel Association,** commonly known as **STA** (www.sta.com). This web page links to STA representatives in nearly 75 countries and has a search engine for cheap fares. Students under 26 can purchase a $22 student ISIC card that entitles you to trip insurance, student airfares, and a range of discounts from buses to museums. Student discounts are very common in Peru—get this card if at all possible.

From North America

Direct flights from Miami are available on **American** (www.aa.com) and **LanPeru**(www.lan-Peru.com). Flights from Miami with one layover to Lima include Avianca (www.aviancaPeru.com) with a stop in Bogotá, Colombia; Copa (www.copaair.com) with a stop in Panama City, Panama; Lacsa and Taca (www.taca.com) with stops in San José, Costa Rica.

Direct flights from Los Angeles are available through LanPeru, from Dallas through American, through Houston and Newark through **Continental** (www.continental.com), from Atlanta through **Delta** (www.delta.com) and **Air France** (www.airfrance.com), and through New York from LanPeru and American.

Recommended U.S. agencies that deal with a number of consolidators include **World Class Travel** (800/771-3100 in the U.S., info@peruPeru.com, www.peruPeru.com), **eXito**

Latin American Travel Specialists (800/665-4054 in the U.S., try Marie at ext. 8514, www.exitotravel.com) and **Big Sky Travel** (800/284-9809).

Good North America–specific web pages for consolidator tickets include **Orbitz** (www.orbitz.com), **Hot Tickets** (www.hottickets.com), and the bid-your-price option, **Priceline** (www.priceline.com).

There are also several courier companies from the Unites States where travelers may be able to find even cheaper fares in exchange for carrying packages to and from Peru. These fares come with heavy restrictions on flying times and luggage limits. The bigger companies are **Air Courier.org** (800/280-5973 in U.S., www.air-courier.org), **Air Courier International** (800/682-6593 in U.S.) and **International Association of Air Travel Couriers** (308/632-3273 in U.S., www.courier.org).

From Mexico, Central America, and the Caribbean

Direct flights from Mexico City are available from **Aeromexico** (www.aeromexico.com) and **Taca** (www.grupotaca.com). Taca, Copa, Avianca, and other airlines operate a range of direct Lima flights from Cancún, Mexico; Santo Domingo, Dominican Republic; La Havana, Cuba; Panama City, Panama; San José, Costa Rica; and San Salvador, El Salvador.

From Europe

The only direct flights to Lima from Europe are from Amsterdam and Madrid (no longer London at this time), though the cheapest fares include a layover in the U.S. or Caribbean. The carriers that fly direct between Europe and Peru are **KLM** (www.klm.com), **British Airways** (www.britishairways.com), and **Iberia** (www.iberia.com). Carriers that make one stopover en route to Lima include LanChile, American, Delta, Continental, Air France, and Varig (www.varig.com).

In the UK, good consolidators include **North-South Travel** (tel. 01245/608291 in the UK, www.northsouthtravel.co.uk), which gives part of its proceeds to an international development trust it has set up. There is also **Bridge the World** (tel. 0870/443-2399 in the UK, www.b-t-w.co.uk) and **Quest Travel** (www.questtravel.com, tel. 0870/442-3542 in the UK). **Flight Centre International** (tel. 0870/890-8099 in the UK, www.flightcentre.co.uk) is good for tickets between the UK and the U.S. only.

From France good consolidators include **Last Minute** (tel. 0tel. 892/70-5000 in France, www.fr.lastminute.com), **Nouvelles Frontiéres** (www.nouvelles-frontieres.fr), and **Voyageurs de Monde** (te. 0140/151115 in France, www .vdm.com).

From Germany a good option is **Last Minute** (tel. 01805/777-257, www.de.lastminute.com) or **Just Travel** (tel. 089/747-3300, www.just-travel.de). In the Netherlands try **Airfair** (tel. 020/620-5121, www.airfair.nl), and in Spain there is **Barcelo Viajes** (tel. 902/116-226, www.barceloviajes.com).

From Asia, Africa, and the Pacific

From Asia there are no direct flights at this time to Lima. All flights from Hong Kong, Tokyo, and other Asian cities first stop in the United States. Good Asian consolidators include **Japan's No 1 Travel** (tel. 03/3205-6073, www.no1-travel.com), Hong Kong's **Four Seas Tours** (tel. 2200-7760, www.fourseastravel.com/english) and India's **STIC Travels** (www.stictravel.com).

From New Zealand and Australia, travelers usually lay over in Los Angeles or Miami before heading to the United States. A good agency for flights to the U.S. is Flight Centre International (tel. 0870/890-8099, www.flightcentre.co.uk).

From Africa, travelers to Lima head to Europe first, though **South African Airways** (www .flysaa.com) has a flight from Johannesburg to São Paolo, Brazil. A good African agency is **Rennies Travel** (tel. 0861/100-155 from South Africa, www.renniestravel.com).

Within South America

More than a dozen South American cities have daily flights to Lima. **LanChile** (www.lanchile.com) and **Taca Peru** (www.grupotaca.com) generally have the cheapest flights. Taca Peru flies from Bo-

gotá in Colombia, Quayaquil in Ecuador, Caracas in Venezuela, Buenos Aires in Argentina and São Paolo in Brazil. LanChile flies from Santiago in Chile as well as Quito and Bogotá. Aerolineas Argentinas (www.aerolineas.com) flies from Buenos Aires. Avianca (www.avianca.com) flies from Bogotá, Varig (www.varig.com) flies from Brazil, and Lloyd Aero Boliviano (www.labairlines.com) flies from La Paz.

BUS

It is possible to reach Peru by international bus service from the surrounding countries of Paraguay, Uruguay, Ecuador, Bolivia, Chile, Brazil, and Argentina. The major buses that run these routes can be quite comfortable, with reclining seats, movies and meals. The longest international bus trips leave from Lima. Some major neighboring cities from which buses travel to Lima are; Santa Cruz in Bolivia, Asuncion in Paraguay, Córdoba and Buenos Aires in Argentina, Montevideo in Uruguay, São Paulo and Rio de Janeiro in Brazil, and Santiago in Chile. Buses leave frequently leave from La Paz, Bolivia, for the five-hour direct journey to Puno and on to Cusco. The main international bus companies are **Ormeño** (in Lima tel. 01/472-1710, www.grupo-ormeno.com), **Caracol/Cruz del Sur** (tel. 01/431-1400, www.peru-caracol.com) and **El Rápido** (in Lima tel. 01/422-9508).

BOAT

Some shipping lines offer regular departures from the U.S. or Europe to the Lima's port of Callao. Some cruises also include Peru in their itineraries, arriving in Callao or Pisco. Caribbean Cruises Vacations (www.caribbean-cruises-vacations.com), Royal Olympia Cruises (www.royal-olympic-cruises.com) departing from San Francisco, and the European Holland America Cruises (www.affordablecruisesweb.com) are some reputable companies to check out.

There are also a variety of vessels, ranging from banana boats to luxury cruisers, that chug up the Amazon River to Iquitos.

Getting Around

Peru's diverse landscape includes long stretches of desert, high Andean passes, and endless tracts of swampy jungle. Not surprisingly, Peru can be a complicated country to navigate. Nearly all of Peru's major jungle destinations require a flight unless you want to spend a few days on a cargo boat or one day, sometimes three, riding in a bumpy bus. Train service is limited, except in the Cusco area, but new highways have made traveling by bus much faster and more comfortable than it was a decade ago.

PLANE

If you are on a tight schedule and want to see a range of places, flying is the best way to go. In Peru, a one-way ticket is always half the price of a round-trip fare, so it makes sense to fly one way (to Cusco, for instance) and then travel overland on the way back. The best way to buy tickets, or reconfirm them, is through the airline's local office or with a recommended agency. Finding tickets around Christmas, Easter, and the national holiday of Fiestas Patrias in the last weekend of July is expensive and difficult.

The major Peru airlines are **LanPeru** (www .lanPeru.com), and **TANS** (www.tansPeru .com.pe), a budget option for Cusco, Iquitos, and Puerto Maldonado. Here are some approximate round-trip fares from Lima: Arequipa ($140), Cajamarca ($120), Chiclayo ($140), Cusco ($120), Iquitos ($120), Puerto Maldonado ($150, includes stop in Cusco), and Puno ($150). AeroCondor offer round-trip day packages from Lima to the Nasca Lines as well as flights to Ayacucho, Trujillo, Andahuaylas, and Cajamarca. More information on Peru flights can be found at www.traficoPeru.com.

LanPeru sells air passes for domestic flights around the country. The passes have complex formulas for coming up with savings, which usually don't amount to much—if you want to have flexibility in your travel plans, you can buy tickets for the same price (or better) in Peru.

Aero Continente, Peru's largest airline was teetering on the edge of bankruptcy at the time of publication. After years of run-ins with the U.S. Drug Enforcement Agency, Aerocontinente's founder, Fernando Zevallos was added to the U.S. White House list of major foreign drug kingpins in June, 2004. It took Zevallos just 25 years to build a small jungle charter plane business into a fleet of Boeing passenger jets. But his rapid rise was not without turbulence. He's faced charges of contract murder, money laundering, and narcotics trafficking along the way. While Zevallos vehemently denies any wrongdoing and is quick to point out that he has never been convicted of a crime, Peruvian and U.S. law enforcement officials contend that he founded Peru's largest airline with $1.5 million in cocaine profits. According to a communiqué from the U.S. State Department, it is illegal for Americans to travel on Aerocontinente flights as of June, 2004. With no passengers and no access to its American suppliers, the future of Aerocontinente seems bleak, though its planes are likely to be purchased by one of its competitors. For up-to-date information on Peru's airlines, see www.traficoperu.com.

BUS

Because nearly all Peruvians travel by bus, the country has an incredible network of frequent, high-quality buses (much better, in fact, that most first-world nations). In preparing this book, we talked to a lot of travelers and tried to recommend only the best bus companies. You will be safer if you avoid the dirt-cheap bus companies, where drivers are so underpaid that they pick up clandestine passengers along the way. Some of these buses have been adapted (stretched) to the point where they are structurally unsound.

Bus companies in Peru have a confusing variety of labels for their deluxe buses, which include Imperial, Royal Class, Ejecutivo, Especial and Dorado. The absolute best service, comparable to traveling business class on an airplane, is Cruz del Sur's Royal Class. Deluxe bus service means fewer stops, more leg room, reclining seats, on-board food and beverage service, videos, safe drivers, and bathrooms—but it's twice or three times more expensive than the chicken buses.

Reputable bus companies in Lima are **Cruz del Sur** (in Lima tel. 01/225-6163 for English-speaking call center, www.cruzdelsur.com.pe), **Ormeño** (tel. 01/472-5000 Spanish-only call center, www.grupo-ormeno.com), and **Movil Tours** (tel. 01/332-0024). Cruz del Sur offer a 10 percent discount to students with an ISIC card. Remember that the times, and even the companies, listed in this book will change frequently.

Bus travel is easiest in cities like Arequipa, Puno, and Cusco, where all the bus companies are consolidated in a main bus station, which is usually known as the Terminal Terrestre. Travelers can arrive there, shop around, and usually be on a bus in an hour or two. In other cities, such as Lima, each bus company has its own bus terminal, and travelers can save time by buying a ticket through an agency or at a supermarket.

Luggage theft is a big problem for bus travelers, especially for those who travel on the less-expensive bus lines. Always keep your hand on your luggage at a bus station. Once on the bus, the luggage that is checked underneath is usually safe because passengers can only retrieve bags with a ticket. The big problem is carry-on luggage. Place it on a rack where you can see it, and whatever you do, don't fall asleep. Some people bring oversized locks to chain their luggage to a rack, but thieves will just razor through your bag and take what they want.

Assaults on night buses continue to be a problem in Peru's mountains. These highway bandits ether hold the bus up by force on the highway or sometimes board as normal passengers and hijack it en route. No one has been recently hurt, though some travelers have been shaken down for their money and passports. Though some companies use a camcorder to film all passengers getting on board, no company can eliminate the risk entirely. Do not travel at night through Peru's mountains, and ask around before doing it on the coast.

TRAIN

The Orient-Express-owned **PeruRail** (www.perurail.com) runs world-class train service from Cusco to Machu Picchu and Lake Titicaca. With a new highway between Arequipa and Lake Titicaca, passenger trains now run on a charter-only basis between Arequipa and Puno. During high season, it is best to reserve tickets online ahead of time. Buying tickets once you arrive in Cusco is a hassle, but many of Cusco's nicer hotels will purchase them for their guests. PeruRail may introduce online ticket purchase in the future. There are three classes of service to Machu Picchu with a tremendous variance in price.

The world's highest railway runs from Lima to Huancayo through the Central Andes at a high elevation point of 4,751 meters (nearly 15,700 feet!). The service was shut down in the early 1990s because of terrorism and has only been recently restored. Departures are about once per month between May and October for this 12-hour ride with stunning views.

COMBIS AND COLECTIVOS

The cheapest way to move around a major city like Lima and to get to destinations outside town such as Trujillo's Huaca de la Luna is by public transportation. There are **buses** (often lumbering old school buses), *combis* (Korean-import vans that dart all the roads), and *colectivos* (old American sedans with room for five passengers). The buses are cheap, slow, and high enough off the ground to offer good views. The *combis* are a bit faster but tend to be very cramped. The *colectivos* are the fastest of all.

Bus ares usually hover around $0.30 (*colectivos* are about twice that), but fares go up on weekends and evenings. You can tell by where buses and *combis* are going by the sticker on the front windshield, *not* by what is painted on the side. Before you take public transportation, ask a

Know Peru

local for specific directions to where you are going. It can be a fun, inexpensive way to travel around. To get off a bus or *colectivo* simply say *baja* ("getting off") or *esquina* ("at the corner"). Have your change ready, as money is collected right before you get off.

TAXI

The fastest, and a not-too-expensive, way to get around Peru's cities is via **taxi** or ***motocar,*** the three-wheeled canopied bikes that buzz around cities in the jungle and the coast (not Lima, though). The typical fare for in-city travel is between $0.75 and $1 for a *motocar* and $1–2 for a taxi.

Assaults on taxi passengers happen as often as once a week in Cusco, Lima, and Peru's other tourist hot spots. The best way to avoid this is to have your hostel call for a taxi or to flag down only registered taxis on the street. Take only yellow-colored taxis with numbers on their side, an insurance or certification sticker on their window, and a taxi sign on the roof. Avoid young, suspicious-looking drivers and beat-up cars with tinted windows and broken door handles.

Bargaining is an essential skill for anyone taking a taxi, because taxis in Peru do not use meters. Know approximately what the fare should be and stand somewhere where your taxi driver can pull over without holding up traffic. Always negotiate the fare before getting in the car. A typical bargaining conversation would be: You: "¿Cuánto cuesta a Barranco (or wherever you're going)?" Taxi driver: "Ocho soles." You: "No seis, pues." You get the picture. If you can't get the fare you want, wave the driver on and wait for the next taxi.

Private drivers can also be hired for the hour or day, or for a long-distance trip. The fee can often be as low as $5 per hour. Ask at your hotel for recommended drivers.

Mototaxis are ever-present on Peru's roadways.

RENTING A CAR OR MOTORCYCLE

Renting a car does not usually make sense cost-wise in Peru because taking taxis or hiring a private car is so cheap. Also, gas is expensive (about $3 per gallon, depending on the grade) and distances between cities are considerable. Your best bet is to get to your destination and then rent a car to get around.

The yellow pages of any major Peruvian city is filled with rental car options, which are usually around $50 per day once you factor in extra mileage, insurance, and other hidden costs. Four-wheel-drive cars are usually $750–100 per day. Major rental companies include **Hertz** (www .hertz.com), **Avis** (www.avis.com), and **Budget** (www.budget.com). All these companies have office in Lima, Arequipa, and Cusco, and smaller companies operate in many other cities. To rent a car, drivers usually need to be at least 21 years of age and have both a driving license from their country and a credit card. Each city's option for

renting cars, and even motorcycles, is found in the *Getting Around* section.

BUYING A CAR

Almost-new cars can be purchased for rock-bottom prices in **Tacna,** the duty-free port that supplies the country with Asian imports. There is a company now in Lima that will take care of the paperwork for you and even allow you to sell the car back to it at the end of your trip. If you are staying in Peru for more than a month and have a traveling companion or two, this may not be much more expensive than taking high-quality buses. Traveling along Peru's remote dirt roads with a four-wheel-drive vehicle is an exhilarating, wild experience.

Peru's highway system is much better than it was a decade ago, though gasoline is expensive and the road hazards are extreme. They include open manhole covers, herds of llama, and rocks that have either rolled from the cliffs or been left by drivers after working on their cars. Night is

YOUR OWN WHEELS

More surprising than the freedom of having your own car in Perú is that it's surprisingly affordable. Even with Perú's expensive gasoline, the cost of driving for two can be about the same as taking buses. And, of course, the more seats you fill, the cheaper it gets. Some travelers sleep in the vehicle as well, to save on hotel bills.

Naturally, the big cost is the car. Shipping your own car to Perú is pricey, and import taxes make Perú's new cars twice the price of North America's—a fact that is also reflected in rental car prices.

Amazingly cheap cars can be purchased, however, over the border in northern Chile—the largest duty-free zone in the Americas. There, used cars from Japan are sold tax-free at a fraction of their value.

Travel writer Brian Hennessey, who has driven his car around the world, was so impressed by the deals he saw there that he started Vineeta (www.vineeta.org, yourwheels@vineeta.org), a service that allows travelers to buy or rent these

cars. Either way, travelers purchase the cars as a way of making a deposit and ensuring legal responsibility (it's also easier to cross borders with papers in your name).

Vineeta has put travelers into mid-1990s Nissan Pathfinders for less than $3,000 (which would cost $6,000 in the States, $10,000 in Europe). The cheapest imported cars start at less than $1,000.

You can re-sell the vehicle or keep and drive it around South America and all the way home, in which case Vineeta will determine if your car needs any modifications to meet your country's emissions and safety standards. Vineeta can also inform you of what taxes to expect. Or you can predetermine a dropoff point and get a refund of what you paid, minus damages and rental fees as low as $5 per day.

This option obviously makes most sense for a group of travelers who want to travel throughout South American in a car or who are planning to spend more than a month in Perú.

even more dangerous, with speeding buses and slow-moving trucks that often have no lights whatsoever, like ghost ships on the highway. Gas stations are far apart, and the only options on dirt roads is low-quality fuel siphoned from a rusting steel drum. So fill up frequently and consider carrying spare gallons of gasoline. Drivers should also be prepared with spare tires, tools, food, water, and sleeping bags.

Speeding or running yellow lights is a bad idea, as police look for the chance to pull over a *gringo,* especially in Lima. After making you wait for 20 minutes, they will threaten jail time and thousands of dollars in fines. Right before hauling you off to the *comisaría* (police station), they will slyly ask for a bribe ranging from $3–10. Many drivers pay the $3 just to move along, while others adamantly refuse and are generally let off the hook. The problem of crooked police is less common now than in the past, and is a result of the poverty-level wages they receive.

A Peru driver's worst nightmare is getting in an accident. The general rule is *quien pega, paga* (whoever hits, pays), but foreigners are going to be hard-pressed to get any money off a Peruvian taxi or truck driver. The best way to protect yourself, if you have a car worth anything, is to buy **car insurance** (about $10 per day, or $30 to $50 per month depending on the car). Because most cars in Peru are uninsured, fender-benders are usually resolved by both drivers heading together to a mechanic to get a repair estimate. In the case of a serious accident, let the courts decide whose fault it was or you will end up paying for everyone's damage and medical bills.

U.S. and European licenses are valid for one month in Peru ,and thereafter **international driving licenses** (available in the United States from **AAA** or www.aaa.com) are required. In practice, however, we drove for eight months with a U.S. license and never had a problem. Drivers should also have the car's registration and their passports with them at all times. or police will offer to *llevarle a la comisaría* (haul you down to the station).

BOAT

There is no better way to experience Peru's Amazon than sitting in a hammock with a cold beer and watching the jungle by. This experience is easy to have on an Amazon cargo boat, which offer bathrooms, plenty of deck space for slinging a hammock, and kitchens that serve palatable meals. You need to be flexible on time, however, because boats wait until they are filled with cargo and rarely depart on the day they say they will.

The most popular routes start from **Yurimaguas** or **Pucallpa** and float toward **Iquitos** on muddy, torpid rivers. An even longer option, which we really want to do someday, is the **Río Urubamba** from **Quillabamba** all the way to Pucallpa. This journey includes incredible stretches of jungle and passes through the Pongo de Mainique, an infamous whitewater gorge.

It is much faster to head downstream, and some routes become dangerous during high water months between January and June. Some rivers are unsafe due to drug trafficking or conflicts with native groups. These include the **Río Huallaga** above Tarapoto, the **Río Marañón** from Bagua to where it joins with the Río Huallaga, and any of the small rivers around Chanchamayo that drain into the **Río Urubamba.**

A more upscale option in the Iquitos area is a river cruise. These comfortable journeys will take you down the Amazon River toward Brazil or into the world-class Reserva Nacional Pacaya-Samiria.

The preferred mode of local travel in the jungle is by **dugout canoe** or *peki-peki,* a name that perfectly describes the sound of the boat's engine. These boats, also used in parts of Asia, are dugout canoes with a long propeller shaft that can be lifted out of the water for maneuvering or avoiding obstacles.

Boats also ply the waters of **Lake Titicaca,** and these are much safer than they were a decade ago. Now the boats are inspected and required to have life jackets for everyone. The captain even carries a cell phone for emergencies. Other boat options in Peru include **deep-sea fishing boats** that can be contracted in places like Órganos and Punta Sal on the north coast, though there is no transport service along Peru's turbulent Pacific coast.

BIKE

Biking is a great way to explore Peru's back roads and get to know local people along the way. Many of Peru's adventure agencies, especially those that offer rafting trips, rent **mountain bikes** for about $20 per day and up, though quality varies tremendously and the bikes are generally meant for local use only. There are adventure agencies in Lima, Arequipa, Huaraz, and Cusco that offer multiday bike expeditions with tents, support vehicle, and a cook. These trips follow fabulous single-track routes up and over the mountains with mind-boggling descents on the other side.

Dozens of cyclists pass through Peru each year on the epic Alaska-to-Chile pilgrimage. Those who want to start their tour from Peru will have to box their bike up and fly it with them, as good bicycles are extremely expensive in Peru. Some airlines provide a box in which your bike will fit once you take the handlebars off. If your bike is or looks new, smear mud on it so you can get through customs without having to pay duty taxes. Most people use mountain bikes to travel on dirt roads, often with slicks for road and highway travel.

When planning your route, keep in mind that the Pan-American Highway (Panamericana) is a dangerous bike route because buses pass at high speeds and the shoulder is cluttered with debris. The same applies for major routes into the mountains, including the Cañon de Pato near Huaraz. The best trips are on remote back roads, which are invariably spectacular and much safer. Keep in mind altitude, weather extremes, drinking water, and the complete lack of repair parts outside of major cities.

Good sources of information include **Bicycle the Americas** (www.bicycletheamericas.com), which is a cooperative effort of long-distance bikers in the Americas. The best adventure bike page in the U.S. is www.adventurecycling.org/, and loads of trip journals from people who have biked in Peru can be found at www.geocities.com/thetropics/island/6810/. Peru's best known biker, **Omar Zarzar Casis** (omarzarzar@aventurarse.com), has written a book available in many Peruvian bookstores describing different bike routes across the country.

HITCHHIKING

People in Peru are not afraid to flag down whatever transport happens to pass by, and drivers usually charge them a bit of money for gas. Instead of sticking their thumb up, Peruvians in the countryside will swish a handkerchief up and down in front of them to attract drivers' attention. We think hitchhiking is fairly safe on country roads where there are no other options. When near cities or large highways, though, always take buses. If you hitchhike, do it with a companion, and make sure your driver is sober before getting in.

DAY TOUR OPERATORS

Because of all the public transport in Peru, independent travelers can usually find their way even to the country's most out-of-the-way sites—if they don't mind waiting around for an hour or two, walking, and sometimes hitchhiking.

No one likes to be in a group of obvious tourists, but taking a day tour is the fastest, easiest, and sometimes cheapest way to see a given area's sights—like taking a **group taxi.** In most cities, tour agencies are clustered together on the main square or along a principal street. Before paying, confirm how good your guide's English is and get tour details confirmed in writing, including sites visited, how many people maximum in the group, and whether the cost includes lunch and admission fees. If your guide does a good job, make sure to give him or her a tip ($1–2). Agencies are recommended in this book under the *Sports and Recreation* section of each area.

Tours

Organized tour groups are a good idea for travelers leery of traveling on their own or who long for a **hassle-free, action-packed tour**. There are a range of excellent, though often expensive agencies that operate in Peru and offer anything from general tours with a bit of soft adventure to well-tailored adventures in out-of-the-way places for trekkers, climbers, bird watchers, spiritual seekers, or just about any other group.

With the right company, tours can be safe, hassle-free, cheap, and enlightening—and a great way to make new friends. Common complaints include a lack of flexibility on meals and lodging options, a go-go schedule that allows no time for relaxation, and a large up-front payment.

Before booking, read the fine print and ask a lot of questions. Find out what hotels you are staying in and then check them with this book. Look for hidden expenses like airport transfers, meals, and single rooms if you are traveling alone. Find out who your guide will be and what his or her experience and language skills are. Ask about the size of the group, the average age of the other passengers, and the cancellation policy. Get everything in writing and add up what all the costs would be using this book. Peru is a relatively inexpensive place to travel in and you may be able to do it cheaper on your own.

PACKAGE TOURS

Package tours typically include airfare, hotels, and some meals—but you choose what to do and where to eat. Many Peru-bound airlines offer package tours, including **American Airlines Vacations** (800/321-2121, www.aavacations.com) and Continental **Airlines Vacations** (800/301-3800, www.covacations.com, operated by Solar Tours). The web page of the **United States Tour Operators Association** (www.ustoa.com) has a search engine to find package tours and specialty tour operators, as does **Online Vacation Mall** (800/839-9851, www.onlinevacationmall.com).

Many of the package operators are based in Miami, including **Analie Tours** (800/811-6027, www.analietours.com, info@analietours.com), which was recently advertising a flight from Miami with two nights in Lima and three in Cusco from $825. To get these rock-bottom prices, however, you have to travel on a specific date and stay in the hotels they have reserved—otherwise expect add-on costs. Resort hotels including Ica, Tarapoto, and Cajamarca often promote specials for Lima weekenders on their web pages. These all-inclusive packages can be an excellent value for foreign travelers.

OVERLAND JOURNEYS

There are a number of companies in the United Kingdom and the UK that offer overland backpacking trips for large groups. You and 39 others hop on a retrofitted Mercedes bus for a one- or two-month tour that could begin in Santiago, Chile (or São Paolo!), and end in Lima, visiting Cusco, Machu Picchu, and all the other sites along the way. These companies strike bargains with hotels ahead of time and take care of all food, lodging, and transport. These trips move like an army, camp on beaches, advance along the Inca Trail, and leave behind a litter of soap opera romances. With a two-month trip costing around $3,000 these trips are about as good a value as you are likely to find. A pair of budget-minded travelers could, however, do the same trip for the same cost or less. Last-minute web specials often offer 25 percent discounts on these trips.

The best agencies to look at are **Kumuka** (www.kumuka.co.uk), **Bukima Adventure Travel** (www.bukima.com), **Encounter** (www.encounter.co.uk), and **South American Safaris** (www.southamericansafaris.com). A final highly recommended option is the Australia-based **Tucan Travel** (www.tucantravel.com), which offers a range of trips including language schools and custom packages for independent travelers.

day three on the Inca Trail

INTERNATIONAL TOUR AGENCIES

Peru has a huge range of good tour operators with overseas agents, who can work with you regardless of what country you are calling from. The operators in Peru will be the ones you meet when you arrive there. The local operators are listed throughout this book in the *Sports and Recreation* section for each area. Contacting these operators directly can sometimes be cheaper, though they are officially supposed to offer the same price to you as their agent overseas does.

The prices quoted below do not include international or domestic flights unless noted, though operators will sometimes book these for you. Many of the agencies listed below will organize a tour for as few as two people, with options for strip extensions. In the Cusco area, for instance, tour operators generally offer trip extensions to Lake Titicaca or the jungle.

Adventure tourism is growing fast in Peru, and new tour operators appear every year. To keep abreast of the latest operators, watch the classified ads sections of adventure magazines such as *Outside* and *National Geographic Adventure* or online resources such as www.andeantravelweb.com/.

World Class Travel Services (800/771-3100 from the U.S., info@peruPeru.com, www.peruPeru.com) is a leading seller of consolidated tickets and arranges professional, well-organized tours. It works with the best operators in Peru, such as **Amazons Explorer** and **InkaNatura.** World Class offers tours all over Peru, including a $279 three-day package that includes all but a few meals for visiting Cusco, Sacred Valley, and Machu Picchu. World Class owner Bob Todd personally inspects all the hotels to which he sends clients and is willing to work with groups as small as two people.

Culture and Soft Adventure
Far Horizons Archaeological & Cultural Trips (800/552-4575 from the U.S., journey@farhorizon.com, www.farhorizon.com), a New Mexico–based agency, is the right choice for those with a passion for archaeology. Tours hit all of Peru's major ruins and are guided by an American university professor. Along the way, guests attend lectures by Peru's most noted archaeologists, including **Walter Alva,** who excavated the Lords of Sipán tombs. Their tours often include a complete tour of the north coast, Chavín ruins in the Cordillera Blanca, Cusco, Machu Picchu, and Lima's main museums. Their trips, with all airfare include, are around $5,000 for two weeks.

Socio Adventures (tel. 01/99-19814 in Cajamarca, www.socioadventures.com, info@socioadventures.com) is the brainchild of Ben Eastwood, an American mountain climber who has spent a lot of time living with remote Andean communities near Cajamarca. He offers five-day cultural treks ($435) from **Cajamarca,** where participants understand Andean life close up and give back by building an innovative cooking stove that Eastwood designed. This is one of the more creative endeavors that we ran across while in Peru—Ben's enthusiasm is contagious!

Nature Expeditions International (800/869-0639 in US or 954/693-8852, info@naturexp.com, www.naturexp.com) has been in business for three decades and runs a range of upscale trips trips throughout Peru. Its 12-day Peru Discovery trip passes through Lima, Arequipa, and the whole Cusco area and includes stays in top-notch hotels like the **Hotel Libertador** in Cusco and the **Pueblo Hotel** near Machu Picchu. Cost is $2,685 per person, not including flights. It works with groups of just two people and can arrange lectures on a range of topics, from natural healing to Peruvian cuisine.

For a more luxurious trip, **Abercrombie & Kent** (800/221-0090 from the US, www.abercrombiekent.com, info@abercrombiekent.com) pampers its travelers with small groups, the top hotels of the country, and luxury train travel. The trips are expensive, but there are occasional discounts available on its website.

Guerba Adventure & Discovery Holidays (01-373/858956 from the UK, info@guerba .co.uk, www.guerba.co.uk) is a long-established UK operator that offers a good range of hotel-based culture tours and gentle treks. Its tours range from one week to four months and have won international awards for environmentally responsible tourism.

Adventure and Nature Tour Operators in North America

Our top choice for treks anywhere in Peru is **Andean Treks** (617/924-1974, 800/683-8148 in the U.S., info@andeantreks.com, www.andeantreks.com). It is affiliated with the highly recommended Peruvian Andean Treks in Cusco, and its treks range from a seven-day **Ausangate** trip ($672), five-day Inca Trail ($499), or an 18-day **Vilcabamba** expedition ($1,950). It has been around since the 1970s and has been leaders in taking care of the environment and porters—it's probably the only agency in Peru that pays retirement to its porters!

Adventure Life International (406/541-2677, 800/344-6118 in the U.S., info@adventure-life.com, www.adventure-life.com) is a five-year-old company based in Missoula, Montana, that is a good bet for budget-minded trekkers. Its nine-day Machu Picchu Pilgrimage

includes Cusco, Machu Picchu, and a well-run Inca Trail trek for $1,495. It also offers affordable trips to the fabulous **Tambopata Research Center.** It uses three-star, family-run hostels and local guides, and gives independent travelers flexibility on where they eat. Maximum group size is 12, though it often sends off groups as small as two people. It has recently set up a fund (www.earthfamilyfund.org) to give back to the countries it visits.

South Winds (800/377-9463 in the U.S., www.southwindadventures.com) is based in Littleton, Colorado, and offers a range of eco-adventures from the jungle to the high Andes. It comes highly recommended from people who have traveled with them.

The Miami-based **Tropical Nature Travel** (877/827-8350 in the U.S., www.tropicalnaturetravel.com) works with a variety of conservation organizations across Latin American to plan jungle trips. In Peru it works with Inka-Natura, the owner of some of Peru's best jungle lodges. Your choices range from the **Manu Wildlife Center** and **Cock of the Rock Lodge** in the Manu Area, or the **Sandoval Lake** and **Heath River** lodges around Puerto Maldonado.

KE Adventure Travel (970/384-0001, 800/497-9675 in the U.S., info@keadventure.com, www.keadventure.com) is based in Glenwood Springs, Colorado, and offers a range of high-quality climbs and treks—at considerably lower prices than its competitor **Mountain Travel Sobek.** It works with top international trekking guides and is best known for treks around the **Cordillera Huayhuash** and **Nevado Ausangate** near Cusco. It also guides peaks in the Cordillera Blanca and leads multi-sport trips that combine rafting, trekking, and mountain biking.

GAP Adventures (800/692-5495 in U.S. or 800/465-5600 in Canada, www.gap.adventures.com) stands for *Great Adventure People* and is one of Canada's lead tour outfits. It is a good choice for independent-minded travelers who prefer small groups. Groups stay in locally owned hotels, and GAP is known for socially responsible tourism that includes a good deal of interaction with communities. Trips run anywhere from four days in the **Manu jungle** for $930 to three weeks through the **central Peruvian Andes** for $1095.

Our vote for best international climbing agency in Peru goes to Seattle-based >**Alpine Ascents** (206/378-1927 in US, www.alpineascents.com, climb@alpineascents.com). Peru guide **José Luis Peralvo** splits his time between Everest, his home in Ecuador, and Peru and has been guiding the world's toughest peaks for nearly two decades. Alpine Ascents is extremely responsible about acclimatization and small rope teams.

Other new adventure options in Peru can be found at the Adventure Center (800/277-8747, www.adventurecenter.com), which sells the packages of various operators from its offices in Emeryville, California.

For esoteric tours and ayahuasca sessions, check out **El Tigre Journeys** (www.biopark.org/peru). This organization has been in business since 1997 and works with the **International Biopark Foundation** in Tucson, Arizona. It leads ayahuasca ceremonies in the Amazon, spirit journeys, and solstice celebrations throughout the year.

Adventure and Nature Tour Operators in the UK

Amazonas Explorer (www.amazonas-explorer.com) has tons of on-the-ground experience in Peru and an unmatched array of adventure trips that integrate kayaking, rafting, mountain biking, and trekking. It is constantly innovating new trips, with a team full-time in Cusco.

Based in Edinburgh, Scotland, **Andean Trails** (tel. 0131/467-7085 from the UK, www.andeantrails.co.uk, info@andeantrails.co.uk) was co-founded in 1999 by a former South America adventure guide. The company has small groups and interesting mountain bike and trekking adventures throughout Peru.

Journey Latin America (tel. 020/8747-8315 from the UK, sales@journeylatinamerica.co.uk, www.journeylatinamerica.co.uk) is the UK's largest operator of specialty tours and been in business for 25 years. It does rafting, kayaking, trekking, and cultural tours that can either be escorted groups or tailored for two people. It also sets up homestays and language classes.

Exodus (tel. 20/8675-5550 from the UK, www.exodus.co.uk, info@exodus.co.uk) is one of the UK's larger adventure tour operators, with 25 years' experience and trips in 80 countries. Its 15 Peru trips often include visits to **Bolivia** or **Ecuador.**

World Challenge Expeditions (tel. 020/8728-7200 from the UK, www.world-challenge.co.uk, welcome@world-challenge.co.uk) is a London-based adventure for student groups in Peru. Its coordinator in Peru, Richard Cunyus, is a full-time resident, takes great care of the students, and tracks down excellent adventures such as trekking in the **Cordillera Huayhuash** or paddling a dugout in the **Reserva Nacional Pacaya-Samiria.** It also works with many students from the United States.

Adventure and Nature Tour Operators in Australia

World Expeditions (tel. 1300/720-000 toll-free in Australia, www.worldexpeditions.com.au, enquiries@worldexpeditions.com.au) is Australia's leader in adventure tours and treks to Peru. It works with Tambo Treks, a small and reputable trekking outfit in Cusco. In Peru, trips include treks through the **Lake Titicaca grasslands,** forays into the **Colca Canyon,** and longer trips that take in Peru, Bolivia, and the Amazon jungle. It has representatives in the United Kingdom (www.worldexpeditions.co.uk), New Zealand (www.worldexpeditions.co.nz), and the U.S. (www.worldexpeditions.net).

Visas and Officialdom

VISAS AND PASSPORTS

Citizens of the United States, Canada, United Kingdom, South Africa, New Zealand, and Australia do not require visas to enter Peru as tourists, nor do residents of any other European or Latin American country. When visitors enter the country, either a 30- or 90-day stay is stamped into both a passport and an embarkation card that travelers must keep until they exit the country. If you plan on staying more than a month, make sure you get the 90-day stamp and be ready to support your argument by explaining your travel plans and showing your return ticket.

Extensions on stays for up to 180 days can be arranged at Peru's immigration offices in Lima, Arequipa, Cusco, Iquitos, Puno, and Trujilo for $28. There are also immigration offices where the Panamericana (Pan-American Highway) enters Chile and Ecuador, though at this point it is easier just to leave the country, stay the night, and re-enter again on a fresh 90-day visa.

Always make a photocopy of your passport and your return ticket and store it in a separate place. Passports, especially those from first-world countries with a lot of travel stamps, are worth thousands of dollars on the black market. Carry yours in a money belt underneath your clothing, or leave it in a security box at your hotel. If your passport is lost or stolen, your only recourse is to head to your embassy in Lima. If you have lost or had your passport stolen before, it may take up to a week while your embassy runs an international check on your identity.

PERUVIAN EMBASSIES AND CONSULATES ABROAD

If you are applying for a work or other type of special visa for Peru, consult www.peruemb.org for the location of the nearest Peruvian embassy or consulate. In the United States, the Peruvian embassy is in Washington D.C. and the Peruvian consulates are in New York, Los Angeles, Miami, Boston, Chicago, Denver, Houston, and San Francisco. The Peruvian Embassy in Canada is in Ontario, with consulates in Montreal, Toronto, and Vancouver. In the U.K. the embassy is in London (www.peru-embassy.uk). In Australia the embassy is in Barton (www.embaPeru.org.au), with a consulate in Sydney. In New Zealand the embassy is in Wellington.

FOREIGN EMBASSIES IN PERU

Many foreign travelers are surprised by how little help their own embassy will provide them during an emergency abroad or a tight situation. If you have been robbed and have no money, expect no help from your embassy, apart from replacing your passport. The same applies if you have broken Peruvian law, even by doing something that would be legal in your own country. Go ahead and contact your embassy in an emergency, but don't wait for them to call back. These embassies are each in Lima: **United States** (La Encalada Block 17, Monterrico, tel. 01/434-3000, 8 A.M.–5 P.M. Mon.–Fri.), **Canada** (Libertad 130, Miraflores, tel. 01/444-4015, 8 A.M.–1 P.M. Wed., 8 A.M.–5 P.M. rest of week), and **United Kingdom** (José Larco 1301, Miraflores, tel. 01/617-3000, 8:30 A.M.–1 P.M. Tues.–Thurs., 8:30 A.M.–noon Mon. and Fri.).

If you find yourself in trouble, your best hope for finding a lawyer, good doctor, or a bit of moral support may not be with your embassy, but with the **South American Explorers Club (SAE)** with offices in Cusco (Choquechaca 188, #4, tel. 084/24-5484, cuscoclub@saexplorers.org, 9:30 A.M.–5 P.M. Mon.–Fri., 10 A.M.–1 P.M. Saturday) and Lima (Piura 135, Miraflores, tel. 01/445-3306, limaclub@saexplorers.org, 9:30 A.M.–5 P.M. Mon.–Fri., 9:30 A.M.–1 P.M. Saturday).

Know Peru

TAXES

Foreign travelers are required to pay a $28 exit tax before boarding an international flight and $4.50 for all domestic flights.

As of 2001, foreigners no longer have to pay an 18 percent **value-added tax,** commonly known as **IGV,** on rooms or meals purchased at hotels. This benefits upper-crust travelers, because back-packer hostels, *hospedajes,* and one- and two-star hotels never charged IGV in the first place. When you check into a nice hotel, make sure the receptionist copies your passport. Check your bill upon leaving.

Foreigners still have to pay the 18 percent IGV at upscale restaurants that are not affiliated with hotels. These restaurants often tack on a 10 percent service charge as well, which can turn an expensive meal into a *really* expensive meal.

CUSTOMS

Peru's Customs *(aduana)* is notorious for hassling travelers come back from Miami with loads of imported goodies. That is why you will see a line of nervous Limeños nervously waiting to pass through the stoplight at Peru's Customs. If you get the unlucky red light, you should know the rules. Travelers are allowed to bring three liters of alcohol and 20 packs of cigarettes into Peru duty-free. You can also bring in $300 worth of gifts, but not to trade nor sell.

Travelers carrying expensive items such as laptops, cameras, bicycles, and climbing gear may be asked to leave a cash bond for 25 percent of the item's value, which insures they don't sell the item in the country. Refuse to pay this and ask to speak to the supervisor if necessary. When you leave the country, you have a slim chance of seeing this money again, especially if you only have an hour or two to board a plane.

On your way home, it is illegal to leave Peru with archaeological artifacts, historic art, animal products from endangered species, or coca leaves—even in tea bags.

BORDER CROSSINGS

Peru has around 10 official border crossings with Chile, Ecuador, Brazil and Colombia. They are open year-round and are not usually a hassle as long as one's passport and tourist card are in order. The hours and operations of these border crossing is described in the *Getting There* section of the closest city.

POLICE

Peruvian police offers are incredibly helpful and, for the most part, honest. Always carry your passport with you, and have some form of identification, like a driving license, when you are walking around. If you are stopped on the street, the only thing police are allowed to do is check your Peru visa or passport. If police hassle you for a bribe for whatever reason, politely refuse and offer to go to the police station or just act like you don't understand. Police will usually just give up and let you go.

Police corruption is much less common in Peru than it was a decade ago. If you have an encounter with a crooked cop, get their name and badge number and call Peru's 24-hour, English-speaking tourist police hotline: tel. 01/574-8000.

Peru has set up tourist police offices in Arequipa, Ayacucho, Cajamarca, Chiclayo, Cusco, Huancayo, Huaraz, Ica, Iquitos, Lima, Nasca, Puno, Tacna, and Trujillo. In Lima, the emergency number for the police is 105 but English-speaking operators are usually not available. Your best bet is to call the 24-hour hotline listed above.

Conduct and Customs

ETIQUETTE

Peruvians invariably exchange a *buenos dias* (good morning) or *buenos tardes* (good afternoon). Women and men greet each other with a single kiss on the right cheek, though highland Indians generally just offer a hand (sometimes just a wrist if they have been working). Whistling can be a form of greeting in the north and other parts of Peru, so women should not mistake it for harassment.

Señora is reserved for married women with children and can be quite insulting if addressed to a younger girl. *Señorita* is for younger, usually unmarried women. *Señor* is used to address men, and *Don* is used for elder men as a sign of respect.

Machismo is very much a part of Peruvian culture. Men will often direct dinner conversation only toward other men. Women can attempt to break this custom by directing conversation at both the men and women alike at the table.

Except for in jungle areas, Peruvians rarely wear short pants in public. Foreigners will call less attention to themselves if they do the same and wear generally inconspicuous clothing. Entering churches with shorts or flashy and revealing clothing is considered highly disrespectful.

CULTURE

Family is the center of Peruvian society. Extended families often live in neighboring houses, and young cousins are raised together as if they were brothers and sisters. Peru's mostly Catholic population is just beginning to use birth control, so families tend to be quite large. Women travelers over the age of 20 should expect to be asked repeatedly whether or not they have children.

Many Peruvians are comfortable with **high noise levels,** a cultural difference that most foreigners find grating. Shops will blare meringue, techno-cumbia, and other Latin pop music to the point where conversation becomes impossible but commerce goes on as usual. Radios tend to be turned up at the first sign of morning light, and workmen start hammering at dawn, so sleeping in is often out of the question.

Peruvians are also used to crowded spaces, and are very comfortable sitting close to one another on buses and *colectivos*. While at the bank, they will stand just inches away from one another even though there is plenty of space around. Houses are small, often with all family members sleeping in the same room. Women travlers often think that men are pressing in on them, when actually they just have a **different sense of space.**

Peruvians also have a very **Latin relationship towar time**—they take things relaxed and slow, and usually arrive late. You will inevitably sit in a restaurant longer than anticipated, waiting for your food, waiting for your bill, and then waiting some more for your change. You are never going to change this, so just sit back, be patient, and smile.

PANHANDLING

Whether or not to give money to beggars is a personal decision. The hardest to turn down are the six-year-old street kids with rosy, dirt-covered cheeks and an outreached hand. In the countryside, children will frequently ask for money in exchange for having their picture taken. Remember that when you give them money, you are encouraging the practice in the future. Also, know that parents often have their children working as teams to collect money in the street. Instead of money, the best-prepared travelers give pens, notebooks, or other useful items.

Tips for Travelers

⚑ ACCOMMODATIONS

Choosing the right place to stay is key to having a relaxed, enjoyable trip to Peru. The quality of lodging ranges dramatically in most Peruvian cities and often has no correlation whatsoever with price. If you plan well, you should usually be able to find a safe and quiet room, with a charming environment and a helpful staff.

Because where you stay makes a huge difference in the quality of your experience, we recommend making advance reservations by email—especially in hot spots like Lima, Arequipa, Huaraz, Cusco, and Puno and especially between the busy months from May to September. Rates go way up during local festivals or national holidays such as the July 28 Fiestas Patrias weekend. Always show up in the morning to claim your room, or call ahead—otherwise you might lose it or get shuffled into a lesser room.

It is true that walk-in travelers often get better rates than those who make reservations over email, but those with a reservation often get the corner room with a view, the quieter space off the street, or the room with a writing desk—especially if you ask for it in advance. Peru is a booming travelers' destination, and there is a shortage of good hotels in many cities. The last thing you want to be doing is lugging your backpack through the streets in search of a room or settling on a hotel that is above your budget.

Lodging rates can be negotiated at all but the busiest of hotels. Ask walk-in travelers what they are paying and ask your hostel to match that. Businesses in Peru almost never refund money, but they might throw in a free breakfast or an extra night to make up the difference. Two- and three-star hotels that work with agencies list their official rates *(tarifas publicadas)* on a small sign in the reception area. These rates invariably include a 20 to 35 percent markup that covers travel agency commissions. If you are a walk-in traveler, ask for the corporate rate *(tarifa cororativa)*, which

is hotel lingo for the official rate minus the agency commission.

First impressions are important in Peru. If you walk into a hotel and get a bad vibe from the staff, chances are you will have an unpleasant visit. Before you pay for a room, ask to see it and any other rooms that are available. Be persistent and picky and keep in mind that most places have rooms that vary dramatically in quality but are the same price. Look carefully at how safe a hotel is, especially what neighborhood it is in. Look for discos, bars, bus stations, or other places nearby that might make your room more noisy at night. Inspect the bathrooms carefully and turn on the hot water to make sure it exists. If you are in a cold area, like Puno or Cusco, ask if the hotel provides electric heaters. If you are in a jungle city, ask if there are fans. If you are planning to make calls from your room, ask if there is direct dial service that allows the use of phone cards—otherwise you will have to wait for the receptionist to make your call at a hefty rate that can be as much as $0.50 per minute for local calls. Once you pay your money, good luck getting it back—though you can always file a complaint with an i Peru government tourist office (or call tel. 01/574-8000).

Budget Hotels

The best value, and often the best quality, can be found in budget hostels, which range in price from $10 to $25 for a double. The cheaper establishments are called *hospedajes,* and the *hostales* are usually a bit fancier. There are government rules that define the difference between a *hospedaje, hostal,* and hotel, but there is a lot of gray area too. Key things to look for with budget place are the quality of the beds, nifty perks like shared kitchen or free Internet, the cleanliness of the bathroom, and how the water is heated. Many hotels use water heaters with a limited supply of hot water. Others use electric showerheads, which heat water with electrical current like a toaster oven does. Often the device needs to be turned on at the showerhead or via a circuit breaker in the bathroom. The whole concept is unnerving, but the devices are surprisingly safe, even though some travelers receive a mild shock. The problem is, they often only make the water lukewarm.

Mid-Range Hotels

This is our least favorite category of lodging, which varies from $25 to $75 for a double. These tend to be modern, charmless buildings with a fancy reception but mediocre rooms with tacky decorations. But they are usually a sure bet for hot water, safe rooms, phones, and refrigerators.

High-End Hotels

Nearly all major Peruvian cities have high-end hotels with the full range of international creature comforts, including spring mattresses, alarm clocks, refrigerators, loads of hot water, bathtubs, and direct-dial phones. The fancier establishments often have kitchenettes, cable computer connections, slippers, bathrobes, and complimentary toiletries. Often suites are just a bit more expensive but much more luxurious. These hotels invariably charge an 18 percent value-added tax, which by law must be refunded to travelers as long as the hotel has a copy of your passport.

DINING

Peruvian food is a double-edged sword. Many travelers bring back fond memories of the exquisite and surprising range of flavors, while others return with their stomachs crawling with bacteria or parasites. Choose where you eat carefully and work from the recommendations in this book or from fellow travelers. Peruvians often recommend hole-in-the-wall restaurants that work well for their hardy stomachs, but not yours. We always take a quick glance at the kitchen before sitting down. If it is clean and well-swept, the food is likely to be safe. If there are pots piled up everywhere and food scraps on the ground, go elsewhere.

Service at Peruvian restaurants is much slower than in Europe and North America, mainly because Peruvians leave only a few small coins as a tip. The service is broken down into various steps, which include receiving the menu, ordering, waiting for food, waiting for the bill, and then waiting for change. To save time, we recommend asking for your bill *(boleta, por favor)* when your food is served, and always keeping a supply of small bills and change (for this reason, seasoned Peru travelers always use large bills when purchasing items at a store and ask for small bills when changing money). If you are eating lunch, you can save money and time by order the fixed menu *(menú)* which is usually pre-prepared and served quickly. À la carte items are generally twice as expensive as the *menú*. Many travelers choose to make their own breakfasts by buying yogurt, cereal, and some fruit. A generous tip in most mid-range restaurants is $1, but we encourage people to always leave 10 percent of the bill.

EMPLOYMENT

Jobs teaching English in Peru are easy to find and can often be arranged in-country without a work visa. You should first scan expatriate bulletin boards in Lima, where language schools often advertise jobs for around $8 per hour. One of Lima's better language schools is El Sol (elsolperu@idiomasperu.com, elsol.idiomasperu.com).

International organizations that help find teaching positions include **Amerispan** (www.amerispan.com) and **TEFL** (www.tefl.com). The following organizations are also worth contacting: **International Schools Services** (609/452-0990 in the U.S., iss@iss.edu, www.iss.edu), **Británico** (tel. 01/221-7550 in Lima, informes@acpb.edu.pe, www.britanico.edu.pe), **American Language Institute** (alisac@terra.com.pe, contact Joseph Phrower in Lima), **Teaching Abroad in the UK** (www.teaching-abroad.co.uk), or **EFL** (efl.institute@terra.com.pe) in Lima. Wherever you work, make sure you get a contract in writing.

Other paid employment can be found through the **International Career and Employment Center** (www.internationaljobs.org). This organization collects information on current international job openings with governments, government contractors, United Nations agencies, private voluntary organizations, and student exchange organizations. Membership, including posting your credentials in its database and access to profiles of major employers, is $26 for six weeks.

For tips on living overseas see **Escape Artist** (www.escapeartist.com), which is a resource guide for expatriates with everything from apartments to tips on how to deal with culture shock. Other ideas may be found in the upcoming guide to live in Peru, *Culture Shock! Peru.*

VOLUNTEERING

There are hundreds of volunteer opportunities in Peru, involving art and culture, community development, disability and addiction services, ecotourism and the environment, education, health care, and services for youth and women. Although these organizations do not pay salaries, they often provide food or accommodation in exchange for your time.

The most common complaint with volunteer work is that the organization is disorganized, there is not enough meaningful work, or that organizations are exploiting eager beavers for their own bottom line. For that reason, do research and try to speak with people who have worked with the organization in the past.

The best source for volunteer information in Peru is the Lima office of the **South American Explorers Club** (Piura 135, Miraflores, tel. 01/445-3306, limaclub@saexplorers.org, www .saexplorers.com, 9:30 A.M.–5 P.M. Mon.–Fri., 9:30 A.M.–1 P.M. Saturday). If you're a member, you can even access its volunteer database online. If you're not, you can send an email or buy a phone card and talk to someone in person. (But if you stay in Peru, you will want to be a member.) Another organization in Lima that hooks up volunteers with organizations is **Trabajo Voluntario** (www.trabajovoluntario.org).

There are many Spanish-language schools that combine teaching with volunteering and are described under *Information and Services* in the appropriate city section in this book. Highly recommended contacts include Tina Smith of the **Tambopata Education Centre** (see *Puerto Maldonado*), Lucho Hurtado of

Incas del Peru (see *Huancayo)* or Richard Webb of **ProPeru** (see *Urubamba*).

Interesting nonprofit groups are profiled regularly on the web page of Cultural Survival (www.cs.org). **Bruce Peru** (www.brucePeru.com), is dedicated to Peru's street children. It lodges and feeds volunteers at its centers in Cusco, Trujillo, and Cajamarca. They can take a huge range of volunteers, from web masters to musicians, and ask volunteers to make a $230-per-month donation.

Cross-Cultural Solutions Peru (800/330-4777 in the U.S., tel. 44845/458-2781 from the UK, www.crossculturalsolutionsorg) runs highly professional volunteer programs mainly for students from the UK and the U.S. in Lima, Trujillo, and Ayacucho. In Lima, the company works in Villa El Salvador, the 350-person shantytown that was a Nobel Peace Prize nominee for its community organization. The program is quite expensive but recommended for its professional staff: costs are $2,174 for two weeks with every additional week costing $250.

Inka Porter Project (porters@peruweb.org, www.peruweb.org/porters) is an initiative to improve the welfare of Peru's porters through education, equipment loans, and a system for regulating abuses. It needs volunteers for policing the Inca Trail and staffing offices in Cusco and maybe Huaraz in the future.

World Youth International (www.worldyouth.com.au, wyi@worldyouth.com.au) organizes volunteer programs around the world. We were very impressed with its Cusco representative, Claire Dean, who can be reached at her swanky café, The Muse. Claire can get you into any one of a variety of volunteer programs in the Cusco area, including the Clínica San Juan de Dios, which is a well-organized resident program for disabled children.

Kiya Survivors (tel. 084/962-5444 in Peru or tel. 440/1273-721092 from the UK, www .kiyasurvivors.com, info@kiyasurvivors.com) works with special-needs children, abandoned women, and young single mothers. It is run by British citizen Suzy Butler out of Cusco and offers volunteer placements of two to six months. A standard six-month placement, including in-country tours and accommodations, costs $3,600, which includes a tax-deductible donation to the organization.

OPPORTUNITIES FOR STUDY

Peru has a variety of great Spanish-language programs in Lima, Huaraz, Cusco, Urubamba, Arequipa, Huancayo, Cusco, and Puerto Maldonado (see *Information and Services* for these cities). These programs offer either private instruction for $5 to $7 per hour or much cheaper group classes that last between a week and a month. Many of these programs will also set up homestays, hikes, classes, and other activities. The schools vary in quality, so we recommend asking the school for email addresses of former students in order to contact them. Many of the schools also involve volunteer projects, which is a great way to immerse yourself in Spanish. When choosing a school, think carefully about what situation will provide the most immersion. We recommend a homestay where you will not be able to speak English and a city where there are few gringos.

Council on International Educational Exchange (www.ciee.org) organizes study-abroad programs and has links to a variety of programs.

BSES Expeditions (tel. 020/7591-3141 from the UK, bses@rgs.org, www.bses.org.uk) runs annual science expeditions for British teenagers, though Americans also sign up. The trips usually include science "base camps" in unusual areas of Peru, along with trekking, rafting, and other adventure activities.

WOMEN TRAVELING ALONE

Machismo is alive and well in Peru, so women traveling in Peru should know what to expect. Because of *Baywatch* and other exemplary products of the U.S. mass media, most Latin men assume that a woman traveling on their own—especially with blonde hair—must be promiscuous. So you have to set the record straight.

At some level, there is the larger issue that some men feel threatened by women who travel abroad, study, work, and are generally independent because it conflicts with their perceptions about how their women should be.

How you interact with men makes a huge difference. Speak with men you do not know in public places only. Treat them neutrally and avoid intimate conversation and behaviors, like friendly touches that might be misinterpreted. Wear modest clothing, and some say a fake wedding ring helps. Some women make a point of referring to a nonexistent husband or boyfriend.

Peruvian men, and often teenagers, will often ingratiate themselves with a group of *gringas* and tag along for hours, even if they are completely ignored. The best way to deal with this is by telling them early on that you want to be alone *(Quiero estar sola, por favor)*. The next step would be a loud and clear request to be left alone *(déjeme, por favor)*. The final step would be to ask passersby for help *(por favor, ayúdeme)*. The bad side of *machismo* is harassment, but the flip side is protection.

Be especially careful at night. Choose a hotel in a safe, well-lit part of town. Take care when flagging down a taxi and do not walk around alone at night, especially in tourist towns like Cusco. Walk with confidence and purpose, even if you do not know where you are going. Women who look lost are inevitably approached by strangers. Peruvian women ignore catcalls, aggressive come-ons, and flirtatious lines called *piropos* that are almost a form of poetry among men. You should do the same.

Do not walk alone in out-of-the-way places in the countryside. We have heard reports of women who have been assaulted while walking alone on popular travelers' routes, such as the trail from Tingo to Kuélap in the Chachapoya area. Trek or hike in the daylight and with at least one other person. If you are robbed, surrender your purse rather than risk physical harm. Mace, whistles, alarms, and self-defense skills are effective tools that are likely to catch most assailants off-guard.

GAY AND LESBIAN TRAVELERS

Peru is far from progressive for gay and lesbian travelers, and Lima's gay scene is considerably smaller than that in other major South American capitals. There are a variety of well-hidden and exclusively gay bars, restaurants, and clubs in cities like Lima, and a growing number in Iquitos and Cusco—though none cater exclusively to lesbians. Most gay men in Peru's *machista* society are still in the closet and maintain heterosexual relationships as well—evidence of this lack of clarity is the dozens of transvestite prostitutes who line the avenue at night on the way to Lima's airport.

The only way to find about gay and lesbian establishments is online. The concept of gay rights in unheard-of in Peru, so gay and lesbian travelers are advised to be discreet and exercise caution, particularly while walking around at night. The best website is **Gay Lima** (http://gaylimape.tripod.com), which is written by an American living in Lima and gives a good overview of gay and lesbian life in Peru. The page is updated constantly with the latest bars, nightclubs, and hotels and also include chat rooms and links. Another good online resource is **Gay Peru** (www.gayPeru.com), a great site on gay travel including gay-oriented package tours, although it is in Spanish only.

The San Francisco–based **Now Voyager** (www.nowvoyager.com) is a worldwide gay-owned, gay-operated full-service travel agency, as is Purple Roofs (www.purpleroofs.com). **International Gay and Lesbian Travel Association** (www.iglta.org) has an extensive directory of travel agents, tour operators, and accommodations that are gay- and lesbian-friendly. **Above Beyond Tours** (www.abovebeyondtours.com) is an Australia-based gay travel specialist offering independent and group travel packages.

For information on the HIV/AIDS situation in Peru, see *Sexually Transmitted Diseases* below.

ACCESSIBILITY

Facilities for the disabled are improving in Peru, but are far from adequate. Most bathrooms are impossible to enter in a wheelchair. Hotel stairways are usually narrow and steep, and ramps are few and far between. Peru's sidewalks are hard to navigate with a wheelchair because they are frequently narrow, potholed, and lack ramps. Cars usually do not respect pedestrians, so cross streets with extreme caution.

The exceptions to the above are airports and high-end hotels. Peruvian hotel chains such as **Sonesta** (www.sonesta.com) and **Casa Andina** (www.casa-andina.com) stand out for handicap rooms in hotels in Lima, Cusco, the Sacred Valley, the Colca Canyon, Arequipa, and Nasca.

PromPeru, the government tourism commission, has launched a major accessibility campaign and now claims that more than a hundred tourist facilities have been handicapped-approved in Aguas Calientes, Cusco, Iquitos, Lima, and Trujillo. PromPeru lists these wheelchair-accessible places on its web page (www.promPeru.gob.pe). Other resources for disabled travelers include **Access-Able Travel Source** (www.access-able.com) and **Society for Accessible Travel and Hospitality** (212/447-7284 in U.S., www.sath.org).

SENIORS

Many organized tours of Peru cater to older people. The major airlines offer discounts for seniors, as do international chain hotels but, other than that, senior discounts in Peru are nonexistent. For visiting the jungle, Amazon cruise boats are an excellent option for people with limited walking abilities.

Good senior agencies include **SAGA Holidays** (800/343-0273 in U.S., www.sagaholidays.com), which offers all-inclusive tours and cruises for those 50 and up. **Elderhostel** (877/426-8056 in U.S., www.elderhostel.org) arranges study programs for people 55 and up in countries worldwide, including Peru. The University of New Hampshire's **Interhostel** (800/733-9753, www.learn.unh.edu/interhostel) offers educational travel for those 50 and up. These tours are packed with seminars, lectures, and field trips with sightseeing led by academic experts.

TRAVELING WITH YOUNG CHILDREN

With the right planning, traveling with kids through Peru can be a blast. Kids tend to attract lots of attention from passersby and can cause interesting cultural interactions. By traveling through Peru, kids learn a great deal and gain an understanding of how different life can be for people across the world.

Experts suggest that children should be involved in the early stages of a trip in order to get the most out of it. Children's books and movies that deal with the history of the Incas and the Spaniards will help your kids better relate to the ruins they will see later on. Parents should explain to children what they will encounter, prep them for the day's activities, and then hear from them how it went afterwards.

Keeping your children healthy means taking precautions. Make sure your children get the right vaccinations, and watch what they eat while they are in Peru, because the major threat to their health is dehydration caused by diarrhea. Bacterial infection can be prevented by washing children's hands frequently with soap or **Purell,** the antibacterial gel.

For very young children, don't bother bringing your own baby food, as it is cheaper in the country. You will have a hard time, however, finding specialty items like sugar-free foods, which should be brought from home. Outside of Peru's major cities, there is not much selection in supermarkets, so stock up while you can. Always carry a good supply of snacks and bottled water with you, as there can be long stretches where nothing to eat or drink is available.

Pack your **medical kit** with everything you will need for basic first aid: bandages and gauze pads, antibacterial ointment, thermometer, child mosquito repellent (vitamin B acts as a natural mosquito repellent), envelopes of hydrating salts, and strong sunscreen. Items like Tylenol (*paracetemol infantil*) can easily be found in the local pharmacies, though quality varies. Medical services are very good in Lima and often quite good in the countryside, where city-trained, English-speaking medical students perform residency. Medical care is so cheap in Peru that parents should never hesitate about seeing a doctor. Bring photocopies of your children's medical records.

Your embassy may be of some help, but the best place to contact for advice or help is probably the **South American Explorers Club** (Piura 135, Miraflores, tel. 01/445-3306, limaclub@saexplorers.org, www.saexplorers.com, 9:30 A.M.–5 P.M. Mon.–Fri., 9:30 A.M.–1 P.M. Saturday).

Think carefully about your travel arrangements. Kids are likely to enjoy a sensory-rich environment like the Amazon jungle much more than back-to-back tours of archaeological ruins. Buses generally allow children to travel for free if they sit on your lap, but choose flights over long bus rides that will make kids crabby. Choose family-oriented hotels, which offer playgrounds and lots of space for children to run around unsupervised. If you ask for a room with three beds you generally won't have to pay extra. If you have toddlers, avoid hotels with pools, because they are rarely fenced off. Children's rates for anything from movies to museums are common and, even if they are not official, can often be negotiated.

Because parents are often distracted by their children, families can be prime targets for thieves in public spaces like bus stations and markets. Even if you have taught your children to be extra careful about traffic at home, you will have to teach them a whole new level of awareness in Peru. Time moves slower in Peru, and families spend a lot of time waiting for buses, tours, or meals. Be prepared with coloring books and other activities.

Health and Safety

It pays to think ahead about your health before traveling to Peru. With the right vaccinations, a little bit of education and a lot of common sense, the worst that happens to most visitors is a bit of traveler's diarrhea.

Things get more complicated if you decide to visit the jungle, because Peru, like parts of Africa and Asia, lies in the tropical zone. Travelers who visit the Amazon should be vaccinated against yellow fever, be taking malarial medicine, and take full precautions against mosquitoes.

VACCINATIONS

Vaccination recommendation can be obtained from the **Centers for Disease Control** (877/FYI-TRIP, www.cdc.gov/travel), which recommends the following vaccinations for Peru: **hepatitis A** and **typhoid. Yellow fever** is recommended for people traveling into the jungle below 2,300 meters. Rabies is recommended if you are going to be trekking through areas where the disease is endemic. **Hepatitis B** is recommended if you might be exposed to blood (for instance, health care workers), plan on staying for more than six months, or may have sex with a local. Travelers should also be vaccinated against **measles** and **chicken pox** (those who have these diseases are already immune) and have had a **tetanus/diphtheria** shot within the last ten years.

Unless you are coming from a region in the Americas or Africa where yellow fever is a problem, you are not required by Peruvian law to have any vaccinations before entering the country. The yellow immunizations pamphlet, which doctors tell you to guard ever so carefully, is rarely checked, but you should carry it with your passport. The shots can be quite expensive, in the United States at least, and many of the shots require second or even third visits. Hepatitis A, for instance, require a booster shot 6–18 months after the initial shot, which most people get after returning from Peru. Hepatitis B is generally received in three doses, and there are new vaccines

now that combine both hep A and hep B in a series of three shots. Rabies is also given in three shots, though both yellow fever and typhoid are single shots.

Most vaccinations do not take effect for at least two weeks, so schedule your shots well in advance. If you are taking multishot vaccinations such as hep B, you will need to receive your first shot five weeks before departing, even under the most accelerated schedule. Getting shots in Peru is easy and a lot cheaper than in the U.S., but you will not be protected for the first two to four weeks. Places to get shots include **Suiza Lab** (Atahualpa 308, Miraflores, tel. 01/444-2288, 9 A.M.–noon), **Oficinas de Vacunación** (Independencia 121, Breña, 8 A.M.–12:30 P.M. Mon.–Sat.), and **International Vaccination Center** (Parque de la Medicina s/n, Dos de Mayo National Hospital, 7:30 A.M.–1:30 P.M. Mon.–Sat.).

TRAVELER'S DIARRHEA

Traveler's diarrhea pulls down even the stoutest of Peru travelers eventually and can be surprisingly unpleasant. It can be caused by parasites or viruses, but most often it is caused by bacteria carried in food or water. Plenty of other diseases in Peru are spread this way, including cholera, hepatitis A, and typhoid. Nothing is more important for you healthwise than thinking carefully about everything you eat and drink.

Only drink bottled water or water that has been previously boiled. Instead of buying an endless succession of plastic bottles, which will end up in a landfill, travel with a few Nalgene bottles and ask your hotel to fill them with boiling water every morning. Refilling bottles is especially easy at hotels that have water tanks, or *bidones,* of purified water. When you order a drink, order it without ice unless you are certain that the water used to make the ice was previously boiled. Wipe the edges of cans and bottles before drinking or carry straws.

Avoid street vendors and buffets served under

the hot sun. Instead, choose restaurants that come well-recommended for taking precautions for foreigners. If the kitchen looks clean and the restaurant is full, it is probably all right. Before and after you eat, wash your hands with soap and water. Because soap is hard to find in all but the best Peruvian restaurants, a good substitute is Purell, the antibacterial gel.

The safest foods in restaurants are those that are served piping hot. Soups, well-cooked vegetables, rice, and pastas are usually fine. Eat salads and raw vegetables with extreme caution and confirm beforehand that they have been previously soaked in a chlorine solution. Better yet, prepare your own salads with food disinfectants for sale in most Peruvian supermarkets.

An exception to the no-raw-foods rule is **cebiche,** which is raw fish marinated in bacteria-killing lime juice. As long as you are in a reputable restaurant, fish **cebiche** is a safe bet. Avoid all types of shellfish, however—bad shellfish, even if it is cooked or marinated in lime juice, will still make you sick.

Be careful with dairy products. Before dumping cream into your coffee, make sure that it has been pasteurized. Only eat ice cream from top manufacturers like D'Onofrio, but avoid it if partially melted

Market foods that are safe include all fruits and vegetables that can be peeled, like bananas, oranges, avocadoes, and apples. Many local fruits are OK as well, including chirimoya, *tuna* (the prickly pear fruit), and *granadilla* (a round, stemmed fruit with a hard skin and gooey insides). Dangerous items include everything that hangs close to the ground and could have become infected with feces in irrigation water. These include strawberries, mushrooms, lettuce, and tomatoes. There are plenty of safe things to buy in the market and, when combined with other safe items like bread and packaged cheese, make for a great lunch.

ALTITUDE SICKNESS

Most people who visit Cusco at 3,400 meters (11,150 feet) feel at least some effect of the alti-tude. The air is even thinner at Lake Titicaca at 3,810 meters (12,500 feet), and trekkers on the Inca Trail head over a pass at around 4,200 meters (13,780 feet).

Symptoms of mild altitude sickness include shortness of breath, quickened heartbeat, fatigue, difficulty sleeping, loss of appetite, headache, and nausea. The best way to prevent this is to avoid heavy exercise, like lugging your bags around, and drink plenty of water. Follow that old Bolivian saying *tome poco, come poco, y duerme solo* ("drink little, eat little, and sleep alone").

Tea made from *coca* leaves helps, as does 100 mgs of the Chinese herb **ginko** twice a day. Many people also take **Acetazolamide (Diamox)** in varying quantities prescribed by the doctor—usually 125 to 250 mg. in the morning and evening.

If you feel sick, you'll be hapy to know that all the hospitals in Cusco have bottled oxygen and the five-star Hotel Monasterio can even pump your room full of oxygen. But the best way to avoid altitude discomfort is to begin your Cusco trip in the Sacred Valley, which is 500 meters lower than the Inca capital.

People with several altitude sickness lose co-ordination and can develop one of two deadly, and poorly understood, conditions. **High Altitude Pulmonary Edema** (HAPE) includes chest pain, a productive cough, and buildup of fluid in the lungs. **High-Altitude Cerebral Edema (HACE)** involves a severe headache coupled with bizarre changes in personality. Either one of these warrants treatment with an oxygen tank and immediate evacuation to a lower altitude.

MALARIA

Malaria starts becoming an issue as the Andes slope into the Amazon below about 1,500 meters. There is a much greater chance of getting malaria in the jungle of northern Peru (such as **Tarapoto, Reserva Nacional Pacaya-Samiria** or **Iquitos**) than there is in the southern jungle (**Parque Nacional Manu, Puerto Maldonado** area).

The four species of parasite that cause malaria are all transmitted by a female mosquito, which bites most frequently at dawn and dusk.

PACKING A MEDICAL KIT

Having a small medical kit will come in handy over and over again in Peru, especially in remote areas. Here's a checklist of what we packed in ours:

- antacid tablets (Tums)
- antihistamine (Benadryl)
- diarrhea medications (Imodium)
- motion-sickness medication (Dramamine)
- lots of ibuprofen (Advil)
- lots of acetaminophen (Tylenol)
- Pepto-Bismol (liquid is better)
- insect repellent (12–35 percent DEET or above)
- insect clothing spray (permethrin)
- water purification tablets
- bandages, gauze pads, and cloth tape
- butterfly bandages or Superglue (for sealing gashes)
- Ace bandage
- decongestant spray (Afrin)
- packages of rehydration salts
- antibacterial ointment (Neosporin)
- fungus cream (Tinactin)
- hydrocortisone cream for bug bites
- Moleskin, both thin and foam
- tweezers
- scissors or knife
- syringe and needles
- thermometer
- CPR shield (if you are CPR-certified)
- latex gloves

Our doctor told us to use **Advil for pain** (no more than 2,000 mgs. per day), **Tylenol for fevers** over 101.5 F (38.6 C), and **Pepto-Bismol for stomach upset** and diarrhea (it apparently has a slight antibiotic effect too).

Our doctor was willing to prescribe to us a few antibiotics before we went as well: **Keflex (Cephalexin)** works for systemic infections, like when a cut causes your foot to swell; **Zithromax or Erythromycin** for respiratory infections; and **Ciprofloxacin** for gastrointestinal issues—though we always consulted a local doctor before taking any of these medines. We also got **Acetazaolamide**, commonly known as Diamox, for altitude sickness. If you want to be super-cautious, an **Epi-Pen** or **Ana-Kit** that contains epinephrine is the best safeguard against severe allergic reaction to insect stings.

Travelers should also put in their medical kit their brief medical history, including recent allergies and illness. If you take prescription drugs, include written instructions for how you take them and the doctor's prescription as well, just in case you get stopped in customs.

Of course, the medical kit only works at the level of the person who is using it. If you can't take a first-aid course, a backcountry wilderness guide like that published by **Wilderness Medicine Institute** (www.nols.edu/wmi/) will come in handy. Nearly all these medicines, including the antibiotics, can be bought in a pharmacy in Peru without a prescription—but stick to high-quality brand names like Laboratorios Chile.

Symptoms include chills, sweats, headaches, nausea, diarrhea, and, above all, spiking fevers. We recommend that travelers heading to the Amazon protect themselves from mosquito bites and take antimalarial medicines.

Peru's mosquitoes, affectionately known as the Bolivian air force, have developed a resistance to **chloroquine,** the traditional malaria medicine. So that leaves three medicines available to travelers: **Mefloquine** is taken weekly both before and after leaving the jungle, but it has a host of side effects (we, for instance, had hallucinatory dreams). **Malarone** is a new drug that is taken daily and has few side effects but is very expensive. And then there is **Doxycycline,** which is also taken daily but is very cheap. Doxycycline's side effects can cause upset stomach and make your skin sensitive to sunlight.

Unfortunately, none of these medicines are completely effective, and many have contra-indications. Consult your doctor as to which is most appropriate for you. After returning from the jungle, finish your malarial meds completely. Malaria symptoms can take months to appear, and you should see your doctor if you experience fevers after your return from Peru. More information is available in the U.S. through the CDC's hotline: 770/488-7788.

AVOIDING MOSQUITO BITES

Apart from malaria, mosquitoes in Peru also transmit **yellow fever** and **dengue,** a flu-like disease that is usually not life-threatening. Ticks and smaller insects can also transmit **Chagas disease.** With a few simple precautions against insects, Amazon visitors greatly reduce their risk of exposure to these diseases.

Begin by wearing long pants, long-sleeved shirts, good shoes, and a hat with a bandanna covering the neck. Clothes should preferably be thick enough to prevent mosquitoes from biting through, but that is hard to do in the jungle. Darker colors for some reason seem to keep mosquitoes away.

Spray your clothes with a **permethrin**-based spray, especially cuffs and sleeves. When arriving at the lodge, spray the mosquito net over your bed with the spray as well and let it dry before sleeping. Studies show that permethrin lasts up to several weeks on clothes, even after having been washed five or six times.

Avoid walking about at dawn and dusk, when mosquitoes are most abundant.

Apply a **DEET**-based solution when mosquitoes are present. Studies have shown that 20–33 percent DEET lasts for six to 12 hours (less if you are perspiring) and that anything over that strength produces only marginal improvements in protection. DEET is a highly toxic substance, so wash it off the skin as soon as possible. Use only 10 percent DEET on kids and none at all on infants. DEET will melt any plastic bag you store it in and will also ruin jewelry.

Many lodges provide a coil that can be lit and then smokes throughout the night, releasing a mild insecticide. These seem to work quite well. Make sure your mosquito bed net is wide enough so that you don't lie against it as you sleep—otherwise the mosquitoes will bite you right through it.

Peruvian mosquitoes, unfortunately, seem to pay no attention to natural repellants such as cit-

ronella or oils made from soybean and eucalyptus. Bring DEET-based lotion at least as a backup.

DOGS AND RABIES

There are lots of wild (or at least surly) dogs in Peru, as trekkers in places like the Cordillera Huayhuash soon find out. If you are planning to spend a lot of time trekking in Peru, you should consult with your doctor about getting a **rabies** vaccine.

There are lots of things you can do to avoid being bitten by a dog. As cute or as hungry as a dog may look, never pet a dog in Peru nor hold your hand out for it to sniff. Many of these dogs have been mistreated and have highly unpredictable behavior.

If you are walking into an area with dogs, collect a few stones. All Peruvian dogs are acutely aware of how much a well-aimed stone can hurt, and they will usually scatter even if you pretend to pick up a stone, or pretend to throw one. This is by far the best way to stop a dog, or a pack of them, from bothering you.

If you do get bit, wash the wound with soap and water and rinse it with alcohol or iodine. If possible, test the animal for rabies. Rabies is a fatal disease. If there is any doubt about whether the animal was rabid, you should receive rabies shots immediately.

HYPOTHERMIA

Peru's snow-covered mountains, highlands, and even cloud forests have plenty of cold, rainy days, which are the conditions in which hypothermia is most likely to occur. If you are out in conditions like this, watch yourself and those around you for early signs of hypothermia, which include shivering, crankiness, exhaustion, clammy skin, and loss of fine coordination. In more advanced hypothermia the person stumbles, slurs his or her speech, acts irrationally, and eventually become unconscious, a state doctors refer to as the "metabolic ice box."

The key to preventing hypothermia is being prepared for the elements, and that starts with clothing. When you go for a hike, pack plenty of different layers in a plastic bag. Remember that cotton is great for evaporating sweat and cooling down on a hot day, but actually works against you in wet, cold weather. Artificial fibers like fleece or polypropylene work when wet because they wick water away from your body. Wool is another good choice because it insulates even when wet. And a waterproof poncho or a Gore-Tex jacket will help keep you dry. Having a lot of food and water is also important, and in demanding conditions you and everyone you are with should be fueling up constantly.

The key to avoiding hypothermia is catching it early. If you or someone in your group is shivering or having a hard time zipping up a jacket, take action immediately. In mild hypothermia, the body is still trying to warm itself, and all you have to do is support that process. Feed the person water and a variety of foods, from fast-burning chocolate to bread and cheese. Have them do vigorous exercises like squatting and standing over and over, or swinging their arms around like a windmill. If the person remains cold, set up a tent and put him or her in a sleeping bag with hot-water bottles. Monitor the person carefully until their body temperature returns to normal. A person who was on the edge of hypothermia one day is more susceptible the next, so allow for at least a day or two of rest and recuperation.

HEAT EXHAUSTION

Peru's tropical sun and its climate extremes, from searing desert to steamy jungle, can be dangerous for those who are unaccustomed to them. Like hypothermia, heat exhaustion is caused by environmental conditions that knock the body temperature out of whack. And like hypothermia, heat-related illnesses can be deadly if not treated in time.

People suffering from heat exhaustion usually have been sweating profusely and have become dehydrated, which causes the person to have a headache. The skin appears pale and the person may vomit or feel dizzy after standing. The heart rate is elevated and, at first glance, the person appears to have the flu.

The most important thing to do is to take care of the problem before it gets worse. Find a shady spot—or create one with clothing—and give the person plenty of water, preferably mixed with electrolytes or at least a pinch or two of salt. Place damp, cool cloths on the person's face and back. Allow them to sleep if they feel drowsy. Another side effect of dehydration is painful heat cramps, which can be relieved by hydration and massage.

People are more prone to heat exhaustion when they are dehydrated, overweight, unaccustomed to a sunny or humid climate, and either very young or old. Taking it easy and drinking plenty of water is the best way to avoid heat exhaustion. Wearing a wide-brimmed hat and loose cotton clothing that cover the body is also important, along with applying plenty of sunscreen. If you exert yourself on a hot day, remember that you should be drinking anywhere from three to five liters per day.

SEXUALLY TRANSMITTED DISEASES

HIV/AIDS is a worldwide health problem that is spreading in Peru along with **hepatitis B** and other sexually transmitted diseases. The United Nations officially classifies Peru's AIDS epidemic as *low-level* and estimated in 2002 that there were approximately 71,200 people in Peru living with HIV/AIDS. About 74 percent of the adults were men, more than half of whom identified themselves as heterosexual. The number of infected women and children is rising.

The concept of *safe sex* has not caught on in Peru, and many men refuse to use condoms. HIV/AIDS and other sexually transmitted diseases may be transmitted just as often in homosexual sex as in heterosexual sex. Travelers should take full precautions before engaging in sex, beginning with the use of condoms.

MEDICAL CARE IN PERU

Peru's health-care system is excellent considering the fact that many Peruvians live in poverty.

Even small villages usually have a medical post, or *posta médica,* which is often staffed with a university-trained medical student completing his or her residency. Midsize cities like Huaraz have a range of health options, including a few government hospitals and a few private clinics. In general, the clinics provide more personalized, high-tech service, but we have been to plenty of state hospitals where we received better health care than we ever get in the United States. And a country doctor in Peru is probably going to identify your particular stomach ailment faster than a specialist in the United States—simply because the Peruvian doctor has seen your condition many times before.

For serious medical problems or accidents, we recommend that people travel to Lima as soon as possible. The best hospitals are here, and insurance companies in the States are often able to handle payments directly with them (elsewhere the patient is expected to shell out the cash and hopefully be reimbursed later).

Nearly all international medical policies will cover a speedy evacuation to your country if necessary, which is one of the main reasons for getting insurance in the first place. A good resource for advice in medical situations is the **South American Explorers Club** in Lima (Piura 135, Miraflores, tel. 01/445-3306, limaclub@saexplorers.org, www.saexplorers.org).

MEDICAL TRAVEL INSURANCE

Most medical insurance will not cover you while traveling abroad, so most Peru travelers buy overseas medical insurance. Go with a reputable insurance company, or you will have trouble collecting claims. Nearly all Peru hospitals will make you pay up front and then it's up to you to submit your claim.

Some U.S.-based companies that have been recommended by travelers include **Medex Assistance** (410/453-6300, www.medexassist.com), **Travel Assistance International** (800/821-2828, www.travelassistance.com), **Health Care Global** by Wallach and Company Inc. (800/237-6615 in U.S., www.wallach.com, info@wallach.com), and

International Medical Group (800/628-4664, www.imglobal.com). Students can get insurance through the **STA** (800/226-8624, www.sta.com), with 12 months costing around $550.

Some companies sell additional riders to cover high-risk sports such as mountain climbing with a rope, paragliding, and bungee jumping. One good company is **Specialty Risk International** (800/335-0611, info@specialtyrisk.com, www.specialtyrisk.com), which insures for as little as 15 days. Membership with the **American Alpine Club** (303/384-0110, getinfo@americanalpineclub.org, www.americanalpineclub.org) is open to anyone who has climbed in the last two years and includes rescue and evacuation for mountain climbers around the world.

PRESCRIPTION DRUGS

Generic medicines are easy to buy in Peru, though quality is often not the same. Many travelers stock up their medical kit in Peru, where pharmacists will sell any antibiotic you can imagine without a prescription (pain meds, however, require a doctor's note). Specific birth control or allergy pills are hard to find in Peru.

Though it's tempting, avoid self-medicating. Visiting a Peruvian doctor costs as little as $3, and they are the world's leading experts on bacteria and parasite conditions specific to Peru. You can waste a lot of time and money, and negatively affect your health, taking Cipro, for instance, when another medicine would have been better.

ILLEGAL DRUGS

Do not take drugs while in Peru. Though smoking **marijuana** is rarely punished these days in parts of the United States, Canada, and Europe, Peru's laws are as strict as ever and tourists have ended up in jail. The penalties are even stricter for **cocaine,** which is common in Peru though it is often cut with all kinds of dangerous chemicals. Under Peruvian law, foreigners in possession of drugs are regarded as international traffickers and can face **jail time** from 15 years to life. There is no bail for drug trafficking cases, and the legal process can drag on for up to two years. Your embassy will most likely decline to get involved.

Peru is well known for confidence scams that involve drugs. One friend we know was sitting in central Lima's Plaza de Armas on his first day in Peru when an attractive young woman approached him. They fell into conversation and then moved to a café. Our friend could not believe his luck at having met such an attractive woman. As they were walking down an alleyway, the woman pulled a joint from her purse, lit it, and offered it to our friend. Within seconds, the pair was surrounded by police and the woman disappeared.

The police explained to our friend that he would spend the next five years of his life in jail. As they were about to take him to the station, our friend offered to pay money to get out of the situation. The police drove him to place where he could cash all of his travelers checks. But that wasn't enough, so they visited a series of ATMs in order to take as much money as possible out of his bank and Visa cards. Several hours later, and $1,100 poorer, our friend was dropped off in the streets of Lima. And the worst part is that the perpetrators were probably not even real police.

CRIME

Peru is generally a safe country, so travelers should not feel paranoid—we traveled for eight months with electronic cameras and laptops and had no worries at all. But you have to follow common-sense rules and realize that thieves target gringos because they have cash, passports, and valuable electronics on them.

Most important, be alert and organized and watch your valuables at all times. Your money and passport should be carried under your clothes in a pouch or locked in a safety box at your hotel. We carried small bills in the front pocket of our pants. Keep a constant eye on your luggage in bus stations. When in markets, place your backpack in front of you so that it cannot be slit open. When in restaurants or buses, keep your purse or bag on your lap.

Make yourself less of a target. Do not wear jewelry or fancy watches, and keep your camera in a beat-up hip bag that is unlikely to draw attention. Be alert when in crowded places like markets or bus stations where pickpockets abound. Go only to nightspots that have been recommended. Walk with a sense of purpose, like you belong exactly where you are. When withdrawing money from an ATM, be with a friend or have a taxi waiting.

Experienced travelers can sense a scam or theft right before it happens and, nine times out of ten, it involves momentary distraction or misplaced trust. If someone spits on you, latch onto your camera instead of cleaning yourself. If someone falls in the street in front of you or drops something, move away quickly. If an old man asks for your help in reading a lottery ticket, say no. If a stranger motions you over or offers a piece of candy, keep going. Be distrusting of people you do not know.

At nightspots, do not accept alcohol from strangers, as it might be laced with a sleeping drug. Do not do drugs. If you have been drinking, take a taxi home instead of walking.

Be careful when hailing taxis and when changing money. When riding to the Lima airport, lock your luggage in the trunk and hold onto your valuables. When traffic becomes heavy on Avenida Marina, teams of delinquents often break windows and snatch bags before speeding away on a motorcycle.

Information and Services

MONEY

Thanks to ATMs, getting cash all over Peru is about as simple, easy, and cheap as it is in your own country. There is usually a $3 fee per transaction, but the benefits of using bank cards outweigh the risk of carrying loads of cash. Banks usually charge hefty commissions for cashing travelers checks, but a modest supply is nice to have along in case your bank cards are stolen (check with your bank before you go if it is even possible to replace your bank cards overseas). Visa credit cards are useful in fancy restaurants and five-star hotels, but other businesses will charge you a commission. If your bank cards get stolen, and you spend all your travelers checks, you can always get a cash withdrawal off your credit card. Bottom line: Rely on your ATM card, and bring some travelers checks and a credit card or two.

Peruvian Money

The official Peruvian currency is the **Nuevo Sol** (S/), which for the last several years has hovered around 3.5 soles per US$ 1. Peruvian bills come in denominations of 10, 20, 50, 100, and 200 soles (we've never seen this last bill, but it apparently exists). The sol is divided into 100 smaller units, called *céntimos,* which come in coins of 5, 10, 20, and 50 *céntimos.* There are also heavier coins for 1, 2, and 5 soles. Currency calculations with today's rate can be made with online currency converters such as XE.Com (www.xe.com). Exchange rates are commonly listed on signs in front of banks and exchange houses and are also posted in daily newspapers.

Changing Money

The U.S. dollar is by far the easiest foreign currency to exchange. It is advisable for travelers to buy U.S. dollars in their home country because the exchange rates in Peru are generally not as good for British pounds, Euros, or other foreign currencies. Many stores, especially supermarkets, will accept dollar bills at exchange rates better than the bank. Inspect your dollar bills carefully before leaving your country and treat them with care—even slight rips will cause them to be rejected everywhere you go. In the best case, you might be able to cash a tattered bill on the street for a lower rate. There are a few **banks** and **money exchange houses** at the airport. Generally speaking, most Peruvians exchange their dollars at exchange houses, called *casas de cambio,* because they give a slightly higher rate than banks and there is less of a wait (Peruvian banks are notorious for long, snaking lines). These *casas de cambio* are usually clustered around the Plaza de Armas or main commercial streets. In major cities, representatives of *casas de cambio* will even come to your hotel to exchange money.

In major cities, there are also money changers on the street who wear orange vests and an ID card. These people are generally safe and honest, though they will sometimes take advantage of you if you don't know the daily exchange rate. Never change money with unlicensed money changers, who will sometimes have rigged calculators. Whenever you change money on the street, check the amount with your own calculator.

When you change money, check each bill carefully to see that it is not counterfeit. Hand back all bills that have slight rips, have been repaired with tape, or have other imperfections. Insist on cash in 10-, 20-, and 50-sol bills. Unless you are at a supermarket, the 100-sol bills are hard to change and you will end up waiting as someone runs across the street to find change for you.

Money Machines

ATMs, known as *cajeros automáticos,* are spreading across Peru like wildfire and most banks, even in small towns, now have one outside on the street. The most secure ATMs are in glass rooms that you unlock by swiping your card at the door. ATMs that accept VISA/Plus are more common than MasterCard/Cirrus, though many machines accept everything. Many machines don't beep

AVOIDING COUNTERFEIT MONEY

Counterfeit money is rampant in Peru, and includes both US and Peruvian bills and even coins. Peruvians can recognize them a mile away, and once you have one you will never get rid of it. Getting money from an ATM or a bank reduces the risk but is still not a guarantee. Here are few tips for avoiding counterfeit bills:

• Feel and scratch the paper. Counterfeit bills are usually smooth and glossy, while real bills are crisp and coarse and have a low reflective surface. For U.S. dollar bills, many Peruvians scratch the neck area of the person pictured on the bill. The lapel should have a bumpy quality, unless it is an old bill. Hold both ends and snap the bill—it should have a strong feel.

• Reject old bills. This includes ones that are faded, tattered, ripped, or taped. You will never get rid of these bills unless you trade them on the street at a lesser rate. Counterfeit bills are made of inferior paper and often rip. Money changers have no problem trading you for a new bill anyway.

• Hold the bill up to a light. In both Peruvian and American bills there should be watermarks and thin ribbons that only show up when put against a light source. In the new U.S. $10 and $20 bills, the watermark is a smaller, though fuzzy replica of the person pictured on the bill. These bills also have thin lines that run across the bill and say *US TEN* or *US TWENTY.*

• With Peruvian bills, look for reflective ink. When you tilt a Peruvian bill from side to side, the ink on the number denomination should change color, like a heliogram. So far, Peruvian counterfeiters have been unable to reproduce this ink.

---

to remind you to take your card back, so remember to take it out of the machine. It will be eaten by the machine and then be very difficult to get back. Thieves sometimes wait for people to take cash out of their ATM and then follow them, sometimes on a motorcycle, to a secluded spot. For this reason, use ATMs during the day and preferably with a friend. If you are taking out a large amount, have a taxi waiting.

Banks and Wire Transfers

Banks are generally open from 9 A.M. to 5 P.M. from Monday to Friday, open mornings only on Saturday, and closed on Sundays. Banks and their hours are listed in each city under *Information and Services.* Banks are useful for cashing travelers checks, receiving wire transfers, and getting cash advances on credit cards (**Visa** works best, but **MasterCard** and **American Express** are also accepted). Bank commissions for all these transactions vary from $5 to $15, so it is worth shopping around.

A cheaper option for wire transfers is often **Western Union,** which has offices in many Peruvian cities. Call the person you want to wire money to you and give them an address and phone number where Western Union can contact

you. Once your money has arrived, you just go to the Western Union office with your passport to pick it up.

Travelers Checks

American Express is the most widely accepted travelers check and can easily be exchanged in banks. From the United States these checks can be ordered over the phone by calling toll-free 800/721-9768. The best place to change travelers checks in Peru is at **Banco de Crédito,** also known as **BCP,** which often charges no fee at all. The other banks charge a 2.5 percent commission or a flat fee that can be as much as $10. *Casas de cambio* charge even higher fees.

Remember to record the numbers of your travelers checks and keep them in a separate place. Some travelers email these numbers to themselves so that they are always available when needed. If you end up not using your travelers checks, they can always be converted into cash back home for their face value.

If your American Express travelers checks get stolen, you can call the company collect either in Peru at 0800/51-531 or in the U.S. at 1-801/964-6665. You can also go online to www.americanexpress.com to find the nearest office. American Express maintains representatives in Peru in Chiclayo, Trujillo, Lima, and Arequipa. In Lima its representative is Viajes Falabella, which has a half dozen offices in the city including Miraflores (Larco 747 tel. 01/444-4239, 9 A.M.–6 P.M. Sun.–Fri.).

Credit Cards

Only high-end hotels, restaurants, and travel agencies will allow you to use your credit card with no surcharge. Other business will charge between 2.5 percent and 12 percent extra. Businesses that are not used to credit cards may delay 20 minutes in making the transaction, so many people end up wishing they had just paid in cash. The best card to have in Peru is **Visa,** though **MasterCard, Diners Club,** and **American Express** are accepted at fancy places. Apart from their in-country toll-free numbers, most credit cards list a number you can call collect from overseas. Carry this number in a safe place or email it to yourself so that you have it in an emergency.

For Visa cards, you can also look online at www.internationalvisa.com or call collect in the U.S. to 410/581-0120. For MasterCard, see www.mastercard.com or call its 24-hour Lima number at tel. 01/444-1891. For American Express, see www.americanexpress.com or call the company in the U.S. at 336/393-1111. To contact Diners Club while in Peru, call tel. 01/221-2050.

Bargaining

Bargaining is common practice nearly everywhere in Peru, especially at markets, hotels, and shops. Bargaining can be fun, but don't go overboard. Have a good sense of what an item should cost beforehand. Ask them how much it costs (*¿Cuánto cuesta?*) and then offer 20–50 percent less, depending on how outlandish the asking prices is. Usually vendors and shoppers meet somewhere in the middle. Some people bargain ruthlessly and pretend to walk out the door to get the best deal. We always found a smile, humor, and some friendly conversation works better.

If you have a reasonable price, accept it gra-ciously. There is nothing worse than seeing a *gringo* bargaining a *campesino* into the ground over a pair of woven mittens. We might go and have a coffee with the money we save, while the vendor might use it to buy shoes for his daughter!

Discounts

Student discounts are ubiquitous in Peru, so get an **ISIC card** (International Student Identity Card) if you can, and flash it wherever you go. If you are in Peru for a week or two it is usually possible to make up the money you spent on that **South American Explorers Club** membership just in the discounts you are entitled to at hotels, restaurants, and agencies—the hardest part is remembering to ask for it before you pay. The SAE in Lima and Cusco has lists of establishments that accept their discounts, and throughout this book we often note the discounts in the parenthetical information given for each business.

Tipping

Tipping is a great way for foreign travelers to get money to the people who need it the most—the guides, waiters, hotel staff, drivers, porters, burro drivers, and other frontline workers of the tourism industry. Though not required, and often not expected, even the smallest tip is immensely appreciated. It's also a good way of letting people know they are doing a great job. Tipping is an ethic that varies from person to person, so we will tell you what we do when in Peru.

In restaurants we leave a tip of 10 percent, even though most Peruvians leave a 1-sol coin at inexpensive restaurants and just a few soles more at fancier places. We think a tip is a good idea even if the restaurant is charging you 10 percent for service, which the waiter will never see. Try to give the tip to the waiter personally, especially when the table is outdoors. It is not necessary to tip taxi drivers in Peru, but you should give a few soles to anyone who helps you carry your bags, including hotel staff or an airport shuttle driver. Assuming you were pleased with their service, you should tip guides, porters, and mule drivers at least one days' wage for every week worked. If they did a great job, we will tip more. If we stay at a particular hotel for more than a few days we give a tip to the receptionist, doorman, and other employees we enjoyed during our stay.

MAPS AND TOURIST INFORMATION

Maps

You can buy a range of maps in Cusco and Huaraz, but the best maps are to be found in Lima. **South American Explorers Club** in Lima and Cusco sells the leading country maps, plus a good selection of military topographic maps. To find topographic maps for out-of-the-way areas you will have to make a trip down to Lima's **Instituto Geográficio Nacional** (for more information, see www.ignPeru.gob.pe.

Good bookstores generally sell the better national maps, and we especially liked the maps in the back of the *Inca Guide to Peru* and the **Lima 2000** series (scale 1:2,200,00). Many hotels and i Peru officies (see below) give out free city maps. If you want to purchase maps before arriving in Peru, the Lima 2000 map is sold for $13 at www.gonetomorrow.com. Antoher online map store is www.omnimap.com/.

Tourist Offices

The Peruvian government has set up tourist offices (known as *i Peru*) in most major cities, including Lima, Arequipa, Ayacucho, Cusco, Huaraz, Iquitos, Puno, and Trujillo. They receive questions and have a website in English, French, German, Portuguese, Italian, and Spanish (tel. 01/574-8000, iperu@promPeru.gob.pe, www.Peru.gob.pe). They can give you brochures, maps, and basic info.

I Peru is also the place to go if you want to file a complaint or need to solve a problem. These can include a bus company not taking responsibility for lost luggage, a tour company that did not deliver what it promised, or an independent guide who is not honest. In an emergency, you should contact the police and also call I Peru's 24-hour hotline: tel. 01/574-8000.

FILM AND PHOTOGRAPHY

Peru is a very photogenic country, and don't be surprised if you snap off twice as many rolls as you were expecting. When available, camera services are listed under *Information and Services* for each area. In Peru, photographing soldiers or military installations is against the law.

Digital Cameras

Memory cards and other accessories are increasingly available in Lima and other large Peruvian cities. These same outfits will usually take a full memory card and burn it onto a compact disk for about $5—but it will need the toggle cable that comes with your camera. Bring a few large-capacity cards and an extra battery. Unless you have your own laptop, there will be long stretches where you will not be able to download. If you are in the jungle or traveling on back roads, you might not be able to charge your battery either.

Film Processing

Nearly every Peruvian city has a photo processing lab, which is usually affiliated with Kodak. Quality varies, however, and if you are looking for professional quality, wait until you return home or get to Lima. Developing black-and-white or slide film is difficult outside of Lima.

Photo Tips

The main issue for photography on the coast and in the highlands is the intense sunlight. The ideal times to photograph are in the warm-color hours of early morning or late afternoon. Bring filters that knock down UV radiation and increase saturation of colors. In the jungle, the main problem is lack of light, so a faster film is recommended. If you want to take pictures of wildlife, you will have to bring a hefty zoom and have a lot of time to wait for the shots to materialize. A good source of information on travel photography is **Tribal Eye Images** (www.tribaleye.co.uk). The author offers free tips on choosing equipment and film, general techniques and composition, photographing people, and selling your work. Other sites in-

YOUR ONE-STOP INFORMATION SHOP

When in Lima or Cusco, do not fail to visit the **South American Explorers,** a gold mine of information about Peru and the rest of South America and the number-one spot in the country to meet people. If you plan on doing anything off the beaten path in Peru, you will want to fork over the $50 for a membership (or $80 for a couple). If this sounds like too much money, read on.

Though nonmembers can enter the elegant clubhouse to sniff around and buy a map or two, only real members can flop themselves across the couch, get wired on real coffee, and read trip reports and guidebooks with reckless abandon. In the Lima clubhouse, we have taken our fair share of naps on the couch upstairs, where there is a private phone, cable TV, and a library of videos to choose from.

A good way to plan your Peru trip, in fact, is to simply buy a ticket to Lima, show up at the club, and pay your dues, and then sit down and plan your trip in one day. There are folders stuffed with travelers' recommendations, a good bulletin board, a huge range of maps, nearly every guidebook written about Peru and the rest of South America, a database of volunteer opportunities, and a well-organized library that has been growing ever since the club was founded in 1977. An inquisitive mind could be distracted here for weeks.

Then there's the social opportunities. Interesting people are always bopping in and out of the club, along with nearly all of Peru's backpackers. There are lectures on Wednesday nights, and club members usually head out each week for beers and danc-

ing. We have known five separate club managers over the years, and they have all been thoroughly enjoyable people.

Other perks include free luggage storage, mail and fax services, flight confirmations, book exchange, and a subscription to the excellent 64-page quarterly *South American Explorer* magazine. There are also trip reports, volunteer opportunities, and bulletin boards, along with loads more info on the SAE website, for those who will be skipping Lima and Cusco.

If the $50 still seems like too much, consider that South American Explorers has worked diligently to procure discounts for its members at a good variety of hotels, restaurants, and travel agencies. If you can remember to ask for the discount—and that is the hard part, believe us—you are likely to recoup your investment.

SAE's web page is www.saexplorers.org and its headquarters are in Ithica, New York (607/277-0488, explorer@saexplorers.org). Most travelers simply drop by the clubhouse in **Lima** (Piura 135, Miraflores, tel. 01/445-3306, limaclub@saexplorers.org, 9:30 A.M.–5 P.M. Mon.–Fri., 9:30 A.M.–1 P.M. Saturday) or **Cusco** (Choquechaca 188, #4, tel. 084/24-5484, cuscoclub@saexplorers.org, 9:30 A.M.–5 P.M. Mon.–Fri., 10 A.M.–1 P.M. Saturday). There is also a clubhouse in **Quito, Ecuador** (Jorge Washington 311, tel. 5932/222-5228, quitoclub@saexsplorers.org). Aside from the clubs, there are SAE representatives in countries where there is not a physical clubhouse.

clude www.photo.net/travel/traveltips and the members-only www.photographytips.com/.

Photographing Locals

Photographing locals poses a real dilemma. On one hand, their colorful clothing and expressions make the best travel photos. But many Peruvian feel uncomfortable with having their picture taken, and foreigners need to respect that. Before you take a picture of someone, take the time to meet them and establish a relationship. Then ask permission to take their photo. In jun-

gle and highland areas, you will be surprised by how many people decline out of beliefs that cameras can steal the soul.

The most compliant subjects are market vendors, especially those from whom you have just bought something. Many children in highland Peru are now asking for money in order to have their picture taken, which we feel is a bad idea.

There are many tricks for taking pictures of people in a discreet way. Digital cameras with a flip screen can be held at your waist or over your head. Other photographers pretend to look at a far-off

Know Peru

object such as a building, before clicking a busy scene in the foreground of people in a market. For other tricks on photographing people, see the Tribal Eye Images website (www.tribaleye.co.uk).

COMMUNICATIONS AND MEDIA

Mail

Peru's national post office is **Serpost,** and there is an office in nearly every village, or at the very least a mailbox (*buzón*). Postal service in Peru is fairly reliable and surprisingly expensive. Postcards and letters cost $1.20 to the U.S. and Europe, and more if you want them certified. Letters sent from Peru take around two weeks to arrive in the U.S., but less time if sent from Lima. Specific post office locations and hours are listed under *Information and Services* in each destination chapter. Shipping packages out of Peru is a risky business—use DHL or some other courier service instead.

If you become a member of South American Explorers, you can receive personal mail at its offices in Lima or Cusco. You can also receive mail at your respective embassy in Lima. Don't even think about having someone send you a package, because they always get held up in customs. This means that you have to go to the airport, wait in line, and then pay duty taxes that are often more than the value of the package itself. Many people allow their packages to be sent back to the country of origin once they realize how much they will have to pay.

Telephone Calls

A number of Internet cards, which can be purchased online, make calling Peru incredibly cheap—as low as $.07 per minute! You will never find a cheaper rate from Peru, so you can get one of these cards for a boyfriend or for your family. Before your trip, you can use them to make cheap calls to Peru. Alosmart (www.alosmart.com) has a search engine for finding the best card depending on the type of calls you are going to make. We have been happy with this service.

Peru's country code is **51** and each department, or region, of Peru has a different code.

Cusco, for instance, is 84. So dialing a Cusco number from the United States would be 01 (used for all international calls) + 51 (country code) + 84 (city code).

Most towns have public phones on the main square and usually an office of **Telefónica,** Peru's main phone company. The phones are coin-operated but most people buy telephone cards.

The most popular prepaid card is called 147 and can be bought in denominations from $2 to $25 at most pharmacies, supermarkets, and from the Telefónica offices themselves. Avoid buying **HolaPeru** cards because they rarely work, and never buy a card off the street. Street hustlers will buy the card, read the number, and then both reseal the plastic and re-cover the number with a fake gray strip. With the **147 phone card,** dialing

PERU'S AREA CODES

Aguas Calientes	84
Arequipa	54
Ayacucho	66
Cajamarca	76
Cusco	84
Chachapoyas	41
Chiclayo	74
Huancayo	64
Huaraz	43
Ica	56
Iquitos	65
Lima	1
Machu Picchu	84
Mancora	73
Nasca	56
Piura	73
Puerto Maldonado	82
Puno	51
Tarapoto	42
Trujillo	44
Tumbes	72

the U.S. is about $1 per minute and a local call is about $0.15 per minute. Surcharges are applied to all calls made from pay phones, so use your hotel phone or walk into any small store in Peru with the green-and-blue phone symbol above it.

All major **international phone cards** can be used in Peru, as long as you know the access code. The access codes are AT&T (0800-5000), MCI (0800-50010), TRT (0800-50030), and Sprint (0800-50020). Worldlink has no direct access in Peru.

The cheapest way to make long-distance calls from Peru, however, are the **net-to-phone** systems available at many Internet places for as low as $0.17 per minute calling to the U.S. or Europe. There is an irritating lag when calling with most of these services, though Internet cafés that have cable service are usually crystal clear—often even better than a phone!

When calling a cell phone in Peru, place a "9" before the number. All long-distance calls in Peru are preceded by a "0" and the area code of that particular region, or department, of Peru. For instance, for calling Cusco all numbers are preceded by "084"—these preceding numbers are listed whenever a number is listed in this book.

Perú's country code is **51** and each department, or region, of Perú has a different code. Cusco, for instance, is 84. So dialing a Cusco number from the United States would be 011 (used for all international calls) + 51 (country code) + 84 (city code). All cities in Peru have two-digit city codes when dialing from overseas, except Lima. For dialing Lima for the United States, dial 011-51-1 and then the number, which should begin with a "2" or a "4". When dialing Lima from within Peru, however, you must first dial "01".

To place a direct international phone call, dial 00 + country code + city code + number. The country code for Argentina is (54), Australia (61), Canada (1), Chile (56), Denmark (45), France (33), Germany (49), Holland (+6), Israel (972), Japan (81), New Zealand (64) Norway (47), Peru (51), Spain (34), Switzerland (41), UK (44), U.S. (1). So for calling the UK from Peru, callers should dial 0044 before any number, and for the US 001.

Collect calls are possible from many Telefónica offices, or you can dial the International Operator (108) for assistance. The correct way to ask for a collect call is: *Quisiera hacer una llamada de cobrado revertido, por favor).*

The following codes can be called for help: Directory Assistance (103), Emergency Assistance in Lima (105), International Operator Assistance (108), National Operator Assistance (109), Fire (116), and Urgent Medical Assistance (117). The chances of finding an English-speaking operator, however, at these numbers is slim. i Peru maintains a 24-hour English-speaking operator at the Lima airport who is trained to handle emergencies: tel. 01/574-8000.

Fax

Sending a fax from Peru to the United States is expensive, ranging from $2 to $9 per page to the United States or Europe. Instead of a fax, scan your document and send it as an attachment. Fax machines are available at most hotels, photocopy stores, and Telefónica offices.

Internet Access

Internet is by far the cheapest and most convenient way to communicate in Peru. Internet cafés are everywhere and are popping up in even tiny towns. Using the Internet is cheap ($0.40–0.90) and often you can also make net-to-phone overseas calls as well, which are cheap but are usually not as satisfying as a crisp telephone call.

There is a lot that goes into choosing an Internet café, however. First off, make sure it is a high-speed connection, which in Peru is generally referred to as "speedy." Some speedy connections, however, are much faster than others. If your email takes more than a minute or two to open up, we suggest you head elsewhere. Another huge factor is noise, especially with Internet places that cater to schoolkids, who show up each afternoon and shout and scream and wrestle with each other over who gets to use what machine.

Besides *speedy,* which is a DSL line, Lima now has faster connections with cable modems—and most important, crystal-clear, dirt-cheap international calls. Sometimes an out-of-the-way jungle town can have a satellite Internet center, which is also amazingly fast.

Newspapers and Magazines

The largest daily newspaper in Lima is **El Comercio** (www.elcomercio.com.pe), which has a variety of supplements and good information on performing arts, etc. We prefer **La República,** however, because it takes more risks with its news coverage, and there is a political column worth reading by analyst Mirko Lauer.

The best magazine by far in Peru is **Caretas** (www.caretas.com.pe), which has been published for a half century by the Zileri family. The magazine was critical of the Fujimori government even when *Fujimorismo* was at its height in the mid-1990s. Though it lost a lot of advertising revenue, the magazine was the first to write about the financial scandals and heavy-handed maneuvers that would end up toppling President Fujimori. Besides political coverage, *Caretas* has sections devoted to art, humorous essays, interesting letters to the editor, jokes, crossword puzzles, and great photographs, including a scantily clad man or woman on the back page.

All these publications are in Spanish only. The *Lima Times,* Peru's English-language newspaper, closed years ago, and a similar recent effort in Cusco flopped soon after it started.

WEIGHTS AND MEASURES

Peru uses the metric system for everything except gallons of gasoline. For conversion information, see the back flap of this book.

Electricity

The electric system of Peru is 220 volts and 60 cycles. If you absent-mindedly plug in a 110-volt appliances from the U.S. into a 220-volt Peruvian outlets (like I did), you will start a small fire. Some high-end hotels have additional outlets of 110 volts, but we were always too nervous to use them.

The only way to use 110-volt appliances in Peru is with a converter, which tend to be quite heavy. You can buy one in an electronics shop, though they are cheaper in Peru. Make sure you get the right type, as a hair dryer needs a more robust converter than, say, a digital camera battery charger. Voltage surges are common in Peru, so it is also a good idea to bring a surge protector from home that can be plugged between your appliance and the converter. Most laptops and digital cameras these days can take either 110 or 120 volts, so check on this before you buy a converter.

TIME ZONES

Peru is in the same time zone as New York, Miami, and the East Coast of the United States. Peru does not use Daylight Savings Time, meaning that its time remains constant throughout the year. The entire country is in the same time zone, though Bolivia is one hour ahead. Other time differences: Argentina is (+2), Australia (+15), Chile (+1), Denmark (+6), France (+6), Germany (+6), Holland (+6), Israel (+7), Japan (+14), New Zealand (+17), Norway (+6), Spain (+6). and the U.K. (+5).

Spanish Phrasebook

Even a beginner's grasp of the Spanish language will make your travels more enjoyable. Studying the basics before your trip so you will be ready to practice once you arrive in Peru.

Spanish commonly uses 30 letters—the familiar English 26, plus four straightforward additions: ch, ll, ñ, and rr, which are explained in "Consonants," below.

PRONUNCIATION

Unlike English, Spanish is a phonetic language. In other words, words are always pronounced exactly as they are spelled. As long as you know how to pronounce the vowels and consonants, you should be able to read Spanish and pronounce it correctly.

Vowels

a — like ah, as in "hah": *agua* AH-gooah (water), *pan* PAHN (bread), and *casa* CAH-sah (house)

e — like ay, as in "may:" *mesa* MAY-sah (table), *tela* TAY-lah (cloth), and *de* DAY (of, from)

i — like ee, as in "need": *diez* dee-AYZ (ten), *comida* ko-MEE-dah (meal), and *fin* FEEN (end)

o — like oh, as in "go": *peso* PAY-soh (weight), *ocho* OH-choh (eight), and *poco* POH-koh (a bit)

u — like oo, as in "cool": *uno* OO-noh (one), *cuarto* KOOAHR-toh (room), and *usted* oos-TAYD (you); when it follows a "q" the **u** is silent; when it follows an "h" or has an umlaut, it's pronounced like "w"

Consonants

b, d, f, k, l, m, n, p, q, s, t, v, w, x, y, z, and **ch** — pronounced almost as in English; **h** occurs, but is silent, not pronounced at all.

c — like k as in "keep": *cuarto* KOOAR-toh (room); when it precedes "e" or "i," pronounce **c** like s, as in "sit": *cerveza* sayr-VAY-sah (beer), *encima* ayn-SEE-mah (atop).

g — like g as in "gift" when it precedes "a" "o," "u," or a consonant: *gato* GAH-toh (cat), *hago* AH-goh (I do, make); otherwise, pronounce **g**

like h as in "hat": *giro* HEE-roh (money order), *gente* HAYN-tay (people)

j — like h, as in "has": *Jueves* HOOAY-vays (Thursday), *mejor* may-HOR (better)

ll — like y, as in "yes": *toalla* toh-AH-yah (towel), *ellos* AY-yohs (they, them)

ñ — like ny, as in "canyon": *año* AH-nyo (year), *señor* SAY-nyor (Mr., sir)

r — is lightly trilled, with tongue at the roof of your mouth like a very light English d, as in "ready": *pero* PAY-doh (but), *tres* TDAYS (three), *cuatro* KOOAH-tdoh (four).

rr — like a Spanish r, but with much more emphasis and trill. Let your tongue flap. Practice with *burro* (donkey), *carretera* (highway), and Carrillo (proper name), then really let go with *ferrocarril* (railroad).

Accent

The rule for accent, the relative stress given to syllables within a given word, is straightforward. If a word ends in a vowel, an n, or an s, accent the next-to-last syllable; if not, accent the last syllable.

Pronounce *gracias* GRAH-seeahs (thank you), *orden* OHR-dayn (order), and *carretera* kah-ray-TAY-rah (highway) with stress on the next-to-last syllable.

Otherwise, accent the last syllable: *venir* vay-NEER (to come), *ferrocarril* fay-roh-cah-REEL (railroad), and *edad* ay-DAHD (age).

Exceptions to the accent rule are always marked with an accent sign: (á, é, í, ó, or ú), such as *teléfono* tay-LAY-foh-noh (telephone), *jabón* hah-BON (soap), and *rápido* RAH-pee-doh (rapid).

BASIC AND COURTEOUS EXPRESSIONS

Most Spanish-speaking people consider formalities important. Whenever approaching anyone for information or some other reason, do not forget the appropriate salutation—good morning, good evening, etc. Standing alone, the greeting *hola* (hello) can sound brusque.

Hello. — *Hola.*
Good morning. — *Buenos días.*
Good afternoon. — *Buenas tardes.*
Good evening. — *Buenas noches.*
How are you? — *¿Cómo está usted?*
Very well, thank you. — *Muy bien, gracias.*
Okay; good. — *Bien.*
Not okay; bad. — *Mal* or *feo.*
So-so. — *Más o menos.*
And you? — *¿Y usted?*
Thank you. — *Gracias.*
Thank you very much. — *Muchas gracias.*
You're very kind. — *Muy amable.*
You're welcome. — *De nada.*
Goodbye. — *Adios.*
See you later. — *Hasta luego.*
please — *por favor*
yes — *sí*
no — *no*
I don't know. — *No sé.*
Just a moment, please. — *Momentito, por favor.*
Excuse me, please (when you're trying to get attention). — *Disculpe* or *Con permiso.*
Excuse me (when you've made a boo-boo). — *Lo siento.*
Pleased to meet you. — *Mucho gusto.*
What is your name? — *¿Cómo se llama usted?*
Do you speak English? — *¿Habla usted inglés?*
I don't speak Spanish well. — *No hablo bien el español.*
I don't understand. — *No entiendo.*
How do you say . . . in Spanish? — *¿Cómo se dice . . . en español?*
My name is . . . — *Me llamo . . .*
Let's go to . . . — *Vamos a . . .*

TERMS OF ADDRESS

When speaking with someone of respect, or someone you do not know, use *usted* for you (formal). Otherwise use *tu* for you (informal).
I — *yo*
you (formal) — *usted*
you (familiar) — *tu*
he/him — *él*
she/her — *ella*
we/us — *nosotros*

you (plural) — *ustedes*
they/them — *ellos* (all males or mixed gender); *ellas* (all females)
Mr., sir — *señor*
Mrs., madam — *señora*
miss, young lady — *señorita*
wife — *esposa*
husband — *esposo*
friend — *amigo* (male); *amiga* (female)
boyfriend/girlfriend — *enamorado* (male); *enamorada* (female)
son; daughter — *hijo; hija*
brother; sister — *hermano; hermana*
father; mother — *padre; madre*
grandfather; grandmother — *abuelo; abuela*

TRANSPORTATION

Where is . . . ? — *¿Dónde está . . . ?*
How far is it to . . . ? — *¿A cuánto está . . . ?*
from . . . to . . . — *de . . . a . . .*
How many blocks? — *¿Cuántas cuadras?*
Where (Which) is the way to . . . ? — *¿Dónde está el camino a . . . ?*
the bus station — *la terminal de autobuses*
the bus stop — *la parada de autobuses*
Where is this bus going? — *¿Adónde va este autobús?*
taxi — *taxi*
public taxi — *colectivo*
public van — *combi*
three-wheeled motorized bike-taxi — *motocar*
jungle boat with raised propeller *peki-peki*
mule driver — *arriero*
mules, burro — *mule, donkey*
the airport — *el aeropuerto*
I'd like a ticket to . . . — *Quisiera un boleto a . . .*
roundtrip — *ida y vuelta*
reservation — *reserva*
baggage — *equipaje*
Stop here, please. — *Pare aquí, por favor.*
the entrance — *la entrada*
the exit — *la salida*
the ticket office — *la oficina de boletos*
is (very) near; far — *está (muy) cerca; lejos*
to; toward — *a*
by; through — *por*

from — *de*
the right — *la derecha*
the left — *la izquierda*
straight ahead — *derecho; de frente*
in front — *en frente*
beside — *al lado*
behind — *atrás*
the corner — *la esquina*
the stoplight — *la semáforo*
a turn — *una vuelta*
right here — *aquí*
somewhere around here — *por acá*
right there — *allí*
somewhere around there — *por allá*
street — *calle*
highway — *carretera*
bridge — *puente*
address — *dirección*
north; south — *norte; sur*
east; west — *este; oeste*

ACCOMMODATIONS

hotel — *hotel*
Is there a room? — *¿Hay cuarto?*
May I (may we) see it? — *¿Puedo (podemos) verlo?*
What is the rate? — *¿Cuál es el tarifa?*
Is that your best rate? — *¿Es su mejor tarifa?*
Is there something cheaper? — *¿Hay algo más económico?*
a single room — *un cuarto sencillo*
a double room — *un cuarto doble*
double bed — *cama matrimonial*
twin beds — *camas dobles*
with private bath — *con baño privado*
hot water — *agua caliente*
shower — *ducha*
towels — *toallas*
soap — *jabón*
toilet paper — *papel higiénico*
blanket — *frazada; manta*
sheets — *sábanas*
air-conditioned—*aire acondicionado*
fan — *ventilador*
key — *llave*
manager — *gerente*

FOOD

I'm hungry — *Tengo hambre.*
I'm thirsty. — *Tengo sed.*
menu — *carta*
glass — *vaso*
fork — *tenedor*
knife — *cuchillo*
spoon — *cuchara*
napkin — *servilleta*
soft drink — *gaseosa*
coffee — *café*
tea — *té*
boiled water for drinking— *agua hervida para tomar*
bottled carbonated water — *agua mineral*
bottled uncarbonated water — *agua sin gas*
beer — *cerveza*
wine — *vino*
milk — *leche*
juice — *jugo*
cream — *crema*
sugar — *azúcar*
salt — *sal*
black pepper — *pimienta*
chili pepper — *aji*
cheese — *queso*
breakfast — *desayuno*
lunch — *almuerzo*
fixed lunch menu — *el menú*
dinner — *comida* (often eaten in late afternoon); *cena* (a late-night snack)
the check please — *la cuenta por favor*
eggs — *huevos*
bread — *pan*
salad — *ensalada*
lettuce — *lechuga*
onion — *cebolla*
tomato — *tomate*
fruit — *fruta*
mango — *mango*
papaya — *papaya*
banana — *plátano*
apple — *manzana*
orange — *naranja*
avocado — *palta*
lime — *limón*

Know Peru

beans — *frijoles*
fish — *pescado*
shellfish — *mariscos*
crab — *cangrejo*
lobster — *langosta*
mussels — *choros*
scallops — *conchas*
sea bass — *corvina*
shrimp — *camarones*
sole — *lenguado*
squid — *calamares*
trout — *trucha*
(without) meat — *(sin) carne*
chicken — *pollo*
pork — *cerdo*
beef; steak — *res; bistec*
bacon; ham — *tocino; jamón*
fried — *frito*
roasted — *asada*
grilled — *a la parrilla*

SHOPPING

money — *dinero*
money-exchange bureau — *casa de cambio*
money changer — *cambista*
I would like to exchange traveler's checks. — *Quisiera cambiar cheques de viajero.*
What is the exchange rate? — *¿Cuál es el tipo de cambio?*
How much is the commission? — *¿Cuánto cuesta la comisión?*
Do you accept credit cards? — *¿Aceptan tarjetas de crédito?*
money order — *giro*
How much does it cost? — *¿Cuánto cuesta?*
What is your final price? — *¿Cuál es su último precio?*
expensive —*caro*
cheap — *barato; económico*
more — *más*
less — *menos*
a little — *un poco*
too much — *demasiado*

HEALTH

Help me please. — *Ayúdeme por favor.*
I am ill. — *Estoy enfermo.*
Call a doctor. — *Llame un doctor.*
Take me to . . . — *Lléveme a . . .*
hospital — *hospital; sanatorio*
drugstore — *farmacia*
pain — *dolor*
fever — *fiebre*
headache — *dolor de cabeza*
stomachache — *dolor de estómago*
burn — *quemadura*
cramp — *calambre*
altitude sickness — *soroche*
nausea — *náusea*
vomiting — *vomitar*
medicine — *medicina*
antibiotic — *antibiótico*
pill; tablet — *pastilla*
aspirin — *aspirina*
ointment; cream — *pomada; crema*
bandage — *venda*
cotton — *algodón*
sanitary napkins — use brand name, e.g., Kotex
birth control pills — *pastillas anticonceptivas*
condoms — *preservativos; condones*
toothbrush — *cepilla dental*
dental floss — *hilo dental*
toothpaste — *crema dental*
dentist — *dentista*
toothache — *dolor de muelas*

COMMUNICATIONS

long-distance telephone — *teléfono larga distancia*
I would like to call . . . — *Quisiera llamar a . . .*
collect — *por cobrar*
credit card — *tarjeta de crédito*
post office — *correo*
general delivery — *lista de correo*
letter — *carta*
stamp — *estampilla, timbre*
postcard — *tarjeta*
air mail — *correo aereo*
registered — *registrado*

package; box — *paquete; caja*
string; tape — *cuerda; cinta*

AT THE BORDER

border — *frontera*
customs — *aduana*
immigration — *migración*
tourist card — *tarjeta de turista*
inspection — *inspección; revisión*
passport — *pasaporte*
profession — *profesión*
marital status — *estado civil*
single — *soltero*
married; divorced — *casado; divorciado*
insurance — *seguros*
title — *título*
driver's license — *licencia de manejar*

GAS STATION

gas station — *gasolinera*
gasoline — *gasolina*
unleaded — *sin plomo*
full, please — *lleno, por favor*
tire — *llanta*
tire repair shop — *llantero*
air — *aire*
water — *agua*
oil change — *cambio de aceite*
My . . . doesn't work. — *Mi . . . no sirve.*
battery — *batería*
radiator — *radiador*
alternator — *alternador*
generator — *generador*
tow truck — *grúa*
repair shop — *taller mecánico*

VERBS

Verbs are the key to getting along in Peru because Spanish is verb-driven. There are three classes of verbss, which end in *ar, er,* and *ir.*
to buy — *comprar*
I buy, you (he, she, it) buys — *compro, compra*
we buy, you (they) buy — *compramos, compran*

to eat — *comer*
I eat, you (he, she, it) eats — *como, come*
we eat, you (they) eat — *comemos, comen*

to climb — *subir*
I climb, you (he, she, it) climbs — *subo, sube*
we climb, you (they) climb — *subimos, suben*

Got the idea? Here are more (with irregularities marked in **bold**).

to do or make — *hacer*
I do or make, you (he she, it) does or makes — ***hago,*** *hace*
we do or make, you (they) do or make — *hacemos, hacen*
to go — *ir*
I go, you (he, she, it) goes — ***voy, va***
we go, you (they) go — ***vamos, van***
to go (walk) — *andar*
to love — *amar*
to work — *trabajar*
to want — *desear, querer*
to need — *necesitar*
to read — *leer*
to write — *escribir*
to repair — *reparar*
to stop — *parar*
to get off (the bus) — *bajar*
to arrive — *llegar*
to stay (remain) — *quedar*
to stay (lodge) — *hospedar*
to leave — *salir* (regular except for ***salgo,*** I leave)
to look at — *mirar*
to look for — *buscar*
to give — *dar* (regular except for ***doy,*** I give)
to carry — *llevar*
to have — *tener* (irregular but important: ***tengo, tiene,*** *tenemos,* ***tienen***)
to come — *venir* (similarly irregular: ***vengo, viene,*** *venimos,* ***vienen***)

Spanish has two forms of "to be." Use *estar* when speaking of location or a temporary state of being: "I am at home." ***"Estoy en casa."*** "I'm sick." ***"Estoy enfermo."*** Use *ser* for a permanent state of being: "I am a doctor." ***"Soy doctora."***

Estar is regular except for **estoy,** I am. *Ser* is very irregular:

to be — *ser*
I am, you (he, she, it) is — **soy, es**
we are, you (they) are — **somos, son**

NUMBERS

zero — *cero*
one — *uno*
two — *dos*
three — *tres*
four — *cuatro*
five — *cinco*
six — *seis*
seven — *siete*
eight — *ocho*
nine — *nueve*
10 — *diez*
11 — *once*
12 — *doce*
13 — *trece*
14 — *catorce*
15 — *quince*
16 — *dieciseis*
17 — *diecisiete*
18 — *dieciocho*
19 — *diecinueve*
20 — *veinte*
21 — *veinte y uno* or *veintiuno*
30 — *treinta*
40 — *cuarenta*
50 — *cincuenta*
60 — *sesenta*
70 — *setenta*
80 — *ochenta*
90 — *noventa*
100 — *ciento*
101 — *ciento y uno* or *cientiuno*
200 — *doscientos*
500 — *quinientos*
1,000 — *mil*
10,000 — *diez mil*
100,000 — *cien mil*
1,000,000 — *millón*

one half — *medio*
one third — *un tercio*
one fourth — *un cuarto*

TIME

What time is it? — *¿Qué hora es?*
It's 1 o'clock. — *Es la una.*
It's 3 in the afternoon. — *Son las tres de la tarde.*
It's 4 A.M. — *Son las cuatro de la mañana.*
6:30 — *seis y media*
a quarter till 11 — *un cuarto para las once*
a quarter past 5 — *las cinco y cuarto*
an hour — *una hora*

DAYS AND MONTHS

Monday — *lunes*
Tuesday — *martes*
Wednesday — *miércoles*
Thursday — *jueves*
Friday — *viernes*
Saturday — *sábado*
Sunday — *domingo*
today — *hoy*
tomorrow — *mañana*
yesterday — *ayer*
January — *enero*
February — *febrero*
March — *marzo*
April — *abril*
May — *mayo*
June — *junio*
July — *julio*
August — *agosto*
September — *septiembre*
October — *octubre*
November — *noviembre*
December — *diciembre*
a week — *una semana*
a month — *un mes*
after — *después*
before — *antes*

—Courtesy of Bruce Whipperman, author of *Moon Handbooks Pacific Mexico.*

QUECHUA BASICS

Quechua is spoken throughout Peru's highlands, but especially in the area including Ayacucho, Cusco, and Lake Titicaca. The following is only intended to get you started.

hello — *napaykullayki*
yes — *riki*
no — *mana*
please — *allichu*
thank you — *añay*
father or sir — *Tayta*
mother or madame — *Mama*
mountain god — *apui*
Inca messenger runners — *chasquis*
rest place for chasquis — *tambo*

lake — *cocha*
dried llama meat (jerky) *charqui*

allichu — please
añay — thank you
apui — mountain god
charqui — dried llama meat (jerky)
chasquis — Inca messenger runners
cocha — lake
tayta — father or sir
mama — mother or madame
mana— no
napaykullayki — hello
riki — yes
tambo — rest place for chasquis

Glossary

abra — high pass
aluvión —mudslide
anticuchos — beef heart brochettes served with an assortment of spicy sauces
arroz con pato — duck with rice, originally from the north coast but now found everywhere
cancha — fried corn kernels, a popular snack to nibble with beer, usually served with cebiche
cañón — canyon
causa — cold casserole of mashed potatoes mixed with hot peppers, onions, and avocado
cebiche — the trademark of Peruvian cuisine. Fish, shrimp, scallops, or squid, or a mixture of all four, marinated in lime juice and chili peppers for 10 minutes. Traditionally served with corn, sweet potatoes, onions, yucca, and cancha.
cebiche mixto — cebiche with fish and shellfish
chicha — fermented beer made from different colors of corn
chicha morada — sweet, refreshing drink made from purple corn, served chilled
chirimoya — sweet, juicy fruit with mushy texture and a bitter skin
choclo — large-grained ears of maize, which are sold steamy hot with slices of cheese and chili sauce on street corners
cocha — lake in Quechua
conchitas negras — black scallop delicacy common in northern Peru
cordillera — mountain range
Cuy — guinea pig stewed, fried or spit-roasted
granadilla — sweet, pulpy passion fruit with a hard shell
guanabana — indescribably delicious jungle fruit
guayaba — guava
juanes — tamale stuffed with chicken and rice
kiwicha — purple-flowered grain high in protein, folded into breads, cookies, and soups
lúcuma — small brown fruit recognizable by its dark peach color and smoky flavor A popular ice cream, yogurt, and milkshake flavor.
lago — lake
laguna — smaller lake
lomo saltado — french fries combined with strips of steak, a spicy orange pepper, onions, and tomatoes stir-fried and served over rice. This dish is inexpensive and popular all over Peru.
maracuya — seedy passiofruit, often served as a juice

masato — alcoholic drink made from fermented yucca

mazamorra morada — pudding-like dessert made from purple corn

mirador — lookout point

nevado — mountain

paca — fish steamed inside a bamboo tube

papa a la Huancaina — cold appetizer of potatoes in a spicy light cheese sauce from the Huancayo region

papa ocopa — Arequipeña dish of sliced and boiled potatoes, smothered in a spicy peanut sauce, garnished with hard-boiled eggs and olives

papa rellena — fried oblong of mashed potatoes stuffed with meat, onions, olives, boiled eggs, and raisins

papaya — papaya

pachamanca — beef, pork, and chicken mixed with a variety of vegetables, and cooked together over heated stones in a hole in the ground. This is a popular Sunday dish in the sierra region.

paiche — huge, succulent river fish

palmito — ribbons of palm heart that look like pasta when served

Panamericana — Pan-American Highway

plítano frito — fried bananas

playa — beach

pirañas — small, sharp fanged fish found in oxbow lakes and rivers

pongo — river gorge that is often dangerous in high water

puna — high plains, often grasslands

quebrada — narrow valley, ravine

quinoa — golden-brown, round grain

río — river

seco de cabrito — roasted goat marinated with fermented chicha, served with beans and rice

tiradito — a cebiche of longer fish strips without onion or sweet potato

tuna — prickly pear from desert cactus

valle — valley

yucca — cassava root

Suggested Reading

HISTORY

Bowen, Rally and Jane Holligan. *El Espá Imperfecto. La Telaraña Siniestra de Vladimiro Montesinos* (*The Imperfect Spy: The Sinister Spiderweb of Vladimiro Montesinos*). Lima: Peisa Editores, 2003. This is the latest work of two foreign correspondents who spent two years piecing together a profile of Alberto Fujimori's head of intelligence, Vladimiro Montesinos. This Rasputin-like character ordered secret assassinations, bribed half of the TV channels in Lima, and absconded with millions of dollars. The English-language version of this books is available in Lima bookstores.

Burger, Richard. *Chavín and the Origins of Andean Civilization.* Thames and Hudson: London, 1995. A groundbreaking investigation of the Chavín culture, which spread across Peru's highlands 2,000 years before the Incas.

Hemming, John. *Conquest of the Incas.* New York: Harcourt Brace & Company, 1970. This is a masterpiece of both prose and history, in which famed Peru historian John Hemming lays out a gripping, blow-by-blow account of the Spanish conquest of Peru. Hemming, who was only 35 when *Conquest* was published, has written nearly a dozen books about Inca architecture and the native people of the Amazon.

Heyerdahl, Thor and Daniel Sandweiss. *The Quest for Peru's Forgotten City.* London: Thames and Hudson: 1995. Norwegian explorer Thor Heyerdahl was most famous for piloting the *Kon-Tiki* balsawood raft from Callao, Peru, to the Polynesian Islands in 1947. From 1988 until he died in 2002, Heyerdahl's obsession with early ocean travel focused on the inhabitants of Túcume, a complex of 26 pyramids north of present-day Trujillo that was built by the Sicán culture around 1050 A.D. This remains the best work on Túcume.

Kirkpatrick, Sidney. *Lords of Sipán: A True Story of Pre-Inca Tombs, Archaeology, and Crime.* New York: William Morrow, 1992. Shortly after grave robbers unearthed a royal tomb of the Sipán culture near present-day Trujillo, Sydney Kirkpatrick documented the underworld of artifact smugglers and their Hollywood clients. At the center of this real-life drama is Peruvian archaeologist Walter Alva, who struggles against an entire town as he fights to preserve his country's heritage.

Mosley, Michael. *The Incas and Their Ancestors.* London: Thames and Hudson, 1993. This masterly work is still the best general introduction to the history of Peru's early cultures, including the Nasca, Moche, Wari, and Tiahuanaco.

Muscutt, Keith. *Warriors of the Clouds: A Lost Civilization in the Upper Amazon of Peru.* Albuquerque: University of New Mexico, 1998. This book provides a good overview of what archaeologists know of the Chachapoya, a cantankerous cloud-forest empire that was never dominated by the Incas, and is replete with beautiful images of ruins in the remote cloud forest of northeastern Peru.

Protzen, Jean-Pierre. *Inka Architecture and Construction at Ollantaytambo.* Oxford, UK: Oxford University Press, 1993. Jean-Pierre Protzen spent years at the Inca site of Ollantaytambo in order to understand its historical significance and construction. This hard-to-find book is the best single work on Ollantaytambo, the most important Inca ruin next to Machu Picchu. A copy can be perused at Wendy Weeks' *El Albergue* in Ollantaytambo.

Savoy, Gene. *Antisuyo: The Search for the Lost Cities of the Amazon.* New York: Simon & Schuster, 1970. Gene Savoy, who is second only to Hiram Bingham in his knack of sniffing out lost cities, describes in somewhat stilted prose his search for Espíritu Pampa, the last stronghold of the Incas.

Starn, Orin, ed., Carlos Iván Degregori, and Rob Kirk. *The Peru Reader.* Duke University Press, 1995. This is a great paperback to bring on the airplane or a long train ride, stuffed with an endlessly entertaining and eclectic collection of short stories, anthropological essays, translated chronicles, and a bit of poetry.

Von Hagen, Adriana and Craig Morris. *The Cities of the Ancient Andes.* Thames and Hudson: London, 1998. Lima-based writer Adriana von Hagen and a curator of New York's America Museum of Natural History teamed up for this highly recommended introduction to Peru's major archaeological sites. This is the most concise and accessible history of Peru's ancient cultures, written around the centers and cities they left behind.

CHRONICLES

Cieza de León, Pedro. *The Discovery and Conquest of Peru: The New World Encounter.* Durham, North Carolina: Duke University Press, 1999. Pedro Cieza de León arrived in Peru in 1547, wide-eyed at the age of 27, and proceeded to explore every nook and cranny, describing everything as he went. He is the first Spaniard to describe Spanish mistreatment of Peru's natives. His reliable voice paints the Spanish-Inka encounter in simple and clear language.

Garcilaso de la Vega, Inca and Harold Livermore, translator. *Royal Commentaries of the Inca and General History of Peru.* Austin, TX: University of Texas Press, 1966. Inca Garcilaso was the son of a conquistador and an Inca princess who moved to Spain in his youth and spent the rest of his life documenting the myths, culture, and history of the Incas. Though criticized for historical inaccuracies and exaggeration, Inica Garcilaso's 1,000-page *Royal Commentaries* contains subtitles that make this work easy to thumb through.

Poma de Ayala, Felipe Guamán. *Nueva Croónica y Buen Gobierno.* This magnificent 16th-century manuscript has become the New World's best-known indigenous chronicle since it was discovered in the Royal Library of Copenhagen in 1908. It is a 1,200-page history of the Spanish conquest, told from the Andean point of view in an eclectic mixture of Quechua and Spanish. Its harangues against Spanish injustice are complemented by 400 drawings made by Poma de Ayala, which accompany the text. Parts of this text, which was intended as a letter to Spanish King Phillip III, have been translated into English and are published on the Internet at www.personal.umich.edu/~dfrye/guaman.htm.

LITERATURE

Alegria, Ciro. *Broad and Alien Is the World.* Chester Spring, PA: Dufour Editions. This award-wining, lyric novel (*El Mundo Es Ancho y Ajeno,* 1941) was written by a celebrated Peruvian novelist who spent his career documenting the oppression of Peru's indigenous peoples. Look also for Alegria's other classic, *The Golden Serpent (La Serpiente de Oro).* The Spanish versions of these works are ubiquitous in Peru.

Galeano, Eduardo and Cedric Belfrage, translator. *The Open Veins of Latin America. Five Centuries of the Pillage of a Continent.* Monthly Review Press, 1998. Though written three decades ago, this classic work of Latin American social conscience still rivets readers today. Written in "90 nights" when Galeano was 31 years old, it paints the warped evolution of Latin America's republics during five centuries of subjugation to more powerful Western nations.

Vargas Llosa, Mario. *Aunt Julia and the Scriptwriter.* New York: Penguin, 1995. This tale of taboo mixes radio scripts with the steamy romance that a young radio writer carries on with his aunt. This was one of Vargas Llosa's first novels and offers a revealing glimpse into highbrow Lima society.

Vargas Llosa, *Captain Pantoja and the Secret Service.* New York: Harper Collins, 1978. This wins our vote for funniest Peruvian novel of all time. It tells the story of a faithful soldier, Pantaleón Pantoja, and his mission to begin a top-secret prostitution service for Peru's military in Iquitos, Peru. His problem is that he is too successful.

Vargas Llosa, Mario. *The Green House.* New York: Harper Collins, 1984. This epic saga of Faulknerian blackness narrates the lives of Ashaninka Indians and jungle colonists whose lives converge into a brilliant evocation of the Amazon.

Wilder, Thornton. *The Bridge of San Luis Rey.* Perennial, 2003. This 1927 Pulitzer Prize winner begins with the death of five people when a bridge collapses over Peru's Apurímac River in 1714. A monk, who witnessed the tragedy, embarks on an existential investigation of the human condition.

TRAVEL AND EXPLORATION

Bingham, Hiram. *Phoenix: Lost City of the Incas.* Hugh Thomson, editor. London: Phoenix Press, 2003. Bingham's classic description of how he discovered Machu Picchu lends historical detail to Peru's stand-out attraction and also explains why Bingham went on to become the leading inspiration for movie character Indiana Jones.

Kane, Joe. *Running the Amazon.* New York: Vintage, 1990. Starting from a glacier at 17,000 feet, Joe Kane and a team of adventurers attempted the never-before-done feat of navigating the entire length of the Amazon River from source to mouth. The story begins as an accurate description of life in Peru's highlands and ends with the difficulties of managing personalities in a modern-day expedition.

Lee, Vincent. *Sixpac Manco: Travels Among the Incas.* This self-published book is a must-read for Vilcabamba explorers and is available at the

South American Explorers Club in Lima. The book comes with highly accurate maps of the area around Espíritu Pampa and Lee's amusing, shoot-from-the-hip adventurer's attitude.

Mathiessen, Peter. *At Play in the Fields of the Lord.* New York: Vintage, 1991. Set in a malarial jungle outpost, this Mathiessen classic depicts the clash of development and indigenous peoples in the Amazon jungle (It was made into a motion picture as well).

Muller, Karin. *Along the Inca Road, A Woman's Journey into an Ancient Empire.* National Geographic, 2000. The author traces her 6,000-mile journey along Inca roads in Ecuador, Peru, Bolivia, and Chile. Along the way she shares her insights about modern exploration and Inca history.

Schneebaum, Tobias. *Keep the River on Your Right.* New York: Grove Press: 1998. In 1955, New York intellectual Tobias Schneebaum spent eight years living with the Akarama tribe in the remote Madre de Dios jungle. His book describes his participation in homosexual and cannibalistic rituals and became an immediate jungle classic when it was published in 1969.

Shah, Tahir. *Trail of Feathers: In Search of the Birdmen of Peru.* London: Orion Publishing, 2002. A 16th-century mention of Incas who "flew like birds" over the jungle leads one journalist on a quest to unlock the secret of Peru's so-called birdmen. His journey takes him to Machu Picchu, the Nasca Lines, and finally into the Amazon itself.

Simpson, Joe. *Touching the Void.* New York: Harper Perennial, 2004. In 1985, Joe Simpson and Simon Yates attempted a first ascent of Siulá Grande, a forbidding peak in Peru's Cordillera Huayhuash. Simpson's subsequent fall into a crevasse, and his struggle to survive, will grip even non-climbers. This book was recently made into a motion picture of the same name.

Thomson, Hugh. *The White Rock, An Exploration of the Inca Heartland.* New York: Overlook Press, 2001. British documentary filmmaker Hugh Thomson returns to Vilcabamba, where he explored in his early 20s, to weave a recollection of his travels together with an alluring blend of Spanish chronicles and Inca history. It contains vivid, sometimes scathing, depictions of local personalities and makes for a fast, exciting way to read up for a Peru trip.

TRAVEL GUIDES

Bracco, Felix and Matias Guzman. *Peru Surfing Travel Guide.* Buenos Aires: Gráficas Boschi, 2002. These Argentines had a tremendous time searching out Peru's breaks and writing the first book in English to South America's surfing mecca. This book can be found in Lima bookstores and sometimes ordered online in the United States.

Frost, Peter. *Exploring Cusco,* 5th ed. Lima: Nuevas Imágenes, 1999. This book, recently updated, continues to be the best-written, most readable historical and archaeological approach to the Cusco area, written by long-time Cusco resident Peter Frost.

Johnson, Brad. *Classic Climbs of the Cordillera Blanca.* Montrose, CO: Western Reflections, 2003. Johnson has been guiding in the Cordillera Blanca for nearly two decades and presents detailed descriptions of the area's major climbing routes, together with three-dimensional maps and vibrant color photos. This is a brand-new, award-winning guide to one of the world's top mountaineering destinations.

Wust, Walter et al. *Inca Guide to Peru.* Lima: Peisa, 2003. This excellent highway guide, sponsored by Mitsubishi, contains the country's best road maps and detailed descriptions of all the driving routes. There is also some historical and cultural information on each of Peru's main destinations, though little information on hotels and restaurants. This company has also published *Guia Inca de Playas,* which runs down all the remote camping and surfing spots along Peru's coast from Tumbes to Tacna. These books are for sale in Ripley department stores and most Lima bookstores.

Zarzar, Omar. *Por los Caminos de Peru en Bicicleta.* Lima: Editor SA, 2001. This is a guide to Peru's best mountain-biking routes. Though written in Spanish, the maps and itineraries are useful even for non-Spanish speakers.

NATURE AND THE ENVIRONMENT

Beaver, Paul. *Diary of an Amazon Guide: Amazing Encounters with Tropical Nature and Culture.* AE Publications, 2001. Paul Beaver, owner of the Tahuayo Lodge near Iquitos, holds a Phd from the University of Chicago and has spent two decades exploring the upper Amazon. He provides a fast-moving, insightful and humorous glimpse into both the nature and people of the area.

Forsyth, Adrian and Ken Miyata. *Tropical Nature, Life and Death in the Rain Forests of Central and South America.* New York: Simon & Schuster, 1984. This well-written and at times humorous book lays out the principles of rain forest ecology in easy-to-ready, entertaining prose. First-time jungle visitors will understand much more of what they see in the Amazon after reading this book.

Kricher, John. *A Neotropical Companion,* 2nd ed. Princeton, NJ: Princeton University Press, 1999. Compared to *Tropical Nature,* this book offers a more detailed, scientific look at rainforest ecology, though it is still designed for non-biologists. This is the bible for the Amazon enthusiast, with a good listing of animals, plants, and ecosystems and theoretical discussions of evolutionary biology and other advanced topics.

MacQuarrie, Kim and André Bärtschi, photographer. *Peru's Amazonian Eden: Manu Na-* *tional Park and Biosphere Reserve,* 2nd ed. Barcelona, Spain: Francis O. Patthe, 1998. This book of stunning photos is more than just a coffee-table book. Kim MacQuarrie spent six months living with a previously uncontacted tribe in the Manu and writes an eloquent evocation of the people and wildlife of Peru's most pristine patch of Amazon.

MacQuarrie, Kim with Jorge Flores Ochoa and Javier Portós. Photos by Jaume and Jordi Blassi. *Gold of the Andes: The Llamas, Alpacas, Vicuñas, and Guanacos of South America.* Barcelona, Spain: Francis O. Patthe, 1994. This is another well-written book with large-format pictures of Peru's highlanders and the animals on which they depend.

Stap, Don. *A Parrot Without a Name.* Austin, TX: University of Texas Press, 1991. Poet-naturalist Don Stap accompanied two of Latin American's more renowned ornithologists, Ted Parker and John O'Neil, on birding expeditions into unexplored corners of the Amazon. The book blends Amazon adventure with a close look at the odd, obsessive life of ornithologists.

BIRDING

Clements, James and Noam Shany. *A Field Guide to the Birds of Peru.* Temecula, CA: Ibis Publishing Company, 2001. Though much criticized by bird watchers for its faulty pictures of certain birds, this $60 tome catalogs nearly 1,800 birds known to reside, or migrate to, Peru.

Krabbe, Nils and John Fjeldsa. *Birds of the High Andes.* Copenhagen: Denmark Zoological Museum of the University of Copenhagen, 1990. Real birders consider this such a must-have masterpiece that they are willing to shell out $150 for this classy tome. It includes all the birds you are likely to encounter in the temperate and alpine zones of Peru.

Walker, Barry and Jon Fjeldsa, illustrations. *Field Guide to the Birds of Machu Picchu.*

Lima: Peruvian National Trust for Parks and Protected Areas. This portable guide, written by Cusco's foremost bird expert and owner of Manu Expeditions, is widely available in Cusco. At $30 it is an excellent value with 31 superb color plates and descriptions of 420 species.

Valqui, Thomas. *A Bird-Finding Guide to Peru,* 1st ed. This is the long-awaited new comprehensive bird guide to Peru, which is likely to replace *A Field Guide to the Birds of Peru.* This paperback tackles the Herculean task of cataloging Peru's entire bird population. More information about this book may be found at www.tvalqui.com.

PHOTOGRAPHY

Wust, Walter and Marie Isabel Musselman. *Land of a Thousand Colors.* This coffee-table book sparkles with the prose of Peruvian writer Antonio Cisneros and painter Fernando de Szyslo. It captures Peru's diversity in large-format, color prints that are organized not by content, but by their color.

Chambi, Martín. *Photographs, 1920–1950.* Foreword by Mario Vargas Llosa. Washington, DC: Smithsonian Institution Press, 1993. This high-quality collection of black-and-white stills were taken by Martín Chambi, a major unsung photographer of the mid-20th century whose life work is based on Inca stonework and the rhythms of life in Cusco. There is another Chambi book as well, published in 1994 by Lunweg Editores in Barcelona.

Milligan, Max. *Realm of the Incas.* New York: Universe Publishing, 2001. English photographer Max Milligan spent years trekking to the remote corners of Peru to capture images that range from the sacred snows of Nevado Ausangate to the torpid meanderins of the Río Manu.

FOOD

Acurio, Gastón. *Peru: Una Aventura Culinaria.* Lima: Quebecor World Peru, 2002. This large-format photo book profiles Peru's array of foods in chapters titled Water, Land, and Air. It includes a range of recipes and profiles of Peru's leading chefs and is available in Lima bookshops.

Custer, Tony. *The Art of Peruvian Cuisine.* Cimino Publishing Group, 2003. This brand-new book has high-quality photos and an excellent selection of Peruvian recipes in both Spanish and English.

Morales, Edmund. *The Guinea Pig: Healing, Food, and Ritual in the Andes.* Tucson, AZ: University of Arizona Press, 1995. This is the first major study, with good pictures, of how Andean highlanders not only eat guinea pig but also use it for medicinal and religious purposes.

SPIRITUAL AND ESOTERIC

Milla, Carlos. *Genesis de la Cultura Andina,* 3rd edition. If you can read Spanish, this book presents esoteric theories based on many of Peru's ancient ceremonial centers. His latest book, 2003's *Ayni: Semiotica Andina de los Espacios Sagrados,* focuses on astrology. Carlos Milla can be reached in Cusco at cmilla@viabcp.com

Villoldo, Alberto and Erik Jendresen. *The Four Winds: A Shaman's Odyssey into the Amazon.* New York: Harper Collins, 1991. Even Peru's shamans respect this work, which documents the author's spiritual initiation into Amazon rituals.

WEAVING

Pollard Rowe, Anne and John Cohen. *Hidden Threads of Peru: Q'ero Textiles.* London: Merrell Publishers, 2002. In vibrant pictures and concise prose, this book documents the extraordinary weavings of Q'ero, a remote town in south Peru where the authors have been researching for nearly four decades.

Heckman, Andrea. *Woven Stories: Andean Textiles and Rituals.* Albuquerque, New Mexico: University of New Mexico Press, 2003. A series of ethnographic essays on Andean life and weaving by a researcher with two decades in the field.

CHILDREN

Hergé, *The Adventures of Tintin: Prisoners of the Sun,* 1949. In this Hergé classic, a sequel to "The Seven Crystal Balls," Tintin, Captain Haddock, and Milou catch a steamer to Peru to rescue a kidnapped professor. The adventure leads them through the Andes and the Amazon, which are depicted in fascinating detail and through the romanticized lens of the mid-20th century.

Internet Resources

TRAVEL INFORMATION

South American Explorers
www.saexplorers.org

This fabulous web page has books for sale, information on insurance providers, an online bulletin board with cars for sale and apartments for rent and interesting links. There are a few services, such as trip reports and the volunteer database, that members can access online with a password.

PromPeru
www.peru.org.pe

The government's tourist agency has a web page that is getting better and better each year.

The Peruvian Times
www.peruviantimes.com

Lima's oldest English-language publishing house, which until recently published the *Lima Times,* has an interesting website with tips on arriving in Lima, photos, links, and a directory of expatriate associations.

Andean Travel Web
www.andeantravelweb.com

This is the best of several websites in Peru that evaluate hotels, restaurants, and agencies.

The Latin American Network Information Center
www.lanic.utexas.edu/la/peru

The largest single list of links to information on Peru has been compiled by the University of Texas.

Peru Links
www.perulinks.com

This huge page of links offers less formal entries like gay and lesbian clubs, alternative medicine, chat rooms, etc.

FLIGHT INFORMATION

Tráfico
www.traficoperu

This agency newsletter is an updated list of all international and domestic flights in Peru.

Lima Airport
www.lap.com.pe

The home page of the Lima airport contains up-to-the-minute travel information and good information about airport services.

WEATHER

Senamhi
www.senamhi.gob.pe

This is the Peruvian government's Spanish-only guide to Peru's weather.

ECOTOURISM

GORP
www.gorp.com
> This joint production of Away.com, Gorp, and Outside Online has hundreds of travel stories on Peru, a list of top 20 travel destinations, and links to tour operators.

Planeta
www.planeta.com
> he world's largest ecotourism site includes articles, essays, and links to responsible tour operators.

LIMA

El Sol
www.elsol.idiomasperu.com
> Lima's largest language school runs a mailing list for expatriates in Peru with offers for housing, services, and jobs. You can sign up from overseas and the messages will be sent automatically to your email.

SURFING

Peru Azul
www.peruazul.com
> Peru's most popular website for surfing and ocean conditions along the coast though is for Spanish speakers only.

Wanna Surf
www.wannasurf.com/spot/South_America.
> This is another good website for wave riders—in English.

CURRENT AFFAIRS

Peruvian Graffiti
http://gci275.com/peru
> Peru's best English-language current-affairs site I written by a Lima-based foreign correspondent. Peruvian Graffiti includes a straightforward explanation of Peru's history, links to every imaginable organization, photo galleries, blogs—you name it.

ANDEAN CULTURE

Culture of the Andes
www.andes.org
> A labor of love from Peru fanatics Russ and Ada Gibbons, this site focusing on Andean culture includes short stories, jokes, music, songs in Quechua, poetry, and riddles.

Machu Picchu Library
www.machupicchu.org
> This is another good Andean site; though unfortunately, many of the links are now outdated.

Index

Ancient Cultures

Hiking/Backpacking

Reserves and Protected Areas

Acknowledgments

In preparing *Moon Handbooks Peru,* we spent eight months bumping around in a borrowed jeep, exploring every nook and cranny of the country. The book came alive because of the extraordinary people we met along the way. The project remained a labor of love for us, even after we had left Peru behind and were typing away furiously in a snowbound log cabin in Evergreen, Colorado.

In Lima, our dear friend Ramsay Ross lent us his jeep just as we were carrying our laptops and digital cameras onto a bus out of Lima. Sara Mateos and Marco Zileri gave us political insight and plied us with pisco sours, Ramiro Garay plugged us into the best new restaurants and night spots, Javier and Susan Torre rolled up their sleeves and got to work and Radiq and Brian Hennessey kept us laughing. Richard Cunyus and Rick Vecchio supplied key bits of wisdom and Yolanda Portugal in the Foreign Ministry and Fernando Lopez in PromPeru went out of their way to help us. Leda Duif of the South American Explorers Club is not only a generous friend but a source of inspiration.

In the north of Peru, David Wroughton insisted we cool our heels at the beach while Rodrigo Costodio and Patricia Vargas eased us into Chiclayo. In Cajamarca, John Herdin, Carlos Diaz, and Nora Regalado opened our eyes to the tremendous beauty and fabulous network of Inca trails in the area. Likewise, Tarapato became an endlessly interesting place once we met Dr. Carlos Alejandro Gonzalez and Dr. Jacques Mabit. The Northern Highlands chapter was much improved thanks to careful edits by Rob Dover and Tina and Charles Motley.

In the Huaraz area, where we lingered for more than a month, we owe eternal gratitude to Isabel and Chris Benway, Julio Olaza, John Lockwood, Pocha and Ario Ferri, Alcides Ames and star mountain guide Richard Hidalgo. Val Pitkethly, one of the most experienced mountain guides in Peru, made infinite suggestions

for all of Peru's mountain areas. Our ascent of Tocllaraju would not have been nearly so pleasurable were it not for the humor and perseverance of Sam Schlehuber, Mike Lindley, and Melky Bedón.

Another mind-blowing adventure was a two-week float in homemade balsa rafts down the Río Chilive near the Parque Nacional Manu. Special thanks to New York-based photographer Joshua Paul, Stephanie Pearson of *Outside* magazine, Raúl Montes and especially the inimitable Hugo Pepper for pulling the trip together. In the Cusco area, we also want to thank Richard Webb, Eric Arenas, Franco Negri, Wendy Weeks, Joaquin Randall, José Ignacio Lambarri, Rafael Casabonne, and Ulrike in Pisac, along with her next-door neighbors Fielding and Roman Vizcarra. Based in Urubamba, Nicholas Asheshov is one of the great experts on Peru. Along with his wife María del Carmen, he contributed immeasurably to this project.

We gained a new perspective on Lake Titicaca thanks to Eliana Pauca and on the Colca Canyon because of Lourdes Pérez Wicht and César Torres Bazán. We got oriented in Arequipa thanks to Rafael of Los Balcones de Moral and Gian Marco Vellutino. We will never forget the red wines and homemade pastas enjoyed in Nasca with Enzo Destro and local archaeologist Giussepe Orefici, nor the energy and optimism of Bruno Pegorer, Mario Urbina, and Roberto Penny Cabrera in Ica. We experienced the point breaks of Punta Hermosa thanks to Mario León Villarán and his talented son Daniel.

The most difficult area in all of Peru to explore, and to write about, is the rain forest. The section was greatly improved thanks to the insight and guidance of a series of Amazon readers including Dr. Charles Mango, Paul Beaver, Peter Jensen, Analía and Percy Sánchez, María Elena Lau, Barry Walker, Boris Gomez, Max Gunther, and Rudi von May. José Koechlin, a gentle but powerful voice in Peru's fight to conserve the Amazon, was a huge help as always.

We also want to thank the kind and professional staff at Avalon Travel Publishing. Publisher Bill Newlin placed his complete trust in us and our editor Kevin McLain guided us expertly, and with unflappable patience, through the whole process. Thanks also to those who helped key aspects of the book, including Sarah Coglianese, Amber Pirker, Olivia Solís, and Mike Morgenfeld.

Our parents, George del Gaudio, and Harrison and Joan Wehner, encouraged us every step of the way. This book is dedicated to them.

ALSO AVAILABLE FROM

MOON HANDBOOKS®
The Cure for the Common Trip

USA

Acadia National Park	O`ahu
Alaska	Ohio
Arizona	Oregon
Big Island of Hawai`i	Pennsylvania
Boston	Rhode Island
California	San Juan Islands
Cape Cod, Martha's	Santa Fe-Taos
Vineyard & Nantucket	Silicon Valley
Charleston & Savannah	Smoky Mountains
Chesapeake Bay	South Carolina
Coastal California	Southern California
Coastal Carolinas	Tahoe
Coastal Maine	Tennessee
Coastal Oregon	Texas
Colorado	Utah
Columbia River Gorge	Virginia
Connecticut	Washington
Florida Gulf Coast	Wisconsin
Four Corners	Wyoming
Georgia	Yellowstone & Grand
Grand Canyon	Teton
Hawaii	Yosemite
Hudson River Valley	Zion & Bryce
Idaho	
Kaua`i	
Maine	
Maryland & Delaware	
Massachusetts	
Maui	
Michigan	
Minnesota	
Montana	
Monterey & Carmel	
Nevada	
New Hampshire	
New Mexico	
New Orleans	
New York State	
North Carolina	
Northern California	

THE AMERICAS

Alberta
Atlantic Canada
British Columbia
Canadian Rockies
Vancouver & Victoria
Western Canada

Acapulco
Baja
Cabo
Cancún
Guadalajara
Mexico City
Oaxaca
Pacific Mexico
Puerto Vallarta
Yucatán Peninsula

Argentina
Belize
Brazil
Buenos Aires
Chile
Costa Rica
Cuba
Dominican Republic
Ecuador
Guatemala
Havana
Honduras
Nicaragua
Panama
Patagonia
Peru
Virgin Islands

ASIA & THE PACIFIC

Australia
Fiji
Hong Kong
Micronesia
Nepal
New Zealand
South Korea
South Pacific
Tahiti
Thailand
Tonga-Samoa
Vietnam, Cambodia &
Laos

www.moon.com

With expert authors, suggested routes and activities, and intuitive organization, Moon Handbooks ensure an uncommon experience—and a few new stories to tell.

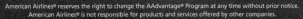

U.S.~Metric Conversion

1 inch	=	2.54 centimeters (cm)
1 foot	=	.304 meters (m)
1 yard	=	0.914 meters
1 mile	=	1.6093 kilometers (km)
1 km	=	.6214 miles
1 fathom	=	1.8288 m
1 chain	=	20.1168 m
1 furlong	=	201.168 m
1 acre	=	.4047 hectares
1 sq km	=	100 hectares
1 sq mile	=	2.59 square km
1 ounce	=	28.35 grams
1 pound	=	.4536 kilograms
1 short ton	=	.90718 metric ton
1 short ton	=	2000 pounds
1 long ton	=	1.016 metric tons
1 long ton	=	2240 pounds
1 metric ton	=	1000 kilograms
1 quart	=	.94635 liters
1 US gallon	=	3.7854 liters
1 Imperial gallon	=	4.5459 liters
1 nautical mile	=	1.852 km

To compute Celsius temperatures, subtract 32 from Fahrenheit and divide by 1.8. To go the other way, multiply Celsius by 1.8 and add 32.

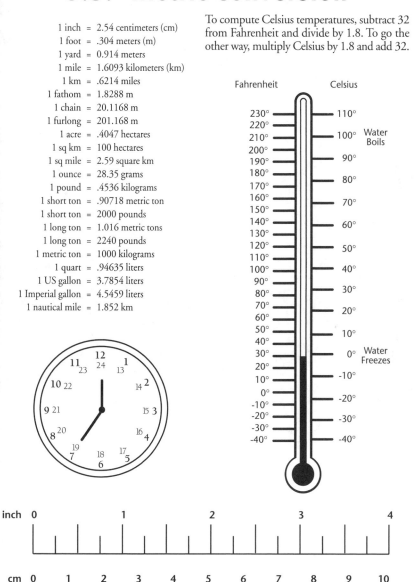

Keeping Current

Although we strive to produce the most up-to-date guidebook humanly possible, change is unavoidable. Between the time this book goes to print and the moment you read it, a handful of the businesses noted in these pages will undoubtedly change prices, move, or even close their doors forever. Other worthy attractions will open for the first time. If you have a favorite gem you'd like to see included in the next edition, or see anything that needs updating, clarification, or correction, please drop us a line. Send your comments via email to atpfeedback@avalonpub.com, or use the address below.

Moon Handbooks Peru
Avalon Travel Publishing
1400 65th Street, Suite 250
Emeryville, CA 94608, USA
www.moon.com

Avalon Travel Publishing,
An Imprint of
Avalon Publishing Group, Inc.
AVALON
publishing group incorporated

Editor and Series Manager: Kevin McLain
Acquisitions Editor: Rebecca K. Browning
Copy Editor: Emily McManus
Graphics and Production Coordinator:
    Amber Pirker
Cover Designer: Kari Gim
Interior Designers: Amber Pirker,
    Alvaro Villanueva, Kelly Pendragon
Map Editor: Olivia Solís, Naomi Adler Dancis
Cartographers: Mike Morgenfeld,
    Kat Kalamaras, Suzanne Service
Indexer: Rachel Kuhn

ISBN: 1-56691-674-7
ISSN: 1549-7445

Printing History
1st Edition—November 2004
5 4 3 2

Text © 2004 by Ross Wehner and
    Renée del Gaudio.

Maps © 2004 by Avalon Travel Publishing, Inc.
All rights reserved.

Some photos and illustrations are used by permission and are the property of the original copyright owners.

Front cover photo: © John Borthwick/Lonely Planet Images

Printed in the USA by Worzalla